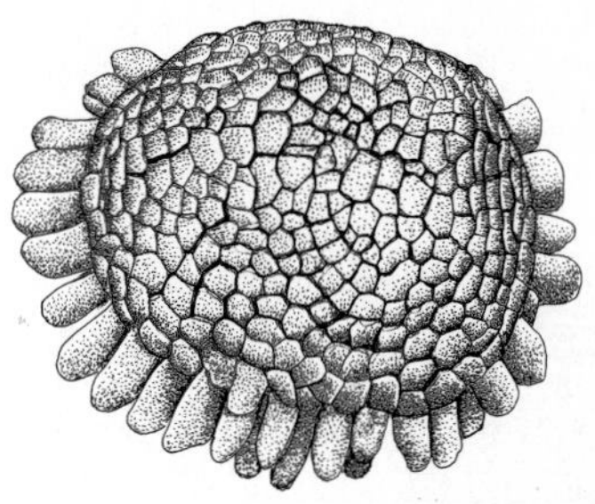

There are more important things in life
than continually trying to speed it up.
(Mahatma Gandhi)

PHILIPPINES TRAVEL GUIDE

Jens Peters

Philippines Travel Guide

2nd edition 2005

ISBN 3-923821-32-8

Published by *Jens Peters Publications*

Translation by *Colin Hall*
Layout, maps & photos by *Jens Peters*
Illustrations by *Boy Diego Jr*
Cover design by *Hans Ott*

Printed in Germany
by *Fuldaer Verlagsaanstalt*

Main distributor
Jens Peters Publications
Osterholzer Dorfstrasse 45
D-28307 Bremen
Germany

Tel +49 (421) 451743
Fax +49 (421) 455406
E-mail: KnopVA@aol.com

www.travelphil.com

Notes on This Book

Compared with other countries of South-East Asia, the Philippines only make rare appearances in the catalogues of the major travel companies - if at all. There's no doubt this means a huge loss of revenue for the country, but it actually turns out to be an advantage for the Filipino people, constantly battered as they already are by all kinds of natural and political upheavals. The truth is, they still have a long way to go before they can handle the consequences of organised, modern mass tourism.

If you travel on your own through the Philippine archipelago, be prepared to be flexibile from time to time. But you can look forward to a rewarding experience all the same, for nowhere else in the world will you come across people who are as hospitable as the Filipinos. Nowhere else will you find such natural, unaffected openness, which makes it so easy to meet people and have a good time together with them.

Transport on and between the larger islands is usually good, and there are more than enough hotels and restaurants to fit every budget. However, don't look for speed, exactness and punctuality here, just relax and learn to be as laid-back as the locals.

This guide will help you to plan and enjoy your trip to the Philippines. It contains important information on the country and its people, ideas on how to prepare for your journey, travel tips for the Philippines, as well as pre-planned routes with descriptions of the islands, towns and cities, sights, hotels and restaurants you will encounter there.
Manila and the main island Luzon are covered first in the travel section, followed by the islands around Luzon, the Visayas, Mindanao and the Sulu Islands, with Palawan rounding it all off.

Most of the information in the guide was personally gathered by myself and updated during 2004. Although I can't guarantee every last detail one hundred percent, I did my level best to strive for accuracy throughout the book, of that you can be sure.

I would like to express my sincere gratitude to friends and others who gave me tips, ideas and encouragement for this edition of the book. A special thank you goes to Freddie Fritsche who helped me with the research, and of course to Colin Hall for his professional translation of the original German *Philippinen Reise-Handbuch*. It was a real pleasure to work together with them while producing and independently publishing my very own English edition of the *Philippines Travel Guide*.

Have a good journey and above all, have fun!

Jens Peters

Contents

Info-Boxes

Maps

@ E-mail (This symbol in the text means that the hotel etc can be contacted by e-mail. The address can be found in the E-mail Directory at the back of the book.)

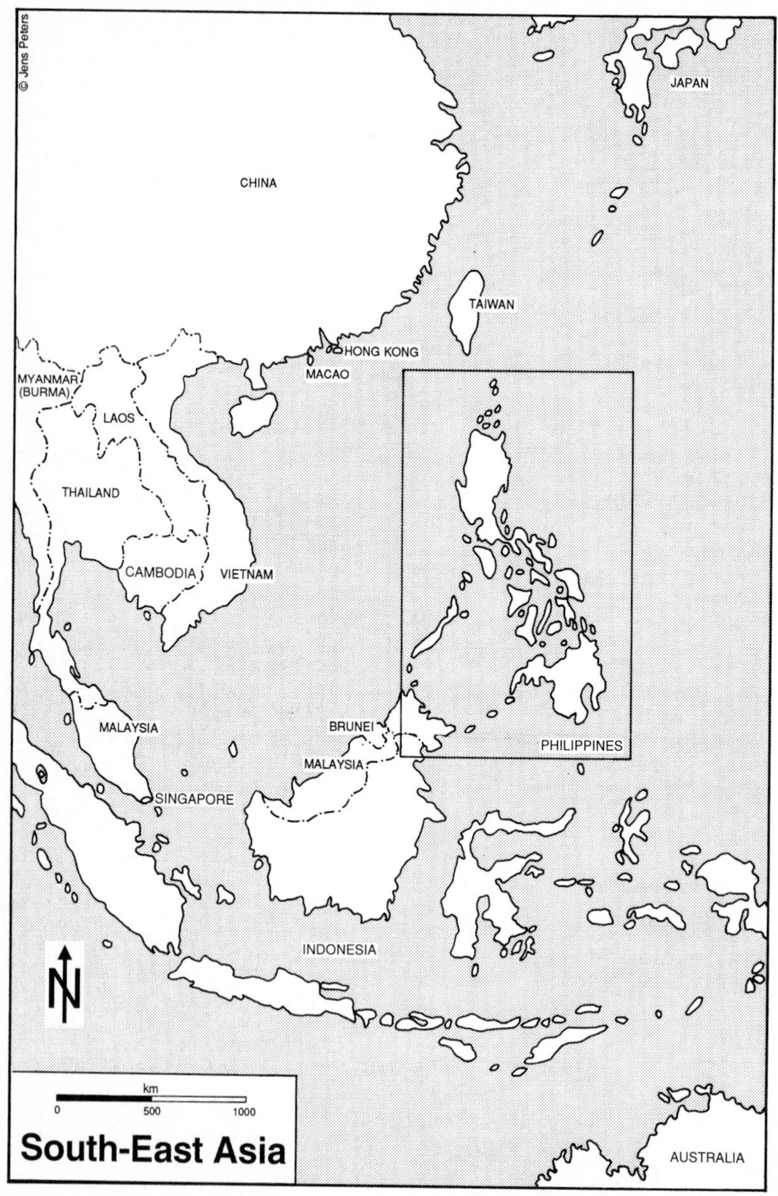
© Jens Peters
JAPAN
CHINA
TAIWAN
HONG KONG
MACAO
MYANMAR
(BURMA)
LAOS
THAILAND
CAMBODIA
VIETNAM
MALAYSIA
BRUNEI
MALAYSIA
PHILIPPINES
SINGAPORE
INDONESIA
N
km
0
500
1000
South-East Asia
AUSTRALIA

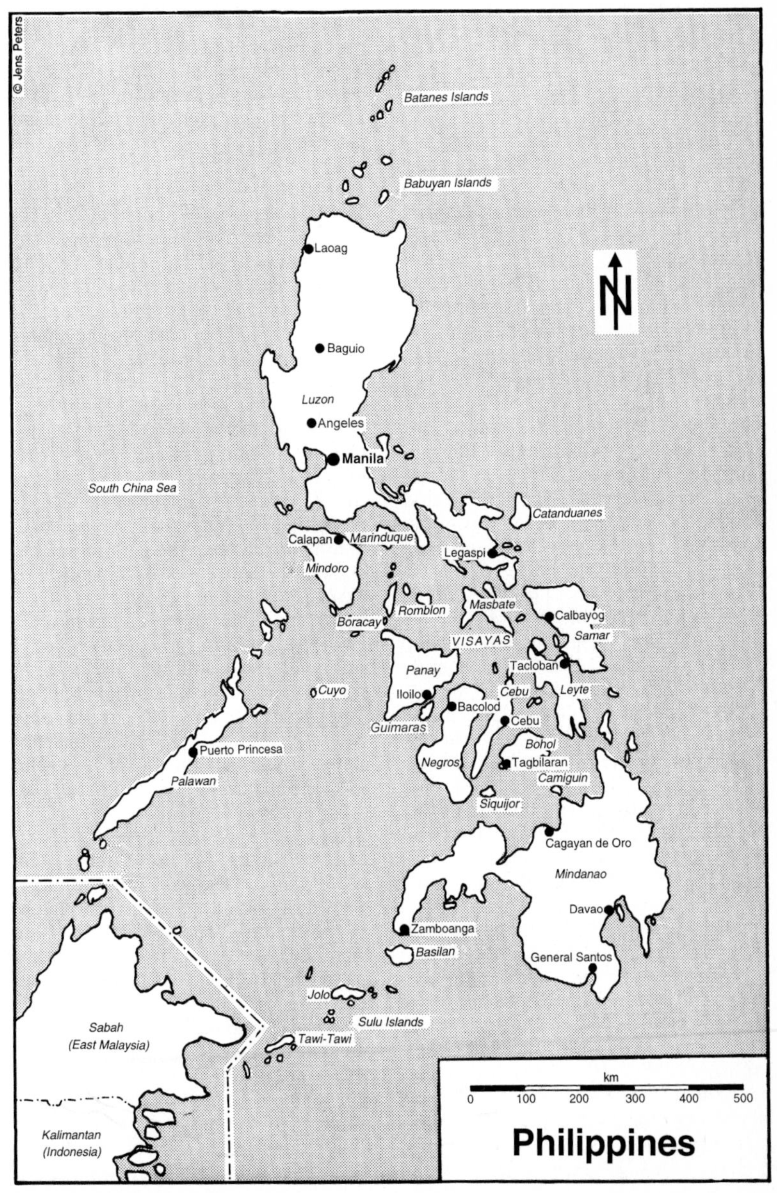
© Jens Peters
Batanes Islands
Babuyan Islands
Laoag
Baguio
Luzon
Angeles
Manila
South China Sea
Catanduanes
Calapan
Marinduque
Mindoro
Legaspi
Boracay
Romblon
Masbate
Calbayog
Samar
VISAYAS
Panay
Tacloban
Cuyo
Iloilo
Cebu
Leyte
Bacolod
Cebu
Guimaras
Bohol
Puerto Princesa
Negros
Tagbilaran
Camiguin
Palawan
Siquijor
Cagayan de Oro
Mindanao
Davao
Zamboanga
Basilan
General Santos
Jolo
Sulu Islands
Sabah
(East Malaysia)
Tawi-Tawi
km
0
100
200
300
400
500
Kalimantan
(Indonesia)
Philippines

Country & People

Facts about the Country

Location

Five to 21 degrees north of the equator; 160 km south of Taiwan; 25 km north of Sabah (Borneo); 960 km east of Vietnam.

Area

The total area of the Philippines is 299,404 sq km. From north to south the Philippines stretches for 1850 km and from east to west for 1100 km.

Islands

The Philippines officially consists of 7107 islands of which only 2000 are inhabited. Only about 500 of the islands are larger than one sq km and 2500 aren't even named. In descending order of size the biggest islands are Luzon (104,688 sq km), Mindanao (94,630 sq km), Samar (13,080 sq km), Negros (12,710 sq km), Palawan (11,785 sq km), Panay (11,515 sq km), Mindoro (9,735 sq km), Leyte (7,214 sq km), Cebu (4,421 sq km), Bohol (3,864 sq km) and Masbate (3,269 sq km).

The islands of the Philippines can be divided conveniently into four groups. First there's Luzon, the largest and northernmost island and the site of the capital, Manila. The nearby islands of Batanes, Catanduanes, Mindoro, Marinduque, Masbate and Romblon are generally included with Luzon.

At the other end of the archipelago is the second largest island, Mindanao. From Mindanao's south-western tip, the islands of the Sulu archipelago form stepping stones south to Borneo.

Third is the tightly packed island group known as the Visayas, which fills the space between Luzon and Mindanao. Seven major islands make up this group: Panay, Negros, Cebu, Bohol, Leyte and Samar.

Finally, off to the west, there's the province of Palawan with more than 1700 islands. The main island is Palawan, which is long and narrow and forms another bridge from the Philippines to Borneo.

Population

In 2001 the population stood at 78.2 million. The trend is for the number of inhabitants of the Philippines to grow at a rate of 2.3% a year. The Philippines' family planning programmes are hampered not only by the strong Catholicism of the Filipinos but also by the usual Asian wish for the 'insurance' of a large family in old age. Filipinos are inclined to be very fond of children and have on average six children to a family. Consequently, you will hear of 'family planting' rather than 'family planning', although the government is putting a great deal of effort into popularising the concept of birth control.

Nearly 40% of the population of the Philippines live in the city, while the other 60% live in the country. Thirty-seven percent of Filipinos are under 14 years of age, while those who are 65 or over account for only 3.8% of the population. The ratio of males to females is almost even, averaging out at 100 males to 98.4 females.

Cities

Although there is more hope than opportunity of getting a job, migration from rural into urban areas is a feature of the country. The largest cities are Manila, Davao, Cebu, Iloilo, Zamboanga, Bacolod, Angeles, Butuan and Cagayan de Oro. In 1980, Manila on its own had a population of 1.6 million, although a previous amalgamation in the 1970s had brought together 17 cities and districts (including Quezon City, Caloocan City, Pasay City etc) to form Metropolitan Manila (better known as Metro Manila). The present population of Metro Manila is over 10 million. Manila is the seat of government. The National Assembly (Batasang Pambansa) meets in Quezon City.

Mountains

The highest mountains are Mt Apo, near Davao in Mindanao, at 2953m and Mt Pulag, north-east of Baguio in North Luzon, at 2922m.

One official publication lists 37 volcanoes in the Philippines, 18 of which are classed as being active; another lists as many as 88 inactive volcanoes. Mt Mayon near Legaspi in South Luzon is said to be the most beautiful volcano in the world because it is almost a perfect cone, while Mt Pinatubo north-west of Manila in Central Luzon is one of the most dangerous.

Rivers

The longest rivers are the Cagayan River, the Rio Grande de Pampanga and the Agno River in Luzon, and the Rio Grande de Mindanao and the Agusan River in Mindanao.

Geology

Islands, islands, everywhere - the Philippine archipelago has over seven thousand of them. Even if you only spent one day on each one, you would need 20 years to do it. Travelling in the Philippines means island hopping, covering a remarkable range of land formations. On the main island of Luzon it's the gigantic rice terraces of the Central Cordillera, and in the south the majestic, classically shaped Mayon volcano. Although less impressive, the Chocolate Hills on the island of Bohol are all the more mysterious. This bizarre, bumpy landscape has piqued the curiosity of many an observer. Then there are the extensive flat areas on the island of Negros, ideal for planting sugar cane. But Negros, like most Philippines islands, also has its fair share of volcanoes. Some, for example the relatively small islands of Biliran and Camiguin to name just two, are positively crowded with them. The only exception is mountainous Palawan - at least there is absolutely no sign of volcanic activity there at the moment. To make up for it, around El Nido on the north-west coast weirdly shaped chalk cliffs rise steeply out of crystal clear water. Those are the islands of the Bacuit archipelago, just as popular a destination as the small dream islands of Boracay, North Pandan and Malapascua. Pearls in the sea, a few of the many that invite you to island hop.

History

Philippine history is classified as beginning somewhere between 150,000 and 30,000 years ago. From this epoch stem the stone artefacts (palaeoliths) which have been found together with fossils of long-extinct mammals in Solana in Cagayan Province. These primitive stone tools were probably used by hunters who migrated over a land bridge from the Asiatic mainland.

The oldest human bones which have so far been excavated have been dated at 50,000 years of age. However, many historians consider the Negrito or Aeta, who arrived about 25,000 years ago from the Asian continent, as the aboriginal inhabitants of the Philippines. They were later driven back by several waves of immigrants from Indonesia.

Immigration

In about 5000 BC the last land bridge sank into the ocean. Five immigration periods from Indochina between 1500 and 500 BC have been recorded. The last of these groups to arrive in their long canoes brought the first copper and bronze articles, and they are also credited with building the gigantic rice

Magellan reached the Philippines in 1521

terraces at Banaue (Banawe), North Luzon. The immigration of Malayan peoples from 500 BC to 1500 AD brought further cultural changes, particularly in house construction (they built on piles), agriculture (they introduced plants and trees) and animal husbandry (they used water buffalo).
Indian influences came from the Buddhist-Hindu empire of Srivijaya (800-1377 AD) in Sumatra, and Majapahit (1293-1478 AD) in Java. During this period, trade also began with Indochinese states. In particular the merchants of the Sung Dynasty (960-1280 AD) visited the main island, Luzon, and the islands of the Visayas with their merchant ships. They mainly exchanged Chinese products like porcelain for native wood and gold. In 1380 the Arab-taught Makdum arrived in the Sulu Islands in the south of the Philippines and began the 'Propagation of Islam. His mission was most successful in Bwansa, the old Sulu capital, and Tapul Island. A powerful Islamic centre was finally established in 1475 by Sharif Mohammed Kabungsuwan, a Muslim leader from Johore. He married the very influential native princess Putri Tunoma, converted many tribes and was the first sultan of Mindanao.

The Spanish

The Muslims had already extended their power to a part of Luzon, when Ferdinand Magellan, a Portuguese seafarer in the service of Spain, arrived on the scene on 16 March 1521. His first landfall was on Homonhon, an uninhabited island near Leyte, but it was on Mactan that he erected a cross and claimed the whole archipelago for Spain - with the blissful disregard typical of early European colonisers for the local inhabitants' claim to their country. Lapu-Lapu, a proud Filipino chief, opposed the Spanish authority and this led to a battle in which Magellan was killed.
Ruy Lopez de Villalobos was the next to try and claim the islands for Spain. He reached the island realm with an expedition in 1543 and named it 'Filipinas' after King Philip II of Spain. The permanent Spanish colonial occupation of the Philippines began in 1565. In

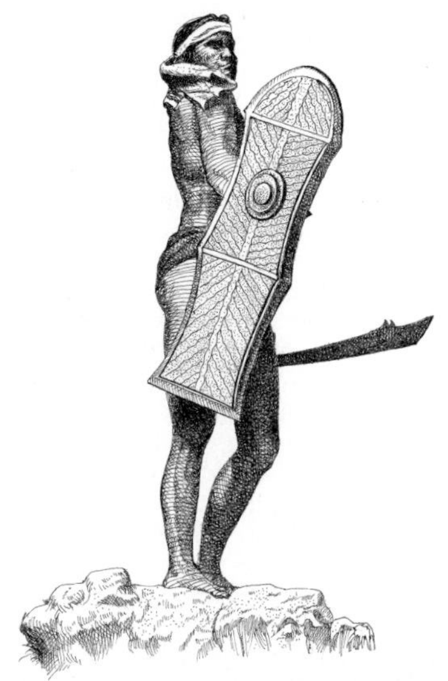
Chief Lapu-Lapu defeated Magellan in battle

November of that year Miguel Lopez de Legaspi landed with his fleet at Bohol. In Tagbilaran he sealed a blood friendship with the island ruler Rajah Sikatuna, conquered Cebu a short time later and erected the first Spanish fort in the Philippines.

In 1571 Legaspi conquered Manila and a year later the whole country, with the exception of the strictly Islamic Sulu Islands and Mindanao, was under Spain's domination. With the zeal typical of the Spanish at the time, churches were built and the propagation of Catholicism began.

The Push for Independence

Until 1821 the Philippines was administered from Mexico. Attempts by the Dutch, Portuguese and Chinese to set foot in the Philippines were successfully repelled by the Spanish, though the British managed to occupy Manila for a short time in 1762 during the Seven Years' War. They reluctantly handed it back to Spain under the conditions of the Treaty of Paris signed in 1763.

After the opening of the Suez Canal in 1869, many young Filipinos left their country to study in Spain and other European countries. They brought back with them new ideas and thoughts of freedom. In 1872 there was a revolt in Cavite by about 200 Filipino soldiers against their Spanish masters. It was quickly put down, but it signalled the start of a determined struggle for freedom and independence.

The spiritual founders of the independence movement were the Filipino thinkers and patriots Marcelo H del Pilar, Graciano Lopez Jaena, Juan Luna and Dr Jose Rizal. The critical writings and poems of Rizal inspired many Filipinos in their fight for freedom. When Jose Rizal founded the 'Liga Filipina' in 1892, he was exiled as a revolutionary agitator to Dapitan, Mindanao. Andres

Dr Jose Rizal

Bonifacio then founded the secret organisation Katipunan. In August 1896 the armed struggle for independence broke out, first in Manila and later throughout the country. On 30 December 1896, after an absurd mockery of a trial, Rizal was executed by the Spanish authorities. He spent the last weeks before his death in the dungeon of Fort Santiago in Manila. In March 1897, Emilio Aguinaldo replaced Bonifacio as leader of the revolution.

The USA

In 1898, as a result of a dispute over Cuba, a war between Spain and the USA broke out. Under Admiral Dewey the Spanish fleet was decisively beaten in Manila Bay. The Filipinos, seizing their chance to strike against the Spanish, fought on the side of the USA, and on 12 June 1898 General Aguinaldo declared the Philippines independent. The Americans, however, ignored the role the Filipinos had played in the war and paid the Spanish US$20 million for the latter's ex-possession: this was ratified by the Paris Peace Treaty of 10 December 1898. The USA refused to

recognise General Aguinaldo as president of the revolutionary government, so once more, the Filipinos had to begin the struggle against foreign domination. But this time they failed, and in the end they came to an arrangement both sides could accept.
Finally, after President Roosevelt recognised the newly drawn-up Philippine constitution, Manuel L Quezon was sworn in as President of the Philippine Commonwealth.

World War II

After the attack on Pearl Harbour, Japanese troops landed on Luzon and conquered Manila on 2 January 1942. The Filipino and US troops suffered defeats with high casualty rates in battles at Corregidor Island and on the Bataan Peninsula. This brought about the brutal Japanese military rule which continued until 1944, when General Douglas MacArthur fulfilled his promise to return and liberate the Philippines from the Japanese. US troops landed at Leyte and, under their lead, the islands were recaptured from the Japanese forces.
On 4 July 1946 the Philippines received full independence as had been promised in 1935 by the US. The first president of the republic was Manuel Roxas. His successors were Elpidio Quirino, Ramon Magsaysay, Carlos Garcia and Diosdado Macapagal.

The Marcos Years

Ferdinand E Marcos was elected to power in 1965 and, unusually for the Philippines, was re-elected in 1969. The Marcos government found the country in a chaotic state. Corruption and crime had become the order of the day. People talked of the 'Wild East'.
In 1972 Marcos declared martial law and began to implement his concept of the 'New Society'. Within a short time some changes were apparent - guns disappeared from the streets, crime decreased and improvements in public health were made, but the land reform law of October 1972 only partly abolished land rents.
In foreign policy, the joining of international organisations like the Economic & Social Commission for Asia & the Pacific (ESCAP), Asian & Pacific Council (ASPAC), Association of South-East Asian Nations (ASEAN) and the Colombo Plan was successful. The Philippines was also a provisional member of the General Agreement on Tariffs & Trade (GATT).
Political peace, tax abatement and low wages were reasons for foreign companies to invest money again in the Philippines from the mid-1970s on. Not all Filipinos agreed with this political peace, and communist guerrillas of the New People's Army (NPA) and members of the Moro National Liberation Front (MNLF) tried to force change through violence. The opposition parties, the Democratic Socialist Party and the Philippine Democratic Party, had no influence on internal politics. The Communist Party of the Philippines was prohibited. Although martial law was abolished in January 1981, Marcos could continue his dictatorial form of government with so-called presidential decrees.
In the presidential election of June 1981, Marcos was confirmed as head of state for another six years, but the result was contested and allegations of vote-rigging were loud and many. Parliamentary elections were held in 1984 and the opposition United Nationalist Democratic Organisation (UNIDO, an amalgamation of 12 parties) won 63 of the 200 seats. The independent candidates won eight seats, and the government party, Kulisang Bagong Lipunan (KBL) - New Society Movement -, won 125, including the mandate for 17 which were directly decided by Marcos.

Dr Jose Rizal

The Philippine National Hero

Jose Rizal was born on 19 June 1861 in Calamba, Laguna. Prior to moving to Manila in 1872, where he studied painting and sculpting, he was educated by his mother and private tutors. Once at the Santo Tomas University, he started his studies in medicine, philosophy and literary science. He continued at Madrid in 1882, where he also finally graduated. To further his education, he spent the next few years amongst others in Paris, Heidelberg, London and Berlin. During this time he came into contact with European scholars and Philippine artists and patriots of the same political persuasion as himself, who shared his dream of independence and a sense of national dignity. In 1887 his famous book *Noli Mi Tangere* (Do Not Touch Me) was published in Berlin. This socio-political work was written as a *roman à clef* and grappled with the issues of the Philippine reality and the suppressive policies of the Spanish colonial power. Although the Spanish censor banned the dissemination of the book, its stirring message achieved its aim. His second book, *El Filibustrismo*, as well as scores of inflammatory essays calling for an uprising against the Spanish were secretly distributed in the Philippines, finding a powerful resonance there.

In 1892 Rizal risked returning home and together with friends he founded the reform movement, the Liga Filipina, on 3 July. After his arrest only four days later, Rizal was exiled for four years to Dapitan on Mindanao. He used the time in exile to develop his artistic and scientific skills and for developing various pieces of technical apparatus and equipment. He also learned several Philippine languages and worked as a teacher and doctor.

When the Philippine Revolution broke out in 1896, Rizal was condemned to death by a military tribunal in Manila for inciting people to revolt. On 30 December 1896, in front of the walls of Intramuros, now known as Rizal Park, he was executed by firing squad.

In the night before his execution Jose Rizal sat in his cell in Fort Santiago, Manila, and penned a farewell poem to the Philippine people and to his country:

My Last Farewell *(Mi Ultimo Adios).*

Farewell, my adored land, region of the sun caressed,
Pearl of the Orient Sea, our Eden lost,
With gladness I give you my life, sad and repressed;
And were it more brilliant, more fresh and at its best,
I would still give it to you for your welfare at most.

If over my tomb some day, you would see blow,
A simple humble flow'r amidst thick grasses,
Bring it up to your lips and kiss my soul so,
And under the cold tomb, I may feel on my brow,
Warmth of your breath, a whiff of your tenderness.

Cory Aquino

A deciding factor in the surprise success of the opposition was not only the dissatisfaction of a large proportion of the population over the state of the economy, but also the response of many voters to the murder of the liberal opposition politician and popular former senator Benigno Aquino upon his return from exile on 21 August 1983. This, more than anything, sharpened the political awareness of all levels of society and moved hundreds of thousands of people to protest. The snap election planned for 7 February 1986 saw the opposition unite for the first time under Aquino's widow, Corazon 'Cory' Aquino of the Philippine Democratic Party (PDP-Laban), and her vice-presidential running mate Salvador Laurel, leader of UNIDO. They were pitted against the team of Marcos and Tolentino.

In the past Marcos had been in a position to decide more or less the outcome of the election, but this time events were being closely monitored by both internal and external sources. Cory Aquino rallied the people in a campaign of civil unrest and national protest of the non-violent Gandhian kind. Banks, newspapers and companies favoured by Marcos were boycotted and 'People Power' began to make itself felt.

The last straw for Marcos came when Defence Minister Juan Ponce Enrile and Armed Forces Vice-Chief of Staff Fidel Ramos joined the Aquino camp together with military units. Tens of thousands of unarmed civilians barricaded the streets, preventing loyalist soldiers from intervening and causing a major bloodbath.

Following the election, both candidates claimed victory and on 25 February both Ferdinand Marcos and Cory Aquino were sworn in as president in separate ceremonies. Later that same day Marcos fled into exile in Hawaii and Cory Aquino stood unopposed. She annulled the constitution and abrogated parliament.

This historic change of leadership was not really a revolution and it hardly touched the country's elite and the structures of power. Nevertheless, through her ousting of the dictator, Corazon Aquino became a national hero and an international celebrity. She restored democracy to the Philippines by re-establishing the political institutions of a democratic parliament and a supreme court. Although she commanded considerable political power at the beginning of her presidency, she did not manage to bring either the military or the feudal families under control. The president could only partly fulfil the Filipinos' hopes for well-being and democracy. The overwhelming majority of the population, who live under conditions of appalling poverty barely above the survival line, did not profit in any way from the short-lived period of economic expansion in 1987 and 1988. Exactly the opposite: their economic misery became more pronounced from year to year. The much vaunted land reform, eagerly awaited by the numerous landless Filipinos, never really got off the ground.

During her period of office as president and commander-in-chief of the Armed Forces, Corazon Aquino survived seven attempted coups. However, it is clear she would not have survived until the last day of the six-year legislative period as head of state without the support of her defence minister General Fidel Ramos, and his influence on the military establishment. As a demonstration of her gratitude for his loyalty, she proposed Ramos to the Filipino voters as her candidate of choice to succeed her as president.

Ramos' Effective Term of Office

As a Protestant, Fidel Ramos could not count on the support of the influential

Catholic Church as he went into the election campaign that led to his narrow victory in mid-1992. The favoured candidate of the clergy, the legal expert and former judge Miriam Defensor Santiago, and the government spokesman Ramon Mitra failed to get elected, as did the candidates from the camp of the late President Marcos, who had died in exile: the magnate Eduardo Cojuanco and the eccentric Imelda Marcos.

President Ramos took office on 1 July 1992 and shortly thereafter announced his cabinet, an able group of experts in their respective fields. The goals announced by the government were ambitious. The main areas to be tackled were the creation of jobs, revitalisation of the economy, reduction of the enormous foreign debt of US$32 billion and the re-establishment of a political climate in which corrupt civil servants could have no opportunity to get rich by plundering the state.

In addition, a reliable electricity service had to be established as soon as possible. In the early 1990s so-called brownouts paralysed the country daily for several hours. The responsibility for this economically unacceptable state of affairs lay with the antiquated and badly (if at all) serviced power stations that broke down regularly. The failure of the Aquino administration to produce a far-sighted energy policy was one of the most serious negative points in the sobering catalogue of problems the President inherited from his predecessor.

Equipped with sweeping new powers, he soon moved to secure the ailing energy sector, encourage foreign investment and, in a surprise move, even lifted the ban on the Communist Party of the Philippines in an attempt to end the guerrilla war draining the resources of the country. In 1996, Ramos finally succeeded in concluding a peace agreement with the Moslem freedom movement, the Moro National Liberation Front (MNLF), after much tough negotiating. The agreement foresaw the rebels being granted considerable autonomy in several provinces on the island of Mindanao. With a stroke of the pen, a quarter century of underground fighting was ended in the southern Philippines - on paper, at least. In reality, however, the apparent peace was only the calm before the storm, for fundamentalist Moslem splinter groups, above all the extremist MILF (Moslem Islamic Liberation Front), have no intention of giving up their avowed goal of creating an independent Islamic state on Philippine territory. They will not be satisfied with the autonomy granted by the Philippine government to the Moslems in the Autonomous Region of Moslem Mindanao (ARMM), comprising the provinces of Lanao del Sur, Maguindanao, Sulu and Tawi-Tawi.

Joseph Erap' Estrada

In his six-year term of office, President Fidel Ramos was able to bring about visible progress in the country's affairs and would most probably have been re-elected if this had been possible. However, the Philippine Constitution does not permit the incumbent a second period in office. During the run-up to the presidential election in 1998, it soon became clear that President Ramos's populist vice-president Joseph Ejercito Estrada was going to be his successor. On polling day Estrada received a convincing 27% more of the vote than his nearest competitor Jose de Venecia. The ever-popular Gloria Macapagal-Arroyo was elected vice-president of the country. Estrada received most of his votes from simple citizens, almost definitely because of the Robin Hood image he had earned in his former career as a film star. (Erap' is backwards slang for pare', meaning buddy, or pal.) On the other hand, the cultural

Provinces

1 Batanes *(Capital: Basco)*
2 Ilocos Norte *(Laoag)*
3 Apayao *(Kabugao)*
4 Cagayan *(Tuguegarao)*
5 Abra *(Bangued)*
6 Kalinga *(Tabuk)*
7 Ilocos Sur *(Vigan)*
8 Mountain Province *(Bontoc)*
9 Isabela *(Ilagan)*
10 Ifugao *(Lagawe)*
11 La Union *(San Fernando)*
12 Benguet *(La Trinidad)*
13 Nueva Vizcaya *(Bayombong)*
14 Quirino *(Cabarroguis)*
15 Pangasinan *(Lingayen)*
16 Zambales *(Iba)*
17 Tarlac *(Tarlac)*
18 Nueva Ecija *(Palayan)*
19 Aurora *(Baler)*
20 Pampanga *(San Fernando)*
21 Bulacan *(Malolos)*
22 Bataan *(Balanga)*
23 Rizal *(Antipolo)*
24 Cavite *(Tres Martires)*
25 Laguna *(Santa Cruz)*
26 Quezon *(Lucena)*
27 Batangas *(Batangas)*
28 Camarines Norte *(Daet)*
29 Camarines Sur *(Naga)*
30 Catanduanes *(Virac)*
31 Marinduque *(Boac)*
32 Mindoro Oriental *(Calapan)*
33 Mindoro Occidental *(Mamburao)*
34 Albay *(Legaspi)*
35 Sorsogon *(Sorsogon)*
36 Romblon *(Romblon)*
37 Masbate *(Masbate)*
38 Northern Samar *(Catarman)*
39 Samar *(Catbalogan)*
40 Eastern Samar *(Borongan)*
41 Biliran *(Naval)*
42 Aklan *(Kalibo)*
43 Capiz *(Roxas)*
44 Antique *(San Jose)*
45 Iloilo *(Iloilo)*
46 Guimaras *(San Miguel)*
47 Leyte *(Tacloban)*
48 Southern Leyte *(Maasin)*
49 Cebu *(Cebu)*
50 Negros Occidental *(Bacolod)*
51 Negros Oriental *(Dumaguete)*
52 Bohol *(Tagbilaran)*
53 Palawan *(Puerto Princesa)*
54 Siquijor *(Siquijor)*
55 Camiguin *(Mambajao)*
56 Surigao del Norte *(Surigao)*
57 Surigao del Sur *(Tandag)*
58 Agusan del Norte *(Butuan)*
59 Misamis Oriental *(Cagayan de Oro)*
60 Misamis Occidental *(Oroquieta)*
61 Zamboanga del Norte *(Dipolog)*
62 Zamboanga del Sur *(Pagadian)*
63 Zamboanga Sibugay *(Ipil)*
64 Lanao del Norte *(Tubod)*
65 Lanao del Sur *(Marawi)*
66 Bukidnon *(Malaybalay)*
67 Agusan del Sur *(Prosperidad)*
68 Davao del Norte *(Tagum)*
69 Compestela Valley *(Nabunturan)*
70 Davao Oriental *(Mati)*
71 Maguindanao *(Shariff Aguak)*
72 Cotabato *(Kidapawan)*
73 Davao del Sur *(Digos)*
74 Sultan Kudarat *(Isulan)*
75 South Cotabato *(Koronadal)*
76 Sarangani *(Alabel)*
77 Basilan *(Isabela)*
78 Sulu *(Jolo)*
79 Tawi-Tawi *(Bongao)*

Regions

I Ilocos
II Cagayan Valley
III Central Luzon
IV Southern Tagalog
V Bicol
VI Western Visayas
VII Central Visayas
VIII Eastern Visayas
IX Western Mindanao
X Northern Mindanao
XI Southern Mindanao
XII Central Mindanao
A Cordillera Autonomous Region
B Caraga
C Autonomous Region in Muslim Mindanao

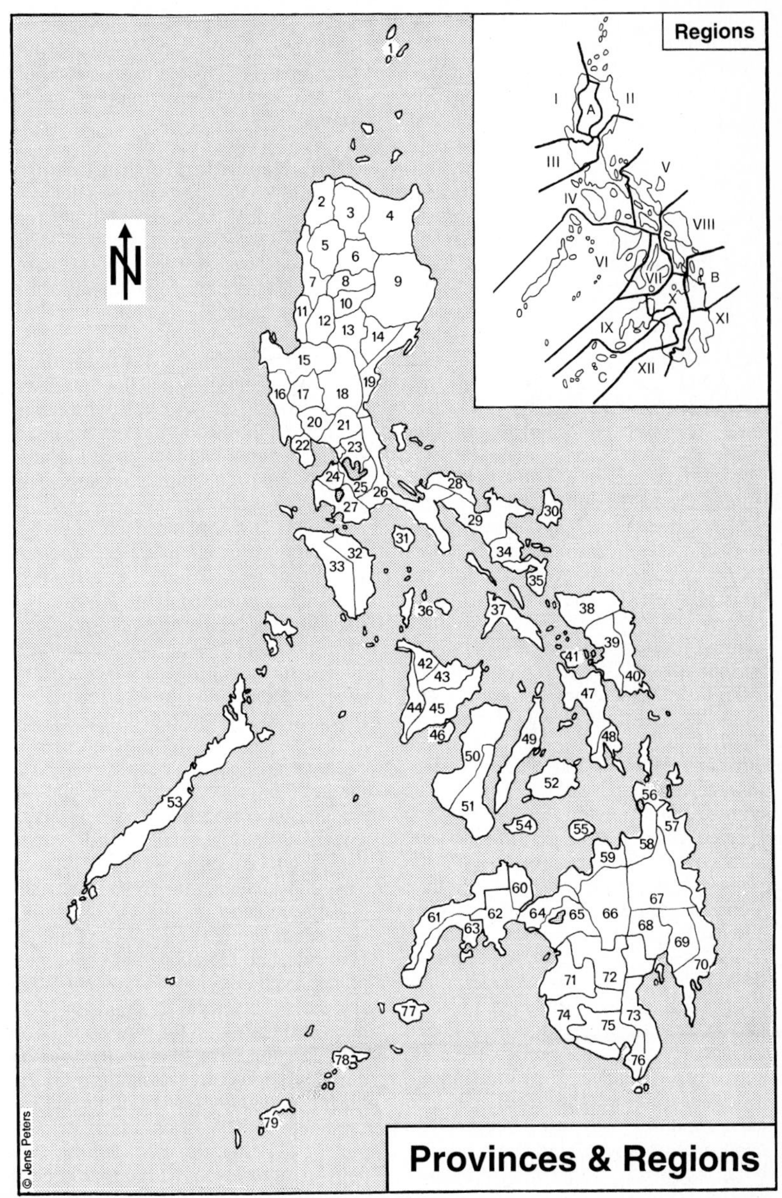

Regions
I
II
A
III
V
IV
VIII
VI
VII
B
X
XI
IX
XII
C
N
1
2
3
4
5
6
7
8
9
10
11
12
13
14
15
16
17
18
19
20
21
22
23
24
25
26
27
28
29
30
31
32
33
34
35
36
37
38
39
40
41
42
43
44
45
46
47
48
49
50
51
52
53
54
55
56
57
58
59
60
61
62
63
64
65
66
67
68
69
70
71
72
73
74
75
76
77
78
79
© Jens Peters
Provinces & Regions

and economic elite of the country remained sceptical about him.
Estrada declared his most important priorities as president to be the fight against corruption and nepotism, economic reforms to improve inward investment, and improving the situation of the poor and rural citizens. His heart was obviously not in the fight, for President Estrada never missed an opportunity to fill his own pockets. Eventually, Luis Singson, a former drinking buddy of the president and governor of the province of Ilocos Sur, publicly accused him of diverting large amounts of money from tobacco tax to his own accounts and of being involved in running the popular, and illegal, gambling game Jueteng. Shortly thereafter, the opposition against Estrada solidified. Under the leadership of Gloria Macapagal-Arroyo, who had demonstratively resigned from the cabinet, the opposition initiated proceedings for the impeachment of the president. Witnesses were willing to confirm their claims in court that the president had stashed away 3.3 billion pesos (around US$70 million) in several secret bank accounts. Documentary evidence was handed over to prosecutors in a sealed envelope. However, 11 of the 21 senators voted against the opening of the controversial envelope, and Estrada seemed to be about to get off scot-free. But he was not reckoning with the power of the people. They showed they were not going to stand by passively, and within a few hours the streets of Manila were filled with hundreds of thousands of protestors demanding his resignation. As had happened 15 years previously when 'People Power' hounded President Marcos out of office, the pressure on the president grew until finally his cabinet resigned, the military changed sides, and the way was free for the hand-over of power. Three months after being removed from office, Estrada was arrested and a legal investigation into the accusations made against him was initiated. This led to massive public demonstrations of support by his supporters.

GMA - New Hope for the Country

Gloria Macapagal-Arroyo was declared new president of the Philippines as 'Edsa-Dos', the second People Power movement, was still making itself felt. On her way to power the devout Christian was crucially supported by the Catholic Church which had always been offended by the feudal way of life of her drinking, gambling and womanising predecessor. Her top priority on taking office was to restore order in the country, for Estrada had instigated the most serious crisis in confidence since the Marcos years.
Although GMA as head of state was not going to be able to solve the economic problems overnight, her competence as an economist and the fact she was the daughter of an eminent ex-president of the country meant she was initially able to spread confidence. But it didn't take long for reality to assert itself, for it's particularly difficult in the Philippines to force through sweeping changes against the people who hold the real power. So her high hopes of rooting out corruption, attracting major inward investment and turning round the ailing economy were all dashed. This may be one of the reasons why she announced early on that she would not be a candidate in the 2004 election.
However, in October 2003 she surprised everybody by announcing that she *did* in fact want to stand for election (Remember: In the Philippines you have to expect the unexpected!). Over the course of the campaign Gloria Macapagal-Arroyo overtook her fellow candidate and the strongest of her opponents, Fernando Poe Junior, the popular actor who had initially been

leading in the polls. But victory was hers and she can now remain in office until 2010. The TV journalist and senator, Noli de Castro, was elected Vice-President.

Government & Politics

The Philippines has a constitutional form of government. The legislative power is vested in Congress, composed of the Senate (Upper House; 24 senators) and the House of Representatives (Lower House; 250 members of congress). The president is elected directly by the voters for a six-year term.

The administration of the Republic of the Philippines (Republica ng Pilipinas) is subdivided into 15 regions (plus Metro Manila as the National Capital Region) consisting of 79 provinces. Every province coomprises a provincial capital and several municipalities, which are in turn made up of village communities or barangays.

A barangay with an elected head/administrator, the 'barangay captain', is the smallest socio-political administration unit in the Philippines. The term 'barangay' originates from the time the archipelago was settled between 500 BC and 1500 AD. During that time, a barangay (or balanghai) was a large seaworthy outrigger boat which could carry up to 90 passengers and was used by Malayan peoples to migrate to the Philippines. The crews of these boats were probably social groups like village communities or extended families.

National Flag & National Anthem

The national flag of the Philippines has a white triangle on the left. On either side tapering off to the left are two stripes, the top one blue, the bottom one red. The white triangle contains three five-point stars and a sun with eight rays. The sun symbolises freedom and its eight rays represent the first eight provinces that revolted against Spanish colonial rule. The stars symbolise the three geographical divisions of the Philippines: Luzon, the Visayas and Mindanao. The blue stripe stands for the equality and unity of the people. The red stripe (placed on top in wartime) symbolises the readiness of the Filipinos to fight to the death for their country.

On 12 June 1898, from the balcony of his house in Cavite, General Emilio Aguinaldo declared the independence of the Philippines. On this day the Philippine national flag was raised and the Philippine national anthem played for the first time. In the form of a march, the *Marcha Nacional Filipina* anthem was composed by Julian Felipe and the words were written by Jose Palma.

Economy

The politics of stability of the Ramos government in the 1990s were responsible for impressive growth in both inward and internal investment, leading to a remarkable period of economic growth in the country. These well thought-out, prudent policies showed their value when in mid-1997 Thailand experienced a serious economic and currency crisis that threatened to drag the Philippines down with it. The peso did lose around 20% in value, but the country was well able to weather the storm. Thanks to high foreign currency reserves, the government was neither forced to introduce swingeing spending cuts nor negotiate expensive loans. On the other hand, the 21st century began modestly for the Philippine economy, with a flattening off in growth due largely to the Mindanao conflict and the high price of crude oil.

In May 2004 the rate of inflation was 4.5%.

Fishing & Agriculture

About two-thirds of Filipinos live by fishing, agriculture and forestry. A significant contribution to their diet comes from ocean, coast and freshwater fishing. Rice is the most important agricultural product. The development of new varieties of rice at the International Rice Research Institute in Los Baños, improvements in methods of cultivation and enlargement of the area of cultivation have brought the Philippines closer to self-sufficiency in food production.

The main products for export are coconuts (copra), abaca (Manila hemp), tobacco, bananas, pineapples and recently also cut flowers, including orchids.

Cattle Farming

Cattle farming is still relatively undeveloped. Poultry, pigs, sheep and goats are reared for meat, while buffaloes serve mainly as work animals.

Mineral Resources

The most important minerals are chrome, iron, copper, coal, nickel, gypsum, sulphur, mercury, asbestos, marble and salt. Test drillings for oil have proved successful. Positive development in this sector, so important for providing the country's energy requirements, could considerably reduce their dependence on imports. Every year about US$2 billion has to be spent on crude oil imports. It is hoped that hydroelectric and geothermal power projects will also go some way towards improving the energy situation. The Philippines is second only to the USA in harnessing geothermal energy sources.

Manufacturing

Manufacturing occurs principally in and around Manila, and contributes 25% of Gross National Product. Leading industries include the production of luxury goods, food, textile and leatherware, although the Philippines also manufactures automobile components. New, growth industries are steel and shipbuilding, while wood processing plants are becoming increasingly important.

Tourism

Tourism is a further source of income and from 1970 to 1980 the tourist flow increased from just 14,000 visitors to over a million. In the years of political unrest from 1983 to 1986 the tourist figures declined, only to shoot up again in 1987, and in 1993 over 1.3 million tourists visited the country. According to official statistics, the number of tourists passed the 2 million mark for the first time in 1996.

Income

The basic level of income is fixed by the state. According to law, the minimum wage in 2004 was P225 per day in the provinces and P275 in Manila, equivalent to about US$4 and US$5 respectively.

There are a number of nationally agreed wage rates but these exist only on paper, considerably few of them being in fact observed. There are also clear discrepancies in income between city and country. Here are some examples of average monthly wages in Manila (in the provinces the wages are on average 30% lower): blue collar workers, US$110; restaurant staff US$85 (without tips); office workers, US$160; policemen, US$200; teachers, US$250; and engineers, US$300. To cover the basic necessities of life in Manila a family of five needs at least 8000 pesos (US$145) per month.

Cost of Living

Prices are considerably higher in the cities than in rural areas. In the country a Filipino meal costs no more than US$2. A bottle of rum (70cl) will set you back all of US$0.90, beer (.33 litres)

Overseas Filipino Workers

Over 7.5 million Filipinos live outside the Philippines. About 3.2 million of them earn sought-after hard currencies as foreign workers, mostly as seamen, housemaids, construction workers, nurses and entertainers. About 2.8 million Filipinos are permanent overseas residents and 1.6 million are temporarily resident in other countries. All together they officially repatriate around US$8 billion every year, and added to this are the considerable sums of money they hold as personal savings. The money the Overseas Filipino Workers (OFW) send home every year makes up about half the annual Philippine turnover in overseas trade. So the 'export' of workers represents an important economic sector, without which living standards in the country would be visibly poorer.

can be bought for the equivalent of US$0.25, and about US$0.20 is charged for soft drinks like Coca-Cola. Naturally everything is a good deal dearer in exclusive restaurants and bars. For instance, you'll pay about US$1.50 for a Coke at the swimming pool of a five-star Manila hotel, while a beer in one of the Makati nightclubs will cost around US$2. See also the chapter 'Travel Planning': *Examples of Costs*.

Ecology & Environment

'What do I care about posterity, what did posterity ever do for me?' You won't hear this on Palawan. On this, the third largest island in the Philippine archipelago, posterity will still be able to enjoy the forests, illegal fishing is mercilessly prosecuted, and the trade in protected animals rigorously prevented. Nowhere else in the country do people show so much consideration for the environment. Friends of nature got wind of the exemplary protection of the Palawan forests, coastal waters and coral reefs, leading to a boom in so-called eco-tourism. Things could be the same in the rest of the country - *could*, and *should*, be.

As with many other areas of South-East Asia, the Philippines environment suffered heavily after WWII with the introduction of large-scale logging and mining operations. Some islands, notably Cebu, were so badly damaged that many of the more vulnerable species became extinct. Most of the larger islands retain their original forest cover only on the rugged mountain tops, which form havens for the plants and animals. Other islands, like Palawan, remain relatively untouched and visitors there can still experience the original Philippines. Tree-felling and slash-and-burn clearing did not take long in the 80s to reduce vast wooded areas to shadows of their former splendour. Only the visible consequences of this selfish plundering of nature - erosion, soil dehydration and climatic changes - managed to rouse the politicians from their torpor.

At the beginning of 1989, all further deforestation was prohibited countrywide by law. Still, in the absence of an effective means of control, it remains to be seen whether this logging ban can bring a halt to the depredations caused by the profiteering timber industry and stop drastic deforestation by *kaingineros* (clearers so called because they create farming land through the *kaingin*, or the slash-and-burn method). On the other hand if there were not so many timber orders from industrialised countries, fewer trees would be felled and whole forests could be saved.

Perhaps it was the catastrophe in Ormoc on the island of Leyte in November 1991 that shook the Filipinos out of their traditional complacency concerning the environment. In the aftermath of a destructive typhoon, enormous masses of water thundered down to the plains from the mountains and caused havoc in the town of Ormoc, killing 5000 and leaving 50,000 homeless. Years of illegal tree-felling in the hills above the town had left the slopes bare and incapable of supporting vegetation. There was nothing left to prevent the topsoil from being swept away by floods, a disaster waiting to happen in a country where massive amounts of rain can fall in short periods.

Although there is a long way to go, government agencies like the Department of Environment and Natural Resources (DENR) are trying to reverse the trend towards putting the economy before the environment - a problem even developed countries are only now coming to terms with. Perhaps it will take a few more natural catastrophes with their painful financial aftermaths, to force the last ignorant person to change their mind.

Another serious problem, again made worse because large amounts of money are involved, are fishing methods using cyanide and dynamite. In the former, cyanide is used to stun tropical fish living amongst coral reefs so they can be collected and shipped off - mostly to Japan. Apart from killing about half of the fish which had been living in the reef, the poison also has a deadly effect on the coral itself. It gradually turns white as it dies and finally ceases to exist as a living entity; an algae-covered corpse. Dynamite has the same effect, but is only apparently more destructive because the damage is immediately obvious to the observer. Both have the result of destroying entire coral reefs, irreplaceable for themselves, but also as a habitat for countless species.

But awareness of the importance of an intact, clean environment is becoming apparent in more and more sections of society. The newspaper *Today* together with other sponsors has published full-page ads with photos of dead fish, appealing to people to stop polluting 'before toxic wastes lead our rivers and lakes to extinction'. The TV station ABS-CBN in its programme *Bantay Kalikasan* (Environmental Watch) regularly gets on the case of polluters and other despoilers of the environment who have been reported to their hotline by concerned citizens. The Department of Interior and Local Government (DILG) has also developed an effective way of awakening environmental awareness. They publish a yearly list of the 'cleanest and greenest towns, cities and provinces'. And it is beginning to matter to people whether their town, city or province comes near the top of the list as clean and green, or at the bottom among the 'dirty dozen'.

As the affluent countries have shown, no country can afford to be complacent about the environment. None of us have been paragons of virtue. The Philippines, with their seemingly intractable problems of poverty and unemployment, can only be commended and encouraged by visitors in their attempt to turn things round.

Flora & Fauna

For many years the Philippine archipelago remained relatively isolated from the rest of the world. This meant that the existing plants and animals could evolve in their particular environment to become unique species.

Flora

The flora includes well over 10,000 species of trees, bushes and ferns, many of

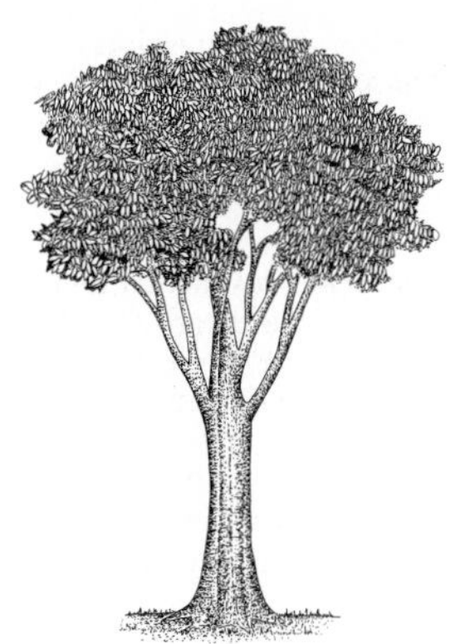

Narra, the Philippine national tree

which are endemic to the Philippines. Most common are pines (in the mountains of North Luzon), palm trees and various kinds of bamboo (along the coasts and in the flat interior). In spite of uncontrolled tree felling in the 80s, the islands of the Philippines are still covered with around 10% tropical rainforest.

The variety of tropical flowers and plants is remarkable. Over 900 species of orchid alone have been counted here, the most strikingly beautiful of which must be the Cattleya and Vanda varieties.

The sweet-scented *sampaguita* was chosen to be the national flower. Filipinos like to wear chains of it around their necks and drape them round the necks of important guests when they greet them.

There is also a broad palette of economically important cash crops, from the coconut palm to rice and sugar cane, as well as many different kinds of tropical fruits.

Fauna

According to the latest estimates of fauna in the Philippines there are over 200 species of mammals, around 580 species of birds, 200 species of reptiles and 100 species of amphibious animals. Amongst those are a handful of unusual and rare species only to be found on one or two islands. It is very likely that others are yet to be discovered.

Mouse Deer *(Tragulus nigricans)*

There are no large predators, and a noticeable number of the endemic species on the islands are smaller animals, like the rare mouse deer in Palawan, which is a midget deer and the smallest species of red deer in the world. Lake Buhi, South Luzon, is the home of the *sinarapan*: they are the smallest edible fish in the world and are not even one cm long. The *tamaraw*, a wild dwarf buffalo with relatively short horns, lives in the mountains of Mindoro. The

Tamaraw *(Anoa mindorensis)*

Love of Animals

The average Filipino doesn't have a close relationship with animals, unlike Western animal lovers, who spoil their little darlings as we all know. The Filipinos don't usually have enough spare money for this kind of luxury. If they do look after animals voluntarily, then only ones that are useful to them: pigs, fish, chickens and - in some regions - dogs, which all end up in the pot, or the lumbering water buffalo, which they set to work for them. Only the latter are actually treated in a friendly fashion.

fist-sized *tarsier*, the smallest primate in existence, and the *tabius*, the second smallest, are likewise at home in the Philippines. Both are on the endangered list, and likely to remain on it, as they are also on the menu of the *haribon*, or Philippine eagle, one of the largest eagles and rarest in the world. It's their bad luck that the country's national bird - of which only 100 are left in the wild - is partial to small primates.

Parrots are mainly found in Palawan, and colourful butterflies abound in Cebu, Mindanao and Palawan. Also well represented in the Philippines are the ubiquitous cockroaches and mosquitoes. The latter are a favourite food of the little gecko, which is very popular as a household pet. The largest reptile of the lizard family found in the Philippines is the *waran* monitor which can grow to be two metres long.

Philippine crocodiles, the largest of the wide range of reptiles here, are rare. Although they still exist on Mindanao and Palawan, they are on the endangered list. As in all tropical biotopes, there is a great variety of snakes: especially noteworthy are the metre-long python which kills its victims by suffocation, and the poisonous sea snake.

There is an unbelievable array of fish, seashells and corals. Sea cows, whale sharks, dolphins and whales are amongst the largest sea animals in Philippine waters. The cumbersome water buffalo, the *carabao*, is the most important domestic animal of the Filipinos and is not called the 'farmer's friend' for nothing.

Endangered Species

Apart from those already mentioned under Fauna, the following animals are on the endangered list: the scaly anteater, Palawan peacock pheasant, Luzon bleeding-heart dove, Palawan bearcat, flying lemur, flying fox, hawksbill turtle, green sea turtle and estuarine crocodile.

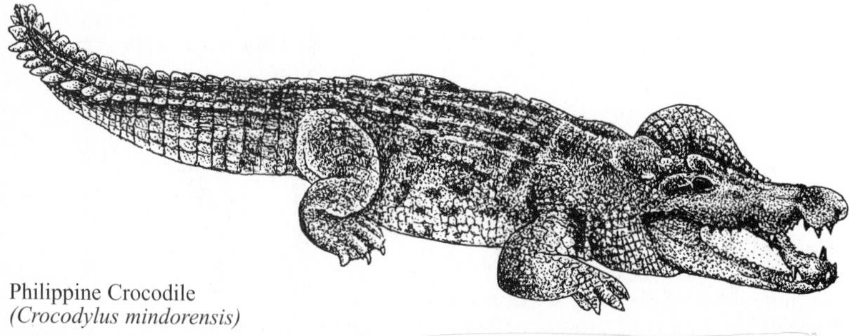

Philippine Crocodile
(Crocodylus mindorensis)

Philippine Orchids

Amasiella philippinensis

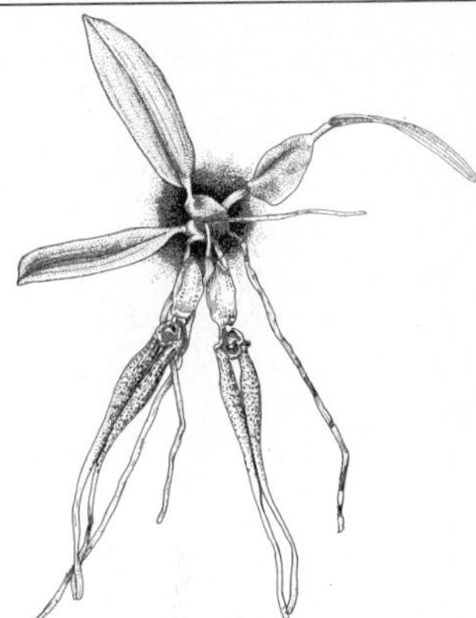

Cirrhopetalum biflorum

Dipodium paludosum

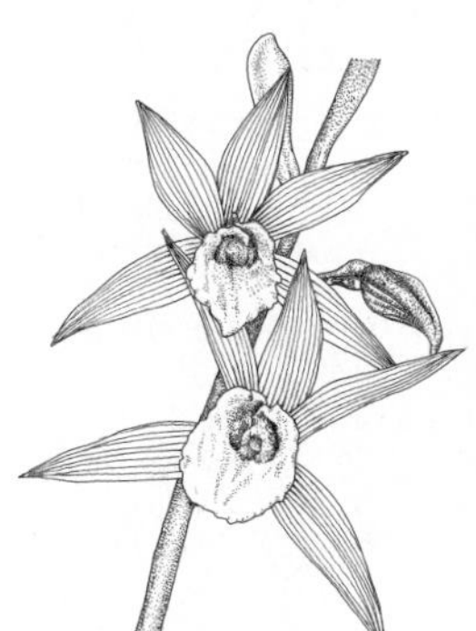

Phajus tankervilleae

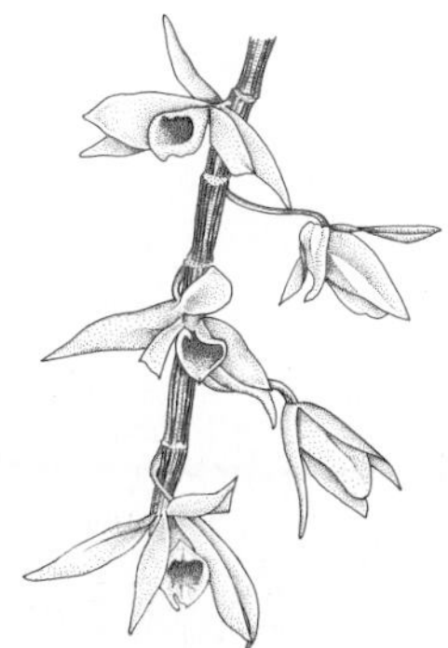

Dedrobium anosmum

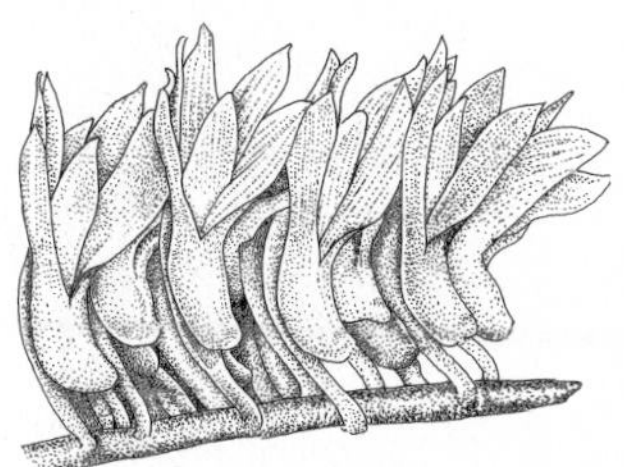

Dendrobium secundem

Palm trees of the Philippines

Screw Palm *(Pandanus tectorius)*

Sago Palm *(Metroxylon sagu)*

Pitogo Palm *(Cycas rumpii)*

Coconut Tree
(Cocos nucifera)

Nipa Palm *(Nypa fruticans)*

Fan Palm
(Corypha elata)

Royal Palm *(Roystonia regia)*

Butterflies of the Philippines

Papilio trojana

Papilio doson gyndes

Pantoporia maenas semperi

Graphium agamemnon agamemnon

Salatura genutia

Demoleus demoleus

Troides magellanus

Papilio idaeoides

Graphium anthipathes itamputi

Zeuxidia semperi

Fish of the Philippines

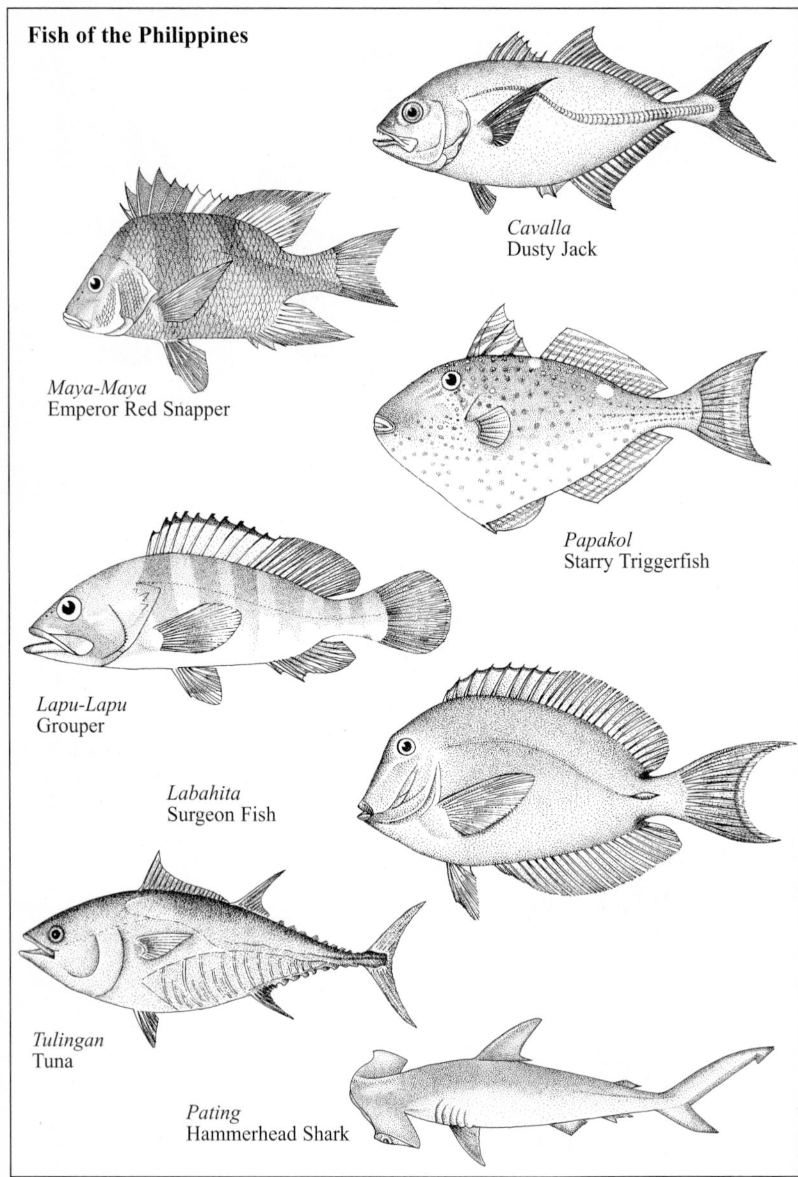

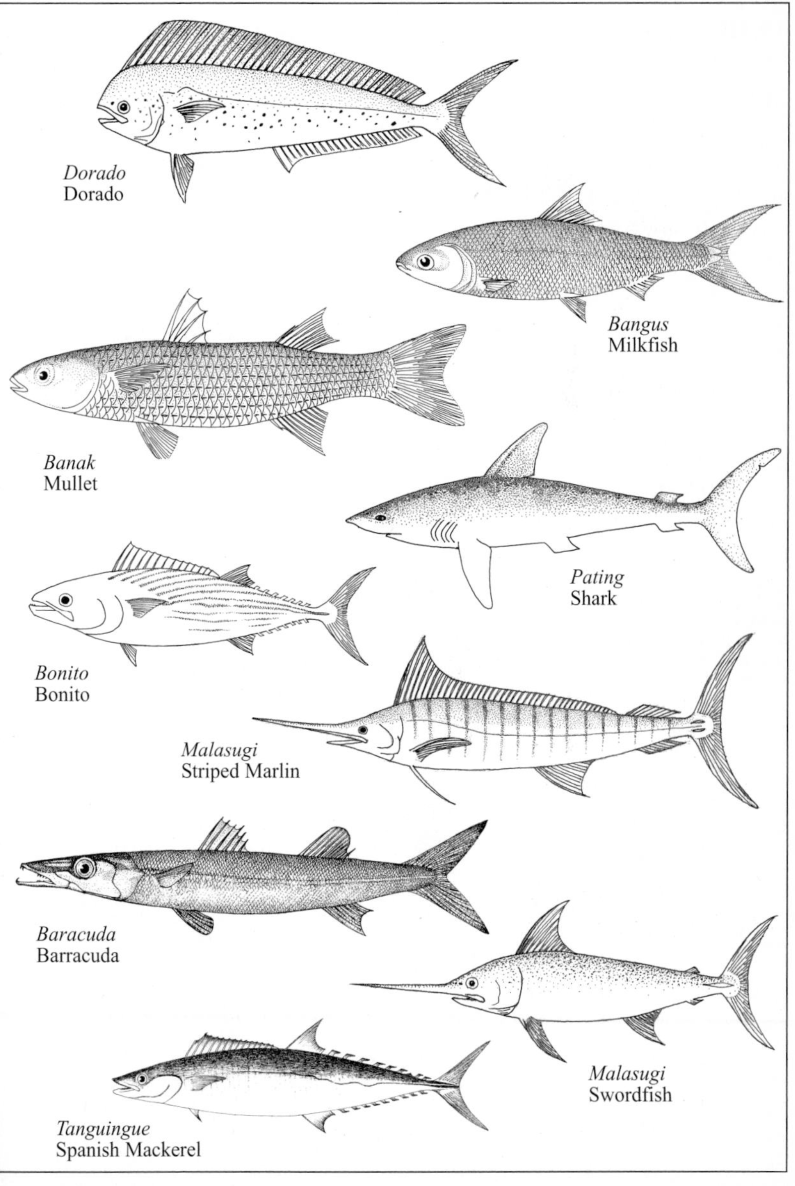
Dorado
Dorado
Bangus
Milkfish
Banak
Mullet
Pating
Shark
Bonito
Bonito
Malasugi
Striped Marlin
Baracuda
Barracuda
Malasugi
Swordfish
Tanguingue
Spanish Mackerel

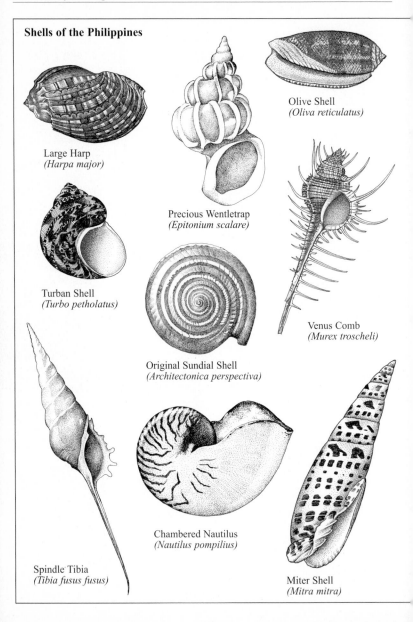

Shells of the Philippines

Large Harp
(Harpa major)

Precious Wentletrap
(Epitonium scalare)

Olive Shell
(Oliva reticulatus)

Turban Shell
(Turbo petholatus)

Original Sundial Shell
(Architectonica perspectiva)

Venus Comb
(Murex troscheli)

Spindle Tibia
(Tibia fusus fusus)

Chambered Nautilus
(Nautilus pompilius)

Miter Shell
(Mitra mitra)

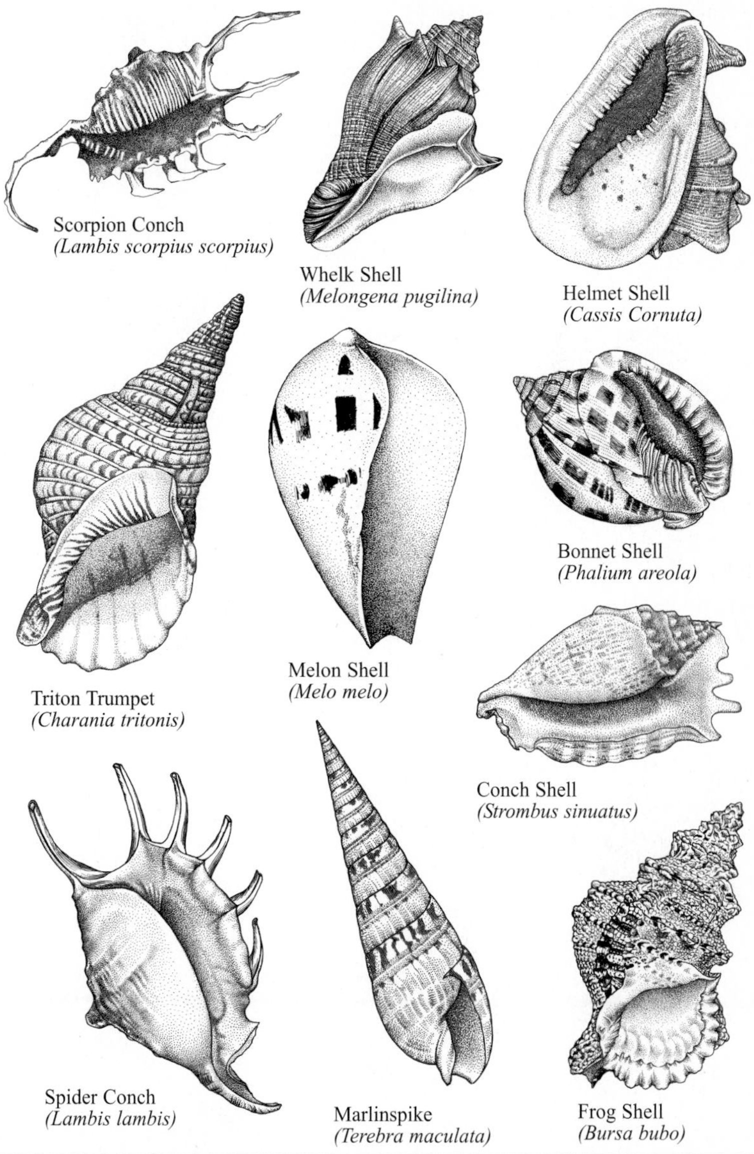

Scorpion Conch
(Lambis scorpius scorpius)

Whelk Shell
(Melongena pugilina)

Helmet Shell
(Cassis Cornuta)

Triton Trumpet
(Charania tritonis)

Melon Shell
(Melo melo)

Bonnet Shell
(Phalium areola)

Conch Shell
(Strombus sinuatus)

Spider Conch
(Lambis lambis)

Marlinspike
(Terebra maculata)

Frog Shell
(Bursa bubo)

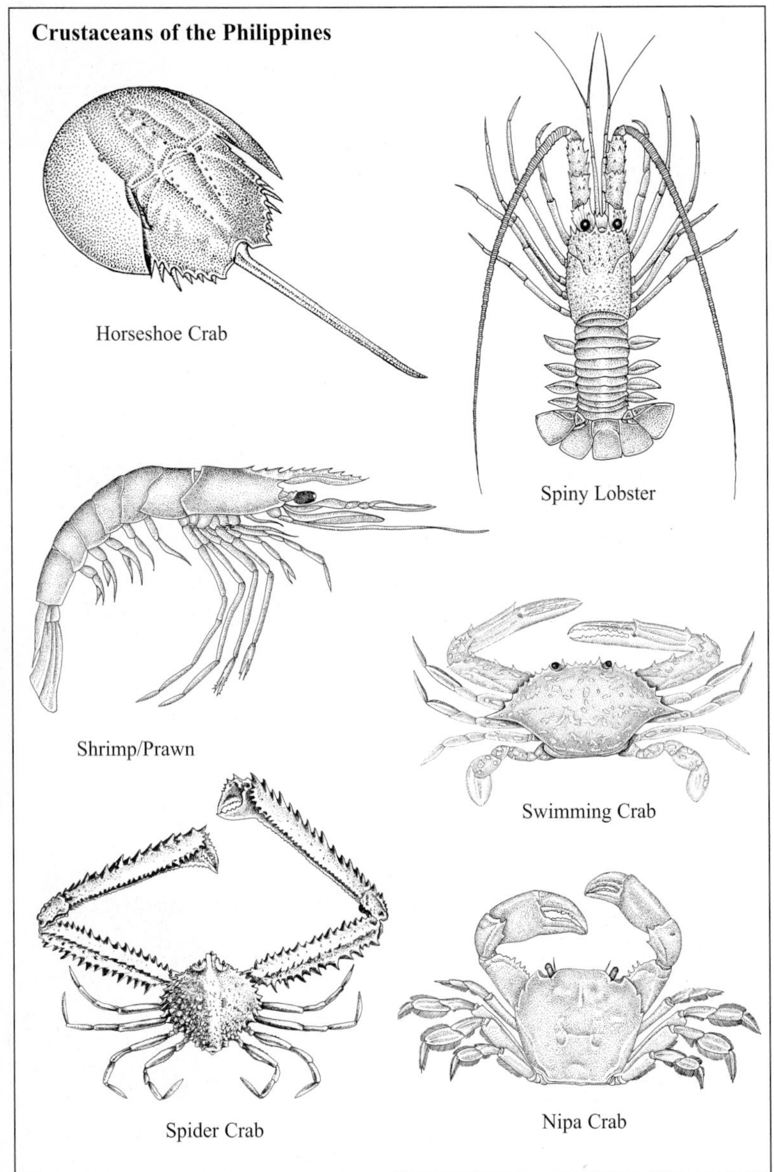
Crustaceans of the Philippines
Horseshoe Crab
Spiny Lobster
Shrimp/Prawn
Swimming Crab
Spider Crab
Nipa Crab

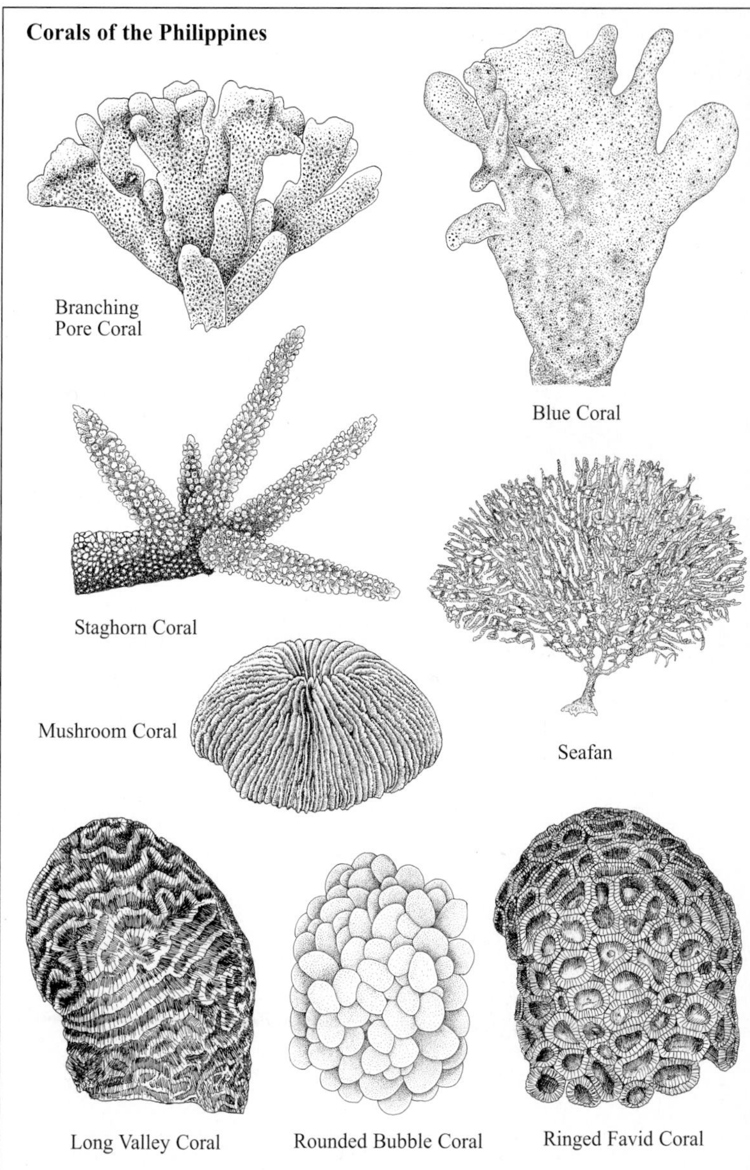
Corals of the Philippines
Branching
Pore Coral
Blue Coral
Staghorn Coral
Seafan
Mushroom Coral
Long Valley Coral
Rounded Bubble Coral
Ringed Favid Coral

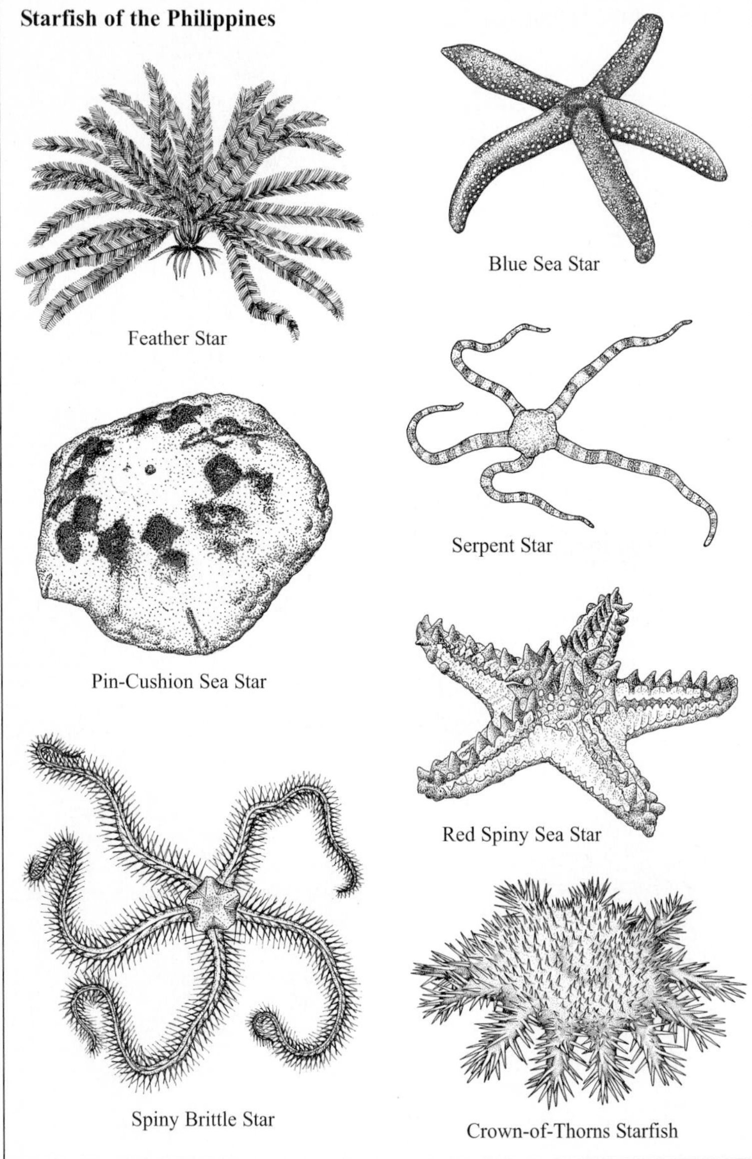
Starfish of the Philippines
Feather Star
Blue Sea Star
Serpent Star
Pin-Cushion Sea Star
Red Spiny Sea Star
Spiny Brittle Star
Crown-of-Thorns Starfish

Birds of the Philippines

Philippine Trogon
(Harpactes ardens)

Philippine Eagle
(Pithecophaga jefferyi)

Palawan Hornbill
(Anthracoceros marchei)

Seloputo Owl
(Strix seloputo wiepkeni)

Philippine Kingfisher
(Halcyon chloris qullaris)

1 Balbalasang Balbalan NP
2 Mt Data NP
3 Mt Pulag NP
3 Hundred Islands NRA
5 Aurora Memorial NRA
6 Mt Arayat NRA
7 Bataan NP
8 Taal Volcano NP
9 Mt Banahaw-Cristobal NRA
10 Quezon NP
11 Bicol NRA
12 Mt Isarog NP
13 Mayon Volcano NP
14 Bulusan Volcano NP
15 Calavite NWS
16 Lake Naujan NP
17 Mt Ilig-Mt. Baco NWS
18 Calauit SNR
19 Apo Reef NP
20 Mt Guiting-Guiting NP
21 Cuyo 'English Game' SNR
22 Cleopatra Needle NWS
23 St Paul Subterranean NP
24 Mt Bantalingahan NWS
25 Ursula Island SNR
26 Tubbataha Reefs NP
27 Turtle Island NWS
28 Sohoton Natural Bridge NRA
29 Lake Danao NRA
30 Mahagnao Volcano NRA
31 Mt Kanlaon NP
32 Twin Lakes NP
33 Datu Sikatuna NP
34 Mt Malindang NP
35 Mt Kilanglad NP
36 Agusan Marsh NWS
37 Philippine Eagle NWS
38 Mt Apo NP
39 Liguasan Marsh NWS

National Parks

One job given to the Bureau of Forest Development (BFD) which was established in 1973 as the central environmental authority, was to take care of and maintain certain forested areas. Their solution was to set up over 30 protected areas, including rainforests, coral reefs and game reserves. These areas are classified as follows:
NP = National Park/Marine Park; a relatively large area with largely intact nature.
NRA = National Recreation Area; an official leisure and recreation area.
NWS = Nature Reserve/Wildlife Sanctuary; a protected area for wildlife, only accessible to the public in exceptional cases.
SNR = Strict Nature Reserve; a nature reserve established for research into flora and fauna, only accessible to visitors under exceptional circumstances.
The state of the national parks varies from place to place. Mt Apo National Park on Mindanao and St Paul Subterranean National Park on Palawan belong to those where nature is to a large extent still intact. In stark contrast to this, illegal tree felling has left a large area of Bicol National Park totally denuded of any growth.

Forces of Nature

Earthquakes & Volcanoes

The earth's crust, the lithosphere, is only about 70 km thick and is composed of several small and large plates. Earthquakes occur depending on the amount of friction between these horizontal plates. Among the six large plates, also called continental or tectonic plates, are the Eurasian and the Pacific plates and in between is squeezed the small Philippine plate. Strong earthquakes are fairly rare, but there are light tremors from time to time.
One of the worst earthquakes to strike the Philippines last century hit large parts of the country on 16 July 1990.

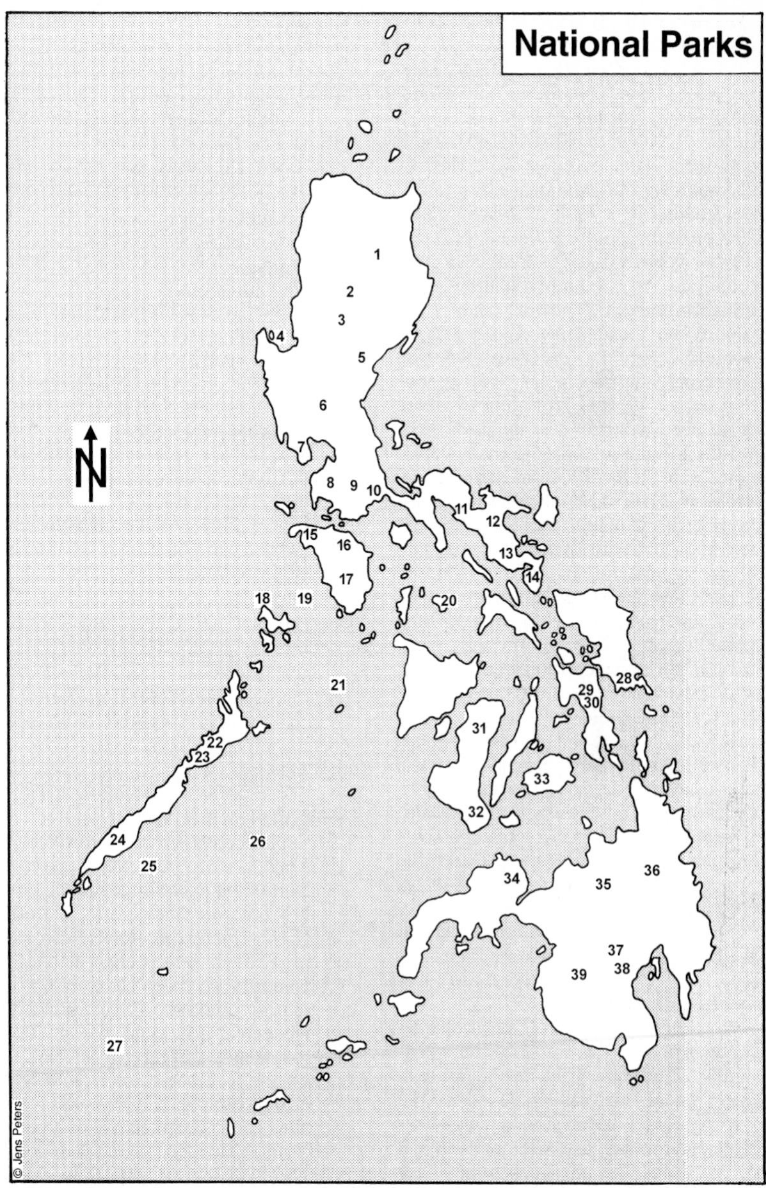
National Parks
1
2
3
4
5
6
7
8
9
10
11
12
13
14
15
16
17
18
19
20
21
22
23
24
25
26
27
28
29
30
31
32
33
34
35
36
37
38
39
N
© Jens Peters

Measuring 7.7 on the Richter scale, the trembler killed over 1600 people and destroyed over 20,000 buildings, leaving more than 100,000 people homeless. Several strong aftershocks caused further damage to roads and houses. The worst affected cities were Baguio, Cabanatuan and Dagupan, all in northern Luzon.

The breaking points in the earth's crust are marked by deep trenches, high mountain ranges and volcanoes. The most prominent volcanic chain ('the ring of fire') leads from Alaska and the Aleutian Islands, past the Siberian Kamchatka Peninsula, the Kuril Islands and Japan to the Philippines, where there are 37 volcanoes, at least 18 of which are active. That dormant volcanoes can suddenly turn dangerously active was proved by the massive eruptions of Mt Pinatubo in June 1991. After 600 years of peace the volcano erupted again, ejecting up to 40 km into the stratosphere huge amounts of ash, mud and rocks, most of which then rained down on the provinces of Pampanga, Tarlac and Zambales, causing widespread destruction in the process. Nearly 900 people lost their lives as a result of the eruption, thousands more lost everything they owned. And there will be more victims in the future when the accumulated detritus from the eruption is loosened by the monsoon rains and pours down from the slopes of the Zambales Mountains into the plains as an avalanche of mud *(lahar)*, to bury countless villages and whole tracts of the countryside.

Typhoons & Fires

Luzon and the northern Visayas also lie in the typhoon belt. Some of the whirlwinds wandering from the Pacific to the Chinese mainland also affect the Philippines. Violent storms can occur from June to January. Although August to November are the peak months for typhoons, there have been rogue typhoons noted as early as March.

Typhoons nearly always cause power failures, and fires (often caused by candles being blown over) frequently follow. Overloaded electrical points, open fires, exploding gas bottles and arson are other causes of the many fires in the Philippines.

Climate

The climate in the Philippines is typically tropical - hot and humid year-round. Although the weather pattern is fairly complex, it can be roughly divided into the dry season - January to June - and the wet season - July to December. January is usually the coolest month and May the hottest, but the average temperature is usually around 25°C throughout the year. However, like everywhere in the world, the Philippines weather is not 100% predictable.

There are five basic climatic zones in the Philippines:

1. Typical South-East Asian monsoon climate. Long dry season from November/December to May and intense rainy period from June to November/December.
2. Short dry season from March to May. Although the rainy season from June to February is long, it is not very intense.
3. No clear-cut dry season, with rain falling during most of the year. The heaviest showers are in the months of November, December and January.
4. No clearly defined dry season. The heaviest rainfall is in the months of April to September.
5. No clearly defined wet or dry season.

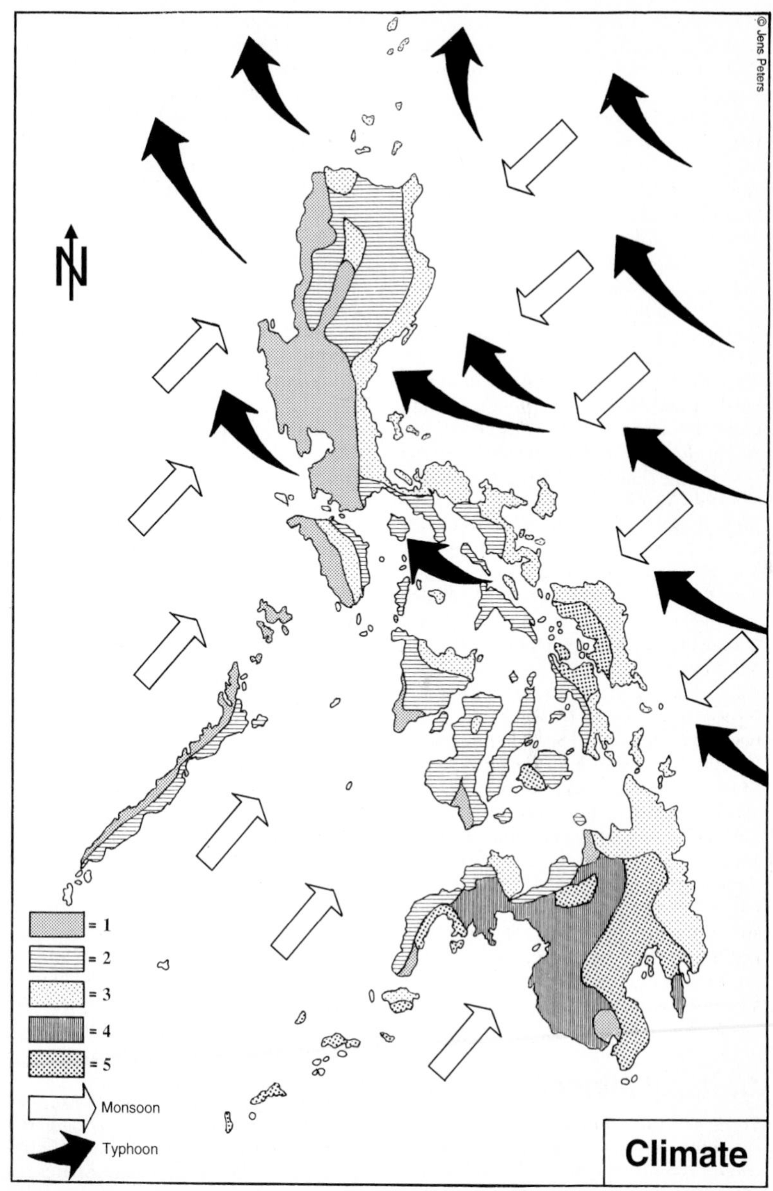

© Jens Peters
N
= 1
= 2
= 3
= 4
= 5
Monsoon
Typhoon
Climate

December to February is the 'cool dry' period while March to May is the 'hot dry' period. You can expect rain every day in July, August and September. In May, Manila usually has daytime temperatures of 35ºC to 39ºC; towards morning it cools to about 25°C. It's not so warm in the mountains of North Luzon. People consider the ideal climate to be that in Baguio, and well-to-do Filipinos have their summer home here.

The Pacific Ocean coastline, comprising Luzon, Samar, Leyte and Mindanao, lies in the path of the north-east tradewinds, ensuring a mild oceanic climate. The north-east monsoon (*amihan*) occurs around December/January to May and brings rain to the Pacific coast but primarily dry pleasant weather to the rest of the land. In North Luzon the Central Cordillera acts as a natural climate divider. During the first weeks of the north-east monsoons in December and January, it may rain on the eastern side of this mountain range, for example, in Banaue; while a little to the west it may be dry, for example, in Bontoc and Sagada.

The south-west monsoon *(hagabat)* blows from June to November/December and brings rain. The typhoons in the Pacific region are predominantly in the Marshall Islands and Caroline Islands. They travel in a north-westerly direction to the Chinese mainland between June and November, mainly in August/September. Typhoons are rare in November, but almost always have catastrophic consequences if they do occur. Including the outer reaches of the typhoon, which precede and follow the storm itself, it only takes a few days to pass through an area.

Cultural Minorities

Some six million Filipinos make up the so-called cultural minority groups or tribal Filipinos, which collectively comprise 12% of the total population. This figure includes the four million Muslims. There are 60 ethnological groups altogether distributed mainly around North Luzon (Bontoc, Ibaloy, Ifugao, Ilokano, Kalinga, Tingguian), Central Luzon (Negritos), Mindoro (Mangyan), and western Mindanao and the Sulu Islands (Muslim). The native people of the Central Cordillera in North Luzon are often referred to collectively as Igorot, which roughly translates as 'people of the mountains'.

It would be beyond the scope of this book to describe all the ethnological groups in the Philippines, but a selection of those which represent an important part of the population structure and which are accessible to foreign travellers follows.

Warning: Before you go into areas set aside for the indigenous people, please examine your motives carefully. If you just want to 'check out the natives' and take pictures for your slide night, you are very misguided. You won't be welcome, and will recognise this fact fairly promptly.

Most cultural minorities are quite friendly to strangers and foreigners. Should you be invited to eat with them, don't refuse without good (for example, religious) reasons, as it could be taken as an insult to the host. On the other hand don't eat too much as the first invitation is usually followed by a second, then a third and so on. If they sing a song for you in the evening, you should have a song on hand to sing in return. Saying that you can't sing or don't know any songs will not get you off the hook as they won't believe you. A song book may be useful if you intend visiting many minorities.

Don't refer to Muslims as Moro. The tag 'Moro' was first used by Spaniards who viewed the Muslims with contempt, probably because the Spaniards resented not being able to bring them under their yoke, as they did with the other population groups. Although many Muslims today proudly name themselves Moro, there are still some who feel discriminated against when a foreigner calls them by this name.

Apayao

The Apayao prefer to live close to the rivers, particularly along the shores of the Apayao and Matalang rivers in the highlands of the Ilocos and Abra provinces in north-west Luzon. They call themselves *isneg* and are the descendants of the feared head-hunters in the Central Cordillera. Their leaders, named *mengal*, are celebrated, wealthy warriors with appropriately large followings. Positions of leadership are not inherited but are accorded the warrior with the greatest ability and charisma. The Apayao believe in ghosts which may take the form of people, animals, giants and monsters. They are protected by Anglabbang, the best and highest god of the head-hunters.

Badjao

The Sulu archipelago in the south of the Philippines, as well as the coast and waters of north-east Borneo and east Indonesia, are the domain of the Badjao (or Bajau, Badjaw). They are sea gypsies, many of whom still live in small boats as extended families. Today, however, most of them have given up a nomadic way of life and have settled in houses built on stilts on coral reefs far out in the ocean or on sandbanks near the coast. No-one knows exactly how many Badjao there are, but the figure is estimated at about 30,000, two-thirds of them living in Philippine waters. They are said in legend to have originated in Johore in Malaysia.

A Badjao boat, or *lipa* (pronounced 'leepa'), is made of wood, is seven to 12m long, and has a removable roof over its central section. The long, thin hull is fitted with individual slats, serving as a flat base on which to stand when punting or spearing fish. The catch is then hung out to dry in the stern. There is a little oven over the stern where fish can be cooked. Apart from seafood, the mainstay of the Badjao diet is cassava: a nourishing stew that is prepared using the cassava tuber, which is rich in starch.

Sea cucumbers are gathered to be sold for use in Chinese restaurants but before they are sold they are cooked, cleaned and dried. In recent years seaweed has developed into a marketable crop. The Badjao, having adopted a settled lifestyle, have planted regular fields of seaweed grown on long stalks under the water around their homes. After the harvest it is stretched out on the platform of the villages to dry, and is later sold to chemical and pharmaceutical companies.

The Badjao try to fit in with their neighbours who, in the Sulu Islands, are the Samal and the Tausug. On the sea the Badjao consider themselves part of a mystical animist world ruled by the great god Tuhan, but many of them closer to land have adopted Islam. Despite Mecca, they are still afraid of *saitan*, the spirits of the winds, the fish, the trees, the hills and so on, because these will cause sickness if they are angry. Only the *jin*, a sort of magician or medicine man, can make contact with these spirits and try to appease them or drive them out and thereby eventually heal the sick.

A marriage celebration lasts for two days and only takes place when there is a full moon. The whole village joins in. After much clanging of *kulintangan* (xylophones), *tambol* (drums) and *agung* (gongs) men and women dance the *igal*, a traditional dance. Polygamy is allowed but is seldom practised. Couples rarely have more than five children.

1 Ita (Negritos)	17 Tagbanua
2 Ilokano	18 Batak
3 Apayao Tingguian	19 Pala'wan
4 Kalinga	20 Tau't Batu
5 Bontoc	21 Jama Mapun (Muslim)
6 Ifugao	22 Manobo
7 Ayta (Negritos)	23 Bagobo
8 Dumagat (Negritos)	24 Mandaya Mansaka
9 Agta (Negritos)	25 T'boli
10 Iraya (Mangyan)	26 Tasaday
11 Alangan (Mangyan)	27 Maranao (Muslim)
12 Tadyawan (Mangyan)	28 Subanon
13 Buhid (Mangyan)	29 Samal (Muslim)
14 Hanunoo (Mangyan)	30 Yakan (Muslim)
15 Ati (Negritos)	31 Badjao
16 Ata (Negritos)	32 Tausug (Muslim)

The dead are buried on special islands which serve as graveyards and these are only visited for burials. Because contact with the spirits of the dead is maintained, the sea people are tied to the land. Before burial the corpse is washed and wrapped in a white sheet. As well as personal treasures, provisions are placed in the grave for the journey to the beyond.

Batak

The Batak are semi-nomadic hunter-gatherers. They live together in many small groups in the hills and coastal regions of north-east Palawan. During the rainy season, groups join together to form larger communities. The *kapitan* (leaders) of the small groups nominate one person, also known as a kapitan, to lead the larger community during this time. The kapitan makes all the important decisions, such as choice of settlement, sharing of work and organisation of gathering activities. During this settled period the Batak also plant crops.

Encroaching civilisation and disease have tragically decimated these shy indigenous people. One can only hope that international attempts being made to stop these people disappearing entirely are successful.

Bontoc

The Bontoc live in thoroughly organised village communities in the Central Cordillera. Their houses are built close to the ground, and every *iti* (village) has two further important accommodation arrangements - *ato* and *olog*. The village elders live in the ato, where social and political decisions are made and religious ceremonies prepared. An ato also serves as a guesthouse and as sleeping quarters for young bachelors. Women are strictly prohibited from entering.

About 10 girls of marriageable age live in the olog, a flat house with an extraordinarily small entrance. This building is taboo to married men: only bachelors are allowed to enter an olog and spend the night with their intended wives. Before they get that far, both partners must fulfil certain rules of the game - the man must promise to marry his partner in the event of pregnancy; if he

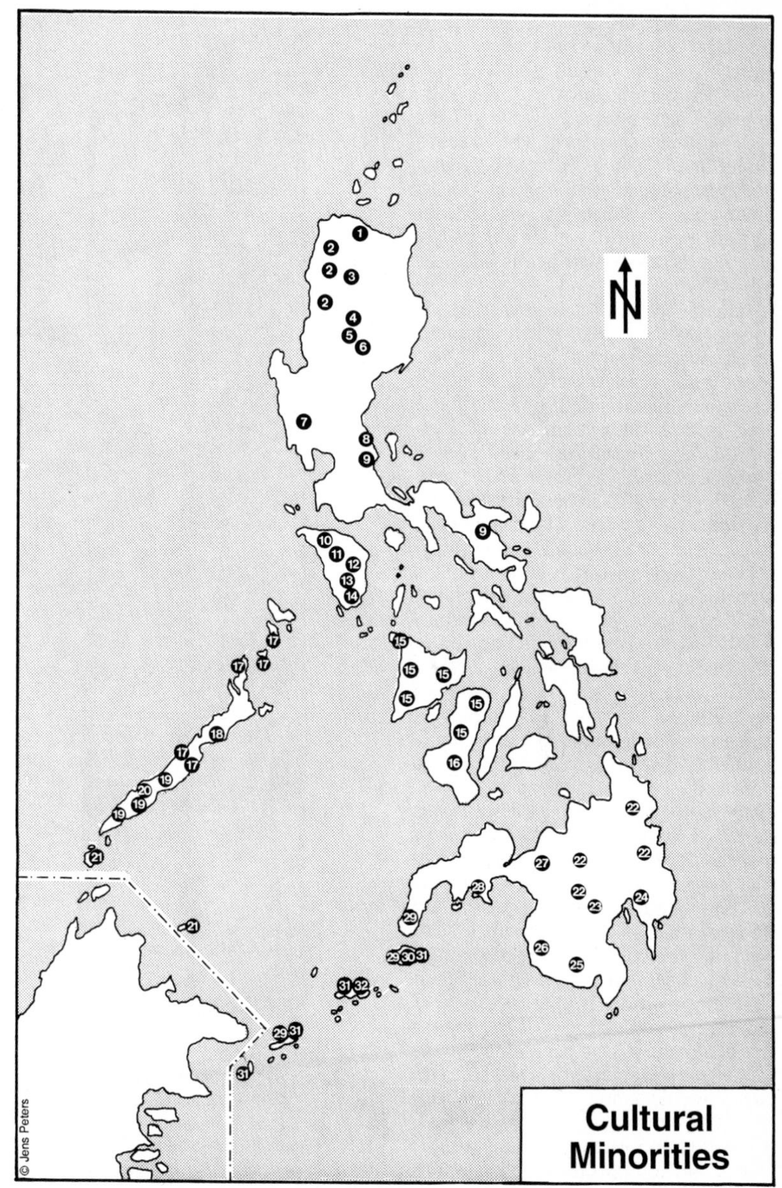
N
Cultural
Minorities
© Jens Peters

doesn't keep his promise, he will be socially isolated and not permitted to enter the ologs again. The invitation and permission to spend the night together must be issued by the girl, and as a sign of her consent, she 'steals' a small item of his property. Every Bontoc understands this hint, and when many tobacco pouches or pipes are purloined during the day in the village, you can bet the ologs will be crowded that night.

Although the days are gone when the Bontoc were feared as head-hunters, even today this act of revenge has not been completely wiped out. Justice in the mountains is strictly 'an eye for an eye, a tooth for a tooth', or more appropriately, 'a head for a head'. *Tuf-ay* (spear), *kalasag* (shield), *kaman* (head-axe) and *sangi* (satchel) comprise the equipment of a warrior. The sangi serves as a carrier for the enemy's head. When a successful warrior returns from his expedition, there is a great celebration for two days in the village. As a sign of his heroic deed the hero is tattooed on the chest: this is known as *chak-lag* and is much coveted, as it symbolises strength and bravery. The tattooing on the arms of male and female Bontoc is called *pango*. *Fatek* simply means tattoo.

The Bontoc believe in a better life after death; their funerals are not sorrowful occasions and only the heads of the family are in mourning. The most important requisite of the ceremony, which lasts for several days, is a death seat, the *sungachil*. A short time after a person's death, the body is placed in an upright position in the death seat, bound fast and placed so as to be visible to all who pass in front of the house. The shroud is selected according to the status of the family. Old women sing the *anako*, the death song, and a pig is sacrificed and eaten. After nightfall, a sort of recitation begins, called *achog*,

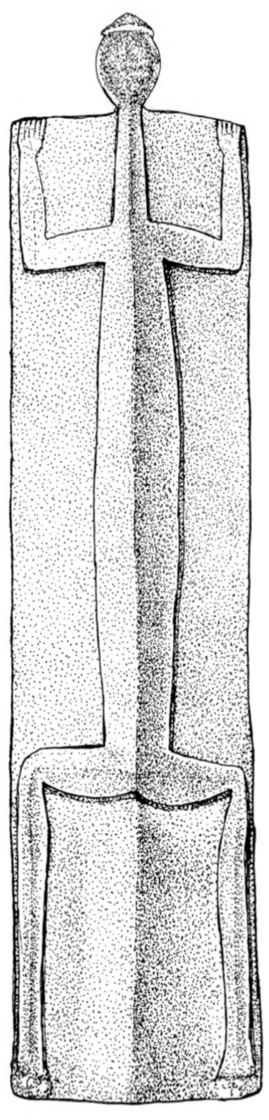

Bontoc Shield
Filipino warriors used shields made of engraved buffalo leather or carved out of wood to protect themselves in battle long before the well-armed Spanish reached the archipelago.

in which the life history of the dead person is reflected upon. This ritual can be quite merry as it is very difficult to get a coherent, objective account of the deeds accomplished by the deceased during their lifetime. Daybreak or exhaustion of the participants ends this part of the funeral ceremony.

Ifugao

No other people of the Philippines apart from the Tasaday have attracted more attention than the Ifugao. They are the builders of the gigantic rice terraces of Banaue and the surrounding area. Over the last 2000 years they have shaped a technical and architectural masterpiece with bare hands and primitive tools. The imposing terraced landscape was constructed step by step from the bottoms of the valleys up to heights of 1000m or more. These are productive rice fields with a perfectly functioning irrigation system on the steep mountain slopes. The boundary walls have a total length of about 20,000 km. From this measurement the rice terraces of the Ifugao exceed by far those of the Bontoc and Kalinga. They are often justifiably referred to as the eighth wonder of the world.

The life of the Ifugao is full of ceremonies and celebrations at which *tapuy*, a rice wine, plays an important part, whether it's at a funeral or at the carving up of a wild pig brought in by the hunters. They originally learned the rice wine manufacturing process from Chinese traders. Rice harvested under the full moon is preferred, and, in order to accelerate the process of fermentation, the rice is partly boiled in fresh, clean water. After adding a minimal quantity of sugar, the promising pot contents are emptied into an earthenware vessel, sealed and left for six months to ripen. After this period, the Ifugao can enjoy themselves over a pleasant-tasting tapuy. It is also possible that an undrinkable, sour liquid will result from mistakes made in the manufacturing process.

The Ifugao build their houses on piles; the windowless space under the pyramid-shaped roof is used as a bedroom, kitchen and storeroom. In order to please the gods, the skull of a sacrificed pig is fixed on the outside of the house.

The Ifugao, too, were feared head-hunters in their day. Even today, although now becoming increasingly rare, head-hunting is considered a legitimate way of executing tribal judgements. Amongst the old laws which have survived through the centuries they also have one involving a kind of blood feud. This demands a life, or appropriate damages, in exchange for a wrong committed. For example, in the late 80s, a bus driver caused a serious traffic accident with fatal consequences for several Ifugao near Banaue. When the bus company refused to admit responsibility for the deaths and injuries, axes were sharpened in the villages in question. After that no bus driver would drive into the Ifugao district for fear of getting an axe in his neck, and, until the last damages payment was made, the bus company had to hand over the last 50 km section of the Manila to Banaue route to local jeepneys.

The *bangibang* (war dance) is a component of this traditional vengeance. Equipped with spears, shields and axes, the warriors dance on the walls of the rice fields, their heads adorned with *katlagang*, a form of head-dress made of leaves. The person who will carry out the act of vengeance is determined by using a chicken. The warriors form a circle, kill a chicken and leave it to die in the circle. The one chosen is the one closest to the chicken when it finally comes to rest after its final death throes.

Ilokano

The Ilokano are of Malay ancestry. About 200 to 300 BC they came through

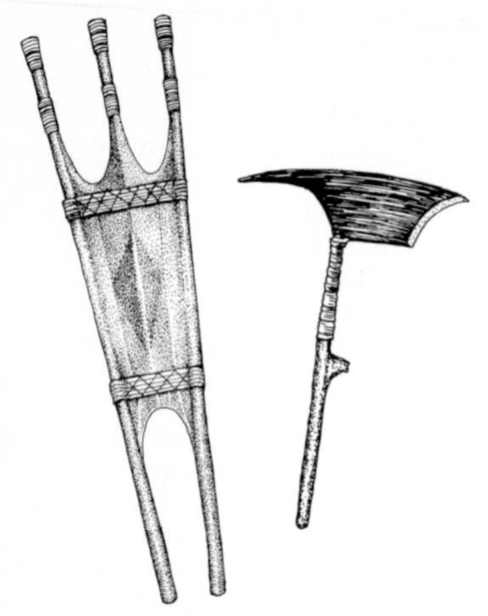

Head-axe and shield of the Kalinga

Borneo, Palawan and Mindoro to Luzon where they settled. The most significant part of the group settled the coastal strips and the adjoining mountain regions in northern and north-western Luzon.

Already settled ethnic groups like the Isnega and Tingguian could not resist the new wave of immigration and were pushed into the hinterlands. Before the Ilokano were confronted with Christian beliefs, they had a multi-tiered and complicated system of gods and spirits. Only fragments of their superstitions have persisted, however, and these are mainly ornamental - such as amulets and lucky charms which are generally only worn by the inhabitants of outlying Ilokano villages.

Kalinga

The Kalinga live north of the Bontoc. They are also head-hunters. Wars and head-hunting expeditions have been largely restricted through the peace pact, *budong*, which they have worked out. This treaty declares above all that a Kalinga whose honour has been impugned does not lose the respect of the tribe if, instead of beheading the enemy, he accepts a water buffalo, for example, as payment. A significant effect of this ruling is the initiation of social and family ties between different groups.

Like the Bontoc, the Kalinga also have a house for the men and village elders. They call it *dapay*. However, there is not a typical house for marriageable girls and women. It can be any house and is indistinguishable from the others from the outside; the Kalinga name for it is the *ebgan*. Here the evening courtship takes place, the initiation songs are sung, stories told or flutes played. Successful suitors spend the night with their women in the ebgan and both partners have the opportunity to consider a common future together. If they decide to separate, the event of a pregnancy is no hindrance as there are no disadvantages for the parents or the child, who is later declared legitimate by the tribal community.

A marriage is prepared for over a long period by different ritual acts. Earthquakes, landslides and other bad omens can draw out the required ceremonies for months. When all the formalities have at last been accomplished, a house is built for the engaged couple. According to Kalinga tradition, marriages can only be celebrated in the *dadawak* (the season for marriages) months of March, September or October.

Mandaya & Mansaka

The Mandaya live in the north-eastern and south-eastern part of Davao del Norte on Mindanao. Mandaya means 'inhabitant of the highlands'. The Mansaka are classified ethnologically with the Mandaya. They were originally highland people who settled in clearings deep in the mountains, though today many Mansaka live in the eastern coastal regions of Davao Bay.

Baskets
Baskets in all sorts of different shapes, sizes, patterns and colours are normally made and used by ethnic minorities. The materials most often used to make hand baskets, panniers, hampers, trays and fish traps are bamboo, rattan and pandanus. Older baskets from the Central Cordillera often have a dark patina, which is a result of heavy use and being exposed to the smoke from cooking stoves in windowless houses. This characteristic of antique baskets is often reproduced in record time to be able to charge unsuspecting buyers a higher price. Hand-made, and if possible antique, utensils used by mountain tribesmen are not only popular as souvenirs with foreign and native tourists alike, but are also frequently used for decoration in big hotels and restaurants with a folk decor.

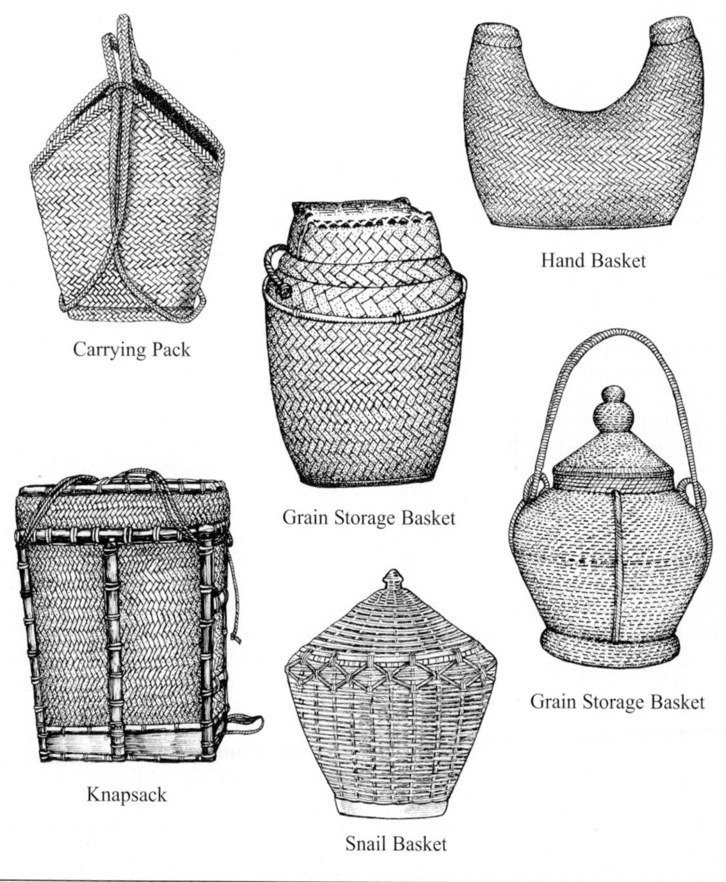

Carrying Pack

Hand Basket

Grain Storage Basket

Grain Storage Basket

Knapsack

Snail Basket

Animism is strongly practised by both groups, as demonstrated by the many idols carved out of wood which stand in their houses and fields. Also noteworthy are the numerous examples of silver work. Hardly any other ethnic group would use more silver to produce ornaments than the Mandaya. Even more striking than the ear adornments and finger rings are the large round chain pendants which are worn by men and women and are frequently made from coins.

Mangyan

Over 80,000 Mangyan live on Mindoro. The majority of them live in the dense jungles of the mountainous interior. The Mangyan are subdivided into the Iraya, Hanunoo, Alangan, Tadyawan, Batangan, Buhid and Ratagnon.

In earlier times the majority of the Mangyan lived and fished along the coast, but later they retreated to the hills, changed their lifestyle and took up agriculture. They did not go there of their own free will but were driven back by new settlers. In their culture land belongs to everyone. If someone approaches them with deeds of title, these peace-loving people simply withdraw.

Despite the inevitable influences of civilisation, the traditions and culture of the Mangyan have survived. Distances are measured in yells - the distance over which one scream is audible.

In the south of Mindoro there are settled Hanunoo who are often referred to as 'true Mangyan'. They have their own form of writing in an elaborate syllabic script. Hanunoo means 'real' and 'true'. They also have their own postal system. If they want to send messages across great distances, they carve the text into a piece of bamboo and place it into a particular bamboo post. These 'post boxes' are spread over the entire area in specially designated or well-known positions. If the Mangyan come across one of them they read all the letters and deliver those with destinations which are on their route, either personally or by placing them in a more advantageous 'post box'.

The *ambahan*, the stories told by the Mangyan, are also recorded by being carved in bamboo. A typical ambahan has each line made up of seven syllables. These poems are of a social nature. Thus they may be read to children to discipline them, or they may be given to an adult to read in cases where speaking directly with the person may be embarrassing or painful.

Maranao

The province of Lanao del Sur in the north of Mindanao is the homeland of the Maranao (or Maranaw). They are the 'people of the lake' - Lake Lanao. Of all the Philippine Muslim groups, the Maranao were the last to be converted to Islam. They successfully defended themselves against all colonisation attempts by the Spaniards and Americans, for which their natural environment provided a not inconsiderable protection. Their culture and religion have both developed without interference.

Today the Maranao are concerned with preserving and maintaining their cultural identity. Marawi, lying on the northern tip of Lake Lanao, is an important spiritual centre for Muslims. Several Islamic-oriented schools and the Mindanao State University (MSU), a southern branch of the University of the Philippines, are here.

Maranao are skilled artisans and capable merchants. Cloth, wood and metal work collectively is the second most important sector of their economy; only agriculture is more important. They have a leading position in the country in the production of brass work.

Houses of the Central Cordillera
Apayao
Bontoc
Bontoc
Ifugao
Ibaloy
Kalinga
Kalinga

Negritos

There are said to be 15,000 to 50,000 pure Negritos living in the Philippines; estimates vary wildly. The number for people with Negritos blood in them, including those of mixed race, would obviously turn out much higher.

The various Negritos groups call themselves names like Agta, Alta, Ita, Ati, Ata and Aeta, which all mean 'man' or 'person'. They live dispersed over many islands but are principally found in eastern Luzon. They can be readily distinguished from all other Filipinos by their physical characteristics: they are darker and rarely taller than 1½ m. Their hair is short and woolly-crinkly, often decorated with a bamboo ornament. Sometimes they still wear scanty clothing made out of tree bark.

The Negritos are nomads and only a few of them have settled in one place. Instead of living in solid houses, they live in huts built from twigs, branches, foliage and grass. Sometimes they lay out small fields in which they plant sweet potatoes, rice and vegetables; they also hunt and gather fruit. Bows and poison-tipped arrows are their weapons.

Seafaring Negritos are called Dumagat. You meet them occasionally on secluded beaches on the Pacific coast of North Luzon, where they settle temporarily in hastily built huts.

The Negritos do not have laws, nor do they feel themselves bound to any authority. When decisions have to be made, the decision of the head of the family is accepted and followed.

Pala'wan

The Pala'wan live in the highlands of south Palawan. Their villages consist of three to 12 houses. They are led by a number of *panlima*, who are administrators and are also meant to help maintain the peace. The Pala'wan's religion has been influenced by Hindu and Islamic elements. The highest deity is Ampo, who is believed to pass on responsibility for the regulation of the affairs of humanity to his subordinate gods, the *diwata*. The practice of the religion also includes social activities such as communal dancing, singing and drinking of rice wine. A marriage is only agreed upon after lengthy negotiations between the two families concerned and is often arranged when the couple are still children.

Tasaday

The Tasaday live in the mountains deep within the tropical rainforest of South Cotabato Province on Mindanao. The discovery of the Tasaday by the outside world has caused considerable controversy.

They were first discovered in the early 1960s by a hunter named Dafal, but the first 'official' meeting didn't take place until June 1971. Their good health was remarkable; from the dawn of time until their discovery, these semi-naked cave and forest dwellers lived only on the fruit they gathered and the fish, frogs, tadpoles and crabs they caught. They had not yet discovered hunting or agriculture and used only primitive stone tools.

Because of their isolation, at least 50,000 years of evolution had completely passed them by. According to some reports, the 25 clan members had no contact at all with the outside world until they met Dafal. They did not even know of the existence of other groups of people outside their forest. It's worth reading John Nance's book *The Gentle Tasaday* (Harcourt Brace Jovanovich, New York, 1975; Victor Gallancz, London, 1975), which offers a fascinating eyewitness account with many photos.

However, in early 1986, Dr Oswald Iten of Switzerland, *Stern* reporter Walter Unger and Jay Ullal published some disconcerting revelations suggesting

Maranao Art

The Maranao, who live on Lake Lanao on Mindanao, are well known for their skills as artists. Maranao art is known as okir. A distinction is made between okir-a-bai, the geometric decor in the weaving work produced by women, and okir-a-datu, the mainly organic motifs such as leaves, creepers, flowers and buds employed in the woodcarvings and brasswork produced by men.

Kulintang
Musical instrument comprising brass gongs on a wooden stand

Panolog
A floor beam extension for a Maranao house

Brass Arm Band

Decorative Motif

Sarimanok
The `imitation cockerel' is a symbolic representation of a bird to the Maranao

Baong
Brass Vessel

Langguay
Brass Vessel

Brass Betelnut Container

that the sensational discovery of the Tasaday had been nothing but a publicity stunt cleverly staged by Manuel Elizalde, who at the time was chief of Presidential Assistance on National Minorities (PANAMIN; the bureau has since been disbanded).
It was quite a pickle for everyone involved. Scholars and journalists from all over the world who had been convinced that the Tasaday were genuine demanded further proof and explanations. The Department of Anthropology convened an ultimately inconclusive symposium, and only a testimonial issued by the Philippine Congress, which had arranged for some Tasaday to be flown to Manila in order to clarify the question, could bring about a provisional settling of the heated debate. The authenticity of the Tasaday as an ethnic group was then officially confirmed by the highest government authorities. The most recent confirmation of the authenticity of the Tasaday was presented at the International Congress of Anthropological & Ethnological Sciences in early 1992 in Washington, DC.

Tausug

The majority of Tausug live on the island of Jolo in the Sulu archipelago. They describe themselves as 'people in the current' and were the first in the Philippines to accept Islam. Nevertheless, traditional customs are still maintained. Thus a Tausug wedding, *pagtiaun*, is among the richest, most colourful festivals celebrated anywhere on the Sulu Islands. The ceremonies and celebrations last a week. An important part of the activity is the *pangalay*, a wedding dance to the sound of gongs and drums.
The Tausug love freedom and are proud of their bravery. They are renowned as skilled seafarers, diligent traders and excellent business people. Prosperity and pride have helped make the Tausug the dominant tribe from Zamboanga to Sitangkai. Their cultural wealth is exhibited through their dress, the architecture of their houses and in the style of their brass artefacts, jewellery and weapons.

Tau't Batu

The Tau't Batu are referred to as 'people of the rock'. They live in caves in the Signapan Basin, north-west of Mt Mantalingajan, the highest peak in Palawan. They only leave their caves to hunt, gather fruit or harvest cassava and rice in unobtrusive fields. Other sources of nutrition, such as bats and birds, are found inside the caves. Their belief demands that nature be compensated for the death of any of the animals. Animals which have been killed will therefore be replaced by a representation in stone or wood.
A particular social custom is *bulun-bulun*, the communal living of several families brought about through the necessity to share nourishment. The Tau't Batu were not officially discovered until 1978. In order to protect the lifestyle and habitat of this peaceful group, the Signapan Basin has been declared off limits to outsiders and this is strictly enforced.

T'boli

An estimated 60,000 T'boli live in about 2000 sq km in the south-western corner of Mindanao. The area is known as the Tiruray Highlands and their culture is centred in the triangle formed by the villages of Surallah, Polomolok and Kiamba, near Lake Sebu.
The T'boli do not have a village community structure. They live in houses set well apart from each other along the ridges of the highlands. In some cases, when there are close family ties, three or four houses are clustered together. Called long houses, or more colloquial-

Swords

Single- and double-edged swords of various designs are an integral part of the arts and crafts of the Muslims in the south of the Philippines. In Mindanao and the Sulu Islands in particular, the art of forging blades and shaping handles remains important. In Sulu, the classical type is the kris, called kalis seko, and the kampilan. Although they are rarely used in battle these days, swords are still of social and symbolic significance to the wearer.

1 Barong: a leaf-shaped, single-edged blade
2 Kampilan: the handle is supposed to represent the open mouth of a crocodile
3 Kris: a wavy-shaped blade
4 T'boli Bolo: the handle is decorated with brass curls
5 Dragger Kris: a weapon preferred by women
6 Talibong: a sabre with a single-edged, curved blade

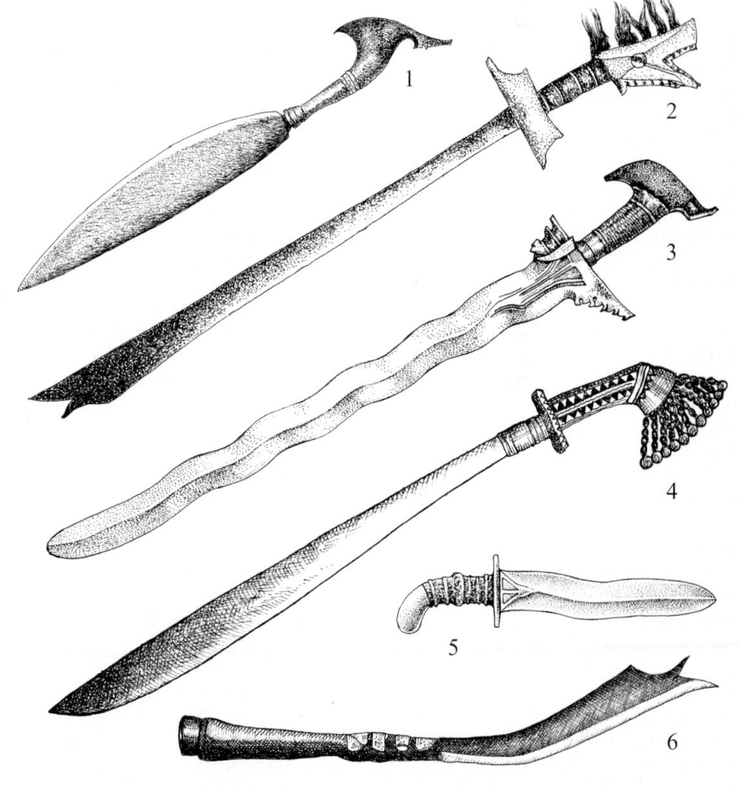

ly, *gunu bong*, they stand on two-metre-high posts and are about 15 m long and 10 m wide. The T'boli are monogamous people, but polygamy is allowed and is sometimes practised by the more prosperous as a status symbol. T'boli women have a passion for decoration and adorn themselves with ornamental combs, earrings, necklaces and chains, arm and foot bracelets, finger and toe rings and heavy, bell belts. You seldom see one without a head covering, either a *kayab*, originally a turban of abaca, more often today a simple towel; or a colourful *s'laong kinibang*, a large, round hat with a diameter of about half a metre. The traditional clothing of both men and women consists of *t'nalak* - a material woven from abaca with a dark brown background lightened by red and beige designs. It takes several months to weave, but the weaving of the *kumo*, the wedding dress, takes even longer. This typical metre-long T'boli covering has great significance in the wedding ceremony.

Yakan

The Yakan mainly live on Basilan Island in the south of the Philippines, although some have settled near Zamboanga on Mindanao. They are peace-loving Muslims who live by agriculture and cattle breeding. The most important house in a village is the *langgal*, or prayer house, which is run by an *imam*. All larger annual ceremonies take place here, too. Absolutely essential elements to any festival are music and games, with water buffalo fights being particularly thrilling.

The Yakan are famous as exceptional weavers. A part of their unusual traditional clothing is the *kandit*, a red belt several metres long which is wrapped around the hips to hold up skin-tight trousers, called *sawal*. Adornments men wear include a colourful turban known as a *pis*, or a helmet-shaped hat called a *saruk*. Old women can still be found with overlong artificial fingernails known as *suploh*.

Religion

The Philippines is unique for being the only Christian country in Asia - over 90% of the population claim to be Christian, more than 80% of whom are Roman Catholic. The Spanish did a thorough job!

Largest of the minority religious groups are the Muslims (about 8%) who are found chiefly on the island of Mindanao and along the Sulu archipelago. When the Spanish arrived toting their cross, the Muslims were just getting a toehold in the region. In the northern islands their influence was only small and was easily displaced, but in the south, the people had been firmly converted and Christianity was never able to make a strong impression.

About 4% of Filipinos belong to the Philippine Independent Church, which was founded by Gregorio Aglipay in 1902 as a nationalist Catholic church. The Iglesia ni Kristo is the largest community of Protestant believers, to which 4% of the population belong. Baptists, Methodists, Mormons, Jehovah's Witnesses and members of other religious groups and sects make up about 2%. Except for a tiny percentage of Buddhist believers, the remainder of the population are animists.

Arts

Traditional Culture

The Philippines has developed a unique mixed culture from the historical blending of foreign influences with indigenous elements. Today, the Muslims and some of the isolated tribes are the only people whose culture remains unadulterated by Spanish and American influences.

Money, Money, Money

The Filipinos were quick to understand that money is worthless unless and until you spend it. They are not keen on saving. Saving means providing for the future, which itself means actually thinking about future problems. But you will hardly find a Filipino who will voluntarily worry about something that is not just about to happen. Why worry about the day that might never come?
'Study Now, Pay Later' is the exhortation on every P500 note, which makes no bones about the general Philippine attitude to sordid Mammon. In other words: 'If you don't have it, borrow it'. No wonder pawn-shops do a land office business all over the country. It's also no surprise that housewives prefer to do their daily shopping in shops that will give them credit (*utang*). Filipinos also like to practise what they call *lista na tubig*, which could be loosely translated as 'writing a debt on water' (liquidity takes on a whole new meaning...).
It's not unusual for somebody to borrow a large sum of money for a sure-fire business idea. Plans are drawn up with great enthusiasm, and maybe even promising first steps are taken. But then the initial burst of enthusiasm suddenly dies down, and the project simply fails. This phenomenon is known as *ningas cogon*, a process which illustrates the wildfire nature of the Philippine mentality most clearly. Ningas cogon is also the reason why a financial enterprise that requires a bit of patience and doesn't bring in the money straight away rarely leads to success in the Philippines.

The results of this foreign influence can be seen every day in the Philippines, for example every afternoon when even the smallest village square is converted into a basketball court. Ever since American colonial times the entire country has been crazy about this sport of giants - even though the Filipinos themselves tend to be shorter. They also love to gamble, and cockfighting gives them a great chance to indulge in this. It's also not unusual for sums of pesos to change hands after a game of Jai-alai, the fast ball game from the Basque country, also popular here. The average Filipinos are not great savers anyway; they live more to enjoy today and survive it if they can. Tomorrow will take care of itself.
The ability of the Filipinos to improvise and copy from their previous colonial masters is nowhere more apparent than in the jeepney. The army jeeps left behind by the Americans after WWII were converted into colourful, shining-chrome taxis through painstaking detailed work. Nowadays, these vehicles are produced locally, and what would a typical Philippine city look like without these unique jeepneys?
The ideas of the New Society propagated by Marcos really caught the national consciousness of the Philippines in the 1970s, just as People Power did in the 1980s. Perhaps as a reaction against the residual influence of occupying foreign powers, people began to rediscover their own cultural heritage and began to care about their traditional arts and crafts. As a direct result of this, the national language began to find more and more favour and is strongly used today in theatre and literature.

Music

Up until recently, traditional Philippine music was considered to be almost exclusively restricted to ethnic minorities.

The Aegis Phenomenon

No Philippine band has ever made it to the top as quickly as Aegis, and they look like they're here to stay. Practically overnight, they burst onto the Philippine music scene in 2000, rocketing to the top with their first album *Halik* and songs like *Luha* and *Sinta*. The unmistakeable sound of their catchy folk-rock music is immediately recogniseable from their edgy guitar riffs, but especially from the powerful voices of the two lead singers Juliet and Mercy Sunot. In addition to the two likeable sisters from Cagayan de Oro the following members make up this mostly female band: Rowena Pippin (bass), Stella Galindo (keyboards), Vilma Goloviogo (drums) and the only man in the outfit, Rey Abenoja (guitar). Aegis is a *must-see* band. Their professional yet intimate stage show with Juliet's funny remarks between the songs, is an experience you just don't want to miss.

The 'civilised' Filipinos had fallen for American and British style pop music and imitated it astonishingly well. In fact, the Filipino bands' ability to imitate pop and folk music from the West so perfectly has put them in great demand in South-East Asia, from Jakarta all the way to Tokyo. But now more and more musicians are rediscovering their cultural heritage and bringing old melodies back to life, using traditional instruments like bamboo flutes, gongs and wooden drums. Singing Philippine folk songs in the original Tagalog has enjoyed more and more popularity, even bringing stardom in the case of the Mabuhay Singers. It was such a song, *Bayan Ko* ('My Country'), sung by the most popular social critic in the Philippines, Freddie Aguilar, which became the anthem of the Marcos opponents during the uprising of 1986.

Dance

Filipinos are talented dancers. They just can't suppress their enthusiasm for music and vibrant dancing, whether it be disco dancing or cha-cha at a fiesta, colourful folk dancing, or modern and classical ballet. Philippine dances are mainly derived from Malay, Spanish and Muslim origins. Amongst the most beautiful Malay dances are *tinikling* (bamboo or heron dance) and *pandanggo sa ilaw* (dance of lights); the best known Filipino-Muslim dance is *singkil* (court dance). You will also often see performances of the Philippine variations of the Spanish dances *habanera, jota* and *paypay* (the fan dance).

The good old folk dances, foremost among them the national dance tinikling mentioned above, have even become a new tourist attraction. Well-known dance troupes such as Barangay, Bayanihan (National Folk Dance Company), Filipinescas, Karilagan or Ramon Obusan have even found a spot on popular TV shows. Even the Ballet Philippines, the leading troupe in the country for classical and modern repertoire, will occasionally present their interpetation of traditional dances.

Film

Filipino films are produced in great number, dealing mainly with variations on the themes of violence and clichéd love stories. Productions like the socially critical film *Mababangong Bangungot* by Kidlat Tahimik are rare. One of the best-known Philippine films, and the recipient of many awards, is *Oro, Plata, Mata* (Gold, Silver, Death) by Peque Gallaga, which was filmed on the island of Negros in 1982.

In January 1981 the first film festival in Manila took place at the Philippines

International Convention Center. After the success of this trial run and the two first, official festivals of 1982 and 1983 in the specially built film theatre, the organisers hoped that the Manila International Film Festival (MIFF) would be recognised internationally as are the festivals in Cannes, Berlin and Venice and that these cities would send their representatives. But further MIFFs, for economic and probably political reasons, have not taken place. In 1999 the Independent Cinema Association of the Philippines created the first Cinemanila International Film Festival, which is to be held annually in July from now on.

Painting

The best known of the Philippine painters of the 19th century were Felix Hidalgo and Juan Luna. Both were honoured with awards on many occasions. The famous painting *Spoliarium* by Juan Luna was even awarded a gold medal at the 1884 Exposicion General de Bellas Artes in Madrid.

From 1920 until 1940 was the most creative time for Fernando Amorsolo, whose romantic style is best represented by his paintings *Planting Rice* (1921) and *Women Bathers* (1933). A contemporary of Amorsolo was Victorio Edades, who burst onto the scene with his modern works. He is said to be the 'father of Philippine modern art' and was a role model for Vicente Manansala, Hernando R Ocampo and Cesar Legaspi, who achieved international acclaim with their abstract works, above all in the 1950s.

The small gallery shops in Makati and Ermita reflect the high level of Filipino painting: from impressionism to realism, virtually all styles are represented.

Sports & Betting

The Filipinos are enthusiastic sportspeople and gamblers. Basketball is their favourite sport and there has been a professional league since 1975. On the popularity scale, ballroom dancing, billiards, bowling, boxing and chess come near the top. Consequently, a lot of money was wagered on the outcome of the world heavyweight boxing championship back in 1975 (when Mohammed Ali fought Joe Frazier in the 'thriller in Manila'), the World Basketball Championships in 1978, and the chess championship in 1978 (between Korshnoi and Karpov).

Tennis, golf, horse racing, bicycle races and motor racing do have some followers, but are not in the category of a national sport. As a team sport in

Crack Billiard Players

If there's a billiards tournament on TV, no matter where on the planet it's being held, half the population of the nation will be found glued to their sets. For there's almost always a professional from the Philippines amongst the front runners, and names like Efren 'Bata' Reyes, Francisco 'Django' Bustamente, Rudolfo 'Boy Samson' Luat, Leonardo 'Dodong' Andam and Jose 'Amang' Parica are household words. Masters of both the 8-ball and the 9-ball game, they are respected and emulated all over the country. The most successful are Efren Reyes ('The Magician'), winner of the 9-ball World Championship in 1999 and World Pool League champion in 2001 and 2002, and Franciso Bustamente, who was declared Player of the Year worldwide by the US fanzine *Billiards Digest* in 1998 (Reyes held the title in 1995). The best Canadian player and 9-ball world champion in 2004, Alex Pagulayan ('The Lion') was also born in the Philippines.

schools, volleyball is second in popularity to basketball.
The Filipinos show an infectious enthusiasm for betting on sports events, and large amounts of pesos hang in the balance during cockfights and Jai-alai games.

Sipa
Only rarely will you see a game of the once popular *sipa* being played. It's a game played with a plaited rattan ball which is kicked over a net using feet, knees, elbows or the head (a similar idea to volleyball). It is now only played in a few areas in Mindanao and occasionally in Rizal Park in Manila.

Jai-alai
Many pesos are risked at Jai-alai (pronounced 'high-aligh'), the frantically fast ball game of Basque origin. It is played in a court rather like a squash court. The two players have a shovel-like holder called the *cesta* with which they hurl a small, hard ball called the *pelota* against the wall. Their opponent must try to catch the rebounding ball and then hurl it back. The final winner is decided by a knock-out competition and bets are placed on the outcome. Games are held every evening in the Jai-alai stadium in Manila, although it's quite frequently closed because of 'irregularities' and corruption.

Cockfights
The real passion is reserved for games that involve betting. Those who wish to bet on Sunday and public holidays can go to a *sabong* (cockfight). The fights take place in a wooden arena known as a cockpit and there is great activity as early as 8am. Before each fight several *kristos* (bookkeepers) come into the ring to encourage the spectators to part with their money and to take the bets. They use a sign language for betting and, amazingly, nothing is noted down - it's all committed to memory. Four fingers raised means P40, horizontal fingers signify hundreds and fingers pointed downwards means thousands - but check this first if you intend to participate!
While bets are being taken, the very expensive cocks are brought out and stirred up for the fight. Like boxers they fight in different weight classes. Each cock is equipped with a razor-sharp spur fastened behind the leg. This deadly spur usually brings a fight to an end after a few seconds.
A 'non-pro', injured or sickly cock must be pecked twice by the winner. Only then is the fight officially over. Should the champion cock choose not to perform this concluding rite, the fight may be declared a draw. Wounded cocks are 'patched up' by experts behind the cockpit; the dead ones end up in the pot.

Public Holidays & Special Events

Official offices and banks are closed on public holidays; shops and department stores remain open. Good Friday is the only time in the year when the entire country closes down. Even public transport stops running, and domestic airlines remain grounded on that day.

The public holidays are: New Year's Day (1 January); People Power Day (25 February); Maundy Thursday, Good Friday and Easter Sunday (March/April); Bataan Day (9 April); Labour Day (1 May); Philippine Independence Day (12 June); All Saints' Day (1 November); Bonifacio Day (30 November); Christmas Day (25 December); Rizal Day (30 December).

Town Fiestas
There are many town fiestas which take place on the numerous national holidays over the whole year (see Miscel-

Miss Philippines

In no other country are there so many beauty contests as in the Philippines, where the cult status of women has deep roots in Filipino culture. 'Miss' contests are a social event here, beauty queens are respected, admired and feted as celebrities wherever they go.

In the interest of getting to the top of the career ladder as quickly as possible, ambitious and beautiful young women of all social backgrounds exploit their own appearance and intelligence by presenting themselves to the public and judges in scores of beauty contests. The bigger contests at national level are always attended by VIPs, who often sit on the jury as well. Apart from good looks, a candidate in the battle for the crown and a chance at the honour of being voted the 'fairest of them all' has to be of a minimum height and be able to produce at least a high school leaving certificate.

In the struggle for emancipation Filipinas have not modelled themselves on men's behaviour, but have sensitively and skilfully retained their femininity, which by no means implies accepting men's claim to superiority. So the Filipina not only rules the roost in the family and at home, but confidently wields power when in public office and has considerable influence in the workplace and the business world.

laneous in the individual island chapters). An expensive festival is held for two or three days in honour of the appropriate patron saint. It is hard to understand how some of the families shoulder the financial burden: the enormous expenses incurred bear no relation to the poverty and hardship of everyday life in the Philippines. Food and drink are offered with lavish generosity and at the end of the fiesta some visitors even get the money for their journey home pressed into their hands. One or more bands are hired, and musicians and entertainers add to the atmosphere of a people's festival. There is also usually a beauty contest in which the contestants are heavily sponsored. Foreigners and visitors from distant towns get the same royal treatment as friends and relatives.

January
Appey
This is a three-day thanksgiving festival of the Bontoc for a bounteous harvest. Countless chickens and pigs are slaughtered and sacrificed for this festival.

1 January
New Year's Day (public holiday)
As in Western countries the new year is colourfully and loudly welcomed. Families come together to celebrate the traditional *media noche*, the midnight meal. The streets are incredibly noisy and can be dangerous: fireworks are shot off for several days before New Year, often resulting in the loss of fingers and thumbs. Every year unintended and premature explosions of illegally produced fireworks result in chaotic scenes at the hospitals.

First Sunday in January
Holy Three Kings' Day
This is the official end of the Christmas season. The children receive their last Christmas presents on this day. In Santa Cruz and Gasan on Marinduque, the imitation kings are led on horseback

through the town. Spectators throw coins and sweets to the children who run alongside the procession.

9 January
Black Nazarene Procession
What is probably the largest procession of the Philippines begins early in the afternoon in Quiapo at the Quiapo church. Thousands of Catholics crowd the streets in this part of Manila when the 'Black Nazarene', a life-size statue of Christ made of blackwood, is dragged through the town by unbelievably long ropes.

Third Weekend in January
Ati-Atihan
This festival in Kalibo on Panay is the Rio de Janeiro or New Orleans Mardi Gras of the Philippines. It's an important and spectacular festival, when the town raves for three days. People dance, sing and play drums. Thousands of people, outrageously costumed and cleverly masked, celebrate around the clock until the last evening, when a long procession of excited participants ends the intoxicating festivities.
The origins of the festival date back to the middle of the 13th century, when 10 Datu families had to flee from Borneo. They sailed north-east and landed on the Philippine island of Panay, where the resident Ati - small, dark Negrito people - gave them a piece of land on which to settle. A festival was celebrated and the newly arrived people blackened their faces so they would look just like the local Ati.
Many years later the Spaniards, who had converted much of the country to Christianity, used this ritual to deceive unfriendly Muslims and counter their attempts to influence Kalibo. They got the inhabitants to dye their skin black, wear warlike clothing and pretend they were Ati. The victory against the Muslims was interpreted as being achieved through the intervention of Santo Niño, the child Jesus, and thus the festival started to take on a religious significance.

Third Sunday in January
Sinulog - Santo Niño de Cebu
This is the climax of the week-long festival of Pasundayag sa Sinulog. Groups of people, all dressed in costume, gather in Downtown around the junction of Colon St and Osmeña Blvd until about 9.30am when they make their way through the streets of Cebu City, sometimes marching, sometimes dancing the peculiar Sinulog steps and shouting 'Pit Señor'. The procession takes several hours to go past.
Sinulog is the traditional dance of the old women followers, who can also be seen dancing by themselves in front of the Basilica Minore del Santo Niño and Magellan's Cross any day of the week. 'Pit Señor' means 'viva el Señor', by which is meant 'long live Santo Niño' (the child Jesus). Hotels are nearly always booked out on the holiday weekend.
Sinulog is also celebrated in Kabankalan on Negros during this weekend.

Fourth Weekend in January
Ati-Atihan in Ibajay
One weekend after the festival in Kalibo, another festival takes place in Ibajay (pronounced *eebahigh*), 30 km to the north-west. According to what the people of Ibajay say, their Ati-Atihan is the original and only true one - maybe they're correct. At least it's fair to say that though this festival is not supported financially by commercial interests or attended by hordes of tourists, the locals, dressed in their simple but original costumes, celebrate with as much enthusiasm as the people in Kalibo.

Fourth Weekend in January
Dinagyang
This Ati-Atihan look-alike festival in Iloilo City, the biggest city on the island

of Panay, features magnificent parades, but the spectators are quiet and passive, unlike the crowds at the similar Ati-Atihan activities in Kalibo.

January/February
Chinese New Year
Depending upon the lunar calendar, Chinese New Year celebrations take place some time between 21 January and 19 February. Manila's Chinatown is the scene of ritual and traditional dragon and lion dances in the afternoon.

February
Saranggolaham
In many villages and towns this is the beginning of the kite-flying season. People of all ages take part in competitions with kites of the most varied forms, colours and sizes.

Panagbenga (Baguio Flower Festival)
Every year in the second half of February, Baguio features the one-week long Baguio Flower Festival. It opens in a blaze of colour with a flower parade. On the following days, shows, parades and sports events are on the programme. The whole festival is brought to a close with a grand ball and a huge fireworks display.

2 February
Feast of Our Lady of Candelaria
This is a town festival with processions and parades in honour of Nuestra Señora de Candelaria (Our Lady of Candelaria), the patron saint of Jaro, a district of the city of Iloilo. It's the biggest religious event in the western Visayas.

11 February
Feast of Our Lady of Lourdes
This celebration is held in memory of the appearance of the 'Lady of Lourdes' in Lourdes, France. It takes place on Kanlaon St, Quezon City, and includes processions in the evening. The feast is also celebrated in San Juan del Monte, Bulacan Province.

14 February
St Valentine's Day
This is a day for lovers - an important date for the romantic Filipinos. Small gifts and Valentine's cards are personally delivered or sent, and couples dress up to go to a nice restaurant, dance in a disco or go to the movies (or even a motel). Filipinos are deeply upset if they have to spend St Valentine's Day without a Valentine.

22 to 26 February
People Power Days (Fiesta sa Edsa)
These are thanksgiving days for the end of the Marcos era, peacefully brought about by the people. The Epifanio de los Santos Ave (Edsa) in Quezon City and Mandaluyong City was the main scene of the so-called People Power revolution, and on this wide street the reinstalment of democracy is now celebrated every year. The 25th is an official holiday.

26 February
Dia de Zamboanga
This is a festival held by and for Muslims and Christians with cultural offerings, exhibits, regattas and religious ceremonies, in which the old Spanish and Muslim traditions of the city are given expression.

February/March/April
Hariraya Hajji
This is the time of pilgrimages to Mecca. Muslims spend most of the 10th day of the 12th month of their calendar in mosques.

March/April
Moriones Festival
Around Easter there are many passion plays in the Philippines. The most pop-

ular and colourful is the Moriones Festival on the island of Marinduque. The Roman soldier Longinus, not Jesus, is the focus of the week-long play.
Longinus is blind in one eye and as he pierces the right side of the crucified Jesus with his spear, blood drops on his blind eye and suddenly he can see again with both eyes. The first thing he sees is Christ's passage to heaven; Longinus announces the incident and must flee. The Roman warriors want to stop this 'rumour' and capture him on Easter Sunday. His execution by beheading is the climax of the passion plays.

Maundy Thursday (public holiday)
Apart from Good Friday, Maundy Thursday is the most intensively celebrated day of the holy week. Deep in thought, people attend church, most of the traffic comes to a halt and a perceptible silence reigns throughout the country.

Good Friday (public holiday)
The many crucifixions and scourges which take place throughout the country have grown into a real tourist attraction. The best known places for this are San Fernando (Pampanga Province), Antipolo (Rizal Province), Manila and Jordan (Guimaras Island).
On Good Friday all public transport stops running completely, including the Metrorail and Metrostar and inland flights. To cap it all, the cinemas are closed too.

March/April
Easter Sunday (official holiday)
At daybreak throughout the land, church bells are rung to herald the resurrection of Christ. Also at dawn, separate mother and son processions - symbolising the risen Christ's meeting with his mother - begin, concluding under a bamboo and flower arch.

March/April
Maulod-En-Nabi
As this is the prophet Mohammed's birthday, it is a Muslim holiday with ceremonial readings from the Koran in all mosques.

9 April
Bataan Day (public holiday)
This is a national remembrance day at the Mt Samet Shrine recalling the disastrous battle against the Japanese in 1942 and the degrading 'death march' from the Bataan Peninsula to Capas in Tarlac Province.

27 April
Bahug-Bahugan sa Mactan
Magellan's landing and the battle which led to his death are acted out on the beach at Mactan, on Mactan Island, Cebu. There are fights in the water, but be early: as everything depends on the tides, some years the activities start at 8am and are all over a couple of hours later.

April, May or June
Turumba Festival
Turumba means falling, leaping, jumping, skipping or dancing. This describes the behaviour of the participants in the procession in Pakil, Laguna Province.

1 May
Labor Day (public holiday)
This is a national holiday but no important activities are held.

First Week in May
Viva Vigan
One of North Luzon's most attractive festivals, with dancing in the streets, cultural shows and a colourful Calesa parade in the Vigan Heritage Village, the historical old section of town.

1 to 30 May
Flores de Mayo - Santacruzan
Throughout the whole country, proces-

sions in honour of the Virgin Mary take place in the afternoon and evening. Young girls in white dresses decorate the statues of Mary with flowers. An attractive focus of the processions in the flowering month of May are the most beautiful Filipinas from the local villages.

3 May
Carabao Carroza
Water buffalo races are held in Pavia, a few km north of Iloilo City on Panay Island. The fastest water buffaloes from the surrounding 18 *barrios* (neighbourhoods) run against each other in a final deciding race. The beauty queens are carried to the race track on festively decorated sleds. Be there by 8am. There is a town fiesta on the following day.

6 May
Araw ng Kagitingan
A day on which all Filipinos who have shown exceptional courage, either in their private lives or while serving their country are honoured. War veterans and nostalgia seekers visit the fortified island of Corregidor in Manila Bay in memory of the battle against the Japanese (The Fall of Corregidor) in 1942.

14 & 15 May
Carabao Festival
This is a two-day celebration in honour of the farmers' patron saint, San Isidro. Farmers lead decorated water buffaloes to the church square in a long procession on the afternoon of 14 May. There they kneel and are blessed. The next day the water buffalo races take place. Festivals are held in Pulilan (Bulacan Province), San Isidro (Nueva Ecija Province) and Angono (Rizal Province).

15 May
Pahiyas
The patron saint San Isidro is also honoured in Lucban and Sariaya, Quezon Province. On the day of the harvest festival, the house façades are attractively decorated with agricultural products. There is a procession in the afternoon. The huge leaves and blooms, which look like coloured glass and shine in the sun, are particularly decorative on Lucban. They are made out of *kiping*, a rice dough from a traditional recipe, and are eaten at the end of the festival, or given to the guests. The procession takes place in the afternoon.

17 to 19 May
Fertility Rites
This three-day festival in Obando (Bulacan Province) is dedicated to the three patron saints of the city. The Obando Festival became famous for its procession, a series of dances based on earlier fertility rites. On 17 May young unmarried men dance through the streets in the hope of soon finding a bride. The following day, unmarried women try their luck. The last day is given to childless couples who show their desire to have children through their participation in this festival.

12 June
Philippine Independence Day
This is a national public holiday, and a big military parade takes place in Rizal Park in Manila.

24 June
Feast of San Juan Bautista
The deeds of St John the Baptist are reenacted on this day in San Juan, Manila. Friends, relatives and curious spectators are 'baptised'. Water is thrown from, and at, passing cars - keep your camera in a plastic bag!

24 June
Parada ng Lechon
In Balayan, Batangas Province, St John's Day is celebrated with a 'suckling pig parade'.

28 to 30 June
Apung Iro (Apalit River Parade)
The inhabitants of Apalit (Pampanga Province) show their reverence for St Peter with a boat parade.

First Sunday in July
Pagoda sa Wawa
A river procession with the Holy Cross of Wawa in the pagoda boat. It takes place in Bocaue, Bulacan Province, just 30 km north of Manila.

22 July
Sandugo Festival
Commemorates the peace pact between Rajah Sikatuna and the Spanish conquistador Legaspi sealed on 16 March, 1565. The population of the island of Bohol celebrate the so-called 'Blood Compact' in the capital Tagbilaran and a few of the surrounding towns with dancing in the streets, theatre performances and concerts.

29 July
Pateros River Fiesta
Pateros, a suburb of Manila, is the centre of duck breeding. From here Manila is supplied with the Filipino delicacy *balut* (see Snacks in the Food & Drinks section later in this chapter). The fiesta recalls the killing of a legendary crocodile which threatened the existence of the balut suppliers.

August
Kadayawan sa Dabaw
For two weeks in August, Davao on Mindanao celebrates the Orchid Festival, the Fruit & Food Festival and the Tribal Festival.

Third Weekend in September
Peñafrancia Festival
The ceremonious river festival in Naga, South Luzon, has become a great tourist attraction. The climax is the spectacular boat parade on the Naga River in honour of the Blessed Virgin of Peñafrancia.

7 to 12 October
Zamboanga Hermosa
A popular festival with cultural performances, religious ceremonies, exhibitions, regattas and the choosing of Miss Zamboanga. It is dedicated to the patron saint of the city, Nuestra Señora del Pilar.

Second Weekend in October
La Naval de Manila
This procession goes along the main streets of Quezon City to the Domingo Church. It commemorates the victorious sea battle against the Dutch plunderers in the year 1646.

19 October
MassKara Festival
On the weekend closest to 19 October, the largest festival on Negros takes place in Bacolod. There are street dances and groups of people wearing costumes and friendly, smiling masks.

1 November
Undas (public holiday)
On All Saints' Day, families meet at the cemetery and stay there the whole night and even the night before. Numerous lights, candles and flowers on the graves make an impressive sight. There are booths and stalls in front of the cemetery.

23 November
Feast of San Clemente
On this feast day a boat parade takes place in Angono, Rizal Province. It is a thanksgiving by the fishing people in honour of their patron saint, San Clemente.

30 November
Bonifacio Day (public holiday)
A national holiday in tribute to Filipino

heroes, most especially in honour of Andres Bonifacio, who headed the Katipunan, the revolutionary movement formed to fight the Spaniards.

8 December
Feast of Our Lady of the Immaculate Conception
An impressive boat procession is held at night on the Malabon River and Manila Bay at the fishing community of Malabon in the north-west of Metro Manila. In the afternoon, there is a procession through the streets of Malabon which leaves from the Immaculate Conception Church.

16 to 25 December
Simbang Gabi
You can hear Christmas carols practically all over the Philippines from about the beginning of November. Officially, however, the Christmas season begins on 16 December. Following the old traditions, religious Filipinos go to *simbang gabi* (night masses) which are held before dawn.

24 December
Giant Lantern Festival
The most spectacular lantern festival in the Philippines takes place in San Fernando, Pampanga Province. Some of the *parol* (coloured Christmas stars) are so large they need a tractor to pull them. Contact the City Tourist Office in San Fernando from around the middle of December for further details, Tel +63 (0)45 9612872.

25 December
Christmas (public holiday)
This family day, as in practically all Christian countries, is awaited with great excitement by children. However, grown-ups also seem to wait for a Christmas present impatiently, and ask repeatedly for a week beforehand: 'Where is my Christmas?'

28 December
Holy Innocents' Day
Just as people in the West play April Fools' Day tricks on 1 April, Filipinos try to catch one another out on this day, which is also known as *Niños Inocentes*.

30 December
Rizal Day (public holiday)
A national holiday with street parades in memory of the Filipino national hero, Dr Jose Rizal, who was executed by the Spaniards on this day in 1896. Statues of him are decorated with flowers, and national flags are lowered to half-mast.

National Clothing

For men, there is no obligation to wear either a tie or a suit, even at highly official political receptions. The *barong tagalog* is the sensible alternative: it is a long-sleeved shirt which lets the air through and is worn over the trousers. Underneath, it is customary to wear a T-shirt. At weddings, the men of both families consider it their duty to wear a *wedding barong tagalog*. The short-sleeved style is known as a *polo barong*. These cool, semi-transparent shirts with their fine embroidery date from the Spanish era when Filipinos were required to wear their shirts untucked, and the barong became a symbol of national consciousness. Fine barongs are made from *piña*, a fibre made from the pineapple plant. The *terno* is the typical Philippine dress worn by women, recognisable by its stiff butterfly sleeves. It is only worn on formal occasions. The general fashion for women follows Western trends.

Health Service

Thanks to the ongoing, intensive programme initiated by the Department of Health (DOH) to combat ill-health and epidemics, the state of public health has vastly improved in recent years.

The emphasis of this campaign has been on preventative medicine, producing food which keeps fresh longer, and raising people's awareness of the importance of good nutrition. These measures are backed up by a network of local health centres, mobile patient care stations, free medical treatment in some cases, and the distribution of urgently needed medicines.
In addition to a general decline in mortality, a drastic reduction has been achieved in the mortality of mothers and infants. The most serious illnesses are still pneumonia, TB, heart disease, gastric illnesses and bronchitis.

Medical Services
Most Philippine hospitals are privately run. State-owned hospitals and provincial private practices are often badly equipped. In an emergency, you should try to reach the nearest town and check into a private hospital.
The best and most well-known hospitals in Metro Manila are the Makati Medical Center and St Luke's Medical Center, both of which have above-average staff and are equipped with the most up-to-date equipment available.
Dental treatment is adequate, at least in the towns and cities. In country areas on the other hand, dental problems are often simply solved by pulling the tooth.

Education

The Philippine education system is largely based on the American model: Primary education (elementary schools), secondary education (high schools) and higher education (colleges, universities). School attendance is compulsory for the first four years of the six-year elementary school. In addition to the state education institutions there is a large number of private schools, mainly run by religious groups.
With an illiteracy rate of only 12% of the population over fifteen, the standard of education is high compared with other developing countries, even if there is a noticeable drop in standard in non-urban areas.

Media

Newspapers & Magazines

After 20 years of press censorship under Marcos, the change of government in February 1986 brought a flood of new national and local newspapers and magazines indulging in a marvellous journalistic free-for-all. Before, there was a group of four big government-friendly national dailies. Now about 20 publications, including the *Manila Bulletin*, the *Inquirer*, *Malaya*, *Manila Standard*, *Newsday*, *The Manila Chronicle*, *Today*, *Daily Globe*, *The Philippine Star* and *The Journal* fight for their share in a free market. All are in English. In contrast to the unilateral reporting during Marcos's time the media today represent a fair, critical and objective difference of opinion. *Tempo* and *People's Journal* are vigorous tabloid papers, which appear in both English and Tagalog.
A lesser role is played by the Philippine papers *Balita*, *Taliba* and *Ang Pilipino Ngayon*, in keeping with their circulation and layout. In the Sunday editions of various newspapers a magazine is included. Newspapers printed in Manila but sold outside the capital are more expensive because of transport costs.
There are also a few magazines which appear weekly, amongst which the *Free Press*, with its irreverent and quite critical articles, stands out.
International events are meagrely reported or analysed in the Philippine mass media. If you want to know more you can get *Newsweek, Time* and the *International Herald Tribune*. They

can be found on sale in the larger hotels.

The English-language newspapers *What's On & Expat* and *Foreign Post* appear weekly and are free of charge in many hotels. These publications are aimed towards foreigners living in the Philippines, and tourists.

The number of comics published and read each week is quite phenomenal.

Radio & TV

Radio and TV almost all operate on a commercial basis and the programmes are continually interrupted by advertisements. Game shows and soap operas *(Tele Novelas)* are very popular on TV, and dubbed Mexican series such as *Rosalinda* and *Maria La Del Barrio* are followed avidly.

Many hotels now offer cable TV with international programmes such as BBC World and CNN.

Radio Veritas is a non-commercial station, as is FEBC on 98.7 Mhz, the only VHF radio station in Manila with classical music.

Lovers of so-called smooth jazz will be pleased to find the station Citylite 88.3, which transmits in Manila round the clock on 88.3 MHz with a quality programme of jazz, new age, rhythm and blues, and regular special news bulletins for expats. Citylite 88.3 can also be heard in Baguio, Cebu City, Cagayan de Oro and Davao, although on different frequencies.

Sex Bombs for Lunch

At twelve o'clock on the dot, every day apart from Sunday, Channel 7 screens the highly popular noontime show *Eat Bulaga*. Broadcast live since 1979 by the influential GMA network, it's the longest running TV show in the Philippines. The idea of presenting a mixture of comedy, music, dance and games with audience participation might be simple, but it's successful. After two hours of fun and entertainment, seasoned with the occasional *double entendre* and cheeky comments from the presenters, everyday worries are soon forgotten. And all the more so when the attractive Sex Bomb Girls appear on the scene. This absolutely riveting troupe of singing and dancing young ladies in their sexy outfits are not only what every Philippine male dreams about, they are also the idols of hordes of Filipinas who can often be seen copying their delightfully suggestive dance movements on the dance floor. Only a few bars of their hit *Spageti Song* (that's how they spell it) are enough and, wherever they are, there's no way their female fans can stand or sit still.

Food & Drinks

Some Western travellers consider the Philippine diet to be monotonous. Many dairy products are lacking and the daily fare consists of rice and fish, but if you are flexible you can add some variety. There are dairy products like milk, yoghurt, cheese and ice cream in most supermarkets, and meals can be varied by checking out the contents of the cooking pots in restaurants. In a turo-turo restaurant (*turo* means 'point') there is no menu: the food is displayed and customers point to what they would like to eat.

Of course the choice is more restricted in the country than in the city. In larger towns there are usually a number of Western and Chinese restaurants.

Filipino cuisine - with its Chinese, Malay and Spanish influences - is a mixture of Eastern and Western cuisine. It is usually referred to locally as 'native' food and can be really delicious. The different dishes in a meal are all served at the same time with the result that certain dishes end up being eaten cold, something which Filipinos normally don't mind. It is not unusual to be offered cold fried eggs for breakfast; enough to turn most Western appetites off.

Westernised Filipinos usually eat with a spoon and fork; knives are not often used. However, the original *kamayan* mode, namely eating with the fingers off a banana leaf, has come back into fashion, so there is no cutlery laid on the table in a kamayan restaurant.

When travelling around, go ahead and ask for the speciality of the province, which can be surprisingly good. As a rule of thumb, it is cheap and worthwhile eating where the locals eat, but even Western food is not that expensive. In some restaurants you can get a complete Western meal for around P150.

Snacks

Filipinos eat five times a day if possible. Apart from the regular meals of breakfast, lunch and evening meal, in the mornings and afternoons a more or less extensive snack called *merienda* is taken. Besides this, *pulutan* (small morsels) appear on the table when alcoholic drinks are served.

At the eateries in the larger towns, barbecues are very popular in the evenings. You can get pork, liver, whole chickens (*lechon manok*), chicken legs, various seafoods and other tasty snacks in the form of barbecue sticks. In the warm summer months of April and May, when selecting your choice of fresh meat for barbecuing, check it out with your nose first.

The Filipinos have taken to US fast foods wholeheartedly, so there are plenty of hamburgers and hot dogs.

Snack favourites include:

Bagoong - Although not a snack itself, this pungent smelling, fermented, salty sauce or paste made of fish or shrimp is often served with snack food. It is frequently prepared according to traditional folk recipes and people like to eat it with snacks like green mango, for example.

Balut - A popular Filipino snack for between meals, said to make you fit. Before a Filipino suitor invites a woman up to see his stamp collection, he'll usually partake in a couple of baluts washed down with beer. Baluts can be purchased from street sellers and markets. A balut is a half-boiled, ready-to-hatch duck egg. You can distinguish the beak and feathers! Some baluts still contain some liquid so don't break open the whole egg: make a small hole first.

Kilawin - Small cuts of raw meat lightly roasted, then marinated in vinegar and other spices (ginger, onion, salt).

Kinilaw - Small cuts of raw fish or cuttlefish marinated with spices (ginger, onion, chili) in vinegar or lemon.

Siopao - A white, steam heated dough ball with a filling such as chicken or pork. A quick snack.

Tapa - This is baked dried beef served with raw onion rings. Tapa is also available as a vacuum-packed preserved food but this tastes dreadful - remarkably like plastic.

Vegetarian Food

Exclusively vegetarian restaurants are pretty thin on the ground in the Philippines. However, there are a number of places which have vegetarian fare on their menu as well as fish and meat dishes. You have to watch though: some Filipino restaurants are fairly liberal with their use of the word 'vegetarian' and might serve, for example, 'vegetable soup' with both vegetables and meat.

This is also not the only place in the world where the word 'meat' is taken to mean 'beef'. So a 'meatless dish' may contain pork, chicken or any other meat that is not beef. You have to make clear to the person serving you that you do not eat any beef, chicken, pork etc before you order. To be on the safe side, every restaurant that serves Japanese food, specifically tempura, will prepare you a guaranteed meatless yasaii tempura (deep fried vegetables in batter).

Main Dishes

Rice is the staple food and will be served with most meals, even breakfast where it is served with one or two side dishes (Filipino Breakfast). If you ask for bread, you will usually be given a couple of slices of untoasted, basically tasteless white bread. If you actually want toast, you have to ask for 'toasted bread'.

Whatever the dishes are called that make up the meal, there are generic expressions to describe how the dish is cooked. Dishes with *ginataan* after them are cooked in coconut milk, while *inihaw* refers to grilled fish or meat.

The following description of Philippine foods may make it a little easier to choose when confronted with a menu.

Adobo - A national standard dish made from chicken *(chicken adobo)*, pork *(pork adobo)*, squid *(pusit adobo)* and/or vegetables and cooked with vinegar, pepper, garlic and salt.

Adobong Pusit - Cleaned cuttlefish is prepared with coconut milk, vinegar and garlic. The ink is used as a special seasoning.

Ampalaya con Carne - Beef with bitter melon, prepared with onions, garlic, soy sauce and some sesame oil. Served with rice.

Arroz Caldo - Thick rice soup with chicken cooked with onions, garlic and ginger, and black pepper added afterwards.

Asado - Seasonal smoked meat, served with sour *atchara* (papaya strips).

Atchara (Atsara) - A very healthy and vitamin-rich side dish, the Philippine sauerkraut - made from unripe papayas.

Bangus (Milkfish) - Herring-size fish that are lightly grilled and baked with a stuffing made with grated carrot, potato, raisins, tomatoes and onions.

Batchoy - Beef, pork and liver in noodle soup. A speciality of the western Visayas (Bacolod, Iloilo City).

Bulalo - A substantial soup of boiled beef (kneecap), marrow and vegetables.

Calamares Fritos - Fried squid.

Caldereta - A stew of goat's meat, or beef, peas and paprika.

Crispy Pata - Pig skin first cooked then seasoned with garlic, salt, pepper and vinegar, and then baked in oil till crispy. There are many ways of seasoning and preparing it. Crispy pata is often served cut into small pieces. There is usually more crackling than meat - which is how the Filipinos like it!

Dinuguan - Finely chopped offal (pork or chicken) roasted in fresh blood and usually seasoned with whole green pepper corns. This dish is also called chocolate meat on account of its dark colour.

Gambas al Ajillo - Shelled raw shrimps prepared with olive oil, pepper, salt, some paprika and a lot of garlic. Served with white bread.

Kare-Kare - A stew of oxtail, beef shank, vegetables, onions and garlic. The stock can be enriched with peanuts and lightly fried rice, both finely ground.

Lapu-Lapu Inihaw - Grilled grouper, seasoned with salt, pepper, garlic and soy sauce. Lapu-Lapu is the most popular fish dish in the country, but is expensive. It was named after the Filipino chief who killed Ferdinand Magellan in battle.

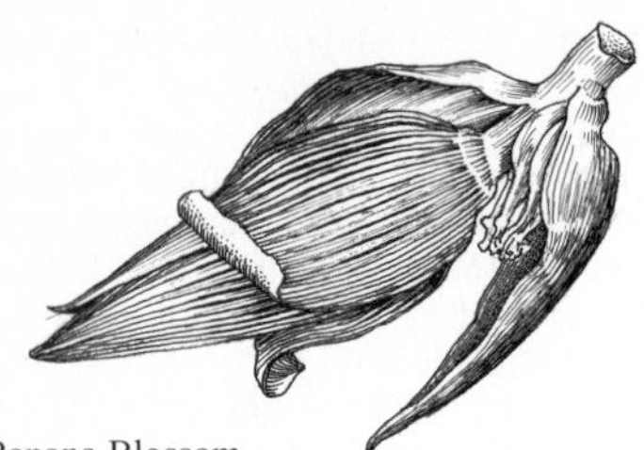

Banana Blossom
The »heart of the banana« *(puso ng saging)* is popular cooked as a vegetable

Lechon - Suckling pig served with a thick liver sauce. Lechon *(litson)* is an important dish at fiestas.
Lechon Kawali - Pork leg, baked and seasoned with green papaya, ginger, vinegar and sugar.
Lumpia - Spring rolls filled with vegetables or meat. They are served with soy sauce, vinegar or a slightly sweet sauce. *Lumpia Shanghai* are fried spring rolls filled with meat, whereas the bigger *lumpia sariwa* are filled with vegetables and served uncooked.
Mami - Noodle soup; when made with chicken it's *chicken mami*, with beef it's *beef mami* etc.
Menudo - Stew made from either small liver pieces or chopped pork, with diced potatoes, tomatoes, paprika and onions.
Misua Soup - Soup made from rice noodles, beef, garlic and onions.
Nilaga - Soup with cabbage, potatoes and meat. With beef it's *nilaga baka*.
Pancit Canton - A noodle dish made with thick noodles which are baked, then combined with pork, shrimps and vegetables. The pork is cooked in soy sauce beforehand.
Pancit Guisado - Like pancit canton but thinner Chinese noodles are used and it's often not so spicy.
Pork Apritada - Pork is cut into small pieces and baked. The sauce includes pieces of tomato, onion, potatoe, pepperoni and garlic.
Shrimp Rebosado - Shrimps are baked in butter then cooked in a roux.
Sinigang - Sour vegetable soup with fish *(sinigang na isda)* or pork *(sinigang na baboy)*. Can be served with rice.
Sisig - Hearty stew made with pork cheek, which is first boiled then grilled until crispy. It is then diced and sauteed in oil together with onions and pieces of liver seasoned with chili, salt and pepper. A speciality of Pampanga Province served on a cast-iron platter.
Tahong - Large green mussels baked or cooked in sauce.
Talaba - Raw oysters soaked in vinegar and garlic.
Tinola - A stew with chicken, vegetables, ginger, onions and garlic.

Desserts

Ice Cream - I would advise against ice cream in open containers from a travelling vendor. It would be better to buy the packaged Dairy Bars or cartons of excellent ice cream from Nestlé or Selecta.
Halo-Halo - Popular dessert made from crushed ice mixed with coloured sweets and fruits, smothered in evaporated milk and mixed together (halo-halo means 'all mixed together'). It tastes noticeably better with a little rum.

Fruits

There's a wide selection of tropical fruits available, depending on the season, at markets and from a few street stalls.

Avocado *(abukado)* - A pear-shaped fruit, with a green skin which turns maroon then purple as it ripens. The soft, very oily flesh has a taste reminiscent of nuts and surrounds a big, smooth stone in the middle. Avocados are in season from May until July.

Banana *(saging)* - There are over 20 known varieties. Bananas are available

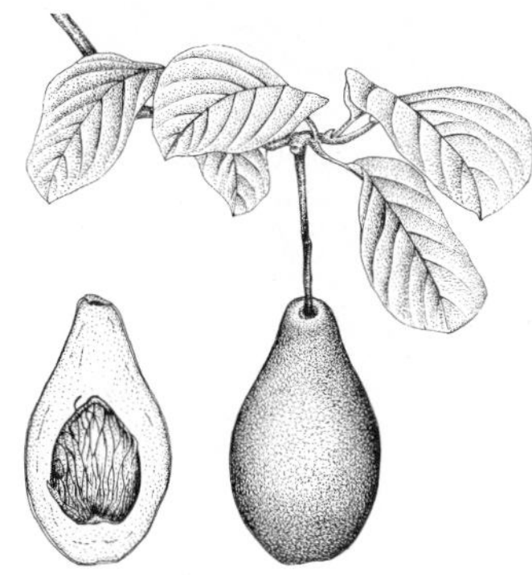

Avocado *(abukado)*

all year-round. You can have them not only as freshly picked fruit, but also cooked, grilled, baked or roasted.

Banana *(saging)*

Carambola or **Star Fruit** *(balimbing)* An egg-shaped fruit with five segments which form a star shape in cross-section. The skin is yellow and has a shiny, polished appearance. The flesh is crisp and juicy, with a tartness to its taste. It's in season from March until June.

Carambola *(balimbing)*

Coconut *(niyog)* - A versatile fruit. While the hard flesh of older coconuts is dried in the sun and processed as copra, the young, green ones *(buko)* with their refreshing juice and soft flesh are sold to be eaten. Here's a tip on one way to enjoy them: Pour out a little of the juice, fill the nut up with small pieces of papaya, pineapple or maybe mango, together with up to half a bottle of rum, and leave it to in the refrigerator for about twelve hours to soak in! Coconuts are available all year round.

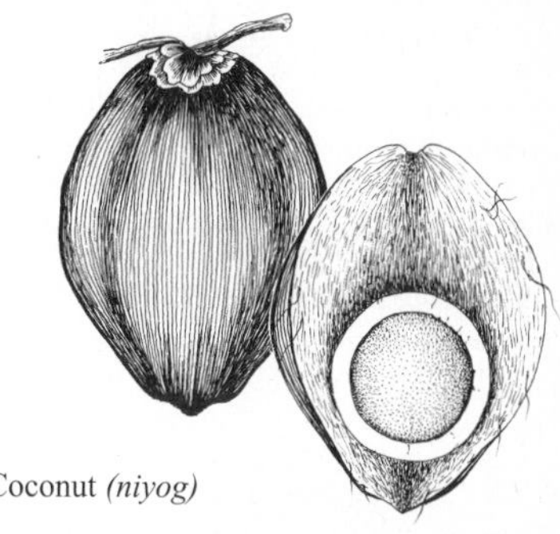

Coconut *(niyog)*

Custard Apple *(atis)*

Custard Apple *(atis)* - Also known as 'sugar apple' or 'cinnamon apple', this fruit has a scaly, grey-green skin and looks rather like a hand grenade. To get at its soft white flesh it's best to cut the custard apple in half and remove its kernel with a knife. The skin is not palatable. The fruit is in season from August to October.

Durian *(durian)* - A thick, prickly fruit, about which opinions are sharply divided: either you're crazy about it or you can't stand it. There's no in-between. Cutting open the outer shell reveals four segments with several large seeds surrounded by the flesh of the fruit. Depending on how ripe it is, the creamy, yellowish-white flesh either has a very pleasant aroma, or stinks terribly (over-ripe). This fruit, with its 'hellish stench and heavenly taste', is in season from August to October.

Durian *(durian)*

Giant Orange *(suha)* - This fruit is also known internationally as pomelo or ugly fruit and resembles a huge grapefruit. It tastes rather like a grapefruit too, except that it's somewhat sweeter. You'll have to peel away a very thick skin to get at the flesh, which is usually fairly dry. You can get giant oranges right through the year.

Giant Orange *(suha)*

Guava *(gayabas)* - A round, egg-sized to apple-sized fruit with light, crispy, faintly acidic flesh and numerous small, hard seeds. Rich in Vitamin C, it is greenish to yellowish in colour and is in season from July to January.

Guava *(bayabas)*

Jackfruit *(langka)* - This is a colossus among fruit. Greenish yellow with coarse skin, it can weigh up to 20 kg and may be as big as a blown-up balloon. The pale yellow flesh is split into portions and eaten as a dessert (sweet), salad or vegetable, depending on how ripe it is; the seeds should be cooked before being eaten. The jackfruit season is from February to July.

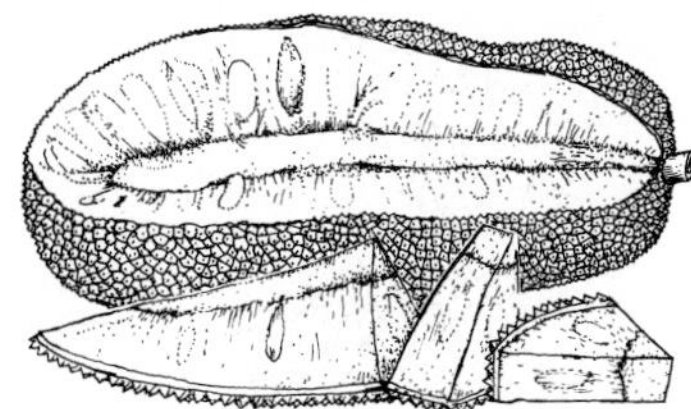

Jackfruit *(langka)*

Kalamansi *(kalamansi)* - This juicy, green lemon-like fruit is about the size of a pinball. It goes beautifully with black tea and is indispensable in the Filipino kitchen as well as for the preparation of 'happy hour' drinks at sunset or whenever. Kalamansi are available all year round.

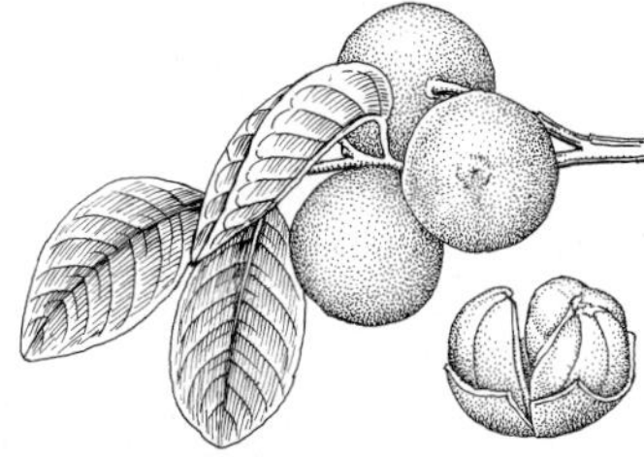

Kalamansi *(kalamansi)*

Langsat/Lanson *(lanzones)* - Looks like a little potato. Under its easily peeled, yellow-brown skin is a delicious, translucent flesh. But be careful: occasionally one of the flesh segments will contain small, very bitter inedible seeds. It's in season from August to November, or April/May in the Visayas.

Langsat *(lanzones)*

Mango *(mangga)* - An oval shaped fruit which can be up to 20 cm long and has a large, flat stone. When the skin is green it is unripe, hard and very sour, but tastes marvellous with salt or a bitter, salty shrimp-paste called bagoong. The flesh of a ripe mango is yellow, juicy and vaguely reminiscent of the peach in taste. The mango is split into three by cutting the fruit lengthwise along the flat stone. The two side sections are eaten with a spoon, the centre piece should be speared with a pointed knife and the flesh gnawed off. The skin is inedible. Mango is in season between April and June.

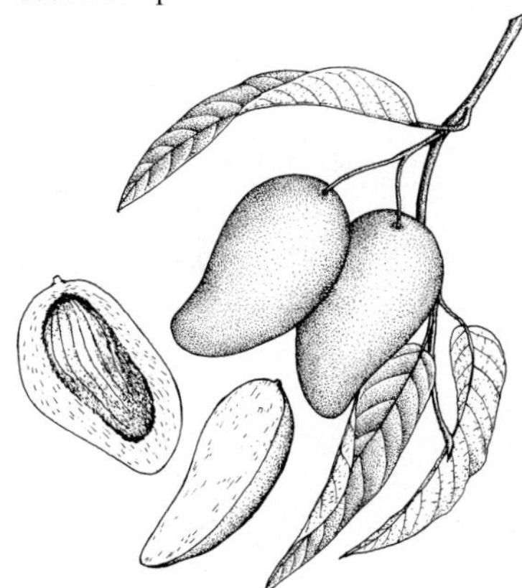

Mango *(mangga)*

Mangosteen *(mangostan)* - This dark purple fruit is about the size of a mandarin orange and has a tough skin. To get to the sweet-sour, white flesh you break it open or use a knife. It's in season from May to October.

Mangosteen *(mangostan)*

Papaya *(papaya)* - A species of melon which, when ripe, reveals a delicious, orange-red flesh under a shiny green to orange-coloured skin. It's best to cut it lengthways, remove the black seeds, sprinkle a little kalamansi juice over the halves and spoon out the pulp. Papaya are in season right through the year.

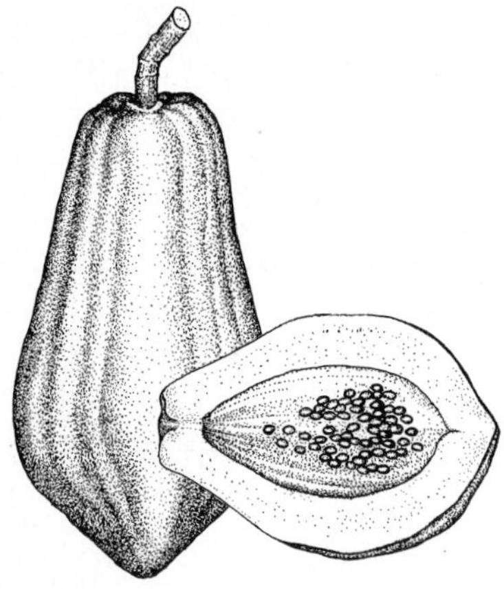

Papaya *(papaya)*

Pineapple *(piña)* - Pineapples can be bought the whole year-round. They're at their juiciest and sweetest during the main season from March to May.

Pineapple *(piña)*

Pomegranate *(granada)* - A thick-skinned, brownish-red fruit about the size of an orange. The numerous fleshy seeds inside are crimson in colour and can be eaten fresh by spooning them out, or used to make jam or grenadine syrup.

Pomegranate *(granada)*

Rambutan *(rambutan)* - Shaped rather like an egg with a reddish, hairy skin - a funny looking fruit. Under the cute packaging you'll find a delicious translucent sweet pulp. Rambutans are sold in bunches and are picked from August to October.

Roseapple *(makopa)* - This small, pear-shaped fruit has an appetising appearance and can be eaten whole, including the skin. Depending on ripeness, its taste ranges from sweet (green, white,

Rambutan *(rambutan)*

light pink) to sour (dark pink, reddish). Best eaten between March and July.

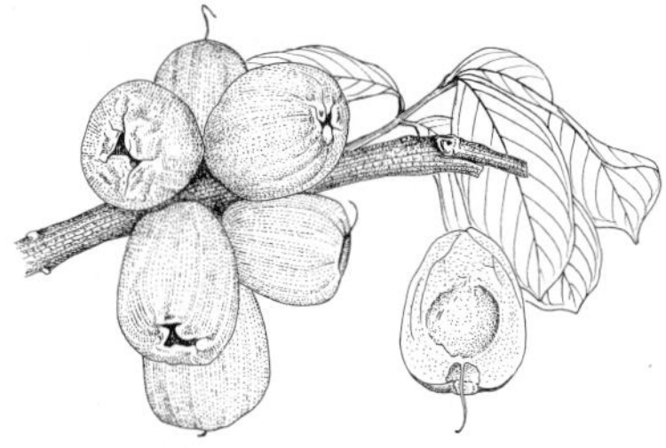

Roseapple *(makopa)*

Sapodilla *(chico)* - A roughly egg-shaped fruit with a brown skin which

Sapodilla *(chico)*

contains a soft, sweet, brownish coloured flesh that looks like wet sand. The skin is normally peeled off but you can also eat it. It's in season from November to February.

Sour Sop *(guayabano)* - The fibrous, juicy flesh of this thorny fruit, which can weigh up to two kg, has a tart, tangy taste and is ideal for making tasty juices and mixed drinks. It's in season from August to November. Try guayabano juice with rum - it's an excellent combination!

Sour Sop *(guayabano)*

Star Apple *(kaimito)* - Slicing a star apple reveals an arrangement of several star shaped segments, hence its name. Soft and very juicy, it is best eaten with a spoon. There are green and violet kinds of star apple, both of which are ripe and edible. The violet ones are sweeter. It's in season from January/ February to March.

Watermelon *(pakwan)* - The size of a football, the flesh of this dark-green melon is red and watery. For a wonder-

Star Apple *(kaimito)*

fully refreshing dessert, pour a small glass of Cointreau over a chilled slice of watermelon. Available all year-round, but especially from April to November.

Watermelon*(pakwan)*

Drinks

Perspiration and thirst are part and parcel of a stay in the tropics. Especially during the hot Philippine summer from March until May, you can be drenched with sweat in no time at all. Your body needs to replace all the fluid it has lost. After you've taken care of that basic need, your thoughts might turn to drinks that do more than just quench a tropical thirst. And you imagine them, of course, ice-cold or on the rocks. Just what your stomach doesn't need, say the doctors. And they're probably right. But can you think of a drink that tastes good lukewarm? At any rate, ice cubes are generally harmless in the Philippines as they are usually produced in ice factories. However, the big ice blocks which are also produced in these factories often get dirty in transport, and are sometimes not smashed up into drink-size bits in the most hygenic way. If you're not sure, remember the old saying: When in doubt, leave it out!

Non-alcoholic Drinks

Most of the drinks in the Philippines are safe as they are in bottles or cartons, including milk and chocolate drinks.

Coffee & Tea - Unlike in other Asiatic countries, people seldom drink tea in the Philippines. About the only way you will see it made is with a Lipton's teabag. However, real Chinese restaurants do serve proper tea made with tea-leaves along with your meal.
Instead of tea, you will usually be served with instant coffee in the Philippines - what would the world do without Nescafé? First class hotels do provide good coffee made from top name brands of imported beans. The local Batangas coffee, also called Barako, is made from locally-grown beans. This is good enough coffee, but the multis are forcing it off the market.

Coconut Juice - If you want to enjoy the delicious, refreshing juice of a very young coconut *(buko)*, get the fruit seller to open it for you to drink. A nut will contain up to a litre of buko juice, which is pure and easy to digest.

Kalamansi Juice - The tiny lemons known as kalamansi provide a sour extract when squeezed, which can be made into a healthy drink with the addition of a little sugar. Kalamansi juice can be drunk hot or cold.

Soft drinks - Internationally known drinks such as Coke, Sprite, 7-Up and a few Philippine products such as Royal and Tru Orange are available on every corner.

Water - Outside of towns and cities it's better not to use the drinking water on offer as it could come out of a well, or be of otherwise dubious origin. In the cities where it is adequately chlorinated, tap water is generally clean and safe to drink, although even there it pays to be careful.
So-called Purified Water Stations are becoming more and more widespread (clearly there's a reason for this), where processed 'drinking water' is on sale in plastic canisters (20 litres/P40). They are also prepared to fill bottles which people have brought with them (1 litre/ P5).
In many shops and restaurants quite expensive mineral water is available these days in the form of plastic bottles filled with safe, uncarbonated drinking water. On the other hand, bottled soda water is only available in a handful of tourist resorts. It's adviseable not to try the mineral water offered on sale by wandering salesmen in harbours and on buses. It's often simply tap water sold in a bottle with a bogus seal on it.

Alcoholic Drinks
Basi - An alcoholic drink made from fermented sugar cane juice is *basi*, an ice-cooled sweet variant of which has a taste reminiscent of sherry or port.

Beer - There are several brands of beer. Apart from the strong Red Horse beer, they are all light and, with a few exceptions, very drinkable. San Miguel is the best known beer and, with over a 90% share of the market, is also the most successful. It's also available as San Mig Light. Competition is provided by Beer na Beer from the Asia Brewery. It is cheaper than San Miguel and is gradually building up its market share.

Hard Drinks - Rum, whisky, gin and brandy of local manufacture are very good value. The well-aged rums of particularly fine quality are Tanduay, Anejo and Tondeña.

Palm Wine - *Tuba* is a palm wine made from the juice of coconut palms. It is tapped from the crown of the tree. Tuba is drunk fresh or after a fermentation process. When distilled it is called *lambanog*.

Rice Wine - *Tapuy (tapey)* is a rice wine and the end of its six-month fermentation process is eagerly anticipated. Only after this period can you discover whether the taste aimed for has been achieved or if the wine has become sour and undrinkable.

Wine - Spirits are often called wine in the Philippines. If it is literally red or white wine you want, then you might have to try ordering 'grapes wine' if all else fails.

Language

History

Historically, the waves of immigration of alien peoples (Indonesians, Chinese, Malays etc) and the structure of the country (a series of islands) have brought about a multiplicity of languages and language groups. Today there are about 80 significantly different dialects spoken.
During the period of Spanish occupation, Spanish was taught in schools and, since education is mainly a prerogative of the wealthy, it developed as the language of politicians and the business

community. Though small, the influence of Spanish on the local languages is still present today (for instance, in the numerical system and in the Zamboangan language of Chavacano). Spanish was abolished in 1968 as a compulsory subject in higher schools, but is still the mother tongue of a small percentage of the population, mainly the upper class.
English became very important in the Philippines with the beginning of the US era on the islands, and has remained the language of commerce and politics even since the declaration of total independence from the United States in 1946. Newspapers, TV, radio announcements and even government statistics are evidence of this.

National Language
The concept of a national language was formed after the Spanish-American War in 1898, but it wasn't until 1936, a year after the formation of the Philippines Commonwealth, that the Institute of National Language was established. President Manuel Quezon declared Tagalog the national language in that year and the appropriate bill was incorporated into the Philippine constitution in 1946.
There were several other contenders for the role of the main language in this multilingual country - among them Cebuano, Hiligaynon and Ilocano. The compromises reached during the 1970s still hold; the constitution of 1973 confirms Filipino as the national language. It is based on Tagalog but contains certain linguistic elements from other Philippine languages. Since 1978 Filipino has been taught in schools and universities.

Gestures & Signs
As well as the spoken and written language, the Filipinos use various gestures and signs.

- The hand movements which mean 'go away' to us signify 'come here' in the Philippines.
- Instead of pointing with your finger, you indicate discreetly by pointing pursed lips in the direction you want.
- The brief raising of the eyebrows is generally meant positively.
- People used to hiss to gain attention, for example, when calling one of the waiters in a restaurant. Nowadays, it's not so common and may even cause offence.
- The thumb is not used to indicate numbers; you indicate two beers, for example, with the ring finger and the little finger.
- When you want to pay the bill, look out for one of the waiters and draw a rectangle in the air with your index finger and thumb. Should the waiter or waitress be looking the other way, just clap your hands two or three times. The bill is called a 'chit' in the Philippines.
- If Filipinos don't understand a question, they open their mouths.

Communicating
It is important to remember that English as spoken in the Philippines sometimes varies wildly from Standard English. The correct answer to a negative question is Yes, and not No as would be normal in English-speaking countries. For example, if asked the question: 'You don't smoke, do you?' the answer 'Yes' means 'Yes, that's correct, I don't smoke'! Although we laugh, it's not difficult to imagine a situation when offence could be given inadvertently, and you might never know. Imagine, for instance, what could happen if your host were to ask: 'You don't like Philippine food?'.
It is not vital to know the local language, as English will get you through most situations, but as in any country, locals will be pleased and surprised if you have learned even a few fragments of their language. The following may help.

Some Notes on Pronunciation

- In Filipino *p* and *f* are often interchanged (Filipino = Pilipino). This means that a written *p* can be pronounced as an *f*. This interchange is sometimes carried over into English by Filipinos (April = Afril) but it in no way impairs understanding.
- Double vowels are pronounced separately (paalam = pa-alam).
- The combination *ng* is pronounced 'nang' and *mga* is pronounced 'manga'.
- The syllable *po* underlines courtesy towards elders and persons of respect (eg, *Salámat po Ginang Santos*, Thank you Mrs Santos).
- In the words and phrases below, an accent over the vowel of a syllable means that this syllable is stressed. Alternative forms have been added in brackets.

Filipino

Greetings & Civilities

Hello, greetings	*mabúhay*
Good morning	*magandáng umága*
Good day	*magandáng tangháli*
Good afternoon	*magandáng hápon*
Good evening/night	*magandáng gabí*
Goodbye	*paálam (adyós, bye)*
How are you?	*kumustá (ka)?*
How are you? (plural)	*kumustá (po) kayá?*
Good/well	*mabúti*
Well, thank you, and you?	*mabúti salámat, at ikáw?*
Also good/well	*mabúti rin*
Where have you been?	*saán ka gáling?*
Where are you going?	*saán ka pupuntá?*
I'm coming from Bato	*gáling akó sa Bato*
I'm going to Talisay	*pupuntá akó sa Talisay*
Thank you	*salámat*
Thank you very much	*maráming salamat*
Please	*pakí*
You're welcome	*waláng anumán*
Yes/no	*oó/hindí*
Yes/no (polite)	*opó/hindí po*
And	*at*
OK	*síge*
Only, merely, simply	*lang (lamang)*
Just a minute	*sandalí (sandalí lang)*
Again, similarly	*namán (na namán)*
Always, of course	*siyémpre*
No problem	*waláng probléma*
It's all right	*ayós ang lahát*

Small Talk

Wait *téka*	*(téka muna)*
Come here	*halíka díto*
Slowly, take your time	*dahán-dahán*
What is your name?	*anóng pangálan mo?*
How old are you?	*iláng taón ka na?*
Where do you come from?	*tagásaáng bayán ka?*
I like you	*gustó kitá*
I love you	*mahál kitá (ini-íbig kitá)*
You are beautiful	*magandá ka*
What did you say?	*anó po? (anó?)*
Is it true?	*totoó ba?*
I don't know	*áywan ko (hindí ko alam)*
I like (that)	*gustó ko (itó)*
I don't like...	*ayaw akó... (ayóko)*
I'll do it (I'll get it)	*akó na lang*
You do it (you get it)	*ikáw na lang*
Let's go	*táyo na (síge na)*
It's too late	*hulí na*
I have no time	*walá akóng panahón*
Are you sure?	*siguradó ka ba?*
Wake up	*gísing na*
Not yet	*hindí pa*
Maybe/perhaps	*sigúro*
What a pity	*sáyang*
Really	*talagá*
That's not true (flatterer)	*boléro*
Crazy	*lóko-lóko*
Fool (you)	*gágo (ka)*
Mad	*galít*
Are you mad?	*galít ka?*
Rude, insolent	*bastós*
Braggart	*mayábang*
It's none of your business	*walá kang pakíalam*
Get lost!	*alís diyán!*
Later on	*mamayá na*
Never mind	*hindí bále*

People & Pronouns

Man	*laláki (laláke)*
Woman	*babáe*
Unmarried man	*binatá*

Unmarried woman	*dalága*
Mr	*Ginoó*
Mr Santos	*Ginoóng Santos*
Mrs	*Gínang*
Mrs Santos	*Gínang Santos*
Miss	*Binibíni*
Miss Santos	*Binibíning Santos*
Child (general)	*batá*
Child (own)	*anák*
Boy	*bátang laláki*
Girl	*bátang babáe*
Grandmother/grandfather	*lóla/lólo*
Friend	*kaibígan*
I	*akó*
You	*ka (ikáw)*
He/she	*siyá*
They	*silá*
We (I and you)	*táyo*
We (I and others)	*kamí*
You (plural)	*kayó*
Old	*matandá*
Young	*batá*
Tall	*mataás*
Short	*pandák*
Fat	*matabá*
Slim, sexy	*balingkinitán*
Happy	*maligáya*
Sad	*malungkót*
Intelligent	*matalíno*
Stupid	*tangá*
Handsome, pretty	*pógi, guwápo/guwápa*
Ugly	*pángit*
Drunken	*lasíng*
Sober	*hindí lasíng*

Common Questions

Do you have...?	*mayroón...?*
How?	*paáno?*
How many?	*ilán?*
How much?	*gaáno (magkáno)?*
How much is one coffee?	*magkáno isáng kapé?*
How far is it?	*gaáno kalayo?*
What?	*anó?*
What is this/that?	*anó itó/iyán?*
What did you say?	*anó ang sabi mo?*
Who (singular)?	*síno?*
Who (plural)?	*sinu-síno?*
Who is there?	*síno iyán?*
When?	*kailán?*
When will it be ready?	*kailán matatápos?*
Where?	*saán*
Where is the post office?	*saán ang koréyo (saán ang post office)?*
Why?	*bákit?*
Why not?	*bákit hindí?*

Accommodation

Bathroom	*bányo*
Bed	*káma*
Blanket, cover	*kubrekáma*
Hotel	*oté'l*
Key	*susí*
Mosquito net	*kulambó*
Pillow	*únan*
Room	*kuwárto*
Room with bath	*kuwáto na may bányo*
Toilet	*kubíta*
Do you have air-con?	*mayroón bang air-condítión?*
There is no water	*waláng túbig*
How much is a room?	*magkáno ang isáng kuwárto?*
I'll take the room	*síge kukúnin ko ang kuwártong itá*

Food & Drink

Food, meal	*pagkaín*
Breakfast	*almusál*
Lunch	*panánghalían*
Dinner	*hapúnan*
I am hungry	*gutóm na akó*
I am thirsty	*naúuhaw akó*
I am full	*busóg pa akó*
I have no appetite	*walá akóng gana*
It is cold	*malamíg íto*
I want rice & fish	*gústo ko ng kánin at isdá*
That was a good meal	*ang saráp ng pagkaín*
Bill	*kuwénta (chit, recibo)*
The bill, please	*áki na ang kuwénta (chit/recibo) ko*
Pay	*bayad (magkáno)*
Cup	*tása*
Glass	*báso*
Fork	*tinidór*
Knife	*kutsílyo*
Plate	*pláto*
Serviette/napkin	*serbilyéta*
Spoon	*kutsára*
Teaspoon	*kutsaríta*
Cold	*malamíg*
Cooked, steamed	*nilága*
Delicious	*masaráp*
Fried	*pritó*
Grilled	*iníhaw*
Hard	*matigás*

Hot, warm	*mainít*
Marinated	*kilawín (kiniláw)*
Salty	*inasinán*
Soft	*malambót*
Sour	*maásim*
Spicy	*maánghang*
Spoiled	*sirá*
Sweet	*matamís*
Apple	*mansánas*
Banana	*ságing*
Beans	*sítao*
Beer	*serbésa*
Bread	*tinápay*
Chicken	*manók*
Coconut young/ripe	*bukó/niyog*
Coffee	*kapé*
- Black coffee	*kapéng matápang*
Crab	*alimángo*
Egg	*ítlog*
- Fried egg	*prítong ítlog*
- Soft-boiled egg	*malasádong ítlog*
Eggplant	*talóng*
Fish	*isdá*
- Grouper	*lápu-lápu*
- Snapper	*máya-máya*
- Spanish Mackerel	*tanguíngue (tanguígui)*
- Tuna	*tulíngan*
Garlic	*báwang*
Ginger	*lúya*
Grapes	*ubás*
Guava	*bayábas*
Ice, ice cubes	*yelo*
Ice cream	*sorbetes (surbétes)*
Jackfruit	*langká*
Mango	*manggá*
Meat	*karné*
- Beef	*karnéng báka*
- Pork	*karnéng báboy*
Milk	*gátas*
Mussel	*táhong*
Onion	*sibúyas*
Orange	*kahél*
Papaya	*papáya*
Peanut	*maní*
Pepper (grains)	*pamintá*
- Pepper (powdered)	*pamintáng duróg*
Pineapple	*pinyá*
Potato	*patátas*
- sweet potato	*kamóte*
Prawn	*gámbas*
Rice (uncooked)	*bigás*
- Rice (cooked)	*kánin*
Salad	*insaláda*
Salt	*ásin*
Shrimp	*hípon*
Soup	*sabáw*
Soy sauce	*toyó*
Squid	*pusít*
Sugar	*asúkal*
Tea	*tsa*
Tomato	*kamátis*
Vegetables	*gúlay*
Vinegar	*suká*
Water	*túbig*
Water melon	*pakwán*

Getting Around

Back	*pauróng (pabalík)*
Left	*kaliwá*
Right	*kánan*
Straight on	*dirétso*
Here	*díto*
There	*diyán (doón)*
Near	*malápit*
Far	*malayó*
Turn-off	*lumikó*
Stop	*pára*
Aeroplane	*eropláno*
Boat	*bangká*
Bus	*bus*
Car	*kótse*
Ship	*barkó*
Taxi	*taksi*
Tricycle	*traysikel*
Airport	*airport*
Bus station	*estasyón ng bus*
Embassy	*embassi*
Petrol station	*estasyón ng gas*
Police station	*estasyón ng pulis*
Road	*daán (kálye)*
Street corner	*kanto*
Town/city	*bayán/lungsód*
Village	*báryo*
Bay	*loók*
Beach	*baybáy*
Coast, shore	*tabíng-dágat*
Creek	*sápa*
Forest, jungle	*kagubátan*
Hill	*buról*
Island	*puló*
Lake	*láwa*
Mountain	*bundók*
Ocean, sea	*dágat*
River	*ílog*
River mouth	*wáwa*
Waterfall	*talón*

Which is the bus for Manila?	*alíng bus ang papuntáng Maynila?*
Where is the bus stop?	*saán ang hintáyan ng bus?*
Where do I catch the jeepney?	*saán ang sasakay ng jeepney?*
Where does this bus go?	*saán papuntá ang bus na itó?*
Where do I get off?	*saán akó dapát babá?*
How much is the fare?	*magkáno ang pamasáhe?*
What town is this?	*anóng báyan íto?*
How many km to...?	*ilán ang kilometro hanggáng...?*

Weather

Clear, bright	*malinawág*
Clouds, fog, mist	*úlap*
Cloudy	*ulap (maúlap)*
Cold	*malamíg*
Lightning	*kídlat (lintík)*
Rain	*ulán*
Rainy	*maulán*
Storm/typhoon	*bagyó*
Sun	*áraw*
Thunder	*kulóg*
Warm	*mainít*
Wind	*hángin*
Windy	*mahángin*

Shopping

All	*lahát*
Big	*malakí*
Broken, destroyed	*sirá*
Cheap	*mura*
Closed	*sarado*
Entrance	*pasukán*
Exit	*lábasan*
Expensive	*mahál*
Too expensive	*masyádong mahál*
Few	*kauntí*
Heavy	*mabigát*
Less	*tamá na*
Many	*marámi*
Money	*péra*
More	*kauntí pa*
New (things)	*bágo*
Old	*lumá*
Open	*bukás*
Small	*maliít*

What is this?	*ano itó?*
How much is this? (touch)	*magkáno itó?*
How much is this? (point)	*magkáno iyán?*
How much is one kilo?	*magkáno isáng kilo?*
Do you have/is there...?	*mayroón...?*
Do you have any...?	*mayroón ba kayong...?*
Do you have anything cheaper?	*mayroón bang mas múra?*
Too expensive	*masyádong mahál*
This is cheap	*múra na itó*
Could you wrap it?	*pakí balot*
I'd like to pay now	*magbabáyad na akó (magkáno ang babáyaran ko)*

Numbers

0	*walá*
1	*isá*
2	*dalawá*
3	*tatló*
4	*apát*
5	*limá*
6	*ánim*
7	*pitó*
8	*waló*
9	*siyám*
10	*sampú*
11	*labing-isá*
12	*labíndalawá*
13	*labíntatló*
20	*dalawampú*
21	*dalawampút isá*
22	*dalawampút dalawá*
30	*tatlumpú*
31	*tatlumpút isá*
40	*ápatnapú*
50	*limampú*
60	*ánimnapú*
70	*pitumpú*
80	*walampú*
90	*siyámnapú*
100	*isáng daán*
101	*isáng daán at isá*
200	*dalawáng daán*
201	*dalawáng daán at isá*
500	*limáng daán*
1000	*isáng libo*
5000	*limáng libo*

1 kg	*isáng kilogram (kilo)*
2 pesos	*dalawáng píso*
3 km	*tatlóng kilométro*
5 litres	*limáng lítro*

One-half	*kalahatí*
One-third	*isáng-katló*
One-quarter	*isáng-kapat*

Once	*minsan*
Twice	*makálawá*
Three times	*makatatló*
Often	*madalás*
Seldom	*bihirá*
Always	*lagí (palagí)*

Time & Dates

Today	*ngayón*
Tomorrow	*búkas*
Every day	*áraw-áraw*
Every night	*gabí-gabí*
Tonight	*ngayóng gabí*
Last night	*kahapong gabí*
Anytime	*maski kailán*
A day	*isáng áraw*
A night	*isáng gabí*
Day & night	*áraw-gabí*
Every Thursday	*túwing Huwébes*
Every afternoon	*túwing hápon*
Yesterday	*kahápon*
Day before yesterday	*noáng kamakalawá*
Day after tomorrow	*sa makalawá*
What time is it?	*anóng óras na?*
Week	*linggó*
Last week	*noóng nakaraáng linggó*
This week	*ngayóng linggóng itó*
Next week	*sa linggóng daratíng*
Month	*buwán*
A month	*isáng buwán*
This month	*ngayóng buwáng itá*
Year	*taó*
A year	*isáng taón*
Every year	*taón-taón*
Last year	*nakaraáng taón (nagdáan na taón)*
Next year	*sa sunód sa taón*

Days

Monday	*Lúnes*
Tuesday	*Martés*
Wednesday	*Miyérkoles*
Thursday	*Huwébes*
Friday	*Biyérnes*
Saturday	*Sábado*
Sunday	*Linggó*

Months

January	*Enéro*
February	*Pebréro*
March	*Márso*
April	*Abril*
May	*Máyo*
June	*Húnyo*
July	*Húlyo*
August	*Agósto*
September	*Setyémbre*
October	*Oktúbre*
November	*Nobyémbre*
December	*Disyémbre*

Animals

Ant	*langgám*
Butterfly	*parú-paró*
Cat	*pusá*
Chicken	*manok*
Cow	*báka*
Dog	*áso*
Duck	*páto*
Flea	*pulgás*
Fly	*lángaw*
Frog	*palaká*
Gecko	*tukó*
Goat	*kambíng*
Horse	*kabáyo*
Louse	*kúto*
Monkey	*unggóy*
Mosquito	*lamók*
Mouse, rat	*dagá*
Pig	*báboy*
Rabbit	*kuného*
Sheep	*túpa*
Snake	*áhas*
Spider	*gagambá*
Water buffalo	*kálabaw (carabao)*
Worm	*uód*

Colours

Black	*itím*
Blue	*asúl*
Brown	*kulay-kapé*
- Brown (complexion)	*kayumanggí*
Green	*bérde*
Grey	*abuhín (gris)*
Orange	*kulay-dalandán*
Red	*pulá*
White	*putí*
Yellow	*diláw*

Cebuano

After Filipino, Cebuano is the second most widely spoken language in the Philippines. It's spoken in the Visayas and in many parts of Mindanao. There follows a short selection of words, phrases and sentences:

Greetings & Civilities

Hello, greetings — *mabúhay*
Good morning — *maáyong búntag*
Good day — *maáyong udtó*
Good afternoon — *maáyong hápon*
Good night — *maáyong gabií*
Goodbye — *babáy (síge)*

How are you? — *kumustá (na)?*
How are you? (plural) — *kumustá (na) kamó?*
Good, well — *maáyo*
Well, thank you, and you? — *maáyo man salámat, ug ikáw?*
Also good/well — *maáyo sab (maáyo man)*
Where have you been? — *diín ka gíkan (asá ka gíkan?)*
Where are you going? — *asá ka muadtó (asá ka páingon?)*
I'm coming from Bato — *gíkan ko sa Bato (tayá Bato ko)*
I'm going to Talisay — *muadtó ko sa Talisay (páigon ko sa Talisay)*

Thank you — *salámat*
Thank you very much — *dagháng salámat*
Please — *palihóg*
You're welcome — *waláy sapayán*

Yes/no — *oó/díli*
Yes/no (polite) — *opó/dilagí*
And — *ug*
OK — *síge (síge taná)*
Only, merely, simply — *lang*
Just a minute — *kadalí lang*
Again, similarly — *napúd*
Always, of course — *siyémpre*
No problem — *walá probléma*
It's all right — *maáyo ang tanán*

Small Talk

What is your name? — *unsay pangalan mo?*
How old are you? — *píla na may ímong idad?*
Where do you come from? — *tagá diíng lúgar ka?*
I like you — *gústo ko nimó (nagustuhán ko ikáw)*
I love you — *gihigúgma ko ikáw*
I don't know — *ámbot lang (walá ko kahibaló)*
I like (that) — *gustó ko (niána)*
I don't like... — *díli gustó ko...*
I'll do it/I'll get it — *akó na lang*
You do it (you get it) — *ikáw na lang*
Come here — *dalí díri*
Let's go — *dalí na (síge na)*
It's too late — *awáhi na*
I have no time — *wa koy panáhon*
Are you sure? — *siguradó ka ba?*
Not yet — *walá pa*
Maybe/perhaps — *tingáli*
What a pity — *anugon*
Really — *tínuod*
That's not true (flatterer) — *boléro*
Fool (you) — *búgok (ka), bangak*
Crazy, mad — *lúku-lúko (buáng-buang)*
Rude, insolent — *bastós*
Braggart — *hambugéro*
It's none of your business — *walá kay labot*
Get lost! — *paháwa dihá!*
Later on — *pagkátaud-taud*
Never mind — *síge na lang*

People & Pronouns

Man — *laláki*
Woman — *babáye*
Unmarried man — *ulitawó (soltéro)*
Unmarried woman — *dalága (dalagíta)*
Mr — *Ginoó*
Mr Santos — *Ginoóng Santos*
Mrs — *Gínang*
Mrs Santos — *Gínang Santos*
Miss — *Dalága*
Miss Santos — *Dalagáng Santos*
Child — *báta*
Child (own) — *anák*
Boy — *binatilo*
Girl — *balagíta*
Grandmother/grandfather — *lolá/loló*
Friend — *amígo/amiga*

I — *akó*
You — *ikáw*
He/she — *siyá*
They — *silá*
We (I and you) — *kitá*

We (I and others)	*kamí*
You (plural)	*kamó*
Drunken	*hubóg*
Handsome, pretty	*gwápo/gwápa*
Happy	*malipáyon*
Intelligent	*hawód*
Old	*tigúlang*
Sad	*magu-ol*
Short	*mabú*
Sober	*walá mahubóg (díli hubóg)*
Tall	*taás*
Ugly	*ngíl-ad*
Young	*batán-on*

Common Questions

Do you have …?	*adúnay …?*
How?	*unsaón?*
How much?	*tagpila (pila)?*
How far is it?	*unsa kaláyo (layo)?*
What?	*unsa?*
What did you say?	*unsa tó?*
Where?	*asá?*
Where is the post office?	*asá man ang post office?*
When?	*kánus-a?*
When will it be ready?	*kánus-a matápos?*
Who? (singular)	*kinsá?*
Who? (plural)	*kinsá-kinsá?*
Who is there?	*kinsá ná?*
Why?	*nganóng (ngáno)?*
Why not?	*nganóng díli?*

Accommodation

Bath	*bányo*
Bed	*katré*
Blanket, cover	*hábol*
Hotel	*otél*
Key	*yáwi*
Mosquito net	*muskitéro*
Pillow	*únlan*
Room	*kuwárto*
Room with bath	*kuwárto nga anaáy bányo*
Toilet	*kasílyas*
Do you have air-con?	*nabáy air-condítión?*
There is no water	*walá túbig*
How much is a room?	*pilá ang usá ka kuwárto?*
I'll take the room	*síge kuhaon ko ang kining kuwárto*

Food & Drink

Food, meal	*pagkaón*
Breakfast	*pamaháw*
Lunch	*paniúdto*
Dinner	*panihápon*
I am hungry	*gigútom na akó (gigútom ko)*
I am thirsty	*guiháw ko (guiháw na akó)*
I am full	*busóg na akó (busóg ko)*
I have no appetite	*walá koy gana*
That was a good meal	*kalami sa pagkaón*
The bill please	*ang báyronon palíhog (ambi na ang chit)*
Pay	*bayad*
Cup	*tása*
Fork	*tinidór*
Glass	*báso*
Knife	*kutsílyo*
Plate	*pláto*
Serviette/napkin	*serbilyéta*
Spoon	*kutsára*
Teaspoon	*kutsaríta*
Cold	*bugnáw*
Cooked, steamed	*nulúto*
Delicious	*lamí*
Fried	*gisádo (piniríto)*
Grilled	*tinápan (sinúgba)*
Hot, warm	*inít*
Marinated	*kilawín (kiniláw)*
Salty	*parát*
Sour	*aslum*
Spicy	*hang*
Spoiled	*pános*
Sweet	*tamís*
Apple	*mansánas*
Banana	*ságing*
Beans	*sítao*
Beer	*serbésa*
Bread	*tinapáy (pan)*
Chicken	*manók*
Coconut young/ripe	*butóng/lubi*
Coffee	*kapé*
- Black coffee	*maisóg na kapé*
Crab	*alimángo*
Egg	*ítlog*
- Fried egg	*prítong ítlog*
- Soft-boiled egg	*malasádong ítlog*
Fish	*isdá*
- Grouper	*lápu-lápu*

- Snapper	*máya-máya*
- Spanish Mackerel	*tanguígue*
- Squid	*nókos*
- Tuna	*tulíngan*
Garlic	*áhos*
Ginger	*lúya*
Grapes	*ubás*
Guava	*bayábas*
Ice, ice cubes	*ápa*
Jackfruit	*nangká*
Mango	*manggá*
Meat	*karné*
- Beef	*karnéng báka*
- Pork	*karnéng báboy*
Milk	*gátas*
Onion	*sibúyas*
Orange	*kahíl*
Papaya	*kapáyas*
Peanut	*maní*
Pepper (grains)	*pamintá (síli)*
- Pepper (powdered)	*pamintáng ginalíng*
Pineapple	*pinyá*
Potato	*patátas*
- Sweet potato	*kamóte*
Prawn	*lokón*
Rice (uncooked)	*bugas*
- Rice (cooked)	*kanú*
Salad	*salad*
Salt	*ásin*
Shrimp	*uláng (pasáyan)*
Soup	*sabáw*
Soy sauce	*toyó*
Sugar	*asúkar*
Tea	*tsaa*
Tomato	*kamátis*
Vegetables	*utan*
Vinegar	*suká*
Water	*túbig*
Water melon	*milón*

Getting Around

Left	*walá*
Right	*tuó*
Straight on	*dirétso*
Back	*luyó (mobalík)*
Here	*dínhi*
There	*dínha (dídto)*
Near	*dúol*
Far	*layó*
Turn-off	*molikó, (nilikó, likó)*
Stop	*pára*
Aeroplane	*eropláne*
Boat	*sakayán*
Bus	*track (bus)*
Car	*kótse (sakyanán)*
Ship	*bárko*
Bay	*look*
Beach	*baybáyon*
Coast, shore	*hunásan*
Creek	*sápa*
Forest	*lasáng*
Hill	*búngtod*
Island	*puló*
Lake	*línaw*
Mountain	*búkid*
Ocean, sea	*dágat*
River	*subá*
River mouth	*bába sa subá*
Road	*dálan*
Town/city	*lungsód (siyudád)*
Village	*báryo*
Waterfall	*busáy*
Which bus for Cebu?	*únsang bus ang maodtong Cebu?*
Where is the bus stop?	*asa man ang hulatán ug bus?*
Where do I catch the jeepney?	*asa ko musakay ug jeepney?*
Where does this bus go?	*asa man moadto kíning bus?*
Where do I get off?	*asa ko manaóg?*
How much is the fare?	*tagpíla ang pléte?*

Weather

Clear, bright	*hayag (kláro)*
Clouds, fog, mist	*pangánod*
Cloudy	*panganod (dághang)*
Cold	*túgnaw*
Lightning	*kílat (lintí)*
Rain	*ulán*
Rainy	*ting-ulá'n*
Sun	*ádlaw*
Thunder	*dúgdog (dalúgdog)*
Typhoon	*bagyó*
Warm	*inít*
Wind	*hángin*
Windy	*mahángin*

Shopping

All	*tanán*
Big	*dako*
Broken, destroyed	*gubá*
Cheap	*baráto*
Expensive	*mahál*
Too expensive	*kamahál (mahál kaáyo)*
Few	*diyútay*

Less	*hustó na (diyutay)*
Many	*dághan*
Money	*kuwárta*
More	*gamáy pa*
New (things)	*bágo*
Old	*dáan*
Small	*gamáy*
What is this?	*unsa ni?*
How much is this? (touch)	*tagpíla na?*
How much is this? (point)	*tagpíla kaná?*
How much is one kilo?	*tagpíla ang usa ka kilo?*
Too expensive	*kamahál (mahál kaáyo)*
This is cheap	*baráto na kiní*
Could you wrap it?	*pustá palihog*
I'd like to pay	*mobayád na akó*

Numbers

0	*walá*
1	*usá*
2	*duhá*
3	*tuló*
4	*upát*
5	*limá*
6	*únom*
7	*pitó*
8	*waló*
9	*siyám*
10	*napuló*
11	*únsi*
12	*dóse*
13	*trése*
20	*báynte*
21	*báynte úno*
22	*báynte dos*
30	*tranta*
31	*tranta'y úno*
40	*kuwarénta*
50	*singkuwénta*
60	*sayesénta (sisénta)*
70	*siténta (seténta)*
80	*otsénta*
90	*nobénta*
100	*usá kagatós*
101	*usá kagatós ug usá*
200	*duhá kagatós*
201	*duhá kagatós ug usá*
500	*limá kagatós*
1000	*usá kalíbo*
5000	*limá kalíbo*

1 pound (weight)	*usáng librá*
2 pesos	*duhá ka píso*
3 km	*tuló ka kilométro*
5 litres	*limá ka lítro*
One-half	*tungá*
One-third	*tuló ka tungá*
One-quarter	*upát ka tungá*
Once	*usaháy*
Twice	*kaduhá (ikaduhá)*
Three times	*katuló*
Often	*pirme (síge síge)*
Seldom	*tág-sa (tagsa-ón)*

Time & Dates

Today	*karón*
Tomorrow	*ugma*
Every day	*káda ádlaw (ádlaw-ádlaw)*
Every night	*káda gabií*
Last night	*kagabií*
A day	*usá kaádlaw (úsang ádlaw)*
A night	*usá kagabií (úsang gabií)*
Day & night	*ádlaw-gabií*
Every Thursday	*káda Huwébes*
Every afternoon	*káda hápon*
Day before yesterday	*sa úsang ádlaw*
Yesterday	*gahápon*
Day after tomorrow	*sunód ugma*
What time is it?	*unsang orása na?*
Week	*semána (dominggó)*
Last week	*niáging semána*
This week	*károng semanáha (károng dominggó)*
Next week	*sa sunód semána (dominggó umáabot)*
Month	*bulán*
A month	*usá kabúlan*
This month	*károng bulána*
Year	*tuíg*
A year	*usá kátuig*
Every year	*tuíg-tuíg (káda tuíg)*
Last year	*niáging tuíg*
Next year	*sa sunód tuíg*

Days

Monday	*Lunés*
Tuesday	*Martés*
Wednesday	*Miyérkoles (Miércules)*

Thursday	*Huwébes (Juéves)*
Friday	*Biyérnes (Viérnes)*
Saturday	*Sábado (Sábao)*
Sunday	*Dominggó*

Months

January	*Enéro*
February	*Pebréro*
March	*Márso*
April	*Abril*
May	*Máyo*
June	*Húnyo*
July	*Húlyo*
August	*Agósto*
September	*Setyémbre*
October	*Oktúbre*
November	*Nobyémbre*
December	*Disyémbre*

Animals

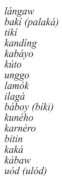

Ant	*hulmigás*
Butterfly	*kabkába*
Cat	*iríng*
Chicken	*manok*
Cow	*báka*
Dog	*iró*
Duck	*ítik*
Flea	*pulgás (tungáw)*
Fly	*lángaw*
Frog	*bakí (palaká)*
Gecko	*tikí*
Goat	*kandíng*
Horse	*kabáyo*
Louse	*kúto*
Monkey	*unggo*
Mosquito	*lamók*
Mouse, rat	*ilagá*
Pig	*báboy (bíki)*
Rabbit	*kuného*
Sheep	*karnéro*
Snake	*bitin*
Spider	*kaká*
Water buffalo	*kábaw*
Worm	*uód (ulód)*

Colours

Black	*itím*
Blue	*asúl*
Brown	*brawn (kapé)*
- Brown (complexion)	*itúm*
Green	*bérde*
Grey	*abuhon*
Orange	*orins*
Red	*pulá*
White	*putí*
Yellow	*yélo (dalág)*

Travel Planning

Getting There & Away

With only a few exceptions, the only way to get to the Philippines and away again is by air. Some airlines will only allow you to board a flight going there if you have an onward or return ticket. On one occasion, the author had to convince an Egyptair official in Bangkok that he would eventually be leaving the Philippines by yacht. Even then, the matter was only brought to an end when a document was produced and signed saying that the author would pay any costs incurred if he was refused permission to enter the Philippines and had to fly back immediately.

Manila

Air: Although Angeles (Clark), Cebu City, Davao, Laoag, Olongapo (Subic) and Zamboanga have international airports, Manila is virtually the only international gateway, so, for probably 99% of visitors to the Philippines, Manila is their first experience of the country.
There are flights to Manila from most of the Philippines' Asian neighbours, including Japan, Hong Kong, Malaysia, Singapore and Thailand, as well as from Australia, the USA and Europe.
It has recently been reported that immigration officials in Manila have been denying entry to travellers who are unable to produce a departure ticket, especially when they don't have a visa stamped in their passport. If this happens, you can only hope to find some friendly person nearby who can quickly arrange the necessary ticket for you. You will find the airline offices upstairs in the airport building.
Various airlines which fly to Manila offer a stopover programme when they sell you the ticket. See also the chapter 'Travel Tips': *Accommodation - Prices.*

Left Luggage: There are no left luggage facilities at Manila's Ninoy Aquino International Airport.

Angeles/Central Luzon

Air: The following airlines offer non-stop or direct flights to Angeles (Clark): Asiana Airlines on Monday, Wednesday, Thursday, Saturday and Sunday from and to Seoul, South Korea; CR Airways on Wednesday, Friday and Sunday from and to Hong Kong; Tiger Airways daily from and to Singapore. Air Asia three or four times weekly from and to Kuala Lumpur (Malaysia).

Laoag/North Luzon

Air: The following airlines offer non-stop or direct flights to Laoag: China Southern from and to Guangzhou; CR Airways from and to Hong Kong; Far Eastern Air Transport from and to Kaohsiung (Taiwan).

Cebu & Mindanao

Air: The following airlines offer non-stop or direct flights to Cebu City: Cathay Pacific from and to Hong Kong; Malaysia Airlines from and to Kuala Lumpur (via Kota Kinabalu); Philippine Airlines from and to Seoul and Tokyo; Qatar Airways and Singapore Airlines (Silkair) from and to Singapore; Mandarin Airlines from and to Taipei.
There are also regular flights operating once a week with the Indonesian airlines Bouraq or Merpati between Davao in the south of Mindanao and Manado in the north of Sulawesi in Indonesia (one-way US$135; tickets available from Anstar Travel in Davao).
Malaysia Airlines flies to Davao from Malaysia (Kuala Lumpur via Kota Kinabalu), and Silkair from Singapore.
South Phoenix Airways flies on Wednesday and Saturday from Sandakan, Sabah, Malaysia, to Zamboanga, Mindanao.

Boat: Twice a week a fast ferry belonging to SRN Fast Seacrafts sails between Zamboanga, Mindanao, and Sandakan, Sabah, Malaysia. Departure from Zamboanga on Monday and Thursday at 5am, leaving Sandakan on Tuesday and Friday at 7am (US$42; 14 hrs; via Bongao/Tawi-Tawi, 1-hr stopover there). Information and tickets can be obtained from:
SRN Fast Seacrafts, Amil's Tower, 7000 Zamboanga, Pilar St, Tel +63 (0)62 9923756;
SRN agent in Sandakan: Hotel New Sabah, Jalan Singapura, Tel. +60 (0)89 212872.
The Aleson Shipping Lines' MV *Lady Mary Joy* regularly serves the cities of Zamboanga, Mindanao, and Sadakan, Sabah, Malaysia twice a week. Departure from Zamboanga on Monday and Thursday at 2pm, leaving Sandakan on Tuesday and Friday at 5pm (economy US$33, cabin US$36; 20 hrs). Information and tickets can be obtained from:
Aleson Shipping Lines, Veterans Ave, 7000 Zamboanga, Tel +63 (0)62 9912687, Fax: +63 (0)62 9912099;
VHV, Lot 22v, Ground Floor, Block A, Hsiang Garden, Jalan Leila, 90000 Sandakan, Tel. +60 (0)89 212063.

Palawan

Air: The flight connection Kota Kinabalu (Sabah, Malaysia) - Puerto Princesa (Palawan), with the Malaysian airline Layang Layang Aerospace has been discontinued (temporarily?). Further information from:
Layang Layang Aerospace, Terminal 2, Old Airport Rd, 88100 Kota Kinabalu, Tel +60 (0)88 238616, Fax +60 (0)88 239616, @.

Departure

Make absolutely certain you confirm your onward flight with the airline at least 72 hours before departure. It's even better to confirm your outward flight when you arrive. That way you can be fairly certain that your booking has been registered on the computer. Don't check in at the last minute; flights are often overbooked and, in spite of a confirmed ticket, you can find yourself bumped from the flight!

Departure Tax

The current airport tax for international flights is P550 (US dollars can be used for payment).

Airfares from Manila

The following sample prices are for one-way flights only. Long-haul flights (Australia, Europe, USA) cost roughly twice as much for a return ticket; within South-East Asia round trips usually only cost 75% more. These prices were checked with Interisland Travel & Tours and Mr Ticket. Both travel agents offer a good deal, however on some routes there are definite differences in price - it pays to shop around.
Amsterdam US$413 (Kuwait Airways); Bangkok US$187 (Kuwait Airways); Darwin US$393 (Royal Air Brunei); Frankfurt US$500 (Emirates); Guam US$509 (Continental Micronesia); Hong Kong US$190 (Cathay Pacific); Honolulu US$445 (Continental Micronesia); Jakarta US$332 (Garuda); London US$500 (Emirates); Los Angeles/ San Francisco US$465 (Northwest Airlines); New York US$540 (Continental Micronesia); Paris US$500 (Emirates); Perth US$403 (Cathay Pacific); Rome US$500 (Emirates); Singapore US$250 (Singapore Airlines); Stockholm US$650 (British Airways); Sydney US$450 (Malaysia Airlines); Taipei US$228 (Eva Air); Tokyo US$500 (Northwest Airlines); Toronto US$500 (Northwest Airlines); Vancouver US$482 (Cathay Pacific); Vienna US$473 (Eva Air); Zurich US$500 (Emirates).

Bucket Shop Prices in Manila

Interisland Travel & Tours, Marc 2000 Building Annex, Taft Ave corner San Andres St, Malate, Tel +63 (0)2 5238720-24, Fax +63 (0)2 5224795, @.
Filipino Travel Center, 1555 Adriatico St, Ermita, Tel +63 (0)2 5284507-09, Fax +63 (0)2 5284503, @.
Mr Ticket, Park Hotel (Lobby), 1030 Belen St, Paco, Tel +63 (0)2 5212371-75, Fax +63 (0)2 5212393, @.

Warning

The information in this chapter is especially vulnerable to change - prices for international air travel are volatile, routes are introduced and cancelled, schedules change, rules are amended and special deals come and go. The details given in this chapter should be regarded as pointers and not as a substitute for your own careful, up-to-the-minute research.

When to Go

Weather

Generally, the best time to travel is from the middle of December to the middle of May. That's off season for typhoons. In December and January, however, you can expect rain.
In the provinces along the Pacific coast, where vast amounts of rain can fall between November and January, the dry season usually begins by the first half of March at the latest.
March, April and May are the pleasant, warm and sunny summer months. But it really heats up in May, when you'll be glad of the slightest breeze.
Normally, for large areas of the Philippines, the rainy season starts in June, however this does sometimes hold off till the middle of July these days.
Travelling around isn't really affected by the occasional downpour, but more by the unpredictable typhoons, which usually come with the wet monsoon season from June to November. The south-west Visayas and Mindanao lie beneath the typhoon belt, but can occasionally be hit by a crosswind. Typhoons usually blow in from the south-east.

Mini High Seasons

Apart from Christmas, the tourism industry in the Philippines looks forward to doing good business at Chinese New Year and Easter, when hotels, flights, buses and ships will all be fully booked. It's a good idea to book well in advance. The next dates are:

Chinese New Year	Easter
2006: 29 - 31 January	13 - 16 April
2007: 18 - 20 January	5 - 8 April
2008: 7 - 9 February	20 - 23 March

Time

Anyone who wants to travel intensively around the Philippines needs plenty of time. Days and weeks pass very quickly, particularly if you want to go island hopping. You should plan a two or three-week stay fairly well if you want to experience some of the country's more unusual aspects. If you only have a little time, say a week, and don't particularly want to get to know Philippine airport architecture intimately, you would do well to restrict yourself to a round trip of North Luzon.
You would be well advised not to travel more than necessary during the Christmas and Easter holiday periods. So, find yourself a pleasant base to stay at. The entire country is on the move at these times and you will hardly find a seat on any form of transport.
January and May are the months with the most colourful festivals. The rice terraces in North Luzon show themselves from their best side in March and April, and island hopping is most fun in these pleasant summer months.

Where to Go

There are all sorts of possible routes around the Philippines and it really is up to individual taste how you explore this fascinating archipelago. More detailed information on sightseeing, accommodation and transport can be found in the individual island chapters.

Suggested Itineraries

The following is a list of a few of the possibilities, but there are of course endless opportunities to discover the island world for yourself.
See also the Island Hopping section of the Visayas chapter later in this book (the Visayan islands are particularly suitable for island hopping because of the good transport connections).

- From Manila via Batangas to Mindoro (Puerto Galera). Along the coast from Mindoro via Calapan to Roxas. Carry on from there to Boracay and Panay. From Kalibo or Iloilo City back to Manila.
- From Panay to Cebu via Negros going south with a detour to Bohol, then back to Manila direct from Cebu City.
- From Cebu (Cebu City) to Palawan (Puerto Princesa), then travel to northern Palawan, returning to Manila from El Nido or from Busuanga.
- From Cebu directly or via Bohol to Leyte and Samar, then through South Luzon to Manila.
- From Cebu to Mindanao (Cagayan de Oro) with a short excursion to Camiguin. Then from north-eastern Mindanao (Surigao and Siargao Island) on to Leyte and Samar, returning to Manila via South Luzon.
- A popular round trip through North Luzon takes you from Manila via Angeles (Pinatubo hike) to Baguio (the summer capital). There you start the impressive tour of the terraces: via the hair-raising Halsema Road up into the mountains to Sagada and Bontoc. Then carrying on to Banaue, Bangaan and Batad (rice terraces). From Banaue back to Manila.

Highlights

- One of the most magnificent pieces of scenery in the Philippines is the Central Cordillera in the north of the country. The journey through the mountains, although not the easiest, is unforgettable. And then you have the absolute highlight: the magnificent rice terraces of Banaue.
- Not man-made, the impressive countryside around Mt Pinatubo was created by the forces of nature. Guided tours operate mostly from Angeles.
- The active, cone-shaped Mayon volcano at Legaspi in South Luzon, is considered to be one of the most beautiful volcanoes in the world. You can make it to the summit and back in three days.
- In spite of the first signs of its moving in the direction of up-market tourism, the little island of Boracay still has that 'certain something'. Up till now, anyway. In another few years it'll just be one among many.
- Perhaps not everyone's idea of a highlight, but unique at any rate, the Chocolate Hills on the island of Bohol are worth a visit. You can make a little detour there when island hopping through the Visayas.
- Lake Sebu in the southern Tiruray Highlands, where the T'boli live, must be the most beautiful inland lake in the Philippines. Unfortunately this area, as well as other areas of Mindanao, is a region of conflict and not always safe.
- On Palawan, St Paul Subterranean National Park & Underground River as well as El Nido & Bacuit Archipelago are two attractive places worth going to see, especially for nature lovers.
- The Philippines without fiestas? - unimaginable. The colourful Ati-Atihan

Festival in Kalibo on the island of Panay is the most spectacular in the country. But even less loud, less wild local town fiestas have a fascination of their own.

What Kind of Trip?

If you travel on your own in the Philippines, you'll often be asked solicitously: 'Don't you have a companion?' In fact, it's a good way to meet the locals, so travelling alone doesn't mean actually being alone.

Amongst other things, the advantage of travelling in twos or threes is that taxi costs can be shared, hiring a boat is more affordable, and jobs can be shared. For example, one person can look after baggage while the other gets tickets or looks at a hotel room.

Do-it-yourself travelling in the Philippines almost always means leisurely going from island to island, and forgetting time while you're at it. That, after all, is what makes this country so special for the tourist. However, if you have a specific interest in mind, you might want to spend time at one place with other like-minded people. Some visitors stay for months on Boracay because the windsurfing conditions are ideal; others find wreck diving so fascinating they won't leave the Calamian Group in North Palawan until they have inspected every last sunken ship.

Package tours are especially handy for people who only have a limited amount of time. However, compared to other Asian countries, there is not a wide choice of them available in the Philippines.

Organised Tours

For Philippine package tours check with the following Manila based travel agents:

Blue Horizons Travel & Tours, Trafalgar Plaza, Dela Costa St, Salcedo Village, Makati, Tel +63 (02) 8483901, Fax +63 (02) 8483909, @.

Filipino Travel Center, 1555 Adriatico St, Ermita, Tel +63 (02) 5284507-09, Fax +63 (02) 5284503, @.

Interisland Travel & Tours, Marc 2000 Building Annex, Taft Ave corner San Andres St, Malate, Tel +63 (0)2 5238720-24, Fax +63 (0)2 5224795, @.

Marsman Tours & Travel, Marsman-Dyrsdale Building, 2246 Chino Roces Ave, Makati, Tel +63 (02) 8402121, 8921817, Fax +63 8156228, @.

Rajah Tours, Physicians' Tower, 533 United Nations Ave, Ermita, Tel +63 (02) 5220541-48, Fax +63 (02) 5212831, @.

Visas

Passport

It is necessary to have a valid passport; however, your passport has to be valid at least six months beyond the period you intend to stay.

Visa Regulations

Entry without Visa

Visa regulations vary with your intended length of stay. The easiest procedure is simply to arrive without a visa. To make the most of this length of stay it's important to remember that the days of arrival and departure count as one day. If, for example, you arrive on a Saturday, then you can remain until the Saturday three weeks later, without paying a fee. It is possible to extend your visa: see below under 'Visa Extensions': *21 to 59 Days*.

Tip: If you enter the Philippines without a visa and can only produce an open-ended ticket (ie without an exact day of departure) for the rest of your journey, it is possible you may have to leave the country after 21 days. Your passport will be stamped with this in-

Batanes & Luzon Route (minimum two weeks)

Manila - Batanes Islands (flight), Batanes Islands - Laoag (flight), Laoag - Vigan (bus), Vigan - San Juan or San Fernando (bus), San Fernando - Baguio (bus), Baguio - Sagada (bus), Sagada - Bontoc (jeepney), Bontoc - Banaue (bus or jeepney), Banaue - Manila (bus)

or: Banaue - Angeles (bus; via Santa Rosa), Angeles - Manila (bus or flight)

Manila - Batangas (bus), Batangas - Puerto Galera/Mindoro (boat)

or: Manila - Legaspi (flight), Legaspi - Samar (bus and boat)

This route includes several scenic and historical highlights: the remote and secluded Batanes Islands, the sand dunes and old Spanish churches at Laoag, the old colonial town of Vigan, the surf beach at San Juan just north of San Fernando, the mountain town of Baguio, starting point of the hair-raising Halsema Road, the caves and hanging coffins of Sagada and the rice terraces of Bontoc and Banaue. On the return journey from Banaue to Manila you could also make a detour via Angeles, departure point for impressive Pinatubo tours.
If you want to add a couple of days at the beach, you could leave Manila for Puerto Galera on the island of Mindoro. Another idea would be to fly from Manila to Legaspi in the south of Luzon where you could explore the volcano Mt Mayon, then go from Legaspi to Samar, Leyte and Cebu.

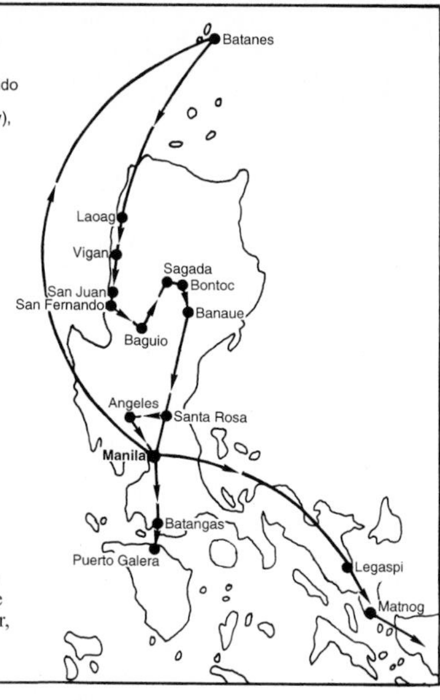

North Luzon & Palawan Route (minimum four weeks)

Manila - Angeles (bus or flight), Angeles - Baguio (bus), Baguio - Sagada (bus), Sagada - Bontoc (jeepney), Bontoc - Banaue (bus or jeepney), Banaue - Manila (bus), Manila - Busuanga (boat or flight), Busuanga - El Nido (boat or flight), El Nido - Taytay (bus or jeepney), Taytay - Roxas (bus or jeepney), Roxas - Port Barton (jeepney), Port Barton - Sabang (boat), Sabang - Puerto Princesa (bus or jeepney), Puerto Princesa - Cebu City (flight), Cebu City - Tagbilaran - Cebu City (boat), Cebu City - Caticlan (flight), Caticlan - Boracay (boat), Caticlan - Manila (boat or flight)

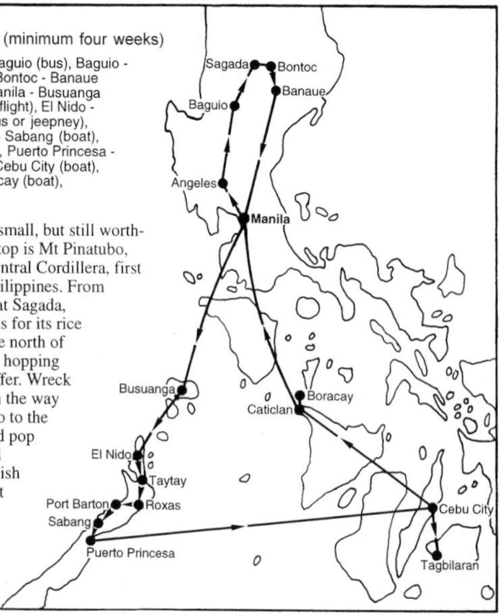

The first half of this route consists of a small, but still worthwhile, tour around North Luzon. First stop is Mt Pinatubo, near Angeles. Then you head for the Central Cordillera, first to Baguio, the summer capital of the Philippines. From there your route takes you to the caves at Sagada, followed by Bontoc and Banaue, famous for its rice terraces. Busuanga is the first stop in the north of Palawan, where it's hard to resist island hopping around the huge variety of islands on offer. Wreck divers are also in their element here. On the way from the picturesque location of El Nido to the Underground River at Sabang you could pop in for a look at the pleasant little coastal towns of Taytay and Port Barton. To finish off, you could simply take a direct flight to Manila from Palawan's neat and tidy capital, Puerto Princesa, or for example fly first to Cebu City, make a short detour to Bohol, and then head for Boracay for a few days on the beach.

Visayas Route (minimum three weeks)

Manila - Caticlan (boat or flight),Caticlan - Kalibo - Iloilo City (bus), Iloilo City - Bacolod (boat), Bacolod - Sipalay (bus), Sipalay - Dumaguete (bus),Dumaguete - Siquijor (boat), Siquijor - Tagbilaran (boat), Tagbilaran - Cebu City (boat), Cebu City - Malapascua (bus and boat), Malapascua - Bantayan (boat), Bantayan - Cadiz (boat), Cadiz - Bacolod (bus or jeepney), Bacolod - Manila (boat or flight)

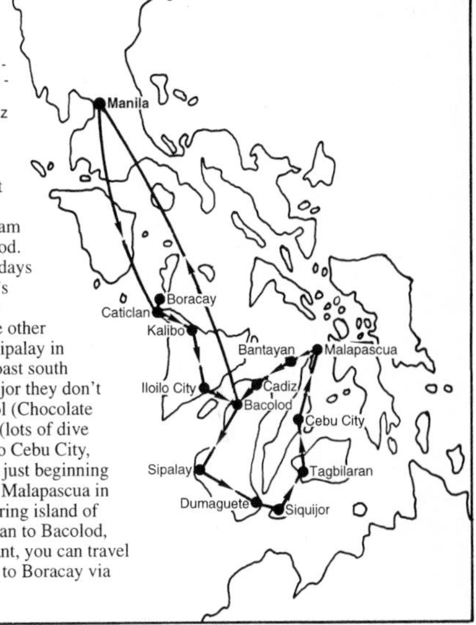

This interesting round trip includes nine different islands of the Visayas, and can be punctuated as often as you want by short breaks on various dream beaches. Boracay is perfect for getting in the mood. If you like the atmosphere, you can spend a few days there before heading off. If, on the other hand, it's solitude you're after, take your pick from a wide selection of less well-known places on one of the other islands. Good alternatives are the beaches near Sipalay in the south-west of Negros and on the stretch of coast south of Dumaguete. On the "witches' island" of Siquijor they don't understand the meaning of the word stress. Bohol (Chocolate Hills) and the nearby offshore island of Panglao (lots of dive shops) are good ideas for stopovers on the way to Cebu City, the second largest city in the country. Tourism is just beginning to get established on the beautiful little island of Malapascua in the north of Cebu and on the attractive neighbouring island of Bantayan. It's only a few hours trip from Bantayan to Bacolod, the capital of Negros, the sugar island. If you want, you can travel straight back to Manila from there, or head back to Boracay via Iloilo City, traversing Panay on the way.

Visayas & East Philippine Route (minimum four weeks)

Manila - Dumaguete (boat or flight), Dumaguete - Moalboal (boat and bus), Moalboal - Cebu City (bus), Cebu City - Siargao (flight), Siargao - Surigao (boat), Surigao - Butuan - Balingoan (bus), Balingoan - Camiguin (boat), Camiguin - Cebu City (flight), Cebu City - Ormoc (boat), Ormoc - Tacloban (bus), Tacloban - Legaspi (bus and boat), Legaspi - Lucena (bus), Lucena - Marinduque (boat), Marinduque - Manila (flight)

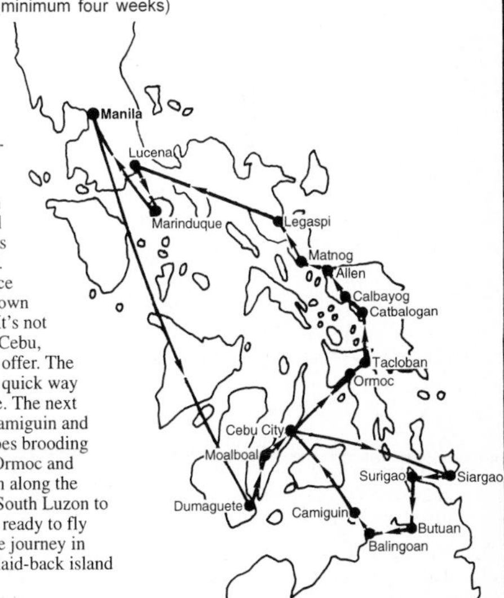

The best time to travel around the islands in the east of the Philippines is from May until September, while the south-west monsoon is drenching the west and north of the country. As long as the weather is agreeable, the place to start this route is the friendly university town of Dumaguete in the south-east of Negros. It's not far from there to Moalboal on the island of Cebu, where all kinds of sporting activities are on offer. The flight from Cebu City to Siargao Island is a quick way of getting to the Philippine surfers' paradise. The next destination is the pleasant little island of Camiguin and its numerous waterfalls, with seven volcanoes brooding over them. Then it's off, via Cebu City, to Ormoc and Tacloban on the island of Leyte, carrying on along the beautiful west coast of Samar and through South Luzon to Legaspi (Mt Mayon volcano). If you're not ready to fly directly back to Manila, you could break the journey in Lucena and nip over to enjoy the pleasant, laid-back island of Marinduque.

formation and you will not be allowed to extend your visa.

Entry with Visa

If you wish to spend between 21 and 59 days in the Philippines, you should request a 59-day visa from any Philippine embassy or consulate. This will normally be granted for about US$35. If you're unable to make your application in person, you should send a letter of request asking for the application forms, and enclose a stamped, self-addressed envelope. Don't send in your passport straight away. Some Philippine embassies and consulates offer downloadable visa application forms on their websites.

You will be issued with a 59-day or 90-day visa, although the latter will almost definitely be changed when you enter the country and a 59-day residence permit stamped in your passport. Anyone entering the country with a 90-day visa who stays in the country longer than 59 days has to pay a fee; see below under 'Visa Extensions': *59 Days to Six Months*.

You have to enter the Philippines within three months of the visa's being issued, otherwise it automatically expires.

Visa Extensions

It is possible to get an extension from the Immigration Office (Bureau of Immigration/Commission on Immigration and Deportation - CID), Magallanes Dr, Intramuros, Manila. Extensions are also available from immigration offices in other cities (Angeles, Cebu City, Dumaguete, Iloilo City, Puerto Princesa, San Fernando La Union, Tacloban etc) although they may send your passport and application form to Manila to be processed. The cost of extensions is regulated according to the time period proposed. As a rule, the visa will only be extended by two months per application.

At the conclusion of the period stipulated by the visa, you present your extension application and passport to the various immigration officials, and these documents remain up to three days with the Immigration Office for processing (regular service). However, you can get your extension in about one day if you pay an 'express service' fee of P500. Keep all receipts, as they are likely to be checked at the airport when you leave the country. Incidentally, anyone applying for a visa extension dressed in thongs (flip-flops), shorts and singlet/undershirt can expect to be refused service. A number of travel agencies and restaurants run by foreigners will offer to take care of your extension application for a reasonable sum, normally between P200 and P300.

Warning: Don't overstay! If you do not extend your visa within the deadline you will have to pay a fine of P500 for every month or part of month you are in the country. They may inform you that you have one week to leave the country (and they may put a stamp in your passport that confirms this!). So make sure you apply for an extension a few days before your valid one expires.

21 to 59 Days

Anyone entering the Philippines without a visa or with only a 21-day visa and wishing to remain in the country for up to 59 days must pay P1520 for a 38-day extension (P1000 Visa Waiver Application Fee, P500 Visa Waiver Fee, plus a P20 'legal research fee'). In addition there's an express service fee of P500.

59 Days to Six Months

Anyone wishing to stay in the country for more than 59 days, but no longer than six months, has to pay the following fees:

Application Fee (P300).

Visa Fee (P1000) - not applicable in the case of previously paid visa fees.
Alien Head Tax (P250) - applicable only to persons over 16 years of age.
ACR: Alien Certificate of Registration (P1000) - in the case of a second application within the same calendar year; this only costs P250.
Extension Fee (P500) - for each month of the extension period already begun.
ECC: Emigration Clearance Certificate (P700) - the fee can be paid at the airport on departure; you can also make the payment at the Immigration Office, though this must be done no sooner than 30 days before departure.
LRF: Legal Research Fee (P10) - additional to every other payable fee with the exception of the Alien Head Tax.

Six Months & Longer
Anyone wishing to remain in the country over six months must, in addition to the extension fees listed earlier, pay the following fees:
CRTV: Certificate of Residence/ Temporary Visitor (P700).
Application Fee for CRTV (P1400).
Application Fee for ACR (P1000).
LRF: Legal Research Fee (P50).
When departing after a stay of one year or longer, there is a further travel tax to pay to the tune of P1620.
The Immigration Office can order anyone applying for a visa extension of over six months to undergo an AIDS test, and can grant or refuse the application on the basis of the result.
On leaving the country after a stay of more than six months you will need an Exit Clearance, which is issued by the Immigration Office. You will need to include four passport photos with the application.

Balikbayan

Balikbayan (Filipinas/Filipinos living abroad and their foreign dependants) can stay in the Philippines up to one year without a visa. They must produce the following documents when entering the country:
Former Filipinos: birth certificate, old Philippine passport or naturalisation papers.
Accompanying spouse: marriage certificate (extract from the Register of Marriages).
Accompanying child: birth certificate (extract from the Register of Births).

Embassies & Consulates

Philippine Embassies & Consulates Abroad

Australia
1 Moonah Place, Yarralumla ACT 2603 Canberra, Tel (06) 2732535, @.

Consulates
7 Hamilton St, Erindale, Adelaide, SA 5066, Tel (08) 83317311.
126 Wickham St. Fortitude Valley, Brisbane, Qld 4006, Tel (07) 32528215.
2 Coolibah St, Nightcliff, Darwin, NT 0810, Tel (08) 89844411.
45 Murray St, Hobart, TAS 7000, Tel (03) 62304000.
250 Gores St, Fitzroy, Melbourne, VIC 3065, Tel (03) 94197337.
127 Melville Parade, Como, Perth, WA 6152, Tel (09) 93674189.
Philippine Center, 27-33 Wentworth Ave, Sydney, NSW 2000, Tel (02) 92627831, @.

Cambodia
Sangkat Tonle Bassac, Khan Chamcar Mon, Phnom Penh, Tel (05) 23428592, @.

Canada
130 Albert St, Ottawa, Ontario, Tel (613) 2331121, @.

Consulates
151 Bloor St West, Suite 365, Toronto, Ontario, M5S 1S4, Tel (416) 9227181, @.
700 West Pender, Suite 1405, Vancouver, BC, V6C 1G8, Tel (604) 6851619, @.

China
23 Xiu Shui Bei-jie, Jiangoumenwai, Beijing, Tel (010) 65322518, @.

Consulates
United Centre, 95 Queensway, Central, Hong Kong, Tel (852) 28238500, @.
Shanghai Centre, 1376 Nanjing West Rd, Shanghai 200040, Tel (21)62798337, @.

France
4 Hameau de Boulainvilliers, 75016 Paris, Tel (01) 44145700, @.

Germany
Uhlandstrasse 97, 10715 Berlin, Tel (030) 8649500, @.

Indonesia
Jalan Imam Bonjol 6-8, Menteng, Jakarta, Tel (021) 3155118, @.

Consulate
J1n Tikala Satu No 12, Tikala Ares Lingkungan 1, 95124 Manado, Tel (0431) 861178, @.

Italy
Via delle Medaglie d'Oro No. 112-114, 00136 Rome, Tel (06) 39746621, @.

Japan
5-15-5 Roppongi Minato-ku, Tokyo 106-8537, Tel (03) 55621600, @.

Korea
Diplomatic Center, 1376-1 Seocho 2-dong. Seocho-ku, Seoul, Tel (02) 5776147.

Malaysia
1 Changkat Kia Peng 50450, Kuala Lumpur, Tel (03) 21484233, @.

Netherlands
125 Laan Copes Van Cattenburch 2585 EZ, The Hague, Tel (070) 3604820, @.

New Zealand
50 Hobson St, Thorndon, Wellington, Tel (04) 4729921, @.

Papua New Guinea
Lot 1, Section 440, Islander Village, Hohola, Port Moresby, Tel (05) 3256577, @.

Singapore
20 Nassim Rd, Singapore 258395, Tel 7373977, @.

South Africa
154 Nicolson St, Muckleneuk 0181, Pretoria, Tel (012) 3420451, @.

Sweden
Skeppsbron 20, 11130 Stockholm, Tel (08) 235665, @.

Switzerland
Kirchenfeldstrasse 73-75, 3005 Berne, Tel (031) 3501717, @

Thailand
760 Sukhumvit Rd, Bangkok 10110, Tel (02) 2590140, @.

UK
9A Palace Green, London W8 4QE, Tel (0171) 9371600, @.

USA
1600 Massachusetts Ave NW, Washington DC 20036, Tel (202) 4679300, @.

Consulates
30 North Michigan Ave, Suite 2100, Chicago, IL 60602, Tel. (312) 3326458, @.
2453 Pali Highway, Honolulu, HI 96817, Tel (808) 5956316, @.
556 Fifth Ave, New York, New York 10036, Tel (212) 7641330, @.
3600 Wilshire Blvd, Suite 500, Los Angeles, CA 90010, Tel (213) 6390980, @.
445-447 Sutter Blvd, San Francisco, CA 94108, Tel (415) 4336666, @.

Vietnam
27-B Tran Hung Dao St, Hanoi, Tel (04) 9437873, @.

Foreign Embassies in the Philippines

Australia
RCBC Plaza, Tower 2, 6819 Ayala Ave, Makati, Tel 7578100, @.

Austria
Prince Building, 117 Rada St, Makati, Tel (02) 8179191.

Belgium
Multinational Bancorporation Center, 6805 Ayala Ave, Makati, Tel (02) 8451869, @.

Canada
RCBC Plaza Tower 2, 6819 Ayala Ave, Makati, Tel. (02) 8579001, @.

Denmark
PBCom Tower, 6795 Ayala Ave corner Herrera St, Makati, Tel 8158015, @.

Finland
BPI Buendia Center, Gil Puyat Ave, Makati, Tel (02) 8915011-15, @.

France
Pacific Star Building, Gil Puyat Ave corner Makati Ave, Makati, Tel (02) 8101981-88, @.

Germany
RCBC Plaza, Tower 2, 6819 Ayala Ave, Makati, Tel (02) 7023000, @.

India
2190 Paraiso St, Dasmariñas Village, Makati, Tel (02) 8430101, @.

Indonesia
Indonesia Building, 185 Salcedo St, Makati, Tel (02) 8925061-68.

Italy
Zeta II Building, 191 Salcedo St, Makati, Tel (02) 8924531-34, @.

Japan
2627 Roxas Blvd, Pasay City, Tel (02) 5515710.

Korea
Trafalgar Plaza, Dela Costa Street, Makati, Tel (02) 8116139-46.

New Zealand
BPI Buendia Center, Gil Puyat Ave, Makati, Tel. (02) 8915358-67, @.

Netherlands
King's Court Building, Chino Roces Ave, Makati, Tel (02) 8125981, @.

Norway
Petron Mega Plaza Building, 358 Gil Puyat Ave, Makati, Tel (02) 8863245, @.

Sweden
Equitable PCI Bank Tower II, Makati Ave corner Dela Costa St, Makati, Tel (02) 8191951, @.

Switzerland
Equitable PCI Bank Building, 8751 Paseo de Roxas, Makati, Tel 7579000, @.

Thailand
Royal Thai Embassy Building, 107 Rada St, Makati, Tel (02) 8154219.

UK
LV Locsin Building, 6752 Ayala Ave, Makati, Tel (02) 8167116, @.

USA
1201 Roxas Blvd, Ermita, Tel (02) 5321001.

Vietnam
554 P Ocampo St, Malate, Tel (02) 5240364.

Customs

Imports

Visitors may bring in 200 cigarettes, 50 cigars, or two tins of tobacco and two litres of alcohol free of duty.
Personal effects, a reasonable amount of clothing, toiletries, jewellery for normal use and a small quantity of perfume are allowed in duty free. The same applies to cameras and films, although there may be a problem if you have a large amount of electronic or optical equipment. It is up to the individual customs official whether they count as personal effects or tradeable goods and/or professional equipment. You may have some convincing to do!
It is strictly prohibited to bring illegal drugs, firearms, obscene and pornographic media into the country. (Beware: Even the likes of *Playboy* count as pornographic magazines in the Philippines.)

Exports

It is strictly forbidden to export drugs. In addition, coral, certain types of orchid and parts of animals such as turtle shells and python skins may not be exported.

Currency Regulations

On entering or leaving the Philippines, visitors are allowed to import and ex-

port up to 10,000 Philippine pesos in bank notes or other form. The import or export of larger amounts must be pre-approved by the Central Bank (Bangko Sentral ng Pilipinas).
Foreign currencies up to a value of US$10,000 can be imported and exported. A declaration is required for amounts over this limit.

Money

Currency

The Philippine currency is the peso (P) - correctly spelt piso but always referred to as the peso. It's divided up into 100 centavos (c). There are coins of 1, 5, 10, 25 and 50 centavos and of 1, 5 and 10 pesos. Banknotes are available in denominations of 10, 20, 50, 100, 200, 500 and 1000 pesos.

Changing Money

The only foreign currency to have in the Philippines is US dollars - it's no longer true to say that nothing else is considered to exist but the US dollar certainly exists more than most.
When you do change money try to get a reasonable amount of it in smaller denominations: taxi drivers hardly ever have change of big notes. In more remote areas it can be difficult to change even P100 notes.
In some smaller regional towns there may be no bank at all and the only possibility of changing money may be at a hotel and then at a poor exchange rate.
Moneychangers are often faster and more efficient than banks, although it's wise to shop around since their rates do vary.

Banks

You'll get the best exchange rate in Manila. In the provinces you may lose as much as 20%. In remote districts only the peso and, possibly, the US dollar will be accepted; in those areas no other currency can be relied upon. Sometimes a bank will give you a better rate for your currency than a moneychanger, at other times the opposite will be the case. You could also be charged for a quick comparison of exchange rates.
You are not permitted to take more than P10,000 out of the country. Unused pesos can only be changed at the banking counter in the departure hall of Ninoy Aquino International Airport (NAIA); you have to produce an official white (or yellow) exchange slip. These can be obtained from a bank or a licensed money exchange office.
Opening hours in Philippine banks are Monday to Friday from 9am to 3pm; a few banks close at 3.30pm. Most banks will only cash travellers' cheques after 10.30am after the new rates of exchange for the day have been issued.
The bank counters at the airport are closed during night hours.

Exchange Rates (October 2004)

Australia	A$1	P40.95
Canada	C$1	P44.90
Euro	€1	P69.65
Hong Kong	HK$1	P7.25
Japan	¥100	P51.40
New Zealand	NZ$1	P38.20
Switzerland	Sfr1	P45.05
UK	UK£1	P101.20
USA	US$1	P56.40

Moneychangers

You'll get a fairly good exchange rate for cash in all SM department stores or from licensed moneychangers. In Manila these will be found on Mabini St (between Padre Faura and Pedro Gil) in Ermita - eg 'Edzen'. The rate varies with the size of the bill - US$100 and US$50 bills are best, US$1 bills are hardly wanted at all. Some of the money-

changers will change travellers' cheques as well, although the rate is usually not as good as a bank will give you. Besides your passport (a photocopy of which is taken on your first transaction), you will need to produce the receipts from your purchase of travellers' cheques showing the certified number of each cheque.
Most moneychangers are open daily to 10pm. After 9pm the rates of exchange are not so good, especially at weekends and on public holidays.

Warning: In the last few years there have been repeated examples of money-changers ripping customers off. The trick is that they count out the correct sum, then discretely stash the lower part of the bundle as it's being handed over.

Black Market

There is said to be a small black market but the rate is apparently only minimally better, so it's not worth the risk. The risk is real - there are a lot of money rip-off scams in Manila and any offer of a spectacular exchange rate is bound to be a set-up. The scam artists have a wide and interesting variety of tricks involving sleight of hand and other subterfuges, and they usually approach you in a seemingly innocent way. For example, somebody comes up to you in the street in Ermita or Malate and shows you a piece of cardboard with an enticingly high exchange rate written on it. Don't fall for it.
Beware, plenty of gullible tourists have been taken for a ride! You can be sure you won't gain anything if you let a persuasive dealer convince you to change money.
The illegal moneychangers ply their trade in the following way. To begin with they'll offer you a perfectly correct rate of exchange. You receive your pesos, the dealer takes the dollars. Then, all of a sudden, the dealer will apologise for having short changed you P50. The dealer takes the pesos back, counts them out again and ostentatiously places the allegedly missing P50 on top of the pile while stealthily removing some other notes from the bottom!
Another favourite trick is not to pay out in full the agreed sum so as to provoke the irritated customer into cancelling the deal. The customer then gets counterfeit dollars handed back while the dealer keeps the good dollars and pesos! There's no getting away from the fact that most black marketeers are consummate artists when it comes to fraud. This also goes for the pretty young Filipinas who use their charms to lure male tourists. The tourist wanting to change money is taken in by their tale of poverty and woe, and soon finds himself dealing with their well-fed moneychanging 'brothers'.

Cash

In the Philippines, unlike many other countries, the rate of exchange is somewhat higher for cash than it is for travellers' cheques. You'll get the best value for large US denominations like US$50 and US$100 bills. When selling currency, bear in mind that only clean banknotes are acceptable. Crumpled, torn or dirty ones will be rejected by moneychangers.
The US dollar is by far the most recognised foreign currency in the Philippines. Although the safety consideration with travellers' cheques applies as much in the Philippines as anywhere else, cash does, as usual, have its advantages. You will often find it easier to change a small amount of cash rather than a cheque.

Travellers' Cheques

If you want to keep on the safe side of the law and are prepared to accept an exchange rate about 5% lower, you should take travellers' cheques rather than cash with you. Travellers' cheques in US dollars issued by American Express (the easiest to exchange), the Bank of America and Thomas Cook will be cashed by almost every Philippine bank, and certainly by the Philippine National Bank (PNB).

According to the Philippine National Bank it is not a good idea at the moment to depend on Euro travellers' cheques. Apparently, they are not yet widely enough known in Philippine banks, especially in the provinces.

Hold on to your original purchase receipts, as most moneychangers and banks will not cash cheques unless you can produce this documentation. Some branches insist on having a copy of your passport and receipt of purchase, but don't have a photocopier themselves. To avoid long delays, take a few copies with you.

Most banks will not change money until after 10.30am, when the new exchange rates become available. Before changing money you should first find out how much they charge per cheque, as there are wide differences between banks.

The main problem is that changing travellers' cheques can be slow, particularly outside of Manila, due to the endless amount of red tape you have to go through. It can take up to an hour, so don't be in a hurry.

Many provincial banks only exchange travellers' cheques to a total value of US$100 or less. Cheques for larger amounts can only be cashed with the consent of the bank manager. So don't countersign them until he has given his approval.

Credit Cards

Well-known international cards such as American Express, Diners Club, MasterCard and Visa are accepted by many hotels, restaurants and businesses in the Philippines, although they are still not an everyday form of payment outside of Manila and the tourist areas. One downside to paying by credit card is that businesses almost always demand a service charge of between three and 10 (!) percent. If you can persuade them to state this charge separately on the receipt you can try to reclaim this amount later from the credit card company. Some hotels require guests to sign a blank credit card form which will be filled in later by the hotel. If you have any reason at all to doubt the honesty of the hotel staff, then it would be better to pay a reasonable amount in advance to avoid any unpleasantness later.

Cash advances

You can buy or withdraw:

- US dollars, travellers' cheques or pesos with your American Express card only at an American Express office, eg in Manila in the Ace Building, Rada St, Legaspi Village, Makati. Every 21 days you can abtain US$1000 in travellers' cheques, but you must have a personal cheque as well. Without a personal cheque for any 30-day period, card members may not exceed US$500 (US$1000 for Platinum Card members) or its equivalent in local currency;
- cash in pesos at any branch of the Equitable PCI Bank with your Visa or MasterCard (P20,000 minimum). There are plenty of these all over the country, with around 200 in Metro Manila only.
- cash with your Visa at the Citibank in Manila or Cebu City (US$300 minimum);

Bank Account

For those who intend to stay for an extended period in the Philippines, it would be worthwhile opening a bank account there and applying for an ATM card. But be aware that only the first P250,000 are insured. By law larger amounts do not have to be reimbursed should the bank suffer bankruptcy. Even two or more accounts at the same bank are not insured beyond a total amount of P250,000 when the holder of each account is the same person.

When opening an account, two pieces of ID are required, eg your passport and your driving licence, two passport photos (2×2 inches), and some banks also require a rental agreement for a house or apartment. It's possible to open peso accounts (with a minimum amount of 3000 to 5000, depending on the bank), and US$ accounts (500 to 1000, depending on the bank).

The Hongkong and Shanghai Banking Corporation (HSBC) in Manila permits customers to open an account in other currencies, eg A$ (minimum 8000), Euro (minimum 5000) and Sfr (minimum 8000) and will issue an ATM card for that account.

ATMs

Holders of a plastic keycard are not limited by the opening hours of the bank if they wish to withdraw money from their account. You will find ATMs not only inside and outside of bank branches but also in some public buildings, shopping centres and hotels. Information on the location of ATMs can be obtained on bank websites under 'ATM Locator' or 'Branch Directory' (Jens Peters' website www.travelphil.com has a good selection of links to bank websites under 'Money').

ATM Networks

There are three ATM consortia in the Philippines: BancNet, ExpressNet and MegaLink.

MegaLink is linked to both BancNet and ExpressNet, ie holders of a MegaLink card can draw money from ATMs belonging to banks associated with BancNet and ExpressNet, albeit for a small fee of around P10. All in all, the best thing to do is have an ATM card from one of the leading MegaLink banks.

BancNet: Over 30 member banks, including Allied Bank, Banco Filipino, Bank of Commerce, Citibank, Metrobank, Equitable PCI Bank, Security Bank and Union Bank.

ExpressNet: Seven member banks, including Hongkong & Shanghai Banking Corporation (HSBC), Banco do Oro, Bank of the Philippine Islands (BPI) and Landbank.

MegaLink: Over 20 member banks, including Development Bank of the Philippines, Equitable PCI Bank, Philippine National Bank (PNB), Union Bank and United Coconut Planters Bank (UCPB).

Cash withdrawals

Providing they have one of the following logos on the front or back, you can withdraw money with the following ATM and international credit cards using your PIN, and the amount will be debited from your account back home.

- **American Express:** Bank of the Philippine Islands.
- **Cirrus:** Citibank, Metrobank, Hongkong & Shanghai Banking Corporation (HSBC).
- **EC:** Citibank, Bank of the Philippine Islands, Equitable PCI Bank, Metrobank.
- **Maestro:** Metrobank, Hongkong & Shanghai Banking Corporation (HSBC).
- **MasterCard:** Citibank, Equitable PCI Bank, Hongkong & Shanghai Banking Corporation (HSBC), Metrobank.
- **Plus:** Equitable PCI Bank, Hongkong & Shanghai Banking Corporation (HSBC), Metrobank.
- **Visa:** Citibank, Equitable PCI Bank, Hongkong & Shanghai Banking Corporation (HSBC), Philippine National Bank.

How much?
The daily limit basically depends on the individual card limit. However, the upper limit from most ATMs is P20,000 (5 × P4000, 4 × P5000 or 2 × P10,000).

● At the Equitable PCI Bank the daily limit is P50,000 (5 × P10,000), although some of their ATMs only allow individual transactions of P4000 or P5000.

● If you have an EC card with the Maestro logo you can draw up to P50,000 daily from Bank of the Philippine Islands ATMs (5 × P10,000).

● Hongkong and Shanghai Bank Corporation (HSBC) ATMs allow you to draw up to P40,000 daily (2 × P20,000).

● Citibank ATMs allow you to draw up to P150,000 daily (10 × P15,000).

When?

● Don't wait until the last minute to replenish your travel money, as ATMs could be empty or offline, especially on Sundays and public holidays.

● Try only to draw money during normal banking hours, as some ATMs are obviously only connected to their headquarters in Manila during these hours.

● If possible, draw money in the early forenoon while there is still enough money available in the ATMs.

● When using an international card, it is possible that the machine will be unable to establish a connection to the global network, while there's still no problem drawing money using a Philippine card. In that case, just try another machine.

● **Important note:** Some banks count Saturday, Sunday and Monday as one banking day (eg the Equitable PCI Bank does this). So if you draw up to the limit on Saturday, you'll have to wait until the following Tuesday before you can draw money again.

International Transfers
Depending on the bank, money orders can take up to ten days or even more. It's advantageous to have a safe-deposit account, as that way you can arrange for the desired sum of money to be sent by telex. Costs are in the vicinity of US$15 and the waiting time is two days.
Some banks are unwilling to pay out dollars in bills. If anything, they might offer you the amount in very small bills, which you're better off refusing.

Western Union
Western Union money transfer is fast, and worldwide. Just a few minutes after someone has paid money into a Western Union agent the addressee can pick up the money at any Western Union agent in the world. There are over 5000 Western Union agents in the Philippines, including the offices of Aboitiz Express, Philcom, RCPI and Swagman Travel.
To find out where the nearest agent is, phone 8190538 in Metro Manila; outside of Metro Manila dial 1-800-1-8880102 (freephone).

Other Methods
If you wish to send money in a letter to the Philippines, you should only do so by registered letter, otherwise its safe arrival can't be guaranteed. To keep on the safe side, camouflage the valuable item with a piece of carbon paper and then fasten the contents to the envelope with a staple on the outside: there are postal employees with X-ray vision! In fact, it's not uncommon for envelopes also stamped on the back to be opened (registered letters are known to carry valuable items!). Post office crooks are capable of removing most of the enclosed money and leaving just a token remainder; or they might switch a US$5 bill for a US$50 one before passing the letter on for 'regular' delivery.

Postal money orders present no problem. These take about 10 days.

Documents

Travel Insurance

If available in your country then it would be advisable to arrange for the following insurance cover: Travel health insurance (including repatriation cover in case of serious illness), and baggage insurance (including belongings).

Driving Licence & Permits

If you want to hire a car, you will need a valid driver's licence from your country of origin or an International Driver's Permit. After a stay of more than 90 days you will need a Philippine driving licence. See also the Car section in the Getting Around chapter.

Hostel Card

There is only a handful of youth hostels and Y's in the Philippines; card holders are given a small discount.

Student & Youth Cards

Some bus and ship companies give student discounts, although not during vacation time.

International Health Card

Vaccinations and immunisations are noted on the International Health Card. Even if it has not been necessary to show the card on arrival in recent years, it wouldn't harm to have it with you. However, if you are arriving in the Philippines from an area with yellow fever, you must have proof of immunisation.

Photocopies

Make two copies of your documents and of the receipts of your travellers' cheques and leave one copy at a permanent address so you can send for it if necessary. Either exchange the other copy with your travelling companion for theirs or keep it in your luggage, quite separate from the originals. Identification problems and document replacement in the case of loss or theft will be a lot easier if you take these precautions.

If you take a personal address book containing important addresses and telephone numbers, you should make a copy of them and store them separately from the originals.

What to Bring

Bring as little as possible is the golden rule - it's almost always possible to get things you might need and that's far better than carrying too much with you. T-shirts and shoes are good value, although shoe sizes 10 and upwards are quite rare and are as expensive as they are in Europe. You can have jeans made for about US$15. Most hotels have towels, so two extra towels would be enough. Many hotels and hostels have mosquito nets available on request.

A backpack is probably the best way of carrying your gear but try to thief-proof it as much as possible and remember that backpacks are prone to damage, especially by airlines, where they easily get caught up in loading equipment. Travel packs are a relatively recent innovation that combine the advantages of a backpack and a soft carry bag. The shoulder straps either detach or can be hidden away under a zip-fastened flap so they do not catch on things.

The Philippines has enough climatic variations to require a fairly wide variety of clothing. At sea level you'll need lightweight gear, suitable for tropical temperatures. In Mountain Province or when scaling the odd volcano, you'll need warmer clothing - jumpers (sweaters) and a light jacket. Bring thongs (flip-flops) for use in hotel bathrooms and showers.

Examples of Costs

Beer (small bottle) P15
(about US$0.28)
Big Mac P55
(about US$1)
Blouse/shirt washed and ironed P20
(about US$0.36)
Cigarettes (Marlboro, local) P22
(about US$0.40)
Coke (small bottle) P9
(about US$0.16)
Daily newspaper P15
(about US$0.28)
Doctor's consultation P200-P500
(about US$3.60-9)
Film (Ektachrome 100) P250
(about US$4.55)
Milk (1 litre) P42
(about US$0.76)
Mineral water (0.5 l) P10
(about US$0.18)
Postcard to Europe P11
(about US$0.20)
Rice (1kg) P25
(about US$0.45)
Shampoo (100ml) P35
(about US$0.65)
Soap (100g) P35
(about US$0.65)
Telephone call (local) P5
(about US$0.09)
Toothpaste (25ml) P15
(about US$0.28)
100 km by ordinary bus P100
(about US$1.80)
100 km by air-con bus P120
(about US$2.20)
One hour domestic flight P2900
(about US$52)
Litre of petrol P25
(about US$0.45)

Soap, toothpaste and other general toiletries are readily available, but out in the sticks, toilet paper can be difficult to find.

Suggested Equipment

- A first-aid kit is useful (see the Health section later in this chapter).
- As opposed to sanitary napkins, tampons are not very well known in the Philippines and are only available in drugstores in larger cities and tourist centres, if at all. So women travellers should stock up before they go if they're planning an extended trip in the provinces.
- The third class on the inter-island boats is equipped with bunks or camp beds. A big cloth towel or a thin sleeping bag can really help you feel more comfortable on the rubber sheets covering them. Trips on outrigger boats can turn out to be quite splashy. A big plastic rubbish bag will save your bags from getting wet.
- For longer bus and ship journeys, it's useful to take an inflatable cushion with you for your extra comfort. For example, on an overnight bus journey you could use it to lean your head on.
- If you're a keen snorkeller, bring your mask and snorkel; there are many superb diving areas around the islands.
- Especially in country areas electricity cannot be taken for granted, so don't forget to take along a torch (flashlight). A dynamo version will save taking batteries and avoid the problem of their disposal when flat.
- A padlock is always worth carrying: you can often use it to add security to your hotel room.
- A pocket calculator can come in handy for checking the addition on dubious bills and for working out exchange rates.
- When it rains in the Philippines, it really rains, so bring an umbrella (it can also double up as a parasol if need be).

● Other possibilities include a sewing kit, a Swiss army knife, and a travel alarm clock - the list goes on.

Film

Take sufficient slide film with you as there is not a lot of choice in the Philippines. This is especially true of the provinces, where the use-by date has often expired. Kodak Ektachrome 100 costs about P250 (US$4.50).

There's no problem with normal colour film, which is often preferred by Filipinos. Development is fast and good value. Highgloss prints (nine cm by 13 cm) can be processed in an hour at a cost of P5 per print.

Officially you are only allowed to bring five cartridges of film in with you, but the customs officials usually turn a blind eye in the case of tourists.

Presents

You can bring a lot of happiness to children and adults in the Philippines through small tokens of appreciation, but don't overdo it. Filipinos are very inquisitive and interested in where the visitor comes from and what it's like there. To show them, or to offer them a gift in return for hospitality you have received, you can make good use of postcards from your country. People also like to look at pictures of your home, family, animals and plants. These things are good conversation starters.

You will be well liked if you're friendly - it doesn't cost anything. There's a fine local saying: 'A smile gives more light than electricity'.

Health

Pre-departure Preparations

Travel health depends on your pre-departure preparations, your day-to-day health care while travelling and how you handle any medical problem or emergency that does develop. While the list of potential dangers can seem quite frightening, with a little luck, some basic precautions and adequate information you will experience little more than an upset stomach.

If you are embarking on a long trip, for example, make sure your teeth are OK: there are lots of places where a visit to the dentist would be the last thing you'd want to do.

If you wear glasses take a spare pair and your prescription. Losing your glasses can be a real problem, although in many places you can get new spectacles made quickly, cheaply and competently.

If you require a particular medication take an adequate supply, as it may not be available locally. Take the prescription, with the generic rather than the brand name (which may not be locally available), as it will make getting replacements easier. It's a wise idea to have the prescription with you to show you legally use the medication.

Medical Kit

A good medical kit is essential, particularly if you are going off the beaten track. Because you can't always get to your main luggage when travelling, for example on a flight, it's recommended that you keep a small medical kit in your hand luggage with medications such as pain-relieving tablets, diarrhoea tablets, eye drops and perhaps Alka Seltzer. Consult your doctor about individual medicines.

A possible kit list would include:

● Pain and fever tablets. Something to help toothache.

● Antihistamine - useful as a decongestant for colds, allergies, to ease the itch from insect bites or stings or to help prevent motion sickness.

● Antibiotics - useful if you're travelling off the beaten track. Choose a good broad-spectrum antibiotic.

- Tablets for stomach upsets or diarrhoea.
- Rehydration mixture - for treatment of severe diarrhoea, this is particularly important if travelling with children.
- Antiseptic, mercurochrome and antibiotic powder or similar 'dry' spray - for cuts and grazes.
- Calamine lotion - to ease irritation from bites or stings.
- Bandages and Band-aids - for minor injuries.
- Scissors, tweezers and a thermometer (note that mercury thermometers are prohibited by airlines).
- Insect repellent, sunscreen, suntan lotion, chapstick and water purification tablets.
- Condoms - to avoid sexually transmitted diseases.

Medicines

In the Philippines many medicines will generally be available over the counter and the price will be much cheaper than in the West, but they may be marketed under a different name. Some medicines are supposedly available only with a prescription form, but, it seems, it's not compulsory for every pharmacy to see one. Antibiotics are available in Philippine pharmacies without prescription. Manila is the best place to buy antibiotics.

Popular medicines for a cold are Nafarin A and Neozep.

'Off' is a good mosquito repellent. If you're coming from Thailand, buy some Jaico mosquito repellent there - it's made in Belgium - for about US$5. In the opinion of the author, it feels more pleasant on the skin and lasts longer than all the other well-known brands.

Medical Services

Doctors charge around P300 (US$5.50) for a consultation. Your embassy will provide you with a list of recommended doctors, who are usually multilingual. See also under *Miscellaneous* for the individual areas.

Immunisations

For the Philippines in general no immunisations are required, but the further off the beaten track you go the more necessary it is to take precautions. However, tropical institutes recommend travellers take a malaria prophylaxis. Up to date information on preventative measures is available on the CDC website Travelers' Health page (www.cdc.gov/travel/seasia.htm).

You only need a yellow fever vaccination if you're coming from an infected area. Nevertheless, all vaccinations should be recorded on an International Health Certificate, available from your physician or government health department.

When organising your vaccinations make sure you plan ahead as some of them require an initial shot followed by a booster, while some vaccinations should not be given together. Most travellers from Western countries will have been immunised against various diseases during childhood, but your doctor may still recommend booster shots for measles or polio, diseases still prevalent in many developing countries. The period of protection offered by vaccinations differs widely and some are contraindicated if you are pregnant. The possible list of vaccinations includes: Tetanus & Diphtheria, Typhoid, Hepatitis A and Hepatitis B.

Health Insurance

A travel insurance policy to cover theft, loss and medical problems is a wise idea. There is a wide variety of policies and your travel agent will have recommendations. Some policies offer lower and higher medical expense options, but the higher one is chiefly for countries like the USA which have extremely high medical costs. Check the small print:

- Some policies specifically exclude 'dangerous activities' such as scuba diving, motorcycling, or even trekking. If such activities are on your agenda you don't want that sort of policy.
- You may prefer a policy which pays doctors or hospitals direct rather than you having to pay on the spot and claim later. If you have to claim later, make sure you keep all documentation. Some policies ask you to call back (reverse charges) to a centre in your home country where an immediate assessment of your problem is made.
- Check if the policy covers ambulances or an emergency flight home. If you have to stretch out you will need two seats and somebody has to pay for them!

Post

Letters to and from the Philippines take from about four to 14 days, depending on where the sender is.
During the Christmas period, from mid-December to mid-January, mail is delayed by up to a month.

Mail to the Philippines

The Philippine postal system is generally quite efficient. You can get mail sent by poste restante at the GPO in all the major towns. Ask people who are writing to you to print your surname clearly and to underline it - most missing mail is simply misfiled under given names. Any mail which remains uncollected after about three months will be sent back free of charge.
You can also have mail sent to an American Express office if you're using American Express travellers' cheques or carrying an American Express card. American Express has offices in Manila and Cebu City. The Manila address is Clients' Mail, American Express, Ace Building, Rada St, 1200 Makati, Metro Manila. You can get information by calling Tel 8144777 (ask to be connected).

Mail from the Philippines

Letters
So far all letters from the author have arrived home safely. If you are sending important items (such as film) out by mail, it is best to send it by registered post. Registered express letters will be delivered - all going well - within five days. Around Christmas especially, you should make sure your letters are stamped immediately so that no-one can remove your postage stamps and use them again.

Parcels
Only parcels weighing less than 20 kg will be dispatched by the Philippine postal service. The parcel post rates are calculated in kilograms. There is a basic rate for the first kg, thereafter you are charged for every kg or part thereof. Parcels sent to Europe by surface (sea) mail take from two to four months to reach their destination.

Mail within the Philippines

A letter sent by regular post within the Philippines can take about one or two weeks to be delivered. For P60 you can use LBC, the efficient courier service, which can be found in every town or city. LBC delivers within 24 hours all over the country. You can search for the addresses of LBC branches by SMS, eg for Angeles enter LBCFIND Angeles, then send to 2333 (Globe) or 211 (Smart).

Postal Rates

Letters
Airmail letters (per 20g) within the Philippines cost P6 (ordinary/two weeks) and P15 (priority/one week).

Airmail letters (per 20g) cost P17.50 to South-East Asia, P21 to Australia and the Middle East, P22 to Europe and North America and P23 to Africa and South America.

Aerograms and postcards cost P11 regardless of the destination.

Some postal workers will, on their own initiative, add a P2 donation stamp in aid of the TB Society to your letter. This is not an official stamp but a voluntary payment.

Parcels

Airmail: To Australia P600 for the first kg (for each additional kg or part thereof P335); UK P792 (P442); USA P685 (P461).

Surface mail: To Australia P457 for the first kg (for each additional kg or part thereof P158); UK P693 (P343); USA P432 (P202).

Opening Hours

Opening hours in Philippine post offices are not the same everywhere. Many close at noon for an hour, others are shut all day Saturday. The following opening hours can usually be relied upon: Monday to Friday from 8am to noon and 1 to 5pm.

With few exceptions, post offices are closed on Sundays and public holidays, and at the end of the year there are at least three public holidays: Rizal Day (30 December), New Year's Eve and New Year's Day.

Freight

For consignments which are too large for airmail or even surface mail, an air or sea carrier is the alternative. The freight company Royal Cargo, Sta Agueda Ave, Pascor Dr, 1704 Parañaque, Manila, Tel (02) 8516229, Fax (02) 8516202, @, is reliable and efficient. They also go under the name of Royal Moving & Storage and have branches in several cities, including Angeles, Baguio and Cebu. Other freight companies can be found in the Yellow Pages under 'Movers'.

In the case of air freight, a good alternative is a combined shipment. Although it takes a bit longer than shipping individually, it costs a lot less money.

Telephone & Fax

Telephone

You won't find telephones everywhere in the Philippines; in an emergency try the nearest police station, which in many areas will have the only telephone. Telephone numbers are always changing so get hold of a local directory before calling, or you can call information on 114.

In contrast to overseas calls, local calls in the Philippines are full of problems. It can take a ridiculously long time to be connected and the lines over long distances are bad. International calls are a breeze in comparison.

Long-distance overseas calls can be made from most hotels (operator or direct dialling; it depends on their equipment). A three minute station to station call to Europe costs about P300. It's a few pesos cheaper if you call directly from any PLDT (Philippine Long Distance Telephone Company) office.

Note that it is far cheaper to make station to station rather than person to person calls from the Philippines: the charges are about 25% less.

Try to call outside business hours (of the country you are ringing) when the waiting time will be considerably less. On Sunday there is a 25% reduction in the charge.

Telephone cards

The telephone companies Digitel and Globe Telecom have begun installing

SMS - PTMM...

The Filipinos are world leaders in texting (SMS) and sending pictures (they send more of both per day than the whole of Europe together). Here, as elsewhere, text shortcuts are used, some of which are quite creative. A text message could look something like this:

HI QT, GUD AM. HW R U? IB IN MLA, CAN I C U L8R 2NYT? M TOY 24/7 - HHOK. K, I G2GN, PTXTB. B4N, ILU2.

Here are a few of the more popular shortcuts:

2NYT	Tonight	IDTS	I Don't Think So
2 U	To You	ILU	I Love You
24/7	24 Hours A Day, 7 Days A Week	ILU2	I Love You Too
		K	Okay
6E	Sexy	L8R	Later
AM	Morning	LTNS	Long Time No See
BBL	Be Back Later	M	I Am
BCS	Because	MLA	Manila
BC	Busy	N/M	Never Mind
B4	Before	NE1	Anyone
B4N	Bye For Now	NP	No Problem
BION	Believe It Or Not	NW	Now
BTW	By The Way	QT	Cutie
CB	Call Back	PCB	Please Call Back
C U	See You	PRMIZ	Promise
DIKU?	Do I Know You?	PTMM	Please Tell Me More
EOM	End Of Message	PTXTB	Please Text Back
ESP	Specially	R	Are
F2F	Face To Face	R8	Right
FOAF	Friend Of A Friend	TNX	Thanks
FYI	For Your Information	TOY	Thinking Of You
G2GN	Got To Go Now	TTYL	Talk To You Later
GF	Girlfriend	TXTM8	Textmate
GUD	Good	TY	Thank You
GV	Give	U	You
HHOK	Ha Ha Only Kidding	UR	Your
HW	How	URLCM	You Are Welcome
IB	I'M BACK	W8	Wait
I C	I See	ZZZZ	Sleeping

payphones in well-frequented places in the Philippines, which can be used to make low cost national and international calls with the DigiKard or the Globe Telcard.
Globe Telcards are available for P100, P150 and P200. Inland calls cost P1.50 to P4.50 per minute (landlines) or P12.50 per minute (mobile network). International calls cost US 40¢ (around P20) per minute.

Mobile Phones

The digital mobile phone network doesn't cover the whole country yet, although the gaps in coverage are being filled quite quickly. Occasionally the radio contact is too weak for telephone

New telephone numbers
Starting soon, all Manila telephone numbers will have an additional digit, an 8, which will be added to the beginning of the present numbers.

conversations, but is still usually strong enough to send a text message. There are no problems in cities and tourist centres.
In the Philippines, mobiles are called cellphones (cellular telephones). They are very popular and are used mainly for sending cheap text messages. If you want to bring your mobile with you (handy for booking a room, for example), a Philippine prepaid phone card is a good idea. You can get them without any formalities from Globe Telecom, for example, who are good value for overseas calls. Smart might be better when you're travelling, as they have better coverage on many islands, eg in the south of Negros, in the north of Palawan and on some of the inter-island ships, Negros Navigation for instance.
You do have to remember that your normal number is not available while you're using the Philippine card, so you will have to inform people of your temporary Philippine number if you want to receive calls. Connection (Sim Pack/Sim Card) costs P200 to P300, which includes P100 calling credit.
A huge variety of mobiles is available in the Philippines. A basic model, eg the Nokia 3210, costs P3000 (around US$55).

Fax
Many hotels and offices are equipped with fax machines. Sending a fax from a hotel to overseas can be quite expensive (eg P350 for one page to Europe). On the other hand, private telecommunication companies, including Eastern Telecoms and PLDT charge about P95 for the first minute (one page) and P85 for the following minutes.
Domestic fax transmissions are relatively cheap, eg from Manila to Cebu City the first minute costs P25 and the following minutes are P20.

Area Codes
The Philippine telephone area codes can be found in the individual chapters under 'Miscellaneous': *Post & Telephone*. Here are the most important ones for your convenience:
Angeles (045); Bacolod (034); Boracay (036); Cebu City (032); Davao (082); Iloilo City (033); Manila (02); Puerto Princesa (048); San Fernando/La Union (072).
The country code for the Philippines is 0063.

Internet & E-mail
A lot of information on the Philippines can also be found on the Internet. A great number of cities have their own websites, as do daily newspapers, hotels and diving schools. The author's website *www.travelphil.com* offers links to a lot of websites which can help you with your travel preparations.
There are more than enough internet cafés in the Philippines, not only in the larger cities. In addition, many hotels are equipped with a business centre where guests can take care of e-mails and surf the net. You'll pay around P25 to P60 per hour in the provinces, from P50 to P90 in Manila. Usually 15 minutes is the minimum deducted time.

Tourist Offices
The vast Department of Tourism (DOT) office in Manila could be more aptly called the Temple of Tourism. Computer printouts with completely up-to-date information on various places are handed out.

The regional DOT offices are smaller operations - but the staff are often very knowledgeable, have all the facts at their fingertips and can provide useful information sheets on their localities.
Several cities which don't have an official DOT office have opened up a tourist office of their own, responsible for the local area. Usually this office can be found in the town hall.

Local Tourist Offices

Bacolod: City Tourist Office, San Juan Street, Tel +63 (0)34 4346751.
Provincial Tourist Office, South Capitol Rd, Tel +63 (0)34 4332515.
Baguio: Department of Tourism Complex, Governor Pack Rd, Tel +63 (0)74 4426708, @.
Butuan: D&V Plaza II Building, JC Aquino Ave, Tel +63 (0)85 2255712, 3416371, @.
Cagayan de Oro: Pelaez Sports Complex, Velez St, Tel +63 (0)8822 723696, 723696, +63 (0)88 8564048, @.
Cebu City: LDM Building, Lapu-Lapu St, Tel +63 (0)32 2542811, 2546077, @.
Cotabato: Cosme Building, Quezon Ave, Tel +63 (0)64 4211110, @.
Davao: Magsaysay Park Complex, Tel +63 (0)82 2216798, 2216955, @.
Iloilo City: Bonifacio Dr, Tel +63 (0)33 3375411, 3350245, @.
Legaspi: Regional Center Site, Rawis, Tel +63 (0)52 4820712, @.
Manila: Department of Tourism (DOT), TM Kalaw Street, Rizal Park, Ermita, Tel +63 (0)2 5242384, 5252000, @.
San Fernando (La Union): Oasis Country Resort, Sevilla, National Highway, Tel +63 (0)72 8882411, @.
San Fernando (Pampanga): Hilaga, Tel +63 (0)45 9612665, 9612621, @.
Tacloban: Magsaysay Blvd, Tel +63 (0)53 3212048, 3214333, @.
Tuguegarao: Tuguegarao Supermarket, Gonzaga St, Tel +63 (0)78 8441621.
Zamboanga: Lantaka Hotel, Valderroza St, Tel +63 (0)62 9910218, @.

Tourist Offices Abroad

Overseas offices of the Philippines Department of Tourism include:

Australia: Philippine Centre, Level 1, 27-33 Wentworth Ave, Sydney, NSW 2000, Tel (02) 92830711, @.
China: Philippine Consulate, 6F United Centre, 95 Queensway, Central, Hong Kong, Tel (852) 8667643, @.
France: Ambassade des Philippines, 3 Faubourg Saint Honoré, 75008 Paris, Tel (01) 42650234, @.
Germany: Kaiserhofstrasse 7, 60313 Frankfurt/M, Tel (069) 20893, @.
Japan: 5-15-5 Roppongi Minato-ku, Tokyo 106-8537, Tel (03) 55621583, @.
Singapore: Orchard Towers, 400 Orchard Rd, Singapore 238875, Tel (065) 7387165, @.
UK: Philippines Tourism & Cultural Office, 146 Cromwell Rd, London SW 7 4EF, Tel (020) 7835100, @.
USA: 30 North Michigan Ave, Suite 913, Chicago, IL 60602, Tel. (312) 7822475, @.
- Philippine Center, 556 Fifth Ave, New York, NY 10036, Tel (212) 5757915, @.
- 3660 Wilshire Blvd, Suite 216, Los Angeles, CA 90010, Tel (213) 4874527, @.
- 447 Sutter St, Suite 507, San Francisco, CA 94108, Tel (415) 9564060, @.

@ E-mail (This sign in the text means that the hotel etc can be contacted by e-mail. The address can be found in the E-mail Index at the back of the book.)

Travel Tips

Accommodation

Prices

If your budget for a night's accommodation only stretches up to P100, then there are only a few hotels available. Prices for quite inexpensive accommodation start at around P200 (about US$4).

The cheapest are the guesthouses in the mountains of North Luzon which can cost as little as P100 (US$2), although some will be pretty basic - with no electricity for example. The best selection of well-equipped, medium-priced hotels with air-con, TV, hot water and swimming pool can be found in Angeles, near Mt Pinatubo for about P800 (US$16).

On the popular little island of Boracay during the on season from December until May, only a handful of resorts offer cottages for less than P500. Most cost between P800 and P1500 (about US$16 to US$30); however, during the off season all sorts of attractive discounts are available.

Throughout the Philippines you will find that prices for single and double rooms are sometimes the same. This is because single rooms sometimes have a double bed and can therefore be used by two people; to the Filipinos this is the same as a double room. Double rooms usually have two beds. If you intend staying anywhere for some time ask about weekly and monthly rents.

Hotels in the top category charge around 20% for service and tax on top of the price of the room. It's always worth the effort to ask if they have promo rates available. Sometimes they'll even throw in breakfast.

Almost all airlines that fly to Manila offer a stopover programme when they sell you a ticket. This is often a good way to get inexpensive accommodation in first class hotels; they may even pick you up in a limo at the airport.

However, the best deals of all can be had from online travel agents, who can offer up to 70% discount if you pay in advance by credit card. A good example is Asia Travel:
www.asiatravel.com/philippines.html

Hotels

Basic hotels and so-called pensions (guesthouses) are usually only furnished with the bare necessities, and are often not completely up to standard. Medium-priced hotels come in varying degrees of quality. They are usually equipped with aircon, telephone and TV, frequently also with a refrigerator (minibar). The better hotels of this category also have a business centre (with internet access, photocopier and fax machine), and sometimes also a fitness room and swimming pool as well.

First-class hotels offer their guests top comfort. They usually belong to an international luxury hotel chain and the staff are trained to the highest of standards.

If the hotel of your choice is booked out, depending on the time of day, you might consider waiting in the lobby to see if a room becomes available. There is less chance of someone checking out after 12 noon, however. If you ask nicely, the staff will almost definitely phone around and see if anywhere else has a room for you. As a general rule, room reservations will only be held until 6pm if you haven't paid in advance.

Maintenance in many hotels is a little lackadaisical so it's a good idea to check if the electricity and water (shower and toilets) are working before you sign in. Also keep in mind that there are often cheaper rooms without windows in the inner part of the building.

The lighting in hotel rooms is often rather dim. If you want to read or write in the evenings you should get a light bulb of at least 60 watts beforehand.

Beware of fires in hotels - Philippine hotels don't close down, they burn down. Check fire escapes and make sure windows will open.

It might be advisable to deposit any valuables in the hotel safe. If a simple drawer is used as a locker, don't entrust your things to the hotel. It is also inadvisable to leave large amounts of cash with the hotel reception. If you do deposit your valuables in the hotel safe, get a receipt with an exact account of the details. Also ask whether there are certain times when you can't get them back. The night shift is not always entrusted with a key. When you do get your valuables back, check your cash and travellers' cheques carefully.

The term 'bath' has generally been used throughout the book to mean a bathroom that is equipped with a toilet and shower. It is only in first-class international hotels that you can expect a bathtub. Private Filipino homes normally have a shower and not a bathtub.

Motels

In the Philippines, a motel is not a hotel for people in cars as is normal in most countries, but a short-stay hotel (known as a 'shorttime hotel' in Philippine English). Rooms with discrete adjacent garage can be rented for three, six or more hours. Depending on price class, the furnishings are comfortable, occasionally with erotic fittings, glass-front showers and equipped with a porn channel on the TV.

Cottages

On most beaches, cottages are the usual form of accommodation. They are little holiday chalets made of bamboo or stone. The price depends on the size and furnishings and is usually meant to be for two people. An inexpensive cottage is nothing more than a very simple hut made of bamboo and leaves, crudely furnished with a basic bed, mosquito net and petroleum lamp. More expensive cottages will have a fan and bath, better furniture and a veranda. The most expensive are stone-built, comfortably furnished with one or two beds, air-con and bath.

Rental Accommodation

For a long stay it's worth taking a furnished apartment. This greatly reduces the expense. See also the chapter Manila: *Apartments*.

Private Accommodation

Should you have difficulties finding accommodation in smaller towns, go to the mayor or barrio captain. He will quickly arrange some shelter for you and may even find a place for you in the government resthouse.

In the provinces you may often be invited into private homes. It is the custom in the Philippines to offer guests the best food and lodging, but this can be very expensive for the family. By all means accept their hospitality, but don't offer money directly for your board and keep either - say it's to educate their children, for example.

Camping

As a general rule, you can pitch a tent anywhere you want in the Philippines. Needless to say, it is customary to ask politely for permission if your place for the night is obviously on private land. You will seldom get No for an answer. The ideal site is under the shade of a big, leafy tree. Never put your tent under a coconut palm, because a falling nut can cause serious problems. On a beach you can orient yourself by looking for the high water line, which is marked by flotsam and jetsam. If you are in the mountains, do not camp underneath a steep rock face, where things that go bump in the night could be extremely dangerous loose stones and rocks. The middle of a dry river bed is

also not as good a place as it might look: one heavy rain shower upstream and you could find yourself waking up in the middle of a raging torrent.
Ants can be a real pain if they decide to share your tent, so put all your provisions into tightly sealed containers, and keep them outside of the tent. If you spread ash from a wood fire in a ring around your campsite this should manage to ward off the little pests for a while.

Tipping & Bargaining

Just as in other countries, whether or not to tip is a personal decision. If you stay in the same hotel for a few days however, there is no doubt that hotel staff would appreciate a P20 to P50 tip. Restaurant staff generally expect a tip (it is part of their wage), even if the menu states that a service charge is included. The money then almost always goes into a kitty and is shared later with the cook and the cashier. If the service was particularly good, a tip of around 5% of the bill will show your appreciation.
Taxi drivers will often try to wangle a tip by claiming not to be able to give change. If the charge on the meter appears to be accurate, the passenger should voluntarily round up the amount: for example, if the fare is P44, then P50 would be appropriate.
When shopping in public markets or even shops, Filipinos try to get a 10% discount. They almost always succeed. Foreign customers will automatically be quoted a price that is around 20% more than normal or, in places which deal mainly with tourists, up to 50% more. On the other hand, department stores and supermarkets offer set prices, and it is not customary to bargain.

Electricity

The electric current is generally 220V, 60 cycles, although the actual voltage is often less, in some areas the standard current is the US-style 110V.
Blackouts are common even in the tourist centres. A pocket torch (flashlight) is very useful for such occasions.
An adapter may be needed for Philippine plugs which are usually like the US flat, two-pin type.

Laundry

There are only a few laundries in the Philippines open to the public which are equipped with modern machinery. Self-service launderettes with coin-operated machines are completely unknown.
If you don't want to wash your clothes yourself, hand them in to your hotel or guesthouse and you'll get them back within two to three days. They will not always be ironed though. It costs about P20 to have a shirt or blouse washed and ironed.

Toilets

The toilets are known as comfort rooms or CRs - *lalake* means 'gentlemen' and *babae* 'ladies' in Filipino. The toilets in restaurants and bars are usually dirty and there is seldom toilet paper, but you will always find clean toilets in the lobbies of the larger hotels and in restaurant chains such as McDonald's (at least if they've just been cleaned). Western-style sit-down toilets are the norm, although the Philippine variety is smaller.

Time

The Philippines is eight hours ahead of GMT/UTC, 13 hours ahead of US Eastern Standard Time, 16 hours ahead of US Pacific Time, and two hours behind Australian Eastern Standard Time. Adjustments would obviously have to be made for countries with Daylight Savings Time.

Do's & Don'ts

Historically, foreigners have generally not come to the Philippines with the best of intentions. In spite of this, every visitor is heartily welcomed: the Filipinos are very sociable and tolerant and their natural openness charms many visitors.

But to say every visitor is welcome, is not strictly true. There is in particular one type of visitor they can do quite well without: the pedophiles. The Philippines has the dubious distinction of being on the list of places where child abusers feel they can exploit the poverty of the people. Most of them are men from rich countries, whose foremost thought is to have pleasure at the expense of a defenceless child. To call it decadence is to condemn it too lightly. The organisation End Child Prostitution in Asian Tourism (ECPAT) has been active for a considerable time in supporting the rights of children and youths (who do not come of age until their 18th birthday in the Philippines). Investigators have arrested large numbers of foreigners for sexually molesting children.

On a lighter note, but still not unimportant: In the Philippines, as elsewhere, there are lots of toes you can accidentally tread on unless you're careful. Here are a few tips to help you avoid potentially embarrassing situations while you're travelling:

● Don't get annoyed if people stare at you. If they find you interesting - even exotic - then they want to get a good look at you.

● Do treat senior citizens with particular respect. Always greet the elderly if there are any present.

● Do allow Filipinos a way out of an awkward situation. Especially, for example, when they may risk a possible 'loss of face' - a painful and embarrassing situation which the Filipino will try to avoid. Be mindful that they may give completely false information rather than admit they don't know - or they will just grin at you benignly pretending not to understand your question.

● Don't be punctual if you are invited to a social occasion! Turn up at least thirty minutes after the arranged time if you want to be a really polite guest. It is normal to remove your shoes before entering someone's home.

● Do take at least a taste of food if offered. If you like it, remember to leave some food on the plate to show you've had plenty.

● Don't remain silent in company, unless you want to imply that you are unhappy with the situation, or don't like somebody present. Attempts to spend time alone in a restaurant or pub are doomed to failure from the start. Chatty people ready to ask questions are always close at hand, especially if there is a possibility of alcohol. If you really need peace and quiet, go somewhere you can literally be alone.

● Don't be belligerent, even if an idiosyncrasy of the Filipinos seems unpleasant or uncomfortable to you. You will achieve a lot more by being polite or making light of problems. Foreigners who indulge in exaggerated reticence, arrogance or who take the opportunity to lord it over the locals financially or culturally, will never find a friend in the Philippines. They will have to make do with being ignored or mistreated.

● Do remember that there are black sheep among the Filipinos, just like everywhere else. For important information on this see Security later on in this chapter.

'Filipino time' has a curious nature - it includes lack of punctuality and a need for patience. A rendezvous à la Filipino time is basically very loose. Either you are waited for, or you wait. Don't get too upset - tomorrow is another day. Remember this warning when you've missed a 7 o'clock bus because it had already left at 6.30! In the Philippines the only reliable times are sunrise and sunset.

Business Hours

Businesses first open their doors in the morning between 8 and 10am (shopping malls open at 10am). Offices, banks and public authorities have a five-day week. Some offices are also open on Saturday morning.

Banks open at 9am and close at 3 or 3.30pm. Embassies and consulates are open to the public mainly from 9am to 1pm. Offices and public authorities open at 8am and close at 5pm. Large businesses like department stores and supermarkets continue until 8pm. Smaller shops are often open until 10pm and some, eg 7-Eleven, are even open around the clock.

Security

If you throw your money on the table in bars and restaurants, or flash large banknotes around, don't be surprised if you get mugged on the corner when you leave. Carelessness gets punished, and the big and small-time gangsters in Manila are waiting for opportunities, just like their counterparts anywhere else in the world.

Look after your valuables and don't even let on that you have them. You will be taken for a wealthy foreigner regardless, even if you are not well off by Western standards and have saved for ages for your trip. Irresponsible behaviour will only provoke a challenge. This is particularly the case at Christmas, when the time of peace and goodwill mobilises a whole army of thieves and beggars to pay for their gifts with the help of money from tourists and locals alike.

Here are some hints on how to guard your possessions and look after your own safety:

- Money belongs in your front trouser pockets, in a pouch worn around your neck and under your clothes, or in a concealed money belt. Don't make it easy for pickpockets, as they are often very skilful.
- Keep shoulder bags or camera bags in body contact; don't let them out of your sight. Develop the habit of keeping your hand underneath them: Filipinos with razors are quiet and quick.
- Avoid dark alleys at night, especially if you have been enjoying San Miguel beer or Tanduay rum.
- Don't pay your taxi fare until all of your luggage is unloaded.
- Deposit valuables in the hotel safe, or rent a safe-deposit box at a large bank: it will cost about P1000 a year. This is recommended if you want to deposit tickets, documents, travellers' cheques or souvenirs for any length of time while travelling around the country. An important thing to remember when leaving is that all the banks are closed on public holidays. Unfortunately, it's very difficult to get an empty safe-deposit box: either they are all allocated or the bank will not accept deposits for only a short time.
- Don't reveal the name of your hotel and especially not your room number to just anyone who asks for it. If necessary, give a false address spontaneously and believably.
- Look over your hotel room carefully before you check out: anything left behind becomes the property of whoever finds it.
- Wherever there are tourists there are thieves: for example, pickpockets

and transvestites on Ermita and amateur and professional thieves in the buses to Batangas and the Puerto Galera pier. Be particularly cautious around Ermita, especially on Mabini St and Rizal Park.

Traveller beware!

Recently there appears to have been an upsurge of thieves who specialise in robbing travellers, so beware. Usually these situations are provoked by gullibility and misplaced trust. It's only a small percentage of Filipinos who should be avoided and if you keep your wits about you, there should be no problems. It's not necessary to become totally insecure, but the following ruses have all been used:

- If someone runs up to you, anxiously advising you that your money has been stolen, stay calm and don't immediately reach for the place where you keep your money. The pickpocket is just waiting for you to give your hiding place away.
- Newspaper vendors usually have a thick bundle of newspapers tucked under their arm. Pickpockets on the other hand will usually only offer one newspaper for sale, holding it up with one hand far closer than normal to their victim's face, while the other takes advantage of the cover and cleans out their pockets. Now and then these mostly youthful thieves will employ their tricks in restaurants, taking with them anything useful such as cigarettes and lighters, or even a wallet carelessly left on the table.
- There have also been reports of fraud in Baguio and Banaue. Tourists are approached by one or two attractive young Filipinas (or two friendly Filipino men) who are well dressed and speak good English, and are invited for coffee, which tastes a bit strange (not uncommon for native coffee in this area). After five or 10 minutes the visitors are out cold, and wake up 12 hours later in a park or field somewhere with all their valuables gone.
- If a complete stranger comes up to you, especially in the Ermita district (Mabini St, Rizal Park) and hands you a line about remembering you (for example 'Hello my friend, do you remember me from the airport... San Fernando... I was your bus driver' etc) and suggests showing you the town or inviting you to dinner, don't accept. Others may claim that they were the customs or immigration officer when you arrived at NAIA recently. They weren't. Another line is: 'We're also strangers here, but we know people who can show us the town together'. Invitations to a party from such a stranger will usually end up with you being drugged, robbed and abandoned. Another is to claim that a sister will be flying next week to, for example, Germany, Australia or the USA and - what a coincidence - will be working as a nurse in the same town as you come from. However, before her departure she would like to be reassured by hearing something more about the country and the town. This is merely a pretext to lure you to a house and rob you. It's a well-practised trick in Baguio.

Once more: always be wary of sudden invitations, even at the risk of condemning innocent Filipinos. Don't accept drinks and food from strangers, not even on bus trips (sweets can be doctored as well!)

- Beware also of Westerners who either can't or don't want to go home, and talk about 'extremely promising' ideas or having good connections. They will tell you that all they need is an investor and will assure you they're not in the least worried about how small or large the investment might be.
- If someone tries to get hold of the name of your bank or your account number under some pretext, be careful.

If, as well, either before or after this attempt, you are asked if they can leave some of their stuff with your things, look out. Now they have an excuse to look through your things as well as theirs and possibly find your bank account number, and with this information they can telex your bank to send money to an account they have set up in your name.

● Calesas (horse-drawn cabs) in the Ermita district, for example, along Roxas Blvd, are almost always on the lookout fur unsuspecting tourists. The favourite trick is to invite the tourist into the cab to take a picture of him with his own camera. While this is happening two Filipinos get in and tell the driver, who is in the know, to take them on a 'city tour'. After 200 to 300 metres the 'tour' is over, and the tourist has a tough time trying to get out of paying P250 for it.

● Never join a card game with Filipinos - you'll always lose. If the 'cousin' of your host allegedly works at the casino, and offers to coach you in tricks, don't be taken in. I've met people who, after losing three games, still haven't realised the syndicate was working against them.

● And then there are the fake police who cruise through the tourist quarters of Manila in twos or threes in a new limousine. They stop tourists from their 'squad' car, showing them a false police badge and, on the pretext of checking for counterfeit currency allegedly in circulation, ask them to step into the vehicle for a few minutes. Then these very experienced and terribly obliging gentlemen will kindly offer to check your money to make sure it's genuine. While doing this they skilfully and swiftly help themselves to some of the cash, and on handing back the rest, will reassure you that the notes are perfectly good. And just to complete the trick, as you alight they'll helpfully draw your attention to the pickpockets and petty criminals allegedly waiting for you on every street corner...

There are a few points you should be aware of so you'll know who you're dealing with. It is extremely rare for Filipino police officers to show a badge as ID: usually their mark of authenticity is the neatly pressed uniform or the revolver hanging loosely from their belt. Plain-clothes police officers are more likely to go about in a T-shirt, jeans and gym shoes, than in smart fashionable suits. Number plates on police cars are, as on all government vehicles, white with red letters and numbers, and the first letter is as a rule 'S'. Number plates of licensed taxis are yellow with black lettering, and those of private vehicles are white with green lettering.

● As well as meeting fake police officers, you may come into contact with a related species: false immigration officials, whose favourite haunt is the Intramuros/Rizal Park district. Their game is to demand to inspect tourists' passports, and then to return them only on payment of a handsome sum. In reality genuine immigration officials make only occasional random checks of tourists' passports. In any case they are normally satisfied with a photocopy: there's no need to have the original on you night and day.

● Finally, remember that there will be new ideas and variations each year. Filipino thieves do not lack ingenuity or imagination. Don't let them spoil your trip.

Drugs

According to the Drug Enforcement Agency (DEA) based in the US, the Philippines is the second largest marijuana producing country in the world after Mexico. International drug syndicates also use the country as a trans-shipment hub for illegal drugs such as shabu (methamphetamine hydrochloride) which is a cheap version of crack cocaine, presumably manufactured in China.

Due to the drastic increase in all kinds of drug abuse and the resulting drug-related crime, the laws governing drug abuse have grown increasingly severe in the Philippines since the 1980s. Political pressure has forced prosecutors to deal with offenders increasingly harshly. Whereas previously drugs offenders usually received fines and were deported if foreigners, nowadays the law is applied in its full severity.

Unauthorised people are absolutely forbidden to handle, own or traffic in drugs - regardless of the amount involved. So-called dangerous drugs are divided into two categories: prohibited drugs (opium, heroin, morphine, cocaine, LSD, marijuana); and regulated drugs (pharmaceutical drugs, sleeping pills, pain killers etc).

Transgressions are punished very severely. Penalties range from six to 12 years imprisonment plus a fine of P6000 to P12,000 for possession of marijuana and go up to P14,000 to P30,000 plus the death penalty for manufacture, trafficking, or import or export of any of the prohibited drugs.

Under Philippine law too, people found in possession of over 750 grams of marijuana, 50 grams of hashish, 200 grams of shabu or 40 grams of heroin, cocaine, opium and morphine will be given the death sentence.

The laws also impose these sorts of penalties for the abuse of regulated drugs, if possession and use is not certified by a doctor's prescription.

If a fine can't be paid in the time allowed, the accused is free to bring in a lawyer, or to obtain the services of a Legal Assistance Office who, although paid by the state, should also receive appropriate encouragement to do his job!

The drugs squads in the Central Cordillera of North Luzon are particularly active. Frequently, buses and private vehicles from Sagada and other areas of Mountain Province are stopped by the military or NARCOM (Narcotic Commission) personnel who then search the passengers' baggage for marijuana, which is covertly grown in the mountains.

Legal Matters

If you are arrested, contact your nearest embassy or consulate immediately. However, they may not be able to do much more than provide you with a list of local lawyers and keep an eye on how you are being treated. Remember you are subject to Philippine law when in the Philippines.

Work

Non-resident aliens are not allowed to be employed at all, nor theoretically even look for work, without a valid work permit, while foreign residents need the necessary work registration; both can be obtained from the Department of Labor and Employment.

Women Travellers

Attitudes to Women

Many Filipinos like to think of themselves as being irresistible macho types, but can also turn out to be surprisingly considerate gentlemen. They are especially keen to show their best side to foreign women. They will address you respectfully as 'Ma'am', shower you with friendly compliments ('you are so beautiful' etc) and engage you in polite conversation.

But Filipinas too (for instance if travelling next to a foreign women on a bus) will not miss the chance to ask a few questions out of curiosity: for example, about your home country, reason for and goal of your journey, and of course

about your husband, how many children you have etc. It is then not unusual for the Filipina to get out of the bus after a few km and be replaced by another one, who will then proceed to ask exactly the same questions all over again.
So it would be a good idea to be prepared and have a few polite answers ready. After a few days on the road you'll be grateful for them.

Safety Precautions

If drunken Filipinos pester you, it is best simply to ignore them. Simulated friendliness could easily be misunderstood as an invitation to get to know each other better. If a group of Filipinos starts a drinking session in a restaurant, it is not exactly recommended practice to sit down at a table next to them. In such cases, the best thing to do is just to change restaurants.
There have been cases reported of Filipinos sexually harassing foreign women, but they are very, very rare. In the absence of alcohol, frightening naivety and simple stupidity, probably the vast majority of cases could have been avoided.
Another word of advice: inspect hotel rooms with thin walls for strategic peepholes, and remember, don't accept cigarettes, food, drinks or sweets from friendly strangers as these gifts might be drugged.

What to Wear

Women are very fashion conscious in the Philippines and place a great deal of emphasis on being neat and tidy in their dress. Visiting foreign women should also pay more attention to their outward appearance if they want to be looked at with respect. Clothing can be practical, eg shorts and a blouse or T-shirt are quite acceptable while travelling. If you are swimming in a place where there are not many tourists, or you have Filipino friends with you, it is better to wear shorts and a T-shirt over your swimsuit. That way you will not draw unwanted attention to yourself or embarrass your friends on your behalf. Particular care should be taken in Muslim areas, where wearing revealing clothing can cause real unpleasantness. It's better to wear a knee-length skirt, especially if you intend to visit a mosque.

Travel with Children

A Philippine child is never alone, so an 'exotic' foreign child will definitely never spend a moment without someone to play with. Filipinos are simply crazy about children. If you travel with a child, people will often strike up a conversation with you and you'll have to talk a lot.
It's a good idea when travelling with children to include as many specific activities for them as you feel comfortable with yourself. For instance, in Manila a visit to the Museo Pambata will keep them occupied and challenged for quite some time. This can help make up for the more 'boring adult' places you visit.

Senior Travellers

The older generation is treated with respect and deference in the Philippines and this applies equally well to visitors. On the practical side, if you are a senior over 60 years of age, you could try to get a 20% rebate on inland flights, bus and ship journeys and museum visits. Just present an official form of identification with your date of birth when purchasing your ticket.

Gay & Lesbian Travellers

Homosexuality is viewed tolerantly in the Philippines. Even if jokes are told about them (never meant in an insulting or prejudiced way), gay men ('bakla') and lesbians ('tomboy', 'binalaki' or 'binalalaki') are almost universally accepted as part of everyday Philippine society. An exception is made in the armed forces, where gays and lesbians are banned from military service.

Disabled Travellers

If you only look at what provisions have been made in buildings, then the Philippines are really not suited for disabled people. Only a few hotels and guesthouses are equipped with a suitable ramp for wheelchairs, and only rarely has an architect thought of providing roomy toilets with big doors.
On the other hand, these deficits are largely made up for by the sheer humanity of the people. When they see a disabled person, Filipinos are not stunned into inaction because they're so concerned, nor do they turn away helplessly. They behave perfectly naturally, without ingratiating themselves in an embarrassing way. And if needed, there's always someone there with a helping hand.

Photography & Video

Photography
The usual rules for tropical photography apply in the Philippines. Remember to allow for the intensity of the tropical light, try to keep your film as cool and dry as possible and have it developed as soon as possible after exposure.

Video
The Philippines are full of colour and motion, providing an endless palette of themes for the amateur and professional camera buff. Remember to use your zoom sparingly - there is usually enough action going on in front of the camera lens, it doesn't need any additional help.

Photographing People
Filipinos are extremely fond of having their picture taken, but always remember that cameras can be one of the most intrusive and unpleasant reminders of the impact of tourism - it's polite to ask people before you photograph them. A smile always helps. Under no circumstances should photographs be taken of soldiers or military installations.

Airport Security
Although airport X-ray equipment is said to be safe for film, it's certainly not good it. If you're passing through airport security checks on a number of occasions, have it inspected separately.

Travel Tips

Entertainment

Cinemas
Cinemas are good value - for a few pesos (from P30 in the provinces to P150 in Manila) you sometimes even get a double feature. There are particular starting times but not always fixed entry times, which means there is a constant coming and going during the programmes. To add to the turbulence, the Filipino audience really gets carried away, and enthusiastically participates in the action on the screen (especially during sensational films about natural catastrophes, killer sharks, vampires and such like). In some first-run cinemas in Manila however, cinema-goers are not allowed in until the official admission time and have to leave after the end of the film.
Watch out for the national anthem - sometimes they play it at the end, sometimes at the beginning, usually not at all. If they do play it, all the Filipinos will stand up. It's best to join them. Cameras are not allowed in cinemas.

Discos
There is scarcely a town in the Philippines that does not have at least one

disco. Even in the depths of the provinces far from the nearest power station the Filipinos don't have to do without their dearly loved pleasure. Once a month, or even once a week, travelling discos drop in to the community to the immense pleasure of young and old, who can then boogie together to their hearts' content on the village square under the stars.

Nightclubs

The Filipinos are very keen on their nightlife - it certainly does not depend solely on tourists. There are bars and clubs in the provinces where foreigners seldom go, but in the big cities tourism has certainly contributed to the booming nightlife. Wherever you go you'll find karaoke bars, also known locally as videoke, which are full of Filipinos parading their singing talents.
Although they are more enticing after dark, you can, of course, frequent the bars during the day. However, serious drinkers will hang on to their money until the happy hour when the price of drinks is reduced. Most nightclubs demand a cover charge and/or a table charge. It's justifiable if there's a good programme, but it's also advisable to enquire beforehand how much you are likely to be up for in the end. The bars and clubs in the big hotels can be excellent places for meeting people.
There are many bars with go-go girls and GROs ('guest related officers') who are always ready for a 'chat' and happy to let men buy them a 'lady's drink' - which is usually little more than cola and two to three times more expensive than beer. The bar and the girls both profit from this. In an expensive club, conversation with one of the hostesses can cost P300 an hour - not bad for the conversational skills of the young 'student'. If one of these girls wants to leave early with a customer, the barkeeper will demand a so-called bar fine from the customer before she is free to go.
Women from overseas should not be misled by notices saying 'unescorted ladies not allowed': this only refers to the local professionals.

The Aids issue

Is Aids prevalent in the Philippines? Yes, and the trend is unfortunately upwards. According to the Philippine Department of Health (DOH) there were 1921 HIV/Aids cases with 255 deaths reported between 1984 and 2003. The National Aids Prevention Program estimates there are 40,000 cases of HIV-infected Filipinos at the moment.
Education concerning this deadly disease is still in its early stages in the Philippines; the decision on whether to use a condom or not is usually left up to the man.

Activities

> *'Few countries in the world are so little known and so seldom visited as the Philippines, and yet no other land is more pleasant to travel in than this richly endowed island kingdom. Hardly anywhere does the nature lover find a greater fill of boundless treasure.'*

This was written about 130 years ago by Fedor Jagor, a German ethnographer. Today Jagor would be astonished - basically nothing in his assessment has changed. Although the Philippines is not so unknown any more, it still surprises adventurers and discoverers with remarkable experiences: buried gold, unexplored caves, undamaged diving holes, sunken Spanish galleons, dense jungles with rare plants and animals, primeval people, active volcanoes of all sizes and completely uninhabited paradise islands.

Caving
Compared with the number of caves in existence, only a handful could have so far been explored. This is because very few Filipinos would willingly go into the unknown depths of the earth! The reasons are fear and superstition or just plain lack of interest.
In earlier times many caves served as burial grounds. It is not unusual to find bones and skulls, although you seldom find artefacts like vessels, tools, arms or jewellery. These have all been gathered up during earlier explorations.
If you shine a light in completely unknown caves you might find some war spoils left by the Japanese, which, according to the calculations of the American columnist Jack Anderson, are distributed over 172 hiding places in the Philippines and are worth close to US$100 billion.

Cycling
If anybody were to doubt how popular mountain biking is becoming in the Philippines, they would just have to take a look at the incredible increase in membership of the recently founded clubs and organisations dedicated to it. Regional associations have sprung up all over, often with belligerent sounding names like COMBAT (Cagayan de Oro Mountain Bikers & Trekkers, Tel +63 (0)8822 726545), M-BOMB (Mountain Bike Organisation of Metro Bacolod, Tel +63 (0)34 29525) and RAMBO (Road & Mountain Bikers Organisation of Cebu, Tel +63 (0)32 2533424). Others stick to short names like BME (Butuan Mountainbike Enthusiasts, Tel +63 (0)85 2555408), DATBA (Davao All Terrain Bikers Association), IMBA (Iloilo Mountain Bike Association, Tel +63 (0)33 3201272) and PACA (Philippine Amateur Cycling Association). They are all incredibly enthusiastic and genuinely glad to make contact with foreign bikers. They especially welcome fellow enthusiasts when there is a competition involved, eg the Guimaras International Mountain Bike Festival which was started as an annual event in February 1995, where international participation is actively encouraged.

Desert Islands
There are 7107 islands in the Philippines and more than 60% of them are uninhabited. One would think that this would be music to the ears of a modern-day Robinson Crusoe, but unfortunately most of these godforsaken islands are stark rocks or simply sandbanks sticking uninvitingly out of the sea. If you search for it, however, you will almost certainly find an idyllic spot with white sand and palm beaches. Try north of Bohol, or in Gutob Bay between Culion and Busuanga. I found 12 isolated islands there in one day!
To really go à la Robinson Crusoe and enjoy it you need something to do, otherwise you'll get bored very quickly in paradise. If you take few supplies, you will soon find your days filled with trying to find more. The sea offers most things: fish, crayfish, sea porcupines, mussels, snails, algae and seaweed.
After just a few days of complete isolation, most budding Crusoes come to the conclusion that it is better to be isolated in pairs or groups. Of what use is the most beautiful place in the world if there is no-one to share it with?

Diving
Diving has become a very popular activity in the Philippines and not without reason. This country possesses a large selection of major diving areas, although many underwater sites in recent times have suffered violent ecological damage. To get first-class dives you should use proven diving operators who know the remaining good diving sites.
Lots of diving businesses have grown over the last few years and an almost

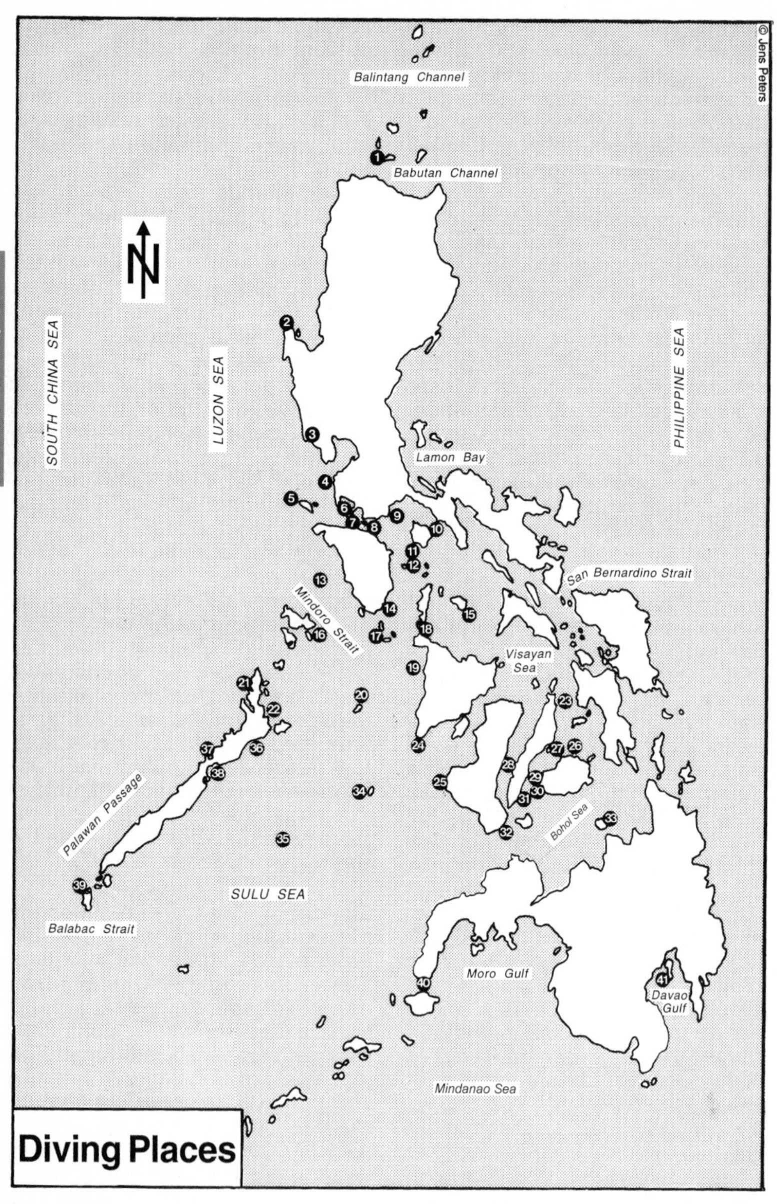

© Jens Peters
Balintang Channel
Babutan Channel
SOUTH CHINA SEA
LUZON SEA
PHILIPPINE SEA
Lamon Bay
San Bernardino Strait
Mindoro Strait
Visayan Sea
Palawan Passage
Bohol Sea
SULU SEA
Balabac Strait
Moro Gulf
Davao Gulf
Mindanao Sea
Diving Places

Diving Places		Diving Season	Entry Point
1	Fuga Island	April - Mai	Fuga Island
2	Santiago Island	November - Juni	Bolinao
3	Subic Bay	November . Juni	Olongapo
4	Nasugbu	November - Juni	Nasugbu Town
5	Lubang Islands	März - Juni	Catalagan (Batangas Province)
6	Balayan Bay	All Year	Anilao
7	Puerto Galera	All Year	Batangas City
8	Verde Island	All Year	Batangas City
9	Sigayan Bay	All Year	San Juan
10	Mopog Island	April - October	Lucena City, Gasan
11	Tres Reyes Islands	April - October	Gasan
12	Dos Hermanas Islands	April - October	Gasan
13	Apo Reef	March - Juni	San Jose (Mindoro)
14	Buyallao	April - October	Mansalay
15	Cresta de Gallo	March - June	Romblon, Sibuyan
16	Calamian Islands	All Year	Coron
17	Semirara Island	March - June	San Jose (Mindoro)
18	Boracay Island	All Year	Kalibo
19	Batbatan Island	April - June	San Jose (Panay)
20	Cuyo Islands	March - June & Oct	Cuyo Town
21	Bacuit Bay	November - June	Liminangcong, El Nido
22	Taytay Bay	April - October	Taytay
23	Capitancillo Island	April - October	Sogod
24	Nagas Island	All Year	San Joaquin
25	South-west Negros	All Year	Sipalay
26	Danajon Island	All Year	Mactan
27	Mactan	All Year	Cebu City, Mactan
28	Pescador Island	All Year	Moalboal
29	Cabilao Island	All Year	Tagbilaran, Panglao Island
30	Panglao Island	All Year	Tagbilaran, Panglao Island
31	Sumilon Island	All Year	Dumaguete
32	Apo Island	All Year	Dumaguete
33	Mambajao	All Year	Balingoan, Camiguin
34	Cagayan Islands	March - June	Cagayancillo
35	Tubbataha Reef	March - June	Puerto Princesa
36	Green Island Bay	April - October	Roxas
37	Ulugan Bay	November - June	Bahile
38	Honda Bay	April - October	Puerto Princesa
39	Balabac Island	All Year	Balabac
40	Santa Cruz Island	All Year	Zamboanga
41	Talikud Island	All Year	Davao

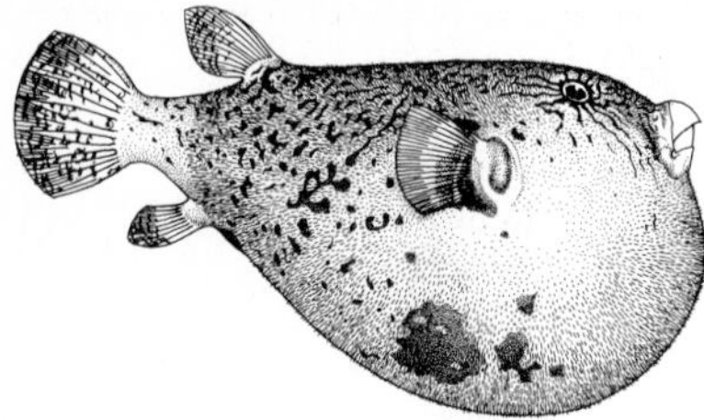
Pufferfish

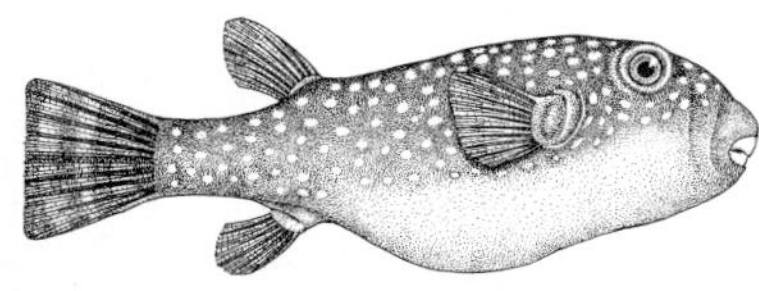
Blowfish

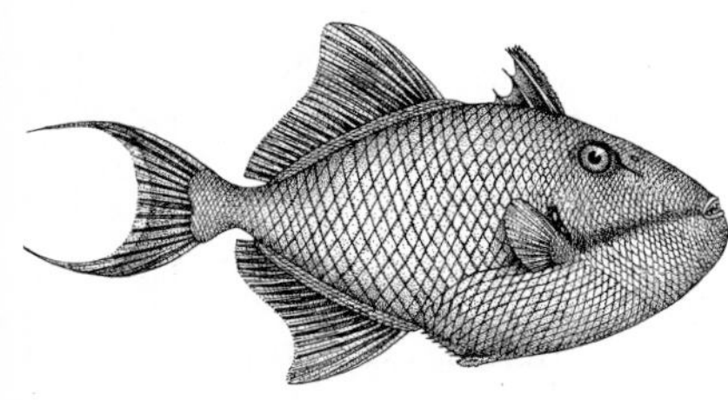
Triggerfish

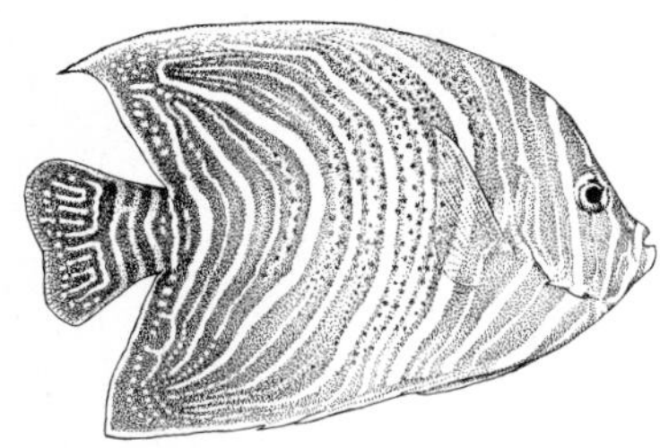
Angelfish

Amongst the best-known diving operators with branches all over the country are:
Aquaventure, Almeda Building, Chino Rocos Ave, Makati, Manila, Tel +63 (0)2 8992831, Fax +63 (0)2 8992551, @.
Dive Buddies, Robelle Mansion, 877 JP Rizal St, Makati, Manila, Tel +63 (0)2 8997388, Fax +63 (0)2 8997393, @.
Sea Explorers, Archbishop Reyes Ave, Cebu City, Tel +63 (0)32 2340248, Fax +63 (0)32 2340245, @.
Whitetip Divers, Jancor II Building, 1362 Mabini St, Ermita, Manila, Tel +63 (0)2 5210433, Fax +63 (0)2 5221165, @.

endless variety of programmes is available. During the high season (mid-March to mid-May) mobile dive bases are set up on various islands. You can hire completely equipped diving boats at any time of the year and you can rent anything you need from Manila's diving shops, although it is better to bring some of your own equipment. Philippine Airlines will raise your baggage limit to 30 kg to allow for this, but any oxygen tanks you bring with you must be empty.
If you need to buy diving equipment, there are some well-equipped shops in Manila (see the chapter Manila: *Shopping - Diving Equipment*).
Technical diving with nitrox is starting to be available in the Philippines, although only a few dive shops offer it at the moment. This will cost you US$5 more per dive than a conventional dive.
The most beautiful diving sites are far from the settled areas where the underwater scenery is likely to have been destroyed by drainage and dynamite. In the Mindoro Strait, east of the little is-

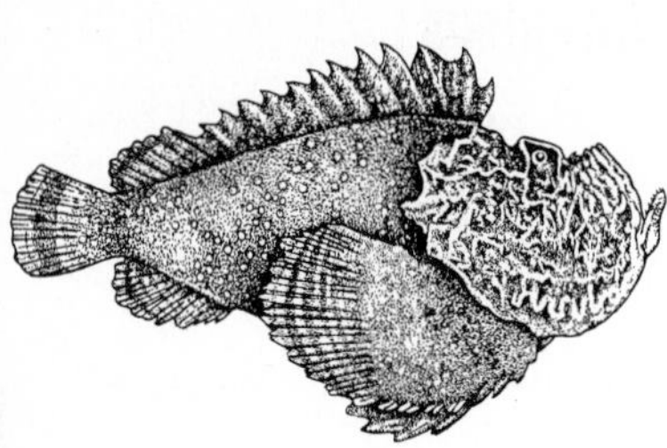

Stonefish *(Synanceja verrucosa)*
The dorsal spines of this well-camouflaged fish contain a deadly poison

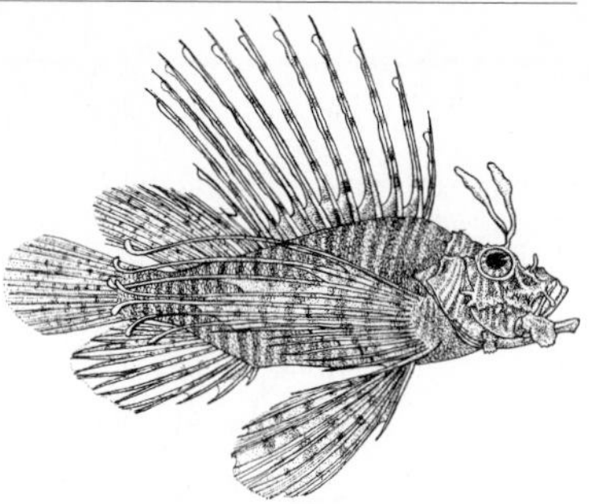

Lionfish *(Pteroi volitans)*
This elegant swimmer is equipped with extremely poisonous spines

land of Apo, you will find the Apo Reef. At low tide this reef is partly exposed and is among the most spectacular diving areas in the Philippines.

Probably the best place for diving is in the Sulu Sea on the little-explored Tubbataha Reef. Because of the long distance from the port of departure - it's about 185 km from Puerto Princesa in Palawan - and because of the resultant high costs involved, very few companies offer expeditions to this area. The island world of the Calamian Group (Busuanga, Culion, Coron), the Bacuit Archipelago (El Nido) and Honda Bay (Puerto Princesa) is relatively easy to get to and one of the most popular diving areas in Palawan.

Year-round favourites are Puerto Galera on the north coast of Mindoro, Moalboal in the south west of Cebu, Apo Island off the south coast of Negros, and Cabilao Island and Panglao Island off Bohol.

There's one thing they don't have to do in the Philippines that diving areas in other parts of the world find necessary: sinking ships deliberately, so adventure-hungry divers can have tempting targets to explore. Hundreds of years of maritime activity have made sure that the floor of the archipelago is littered with wrecks from typhoons, wars and collisions with reefs. Ideal conditions for exploration are found in the sound between the islands of Busuanga and Culion; in 1944 a fleet of 12 Japanese ships went down here, seven of them in a small protected bay, where the wrecks now lie in 30 to 40 metres of crystal clear water. Subic Bay, which was a restricted military area for years, is a new area for wreck divers. Shortly after the Americans had left, the first divers were there exploring the wrecks, some of which had lain undisturbed for 50 years. There are said to be at least 20 merchant marine and naval ships sunk in the bay.

For 250 years Spanish galleons travelled between Manila and Acapulco in Mexico, laden with silver coins, gold, silk, porcelain, pearls, precious stones and other objects of value. Of the more than 40 trading vessels which were lost during this era, 21 sank in the coastal waters near the Philippines, mostly near Catanduanes, Samar and South Luzon. Fabulous treasures are said to be spread over the ocean floor for up till now neither the remains nor the cargoes of 13 of these wrecks have been located.

There is no law in the Philippines against searching for lost galleons. If you find one, however, you must inform the National Museum. If there is a recovery, the discoverer will get a share of the spoils. If you want to explore or photograph a known wreck, you should inform the National Museum of your intentions in writing. It is all too easy as a stranger to be charged with illegal plunder of treasure.

If you want to find out more about diving opportunities in the Philippines, contact the Philippine Commission of Sports/Scuba Diving, Department of Tourism Building, TM Kalaw St, Rizal Park, Manila, Tel +63 (0)2 5254413.

A very informative book on the subject is *The Dive Sites of the Philippines* by Jack Jackson (New Holland Publishers Ltd, London 1995). You will also find invaluable tips in the *Asia Diver Scuba Guide Philippines* by Gretchen Hutchinson and Edgar Venture (Sports Asia Media Pte Ltd, Singapore, 1993), and in the *Philippine Diving* by Ronald van de Vooren (PDP Digital Inc, Cebu City, 2003), that describes the diving areas round Apo Island, Bohol, Cebu and Siquijor.

Gold Hunting

There is so much that wasn't found by the gold-hungry Spaniards. For over 300 years they ruled these islands, yet compared to the pillage of South and Central America, their excesses here were humble indeed. Today the Philippines has an output of 30 tonnes of pure gold annually, placing it at number six on the world scale. Less than 10% of the land mass has been explored using the detailed methods of modern mineralogy, so there is still a lot of ground to be covered.

Visitors to the Philippines are allowed to search for gold, the only drawback being that they are not allowed to keep or take out of the country any gold that they might find, as all wealth belongs to the state. In practice this is not always adhered to very strictly.

The best way to go fossicking is to get in touch with small-claim holders and make yourself known to local gold panners. If you want to follow a hot tip absolutely legally then you must find a Filipino partner for the business and use their name to contract mining rights with the Bureau of Mines & Geo-Sciences.

Hiking & Trekking

There is always an alternative route available in the Philippines - not just on the freeways and asphalt-covered roads but along the paths and byways which criss-cross the entire archipelago. It's possible to go from the far north to the deep south with minimum contact with motorised transport. On some islands in fact, it is practically impossible to see a car. Batan Island is an example. You can go right round it on a wonderful semi-surfaced coast road. Alternatively, there is Lubang where high-wheeled horse carts still dominate the traffic in spite of the introduction of a few jeeps. It is the same in Busuanga. There, only twice a day, a rattling old bus travels along the dirt road from Coron to Salvacion. The centre and the north of this island are practically free of cars.

There are wonderful opportunities for trekking along the Pacific coast in the Bikol provinces and Quezon Province in Luzon. If you want to get to know the primeval landscape of Palawan, then you can try some of the many first-class treks there.

It is also tempting to read the recollections of the treks undertaken by European travellers in the last century, recorded in books which are witness to their love of the Philippines. Two of these are Fedor Jagor's *Travels in the Philippines* (London, 1873) and Paul de la Gironnière's *Adventures of a Frenchman in the Philippines* originally published in 1853 and republished in 1972 by Rarebook Enterprises, Caloocan City.

Older, but still useful, topographical maps on a 1:250,000 scale are available from Namria in Fort Bonifacio in Makati and in the well-stocked Namria branch in Barraca St, San Nicolas, Manila (see also the chapter Manila: *Shopping - Books & Maps.*

Mountaineering

There are no alpine summits in the Philippines, although there are volcanoes worth climbing. One official list records 37 volcanoes, 18 active and 19 dormant, but all unpredictable; another lists as many as 88 inactive volcanoes. The most dangerous include Mt Mayon, Mt Pinatubo and Mt Taal, which are all known to be explosive and potentially highly destructive. Various hotels in Angeles offer tours to Mt Pinatubo (1450m).

Other appealing challenges for climbers are the volcanoes Mt Makiling (1144m) and Mt Banahaw (2177m) on Luzon; Mt Hibok-Hibok (1322m) on Camiguin; Mt Kanloan (2465m) on Negros; and Mt Apo (2954m - the highest mountain in the Philippines) on Mindanao.

All dangerous volcanoes are overseen by the Philippine Institute of Volcanology & Seismology (Phivolcs), Hizon Building, 29 Quezon Ave, Quezon City, Manila. This is where you can learn whether or not an eruption is predicted in the foreseeable future.

Specific questions about climbs can be answered by the Mountaineering Federation of the Philippines, 12 J Francisco St, Krus na Ligas, Diliman, Quezon City, Manila.

Sailing

Every two years Manila is the destination of the China Sea Race, a classic 1200 km regatta which starts in Hong Kong. This event not only serves to guide the participants through some exotic islands, but also brings with it thousands of spectators from the international yachting scene.

The monsoon which blows steadily from September to May in the north-east guarantees good sailing conditions and many natural harbours invite sailors to rest. It is not uncommon for a crew to decide to spend the winter in one of the beautiful bays of Puerto Galera or Balanacan.

Favourite spots for yachts include the anchorages in the Visayas. For sailing enthusiasts there is also the opportunity to take part in a round trip. You can ask about this at the Manila Yacht Club (MYC) on Roxas Blvd, Tel +63 (0)2 5267868, Fax: +63 (0)2 5237183, @. The MYC is helpful to foreign yachts as well, and will organise guides or an escort from the coastguard when sailing through pirate-infested waters.

Surfing

Surfing in the Philippines is still a relatively new phenomenon. Although American GIs stationed in Angeles and Olongapo were already looking for big waves in the 80s, it wasn't until the 90s that it really became widely popular. Enticing photos in glossy international surf magazines gave the final push, until finally the Surfers Association of the Philippines (SAP) was founded and surfing competitions were organised.

The best known surfing beaches can be found at places like San Juan on the north-west coast of Luzon; Baler and Daet (Bagasbas Beach) on the Pacific east coast of Luzon; Puraran on Catanduanes; and, most important of all, on Siargao Island in the north-east of Mindanao. The east coast of Mindanao (eg Tandag) and the south-east coast of Samar also have a few interesting places to offer.

Surf season on the beaches of the South China Sea is from November until

March, while the Pacific beaches have their best conditions from May until November when the wind blows steadily from the south-west. That's the time for first class waves to roll in and, if nature is on her best behaviour, for the surfer to be blessed with a tube.

Whitewater Rafting

On Luzon and Mindanao you can take an action-packed, several hour-long journey in a rubber dinghy, rocking and rolling through the bubbling white foam of a roaring river. The most popular and exciting are the whitewater tours on the Chico River in Kalinga Province in North Luzon, and, although not quite so spectacular, on the Cagayan de Oro River in Misamis Oriental Province, North Mindanao. Organisers include:

Adventure & Expeditions Philippines, Tuguegarao, Cellphone +63 (0)917-5327480, @.
www.geocities.com/aephils

Chico River Quest, Tabuk, Cellphone +63 (0)917-9668081, @.
www.chicoriverquest.com

Tribal Adventure Tours, Boracay, Tel. +63 (0)36 2883207, @.
www.tribaladventures.com

Whitewater Rafting Adventure, Cagayan de Oro, Cellphone +63 (0)917-3863195, @.

Windsurfing & Kitesurfing

Some time in the mid 80s the first colourful sails could be seen darting back and forward at White Beach on Boracay, and it was not difficult to predict that this new sport would quickly attract enthusiasts. Nowadays you couldn't imagine Boracay without windsurfers. From November until March, the time when the north-east monsoon *(amihan)* blows, the island is the unchallenged number one spot for windsurfing in the Philippines. The highlight of every season is the annual Boracay International Funboard Cup, held in January. It is Asia's most important windsurfing competition, which is reflected in the number of international entries.

The new fad on Boracay is the latest action sport, kitesurfing (aka kiteboarding), which involves the kitesurfer being pulled along over the water on a steerable kite, soaring up every now and then in incredible jumps.

A favourite destination for the boardsailing community is also Lake Caliraya, home of the Caliraya Windsurfing Fleet (CWF), about 80 km south-east of Manila, in the rolling foothills of the Sierra Madre mountains.

Wellness

Relaxing under palm trees in an exotic setting refreshes both body and soul. Various Philippine spas have recognised this trend and are offering wellness holidays, with or without accommodation. The prices depend on the range of treatment, but they're almost always on the high side. Most arrangements include wellness treatments such as massages and baths in the basic price.

Links to the websites of the following spas can be found on the author's website www.travelphil.com on the 'Health' page.

Mandala Spa, Boracay, Tel +63 (0)36 2885858, @;

Meddah Spa, Cebu City, Cebu, Tel +63 (0)32 2342080, @;

Subic Bay Wellness Center, SBFZ, Olongapo, Tel +63 (0)47 2529280-85, @;

The Farm at San Benito, Lipa, Batangas, Cellphone +63 (0)917-5368879, @;

The Spa, Metro-Manila, @. branches in Alabang, Tel. +63 (0)2 8503490, Makati and Quezon City, Tel +63 (0)2 6342848.

Books & Maps

Manila has several good book stores. If you are looking for literature on a specialised subject you should be able to find it after a short search. The only problem is with travel books, especially travel guides on other countries. It would be better to stock up with that kind of thing in Bangkok, Hong Kong or Singapore.

Road maps covering the entire Philippines are published by the oil companies Petron and Mobil. The *Philippine Motorist's Road Guide* from Petron is available in some book stores. Nelles Verlag, Munich, Germany publishes the *Philippines* (1:1,500,000) and *Manila* (1:17,500) maps in their Nelles Map series.

United Tourist Promotions have published a whole series of town plans and island maps (E-Z Maps), which are widely available and on sale in many hotels. Reduced-size versions of these maps have been combined and are on sale as the *Philippines Travel Atlas*. It costs P495 (roughly US$9) in the Philippines. A practical aid when you're on the road is the *Philippines Road Atlas & Stopover Guide* which is available in both a Luzon and a Visayas edition (P295).

Asiatype Inc publishes the *Metro Manila Citiatlas* (P330; handy book format), as well as the *Cavite-Laguna-Batangas-Quezon-Rizal Road Map* (P185) and the *Makati-Ortigas Building Map* (P90).

Detailed maps and nautical charts are available at Namria (see the chapter Manila: *Shopping - Books & Maps*).

Information

Probably your best bet for further travel tips and up-to-the-minute news about prices, departure times etc is to ask fellow travellers. Specific, local information can be obtained from the employees of the Department of Tourism (DOT).

In several towns which do not have their own DOT office, the local town council has set up a Tourist Office for the area. You can usually find them in the City Hall (Municipal Hall) wherever you are.

For the directory of local tourist offices see Tourist Offices in the Travel Planning chapter.

@ E-mail (This symbol in the text means that the hotel etc can be contacted by e-mail. The address can be found in the E-mail Directory at the back of the book.)

Getting Around

Calesa

These two-wheeled horse-cabs are found in Manila's Chinatown, in Vigan, where they fit the local scene very well, and in Cebu City, where they are called *tartanillas*. In Manila, Filipinos pay about P20 for short trips; tourists are usually charged more (sometimes a *lot* more). Establish beforehand if the price is per person or per calesa.

Bicycle

Although it's dangerous on busy roads, travelling by bicycle can be another interesting way to explore the Philippines, even if considered a bit unusual. A German couple who rode from Davao in the south of Mindanao via the islands to Manila in four weeks caused quite a stir.
Buses and jeepneys will transport bikes for a small fee. Inland flights should also present no problem, apart from your having to remove the front wheel and turn the handlebars.

Rental

A few hotel and resort owners rent out mountain bikes, eg on Boracay, Camiguin and Cebu (Moalboal). Depending on the quality of the bike it should cost around P150 to P300 a day.

Purchase

A good mountain bike costs about P7000 to P9000 in the Philippines. There are several bike shops in Manila at the Cartimar Market in Pasay City. There you will find a good selection of bikes in all price categories at fair prices. The shops in Cebu City are a bit more expensive.

Pedicab

Also known as trisikads, these are bicycles with sidecars for passengers. No longer so frequent a sight in the big cities, pedicabs still hang on to their popularity in the provinces, where they are even experiencing a bit of a comeback. Fares start at about P3 per person for a short trip.

Tricycle

These are small motorbikes or mopeds with sidecars for passengers, and which hold more people than you might think. The fare must be negotiated, and is usually around P4 per person for a short ride.

Habal-Habal

Motorbikes with an extended seat for up to four passengers. In some areas, such as on Camiguin and in the north of Mindanao, they are only used for shorter journeys. Depending on the distance and number of passengers the fare is between P5 and P20 per person.

Motorcycle

Motorbike tours are getting more and more popular, especially in North Luzon and in the Visayas.

Travelling Around

Before you start off, make sure you have the owner's manual with you. A tool set, including screwdriver and spark plug key is essential for all types of bike; for the 600 cc it is imperative to take a spare tube, patching kit, spark plugs and chain with you. The traffic police insist on a helmet.
If you are island hopping, you will require the following papers: Certificate of Registration and/or the Deed of Sale (best take several photocopies with you). You should also carry the insurance documents with you.
Only motorbikes over 600 cc are allowed to use the North Luzon Expressway and the South Luzon Tollway.

Rental

Only a few tourist spots have places which rent out motorbikes. A good place

Which Driving Licence?
The International Driving Licence is recognised in the Philippines for the duration of its validity. Foreign driving licences that are issued *in English* may be used up to 90 days from entry into the country (foreign driving licences issued in any language *other than English* are not considered valid). After that, a Philippine licence, which can be obtained at any Land Transportation Office (LTO) for P235, is obligatory. Smaller LTO offices are usually unable to issue the driving licence on the spot. In this case, they will only initially provide the applicant with a temporary licence, and the driving licence itself is not issued for up to two to four months. It is valid for three years (valid from the applicant's birthday). An application for a Philippine driving licence made with a foreign licence not issued in English, must be presented to the LTO together with an official translation, approved by the embassy of the issuing country. In addition, the applicant has to take a drug test (urine) and a health check-up (eyes, blood pressure), for which there is a charge of a few pesos.

to start looking is Angeles City, where there is a good choice of companies hiring out various makes of bike. For a Honda 125 cc, expect to pay P350 to P650 a day.
When renting a bike you should check that the sticker on the licence plate is still in date and that the papers are still valid.

Purchase
You'll find motorcycles for sale in the advertisements under 'Classified Ads - For Sale' in the *Manila Bulletin*, especially in the Sunday edition. The most common bike is a 125 cc, but it's better though dearer to buy a 600 cc, as you can overtake faster and more safely. However, outside Manila, parts are hard to come by. A new Honda XLR 200 (Enduro) costs about P105,000, a Honda 125 cc (Wave) about P55,000.
If you buy a motorcycle or car, make sure you obtain the originals of the following documents:
1 Deed of Sale - have it drawn up by a lawyer.
2 Certificate of Registration - endorsed by the Land Transportation Office (LTO).
3 Official Receipt - you need this for the tax authorities. Get it at the LTO.

Selling
If you want to sell your motorcycle or car before leaving the country, you'll be paid in pesos. You can only exchange these (with difficulty) for foreign currency on the black market. It is recommended that you change dollars into pesos before you buy. You can do this officially at the Central Bank, which will give you a receipt for the transaction. With this receipt you can then change the pesos back into dollars without problems.

Car
Travelling by private car is a great way to explore the country. A two-week round trip round North Luzon can be highly recommended. It will take you through many different kinds of impressive scenery, offer a variety of cultural attractions and allow you to visit many of the highlights for the tourist.

Rental
Apart from various local firms, the internationally known, reputable companies Avis, Budget and Hertz have good, reliable vehicles. Avis has offices in Metro Manila, Angeles, Baguio, Cebu City and Davao.

You can rent cars by the day, week or month. The cheaper cars are usually booked, so it's worth reserving one if you want a particular model. A Toyota Corolla XL 1.3 with air-con and a radio costs P2760 (US$50) a day, or P16,850 (US$306) a week, including unlimited km. Petrol costs about P25 (US$0.45) a litre.

The person hiring the car must be at least 21 and no older than 65.

One important stipulation in the small print is that hire cars may only be driven on surfaced roads, which cramps your style if you stick to it. For example, the road from Baguio through the mountains via Bontoc to Banaue (rice terraces) is one of the many unsurfaced roads.

Note: You are not allowed to take a hire car from one island to the next.

Purchase/Selling: See 'Motorcycle' above. The weekly magazine *Car Finder* provides a good bird's eye view of the used car market. See also the Jens Peters website www.travelphil.com page 'Cars & Bikes'.

Beware of the Crocodiles!

The farther away payday is, the more likely you are to be stopped by the police who will check your vehicle's indicators and lights, or point out some traffic infringement you have just committed. Rest assured, they will find some offence that costs a spot fine of between P100 and P500. If you ask for a receipt, you'll have to give them your driving licence. You can get it back later on that day, or maybe not until the next day, after you've paid the fine and received your receipt. Filipinos call the police crocodiles (*buwaya*), but definitely not because of their twinkling eyes.

Official Fines & Penalties:
Driving without a seatbelt: P250; faulty horn or indicator: P150; all parking violations: P150; invalid registration: P300; failure to show or surrender driver's license: P150; expired driver's license: P375.

Road Rules

Traffic drives on the right in the Philippines. However much you may enjoy driving, there are laws to be respected on the roads in the Philippines, written and unwritten ones. Traffic signs conform to international standards, Filipinos pay scant attention to them however. Within town boundaries it seems everything is allowed that gets you closer to your destination. On country roads survival of the fittest is the maxim; in other words, buses and trucks have the right of way at all times.

Whatever happens, do not allow yourself to be influenced by the overtaking antics of the local drivers. Drive defensively. It is probably not a good idea to drive at night, first of all because you don't know what condition the roads are in. What's more, other drivers often have no lights at all, or insufficient lighting, on their vehicles.

Note: If you are driving in Manila or Baguio, be aware that there are restrictions (color-coded day) for certain vehicles from Monday to Friday. Vehicles with the following last numbers on their plates are not allowed to drive on the respective days: 1 and 2 on Mondays; 3 and 4 on Tuesdays; 5 and 6 on Wednesdays; 7 and 8 on Thursdays and 9 and 0 on Fridays. Violations incur a P300 fine.

Hitching

As transport costs are so low, it's hardly worth anyone's while to hitchhike.

No Filipino would ever dream of sticking his thumb out for a lift, even if he didn't have the money for a ticket. And anyway, drivers usually expect a few pesos if they do give lifts 'because of the high price of petrol'.

Taxi

Taxis are equipped with air-conditioning and also have meters. Under no circumstances should taximeters be switched off. Flat fare arrangements always favour the driver. It doesn't hurt to show taxi drivers that you know more than they think, so that they won't take roundabout routes.
The flag-down charge is P30, thereafter P2.50 for every further 300m.
If possible, have small change handy as it is difficult to get change for anything over P50. If a taximeter has obviously been rigged and is running too fast, the only sensible thing is to stop and take another taxi. The taxis that wait outside the big hotels, bus stations, wharves and air terminals almost always have meters that run fast or the drivers want to negotiate a flat fare. It usually pays to walk to the next street.

Jeepney

These are the most popular form of transport for short journeys. Originally they were reconstructed Jeeps which were left in the Philippines by the US army after WWII. Few of these old models are left. The new jeepneys, which may be Ford Fieras, are brightly painted in traditional designs and the bonnets are decorated with a multitude of mirrors and figures of horses. They are part of any typical Philippine street scene.
The jeepneys' route is indicated and the official charge is P7.50 for the first four km, and P1,25 for each extra km. When you want to get out, just bang on the roof, hiss or yell *pará* (stop).

In the provinces, it is important to negotiate a price before setting out on a long trip over unfamiliar territory. Before you start, ask other passengers about the price or check in a nearby shop, and then confirm the price with the driver. This may save you an unpleasant situation when you reach your destination. Jeepneys usually only leave when full (or overflowing) with passengers, so you must allow for long waiting periods, especially if time is tight. You can get the driver to leave immediately, but you'll have to pay for the empty 'seats'.
If, when you climb into an empty jeepney, the driver takes off straight away, it usually means you'll be charged for a Special Ride. Unless that's what you actually want, you must make it clear that you are only prepared to pay for a regular ride. You might need to get the driver to stop straight away, especially if no more passengers are getting on.
It costs about P2000 to rent a jeepney for a day and more if the roads are in bad condition; petrol is extra.

Safety Tip

If several men get into the jeepney straight after you and try to sit near you or get you to change seats under some pretext, they may be intent on relieving you of your valuables. Get out immediately.

Multicabs

Also called mini vans, multicabs are roofed transporters with a driver's cabin which has room for two passengers, and a cargo space with two rows of seats for up to 12 passengers. They can be seen in cities, mostly in Mindanao, but more and more often on other islands.
The fare is P5.50 which is handed to the driver through an opening in the rear window of the driver's cabin.

Minibus

On busy routes the regular bus services are supplemented by aircon minibuses, also called vans, L300 (Mitsubishi) or FX (Toyota Tamaraw). They transport ten to 15 passengers fast and non-stop from A to B. The fare is a little more than the regular bus fare.

Bus

There are buses with or without aircon (described as aircon and ordinary or regular buses). Night journeys with aircon buses can be really cold, so it's worth remembering to take along a sweater or jacket.

If you have long legs, you will find the most comfortable seats in smaller buses are those beside the driver. In the large overland buses, the back seats may be your best choice, mainly because you get to sit close to your luggage, although it can be more bumpy than in the middle of the bus. On many buses it's possible to pack away your luggage in a compartment at the back if it doesn't fit into the luggage net.

Like most Asians, Filipinos are often travel-sick so being at the back has the further advantage of having no-one behind you. Of course, the weak stomachs may be the result of drivers from competing companies trying to race each other off the roads, which are often bumpy and not at all suited to Le Mans-type speeds.

Street vendors flock to the buses with all kinds of edibles at each stop, so it's not necessary to carry food on long trips. On offer are bananas, cakes, eggs, ice cream, drinks etc, and the drivers also make lunchtime stops and other breaks for food to look after their passengers who are obviously all dying of hunger. All in all, apart perhaps from a little bottle of rum to take care of a queasy stomach, you don't need to take any sustenance with you on the average Philippine bus journey.

Buses often set off before the scheduled departure time if they are full - especially if there is only one bus a day, it's wise to get there early! In country areas, even when the buses are full, they may go round the town several times, picking up freight or making purchases, which may take up to an hour. For shorter trips of up to 20 km, it's quicker to take a jeepney if you are in a hurry.

Reservations

Some bus companies accept reservations, either personally or on the phone. However, you can never depend one hundred percent on them to actually keep a seat for you.

Costs

The fare is reckoned by the number of km travelled but it costs more to travel on gravel road than on surfaced road. On long stretches, fares are always collected fairly late. First the conductors ask passengers their destinations, then dispense the tickets; these will be inspected several times by different inspectors. Finally they get around to collecting the fares. If you have an international student card, show it when you state your destination. Discounts are not available during school holidays or on Sundays and public holidays.

One-hundred km by ordinary bus should cost around P100 (US$1.80), by aircon bus around P120 (US$2.20).

Ordinary bus/aircon bus fares from Manila are: to Alaminos (237 km) P200/260; to Baguio (250 km) P190/260; to Batangas (110 km) P100/120; and to Legaspi (544 km) P460/510.

See the Getting There & Away section of the Manila chapter for details of where the bus terminals are and for information about local buses.

Train

After the closure of the railway lines on Panay and North Luzon, there is only

one route run by the Philippine National Railways (PNR), and that's from Manila to Legaspi. The Southern Line from Manila leaves from Tayuman Railway Station and runs via Calamba, San Pablo, Lucena, Naga and Iriga to Legaspi in South Luzon.
Typhoons damage bridges almost every year so journeys on this stretch can either be frequently interrupted or only partly completed.
See also the Getting There & Away section at the beginning of the South Luzon chapter.

Boat

Wherever you go, there's always a boat ready to take you to the next island. You don't have to be on board until an hour before departure, although departure times given by the shipping companies are not always strictly adhered to. So it makes sense to go down to the wharf even if you think you have already missed a boat.
If you are travelling long distances by freighter, you have to put up with the possibility of long, unscheduled stops in the different ports.

Note: In the Philippines, it seems that boats are seldom used on the same route for much more than six months at a time. Another problem is that shipping companies seem to change sailing schedules at random. So please only use departure days and times given in this book as a rough guide (as it were) - there's no way we can make them 100% accurate.
It makes sense in a larger city to phone the shipping line or pop by personally and check departure times at their ticket office.
It's also a good idea to check the shipping company adverts in the local daily newspapers as well as their respective websites (links can be found on the author's website www.travelphil.com).

Outrigger Boats

For short trips, outrigger boats, pumpboats or *bangkas* (English: *bancas*) are used. The motor is at the back - a very noisy arrangement. A 16 hp pumpboat uses five litres of fuel for an hour's speedy motoring, so you can work out the cost of chartering.

Fast Ferries

Fast ferries have brought about a real improvement to the inter-island service. These aircon ships, mostly catamarans, have names like *Bullet Xpress*, *Delta Ferry*, *Oceanjet* and *Supercat* and mainly cover routes in and around the Visayas, eg Cebu-Ormoc, Cebu-Tagbilaran-Dumaguete and Dumaguete-Siquijor. The Cebu-Tagbilaran crossing only takes 1½ hrs and costs P400. The ferries are fitted with aircraft seats, with a small bar and videos, which makes them a real alternative to flying.
Tip: Some of these fast ferries have the aircon turned up full blast, so it's a good idea to have a jacket or thin blanket handy on board, especially if you've worked up a sweat dragging your bags to the pier.

Supercat via SMS: If you have a mobile phone (cellphone) with a Globe Card (see chapter: Planning: Telephone & Fax) you can request current Supercat departure times and fares via SMS. Simply press Supercat and the first three letters of the place of departure and destination respectively, then send that to 2333. Example: from Cebu to Ormoc: Supercat Ceb Orm.

Passenger Ships

The quality of the passenger ships of the inter-island operators varies greatly. The flagships of several companies run on the prestigious Manila-Cebu route. They are punctual and fast and the service is relatively good. Some ships even have a disco on board.

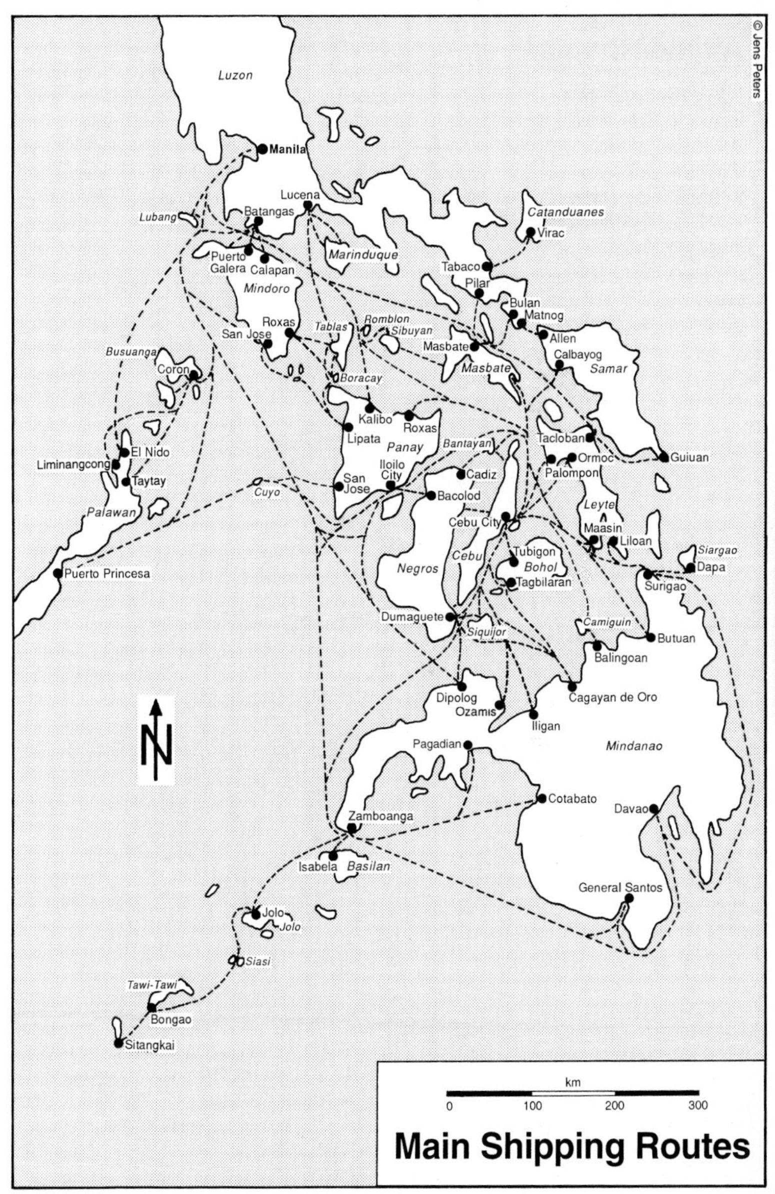
© Jens Peters
Luzon
Manila
Lucena
Lubang
Batangas
Catanduanes
Virac
Puerto Galera
Calapan
Marinduque
Tabaco
Mindoro
Pilar
Bulan
Matnog
Roxas
Romblon
San Jose
Tablas
Sibuyan
Allen
Masbate
Busuanga
Calbayog
Samar
Coron
Boracay
Kalibo
Roxas
Tacloban
Lipata
Panay
Bantayan
El Nido
Ormoc
Guiuan
Liminangcong
Palompon
Taytay
Iloilo City
Cadiz
San Jose
Cuyo
Bacolod
Leyte
Palawan
Cebu City
Maasin
Liloan
Tubigon
Siargao
Cebu
Dapa
Puerto Princesa
Negros
Bohol
Tagbilaran
Surigao
Dumaguete
Camiguin
Siquijor
Butuan
Balingoan
Dipolog
Cagayan de Oro
Ozamis
Iligan
Pagadian
Mindanao
Cotabato
Davao
Zamboanga
Isabela
Basilan
General Santos
Jolo
Jolo
Siasi
Tawi-Tawi
Bongao
Sitangkai
km
0
100
200
300
Main Shipping Routes

Getting Around

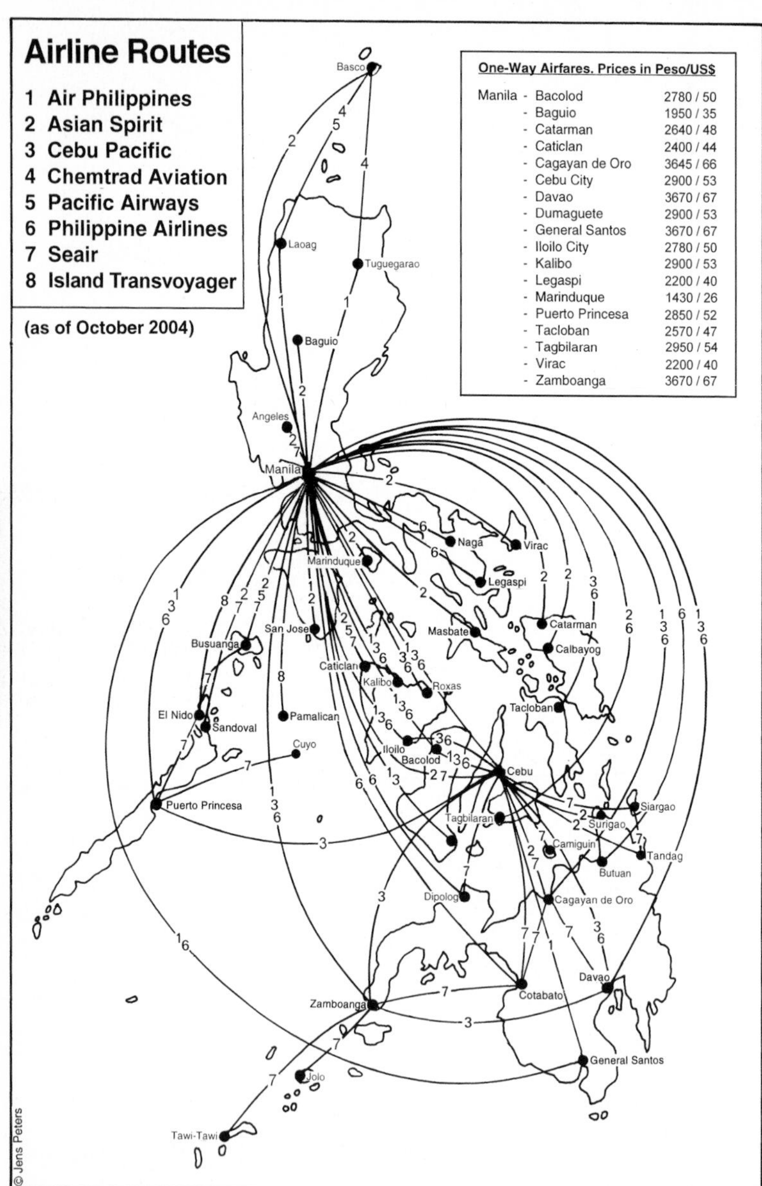

One-Way Airfares. Prices in Peso/US$

Manila	- Bacolod	2780 / 50
	- Baguio	1950 / 35
	- Catarman	2640 / 48
	- Caticlan	2400 / 44
	- Cagayan de Oro	3645 / 66
	- Cebu City	2900 / 53
	- Davao	3670 / 67
	- Dumaguete	2900 / 53
	- General Santos	3670 / 67
	- Iloilo City	2780 / 50
	- Kalibo	2900 / 53
	- Legaspi	2200 / 40
	- Marinduque	1430 / 26
	- Puerto Princesa	2850 / 52
	- Tacloban	2570 / 47
	- Tagbilaran	2950 / 54
	- Virac	2200 / 40
	- Zamboanga	3670 / 67

Third class (deck-class or sun deck) is quite acceptable. Bunks or camp beds (depending on the quality of the vessel) are under cover and protected from sun and rain, whereas the cabins and dormitories below deck are often cramped and stuffy. Down there, the aircon can also freeze you with an unhealthy, continuous blast of cold air.

At the beginning of 1996, three of the biggest Philippine shipping companies, William Lines, Gothong Lines and Aboitiz Lines amalgamated and now trade under the name of WG & A. Their inter-island ships were refitted and renamed; they are now called *Superferry 1*, *Superferry 2* etc. WG & A now have by far the best equipped fleet in the Philippines; their service is well above average, the quality of the food on board has been markedly improved, and to top it all off, the ships are surprisingly punctual. The three companies also set up a second company for the area around the Visayas, called Cebu Ferries.

The major shipping lines include WG & A, Sulpicio Lines, Negros Navigation, Cebu Ferries, George & Peter Lines and Trans-Asia Shipping Lines. You will find others listed in the Yellow Pages under 'Shipping'.

Booking

If possible, buy tickets a few days before sailing as the ships are quickly booked out, especially around Christmas. It is possible to book WG & A and Supercat Fast Ferry tickets online.

On longer trips, basic meals (fish and rice, coffee and water) are usually included in the fare although some shipping lines now offer tickets with or without meals. If this is the case, then it's best to buy a ticket without meals as there will be a good, inexpensive restaurant on board where you can choose your own food and also not be tied to specified mealtimes.

It's a good idea to be on board one hour before the scheduled departure time.

Costs

Examples of average 3rd-class (deck-class, without meals) fares from Manila are as follows: to Bacolod on Negros P1460; to Cebu City on Cebu P1410; to Kalibo on Panay P1010; to Coron on Palawan P980; to Puerto Princesa on Palawan P1320; to Cagayan de Oro on Mindanao 1790 P; and to Davao on Mindanao P1870.

Cabin: A luxury cabin for two people with a wide bed, bath and TV, full board, costs about the same as two plane tickets.

Air

After practically monopolising the air traffic scene for many years, Philippine Airlines (PAL) is now facing a bit of competition from the relatively new companies Air Philippines and Cebu Pacific. Some PAL flights are now being serviced by Air Philippines, eg Cebu City-Bacolod, Cebu City-Davao, Cebu City-General Santos und Cebu City-Iloilo City.

Smaller airlines such as Asian Spirit, Pacific Airways and Seair offer quite a few interesting short-haul services. Seair are especially active in this area as they have an ongoing programme of expanding their flight network to places of interest to the tourist. They also have a well-maintained, young fleet of aircraft.

A word of warning: It is possible you will be asked for proof of identity at check-in. It pays to have your passport or a copy of it with you.

Flight Schedules

Inland flight schedules are usually revised at least twice and up to four times a year. The larger airlines publicise their new departure days and times in the local daily newspapers.

Note: Especially during the rainy season some flights might well be cancelled. If you have to catch an international flight in Manila, Cebu City or Davao, you should take this into consideration when you are planning. It can be handy to have written confirmation from the airline if the flight was in fact cancelled. This will most likely save your having to pay a fee to have your ticket changed by the international airline.
In Manila, Cebu Pacific organises a free transfer from the Domestic Airport to the International Airport, if the passenger lands in Manila on one of their flights and will be leaving on the same day on an international flight. Important: Ask for this service as you're checking in.

Aircraft in Service
Air Philippines flies Boeing 737s, Philippine Airlines Airbus 330s and Boeing 737s, while Cebu Pacific prefers the Boeing 757 and DC9.
Propeller aircraft are flown by Asian Spirit (Dash 7, YS-11, LET 410, CN-235), Pacific Airways (Cessna) and Seair (LET-410).
Smoking is not permitted on board the aircraft.

Booking
Tickets are available at the airline offices or can be arranged at short notice by travel agents. Some travel agents are agents for several airlines and can issue tickets themselves. It is possible to book Asian Spirit and Philippine Airlines tickets online. It's a good idea to book early.
Over the Christmas period, between 15 December and 4 January, and during Holy Week, all flights are usually fully booked although it might be worthwhile to try your luck on the waiting list.
Bookings can be changed free of charge only if made before noon on the day before the flight. After that, you'll have to pay a processing fee of about P50 to P100.

Costs
Sample prices of one-way fares from Manila are: to Baguio P1950 (US$36); to Cebu City P2900 (US$52); to Davao P3670 (US$67); to Kalibo P2570 (US$57); and to Puerto Princesa P2850 (US$52).

Baggage
Passengers on domestic flights are officially allowed only 18 kg of baggage free of charge; 10 kg on smaller aircraft. Extra baggage costs about P25 per kg (depending on the route).

Departure Tax
The current airport tax for inland flights is P200 and for international flights, P550.

Charter Service
Independently of scheduled flights, internal flights within the Philippines are possible with the following charter companies:
Interisland Air Services, Manila, Tel +63 (0)2 8528010, Fax +63 (0)2 8527793, @.
www.interislandairservices.com

Navion Air Service, Angeles, Tel & Fax +63 (0)45 3317181, Cellphone +63 (0)917-8260251, @.
www.navionair.com

Omni Aviation, Angeles, Tel & Fax +63 (0)45 8926664, @.
www.omniaviation.com.ph

Subic Seaplane, Olongapo, Tel +63 (0)47 2522230, Fax +63 (0)47 2521844, Cellphone +63 (0)919-3251106, @.
www.seaplane-philippines.com

Manila

Manila is the capital of the Philippines. In 1975, 17 towns and communities were combined to form Metropolitan Manila. Known as Metro Manila, this conglomeration is home to a population of more than 10 million people, far too many cars, daily traffic chaos and an alarming amount of air pollution. San Nicolas, Binondo, Santa Cruz, Quiapo and San Miguel form the nucleus of the city, where you will find markets (Divisoria Market, Quinta Market), churches (Quiapo Church, Santa Cruz Church), busy shopping streets ('Avenida' Rizal Ave, Escolta St), Chinatown (Binondo, Ongpin St), the official home of the president (Malacañang Palace in San Miguel) and lots and lots of people.

Rizal Park, better known as Luneta Park, is is one of Manila's most important meeting places, and is flanked by the two most popular areas for tourists. To the north is Intramuros, the Spanish walled city which was badly damaged during fierce fighting in WWII. To the south is the area where the more peaceful modern invaders are drawn - Ermita and Malate. Here you will find most of Manila's hotels and international restaurants. It is known as the 'tourist belt', and its main street is the waterfront Roxas Blvd. Ermita is about seven km north-west of Ninoy Aquino International Airport (NAIA).

Manila's business centre is Makati, where the banks, insurance companies and other businesses have their head offices. The embassies of many countries and many airline offices can also be found here. At the edge of Makati, along E de los Santos Ave (almost always called Edsa), closed off from the rest of the city, the upmarket districts of Dasmariñas, Forbes Park and Urdaneta (so-called 'villages') each have their own police force to patrol the palatial mansions.

At the other extreme is Tondo, Manila's main slum. It's estimated that 1½ million Filipinos live in slums in Metro Manila, and Tondo alone has around 200,000 inhabitants living in huts in just 1½ sq km.

Other areas of Manila which may be of interest to the incurably curious traveller include Caloocan City, a centre of light-industrial engineering and food processing. At the end of Rizal Ave Extension stands a monument to Andres Bonifacio. This statue, known as 'Monumento', is a stopping or turning point for many buses and jeepneys.

Quezon City is the centre of government, where you'll also find the Philippine Heart Center for Asia, the 25,000 seat Araneta Coliseum and the four km^2 campus of the University of the Philippines (UP).

The name Manila was originally two words: *may* and *nilad*. *May* means 'there is' and *nilad* is a mangrove plant which used to grow on the banks of the Pasig River. The bark of the mangroves gave a natural soap which the locals used for washing their clothes.

Three years after he founded the colony, King Philipp II of Spain called the town '*Isigne y Siempre Leal Ciudad*', meaning 'Distinguished and Ever Loyal City'. This charming name could not, however, replace the name Maynilad. If you want to know what Maynilad looked like in the middle of the last century, read Fedor Jagor's classic book *Travels in the Philippines*, published in 1873.

Rizal Park

This is a real oasis in the centre of the city and is popularly known as Luneta Park. There are flowers, fountains, wide lawns and, of course, plenty of music attracting thousands of strolling Filipinos every day in the late afternoon and evening. If you're there at 5am, you can see the first eager Chinese do-

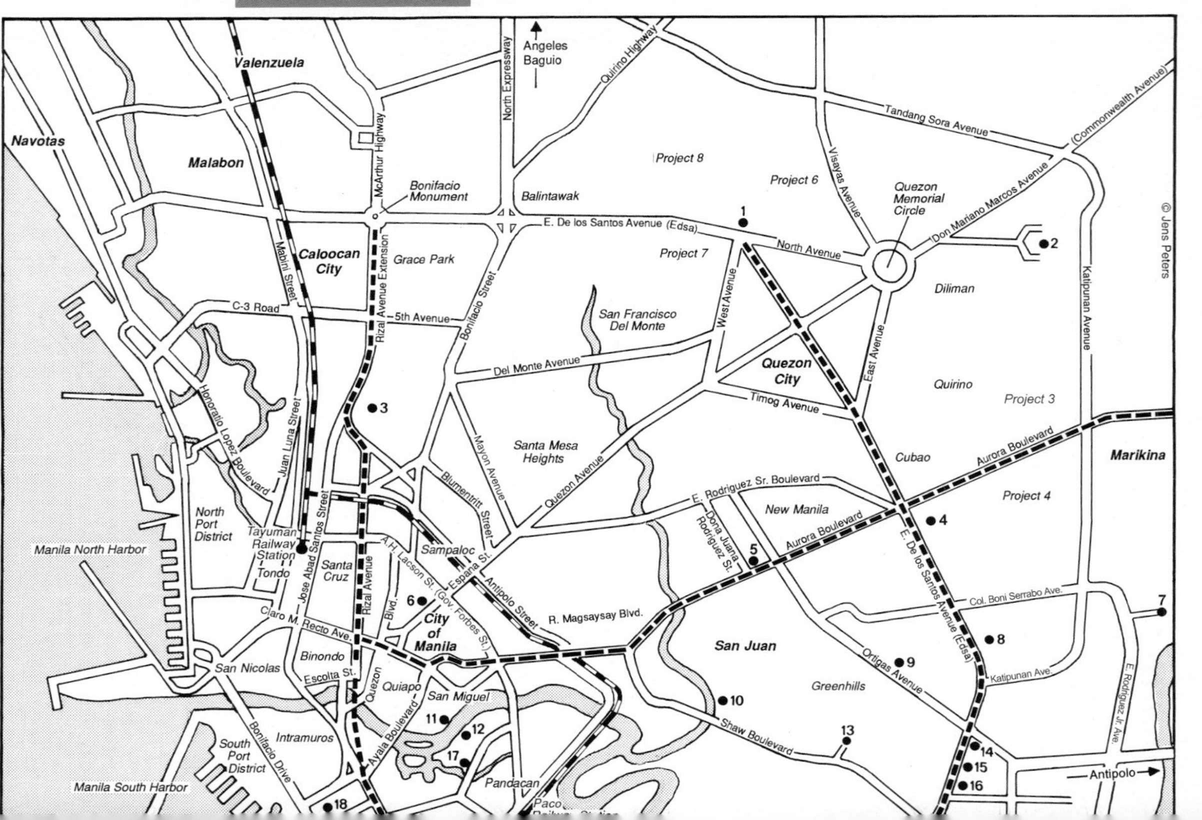

© Jens Peters
Valenzuela
Angeles
Baguio
North Expressway
Quirino Highway
Tandang Sora Avenue
(Commonwealth Avenue)
Navotas
Malabon
McArthur Highway
Bonifacio Monument
Balintawak
Project 8
Project 6
Visayas Avenue
Quezon Memorial Circle
Don Mariano Marcos Avenue
E. De los Santos Avenue (Edsa)
North Avenue
Caloocan City
Grace Park
Project 7
Mabini Street
Rizal Avenue Extension
Bonifacio Street
Diliman
Katipunan Avenue
C-3 Road
5th Avenue
San Francisco Del Monte
West Avenue
Del Monte Avenue
Quezon City
East Avenue
Quirino
Project 3
Timog Avenue
Honoratio Lopez Boulevard
Juan Luna Street
Santa Mesa Heights
Mayon Avenue
Quezon Avenue
Blumentritt Street
Cubao
Aurora Boulevard
Marikina
Project 4
E. Rodriguez Sr. Boulevard
New Manila
North Port District
Jose Abad Santos Street
Tayuman Railway Station
Manila North Harbor
Sampaloc
España St.
Santa Cruz
Tondo
A.H. Lacson St. (Gov. Forbes St.)
Dona Juana Rodriguez St.
Antipolo Street
R. Magsaysay Blvd.
Rizal Avenue
Blvd.
City of Manila
Claro M. Recto Ave.
Col. Boni Serrabo Ave.
San Juan
Ortigas Avenue
Katipunan Ave.
Binondo
San Nicolas
Escolta St.
Quezon
Quiapo
San Miguel
Greenhills
E. Rodriguez Jr. Ave.
Shaw Boulevard
Intramuros
Ayala Boulevard
South Port District
Bonifacio Drive
Manila South Harbor
Pandacan
Paco
Antipolo
1
2
3
4
5
6
7
8
9
10
11
12
13
14
15
16
17
18

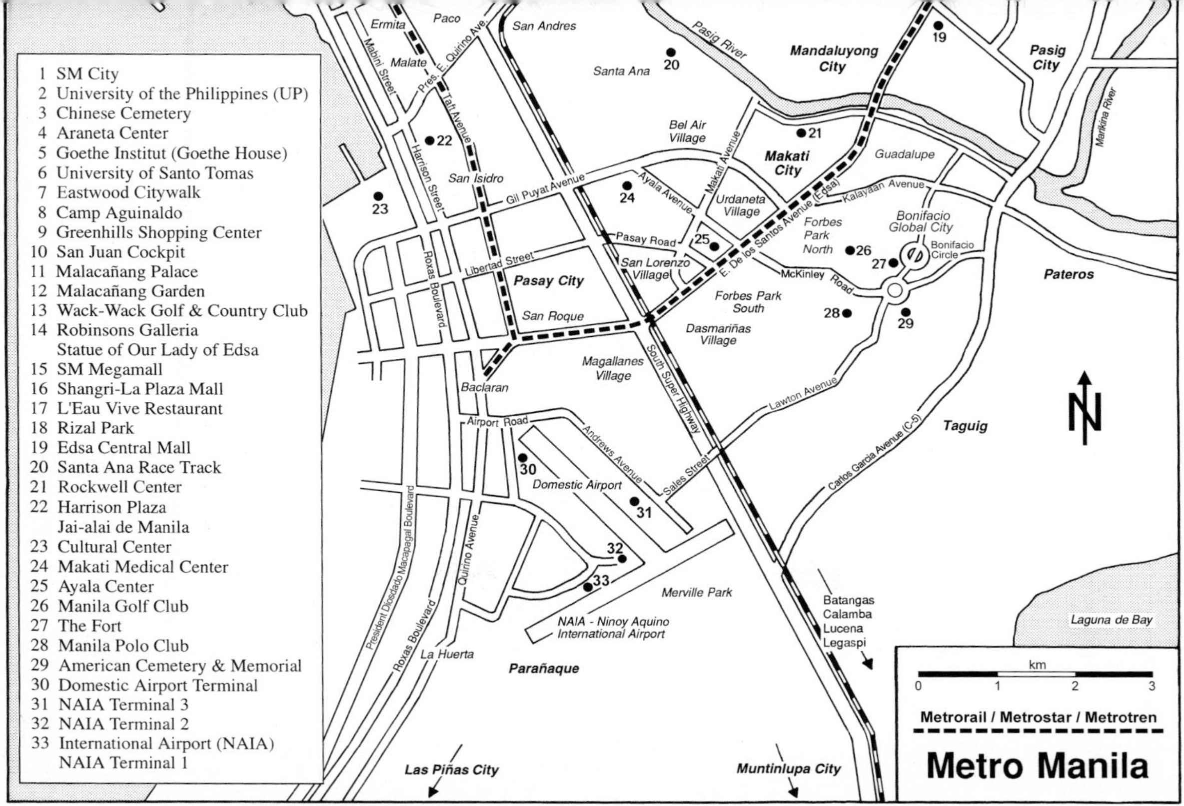

Metro Manila

Metrorail / Metrostar / Metrotren

km 0 1 2 3

1 SM City
2 University of the Philippines (UP)
3 Chinese Cemetery
4 Araneta Center
5 Goethe Institut (Goethe House)
6 University of Santo Tomas
7 Eastwood Citywalk
8 Camp Aguinaldo
9 Greenhills Shopping Center
10 San Juan Cockpit
11 Malacañang Palace
12 Malacañang Garden
13 Wack-Wack Golf & Country Club
14 Robinsons Galleria
Statue of Our Lady of Edsa
15 SM Megamall
16 Shangri-La Plaza Mall
17 L'Eau Vive Restaurant
18 Rizal Park
19 Edsa Central Mall
20 Santa Ana Race Track
21 Rockwell Center
22 Harrison Plaza
Jai-alai de Manila
23 Cultural Center
24 Makati Medical Center
25 Ayala Center
26 Manila Golf Club
27 The Fort
28 Manila Polo Club
29 American Cemetery & Memorial
30 Domestic Airport Terminal
31 NAIA Terminal 3
32 NAIA Terminal 2
33 International Airport (NAIA)
NAIA Terminal 1

Ermita
Paco
San Andres
Pasig River
Mandaluyong City
Pasig City
Marikina River
Malate
Mabini Street
Pres. E. Quirino Ave.
Taft Avenue
Santa Ana
Bel Air Village
Makati City
Guadalupe
Harrison Street
San Isidro
Gil Puyat Avenue
Ayala Avenue
Makati Avenue
Urdaneta Village
Kalayaan Avenue
Bonifacio Global City
Bonifacio Circle
Forbes Park North
E. De los Santos Avenue (Edsa)
Pasay Road
San Lorenzo Village
Libertad Street
Pasay City
McKinley Road
Pateros
Roxas Boulevard
Forbes Park South
Dasmariñas Village
San Roque
Magallanes Village
South Super Highway
Baclaran
Lawton Avenue
Taguig
Airport Road
Andrews Avenue
Sales Street
Carlos Garcia Avenue (C-5)
Domestic Airport
President Diosdado Macapagal Boulevard
Quirino Avenue
Merville Park
NAIA - Ninoy Aquino International Airport
Batangas
Calamba
Lucena
Legaspi
Laguna de Bay
La Huerta
Parañaque
Las Piñas City
Muntinlupa City

Orientation

Although Manila is a fairly sprawling city, it's quite easy to find your way around. Like Bangkok, however, Manila has a number of 'centres'. Makati, for example, is the business centre, while Ermita is where tourists tend to go. The area of most interest to visitors can be defined by the Pasig River, Manila Bay and Taft Ave. The river forms the northern boundary of this rectangular area, while the bay and Taft Ave form the western and eastern boundaries.

Immediately south of the river is the oldest area of Manila, which includes Intramuros. This is where you'll find most of the places of historic interest in the city. The General Post Office (GPO) and the Immigration Office are also located here. Farther south is the open expanse of Rizal Park which extends from Taft Ave to the bayside Roxas Blvd. This is the central meeting and wandering place in Manila. South of the park is Ermita, the tourist centre, which has cheaper (and some more expensive) accommodation, restaurants, airline offices, and pretty much everything else you'll need. Farther south again are Malate and Pasay City, where there are a lot of up-market hotels, particularly along the bay, on Roxas Blvd. The modern Cultural Center is built on reclaimed land jutting into the bay. Continue down Taft Ave to the airport or travel south-east from Taft Ave to Makati.

North of the river is the crowded and interesting Chinatown area and the sprawling slums of Tondo.

ing their t'ai chi. Sunday is family day, with a chance to listen to the free concert at 5pm, the Concert at the Park. On New Year's Day there are great celebrations here.

It is interesting to watch the changing of the guard at the Rizal Memorial, which is close to where the national hero Dr Jose Rizal was executed by the Spaniards on 30 December 1896. The dramatic scene of the execution squad pointing their weapons at Rizal is the theme of a group of statues near the Rizal Memorial and forms the centrepiece of a lightshow based on the execution. As this is not a regular event, it's best to check first with the Tourist Office when it'll next take place. You can also view the statues during the day. His farewell poem, *Mi Ultimo Adios* (My Last Farewell), is inscribed on a brass plaque in different languages.

Tucked away between the monument and the fishpond (towards TM Kalaw St) is Rizal's Fountain - a well from Wilhelmsfeld, a village near Heidelberg in Germany. They say that Rizal used to drink from this well during his days as a student in Heidelberg.

At the side of the park nearest the water is the Luneta Boardwalk, where you can enjoy the colourful Manila Bay sunsets. On the opposite side, near the big Department of Tourism building, the roller-skating rink and the topographical model of the Philippines, there is another playground (Pistang Pambata), with wonderful large stone statues of dinosaurs and monsters to climb on; admission P10.

On either side of the open-air auditorium (Teatro at Pelikula) and planetarium are the Chinese and Japanese gardens, which are popular meeting places for couples; admission P5 to each garden.

Between the Japanese Garden and the Museum of Filipino People, tucked away so it's scarcely visible from the outside, is the horticultural highpoint of

Rizal Monument

Rizal Park, the Orchidarium & Butterfly Pavilion. It is a masterpiece of design, with winding pathways and little bridges leading over romantic fishponds. As if a huge variety of orchids was not enough, there is also a wide variety of other exotic flowers, ferns and trees, a man-made waterfall, a climbing wall, and right in the middle of it all, the Lush Life Restaurant. Open daily from 9am to 5pm. Admission P100; students and senior citizens P60.

Luneta Boardwalk

Luneta Boardwalk is the extension of Rizal Park out to sea. To make this possible, an enormous platform has been built in Manila Bay. Supported by stilts, it can be reached by three pedestrian bridges. When it is completely finished - estimated to be by the end of 2004 - it will house four buildings which will accommodate a wide selection of shops and restaurants. What's more, this attraction will also feature a place for cultural events and of course a promenade for visitors to feast their eyes on the sunsets.

Manila Baywalk

The pedestrian zone along the paved promenade reaching from the US embassy to the Manila Yacht Club is the pride and joy of Roxas Boulevard. Numerous park benches under the palm trees invite you to rest your legs, and at about 5pm, in good time for the magnificent display of the sunset, the open air restaurants raise their shutters to serve barbecued delights and cold drinks. Later in the evening, when the strip is illuminated by lamps and the air reverberates with the sound of live music, eg in Anthology by the Bay, it doesn't take long for the party atmosphere to take hold.

Intramuros

Literally the city 'in walls', Intramuros is the Manila of the past. This is where Legaspi erected a fortress in 1571 after his victory over the Muslims. Following attacks by the Chinese fleet and a fire, the Filipinos were forced to build the wall. A wide moat all around made the bulwark complete. Within the walls, the most important buildings were the numerous feudal lords' houses, 12 churches and several hospitals. Only Spaniards and Mestizos were allowed to live within the walls; Filipinos were settled on what is now the site of Rizal Park. Likewise, the Chinese were housed within the range of the cannon, about where the City Hall stands today. Neither the Dutch nor the Portuguese managed to storm this fortress and the attacks of the Sulu pirates were also unsuccessful.

Intramuros was almost totally destroyed by bomb attacks in WWII. The San Agustin Church remained relatively undamaged and the Manila Cathedral

from map page 167

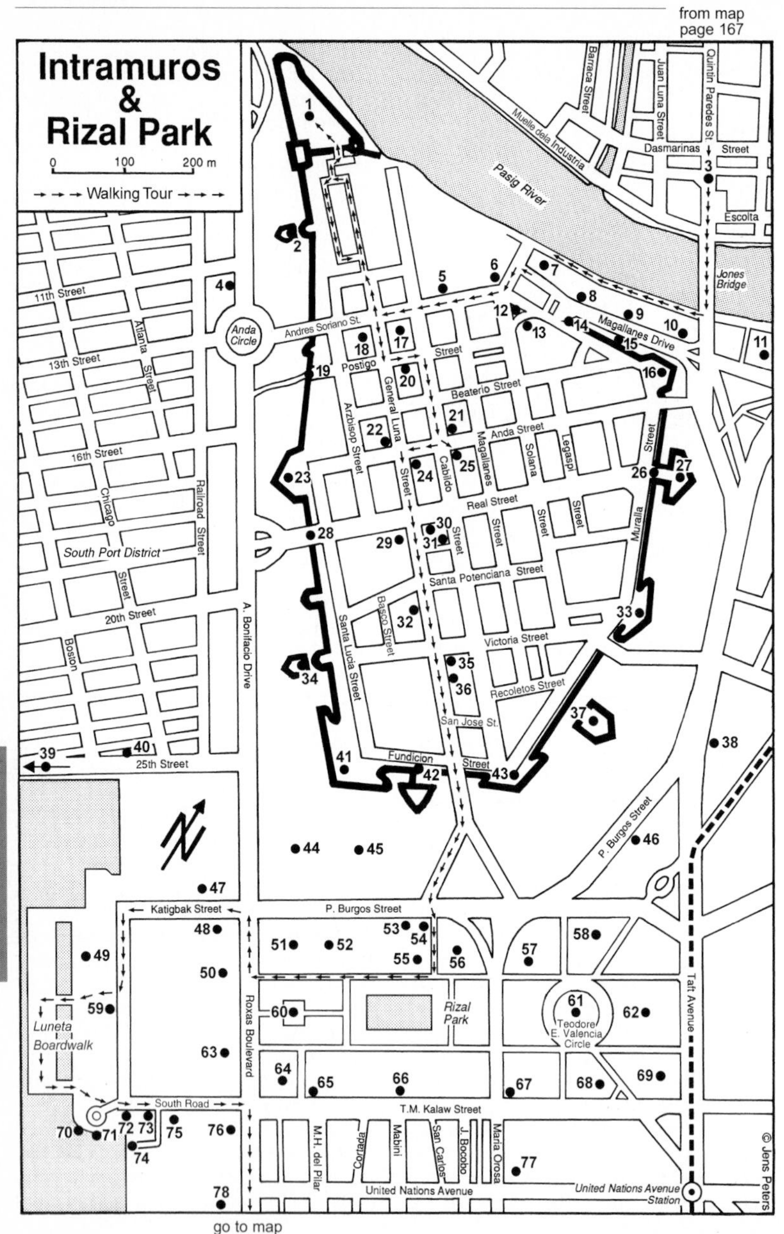

go to map page 184

Manila

Getting There & Away
27 Super Terminal

Places to Stay
31 Hotel Intramuros
47 Manila Hotel
77 Manila Pavillon Hotel

Places to Eat
5 Bacolod Chicken House
6 Jollibee
14 Starbucks
22 Orchidas Restaurant
Swan Restaurant
30 Barbara's Restaurant
Café Luna
36 Ilustrado Restaurant
67 Jollibee
70 Harbor View Restaurant
71 Golden Horizon Restaurant
72 Pantalan Maynila Restaurant
Sanbashi Restaurant
Banda Forest Restaurant
73 Blue Bay Grill
Lami Barbecue
74 Seafood Wharf Restaurant

Miscellaneous
1 Fort Santiago
Rizal Shrine
2 Revellin de San Francisco
3 First Welcome Marker
4 Seamen's Club
7 Philippine-Mexican Marker Plaza
8 Immigration Office
9 Equitable PCI Bank
10 National Press Club
11 General Post Office
12 Felipe II Monument
13 Bank of the Philippine Islands
15 Puerta Isabel II
16 Bastion de San Gabriel
17 Plaza de Roma
18 Palacio del Gobernador
19 Puerta del Postigo
20 Manila Cathedral
21 Palacio del Sana
22 Palacio Grande
23 Bastion de Santa Lucia
24 Plazuela de Sta Isabel
25 Bahay Tsinoy
Kaisa Angelo King Heritage Center
26 Puerta del Parian
27 Revellin del Parian
28 Puerta de Santa Lucia
29 San Agustin Church
30 Plaza San Luis Complex
Casa Manila Museum
32 NCCA Building
33 Bastion de Dilao
34 Fortin San Pedro
35 Patio Victoria
36 El Amanecer Compound
Silahis
37 Revellin de Recoletos
38 Manila City Hall
40 Bureau of Quarantine
41 Bastion de San Diego
42 Puerta Real
43 Bastion de San Andres
44 Legaspi & Urdaneta Monument
45 Golf Course
46 National Museum
48 Rizal Park Post Office
49 Children's Playground
50 Carabao Statue
51 Rizal's Execution Spot
52 Chinese Garden
53 Planetarium
54 Rizal Park Library
55 Concert at the Park
56 Japanese Garden
57 Orchidarium & Butterfly Pavilion
58 Museum of Filipino People
59 Quirino Grandstand
60 Rizal Monument
61 Skating Rink
62 Philippines Model
63 Tamaraw Statue
64 Rizal's Fountain
65 Philippine National Bank (PNB)
66 National Library
68 Department of Tourism (DOT)
Tourist Office, Tourist Police
69 Children's Playground
75 Museo ng Maynila
76 Museo Pambata
78 US Embassy

was rebuilt after the war. During the restoration, Puerta Isabel II and Puerta Real, two of the original seven gates of the city, were also restored.
A few houses are also well worth seeing, like the Casa Manila in the Plaza San Luis Complex and the El Amanecer Compound, both in General Luna St (see also below under 'Museums': *Casa Manila*).

Fort Santiago

The most important defence location of the Intramuros fortress-city was Fort Santiago, Tel 5271572. From this strategic location, at the mouth of the Pasig River, all activity in Manila Bay could be observed. During the Japanese occupation in WWII, innumerable Filipino prisoners lost their lives in the infamous dungeon cells which lay below sea level - at high tide there was no escape. Dr Jose Rizal also spent his last days in a cell at this fort before his execution by the Spaniards in 1896.
Today Fort Santiago is a national monument. Inside the grounds there is an open-air theatre (the Rajah Sulayman Theater) and a Rizal museum (the Rizal Shrine; only open until 5pm - see also below under 'Museums').
In early 1988, Fort Santiago was turned inside out, with government permission, by US goldseekers who, by excavating, hoped to uncover the legendary war treasure of the Japanese general Yamashita, which was rumoured to have been hidden in the Philippines. Naturally, the excavations drew a blank in every case.
The fort is open daily between 8am and 6pm, and admission is P40 (students P5), including the Rizal Shrine.

San Agustin Church

The first constructions of the San Agustin Church were destroyed by fires in 1574 and 1583. In 1599 the foundation stone for the present construction was laid. The massive church

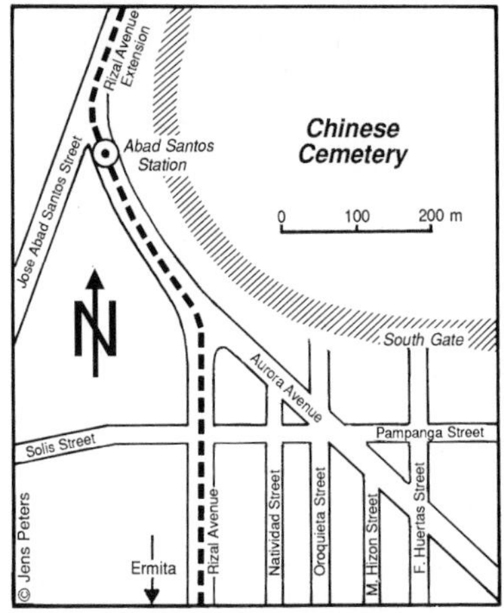

was not damaged by the earthquakes of 1645, 1754, 1852, 1863, 1880, 1968 and 1970, nor by the bombardment in the fighting around Manila in February 1945. San Agustin is one of the oldest existing stone churches in the Philippines. In 1879 and 1880, the crystal chandeliers were brought from Paris, the walls and roofs were masterfully painted by two Italian artists and the choir stalls were carved by the Augustinian monks themselves. In a small chapel to the left of the high altar lie the mortal remains of Legaspi. There is a museum and a contemplative inner courtyard adjoining the church.

Manila Cathedral

This cathedral, with its great cupola, is the Philippines' most significant Catholic church. It is in the Plaza Roma at Intramuros. The building, which was destroyed in WWII, was rebuilt with the help of the Vatican from 1954 to 1958; some old walls were restored and integrated into the new construction. The large organ with its 4500 pipes came from the Netherlands and is apparently the largest in Asia.

Every Sunday, the cathedral echoes to the sound of young couples exchanging their vows. The doors are open to all, and this is a good opportunity to witness a genuine Philippine wedding.

Quiapo Church

This church became famous because of its large crucifix of black wood. The Black Nazarene was carved in Mexico and brought to the Philippines by the Spaniards in the 17th century. Each day, especially on Friday, thousands of Catholics come to the church to pay homage to the crucifix. The climax of the adoration is the procession on 9 January and in Passion Week (the week between Passion Sunday and Palm Sunday, before Easter) on Monday and Friday.

Chinese Cemetery

It may seem irreverent to recommend a cemetery as a tourist attraction but this one should not be missed. It contains some of the most ostentatious tombs in the world. There are actual houses with mailboxes and toilets - some even have air conditioners.

Things get lively on All Saints' Day (1 November), when the descendants of the dead come to visit their ancestors, just as Catholic Filipinos do. Most Sundays, in fact, it's a fascinating place to visit. Attendants, who also live in the cemetery, have started to offer guided tours. They charge a hefty P200 to P300 for a one-hour tour, but they do show the visitor the most impressive buildings and crypts. If asked, they will also open some of them up - and tell the most amazing stories while they're at it. It's also just as well to have their company for safety reasons if it is a quiet day and you are walking round the area, which is crossed by several streets and is about as big as Rizal Park. The Chinese Cemetery is in the north of the district of Santa Cruz, just where Rizal Ave becomes Rizal Ave Extension. It has two entrances: the North Gate, which is almost always closed, and the South Gate, which is tucked away and can be reached from Aurora Ave via Pampanga St and F Huertas St. Apart from taxis, the best way to get there from Ermita is by Metrorail to Abad Santos Station. From there it is about 600m to the South Gate.

There is a P50 charge if you want to drive your car through the cemetery.

Chinatown

Chinatown is not a clearly defined suburb but a cultural and business district that takes in parts of Santa Cruz and Binondo, roughly the area between the three Chinese-Philippine friendship arches called the Welcome Marker. From Ermita you cross the Pasig River over the Jones Bridge, between the Immigration Office and the GPO, to the First Welcome Gate. The southern part of Chinatown begins here. From Quintin Paredes St, which runs through the gate, several little streets seem to wind crazily towards the big east-west curve of Ongpin St, the eastern end of which is marked at Plaza Santa Cruz by the Third Welcome Gate (Arch of Goodwill). Ongpin St is the main business street of Chinatown, with well-stocked Chinese grocers, herb-scented drug stalls and spacious restaurants. However, you can also find exotic shops and little teahouses in the sidestreets leading off Ongpin St, eg in the narrow confines of Carvajal St. Unlike the Chinatowns in other Asian cities, this one is very busy on Sunday.

Malacañang Palace

The Malacañang Palace is the single most noteworthy attraction in the district of San Miguel. It is in Jose P Laurel St, on the banks of the Pasig River. Malacañang is a derivation of the old Filipino description *'may lakan diyan'*

Getting There & Away
16 Genesis Transport Bus Terminal
17 Philippine Rabbit Bus Terminal
44 Park 'n' Ride Lawton Bus Terminal

Places to Stay
8 First Hotel
11 Binondo Suites
15 Merchant's Hotel

Places to Eat
1 Bodhi Vegetarian Restaurant
9 President Restaurant
10 Mandarin Palace Seafoods
11 Café Chino
12 Lai Lai Palace Restaurant
Lok Fu Seafood Restaurant
14 Maxim's Tea House
22 Wan Tsi Tea House
23 Emperor Villa Seafood Restaurant
28 McDonald's

Miscellaneous
1 Tutuban Mall
2 Divisoria Market
3 Seng Guan Buddhist Temple
4 Plaza Lorenzo Ruiz
5 Binondo Church
6 Statue of Roman Ongpin
7 Carvajal Street Shops
11 Equitable PCI Bank
13 Small Temple
18 Manila City Jail
19 National Bookstore
20 Namria
21 Young's Sporting Goods
24 International Exchange Bank
25 Philtrust Bank
26 Union Bank
27 First Welcome Gate
29 Third Welcome Gate
30 Carriedo Fountain
Plaza Santa Cruz
31 Santa Cruz Church
32 Statue of Arsenio Lacson
Plaza Lacson
33 SM Department Store
34 Hidalgo Street Photo Shops
35 Quiapo Church
36 Plaza Miranda
37 Mercury Drug
38 Philippine-Mexican Marker Plaza
39 Immigration Office
40 General Post Office
41 Quinta Market
42 Ilalim Tulay Market
43 Metropolitan Theatre
45 Globo de Oro Mosque

Manila Walking Tour

Many visitors to the Philippines don't have a good word to say about Manila, often however without having made the effort to have a proper look at the city itself. Admittedly, Manila doesn't have the immediate charm of other world cities such as Sydney, Prague or Rio de Janeiro, but a closer look will reveal that the once glamourous capital still has many attractions to its name.

If you want to get a feeling for the variety on offer in the different areas of the city, you could do worse than take the city walking tour which follows. It begins in Quiapo and takes about five to eight hours, depending on how much time you take out for sightseeing, museum visits and breaks. The best time to arrive at Roxas Blvd is 5pm, because there, at the end of the tour, the street cafés and restaurants on the Manila Baywalk open, just in time for the setting of the sun.

Note: With the exception of the San Agustin Museum all the museums mentioned below are closed on Mondays.

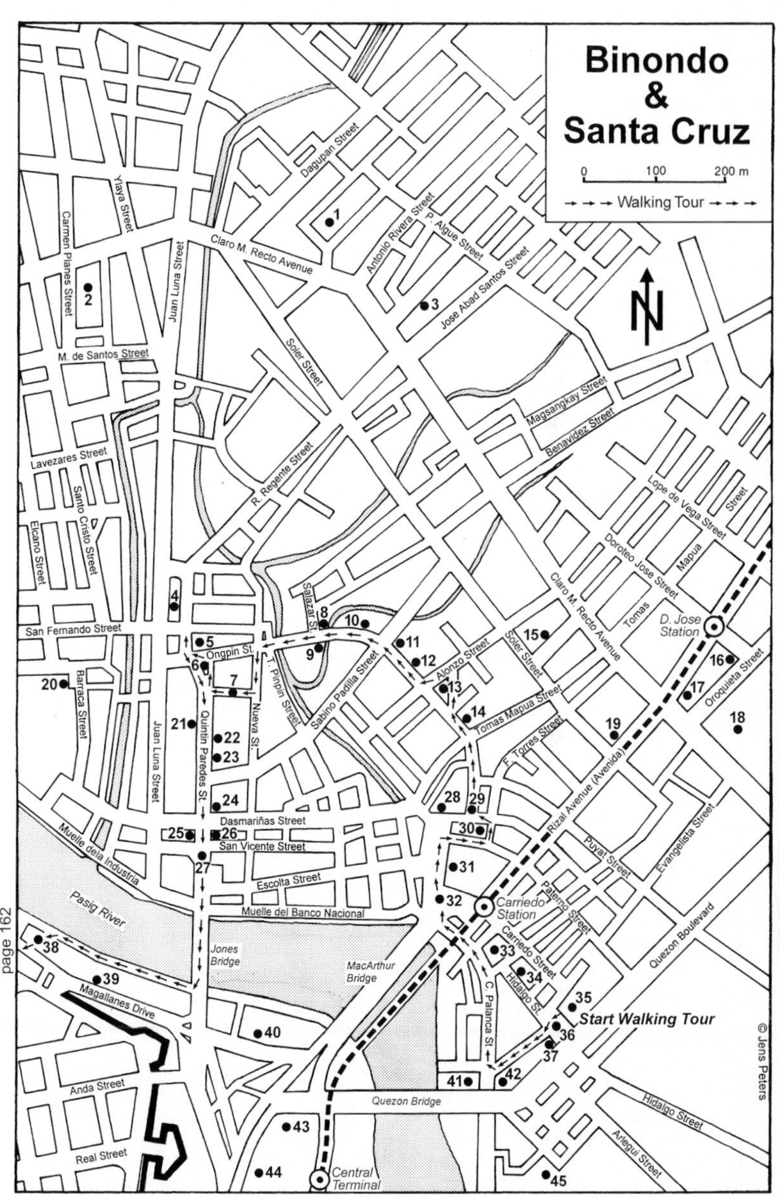

go to map page 162

From the Quiapo Church to the Philippine-Mexican Marker Plaza (see 'Binondo & Santa Cruz' map on page 167):

The starting point for the tour is the big Quiapo Church with its famous 'Black Nazarene', a crucifix hewn from black wood. It's best to take a taxi there, or take the Metrorail to Carriedo Station and walk from there through Carriedo St (lots of market stalls in the middle of the road with textiles, toys, CDs and costume jewelry) to Quiapo Church. After visiting the church - the west side door on Carriedo St is usually open - cross the square in front (Plaza Miranda) and take the little street which runs parallel to the wide Quezon Blvd to the Ilalim Tulay Market (handicrafts on sale under the Quezon Bridge), turn right there into C Palanca St, passing by the Quinta Market and the profusion of market stalls selling fruit, under the Metrorail to Plaza Lacson with its statue of the ex-mayor, Arsenio Lacson, in his time an effective local polititian.

A street leads from Plaza Lacson past the big Santa Cruz Church to Plaza Santa Cruz with its centre point, the circular Carriedo Fountain (dedicated to Francisco Carriedo y Pedoro, the benefactor who financed Manila's first waterwork system with an impressive donation). Not far from there an ornately decorated arch (Arch of Goodwill: Third Welcome Gate) frames the beginning of Ongpin St, leading the way into the heart of Chinatown. Amongst other things, you'll find chemists with all kinds of exotic Chinese medicine, and quite a few inviting restaurants as well. In little Kipuja St, which connects Fernandez St (leading off Ongpin St) and Teodora Alonzo St, there's a small temple where Kuan Yin, the goddess of mercy, and Kuan Te Ya, the god of businessmen, are worshipped. After crossing Ongpin North Bridge and Ongpin South Bridge, both decorated with Chinese arches, you come to the junction with Nueva St (turn left) and after about 70m to Carvajal St (turn right). This quaint alleyway boasts several teahouses and even more tropical fruit and vegetable stands, and is well worth having a look at. Carvajal St finally opens out into Quintin Paredes St, which then leads you to the Binondo Church (turn right). The main entrance to this massive church dating from Spanish colonial times is on the Plaza Lorenzo Ruiz.

From the Binondo Church head back towards Quintin Paredes St, past the statue of the important Filipino-Chinese merchant Roman Ongpin, who gave his name to the nearby shopping street. Several bank buildings around the junction of Quintin Paredes St and Dasmariñas St are witness to the fact that this was once the most important financial centre in the country (nowadays Makati has that title). After walking through the First Welcome Gate at the entrance to San Vicente St you leave Chinatown behind you, and after about 150m you reach Jones Bridge, which leads over the broad Pasig River. On the bridge you can enjoy the cool, refreshing breeze which reminds you that Manila Bay isn't far away. On your left on the other bank of the river you'll see a neoclassical building, the General Post Office, and on the right the Bureau of Immigration. At the end of Jones Bridge steps lead down to the river, where you can walk past the back of the National Press Club and Bureau of Immigration, ending up in the beautifully laid out Philippine-Mexican Marker Plaza. In the shade of this little park a monument with a memorial plaque reminds passers-by of the trade carried out by the galleons of the colonial power, Spain, between Acapulco in Mexico and Manila, a trade which lasted exactly 250 years (1565-1815).

From the Philippine-Mexican Marker Plaza to the Manila Baywalk (see 'Intramuros & Rizal Park' map on page 162 and 'Ermita, Malate & Paco' map on page 184):

The next stop is Fort Santiago in the north-west corner of Intramuros, the historical 'town within walls' erected by the Spanish in the 16th century. So, after you have left the Philippine-Mexican Marker Plaza turn right behind the Jollibee into Andres Soriano St. If you feel like a quick break for a coffee first, there's a Starbucks across from the Bureau of Immigration. Not far from there, where Andres Soriano St leads into Solana St, there's a small traffic island with a statue on it of the Spanish King Philipp II (Felipe II, Rey de España), after whom the Philippines are named.

The extension of General Luna St, which crosses Andres Soriano St at the Plaza de Roma near Manila Cathedral, leads to Fort Santiago, which was the most important Spanish fortification in the Philippines during the colonial period. It is now a protected building and houses amongst other things an interesting Rizal Museum (Rizal Shrine). After looking around the fort and taking a short walk through the well-kept park in front, head back towards Plaza de Roma and the monumental Manila Cathedral with its striking dome.

By way of Cabildo St, past the cathedral, you come to the Kaisa Angelo King Heritage Center which houses the Bahay Tsinoy, a little museum dedicated to the history of the Chinese in the Philippines. It's only a few steps along Anda St over to General Luna St, which runs west of Cabildo St. There you'll turn left and at the next crossing decide whether you first want to have a quick look at the San Agustin Church with its adjacent museum, or whether you'd prefer to see the restored Plaza San Luis Complex. In the latter you'll find the Casa Manila Museum, Barbara's Restaurant, the pleasant Café Luna (with tables outside in the patio; great place to while away some time) and the elegant, fittingly designed Hotel Intramuros (entrance in Urdaneta St).

Three blocks further south, past the NCCA Building (National Commission for Culture and Arts) and Patio Victoria (where weddings take place) Silahis in the El Amenecer Compound has a wide selection of Philippine art handicrafts. And in the pleasantly designed inner courtyard the noble ambience of the Ilustrado Restaurant radiates its old world charm.

Just outside the stronghold, a covered walkway leads from Intramuros to P Burgos St. On the right-hand side in the distance you can't miss the Manila Hotel with its green roof and yellow lettering. After crossing P Burgos St, you walk past the Rizal Park Library, Andres Soriano Jr Library and the Japanese Garden to the Big Lagoon in Rizal Park, which is lined with busts of historical personalities of the country. Tucked away behind the Chinese Garden, is the Bulwagan ng Kigitingan (Memorial to Heroism). It's easy to overlook the sign 'Do Not Enter', and a few metres to the left of it you can make out the first statues of the dramatic scene, which depicts Rizal being shot by the Spanish firing squad.

It's only 200m from the centrally located Rizal Monument on Roxas Blvd to the upmarket Manila Hotel. All manner of heads of state, actors and military men have stayed at this historic hotel which was opened in 1912. General MacArthur even made it his headquarters for several years, and for the German actor Gustav Gründgens, who famously played Mephisto in Goethe's Faust, it was the last stop on his world tour. He was found dead in his room on 7th October 1963 – allegedly meeting his death from an overdose of sleeping pills.

On the way from the Manila Hotel to the Quirino Grandstand you come across a little gate, through which you can get to the Luneta Boardwalk. When construction work is finished - estimated to be by the end of 2004 - this giant platform on stilts in Manila Bay, with a promenade, shops and restaurants, is predestined to be the social focal point of the city. Cheek by jowl with the Luneta Boardwalk, on South Blvd, several restaurants offer a wide selection of culinary delights, including Harbor View (Philippine), Sanbashi (Japanese), Blue Bay Grill (Spanish), Lami Barbecue (Cebuano) and the Seafood Wharf Restaurant. South Blvd is also the location of the informative Museo ng Maynila, housed in a beautiful old building, and 100m away from that, round the corner on Roxas Blvd, the instructive Museo Pambata (Children's Museum) invites visitors.

The final part of this walk leads from the US Embassy along Manila Bay to the Manila Yacht Club. This broad, pedestrian-friendly paved walkway along Roxas Blvd is called the Manila Baywalk. It starts to reveal its glories in the late afternoon, when the open-air restaurants and cafés open and the sun sinks spectacularly into the sea - just the right time for a sundowner.

meaning 'here lives a nobleman' and referring to the Spanish aristocrat Luis Rocha, who built the palace. In 1802 he sold it to an important Spanish soldier. From 1863 the nobleman's house was used as the domicile of the Spanish heads of government. Later, the Americans also used the palace as their residence, as did the first Philippine head of state, Manuel Quezon, in 1935.

Cultural Center

The Cultural Center of the Philippines (CCP) was built in 1969 under the umbrella administration of the ex-first lady Imelda Marcos. It was designed by Leandro Locsin, a leading Filipino architect. The CCP includes a theatre, art gallery and museum. It was designed as a symbol of national cultural development and is open for public viewing daily between 9am and 5pm.

In the vicinity of the CCP are the Folk Arts Theater, the Philippine International Convention Center (PICC), the Amazing Philippine Theatre (formerly the Manila Film Theater), the Coconut Palace (former government guesthouse) and the Westin Philippine Plaza Hotel that houses what must be one of the finest swimming pools in the country. The Folk Arts Theater was built in the record time of only 70 days. Anyone interested in seeing the conference rooms of the Convention Center can take a tour.

Zoo

You will find the Manila Zoological & Botanical Gardens at the southern end of Mabini St and Adriatico St (entrance), in Malate district. The Philippine eagle which you can see there and the tamaraw, a dwarf buffalo from Mindoro, are of great interest. But otherwise the miserable accommodation (small enclosures, no shade, no plants) and the obvious neglect suffered by most of the creatures on display illustrate the usual Asian attitude to animals. Animal lovers are advised to give it a miss. If you do want to visit the zoo, it is open daily from 7am to 6pm. Admission is P10.

Forbes Park

Such a cluster of opulent mansions as you can see in Forbes Park and its neighbouring Dasmariñas Village is almost unique. There is even a special police unit to guard this luxury neighbourhood.

Forbes Park is located in the south-east part of Makati. Buses marked 'Ayala (Ave)' go from Taft Ave in Ermita to the Ayala Center. You then do the remaining one km by taxi as visitors on foot wouldn't stand much chance of getting in. However, even taxis are known to have been turned away if their passengers could not give a definite destination which could be verified. Photography is allowed in Forbes Park but not of embassies.

American Cemetery & Memorial

The trim American Cemetery is directly east of Forbes Park. Here, in rank and file, are the bodies of 17,000 US soldiers who died in the Philippines during WWII. Countless big, informative mosaics depicting the battles of the Pacific can be found in this hillside memorial. Another plaque shows the events of the war in Europe after the US invasion in June 1944.

The hill also provides a good view of Manila and the grand sweep of the cemetery is also a good place for a relaxing walk under the shade of the old trees.

It's about two km from where Ayala Ave meets Edsa. The extension of Ayala Ave is called McKinley Rd and leads through Forbes Park, past San Antonio Church, the Manila Golf Club and the Manila Polo Club directly to the cemetery.

Faith Healers

The unorthodox and controversial methods of the Filipino faith healers have achieved world notoriety through mass media coverage. Clearly some of these 'doctors' are no more than dilettantes and charlatans out to make a buck, but others are so fast and skilful that even sceptics are astounded in spite of themselves.

Many patients travel to Baguio, some to Pangasinan Province, but there are also healers in Metro Manila. Anyone can watch after obtaining the consent of the patient.

For further information, get in touch with the Philippine Spiritual Help Foundation Inc. The founder of this organisation is the famous and businesslike faith healer Alex Orbito, who also owns the travel agency Orbit Tours, Bayview Park Hotel, Roxas Blvd, Ermita, Tel 5216690.

Museums

You will find many interesting museums in Manila; they are listed here in alphabetical order.

Ayala Museum, Makati Ave, Makati, Tel 8121192. Open Tue-Sat 9am-6pm. Admission P120; students P45. Specialises in high points of Philippine his-

New Telephone Numbers
Starting sometime in the future, all Manila telephone numbers will have an additional digit, an 8, which will be added to the beginning of the present numbers.

tory, chronologically presented in over 60 showcase dioramas. There is also an ethnographic section which features artefacts, weapons and ships.

Note: The Ayala Museum is closed at the moment and will probably not be open again until some time in early 2005, when work on a new and bigger building should be completed. Until then, the Historical Dioramas can be seen in the Glorietta 2 Mall (3rd level) behind the Landmark Department Store; the art gallery has been temporarily housed in the building of the Manila Stock Exchange, Ayala Avenue.

Bahay Tsinoy, Anda St corner Cabildo St, Intramuros, Tel 5276083. Open Tue-Sun 1-5pm. Admission P100; students P60. A small museum in the Kaisa Angelo King Heritage Center which is dedicated to the history of the Chinese in the Philippines, starting with the early immigration in pre-colonial times through to their integration into Philippine society nowadays.

Casa Manila Museum, Plaza San Luis Complex, General Luna St corner Real St, Intramuros, Tel 5274084. Open Tue-Sun 9am-6pm. Admission P40; students P15. One of the first examples of the restoration which Intramuros is undergoing. With its beautiful inner courtyards and antique furnishings, it is a faithful reproduction of a typical Spanish residence.

Coconut Palace, Cultural Center Complex, Roxas Blvd, Malate, Tel 8320223. Open Tue-Sun 9-11.30am and 1-4.30pm. Well worth the visit, admission costs P100, including a guided tour which takes just under an hour. This former guesthouse of the Marcos regime, superbly made of the best tropical timbers, was erected in 1981 especially for the first visit of Pope John Paul II who, in fact, refused to use it.

Cultural Center Museum (Museo ng Kalinangang Filipino), Roxas Blvd, Malate, Tel 8321125. Open Tue-Sun 10am-6pm. Admission P20; students P10. Oriental and Islamic art are on permanent display on the 4th floor. The art displays in the main gallery are changed from time to time.

Lopez Memorial Museum, Benpres Building, Meralco Ave corner Exchange Rd, Ortigas Center, Pasig City, Tel 6312417. Open Mon-Fri 8am-5pm, Sat 7.30am-4pm. Admission P70. This is a private museum with the most valuable and comprehensive library of Filipiana anywhere, comprising more than 16,000 books. The collection of historical travel literature is remarkable and includes one of three existing copies of *De Moluccis Insulis* (The Moluccan Islands) by Maximillianus Transylvanus. The work dates back to 1524 and contains the first printed account of Magellan's voyage to the Philippines. There's also a Map Room with maps from 1570 to 1910 and a Rizaliana Room with some of the personal belongings of this national hero. Also on display are some important oil paintings, some of them award-winning works by the well-known classical Filipino artists Felix Resurreccion Hidalgo and Juan Luna, as well as works by Amorsolo, Legaspi, Manansala and Navarro.

Metropolitan Museum of Manila, Central Bank Compound, Roxas Blvd, Malate, near the Cultural Center, Tel 5237855. Open Mon-Sat 10am-6pm. Admission P50; students P30. It has changing displays of various art forms, including some 'old masters', and related documents. There is also a small souvenir shop and the pleasant Met Café.

Museo ng Manila, South Rd, Ermita, Tel 5367388. Open Tue-Sat 9am-4pm. Admission free. Located near Manila Bay and Rizal Park, the museum is housed in a beautiful old building which was constructed in 1911. It was originally the Army & Navy Club, Manila's first social club, but now displays photographs, postcards, engravings and objects from the Spanish and American colonial periods in several rooms, arranged by subject. To round off these examples of Manila's cultural heritage, there is also an exhibition of traditional costumes.

Museo ng Sining, GSIS Building, Cultural Center Complex, Pasay City, Tel 5511301. Open Tue-Sat 8-11.30am and 1-4.30pm. Admission is free. This is the biggest museum of contemporary art in the country, and well worth a visit. Amongst the objects on display are big tapestries and, in separate rooms, paintings by the famous Philippine artists Fernando Amorsolo and Hernando Ocampo.

Museo Pambata, Roxas Blvd, Ermita, Tel 5231797. Open Tue-Sat 9am-5pm, Sun 1-5 pm. Admission P50; children P30. Just the thing for kids, as it was designed to be a hands-on experience for them. Children can go on their own voyage of discovery here, and there is not a 'Do not touch' sign to be seen. The friendly staff are also on hand to explain everything to them if needed. Amongst the many attractions are a reproduction of a rain forest, and a tram (streetcar) and fire engine from old Manila. This museum is simply charming.

National Museum, Burgos St, Rizal Park, Tel 5271216. Open Tue-Sat 9am-5pm. Admission P100, students P30. This wonderfully renovated museum has on display many prehistoric finds, including a piece of the skull of 'Tabon Man' found in the Tabon Cave, Palawan. There are also displays of pottery, jewellery, traditional costumes, weapons, ornaments and much more. The famous painting *Spolarium* by Juan Luna can be seen here in the Museum of Filipino Art department. Some of the exhibits are in the nearby Museum of Filipino People in Rizal Park, including the artefacts of particular historical value recovered in 1992 from the wreck of the Spanish galleon *San Diego* which sank in 1600 off Fortune Island.

Rizal Shrine, Fort Santiago, Intramuros. Open Tue-Sun 9am-noon and 1-5pm, closed on public holidays. Admission is free. A memorial to the national hero, Dr Jose Rizal. On display are some personal effects and his death cell.

San Agustin Museum, San Agustin Church, General Luna St, Intramuros, Tel 5274060. Open daily 9am-noon and 1-5pm. Admission P45; students P20. Established since 1973 in the Augustinian monastery. You can see frescoes, oil paintings, antique choir stalls, precious robes and other liturgical items.

UST Museum (Museum of Arts & Sciences), University of Santo Tomas (UST), España St, Sampaloc, Tel 7811815. Open Tue-Fri 9am-4.30pm. Admission P30; students P20. The oldest university in the Philippines houses an exhibition of ethnological objects, stuffed animals, mussels and paintings. It also has an extensive collection of historic documents and a noteworthy library with more than 180,000 volumes.

Shopping

Markets

Baclaran Flea Market, Roxas Blvd, Baclaran, near the Baclaran Church. One of the biggest markets in Manila, located at the Metrorail South Terminal (the LRT 1 terminus in Baclaran). Every day, from Roxas Blvd up as far as Harrison St, good-value clothing, food,

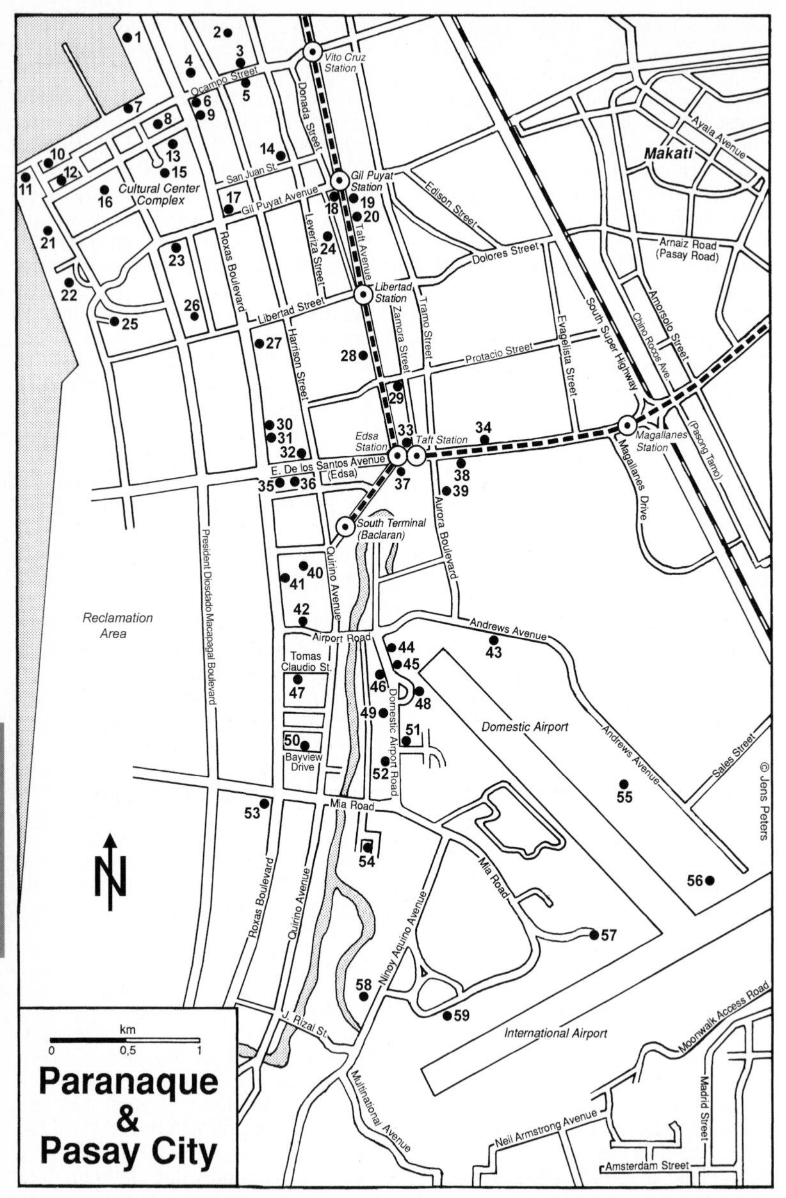
Paranaque & Pasay City
km
0 0,5 1
Vito Cruz Station
Gil Puyat Station
Libertad Station
Edsa Station
Taft Station
Magallanes Station
South Terminal (Baclaran)
Ocampo Street
Donada Street
San Juan St.
Gil Puyat Avenue
Cultural Center Complex
Roxas Boulevard
Leveriza Street
Taft Avenue
Libertad Street
Harrison Street
Zamora Street
Tramo Street
Edison Street
Dolores Street
Protacio Street
Evagelista Street
South Super Highway
Makati
Ayala Avenue
Arnaiz Road (Pasay Road)
Amorsolo Street
Chino Roces Ave.
(Pasong Tamo)
Magallanes Drive
E. De los Santos Avenue (Edsa)
Aurora Boulevard
Quirino Avenue
President Diosdado Macapagal Boulevard
Reclamation Area
Airport Road
Andrews Avenue
Tomas Claudio St.
Domestic Airport Road
Domestic Airport
Bayview Drive
Sales Street
Mia Road
Ninoy Aquino Avenue
International Airport
J. Rizal St.
Multinational Avenue
Moonwalk Access Road
Madrid Street
Neil Armstrong Avenue
Amsterdam Street
© Jens Peters

Getting There & Away

6 Malaysia Airlines
7 Corregidor Ferry Terminal
9 Avis
19 JAM Transit Bus Terminal
20 Tritran Bus Terminal
34 Victory Liner Bus Terminal
37 Crow Lines Bus Terminal
Genesis Transport Bus Terminal
38 Partas Bus Terminal
Philtranco Bus Terminal
39 Five Star Bus Terminal
43 Island Transvoyager
44 Air Philippines
Asian Spirit
Cebu Pacific
45 Seair
46 Philippine Airlines
48 Domestic Airport
51 Pacific Airways
56 NAIA Terminal 3
57 NAIA Terminal 2
Philippine Airlines
59 Ninoy Aquino International Airport - NAIA Terminal 1

Places to Stay

3 Century Park Hotel
5 Orchid Garden Suites
9 Traders Hotel
17 Networld Hotel
18 Atrium Hotel
21 The Westin Philippine Plaza Hotel
29 Lemuria Inn
31 Hyatt Regency
33 Kabayan Hotel
35 The Heritage Hotel
36 Copacabana Apartment Hotel
37 Rotonda Hotel
42 Hotel Carlston
47 Manila International Youth Hostel
50 The Townhouse
54 Euro Apartment

Places to Eat & Entertainment

11 Gloriamaris Shark's Fin Restaurant
32 Edsa International Entertainment Complex
41 Seaside Market
44 Lin-Lu Restaurant
Maranaw Restaurant
49 Entertainment Complex

Miscellaneous

1 Manila Yacht Club
2 Harrison Plaza
4 Central Bank
Metropolitan Museum of Manila
5 Vietnamese Embassy
6 Legaspi Towers
8 Cultural Center
10 Folk Arts Theater
12 Coconut Palace
13 Star City (Star Theater)
14 Ballet Manila Office
Manila Sanitarium & Hospital
15 Philcite Trade Center
16 International Convention Center
22 Amazing Philippine Theater
Manila Film Center
23 World Trade Center
24 Cartimar Market
25 GSIS Building
Museo ng Sining
26 Philippine National Bank (PNB)
27 Cuneta Astrodome
28 Pasay Market
30 Japanese Embassy
40 Baclaran Church
41 Seaside Market
52 Post Office
53 Coastal Mall
55 Villamore Air Base
58 Duty Free Shop

flowers and household goods are on sale. The busiest time is on Wednesday, when crowds of churchgoers come looking for bargains after mass. Watch out for pickpockets at this time too.

Cartimar Market, A Luna St, Pasay City could be compared to the Divisoria Market mentioned below, although it's quite a bit smaller and easier to find your way around. This is just the place for you if you're looking for a pet.

Central Market, Quezon Blvd, Santa Cruz. A big market hall full of clothing and accessories such as T-shirts, bags and shoes.

Divisoria Market, Santo Cristo St and the side streets nearby, San Nicolas. It is a bright, lively market where examples of almost everything produced in the Philippines (except handicrafts) are sold at reasonable prices. There is a good vegetable and fruit section. Watch out for pickpockets here!

Quinta Market, Carlos Palanca St, Quiapo is also called the Santa Cruz or Quiapo Market. It takes place at the Quezon Bridge, near Quiapo Church, and sells textiles, household goods and many other things. A broad selection of handicrafts are sold in the Ilalim ng Tulay Market under the bridge.

San Andres Market, San Andres St, Malate, has a wide range of top-quality tropical fruit. Perhaps the best and certainly the most expensive fruit market in Manila, it is also open at night.

Shopping Centres

Araneta Center, Edsa corner Aurora Blvd, Cubao. There are nearly 2000 speciality stores in this moderately priced shopping centre around the Araneta Coliseum, including lots of shoe shops (Marikina Shoe Expo etc), 12 department stores (SM, Rustan's Superstore etc), 200 restaurants (McDonald's, Shakey's etc), 21 cinemas (Ali Mall Theaters, the New Frontier Cinema etc), 38 banks and the Farmers' Market, with its wide palettes heaped with reliably fresh farm produce and seafood.

Ayala Center, Makati. A modern shopping district between Ayala Ave, Makati Ave, Pasay Rd and Edsa. There is plenty to choose from, including imported

Places to Stay
- 9 Manila Galleria Suites
- 12 Discovery Suites
- 20 Edsa Shangri-La
- 22 Richville Hotel
- 24 The Richmonde Hotel
- 26 Horizon Edsa Hotel
- 27 The Legend Hotel

Places to Eat & Entertainment
- 2 Bistro Lorenzo
- 3 Gloriamaris Seafood Restaurant
- 4 Music Museum
- 13 McDonald's
- 14 Chateau 1771
  Tequila Joe's
  TGI Friday's

Miscellaneous
- 1 Camp Crame
- 4 Greenhills Shopping Center
- 5 Cardinal Santos Hospital
- 6 Wack-Wack Golf & Country Club
- 7 Statue of Our Lady of Edsa
- 8 Robinsons Galleria
- 10 Asian Development Bank
- 11 SM Megamall
- 13 St Francis Square
- 15 Taipan Place Building
  British Council
- 16 Metrobank
- 17 Star Mall
- 18 San Miguel Corporation
- 19 Lopez Memorial Museum
- 21 Shangri-La Plaza Mall
- 23 Edsa Central Mall
- 25 Philsports Arena (Ultra Stadium)

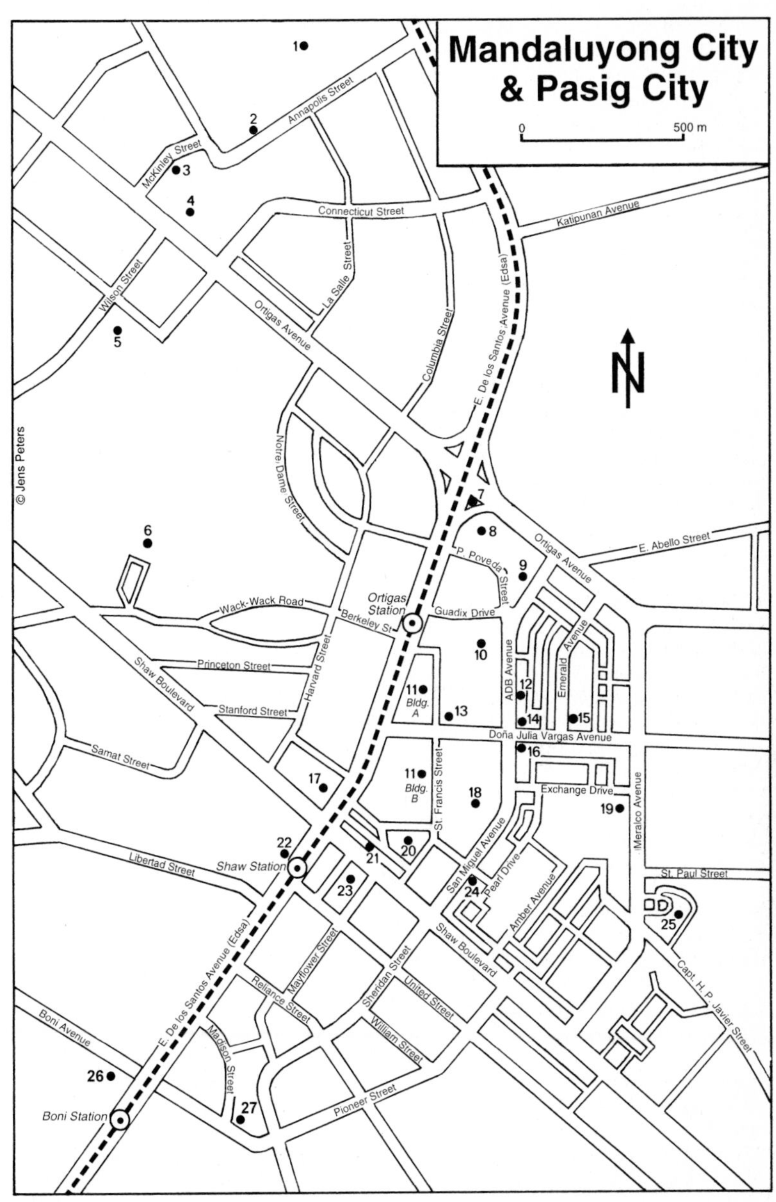
Mandaluyong City & Pasig City
0
500 m
© Jens Peters
Annapolis Street
McKinley Street
Connecticut Street
Katipunan Avenue
La Salle Street
Wilson Street
Ortigas Avenue
Columbia Street
E. De los Santos Avenue (Edsa)
Notre Dame Street
P. Poveda Street
E. Abello Street
Wack-Wack Road
Ortigas Station
Guadix Drive
Berkeley St.
ADB Avenue
Emerald Avenue
Princeton Street
Harvard Street
Shaw Boulevard
Stanford Street
Bldg. A
Doña Julia Vargas Avenue
Samat Street
St. Francis Street
Bldg. B
Exchange Drive
Meralco Avenue
San Miguel Avenue
Pearl Drive
Libertad Street
Shaw Station
St. Paul Street
Amber Avenue
Mayflower Street
Sheridan Street
United Street
Reliance Street
Capt. H. P. Javier Street
William Street
Boni Avenue
Madison Street
Pioneer Street
Boni Station
Manila

goods, and some good bookshops. Restaurants and rest areas are interspersed among the shops. The best department stores in Makati are probably SM Shoemart, The Landmark and Rustan's, all in the Ayala Center.

Other shopping centres in Makati are the ***Atrium of Makati*** (Atrium Shopping Mall) in Makati Ave, ***Makati Cinema Square*** between Chino Rocos Ave and Amorsolo Sts and ***Greenbelt*** between Makati Ave and Paseo de Roxas.

Greenhills Shopping Center, Ortigas Ave, San Juan, has a large selection of restaurants, a supermarket, several cinemas and banks, as well as spotless arcades with small, elegant boutiques. All of this is housed in a pleasant complex.

Harrison Plaza, Harrison St, Malate, has many different shops and restaurants under one roof. Rustan's has a good bakery department.

Robinsons Place, Adriatico Street, Ermita, is a big shopping complex with a fine selection of shops, several restaurants and cinemas.

Robinsons Galleria, Ortigas Ave corner Edsa, Mandaluyong City, features several floors of shops and a wide selection of restaurants.

SM Megamall, Edsa, Mandaluyong City. Giant shopping centre with a huge variety of shops, over 200 restaurants and even an ice-skating rink; ice skates are available for rent. It's a popular place to 'see and be seen' at. The SM group of companies also includes the ***SM Centerpoint*** on Aurora Blvd, Santa Mesa, the ***SM City*** and the ***SM City Annex***, Edsa corner North Ave, Quezon City.

Books & Maps

Bookmark, Greenbelt Dr, corner Makati Ave, Makati. This bookshop has relatively little popular literature, but all the more scientific works and books on the Philippines. They also sell magazines and stationery.

Namria, Barraca St, San Nicolas, has a wide selection of maps of all different scales, covering the Philippines but also including aeronautical and sailing maps. This is actually the former Bureau of Coast and Geodetic Survey which was renamed the National Mapping and Resource Information Authority (Namria for short). There is also a Namria in Lawton Ave in Fort Bonifacio in Makati (head office). Open Mon-Fri, 8am-noon and 1-5pm.

National Book Store, 701 Rizal Ave, Santa Cruz. The biggest, and best-stocked bookshop in the Philippines with branches in various areas of Metro Manila, for example in the Araneta Center in Cubao, and in the Harrison Plaza in Malate.

Solidaridad Book Shop, Padre Faura (between Mabini St and J Bocobo St), Ermita. 'An intellectual's delight' - with excellent sections on religion, philosophy, politics, poetry and fiction. This small, well-stocked bookshop specialises in scholarly publications, with an emphasis on Asia and the Philippines. Economics subjects and almanacs are also available.

Tradewinds Bookshop, El Almanecer Building, General Luna St, Intramuros, specialises in Philippine literature, history, art and culture. They also have a small selection of new and old maps.

Food

7-Eleven, Padre Faura corner Adriatico St, Ermita, is one of the many branches of these small convenience stores found all over Manila which offer fast shopping and are open 24 hours a day. There are three of them in Ermita alone.

Century Park Hotel Deli Snacks, P Ocampo St, Malate. You can buy, among other things, European specialities like bread and sausages. The entrance is on the Harrison Plaza side of the hotel.

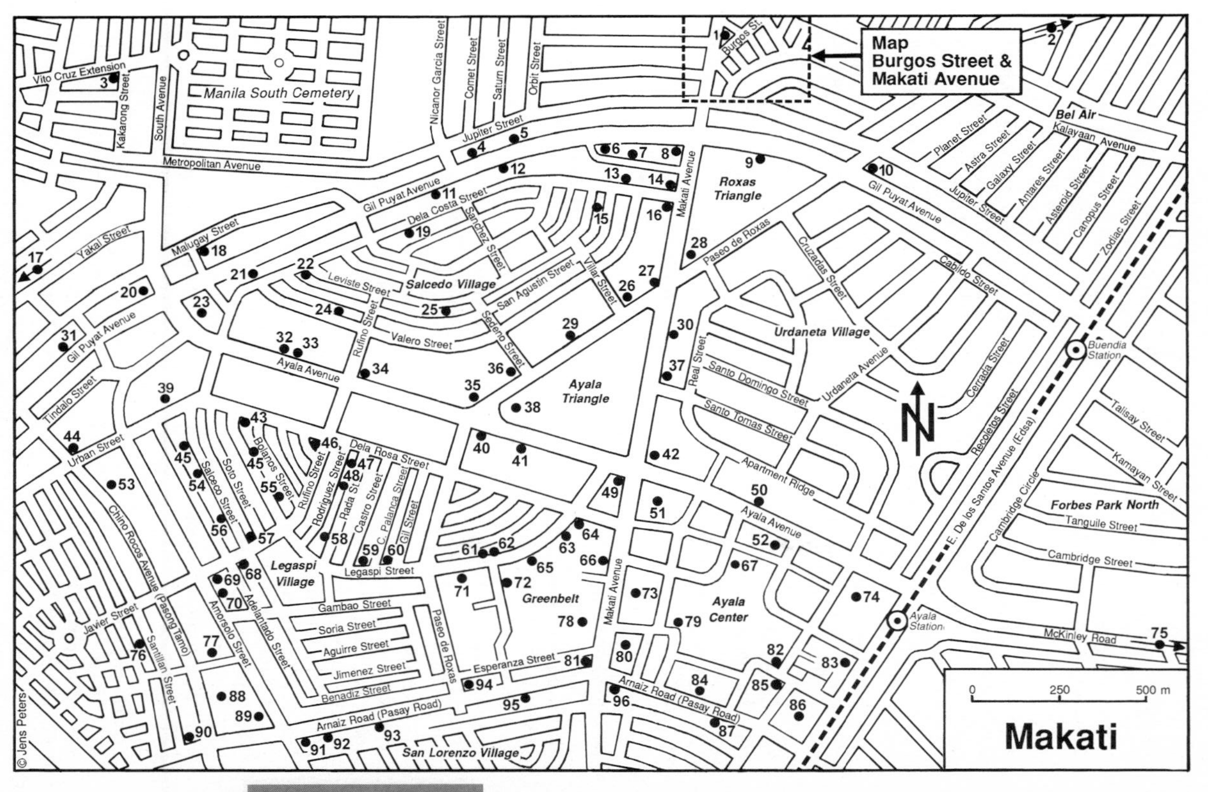
Map
Burgos Street &
Makati Avenue
Makati
0 250 500 m
Bel Air
Forbes Park North
Urdaneta Village
Roxas Triangle
Ayala Triangle
Ayala Center
Greenbelt
Salcedo Village
Legaspi Village
San Lorenzo Village
Manila South Cemetery
Buendia Station
Ayala Station
E. De los Santos Avenue (Edsa)
Gil Puyat Avenue
Makati Avenue
Ayala Avenue
Paseo de Roxas
Metropolitan Avenue
South Avenue
Chino Rocos Avenue (Pasong Tamo)
Arnaiz Road (Pasay Road)
McKinley Road
Kalayaan Avenue
Jupiter Street
Nicanor Garcia Street
Comet Street
Saturn Street
Orbit Street
Planet Street
Astra Street
Galaxy Street
Antares Street
Asteroid Street
Canopus Street
Zodiac Street
Cabildo Street
Cerrada Street
Recoletos Street
Cambridge Circle
Cambridge Street
Tanguile Street
Talisay Street
Kamayan Street
Cruzadas Street
Urdaneta Avenue
Santo Domingo Street
Santo Tomas Street
Real Street
Apartment Ridge
Villar Street
San Agustin Street
Sedeno Street
Sanchez Street
Dela Costa Street
Valero Street
Leviste Street
Rufino Street
Dela Rosa Street
Gil Street
C. Palanca Street
Castro Street
Rada St.
Rodriguez Street
Legaspi Street
Bolanos Street
Soto Street
Salceco Street
Adelantado Street
Amorsolo Street
Gambao Street
Soria Street
Aguirre Street
Jimenez Street
Benadiz Street
Esperanza Street
Santillan Street
Javier Street
Urban Street
Tindalo Street
Yakal Street
Malugay Street
Kakarong Street
Vito Cruz Extension
Burgos St.
© Jens Peters

Getting There & Away

2 Lufthansa
3 Budget
5 Saudi Arabian Airlines
8 Emirates
10 Avis
Royal Brunei Airlines
11 Malaysia Airlines
12 Thai Airways International
13 Cathay Pacific
15 KLM Royal Dutch Airlines
18 Swiss Air
19 Singapore Airlines
21 Air France
Asiana Airlines
22 Gulf Air
23 Egypt Airlines
25 Air India
Korean Air
27 CSA Czech Airlines
SAS
33 Eva Air
37 American Airlines
40 Air Canada
United Airlines
41 Continental Micronesia
43 British Airways
Qantas
45 Air Nuigini
51 Avis
55 Kuwait Airways
57 Aeroflot
59 Vietnam Airlines
60 Cebu Pacific
Qatar Airways
61 Philippine Airlines
62 Air Philippines
Asian Spirit
68 Northwest Airlines
70 Alitalia
80 Ayala Center Terminal
87 Seair

Places to Stay

1 Travelers Inn
28 Mandarin Oriental
42 The Peninsula Manila
50 The Gilarmi Apartments & Suites
51 The Makati Shangri-La
62 Charter House Apartelle
69 Amorsolo Mansion
74 Hotel Inter-Continental
76 Saint Illian's Hotel
81 New World Renaissance Hotel
86 Dusit Hotel Nikko
92 El Cielito Tourist Inn
93 Pensionne Virginia
95 The Copa Businessman's Hotel
96 Tower Inn

Places to Eat & Entertainment

30 Schwarzwälder
37 Old Swiss Inn Restaurant
44 Maxim's Tea House
63 Nandau Restaurant
64 Mario's
65 La Tasca Restaurant
67 Hard Rock Café
Studebaker's
77 Little Tokyo
78 Greenbelt 3
79 Kimpura Restaurant
84 Kowloon House
85 Jollibee
Pizza Hut
Wendy's
86 Paulaner Bräuhaus
90 Kamayan Restaurant
91 Racks Bistro
92 Probinsiya Restaurant
93 Goldilocks Bake Shop
Kashmir Restaurant
94 El Comedor Restaurant
L'Opera Restaurant

Banks

9 Metrobank
14 Equitable PCI Bank
24 Diners Club International
26 Citibank
29 Equitable PCI Bank Building
31 Thomas Cook Travel
35 Bank of America
38 Deutsche Bank

40 Hongkong & Shanghai Banking Corporation (HSBC)
47 American Express
56 Equitable PCI Bank

Embassies

6 Norwegian Embassy
7 Finland Embassy
New Zealand Embassy
8 French Embassy
Taiwanese Embassy (Teco Office)
13 Korean Embassy
14 Swedish Embassy
23 Australian Embassy
Canadian Embassy
German Embassy
29 Swiss Embassy
32 Belgian Embassy
34 Danish Embassy
45 Indonesian Embassy
48 Thai Embassy
49 UK Embassy
53 Dutch Embassy
54 Italian Embassy
58 Austrian Embassy

Shopping

3 Scuba World
17 Säntis Delicatessen
18 Zuellig Wine & Spirits
31 Atrium Shopping Mall
52 Rustan's Department Store
71 Greenbelt Mall
73 The Landmark Department Store
77 Makati Supermarket
82 National Book Store
83 SM Department Store

Buildings

4 ITC Building
5 Metro House
6 Petron Mega Plaza Building
7 BPI Buendia Center
8 Pacific Star Building
9 Metrobank Plaza Building
10 Saville Building
11 Country Space I Building
13 Travalgar Plaza
14 Equitable PCI Bank Tower II
15 Athenaeum Building
16 Equitable PCI Bank Tower I
21 Alcedo Tower
Trident Tower
23 RCBC Plaza
24 LPL Plaza
Philam Life Building
30 Atrium of Makati
31 Skyland Plaza Building
32 Multinational Bancorporation Center
33 LKG Tower
34 PBCom Tower
35 Philamlife Tower
36 PS Bank Center
37 Olympia Condominium
38 Ayala Tower I
40 The Enterprise Center
41 SGV Building
45 Fortune Building
46 Medical Towers Makati
47 ACE Building
49 Locsin Building
53 King's Court Building
54 Zeta II Building
55 Jaka II Building
57 YL Holding Building
60 Colonnade Building
68 La Paz Centre
72 New Garden Square
88 Makati Cinema Square
89 Sunvar Plaza

Miscellaneous

2 Rockwell Center
13 Blue Horizons Travel & Tours
20 Makati Central Post Office
23 General Carlos P Romulo Theater
39 Makati Medical Center
46 GP Dr Peter Kaliski
66 Ayala Museum
75 American Cemetery & Memorial

Säntis Delicatessen, 7431 Yakal St, Makati, Makati, Tel 8441154, offers a wide range of European delicacies such as cheeses, cold meats, ham, smoked goods, olives and much more.

Photo Requisites

Mayer Photo, Carlos Palanca St, Quiapo. In the author's opinion, this is the place for the best value films in Manila. There are other, inexpensive photo shops like Avenue and Mega Colours just round the corner in Hidalgo St.

Travel Equipment & Outdoor Gear

Bombproof Gear, Robinsons Galleria, 3rd Level, Edsa corner Ortigas Ave, Pasig City, Tel 6341760.
Habagat, SM Megamall, Ground Floor A, Mandaluyong City, Tel 6375492.
Mike's Outdoor Shop, Park Square 1, Ground Floor, Ayala Center, Makati, Tel 8128384.

Diving Equipment

Aquaventure Philippines, 7805 St Paul St corner Mayapis St, San Antonio Village, Makati, Tel 8992831, Fax 8992551, @.
Dive Buddies, Robelle Mansion, 877 JP Rizal St, Makati, Tel 8997388, Fax 8997393.
Dive Shoppe, Constancia Building, 71 Timog Ave, Quezon City, Tel 9212020.
Scuba World, 1181 Vito Cruz Extension corner Kakarong St, Makati, Tel 8953551, Fax 8908982.
Whitetip Divers, Joncor II Building, 1362 Mabini St, Ermita, Tel 5210433, Fax 5221165.

Souvenirs

Silahis, General Luna St, Intramuros. Wide selection of art handicrafts from all over the country (quite expensive). Located in the El Amanecer Compound; above it you'll find the Chang Rong Antique Gallery and the Galeria de las Islas for paintings and sculptures.

Places to Stay

All over Metro Manila there's a wide range of accommodation on offer and it shouldn't be too hard to find something to suit you. Having said that, there are certain areas where the variety of hotels means they are especially well equipped to cater for the needs of any guests.

Binondo & Santa Cruz

Just north of the Pasig River is the old business centre of Manila. Many of the long established shops and trading houses can no longer hide the outward signs of their advancing years, but they have also gained in character compared with some of the glitzy, modern boutiques you see. In spite of the giant new shopping malls in other parts of the city, Binondo with its Chinatown and Santa Cruz with its shopping street 'Avenida' (Rizal Ave) are still very popular areas. But very few foreign visitors stay overnight around here, and the choice of hotels is limited.

Ermita, Malate & Paco

Ermita and Malate are particular favourites with visitors from all over the world. Consequently, everything needed to provide services to these visitors is also available here: from inexpensive accommodation to the finest hotels, restaurants, shops, travel agents, moneychangers, you name it. The area may not be crowded with travellers like Khao San Rd in Bangkok, but that's not necessarily a bad thing. In the last few years Malate has become a favourite with those in the know, and the wide selection of pubs, music bars and bistros is especially popular with better-off Filipinos.

Makati

To put it simply, Makati equals business. It has it all: stereotypical skyscrapers filled with banks, embassies and offices, big international hotels with little oases nestled in between them, and streets filled with the finest restaurants. This is the new Manila, the pride and joy of many Filipinos.

Mandaluyong City & Pasig City
This is another showcase area that Manila is proud of, especially along the Edsa (roughly between Pasig River and Ortigas Ave), the northern part of which is called Ortigas Center, with its big shopping centres. There are not many hotels here, but if you find one, it almost definitely belongs to the upmarket category. The only problem if you stay here is that you have to put up with the politically incorrect question: "Where in Mandaluyong, inside or outside?" The explanation can be found in the Philippine National Mental Hospital, the biggest and best known psychiatric clinic in the country.

Parañaque & Pasay City
South of Malate you come to Pasay City, with its important cultural and sports facilities such as the Cultural Center of the Philippines, the Folk Arts Theater, Cuneta Astrodome and Jai-alai de Manila, as well as a few important bus terminals. Neighbouring Parañaque is home to the Ninoy Aquino International Airport (NAIA) and the Domestic Airport. In addition to the wide selection of inexpensive motels, especially in Pasay City, there is accommodation to suit every budget here.

Quezon City
Quezon City, in the north-east of Metro Manila, is the location of dozens of state offices and headquarters of various national organisations. The University of the Philippines (UP) can also be found here, as well as several respected hospitals and a few impressive shopping centres. Along the Edsa in the Cubao district, almost all of the big bus companies have their own terminals.

Saving Money
Several hotels offer up to 40% discount off the regular published rates in the off-season from June till September. Others offer special rates now and then (promo rates), so it's worth asking if they have any available. Filipinos and resident foreigners pay a special rate at many five-star hotels. One method available to every traveller is to book rooms via a local travel agent who can offer rates at first-class international hotels up to 50% cheaper. A good example would be Marsman Tours & Travel, Marsman-Dyrsdale Building, 2246 Chino Roces Ave, Makati, Tel (02) 8921817, Fax 8156228, @. Online reservations are another way of staying within your travel budget, eg with Asia Travel:
www.asiatravel.com/philippines.html

Places to Stay - bottom end

Binondo & Santa Cruz
First Hotel, Ongpin St, Binondo, Tel 2431855, Fax 2440326. SR/ac/bath P650, DR/ac/bath P750 and P800. Reasonable, fairly clean rooms with TV.

Ermita, Malate & Paco
Friendly's Guest House, Adriatico St corner Nakpil St, Malate, Cellphone 0917-3331418. Dorm/ac 250 P, EZ/DZ/fan 350, 420 und 470 P. Basic, but neat and clean accommodation on the 4th floor. Free use of kitchen. Cosy guest lounge with balcony (beautiful view).
Stone House Hotel, 1529 Mabini St, Ermita, Tel 5240302. SR/fan P250, SR/DR/fan P450, SR/DR/ac/bath P800 and P1000. Nice, well-kept rooms of different sizes, the aircon ones with TV. Restaurant.
Mabini Pension, 1337 Mabini St, Tel 5245404, Fax 5234213. SR/DR/fan

from map page 162

© Jens Peters

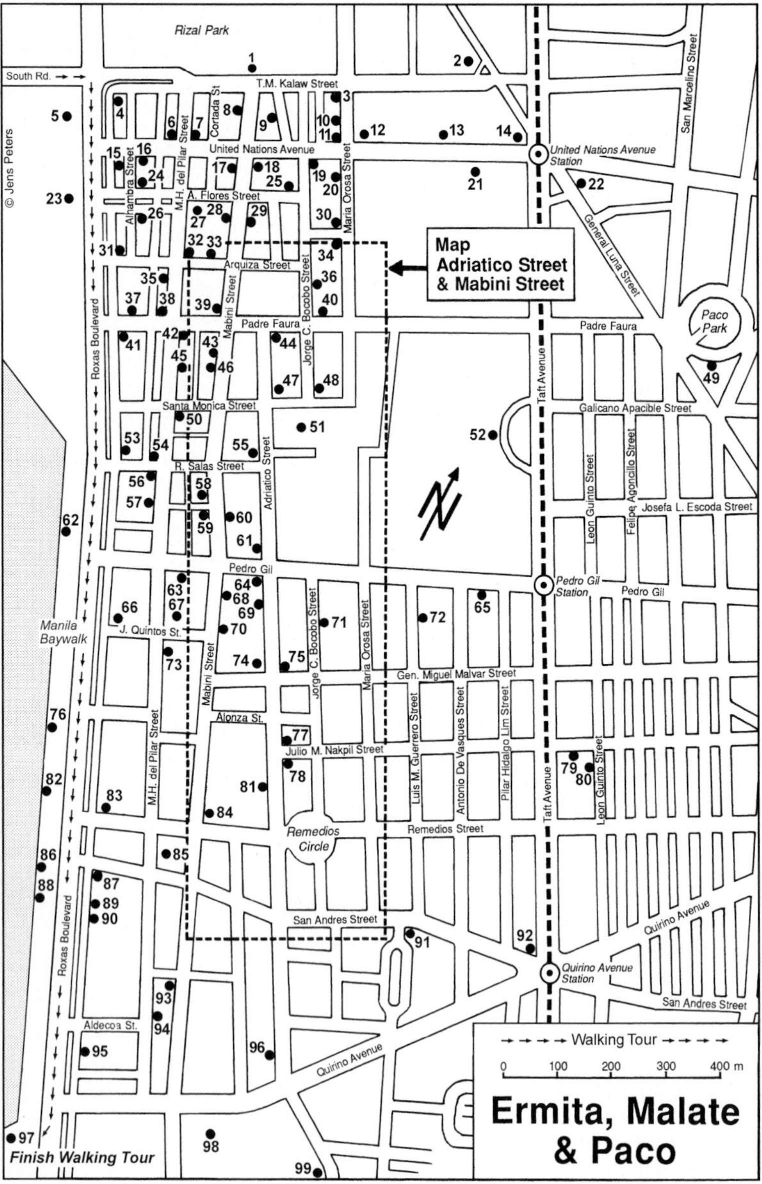

Rizal Park

South Rd.

T.M. Kalaw Street

United Nations Avenue

A. Flores Street

Arquiza Street

Padre Faura

Santa Monica Street

R. Salas Street

Pedro Gil

J. Quintos St.

Gen. Miguel Malvar Street

Alonza St.

Julio M. Nakpil Street

Remedios Street

Remedios Circle

San Andres Street

Quirino Avenue

Aldecoa St.

Alhambra Street

M.H. del Pilar Street

Cortada St

Mabini Street

Jorge C. Bocobo Street

Maria Orosa Street

Adriatico Street

Luis M. Guerrero Street

Antonio De Vasques Street

Pilar Hidalgo Lim Street

Taft Avenue

Leon Guinto Street

Felipe Agoncillo Street

San Marcelino Street

General Luna Street

Galicano Apacible Street

Josefa L. Escoda Street

Paco Park

United Nations Avenue Station

Pedro Gil Station

Quirino Avenue Station

Roxas Boulevard

Manila Baywalk

Finish Walking Tour

Map Adriatico Street & Mabini Street

Walking Tour

0 100 200 300 400 m

Ermita, Malate & Paco

Manila

Getting There & Away
4 Avis
6 Gulf Air
14 WG & A
17 WG & A
41 China Airlines
Northwest Airlines
Thai Airways International
42 Air Philippines
43 Si-Kat Ferry
44 Philippine Airlines
60 WG & A (Filipino Travel Center)

Places to Stay
3 The Corporate Inn Hotel
8 Mabini Mansion
9 San Carlos Mansion
12 Manila Pavillon Hotel
15 Bayview Park Hotel
24 Swagman Hotel
25 Hotel Soriente
26 Celestine Citadel Hotel
29 City Garden Hotel
32 Hotel La Corona
Rosas Garden Hotel
33 Yasmin Apartelle
34 Ralph Anthony Suites
36 Tropical Mansion Hotel
37 Golden Bay Hotel
38 Iseya Hotel
39 Lotus Garden Hotel
40 Midtown Inn
43 Citystate Tower Hotel
46 Mabini Pension
47 Midland Plaza
48 Cherry Blossoms Hotel
49 The Garden Plaza Hotel
Park Hotel
53 Boulevard Mansion
55 Casa Blanca I
58 Stone House Hotel
59 Ermita Tourist Inn
60 Hotel Frendy
63 Sheraton Marina Square Hotel
64 Palm Plaza Hotel
65 Hotel Kimberly
66 Manila Diamond Hotel
67 Marina Richmonde Hotel
68 Las Palmas Hotel
69 Rothman Hotel
70 Executive Plaza Hotel
Riviera Mansion
71 Manila Manor Hotel
72 Tropicana Apartment Hotel
73 Pension Natividad
74 The Pan Pacific Hotel
75 Dakota Mansion
77 Adriatico Arms Hotel
78 Friendl'y Guest House
80 New Solanie Hotel
81 Malate Pensionne
89 Grand Boulevard Hotel
90 Euro-Nippon Mansion
93 Ambassador Hotel
95 Aloha Hotel
96 Bianca's Garden Hotel

Places to Eat & Entertainment
7 Dragon Noodle Center
May Sum Seafood Restaurant
Maxim's Tea House
10 KFC
11 McDonald's
16 Barrio Fiesta
18 Speedy Bar
20 Max's
24 Swagman Outback Café
30 Barrio Fiesta
31 Emerald Garden Restaurant
35 Duck Inn
38 Iseya Restaurant
Rooftop Restaurant
45 Guernica's
Juri's
49 Old Swiss Inn Restaurant
50 Amazonia
54 LA Café
56 Jurassic Bar
57 Jerusalem Restaurant
Red Sea Bar & Restaurant
62 Lami Barbecue
Yakitori Dori
76 Anthrology by the Sea
79 Sala-Thai

82 Café Adriatico by the Sea	24 Swagman Travel
83 Max's, Shakey's	25 Value Point Supermarket
86 Pinoy Fiesta by the Bay	27 Ermita Church
87 Aristocrat	28 Metrobank
88 Koryo House Grill	49 Mr Ticket
Red Cup Café	51 Robinsons Place
94 Endangered Species Café Bar	52 Philippine General Hospital
	61 Filipino Travel Center
Miscellaneous	84 Adventure International Tours
1 National Library	American Express
2 Tourist Office	85 Malate Church
5 Museo Pambata	89 Casino Filipino
13 Manila Doctors Hospital	91 San Andres Market
19 Equitable PCI Bank	92 Interisland Travel & Tours
21 Western Police Station	97 Manila Yacht Club
22 Manila Medical Center	98 Manila Zoo
23 US Embassy	99 Jai-alai de Manila

P500, SR/DR/fan/bath P550, SR/DR/ac/bath P850. Basic rooms with different kinds of furnishings. They will arrange air tickets and visa extensions and will also look after left luggage.

Pension Natividad, 1690 MH del Pilar St, Malate, Tel 5210524, Fax 5223759. Dorm/fan P280, SR/DR/fan P600 and P680, SR/DR/fan/bath P780, SR/DR/ac/bath P980. Good, well-kept rooms. This pension is a sort of oasis in this sometimes hectic city. You can enjoy a relaxing escape from the chaos all around; also, unlike in most of the other pension houses, you can sit outside. There's a pleasant atmosphere in this well-run place. They have a coffee shop and will look after left luggage.

Malate Pensionne, 1771 Adriatico St, Malate, Tel 5238304, Fax 5222389, @. Dorm/fan P250, SR/DR/fan PP550, SR/DR/fan/bath P850, SR/DR/ac/bath P1050 to P1300. Immaculate, well-kept rooms, the aircon ones with TV and some have a refrigerator. Popular place to stay (good idea to make a reservation). Beautiful little garden and restaurant. Lockers are available for rent. They will look after left luggage for P25 per day, and the airport service costs P300.

Ermita Tourist Inn, 1549 Mabini St corner Soldado St, Ermita, Tel 5218770, Fax 5218773. SR/DR/ac/bath P660/720, including breakfast. Reasonable rooms, although those overlooking Mabini St are more than a bit loud. Restaurant. Travel agency.

Yasmin Apartelle, Arquiza St, Ermita, Tel 5245134, Fax 5217225. SR/DR/ac/bath P700. A quiet building with OK rooms, all with TV and refrigerator. Really good value.

Iseya Hotel, 1241 MH del Pilar St corner Padre Faura, Ermita, Tel 5238166, Fax 5262778, @. SR/DR/ac/bath P1100. Quite good rooms with refrigerator and TV. Problem is, it's located at a busy traffic junction, so ask for the quiet rooms. Restaurant.

Rosas Garden Hotel, 1140 MH del Pilar St, Ermita, Tel 4041622, Fax 5220281, @. SR/DR/ac/bath P1300 to P1850; including breakfast. Good rooms of different sizes, all with TV, the more expensive ones also have a refrigerator. Coffee Shop.

Makati

Durban St Inn, 4875 Durban St, Tel 8971866-68, Fax 8954838, @. SR/DR/

Manila

ac/bath P800 (small, cold water), P900 (small) and P1000 (good value). Clean, acceptable rooms with refrigerator and TV.

680 Apartelle, 5021 Burgos St, Tel 8968898, Fax: 8971963. SR/DR/ac/bath P1000. All right, but slightly ageing rooms with TV, refrigerator and cooking facilities. Located next to the Mascara Bar. Entrance through the grocery store (open 24 hrs) to the lift.

Pensionne Virginia, 816 Pasay Rd, Tel 8445228, Fax 8932243. SR/ac/bath P1050, DR/ac/bath P1540. Well-kept, quiet rooms with refrigerator and TV. Pleasant atmosphere.

Robelle House, 4402 Valdez St, Tel 8998061, Fax 8998064. SR/ac/bath P1100, DR/ac/bath P1225, suite P1450. Quiet, reasonable rooms with TV. An older hotel with a pleasant, real Philippine feeling. Restaurant, swimming pool.

Inn Suites Hotel, 5012 Burgos St, Tel 8972053, Fax 8971965, @. SR/DR/ac/bath P1200 and P1500. With refrigerator and TV. The stairway is lined with posters of late, great stars like Marilyn Monroe, James Dean and Elvis. Pleasant little hotel with well-furnished rooms. Their delightful restaurant-bar, the Filling Station, is open 24 hours.

Saint Illian's Inn, 7461 Santillan St, Tel 8930754, @. SR/DR/ac/bath P1350 and P1750. Good, quiet rooms, if a bit small, all with TV. Coffee shop.

Parañaque & Pasay City

Manila International Youth Hostel, 4227 Tomas Claudio St, Parañaque, Tel 8320680, Fax 8187948. Dorm P180, YHA members P150. Tidy place with a garden. Cooking facilities are available. Located next to the Excelsior Building, on Roxas Blvd corner Tomas Claudio St.

The Townhouse Hotel, Villa Carolina Townhouse, 201 Roxas Blvd, Unit 31, Parañaque, Tel 8543826, Fax 8040161, @. Dorm/fan P180, SR/DR/fan P300 and P500, SR/DR/fan/bath P550 and P700, DR/ac/bath P950 (TV). Weekly rates can be arranged. There is also a good and inexpensive restaurant. Pleasant place, with a friendly atmosphere created by Bill and Lorna, who like travelling themselves. Located in a small side street called Bayview Drive almost at the corner of Roxas Blvd, only about five minutes by taxi from the Domestic Airport and NAIA.

Rotonda Hotel, 2921 Taft Ave, Pasay City, Tel 8316504, Fax 8317614. SR/DR/fan/bath P310. Also available for three hours (P100) and 10 hours (P170) A basic place with simply furnished, practical rooms, OK for the money. Conveniently located near the Edsa and Taft Stations and various bus terminals.

Lemuria Inn, 350-C Protacio St, Pasay City, Tel 8311417, Fax 8319167, @. SR/DR/fan P400, SR/DR/ac/bath P800. Small, basically furnished rooms. Friendly, Swiss run place with coffee shop and garden. Also accessible from Zamora St.

Hotel Carlston, Airport Rd corner Roxas Blvd, Parañaque, Tel. 8321167. SR/DR/fan/bath P850, SR/DR/ac/bath P1200 (with TV). Some rooms are a little run-down. Conveniently located for the Domestic Airport. Restaurant, disco.

Places to Stay - middle

Binondo & Santa Cruz

Binondo Suites, Ongpin St corner Sabino Padilla St, Binondo, Tel 7366501, Fax 7365780, @. SR/DR/ac/bath P1330 to P2400, suite P2550 to P4800, including breakfast. Well-appointed, spacious rooms with TV, the more expensive ones also have a refrigerator. Clean and tidy hotel in the heart of Chinatown. Restaurant.

Ermita, Malate & Paco

Bianca's Garden Hotel, 2139 Adriatico St, Malate, Tel & Fax 5260351. SR/DR/fan P800, SR/DR/ac/bath P1800 and P2000 with TV. Formerly known as the True Home Hotel, it is a beautiful building, which you might not expect in this poorer looking part of Adriatico. Tastefully furnished rooms. All rooms have a different decor, and there is a restaurant and swimming pool.

Hotel Soriente, 545 A Flores St corner J Bocobo St, Ermita, Tel 5257304, Fax 5223913. SR/DR/ac/bath P1000. Good rooms with TV. Directly above the Value Point Supermarket.

Park Hotel, 1032-34 Belen St, Paco, Tel 5212371-75, Fax 5212393, @. SR/DR/ac/bath P1200 to P2200, suite P3000. Excellent rooms with refrigerator and TV. Suites with jacuzzi. Restaurant, swimming pool, airport service.

Citystate Tower Hotel, 1315 Mabini St, Ermita, Tel 4007351, Fax 5262758, @. SR/DR/ac/bath P1250 to P1850, suite P2500, all including breakfast. Good rooms, all right for the money, with refrigerator and TV. Restaurant. Located near the corner of Padre Faura.

Cherry Blossoms Hotel, 550 J Bocobo St, Ermita, Tel 5247631, Fax 5224172, @. SR/DR/ac/bath P1250 to P1860, suite P1915 and P3025, all including breakfast. Immaculate rooms with TV, the more expensive ones also have a refrigerator. Well-kept hotel in a quiet location. Coffee shop.

Rothman Inn Hotel, 1633 Adriatico St, Malate, Tel 5234501, Fax 5222606, @. SR/DR/ac/bath P1275 and P1350. Good rooms with TV and refrigerator. Restaurant.

Hotel Frendy, 1548 Mabini St, Ermita, Tel 5264211, Fax 5264213. SR/DR/ac/bath P1300 to P1900, suite P2500, including breakfast. Well-kept, friendly, spacious rooms with refrigerator and TV. Restaurant.

Lotus Garden Hotel, 1227 Mabini St corner Padre Faura, Ermita, Tel 5221515, Fax 5220768, @. SR/ac/bath P1300 to P1900, DR/ac/bath P1500 to P2100, including breakfast. Good rooms of different sizes with refrigerator and TV; the new ones facing Mabini St are fairly loud. Restaurant.

Riviera Mansion, 1638 Mabini St, Malate, Tel 5234511, Fax 5222606. SR/DR/ac/bath P1350 to P1800, suite P2625. Monthly rates available (25% discount). Cosy, pleasantly decorated rooms with TV, the more expensive ones also have a kitchen. Coffee shop.

The Garden Plaza, 1030 Belen St, Paco (near Paco Park), Tel 5224835, Fax 5224840, @. SR/DR/ac/bath P1400 to P2350, suite P3200 and P4200. Comfortable, spacious rooms with refrigerator and TV. The more expensive ones have cooking facilities. Restaurant, swimming pool.

Palm Plaza Hotel, Pedro Gil corner Adriatico St, Malate, Tel 5221000, Fax 5258013, @. SR/DR/ac/bath P1500, including breakfast. Weekly and monthly rates available. Well-kept hotel with comfortable rooms, all with refrigerator and TV. Restaurant, swimming pool.

Las Palmas Hotel, 1616 Mabini St, Malate, Tel 5211000, Fax 5236917, @. SR/DR/ac/bath P1500 to P2000. An older place, but attractively renovated. The rooms are comfortable and all have refrigerator and TV. Restaurant, swimming pool.

Hotel La Corona, 1166 MH del Pilar St, Ermita, Tel 5242631-38, Fax 5213909, @. SR/DR/ac/bath P1500, suite P2800 and P3500, breakfast included. With refrigerator and TV; the suites with jacuzzi. The rooms on to MH del Pilar St are quite loud. A well-run, clean and tidy hotel. Restaurant.

Adriatico Arms Hotel, J Nakpil St corner Adriatico St, Malate, Tel 5210736, Fax 5256214. SR/DR/ac/bath P1500 and P1800. Small hotel with well-kept rooms, all with TV and some with refrigerator. Coffee shop.

Swagman Hotel, A Flores St, Ermita, Tel 5238541-45, Fax 5223663, @. SR/DR/ac/bath P1500 to P2270, including one breakfast. All rooms with refrigerator and TV. There is a 24-hour restaurant, airport service, and a bus leaves three times a day for Angeles. This hotel is a favourite with the Aussies.

New Solanie Hotel, 1811 Leon Guinto St, Malate, Tel 5248641, Fax 5248647, @. SR/DR/ac/bath P1530 to P2050. A quiet place to stay. All rooms have refrigerator and TV, and the more expensive ones have cooking facilities. Coffee shop.

Executive Plaza Hotel, 1630 Mabini St, Malate, Tel 5231000, Fax 5258979, @. SR/DR/ac/bath P1600 to P2000. Well-appointed rooms with refrigerator and TV. Restaurant.

Aloha Hotel, 2150 Roxas Blvd, Malate, Tel 5268088, Fax 5215328 (@). SR/DR/ac/bath P1650 and P1875. Cosy, inviting rooms with TV, the more expensive ones have a view of Manila Bay. Restaurant.

Orchid Garden Suites, 620 P Ocampo St, Malate, Tel 5239870, Fax 5239829, @. SR/DR/ac/bath P1800 and P2200, suite P2500 and P3000. Well-kept, pleasantly furnished rooms with refrigerator and TV, the suites also with a kitchen. Restaurant, swimming pool. (Can be found on the Parañaque & Pasay City map.)

City Garden Hotel, 1158 Mabini St, Ermita, Tel 5361451, Fax 5244844, @. SR/DR/ac/bath P1870 to P2970. With refrigerator and TV. Pleasant rooms in an immaculately run hotel; they are often fully booked. Restaurant.

Hotel Kimberly, 770 Pedro Gil, Malate, Tel 5211888, Fax 5267270, @. SR/ac/bath P1870 to P2640, DR/ac/bath P1990 to P2860, suite P3400. Good hotel with tidy rooms, all with TV, some also with cooking facilities. Restaurant, fitness room, sauna.

Makati

Oka Hotel, 8459 Kalayaan Ave, Tel 8902014, Fax 8902077. SR/ac/bath P1330, DR/ac/bath P1500 and P1800. Friendly rooms with refrigerator and TV. Conveniently located for Burgos St.

El Cielito Tourist Inn, 804 Pasay Rd, Tel 8158951, Fax 8179610, @. SR/DZ/ac/bath P1500 and P1900, suite P2375 (with refrigerator). A pleasant, very clean place with a restaurant and a coffee shop. The staff are friendly.

Tower Inn, 1002 Pasay Rd, Tel 8885170, Fax 8434837, @. SR/ac/bath P1500, DR/ac/bath P2100 and P2400, suite P2800. Well-kept, pleasantly furnished rooms with TV, the more expensive ones also have a refrigerator. Restaurant, roof garden with whirlpool.

Millenium Plaza Hotel, Makati Ave corner Eduque St, Makati, Tel 8994718, Fax 8994755. SR/DR/ac/bath P1800 and P3260, suite P3625, including breakfast. Elegant, attractive rooms. Restaurant, swimming pool, sauna.

Sunette Tower Hotel, Durban St, Tel 8971804, Fax 8966407. SR/DR/ac/bath P1850 to P2750. Comfortably furnished rooms with TV, refrigerator and small kitchen. Only a few steps away from Makati Ave.

Century Citadel Inn Makati, 5007 Burgos St, Makati, Tel 8972370, Fax 8972666, @. SR/DR/ac/bath from P1950, including breakfast (normally from P3000, but this offer seems to have been extended indefinitely). Friendly, neat rooms with TV, refrigerator and small kitchen. Swimming pool.

Astor Hotel, Makati Ave corner Eduque St, Tel 7507564, Fax 7506783, @. SR/DR/ac/bath P2250 and P2500, suite P5200. All including breakfast. Well-kept, comfortably furnished rooms

with refrigerator and TV. Restaurant, swimming pool.
City Garden Hotel Makati, Makati Ave corner Durban St, Tel 8991111, Fax 8991415, @. SR/ac/bath P2320 to P2650, DR/ac/bath P2540 to P2870. Well-maintained, nicely decorated rooms with refrigerator and TV. Coffee shop, swimming pool.

Mandaluyong City & Pasig City
Horizon Edsa Hotel, 778 Boni Ave, Mandaluyong City, Tel 5323021, Fax 5323026, @. SR/ac/bath P2000, DR/ac/bath P2200, suite P2900 and P3900, all including breakfast. Comfortable, well-run hotel. Restaurant.
The Legend Hotel, Pioneer St corner Madison St, Mandaluyong City, Tel 6331501, Fax 6320845, @. SR/DR/ac/bath P4200 and P5000, including breakfast. Comfortable, tastefully decorated rooms with TV, the more expensive ones also have a refrigerator and jacuzzi. Restaurant, swimming pool, fitness room.

Parañaque & Pasay City
Euro Apartment, Lockheed St, Concorde Subdivision, Parañaque, Tel & Fax 5510723, @. SR/DR/fan/Bad P1100, SR/DR/ac/bath P1600 to P2200, including breakfast. Fairly good rooms, all of different sizes and furnishings. Belgian owner. The staff will look after left luggage. Phone them from the airport and they'll be glad to pick you up, as they are quite close.
Kabayan Hotel, 2878 Zamora St, Pasay City, Tel 8917874, Fax 8315152, @. Dorm/ac 450 P, SR/DR/ac/bath P1800 to P2200, all including breakfast. Several dormitories with three bunk beds each, and well-furnished rooms with TV. Quiet hotel, handy for Edsa Station (LRT 1), Taft Station (MRT 3), several bus terminals, and also for the airport. Restaurant, buiness centre, airport service.
Atrium Hotel, Gil Puyat Ave corner Taft Ave, Pasay City, Tel 5520351, Fax 5520182, @. SR/DR/ac/bath P1980 and P2500. Attractive, well equipped rooms with refrigerator and TV, all with a beautiful view (located between the 15th and the 25th floors; with an atrium). Really good value. Coffee shop.

Quezon City
Villa Estela Hometel, 33 Scout Santiango St corner Scout Dr Lazcano St, Tel 3712279. SR/DR/ac/bath P850 to P1280. Roughly 30% discount for a twelve-hour stay. Weekly and monthly rates available. Really good rooms with refrigerator and TV. Restaurant, swimming pool.
Camelot Hotel, 35 Mother Ignacia St, Diliman, Tel 3732101, Fax 3724523, @. SR/DR/ac/bath P1200 to P1500, suite P3200. Reasonable, quiet rooms with refrigerator and TV. Restaurant. As the name suggests, the hotel has been designed to resemble King Arthur's court. Located across from the Danarra Hotel & Resort.
Danarra Hotel & Resort, 121 Mother Ignacia St, Diliman, Tel 3733601, Fax 3724426, @. SR/DR/ac/bath P1200 and P1600, suite P3000. Well-maintained place with good rooms, all with refrigerator and TV. There is also a swimming pool on the trim hotel grounds. The hotel entrance is on Panay Ave.
Great Eastern Hotel, 1403 Quezon Ave, Tel 3718282, Fax 3713312, @. SR/DR/ac/bath P1400 and P1600, suite P2800 and P7200. Good rooms with refrigerator and TV. Coffee shop, swimming pool, fitness room.
Sulo Hotel, Matalino Rd, Diliman, Tel 9245051, Fax 9222030, @. SR/ac/bath from P2200, DR/ac/bath from P2600, suite from P5000. Attractive hotel with comfortable rooms, all with refrigerator and TV. Restaurant, swimming pool.

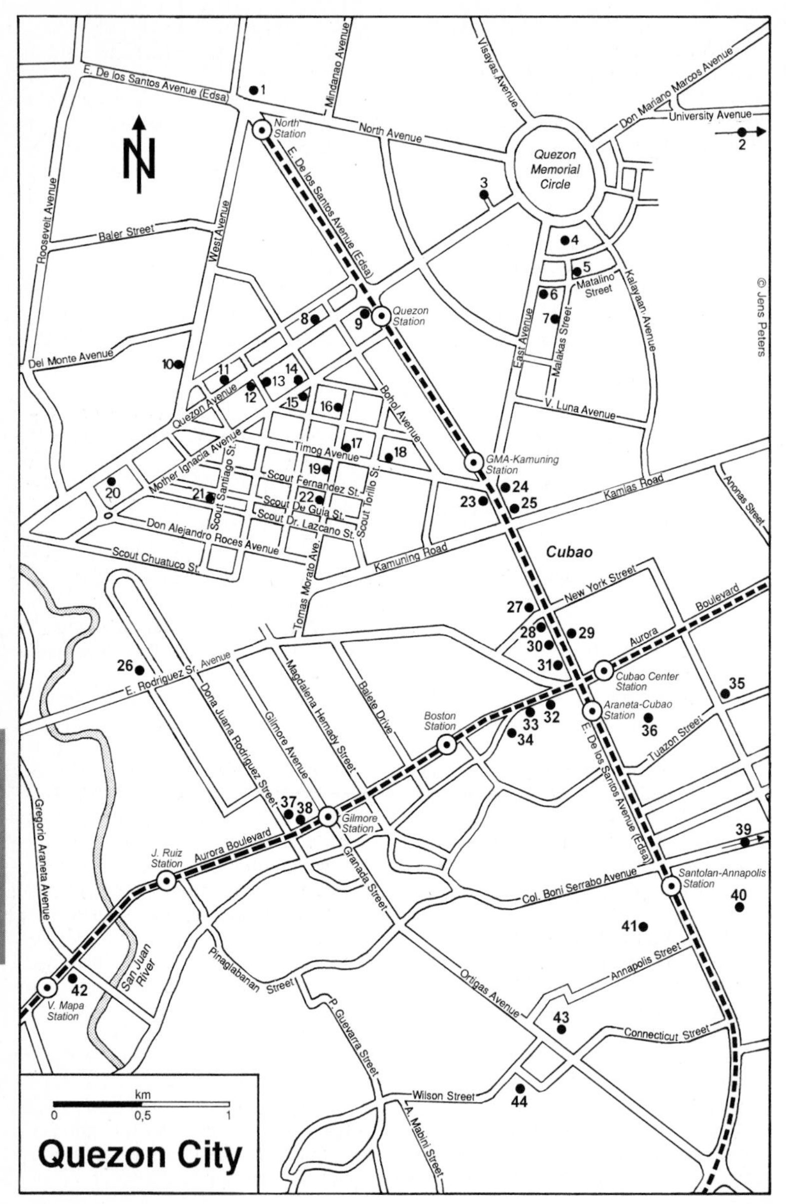
E. De los Santos Avenue (Edsa)
Mindanao Avenue
Visayas Avenue
Don Mariano Marcos Avenue
University Avenue
North Station
North Avenue
Quezon Memorial Circle
Roosevelt Avenue
West Avenue
Baler Street
E. De los Santos Avenue (Edsa)
Matalino Street
Kalayaan Avenue
Quezon Station
East Avenue
Malakas Street
Del Monte Avenue
Quezon Avenue
Bohol Avenue
V. Luna Avenue
Mother Ignacia Avenue
Scout Santiago St.
Timog Avenue
GMA-Kamuning Station
Scout Fernandez St.
Scout Torillo St.
Scout De Guia St.
Scout Dr. Lazcano St.
Kamias Road
Anonas Street
Don Alejandro Roces Avenue
Scout Chuatuco St.
Tomas Morato Ave.
Kamuning Road
Cubao
New York Street
Aurora Boulevard
E. Rodriguez Sr. Avenue
Dona Juana Rodriguez Street
Gilmore Avenue
Magdalena Hemady Street
Balete Drive
Boston Station
Cubao Center Station
Araneta-Cubao Station
Tuazon Street
Gilmore Station
J. Ruiz Station
Aurora Boulevard
Granada Street
Col. Boni Serrabo Avenue
Santolan-Annapolis Station
Gregorio Araneta Avenue
Pinaglabanan Street
Ortigas Avenue
Annapolis Street
San Juan River
V. Mapa Station
P. Guevarra Street
Connecticut Street
Wilson Street
A. Mabini Street
km
0
0,5
1
Quezon City
© Jens Peters

Manila

Getting There & Away
23 Tritran (Kamias Terminal)
24 Victory Liner (Kamias Terminal)
25 JAC Liner Bus Terminal
27 Dagupan Bus Terminal
28 Dominion Bus Line (Cubao Terminal)
29 Baliwag Transit (Cubao Terminal)
30 Victory Liner (Cubao Terminal)
31 JAM Transit (Cubao Terminal)
32 Dangwa Tranco (Cubao Terminal)
33 Partas (Cubao Terminal)
35 Philtranco (Cubao Terminal)

Places to Stay
5 Sulo Hotel
7 Metropolitan Apartment Hotel
11 Great Eastern Hotel
14 Danarra Hotel & Resort
15 Camelot Hotel
16 Hotel Rembrandt
17 Century Imperial Palace Suites
21 Villa Estela Hometel & Clubhouse
37 Broadway Court

Places to Eat & Entertainment
8 Barrio Fiesta
9 McDonald's
10 Alavar's House of Seafood
11 Café de Chine
19 Don Henrico's
20 Nightclubs
22 Mario's
Tia Maria's Mexican Restaurant
39 Eastwood Citywalk (3 km)

Miscellaneous
1 SM City
2 University of the Philippines (UP)
3 National Parks & Wildlife Center
4 Quezon City Hall
6 Philippine Heart Center for Asia
12 Mercury Drug
13 National Book Store
18 Dive Shoppe
26 St Luke Medical Center
34 Buddhist Temple
36 Araneta Center
38 Goethe Institute (Goethe House)
40 Camp Aguinaldo
41 Camp Crame
42 SM Centrepoint
43 Greenhills Shopping Center
44 Cardinal Santos Hospital

Hotel Rembrandt, 26 Tomas Morato Ave, Tel 3733333, Fax: 3720401. SR/DR/ac/bath from P2700, suite P3900. Pleasant, comfortably furnished rooms with refrigerator and TV. Restaurant, swimming pool.

Places to Stay - top end

Manila has plenty of first-class hotels. The elegant Manila Hotel can be ranked with Raffles in Singapore, the Oriental in Bangkok and the Peninsula in Hong Kong as among the oldest and most reputable hotels in South-East Asia.

A selection of 20 of the best luxury hotels in Manila are listed immediately below. All contain numerous bars, restaurants and nightclubs. The guests have the use of swimming pools, saunas and tennis courts. The rooms are all of excellent international standard and, of course, with TV, fridge, aircon and bath. A breakfast buffet and airport service are almost always included in the price. You have to add a 10% service charge and a 10.7% government tax to the price given in US dollars.

Ermita, Malate & Paco

Bayview Park Hotel, Roxas Blvd, Ermita, Tel 5261555, Fax 5212674, @. SR/DR from US$55, suite from US$100.

Century Park Hotel, Ocampo St, Malate, Tel 5288888, Fax 5281811, @. SR

from US$114, DR from US$120, suite from US$200.
Grand Boulevard Hotel, Roxas Blvd, Malate, Tel 5268588, Fax 5260111, @. SR/DR from US$180, suite US$300.
Manila Diamond Hotel, Roxas Blvd corner J Quintos St, Malate, Tel 5283000, Fax 5262255 (@). SR/DR from US$260, suite from US$400.
Manila Hotel, Rizal Park, Ermita, Tel 5270011, Fax 5270022, @. SR/DR from US$100, suite from US$350, penthouse US$2,500.
Manila Pavillon Hotel, United Nations Ave, Ermita, Tel 5261212, Fax 5262552, @. SR/DR US$73, suite US$120.
The Pan Pacific, Adriatico St corner Malvar St, Malate, Tel 5360788, Fax 5266503, @. SR/DR from US$190, suite from US$280.
The Westin Philippine Plaza Hotel, Cultural Center Complex, Roxas Blvd, Malate, Tel 5515555, Fax 5515601, @. SR/DR from US$225, suite from US$375.

Makati
Dusit Hotel Nikko, Ayala Center, Makati, Tel 8673333, Fax 8673888, @. SR/DR from US$140, suite from US$175.
Hotel Inter-Continental, Ayala Ave, Makati, Tel 8159711, Fax 8171330, @. SR/DR from US$140, suite from US$175.
Makati Shangri-La, Ayala Ave corner Makati Ave, Tel 8138888, Fax 8135499, @. SR from US$210, DR from US$235, suite from US$360.
Mandarin Oriental, Makati Ave, Makati, Tel 7508888, Fax 8172472, @. SR/DR from US$100, suite from US$195.
New World Renaissance Hotel, Esperanza St corner Makati Ave, Makati, Tel 8116888, Fax 8116777, @. SR/DR from US$75, suite US$213.
The Peninsula Manila, Makati Ave corner Ayala Ave, Makati, Tel 8872888, Fax 8154825, @. SR/DR from US$125, suite from US$220.

Mandaluyong City & Pasig City
Edsa Shangri-La, Garden Way, Ortigas Center, Mandaluyong City, Tel 6338888, Fax 6311067, @. SR US$195, DR US$220, suite US$340.
Manila Galleria Suites, ABN Ave, Ortigas Center, Pasig City, Tel 6337111, Fax 6332824, @. SR/DR US$110, suite from US$120.
The Richmonde Hotel, San Miguel Ave corner Lourdes St, Ortigas Center, Pasig City, Tel 6387777, Fax 6388567, @. SR US$94, DR US$104, suite from US$120.

Parañaque & Pasay City
Hyatt Regency, 2702 Roxas Blvd, Pasay City, Tel 8331234, Fax 8318076, @. SR/DR from US$90.
The Heritage Hotel, Edsa corner Roxas Blvd, Pasay City, Tel 8548888, Fax 8548833, @. SR/DR from US$220, suite from US$350.
Traders Hotel, 3001 Roxas Blvd, Pasay City, Tel 5263971, Fax 5223985, @. SR from US$100, DR from US$120.

Apartments

If you're going to stay in Manila for a while it may be worth considering apartments instead of hotel rooms. It's possible to find apartments with cooking facilities, aircon, fridge, TV and so on for a monthly rent of around P15,000 to P30,000, depending on what's provided. A month's rent must be paid in advance, and a deposit is required for the electricity. Rentals are available on a monthly, weekly, and sometimes even daily basis. The daily rates include electricity and are around P1000 to P1500. Apartments in Makati are often very expensive, while those in Ermita and Malate are seldom available, especially the cheaper ones, so it's a good idea to book early.

Ermita, Malate & Paco

San Carlos Mansion, 777 San Carlos St, Ermita, Tel 5238110, Fax 5213768. One-room apt. per day P800, per month P16,200; two-room apt. per day P900, per month P18,500.

Casa Blanca I, 1447 Adriatico St, Ermita, Tel 5238251, Fax 5260466. One-room apt. per day P1000, per month P12,900; two-room apt. per day P1650, per month P22,000.

Boulevard Mansion, 1440 Roxas Blvd, Ermita, Tel 5218888, Fax 5215829, @. Studio per day P1300, per month P25,500; one-room apt. per day P1600, per month P25,500; suite per day P2000, per month P37,500. Coffee shop.

Mabini Mansion, 1011 Mabini St, Ermita, Tel 5214776, Fax 5211646, @. One-room apt. per day P1500, per month P24,500; two-room apt. per day P3150, per month P38,800. Coffee shop.

Dakota Mansion, 555 General Malvar St corner Adriatico St, Malate, Tel 5210701, Fax 5218841, @. One-room apt. per day P1500, per month P25,000; two-room apt. per day P3200, per month P30,500. Restaurant, swimming pool.

Tropicana Apartment Hotel, 1630 Luis M Guerrero St, Malate, Tel 5255555, Fax 5255577, @. One-room apt. per day P1925, per week P12,650, per month P45,100; two-room apt. per day P3300, per week P20,900, per month P68,200. Restaurant, swimming pool.

Ralph Anthony Suites, Maria Orosa St corner Engracia Reyes St, Tel 5211107, Fax 5210203, @. Studio per day P1650; one-room apt. per day from P3000, per month from P77,000; two-room apt. per day from P5500, per month from P126,500 P.

Makati

Robelle Mansion, 877 JP Rizal St, Makati, Tel 8997388, Fax 8997390, @. One-room apt. per day P1075 and P1250, per month P19,500 and P22,500.

Travelers Inn, 7880 Makati Ave, Makati, Tel 8957061, Fax 8962144. One-room apt. per day P1500, per month P25,000. Conveniently located for Burgos Street.

Amorsolo Mansion, 130 Amorsolo St corner Herrera St, Makati, Tel 8186811, Fax 8172620, @. Studio per day P1200, per month P29,200; one-room apt. per day P1500, per month P31,600; two-room apt. per day P4000, per month P45,360.

The Gilarmi Apartments & Suites, 6749 Ayala Ave, Makati, Tel 8129311, Fax 8183848. Studio per day P1900, per month P40,700; one-room apt. per day P2700, per month P57,800; two-room apt. per day P3700, per month P77,000.

Regine's Apartelle, 8429 Kalayaan Ave corner Makati Ave, Makati, Tel 8973888, Fax 8906162, @. Studio per day P2300, per month P50,000; one-room apt. per day P3500, per month P70,000; two-room apt. per day P4700, per month P90,000.

Mandaluyong City & Pasig City

Discovery Suites, ADB Ave, Ortigas Center, Pasig City, Tel 6352222, Fax 6838111, @. One-room apt. per day P12,000, per month P152,000; two-room apt. per day P17,820, per month P231,000.

Parañaque & Pasay City

Copacabana Apartment Hotel, 264 Edsa Extension, Pasay City, Tel 8318711, Fax 8314344, @. One-room apt. per day P1800, per month P33,600; two-room apt. per day P2700, per month P54,000; three-room apt. per day P5600, per month P64,000. Coffee shop, restaurant, sauna, swimming pool.

Quezon City

Broadway Court, 16 Doña Juana Rodriguez St, New Manila, Tel 7227411,

Fax 7217795, @. One-room apt. per day P1200, per month P18,000. Coffee shop, tennis courts.

Places to Eat

Manila's restaurants feature an impressive diversity of cuisines and prices. Amongst the popular streets and squares with an above average selection of places to eat are Jupiter St, Pasay Rd, Power Point Mall in the Rockwell Center and Greenbelt 3 in Makati, Tomas Morato Ave and Eastwood Citywalk in Quezon City, St Francis Square and SM Mega Mall (over 200 restaurants!) in the Ortigas Center in Mandaluyong City, The Fort in the burgeoning, up-market Bonifacio Global City development in Taguig, Adriatico St and J Nakpil St in Malate and South Blvd at the Rizal Park in Ermita.

Gourmets have the opportunity to try the local fare as well as the pleasures of other Asian cooking and European, American and Australian dishes. Fast food is available, or you can enjoy the generous fixed-price buffets provided by the top-class hotel restaurants at your leisure.

In most restaurants in Ermita you can get a decent meal for roughly P150. In Adriatico St, where there is a wide range of Asian places, prices are a bit higher. For a meal with several courses you can expect to pay from P200 to P400.

The top restaurants in Makati and in the luxury hotels are expensive, but a real gourmet would probably be prepared to pay the P500 to P1000 or more charged for the excellent food, service and atmosphere. Sometimes these meals are accompanied by cultural entertainment or a fashion show. A lunch buffet costs about P400 to P600.

A decent bottle of wine in a good restaurant will cost at least P800. Wine is imported and transport costs and import duties make it very expensive, so maybe San Miguel beer is a better choice.

Only a few top restaurants insist on formal dress such as ties, jackets or barongs. Otherwise casual clothes are the order of the day. However, even in a middle-range restaurant, thongs (flip-flops), shorts or singlets would be pushing their tolerance a bit far.

The prices given for the following restaurants are the approximate current costs of dinner for one person. Drinks are not included, nor are extra helpings or expensive items like lobster tails by the dozen or caviar by the kg. With buffets in top hotels, about 20% is added for government tax and the service charge.

Filipino Food

Aristocrat, Roxas Blvd corner San Andres St, Malate, Tel 5247671. Open daily 24 hrs; P200. A long established, big, popular restaurant in the mid- price range. Many locals eat here.

Barrio Fiesta, Maria Orosa St corner Arkansas St, Ermita, Tel 5217884. Open daily 9am-11pm; P250. One of a chain of good, medium-priced restaurants with branches all over the country. It has an extensive menu with specialities like crispy pata and kare-kare (stew) together with a Filipino Buffet. There are 14 *Barrio Fiestas* all together in Metro Manila, including on United Nations Ave corner Alhambra St and in Robinsons Place, Adriatico St, both in Ermita, and on Makati Ave in Makati.

Bistro Remedios, Adriatico St, Malate, Tel 5239153. Open daily 6am-3pm and 6-11pm; P200. This elegant restaurant serves special dishes from Pampanga Province. Traditional live music in the evenings.

Harbor View, South Rd, Ermita, Tel 5241532, at the end of Rizal Park. Open daily 11am-midnight; P250. Thongs (flip-flops) are not allowed. This pleasant, half-open restaurant on Manila Bay

right on the waterfront is an ideal place to watch the sun go down and enjoy the fresh breeze while having a cold beer and enjoying good Filipino food like sinigang (a sour soup) or bangus (fish).
Kamayan Restaurant, Padre Faura, Ermita, Tel 5219490. Open daily 11am-2pm and 6.30-10pm; P400. The name means 'bare hands' because knives and forks are not used, and you eat with your fingers here in true Filipino style. They serve a wide range of authentic and tasty dishes from all over the Philippines, and both a Lunch and a Dinner Buffet. There are eight *Kamayan Restaurants* in Manila, including one in Pasay Rd corner Santillan St in Makati.
Max's, Maria Orosa St, Ermita. Open daily 7am-1am the next day; P150. Not just good roast chicken served various ways, but Philippine standards as well. There are over 20 *Max's* in Manila.
Seafood Market, J Bocobo St, Ermita. Open daily 10am-midnight; P600. Fairly expensive, but an excellent place to eat. You select your own fish or other seafood from a display area on one side, and it's cooked up by a squad of short-order cooks lined up along an open window on the street side. They're all frantically stirring woks, scooping pots and juggling frying pans while flames leap high all around them. It's excellent entertainment for passers-by. But beware: Fish, shrimps, crabs etc are sold by weight and the prices given are per 100 grams. Many a guest has piled his or her plate high, only to have a rude awakening after reading the bill. Don't forget that both the preparation of the food and the damp cloths generously handed out are all charged for. Especially in the evening there can be a crowd, so expect a short wait. You can round off the menu with coffee and cake at the *Café Alps* next door in Bocobo St.
Seaside Market, Roxas Blvd, Baclaran (near Baclaran Church), is a real market.

Greenbelt Rendezvous

More and more Filipinos are turning to the latest fad in going out: patronising bars, cafés and restaurants that are all lined up door to door in a newly built complex. Eastwood Citywalk in Libis, Quezon City, quite near the Marikina River, is just one such attraction. This 1.5 hectare mini-city and car free zone is where pedestrians and not vehicles rule the streets. But the hottest address at the moment for night owls is undoubtedly Greenbelt 3 in Makati. Built next to a neat little park, this complex with nearly 50 cafés and restaurants and a foodhall with about 30 food stands is a joy for all the senses.

On the ground floor, most of the guests sit outside, enjoying freshly brewed coffee at Seattle's Best Coffee, Starbucks or the Coffee Bean, drinking Corona and Tequila in the Café Havana (Latino Club with live music) or savouring the exquisite taste of the crepes at Café Breton.

On the first floor you'll mainly find restaurants such as Big Buddha (Thai), Bubba Gump (shrimps, American), Haiku (Japanese), Hue (Vietnamese), Oody's (Asian rice and noodle dishes), Pasha (Mediterranean) und Soul Food (Filipino).

On the second floor next to the cinemas there's a foodhall called Food Choices with a variety of stands with international specialities, eg Auntie Anne's (pretzels), Ceya (Mongolian), Circo (seafood & steaks), Shin Kanzen (Japanese), Thai BBQ and the wonderful little Ice Monster.

Open daily 6am-midnight; P300. You can buy freshly caught fish here and have it prepared cheaply at the little adjoining restaurants for about P50.
The Red Crab, Remedios St, Malate, Tel 4009979. Open daily 11am-3pm and 6-11pm; P400. Serving mainly crabs as the name suggests, which can be prepared in several different ways, they also have seafood and steaks on the menu.
Zamboanga Restaurant, Adriatico St, Malate, Tel 5258828. Open daily 8am-midnight; P400. Seafood dishes like 'fisherman's delight' are a speciality. It has Filipino and Polynesian dancing with dinner at 8.30pm.

Chinese
Gloriamaris Shark's Fin Restaurant, Cultural Center Complex, Malate, Tel 8313812. Open daily 11am-2.30pm and 6-10pm; P400. Chinese and Philippine food. An attractively decorated place, specialising in seafood. Located on Manila Bay near Coconut Palace and Folk Arts Theater.
Maxim's Tea House, MH del Pilar St corner United Nations Ave, Ermita, Tel 5237908. Open daily 24 hrs; P100. Good food at reasonable prices. There are 13 *Maxim's Tea Houses* in Manila, including several in shopping centres and one in Ongpin St, Chinatown.
Sea Palace, Mabini St, Malate, Tel 5216427. Open daily 10.30am-2.30pm and 6-11.30pm; P200. Good, and relatively cheap Chinese restaurant which also serves Filipino food.

Indian & Middle Eastern
Kashmir, Padre Faura, Ermita, Tel 5231521. Open daily 11am-11pm; P400. As the name would suggest, they serve mainly north Indian and Pakistani dishes, hot or mild as required. They also serve vegetarian dishes. There is another *Kashmir* restaurant in Pasay Rd in Makati.

Japanese
Kimpura, West Dr, Makati in the Makati Supermarket building, Tel. 8924456. Open daily 11.30am-2.30pm and 6-10.30pm; P500. Very popular, definitely first class, but nevertheless fairly inexpensive.
Tempura-Misono, Roxas Blvd, Pasay City, Tel 9331234. Open daily 11am-2.30pm and 6-10pm; P800. A lot of people like this Japanese restaurant in the Hyatt Regency Hotel.
Little Tokyo, Chino Roces Ave (Pasong Tamo) corner Fernando St, Makati. In a complex across from the Makati Cinema Square you'll find a few Japanese shops and lots of restaurants (*Genroko, Kaasan, Miyakodori, Robata-Fuji, Sachiko, Teppanyaki Matsuya* etc), which form a kind of Far-East enclave. Various restaurants have specialised in snacks, such as ramen (noodles), sashimi (raw fish), sushi (raw fish and rice) or yakiniku (grilled beef with vegetables), others offer more substantial meals.

Korean
Korean Garden, Jupiter St, Makati, Tel 8955443. Open daily 11am-2pm and 5.30-10.30pm; P300. One of a group of 10 roughly comparable Korean restaurants in Makati.
Korean Palace, Adriatico St, Malate, Tel 5216695. Open daily 10am-2am; P250. Tries to compete with the Korean Village next door. In addition to Korean, they also serve food from other Asian countries.
Korean Village, Adriatico St, Malate, Tel 5244958. Open Mon-Sat 11.30am-2.30pm and 5.30-10pm; P300. Said to be the biggest Korean restaurant in Manila, the specialities here are spare ribs and beef stew.

Thai
Sala Thai, J Nakpil St, Malate, Tel 5224694. Open Mon-Sat 11am-2.30pm

and 6-10.30pm; P200. A popular, fairly inexpensive place to eat. Amongst the dishes most ordered here are Thai curries, tom yum (a spicy, sour soup) and egg rolls.

Sukhothai, Level 4, Building A, SM Megamall, Edsa, Mandaluyong, Tel 6341280. Open Mon-Fri 11am-3pm and 8-9.30pm, Sat-Sun 11am-10pm; P250. Excellent, inexpensive Thai restaurant. A specialty of the house is Chicken Pandan (chicken prepared in pandan leaves).

American

Café Adriatico, Adriatico St corner Remedios Circle, Malate, Tel 5252509. Open Mon-Sat 10am-6am the next day, Sun 11am-5am the next day; P300. A good place to go for a drink or a meal. The usual menu features steaks, salads and seafood, topped off with various kinds of coffee and a good choice of cocktails. A favourite watering hole of the in-crowd, especially after the movies, disco or a party.

Mario's, St Francis Square, Ortigas Center, Mandaluyong City, Tel. 6343417. Open daily 7am-2.30pm and 5-11pm; P600. The steaks and salads are good here, and they also serve seafood, French and Spanish soups as well as Californian wines. There is another *Mario's* on Tomas Morato Ave corner Scout Gandia St, Quezon City.

Steak Town, Adriatico St, Malate, Tel 5222631. Open daily 11am-midnight; P400. Good steaks and seafood, soup, salad, bread, dessert and coffee.

Filling Station, Burgos St, Makati, Tel 8972053. Open daily 24 hrs; P200. Beautifully decorated restaurant, attentive staff and first rate food ranging from a generous breakfast to their Sinatra Chicken Pesto.

Kenny Rogers, Robinsons Place, Adriatico St, Ermita, Tel 5367876. Open daily 10am-10pm; P100. This restaurant chain (24x in Manila alone) specialises in roast chicken with corn muffins.

Australian & UK

Rooftop Restaurant, Padre Faura corner MH del Pilar St, Ermita. Open daily 24 hrs; P200. An Australian restaurant and beer garden on top of the Iseya Hotel. On Sunday there's an Aussie barbecue from 5 to 9pm for P245.

Swagman Outback Café, 411 A Flores St, Ermita. Open daily 24 hrs; P250. Ever-popular restaurant belonging to the Australian Swagman Hotel.

German & Swiss

Donau Stube, Adriatico St, Malate, Tel 5210701. Open daily 7am-11pm; P175. Wide range of outstanding German dishes and a menu of the day. Well-run place, which also sells cold meats to be taken away.

München Grill Pub, Mabini St, Ermita, Tel 5223955. Open daily 7.30am-midnight; P150. Not only Bavarian dishes as you would expect, they also have good value meals of the day with several courses.

Old Swiss Inn Restaurant, Garden Plaza Hotel, Belen St, Paco, Tel 5262741. Open daily 6am-11pm; P400. Come here for excellent Swiss food, such as fondue and other Alpine specialities. There is another *Old Swiss Inn Restaurant* in the Olympia Towers, Makati Ave, Makati.

Schwarzwälder, Atrium of Makati, Makati Ave, Tel 8935179. Open Mon-Sat 7am-10.30pm, Sun 11am-10.30pm; P500. An established restaurant with German dishes like Bratwurst, or even Eisbein and Sauerkraut. All topped off with a salad bar, and a wide range of coffees.

French

L'Eau Vive, Paz Mendoza Guazon Ave, Paco, Tel 5638559. Open Mon-Sat 11am-3pm and 7-11pm; P500. This

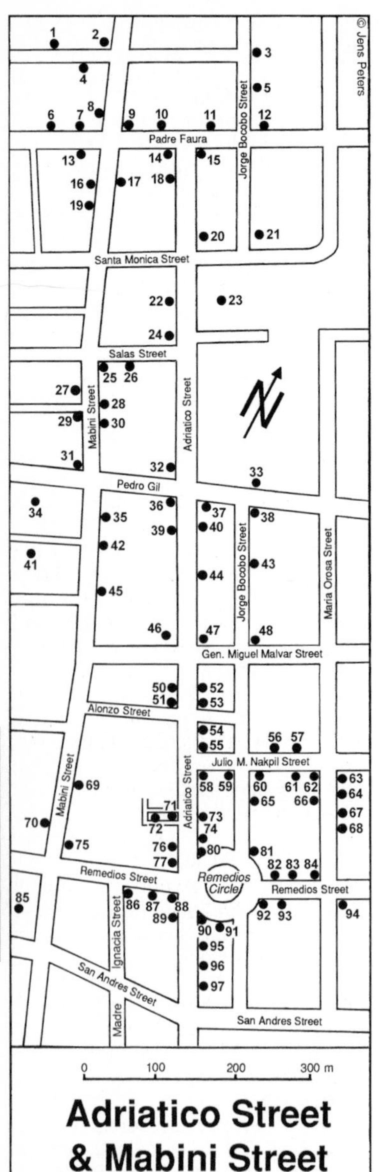

Getting There & Away
15 Philippine Airlines
16 Si-Kat Ferry Office
23 Cebu Pacific Airlines
32 WG & A (Filipino Travel Center)

Places to Stay
1 Yasmin Pension
5 Tropical Mansion Hotel
8 Lotus Garden Hotel
12 Midtown Inn
16 Citystate Tower Hotel
19 Mabini Pension
20 The Midland Plaza
21 Cherry Blossoms Hotel
24 Casa Blanca I
25 Stone House Hotel
28 Santos Pension House
29 Ermita Tourist Inn
30 Hotel Frendy
34 Sheraton Marina Square Hotel
35 Las Palmas Hotel
36 Palm Plaza Hotel
37 Dak's Inn
39 Rothman Hotel
41 Marina Richmonde Hotel
42 Executive Plaza Hotel
Riviera Mansions
43 Manila Manor Hotel
46 The Pan Pacific Hotel
47 Dakota Mansion
54 Joward's Pension House
55 Adriatico Arms Hotel
58 Friendly's Guest House
60 Victoria Mansion
71 Malate Pensionne
72 Juan's Place
93 Clé Dor Hotel
94 Royal Plaza Condominium

Places to Eat & Entertainment
2 Cowboy Grill
3 Café Alps, Sea Food Market
4 Holandia
7 Chowking
10 Jollibee
Kamayan Restaurant
Kashmir Restaurant

14 G-Point Bar
17 Calle 5
München Grill Pub
18 Alda's Pizza Kitchen
22 Wah Yuen Seafood Restaurant
31 Don Henrico's
38 Gloria Maris Restaurant
39 Chia Sian Lou Restaurant
Zamboanga Restaurant
46 Adriatico Square Restaurants
47 Country Style Restaurant
Donau Stube
48 Elite Seafood Restaurant
50 Lavazza Restaurant & Café
51 Rickshaw Café & Resto
52 Hwang's Korean Cuisine
53 Sururbia Music Bar
54 Joward's Seafood Restaurant
Steak Town Restaurant
The Chronicle Café
55 Bravo Restaurant
56 Episode Bar
57 Jazz Rhythms, Wave Bar
Make Love Not War
58 Ping Yang Hot Pot Restaurant
Satu Lagi Music Bar & Bistro
59 Spirits Coyote Bar
61 Bar 8 Zero, Insemnia
Scotch House, The Blue Frog
The Common Ground Café
62 Bargo Restaurant
63 Café Rosa Ladida
64 Mama
Pepe & Pilar
65 Forbest Bar & Grill
66 New York Shop Café
Sonata Bar & Café
67 Café Breton
68 Courtyard, Mint
Raj Indian Restaurant
69 Sea Palace Restaurant
70 Hobbit House
71 Chateau 1771 Restaurant
Portico Restaurant
Starbucks
73 Causeway Seafood Restaurant
Classic Fat Burgers
Rolling Stone Billiard & Bar
74 Anthology
Bedrock Bar & Restaurant
Padi's Point Restaurant
Unplugged
76 Korea House Restaurant
Korean Village Restaurant
77 Korean Palace Restaurant
80 Café Adriatico
81 Patio Guernica
82 Golden Malate KTV Club
Taza Bar & Grill
83 Empress Garden Restaurant
84 Café Rio
86 Tia Maria's Mexican Restaurant
87 The Red Crab Restaurant
88 Café Havana
89 Bistro Remedios
90 In The Mood Dance Bar
91 Cloud 9
Fussion Bar & Restaurant
92 Ciboney Café & Bar
93 Dean St Café
95 Aquistic Village
96 Ciudad Virginia Ballroom Dancing

Miscellaneous

6 Mercury Drug
9 Equitable PCI Bank
11 Solidaridad Book Shop
13 Philippine National Bank (PNB)
14 7-Eleven
22 Metrobank
23 Robinsons Place
25 7-Eleven
26 Laundromat
29 Scenic View Travel
31 Equitable PCI Bank
32 Filipino Travel Center
33 National Book Store
39 Metrobank
40 The Ritz Spa Malate
44 Chinese Temple
45 Sining Pilipino (paintings)
75 Adventure International Tours
American Express
85 Malate Church
97 Equitable PCI Bank

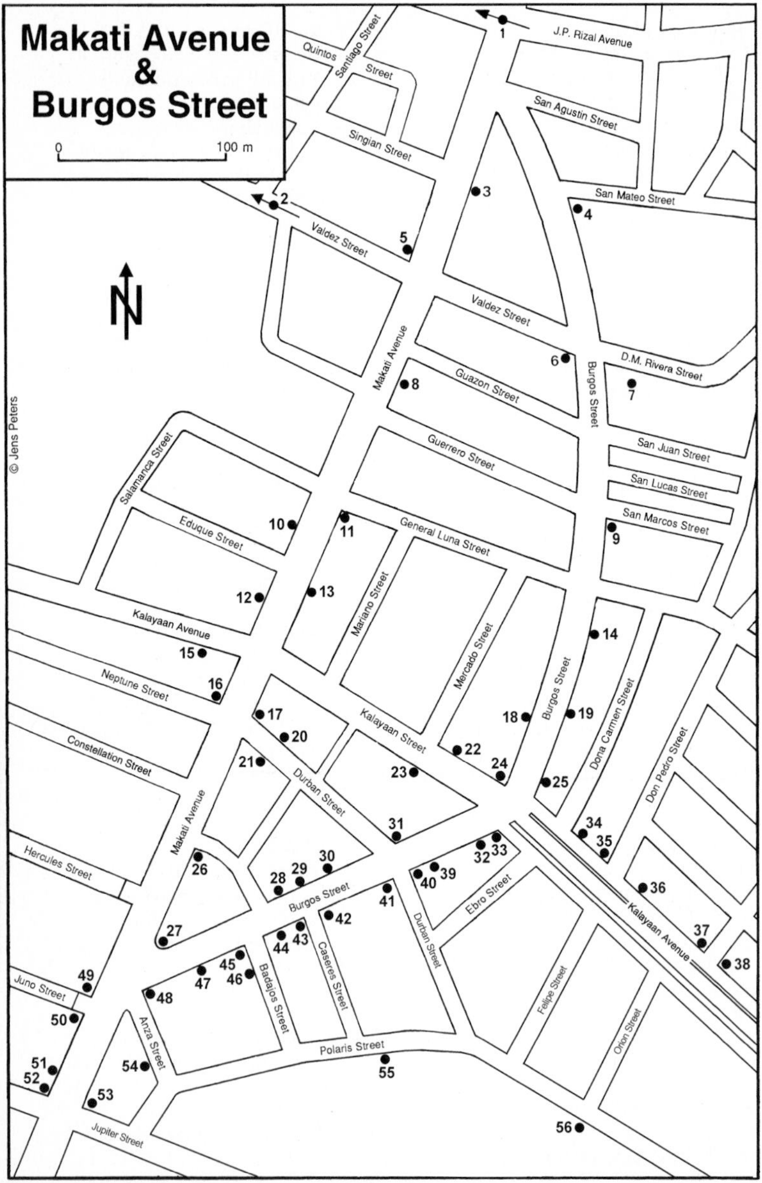
Makati Avenue & Burgos Street
0
100 m
© Jens Peters
J.P. Rizal Avenue
Quintos
Santiago Street
Street
San Agustin Street
Singian Street
San Mateo Street
Valdez Street
Valdez Street
Makati Avenue
D.M. Rivera Street
Guazon Street
Burgos Street
San Juan Street
Guerrero Street
San Lucas Street
Salamanca Street
San Marcos Street
Eduque Street
General Luna Street
Mariano Street
Kalayaan Avenue
Mercado Street
Neptune Street
Burgos Street
Dona Carmen Street
Kalayaan Street
Don Pedro Street
Constellation Street
Durban Street
Makati Avenue
Hercules Street
Burgos Street
Ebro Street
Kalayaan Avenue
Durban Street
Caseres Street
Badajos Street
Felipe Street
Juno Street
Anza Street
Polaris Street
Orion Street
Jupiter Street
1
2
3
4
5
6
7
8
9
10
11
12
13
14
15
16
17
18
19
20
21
22
23
24
25
26
27
28
29
30
31
32
33
34
35
36
37
38
39
40
41
42
43
44
45
46
47
48
49
50
51
52
53
54
55
56

Places to Stay
1 Robelle Mansion (150m)
2 Robelle House (150m)
8 Great Eastern Hotel
10 Astor Hotel
12 Millennium Plaza Hotel
15 Regine's Apartelle
17 City Garden Hotel Makati
20 Durban St. Inn
21 Sunette Tower Hotel
22 Makati Prime Tower Suites
26 Travelers Inn
29 Virra Apartments
30 Inn Suites Hotel
31 Oxford Suites
35 Oka Hotel
39 680 Apartelle
41 The Bel-Air Place
42 Makati Palace Hotel
44 Citadel Inn Makati

Places to Eat & Entertainment
3 Andok's Dine-in
4 Salomon's Grill
5 Barrio Fiesta
6 Friend's & Neighbours
9 Korean BBQ
11 Wendy's
13 Café Oceanic
16 Shakey's Makati
18 Fridays
19 Jools
The Woodman's Head
23 Jungle Room
24 Go Go Bananas
Papillon
25 Montana
26 Wild West Bar
27 Flamingo
Manila Nomads
28 Santa Fe Coffee Shop & Restaurant
30 Bottoms Bar
Dimples
Filling Station Restaurant & Bar
32 Rascal's Bar
33 Korean Palace Restaurant
34 Foxy's
36 JJ's Bar
37 Danish Connection
38 Galleon Club & Restaurant
Cathouse Pub & Restaurant
39 Mascara Bar
40 Billboard Club
Shampoo Bar
41 Bar Bandido
Tickles Bar
43 The Matrix Restaurant
45 Crawdaddy's Restaurant
46 Bar Café Mogambo
47 Bar Hollywood
48 Pizza Hut
Rogues Bar
49 Hossein's Persian Kebab
50 A & W
51 Jollibee
52 McDonald's
53 Papagayo Thai & Mexican Cuisine
54 Heckle & Jeckle
55 La Taverna
56 The Handlebar

Miscellaneous
1 Dive Buddies (150m)
7 St Peter & Paul Church
14 7-Eleven, Insular Bakery
22 Metrobank

unique restaurant is run by nuns and missionaries, and offers international and French cuisine.

Café Breton, Maria Orosa St, Malate, Tel 5360953. Open Mon-Sat 5pm-midnight, Sun 2.30-10pm; P150. Specialises in crepes. There's another *Café Breton* in Greenbelt 3 in Makati.

Dutch

Holandia, Arquiza St, Ermita. Open Mon-Sat noon-1am, Sun 4pm-1am. P200. Dutch and other European specialities.

Italian

Bravo, Adriatico St corner J Nakpil Street, Malate, Tel 3033508. Open daily

Coffee - an Instant Success

The giant multi Nestlé nearly managed to persuade the Filipinos to give up their traditional fresh-brewed coffee in favour of the more practical, globally-known instant brand. All over the country Nescafé became the synonym for coffee and many young Filipinos only know coffee in the form of powder you buy in a glass container. And the amazing thing is, the Philippines produces a huge amount of high-quality coffee beans every year which are almost all destined for export because of the lack of local demand. The best-known is Barako, coffee from the province of Batangas, which is sold in four different versions.

From the mid-1990s onwards more and more big shopping centres were opened up and with them arrived the internationally known coffee shops. So the likes of ***Starbucks*** and ***Seattle's Best Coffee*** encouraged the trend back to fresh coffee brewed from beans. In Manila, speciality cafés managed to get their foot in the door, offering cakes and biscuits together with only one kind of coffee, or a select few types at most. Examples are ***Allegro Café*** (Danesi from Italy), ***Figaro Coffee Company*** (Barako) and ***Old Manila Coffee House*** (Mt Apo arabica from Mindanao).

noon-3pm and 6pm-1am (Fri-Sat until 3am); P300. Try the excellent pizzas from their varied menu. Seating inside and out.

La Taverna, Polaris St, Bel-Air, Makati, Tel 8909648. Open Mon-Sat 11am-2.30pm and 6-11pm, Sun 6-11pm; P600. Offers specialties from Tuscany and northern Italy.

L'Opera, Anson's Arcade, Paseo de Roxas corner Esperanza St, Makati, Tel 8443283. Open daily 11am-2.30pm and 6.30-10.30pm; P500. The menu has a good selection of risottos, pizzas and pasta dishes.

Sbarro, Robinsons Place (3rd floor), Adriatico St, Ermita. Open daily from 10 am to 11 pm; P75. A friendly restaurant with a wide selection of good value dishes ranging from mushroom pizza to baked maccaroni with tomato sauce. There are several *Sbarros* to be found in shopping centres.

Mexican

Don Henrico's, Pedro Gil corner Mabini St (above the Equitable PCI Bank), Malate, Tel 5249141. Open daily 9am-1am the next day; P250. Mexican and Italian food (pizzas and pasta dishes). There are eight *Don Henrico's* in Manila, including one on Tomas Morato Ave corner Limbaga St in Quezon City.

Tia Maria's, Remedios St corner Madre Ignacia St, Malate, Tel 5220429. Open daily 4pm-4.30am; P300. Serves cocktails and good Mexican food. There are four *Tia Maria's* in Manila, including one in Jupiter St, Makati.

Spanish

El Comedor, Anson's Arcade, Paseo de Roxas corner Pasay Rd, Makati, Tel 8925071. Open Mon-Sat 7am-2.30pm and 6.30-10.30pm; Sun 11.30am-2.30 pm and 6.30-10.30pm; P700. Good standard Spanish fare and wines.

Guernica's, MH del Pilar St, Ermita, Tel 5240936. Open Mon-Sat 6pm-2am; P400. Offers typical Spanish dishes like paella, but also serves steaks and seafood. Guitar music provides the atmosphere.

Barbara's Restaurant, Plaza San Luis Complex, General Luna St, Intramuros, Tel 5274086. Open Mon-Sat 11am-2pm and 6-11pm; P500. Traditional

Spanish and Filipino food, served in 19th century surroundings.
Ilustrado, El Amanecer Compound, General Luna St, Intramuros, Tel 5272345. Open Mon-Sat 11am-3pm and 6-10pm, Sun 6-10pm; P800. Spanish and Filipino food in an authentic atmosphere. One specialty of the house is Paella Ilustrado, followed by Sampaguita Ice Cream for dessert.
Patio Guernica, J Bocobo St, near Remedios Circle, Malate, Tel 5214415. Open Mon-Sat 11am-2pm and 5.30-11pm, Sun 5.30-11pm; P500. A well-run place with typical Spanish dishes, as well as steaks and pizzas.

Vegetarian Food

Bodhi, Tutuban Mall, Claro M Recto Ave, Tondo, Tel 3632582. Open daily 10am-8pm; P75. The place calls itself a 'vegetarian health food restaurant' and serves a wide selection of exclusively vegetarian food and drinks. The Tutuban Mall is the long building, slightly set back behind the somewhat larger Tutuban Center on the street. There is another *Bodhi* in Banawe St in Quezon City and one in the SM Megamall, Edsa, Mandaluyong City.
Kashmir, Padre Faura, Ermita, Tel 5231521. Open daily 11am-11pm; P400. Serves mainly north Indian and Pakistani dishes as well as a wide range of vegetarian foods. There is another *Kashmir* restaurant in Pasay Rd in Makati.
Patio Guernica, J Bocobo St, near Remedios Circle, Malate, Tel 5214415. Open Mon-Sat 11am-2pm and 5.30-11 pm, Sun 5.30-11pm; P400. An excellent restaurant which serves mainly Spanish food, as well as some vegetarian dishes.
Sala Thai, J Nakpil St, Malate, Tel 5224694. Open Mon-Sat 11am-2pm and 6-10.30pm; P150. Popular for their Thai food, they also serve vegetarian dishes.
Tia Maria's, Remedios St corner Madre Ignacia St, Malate, Tel 5220429. Open daily 4pm-3am; P300. Good Mexican food which can also be prepared in a vegetarian manner if requested (eg by substituting beans for meat in an enchilada). There are four *Tia Maria's* in Manila, including one in Jupiter St, Makati.

Fast Food

There is a variety of national and international burger and pizza chains in every part of the city, especially in the larger shopping centres. ***McDonald's***, ***Jollibee*** and ***Wendy's*** compete with hamburgers, ***Pizza Hut*** and ***Shakey's*** with pizzas. ***Goldilocks*** serves cakes as well as good value Philippine and Chinese food, eg noodle dishes, spring rolls, caldareta and pork adobo. The restaurant chain ***Chowking*** is very successful with its Chinese fast food.
Both ***Dunkin Donuts*** and ***Mister Donut*** have a good choice of excellent doughnuts and good coffee - not a bad breakfast alternative.

Buffets

Nearly all the big hotels have opulent buffets on offer. Although they might draw you in by appearing inexpensive, they always end up costing you more than you expected. Not only are taxes and gratuity added on top, drinks are extra, and they're not exactly cheap either.
Regular buffet times and prices: Breakfast buffet 6-10am, P400; lunch buffet 11.30am-2pm, P600; dinner buffet 6-10pm, P700.

Entertainment & Events

Basketball

Games of the professional basketball league, the Philippine Basketball Association (PBA), are usually played in Manila at the Araneta Coliseum (22,000 seats), Edsa, Quezon City, at

the Cuneta Astrodome (10,000) on Roxas Blvd, Pasay City and at the Philsports Arena (15,000), also called Ultra, Pasig City.
Admission costs from P30 to P500. The sheer enthusiasm of the spectators alone makes it worth a visit. The team names are unashamed references to commercial products: Gordon's (gin), San Miguel (beer), Alaska (tinned milk) are just a few examples.

Casinos
The extremely profitable Casino Filipino company runs local casinos all over the country and simply rakes in the money. In Manila you can play at the Grand Boulevard Hotel, Roxas Blvd, Malate, at the Manila Pavillion Hotel, United Nations Ave, Ermita and at The Heritage Hotel, Edsa, Pasay City. Admission is P100 and players in too casual clothes or even beachwear will not be admitted.

Cinemas
Amongst other places, there are cinemas in the large shopping centres such as Araneta Center, Ayala Center (Glorietta 1 and 4), SM Megamall and Robinsons Place. Films are advertised in the daily papers. Admission costs between P50 and P150.

Cockfights
There are several cockpits in Manila - the Philippine Cockers Club in Santa Ana; the Olympic Stadium at Grace Park, Caloocan City; Libertad on Dolores St, Pasay City; Elorde on Santos Ave, Parañaque; and La Loma on Calavite St, Quezon City. Fights are staged on Sunday and feast days. Admission is from P20 to P200.

Concerts
In idyllic Paco Park, San Marcelino St, 'Paco Park Presents' puts on free chamber music at 6pm on Friday.
The 'Puerta Real Evenings', which take place every Saturday night at 6pm in Intramuros, offer free musical entertainment in the greenery at the old fortress wall near the Puerta Real.
The free 'Concert at the Park' takes place every Sunday at 5pm in Rizal Park with a different kind of music every week.

Dances
Cultural Center of the Philippines, Roxas Blvd, Malate, Tel 8321125. Events are announced in the CCP display case on Roxas Blvd. Especially popular are performances by the Ballet Philippines, whose repertoire not only includes classical ballet but also jazz interpretations and modern versions of ethnic dances. Tickets, costing between P600 and P1000, can be obtained on the fourth floor, Tel 5511003.
Star Theater, Star City, Cultural Center Complex, Pasay City, Tel 8320796. Not only classical ballet such as the Nutcracker Suite, Swan Lake etc, but also Filipino choreographies (Gabriela ng Vigan, Paalam Maria Clara), performed by the Ballet Manila under their Artistic Director, prima ballerina Lisa Macuja-Elizalde. Tickets for P300 available on the night or at Ballet Manila, Donada St (near the Manila Sanitarium & Hospital), Pasay City, Tel 4000292.
Zamboanga Restaurant, Adriatico St, Malate, Tel 8258828. Filipino and Polynesian dancing with dinner at 8.30pm.

Jai-alai
If not temporarily banned yet again because of game-rigging and betting irregularities, super-fast jai-alai games take place seven days a week from 5pm to 2am at the Jai-alai de Manila stadium on Adriatico St in Malate next to the Harrison Plaza. Admission P50.

Theatre

Amazing Philippine Theatre, Manila Film Center, Cultural Center Complex, Pasay City, Tel 8335785, 8335758. Shows daily at 7.30 and 9pm, admission P1100. Elaborately staged transvestite show with Chinese, Hawaiian, Japanese, Korean and Filipino dances and acts. Top quality choreography.

Cultural Center of the Philippines (CCP), Roxas Blvd, Malate, Tel 8321125. From July until March, the Tanghalang Pilipino Ensemble performs Philippine plays here.

General Carlos P Romulo Theater, RCBC Plaza, Ayala Ave corner Gil Puyat Ave, Makati. Information on the current programme and reservations are available at Tel 8870710. The ticket office is open Mon-Sat 10am-7pm, Sun 2-4pm. The performances are a real pleasure to watch, covering musicals, comedies, classics and children's plays from the repertoire of the Repertory Philippines ensemble every Thu, Fri and Sat at 8pm, as well as Sat and Sun at 3.30pm. This is the best English language theatre in the Philippines.

Rajah Sulayman Theater, Fort Santiago, Intramuros, Tel 7479637, 5271572. Performances in the historical surroundings of the PETA (Philippine Educational Theater Association, Tel 7249637) are dependent on the weather (open-air theatre). Their season normally runs from November until March.

Nightlife

Manila's nightlife is concentrated mainly in Ermita, Makati, Malate, Pasay City and Quezon City. In addition, all the bigger hotels have their own bars and nightclubs.

Ermita: After the go-go bars were closed down in the early 1990s by the then mayor Lim, the lights went out for a long time in Ermita. Although there's not exactly pole dancing nowadays, various pubs and music bars in MH del Pilar St have brought a bit of life back into the former red light district.

Makati: There are lots of nightclubs with go-go girls and a few pubs in Burgos St and the sidestreets leading off it. The bistros and cafés in Greenbelt 3 in Makati Ave are a popular meeting place to see and be seen' in the evenings. Most of the guests sit outside, thus avoiding the smoking ban in Makati's bars and restaurants.

Malate: There's a remarkable phenomenon taking place around Adriatico St, J Nakpil St, Maria Orosa St and Remedios Circle in Malate. In old, restored buildings in this area an upmarket pub/bistro scene has established itself which has a genuine, nostalgic feel to it.

Pasay City: On Roxas Blvd between Gil Puyat Ave and Edsa as well as in the Edsa International Entertainment Complex on Edsa at the corner of Harrison St diagonally across from the Heritage Hotel, there are a few nightclubs with go-go girls. You'll also find some in the Entertainment Complex (drive-in) on Domestic Airport Rd across from the Domestic Airport.

Quezon City: Filipinos like clubs which have stimulating entertainment - say, a model show. These so-called disco-theatres are mainly on Quezon Ave and Timog Ave. In the Eastwood Citywalk complex in Libis there is not only a large selection of restaurants, but cafés, pubs and music bars.

Bistros & Music Lounges

Bistros are enjoying growing popularity in Manila. All the trendy people go there to be with the 'in' crowd. The classic watering holes are constantly being joined by new ones, others disap-

Parties with spirit(s)

On 31 October, the night before All Saints' Day, clubs all over Manila celebrate Halloween, eg in the Hard Rock Café. The focus of all these horrorfests are the party-goers dressed up as ghosts, monsters, witches and vampires, going about their vile business at the witching hour. The best, and craziest, costumes are rewarded with attractive prizes in the clubs.

The word Halloween stems from the expression All Hallows Eve, the night before All Hallows Day (now better known as All Saints' Day). According to an old Celtic tradition, on that night - back then, the Celtic New Year - the dead could be seen abroad, looking for a living body to possess and live in. To scare off such attacks and hopefully remain in possession of their own bodies, the living dressed up to look as frightening as possible and indulged in scary behaviour. That was the origin of Halloween, a custom celebrated not only in the Anglo-Saxon culture nowadays (they borrowed it from the Celts), but all over the world.

pear after a short interval from the scene, leaving the stage for others to strut on. The ones given here are well established and should survive for some time to come. It's considered important for guests to be properly attired, for example, the Café Adriatico and the Hard Rock Café will not allow anyone in wearing shorts and thongs (flip-flops). Admission is nearly always free.

Café Adriatico, Adriatico St at Remedios Circle, Malate, started Manila's craze for bistros and is still a favourite. Open Mon-Sat 10am-6am and Sun 2pm-6am.

Café Havana, Adriatico St at Remedios Circle, Malate. Open daily 11.30am-3pm and 6pm-2am (Fri-Sat until 4am) is where salsa meets Manila: enjoy the laid-back Latin American atmosphere, especially on Friday and Saturday late at night. The *Café Havana* in Makati (Greenbelt 3) has gradually established itself as the number one club there.

Bedrock, Adriatico St, Malate. Open nightly 6pm-4am. Popular bar, with live bands performing every night. There's also a *Bedrock* in Jupiter St in Makati.

Padi's Point, Adriatico St, Malate. Open nightly 6pm-5am. It's always party time here, with events such as drinking contests and dancing competitions. There are several branches in Manila, including one in Jupiter St in Makati.

Hobbit House, Mabini St, Malate. Open nightly 5.30pm-2am. Admission P100. Well-known Philippine artists perform here. Mostly folk music. Good international atmosphere and genuine hobbit-sized waiters who are all dwarfs.

Calle 5, Mabini St, Ermita. Open nightly 5pm-5.30am. Popular, half open-air dancing bar with several good live bands, you can't miss hearing. They sometimes have funky female bands. Most guests start trickling in by late evening.

Cowboy Grill, Mabini St coner Arquiza St, Ermita. Open nightly 6pm-5.30am. The mostly younger guests are entertained by three live bands every evening.

Hard Rock Café, Glorietta 3, Ayala Center, Ayala Ave, Makati. Open daily 11am-2am. Live music from 9pm. Admission P300 (special show P400 to P500), including two drinks. This place was a success story waiting to happen. When the two Americans Peter Morton and Isaac Tigrett opened their first one in 1971 in London they couldn't have foreseen how successful their idea would become all over the world. But, take a restaurant dedicated as a cult shrine to rock 'n' roll, decorate it with genuine memorabilia from famous stars, all accompanied by raunchy music, and you're guaranteed to pull in as big a crowd in Manila as anywhere else.

Pubs

The ***L.A. Café*** in MH del Pilar St, is very popular in Ermita and is already getting into the mood in the afternoon. The friendly service, billiard tables, cold drinks and fantastic food (try the chicken curry) are obviously just the right mixture to keep the customers coming back. In the same building upstairs they have live music from 9pm until 2am, and lots going on late in the evening. Right on the next corner you'll come to the ***Jurassic Bar*** with billiards and videoke, and ***Amazonia***, also offering billiards, live music at the weekends and loads of entertainment, is only 100m away. You could also try the somewhat smaller ***G-Point*** in Padre Faura, near the junction with Adriatico St. It's a pub and restaurant with billiards, live music in the evenings, and the chance of a dance.

Amongst the best-known pubs in Makati, all in the Burgos St area, are ***Danish Connection*** on Kalaayan Ave, ***Heckle & Jeckle*** on Anza St, ***Rogues Sports Bar*** on Anza St corner Burgos, and ***The Handlebar*** in Polaris St, a friendly motorcycle bar that doesn't only welcome bikers. They have all the appropriate furnishings (even a few Harleys on show), plus billiards, and a tattoo studio on the first floor.

Also in Makati, in the Dusit Hotel Nikko, Edsa corner Pasay Rd, the ***Paulaner Brauhaus*** will tempt you in with its fresh, top-brewed beer and Bavarian style atmosphere.

Swimming Pools

Some hotels allow non-residents to use their swimming pools for an admission fee; most are open from 8am till 7pm.

Bayview Park Hotel, Roxas Blvd, Ermita, Tel 5261555. Open daily 7am-5pm. Admission P150.

Century Park Hotel, P Ocampo St, Malate, Tel 5288888. Open daily 2am-8pm. Admission P300.

Seamen's Club, Bonifacio Dr, Port Area, South Harbour. Open Mon-Sat 10am-10pm, Sun 9am-9pm. Admission P110. The official name for this complex, which comprises a large swimming pool, table tennis, billiards, library and restaurant, is the United Seamen's Service.

Medical Services & Wellness

The addresses of reliable doctors and hospitals in Metro Manila include:

General Practitioner (GP): Dr Peter Kaliski, Medical Towers Makati, Rufino St corner Ormaza St, Legaspi Village, Makati, Tel 8402792, Cellphone 0918-9050515, speaks German and English and consults Mon, Tue, Thu and Fri 9am-noon and 2-5pm. Telephone appointment required. Consultation: P1000.

Makati Medical Center, 2 Amorsolo St corner of Dela Rosa St, Makati, Tel 8159911.

Manila Doctors Hospital, 667 United Nations Ave, Ermita, Tel 5243011.

Medical Center Manila, 1122 General Luna St, Ermita, Tel 5238131.

St Luke Medical Center, 279 E Rodriguez Sr Blvd, Quezon City, Tel 7230301.

Mabuhay Spa Experience, Makati Golf Club, Makati, Tel 8302222.

The Spa, Acropolis Center, E Rodriguez Jr Ave, Quezon City, Tel 6342848. Branches in Alabang, Muntinlupa, and Bel-Air, Makati.

Money

The following banks (headquarters) and their branches will change cash and travellers' cheques as well as arrange money transfers:

Bank of America, Philamlife Tower, Paseo de Roxas, Makati, Tel 8155000.

Bank of the Philippine Islands, BPI Building, Ayala Ave, Makati, Tel 8185541.
Citibank, Citibank Center, Paseo de Roxas, Makati, Tel 9959999.
Deutsche Bank, Tower One, Ayala Triangle, Paseo de Roxas corner Ayala Ave, Makati, Tel 8946900.
Equitable PCI Bank, Equitable PCI Towers, Makati Ave corner Dela Costa St, Makati, Tel 8407000.
Hongkong & Shanghai Banking Corporation (HSBC), The Enterprise Center, Ayala Ave corner Paseo de Roxas, Makati, Tel 8305300.
Metrobank, Metrobank Plaza Building, Gil Puyat Ave, Makati, Tel 8103311.
Philippine National Bank, PNB Financial Center, Roxas Blvd, Pasay City, Tel 8916040-79.

Credit Cards & Travellers' Cheques
American Express, ACE Building, Rada St, Legaspi Village, Makati, Tel 8144777 (open Mon-Fri 9am-4.30pm); 24-hr emergency assistance: Tel 8154159.
- Adventure International Tours, 1810 Mabini St corner Remedios St, Malate, Tel 5268960 (open Mon-Fri 8.30am-4pm, Sat 9am-noon).
Bank of America, Philamlife Tower, Paseo de Roxas, Makati, Tel 8155000.
Diners Club International, 114 Valero St, Salcedo Village, Makati, Tel 8104521.
Thomas Cook Travel, Skyland Plaza Building, Gil Puyat Ave, Makati, Tel 8163701.
Visa & MasterCard, Equitable PCI Bank, United Nations Ave corner JC Bocobo St, Ermita, Tel 5212721.
- Paseo de Roxas corner Gil Puyat Ave, Makati, Tel 8972971-75.
- 203 Salcedo St, Legaspi Village, Makati, Tel 8126871.
- Ongpin St corner Sabino Padilla St, Chinatown, Santa Cruz Tel 7331454.

Miscellaneous
Cultural Centres: Alliance Française, Nicanor Garcia St, Bel-Air 2, Makati, Tel 8957441, Fax 8993654, @.
Australia Centre, Tower 2, RCBC Plaza, 6819 Ayala Avenue, Makati, Tel. 7578132, @.
Goethe Institut Manila, 687 Aurora Blvd, Quezon City, Tel 7224671-73, Fax 7224673, @.
The British Council, Taipan Place Building, Emerald Ave, Ortigas Center, Pasig City, Tel 9141011-14, Fax 9141020, @.
Thomas Jefferson Cultural Center, US Embassy, Roxas Blvd, Ermita, Tel 5231001.
Foreign Consulates: See the Visa section in the Travel Planning chapter earlier in this book.
Immigration Office (Bureau of Immigration - BI/Commission on Immigration and Deportation - CID), Magallanes Dr, Intramuros, Tel 5273257, 3384552. Open Mon-Fri 8am-noon and 1-5pm.
Online: Internet access is no problem anywhere in the city, every shopping centre has at least one internet café.
Post & Telephone: The quickest way to send mail from the Philippines is to take it to the Air Mail Distribution Center near the Domestic Airport.
Unlike the General Post Office (GPO), the Rizal Park Post Office is less frequented, and you may only have to wait there a little while or not at all.
A tip for stamp collectors: at the GPO you can get special release stamps. Go to the special room at the rear on the left-hand side of the building.
GPO, Liwasang Bonifacio, Intramuros (open Mon-Sat 8am-5pm, Sun 8am-noon; parcel service only Mon-Sat 8am-4pm). You'll find the poste restante to the left, at the back of the GPO.
Rizal Park Post Office, Rizal Park, near the Manila Hotel, Ermita (open Mon-Fri 8am-5pm, Sat 8am-noon).
Makati Central Post Office, Gil Puyat Ave, Makati (open Mon-Fri 8am-5pm,

Sat 8am-noon; parcel service and registered mail service is available Mon-Fri 8am-4.30pm only).
Domestic Airport Post Office, Domestic Airport Rd, Pasay City (open Mon-Fri 8am-5pm, Sat 8am-noon; parcel service and registered mail service is available Mon-Fri 8am-4.30pm only).
NAIA Post Office, International Airport, Parañaque (open Mon-Fri 8am-5pm, Sat 8am-4pm; parcel service and registered mail service is available Mon-Fri 8am-noon only).
Post Code: 1000 (City of Manila), 1100 (Quezon City), 1200 (Makati), 1300 (Pasay City), 1400 (Caloocan City), 1550 (Mandaluyong City), 1600 (Pasig City), 1700 (Parañaque), 1800 (Marikina).
The area code for Manila is 02.
Travel Agencies: Blue Horizons Travel & Tours, Trafalgar Plaza, Dela Costa St, Salcedo Village, Makati, Tel 8483901, Fax 8483909, @ .
Filipino Travel Center, 1555 Adriatico St, Ermita, Tel 5284507-09, Fax 5284503, @.
Interisland Travel & Tours, Marc 2000 Building Annex, Taft Ave corner San Andres St, Malate, Tel 5238720-24, Fax 5224795, @.
Mr Ticket, Park Hotel (Lobby), 1030 Belen St, Paco, Tel 5212371, Fax 5212393, @.
Swagman Travel, 411 A Flores St, Ermita, Tel 5238541-45, Fax 5223663.
Tourist Office: Department of Tourism Building, TM Kalaw St, Rizal Park, Tel 5242384, 5252000, @. Open daily 7am-8pm.
Tourist Police: Tourist Assistance Unit (TAU), Department of Tourism Building, TM Kalaw St, Rizal Park, Tel 5224372, 5241728, 5241660; police emergency number: 166.

Getting Around

Traffic in Manila is chaotic and noisy, especially to someone who is used to fairly strict traffic controls. There are few bus stops and these are not always used. Buses and jeepneys stop wherever they see a fare to pick up and then taxis of various companies try to get in ahead of them. Horns and hand signals are used most often, brake lights and blinkers rarely, and traffic-lane markings seem to be thought a waste of paint. However, the Filipinos are used to these conditions and there are few accidents - the battered vehicles usually last longer than their appearance would lead you to believe, so you don't need to be nervous.
A pleasant alternative for local journeys is to use the fairly inexpensive, fast Metrorail (LRT 1), Metrostar (MRT 3) and Megatren (LRT 2).

Car

If you are interested in renting a car the following international companies can be recommended:
Avis, Ninoy Aquino International Airport, Arrival Area: NAIA Terminal 1, Tel 8312681, and NAIA Terminal 2, Tel 8796245.
Further branches: Bel-Air Building, Roxas Blvd corner Kalaw St, Ermita, Tel 5281532; Traders Hotel, Roxas Blvd, Pasay City, Tel 5237019, (ext 2501); Makati Shangri-la Hotel, Ayala Ave, Makati, Tel 8671047; Saville Building, Gil Puyat Ave corner Paseo de Roxas, Tel 8998682.
Budget, Ninoy Aquino International Airport, Arrival Area: NAIA Terminal 1, Tel 8318247, 87713137, and NAIA Terminal 2, Tel 87712266.
Further branches: ITC Building, Gil Puyat Ave, Makati, Tel 8890189; West Service Rd, South Super Highway, Parañaque, Tel 7668118.
Hertz, Ninoy Aquino International Airport, Arrival Area, NAIA Terminal 1, Tel 87714063.
Further branch: Sunette Tower, Makati Ave corner Durban St, Makati, Tel 8975161.

Further companies can be found in the yellow pages under 'Automobile'.

Bus
Around Manila, city buses only display their final destination on the front of the bus. That can be a large complex like the NAIA (Ninoy Aquino International Airport), a street name like Ayala (for Ayala Ave or Ayala Center in Makati) or a whole district like Quiapo (north of Pasig River).
The fare is P8 for the first five km and P1.75 for every km after that.

Jeepney
You need to get to know Manila a bit before you can travel through the city by jeepney without problems. Crowding and the limited view make it hard to see where you are going, so a seat by the driver is desirable. Jeepney routes are fixed. Their main streets and stops are shown on the side of the vehicle and mostly on the windscreen as well. For example, jeepneys with the sign 'Baclaran, Harrison, Santa Cruz, Rizal, Monumento' will go from Baclaran in Pasay City, through Harrison St to Harrison Plaza, then down Mabini St, back down MH del Pilar St - both one-way streets - past the Manila City Hall (Lawton), to the district of Santa Cruz, then down Rizal Ave and Rizal Ave Extension to Monumento in Caloocan City.
Jeepneys on the north-south route are almost always marked 'Baclaran' or 'Libertad' to show the southern end of their route, both in Pasay City. The northern end could be 'Monumento' (Caloocan City, at the end of the Rizal Ave Extension); 'Blumentritt' (a street in northern Santa Cruz, by the Chinese Hospital and near the Chinese Cemetery); or 'Divisoria' (the Divisoria Market in the district of San Nicolas). Jeepneys in Ermita run along MH del Pilar St and Mabini St (those marked 'Harrison') or Taft Ave (those marked 'Taft'). Jeepneys whose north-eastern destination is shown as 'Project 2', 'Project 3' or 'Project 4' are going to Cubao (Quezon City), while those marked 'Project 6' and 'Project 8' are heading to the north of Quezon City. The fare is P7.50 for the first four km, and P1.25 for each extra km.
For further information see also the Jeepney section of the Getting Around chapter earlier in this book.

Taxi
Manila is crawling with taxis. The flag-down charge is P30, it's P2.50 for every 300m after that. Always have some change ready when you board a taxi in Manila, as there's no guarantee the driver will have any.
For further information see also the Taxi section of the Getting Around chapter earlier in this book.

Examples of fares: From Ermita (corner of Mabini St and Padre Faura) to Domestic Airport P120; International Airport P140; Intramuros/GPO P50; Makati P100; North Harbour P60; Pasay City (Edsa bus terminals) P100; and Santa Cruz (Philippine Rabbit Bus Terminal) P80.

Metrorail, Metrostar & Megatren
The Metrorail (LRT 1 - Light Rail Transit -, Yellow Line) is an overhead railway which runs on concrete pylons several metres high, linking the districts of Caloocan City and Pasay City. The line runs from North Terminal (Monumento) in Caloocan City, via Rizal Ave to Central Terminal near the Manila City Hall and on via Taft Ave to South Terminal in Baclaran, Pasay City.
A second, independent line, the Metrostar (MRT 3 - Metro Rail Transit) runs from North Ave in Quezon City along Edsa to Taft Ave in Baclaran, Pasay City.

A third line, the Megatren (LRT 2 - Purple Line) is being built at the moment and should be fully operational by the end of 2004. It runs from Santolan Station in Pasig City via Marikina, Quezon City and San Juan mostly along Aurora Blvd to Recto Station in Santa Cruz. A section of the line, from Santolan Station to Cubao Center Station, was opened in April 2003.

Times: With the exception of Good Friday, the Metrorail and Metrostar services run from 5.30am until 9pm, and the Megatren from 5am until 8pm. Smoking, eating and drinking are not allowed, either on the platforms or in the trains. Bulky objects which may cause obstruction will not be carried. Watch out for pickpockets!

Fares: The fare for the Metrorail is a flat rate of P12, irrespective of how far you go, with the exception being that you only pay P2 if you are only travelling the last three stations to the terminus.
The Megatren fare is also a flat rate of P12; however, once the line is fully operational there will be range of fares. The fare for the Metrostar depends on how many stops you go before you get off (it's P9.50 to P15, which is 50 centavos per stop on top of the basic fare). In addition to single tickets, so-called SVTs (Stored Value Tickets) for a value of P60 and P120 are available, which must be used up within six months of purchase.

The following are the stations from north to south (Metrorail, Metrostar), and west to east (Megatren), and some of the prominent city features near each one (see also map on page 224):

Metrorail (LRT 1)

North Terminal (Monumento)
for: Andres Bonifacio Monument, Philippine Rabbit Bus Terminal (Edsa), Victory Liner Bus Terminal (Caloocan).

5th Ave Station
for: Caloocan City.

R Papa Station
for: Baliwag Transit Bus Terminal (Caloocan).

Abad Santos Station
for: Chinese Cemetery.

Blumentritt Station
for: Chinese Hospital, Eagle Star Bus Terminal, San Lazaro Hippodrome.

Tayuman Station
for: Autobus Transport Bus Terminal, Dangwa Tranco Bus Terminal (Dimasalang), Fariñas Trans Bus Terminal, San Lazaro Hippodrome.

Bambang Station
for: Dominion Bus Line Bus Terminal (Sampaloc), University of Santo Tomas.

D Jose Station
for: Claro M Recto Ave, Genesis Transport Busterminal (Santa Cruz), Philippine Rabbit Bus Terminal (Avenida), Central Market.

Carriedo Station
for: Chinatown, Escolta St, Ilalim ng Tulay Market, Quinta Market, Quiapo Church, Santa Cruz Church.

Central Terminal
for: GPO, Immigration Office, Intramuros, Manila City Hall.

United Nations Ave Station
for: Manila Doctor's Hospital, Manila Medical Center, Manila Pavillon Hotel, Paco Park, Rizal Park, Tourist, Office, Western Police District.

Pedro Gil Station
for: Manila Midtown Hotel, Philippine General Hospital.

Quirino Ave Station
for: Malate Church, San Andres Market.

Vito Cruz Station
for: Central Bank, Century Park Hotel, Cultural Center, De La Salle University, Harrison Plaza, Star City.
Gil Puyat Station
for: Atrium Hotel, Cartimar Market, JAM Transit Bus Terminal, Tritran Bus Terminal (Pasay), Manila Film Center.
Libertad Station
for: Pasay Market (Libertad Market).
Edsa Station
for: Metrostar (MRT 3) Taft Station, Crow Lines Bus Terminal, Five Star Bus Terminal, Genesis Bus Terminal (Pasay), Partas Bus Terminal (Pasay), Philtranco Bus Terminal (Pasay), Victory Liner Bus Terminal (Pasay).
South Terminal (Baclaran)
for: Baclaran Church, Baclaran Flea Market, Seaside Market.

Metrostar (MRT 3)

North Station
for: SM City, Philippine Rabbit Bus Terminal (Edsa).
Quezon Station
for: National Parks & Wildlife Center, Camelot Hotel, Danarra Hotel & Resort, Hotel Rembrandt.
GMA-Kamuning Station
for: Dagupan Bus Bus Terminal, Dominion Bus Line Bus Terminal (Cubao), JAC Liner Bus Terminal, Tritran Bus Terminal (Kamias), Victory Liner Bus Terminal (Kamias),
Araneta-Cubao Station
for: Araneta Center, Baliwag Transit Bus Terminal (Cubao), Victory Liner Bus Terminal (Cubao), Dangwa Tranco Bus Terminal (Cubao), Partas Bus Terminal Cubao), Philtranco Bus Terminal (Cubao).
Santolan-Annapolis Station
for: Camp Aguinaldo, Camp Crame, Greenhills Shopping Center.
Ortigas Station
for: Ortigas Center, Asian Development Bank, SM Megamall, Robinsons Galleria, Statue of Our Lady of Edsa (Edsa Shrine).
Shaw Station
for: Shangri-La Plaza Mall, Edsa Shangri-La Hotel, The Richmonde Hotel.
Boni Station
for: Horizon Edsa Hotel, The Legend Hotel.
Guadalupe Station
for: Guadalupe Commercial Center.
Buendia Station
for: Equitable PCI Bank.
Ayala Station
for: Ayala Ave, Ayala Center, Pasay Rd, Dusit Hotel Nikko, Hotel Inter-Continental.
Magallanes Station
for: South Super Highway, Magallanes Village.
Taft Station
for: Metrorail (LRT 1) Edsa Station, Crow Lines Bus Terminal, Five Star Bus Terminal, Genesis Transport Bus Terminal (Pasay), Partas Bus Terminal (Pasay), Philtranco Bus Terminal (Pasay), Victory Liner Bus Terminal (Pasay).

Megatren (LRT 2)

Recto Station
for: Claro M Recto Ave, Rizal Ave, Genesis Transport Bus Terminal (Santa Cruz), Philippine Rabbit Bus Terminal (Avenida), Central Market.
Legarda Station
for: Sampaloc Market, Malacañang Palace.
Pureza Station
for: National Statistics Office.
V. Mapa Station
for: SM Centrepoint.
J. Ruiz Station
for: Quadrillion Mansion.
Gilmore Station
for: Broadway Centrum, Broadway Court, Goethe Institute.

Boston Station
for: Dangwa Tranco Bus Terminal (Cubao), Partas Bus Terminal (Cubao).
Cubao Center Station
for: Araneta Center, Baliwag Transit Bus Terminal (Cubao), Victory Liner Bus Terminal (Cubao), Dangwa Tranco Bus Terminal (Cubao), Partas Bus Terminal (Cubao), Philtranco Bus Terminal (Cubao).
Anonas Station
for: Quezon City Medical Center.
Katipunan Station
for: Philippine School of Business Administration, St Bridget's School.
Santolan Station
for: LRT Santolan Administration Building.

Getting There & Away

Air

The Ninoy Aquino International Airport (NAIA), Tel 8795964, is located about seven km south of the areas important for the tourist, ie Ermita/Malate and Makati. Almost all international flights are processed here, at the NAIA Terminal 1, and all information below on arrival etc. refers to this terminal alone.
One km east of NAIA Terminal 1, in NAIA Terminal 2 (aka Centennial Terminal), Philippine Airlines processes its inland and overseas flights.
The construction of NAIA Terminal 3 in Andrews Ave near the Villamor Air Base is almost completed, but arguments over contract details amongst the investors have repeatedly postponed the grand opening, and there is no way of predicting when in fact it is ever going to be operational.

The Domestic Airport is about three km from NAIA Terminal 1, heading into town.

Ninoy Aquino International Airport (NAIA)

Arrival

Immigration: Anyone entering the country with a visa should point this out to the immigration official, just in case. Otherwise, it is possible that only the customary 21 days would be stamped in the passport.

Money: After going through the arrival procedure you have a chance to change money. The Banco de Oro, Landbank and Philippine National Bank (PNB) offer roughly the same rate as the banks in town, not quite as good as the one offered by moneychangers. Don't forget that you will also need some smaller notes as well as big ones; taxi drivers hardly ever have change. If you want to avoid the lines at the foreign exchange counter you could always get up to P20,000 (2 × P10,000) with your plastic keycard from the ATM to the right of the right-hand exit.

Information: Just behind the baggage check you'll find a Department of Tourism (DOT) counter. The nice ladies there will be glad to make enquiries at hotels for you (maybe even make the call yourself).

Reconfirmation: If you want to confirm a connecting flight or your return flight before leaving the airport, you'll find the counters of all the major airlines two floors up; take the staircase in front of the arrival hall exit.

Departure

Reconfirmation: Nearly every international flight has to be reconfirmed by 72 hours before departure at the latest, either by phone or personally. In other words: You inform the airline that you actually do want to take the flight you booked.

If you do not do this, the computer will mercilessly delete you from the passenger list. In view of the number of fully booked flights in high season, this could lead to an unwelcome extension of your holiday by days or even weeks.

Airport Tax: P550 for international flights, and P200 for internal flights.

NAIA Terminal 1 to the City

Taxi: At present, only certain aircon taxis (eg Avis Coupon Taxis) are officially allowed to service the airport. There are set fares for this service: eg P300 to Pasay City, P500 to Ermita, Malate and Makati, and P700 to Quezon City (Cubao). The counters belonging to the various companies can be found outside the arrivals hall, diagonally across the road to the left.
If you don't want to accept the set fare, there is an alternative if you take the stairs up to the departure level. You'll find the nearest staircase before you come to the main exit from the arrival level, and there's another one outside about 50m to the left of the main exit. You can wait for a taxi at the departure level that has just dropped off passengers and would otherwise have to head back to town empty. Mind you, lots of sneaky taxi drivers have hit on this trick and now wait for victims at the departure level with special 'deals'. Normally, a taxi ride from the international airport to Ermita/Malate would cost around P140 (US$2.50), but you will scarcely find a driver who will do it for less than P200.
Another alternative is to walk about 150m along to the bus stop (see 'Bus' below) and ask the guard there to wave down a taxi for you. He will note down the destination and the number of the taxi, so the taxi driver won't be tempted to try on any fiddles.
The meter should be switched on just before the taxi starts off. If the driver tells you that the meter is out of order, you're quite entitled to get out again. However, ordering the driver to stop and let you out after you've gone 500m can be awkward, especially at night. If you agree on a fixed price with the taxi driver, don't forget to specify what currency you mean. It wouldn't be the first time a fare of '200' turned out at the end of the journey to be US$200 instead of P200!
Beware! Certain taxi drivers, however, will proudly hand you typed 'official' fare lists, often impressively set in a leather binder with gold lettering. Be aware that these have no legal validity whatsoever and are simply another crude attempt to defraud unsuspecting tourists.
Keep your cool and don't allow yourself to be provoked if you encounter problems with a driver on the way to the hotel. You're in a much better position to win a fight when you and your luggage are already out of the taxi and you can call on the hotel staff for support.

Bus: Turn right when you leave the NAIA exit, go down the ramp (about 150m) through the underpass and wait at the bus stop on the right hand side of the road for the appropriate bus to come along, eg 'Cubao', 'Quezon City' and 'Monumento' for destinations along Edsa as well as various bus terminals and areas such as Makati and Mandaluyong City (P5 to P10, depending on distance). These buses (some of which are aircon) normally go past the Domestic Airport first.

Jeepney: The cheapest way to get from the NAIA to Mabini St in Ermita is to turn right at the NAIA exit and go down the ramp about 150m to the bus stop (see 'Bus' above). There you catch a jeepney with the sign 'Baclaran' and stay on it until Baclaran itself (P5.50),

Manila

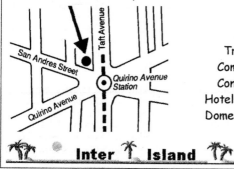

change there onto a jeepney with the sign 'Harrison-Mabini' which will take you to Mabini St (P5.50).
Coming back, catch a jeepney in MH del Pilar St, Ermita, with the sign 'Baclaran', get out in Baclaran and change into a jeepney with the sign 'Sucat-Highway' to the NAIA.

Metrorail/Metrostar: For a jeepney to Baclaran see above. A taxi from NAIA to the Metrorail (LRT 1) South Terminal in Baclaran or the Metrostar (MRT 3) Taft Station is unlikely to cost you more than P50 (providing, that is, a taxi will take you for this short distance). From there it's P12, eg by Metrorail to Pedro Gil Station or United Nations Ave Station in Ermita (for accommodation in Adriatico St and Mabini St) or for P13.50 by Metrostar to the Araneta-Cubao Station in Cubao/Quezon City (various bus terminals). See also the maps on page 184 and page 224.

NAIA Terminal 1 to the Domestic Airport

Travellers landing in Manila and proceeding to another destination within the Philippines have to transfer to the nearby Domestic Airport or to NAIA Terminal 2.
A taxi ride from the NAIA to the Domestic Airport generally costs no more than P50, but you can be charged up to P150. An official airport coupon taxi costs P150 to NAIA Terminal 2 and P300 to the Domestic Airport.

Domestic Airport

In Manila almost all Philippine internal flights are processed at the Domestic Airport. Air Philippines, Asian Spirit and Cebu Pacific use the main building. Smaller airlines such as Island Trans Voyager, Pacific Airways and Seair each have their own little arrival/departure facility. Philippine Airlines processes its flights in NAIA Terminal 2 (between the Domestic Airport and NAIA Terminal 1).
Remember to tell the taxi driver in good time the name of the airline you are flying with and, if necessary, your destination.

Warning: Passengers on the waiting list are accepted 30 minutes before take-off. So, even if you have a fixed reservation, check in with plenty of time to spare, otherwise you risk being deleted from the passenger list and losing your seat.

Domestic Airport to the City

Taxi: Almost all of the taxi drivers waiting at the Domestic Airport will refuse to switch their meter on and will stubbornly demand a ridiculously inflated set price for the journey. Rather than giving in to these latter-day highwaymen, go through the car park until you come to the road which runs from the airport, Domestic Airport Rd, and flag down a passing taxi there. At the time of this book's publication the normal fare to Ermita was around P120.

International Airlines in Manila

Aeroflot Russian International Airlines, YL Holding Building, Herrera St corner Salcedo St, Makati, Tel 8673948.
Air Canada, The Enterprise Center, Ayala Ave corner Paseo de Roxas, Makati, Tel 8848294-95.
Air France, Trident Tower, 312 Gil Puyat Ave, Makati, Tel 8877581.
Air India, Philam Life Building, Leviste St, Makati, Tel 8152441.
Air Nuigini, Fortune Building, Legaspi St, Legaspi Village, Makati, Tel 8913339.
Alitalia, Alexander House, Amorsolo St, Legaspi Village, Makati, Tel 8178894, 8174505.
American Airlines, Olympia Condominium, Makati Ave corner Santo Tomas St, Makati, Tel 8103228.

Asiana Airlines, Salcedo Tower, Dela Costa St, Salcedo Village, Makati, Tel 8925688.
British Airways, Filipino Building, Legaspi St corner Rosa St, Legaspi Village, Makati, Tel 8170361, 8156556.
Cathay Pacific, LKG Tower, Ayala Ave, Makati, Tel 7570888.
Cebu Pacific, Colonnade Building, Palanca St corner Legaspi St, Legaspi Village, Makati, Tel 8939607.
- Robinsons Place, Adriatico St, Ermita, Tel 5269988, 5265516.
China Airlines, Golden Empire Tower, Roxas Blvd corner Padre Faura, Ermita, Tel 5238021.
Continental Micronesia, SGV Building, Ayala Ave, Makati, Tel 8188701.
CSA Czech Airlines, Peninsula Court Building, Paseo de Roxas corner Makati Ave, Makati, Tel 8926006.
Egyptair, RCBC Plaza, Ayala Ave corner Gil Puyat Ave, Makati, Tel 8435901.
El Al, Rajah Sulayman Building, Benavidez St, Legaspi Village, Makati, Tel 8164121.
Emirates, Pacific Star Building, Makati Ave corner Gil Puyat Ave, Makati, Tel 8115278-80.
Eva Air, LKG Tower, Ayala Ave, Makati, Tel 8841135.
Gulf Air, Don Chua Lamko Building, Leviste St, Makati, Tel 8921313, 8178383.
- United Nations Ave corner MH del Pilar St, Ermita, Tel 52577621, 5279535.
Japan Airlines, Standard Chartered Bank Building, Ayala Ave, Makati, Tel 8866868.
KLM Royal Dutch Airlines, Athenaeum Building, Leviste St, Makati, Tel 8154790, 8105817.
Korean Air, LPL Plaza, Leviste St, Makati, Tel 8175705, 8934909.
Kuwait Airways, Jaka II Building, Legaspi St, Makati, Tel 8172778.
Lufthansa, Phinma Plaza, Plaza Dr, Rockwell Center, Makati, Tel. 5806400.
Malaysia Airlines, World Center Building, Gil Puyat Ave, Makati, Tel 8678767.
- Legaspi Towers, Roxas Blvd corner P Ocampo St, Malate, Tel 5259404.
Northwest Airlines, La Paz Centre, Salcedo St coner Rufino St, Makati, Tel 8104716, 8170616 (reservations).
- Golden Empire Tower, Roxas Blvd corner Padre Faura, Ermita, Tel 5211928.
Philippine Airlines, NAIA Terminal 2, Pasay City, Tel 8316541, 8795602-04.
- Adriatico St corner Padre Faura, Ermita, Tel 5214512, 5262597.
- Ali Mall Phase II, Araneta Center, Cubao, Quezon City, Tel 9116666.
- Century Park Hotel, P Ocampo St, Malate, Tel 5231554.
- PAL Building, Legaspi St, Makati, Tel 8558888 (24-hr reservations), 8180111.
Qantas Airways, Filipino Building, Legaspi St corner Dela Rosa St, Legaspi Village, Makati, Tel 8120607.
Qatar Airways, Colonnade Building, Legaspi St, Legaspi Village, Makati, Tel 8121888.
Royal Brunei Airlines, Saville Building, Gil Puyat Ave corner Paseo de Roxas, Makati, Tel 8973309, 8953545.
Saudi Arabian Airlines, Metro House, 345 Gil Puyat Ave, Makati, Tel 8964046.
Scandinavian Airlines System (SAS), Peninsula Court Building, Paseo de Roxas corner Makati Ave, Makati, Tel 8929991.
Singapore Airlines, 138 Dela Costa St, Salcedo Village, Makati, Tel 8104951.
Swiss, Zuellig Building, Malugay St, Makati, Tel 8188351.
Thai Airways International, Country Space I Building, Gil Puyat Ave, Salcedo Village, Makati, Tel 8124744.
- Golden Empire Tower, Roxas Blvd corner Padre Faura, Ermita, Tel 5280122-25.
United Airlines, The Enterprise Center, Tower II, Ayala Ave corner Paseo de Roxas, Makati, Tel 8848272.

Vietnam Airlines, Legaspi Parkview Condominium, Legaspi St corner Castro St, Legaspi Village, Makati, Tel 8302335-36.

Domestic Airlines in Manila

Internal flights are provided by Air Philippines, Asian Spirit, Cebu Pacific, Island Trans Voyager, Pacific Airways, Philippine Airlines and Seair.

Flights for all the above companies can be booked in the following offices (open Mon-Fri 8.30am-5pm, Sat 8.30am-noon) or at the various authorised travel agents.

Air Philippines, Allied Bank Center, Ayala Avenue, Makati, Tel. 8936086.
- Charter House, 114 Legaspi St, Legaspi Village, Makati, Tel 8921459.
- Padre Faura Center, Padre Faura corner MH del Pilar St, Ermita, Tel 5240540.
- Opulent Building, Edsa corner General Roxas Ave, Cubao, Quezon City, Tel 9112122.
- Domestic Airport Rd, Pasay City, Tel 5512180, 5517991.

Destinations: Bacolod, Cagayan de Oro, Cebu City, Davao, Dumaguete, General Santos, Iloilo City, Kalibo, Puerto Princesa, San Jose (Mindoro), Tuguegarao, Zamboanga.

Asian Spirit, LPL Tower, Legaspi St, Legaspi Village, Makati, Tel 8882002-03.
- Domestic Airport Rd, Pasay City, Tel 8518888.

Destinations: Baguio, Batanes, Boac (Marinduque), Busuanga, Calbayog, Catarman, Caticlan (for Boracay), Masbate, San Jose (Mindoro), Sandoval/ Taytay (Palawan), Tagbilaran, Virac.

Cebu Pacific, Domestic Airport Rd, Pasay City, Tel 8521318, 8519182.
- Colonnade Building, Palanca St corner Legaspi St, Legaspi Village, Makati, Tel 8939607.
- Robinsons Place, Adriatico St, Ermita, Tel 5269988, 5265516.

Destinations: Bacolod, Cagayan de Oro, Cebu City, Davao, Dumaguete, Iloilo City, Kalibo, Roxas, Tacloban, Zamboanga.

Island Transvoyager, Soriano Hangar, Andrews Ave, Pasay City, Tel. 8040408.

Destinations: El Nido, Pamalican Island.

Pacific Airways, Domestic Airport Rd, Pasay City, Tel 8322731-32, 8916252.

Destinations: Busuanga, Caticlan (for Boracay).

Philippine Airlines, NAIA Terminal 2, Pasay City, Tel 8795602-04, 8316541. Open daily from 2 am to 9.30 pm.
- Adriatico St corner Padre Faura, Ermita, Tel 5214512, 5262597.
- Ali Mall Phase II, Araneta Center, Cubao, Quezon City, Tel 9116666.
- Century Park Hotel, P Ocampo St, Malate, Tel 5231554.
- PAL Building, Legaspi St, Makati, Tel 8558888 (24-hr reservations), 8180111.

Destinations: Bacolod, Butuan, Cagayan de Oro, Cebu City, Cotabato, Davao, Dipolog, General Santos, Iloilo City, Kalibo, Legaspi, Naga, Puerto Princesa, Roxas, Tacloban, Tagbilaran, Zamboanga.

Seair, Domestic Airport Rd, Pasay City, Tel 8515555, 8841521 (reservations).
- Pasay Rd, Makati, Tel 8437308.

Destinations: Angeles (Clark), Busuanga, Caticlan (for Boracay), El Nido, Puerto Princesa, Sandoval.

Bus

On the main routes, all bus companies use a combination of rustic ordinary buses and more comfortable aircon buses (some with video facilities). You can ring and enquire about exact departure times and possibly reserve a seat at the same time.

Bus Terminals in Manila

There is no central bus terminal in Manila, and those belonging to the individual companies - several of which

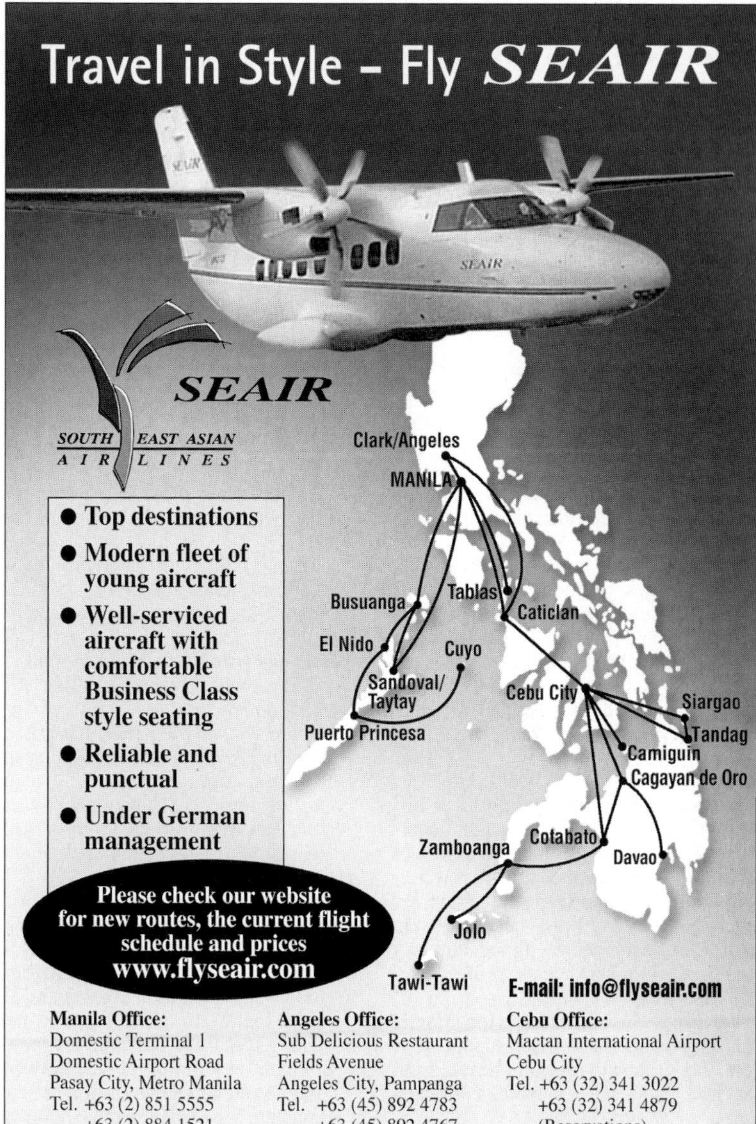

Travel in Style - Fly SEAIR
SEAIR
SOUTH EAST ASIAN AIRLINES
● Top destinations
● Modern fleet of young aircraft
● Well-serviced aircraft with comfortable Business Class style seating
● Reliable and punctual
● Under German management
Please check our website for new routes, the current flight schedule and prices
www.flyseair.com
Clark/Angeles
MANILA
Busuanga
Tablas
Caticlan
El Nido
Cuyo
Sandoval/ Taytay
Puerto Princesa
Cebu City
Siargao
Tandag
Camiguin
Cagayan de Oro
Cotabato
Zamboanga
Davao
Jolo
Tawi-Tawi
E-mail: info@flyseair.com
Manila Office:
Domestic Terminal 1
Domestic Airport Road
Pasay City, Metro Manila
Tel. +63 (2) 851 5555
+63 (2) 884 1521
(Reservations)
Angeles Office:
Sub Delicious Restaurant
Fields Avenue
Angeles City, Pampanga
Tel. +63 (45) 892 4783
+63 (45) 892 4767
Cebu Office:
Mactan International Airport
Cebu City
Tel. +63 (32) 341 3022
+63 (32) 341 4879
(Reservations)

Philippine Rabbit - Hare today, gone tomorrow?

The oldest bus company in the Philippines, Philippine Rabbit, has been laid low since April 2004 by a group of striking workers. Whether their 200 buses and 1,000 employees ever leave the garages again is an open question. They wouldn't be the first Philippine company to end up going bust after prolonged strike action. **Stop press:** The Rabbits are running again.

can be easily reached by Metrorail (LRT 1) or Metrostar (MRT 3) - are scattered all over the city. However, you can find a cluster of bus terminals not far from each other all along Edsa in Cubao (Quezon City).
The Park 'n' Ride Lawton Bus Terminal, Padre Burgos St (next to the Metropolitan Theater not far from Manila City Hall and Quezon Bridge) is used by a few small bus companies that have routes to the south of Manila (Batangas, Lucena, Nasugbu, San Pablo, San Pedro, Tagaytay).

Departures: A few bus companies even have two or three terminals in different parts of the town. After departure, it is possible that buses will first of all drop by a second or third bus terminal to pick up additional passengers. By then of course all the best seats are taken, so it's best to phone and ask where the bus first leaves from.

Warning: Buses heading for Manila hardly ever say so on the front, but show the area of the city they are heading for, such as 'Caloocan', 'Cubao' or 'Pasay'.

Note: There follows a list of the addresses and major routes of the principal bus companies in Manila. The number beside the bus company name refers to its number in the Bus Destinations From Manila map key (page 227).

1 ***Autobus Transport***, España St corner J Tolentino St, Sampaloc, Tel 7358096-98.
Destinations to the north: Aparri, Banaue, Cauayan, Laoag, San Fernando (La Union), Tuguegarao.
Getting there: By Cubao jeepney from Taft Ave.
Nearest Metrorail station: D Jose.

2 ***Baliwag Transit*** (Caloocan Terminal), 199 Rizal Ave Extension corner 2nd Ave, Grace Park, Caloocan City, Tel 3640778.
Destinations to the north: Bulacan Province, Baliwag, Cabanatuan, San Jose.
Getting there: By Monumento jeepney from Mabini St.
Nearest Metrorail station: R Papa.

3 ***Baliwag Transit*** (Cubao Terminal), Edsa, Cubao, Quezon City, Tel 9123343.
Destinations to the north: Aparri, Bulacan Province, Baliwag, Cauayan, San Jose, Tuguegarao.
Getting there: By Cubao jeepney from Taft Ave.
Nearest Metrostar station: Araneta-Cubao.

4 ***Crow Lines***, Taft Ave corner Edsa, Pasay City, Tel 8040623.
Destinations to the south: Nasugbu (Lian/Matabungkay), Tagaytay (Lake Taal).
Getting there: By Baclaran jeepney or bus from Taft Ave or MH del Pilar St and change in or before Baclaran.
Nearest Metrorail station: Edsa.
Nearest Metrostar station: Taft.

© Jens Peters
BONIFACIO MONUMENT
MacArthur Highway
North Expressway
E. De los Santos Ave.
(Edsa)
QUEZON MEMORIAL CIRCLE
Rizal Ave. Ext.
A. Bonifacio
Roosevelt Ave.
C-3 Road
San Francisco del Monte
CHINESISCHER FRIEDHOF
E. De los Santos Ave. (Edsa)
Cubao
Abad Santos
Blumentritt
Quezon Blvd.
E. Rodriguez Sr. Blvd.
Tayuman
TAYUMAN RAILWAY STATION
Jose
Rizal Ave.
Espana
Aurora Blvd.
Moriones
A.H. Lacson St.
North Harbor
Claro M. Recto
Ave
Legarda
R. Magsaysay Blvd.
MACARTHUR BRIDGE
JONES BRIDGE
QUEZON BRIDGE
Laurel
Pasig River
DEL PAN BRIDGE
AYALA BRIDGE
NAGTAHAN BRIDGE
A. Bonifacio
Ayala Blvd.
Drive
South Harbor
P. Burgos St.
RIZAL PARK
T.M. Kalaw St.
United Nations Ave
PACO RAILWAY STATION
Padre Faura
Pedro Gil
Manila Bay
Roxas Blvd.
M.H. del Pilar St.
Mabini St.
Adriatico St.
Quirino Ave
Taft Ave
Manila Yacht Club
Ocampo St.
South Super Highway
Ayala Ave.
Makati
CULTURAL CENTER
Gil Puyat Ave.
Taft Ave.
Pasay City
Harrison St.
Roxas Blvd.
E. De los Santos Ave. (Edsa)
INTERNATIONAL AIRPORT
DOMESTIC AIRPORT
km
0 0,5 1
Manila Bus Terminals
Metrorail Metrostar
1 North Terminal (Monumento)
2 5th Avenue Station
3 R. Papa Station
4 Abad Santos Station
5 Blumentritt Station
6 Tayuman Station
7 Bambang Station
8 D. Jose Station
9 Carriedo Station
10 Central Terminal
11 United Nations Ave. Station
12 Pedro Gil Station
13 Quirino Avenue Station
14 Vito Cruz Station
15 Gil Puyat Station
16 Libertad Station
17 Edsa Station
18 South Terminal (Baclaran)
19 Taft Station
20 Magallanes Station
21 Ayala Station
22 Araneta-Cubao Station
23 GMA-Kamuning Station
24 Quezon Station
25 North Station

Manila

Bus Terminals

1 Philippine Rabbit (Edsa Terminal)
2 Victory Liner (Caloocan Terminal)
3 Baliwag Transit (Caloocan Terminal)
4 Victory Liner (Kamias Terminal)
5 JAC Liner
6 Tritran (Kamias Terminal)
7 Dagupan Bus
8 Baliwag Transit (Cubao Terminal)
9 Dominion Bus Line (Cubao Terminal)
10 Victory Liner (Cubao Terminal)
11 JAM Transit (Cubao Terminal)
12 Partas (Cubao Terminal)
13 Philtranco (Cubao Terminal)
14 Eagle Star
15 Dominion Bus Line (Sampaloc Terminal)
16 Fariñas Trans
17 Genesis Transport (Santa Cruz Terminal)
Philippine Rabbit (Avenida Terminal)
18 Autobus Transport
19 Victory Liner (Sampaloc Terminal)
20 Park 'n' Ride Busterminal
21 JAM Transit (Pasay Terminal)
Tritran (Pasay Terminal)
22 Victory Liner (Pasay Terminal)
23 Partas (Pasay Terminal)
Philtranco (Pasay Terminal)
24 Crow Lines
Genesis Transport (Pasay Terminal)
25 Five Star

5 ***Dagupan Bus***, Edsa corner New York St, Cubao, Quezon City, Tel 7272330.
Destinations to the north: Alaminos, Baguio, Dagupan.
Getting there: By Cubao jeepney from Taft Ave.

6 ***Dominion Bus Line*** (Sampaloc Terminal), Laong Laan St, Sampaloc, Tel 7414146.
Destinations to the north: Bangued, Laoag, San Fernando (La Union), Vigan.
Getting there: By Blumentritt jeepney from Taft Ave.
Nearest Metrorail station: Tayuman.

7 ***Dominion Bus Line*** (Cubao Terminal), Edsa, Cubao, Quezon City, Tel 7272350.
Destinations to the north: Bangued, San Fernando (La Union), Vigan.
Getting there: By Cubao jeepney from Taft Ave.
Nearest Metrostar station: GMA-Kamuning.

8 ***Eagle Star***, Dimasalang St, Sampaloc.
Destinations to the south: Borongan, Calbayog, Catbalogan, Guiuan.
Getting there: By Blumentritt jeepney from Taft Ave.
Nearest Metrorail station: Blumentritt.

9 ***Fariñas Trans***, AH Lacson St, Sampaloc, Tel 7438582.
Destinations to the north: Vigan, Laoag.
Getting there: By Blumentritt jeepney from Taft Ave.
Nearest Metrorail station: Tayuman.

10 ***Five Star***, Aurora Blvd (Tramo), Pasay City, Tel 8334772.
Destinations to the north: Alaminos, Bolinao, Cabanatuan, Dagupan.
Getting there: By Baclaran jeepney or bus from Taft Ave or MH del Pilar

St and change in or before Baclaran. Nearest Metrorail station: Edsa. Nearest Metrostar station: Taft.

11 ***Genesis Transport*** (Pasay Terminal), Taft Ave corner Edsa, Pasay City, Tel 5510842.
Destinations to the north: Baler, Bataan, Cabanatuan.
Getting there: By Baclaran jeepney or bus from Taft Ave or MH del Pilar St and change in or before Baclaran.
Nearest Metrorail station: Edsa.
Nearest Metrostar station: Taft.

12 ***Genesis Transport*** (Santa Cruz Terminal), Oroquieta St corner Doroteo Jose St, Santa Cruz, Tel 7338622.
Destinations to the north: Baler, Bataan, Cabanatuan.
Getting there: By Monumento jeepney from Mabini St.
Nearest Metrorail station: D Jose.

13 ***JAC Liner***, Edsa corner Kamias Rd, Quezon City, Tel 9296943.
Destination to the south: Lucena.
Getting there: By Cubao jeepney from Taft Ave.
Nearest Metrostar station: GMA-Kamuning.

14 ***JAM Transit*** (Pasay Terminal), Taft Ave, Pasay City, Tel 8318264.
Destinations to the south: Batangas, Lucena, Santa Cruz
Getting there: By Baclaran jeepney or bus from Taft Ave.
Nearest Metrorail station: Gil Puyat.

15 ***JAM Transit*** (Cubao Terminal), Edsa corner Monte de Piedad St, Cubao, Quezon City, Tel 4149925.
Destinations to the south: Lucena, Santa Cruz.
Getting there: By Cubao jeepney from Taft Ave.
Nearest Metrostar station: Araneta-Cubao.

16 ***Partas*** (Cubao Terminal) Aurora Blvd, Cubao, Quezon City, Tel 7251740.
Destinations to the north: Bangued, Laoag, San Fernando (La Union), Vigan.
Getting there: By Cubao jeepney from Taft Ave.
Nearest Metrostar station: Araneta-Cubao.

17 ***Partas*** (Pasay Terminal), Edsa, Pasay City, Tel 8514025.
Destination to the north: Baguio.
Getting there: By Baclaran jeepney or bus from Taft Ave or MH del Pilar St and change in or before Baclaran.
Nearest Metrorail station: Edsa.
Nearest Metrostar station: Taft.

18 ***Philippine Rabbit*** (Edsa Terminal), 1240 Edsa, Quezon City, Tel 3643477.
Destinations to the north: Alaminos, Bangued, Laoag, San Fernando (La Union), Tarlac, Vigan.
Getting there: By Monumento jeepney from Mabini St; then catch another jeepney or bus heading for Cubao.
Nearest Metrorail station: North Terminal (Monumento).
Nearest Metrostar station: North.

19 ***Philippine Rabbit*** (Avenida Terminal), 819 Oroquieta St, Santa Cruz, with another entrance on Rizal Ave, Tel 7349836.
Destinations to the north: Alaminos, Angeles, Baguio, Balanga, Laoag, Mariveles, San Fernando (La Union), San Fernando (Pampanga), Tarlac, Vigan.
Getting there: By Monumento jeepney from Mabini St.
Nearest Metrorail station: D Jose.

20 ***Philtranco*** (Pasay Terminal), Edsa, Pasay City, Tel 8518075.

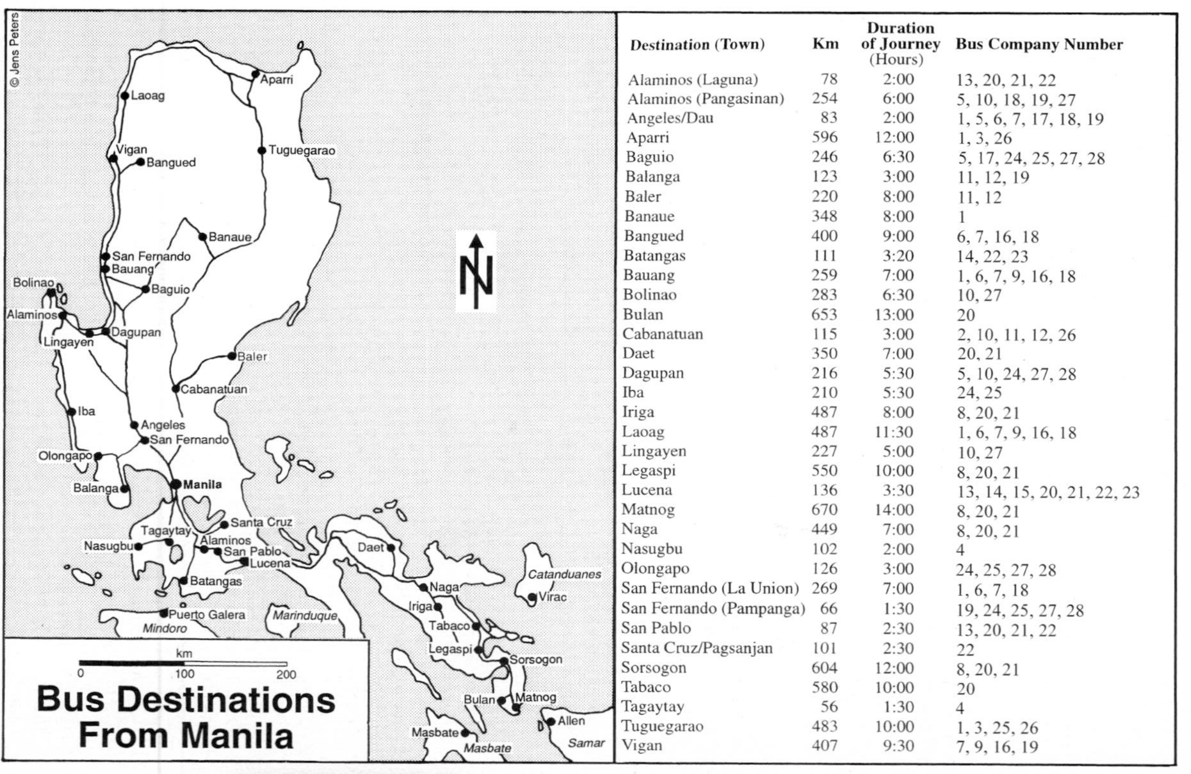

Bus Destinations From Manila

Destination (Town)	Km	Duration of Journey (Hours)	Bus Company Number
Alaminos (Laguna)	78	2:00	13, 20, 21, 22
Alaminos (Pangasinan)	254	6:00	5, 10, 18, 19, 27
Angeles/Dau	83	2:00	1, 5, 6, 7, 17, 18, 19
Aparri	596	12:00	1, 3, 26
Baguio	246	6:30	5, 17, 24, 25, 27, 28
Balanga	123	3:00	11, 12, 19
Baler	220	8:00	11, 12
Banaue	348	8:00	1
Bangued	400	9:00	6, 7, 16, 18
Batangas	111	3:20	14, 22, 23
Bauang	259	7:00	1, 6, 7, 9, 16, 18
Bolinao	283	6:30	10, 27
Bulan	653	13:00	20
Cabanatuan	115	3:00	2, 10, 11, 12, 26
Daet	350	7:00	20, 21
Dagupan	216	5:30	5, 10, 24, 27, 28
Iba	210	5:30	24, 25
Iriga	487	8:00	8, 20, 21
Laoag	487	11:30	1, 6, 7, 9, 16, 18
Lingayen	227	5:00	10, 27
Legaspi	550	10:00	8, 20, 21
Lucena	136	3:30	13, 14, 15, 20, 21, 22, 23
Matnog	670	14:00	8, 20, 21
Naga	449	7:00	8, 20, 21
Nasugbu	102	2:00	4
Olongapo	126	3:00	24, 25, 27, 28
San Fernando (La Union)	269	7:00	1, 6, 7, 18
San Fernando (Pampanga)	66	1:30	19, 24, 25, 27, 28
San Pablo	87	2:30	13, 20, 21, 22
Santa Cruz/Pagsanjan	101	2:30	22
Sorsogon	604	12:00	8, 20, 21
Tabaco	580	10:00	20
Tagaytay	56	1:30	4
Tuguegarao	483	10:00	1, 3, 25, 26
Vigan	407	9:30	7, 9, 16, 19

Destinations to the south: Borongan, Cagayan de Oro, Calbayog, Catarman, Catbalogan, Caticlan (for Boracay), Cebu City, Daet, Davao, Guiuan, Legaspi, Lucena, Naga, Naval (Biliran), Tacloban, Sorsogon, Surigao.
Getting there: By Baclaran jeepney or bus from Taft Ave or MH del Pilar St and change in or before Baclaran.
Nearest Metrorail station: Edsa.
Nearest Metrostar station: Taft.

21 ***Philtranco*** (Cubao Terminal), Araneta Center, Cubao, Quezon City, Tel 9112523, 9135666.
Destinations to the south: Borongan, Cagayan de Oro, Calbayog, Catarman, Catbalogan, Caticlan (for Boracay), Cebu City, Daet, Davao, Guiuan, Legaspi, Lucena, Naga, Naval (Biliran), Tacloban, Sorsogon, Surigao.
Getting there: By Cubao jeepney from Taft Ave.
Nearest Metrostar station: Araneta-Cubao.

22 ***Tritran*** (Pasay Terminal), Taft Ave corner Gil Puyat Ave, Pasay City.
Destinations to the south: Batangas, Lucena, Santa Cruz.
Getting there: By Baclaran jeepney or bus from Taft Ave.
Nearest Metrorail station: Gil Puyat.

23 ***Tritran*** (Kamias Terminal), Edsa corner Timog Ave, Cubao, Quezon City, Tel 9251758.
Destinations to the south: Batangas, Lucena.
Getting there: By Cubao jeepney from Taft Ave.
Nearest Metrostar station: GMA-Kamuning.

24 ***Victory Liner*** (Caloocan Terminal), 713 Rizal Ave Extension, Caloocan City, Tel 3611506, 3611514.
Destinations to the north: Baguio, Dagupan, Iba, Olongapo.
Getting there: By Monumento jeepney from Mabini St.
Nearest Metrorail station: North Terminal (Monumento).

25 ***Victory Liner*** (Sampaloc Terminal), España St corner Galicia St, Sampaloc, Tel 7411436.
Destinations to the north: Baguio, Iba, Olongapo, Roxas, Tuguegarao (via Cabanatuan).
Getting there: By Cubao jeepney from Taft Ave.
Nearest Metrorail station: D Jose.

26 ***Victory Liner*** (Kamias Terminal), Edsa corner East Ave, Quezon City, Tel 9213296.
Destinations to the north: Aparri, Roxas, Tuguegarao (via Cabanatuan).
Getting there: By Cubao jeepney from Taft Ave.
Nearest Metrostar station: GMA-Kamuning.

27 ***Victory Liner*** (Cubao Terminal), Edsa, Cubao, Quezon City, Tel 7274688, 7274534.
Destinations to the north: Alaminos, Baguio, Bolinao, Dagupan, Lingayen, Olongapo.
Getting there: By Cubao jeepney from Taft Ave.
Nearest Metrostar station: Araneta-Cubao.

28 ***Victory Liner*** (Pasay Terminal), Edsa, Pasay City, Tel 8330293, 8335019.
Destinations to the north: Baguio, Dagupan, Olongapo.
Getting there: By Baclaran jeepney or bus from Taft Ave or MH del Pilar St and change in or before Baclaran.
Nearest Metrorail station: Edsa.
Nearest Metrostar station: Taft.

Boat

North Harbor & South Harbor: Nearly all inter-island boats leave Manila from North Harbor. If you have trouble finding it ask a coastguard opposite Pier 8.

Superferries belonging to the shipping company WG & A leave from Pier 4, North Harbor and from the Super Terminal (Pier 15), South Harbor. Find out the pier number when you buy your ticket.

In addition to the North and South Harbor piers there are docking facilities at the Del Pan Bridge (coming from the sea it is the first bridge over the Pasig River). Various small vessels to neighbouring islands depart from here but they don't have any schedules.

Getting there: The Super Terminal is located at the end of 25th St, not far from the Manila Hotel. A taxi there from Ermita shouldn't cost much more than P40.

To get to North Harbor from Ermita by taxi costs about P60. There is a rather roundabout way of getting there by jeepney, although it goes through inner suburbs with heavy traffic and can take up to an hour. From Mabini St or Taft Ave get a jeepney to Divisoria; there you change for a jeepney to North Harbor. In the return direction the drivers can ask for up to P25 per person.

It is extremely difficult to get a taxi with a properly adjusted meter when travelling from North Harbor to Ermita or other districts after a ship has docked. The 'fixed price' is between P150 and P200.

Departures: Schedules are being changed all the time and ships put onto any old route. If you want to travel round the Philippines by boat, then keep your plans flexible and check departure times at the last minute with the shipping company.

The daily newspaper *Manila Bulletin* has a page 'Transportation & Tourism' with a section 'Interisland Shipping Schedules'. There you'll find ship names, ports of call and departure times from Manila. Next to the ship's name you'll see the telephone number of the shipping company (there's a reason for that!).

Tickets: All the shipping companies sell their own tickets in their harbour offices. Negros Navigation and WG & A also have several ticket offices in the city itself. Tickets for WG & A and MBRS Lines can also be bought at the Filipino Travel Center, Adriatico St, Ermita, Tel 5284507.

The prices in this book are valid for the cheapest class (Economy without meals). A two-person luxury cabin costs about the same per person as a plane ticket.

Shipping Companies in Manila

Atienza Shipping Lines, Pier 2, North Harbor, Tel 2438845.
Destination: Palawan (Coron, El Nido).

MBRS Lines, Pier 8, North Harbor, Tel 2435886, 2435888.
Destinations: Palawan (Cuyo), Panay, Romblon.

Moretta Shipping Lines, Pier 6, North Harbor, Tel 7216480.
Destination: Mindoro.

Negros Navigation, Pier 2, North Harbor, Tel 2450601-12.
Destinations: Bohol, Mindanao, Negros, Palawan, Panay.

San Nicolas Lines, Pier 2, North Harbor, Tel 2452830.
Destinations: Lubang/Mindoro, Palawan (Coron, El Nido).

Sulpicio Lines, Pier 12, North Harbor, Tel 2450616-30, 2424258.
Destinations: Cebu, Bohol, Leyte, Masbate, Mindanao, Negros, Panay.

WG & A, Pier 4, North Harbor, and the Super Terminal (Pier 15), South Harbor, Tel 2450660, 5287000, 8943211.
Destinations: Cebu, Bohol, Leyte, Masbate, Mindanao, Negros, Palawan, Panay.

Getting Away from Luzon

On the Nautical Highway to Boracay

The governemt's idea was to make it possible to travel from Manila by bus and car ferry via Mindoro, Panay and Negros to Mindanao, so they established the Strong Republic Nautical Highway in 2003. The main attraction are the individual legs of the route. For example, you can travel every day on a Philtranco bus from Manila to Caticlan (Boracay). The aircon bus leaves Manila at 7.30pm from their Cubao terminal, Araneta Center, and 8.30pm from their Pasay terminal. An ordinary bus leaves an hour later. Arrival in Boracay next day at 2pm. Return journey: Leave Caticlan at 3pm, arrival in Manila the next day at 4.30am. The exact route is as follows:

Manila - Batangas
Philtranco aircon bus (7.30pm; P120; three hrs).
Batangas - Calapan/Mindoro
Montenegro Shipping Lines or Starlite Ferry car ferry (1am; P110; two hrs).
Calapan - Roxas/Mindoro
Philtranco aircon bus (3.30am; P150; 2 ½ hrs).
Roxas - Caticlan (Boracay)/Panay
Montenegro Shipping Lines or Starlite Ferry car ferry (8am; P210; five hrs).

For further departure hours of the Roxas-Caticlan car ferries see the chapters 'Mindoro' and 'Panay': *Getting There & Away.*
Information on current departure times available from Philtranco in Manila, Tel (02) 9112523, and the Tourist Office in Boracay, Tel (036) 2883689.

Note: If you want to save a few pesos and avoid sitting waiting for hours in a bus, then you'd be better off making the trip under your own steam. Get a bus around 4pm from Manila to Batangas Pier (JAM Transit from their Pasay Terminal, or Tritran from their Kamias Terminal/Cubao and Pasay Terminal). Take the 7.30pm car ferry from Batangas to Calapan. Buy the ticket for the minibus from Calapan to Roxas on the boat. A car ferry leaves Roxas for Caticlan at 2am, arriving in Caticlan at either 5.30 or 7am, depending on the boat. So you're in Boracay in time for breakfast.

To Batanes

Air

From Laoag to Basco
Chemtrad Aviation and Pacific Airways fly daily (P2300).
Note: The flight can be cancelled if there are not enough passengers.

From Manila to Basco
Asian Spirit flies on Monday, Wednesday, Friday and Saturday (P3750).

From Tuguegarao to Basco
Chemtrad Aviation flies Monday, Wednesday and Friday (P2450).
Note: Chemtrad flies with Britten Norman Islanders with room for only eight

passengers, so you must reserve a seat about a week in advance. In the summer months from March until May, two to three weeks in advance would be better.

Boat

From Currimao (Ilocos Norte) to Basco

Wednesday with the MV *Ivatan Princess* (P1200; 19 hrs); via Calayan Island.

Note: This route depends on the weather, especially during the rainy season from June to November. Info: Cellphone 0918-6507405, 0917-7930102, 0920-2875003.

To Biliran

Bus/Boat

From Manila to Naval

Daily with Philtranco aircon buses (P970), taking 29 hrs including the ferry from Matnog to Alegria/San Isidro.

To Bohol

Air

From Manila to Tagbilaran

Asian Spirit and Philippine Airlines fly daily (P2950).

Boat

From Manila to Tagbilaran

Monday and Friday with WG & A (P1390; 28 hrs).

Wednesday with Sulpicio Lines (P1100; 29 hrs).

Friday and Sunday with Negros Navigation (P1390; 27 hrs).

To Catanduanes

Air

From Manila to Virac

Asian Spirit flies on Monday, Wednesday, Friday, Saturday and Sunday (P2200).

Boat

From Tabaco to San Andres

Daily at 5.30 and 7am with Regina Shipping Lines (three hrs).

From Tacabo to Virac

Daily at 6.30am and 12.30pm with a Bicolano Lines car ferry (four hrs).

To Cebu

Air

From Angeles to Cebu City

Seair flies on Monday and Thursday.

From Manila to Cebu City

Air Philippines, Cebu Pacific and Philippine Airlines have daily flights (P2900).

Bus/Boat

From Manila to Cebu City

discontinued

Daily with a Philtranco aircon bus, leaving at 3am from the Cubao Terminal, 4am from the Pasay Terminal (39 hrs; P[illegible] plus P70 for the ferry from Luzon to Samar and P150 for the ferry from Leyte to Cebu.

Boat

From Manila to Cebu City

Monday, Tuesday, Thursday, Friday and Sunday with WG & A (P1410; 22 hrs).

Tuesday and Friday with Sulpicio Lines (P1360; 22 hrs).

To Leyte

Air

From Manila to Tacloban

Cebu Pacific and Philippines Airlines have daily flights (P2570).

Bus/Boat

From Manila to Tacloban

Daily with Philtranco aircon buses (P840), taking 25 hrs including the ferry from Matnog to Alegria/San Isidro. Some buses carry on to Ormoc and Maasin.

Boat

From Manila to Calubian, Baybay and Maasin

Wednesday with Sulpicio Lines, taking 32 hrs to Calubian (P740), 40 hrs to Baybay (P835), 44 hrs to Maasin (P905); via Masbate/Masbate.

From Manila to Palompon

Tuesday with WG & A (P820; 32 hrs); via Masbate/Masbate.

From Manila to Ormoc

Friday with Sulpicio Lines (43 hrs; P835); via Masbate/Masbate.

To Lubang

Boat

From Manila to Tilik

Monday and Thursday with San Nicolas Shipping Lines (P250; seven hrs).

To Marinduque

Air

From Manila to Boac

Asian Spirit flies on Monday, Wednesday, Friday and Sunday (P1430).

Boat

From Lucena to Balanacan

Daily at 4 and 8am, 12 noon and 4pm with a Montenegro Shipping Lines car ferry (P90; 2½ hrs).
Daily at 4 and 10.30am with a Blue Magic Ferries fast ferry (P170; 1¾ hrs).
Daily at 11am with Blue Magic Ferries (P150; 2½ hrs).

From Lucena to Cawit

Daily at 4am and 6.30pm with a Phil-Nippon Kyoei Corporation car ferry (P130; three hrs).

Note: The Phil-Nippon Kyoei Corporation car ferries are noticeably better than those belonging to Montenegro Shipping Lines.

From Lucena to Santa Cruz

Daily at 3.30am with a Montenegro Shipping Lines car ferry (four hrs).
Daily at 8.30am with a fast ferry (P160; 2½ hrs).
Arrival is at Buyabod, the Santa Cruz wharf.

To Masbate

Air

From Manila to Masbate

Asian Spirit has daily flights (P2505).

Boat

From Bulan to Masbate

Daily at 1pm with San Pablo Shipping Lines (four hrs); possibly via San Fernando/Ticao Island.

From Lucena to Masbate

Monday, Wednesday and Saturday with a Bluewater Ferry car ferry (P400; 12 hrs).

From Manila to Masbate

Tuesday with WG & A (P500; 18 hrs).
Wednesday and Friday with Sulpicio Lines (P570; 20 hrs).

From Pilar to Masbate

Daily at 5, 8 and 11am, and at 4pm, with a Montenegro Shipping Lines fast ferry (P210; two hrs).
Daily at 7am (big outrigger; P80; four hrs) and at 1pm (wooden boat; P120; three hrs).
Buses and minibuses run between Legaspi (Satellite Bus Terminal) and Pilar (1½ hrs).

To Mindanao

Air

From Manila to Butuan

Philippines Airlines flies daily (P3000).

From Manila to Cagayan de Oro

Air Philippines, Cebu Pacific and Philippines Airlines have daily flights (P3645).

From Manila to Cotabato
Philippines Airlines flies daily except Friday (P3838).

From Manila to Davao
Air Philippines, Cebu Pacific and Philippines Airlines have daily flights (P3670).

From Manila to Dipolog
Philippines Airlines flies daily except Saturday (P3838).

From Manila to General Santos
Air Philippines and Philippines Airlines have daily flights (P3670).

From Manila to Zamboanga
Air Philippines, Cebu Pacific and Philippines Airlines have daily flights (P3670).

Bus/Boat

From Manila to Cagayan de Oro
Daily with a Philtranco aircon bus (P1320), taking 39 hrs including the ferries from Matnog to Alegria/San Isidro and from Liloan to Lipata/Surigao.

From Manila to Davao
Two Philtranco aircon buses daily (P1400), taking 42 hrs including the ferries from Matnog to Alegria/San Isidro and from Liloan to Lipata/Surigao.

Boat

From Manila to Butuan/Nasipit
Monday and Thursday with WG & A; Monday via Cebu City and Surigao (40 hrs), Thursday via Surigao (P1740; 35 hrs).
Wednesday with Sulpicio Lines (P1730; 33 hrs); via Cebu City.

From Manila to Cagayan de Oro
Monday, Wednesday and Thursday with WG & A (P1790; 34 hrs); Wednesday via Dumaguete/Negros (38 hrs).
Monday and Friday with Negros Navigation (P1780; 48 hrs); Monday via Bacolod/Negros, Friday via Iloilo City/ Panay.

From Manila to Cotabato
Friday with WG & A (P1890; 53 hrs); via Iloilo City/Panay and Zamboanga.
Saturday with Sulpicio Lines (P1500; 77 hrs); via Estancia and Iloilo City/ Panay, and Zamboanga.

From Manila to Davao
Monday and Saturday with WG & A; Monday via Zamboanga and General Santos (P1750; 52 hrs), Saturday via Iloilo City/Panay and General Santos (58 hrs).
Thursday and Sunday with Sulpicio Lines; Thursday via Cebu City (P1900; 66 hrs), Sunday via Cebu City and Surigao (52 hrs).

From Manila to Dipolog
Wednesday with Sulpicio Lines (P1100; 37 hrs); via Tagbilaran/Bohol.
Friday with WG & A (P1250; 40 hrs); via Tagbilaran/Bohol.

From Manila to General Santos
Monday and Saturday with WG & A; Monday via Zamboanga (P1870; 42 hrs), Saturday via Iloilo City/Panay (45 hrs).

From Manila to Iligan
Friday and Sunday with WG & A (P1490; 36 hrs).
Sunday with Negros Navigation (P1470; 40 hrs); via Iloilo City/Panay.

From Manila to Ozamis
Wednesday with Sulpicio Lines (P1215; 41 hrs); via Dumaguete/Negros.
Thursday and Sunday with WG & A (P1260; 36 hrs); Sunday via Iligan.
Sunday with Negros Navigation (P1470;

43 hrs); via Iloilo City/Panay and Iligan.

From Manila to Surigao
Monday and Thursday with WG & A (P1550; 28 hrs); Monday via Cebu City (34 hrs).
Wednesday with Sulpicio Lines (P950; 53 hrs); via Masbate/Masbate and Leyte (Calubian, Baybay and Maasin).
Sunday with Sulpicio Lines (P950; 33 hrs); via Cebu City.

From Manila to Zamboanga
Monday and Friday with WG & A (P1460; 28 hrs); Friday via Iloilo City/ Panay (32 hrs).
Tuesday and Saturday with Sulpicio Lines (P1270; 47 hrs); Tuesday via Iloilo City/Panay, Saturday via Estancia and Iloilo City/Panay.

To Mindoro

Air
From Manila to San Jose
Asian Spirit flies Monday, Wednesday, Thursday, Saturday and Sunday (P1400).
Air Philippines flies Tuesday and Friday (P1600).

Bus/Boat
From Manila to Puerto Galera
Daily at 7.30am with an aircon minibus from the Lotus Garden Hotel, Ermita, Tel (02) 3022054, and at 8am from the Swagman Hotel, Ermita, Tel (02) 5238541, to the Island Cruiser ferry from Batangas to Puerto Galera. Arrival in Puerto Galera at around 1pm. Bus/ship tickets are on sale in both hotels (P450).
At least one aircon bus leaves from the Citystate Tower Hotel, Mabini St, Ermita, daily at 8am for Batangas to the fast ferry *Blue Eagle*, which leaves there at 11am. Arrival in Puerto Galera at noon. Reservations and bus/ferry tickets available at the Si-Kat counter in the Citystate Tower Hotel; Tel 5213344. Fare: P500.
Regular buses make the trip from Manila to Batangas roughly every half hour from the JAM Transit bus terminal (Pasay) and Tritran bus terminals (Cubao and Pasay), taking 2½ hrs (P120). Note: 'Batangas Pier' buses which go via the Calabarzon Expressway/Star Tollway (check the destination on the front of the bus) avoid the heavy traffic in Santo Tomas, Tanauan and Lipa.
Aircon minibuses also leave the JAM Transit and Tritran bus terminals in Pasay for the pier in Batangas (P120).
See also chapter 'Central Luzon': *Batangas*.

Warning: The Manila to Batangas route is a favourite with pickpockets; they ply their trade in scheduled buses and usually in teams of three.

Boat
From Batangas to Abra de Ilog
Two times daily, probably at 5am and 2.45pm, with the fast ferry *Supercat* (P180; one hr).
Three times daily, probably at 3 and 8am, and at 1.30pm, with a Montenegro Shipping Lines car ferry (P110; 2½ hrs). After the ship docks a bus leaves about 200m from the wharf in Wawa for San Jose via Mamburao and Sablayan. If you want a seat, you have to hurry.

From Batangas to Calapan
Seven times daily with the fast ferry *Supercat* (P240; 45 min).
From 5am to midnight, roughly every hour with a car ferry (two hrs).
Jeepneys make the trip from Calapan to Puerto Galera, although only until 3.30pm (1½ hrs).

From Batangas to Puerto Galera
Daily at 11am with the fast ferry *Blue Eagle* (one hr) and an Island Cruiser

ferry (two hrs; P150). The ferries can be booked in Manila in combination with an air-con bus ticket; see above (Bus/Boat).

From Batangas to Balatero the fast ferry *Supercat* sails daily at noon (P150; one hr; departure from Balatero at 1.15pm). The car ferry MV *Starlite* leaves Batangas at 4pm (P100; two hrs; departure from Balatero at 6.30am), with an additional departure on Friday, Saturday and Sunday at 9.30am and 1pm from Batangas and Balatero respectively. Balatero is 2½ km west of Puerto Galera. After the arrival of a ferry, jeepneys and tricycles run people to the beaches. A Special Ride with an outrigger from Balatero to Sabang costs P300.

Big outriggers go from Batangas to Sabang daily at 9.30 and 10.30am, noon, 1.30 and 2.30pm, to White Beach at 10.30am and 4pm, at the weekend also at noon and 6pm (P130; 1½ hrs).

A Special Ride with an outrigger from Batangas to Puerto Galera should not cost more than P2000; they will ask for up to P3000.

Note: The departure times are changed frequently, but if you are at Batangas Pier around noon you won't have to wait long for a boat.

From Batangas to San Jose
Daily except Sunday at 6pm with Montenegro Shipping Lines (12 hrs).

From Manila to San Jose
Sunday at 6pm with Moretta Shipping Lines (P330; 14 hrs).

To Negros

Air

From Manila to Bacolod
Air Philippines, Cebu Pacific and Philippine Airlines have daily flights (P2780).

From Manila to Dumaguete
Air Philippines and Cebu Pacific have daily flights (P2900).

Boat

From Manila to Bacolod
Monday, Tuesday, Thursday, Friday and Saturday with Negros Navigation (P1460; 19 hrs).

Thursday and Sunday with WG & A (P1460; 19 hrs).

From Manila to Dumaguete
Monday and Wednesday with WG & A (P1390; 29 hrs); Monday via Tagbilaran/Bohol (33 hrs).

Wednesday with Sulpicio Lines (P1090; 25 hrs).

Sunday with Negros Navigation (P1390; 32 hrs); via Tagbilaran/Bohol.

To Palawan

Air

From Manila to Busuanga
Asian Spirit, Pacific Airways and Seair have daily flights (P2300).

From Manila to El Nido
Island Transvoyager flies daily.

Seair flies three times weekly; via Busuanga (P4400).

From Manila to Puerto Princesa
Air Philippines, Cebu Pacific and Philippine Airlines have daily flights (P2850).

Seair flies three times weekly; via Busuanga and El Nido.

From Manila to Sandoval/Taytay
Seair flies daily (P4400).

Asian Spirit flies Monday, Wednesday, Thursday and Sunday (P4050).

Boat

From Manila to Coron
Monday and Wednesday with Atienza Shipping Lines (P690; 17 hrs).

Tuesday, Thursday and Saturday with San Nicolas Lines (P650; 22 hrs).
Friday with WG & A (P980; 12 hrs).

Note: Almost all the Atienza Shipping Lines and San Nicolas Lines ships are old and rickety freighters, and the trip is only for the adventurous! It is possible that they will soon no longer be allowed to carry passengers.

From Manila to Cuyo
Wednesday with MBRS Lines (25 hrs); via San Jose de Buenavista/Panay.

From Manila to El Nido
Monday and Wednesday with Atienza Shipping Lines; via Coron.
Wednesday and Saturday with San Nicolas Lines (P750; 30 hrs); Wednesday via Coron (42 hrs).

From Manila to Puerto Princesa
Thursday with Negros Navigation (23 hrs).
Friday with WG & A (P1320; 27 hrs); via Coron.

To Panay

Air

From Angeles to Caticlan (Boracay)
Seair flies daily except Saturday and Sunday (P2400); possibly via Manila.
Asian Spirit flies Monday, Wednesday and Friday (P2950); via Manila.

From Manila to Caticlan (Boracay)
Asian Spirit, Pacific Airways and Seair have daily flights (P2400).

From Manila to Iloilo City
Air Philippines, Cebu Pacific and Philippine Airlines have daily flights (P2780).

From Manila to Kalibo
Air Philippines, Cebu Pacific and Philippine Airlines have daily flights (P2900).

From Manila to Roxas
Cebu Pacific and Philippine Airlines have daily flights (P2540).

From Manila to San Jose de Buenavista (Antique)
Asian Spirit flies Monday, Wednesday, Friday and Saturday (P2750).

Bus/Boat

See above: *On the Nautical Highway to Boracay*.

Boat

From Manila to Caticlan (Boracay)
Monday, Wednesday (possibly) and Friday with MBRS Lines (P810; 15 hrs); via Odiongan (Tablas Island)/Romblon. The ship carries on to Lipata on the west coast of Panay.

From Manila to Dumaguit/Kalibo
Monday, Wednesday and Saturday with WG & A (P1010; 15 hrs).
Friday with Negros Navigation (P1010; 17 hrs).

From Manila to Estancia
Saturday with Sulpicio Lines (P815; 17 hrs).
Sunday with Negros Navigation (P1010; 22 hrs); via Roxas.

From Manila to Iloilo City
Monday, Thursday, Friday and Saturday with WG & A (P1460; 21 hrs).
Tuesday and Saturday with Sulpicio Lines (P1090; 25 hrs); Saturday via Estancia (28 hrs).
Wednesday, Friday and Sunday with Negros Navigation (P1460; 19 hrs); Friday possibly via Bacolod/Negros (23 hrs).

From Manila to Roxas
Monday, Wednesday and Saturday with WG & A (P1000; 19 hrs); via Dumaguit.
Tuesday, Friday and Sunday with Ne-

gros Navigation (P1010; 17 hrs); Friday via Dumaguit (21 hrs).

From Manila to San Jose de Buenavista (Antique)
Wednesday with MBRS Lines (16 hrs).

To Romblon

Air

From Manila to Tugdan/Tablas
Seair flies Monday and Thursday (P2790).

Boat

From Batangas to Odiongan/Tablas
Monday, Thursday and Saturday at 5pm with a Shipshape Ferry car ferry (eight hrs).
Wednesday, Friday and Sunday at 5pm with Montenegro Shipping Lines (P265; eight hrs).

From Batangas to Romblon/Romblon
Monday, Thursday and Saturday at 5pm with a Shipshape Ferry car ferry (P330; 12 hrs); via Odiongan/Tablas Island.

From Lucena to Romblon/Romblon
Two times a week, probably Wednesday and Friday at 6pm with Kalaayan Shipping Lines (12 hrs).

From Manila to Odiongan/Tablas
Monday, Wednesday (possibly) and Friday with MBRS Lines (P530; 11 hrs).

From Manila to Romblon/Romblon
Saturday with MBRS Lines (P530; 12 hrs). The ship carries on to Cajidiocan/ Sibuyan Island.

To Samar

Air

From Manila to Calbayog
Asian Spirit flies on Tuesday, Thursday and Sunday (P2750).

From Manila to Catarman
Asian Spirit flies on Monday, Wednesday and Friday (P2640).

Bus

From Manila to Borongan and Guiuan
Daily with Eagle Star and Philtranco buses. Including the ferry from Matnog to Allen or Alegria/San Isidro the trip takes 29 hrs to Borongan and 32 hrs to Guiuan.

From Manila to Calbayog and Catbalogan
Daily with Eagle Star and Philtranco aircon buses. Including the ferry from Matnog to Allen or Alegria/San Isidro the trip takes 23 hrs to Calbayog and 24 hrs to Catbalogan.

From Manila to Catarman
Daily with Philtranco aircon buses. Including the ferry from Matnog to Allen the trip takes 24 hrs.

Boat

From Matnog to Algeria/San Isidro
Daily at 5, 8 and 11.30am and 2, 4 and 8pm with a car ferry (2½ hrs).

From Matnog to Allen
Daily at 4, 4.30. 6.30, 9.30 and 10am and 2.30, 5 and 11pm with a car ferry (P74, including terminal fee; 1½ hrs).

Central Luzon

All the trips described in this chapter can be done as day trips from Manila. The map shows towns that can be reached by bus within three hours. Barrio Barretto/ Subic Bay, Pagsanjan and Matabungkay, however, deserve an overnight stay.
Some destinations can be combined - the volcano at Tagaytay and the beach at Matabungkay, for example. Some places can be visited while heading for other destinations: Olongapo and Subic Bay on the way to the Hundred Islands and San Pablo and Lucena on the way to South Luzon.
In June 1991, 80 km north-west of Manila in the eastern Zambales Mountains, the volcano Pinatubo erupted into life after six centuries of slumber. Violent eruptions continued unabated for several weeks after, making this without a doubt the worst volcanic outburst the world experienced in the 20th century. Pinatubo lost 300m in height as a result, while at the same time, a unique landscape was created in the several thousand square km area which was blanketed by the ash and sand expelled by the eruption. Volcanologists agree that it could be quite some time before the mountain finally settles down again at its new height of roughly 1450m. It has, however, already settled well into its new role as a tourist attraction. Especially popular are hikes through the ravine-like landscape of its lava field at the eastern extremity of the Zambales Mountains, camping tours to the crater, and sightseeing flights.
There is an expressway from Metro Manila north to Dau and Mabalacat, a little beyond Angeles (North Luzon Expressway), and another south just about as far as Calamba (South Luzon Tollway). Both are toll roads (turnpikes) and motorbikes under 600 cc are not allowed on them.

Cavite & Ternate

Cavite is located on a narrow, scythe-shaped peninsula around 35 km south-west of Manila. It has an excellent protected harbour that has been valued since Spanish times. The Philippine navy is stationed there today. The city itself offers no real attractions to the tourist, and this goes for its beaches too, eg Lido Beach. But for those who just want to get out of Manila for a day, it makes a pleasant day trip. The popular resort and leisure park known as Island Cove is located in the small town of Kawit just south of Cavite. The Aguinaldo House Museum is also worth seeing there.
About 40 km south-west of Cavite at the entrance to Manila Bay near Ternate, there are two exclusive, expansively dimensioned resort-hotels. The better-heeled representatives of business, politics and show-biz like to spend their weekends there.

Places to Stay

Novotel Puerto Azul Resort, Ternate, Tel (046) 5240021. SR/DR/ac/bath P2300 and P3500, including breakfast.

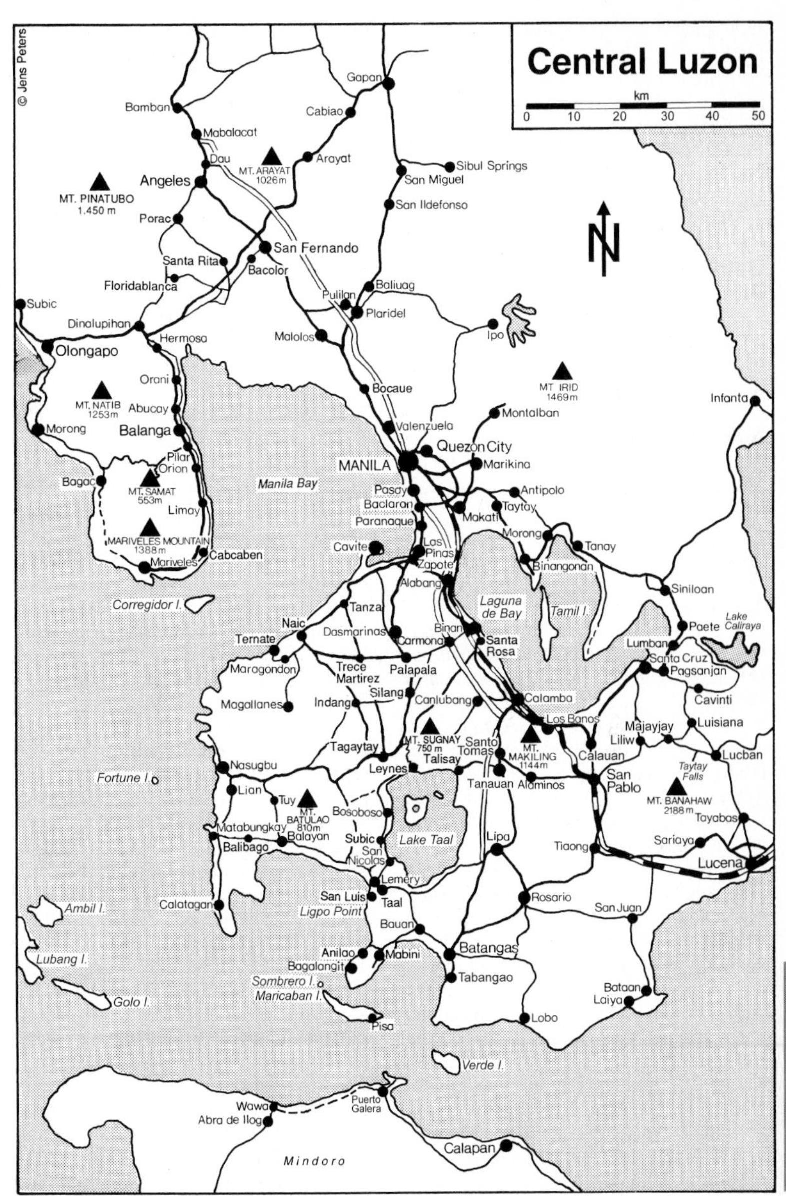
© Jens Peters
Central Luzon
km
0 10 20 30 40 50
N
Gapan
Bamban
Cabiao
Mabalacat
Dau
MT. ARAYAT 1026m
Arayat
Sibul Springs
San Miguel
Angeles
MT. PINATUBO 1.450 m
San Ildefonso
Porac
San Fernando
Santa Rita
Bacolor
Floridablanca
Baliuag
Pulilan
Subic
Plaridel
Dinalupihan
Hermosa
Malolos
Ipo
Olongapo
Orani
MT IRID 1469m
MT. NATIB 1253m
Abucay
Bocaue
Infanta
Montalban
Morong
Balanga
Valenzuela
Quezon City
Pilar
MANILA
Marikina
Orion
Bagac
MT. SAMAT 553m
Manila Bay
Pasay
Antipolo
Limay
Baclaran
Taytay
Paranaque
Makati
MARIVELES MOUNTAIN 1388m
Morong
Cavite
Las Pinas
Tanay
Cabcaben
Mariveles
Zapote
Binangonan
Alabang
Siniloan
Corregidor I.
Laguna de Bay
Tanza
Tamil I.
Lake Caliraya
Naic
Binan
Paete
Dasmarinas
Ternate
Carmona
Santa Rosa
Lumban
Maragondon
Santa Cruz
Trece Martirez
Palapala
Pagsanjan
Silang
Cavinti
Magallanes
Indang
Canlubang
Calamba
Los Banos
Luisiana
Majayjay
Tagaytay
MT. SUGNAY 750 m
Santo Tomas
Liliw
MT. MAKILING 1144m
Calauan
Lucban
Talisay
Nasugbu
Leynes
Taytay Falls
San Pablo
Fortune I.
Tanauan
Alaminos
Lian
Tuy
MT. BATULAO 810m
MT. BANAHAW 2188m
Bosoboso
Tayabas
Matabungkay
Balayan
Subic
Lake Taal
Lipa
Sariaya
Balibago
San Nicolas
Tiaong
Lucena
Lemery
San Luis
Taal
Rosario
Ambil I.
Calatagan
Ligpo Point
San Juan
Bauan
Lubang I.
Anilao
Mabini
Batangas
Bagalangit
Sombrero I.
Tabangao
Maricaban I.
Bataan
Golo I.
Laiya
Pisa
Lobo
Verde I.
Puerto Galera
Wawa
Abra de Ilog
Calapan
Mindoro

Restaurant, coffee shop, swimming pool, tennis courts, squash, golf course, Hobie Cats, windsurfing. Reservations in Manila: Tel (02) 5229382.
Caylabne Bay Resort. SR/DR/ac/bath P4300 and P4800. Restaurant, tennis courts, golf course, swimming pool, Hobie Cats, windsurfing. Reservations in Manila: Tel (02) 8138519-26.

Getting There & Away

Bus: Numerous buses leave Manila for Cavite daily from Taft Ave, either at the corner of P Ocampo St or at the corner of South Super Highway. Travelling time is half an hour.

Note: There is both a city Cavite and a province called Cavite. Not all buses with the destination Cavite automatically go to the city of Cavite.

Corregidor Island

The fortified island of Corregidor ('The Rock'), standing at the mouth of Manila Bay, was the scene of the Filipino last stand after the Japanese invaded in WWII. Even earlier, in 1898, Corregidor was used by the USA in its war against Spain because of its strategic position. Construction of the Malinta Tunnel began 25 years later, and it was used during WWII as an underground arsenal and hospital. It then served as General Douglas MacArthur's HQ from December 1941 to March 1942, as Filipinos and Americans struggled in vain against the Japanese invaders. MacArthur was eventually smuggled out on a PT boat. Today it's a national shrine and you can have a look around the underground bunkers and inspect the rusty relics of the fortress armaments. There are elaborate plans to restore what's left of the WWII junk lying around, as well as the shattered remains of MacArthur's former HQ. On the highest point of the island stands the Pacific War Memorial. Not far away from it, a white lighthouse was rebuilt after the war on the spot where the original was first built by the Spaniards in 1836.

Places to Stay

Accommodation on the island is administered by the Corregidor Foundation Inc. Reservations are preferred: Tel 5235605, 5253420. Package tours can be booked with the organiser Sun Cruises, Tel 8318140, Fax 8341523, @.
Corregidor Youth Hostel. Dorm/ac P450. Near the wharf, not far from the Corregidor Inn.
Corregidor Inn, Cellphone 0917-5276350. SR/DR/ac/bath P1800, suite P3800. From its Visitor's Bar to MacArthur's Suite, this elegant hotel is furnished throughout with traditional Philippine furniture. The modern plastic chairs and tables on the restaurant patio are even more noticeably out of place because of this. There is a swimming pool.
Beach Resort Complex. Cottage/ac/bath P1800. Well-maintained cottages in the south of the island near the Japanese Garden of Peace.

Getting There & Away

Boat: Daytrips are available for P1000 per person from Manila to Corregidor. The price includes the boat trip to the island, sightseeing tour by bus, a guided tour of the island, and a lunch buffet in the restaurant of the Corregidor Hotel. Another P150 can be paid for a light & sound show in the shaft of the Malinta Tunnel, which is largely based on the history of the island. Tickets are available at any travel agency or directly at the pier. Further information is available from Sun Cruises, Tel 8318140.
The MV *Island Cruiser* leaves the ferry terminal (PTA Bay Cruise Terminal) next to the Cultural Center daily at 8am (return trip at 2.30pm), taking 1½ hrs. From October until June, there are two

boats on weekends and holidays, departing Manila at 8 and 10am (return trips 2.30 and 4.30pm respectively).

Note: If you intend to continue your journey from Manila the same evening, check the current weather forecast first. It's possible that the return crossing from Corregidor could be postponed to the next morning because of strong winds and high waves.

Las Piñas

The coast road leaves Manila heading south through built-up areas until, after about 20 km, it reaches Las Piñas. This town is famous for its unique bamboo organ in the San Jose Church. Started in 1816 by the Spanish Father Diego Cerra, the organ was made from bamboo to save money and was finally completed in 1824. Standing over five metres high, it has 832 pipes of bamboo and 122 of metal. From 1973 to 1975 it was overhauled in Germany and now sounds as good as new. A small shop on the church porch sells records and cassettes of bamboo-organ music. The real thing can be heard on Sunday or during the Bamboo Organ Festival which lasts for a week every February. It's a social occasion, with internationally famous organists, choirs and ensembles taking part. On normal weekdays the organ can be seen from 2 to 4pm only.

Getting There & Away

Manila
Bus: In Manila there are plenty of buses to Las Piñas that you can stop in Taft Ave. Destinations shown will be either Zapote or Cavite. The trip takes half an hour.

Jeepney: Take a jeepney to Baclaran (you can get one for example from MH del Pilar St in Ermita), walk to the next crossing where the jeepneys leave for Las Piñas. The destination may be given as Alabang, Cavite or Zapote.

Tagaytay - Matabungkay
Bus: If you want to continue from Las Piñas to Tagaytay or Matabungkay, you can go to the main street and board any of the many buses coming through from Manila on the way to Nasugbu.

Tagaytay

Tagaytay is located about 70 km south of Manila and was once intended to become an alternative to the summer town of Baguio. Its high altitude (600m) and cool climate would seem to make it ideal to take over this role. However, in the end nothing came of it, although the idea was brought up again after a serious earthquake rattled Baguio in mid-1990, and shares in the exclusive apartment buildings which had been built in the meantime were offered.
The sprawling town offers visitors superb views of the volcanic island with its crater lake, but only if the weather is clear. The volcano is one of the smallest and most dangerous in the world. Anyone who wants to climb it can arrange to be taken over to the volcanic island from Talisay, 17 km south-east of Tagaytay.
About 10 km east of Tagaytay, on Mt Sungay (750m) the Viewpoint Complex was built. From the public view deck here you have a marvellous view of Lake Taal to the south, Laguna de Bay to the east and almost as far as Manila to the north. Jeepneys go up there regularly from the Tagaytay Rotonda (Silang Crossing), stopping on the way at the turn-off down to Talisay.

Places to Stay

Almost all the hotels in Tagaytay turn out to be fairly expensive places to stay,

Getting There & Away
6 Jeepneys to Talisay
22 Petron Petrol Station
27 Shell Petrol Station

Places to Stay
1 Royal Taal Inn
4 5 R
5 Nazareth Inn
7 Club Estancia Resort Hotel
9 Country Hotel
14 Days Hotel
16 Royale Parc Hotel
17 Tagaytay Tavern
4 C Apartelle
18 Tagaytay Mahogany Hotel
29 Taal Vista Hotel
31 Gloria de Castro's Store
Natalia's Guest House
32 Mountainside Lake Resort
33 Buco Resort
34 San Roque Beach Resort
Vista Hazel Beach Resort
35 Talisay Green Lake Resort
36 Bougainvillea Resort Inn

Places to Eat
10 Max's
McDonald's
11 Chowking
Jollibee
12 Sizzling King
23 Ronamar Restaurant
25 Viewsite Seafood Restaurant
28 McDonald's
29 Jollibee
30 Josephine Restaurant

Miscellaneous
2 Metrobank
3 City Market
8 Equitable PCI Bank
Olivarez Plaza Mall
12 Grandview Complex
13 7-Eleven
14 Bank of the Philippine Islands
15 Fruit Stalls
18 Tourist Office
19 Mahogany Market
20 City Hall
21 Hospital
24 Philippine National Bank (PNB)
26 Allied Bank
29 Casino Filipino
35 Taal Lake Yacht Club

as they obviously concentrate on well-heeled weekend guests with their own transport. There are a few private places offering rooms, which are also not too cheap, but still put less of a strain on the budget.

5 R, Sungay West. SR/DR/fan/bath P600 and P800. Reasonable, private rooms in Mrs Lumen Austria's house. Located a little off the road in a lane between the school and the church.

Tagaytay Tavern, JP Rizal Ave. SR/DR/fan/bath P800. Small, family accommodation with basic, but acceptable rooms. Located about 150m off the main road.

Tagaytay Mahogany Hotel, JP Rizal Ave, Tel 8600409. SR/DR/fan/bath P1320, SR/DR/ac/bath P1760. Fairly small, but OK rooms, the aircon ones with a refrigerator and TV. All including breakfast. Government hotel near Mahogany Market.

Royal Taal Inn, Calamba Rd, Tel 4131066, @. SR/DR/ac/bath P1540 and P1850 (Mon-Thu), P1850 and P2160 (Fri-Sun). Good rooms with TV and balcony. Pleasant accommodation with only six rooms and a roof terrace (breakfast) with a view of the volcano lake. Located about six km east of the

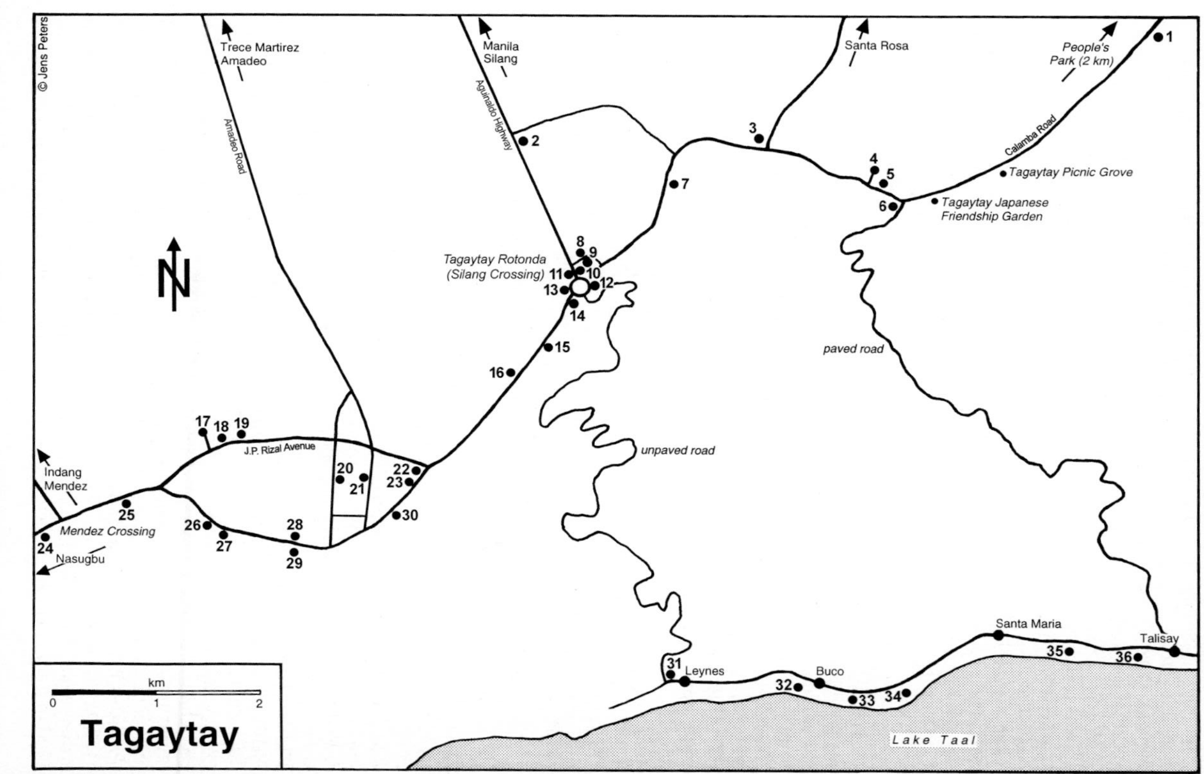
© Jens Peters
Trece Martirez
Amadeo
Amadeo Road
Manila
Silang
Aguinaldo Highway
Santa Rosa
People's Park (2 km)
Calamba Road
Tagaytay Picnic Grove
Tagaytay Japanese Friendship Garden
Tagaytay Rotonda (Silang Crossing)
paved road
unpaved road
J.P. Rizal Avenue
Indang
Mendez
Mendez Crossing
Nasugbu
Santa Maria
Talisay
Leynes
Buco
Lake Taal
km
0
1
2
Tagaytay

Tagaytay Rotonda, on the road to People's Park.

Royale Parc Hotel, Silang Crossing, Aguinaldo Highway, Tel 4130264, Fax 8601474. SR/DR/ac/bath P1800 to P2700. Immaculate rooms with TV, the more expensive ones also have a refrigerator and a veranda. Restaurant.

Club Estancia Resort Hotel, Zone II, San Jose, Tel 4131331, Fax 4131047. SR/DR/ac/bath P2700, cottage/fan/bath P3000, suite P3800. With TV, the suites also have a refrigerator. Comfortable rooms as well as cottages with veranda on the slope below the hotel. Big, quiet place with beautiful view of Lake Taal. Restaurant, swimming pool, jacuzzi, sauna.

Country Inn, Aguinaldo Highway, Tel 4130311, Fax 4132911. SR/DR/ac/bath P2700 to P4500. Comfortable rooms, some quite spacious, with refrigerator and TV. Restaurant.

Taal Vista Hotel, Aguinaldo Highway, Tel 4131000, Fax 4131225, @. SR/DR/ac/bath P4950 and P6600. Tastefully furnished rooms with refrigerator and TV, the better ones have a view of Lake Taal and the volcano. Restaurant. Reservations in Manila: Tel (02) 8671159.

Days Hotel, Aguinaldo Highway, Tel 4132401, Fax 4132323. SR/DR/ac/bath P5450 to P6050, all including breakfast. International hotel with well-maintained, attractively furnished rooms with TV. Restaurant, swimming pool.

Places to Eat

Near the Grandview Complex at the Tagaytay Rotonda (traffic circle) there are several restaurants to choose from, including the ***Sizzling King*** (steaks). Quite near are ***Max's*** (roast chicken) and popular fast food chains such as ***Jollibee***, ***Chowking*** and ***McDonald's***. Well worth recommending is ***Josephine***, where you'll enjoy excellent Philippine food in a pleasant atmosphere.

Miscellaneous

Money: Bank of the Philippine Islands, Equitable PCI Bank and Metrobank, all on Aguinaldo Highway, have ATMs.

Population: 30,000.

Post & Telephone: Post code: 4120. Area code: 046.

Tourist Office, City Hall, Tel 8600697, and Tourist Information Center, JP Rizal Ave, Tel 8601600. Open Mon-Sat 8am-5pm.

Getting There & Away

Manila

Bus: Several Crow Lines buses run daily from Manila to Tagaytay, marked 'Nasugbu'. There are also others that pass through (1½ hrs).

Pagsanjan

Jeepney/Bus: To get to Tagaytay from Pagsanjan you go by jeepney to Santa Cruz. There you get a Manila bus and get out at the junction at Calamba. From Calamba you go by jeepney through Binan to Palapala and from there you get a bus to Tagaytay. It takes about three hrs. As an alternative, instead of getting out at Calamba, you can continue to Alabang and there change to a jeepney to Zapote, where you can catch a bus from Manila heading for Tagaytay.

Talisay

Jeepney: From Talisay to Tagaytay there are several jeepneys (P16). Last one leaves at about 5pm. A Special Ride costs about P200.

Talisay

Talisay is right down on Lake Taal and is a good starting point for trips to the volcanic island. These trips are on offer from various local lodging houses in the Banga and Leynes districts. A boat to the volcano and back costs around

P1000, including guide; without guide P800. It makes sense to have a guide if you go to the lake in the old crater (last eruption 1911), whereas you don't really need one for the new crater (last eruption 1965). You should allow for at least half a day's stay on the island. Warnings made by basically lazy guides about hordes of dangerous snakes at the crater lake should be dismissed with a benign smile! You might have to cope with heavy swells and occasionally get sopping wet, so a plastic bag for your camera is a good precaution.
About five km west of Talisay in Buco, on the edge of Lake Taal, is an old seismological station of the Philippine Institute of Volcanology & Seismology (Phivolc). Its scope has been extended to that of a 'Science House', with staff always on duty and information available on the work of volcanologists, the instruments and the geological history of Lake Taal.

Places to Stay

Gloria de Castro's Store, Leynes, Tel 7730138. SR/DR/fan/bath P300, SR/DR/ac/bath P1000. Small, basic, friendly accommodation with a restaurant.
Mountainside Lake Resort, Leynes, Tel 7730142. Cottage/fan/bath P600. Basic, but clean stone cottages. OK for the money.
Buco Resort, Leynes, Tel 7730306. SR/DR/fan/bath P700, SR/DR/ac/bath P1000 and P2500. Basic, reasonable rooms in a neat house with balcony. Beautiful view.
San Roque Beach Resort, Buco, Tel 7730271, @. SR/DR/ac/bath P1500, cottage/ac/bath P1500 and P3000 (with living room and kitchen). Well-kept rooms and cottages. They also have two guesthouses with three bedrooms, two baths, living room (TV), kitchen and terrace available. Price: P5500 and P6000. Pleasant place directly on the water (bathing possible). Restaurant, garden.
Taal Green Lake Resort, Santa Maria, Tel 7730247. SR/DR/fan/bath P1500, SR/DR/ac/bath P2000 (with TV). Reasonable rooms. Quiet, big grounds. Restaurant, swimming pool.
Bougainvillea Resort Inn. Cottage/ac/bath P2200 and P2500, with refrigerator and TV. Spacious, pleasantly decorated stone cottages with big verandas. Well-kept, extensive grounds. Restaurant.

Miscellaneous

Post & Telephone: Post code: 4220. Area code: 043.

Getting There & Away

Batangas
Bus/Jeepney: From Batangas, it's best to use the many daily Manila buses to get to Tanauan. This route is also served by jeepneys, but buses are more comfortable. In the public market in Tanauan you can get a jeepney to Talisay. The total travelling time is two hrs.

Manila
Bus/Jeepney: From Manila the trip to Talisay is in two stages. First you get one of the numerous daily JAM Transit or Tritran buses marked 'Batangas' and go as far as Tanauan. From there you can get a jeepney at the public market going to Talisay. Total travelling time is two hrs.

Pagsanjan
Bus/Jeepney: To reach Talisay from Pagsanjan you begin by catching a jeepney to Santa Cruz. Then catch a Manila bus and get out at the junction at Calamba. From there, catch a jeepney to Tanauan, where you can pick up a jeepney to Talisay. Total travelling time is about 2½ hrs. Instead of going through Calamba, you can use jeepneys from Pagsanjan and Santa Cruz via San Pablo to Tanauan and Talisay.

Tagaytay
Jeepney: A few km east of Tagaytay a road takes you the 10 km down to the lake and Talisay. Jeepneys wait at the turn-off and leave when they are full. The fare is P16, and a Special Ride costs around P200. The last one leaves at 5pm. Jeepneys also cover the route from the Tagaytay Rotonda to the turn-off.

Nasugbu

The better beaches at Nasugbu are about three to four km to the north, eg White Sands. It can be reached by outrigger boat from Nasugbu or Barrio Wawa.

Places to Stay

Maryland Beach Resort, Tel (043) 2162277, @. Cottage/fan/bath P1000 to P2400, SR/DR/ac/bath P2800 to P4000. Acceptable, but fairly expensive rooms in a big stone building. Restaurant, swimming pool. Admission for non-residents P50. Reservations in Manila: Tel (02) 4310433.

Getting There & Away

Bus: Crow Lines buses leave Manila for Nasugbu hourly from 5.30am (two hrs).

Matabungkay

Matabungkay has the most popular beach in the neighbourhood of Manila, so on weekends there are lots of day trippers. Although the sand is not dazzlingly white, it's not bad and the water is clean, just don't expect some deserted South Sea dream of a beach. Among the main attractions are thatched-roof rafts with tables and chairs which can be hired for around P500 per day and anchored over the reef to act as platforms from which to swim and snorkel. The hirer also brings out food and ice-cold drinks to order. Day trips to nearby Fortune Island can be arranged for P800 to P1000. Some ideas on the origin of the name spring to mind when you hear they charge P500 to set foot on the island!

Note: In Matabungkay persistent touts try to persuade newly-arrived tourists to follow them to accommodation, where they will pocket a sizeable commission for their services. If you know where you are going and object to this kind of inflationary pressure, steer well clear of them.

Places to Stay

Twins Beach Club, Cellphone 0917-2782121, @. SR/DR/ac/bath P1200. Friendly, family-style accommodation with good, well-kept rooms. Restaurant. Under German management.
Coral Beach Club, Cellphone 0917-9014635, @. SR/DR/ac/bath P2400 (TV) and P3400 (refrigerator and TV). Sizeable discount on weekdays. Attractive little place with hospitable rooms. Restaurant, swimming pool. Under Australian management.
Matabungkay Beach Resort & Hotel, @. SR/DR/ac/bath P2300 and P2800, suite P3500 and 4000. Extensive, well-maintained grounds with good rooms, the more expensive ones have a refrigerator and TV. Restaurant, swimming pool, tennis courts. Reservations in Manila: Tel (02) 8193080.
Lago De Oro Beach Club, Balibago, Cellphone 0917-8982685. @. SR/DR/ac/bath P3400. Well-kept, comfortable rooms. Extensive grounds about five km south of Matabungkay, on the road to Calatagan. Good restaurant with Italian and Philippine food, swimming pool, diving. However, the main attraction is a lake where you can enjoy water skiing with a cable ski system; P350/hr.
Punta Baluarte Resort, Calatagan. SR/DR/ac/bath P4000 to P5000. Up-

market place about 10 km south of Matabungkay. It has a restaurant, swimming pool, riding and tennis courts. Reservations in Manila: Tel (02) 8994546. Note: This resort was closed in September 2004 for remodelling.

Getting There & Away

Batangas
Jeepney: From Batangas to Matabungkay and Nasugbu is a three or four-stage trip by jeepney: one from Batangas to Lemery, another one from Lemery to Balayan, and a third one from Balayan to Balibago and jeepney or tricycle (P30) from Balibago to Matabungkay.

Bus: About every two hours a Crow Lines bus leaves from Batangas Pier for Nasugbu/Lian (1½ hrs). Carry on from Lian to Matabungkay by jeepney.

Manila
Bus: From Manila to Matabungkay take a Crow Lines bus with the destination Nasugbu, then get out at Lian and do the last few km by jeepney. These leave about 100m from the bus stop in the direction of the town centre. Total travelling time is 2½ hrs.
From Matabungkay to Manila, take a jeepney to Nasugbu bus terminal and carry on by bus.

Deadly Butterflies

With one hand, quick as a flash, an expert can open a Balisong Knife and transform it, unseen, into a deadly weapon. One practised flick and the harmless looking double handle suddenly produces a razor-sharp blade.

Also known as Butterfly Knives and Batangas Knives, these flick knives are produced in workshops in the outskirts of Taal, mainly in the barrio of Balisong. They have become a trade mark of Batangas Province and achieved country-wide popularity after appearing in countless Philippine films.

Lemery, San Luis & Taal

From Lemery, an unassuming place, you can get to Ligpo Point, eight km to the south, via San Luis. The small Ligpo Island - a popular place with divers - is just offshore.
Taal is about one km east of Lemery. It's a peaceful small town with a few old buildings in colonial style and the impressive Basilica Minore of Saint Martin of Tours, built between 1858 and 1878.

Places to Stay

Rockpoint, Balite, Cellphone 0917-9709812, @. SR/DR/fan/bath P1400 per person, including three meals. Basic rooms in a quiet little place directly on the water (no beach). Located 3½ km south of San Luis and 500m south of Balite.
Casa Punzalan, T Gomez St corner C Ilagan St, Taal, Tel 4213034, Fax 4080577. SR/DR/fan P500, SR/DR/ac/bath P800 and P1000. Five guest rooms are available. Beautiful old building, furnished with antique furniture and

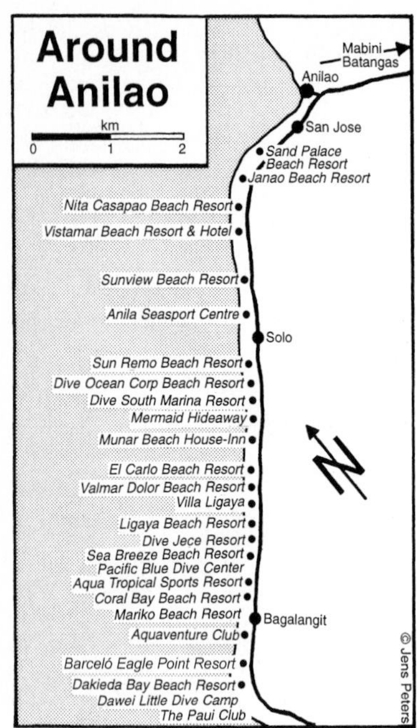

more traditional Capiz windows than you could count. Located near the basilica.

Miscellaneous

Post & Telephone: Post code: 4209 (Lemery), 4210 (San Luis), 4208 (Taal). Area code: 043.

Getting There & Away

Batangas

Jeepney: From Batangas several jeepneys run daily to Lemery via Taal (1½ hrs).

Manila

Bus: Several JAM Transit and Tritran buses run daily from Manila to Lemery (three hrs).

Anilao

South of Anilao, along the west coast of the Calumpan Peninsula which divides Batangas Bay and Balayan Bay, there are over a dozen resorts, most of which have dive shops. Because it's quite close to Manila, and Balayan Bay has good diving spots near Cape Bagalangit and around the islands of Sombrero and Maricaban, this area has become a popular destination for week-end day trippers.

The beach near Anilao is not too impressive. You can, however, hire thatched bamboo rafts (*balsa*) with tables and benches for P300 to P500. These are anchored some distance out from the beach and are good platforms for swimming and snorkelling.

Boat hire for a day trip to Sombrero Island is around P1200.

Places to Stay

Anilao Seasport Centre, Solo. SR/DR/fan/bath P1200. Full board possible. Basic, pleasant rooms. Restaurant, Hobie Cats, windsurfing , diving.

Aqua Tropical Sports Resort, Ligaya. SR/DR/fan/bath P1400, SR/DR/ac/bath P2200 and P2800. Reasonable, quite comfortable rooms, the expensive one with refrigerator and TV. Restaurant, swimming pool, diving.

Vistamar Beach Resort & Hotel, San Jose, Cellphone 0917-5044831, @. SR/DR/fan/bath P1800, SR/DR/ac/bath P2200 and P2600 (with TV). Good, acceptable rooms. Extensive grounds, including even their own chapel. Restaurant, swimming pool, windsurfing, diving. Reservations in Manila: Tel (02) 8218332, Fax (02) 8240755.

Getting There & Away

Bus/Jeepney: From Batangas to Anilao, there are several buses and jeepneys daily, although it may be necessary to change at Mabini. The trip takes 1½ hrs.

Batangas

Batangas is the capital of the province of the same name. There is talk of developing an industrial zone in and around the city, which would provide a convenient location for foreign investors. The South Luzon Tollway is to be extended to Batangas and the possible reopening of the old Manila to Batangas railway is being considered. The depth of Batangas Bay and the ease with which harbour facilities could be extended are also put forward as advantages Batangas has over other regions.
Tourists mainly use Batangas as a transit point on the way to Puerto Galera on Mindoro. However, it's also a good point from which to make day trips to Lake Taal, to the hot springs at Calamba and Los Baños, to Banuan Beach and to Tabangao, further out on the rocky coast seven km from Batangas, which is good for diving and snorkelling.

Places to Stay

Avenue Pension House I, 30 JP Rizal Ave, Tel 3001964. SR/DR/fan/bath P300, SR/DR/ac/bath P400. Basic rooms, OK for the money. Three and 12-hour rates are also available. Fairly centrally located little lodging house.
Mac-Ro Lodge, Panganiban St, Tel 7221030. SR/DR/fan/bath P600, SR/DR/ac/bath P1000, suite P2400. Half price for twelve hours - perfect if you're just passing through. Good rooms.
Alpa Hotel, Kumintang Ibana, Tel 7231025, Fax 7230140. SR/DR/ac/bath P970 to P2420. Spacious rooms with small blemishes, but still OK. Only the more expensive rooms have warm water, TV and refrigerator. An older hotel a little north of the centre. Restaurant, swimming pool.
Batangan Plaza, Kumintang Ibana, Tel 7237701, Fax 9808700, @. SR/DR/ac/bath P3000 to P4200, suite P6000. With refrigerator and TV. Comfortable hotel with well-kept rooms. Restaurant. Located on the way into town coming from Manila, near the Lion Welcome Marker (obelisk) a bit off the National Rd.
Days Hotel, Pastor Village, Pallocan West, Tel 7236931, Fax 7236951, @. SR/ac/bath P3550 and P4200, DR/ac/bath P3800 and P4500, suite P5500. Attractive, comfortable rooms with TV, the suites also have a refrigerator and jacuzzi. Restaurant. Just outside the town to the east.

Places to Eat

In Burgos St, the popular ***Marylyn's Restaurant*** has Philippine food and live music in the evenings. The seafood can be recommended in the pleasant ***Lutong Bahay sa Sawali Restaurant*** in the north-east of town (300m off Herrera St), where they have live music in the evenings. The big ***Gat Polintan Restaurant*** in the Alpa Hotel offers several-course meals of the day and steaks (around P300 with a good selection). In the ***Princesa Kumingtang Restaurant*** in the same hotel, the only people who would feel at home are dedicated karaoke fans.
Friends of fast-food will find branches of all their favourite franchises: ***Chowking, Greenwich*** and ***KFC*** in Rizal Ave, ***Jollibee, McDonald's*** and ***Shakey's*** in Burgos St.

Miscellaneous

Festival: Sublian Festival on 23 July.
Immigration Office, Diversion Rd, Tel 7233032. At the Bauan-Batangas crossroads, about two km from the harbour and the centre respectively.
Money: The branches of the Equitable PCI Bank on Rizal Ave corner Burgos St, and in the Bay City Mall, Silang St corner Tirona St, have ATMs available.
Online: Dalcan Internet Access in the terminal at the pier (P60/hr).

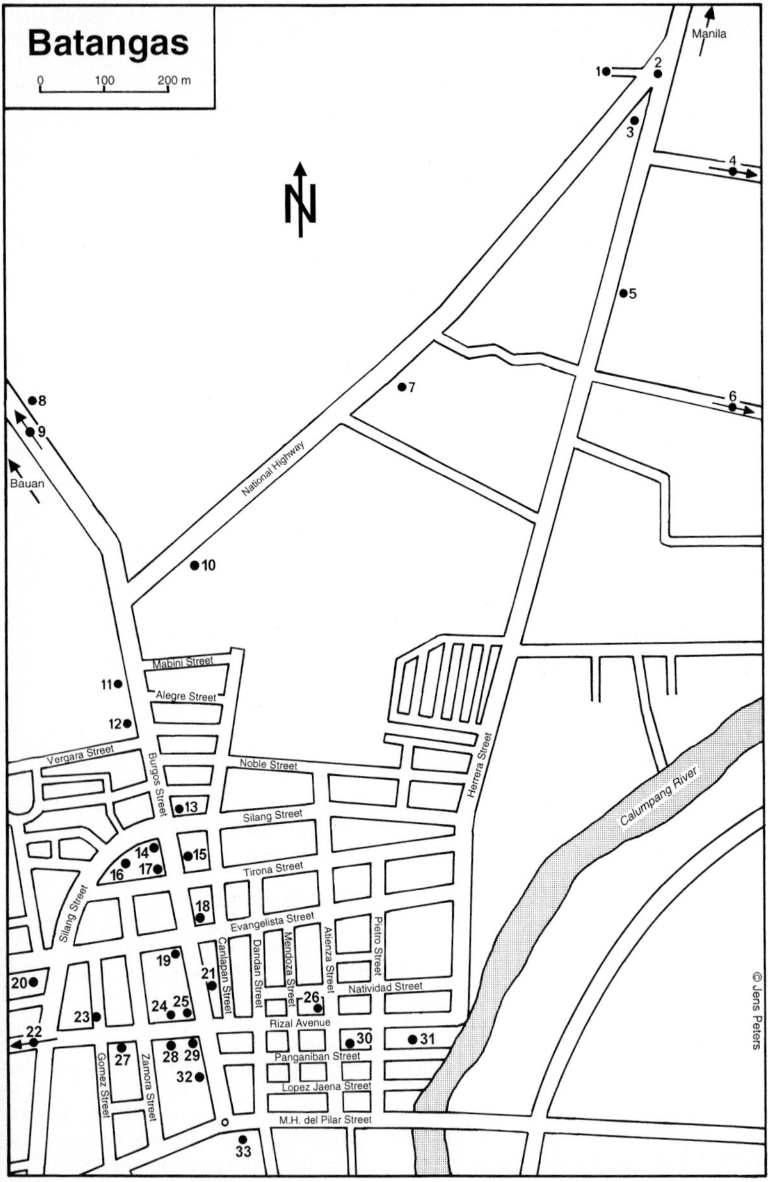
Batangas
0 100 200 m
Manila
Bauan
National Highway
Mabini Street
Alegre Street
Vergara Street
Burgos Street
Noble Street
Herrera Street
Calumpang River
Silang Street
Tirona Street
Evangelista Street
Canlapan Street
Dandan Street
Mendoza Street
Atienza Street
Pietro Street
Natividad Street
Rizal Avenue
Panganiban Street
Lopez Jaena Street
M.H. del Pilar Street
Gomez Street
Zamora Street
1
2
3
4
5
6
7
8
9
10
11
12
13
14
15
16
17
18
19
20
21
22
23
24
25
26
27
28
29
30
31
32
33
© Jens Peters

Getting There & Away
3 Supreme Lines Bus Terminal
8 JAM Transit Bus Terminal
22 Batangas Port (Pier)
23 Jeepneys to Batangas Port

Places to Stay
1 Batangan Plaza
4 Days Hotel
5 Alpa Hotel
26 Avenue Pension House I
30 Mac-Ro Lodge

Places to Eat
4 Lutong Bahay sa Sawali Restaurant (200m)
5 Gat Polintan Restaurant
Princesa Kumingtang Restaurant
11 McDonald's
12 Marylyn's Restaurant
13 Jollibee
14 Max's
16 Chowking
Pizza Hut
18 Shakey's
24 Chowking
Greenwich
28 KFC

Miscellaneous
2 Lion Welcome Marker
6 Provincial Hospital
7 Provincial Capitol
9 Immigration Office (1 km)
10 University of Batangas
15 Bank of the Philippine Islands
16 Bay City Mall
Equitable PCI Bank
17 Philippine National Bank (PNB)
19 Mercury Drug
20 Market
21 Landbank
24 City Mart Shopping Center
25 Metrobank
27 Mercury Drug
29 Equitable PCI Bank
31 Saint Patrick's Hospital
32 City Hall
Police Station
Post Office
33 Basilica Immaculate Conception

Population: 220,000.
Post & Telephone: Post code: 4200. Area code: 043.

Getting There & Away

By Bus: The Supreme Lines Bus Terminal is located on the northern edge of town near the Lion Welcome Marker. The JAM Transit Bus Terminal is about one km north-west of the centre on the road to Bauan. Many buses from Manila drive directly to the pier.

By Boat: Batangas harbour is about 1½ km west of the city centre. Jeepneys leave from Gomez St at the corner of Rizal St.
Montenegro Shipping Lines, Pier, Tel 7238294.
Destinations: Mindoro, Romblon.
Shipshape Ferry, Pier, Tel 7237615.
Destination: Romblon.
Starlite Ferry, Pier, Tel 7239965, 7220162.
Destination: Mindoro.
Supercat Fast Ferry Corporation, Pier, Tel 7238227.
Destination: Mindoro.

Lucena
Bus: Many Supreme Lines buses run every day from Lucena to Batangas (P75; 2½ hrs).

Manila
Bus: Several JAM Transit and Tritran buses leave Manila daily for Batangas (P110; 3½ hrs). If you want the harbour in Batangas, look for the buses for Batangas Pier. Failing that, you'll have

to get a jeepney down to the dock. Note: 'Batangas Pier' buses which go via the Calabarzon Expressway/Star Tollway (check the destination on the front of the bus) avoid the heavy traffic in Santo Tomas, Tanauan and Lipa (P120; 2½ hrs).
In addition, aircon minibuses leave from the JAM Transit and Tritran bus terminals in Pasay for Batangas pier (P120).
If you arrive in Batangas from Mindoro, you can take one of the Manila buses waiting at the pier and carry on directly to Manila.

Beware of pickpockets on these buses - they often operate in teams of three. Forty winks during the journey could cost you dear!

Bus/Boat: If you are going from Manila to Batangas and on towards Puerto Galera, there are daily combined bus and ship services (no scheduled buses) from the Lotus Garden Hotel, Ermita, leaving at 7.30am, from the Swagman Hotel, Ermita, leaving at 8am, and from the Citystate Tower Hotel in Mabini St, Ermita, leaving at 8am sharp (see also the Getting Away from Luzon section in the Manila chapter).

Matabungkay - Nasugbu
Bus: Roughly every two hours, a Crow Lines bus leaves from Lian/Nasugbu for Batangas (1½ hrs). Jeepneys run between Matabungkay and Lian.

Pagsanjan
Jeepney/Bus: To go to Batangas from Pagsanjan quickly, take a jeepney to Santa Cruz; from there, catch a Manila-bound bus as far as Calamba. From Calamba, either take a jeepney directly to Batangas or take a jeepney to Tanauan and then catch a Batangas-bound bus travelling from Manila.

Calamba

The national hero Jose Rizal was born in Calamba, a small town on the southwest shore of the inland lake Laguna de Bay. Rizal House, with its garden, is now a memorial and museum. It is located across from the Town Hall. Open Tue-Sun 8am-noon and 1-5pm.
There is a whole row of resorts along the highway in the Los Baños direction, a few km south of Calamba. These resorts take advantage of the local hot springs and are a popular source of relaxation for stressed-out inhabitants of Metro Manila. Almost all of them offer overnight accommodation, although the facilities can be used by non-residents for an admission fee.
In 1995, an amusement park, the Enchanted Kingdom, was opened 10 km north of Calamba at Santa Rosa, which claims to be 'the country's first and only world-class theme park'. Familiar-sounding rides like the Space Shuttle, Jungle Log Jam, Wheel of Fate, and the 100-foot high Ferris wheel are complemented by interactive displays, an archaeological dig and much more. Open Mon-Thu 2-9pm, Fri-Sat 10am-midnight, Sun 10am-10 pm; admission P400.

Places to Stay

Crystal Springs, National Rd. SR/DR/ac/bath P1500. Good, spacious rooms, each with its own private minipool (2x2 m). This is a generously laid-out place with eight differently sized swimming pools. Five km south of Calamba.

Miscellaneous

Post & Telephone: Post code: 4027. Area code: 049.

Getting There & Away

Batangas
Bus: Frequent buses marked 'Manila' also go from Batangas to Calamba daily (1½ hrs).

Manila
Bus: The buses marked 'Santa Cruz' leaving the JAM Transit and Tritran bus terminals daily in Manila frequently go via Calamba (one hr).

Pagsanjan
Bus: Numerous Manila-bound buses go to Calamba daily from Santa Cruz/Pagsanjan (one hr).

Los Baños

Just south of Calamba, the University of the Philippines (UP) has a forestry institute with botanical gardens in Los Baños. The garden is not so botanical (only trees), but it has a big swimming pool. Look for the sign 'UP Los Baños' on the main road. Not far from the UP is the International Rice Research Institute (IRRI) which was founded in 1960. If you are interested in the history and methods of rice planting in various countries, then the Riceworld Museum is a mine of information.
Los Baños is noted for its hot springs, discovered in 1590, which you can bathe in. Most resorts are outside the town along the highway, and end up running into those at Calamba. About two km along the road to Calamba, between the highway and Laguna de Bay, you will find Alligator Lake, a deep crater lake which has none of the reptiles you would expect to find in it.
Not far from Los Baños is the Philippine Art Center, from where you can get a good view over Laguna de Bay. Only prearranged visits are permitted, and with the express permission of the artists, who want to be given peace to work. At nearby Mt Makiling there is a nice park with a zoo and pool, and good views. Jeepneys to the Scout Jamboree Park go there. Mt Makiling is a 1144m high volcanic massif, the upper slopes of which are covered in jungle, home to a vast variety of flora (watch out for leeches).

Places to Stay

Lakeview Resort Hotel, 728 Lopez St, Tel 5361771. SR/DR/ac/bath P800 to P2000. Adequate rooms, the expensive one with refrigerator and TV. Restaurant, and four swimming pools.
City of Springs Resort Hotel, 147 N Villegas St, Tel 5360731, Fax 5360137, @. SR/DR/ac/bath P660 to P2000. Good rooms furnished in different styles, some with a minipool and jacuzzi. Check-out time at the weekends is 10 am. Restaurant, and several swimming pools. Located directly on the water.

Miscellaneous

Post & Telephone: Post code: 4030. Area code: 049.

Getting There & Away

Batangas
Bus: There is no direct route from Batangas to Los Baños. Best take a bus to Calamba through to the bus terminal, then carry on by bus or jeepney.

Manila
Bus: In Manila, JAM Transit and Tritran buses marked 'Santa Cruz' leave daily, frequently going via Los Baños (two hrs).

Pagsanjan
Bus: From Santa Cruz and Pagsanjan, the numerous buses marked 'Manila' go through Los Baños (one hr).

Alaminos

Alaminos is known for Hidden Valley, a fascinating private property and resort with lush tropical vegetation and several springs. This wonderful natural area is a paradise for botanists and a popular subject for film and photography. Similar to Los Baños, there are hot springs all around here, so don't forget your swimsuit. Although part of Alaminos, it's five km from the town centre. Tricycles will ask for P100 for the short stretch from Alaminos to the gates, where visitors have to pay a whopping admission of P1700. This includes a drink on arrival, buffet lunch, snacks in the afternoon and use of the facilities such as the swimming pool, showers, changing rooms etc.

Places to Stay

Hidden Valley Springs, Cellphone 0919-5401766. SR/ac/bath P5360, DR/ac/bath P8250, all including three meals. The rooms are pleasant enough, although they would cost quite a bit less in other surroundings. The price for overnight accommodation includes the admission fee for the resort. Reservations can be made in Manila: Tel (02) 8184034.

Getting There & Away

Los Baños

Jeepney/Bus: Mt Makiling lies between Los Baños and Alaminos, so the route from Los Baños is a bit roundabout. Go by jeepney from Los Baños to San Pablo, then take either a Manila-bound bus or a Tanauan-bound jeepney to Alaminos. The trip takes an hour.

Manila

Bus: Several JAC Liner, JAM Transit and Philtranco buses leave Manila daily and go through Alaminos, for example, those marked 'San Pablo', 'Lucena', 'Daet', 'Naga' and 'Legaspi', taking two hrs.

San Pablo

San Pablo is known as the City of the Seven Lakes. It's a good centre for walks. There's one around Sampaloc Lake, which has restaurants built on stilts along the lakeside, and others to Pandin and Yambo lakes. The remaining four lakes are Calibato, Mohicap, Palakpakin and Bunot.

Climbers may like to tackle the nearby Mt Makiling, a volcanic mass of 1144m with three peaks. This is best reached from Alaminos or Los Baños. However, if you are starting from San Pablo, the best climb is the 2188m-high Mt Banahaw. This dormant volcano, with its springs and waterfalls, is credited with mystical powers. Especially at Easter, many Filipinos come to meditate and pray in the ravines and drink or bathe in the 'holy water' of the splashing streams. The climb usually begins at Kinabuhayan, which is reached by jeepney from San Pablo. Three days are needed for the climb.

About 10 km south of San Pablo, just before Tiaong, is the Villa Escudero, a coconut plantation and resort combined. Admission is P840 (Friday, Saturday and Sunday P950), including guided tour, lunch buffet, trip on a raft and use of the facilities such as swimming pool and billiards etc. In this complex, reminiscent of the Spanish colonial era, it is worth paying a visit to the museum, which has many valuable historical and cultural artefacts. This is a rewarding daytrip.

Places to Stay

Sampaloc Lake Youth Hostel, Efarca Village, Schetelig Ave, Tel 5623376. Dorm/fan P200. Very basic rooms with bunk beds. Friendly, family-style accommodation with sea view, and steps down to the sea. Located in a residential area at the outskirts of town. Get there by tricycle from the church/plaza in San Pablo (P15).

Pine Rock Hotel, Maharlika Highway, Tel 5627521, Fax 8002295. SR/DR/fan/bath P350, SR/DR/ac/bath P500 to P980. Basic, but acceptable rooms, the more expensive have TV. Coffee shop. Next to the Caltex filling station.

City Inn, Colaga Ave, Tel 5629273. SR/DR/fan P360, SR/DR/fan/bath P380, SR/DR/ac/bath P700 and P1000. Reasonable accommodation, the aircon rooms have TV. OK for the money; to be preferred to the Pine Rock Hotel.
Platinum Lodge, Maharlika Highway, Tel 5612810, Fax 5624279, @. SR/DR/ac/bath P935 to P2200. Immaculate, well-appointed rooms with TV and refrigerator, the expensive ones also have a jacuzzi. Good value. About 30% cheaper for a twelve-hour hire. Restaurant, coffee shop, billards, fitness room. Located about 150m off the highway on the way out of town heading for Manila.
The Coco Palace Hotel, Maharlika Highway, Tel 5612272, Fax 5622254, @. SR/DR/ac/bath P1200 to P2000, all including breakfast. Good, well-kept rooms with TV, the more expensive ones also have a refrigerator. Restaurant. Coffee shop. The best hotel in town, in the outskirts heading for Lucena (next to Max's Restaurant).
Villa Escudero, Tiaong. SR/DR/fan/bath P2170/3340, including three good meals. Attractive, spacious cottages with big veranda on stilts in the water of a tranquil lake. Attentive service. Restaurant, swimming pool. Reservations in Manila: Tel (02) 5232944.

Miscellaneous

Festival: Coco Festival from 8 to 15 January. City Fiesta on 15 January.
Population: 190,000.
Post & Telephone: Post code: 4000. Area code: 049.

Getting There & Away

Los Baños
Jeepney: Numerous jeepneys run daily from Los Baños to San Pablo (30 min).

Manila
Bus: Several JAC Liner, JAM Transit and Philtranco buses leave Manila daily marked 'Lucena', 'Daet', 'Naga' and 'Legaspi'. All of these go through San Pablo (two hrs).

Pagsanjan
Jeepney: From Pagsanjan you get to San Pablo in two stages. First take a jeepney from Pagsanjan to Santa Cruz, then catch another jeepney to San Pablo. The whole trip takes 1½ hrs.

Mt Banahaw & Taytay Falls

To be precise, the gigantic Banahaw-Massiv consists of three peaks: the central Mt Banahaw (2188m), to the west of that Mt San Cristobal (1470m), and Mt Banahaw de Lucban (1875m) in the east. You can get close to the last one fairly easily with your own vehicle.
About two km west of Lucban on the road between Majayjay and Lucban, a road breaks off towards Taytay Falls. It ends after nearly five km in a car park where you pay P10 per person and P20 for parking. It's only 800m on foot to the beautiful Taytay waterfall with its natural pool. There are a few restaurants at the car park and you can also hire guides for the mountain tour there. The climb takes about four hours to the summit. To hire a tent, for example if you want to stay overnight at the waterfall, costs P150 a day.

Pagsanjan

A trip to Pagsanjan (pronounced pag-san-han) is an obvious 'must' on every Philippine tour itinerary. The last section of Francis Ford Coppola's Vietnam War film *Apocalypse Now* was filmed here. The Magdapio Waterfalls are only part of Pagsanjan's attractions; it's the river trip through the picturesque tropical gorge which is the real drawing card.

Two 'banqueros' will paddle you upstream against the strong current in a *banca* (canoe). It's a feat of strength which taxes even two men paddling together. At the last major waterfall you can ride on a bamboo raft for an extra P70. You come downstream at a thrilling speed. Shooting the rapids is at its most exciting in August and September, when the river is high. Don't hold on too tightly to the sides of the boat and keep your hands inside or your fingers may get crushed. Use a plastic bag to keep your camera dry.

All inclusive, the officially fixed price of this harmless bit of fun is P580. (Up to three people can ride in a banca; if you go alone, it costs P1160.) However, tips may be requested, even demanded vehemently. Readers' letters have told of boat operators making most aggressive demands at times - sums of from P500 to P1000 (and more) have been mentioned. According to most reports, anyone who is not prepared to give in to a demand for extra payment made halfway up to the waterfall, is not going to enjoy the rest of the trip. So pay up or suffer. You can, of course, skip the trip, save your money and let others be annoyed. The banqueros, who are arranged through the Pagsanjan Youth Hostel, Pagsanjan Falls Lodge, Pagsanjan Garden Resort and Willy Flores Guesthouse, apparently will not cause an unpleasant scene if challenged. However, there is no guarantee against unpleasant surprises.

Organised day tours from Manila can be arranged for about US$45 at the various travel agencies and the tourist office. This way all costs are covered and you may avoid hassles with banqueros.

If you feel like trying your luck on your own, don't go on weekends, when there are so many tourists it resembles an anthill. If you stay overnight in Pagsanjan and leave for the falls at sunrise, you'll be on the river long before the hordes arrive from Manila between about 10 and 11 in the morning. As sunlight comes late in the deep valleys, photographers will have difficulty taking pictures with normal equipment in the very early morning.

A good view of Pagsanjan and area can be obtained from the water tanks on the hill above the town. From Mabini St, which runs parallel to Rizal St, Pagsanjan's main street, there are steps up to the school where the path up the hill begins.

Day Trips

Visits to the following destinations make good day trips from Pagsanjan. Paete is the best known Philippine centre for wood carving in ebony. The Japanese Garden is a memorial to the Japanese soldiers who died in WWII in and around Pagsanjan. Caliraya Reservoir is a massive artificial lake with resorts like Sierra Lakes and Lake Caliraya Country Club featuring water skiing and windsurfing.

The village of Lucban, halfway along the road to Lucena, is a good example of what villages must have looked like during the era of Spanish rule. Lucban has its harvest festival on 15 May (see the Public Holidays & Special Events section in the earlier Country & People chapter).

Places to Stay

A good rule for most places in Pagsanjan is to find your own way there. The area is not too big and you don't really need a guide, especially since the room will end up costing more because the owner has to pay them a commission!

Willy Flores Guesthouse, 821 Garcia St, Tel 5008203. SR/DR/fan P250/300, SR/DR/fan/bath P350/400. The atmos-

phere is friendly and homely, and the rooms are basic but pleasant and clean. Boat trips to the waterfall.
Pagsanjan Garden Resort, Pinagsanjan, Tel & Fax 8084451, @. SR/DR/fan P400, SR/DR/ac/bath P1200. OK rooms. Beautiful garden grounds with a big swimming pool. Restaurant.
Pagsanjan Rapids Hotel, General Taiño St, Tel 8084180, Fax 8084258. SR/ac/bath P1080 and P1320, DR/ac/bath P1320 and P1680, cottage/ac/bath P1680 and P1920. Tour group hotel with really good rooms, all with TV. Restaurant, swimming pool, boat trips to the waterfall.
Pagsanjan Falls Lodge, Tel 8084209, Fax 8084927. SR/DR/fan/bath P1200, SR/DR/ac/bath P1500 and P1800. Acceptable, but fairly expensive rooms with TV. Restaurant, disco, swimming pool, boat trips to the waterfall. Day visitors can rent a locker for P20.
La Corona de Pagsanjan Resort Hotel, Tel 8081753, Fax 8081725. SR/DR/ac/bath P1800 and P2200, including breakfast. Immaculately decorated rooms with TV. Restaurant. Extensive grounds with plenty room for the three swimming pools. Located a bit outside town, about two km in the direction of Lucban. Reservations can be made in Manila at the Hotel La Corona, Tel (02) 5242631. Fax (02) 5258628.

Places to Eat

There are plenty of good eating places in Pagsanjan, such as the ***Dura-Fe Restaurant*** on General Jaina St which has very good food. It closes early at night. Also recommended are the ***D & C Luncheonette*** on National Rd near the Pagsanjan Falls Lodge and the ***Me-Lin Restaurant*** in Mabini St near the plaza. People find the ***Hidden Café*** in Garcia St a pleasant garden restaurant. It is right alongside the river and serves fairly inexpensive Filipino and European food.

Miscellaneous

Festivals: Bangkero Festival on 27 and 28 May. Town Fiesta on 12 December.
Population: 30,000.
Post & Telephone: Post code: 4008. Area code: 049.

Getting There & Away

Batangas

Bus/Jeepney: To reach Pagsanjan from Batangas, it's quickest to get a Manila-bound bus as far as Calamba. There, catch a bus coming from Manila to Santa Cruz and go on to Pagsanjan by jeepney.

Lucena - South Luzon

Jeepney/Bus: If you are going to South Luzon from Pagsanjan, there are several jeepneys running daily from Santa Cruz to Lucena via Lucban (three hrs). All buses from Manila marked 'Daet', 'Naga', 'Legaspi' etc, go through Lucena, so you don't have to go right back to Manila.

Manila

Bus/Jeepney: Several buses of the companies JAM Transit and Tritran (from their Pasay terminal) leave Manila daily for Santa Cruz (2½ hrs). The last few km from Santa Cruz are done by jeepney. Special Rides by tricycle are not necessary, even when the driver tries to persuade the innocent foreigner to the contrary.

Warning: The route from Calamba to Santa Cruz is very popular with pickpockets. Two or three of them get onto the bus together, usually in Calamba or Santa Cruz, and skilfully distract tourists while their partner is helping himself to their belongings. The young men are around 20, well dressed and look respectable. Obviously there are a few experienced teams at work on this stretch of road.

Tagaytay
Bus/Jeepney: There are two shortcuts when travelling from Tagaytay to Pagsanjan which save you going right back to Manila. One involves travelling by bus to Zapote, then by jeepney to Alabang, by bus to Santa Cruz and by jeepney to Pagsanjan. Alternatively, take a bus from Tagaytay to Palapala, then a jeepney through Binan to Calamba, then a bus to Santa Cruz and a jeepney to Pagsanjan.

Lucena

The capital of Quezon Province has no particular sights for the tourist to get worked up about. The little harbour of Dalahican has more to offer, however, as boats leave here for Marinduque, Masbate and Romblon. It would be worth making a detour to Quezon National Park between Lucena and Atimonan, with its wide variety of birds, especially if you are the kind of birdwatcher who likes adventure. There are interesting walks through the wonderful vegetation with its beautiful flowers, monkeys and so on. About 19 km east of Lucena, the 'Old Zigzag Road' branches off to the right, leading through the park to rejoin the highway after five km.
Lucena would be the place to spend the night if you want to experience the famous Pahiyas Festival in the middle of May, which takes place in Lucban, 25 km to the north.

Places to Stay

Nearly all the hotels in Lucena offer their rooms at a reduced price for short stays (three, six or 12 hours). Most are located west of the centre, in the districts of Iyam and Isabang in ML Tagaro St, the main road out of town.
Anahaw Hotel, ML Tagarao St corner Merchant St, Tel 7103889, Fax 7107197. SR/DR/fan/bath P180, SR/DR/ac/bath P340. Basic rooms, OK for the money. Centrally located.
Tourist Hotel, ML Tagarao St, Iyam, Tel 7104456. SR/fan/bath P150, DR/fan/bath P200, SR/DR/ac/bath P300. Basic, but clean. Very good value. Restaurant. Located 100m off the road.
Lucena Fresh Air Hotel & Resort, ML Tagarao St, Isabang, Tel 7102424, @. SR/fan P195, DR/fan P250, SR/DR/fan/bath P270 to P350, SR/DR/ac/bath P585 and P700. Big place with basic, reasonable rooms which are acceptable for the money, although some of them are not in the best of condition. The rooms at the back are large and quiet. Restaurant, four swimming pools.
Travel Lodge, ML Tagarao St, Iyam, Tel 7104482. SR/DR/fan/bath P200/250, SR/DR/ac/bath P450 and P650, suite P725 and P800. Basic, quiet rooms. Those with fan are OK, but the suites are perhaps a bit pricey. Restaurant, swimming pool.
Lady Luck Hotel, ML Tagarao St, Tel 3711565, Fax 3733575. SR/DR/fan/bath P200, SR/DR/ac/bath P360, P620, P750 and P1200. Squeaky clean, really good rooms all of different sizes and furnishings (some with TV, refrigerator and kitchen). Good value.
The House of Halina, 104 P Gomez St, Tel 7102902, Fax 6603567, @. SR/fan/bath P225, DR/fan/bath P300, SR/ac/bath P540 and P950, DR/ac/bath P640 and P1050, suite P1550 and P1850. A large number of immaculate rooms, some with veranda. The more expensive ones and the very spacious suites also have a refrigerator and TV. Pleasant hotel at the north-east edge of town. Restaurant, big inner courtyard with parking spaces.
Greenview Hotel, ML Tagarao St, Iyam, Tel 6605191, Fax 7107044, @. SR/DR/fan/bath P300 and P500, SR/DR/ac/bath P900 to P1400. Spotless rooms, the aircon ones are very spacious and have a refrigerator and TV.

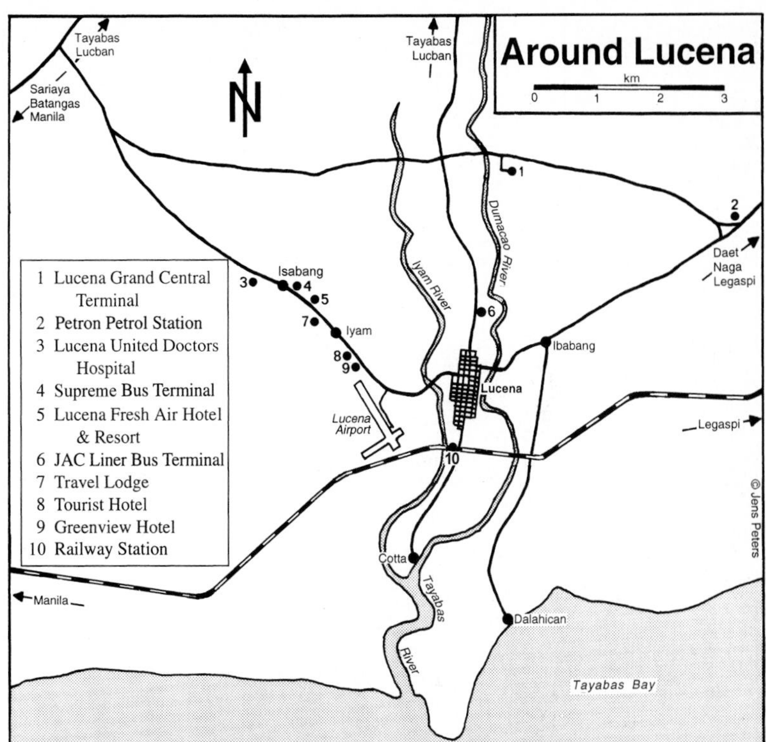

The best accommodation in town (hotel or motel). Big inner courtyard with a small open-air restaurant. Quiet location, set back a bit off the main road.

Places to Eat

There is a whole row of good restaurants in Quezon Ave, Lucena's main shopping street. One speciality of the attractive ***Hacienda Inn*** is Chinese *dim sum*, while in ***Greenwich*** next door it's mainly pizza and pastas people prefer. Friends of fast food will face the familiar choice in Quezon Ave between ***Chowking***, ***Jollibee***, ***KFC*** and two ***McDonald's***. Both branches of ***Coffee Klatch*** will serve you coffee and cake.

In the ***New Cherry Blossom Restaurant*** in Enriquez St, you'll find international, Cantonese, Philippine and Thai food.

Miscellaneous

Festivals: City Fiesta on 30 May. Araw ng Lucena on 20 August.
Money: Bank of the Philippine Islands, Quezon Ave corner Lakandula St, and Granja St corner Zamora St, and Equitable PCI Bank, Quezon Ave corner CT Profugo St, and Enriquez St corner Evangelista St, have ATMs.
Population: 180,000.
Post & Telephone: Post code: 4301. Area code: 042.

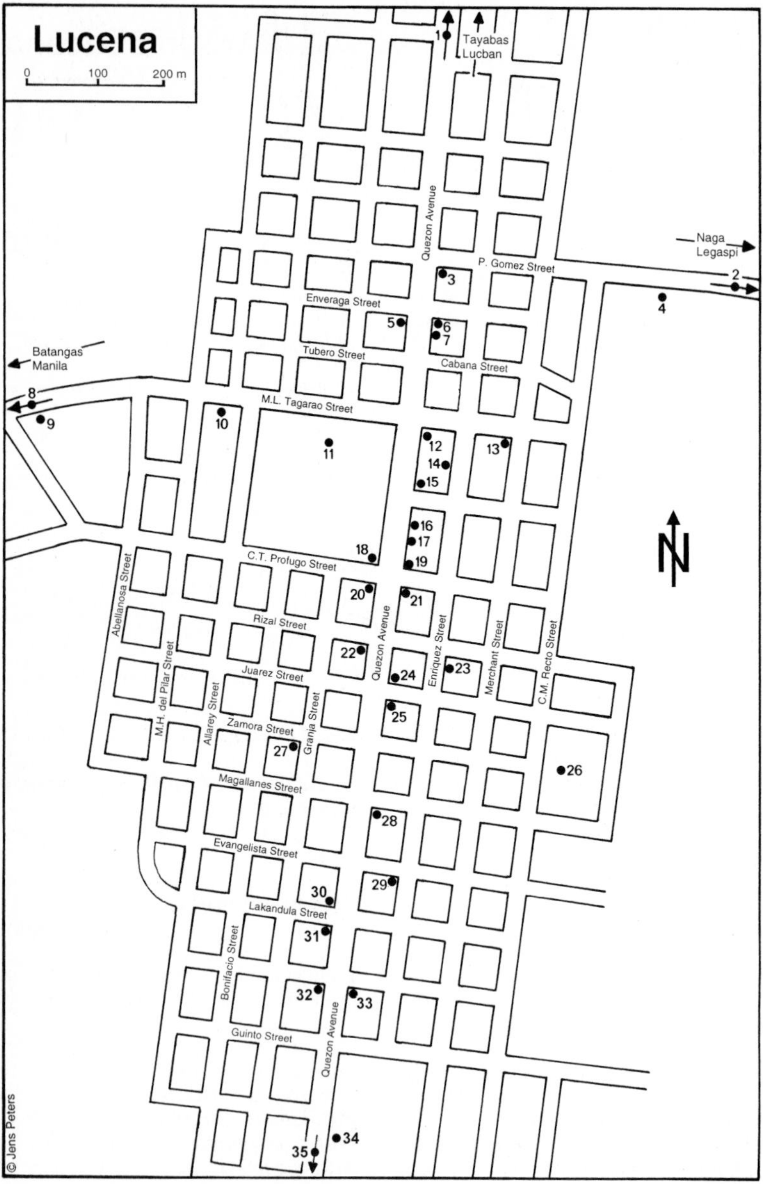

Lucena

0 100 200 m

Tayabas
Lucban
Naga
Legaspi
Batangas
Manila

Quezon Avenue
P. Gomez Street
Enveraga Street
Tubero Street
Cabana Street
M.L. Tagarao Street
C.T. Profugo Street
Rizal Street
Juarez Street
Zamora Street
Magallanes Street
Evangelista Street
Lakandula Street
Guinto Street
Abellanosa Street
M.H. del Pilar Street
Allarey Street
Granja Street
Enriquez Street
Merchant Street
C.M. Recto Street
Bonifacio Street

N

Getting There & Away
1 JAC Liner Bus Terminal (700m)
Lucena Grand Central Terminal (3.5 km)
2 Dalahican Port (6 km)
3 Caltex Petrol Station
4 Shell Petrol Station
8 Supreme Bus Terminal (3 km)
35 Railway Station (500m)
Cotta Port (2.5 km)

Places to Stay
4 The House of Halina
8 Greenview Hotel (1.4 km)
Tourist Hotel (1.5 km)
Travel Lodge (2.3 km)
Lucena Fresh Air Hotel & Resort (2.5 km)
9 Lady Luck Hotel
13 Anahaw Hotel

Places to Eat & Entertainment
7 Coffee Klatch
12 McDonald's
15 Jollibee
16 Coffee Klatch
17 Hacienda Inn
19 Greenwich
21 Antigua Restaurant & Café
22 KFC
23 New Cherry Blossom Restaurant
24 Dunkin' Donuts
25 Dick's Diner
31 Chowking
McDonald's
32 Goldilocks
33 New Cherry Blossom Restaurant

Miscellaneous
5 Internet Access Center
6 Bank of the Philippine Islands
8 Lucena United Doctors Hospital (3.5 km)
10 City Hall
11 Saint Fernand Cathedral
14 Metrobank
18 Equitable PCI Bank
20 Centro Department Store
26 Market
27 Bank of the Philippine Islands
28 Mercury Drug
29 Equitable PCI Bank
30 Bank of the Philippine Islands
31 Ocean Palace Shopping Center
34 Philippine National Bank (PNB)
35 Perez Park & Museum (200m)

Getting There & Away

By Bus: The Lucena Grand Central Terminal is located in Diversion Rd (by-pass), about 3½ km north of the city. Jeepneys run to the city centre and Dalahican Port. JAC Liner operates its own terminal about one km north of the town centre. The Supreme Bus Terminal is located three km north-west of the centre in the area of Isabang.

By Boat: The harbour of Dalahican is about six km south of Lucena. There you will find ticket counters of various shipping lines going to Marinduque and other destinations. Jeepneys leave from the pier for Lucena.
Bluewater Ferry, Tel 7104168.
Destination: Masbate.
Kalaayan Shipping Lines, Tel 7104604.
Destination: Romblon.
Montenegro Shipping Lines, Tel 3737084.
Destination: Marinduque.
Phil-Nippon Kyoei Corporation, Tel 3732458.
Destination: Marinduque.

Batangas
Bus: There are several Supreme Lines buses that make the run from Batangas to Lucena every day (P75; 2½ hrs).

Manila
Bus: Plenty of JAC Liner, JAM Transit, Philtranco and Tritran buses go from Manila to Lucena every day. They may be going only as far as Lucena or be on

Bacolor - Submerged in the Mud

In September 1995 San Fernando narrowly escaped a catastrophe. In the foothills of Mt Pinatubo heavy rain had released enormous mudslides which flowed south-east down the Pasig-Potrero river system, causing tremendous flooding. Wide areas of San Fernando and the province were submerged under the flood waters for days. But much worse: low-lying areas were completely filled up with mud, and whole communities disappeared under the slimy mess. Bacolor, right before the gates of San Fernando, was hit especially badly. Since then, even the big church has remained submerged under the grey mass, with little more than the roof sticking defiantly out. A hastily erected dike is now supposed to prevent San Fernando being next in line to be victim to a mudslide.

their way to Daet, Naga, Legaspi or Matnog (P135; 3½ hrs).

Santa Cruz - Pagsanjan - Lucban

Jeepney: Several jeepneys run daily from Santa Cruz to Lucena, via Pagsanjan and Lucban (three hrs).

The jeepneys from Lucena to Santa Cruz leave from the Lucena Grand Central Terminal.

San Fernando (Pampanga)

Don't confuse San Fernando (Pampanga), the capital of Pampanga Province 50 km north of Manila, with the San Fernando that is the capital of La Union Province, north-west of Baguio on the coast. This town is notorious at Easter and Christmas. On Good Friday at noon you can see at least one fanatic being nailed to a cross in a rice field in the barangay San Pedro Cutud. In 2004 there were 11 such fanatical 'believers'! These imitators of Christ are accompanied on their 'Via Crusis' (way of the cross) to 'Golgotha' by hordes of flagellants, who whip their backs until they bleed, watched by a crowd of curious onlookers.

On the Saturday evening before Christmas, several oversized Christmas stars (*parol*) that would not be out of place as light organs in discos are put on show for people to judge at the SM City shopping centre on the North Expressway. Starting from the next day, the best of these 'giant lanterns' can then be viewed for a week on the town plaza in the city centre. As it is possible the schedule of the lantern festival may be altered at short notice, it would be best to check times and dates with the tourist office in about mid-December. See also the Public Holidays & Special Events section in the earlier Country & People chapter.

The Hilaga is on the Expressway outside the city gates of San Fernando, and is a cultural showcase for Luzon north of Manila. The Ilocos Region (Region I), Cagayan Valley Region (Region II), Central Luzon Region (Region III) and Cordillera Administrative Region (Region IV) are presented here with entertainment such as folk dances, demonstrations of the production of handmade artwork, and examples in several restaurants of the cuisine of North Luzon. Other attractions in this complex include a hotel, an amphitheatre, a bookstore with publications on North Luzon, and the Tourist Office of the Central Luzon Region.

Places to Stay

Boliseum Motel, Juliana Subdivision, Tel 9612040. SR/DR/ac/bath P650. Good rooms, which can also be rented for three hours (P300); all with TV.

Restaurant. It's a bit out of the way on the outskirts of town, but to make up for it, it's quiet.
Hotel Gracelane, MacArthur Highway, San Agustin, Tel 9613696, Fax 9615358. SR/DR/ac/bath P1375 to P1925, suite P3600. Well furnished, really comfortable rooms with TV, the suites also have a refrigerator. Located about 2½ km north of the town centre on the road to Angeles.

Miscellaneous

Festival: Giant Lantern Festival in the third week in December.
Population: 200,000.
Post & Telephone: Post code: 2000. Area code: 045.
Tourist Office: City Tourist Office, City Hall, Tel 9612872.
Central Luzon Tourist Office, Hilaga, Tel 9612665, Fax 9612612, @. Open Mon-Fri 8am-5pm.

Getting There & Away

Angeles
Bus: Victory Liner buses from Baguio to Olongapo go through Angeles and San Fernando, and it is possible to get on them (30 min).

Jeepney: There are several jeepneys from Angeles to San Fernando daily (30 min). Most come from Mabalacat or Dau, north of Angeles.

Manila
Bus: Only a few buses go direct from Manila to San Fernando along the old MacArthur Highway. Most use the quicker Expressway. There are several Philippine Rabbit and Victory Liner buses every day. Buses from Manila to Olongapo almost always go into San Fernando; if necessary, you can get a jeepney from the nearest cross-roads into the town. The buses take about 1½ hrs.

Olongapo
Bus: Numerous Victory Liner buses go from Olongapo through San Fernando daily, almost all on the way to Manila or Baguio, taking 1½ hrs.

Angeles

Until 1991, Angeles was home to Clark Air Base, run by and for the US Air Force. In that year, the Americans had to respect the wishes of the Philippine senate that they leave the country. The withdrawal was accelerated a little by the eruption of Pinatubo, which didn't just destroy the air base, but made a total mess of Angeles itself and the surrounding area. Even considering how much has already been cleaned up and how well life has returned to normal here, it will still take a few years before the area fully recovers from the devastation.
As was the case in Olongapo, the sudden withdrawal of the Americans had serious repercussions for the economy of the town at first. However, the efforts put into converting the huge area of the former base into an industrial, airport and tourism complex have already shown considerable results. In the meantime, several national and international companies are conducting business in the Clark Special Economic Zone (CSEZ), the hotel Holiday Inn Resort Clark Field has been opened, as have the Mimosa Golf & Country Club and Fontana Leisure Parks, a pleasure park with the usual complement of big water slides etc. Sporting/tourist events such as the Clark International Hot Aerosports Festival, go-kart rides, and drag races take place regularly. In addition, a good number of people every day take advantage of the cheap shopping facilities in the FTZ (Free Trade Zone).
Various local hotels now offer Pinatubo tours. The tourists have also meant

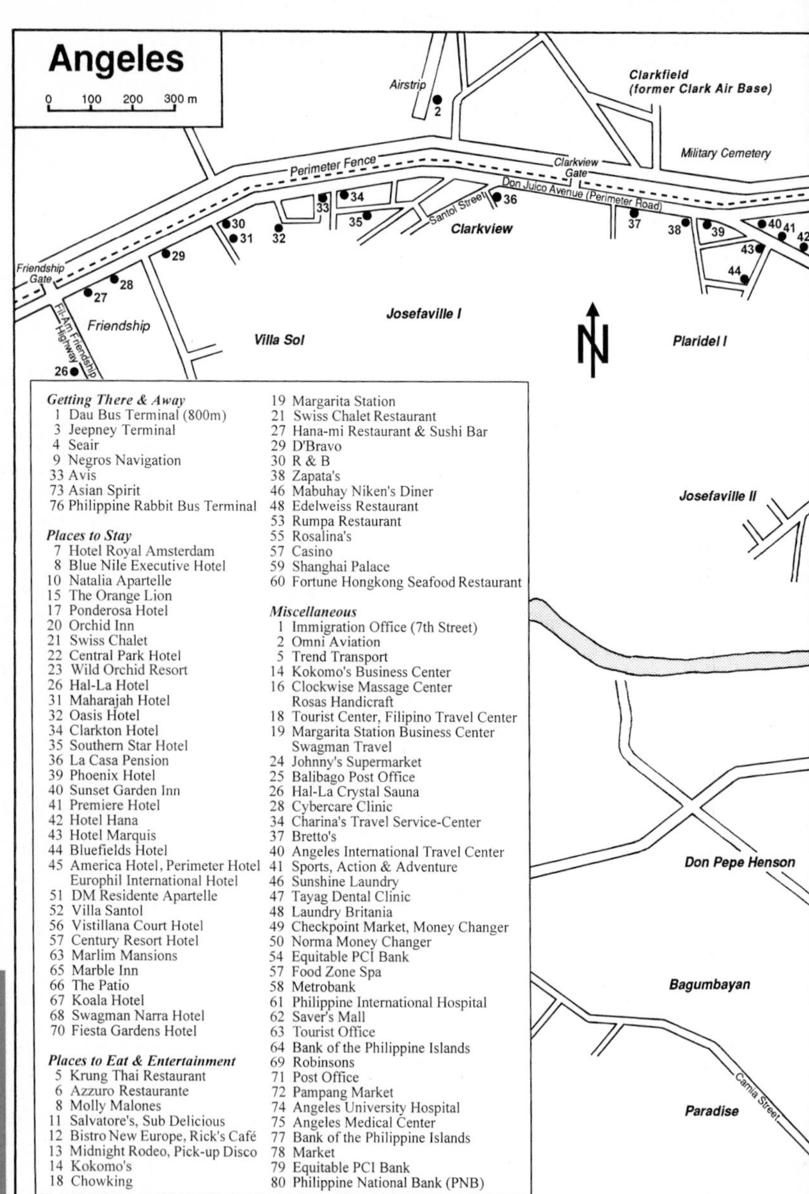
Angeles
0 100 200 300 m
Airstrip
Clarkfield
(former Clark Air Base)
Military Cemetery
Perimeter Fence
Clarkview Gate
Don Juico Avenue (Perimeter Road)
Santol Street
Clarkview
Friendship Gate
Fil-Am Friendship Highway
Friendship
Villa Sol
Josefaville I
Plaridel I
Josefaville II
Don Pepe Henson
Bagumbayan
Camia Street
Paradise
Getting There & Away
1 Dau Bus Terminal (800m)
3 Jeepney Terminal
4 Seair
9 Negros Navigation
33 Avis
73 Asian Spirit
76 Philippine Rabbit Bus Terminal
Places to Stay
7 Hotel Royal Amsterdam
8 Blue Nile Executive Hotel
10 Natalia Apartelle
15 The Orange Lion
17 Ponderosa Hotel
20 Orchid Inn
21 Swiss Chalet
22 Central Park Hotel
23 Wild Orchid Resort
26 Hal-La Hotel
31 Maharajah Hotel
32 Oasis Hotel
34 Clarkton Hotel
35 Southern Star Hotel
36 La Casa Pension
39 Phoenix Hotel
40 Sunset Garden Inn
41 Premiere Hotel
42 Hotel Hana
43 Hotel Marquis
44 Bluefields Hotel
45 America Hotel, Perimeter Hotel
Europhil International Hotel
51 DM Residente Apartelle
52 Villa Santol
56 Vistillana Court Hotel
57 Century Resort Hotel
63 Marlim Mansions
65 Marble Inn
66 The Patio
67 Koala Hotel
68 Swagman Narra Hotel
70 Fiesta Gardens Hotel
Places to Eat & Entertainment
5 Krung Thai Restaurant
6 Azzuro Restaurante
8 Molly Malones
11 Salvatore's, Sub Delicious
12 Bistro New Europe, Rick's Café
13 Midnight Rodeo, Pick-up Disco
14 Kokomo's
18 Chowking
19 Margarita Station
21 Swiss Chalet Restaurant
27 Hana-mi Restaurant & Sushi Bar
29 D'Bravo
30 R & B
38 Zapata's
46 Mabuhay Niken's Diner
48 Edelweiss Restaurant
53 Rumpa Restaurant
55 Rosalina's
57 Casino
59 Shanghai Palace
60 Fortune Hongkong Seafood Restaurant
Miscellaneous
1 Immigration Office (7th Street)
2 Omni Aviation
5 Trend Transport
14 Kokomo's Business Center
16 Clockwise Massage Center
Rosas Handicraft
18 Tourist Center, Filipino Travel Center
19 Margarita Station Business Center
Swagman Travel
24 Johnny's Supermarket
25 Balibago Post Office
26 Hal-La Crystal Sauna
28 Cybercare Clinic
34 Charina's Travel Service-Center
37 Bretto's
40 Angeles International Travel Center
41 Sports, Action & Adventure
46 Sunshine Laundry
47 Tayag Dental Clinic
48 Laundry Britania
49 Checkpoint Market, Money Changer
50 Norma Money Changer
54 Equitable PCI Bank
57 Food Zone Spa
58 Metrobank
61 Philippine International Hospital
62 Saver's Mall
63 Tourist Office
64 Bank of the Philippine Islands
69 Robinsons
71 Post Office
72 Pampang Market
74 Angeles University Hospital
75 Angeles Medical Center
77 Bank of the Philippine Islands
78 Market
79 Equitable PCI Bank
80 Philippine National Bank (PNB)

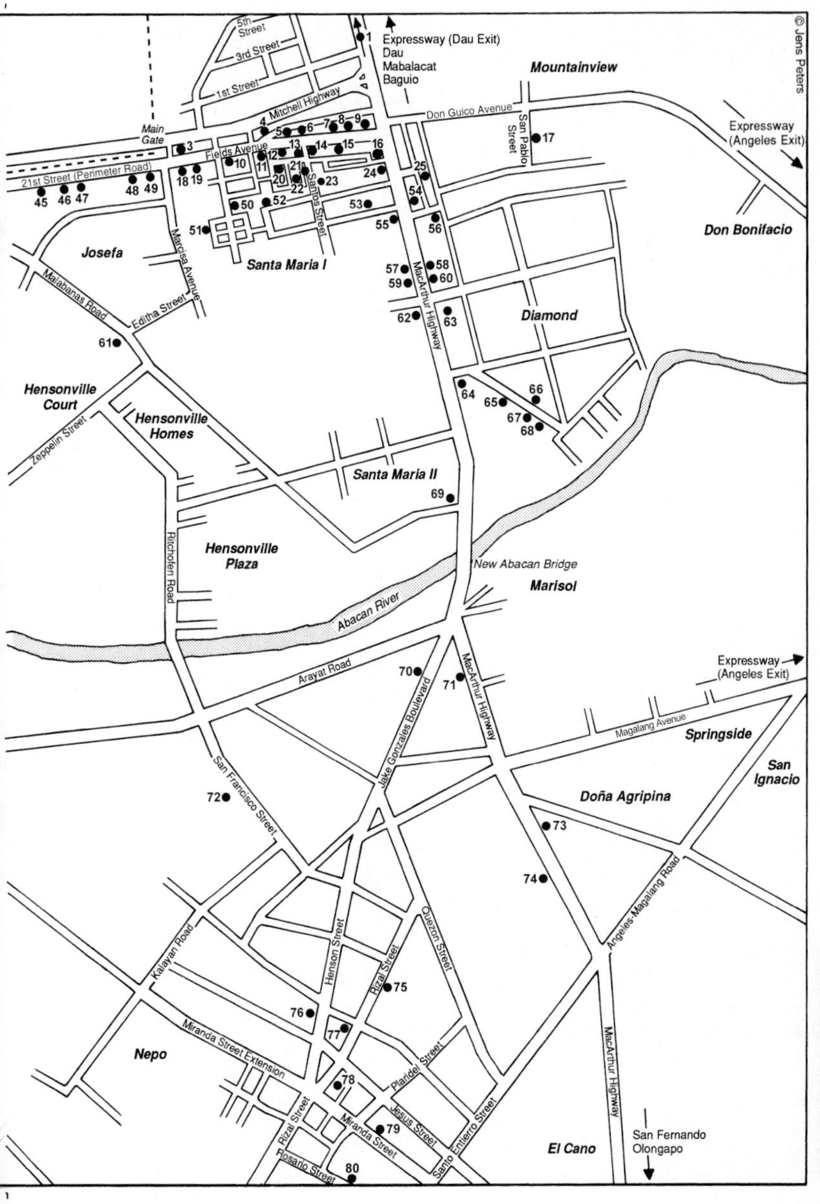

Central Luzon

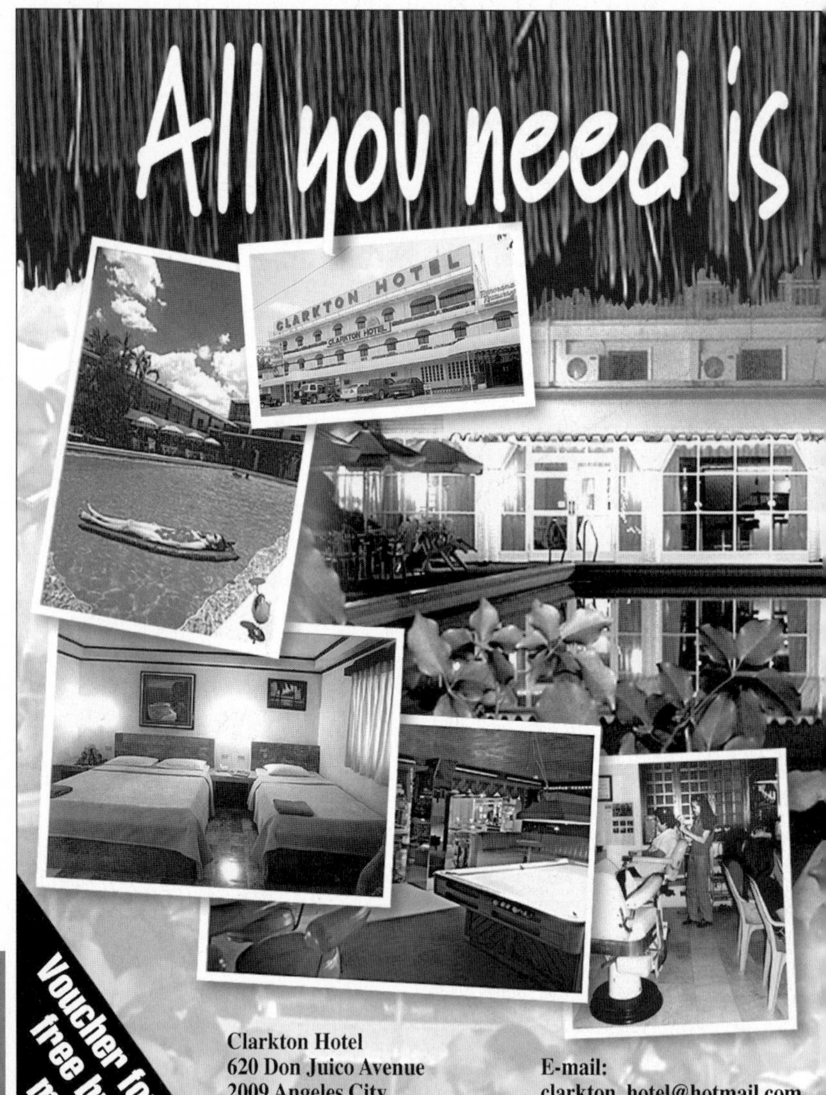
All you need is
CLARKTON HOTEL
Voucher for one free buffet meal
Clarkton Hotel
620 Don Juico Avenue
2009 Angeles City
Tel. +63 (0)45 892 6272 & -6273
Fax: +63 (0)45 625 6887
E-mail:
clarkton_hotel@hotmail.com
clarktonhotel@yahoo.com
info@clarkton.com

Central Luzon

more business for the bars, restaurants and nightclubs that did manage to survive the fateful year of 1991 or have been rebuilt in the meantime.
Unfortunately, the upsurge in business has encouraged the con men to try their luck in the town. With their familiar greeting 'Hello, my friend, I'm from the hotel...' they can be witnessed round the clock doing their level best to relieve unsuspecting tourists of their money, and not taking no for an answer.

Museum

The Clark Museum at the Parade Ground near the Holiday Inn Resort Clark Field provides a good overview of the era of the American Air Base from 1902 to 1991 as well as the metamorphosis of the former military base into the Clark Special Economic Zone. In the upper floor, the Museong Kapampangan houses an interesting exhibition of the Spanish colonial period and is a showcase for artists from the province of Pampanga. Open Mon-Fri 9am-noon and 1-4.30pm. Admission: P20.

Shopping

Philippine arts and handicrafts and Pinatubo souvenirs made from volcanic ash are available at Rosas Handicraft on the MacArthur Highway, Balibago.
For international deli food shopping, Bretto's on Don Juico Ave can be highly recommended. This well-run shop stocks the usual meats and sausages as well as cheeses, wines, müsli and vegetables. They also serve a small selection of tasty dishes.

Places to Stay

Angeles has a large selection of comfortable hotels with restaurants and swimming pools, almost all of which are north of the Abacan River in the Balibao area of town, near Fields Ave with its many bars. In the actual city centre south of the river there are almost no hotels to be found.

Places to Stay - bottom end

Vistillana Court Hotel, Charlotte St, Balibago, Tel 3321408. SR/DR/fan/bath P350, SR/DR/ac/bath P450. Reasonable rooms with TV. Good value for money.
Villa Santol, Fatima St, Santa Maria I, Cellphone 0919-2201143. SR/DR/fan P360, SR/DR/fan/bath P420. Basic, but friendly guesthouse with clean rooms. Small restaurant in the garden.
La Casa Pension, Tamarind St, Clarkview, Tel 3227984, Fax 8926256, @. SR/DR/fan/bath P400/430, SR/DR/ac/bath P580/600. Small, family-style accommodation with well-kept rooms, all with TV.
Koala Hotel, Orosa St, Diamond, Tel & Fax 8920891, @. SR/DR/fan P400, SR/DR/ac/bath P750 and P900 (kitchen). Nice rooms with TV. Small swimming pool. Located next to the Swagman Narra Hotel.
The Patio, Orosa St, Diamond, Tel 8920809, Fax 3321771, @. SR/DR/fan/bath P550, SR/DR/ac/bath P850. Good rooms for the money, all with TV, the more expensive ones also have a refrigerator. Small swimming pool.
Marble Inn, Orosa St, Diamond, Tel 8920901, @. SR/DR/fan/bath P600, SR/DR/ac/bath P700 to P875. Clean, practically furnished rooms with TV, the aircon ones also have a refrigerator. Restaurant.

Places to Stay - middle

Hotel Marquis, Malabañas Rd, Plaridel I, Tel 3224714. SR/DR/fan/bath P650, SR/DR/ac/bath P750 to P1100. OK rooms. Restaurant, and their swimming pool is so small you might miss it.
Bluefields Hotel, Plaridel St, Plaridel I, Tel 8927290, Fax 3223948, @. SR/DR/fan/bath P725, SR/DR/ac/bath P800 and P850. Good, quiet rooms. Restaurant, swimming pool.

Europhil International Hotel, Don Juico Ave, Clarkview, Tel 3222470, Fax 3229520, @. SR/DR/ac/bath P800 and P1100, suite P1300. Fairly basically furnished, standard rooms with TV and better equipped suites. Restaurant, garden with swimming pool.

Swagman Narra Hotel, Orosa St, Diamond, Tel 3225133, Fax 3229467, @. SR/DR/ac/bath P800 to P1300. Reasonable rooms with TV, the more expensive ones also have a refrigerator. Australian management. Restaurant, swimming pool.

Sunset Garden Inn, Malabañas Rd, Clarkview, Tel 8882312, Fax 8882310, @. SR/DR/fan/bath P820, SR/DR/ac/bath P920. Weekly and monthly rates available. Spacious, well-kept rooms with TV. The Swiss management makes sure the rooms are kept spotlessly clean in this friendly place. One of the most popular hotels in town. Reservations are recommended. Restaurant, swimming pool, fitness room.

Premiere Hotel, Malabañas Rd, Clarkview, Tel 8882755, Fax 8882310, @. SR/DR/ac/bath P920. Well furnished rooms with TV. Pleasant grounds with swimming pool and garden. Restaurant. Belongs to the Sunset Garden Inn.

Hotel Hana, Malabañas Rd, Plaridel I, Tel 8926666, Fax 8926001, @. SR/DR/ac/bath P900 and P990. Good rooms with refrigerator and TV. Restaurant, swimming pool. Located next to the Premiere Hotel.

America Hotel, Don Juico Ave, Clarkview, Tel 3321022, Fax 6256106, @. SR/DR/ac/bath P880 (with TV) to P1300 (with refrigerator and TV), suite P3200 (with jacuzzi, refrigerator and TV). Well-kept, comfortable place. The suites are particularly well appointed. Restaurant, swimming pool.

Clarkton Hotel, Don Juico Ave, Clarkview, Tel 3223424, Fax 6256887, @. SR/DR/ac/bath P990 to P1690, suite P1890 and P2190, all with TV, the more expensive ones also have a refrigerator. The rooms are immaculate at this German-run place which has been excellently equipped for wheelchair users. Restaurant, swimming pool, fitness room.

Swiss Chalet, Santos St, Balibago, Tel 8872618, @. SR/DR/ac/bath P1250 to P1450. Well-appointed rooms of various sizes, with refrigerator and TV. Restaurant.

Apartelle Royal, Fields Ave, Balibago, Tel. 8924155, Fax: 8922460, @. SR/DZ/ac/bath P1600 and P2200. Well-kept rooms with refrigerator and TV. Located above the Camelot Bar.

Central Park Hotel, Real St, Balibago, Tel 8920256, Fax 8925680, @. SR/DR/ac/bath P1400 and P1650. Immaculate rooms with refrigerator and TV. Friendly, attentive service. Restaurant, small swimming pool.

Phoenix Hotel, Malabañas Rd corner Don Juico Rd, Clarkview, Tel 8882195, Fax 3322074, @. SR/DR/ac/bath P1300 and P1750, with refrigerator and TV. Good, well-furnished rooms in a Spanish style building. Restaurant, swimming pool.

Woodland Park Resort Hotel, Lizares St, Dau, Tel 8921002, Fax 3323311, @. SR/DR/ac/bath P1400 to P2450. Good rooms with TV, the more expensive ones also have a refrigerator. Pleasant, spread out grounds. Restaurant, and the largest hotel swimming pool in Angeles.

Orchid Inn, 109 Raymond St, Balibago, Tel 8922403, Fax 3222790, @. SR/DR/ac/bath P1400 to P2750. A good, popular hotel with pleasantly furnished rooms, all with refrigerator and TV. Restaurant, swimming pool.

Blue Nile Executive Hotel, Fields Ave, Balibago, Tel 8920120, Fax 8920121. SR/DR/ac/bath P2200 and P3300. Well-appointed rooms, some of them a bit small, with refrigerator and TV. Neat hotel with an impressive, Egyptian-style facade. Restaurant. Swimming pool.

Your place to start an affordable Philippine journey!
SUNSET GARDEN
SUNSET GARDEN HOTEL
Tel. +63 (0)45 888 2312
Fax: +63 (0)45 888 2310
E-mail: sunsetg@mozcom.com
Web: www.sunsetgarden.com
■ Attractive resort with large swimming pool ■ Outdoor-Restaurant (European and Philippine specialities) ■ Cozy bar in Nipa hut style (24-hour service). Popular meeting spot for swapping information and experiences ■ Nice, clean rooms (fan or air-con) ■ Pool billiards. Gym. Golf and tennis facilities close by. ■ The hotel is under the same Swiss management as the Premiere Hotel (150 metres away)
Both hotels accept travellers' cheques and credit cards. Tourist bus service from and to Manila.
PREMIERE HOTEL
Tel. +63 (0)45 888 2755
Fax: +63 (0)45 888 2664
E-mail: premierh@mozcom.com
Web: www.premiere-hotel.com
■ The ideal hotel for those who prefer a quiet and more private atmosphere ■ Beautiful swimming pool (separate paddling pool for children) ■ Attractive garden setting ■ All rooms equipped with air-con and cable TV ■ Restaurant featuring international and Philippine dishes (open around the clock) ■ Internet station ■ Table tennis ■ Pool billiards.

The Orange Lion, Fields Ave, Balibago, Tel 8920998. SR/DR/ac/bath P2300. Nicely decorated rooms with TV, refrigerator and balcony. Restaurant.
Hotel Royal Amsterdam, Fields Ave, Balibago, Tel 8923392, Fax 8923311. SR/DR/ac/bath P900 to P2500, suite P3100 to P8400. Well-kept, spotless rooms with refrigerator and TV, the suites also with jacuzzi. Restaurant.

Places to Stay - top end

Oasis Hotel, Don Juico Ave, Clarkville Compound, Tel 8933301, Fax 8933306, @. SR/DR/ac/bath P1950, suite P2700. Quiet, pleasant place with comfortable, tastefully decorated rooms. Restaurant, swimming pool.
Wild Orchid Resort, Santos St, Balibago, Tel 6256445. SR/DR/ac/bath P3400 to P4500. Attractive hotel with well-appointed rooms, all with refrigerator and TV, the more expensive one also with a balcony onto the swimming pool.
Holiday Inn Resort Clark Field, Mimosa Dr, Clarkfield, Tel 5998000, Fax 5992174, @. SR/DR/ac/bath P7900, suite P12,750 (ask for promo rates). Luxury hotel on the grounds of the former Clark Air Force Base. Next to the casino and Mimosa Golf Course.

Places to Eat

Thanks to the former American air base, Angeles not only has a large selection of comfortable hotels but also a wide range of international restaurants. Almost all the restaurants listed below offer an inexpensive menu of the day and also serve Filipino dishes in addition to their individual specialities.
At ***Mabuhay Niken's Diner*** next to the Sunshine Laundry in Perimeter Rd you can order a good value American breakfast as well as inexpensive Philippine food. A popular expat hang-out, the unpretentious ***Rosalina's*** on MacArthur Highway serves good value, tasty international cooking (meals for less than P100); open for breakfast from 6am, as is ***Rumpa*** in A Surla St.
The cuisine in various hotel restaurants is Australian, eg in the ***Swagman Verandah Restaurant***. Austrian, German and Swiss food can be found at the ***Edelweiss*** (very inexpensive 5-course meals of the day) near the checkpoint, the ***Sunset Garden Inn Restaurant*** in the hotel of the same name (good fondue), and the ***Panorama Restaurant*** at the Clarkton Hotel with its excellent dinner buffet. The ***Bistro New Europe*** on Fields Ave includes a good choice of sandwiches on its menu. Also on Fields Ave, there's an impressive selection of tasty Italian food available at the ***Azzuro Restaurante*** above the Lancelot Bar, and ***Salvatore's*** will serve you what are probably the best pizzas in town.
A first-class place to go for outstanding steaks is the ***Maranao Grill Restaurant*** in the Oasis Hotel, a well-run establishment also frequented by up-market Filipinos. The ***Swiss Chalet Restaurant*** in the hotel of the same name is also well known for good steaks and European food. They have a terrace for guests who prefer to eat outdoors.
The Irish pub & restaurant ***Molly Malones*** at the Blue Nile Executive Hotel on Fields Ave offers excellent international buffets. ***Zapata's*** in Don Juico Ave is the place for Mexican food (closed on Mondays).
Those who are partial to Japanese cooking will appreciate the fairly inexpensive ***Hana-mi Restaurant & Sushi Bar*** on Don Juico Ave (sashimi with five types of fish for P300).
At the ***Shanghai Palace*** on MacArthur Highway the Chinese meals are good value for money. You'll pay more in the ***Fortune Hongkong Seafood Restaurant*** across the road - this has to be the best Chinese restaurant in town.
The ***Krung Thai Restaurant*** and the popular ***Margarita Station*** (open round

the clock), both on Fields Ave, offer good Thai food.

Entertainment

There are countless bars, with and without go-go girls, all along Fields Ave and the sidestreets going off it. In many of them you can play pool or billiards for a few pesos. Now and then you may bump into the 8-ball world champion, Efren 'Bata' Reyes ('The Magician'), who is based in Angeles and likes to play a challenge match for a few hundred pesos in between tournaments.

You will also find a few karaoke clubs in Don Juico Ave which have opened up since the American withdrawal and are mostly frequented by Filipinos. The same goes for the ***D'Bravo*** and the ***R & B*** disco, which also have live music.

In Real St, the elaborately decorated ***Pick-up Disco*** packs them in, especially on Tuesdays, which is ladies' night. Right next door in the ***Midnight Rodeo*** you can enjoy oldies and country & western music every night.

For a very late (or early) drink, ***Margarita Station*** on Fields Ave, is the place to go (try their Frozen Margaritas). It's open 24 hours and busy all the time. A similar place is ***Kokomo's*** at the corner of Fields Ave and Santos St.

Those who like to gamble have two choices of ***Casino*** in Angeles: one at the Century Resort Hotel, MacArthur Highway, and the other next to the Holiday Inn Resort Clark Field, Mimosa Dr, Clarkfield.

Miscellaneous

Festivals: Clark International Aerosports Festival in February. Fiestang Kuliat in October, which reaches a climax with the Tigtigan-Terakan Keng Delan street festival on 30 and 31 October on the MacArthur Highway in Balibago.

Immigration Office, 7th St, Dau, Tel 8926110. Open Mon-Fri 9am-noon and 1-5pm.

Laundry: Britania Launderette and Sunshine Laundry, both on Perimeter Rd, charge about P35 per kg.

Medical Services & Wellness: Angeles Medical Center, Rizal St, Tel 3224632, 3224886.

Cybercare, Don Juico Ave, Tel. 8932459. They have different specialists on different days, so it's better to phone first. Closed on Sunday.

Philippine International Hospital, Malabañas Rd, Tel 8925262

Tayag Dental Clinic, Perimeter Rd, Tel 8927106.

Clockwise Massage Center, Fields Ave corner MacArthur Highway, Tel 3220824 (shiatsu and reflexology; P300/hr). Open daily 10am-10pm.

Food Zone Spa, MacArthur Highway, at the Casino, Tel 6257838 (Chinese foot reflexology, shiatsu and body massage; P500/hr). Open daily 2pm-2am.

Hal-La Crystal Sauna, Friendship Highway, Tel 8932232 (sauna and massage; P240 and P450 P/hr respectively). Open daily 8am-2am.

Money: Money changers at the checkpoint, and the Norma Money Changer in a small side street near the Margarita Station, will all change cash.

Bank of the Philippine Islands, MacArthur Highway (two branches) and Rizal St corner Burgos St, Equitable PCI Bank, MacArthur Highway and Miranda St, Metrobank, MacArthur Highway, and Philippine National Bank, Santo Rosario St, all have ATMs. Kokomo's on Fields Ave has a United Coconut Planters Bank ATM.

The Tourist Center, Fields Ave, Tel 8925107, will change cash and travellers cheques and will also give cash advances on all popular credit cards, albeit for a 7.5% fee (don't forget your passport).

Online: There are several internet cafés along Fields Ave, including Kokomo's Business Center, Rick's Café and Margarita Station Business Center.

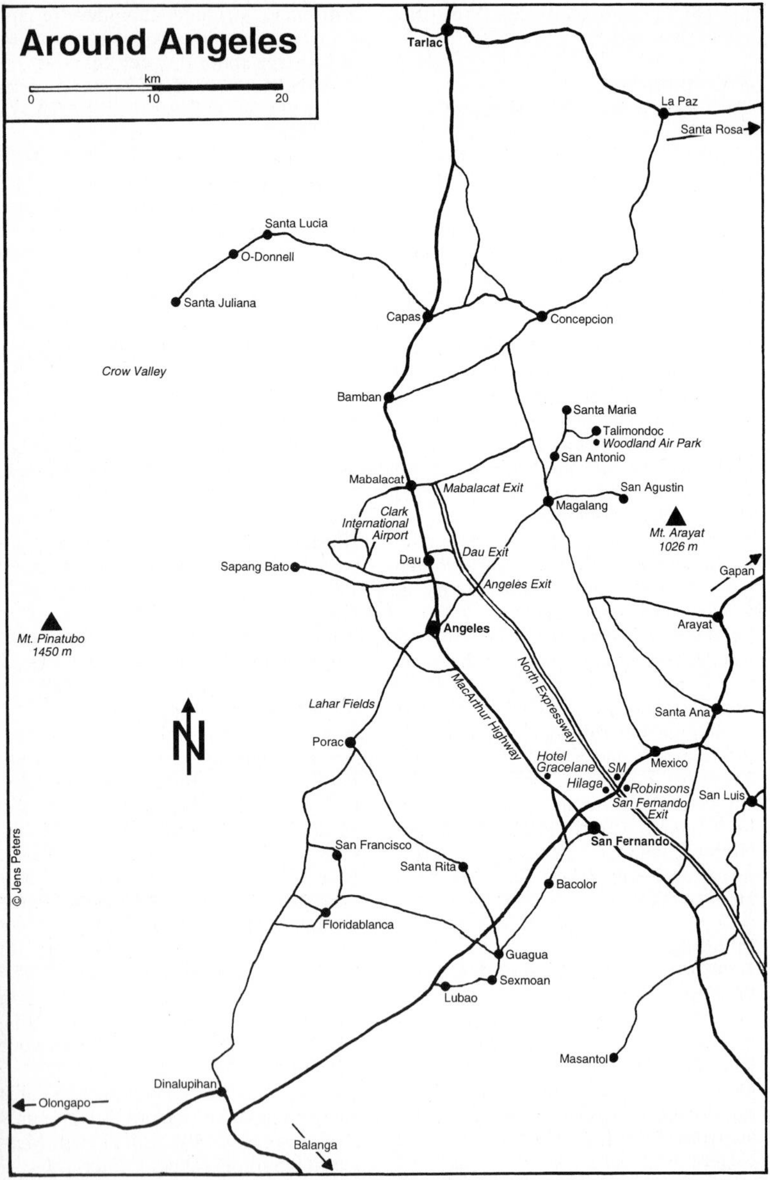
Around Angeles
km
0
10
20
Tarlac
La Paz
Santa Rosa
Santa Lucia
O-Donnell
Santa Juliana
Capas
Concepcion
Crow Valley
Bamban
Santa Maria
Talimondoc
Woodland Air Park
San Antonio
Mabalacat
Mabalacat Exit
San Agustin
Magalang
Clark International Airport
Mt. Arayat 1026 m
Dau
Dau Exit
Sapang Bato
Gapan
Angeles Exit
Arayat
Angeles
Mt. Pinatubo 1450 m
North Expressway
MacArthur Highway
Lahar Fields
Santa Ana
N
Porac
Hotel Gracelane
SM
Mexico
Hilaga
Robinsons
San Luis
San Fernando Exit
San Fernando
San Francisco
Santa Rita
© Jens Peters
Bacolor
Floridablanca
Guagua
Sexmoan
Lubao
Masantol
Dinalupihan
Olongapo
Balanga

Central Luzon

Population: 280,000.
Post & Telephone: Post Office, MacArthur Highway, near New Abacan Bridge. The little Balibago Post Office is in Doña Rosario St not far from Johnny's Supermarket.
Cheap places to phone are Kokomo's, Rick's Café and Margarita Station Business Center, all on Fields Ave.
There are three telephone companies operating in Angeles. If you cannot manage to make a local call, try again, this time adding the area code to the number.
Post code: 2009. Area code: 045.
Tourist Office, Marlim Mansion Hotel, MacArthur Highway, Tel 6258525.
Travel Agencies: Bookings and reconfirmations of national and international tickets as well as visa extensions can be made at Mr Ticket, who can be found every Tuesday, Thursday and Saturday afternoon in the restaurant of the Sunset Garden Inn, and at Swagman Travel, Fields Ave (next to Margarita Station), Tel 8920878.
Cheap international tickets are also available at Charina's Travel Service-Center at the Clarkton Hotel, Don Juico Avenue, Tel 8926272, @, and at the Angeles International Travel Center, Malabañas Rd corner Don Juico Ave, Tel 3225929, Fax 3220801, @; tickets can also be obtained there for inland flights (Air Philippines, Asian Spirit, Cebu Pacific).
The Filipino Travel Center, Fields Ave, Tel 8926247, will accept bookings for ship passages (tickets for Superferries/ WG & A are issued while you wait), national and international flights.
Sports, Action & Adventure in the Premiere Hotel, Malabañas Rd, Tel 8926239, Fax 8926237, @, offers trekking, car tours, historical tours through the former Clark Air Base and sightseeing flights, and will also give independent advice on travel opportunities.
Negros Navigation, Fields Ave, Balibago, Tel 8920259, issues boat tickets for Negros Navigation while you wait.
Ultra-light Flights: Ultra-light aircraft belonging to the Angeles City Flying Club (ACFC), Cellphone 0918-9203090, Fax: 3323311, @, all fly directly from the Woodland Airpark, Sitio Talimundok, Santa Maria, Magalang (about 15 km south-east of Angeles). They offer flights around Mt Arayat. Flights usually last about 20 min and cost P1600 (maximum weight of passenger: 125 kg). One-hour flights that take you further afield are also available. For solo flights a pilot's licence and health certificate are necessary, both of which can be obtained from the ACFC.

Pinatubo Tours

Filipinos don't give up so easily. Although the eruption of Pinatubo had seemed like the end of the world at first, the local population took a quick breather then rolled up their shirt sleeves and got down to making the best of the situation. The idea was to turn the negative event into something positive, and so the concept of having tours to Pinatubo was born. Some said the idea was absurd, but they had to eat their words later.
For, as far as tourism is concerned, the eruption of the volcano has not just brought calamity to the Philippines, but has provided the island state with a new attraction. The ash and sand deposited by the eruption in a wide area around Pinatubo have created a magnificent landscape. To the west of Angeles the grey mass of coagulated material can reach heights of up to 100m. The impressive terrain is criss-crossed with bizarre ravines, through which you can wander for hours.
Other areas can be better explored with a vehicle, and for those who want to have the big picture, an aircraft will provide the perfect vantage point - it can all be arranged.

Mt Pinatubo - The Big Bang of the 20th Century

For many of those involved, the unprecedentedly violent eruption of Mt Pinatubo on 15 June 1991 was like a bad dream. The clouds of steam and detritus produced by the eruption shot up to 40 km into the stratosphere, darkening the sky. Brilliant flashes of lightning rent the daytime darkness eerily, accompanied by rolling thunder and frightening, seemingly endless, earthquakes. Unbelievable amounts of ash and sand settled in wide areas around the volcano, stones the size of fists flew through the air and, to top it all off, a powerful typhoon chose this of all times to lash North Luzon violently. As a result of the heavy rainfall, awe-inspiring avalanches of *lahar* (mud) raced down the hillsides, demolishing bridges, shoving houses aside like toys, and burying entire villages. Most of the Aeta people living on Pinatubo managed to flee down the slopes of the mountain in time to save themselves from being suffocated by the ash falling relentlessly all around them. Many people fled to Manila, unsure whether the volcano would also start to exude deadly, red-hot poisonous gases.

And it had all started so innocently. In April 1991, exactly two months before the big bang, the mountain had quietly rumbled awake, after 600 years of peace nestled into the Zambales Mountains, emitting white clouds of steam which rose gently from a small opening to the side of the actual crater. Yet only one week later the seismometers which had been hurriedly installed by the volcanologists delivered convincing evidence that pressure was building up in a magma chamber deep inside the volcano, and that slowly but surely magma was rising up through a chimney from the underground reservoir, heading for the crater. As the first major eruptions shook the area on 9 June, no-one could have guessed the inferno that was to follow in the next few days. It wasn't until the beginning of September that the volcano finally settled down again, allowing the full extent of this natural catastrophe to be estimated: several thousand hectares of fertile farmland laid to waste, more than 40,000 houses destroyed, nearly 250,000 people left homeless, and nearly 900 fatalities.

Guided tours

Several hotels and travel operators in Angeles offer interesting crater tours and hikes with experienced guides, eg the Sunset Garden Inn, Malabañas Rd, and Trend Transport, Fields Ave, Tel 8920107.

Half-Day Hikes

A half-day tour cost around P950 per person. Four to five hours in the area should be enough to get a first-hand impression of the immense power of nature. It's a good idea to start early, for the heat starts to build up in the ravines from about midday onwards. Ideally you should do this in a small group.

Please note: It is not possible to give a reliable description of a consistent route, as parts of the terrain change out of all recognition during the rainy season due to shifts in the mass of ashes and sand.

Crater Tours

One and two-day crater tours are available for about P2500 to P3000 per person (depending on the size of the group). The trip there leaves from Angeles and heads north to Capas, from there west via O-Donnel to Santa Juliana. You can carry on by jeepney or on foot through Crow Valley to an Aeta village, from where you can only carry on on foot or part of the way by off-road vehicle. It's four hours' walk and climb from the Aeta village to the crater. If you choose the off-road vehicle option you can shorten the walk and climb to around 2½ hours.

Note: Crow Valley used to be a bombing range for the US Air Force and is still used by the Philippine Air Force for training exercises. There's a military checkpoint just after Santa Juliana, where you will be prevented from carrying on if exercises are imminent. So it's a good idea to ask the tour operator when you're booking if there are any manoeuvers planned.

Whole-Day Tours by Car or Motorcycle

The following round trip is no problem with a motorcycle or normal car during the dry season. Heading south-west from Angeles towards Porac the first section is a drive of 75 km in all. This stretch takes you through a broad plain once covered by productive sugar cane plantations, which is now a barren desert stretching as far as the eye can see. The sight of half-buried communities can only begin to give you an impression of what unbelievable quantities of material were spewed out by Pinatubo. From Porac, carry on via Santa Rita to the road for San Fernando. On the right is Bacolor, the half-submerged suburb of San Fernando; a quick detour there and a visit to the buried cathedral could well be the highlight of this tour (see also 'San Fernando' in this chapter). The next stop would be the Hilaga on the Expressway at San Fernando, where the cultures of Central and North Luzon are presented. You can then take the Expressway or the road back to Angeles.

Basic round trips are available at Sports, Action & Adventure, Malabañas Rd (in the Premiere Hotel), and Trend Transport, Fields Ave (next to the Krung Thai Restaurant).

Sightseeing Flights

A one-hour flight from Clark Air Base to the Pinatubo crater with a four-seater Navion-A (built in 1949) costs P6250 (there's room for three passengers). The pilot of this classic propellor aircraft is Jimmy Boyd, a former US Air Force pilot; Cellphone 0917-8260251, @. On request this flight can be extended (eg via Hundred Islands, the Banaue rice terraces and Subic Bay). Reservations directly with the pilot or at Sports, Action & Adventure in the Premiere Hotel (see under 'Miscellaneous': *Travel Agencies*).

Omni Aviation, Tel & Fax 8926664, @, offers one-hour flights with a four-seater Cessna for P3000 per person.

When to Go

For safety reasons, car tours and hikes should only be attempted in the dry season, the best months being February, March and April. After heavy rain, the crater tours in particular will be cancelled for a few days.

Theoretically, sightseeing flights are possible year-round, except during a typhoon. However, rainy days with lots of low clouds could also ruin any plans you may have had. The pilot will decide whether it's OK to fly or not.

Equipment

Those sensitive to the sun should wear long-sleeved clothing and preferably some head protection. When hiking, water is absolutely essential (one to two litres per person for four hours).

Please do not leave empty bottles and rubbish in the area. The best kind of footwear are sturdy, closed shoes that can stand getting wet (eg trainers) and socks (sand can be painfully abrasive). If going by car, in addition to tools remember to take a tow rope and shovel, as well as a board for supporting the jack in case of a flat tyre.

Getting Around

Car: Avis, Don Juico Ave, Clarkview (between Clarkton and Oasis hotels), Tel 6256771, and Holiday Inn Resort Clark Field, Mimosa Dr, Clarkfield, Tel 5992844 (ext 1339).
There are also several local companies on Fields Ave which charge less than Avis.
Motorcycle: There are several companies along Fields Ave between Kokomo's and Margarita Station. The prices range from P500 to P1000 a day, depending on the size of the bike.
Tip: The Angeles police take the regulations regarding crash helmets seriously, at least as far as foreigners are concerned. Only motorbikes over 600cc may use the North Luzon Expressway.
Jeepney: Normally, jeepneys charge the regular fare (P5.50), but beware of Special Rides: they can turn out costly! Watch out also for fellow passengers who are pickpockets.
Taxi: It's a waste of time looking for regular taxis in Angeles, although several are available at the Main Gate to the Clark Special Economic Zone. Normally they serve Clark facilities such as Duty Free Shops etc (P100 to P150) but they will drive other routes.
Tricycle: Tricycles are comparatively expensive: P20 to P50.

Getting There & Away

By Air: Clark International Airport, recently renamed Diosdado Macapagal International Airport, is on the former base at the northern edge of the city. Seair offers a free airport service (from/ to various hotels and the Seair Office on Fields Ave). A taxi from the main gate costs around P150.
Asiana Airlines, Building 2088, Cardinal Santos Ave, Clarkfield, Tel 5996656-57.
Destination: Seoul (South Korea).
Asian Spirit, Ecozone Travel, MacArthur Highway, Tel 8870332.
Destination: Manila.
Seair, Clark International Airport, Clarkfield, Tel 5992384, @.
- Fields Avenue (in the Sub Delicious Restaurant), Tel 8924783, 8924767.
Destinations: Caticlan (for Boracay), Manila.

By Bus: Apart from hotel buses, all buses stop at the Dau bus terminal, roughly two km north of Angeles where you can catch a jeepney back to town. A tricycle from Dau to one of the Angeles hotels listed here will cost P20 to P50, depending on the distance.
Hotel shuttle buses bring passengers to their hotel in Angeles and will pick them up again if a booking is made in time.
The travelling times given below from and to Manila can easily take twice as long at peak traffic times. Sundays usually see the roads fairly uncongested. On Monday mornings the public buses to Manila are very full and it's hard to get a seat.
Fly The Bus, Swagman Travel, Fields Ave, Tel 8926495 (reservations for journeys to Baguio, Bauang/La Union, Manila and Subic).

Baguio

Bus: Victory Liner buses run from Baguio to Angeles hourly every day from 5.30am to 5pm (P110; 4½ hrs). They are the ones marked 'Olongapo'. Buses from other companies such as Philippine Rabbit travel from Baguio to Manila via Dau, but be careful: not every

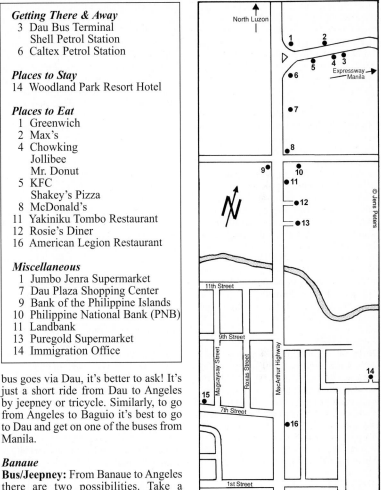

Getting There & Away
3 Dau Bus Terminal
Shell Petrol Station
6 Caltex Petrol Station

Places to Stay
14 Woodland Park Resort Hotel

Places to Eat
1 Greenwich
2 Max's
4 Chowking
Jollibee
Mr. Donut
5 KFC
Shakey's Pizza
8 McDonald's
11 Yakiniku Tombo Restaurant
12 Rosie's Diner
16 American Legion Restaurant

Miscellaneous
1 Jumbo Jenra Supermarket
7 Dau Plaza Shopping Center
9 Bank of the Philippine Islands
10 Philippine National Bank (PNB)
11 Landbank
13 Puregold Supermarket
14 Immigration Office

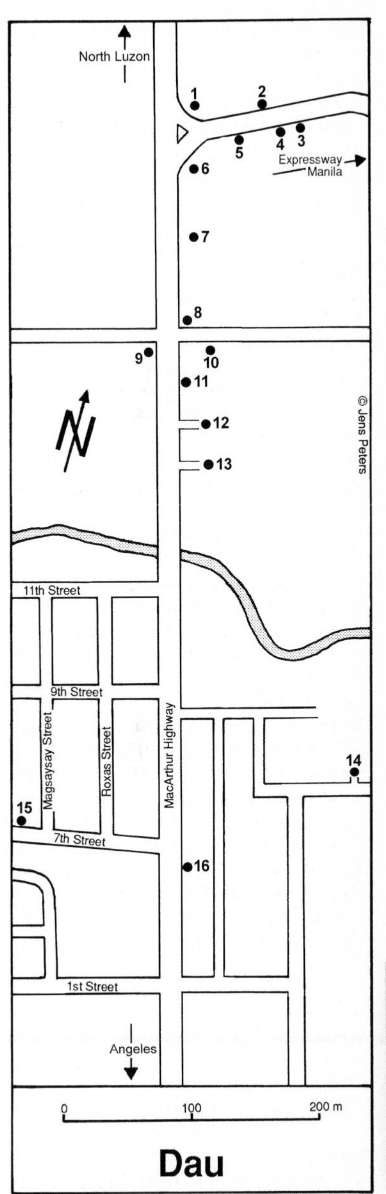

bus goes via Dau, it's better to ask! It's just a short ride from Dau to Angeles by jeepney or tricycle. Similarly, to go from Angeles to Baguio it's best to go to Dau and get on one of the buses from Manila.

Banaue

Bus/Jeepney: From Banaue to Angeles there are two possibilities. Take a Dangwa Tranco bus with the destination 'Baguio', change in Carmen into a bus that is going to Manila via Dau/ Angeles. An alternative is to take the 7am bus with the destination 'Manila' either to Santa Rosa or Gapan (both south of Cabanatuan). Carry on from Santa Rosa by jeepney or bus to Tarlac,

from there you can catch a bus to Dau/Angeles. Or take a bus from Gapan to San Fernando and carry on from there to Angeles by jeepney. Travelling time, including waiting, 10 hrs.
From Angeles to Banaue see the chapter North Luzon: *Banaue - Getting There & Away*.

Bauang - San Fernando (La Union)
Bus: Buses belonging to different companies run from Bauang to San Fernando (La Union) every day with the destination 'Manila', taking 4½ hrs. Get out in Dau, it's only a short trip from there to Angeles (jeepney or tricycle).
From Angeles to Bauang and San Fernando (La Union) it's best to go from Dau, where the buses coming from Manila make a short stop, allowing you to board the bus there.
A minibus (Fly the Bus) also leaves the Swagman Narra Hotel on Monday and Friday at 8am from Angeles to Bauang. Departure from Bauang to Angeles Tuesday and Saturday at 9.30am (P600; four hrs).

Laoag - Vigan
Bus: Numerous buses of various companies travel daily from Laoag and Vigan to Dau on the way to Manila, taking nine hrs (Laoag) and seven hrs (Vigan). If you get out in Dau, it's only a short way by jeepney or tricycle to Angeles.
To go from Angeles to Vigan or Laoag, it's best to go to Dau and get on the buses coming through from Manila.

Manila
Air: Seair flies on Monday Tuesday, Wednesday, Thursday and Friday from Manila to Angeles and vice versa (P850; 30 min).
Asian Spirit flies on Tuesday (P550).

Bus: From Manila, several Philippine Rabbit buses run daily to Angeles (P80; two hrs). Be careful about buses which are not marked 'Expressway/Dau', as these follow side roads and make lots of stops. You can also take a bus from any of the companies - Dominion Bus Line, Fariñas, Five Star, Partas or Victory Liner - to Baguio, Laoag, Vigan, San Fernando (La Union), Dagupan or Alaminos, get out at Dau and go the short way back to Angeles by jeepney or tricycle. To go from Angeles to Manila you can catch a bus in Dau coming from North Luzon.

Hotel bus: Aircon hotel buses (Fly The Bus) from Manila to Angeles leave daily at 11.30am, 3.30 and 8pm from the Swagman Hotel, A Flores St, Ermita, going to the Swagman Narra Hotel. The trip takes 2½ hrs and costs P350.
Departure from Angeles at 8am, noon and 3pm. Passengers who book early will be picked up from their hotel. The airport service from the Swagman Hotel in Manila to the Ninoy Aquino International Airport (NAIA) costs P250.

Taxi: An aircon limo costs about P1500 from the NAIA to Angeles (plus a P100 tip that the driver expects). Several companies have ticket counters a few meters to the right after the exit at the arrivals level (it pays to compare prices).
A regular aircon taxi from Manila to Angeles costs around P600 if the meter is running correctly. Set prices of between P1000 and P1200 are normal and quite acceptable.
In Angeles, several aircon taxis stand at the Main Gate to Clark Field, the former Clark Air Base. The fare to Manila is about P1500 (negotiate).

Olongapo
Bus/Jeepney: Hourly Victory Liner buses run from Olongapo to Angeles daily (2½ hrs). In Olongapo you can also get a Manila bus; get off before

San Fernando (Pampanga) and wait for a bus or jeepney to Angeles.

Subic
Bus: A minibus (Fly the Bus) leaves Angeles for Olongapo, Barrio Barretto and Subic on Monday, Wednesday, Friday and Sunday at 10am (P350; two hrs). Passengers who book in time can be picked up from their hotel.
Departure from Subic at 12.30pm.

Bataan Peninsula

After the completion of construction work on the road between Morong and Olongapo it's now possible to make a trip right round the Bataan Peninsula west of Manila.
On Mt Samat, a little to the south-west of Balanga, the provincial capital, is Dambana ng Kagitingan, a national monument to the victims of the Battle of Bataan. There is a huge cross, over 90m high, with an elevator up to the horizontal section. From there you get a wonderful view over the former battlefield and Manila Bay.
A large part of the south of the peninsula is industrialised. Most of the almost 650 manufacturing plants in the province, including the biggest, are in the Export Processing Zone in Mariveles, where textiles, clocks, electrical appliances and automobile parts are made. Logging will also become important in the future: Tree Resources and Environmental Enterprises (TREE) have already planted half a million trees on Bataan.

Getting There & Away

Manila
Bus: Lots of Genesis Transport and Philippine Rabbit buses leave Manila daily for Balanga (P125; 2½ hrs).

Note: During the rainy season the trip can take longer, as parts of the road from San Fernando to Olongapo are often blocked by mudslides from Mt Pinatubo.

Boat: A Mt Samat Express fast ferry goes from Manila to Orion daily from 6.30am to 5pm roughly every two hours, but not when the sea is rough; Tel (02) 5515290. Departure from the Ferry Terminal at the Cultural Center on Roxas Blvd (P230; one hr).

Olongapo
Bus: Several Victory Liner buses run daily from Olongapo to Balanga (1½ hrs).

Olongapo

Olongapo used to be where the 7th Fleet of the US Navy was stationed. In 1991 the Philippine Senate made the momentous decision not to extend the Military Bases Agreement (MBA) which had regulated the lease of the bases since the end of WWII.
After the US Navy withdrew, the former base itself was turned into Subic Bay Freeport (SBF). Hotels, restaurants, swimming pools, tennis courts, casino, duty-free shops and such like are amongst the attractions. Just like the old days when the Americans were still here, access is over the river bridge at the end of Magsaysay Dr.
In the meantime, effort has been put into turning part of the extensive former military area into a busy industrial zone. Other areas have been earmarked for the development of tourism, amongst them what's left of the rainforest, in fact an area where experienced Ayta tribesmen used to train US marines in jungle survival. It is specifically being set aside for eco-tourists and adventure seekers. This is not a bad idea, considering it would put an end to the total deforestation being planned by the gentlemen with chainsaws. A tour through

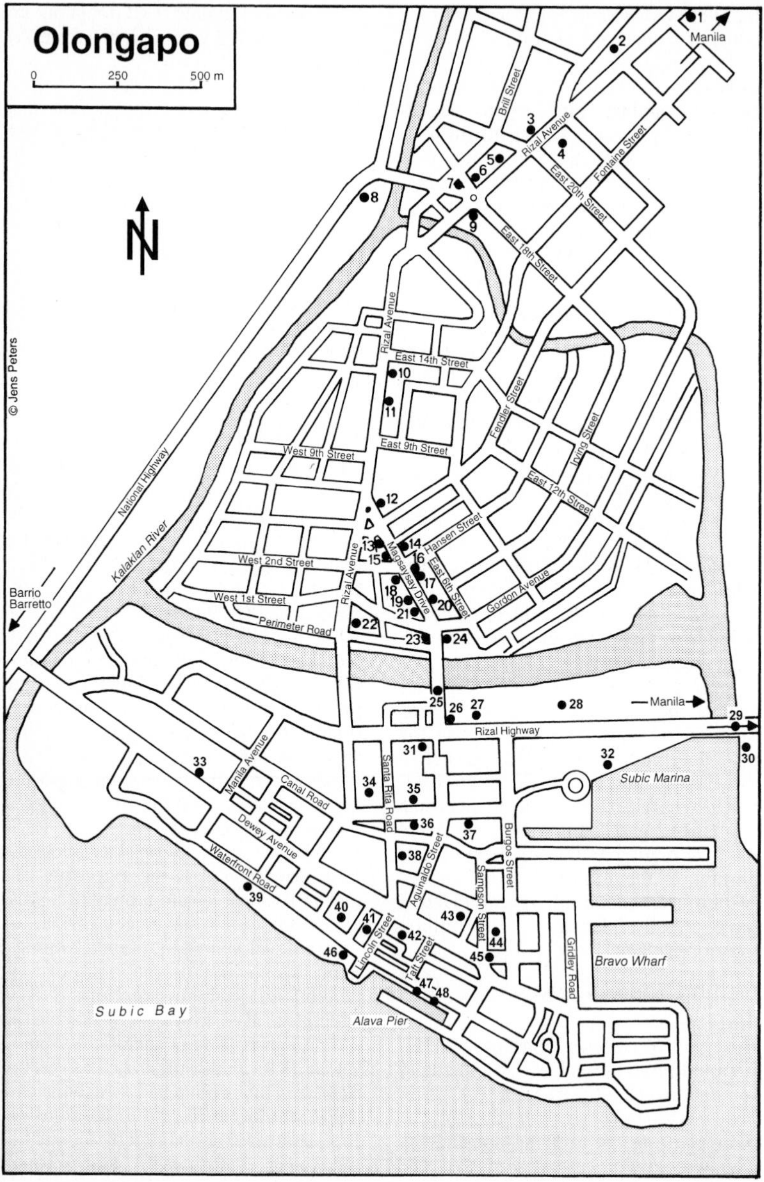

Olongapo

0 250 500 m

N

Manila
Brill Street
Rizal Avenue
Fontaine Street
East 20th Street
East 18th Street
Rizal Avenue
East 14th Street
Fendler Street
Irving Street
East 9th Street
West 9th Street
East 12th Street
Hansen Street
National Highway
Kalaklan River
Magsaysay Drive
East 6th Street
West 2nd Street
Rizal Avenue
Gordon Avenue
Barrio Barretto
West 1st Street
Perimeter Road
Manila
Rizal Highway
Manila Avenue
Santa Rita Road
Subic Marina
Canal Road
Burgos Street
Dewey Avenue
Aguinaldo Street
Waterfront Road
Sampson Street
Lincoln Street
Taft Street
Gridley Road
Bravo Wharf
Subic Bay
Alava Pier

1 2 3 4 5 6 7 8 9 10 11 12 13 14 15 16 17 18 19 20 21 22 23 24 25 26 27 28 29 30 31 32 33 34 35 36 37 38 39 40 41 42 43 44 45 46 47 48

Getting There & Away
6 Victory Liner Bus Terminal
14 Budget
15 Swagman Travel
27 Bus Terminal (Shuttle Buses to Airport & Malls)
29 Airport (6 km)
Subic Seaplane (3 km)
47 Eagle Ferry Landing

Places to Stay
10 Triple Crown Hotel
11 Emperor Hotel
13 Zanzibar Hotel
17 Kong's Hotel
19 Ridgecrest Hotel
21 Let's Inn
23 Anne Raquel's Hotel
29 Crown Peak Garden Hotel (6 km)
Legenda Suites (6 km)
34 Subic International Hotel
37 Grand Seasons Hotel
41 Legenda Hotel

Places to Eat & Entertainment
7 Chowking
9 Jollibee
12 Banaue Disco
16 Pasta Villa
18 Subic Hard Rock
20 Casino Filipino
Blue Note
Shakey's
21 Chatterbox Pizza
24 Jollibee
26 Wimpy's
29 Vasco's (3 km)
30 Hungry Marlin Bar & Grille
33 Dewey's Diner
Sayuri Dragon Restaurant
35 Golden Dragon Restaurant
36 Feng Huang Restaurant
37 Casino
39 Scuba Shack
44 Chowking
Meat Plus Café
46 Seafront Restaurant

Miscellaneous
1 Post Office
2 City Hall
3 Equitable PCI Bank
4 Market
5 Metrobank
8 TLC Medical Center
15 Police Station
22 James L Gordon Memorial Hospital
23 Star City Mall
25 Main Gate
27 Park 'n' Shop
28 Le Mans Go-Kart Track
29 Cubi Bats (6 km)
Magellan's Landing (3 km)
JEST Camp (6 km)
31 Equitable PCI Bank
Times Square Cinema
32 Subic Bay Yacht Club
38 Swimmingpool
39 Subic Bay Aquasport
40 Tappan Park
42 SBMA Office
Tourist Office
43 National Book Store
44 Duty Free Superstore
Freeport Exchange Mall
Metrobank
Sports Unlimited
45 Spanish Gate
48 Bank of the Philippine Islands

the Jungle Environmental Survival Training Camp (JEST) costs P250 per person (minimum five people). Further information can be obtained at Tel (047) 2529072.

Worth seeing near the camp are the swarms of flying dogs (fruit bats, or 'cubi bats') which hang from the gnarled branches of tall trees. They grow as long as 40 cm and have a wingspan of over one metre. The big attraction in the Ocean Adventure near Camayan Wharf is a pool with so-called false killer whales where visitors can swim and dive with the animals for P2500. Another top attraction is the sea-lion show; admission P400. Zoobic Safari, two km to the south-east, is roughly 15 hectares of wildlife park with a serpentarium (snakes), crocodile sanctuary, ostriches, wild hogs and a few tigers which you can get up close to in a safari jeep (P380).

For a day at the beach try a short detour to Grand Island or to Miracle Beach next to Camayan Point, both at the entrance to Subic Bay (see also "Subic Bay" below in this chapter).

From Olongapo you can easily do a day trip to Mt Samat on the Bataan Peninsula. Take a Victory Liner bus from Olongapo to Balanga and from there go on by jeepney or minibus to the Mt Samat turn-off. You'll have to hike the last seven km uphill (good road) as public transport vehicles normally do not go up there. Headware is recommended.

Olongapo is also a good starting point for trips with a rented car, to the Mt Pinatubo area for instance, or along the Zambales coastline.

Places to Stay

In nearby Barrio Barretto the lower and middle category hotels are better than in Olongapo. Within the Subic Bay Freeport Zone, public transport mainly serves the shopping malls and the airport. The best way to reach the hotels there is with your own transport.

Emperor Hotel, 1090 Rizal Ave, Tel 2222191, Fax 2225151. SR/DR/fan P250, SR/DR/ac/bath P400 to P750. Basic, slightly shabby rooms, the more expensive ones with TV. OK for the money though.

Kong's Hotel, 32 Magsaysay Dr, Tel 2241516. SR/DR/fan/bath P400, SR/DR/ac/bath P700 to P2500 depending on size and the number of beds. The walls are a bit thin, but it's otherwise OK for the money. Aircon rooms have a TV, the more expensive ones also have a refrigerator. Chinese restaurant.

Ridgecrest Gardens Hotel, 15 Magsaysay Dr (3rd floor), Tel 2222006, Fax 2237380. SR/DR/ac/bath P600 to P1800. Rooms are of various sizes and furnishings, some with TV and refrigerator; acceptable for the money.

Subic Bay Freeport Zone

Crown Peak Garden Hotel, Cubi Point, Tel 2523144, Fax 2526658, @. SR/DR/ac/bath P900, suite P3500. Well-appointed, spacious rooms with refrigerator and TV. Big hotel in the country with over 800 rooms. Restaurant. Swimming pool. Fitness room.

Grand Seasons Hotel, Canal St, Tel 2522888, Fax 2526831. SR/DR/ac/bath P3200 and P5500. Extensive hotel grounds with immaculate rooms. Restaurant, casino, swimming pool.

Subic Bay International Hotel, Santa Rita Rd, Tel 2526703. SR/DR/ac/bath from P4000. Neat hotel with well equipped rooms. Restaurant.

Legenda Hotel, Waterfront Rd, Tel 2521888. SR/DR/ac/bath P4750 and P5500, suite P8500 to P22,000. Comfortable, tastefully decorated rooms with refrigerator and TV. Restaurant, casino, swimming pool, fitness room.

Legenda Suites, Tarlac Rd corner Sulu Rd, Cubi Point, Tel 2521888, @. SR/DR/ac/bath P7500 and P9000 (ask for promo rates). Suites with kitchen and one or two bedrooms, furnished with comfort in mind. Restaurant. Near the airport.

Places to Eat

Several fast food restaurants and pizzerias can be found in Magsaysay Dr and Rizal Ave, including ***Jollibee*** and ***Shakey's***. On Magsaysay Dr, at the corner of Hansen St, ***Pasta Villa*** is an Italian restaurant with a deservedly good reputation.

To be recommended in the Subic Bay Freeport Zone are ***Seafront Restaurant*** (international), ***Golden Dragon Restaurant*** (Chinese), ***Meat Plus Café*** (steaks) and the cosy ***Scuba Shack*** (great hamburgers). If you want more choice, all hotels in the Subic Bay Freeport Zone have first class restaurants.

There's a gorgeous view onto the Subic Yacht Club from the ***Hungry Marlin Bar & Grille*** restaurant which is open from 7am to 1am. At the weekends they offer a variety of buffets for P300 (Friday: chicken & ribs, Saturday: seafood, Sunday: Mongolian barbecue).

A bit out of town, half-way to the airport, the maritime theme at ***Vasco's*** lends it an air of sophistication. With pleasant terrace dining over the water, it's located on Argonaut Highway in the complex called Magellan's Landing. The international cuisine there is not cheap, but the place is well worth the visit.

Entertainment

The ***Blue Note*** disco on Magsaysay Dr pulls in the crowds, especially at the weekends. Maybe it's their cutting edge sound equipment and excellent live music. The same bands perform in the nearby ***Subic Hard Rock***, although the sound isn't so good there.

Miscellaneous

Diving: Diving trips and information on wreck diving in Subic Bay from Subic Bay Aqua Sports, Building 249, Waterfront Rd, Subic Bay Freeport Zone, Tel 2527343, and from Masterdive, at Magellan's Landing, Argonaut Highway, Tel 2525987, @.

Immigration Office, 7th St, Tel 2242766. Open Mon-Fri 8am-noon and 1-5pm.

Festival: Mardi Gras on 30 December.

Medical Service: James L Gordon Memorial Hospital, Rizal Ave, Tel 2225059; TLC Medical Center, National Highway, Tel 2229299.

Population: 180,000.

Post & Telephone: Post code: 2200. Area code: 047.

Sightseeing Flights: Flights in a seaplane to Mt Pinatubo, Corregidor Island, Puerta Galera etc can be booked at Subic Seaplane, Magellan's Landing, Argonaut Highway, Tel. 2522230, @, and with the pilot, Mike O'Farrell, Tel 2224916.

Tourist Office, Building 662, Taft Street, Subic Bay Freeport Zone, Tel 2524123, Fax 2524194. Open daily 8am-noon and 1-5pm.

Travel Agency: Interisland Tours & Transportation, Legenda Hotel, Waterfront Rd, Subic Bay Freeport Zone, Tel 2523008, Fax 2527800, @. Flight tickets (national and international), inexpensive package tours from Subic International Airport.

Swagman Travel, Magsaysay Dr, Tel 2336240, Fax 2336174 takes care of visa extensions and the booking and reconfirmation of national and international flights.

Getting Around

Car: Budget, 58 Magsaysay Dr, Tel 2232609, 2235279.

Getting There & Away

By Air: The Subic International Airport (Cubi Airport) is on a peninsula five km south of Olongapo. Jeepneys and shuttle buses ply between the main gate to Subic Bay Freeport Zone and the airport (P8). At the moment (2004) there are no scheduled flights to and from Subic/Olongapo, only charter flights.

Alaminos

Bus: There are several Victory Liner buses from Alaminos to Olongapo daily (five hrs).

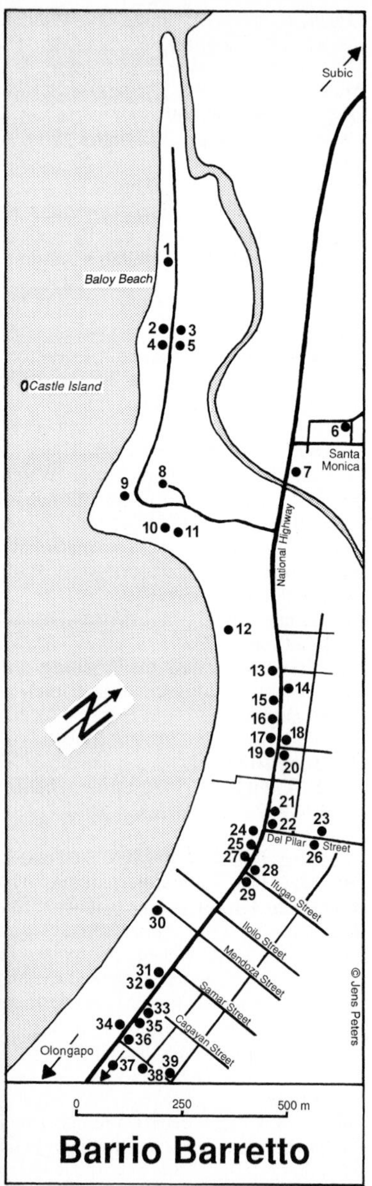

Getting There & Away
6 Mar-Nich Motorcycle Rental
7 Corcel Car & Van Rental

Places to Stay
1 Mynes Inn
2 Johan's Dive Resort
3 Baloy Beach Hotel
4 Beach Boulevard Lodge
8 Zanzibar Resort Hotel
9 Blue Rock Resort
10 Sheavens Hotel
11 The Mangrove Hotel
14 Johansson's Lodge
15 Bart's Resort Hotel
21 Dryden Hotel
22 Mansion House
Subic Garden Hotel
23 Westbay Apartelle
24 By the Sea Resort
28 T-Rose Apartments
29 Anbon Hotel
30 Suzuki Beach Hotel
31 Playa Papagayo Inn
32 Subic Mirage Beach Hotel
34 Arizona International Hotel
37 Halfmoon Hotel

Places to Eat & Entertainment
1 Mynes Restaurant
Seaview Restaurant
4 Beach Boulevard Café
5 Mr. Pumpernickel
13 Midnight Rambler
14 Johansson's Restaurant
16 Mango's Beach Bar
& Restaurant
17 Bos'n Locker
18 Swiss Tavern
19 D'Coconut Barn
21 Dryden Cantina
24 By the Sea Restaurant
26 VFW (The Veterans Bar)
31 Cantina Mexicana
34 Longhorn Steakhouse
36 Coffee Shop

Miscellaneous
2 Johan's Adventure & Wreck Dive Centre
11 Andy & John Downunder Diving
12 Palladium Beach Resort
20 Bretto's Deli Shop
25 Intercity Tours
27 Shraders Travel & Tours
31 Bread Express
33 Swagman Travel
34 HQR Internet
35 Mt Carmel Clinic
38 Small Market
39 Likas Talino Computer Center

Baguio - Angeles
Bus/Jeepney: Victory Liner buses run roughly every hour from 5.30am to 5.30pm daily between Baguio and Olongapo, and it's possible to board them at Angeles (Dau). In Angeles you can also catch a San Fernando jeepney, get out at the turn-off to Olongapo and wait for the next bus. Travelling time from Baguio is six hrs; from Angeles, it takes two hrs.
A minibus (Fly the Bus) leaves Angeles for Olongapo, Barrio Barretto and Subic on Monday, Wednesday, Friday and Sunday at 10am (P350; two hrs). Passengers who book in time can be picked up from their hotel.
Departure from Subic at 12.30pm.

Manila
Bus: From Manila, several Victory Liner buses leave the bus terminal in Caloocan City (Rizal Ave Extension) for Olongapo daily, and also from Pasay City (Edsa), taking three and four hours respectively.

Boat/Bus: From Manila to Olongapo and Barrio Barretto, take the Mt Samat Express fast ferry to Orion (Bataan), which leaves daily at 8.30am and 5pm from the Ferry Terminal at the Cultural Center, carry on from there to your hotel by minibus. The trip takes 2½ hrs and costs P600.
Departure from Barrio Barretto at 6.30am and 3.30pm, from Olongapo at 7am and 3.45pm. Seats can be reserved in most hotels. See also 'Bataan' above in this chapter.

San Fernando (Pampanga)
Bus: Victory Liner buses run several times a day from San Fernando to Olongapo (1½ hrs).

Barrio Barretto & Subic

The withdrawal of the US Navy didn't just mean the end of an era in Olongapo, but also in Barrio Barretto and Subic, both of which were almost completely economically dependent on the American base. Attempts are now being made to attract tourists and investors to the facilities left behind on the former base. Both places have an assortment of hotels and entertainment facilities. Apart from Olongapo, Barrio Barretto and Subic will probably have a future as centres for wreck diving: see also 'Subic Bay' below.
Both places also have an impressive range of different hotels and a modest choice of entertainment.

Places to Stay
Most hotels can be found on either side of the National Highway. There are also a few places to stay at the nearby Baloy Beach, also known as Long Beach, where you can rent cottages and beach houses by the week or month (monthly rates between P4000 and P20,000).

Barrio Barretto along the National Highway
Johansson's Lodge, Tel 2239293, @. SR/DR/fan P300, SR/DR/ac/bath P600 to P1000, depending on size and furnishings (TV). Good value. Restaurant.

Anbon Hotel, Tel 2243141, SR/DR/fan/bath P400, SR/DR/ac/bath P800 (with TV). Good rooms, worth the money. Restaurant.
Subic Garden Hotel, Tel 2224550. SR/DR/ac/bath P550 to P750, depending on size. With TV. Acceptable rooms, although not the newest. Restaurant, small swimming pool.
Mansion House, Tel 2224550. SR/DR/ac/bath P750. Clean, spacious rooms with TV. Well-kept place with a courtyard and a small swimming pool. Quiet location. They share an entrance with the Subic Garden Hotel.
T-Rose Apartments, Tel 2244959, @. SR/DR/ac/bath P600 and P800. Immaculate rooms of different sizes with refrigerator and TV. Good value. Located in a back courtyard behind a bar (entrance through the bar).
Dryden Hotel, Tel 2248701, Fax 2224547, @. SR/DR/ac/bath P600 and P750, depending on size. With TV, some with refrigerator. Good rooms, although a bit stuffy; the ones facing the road are loud. Restaurant. Located next to the Subic Garden Hotel.
Bart's Resort Hotel, Tel 2234148, Fax 2234149, @. SR/DR/fan/bath P600, SR/DR/ac/bath P1000 to P1400, with TV, the expensive ones also with refrigerator. Pleasant little place with nice rooms, although the less expensive, fan rooms are directly under the roof (hot). Restaurant, small swimming pool.
Halfmoon Hotel, Tel 2224987, Fax 2224918, @. SR/DR/ac/bath P950 to P1700. Really good rooms with TV, set in beautiful grounds. The rooms looking down on the pool are the quietest. There is a P30 charge for non-residents to use the swimming pool. Restaurant.
Playa Papagayo Inn, Tel 2223825, @. SR/DR/ac/bath P1000 to P2300, depending on location and size. Immaculate rooms with refrigerator and TV. A tidy beach hotel with idyllic garden. Quiet location, restaurant, boat trips.
By the Sea Inn, Tel 2224560, Fax 2222718, @. SR/DR/ac/bath P1000 to P3500. With TV, some with refrigerator. Good rooms of varying degrees of comfort, the better ones have a sea view. Good restaurant with a sea view, open round the clock.
Westlake Apartelle, Montelibano St, Tel 2224628, Fax 2225571. SR/DR/ac/bath P1320, suite P2800. With TV. It also has monthly rates. The accommodation is comfortable, although parts of the building could use redecorating. Attractive, well-maintained, quiet garden, with idyllic parts on a slope. They have a swimming pool; non-residents pay P50 admission. Formerly the Marmont Hotel, it is located about 100m off the National Highway.
Subic Mirage Beach Hotel, Tel 2239245, Fax 2239254, @. SR/DR/ac/bath P1350 to P1900. Attractive rooms with refrigerator and TV. Restaurant.
Arizona International Hotel, Tel 2244557, Fax 2244993, @. SR/DR/ac/bath P1600 to P2000, depending on location and size. Good hotel with rooms to match, all with TV. Restaurant. Located on the beach in the southern outskirts of town.
Suzuki Beach Hotel, Samar St, Tel 2239965, Fax 2234155. SR/DR/ac/bath P1650 to P2750. Very good rooms with refrigerator and TV, the more expensive ones looking down on Subic Bay. The best beach hotel in Barrio Barretto. Directly on the water a bit off the National Highway. Restaurant.

Barrio Barretto - at Baloy Beach

Mynes Inn, Tel 2225755. SR/DR/fan/bath P400 and P500. Basic, but acceptable rooms, all with beautiful balconies overlooking the bay. Restaurant.
Beach Boulevard Lodge, Cellphone 0919-3526686. SR/DR/fan/bath P500, SR/DR/ac/bath P800 (with kitchen). Basic rooms with TV. Restaurant.

Blue Beach Resort, Tel 2249042, Fax: 2227910, @. SR/DR/fan/bath P500, SR/DR/ac/bath P700 to P2000, depending on location and size. Good rooms, the better ones (refrigerator, TV, veranda) are directly on the beach. Restaurant.
Baloy Beach Hotel, Tel 2249199, Fax 2239389, @. SR/DR/ac/bath P600 and P1500 (with refrigerator and TV). Acceptable rooms. Restaurant.
Sheavens Hotel, Tel 2239430, @. SR/DR/ac/bath P1500 and P1800, suite P2700 (with refrigerator). Three-storey building with different sized, well-kept rooms, all with TV, some with a balcony overlooking the sea. Restaurant. Located about 100m from the beach.
The Mangrove Hotel, Tel 2227909, @. SR/DR/fan/bath P1000, SR/DR/ac/bath P1500. Attractive, spacious rooms with TV and shared veranda. Restaurant overlooking the sea. Small swimming pool.
Zanzibar Resort Hotel, Tel 2245355, Fax 2235895, @. SR/DR/ac/bath P1900 and P2100, suite P2300 to P4100. Big hotel with good, if a bit expensive, rooms with TV, the suites also have a refrigerator. Restaurant, swimming pool.

Subic
White Rock Resort Hotel, Matain, Tel 2322857, Fax 2222398, @. SR/DR/ac/bath P3200 to P4400, all including breakfast. Well-kept grounds with comfortable rooms. Restaurant, swimming pool.

Places to Eat

There are several well-run restaurants on the National Highway. The ***Coffee Shop*** gives you value for your peso with a wide selection of Philippine and international dishes (try the crispy tacos, there's a reason why they're so popular).The ***Dryden Cantina*** in the Dryden Hotel is a popular place to eat. Not exactly cheap, but excellent, is the way to describe the food (including seafood and outstanding steaks) in the small, stylish ***Cantina Mexicana*** in the Playa Papagayo Inn. The ***By the Sea Restaurant*** in the resort of the same name on the National Highway can be recommended. The ***Swiss Tavern*** predictably offers Swiss cuisine, and ***Johansson's Restaurant*** has Swedish specialities. Just over from the Westbay Apartelle, the pub-restaurant ***VFW*** (The Veterans Bar) serves American food. Imported steaks and Australian wines are on the menu in the ***Longhorn Steakhouse*** in the Arizona International Hotel.
There are more restaurants at Baloy Beach, including ***Mr Pumpernickel*** (tasty German food) and the good value ***Seaview Restaurant*** (great breakfast with freshly baked bread).

Entertainment

Along the National Highway a handful of bars has survived the withdrawal of the Americans, fortunately including the ***Midnight Rambler***, with super music, great sound and good drinks. Live music can be heard at ***Bos'n Locker*** (Thursday, Friday and Saturday) and ***D'Coconut Barn*** (Wednesday).

Miscellaneous

Diving: Information on diving courses and wreck diving in Subic Bay is available at:
Andy & John Downunder Diving, Mangrove Hotel, Cellphone 0920-8922203.
Johan's Adventure & Wreck Dive Centre, Midway, Baloy Beach, Tel 2248915, @. Also offers diving instruction in Angeles (hotel swimming pools).
Medical Service: Mt Carmel Clinic on the National Highway for less serious cases, otherwise go to Olongapo.
Money: Swagman Travel, 30 National Highway, will give you a cash advance

on Visa and MasterCard (8% commission). They will also change traveller's cheques (at an unfavourable rate).
Online: The best value are HQR Internet and Likas Talino Computer Center (P1/min, P40/hr).
Post & Telephone: Post code: 2200. Area code: 047.
Tours: All travel agents and Johan's Adventure & Wreck Dive Centre at Baloy Beach offer Subic Bay tours and various Pinatubo tours.
Travel Agency: Reservations and confirmations of national and international flights, as well as visa extensions, can be made at:
Shraders Travel & Tours, 95 National Highway, Tel 2248362, Fax 22490021, @.
Swagman Travel, 30 National Highway, Tel 2234356, 2224610.

Getting Around

Car: Corcel Car & Van Rental, Santa Monica Commercial Complex, Tel 2321229, Fax 2322906, @. Choice of vehicles, eg Mitsubishi Lancer for P1800 per day.
Motorcycle: Mar-Nich, Santa Monica Subdivision, Blk 4, Lot 26, Tel & Fax 2324012, @, rents for P600/day (125 cc).
Tricycle: Within Barrio Barretto P7 per person; from Barrio Barretto to Baloy Beach P15 for the tricycle.

Getting There & Away

Jeepney/Bus: Several Blue Jeepneys run daily round the clock from Olongapo to Barrio Barretto and Subic. But look out - this is a happy hunting ground for pickpockets.
You can also take the Victory Liner buses which go to Iba, Santa Cruz and Alaminos. The trip takes 15 min.

Angeles & Manila

See the Olongapo section earlier in this chapter.

Mt Pinatubo

Just as in Angeles (see there), Barrio Barretto and Olongapo are good starting points for tours of Pinatubo.

Pinatubo Lake

The so-called Pinatubo Lake, or New Lake, at Buhawen was created by damming caused by lava flowing unchecked into the valley after the eruption of the volcano. All that remains to be seen of the little town of Buhawen are a bell tower, the school and the rooftops of various houses sticking forlornly out of the waters. Above the lake a dam can be made out which was constructed by the local Benguet-Dizon Mining Company. If it were to burst, it would probably mean the destruction of all the towns and villages in the valley right down to the coast.
An employee of the company accompanies visitors from the checkpoint to the lake and gives them a little tour when there.

Getting There & Away

Trips to Pinatubo Lake are on offer at various travel agents in Barrio Barretto for around P600. They can also be booked at Baloy Beach in the Mr Pumpernickel restaurant and at Johan's Adventure & Wreck Dive Centre.
It's also possible to make the trip by hire car. From Barrio Barretto, head for San Marcelino via Subic. When there, turn right for San Rafael then go up the road towards Buhawen along the wide riverbed of the Marbella River to the lake. The road from San Marcelino to Buhawen is quite dusty, so it would be better to drive in an enclosed vehicle rather than an open jeep.
Remember: Mudslides on Pinatubo caused by heavy rainfall can change the entire landscape, including the way up to the lake.

Subic Bay

It took over 300 years after they conquered Manila for the Spaniards to decide in 1885 to build an arsenal in Olongapo. Until that time they had simply not taken any notice of the strategic importance of the deep bay at Subic and had anchored their ships near Cavite, where they were also repaired and fitted out. With the outbreak of the Spanish-American War at the end of the 19th century, Subic Bay was planned to be extended and built into the most important naval base in the Philippines. But the idea never got past the planning stage: Before the defensive cannon positioned on Grande Island at the narrow inlet to Manila Bay could be readied to fire, the American admiral Dewey attacked the Spanish fleet in the bay and totally destroyed it.
In 1900 the Americans began to build Subic Bay into a Naval Station. They towed in an enormous floating dry dock and a support base for the navy was constructed. During WWII the Japanese occupied Olongapo and Grande Island but had to retreat at the beginning of 1944 after suffering heavy losses. The victorious Americans consolidated their claim to various bases on the Philippines in the 1947 Military Bases Agreement with the Philippine government which granted them rights to use Subic Bay and the surrounding coastal waters for 99 years.
In the 50s, Cubi Airport was built on an artificial peninsula. A gigantic undertaking for its time, this required not only piling up enormous quantities of earth, but previously hauling away an entire mountain.
The Vietnam War set new standards for Subic Bay. On average, 30 warships anchored daily in the bay, several thousand American military personnel were stationed there, and the number of

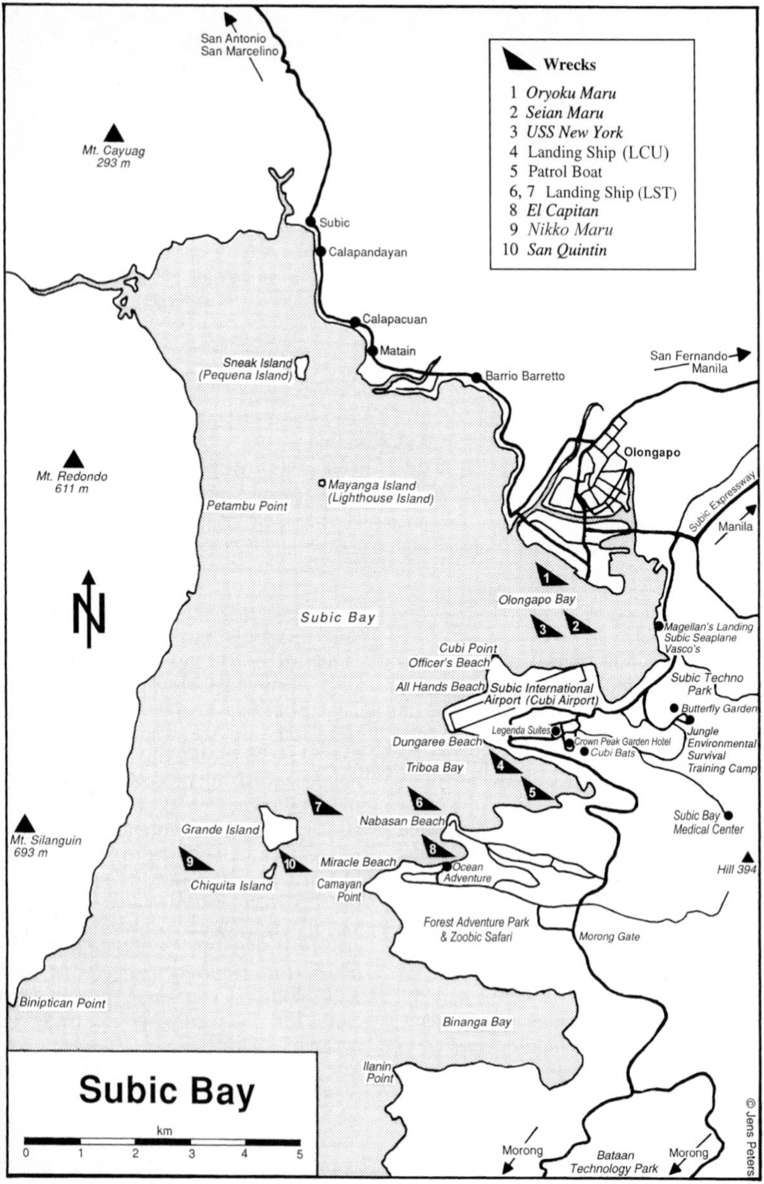

Subic Bay

Wrecks

1 *Oryoku Maru*
2 *Seian Maru*
3 *USS New York*
4 Landing Ship (LCU)
5 Patrol Boat
6, 7 Landing Ship (LST)
8 *El Capitan*
9 *Nikko Maru*
10 *San Quintin*

San Antonio
San Marcelino
Mt. Cayuag 293 m
Subic
Calapandayan
Calapacuan
Matain
Sneak Island (Pequena Island)
Barrio Barretto
San Fernando
Manila
Olongapo
Mt. Redondo 611 m
Mayanga Island (Lighthouse Island)
Petambu Point
Subic Expressway
Manila
Olongapo Bay
Subic Bay
Magellan's Landing
Subic Seaplane
Vasco's
Cubi Point
Officer's Beach
All Hands Beach
Subic International Airport (Cubi Airport)
Subic Techno Park
Butterfly Garden
Legenda Suites
Crown Peak Garden Hotel
Cubi Bats
Jungle Environmental Survival Training Camp
Dungaree Beach
Triboa Bay
Subic Bay Medical Center
Nabasan Beach
Grande Island
Mt. Silanguin 693 m
Miracle Beach
Ocean Adventure
Hill 394
Chiquita Island
Camayan Point
Forest Adventure Park & Zoobic Safari
Morong Gate
Biniptican Point
Binanga Bay
Ilanin Point
km
0 1 2 3 4 5
Morong
Bataan Technology Park
Morong

Philippine support staff rose to 15,000. In 1979 the 1947 agreement was amended: the Americans transferred the sovereign right to the bases to the Filipinos, and their usage rights were codified in a lease agreement which was set to expire in 1991. The use of Subic Bay alone was to bring in US$500 million a year to the Philippine state.

Although the eruption of Mt Pinatubo in June 1991 resulted in the destruction of numerous facilities in the Subic Bay Naval Station, the Americans wanted to continue using the military base there. However, the Philippine government turned down an extension of the agreement in September 1991 but, as a compromise, granted the Americans three years to withdraw from Subic Bay.

Since the lifting of military restrictions Subic Bay has become an interesting diving area for wreck divers. There are at least 20 wrecks lying on the ocean floor, among them the battle cruiser USS *New York*, built in 1891 (sunk in 1941; depth 27m), the Japanese passenger ship *Oryoku Maru* (sunk in 1944; depth 20m), and the Japanese freighter *Seian Maru* (sunk in 1945; depth 27m).

Grande Island & Camayan Point

Grande Island is located at the entrance to Subic Bay, about 20 min by boat from Olongapo. Up until the withdrawal of the US Navy, only Americans were allowed to visit the island, which was used as an R & R Resort. It is now open to the public, although it is used almost exclusively by locals. Admission P15.

Grande Island has a reasonable bathing beach with trees to give shade. Loungers, toilets, showers and a small restaurant are available, as well as a few beach houses with baths and up to six beds (P500 per night). Behind all this there are a few buildings from the time of the Navy, with two cannon and former ammunition depots. A handful of paths lead through the bordering jungle, but they are gradually becoming overgrown.

Not quite 1½ km south-east of Grande Island you come to Miracle Beach, also known as Camayan Beach, at Camayan Point. This beautiful, clean sandy beach, with its drinks kiosk, picnic tables, showers and toilets is only busy at weekends. Admission P50. Parking is available.

At Camayan Wharf not far from Miracle Beach, you'll find Ocean Adventure, an Open Water Marine Park with its sea-lion show. Visitors can also swim with so-called false killer whales (Whale Encounter Program; P2600). Open daily from 9am to 6pm. Admission: P400; children and seniors P320.

Getting There & Away

Boat: The service boat for staff leaves from the Eagle Ferry Landing in Olongapo daily at 8.30am for Grande Island. It will also take day visitors (P60 for a return journey). Departure from Grande Island at 4pm. A Special Ride costs P600.

The boat will stop at Camayan Point if requested on the way from and to Grande Island (arrange to be picked up again).

A big, fast ferry leaves daily at 10am (from next to the Eagle Ferry Landing), returning at 4pm (P120 return; 15 min).

The Zambales Coast

The mountainous province of Zambales borders on the South China Sea to the west. Along the coast between San Antonio and Iba there are several beaches, some of which are over several km long, and some of which have places where you can stay the night. You will find beaches that have not been visited much up to now about 80 km north of Iba, on Dasol Bay. Also remarkable are the extensive salt works north of Santa Cruz. From Manila you can take the direct route to Alaminos and the Hundred Islands National Park, or you can make an interesting detour along the coast road, passing through Olongapo on the way (see the Central Luzon chapter). The catastrophic effects of the Pinatubo eruption are very much in evidence here, especially in the southern section, and will be for years to come.

Getting There & Away

Olongapo - Zambales Coast - Alaminos
Bus: Every day, a number of Victory Liner buses make the trip from Olongapo to Alaminos (five hrs), via San Antonio (45 min), Botolan (two hrs) and Iba (2½ hrs). If you want to start from Manila, first of all take a Victory Liner bus to Olongapo and change there.

San Antonio, Pundaquit & San Miguel

After about an hour's travel from Olongapo, you come to San Antonio, a pleasant little town with a clean market. At least twice a day a jeepney travels over the five km from the plaza there, south-west to Pundaquit.

Pundaquit is a small fishing village on an attractive bay with a long beach. Using that as a base, you can explore the bays cutting deeply into the south coast of Zambales with a boat for about P1500 a day. You could also make a day trip from there to Camera Island or Capones Island. Both islands have white beaches and are rocky, but parts of Capones Island are covered with palms and bushes. There is a lighthouse at the western end of the island which juts out from the sea like a cathedral. Occasionally a few tourists come here to go diving.

From Pundaquit you can walk along the wide beach to San Miguel and beyond, after crossing a fairly shallow river. Tricycles make the trip between San Miguel and San Antonio.

Places to Stay

San Miguel Beach Garden Resort, San Miguel, Cellphone 0919-3337134. SR/DR/fan/bath P400 to P600. Discount available after more than four nights' stay and during the rainy season. Friendly place with good rooms and a beautiful garden. Good value for the money. Restaurant. About 100m from the beach. Boat trips arranged on request (inexpensive). Located five km outside of San Antonio; P20 by tricycle.

Capones Beach Resort, Pundaquit. SR/DR/fan/bath P950, SR/DR/ac/bath P1450. Adequate, practically furnished rooms. Their restaurant is one of these places where you end up spending more than you wanted to. Quiet little place, right on the beach, five km outside of San Antonio.

Botolan

Until the last eruption of Pinatubo, Botolan was a good base to visit the Negritos of the Zambales Mountains. Former weapon carriers (old lorries) used to leave this little place about seven km south of Iba to go inland to Maguisguis or Villar - maybe they have started doing that again. However, the Ayta-Negritos have lost their ancestral living area, some of them having been evacuated to other islands, like Mindoro. There are several beach resorts on the wide beach south of Botolan.

Places to Stay

Rama International Beach Resort, Binoclutan, Cellphone 0918-9101280, @. Dorm/fan P200, SR/DR/fan/bath P700, SR/DR/ac/bath P900 and P1000.

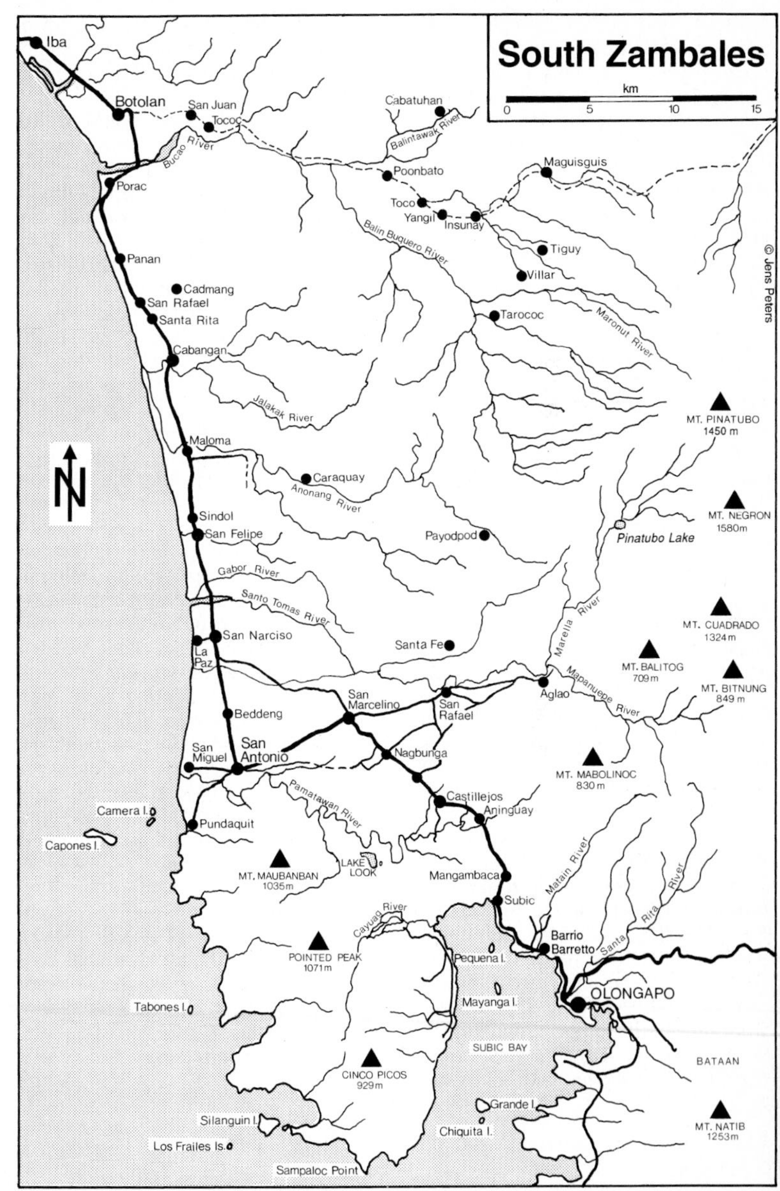
South Zambales
km
0
5
10
15
Iba
Botolan
San Juan
Tococ
Bucao River
Cabatuhan
Balintawak River
Porac
Poonbato
Maguisguis
Toco
Yangil
Insunay
Balin Buquero River
Tiguy
Villar
Panan
Cadmang
San Rafael
Santa Rita
Tarococ
Maronut River
Cabangan
Jalakak River
MT. PINATUBO
1450 m
Maloma
Caraquay
Anonang River
MT. NEGRON
1580m
Sindol
San Felipe
Payodpod
Pinatubo Lake
Gabor River
Santo Tomas River
Marella River
MT. CUADRADO
1324m
San Narciso
La Paz
Santa Fe
MT. BALITOG
709m
MT. BITNUNG
849 m
Aglao
Mapanuepe River
San Marcelino
San Rafael
Beddeng
San Miguel
San Antonio
Nagbunga
MT. MABOLINOC
830 m
Camera I.
Castillejos
Aninguay
Pamatawan River
Pundaquit
Capones I.
MT. MAUBANBAN
1035m
LAKE LOOK
Mangambaca
Matain River
Santa Rita River
Subic
Cayuag River
Barrio Barretto
POINTED PEAK
1071m
Pequena I.
OLONGAPO
Tabones I.
Mayanga I.
SUBIC BAY
BATAAN
CINCO PICOS
929m
Grande I.
Silanguin I.
Chiquita I.
MT. NATIB
1253m
Los Frailes Is.
Sampaloc Point
© Jens Peters

Cottages with two or three bedrooms cost P1250 to P2450. Price reduction from mid-July until end of September. Generously laid-out place with solid stone cottages. Restaurant, swimming pool. Quiet location 500m from the road; about seven km south of Botolan.

Westcoast Beach Resort, Binoclutan, Cellphone 0917-7320716, @. SR/DR/fan/bath P800 and P1000, SR/DR/ac/bath P1100 and P1300. OK rooms, the aircon ones are pleasantly furnished. Very good restaurant with Philippine and international cooking. Swimming pool. Located right next to the Rama International Beach Resort.

Villa Loreto Beach Resort, Binoclutan, Tel 2522157, Fax 2522158, @. SR/DR/ac/bath P3800. Comfortable rooms with TV. A lavishly designed, modern place, which is not what you would expect in this area. They have a big restaurant.

Iba

Iba is the capital of Zambales Province. There are several beach resorts a little outside the town but some of these, unfortunately, have gone a bit downhill - except for the prices. Probably the best beach around Iba is the one slightly north of the centre, just behind the airstrip.

Places to Stay

Palmera Garden Beach Resort, National Rd, Bangantalinga, Tel 8112109, Fax 8111886, @. Cottage/fan/bath P1100, SR/DR/ac/bath P1250 and P1600. Weekly and monthly rates available. They offer a 25% discount from June until October. Popular place, with plants all around, clean rooms and pleasant cottages with TV. Reservations recommended. Under Swiss management. Good restaurant, swimming pool. Located about two km north of Iba.

Lindamar by the Sea, National Rd, Bangantalinga, Tel 8112969, Cellphone 0917-4263836. SR/DR/ac/bath P1200 to P2500. Acceptable, rustically furnished rooms. Attractively laid out grounds, with lots of colour. French-Philippine owners. Restaurant. Billiards. Located about 150m north of the Palmera Garden Beach Resort.

Tammy's Beach Resort, National Rd, Bangantalinga, Tel 8112965. SR/DR/ac/bath P1500. Basic but clean, utilitarian rooms with TV. Three-storey building with billiards on the roof. Inexpensive restaurant. Located right next door to Lindamar by the Sea.

Places to Eat

On the way out of Iba in the north there are a couple of restaurants, including ***Don Guilano's Pizza*** with inexpensive food. On the way out in the south, near the Philippine National Bank, you will find ***Mama Dear Restaurant*** with good local food. ***Bon's Market*** is an inexpensive, air-con restaurant near the market which can be highly recommended (closed in the evenings). Various resort restaurants are closed in the off-season. For self caterers the market and supermarket provide more than enough opportunities to buy food.

Miscellaneous

Festival: Kalighawan Festival in March.

Money: The Philippine National Bank and the Palmera Garden Beach Resort will change travellers cheques.

Population: 35,000.

Post & Telephone: Post code: 2201. Area code: 047.

North Luzon

With over 100,000 sq km, Luzon is the largest island in the Philippines. About half of all Filipinos live there. It plays a leading role in the Philippines' economic and cultural affairs and the number of its tourist attractions is second to none.

Most impressive in North Luzon are the Mountain and Ifugao provinces, with their rice terraces and numerous ethnic minorities. But a number of travellers, especially Filipinos on a short break, are also attracted to the Hundred Islands National Park and the beaches on Lingayen Gulf. On the other hand, the cultivated provinces of Ilocos Norte and Ilocos Sur with its old Spanish churches, extensive sand dunes and the historic town of Vigan are less frequently visited. The most popular town in North Luzon is Baguio in mountainous Benguet Province, also the so-called summer capital of the Philippines. It's a pleasant stopover on the way to Sagada and Bontoc, both of which can be reached by the scenic Halsema Road.

Lingayen Gulf

Lucap & Alaminos

Lucap is a relatively small place on the Lingayen Gulf. It is the starting point for the Hundred Islands National Park. Lots of local tourists come here during Easter week and the hotels can be booked out. There is not much happening here for night owls, as the few restaurants close at 10pm.

Entertainment in nearby Alaminos is limited to bowling and discos. On Sunday there are cockfights a little outside of town. You can do trips from Alaminos to Agno, Sabangan Beach, with its Umbrella Rocks, or Bani, where there is a subterranean river in the Nalsoc Caves. The Nalsoc Caves are in the middle of rice fields about 1½ km outside the small settlement of Colaya. Visitors have to depend on locals to show them the way to the caves. It's important to take a flashlight with you, otherwise only the entrance cavern to the more than one km long cave complex will be visible. To get there, take a jeepney to Bani, then go on to Tiep and continue by tricycle (for about P30) to Colaya. It's best to negotiate a round trip with the driver as there is practically no public transport between Colaya and Tiep, and the journey takes 45 minutes at the best of times (bad road).

Places to Stay

The following prices are valid during the off season. For the high season, which is Easter week and the weekends in April and May, some hotels in Lucap raise their room rates by about 50-100%.

Kilometre One Tourist Lodge, Tel 5512510. SR/fan P200, DR/fan P300. Basic. It also serves as a youth hostel. Restaurant.

Gloria's Cottages, Tel 5512673. SR/DR/fan/bath P350. Generous rooms in cottages on stilts in the sea, some of

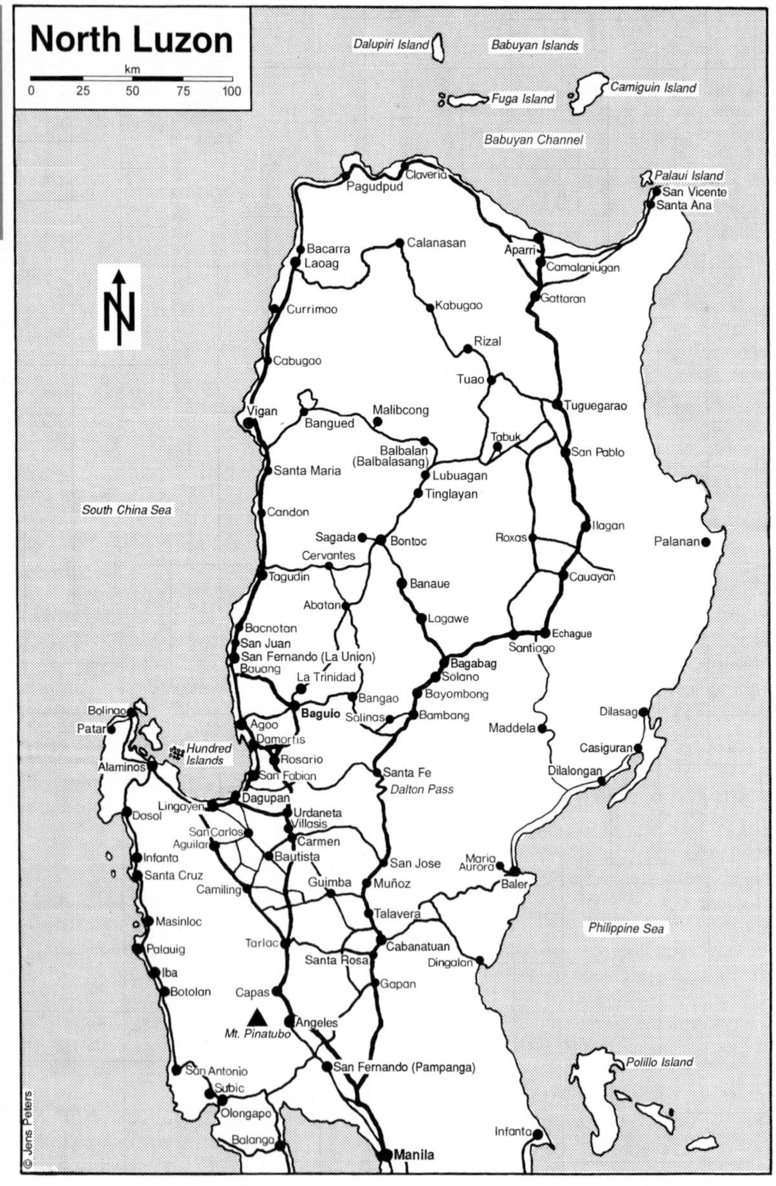
North Luzon
km
0 25 50 75 100
Dalupiri Island
Babuyan Islands
Fuga Island
Camiguin Island
Babuyan Channel
Palaui Island
San Vicente
Santa Ana
Claveria
Pagudpud
Bacarra
Laoag
Calanasan
Aparri
Camalaniugan
Gattaran
Currimao
Kabugao
Rizal
Cabugao
Tuao
Vigan
Bangued
Malibcong
Tuguegarao
Tabuk
Balbalan
(Balbalasang)
San Pablo
Santa Maria
Lubuagan
Tinglayan
South China Sea
Candon
Ilagan
Sagada
Bontoc
Roxas
Palanan
Cervantes
Tagudin
Cauayan
Banaue
Abatan
Lagawe
Bacnotan
Echague
San Juan
Santiago
San Fernando (La Union)
Bauang
Bagabag
La Trinidad
Solano
Bayombong
Bolinao
Bangao
Baguio
Dilasag
Patar
Salinas
Bambang
Maddela
Agoo
Damortis
Hundred Islands
Rosario
Casiguran
Alaminos
San Fabian
Santa Fe
Dilalongan
Dalton Pass
Dagupan
Lingayen
Urdaneta
Dasol
Villasis
San Carlos
Aguilar
Carmen
Infanta
Bautista
San Jose
Maria Aurora
Santa Cruz
Guimba
Muñoz
Baler
Camiling
Masinloc
Talavera
Philippine Sea
Tarlac
Palauig
Cabanatuan
Santa Rosa
Dingalan
Iba
Botolan
Capas
Gapan
Angeles
Mt. Pinatubo
San Fernando (Pampanga)
Polillo Island
San Antonio
Subic
Olongapo
Infanta
Balanga
Manila
© Jens Peters

them no longer in the best condition, but still acceptable for the money. Friendly management.
The Last Resort, Tel 5512440. SR/DR/fan/bath P350, SR/DR/ac/bath P650. Fairly good value. Restaurant. Boating facilities are available.
Ocean View Lodge, Tel 5512501. SR/DR/fan/bath P400, SR/DR/ac/bath P700. Basic, acceptable rooms. Restaurant.
Hundred Islands View Lodge, Tel 5512465, Fax 5512424. SR/DR/fan/bath P550, SR/DR/ac/bath P750. Friendly accommodation with basic, but good rooms. Restaurant and karaoke bar.
Maxine by the Sea, Tel 5512537. SR/DR/ac/bath P700 and P1700. Practically furnished rooms. Beautiful roofed-over patio restaurant right on the water.
VM Pensionne (Villa Milagros), Tel 5513040. SR/DR/ac/bath P750 and P850 (TV). Good, spacious rooms, if a bit spartanly furnished.
Hundred Islands Resort Hotel, Tel & Fax 5515754, @. SR/ac/bath P1100 and P1200, DR/ac/bath 1400 and P1500. Good rooms, the expensive ones with TV. Restaurant, fitness room.
Vista de las Islas, Tel 5512492. SR/DR/ac/bath P1600. Pleasant rooms with refrigerator and TV. Restaurant.

Alaminos
Alaminos Hotel, Quezon Ave. SR/fan P250, SR/DR/fan/bath P350, SR/DR/ac/bath P650. Fairly basic, modestly furnished rooms. Restaurant.

Places to Eat

You can eat cheaply in Lucap at the small ***Canteens*** by the wharf, but some of the lodge restaurants, such as the ***Ocean View Restaurant*** and the airy, two-storey ***Maxine by the Sea Restaurant*** also have good, inexpensive food. Apart from ***The Last Resort Restaurant***, restaurants close quite early on most days, sometimes even by 8pm. In the Hundred Islands Resort Hotel you will also find the rustic ***Boulevard Grill*** and the aircon ***Café Alamos*** which will both serve you seafood and Philippine cooking.
At Alaminos, the ***Plaza Restaurant*** is worth a visit; they also sometimes feature folk singers there. You could also try the ***Imperial Restaurant***.

Demise of Philippine Rabbit?

The bus company Philippine Rabbit, which serves a huge number of destinations in North Luzon, has been laid low since April 2004 by a few dozen striking workers. Who knows whether their 200 buses will ever see service again? It wouldn't be the first time a Philippine company had been put out of business for good by striking employees with the stamina for a drawn-out battle.
Stop press: The Rabbits are running again.

Miscellaneous

Festival: Hundred Islands Festival on 11 and 12 May.
Post & Telephone: Post code: 2404. Area code: 075.
Tourist Office: At the jetty there's a small tourist office, Tel 5512505.

Getting There & Away

Alaminos
Tricycle: Tricycles make the trip between Alaminos and Lucap costing from P20 to P25, regardless of whether you are on your own or are a party of up to four people.

Baguio
Bus: A few Byron Bus buses travel daily from Baguio to Alaminos (four hrs) between 6am and 1pm. You can also go to Dagupan with the Dagupan Bus company and change there.

Banaue
Bus: To travel from Banaue to Alaminos you will have to take the first Baguio bus early in the morning then get off at Rosario and board a Dagupan, Lingayen or Alaminos bus coming from Baguio.

Manila - Angeles
Bus: Dagupan Bus, Five Star and Philippine Rabbit and Victory Liner buses go hourly every day from Manila to Alaminos (P250; six hrs). You may have to change at Lingayen. These buses go via Dau/Angeles, where you can also board them (3½ hrs). It is also possible to take a bus from Manila to Dagupan and change there.

Olongapo
Bus: Several Victory Liner buses travel daily between Olongapo and Alaminos (five hrs).

Hundred Islands

The Hundred Islands are not palm-fringed dream islands, but coral formations of varying sizes with scrub and occasionally small, white beaches. They are of limited appeal for snorkelling as the water is not always crystal clear, often obscuring the reputedly colourful underwater world, which has also been damaged by the long-standing use of dynamite for fishing.

Places to Stay

Take adequate food supplies with you if you want to spend a night or several days on one of the 123 islands. The cheapest place for food is the market at Alaminos and you should be able to get a can of water from the hotel at Lucap. The fee for putting up your own tent is P10 a day on Quezon, Governor's and Children's islands. You can rent a so-called pavilion on Quezon Island for P600. On Governor's Island a cottage for two people costs P400 and a two-roomed cottage for six people P1900. On Children's Island cottages are available for P600 and P1450. Water and cooking facilities are provided and there are toilets. Reservations in Lucap: Tel (075) 5512505.

Getting There & Away

Manila - Olongapo
Bus: To get to Hundred Islands National Park you first have to go to Alaminos and Lucap. There is a direct connection to Alaminos from Manila, but the alternative route along the Zambales coast via Olongapo (see the Central Luzon chapter) should also be kept in mind.

Lucap
Boat: The fare from Lucap to the Hundred Islands National Park by outrigger boat has been fixed officially at P400 plus P15 entry fee per person (P30 for an overnight stay). They can take up to five people, and larger boats are a bit more expensive. It's wise to agree upon the duration of the trip or the driver might return after only 30 minutes. You can also go on an island round trip which will cost you between P100 and P200 extra, depending on the duration and extent of the trip. This makes it possible to choose your own island and be dropped off there, but don't forget to fix a time to be picked up for the return trip. Four or five hours of island life will probably be quite enough, especially when there is no shade. Most day trippers go to Quezon Island, particularly on weekends. You can get drinks at the kiosk there.

Bolinao

Bolinao is a little town north-west of Lucap, which hasn't yet been overrun by tourists, at the far north end of Pang-

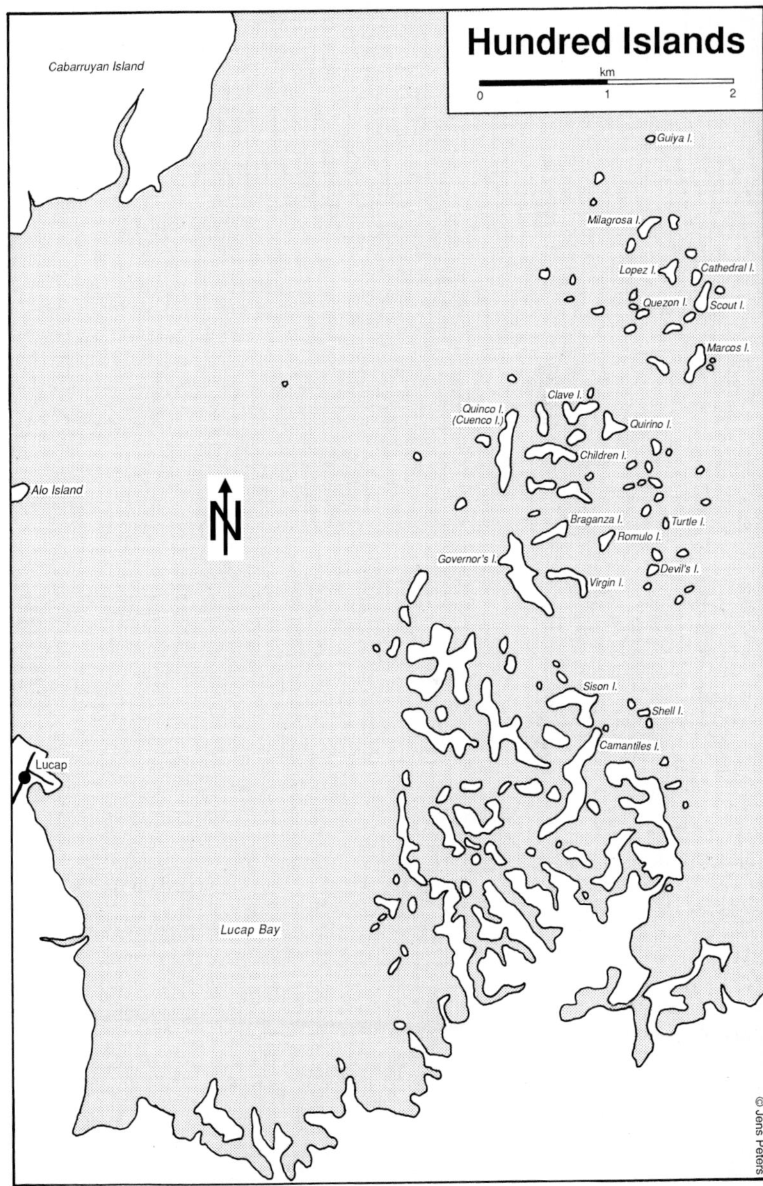

Hundred Islands
km
0
1
2
Cabarruyan Island
Guiya I.
Milagrosa I.
Lopez I.
Cathedral I.
Quezon I.
Scout I.
Marcos I.
Clave I.
Quinco I.
(Cuenco I.)
Quirino I.
Children I.
Alo Island
N
Braganza I.
Turtle I.
Romulo I.
Governor's I.
Devil's I.
Virgin I.
Sison I.
Shell I.
Camantiles I.
Lucap
Lucap Bay
© Jens Peters

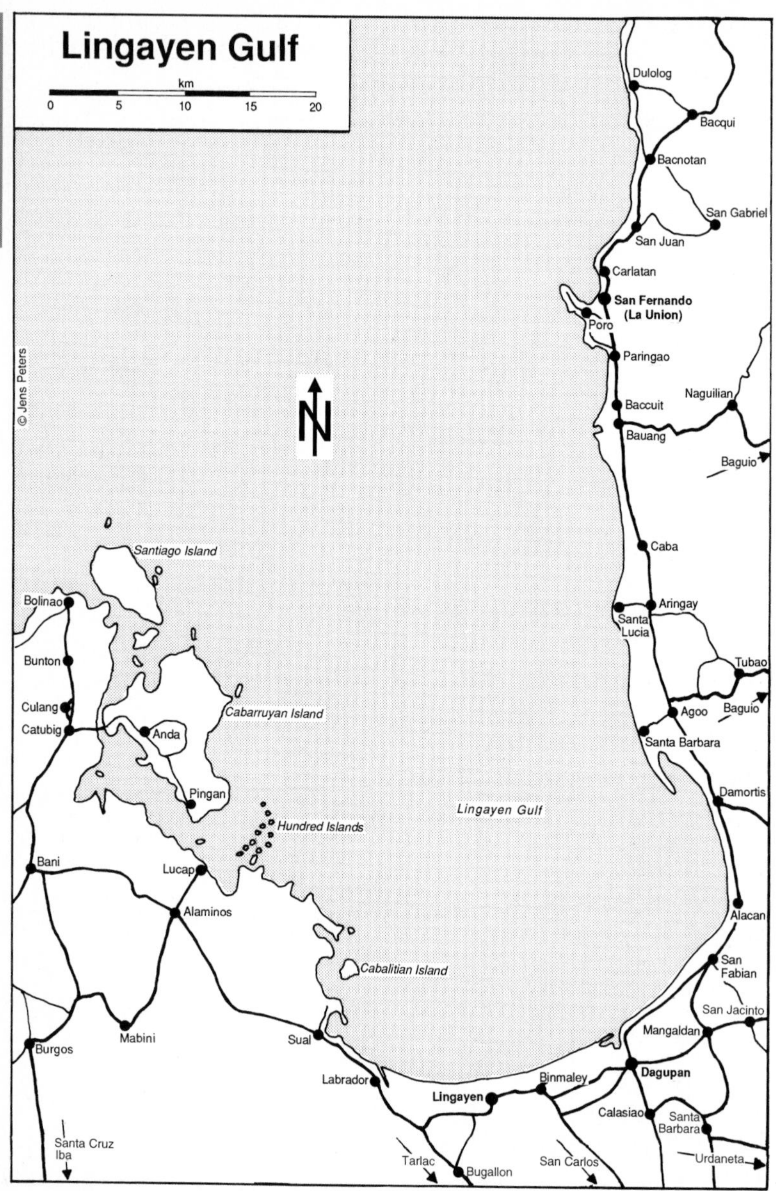
Lingayen Gulf
km
0
5
10
15
20
© Jens Peters
N
Dulolog
Bacqui
Bacnotan
San Gabriel
San Juan
Carlatan
San Fernando
(La Union)
Poro
Paringao
Naguilian
Baccuit
Bauang
Baguio
Caba
Santiago Island
Bolinao
Aringay
Santa
Lucia
Bunton
Tubao
Culang
Cabarruyan Island
Agoo
Baguio
Catubig
Anda
Santa Barbara
Pingan
Damortis
Lingayen Gulf
Hundred Islands
Bani
Lucap
Alaminos
Alacan
San
Fabian
Cabalitian Island
San Jacinto
Mangaldan
Mabini
Sual
Burgos
Dagupan
Labrador
Binmaley
Lingayen
Calasiao
Santa
Barbara
Santa Cruz
Iba
Tarlac
San Carlos
Urdaneta
Bugallon

asinan Province. Unfortunately, there are no acceptable beaches in the area, so you have to drive about 13 km south-west to Patar if it's a beach you're after. Even there it's not exactly a tropical dream beach that awaits you. Of course, if you really want to get away from it all, you could arrange to cross over to one of the offshore islands, although the woodland near the shore slopes steeply for about 10m down to the sea there. Take your own snorkelling equipment as it is next to impossible to find even a pair of goggles in Bolinao. One exception can be found in Pisalayan near Binabalian on the island of Santiago where Jhun Gatchalian rents out snorkelling equipment for P100 per day. He also has two complete sets of diving equipment and a compressor.

In the town centre is the St James Church, which dates back to 1609. It used to double as a fortress during attacks by pirates and by the English, Japanese and Americans. If you can catch the priest when he is not too busy, he might tell you more about those times.

Museum

The Bolinao Museum on the outskirts of town has a collection of Philippine flora and fauna which is worth a look, but, because of the lack of money, it has only a few historical items.

Places to Stay

El Piscador Village Inn, Tel 5542559. SR/DR/ac/bath P1000 to P2000. Good rooms with veranda. Spread out grounds. Big garden restaurant.

Dutch Beach Resort, Patar, Cellphone 0920-7869037. SR/DR/fan/bath P700, SR/DR/ac/bath P1500 and P1800. Pleasantly furnished, small buildings with refrigerators, in a garden directly on the beach. Restaurant. 13 km outside of Bolinao (P100 by tricycle).

Puerto del Sol Beach Hotel, Ilog Malinao, Cellphone 0918-5192147, @. SR/DR/ac/bath P3000, P5000 and P6000 (two bedrooms). Attractive, two-storey building with comfortable rooms, all with refrigerator and TV. Restaurant, swimming pool, jacuzzi. Located about 10 km west of Bolinao, on the way to Patar (P100 by tricycle). Reservations in Manila: Tel (02) 3647874.

Places to Eat

In Don Agaton Celino St at the southern edge of town, about 300m from the National Rd, you'll find the pleasant little, partly open-air ***Tummy Teasers Foodhouse & Bakeshop***. Here you can order pancit malabon as well as pizzas, spaghetti and cakes. ***Whoopee's Garden Restaurant*** next to the Bolinao Central School, National Rd, is open round the clock.

Miscellaneous

Festival: Town Fiesta from 24 to 26 April.

Population: 50,000.

Post & Telephone: Post code: 2406. Area code: 075.

Getting There & Away

Alaminos

Bus/Jeepney: Several jeepneys, minibuses and Five Star buses leave the market at Alaminos for Bolinao daily (one hr).

The last jeepney from Bolinao to Alaminos leaves at about 5pm.

Bauang

Boat: An outrigger leaves Bauang at the east end of Lingayen Gulf for Bolinao daily at 4am (P200; two hrs). Information can be obtained from the Gatchalian family at the entrance to the China Sea Resort; Tel 2420823.

The departure from Bolinao is at 11am. A Special Ride for up to three people costs P600 plus P200 for each additional person.

Manila
Bus: From Manila to Bolinao via Alaminos, Five Star and Victory Liner buses run several times daily (P290; 6½ hrs).

Lingayen

Lingayen, the capital of Pangasinan Province, which dates back to about 1611, has two faces. First there's the historical one with its church and town plaza and the group of spruce buildings around them, dating back to the Spanish colonial time. Then there's the modern one, with its Capitol and other, rather boring buildings. The old town is on the road leading from Alaminos to Dagupan; the new town is about a km north of it towards the coast.
Lingayen Beach is outside the town. As on other well-known beaches at the southern end of the Lingayen Gulf, none of them particularly impressive, you will find many Filipinos from smog-plagued Manila here in search of recreation.
Not quite five km east of Lingayen, the quiet little town of Binmaley is home to an impressive church and numerous little workshops where furniture in colonial style is manufactured.

Places to Stay

Lingayen Gulf Resort Hotel, Provincial Capitol Ground, Tel 5425871. Dorm/fan P200, SR/DR/ac/bath P650, suite P2000. Comfortable rooms with TV and a sea view. A pleasant place, near the beach. Restaurant, swimming pool.

Miscellaneous

Festival: Pista'y Dayat on 1 May.
Population: 80,000.
Post & Telephone: Post code: 2401. Area code: 075.

Getting There & Away
2 Victory Liner Bus Terminal
4 Dagupan Bus Bus Terminal
13 Five Star Bus Terminal

Places to Stay
1 El Piscador Village Inn
17 Dutch Beach Resort (13 km)
Puerto del Sol Beach Hotel (10 km)

Places to Eat
4 Pink Soda Ice Cream Parlour
14 Whoopee's Garden Restaurant
16 Tummy Teasers Foodhouse & Bakeshop

Miscellaneous
5 PLDT
6 Basketball Court
7 Rural Bank of Bolinao
8 Police Station
9 Town Hall
Post Office
10 St James Church
11 Market
12 Plaza
15 Bolinao Central School
18 Bolinao Museum

Getting There & Away

Manila - Angeles
Bus: Dagupan Bus and Five Star run many buses daily from Manila to Lingayen (five hrs) via Dau/Angeles, where you can also board the bus. You can also board buses bound for Alaminos, which go via Lingayen.

Dagupan

In 1590, Augustinian monks declared the community of Bacnotan to be a town and named it Dagupan. It became an important trading and educational centre in Pangasinan, eclipsing the provincial capital, Lingayen.

Only three km north in Bonuan is Bonuan Beach with Tondaligan Beach next to it, neither of which is anything to write home about. There are, however, a noticeable amount of simple kiosks selling cold drinks. The trip there by jeepney costs P6.

Places to Stay

Value Star Inn, AB Fernandez Ave, Tel 5228381, Fax 5228385. SR/DR/fan/bath P250, SR/DR/ac/bath P550 (with TV). Immaculate rooms, good value. Located near the Star Plaza Hotel.

Victoria Hotel, AB Fernandez Ave corner Nable St. SR/DR/fan/bath P390, SR/DR/ac/bath P480 and P600 (TV). Good hotel. Aircon rooms in the new wing are bigger and a bit more comfortably decorated than the more inexpensive ones in the old wing. Restaurant.

Floren Hotel, Rizal St, Tel 5220666. SR/DR/ac/bath P500 and P850. With TV. Trim little pleasant place to stay, with friendly, inviting rooms. Coffee shop.

Star Plaza Hotel, AB Fernandez Ave, Tel 5234888, Fax 5234777. SR/DR/ac/bath P850 and P1050, suite P1500, P1800 and P3000 (with jacuzzi). Comfortable rooms with TV, the suites all facing the river. Located in the centre of

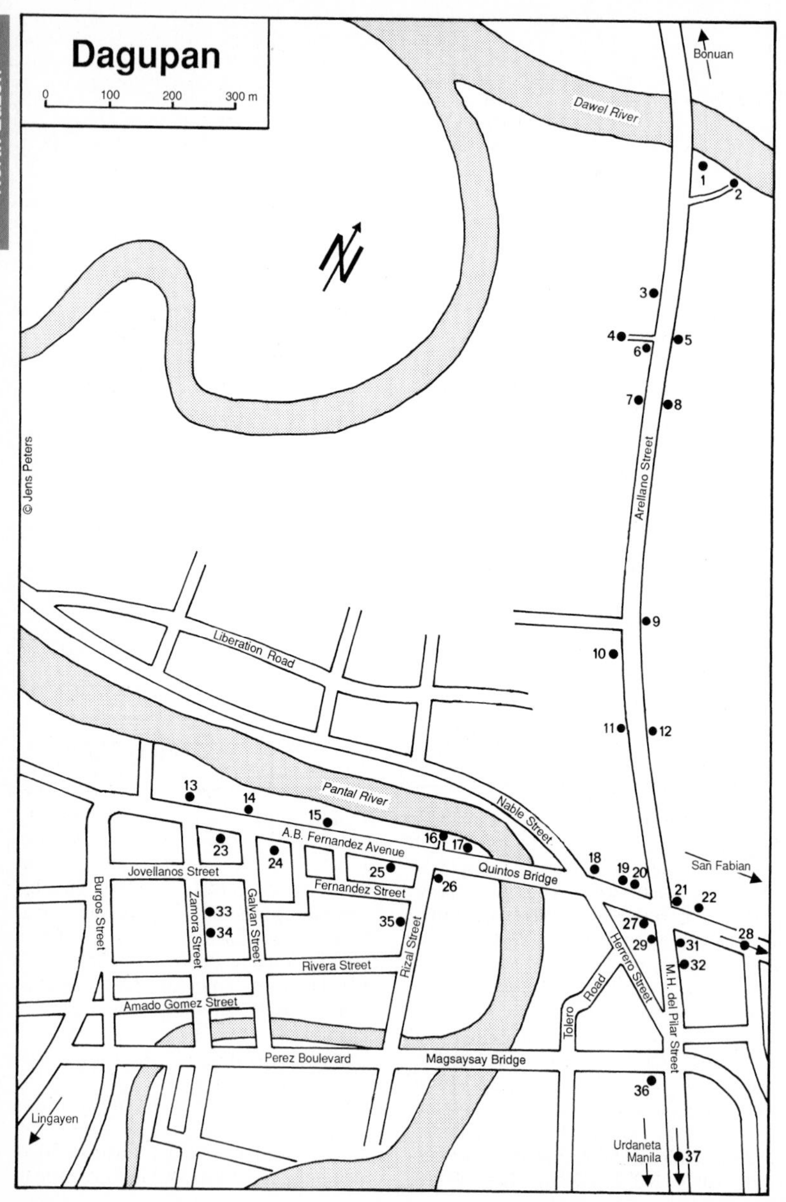
Dagupan
0
100
200
300 m
Bonuan
Dawel River
Arellano Street
Liberation Road
Pantal River
Nable Street
A.B. Fernandez Avenue
Quintos Bridge
San Fabian
Jovellanos Street
Fernandez Street
Burgos Street
Zamora Street
Galvan Street
Rizal Street
Rivera Street
Herrero Street
Road
Tolero
M.H. del Pilar Street
Amado Gomez Street
Perez Boulevard
Magsaysay Bridge
Lingayen
Urdaneta
Manila
© Jens Peters

Getting There & Away
12 Dagupan Bus Terminal
22 Byron Bus Terminal
32 Minibuses to San Fabian & San Fernando La Union
36 Five Star Bus Terminal
Victory Liner Bus Terminal

Places to Stay
16 Value Star Inn
17 Star Plaza Hotel
18 Victoria Hotel
28 Hotel Mil Exel (1 km)
35 Floren Hotel
37 Pangasinan Regency Hotel (4 km)

Places to Eat & Entertainment
1 D'Original Dawel Restaurant
2 Silverio's Seafood Restaurant
3 D'Music Machine Disco
Star City Complex
4 Luzz VI Disco & Pub
5 Goring's Pancit Malabon Restaurant
6 Celebrity House Restaurant
7 Jadelady Disco
8 GG's Restaurant
9 Pedrito's Steak House
11 Giacomino's Pizza
14 KFC
15 Aljas Fastfood Restaurant
20 Chowking Restaurant
21 Dunkin' Donuts
24 Goldilocks
McDonald's
Shakey's
25 Mister Donut
26 Music Box Disco
27 Dagupeña Restaurant
29 McDonald's
31 Jollibee
35 Pedrito's Coffee Shop

Miscellaneous
10 Provincial Hospital
13 Mercury Drug
18 Equitable PCI Bank
23 City Hall
Police Station
24 CSI Market Square Shopping Center
33 Centro Market
34 Post Office

town, this is the best hotel here. Restaurant.

Pangasinan Regency Hotel, Judge Jose de Venecia Sr Ave, Naisian, Calasiao, Tel 5176232, Fax 5230797, @. SR/DR/ac/bath P1280, suite P1350. Tastefully decorated, comfortably furnished, spacious rooms with refrigerator and TV. Really good value. Excellent Chinese restaurant, bar, music lounge, coffee shop. Located about four km south of Dagupan.

Places to Eat

Pangasinan province is known for its excellent bangus (milk fish) - said to be the best in the country. They are bred in countless fish ponds between Dagupan and Lingayen. Nearly all the restaurants in town offer bangus prepared in lots of different ways, eg stuffed or filleted (boneless bangus).

D'Original Dawel is a big, basic, but very popular seafood restaurant at the bridge over the river at the northern end of Arellano St. Mind you, the menu has no prices on it, so when you order don't forget to check the current price of fish, shrimps etc, and how big a portion is. There are more seafood restaurants on the beach in Bonuan, including ***Siapno's Restaurant*** and ***D'Executives Restaurant***, which are mostly patronised after dark.

In town itself the ***Dagupeña Restaurant*** on AB Fernandez Ave can be highly recommended, especially their pleasantly furnished aircon room. They

offer a large selection of Philippine dishes; the house speciality is sizzling boneless bangus. Apart from offering standard Philippine fare like adobo and menudo, ***Aljas Fastfood*** on AB Fernandez Ave has ice-cold beer.
If you have an appetite for fast-food, then ***McDonald's*** and ***Shakey's***, both in the CSI Market Square Shopping Center on AB Fernandez Ave, will take care of it. That is also the location of the popular ***Goldilocks***, where they will serve you coffee and cakes, as will ***Pedrito's Coffee Shop*** in the Floren Hotel, Rizal St.

Entertainment

The nightlife in Dagupan can mostly be found in Arellano St, where there are restaurants and a row of discos. Some of them offer shows after 10pm, others let the guests do the dancing.

Miscellaneous

Festivals: Pistay Dayat (Sea Festival) on 1 May. Agew na Dagupan on 20 June.
Money: The Equitable PCI Bank, AB Fernandez Ave, has an ATM.
Population: 150,000.
Post & Telephone: Post Office, Zamora St.
Post code: 2400. Area code: 075.

Getting There & Away

Baguio
Bus: From Baguio to Dagupan a fleet of buses make the trip daily, including Byron Bus vehicles leaving every half hour between 6am and 4pm, and Dagupan Bus and Philippine Rabbit buses, the last one of which leaves around noon (two hrs).

Bolinao - Alaminos
Bus: From Bolinao to Dagupan, there are many Dagupan Bus buses a day. They take two hrs and go via Alaminos, where you can also board them.
Numerous Dagupan Bus and Victory Liner buses run daily from Alaminos to Dagupan (one hr).

Manila - Angeles
Bus: From Manila to Dagupan, many Dagupan Bus, Five Star and Victory Liner buses travel daily via Dau/Angeles, where you can also board them (P215; 5½ hrs).

Laoag - Vigan
Bus: This is how to get from Laoag and Vigan to Dagupan: First take a bus heading for Manila as far as Damortis, change there into a minibus for Dagupan (six hrs).

San Fabian

San Fabian is a friendly little place, situated a few km north-east of Dagupan. Just outside the town, from Nibaliw West to Bolasi, stretches White Beach, although the old name of Center Beach was more accurate. There are several places to stay here. Like almost all beaches in the Lingayen Gulf, the sand is not dazzling white but brownish-grey. There are a few more resorts four or five km north-east of San Fabian, on the beach at Bolasi and Alacan, which have not been developed much for tourism yet.

Places to Stay

Nibaliw West
Lazy 'A' Resort, Tel 5115014, Fax 5223084. Cottage/fan/bath P800 to P3800, SR/DR/ac/bath P1200 to P2400 (depending on size and season). Good accommodation. The more expensive cottages have two bedrooms and cooking facilities. Restaurant, swimming pool.
Charissa's Beach Houses, Tel 5236861. SR/DR/ac/bath P1000, from the middle of March until the middle of June P1800.

Papaya Tree
This short-lived melon-tree is actually a giant herb. It is one of the commonest fruit trees in the Philippines.

Friendly place Restaurant, swimming pool.
Sierra Vista Beach Resort, Tel 5112023, Fax 5223366. SR/ac/bath P1750, DR/ac/bath P2150, including breakfast. The cottages at this nice little hotel complex are solidly built and pleasantly decorated furnished. Restaurant, swimming pool (P80 for non-residents).

Alacan & Bolasi
San Fabian PTA Beach Resort, Bolasi, Tel 5236504, Fax 5236502. SR/DR/ac/bath P1700 to P2200, presidential suite P4500. Tastefully furnished rooms and the suite is huge. Restaurant, swimming pool. This is the former San Fabian Presidential Resthouse, where the late President Marcos used to stay when he was travelling through northern Luzon.

Miscellaneous

Festival: Town Fiesta from 17 to 20 January.

Post & Telephone: Post code: 2433. Area code: 075.

Getting There & Away

Baguio
Bus: Several Dagupan Bus and Byron Bus buses go from Baguio to San Fabian daily, with the destination 'Dagupan'. The last one probably leaves at about 2pm (two hrs).

Dagupan
Bus: From Dagupan to San Fabian there are also many buses daily. Take either a minibus going to San Fernando (La Union) or one of the Dagupan Bus or Byron Bus buses going to Baguio (30 min). Some of these buses may be coming from Lingayen or Alaminos.

Manila - Angeles
Bus: The best way to get from Manila and Angeles to San Fabian is to take a bus heading for San Fernando (La Union), Vigan or Laoag. Get out at Damortis and cover the remaining 15 km south to San Fabian via Alacan and Bolasi by minibus (see the Getting There & Away section under San Fernando later in this chapter).
It is also possible to travel from Manila and Angeles via Dagupan.

San Fernando (La Union)
Bus: From San Fernando (La Union) to San Fabian there are many minibuses daily, going on to Dagupan (two hrs).

Aringay & Agoo

Agoo and Aringay lie between San Fabian and Bauang. In Aringay, the small Don Lorenzo Museum is opposite the old church.
Worth seeing in Agoo is the Agoo Basilica, which was rebuilt in 1892 after a severe earthquake. Probably the most beautiful church in La Union, it

has a Shrine of Our Lady and is the most important place of pilgrimage in the province during Holy Week. The climax of the Semana Santa (Holy Week) activities is the procession on Good Friday. The large oil painting directly behind the main entrance contains an interesting secret. Commissioned in the 1970s by Jose Aspiras, Secretary of Tourism at the time, who is a native of Agoo, the host of angels includes in the foreground two who are easily recognised as Imelda Marcos and Mrs. Aspiras herself.

Next to the Agoo Municipal Hall is the Museo Iloko. This is a small museum with liturgical objects, antique furniture and china. Next door, in Imelda Park, visitors can pass the time in a beautiful tree house. On the northern outskirts of Agoo a large stone statue of an eagle marks the start of the Marcos Highway, which leads to Baguio.

Several hundred thousand Filipinos congregated on Apparition Hill near Agoo at the beginning of March 1993, to witness the appearance of the Blessed Virgin Mother which had been prophesied. The miracle didn't happen, but even serious newspapers reported that the air there had been filled with a miraculous fragrance and that thousands of pilgrims had seen the sun dancing…

Getting There & Away

Manila - Angeles

Bus: From Manila, take any bus heading for San Fernando (La Union), Vigan or Laoag (six hrs). See also the Getting There & Away sections under San Fernando (La Union) later in this chapter.

San Fernando (La Union)

Bus: There are numerous buses from San Fernando to Agoo (one hr), all going to Manila.

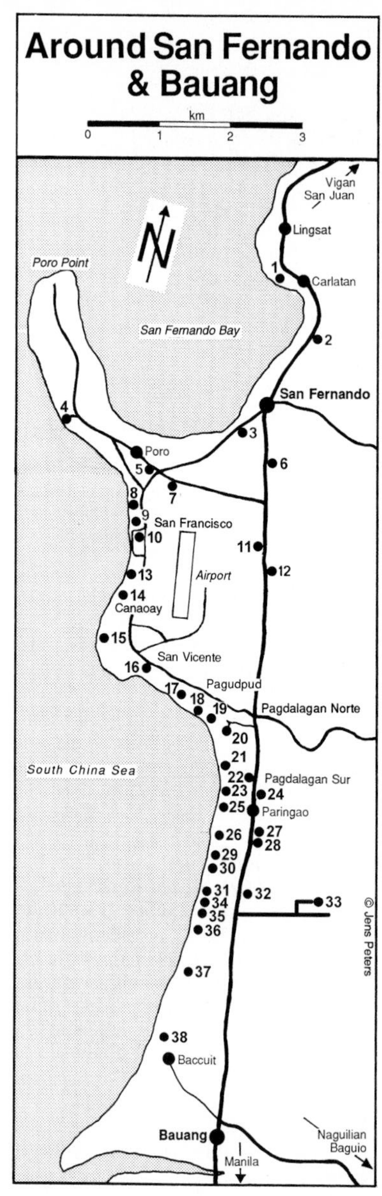

Getting There & Away
6 Philippine Rabbit Bus Terminal

Places to Stay
1 Oceana Apartments
4 Miramonte Beach Resort
8 Driftwood Resort
Sea Park Beach Resort
9 Acapulco Beach Resort
12 Oasis Country Resort
13 Blue Lagoon Resort
14 Sunset Bay Resort
15 Coral Point Beach Resort
16 Lorenza Beach House
18 California Resort
20 Umay Kay Homes
21 Southern Palms Beach Resort
22 Koala Lodge
23 Cesmin Beach Cottages
Ocean Breeze Beach Resort
25 Bali Hai Beach Resort
26 Cabaña Beach Resort
28 Bali Hai East
29 China Sea Beach Resort
Coconut Grove Resort
30 Villa Estrella Hotel Resort
31 Cresta del Mar Hotel
32 Mark Teresa Apartel
33 Schweizergarten Resort
35 Long Beach Resort Hotel
North Palm Beach Resort
36 Nalinac Beach Resort
37 Leo-Mar Beach Resort
38 Hideaway Beach Resort

Places to Eat & Entertainment
5 Nightclub District
7 Gayemm
10 Jochen's Restaurant & Deli Shop
11 Max's
17 Patio del Sol Restaurant
19 Tobacco Road
21 Stiletto's Nightclub
22 Tramps Nightclub
24 Finnegans Restaurant
Footlights Nightclub
28 VFW Canteen
34 Michaela's
Seamen's
36 Cogon Hut Restaurant

Miscellaneous
2 Lorma Medical Center
3 Immigration Office
12 Tourist Office
27 Uni Eastern Travel
29 Ocean Deep Diver Training Center

Bauang

Bauang has developed into the most popular beach resort in North Luzon. The places to stay mentioned here are only a small cross-section, as there are many others. Nearly all of them are on the long, grey beach between Baccuit and Paringao, a little to the north of Bauang proper and about five km south of San Fernando. You can't see much from the road except a few signposts. If you are arriving by bus or jeepney, it is best to warn the driver or conductor that you want to be dropped off at the hotel of your choice. If it is booked out, walk along the beach and you will find plenty of alternative accommodation.

In Naguilian, 10 km east of Bauang, *basi* (an alcoholic drink made from fermented sugar-cane juice) is manufactured, which is reputed to be the best in the country and is especially popular with Ilokanos. The sweet variant of basi tastes a bit like sherry or port.

Places to Stay

The following prices apply during the high season from December to May. They are about 25% cheaper in the off season from June to November, so it is worth haggling a bit.

Cesmin Beach Cottages, Pagdalagan Sur, Tel 8882884. Cottage/fan P250, cottage/fan/bath P250 to P1100, cottage/ac/bath P700 to P1350 with a fridge and cooking facilities. Good value. The monthly rates are favourable.

Koala Lodge, Pagdalagan Sur, Tel 2420863, Fax 8885448, @. SR/DR/fan/bath P295 to P575, SR/DR/ac/bath P395 to P950. Favourable weekly rates. Good rooms for the money, nearly all with refrigerator and TV. Located near the highway, not directly on the beach.

Leo Mar Beach Resort, Baccuit. SR/DR/fan/bath P400 to P600. Basic accommodation without additional comforts. Restaurant.

Ocean Breeze Beach Resort, Paringao, Tel 8883530. SR/DR/fan/bath P550, SR/DR/ac/bath P700. The rooms, which are in attractive stone-built bungalows built a bit too close together, are basic but spacious. Restaurant.

Long Beach Resort Hotel, Paringao, Tel 2420609. SR/DR/fan/bath P700, SR/DR/ac/bath P800 to P1250 (TV). Basically furnished rooms with balconies. Restaurant.

Bali Hai East, Paringao, National Highway, Tel 2420531, Fax 2420528, @. SR/DR/ac/bath P800 to P1600 (with refrigerator and TV). Pleasant rooms. Weekly rates available. Swimming pool. This is the former Eastside Resort Hotel.

Southern Palms Beach Resort, Pagdalagan Sur, Tel 8885384, Fax 8885529, @. SR/DR/ac/bath P795 to P2295. Comfortable rooms of different sizes, nearly all with refrigerator and TV, the more expensive also with a jacuzzi. Restaurant, nightclub, swimming pool.

Coconut Grove Resort, Paringao, Tel 8884276, Fax 8885381, @. SR/DR/ac/bath P1090 to P1750. They offer a 25% discount from June until November. Immaculate rooms with TV, the more expensive also with a refrigerator. Sophisticated resort with a large outdoor lawn bowling complex. Restaurant, swimming pool, diving.

Bali Hai Beach Resort, Paringao, Tel 2425679, Fax 8885480, @. SR/DR/fan/bath P1200, SR/DR/ac/bath P1595 to P2450. Good rooms with TV, the expensive ones also have a refrigerator. Pleasant duplex cottages set in well groomed grounds. Monthly rates can be arranged. Restaurant, swimming pool.

China Sea Beach Resort, Paringao, Tel 2426101, Fax 2420822, @. SR/DR/ac/bath P1375 (TV) and P1600 (TV and refrigerator). Discount from 1 June until 31 October. Pleasant place with well-kept rooms. Restaurant, swimming pool.

Cabaña Beach Resort, Paringao, Tel 2425585, Fax 2423107, @. SR/DR/ac/bath P1620 to P1890. From June until mid-October 15% discount. Good rooms, the more expensive ones also have a refrigerator and TV. Popular with Australians and Germans. Restaurant, swimming pool.

Villa Estrella Beach Resort, Paringao, Tel 2425585, Fax 2423107, @. SR/DR/ac/bath P1600. Friendly rooms with TV, refrigerator P200 extra. Attractive hotel just starting to show its age, built in the Spanish colonial style.

Places to Eat

Try one of the resort restaurants along the beach for a change, though the prices are decidedly higher there. The cuisine at the ***Villa Estrella*** is good, as it is at the ***Bali Hai***. The German and Philippine food in ***Michaela's*** (around P150) is quite inexpensive, and also worth trying is the Mongolian barbecue at the ***Cabaña*** on Saturday night.

At the highway you could always go to the pleasant ***Finnegans Restaurant*** with its excellent Philippine cuisine (eg garlic shrimps, grilled prawns) and international dishes (speciality: Irish stew).

Entertainment

Apart from ***Stiletto's*** nightclub at the Southern Palms Beach Resort the main entertainment available at Bauang is restricted to billiards and videos, eg in ***Michaela's*** and ***Seamen's***. A popular meeting place is ***Tobacco Road*** at the northern end of the beach, with outstanding music (blues in particular) and a beautiful view of the sea. The ***Tradewinds Disco Club*** and ***Kuya's Bar***, both at the Villa Estrella Beach Resort are usually patronised by Philippine nationals.

Not far from the beach, right on the National Highway, the clubs ***Tramps*** and ***Footlights*** are already open for business in the afternoon. There are more discos and a few bars in ***Poro Point*** (junction) near San Fernando; a popular nightclub-disco there is ***Gayyem*** (inexpensive, open till early in the morning). You can get there by tricycle from Bauang Beach for P30.

Miscellaneous

Diving: Ocean Deep Diver Training Center, Tel. 8884440, @, at the Coconut Grove Resort offers good value diving courses and trips.

Festival: Town Fiesta from 26 to 29 April.

Post & Telephone: Post code: 2501. Area code: 072.

Travel Agency: Uni Eastern Travel, National Highway, Paringao, Tel 8885512. Reservation and confirmation of inland and international flights. Visa extensions. Agent for various resorts.

Getting Around

Car: Excel Rent-a-Car, Gov Ortega St, San Fernando, Tel 2420743, rents vehicles at P2000 per day for self-drive. Good idea to book first.

Getting There & Away

Angeles

Bus: See *Manila-Angeles.*

Baguio

Bus/Jeepney: To go from Baguio to Bauang you have a choice of several Philippine Rabbit and Eso-Nice Transport buses bound for San Fernando (1½ hrs). The trip along the winding Naguilian Rd down to the coast is especially attractive in the late afternoon. For the best view, sit on the same side as the driver. You can also go by jeepney, which is a bit faster than the bus.

An aircon minibus (Fly the Bus) goes from Baguio to Bauang Tuesday and Saturday at 8am, leaving from the Aussie Hotel. Departure in Bauang Monday and Friday at 1.30pm (P150; 1½ hrs).

Bolinao

Boat: An outrigger leaves Bolinao for Bauang daily at 11am (P200; two hrs). Information can be obtained at the TV-repair shop The Islander, Arosan St, Bolinao.

Departure from Bauang is at 4am. A Special Ride for up to three people costs P600, with P200 for each additional person.

Laoag - Vigan

Bus: From Laoag and Vigan there are several Autobus Transport, Partas, Philippine Rabbit, Dominion Bus Line, Fariñas Trans, and Maria de Leon buses daily, all going to Manila. The trip to Bauang takes five hrs from Laoag and three hrs from Vigan.

Manila - Angeles

Bus: There are plenty of Autobus Transport, Partas, Philippine Rabbit, Dominion Bus Line, Fariñas Trans, Maria de Leon, Partas, and Philippine Rabbit buses travelling between Manila and Bauang. Take any one going to San Fernando, Vigan and Laoag. These buses go via Dau/Angeles and you can board them there. Travelling time from Manila seven hrs (P250); from Angeles 4½ hrs.

An aircon minibus (Fly the Bus) goes from Angeles to Bauang Monday and

Friday at 8am, leaving from the Swagman Narra Hotel. Departure in Bauang Tuesday and Saturday at 9.30am (P600; four hrs).
The best way to catch a bus on the highway from Bauang to Manila is to stop every bus until you get one that suits you. At Christmas time, when a lot of buses are full, the best idea is to take a jeepney to the bus companies' terminals in San Fernando and try to get a decent seat there.

San Fernando (La Union)
Jeepney: There are many jeepneys daily from San Fernando to Bauang (30 min). You can get off on the highway near the beach resorts.

San Fernando (La Union)

Also called the City of the Seven Hills, San Fernando is the capital of La Union Province. There's a good view over the South China Sea from Freedom Park, also known as Heroes' Hill. The Museo de La Union, next to the Provincial Capitol, provides an even better view from its terrace, as well as giving a cultural overview of the province. It's closed on weekends.
The little Fil-Chinese Pagoda on Gapuz Zigzag Rd and the big Ma-Cho Temple on Quezon Ave, which is really worth seeing, bear witness to the Chinese influence in San Fernando. From 12 to 16 September, the Chinese-Filipino religious community holds an annual celebration of the Virgin of Caysasay at the Ma-Cho Temple.
About three km south-west of San Fernando, on the bay south of Poro, there is a beach with a reasonable stretch around about the Acapulco Beach Resort. The rest of the beach is quite stony and not really suitable for swimming. Most of the hotels there are fairly isolated and not well situated for getting anywhere apart from the airport. In the evening it's a real problem trying to find a tricycle into town.
Set in the forests in the mountains of Cadaclan about seven km east of San Fernando, the La Union Botanical Gardens have an orchidarium, mini-zoo and aviary. However, no regular jeepneys go up there, so you can only get there by Special Ride or private car.

Places to Stay

San Fernando
Hotel Mikka, Quezon Ave, Tel 2425737, Fax 2422688, @. SR/ac/bath P625, DR/ac/bath P750 and P1350. Immaculate rooms with TV. On the first floor of its building. Restaurant. Near the Partas Bus Terminal.
Sea & Sky Hotel, Quezon Ave, Tel 2425579, Fax 2423869. SR/DR/ac/bath P900 and P900, suite (with refrigerator) P1500. Spotless rooms with TV. The quiet ones have a balcony and a beautiful view of the sea. Restaurant, small swimming pool. On the northern edge of town.

Near Airport & Poro
Sunset Bay Resort, Canaoay, Tel 8884843, Fax 2420235, @. SR/DR/ac/bath P700 and P900. Squeaky clean rooms with refrigerator. Pleasant, well-kept, quiet little place set in garden grounds. Good value. Australian management. Good restaurant.
Blue Lagoon Resort, Canaoay, Tel 8882531. SR/DR/ac/bath P1.000. An attractively decorated place with comfortable rooms, some with a little living room attached. Restaurant.
Oasis Country Resort, Sevilla, National Highway, Tel 2425621, Fax 2421469, @. SR/DR/ac/bath P1990 to P3290. Comfortable, friendly furnished rooms with refrigerator and TV. Restaurant, swimming pool. The best hotel in town. Situated two km south of the centre.

North of San Fernando
Oceana Apartments, Carlatan, Tel 2425611-13. SR/DR/ac/bath P800/1600. Two km north of San Fernando, it has indifferently furnished apartments with TV and cooking facilities. This place offers fairly favourable monthly rates.

Places to Eat

Filipino and Chinese meals at the ***Mandarin Restaurant*** and the ***Midtown Food Palace***, both on Quezon Ave near the town plaza and in the ***Crown Food Center*** in P Burgos St at the new market are good and cheap. The ***Sea & Sky Restaurant*** in the hotel of the same name on the northern edge of town, can also be recommended for its international and Filipino cuisine. Head for the town plaza for the ***Café Esperanza,*** a popular place for having a snack between meals which has also made a name for itself with its large selection of cakes. The ***Danish Baker*** on Quezon Ave sells bread and cakes, while ***Jochen's*** in the Sabado Compound, San Francisco (near the airport) is good for German bread, European delicatessen favourites and wine.

Entertainment

In San Fernando, the nightlife mainly centres around Poro Point junction, slightly outside of town. A tricycle from the town plaza costs P10. There you will find the popular nightclub-disco ***Gayyem*** as well as several rustic little bars.

Miscellaneous

Festival: City Fiesta from 7 to 10 February.
Medical Services: Lorma Medical Center, National Highway, Carlatan, Tel. 8882616.
Money: The Equitable PCI Bank and the Philippine National Bank, both in Quezon Ave, have ATMs.
Online: There is an internet café in Quezon Ave near Mr Donut about 30m off the street in the first floor of the back building.
Population: 80,000.
Post & Telephone: Post Office, Rizal Ave and Mabini St (main post office). Post code: 2500. Area code: 072.
Tourist Office, Oasis Country Resort, Sevilla, National Highway (two km south of the centre), Tel 8882411, Fax 8882098, @. Open Mon-Fri 8am-noon and 1-5pm.

Getting There & Away

By Air: The airport is about three km south-west of San Fernando. A tricycle to the town or to the beach in Bauang costs P20 to P30. At the time of writing (2004) there are however no regular flights from and to San Fernando. The nearest airport is in Baguio.

Baguio
Bus/Jeepney: From Baguio to San Fernando, there are several Philippine Rabbit and Eso-Nice Transport buses daily. It's a two-hour trip. Jeepneys also cover this route and are somewhat faster than the large buses. (See also the Getting There & Away section under Bauang earlier in this chapter.) The Eso-Nice Transport Bus Terminal in San Fernando is on the corner of Gov Luna St and Quezon Ave (town plaza).

Dagupan
Bus: From Dagupan several minibuses go to San Fernando daily (two hrs).

Laoag - Vigan
Bus: From Laoag and Vigan to San Fernando, there are several Dominion Bus Line, Fariñas Trans, Partas and Philippine Rabbit buses which go on to Manila daily. The trip takes 4½ hrs from Laoag and 2½ hrs from Vigan.

Manila - Angeles
Bus: A large number of Autobus Transport, Dominion Bus Line, Fariñas Trans,

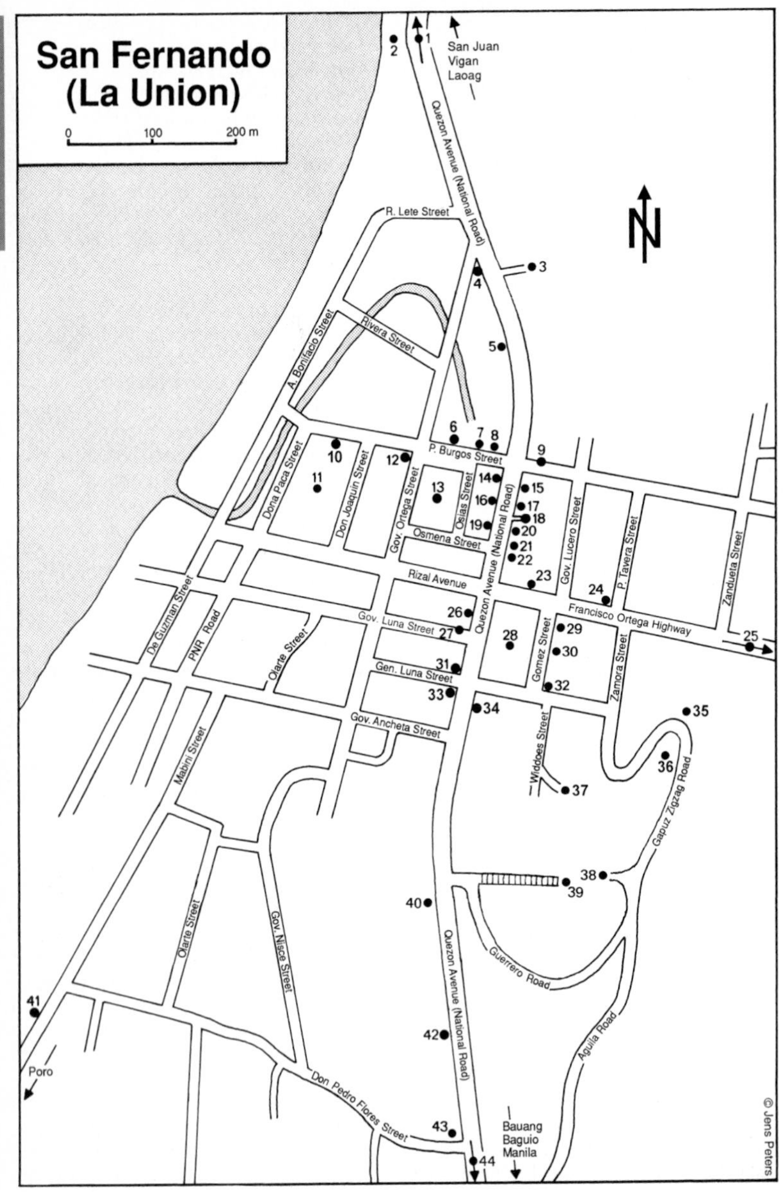
San Fernando
(La Union)
0
100
200 m
San Juan
Vigan
Laoag
Quezon Avenue (National Road)
R. Lete Street
N
Rivera Street
A. Bonifacio Street
P. Burgos Street
Dona Paca Street
Don Joaquin Street
Gov. Ortega Street
Osias Street
Osmena Street
Quezon Avenue (National Road)
Gov. Lucero Street
P. Tavera Street
Zandueta Street
Rizal Avenue
De Guzman Street
PNR Road
Olarte Street
Gov. Luna Street
Francisco Ortega Highway
Gomez Street
Zamora Street
Gen. Luna Street
Gov. Ancheta Street
Widdoes Street
Mabini Street
Gapuz Zigzag Road
Guerrero Road
Olarte Street
Gov. Nisce Street
Quezon Avenue (National Road)
Aguila Road
Poro
Don Pedro Flores Street
Bauang
Baguio
Manila
© Jens Peters
1
2
3
4
5
6
7
8
9
10
11
12
13
14
15
16
17
18
19
20
21
22
23
24
25
26
27
28
29
30
31
32
33
34
35
36
37
38
39
40
41
42
43
44

Getting There & Away
1 Viron Bus Terminal
4 Caltex Petrol Station
5 Partas Bus Terminal
9 Jeepneys to San Juan
27 Eso-Nice Transport Bus Terminal
Buses to Baguio
43 Dominion Bus Line Bus Terminal
44 Philippine Rabbit Bus Terminal (700m)

Places to Stay
2 Sea & Sky Hotel
5 Hotel Mikka
34 Plaza Hotel
35 Bayview Hotel
44 Oasis Country Resort (2 km)

Places to Eat & Entertainment
7 New United Food Palace
12 Dunkin' Donuts
14 Greenwich, Jollibee
16 Midtown Food Palace
17 Mr Donut
20 Mandarin Restaurant
31 Jollibee
32 Café Esperanza
33 KFC
34 Dunkin' Donuts
35 High Altitude Disco
42 McDonald's

Miscellaneous
1 Lorma Medical Center (700m)
3 Ma-Cho Tempel
8 Fiesta Supermart
6 Julie's Bake Shop
10 Malayan Bookstore
11 New Market
13 Old Market
15 Mercury Drug
18 Internet Café
19 The Danish Baker
21 Police Station
22 La Union Trade Center
23 Town Hall
24 Post Office
25 La Union Botanical Gardens (7 km)
26 Philippine National Bank (PNB)
28 Town Plaza
29 Christ the King College
30 St William Cathedral
31 Equitable PCI Bank
36 Fil-Chinese Pagoda
37 Bethany Hospital
38 Provincial Capitol
Museo de La Union
39 Freedom Park (Heroes Hill)
40 Bank of the Philippine Islands
41 Post Office
44 Tourist Office (2 km)

Partas and Philippine Rabbit buses go from Manila to San Fernando daily (P250; seven hrs). Buses going to Vigan and Laoag also go through San Fernando. The route goes through Dau/ Angeles, where you can also board the bus.

San Juan

About five to 10 km north of San Fernando near the small town of San Juan, a wide, long, clean beach with good surfing conditions, not surprisingly known as Surf Beach, stretches along the coast. Surfing season is from July until September and from November until March. Along with Baler, Catanduanes, Daet and Siargao Island, San Juan is one of the most popular surfing areas in the Philippines.

At Tabok, two km north of San Juan, street traders offer a wide variety of locally-made pottery for sale. The Don Mariano State College is located about eight km further north-east, off the main road in wooded mountains at 600m above sea level. The Agricultural Training Development Center (ATDC) there is interesting, where the students

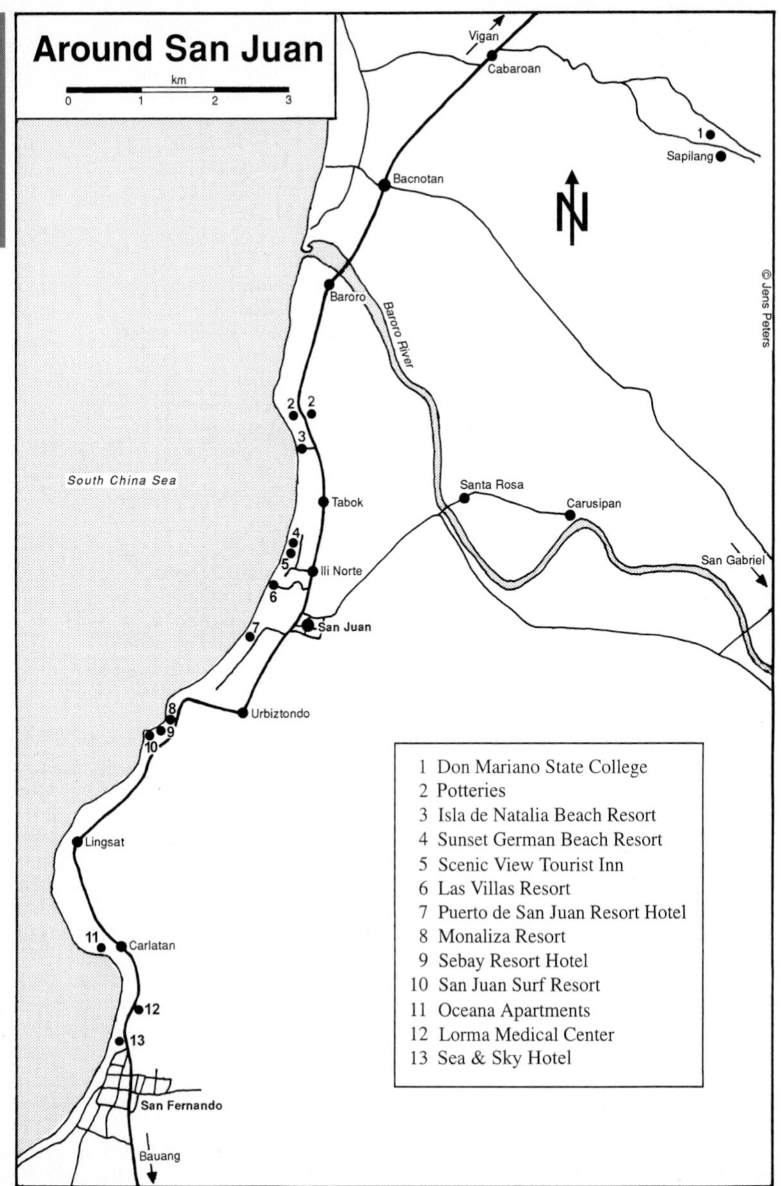

Around San Juan
km
0
1
2
3
Vigan
Cabaroan
Sapilang
Bacnotan
N
Baroro
Baroro River
© Jens Peters
South China Sea
Tabok
Santa Rosa
Carusipan
Ili Norte
San Gabriel
San Juan
Urbiztondo
Lingsat
Carlatan
San Fernando
Bauang
1 Don Mariano State College
2 Potteries
3 Isla de Natalia Beach Resort
4 Sunset German Beach Resort
5 Scenic View Tourist Inn
6 Las Villas Resort
7 Puerto de San Juan Resort Hotel
8 Monaliza Resort
9 Sebay Resort Hotel
10 San Juan Surf Resort
11 Oceana Apartments
12 Lorma Medical Center
13 Sea & Sky Hotel

study bee-keeping. The main kinds of honey gathered here are the dark narra honey and light sunflower honey. Jeepneys with the sign 'Sapilang' go up there from Bacnotan. The whole way directly to the ATDC costs P5 extra.

Places to Stay

San Juan Surf Resort, Urbiztondo, Tel 2424544, Fax 2426149, @. Dorm P150, SR/DR/fan P400, SR/DR/fan/bath P600, cottage/fan/bath with refrigerator and cooking facilities P700, SR/DR/ac/bath P900 and P1100. Discount from April to June. A pleasant little establishment with a good view of the beach.

Scenic View Tourist Inn, Montemar Village, Ili Norte, Tel 2422906. Dorm/fan P250, SR/DR/fan/bath P525, SR/DR/ac/bath P700, all including breakfast. Basically furnished, but OK rooms, most with a veranda. There is no direct access to the beach, so you have to take a short detour. Located directly next to the Sunset German Beach Resort.

Sunset German Beach Resort, Montemar Village, Ili Norte, Tel & Fax 8884719, @. Cottage/fan/bath P550, SR/DR/ac/bath P750, suite P1500. Rugged little stone cottages with friendly rooms. The suite comprises a living room, bedroom and balcony, and has a TV. This is a small, well-tended resort with plants all over the place. They have a very good restaurant which serves excellent Filipino and international cuisine as well as home made bread and their own cold meats. Surfboard hire (only for guests; P40 an hr). Located roughly one km north of San Juan.

Sebay Resort Hotel, Urbiztondo, Tel 2425484, Fax 2425482, @. SR/DR/fan/bath P450, SR/DR/ac/bath P700. Reasonable rooms with no special comforts added. Restaurant, music lounge.

Las Villas Resort, Montemar Village, Ili Norte, Tel 2423770, Fax 2423769, @. SR/DR/ac/bath P1000 to P2500. Pleasant, well looked after rooms. Attractive, Spanish-style buildings. Good restaurant, small swimming pool. Located 700m outside of San Juan.

Puerto de San Juan Resort Hotel, Ili Sur, Tel 2423330, Fax 2423331, @. SR/DR/ac/bath P1800 and P2000, cottage/ac/bath with two bedrooms and a living room P4000. Comfortably furnished rooms with TV. The resort covers a large area and is well-maintained, although it could do with a few plants (lots of concrete). Restaurant, swimming pool. They have their own little church on the premises.

Miscellaneous

Population: 6000.

Post & Telephone: Post code: 2514. Area code: 072.

Getting There & Away

If you want to go to a resort in Montemar Village, best get off about one km north of San Juan at the turn-off in Ili Norte and walk the remaining 500m.

A tricycle from the town centre in San Juan to a resort in Montemar Village costs P10.

Laoag - Vigan

Bus: All buses that travel between Manila and Vigan and Laoag go through San Juan. It takes four hrs from Laoag and two hrs from Vigan.

Manila - Angeles

Bus: The Autobus Transport, Dominion Bus Line, Fariñas Trans, Partas and Philippine Rabbit buses with Bangued, Vigan and Laoag on the front go from Manila to San Juan daily (7½ hrs). The route goes through Dau/Angeles, where you can also board the bus.

San Fernando

Jeepney: Several jeepneys travel every day from San Fernando to San Juan, leaving from the corner of P Burgos St and Quezon Ave (30 min). The signs on them could say 'Bacnotan' or 'Sapilang'.

Tricycle: A tricycle from San Fernando to one of the resorts in Montemar Village should cost no more than P100.

Central Cordillera

Baguio

Baguio (pronounced Bag-ee-o with a hard 'g') is the summer capital of the Philippines. This City of Pines, City of Flowers or City of Lovers, as it is also known, is certainly the most popular place for Filipinos to travel. Filipinos who can afford it move to this town, which is at an altitude of 1500m, during the hot summer months. Easter is the busiest time by a long chalk, and some hotels may raise their prices. There are supposed to be 300,000 visitors, but it's a mystery where they all stay. They rave about the zigzag road (Kennon Rd) and the cooler climate.
From March until May, Baguio shows itself from its best side and displays all the flair of a typical holiday resort. But in the cold months, like December and January, there's not much to hang around there for. The frothy Philippine atmosphere with the relaxed jollity of the lowland Filipinos is missing then: the people you meet in the streets at night are a cheerless lot in their woolly jackets, in contrast to their usual laughing faces and colourful T-shirts with cheeky slogans. Apart from the climate, which is around ten degrees cooler here, most likely the hard life in the mountains is another reason for people to be less laid-back.
A massive earthquake, which shook the north of Luzon on 16 July 1990, also caused a lot of serious damage in Baguio. Roads, schools, hotels and private houses were partially or completely destroyed - the pictures went around the world. Since then most places have either been repaired or demolished and rebuilt, so that visitors will hardly notice any of the damage caused by this natural catastrophe.

Baguio-Benguet Mountain Province Museum

This small museum in Governor Rd, next to the Tourist Office, gives a vivid picture of the life of the cultural minorities in the Central Cordillera. Ethnographic artefacts like wood carvings, baskets, jewellery, pottery and weaving work are on display here. Open Tue-Sun 9am-noon and 1.30-5pm. Admission P20.

Burnham Park

Burnham Park has a small artificial lake in the middle of town. It is named after Daniel H Burnham, the town planner of Baguio. There are boats for hire, a children's playground and an orchidarium (across from the Benguet Pine Tourist Inn). Be careful at night, as people have been attacked here.

St Louis Filigree Shop

Young silversmiths are trained at the St Louis University trade school. You can watch them make the finest filigree. Their work is sold in the St Louis Filigree Shop at fixed prices, but not all have a hallmark. If you want one, arrange to get it while you are there. Open Mon-Sat 8am-noon and 1-5pm.

Easter School of Weaving

The Easter School of Weaving is on the north-western outskirts of Baguio. The weavers make tablecloths and clothing, and you can watch them at work. The prices can be a bit expensive here.
Jeepneys leave from Kayang St or from Chugum St, on the corner of Otek St.

Camp John Hay

Located on the southeast edge of town, Camp John Hay was a Recreation Base

for the US Army. It was given back to the Philippines in July, 1991, and has been run since 1993 as a 'Resort & Recreation Area' by the Bases Conversion Development Authority (BCDA). Despite being renamed Club John Hay, the 695 hectare area is still frequently referred to by its former name.
Camp John Hay and its sports facilities such as a golf course, a swimming pool, and tennis courts, are open to the public. At the heart of the well-maintained former base area are the Baguio Country Club and the stylish Camp John Hay Manor Hotel.
Of special interest is the quirky 'Cemetery of Negativism', left behind by the Americans, where bad habits are 'buried' under amusing gravestones - a piece of real, downhome American philosophy.
Camp John Hay can be reached from the city centre by jeepney from Kayang St or by taxi to the main gate. Jeepneys and taxis also drive on the camp grounds themselves.

Baguio Botanical Gardens, Wright Park & Mines View Park

Unfortunately, all that is left of the different types of houses of the Central Cordillera, which used to be on view in the botanical gardens one km out of town, is a broken-down Ifugao hut. There is also a handicrafts centre with a souvenir shop - a rather touristy affair. You can combine a trip to the botanical gardens with an excursion to Wright Park, where you can go horseback riding, and to the Mines View Park, 2½ km out of town, behind the Baguio Botanical Gardens, for a beautiful panoramic view of the valley and the mountains. (You do have to work your way through crowds of souvenir stalls before you get to the viewpoint.)
To get there, take a jeepney from Magsaysay Ave, opposite the city market, or from Harrison Rd, on the corner of Perfecto St.

Tam-awan Village

About two km north-west of the town centre a replica of an Ifugao village has been built on the side of a hill. It is possible to stay overnight in these original Ifugao houses, the brainchild of the Chanum Foundation, a group of artists who are dedicated to preserving and nurturing the native culture in the Cordilleras. There are demonstrations there of handcraft skills such as weaving and wood carving as well as rice wine production. Admission P20.

Bell Church

There is a Chinese temple a little to the north of town in the direction of La Trinidad (capital of Benguet Province). The temple is run by the Bell Church Sect, which believes in a mixture of Buddhist, Taoist, Confucian and Christian doctrines. You can have your fortune told by one of the priests.
To get to Bell Church, catch a jeepney from Magsaysay Ave, on the corner of Bonifacio St.

Faith Healers

The mass media have given much coverage to the practices of the Filipino faith healers, who 'open' the skin of the patient with their fingers and 'operate' with their bare hands - a dubious business. But as faith can move mountains, there are always sufferers who come from all over the world to Baguio to be saved. If you aren't put off by blood or bad smells, you can always watch one of these miracles.
According to critical reports in some Western mass media, however, most of these healers don't like to be watched too closely. If they do let you, then it is only for a hefty fee. Taxi drivers can usually organise a visit.

Shopping

At the big City Market you can mostly buy local products made or grown in

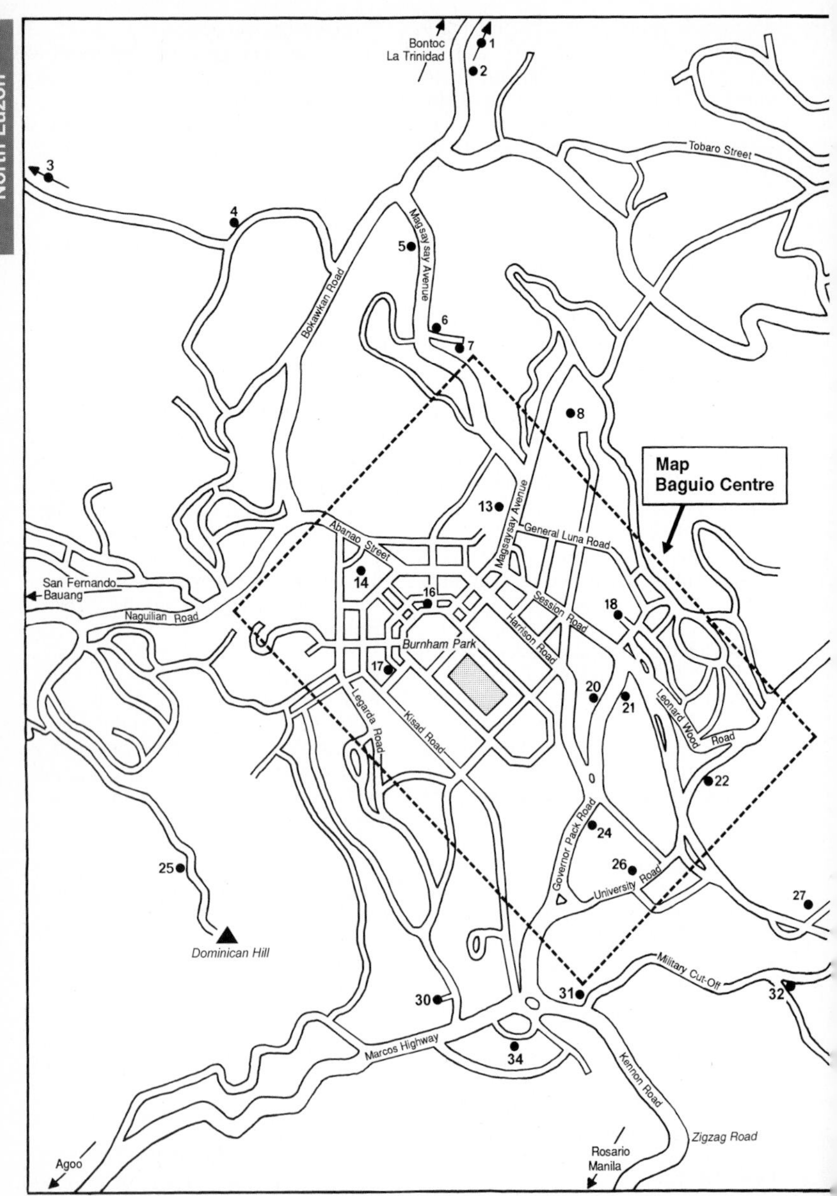

Bontoc
La Trinidad
Tobaro Street
Magsaysay Avenue
Bokawkan Road
Map
Baguio Centre
General Luna Road
Abanao Street
San Fernando
Bauang
Naguilian Road
Session Road
Harrison Road
Burnham Park
Legarda Road
Kisad Road
Leonard Wood Road
Governor Pack Road
University Road
Dominican Hill
Military Cut-Off
Marcos Highway
Kennon Road
Zigzag Road
Rosario
Manila
Agoo

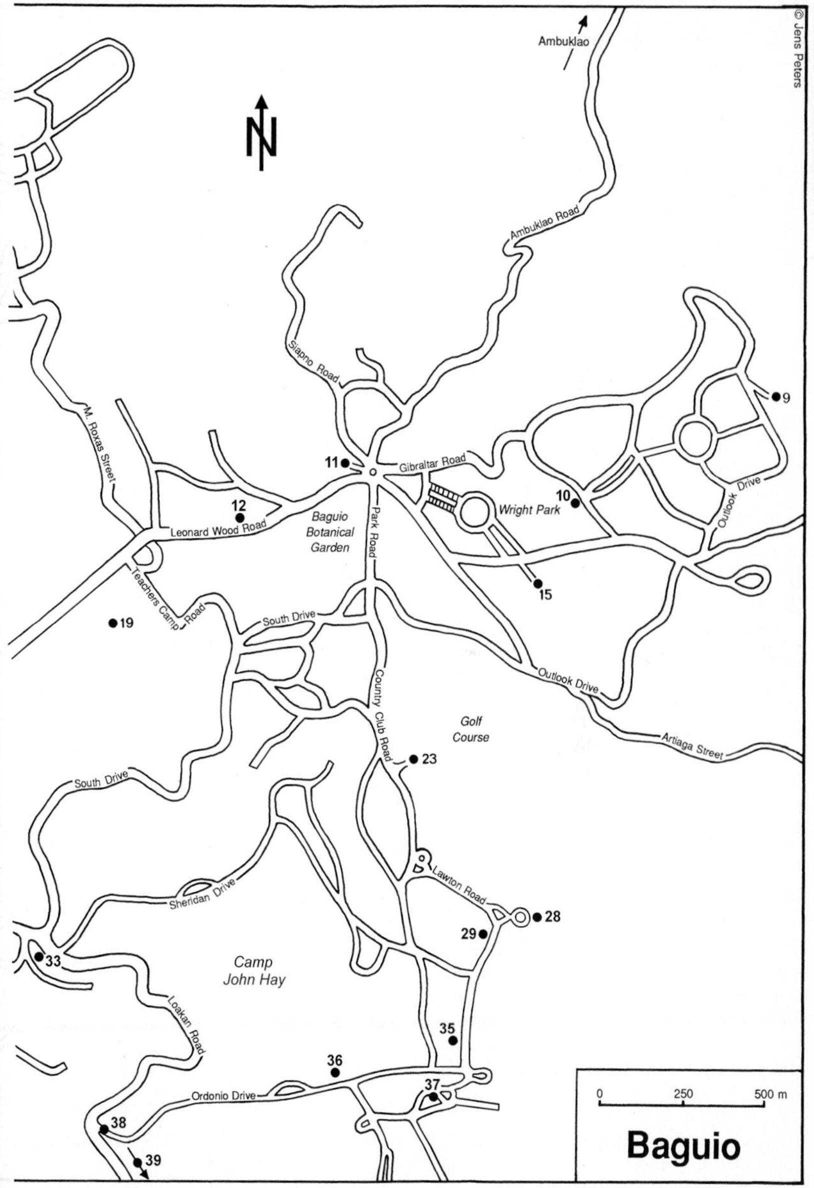
© Jens Peters
Ambuklao
Ambuklao Road
Siapno Road
M. Roxas Street
Gibraltar Road
Leonard Wood Road
Baguio
Botanical
Garden
Park Road
Wright Park
Outlook Drive
Teachers Camp Road
South Drive
Outlook Drive
Country Club Road
Golf
Course
Artiaga Street
South Drive
Lawton Road
Sheridan Drive
Camp
John Hay
Loakan Road
Ordonio Drive
0
250
500 m
Baguio
9
10
11
12
15
19
23
28
29
33
35
36
37
38
39

Getting There & Away

6 D'Rising Sun Bus Terminal
Northern Trans Bus Terminal
Norton Trans Bus Terminal
16 Eso-Nice Transport Bus Terminal
17 KMS Bus Terminal
20 Autobus Transport Bus Terminal
Byron Bus Bus Terminal
Dagupan Bus Bus Terminal
Partas Bus Terminal
Philippine Rabbit Bus Terminal
21 Ohayami Trans Bus Terminal
27 Victory Liner Bus Terminal
39 Loakan Airport (4 km)

Places to Stay

2 Hotel Supreme
5 Baguio Village Inn
10 Richwood Residence Hotel
12 Club Safari Lodge
22 El Cielito Inn
27 Microtel Inn & Suites
30 Concorde Hotel
32 Woods Place Inn
35 Camp John Hay Manor Hotel

Places to Eat & Entertainment

7 Balajadias Restaurant
D'Popular Restaurant
Pilipino First Restaurant
Ramos Restaurant
Tano's Restaurant
22 The Voyagers Restaurant
33 Nevada Square Bars

Miscellaneous

1 Bell Church
3 Tam-awan Village
4 Easter Weaving Room
9 Mines View Park
8 St Louis University
11 St Joseph Church
13 City Market
14 City Hall
Post Office
15 Mansion House
18 Cathedral
19 Teacher's Camp
23 Baguio Country Club
24 Tourist Office
Baguio-Benguet Mountain Province Museum
25 Lourdes Grotto
26 University of the Philippines (UP)
28 MacArthur Park View Point
29 Tennis Courts
31 Baguio Medical Center
34 Baguio General Hospital
36 Swimming Pool, Tennis Courts
37 Liberty Park
Cemetery of Negativism
38 Club John Hay Main Gate
39 Philippine Military Academy (4 km)

Benguet Province, the area around Baguio. You will find basketware, textiles, silver jewellery and woodcarvings as well as vegetables, fruit, honey and so on at this wonderful market. Look out for the strawberries and the sweet, heavy strawberry wine. In the meat section, the grinning dog heads are no longer on sale. After strong international criticism, this highland delicacy was forbidden by the government, so dog meat is no longer prominently displayed at markets where Westerners go.

The traditional arts & crafts of the mountain dwellers are sold in the adjoining Maharlika Livelihood Center, a large complex with numerous shops. You can buy woodcarvings at more reasonable prices there, direct from the makers in the so-called Woodcarver's Village. You'll find it on Asin Rd, about four or five km west of Baguio (jeepney from Kayang St).

Places to Stay - bottom end

Highland Lodge, General Luna Rd, Tel 4427086. SR P200, DR P400, SR/DR/bath P600. Not only because the rooms are small and the walls thin, this is pretty low-end accommodation by any standards, although the people are friendly. There is no restaurant, but there is room service.

Hotel 45, 58 Session Rd, Tel 4426634. SR P250, DR P400, SR/DR/bath P500 and P600 (TV). Quite good rooms, some with no windows. This is the former Baguio Goodwill Lodge.

Benguet Pine Tourist Inn, 82 Chanum St corner Otek St, Tel 4427325. Dorm P300, SR/DR P500, SR/DR/bath P800 and P1000. Basically furnished rooms. Fairly quiet, popular place in this category. Restaurant.

Places to Stay - middle

Burnham Hotel, 20 Calderon St, Tel 4422331, Fax 4428415. SR/DR/bath P985 and P1100. Quiet, cosy rooms, the more expensive ones also have a refrigerator. A fine, tastefully decorated hotel. Restaurant.

Mountain Lodge, 27 Leonard Wood Rd, Tel 4424544, Fax 4426175, @. SR/bath P1000, DR/bath P1200 and P1400 (with TV and open fireplace). East of the town centre, this pleasant hotel is fairly good value, offering quiet and comfortable accommodation in a family atmosphere. Restaurant.

Aussie Hotel, General Luna Rd corner Leonard Wood Rd, Tel 4425139, @. SR/fan/bath P1325, DR/fan/bath P1525. Good rooms with TV. A nice place to stay, popular with expats. Pub and restaurant.

El Cielito Inn, North Dr, Tel 4428743, @. SR/DR/bath P1425 and P1700, suite P2690. Clean, pleasingly furnished rooms with TV, the better ones also have a balcony. Restaurant.

Hotel Veniz, Abanao St, Tel 4460700, Fax 4460704. SR/DR/fan/bath P1300 P, SR/DR/ac/bath P1500 to P2200, suite P2500 to P3600. Good, pleasant hotel with comfortable, nicely furnished rooms with TV. Underground parking.

Belfranlt Hotel, General Luna St, Tel 4425012, 4424298. SR/DR/bath P1500; including breakfast. Spacious, tidy rooms with TV. Restaurant.

Benguet Prime Hotel, Calderon St corner Session Rd, Tel 4427066, Fax 4428132. SR/DR/bath P1500 and P1800. With TV, some with refrigerator; all including breakfast. Prime hotel in a prime location, but sadly past its prime.

Hotel Supreme, 113 Magsaysay Ave, Tel 4432011, Fax 4422855, @. SR/DR /bath P1500, suite P1890; including breakfast. Pleasant rooms with TV, the suites also have a refrigerator and cooking facilities. Quiet, good hotel. Restaurant, heated swimming pool. Located just outside town.

Baguio Palace Hotel, Legarda Rd, Tel 4427734, Fax 4436622. SR/DR/bath P1500 and P1600, suite P2900. Good rooms with TV. Friendly service. Chinese restaurant.

Places to Stay - top end

Prince Plaza Hotel, Legarda Rd, Tel 4425082, Fax 4425093. SR/DR/bath P1700, suite P3000 and P3500 (living room, two bedrooms, cooking facilities). Immaculate rooms with TV, nearly all have a balcony. Good hotel. Restaurant.

Golden Pine Hotel, Legarda Rd corner Cariño St. Tel & Fax 4449965. SR/DR/bath P2000 and P2100, suite P3800; including breakfast. Well-kept hotel with friendly, spacious rooms with TV, the suites also have a refrigerator. Restaurant.

Concorde Hotel, Europa Center, Legarda Rd, Tel 4432058, Fax 4432060, @. SR/DR/bath P1800 to P3000, suite P4000. Rustic, cosily furnished rooms, some with carved furniture. The com-

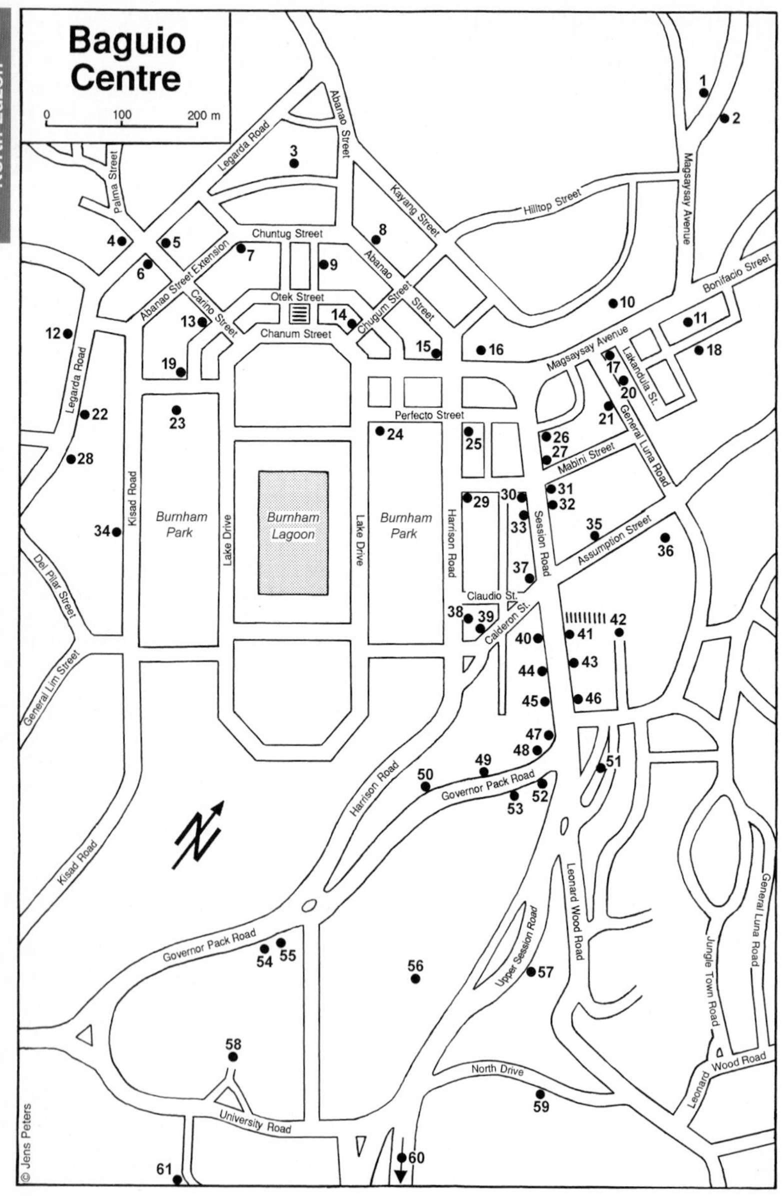

Baguio Centre
0 100 200 m
Legarda Road
Abanao Street
Palma Street
Kayang Street
Hilltop Street
Magsaysay Avenue
Chuntug Street
Abanao Street Extension
Abanao Street
Otek Street
Chugum Street
Carino Street
Chanum Street
Bonifacio Street
Lakandula St.
General Luna Road
Perfecto Street
Mabini Street
Burnham Park
Burnham Lagoon
Lake Drive
Kisad Road
Harrison Road
Session Road
Assumption Street
Claudio St.
Calderon St.
Del Pilar Street
General Lim Street
Governor Pack Road
Leonard Wood Road
Upper Session Road
Jungle Town Road
North Drive
University Road
© Jens Peters

Getting There & Away
14 Eso-Nice Transport Bus Terminal
18 Dangwa Tranco Bus Terminal
   Lizardo Trans Bus Terminal
19 KMS Bus Terminal
38 Avis
46 Asian Spirit
49 Autobus Transport Bus Terminal
   Byron Bus Bus Terminal
   Dagupan Bus Bus Terminal
   Partas Bus Terminal
50 Philippine Rabbit Bus Terminal
53 Ohayami Trans Bus Terminal
60 Victory Liner Bus Terminal (300m)

Places to Stay
1 Leisure Lodge
4 Mount Crest Hotel
5 Golden Pine Hotel
12 Forest Inn Hotel
   Holiday Villa Court Hotel
15 Hotel Veniz
17 Villa Rosal Hotel
19 Benguet Pine Tourist Inn
20 Belfranlt Hotel
21 Highland Lodge
22 Prince Plaza Hotel
26 Mido Inn
28 Baguio Palace Hotel
33 Hotel 45
34 Venus Parkview Hotel
37 Benguet Prime Hotel
39 Burnham Hotel
48 Baden Powell Inn
59 El Cielito Inn
60 Microtel Inn & Suites (300m)

Places to Eat & Entertainment
4 Café Legarda
   Gimbal's Music Lounge
6 Alberto's
7 Café by the Ruins
8 50's Diner
9 Padi's Point
11 456 Restaurant
   Dunkin' Donuts
   McDonald's
12 Joey's Place
13 Spirits
16 Café Teria
   Fast Food Center
24 The New Ganza Steak & Chicken House
25 Rose Bowl Restaurant
26 Chowking
   Sunshine Restaurant
27 Star Café
28 Mr Ching Cuisine Restaurant
30 McDonald's
32 Rumours
33 456 Restaurant
35 Cozy Nook Restaurant
37 Jollibee
39 Cook's Inn Restaurant
40 Sizzling Plate Restaurant
41 Ionic Café
   Swiss Baker
   Mister Donut
   Solibao Restaurant
43 Don Henrico's
44 Le Fondue
   Shakey's Pizza
   Swiss Made
45 KFC
   Kowloon House
46 Kenny Rogers
52 Jollibee
57 Barrio Fiesta

Miscellaneous
2 Equitable PCI Bank
3 City Hall, Post Office
4 Cyberspace Café
10 City Market
11 Center Mall
15 Sunshine Department Store
16 Maharlika Livelihood Center
23 Orchidarium
29 Bank of the Philippine Islands
31 Philippine National Bank (PNB)
36 St Louis Filigree Shop
37 Benguet Supermarket
42 Cathedral
45 Equitable PCI Bank
47 Bank of the Philippine Islands

51 Post Office
54 Tourist Office
55 Baguio-Benguet Mountain Province Museum
56 SM Baguio
58 University of the Philippines (UP)
60 Camp John Hay (1 km)
61 Convention Center

fortable suites have TV, refrigerator and balcony. A very tastefully decorated hotel, set back a little from the road (driveway). Restaurant, fitness room, disco at the weekends.

Microtel Inn & Suites, Upper Session Rd, Tel 6193333, Fax 6193344, @. SR/ac/bath P3200, DR/ac/bath P3800, suite P4600, all including breakfast. Very good hotel with modern furnishings and spotless rooms, all with TV, the suites also with refrigerator and small kitchen. Located next to the Victory Liner Bus Terminal.

Camp John Hay Manor Hotel, Camp John Hay, Tel 4460231, Fax 4450420. SR/DR/bath P4000 to P6000, suite (five people) P9000. Comfortably furnished rooms of various sizes, with refrigerator and TV, nearly all with a balcony. This attractive hotel with its elegantly rustic architecture was designed to blend naturally into the surrounding nature. It's the best place to stay in Baguio. Restaurant. Piano Bar. Palm Garden Health Spa (massage, sauna).

Places to Eat

The simple restaurant in the Dangwa Tranco Bus Terminal serves good and cheap Filipino cuisine. The so-called slaughterhouse restaurants, next to the slaughterhouse on Balajadia St, are also simply furnished. However, they offer excellent meat dishes at reasonable prices, so the locals have every reason to frequent them as often as they do. The ***Balajadias Restaurant*** with its tasty Philippine food can be recommended.

The ***Rose Bowl*** on Harrison Rd and ***Mr Ching Cuisine*** at the Baguio Palace Hotel, Legarda Rd, are two of the best Chinese restaurants in town. The ***New Ganza Steak & Chicken House*** is in Burnham Park and has tables outside.

There are other restaurants of varying quality and price on Session Rd. Head for ***Don Henrico's*** for great pizzas, while the ***Swiss Baker*** is the place for a proper breakfast and tasty cakes. The same goes for the popular ***Star Café*** where they will also spoil you with big portions of Chinese food. The ***Swiss Made*** serves several European specialities, sandwiches, salads and good coffee and cakes.

The Philippine dishes in the ***Barrio Fiesta*** in Upper Session Rd are tasty and good value. Session Rd is also the location for a wide range of fast-food outlets such as ***McDonald's***, ***Chowking***, ***KFC***, and ***Shakey's***. Even more can be found in the ***SM Baguio*** shopping centre in Upper Session Rd. If you would like to try traditional Cordillera cooking and drinks, then the unconventional ***Café by the Ruins*** opposite the town hall is the place to go. This bamboo restaurant is tastefully decorated with plants and traditional artwork, and its menu consists mainly of seasonal specialities, served with tapuy (rice wine), basi or salabat (ginger tea) - a request for San Miguel beer will only get you raised eyebrows here.

Entertainment

A particular favourite with the young folk is ***Padi's Point*** ('The Party Place') near Otek St, with special events such as drinking contests, dancing competitions and live music every night; admission: up to P200, depending on

the entertainment on offer. Live music (three bands in the evening) also in the big and popular ***Alberto's*** in Cariño St corner Legarda Rd. Obviously several places in Legarda Rd have been opened up that offer live music.
You'll always find a good crowd at karaoke bars, eg ***Joey's Place*** on Legarda Rd and the ***Cozy Nook*** on Assumption Rd.
The ***Café Legarda*** in the Mount Crest Hotel in Legarda Rd at the corner of Urbano St provides a sophisticated ambience where the guests are entertained by subdued piano music, while ***Gimbal's Music Lounge*** is quite a few points higher in volume, with live rock from Tuesday to Sunday; admission free.
Popular bars are ***Rumours*** in Session Rd and ***Spirits*** in Otek St, the latter located in a magnificent building that is impressively lit up in the evening. On ***Nevada Square***, a bit out of the town centre heading for Camp John Hay, you'll find a swathe of bars clustered together, with music you won't be able to avoid hearing.

Miscellaneous

Festival: Baguio Flower Festival (Panagbenga) either the whole third or fourth week in February.
Medical Services: The St Louis Hospital (SLU Hospital of the Sacred Heart), Assumption Rd, Tel 4425700 provides good care.
Money: Various textile traders at the market will change US-dollars (cash) at a good rate (shop around though).
Bank of the Philippine Islands, Session Rd and Harrison Rd corner Mabini St, Equitable PCI Bank, Session Rd and Magsaysay Ave, and Philippine National Bank, Session Rd, have ATMs.
Online: Cyberspace Café, Mount Crest Hotel, Legarda Rd corner Urbano St; P100/hr, calculated by the minute.
Population: 230,000.
Post & Telephone: Post Office, Session Rd.
Post code: 2600. Area code: 074.
Tourist Office, Governor Pack Rd, Tel 4427014, Fax 4228848, @. Open Mon-Sat 8am-noon and 1-6pm.

Getting Around

Car: Avis, Padilla Building, Harrison Rd, Tel 4424018.

Getting There & Away

By Air: Loakan Airport is about eight km south of Baguio. If you're catching a flight to Manila, you can get a jeepney from Baguio to the airport which leaves from Mabini Rd, between Session and Harrison Rds. From the airport back into town, the jeepneys leave from Loakan Rd, about 100m from the airport building on the right.
Asian Spirit, Loakan Airport, Tel 4473914.
- Session Rd, Tel 4460001.
Destination: Manila.

By Bus: The bus terminals of the companies Autobus Transport, Byron Bus, Dagupan Bus, Ohayami Trans, Partas and Philippine Rabbit are all in Governor Pack Rd, those belonging to Dangwa Tranco, GL Trans and Lizardo Trans are in Magsaysay Ave (set a bit back). D'Rising Sun, Northern Trans and Norton Trans have their terminals in Balajadia Rd, a little street near the slaughterhouse. Eso-Nice buses leave from Chugum St, KMS buses from Otek St (near the Benguet Pine Tourist Inn), and Victory Liner check people in at their own Baguio Passenger Center in Upper Session Rd.

By Car: If you're arriving by car or by taxi, remember that there are restrictions (color-coded days) in the centre of Baguio (Central Business District) for certain vehicles from Monday to Friday. Vehicles with the following last numbers on their plates are not allowed to drive on the respective days: 1 and 2 on Mondays; 3 and 4 on Tuesdays; 5 and 6 on Wednesdays; 7 and 8 on Thursdays and 9 and 0 on Fridays.

By Motorcycle: Session Rd in Baguios Central Business District is closed to motorbikes.

Banaue
Bus: From Banaue to Baguio buses belonging to various companies take the southern route via Bayombong, San Jose and Villasis (nine hrs). Dangwa Transport used to leave between 6 and 7.30am, but as of early 2004 had (temporarily?) withdrawn from this route; information: Tel (074) 4422449. KMS leaves at 3pm and Ohayami Trans at 4pm.
Departure from Baguio: Dangwa Tranco (if operating) 10am, KMS 7.30am, Ohayami Trans 8pm.

Bauang
See below: *San Fernando (La Union) - Bauang*

Bontoc
Bus: From Bontoc, Dangwa Tranco and D'Rising Sun buses run daily to Baguio, leaving at 6, 7, 8 and possibly 9.15am and 4pm (eight hrs).

Dagupan
Bus: From Dagupan to Baguio, there are plenty of Byron Bus buses every day, leaving every half hour from 6am to 4pm, and Dagupan Bus and Philippine Rabbit also make the trip (two hrs).

Laoag
Bus: Philippine Rabbit buses run from Laoag to Baguio via Vigan and San Fernando (La Union) roughly every hour between 1.30am and 10.30pm. Aircon buses leave at 7.30 and 8.30am and 2.30pm (six hrs).

Manila - Angeles
Air: Asian Spirit flies Monday, Wednesday, Friday and Sunday from Manila to Baguio and vice versa (P1950; one hr).

Bus: From Manila to Baguio, there are plenty of Dagupan Bus, Partas, Philippine Rabbit and Victory Liner buses daily (P260; 6½ hrs). The route goes via Dau/Angeles, where you can also board the bus.
From Baguio to Manila takes about 30 min less than the other way round as the first stretch of road is downhill. Driving down Kennon Rd ('Zigzag Road') you pass a huge lion's head cut into stone on the left-hand side of the road. This is the Lion's Club Welcome Marker.

Olongapo - Angeles
Bus: From Olongapo, you can get to Baguio by Victory Liner bus. These leave hourly (six hrs). They go through Angeles, where you can also board the bus.

San Fernando (La Union) - Bauang
Bus/Jeepney: From San Fernando, several Philippine Rabbit and Eso-Nice Transport buses travel daily to Baguio (two hrs). They go via Bauang, where you can also board the bus. You can also take a jeepney.

Sagada
Bus: From Sagada, GT Trans and Lizardo Trans buses run daily to Baguio, leaving at 5, 6, 6.30, 7, 8, 9 and 10am, and at 1pm (P190; seven hrs).

Tuguegarao
Bus: Three Autobus Transport buses leave Tuguegarao daily in the afternoon for Baguio (P320; 10 hrs).

Warning
Buses and private vehicles from Sagada and other places in Mountain Province have sometimes been stopped

Climbing Mt Pulag

Mt Pulag is 15 km south-east of Kabayan and at 2,922m the highest mountain on Luzon island and the second-highest in the Philippines (after Mt Apo on Mindanao; 2,953m). Four popular trails lead from Kabayan and the surrounding area up to the 11,500 hectare Mt Pulag National Park:

Ambangeg Trail (Babadak Trail)**:** The easist way to the summit, doable as a day trip. From Ambangeg/Bokod, where you first have to register at the Protected Area Office (park entrance fee: P800, Filipinos P100, seniors free) and be allotted a guide (P500), a paved road leads to the Ranger Station in Babadak (12 km). From there it's about another three hrs to the summit (4 km). You can stay the night quite comfortably in the Visitor Center in Ambangeg for P100.

Ellet Trail: From the Ellet Bridge, five km south of Kabayan, via Ellet (aka Eddet), Abukot (sawmill) and past Lake Lebang to the Ranger Station and to the summit.

Kabayan Trail (Akiki Trail)**:** From barangay Akiki, two km south of Kabayan. This is the shortest but most difficult way to the summit. It's also known as the Killer Trail and you definitely have to be fit to manage it.

Tawangan Trail: Nine km north of Kabayan a track leads from the main road to the village of Ballay and from there via Tawangan to Mt Pulag.

Best time to visit: March and April, the rainiest time is in July and August.

by military and Narcotic Commission (NARCOM) officials searching passenger luggage for marijuana.

Kabayan

Kabayan is well known for the many burial caves of the local Ibaloy tribe. There are mummies with their legs hunched up against their bodies lying in hollow tree trunks which serve as coffins. Some are said to be at least 500 years old. Because several caves were plundered in the 1970s, the nearest and best known of them have since been sealed. Those that are still open can only be reached with guides after long hikes. You can also see a few mummies in a small museum in the town hall.

Places to Stay

Multi-Purpose Cooperative (Coop). SR/DR/fan P100 per Person. Basic rooms.

Otherwise, there's only private accommodation available, eg the Berong family accept guests. Payment is voluntary. Mr Berong is an expert on the burial caves.

Getting There & Away

Baguio

Bus: Norton Trans buses leave Baguio for Kabayan at 9.00 and 10.00 am and 12 noon (6½ hrs). There is probably still no connection for Abatan to the north. To get there, you have to walk over to the Halsema road or take the bus back to Baguio the next day at 7, 9 or 10am and 1pm.

Banaue

Bus/Jeepney: There is no direct route between Kabayan and Banaue, but the journey can be done in five stages. First, catch a Norton Trans bus at 7 or 9am heading for Baguio, change in Bangao into a bus belonging to the same company going to Bambang (it will have come from Baguio and waited for your bus from Kabayan). From Bam-

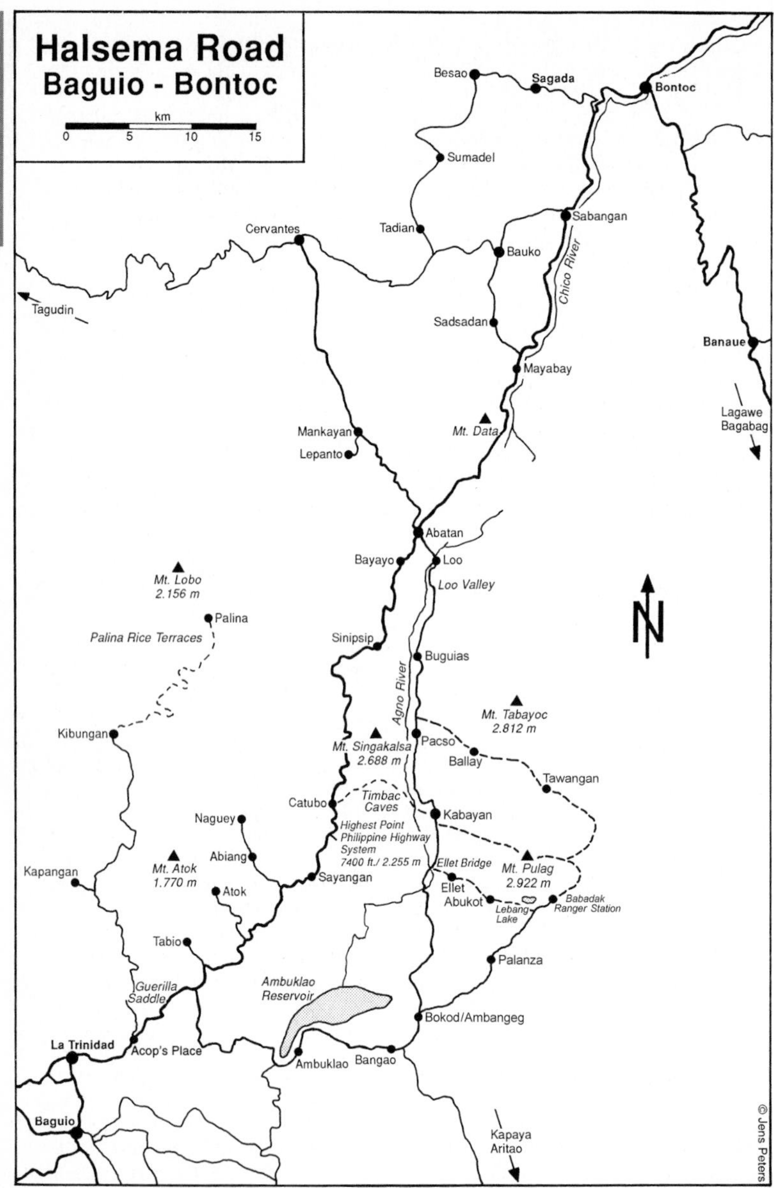
Halsema Road
Baguio - Bontoc
km
0 5 10 15
Besao
Sagada
Bontoc
Sumadel
Sabangan
Tadian
Cervantes
Bauko
Chico River
Tagudin
Sadsadan
Banaue
Mayabay
Lagawe
Bagabag
Mt. Data
Mankayan
Lepanto
Abatan
Bayayo
Loo
Loo Valley
Mt. Lobo
2.156 m
Palina
Palina Rice Terraces
Sinipsip
Buguias
Agno River
Mt. Tabayoc
2.812 m
Kibungan
Mt. Singakalsa
2.688 m
Pacso
Ballay
Tawangan
Catubo
Timbac
Caves
Kabayan
Naguey
Highest Point
Philippine Highway
System
7400 ft./ 2.255 m
Abiang
Mt. Atok
1.770 m
Kapangan
Sayangan
Ellet Bridge
Mt. Pulag
2.922 m
Ellet
Atok
Abukot
Lebang
Lake
Babadak
Ranger Station
Tabio
Palanza
Guerilla
Saddle
Ambuklao
Reservoir
Bokod/Ambangeg
La Trinidad
Acop's Place
Ambuklao
Bangao
Baguio
Kapaya
Aritao
© Jens Peters

The Spectacular Halsema Road

What a road! And what a misleading official name: Halsema Mountain Highway. It runs between Baguio and Bontoc and used to be called the Mountain Trail, which gives you a better idea of what kind of surface to expect. In the 20s, the civil engineer EJ Halsema supervised the widening and improving of the trail through the mountains, and in 1931 a more or less acceptable road was officially opened to traffic. The reason for this enormous undertaking was to provide access to the mineral resources (gold, silver and copper) of the Central Cordillera. To this day however, the work has not been completed. Although much of the road in the south has been surfaced, the majority of the route still is a bumpy, dusty track, winding through sometimes very steep passes.

Actually, the Halsema Road does not begin in Baguio but a few km further east of La Trinidad, the capital of the province of Benguet. From there it twists and winds through 130 km or so of breathtaking mountain scenery in a north-easterly direction until it reaches Bontoc, the capital of Mountain Province.

About seven km east of La Trinidad at Acops Place, a winding road breaks off heading for Kibungan, a small town in a mountain area which is also called the 'Switzerland of Benguet'. Apparently the temperature here can even drop below freezing in December and January. Around Kibungan the area is known as Madaymen, well known for its market gardens, north of which you come to the Palina Rice Terraces.

Shortly after Acops Place the Halsema Road leads over a pass known as the 'Guerrilla Saddle'. From here you can see the Ambuklao reservoir on the right, which is fed by the Agno river. A little further on, a road turns off which takes you there. This road also takes you to Kabayan and, from Ellet Bridge, to Mt Pulag, the second highest mountain in the Philippines.

Further north of Acops Place, around Atok, the so-called 'Salad Bowl of Benguet' begins: vegetable fields as far as the eye can see, most of them in the form of terraces. The Halsema Road really starts to climb here, until just before Catubo the impressive height of 2255m is reached. The point is marked with a plaque announcing tersely 'Highest Point Philippine Highway System - 7400 Ft'.

A trail leads down from Catubo to Kabayan. It crosses the foothills of Mt Singakalsa, also known as Mt Timbac, where some of the famous Kabayan mummies can be found in the Timbac Caves.

In Sinipsip the beautifully laid-out Natubleng Vegetable Terraces stretch away into the distance on both sides of the road. The slopes south of Sinipsip are particularly impressive, with their terraces filling every last inch of ground. From Buguias, the fields then carry on in the Loo Valley.

Abatan is exactly 90 km from Baguio. It's a busy little place at a road crossing, with a big market, loads of shops and stalls. If you take the road that

turns off to the north-west you end up in Mankayan, where two companies run copper mines, and Cervantes. The road that runs south-east goes to Loo and through the Loo Valley along the Agno river to Kabayan.
About 10 km north-east of Abatan the Halsema Road reaches the border to Mountain Province and just after that Mt Data with the comfortable hotel of the same name. It's about another 30 km from here to Bontoc. The rest of the way the road is accompanied on the right by the Chico river in a wide valley. Seven km before Bontoc we come to the last fork in the road. If you want to go to Sagada, then turn off to the left here.

bang take a bus or jeepney to Solano, and from there carry on with a jeepney to Banaue. The whole trip takes eight hrs, and you may have to change in Lagawe.

Sagada

Sagada is a pleasant, tranquil little community in the mountains 18 km west of Bontoc at 1480m above sea level. It is principally known for its caves and the so-called 'hanging coffins'.
St Mary's School next to the church of the same name was established in 1912. The event is celebrated every year from 5 to 10 December, including a procession on 7 December with a dancing competition in traditional costumes afterwards. On 9 December there is a competition involving theatre groups, singing and music.

Museum

A bit further from the town centre, heading towards Bontoc near the turn-off to Banga'an, try a visit to the informal Masferré Gallery, dedicated to the late Eduardo Masferré. The display of his photographs of life in the villages of Mountain Province in the 1930s, 40s and 50s is worth seeing, and a selection of his impressive work has been published in an illustrated book. The museum is in a private house and may be closed to visitors.

Shopping

Weavers make beautiful materials at Sagada Weaving, and you can buy traditional woven goods, but at fairly stiff prices. Josephine's Store sells handicrafts made by local highlanders, such as jewellery, baskets and woodcarvings.

Caves

If you are a climber and are curious to see the caves, you would be well advised to get one of the locals to guide you through them. Most people don't need to be reminded that their curiosity should not get the better of them. Opening coffins is not a sign of respect, and taking bones for souvenirs beggars belief.
The Sagada Environmental Guides Association (SEGA) in the Tourist Information Center will arrange guides for P300 for up to four people, plus P80 for two lamps; P350 for five people; P600 for six to nine people, including two guides. For the Matangkib Cave and Sumaging Cave you will need kerosene lamps, as a torch (flashlight) won't provide enough light. Careful guides will put up ropes for safety at dangerous spots. Good footwear is also important for a visit to the caves.
A guide is not essential for most of the burial caves. They are not very far from the centre of town - at most a 30-minute walk away. Among these is the Lumiang Cave with its cavernous entrance and numerous coffins.

Sumaging Cave (Big Cave) does not contain any coffins. You need a guide to go into this cave, as a thorough exploration can take up to six hours. The water is almost waist high in places and there are a few narrow places to negotiate. Roughly between 11am and 1pm the sun shines quite deeply into the cave and the light is magic.

There is a beautiful view of a vast valley with rice terraces from the path near the Sumaging Cave.

A guide would also be advisable if you were able to visit the Crystal Cave, as it is narrow and involves a difficult climb and descent. However, the Crystal Cave was closed to the public due to visitors insisting on breaking off mineral deposits to take home as a souvenir. The Matangkib Cave has also been closed off with wire mesh.

Hiking

Echo Valley: It's an interesting two-hour hike to Echo Valley. Starting off at St Mary's School behind the church, take the trail up to the cemetery, then go through the cemetery and take the path down into the valley. You can catch your first view down into the valley from the hill next to the cemetery, which has a cross on it. From Echo Valley, where coffins can be seen hanging from the rock face, you go upriver until you come to a cave opening where the Underground River flows out. To the right a path leads to the Matangkib Cave (closed), and from there it's only a few steps to the road. You can also go into the Underground River cave where in a short time you will reach the path that passes by outside. It is possible that the stretch between Echo Valley and Matangkib Cave has been reclaimed by nature and is grown over. In this case it's better to turn round and head back the way you came.

Bokong Waterfall: Although the flow is reduced almost to a trickle in April and May, a visit to Bokong Waterfall with its natural swimming pool is worthwhile and very refreshing after touring the caves in Sagada. It's a little hard to find, so you may have to ask for directions. It takes about 30 min to get there on foot from Sagada. To get there from the centre of the township first walk 300m in the direction of Bontoc, then after Sagada Weaving turn left up the stairs.

Kiltepan Peak: About 1½ km east of the centre of Sagada a bumpy trail turns off the road to Bontoc and leads up to Kiltepan Peak which is 1636m high. There used to be a transmitting tower up here, and the view down on the rice terraces at Kilong and Tetep-an is magnificent.

Banga'an: You can walk from Sagada to Banga'an in not quite two hours through a beautiful landscape with rice terraces. There is also supposed to be a connection by jeepney now. About another two hours on the other side of Banga'an there is a picturesque waterfall, the Bomod-ok ('Big Waterfall'). There is only enough light for sunbathing from morning until noon, so make sure you don't leave Sagada too late. Turn off right after the school in Banga'an and carry on to the village of Fedilisan. For a few pesos one of the children in the village will take you to the waterfall.

Mt Ampacao: The hike to the top of Mt Ampacao (1889m) is more than worth the effort (two hrs). The view of Sagada and its surrounding area from up there is magnificent. You can avoid going back down the same route through Ambasing by taking the path to the little Lake Danum (2½ hrs) and hiking from there back to Sagada (one hr).

Mt Polis: The beautiful hike to Mt Polis (1829m) south of Sagada takes a bit longer. You need about three to four hours if you take the so-called Old Spanish Trail that begins just outside of Ambasing and leads to Bagnen and Mt Polis. Steps that have been hewn into the hillside lead up to the summit.

Places to Stay

The places to stay in this popular little town are all of the basic variety, but inexpensive. If you don't want a cold shower in the morning, order a bucket of warm water for P30 the night before. And when we say cold water, in Sagada it really means cold!

A-Seven House. SR/DR P100/150. Friendly accommodation near the Pines View Inn.

Masferré Country Inn, Cellphone 0918-3416164. SR/DR P100/150. Spacious rooms.

Green House. SR/DR P100/150. A quiet, older private house with a newer building next to it. Both have their own kitchens, and guests may use them for a small fee.

Ganduyan Inn. SR/DR P100/160, SR/DR/bath P600. Friendly accommodation with OK rooms.

Pines View Inn. SR/DR P100/180. A quiet and cosy place with a family atmosphere. There are only three rooms as well as a big living room and kitchen. Located on the road to Banga'an.

Sagada Guesthouse, Cellphone 0918-5141580. SR/DR P100/200. A nice, clean place to stay. Restaurant.

St Joseph's Resthouse. SR/DR P100/200, SR/DR/bath P500 and P1000, cottage/bath P1500. Cosy accommodation in an idyllic setting with variously sized rooms (one to six beds) and attractive cottages for three and four people. Restaurant.

Rocky Valley Inn, Cellphone 0919-4140399. SR/DR P100/200. Pleasant accommodation near the Matangkib Cave, the rooms all have balconies. Good restaurant.

Getting There & Away

6 Buses to Baguio
9 Petron Station
16 Jeepneys to Bontoc

Places to Stay

1 Pines View Inn
2 A-Seven House
4 Sagada Guesthouse
7 St Joseph's Resthouse
11 Rocky Valley Inn
15 Mapiyaaw Sagada Pensione
17 Alfredo's Inn
21 Masferré Country Inn
22 Green House
23 Sagada Igorot Inn
24 Olahbinan Resthouse

Places to Eat

4 Log Cabin
5 Ganduyan Café
12 Rocky Valley Restaurant
17 Alfredo's
20 Shamrock Café
21 Masferré Restaurant
27 Yoghurt House

Miscellaneous

8 St Theodore's Hospital
10 Sagada Weaving & Souvenir Shop
11 Arts & Crafts
13 Josephine's Store
14 Masferré Gallery
18 Police Station
Post Office
Rural Bank
Tourist Information
Town Hall
19 Market
21 Sagada Bakery
25 St Mary's Episcopal Church
26 St Mary's School

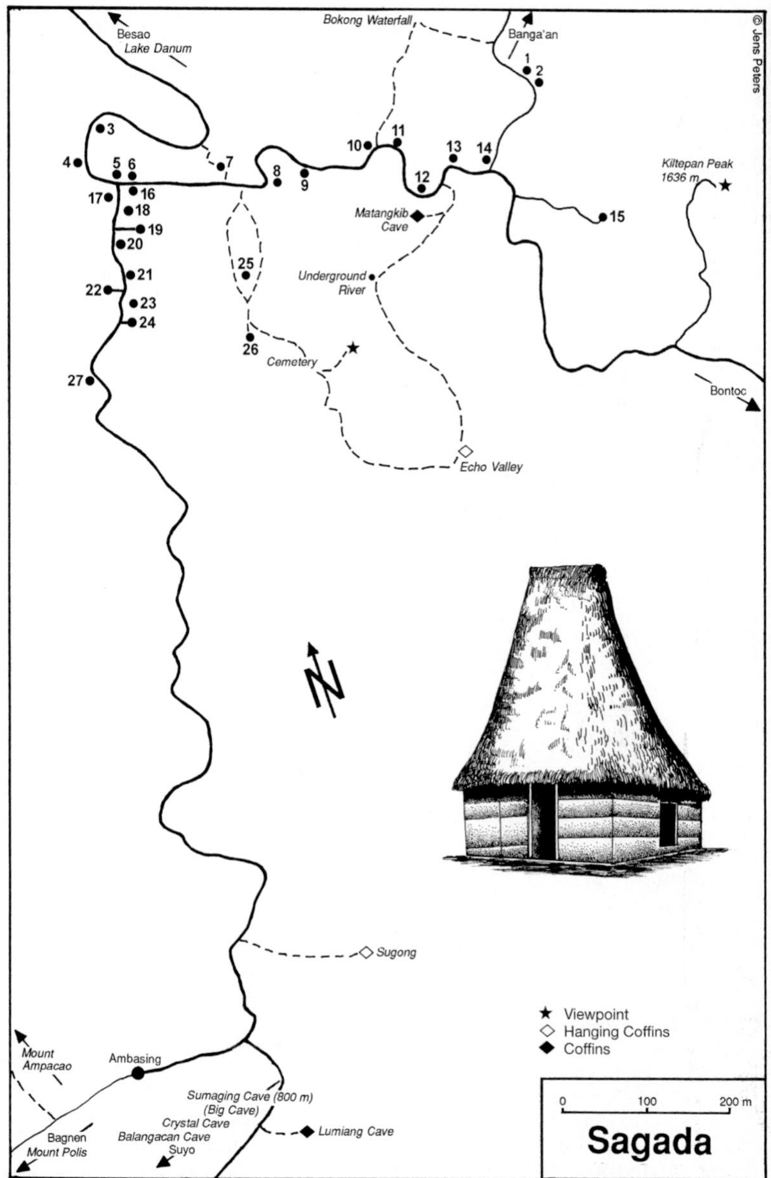

© Jens Peters
Besao
Lake Danum
Bokong Waterfall
Banga'an
Kiltepan Peak
1636 m
Matangkib
Cave
Underground
River
Cemetery
Echo Valley
Sugong
Bontoc
Mount
Ampacao
Ambasing
Sumaging Cave (800 m)
(Big Cave)
Crystal Cave
Balangacan Cave
Suyo
Lumiang Cave
Bagnen
Mount Polis
Viewpoint
Hanging Coffins
Coffins
0
100
200 m
Sagada

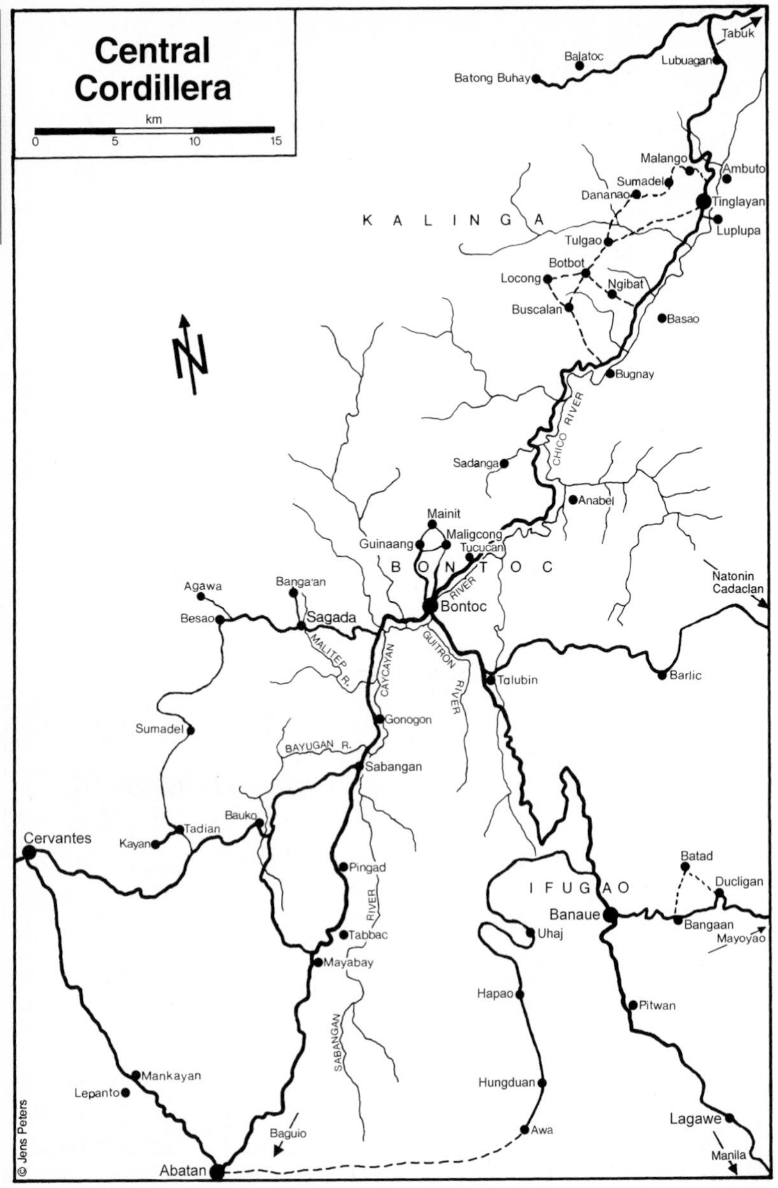
Central Cordillera
km
0 5 10 15
KALINGA
BONTOC
IFUGAO
Tabuk
Balatoc
Lubuagan
Batong Buhay
Malango
Ambuto
Sumadel
Dananao
Tinglayan
Luplupa
Tulgao
Botbot
Locong
Ngibat
Buscalan
Basao
Bugnay
CHICO RIVER
Sadanga
Anabel
Mainit
Maligcong
Guinaang
Tucucan
Natonin
Cadaclan
Agawa
Banga'an
RIVER
Bontoc
Besao
Sagada
MALITEP R.
CAYCAYAN
GUITRON RIVER
Talubin
Barlic
Gonogon
Sumadel
BAYUGAN R.
Sabangan
Bauko
Tadian
Cervantes
Kayan
Pingad
Batad
Ducligan
RIVER
Banaue
Bangaan
Uhaj
Mayoyao
Tabbac
Mayabay
Hapao
Pitwan
SABANGAN
Mankayan
Lepanto
Hungduan
Awa
Lagawe
Baguio
Manila
Abatan
© Jens Peters

Alfredo's Inn, Cellphone 0919-4154653. SR P100, DR P250, DR/bath P500. Beautifully furnished house with basic, but well-kept rooms.
Mapiyaaw Sagada Pensione, Cellphone 0920-5559105. SR/DR P150/300, DR/bath P550 (one bathroom is shared between two rooms). Idyllically located in a natural rock garden 600m from the town centre heading towards Bontoc. It's a three-storey building, but somehow manages to be cosy, with a fireplace, and a balcony on each floor.
Olahbinan Resthouse, Cellphone 0920-2683555. SR/DR P200 to P300, SR/DR/bath P700, suite P1500. Good rooms. Restaurant.
Sagada Igorot Inn, Cellphone 0919-8092448. SR/DR/bath P1000 to P1500. Quite comfortable accommodation for those who want that little bit more.

Places to Eat

You can eat well and cheaply at the ***Masferré Restaurant*** and the ***Shamrock Café***, where in addition to standard Philippine dishes and pancakes, Mountain Province specialities are available. Definitely to be recommended are the attractively decorated ***Alfredo's*** and, a bit south of the centre of town, the ***Yogurt House***, which is also a good place to enjoy a wide selection of breakfast specialties and vegetarian food.
At the ***Log Cabin*** the food is extremely good, but an early reservation is recommended as it can only accommodate a certain number of guests for dinner. Although it's small, it's cosily furnished and a popular place to eat. They even serve wine here.
Several of the guesthouses serve large evening meals and breakfasts, but you should book ahead, say by 4pm. Most restaurants in Sagada close at 9pm.

Miscellaneous

Festival: Town Fiesta in the last week in January or first week in February.
Information: You can get a detailed map, although it's not to scale, of the Sagada area for P10 at various places offering accommodation in town.
Money: The Rural Bank of Sagada will change travellers' cheques (US-dollars); to change cash go to the Masferré Country Inn.
Population: 10,000.
Post: Post code: 2619.

Getting There & Away

Baguio
Bus: Several GT Trans and Lizardo Trans buses leave Baguio daily for Sagada. The departure times are 6.45, 7.30, 8, 9, 10, 11am and 12 noon (P190; seven hrs). Sit next to the driver or on the right side of the bus for the best view. It gets fairly cool, so take a jacket or jumper out of your luggage before it gets stowed away.
The buses leave Sagada for Baguio at 5, 6, 6.30, 7, 8, 9 and 10am, and at 1pm.

Bontoc
Jeepney: From Bontoc to Sagada, every hour from 8.30am to 5.30pm from around the All Saints Mission Elementary School (P25; one hr).

Warning for Self-drivers: The road from the Halsema Rd to Sagada (about 14 km) is in a very bad condition and really only suitable for vehicles with a high clearance from the road.

Bontoc

At an altitude of about 900m, Bontoc is the capital of Mountain Province and is right in the middle of Central Cordillera.
Woven materials are made on old looms in and around Bontoc, for example in the All Saints Mission Elementary School and in Barangay Samoki, a village on the other side of the river. It

takes about 30 min to walk from Bontoc to Samoki.

Museum
You can get a good overview of the differences and similarities between the mountain tribes in the small but excellent Bontoc Museum. The friendly staff are always happy to give detailed information about life in Mountain Province. The opening hours are from 1 to 5pm, although they may be open in the morning from 8am to noon.

Places to Stay
Let's put it this way: accommodation in Bontoc is very basic and most places were obviously at their best a while ago. If, for example, you've come up the Halsema Rd from Baguio by car and are looking forward to a cosy little hotel room in Bontoc, you're out of luck. Your best bet would be stop between Abatan and Bontoc at the ***Mt Data Hotel***, Cellphone 0918-3344701, about 10 km north of Abatan, you can't miss the signs. It's a decent hotel, with a dorm for P150 and very comfortable SR/DR/bath for P1900/2200, including breakfast. The service is friendly and you'll be glad of the open fire in the evening as it's 2250m above sea level. Good restaurant. Reservations in Baguio: Tourist Office, Tel (074) 4426708; in Manila: Philippine Tourism Authority, Tel (02) 5242502. A little less comfortable, but also less expensive, is the ***Golden Pines Hotel*** about three km north of Abatan. Small, well-kept SR/DR/bath with balcony cost P600. It has a restaurant and a lounge with TV.

In Bontoc itself you have the following choice:
Bontoc Hotel. SR/DR P100/200. Basic, older place. Restaurant.
Happy Home Inn. SR/DR P100/200, DR/bath P300. Basic, but all right for the money.

Getting There & Away
7 Jeepneys to Tinglayan
15 Jeepneys to Sagada
25 Vonvon Trans (Buses to Banaue)
26 Dangwa Tranco Bus Terminal
27 Petron Petrol Station

Places to Stay
9 Pines Kitchenette & Inn
12 Ridge Brooke Hotel (500 m)
16 Chico Terraces Inn
17 Churya-a Hotel
19 Village Inn
20 Bontoc Hotel
23 Lynda's Guesthouse
24 Mountain Hotel
29 Happy Home Inn

Places to Eat
9 Pines Kitchenette & Inn
13 New Double Eatery
18 Cable Café
19 Zander's Café
21 Rendezvous Café
25 Country Restaurant
28 Bontoc Diner's Restaurant
30 Beautiful Dreamer Café

Miscellaneous
1 Hospital
2 Church
3 Philippine National Bank (PNB)
Provincial Capitol
4 Town Plaza
5 Landbank
6 Massage Center
8 Post Office
10 Bontoc Museum
11 Market
14 All Saints Mission Elementary School
22 Town Hall
Police Station

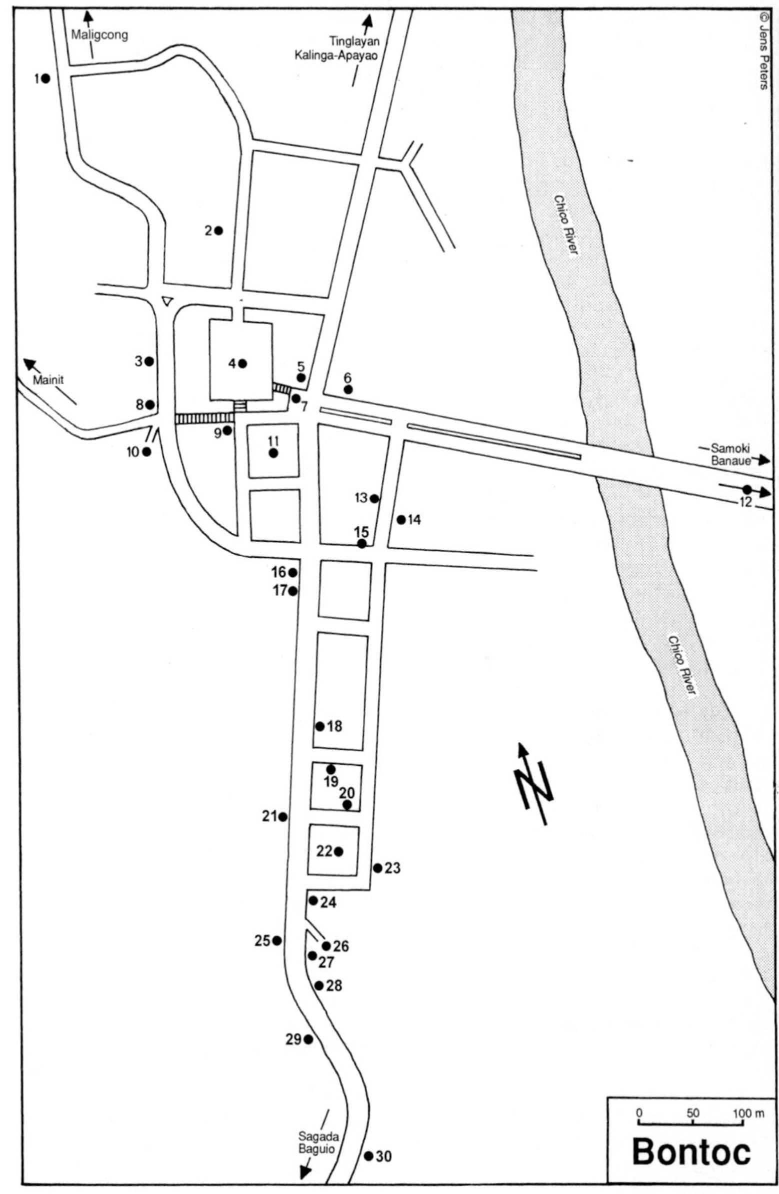
© Jens Peters
Maligcong
Tinglayan
Kalinga-Apayao
Chico River
Mainit
Samoki
Banaue
Chico River
Sagada
Baguio
N
0
50
100 m
Bontoc
1
2
3
4
5
6
7
8
9
10
11
12
13
14
15
16
17
18
19
20
21
22
23
24
25
26
27
28
29
30

Village Inn. SR P100, DR P200 and P300. Friendly accommodation with basic, tiny, clean rooms. Two doubles share a small bath.

Pines Kitchenette & Inn, Tel 6021509. SR/DR P100/200, SR/DR/bath P500. Basic accommodation, the rooms without bath are downright spartan. Restaurant. Near the museum.

Lynda's Guesthouse, Tel 6031053. SR/DR/fan P100/200, SR/DR/fan/bath P350. Pleasant guesthouse with small, friendly, clean rooms. Restaurant.

Churya-a Hotel, Cellphone 0920-7086649. SR/DR/fan/bath P400 to P600. Good rooms, worth the money. To be recommended, centrally located accommodation in a four-storey building with big, prominent balconies. The reception is upstairs on the first floor. Restaurant.

Ridge Brook Hotel. SR/fan P150, SR/DR/fan/bath P600, SR/DR/ac/bath P900 and P1200. Acceptably good rooms for the money. Doubtless the best accommodation in Bontoc, although it's a little bit out of town in Samoki, on the other side of the Chico Rover (tricycle P3.50 per person). Restaurant.

Places to Eat

Almost all of Bontoc's restaurants close at 9pm. You can eat well at the spacious ***Pines Kitchenette & Inn*** where you can also get a good-sized breakfast, and in the ***Cable Café***, which also serves drinks and snacks later in the evening. The food in the pleasant ***New Double Eatery*** across from the All Saints' Mission Elementary School is good and inexpensive, which is also true of the ***Zander's Café*** and the ***Bontoc Diner's Restaurant*** on the southern edge of town where there is a beautiful view of the valley and the river.

Miscellaneous

Festival: Town Fiesta on 21 May.

Massage: If you feel like a soothing massage after your strenuous walks up and down the mountains, go to the Massage Centre (it's a small building). There are two blind masseurs who will give you a professional massage lasting one hour for P150.

Money: The Philippine National Bank (near the museum) and the Landbank both change travellers' cheques.

Population: 25,000.

Post & Telephone: Post Office across from the Bontoc Museum.
Post code: 2616. Area code: 074.

Trekking: The guides Jessie and Kinad will arrange three-day or longer treks (actually, they prefer four-day) to Kalinga villages. Juliet Soria also offers one-day and longer treks and charges P600 per day for up to four people. For five people and more, everybody pays P100 each. They can all be contacted through hotels in Bontoc, eg the Pines Kitchenette & Inn.

Getting There & Away

Baguio

Bus: There are several Dangwa Tranco and D'Rising Sun buses from Baguio to Bontoc a day, leaving from 5am. The last one will probably leave about 12 noon. The 140 km trip takes about eight hrs (P190).

Banaue

Bus: Immanuel Trans and Vonvon Trans buses leave Banaue for Bontoc daily at 10.30 and 11am (two hrs).
Departure from Bontoc to Banaue at 8 and 8.30am.

Jeepney: Several jeepneys leave Banaue for Bontoc daily between 7am and 12 noon (2½ hrs).
Last departure from Bontoc to Banaue between 12 noon and 1pm.

Sagada

Jeepney: Jeepneys leave Sagada for Bontoc roughly every hour from 6am to 12 noon, taking one hr for the trip.

Tabuk

Jeepney: Two jeepneys run daily between Bontoc and Tabuk via Tinglayan, leaving at 6am and 1.30pm (P70; 2½ hrs).

Around Bontoc

Maligcong

The rice terraces at Maligcong are beautifully laid out, some of them even more so than at Banaue. In contrast to the Ifugao, who built their rice terraces with earthen walls, the Bontoc preferred stone walls to separate their fields.

Getting There & Away

Walking: It's about two hours on foot from Bontoc to Maligcong. It can get very hot; take some kind of headcover as well as provisions, including water. From Bontoc, a track goes past the Capitol Building and the hospital, north as far as the valley with the rice terraces below Maligcong. It's a bit of a shortcut if you take the roughly cut, steep stone stairs just outside of town, which lead off right from the track and meet up with it again later. A narrow stone staircase leads off from the end of the track down to the rice terraces. You can then take a path through the rice terraces to the village of Maligcong, which actually isn't particularly interesting.

Jeepney: A jeepney leaves Bontoc at 7am, noon, 2, 4.30 and 5.30pm heading for Maligcong. It stops at the end of the track at a little shelter where people wait it. From there you can make it on foot through the rice terraces to Maligcong.

Return departure at 6.30, 8 and 9am, 2 and 4.30pm.

Mainit

Mainit means hot, probably referring to the bubbling hot springs in this little place where people pan for gold. Some of the springs are even used as natural cooking ranges.

Getting There & Away

Jeepney: A jeepney may leave Bontoc daily for Guinaang at about 6.30 to 7am. From there it is about 45 min on foot downhill to Mainit.

There may be a jeepney in the afternoon from Guinaang back to Bontoc. There is also a track from Mainit to Maligcong. It is hard to find, so a guide may be useful. The track starts before you get into Mainit, at a sulphur spring, which you can smell a long way off. If you are coming from Guinaang, you have to turn right at the sulphur spring and follow the track past the rice terraces to Maligcong.

Natonin

About 35 km east of Bontoc as the crow flies, well off the beaten track in other words, lies the little mountain village of Natonin. It is surrounded by rice terraces that seem to go on for ever in all directions. They were built by the Balangao, a minority group who make this area their home.

Getting There & Away

Jeepney: Once a day, a jeepney goes from Bontoc to Natonin via Barlig. It may only go as far as Barlig or Cadaclan, where another one takes over. It's about 15 km from Cadaclan to Natonin, and you may have to cover them by foot if you're unlucky.

Tinglayan & Kalinga Villages

Tinglayan is about 40 km north-east of Bontoc and is a favourite start-off point for whitewater rafting with kayaks and dinghies on the Chico River downriver to Tabuk. Depending on the water level these trips take about four to seven

Warning
The area around Tinglayan must be regarded as critical because of occasional skirmishes between the three politically distinct units of the Armed Forces of the Philippines (AFP), the New People's Army (NPA) and the Cordillera People's Liberation Army (CPLA). You should check the situation before you go there.

hours. June and July are the best months, as the river calms down noticeably from December/January. The trips can be booked through travel agents in Manila (Marsman Tours & Travel, Tel 02-8870000, @); Tabuk (Chico River Quest, Cellphone 0917-9668081, @); and Tuguegarao (Adventures & Expeditions Philippines, Cellphone 0917-5327480, @).

Tinglayan is also a good starting point for visiting Kalinga villages. Always get a guide to take you from one village to the next, or hire a guide in Tinglayan for the whole trek. One well-known guide is Victor Baculi, the Barangay Captain of the village of Luplupa. He is an experienced guide and a mine of information on the mountains and the Kalinga culture. You get to Luplupa from the road over a long suspended bridge over the Chico River, about 500m south of Tinglayan.

Half-day, one-day or several-day hikes are possible, but you've got to be fit for any of them. The following round trip will take about three days on foot, including stopovers in the villages. You can count on three hours from Tinglayan to Tulgao, 1½ hours from Tulgao to Dananao, two hours from Dananao to Sumadel and one hour from Sumadel to Malango. From Malango you get on to the main road and go back to Tinglayan.

Places to Stay

Sleeping Beauty Inn. SR/DR P150/300. Guesthouse. Nothing to write home about.

Good Samaritan Inn. SR/DR 150/300. Modest accommodation, but OK for the money. Like the Sleeping Beauty Inn located on the road in Tinglayan.

Luplupa Riverside Inn. SR/DR P150/300. Basic, but clean and relatively comfortable rooms in an attractive, unmissable building in the village of Luplupa. Very good value. If you're coming from Bontoc, then get off before Tinglayan at the Lulupa turn-off next to the suspended bridge.

Getting There & Away

Bus: Two or three buses make the trip daily between 6 and 8am from Bontoc to Tinglayan, either direct or heading for Tabuk (3 hrs). Departure from Tinglayan to Bontoc between 9 and 11am.

Jeepney: From Bontoc to Tinglayan there's a daily jeepney which leaves after the arrival of the bus from Baguio between 1 and 2pm, taking three hrs. Departure from Tinglayan for Bontoc at around 7 to 8am.

Banaue

Banaue is at an altitude of about 1200m. The rice terraces around Banaue have been called the eighth wonder of the world. It took the Ifugao tribespeople, with their primitive implements, over 2000 years to create this imposing landscape. Unfortunately, the younger generation no longer feels the call to be rice farmers and carry on the labour-intensive tending of the fields, so the preservation of the rice terraces is in danger. UNESCO could soon provide the necessary financial support to save the terraces, as they now appear on the UNESCO World Heritage list. In 1997, the American Society of Civil Engi-

Lubuagan & Chico Valley Dam

In and around Lubuagan, the former government of president Marcos came into direct conflict with the Kalinga because of the Chico Valley dam project, which was to comprise four single dams and produce 1000 megawatts of electricity. For the government this represents a reduction in oil imports of about ten percent. A source of energy on this scale is of immense importance to a country totally dependent on energy imports. The planning has now been completed but the actual construction has been indefinitely postponed by the National Power Corporation after the World Bank intervened. So the Kalinga have won an important battle, if not the war, in their fight to preserve their way of life.

The Chico Valley dam would have been the largest in South-East Asia and would have flooded the Kalinga's valleys, forcing them to resettle. The Kalinga were opposed to the move as it would have meant the end of their centuries-old culture, which has developed in isolation from the colonised lowlands. The Kalinga's religion was another reason for their opposition to the move. They live in a world of gods and spirits and show great respect to the dead, so their ancestors' resting places must be left undisturbed.

At first there was only scattered fighting against the surveying for the dam. In 1980, however, following the murder of Bugnay's Chief Macliing Dulag, who had been sabotaging the works of the national energy company, the 20 or so groups of Kalinga, comprising about 100,000 members, formed a united front. Macliing was shot by several volleys of machine-gun fire through the thin walls of his hut and it is said that the murderers were wearing military uniforms. The conflict widened and soldiers and construction workers were beheaded and rebellious Kalinga shot. Members of the communist NPA joined the Kalinga and instructed them in the use of modern M-16 rifles.

Today, relations between the mountain dwellers and the NPA, as well as the government, are anything but harmonious. The Kalinga now distrust any power which tries to intrude on them. They continue to be vigilant and regard any stranger as a threat - do not venture into the mountains alone.

neers honoured this unique terrace landscape with the prestigious International Historic Civil Engineering Landmark award.

There are a number of things to do around Banaue. You can visit several Ifugao villages, take some of the paths through the rice terraces, enjoy the panorama from Banaue View Point or take a refreshing dip in the water of the Guihon Natural Pool. On the way there you can make a detour to the bronzesmiths of Matanglag. Set in beautiful surroundings, the village of Poi-tan has kept alive its tradition of wood-carving and weaving. In contrast, the neighbouring village of Tam-an has obviously specialised in selling souvenirs to tourists. Amongst others, Delfin in the Patina Coffee Shop near the Post Office makes

The Ifugao plant rice according to the following calendar:
- In the second half of December, they begin to sow the seed.
- From the beginning of February to the middle of March, they transplant the first seedlings.
- From the middle of April until the middle of June, they weed the fields.
- In July, the harvest takes place.
- From the beginning of August until the middle of December, they work on improvements to the rice terraces and preparing the fields for the next seeding.

artistic woodcuts, including special orders.
A tricycle to Banaue View Point and back costs P80; jeepneys to Bontoc also use this route. Colourfully dressed, elderly Ifugao wait at the view point for photographers, and expect them to pay a few pesos for a photo.
The best time to go to the Banaue area is from January to May. It rains quite frequently in November and December. The rice terraces are irrigated in December and January which produces a beautiful mirror effect. From March until May/June the terraces can be seen in their full verdant glory.

Museum

In the same building as the Banaue View Inn there is a small museum which has traditional Ifugao household objects, jewellery, clothing etc on display. There are also a few interesting books on exhibition. Admission is P20 and don't be afraid to ask them to let you in; they're not actually open on a regular basis. It's worth seeing this museum if you missed the one in Bontoc.

Places to Stay

There are plenty small places to stay, all within walking distance of the market where the buses arrive.
Especially in December and January the nights in the mountains can get bitterly cold, so it would be a good idea to ask for a second blanket when you check in to the hotel. Check-out time is usually at 8am, sometimes 10am.
Brookside Inn. SR/DR P100/200. Basic accommodation.
Jericho Guest House. SR/DR P100/200. Basic, but good accommodation.
Wonder Lodge. SR/DR P100/200. Warm water costs P10 extra. Basic but good quality rooms.
Halfway Lodge, Tel 3864082. SR/DR P100/200, SR/DR/bath P350 an P600. Basic, but clean and cosy. Restaurant.
Stairway Lodge. SR/DR P100/200, SR/DR/bath P350. Basic, but pleasant rooms. Restaurant.
Fairview Inn. SR/bath P300, DR/bath P600. Enjoy the beautiful view of the town from this quiet place.
People's Lodge, Tel 3864014, @. SR/DR P100/200, SR/DR/bath P400 and P500. A wonderful, friendly place with a bakery and restaurant. The rooms are fairly comfortable and good value. If your room doesn't have en-suite facilities, the view of the rice terraces from the shared toilets will more than make up for it! Free left luggage.
Green View Lodge, Tel 3864021. SR/DR P100/200, SR/DR/bath P400 and P550. Good accommodation with tastefully decorated rooms. Restaurant.
Terrace Ville Inn, Tel 3864069. SR/DR/bath P500. Reasonable rooms. Restaurant.
Sanafe Lodge, Tel 3864085. Dorm P150, SR/bath P600, DR/bath P750. The rooms are quite comfortable. Restaurant
Banaue View Inn, Tel 3864078. Dorm P150, SR/DR/bath P600 and P800. As you would expect, there is a beautiful

Places to Stay
1 Terrace Ville Inn
2 Brookside Inn
3 Halfway Lodge
4 Stairway Lodge
6 Wonder Lodge
7 Green View Lodge
9 People's Lodge
10 Valgreg Lodge
12 Banaue View Inn
15 Sanafe Lodge
19 Jericho Guest House
20 Spring Village Inn
21 J & L Pension
22 Fairview Inn
Banaue Hotel
Banaue Youth Hostel

Places to Eat
3 Halfway Restaurant
4 Stairway Restaurant
6 Father's Best Restaurant
8 Las Vegas Restaurant
9 People's Restaurant
11 Cool Winds Restaurant
17 New Look Restaurant

Miscellaneous
5 Church
9 People's Bakery
13 Market
14 School
15 Tourist Information Center
16 RSR Store
18 Municipal Hall
22 Good News Clinic
Post Office

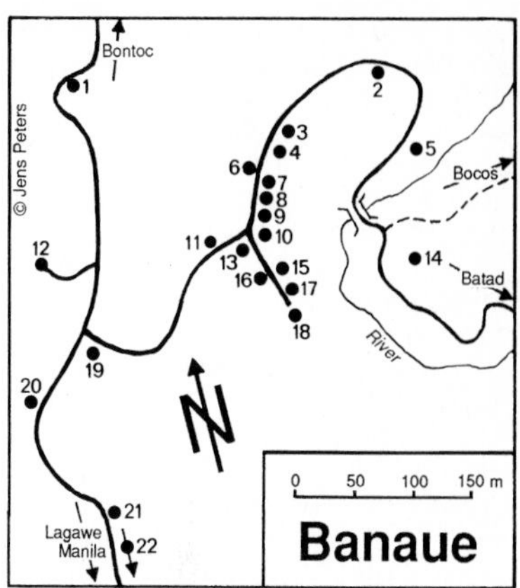

view of Banaue from this pleasant and quiet inn. Coffee shop.

Spring Village Inn, Tel 3864037. SR/DR P500 and P600, SR/DR/bath P1000. Fairly good rooms.

Banaue Youth Hostel. Dorm P200. It is administered by the Banaue Hotel, whose swimming pool is available for use.

Banaue Hotel, Tel 3864087, Fax 3864088. SR/DR/bath P1500 and P2800, suite P6000, all including breakfast. Tastefully decorated throughout and the best place to stay in Banaue. Restaurant, swimming pool. Reservations in Manila: Philippine Tourism Authority, Tel (02) 5242502, Fax (02) 5256490.

Places to Eat

Most hotels have a small restaurant or else the staff will cook meals for guests. The ***Cool Winds Restaurant*** next to the market provides large helpings of good food and local musicians sometimes have a jam session here. The ***New Look Restaurant***, ***People's Restaurant***, ***Halfway Restaurant***, ***Stairway Restaurant*** and the ***Las Vegas Restaurant*** are good and cheap, although they all close at 9pm, as do almost all the restaurants in Banaue.

The restaurant at the up-market ***Banaue Hotel*** is excellent. In the evening, if there are enough guests by say 8.30, then a performance of Ifugao dances will be held. Although these performances are in contrast to the world of international hotels and perhaps seem a little out of place in this setting, they are at least authentic. Admission is P20. On the way back to the village at night it is likely to be very dark, so don't forget to take a torch (flashlight).

The Banaue Hotel also has a pub with a billiard table (P100 per hour for non-residents) which is open until midnight.

Miscellaneous

Information: You can buy a useful map of Banaue's surroundings for P10 at the Tourist Information Center next to the Sanafe Lodge and at several guesthouses. The *Banaue Tour Map* shows the way to various interesting sights and describes them in detail on the back. However, the times given for hikes are at best vague; see also under *Trekking*.

Amongst other things, the Tourist Information Center has lists pinned up with information on Special Rides by jeepney.

Money: There is an authorised foreign exchange counter at the Banaue Hotel. However, the exchange rate is poor and there is a fee of P50 for each travellers' cheque.

The RSR Store across from the Sanafe Lodge will change cheques and cash (US-dollars and possibly other currencies).

Population: 12,000.

Post & Telephone: The Post Office is a little way out of town at the turn-off for the Banaue Hotel. There is also a post box which is emptied daily at the People's Lodge.

Post code: 3601. Area code: 074.

Swimming Pool: Non-residents can use the swimming pool at the Banaue Hotel for P30.

Trekking: Guides who are more than happy to take small groups through the mountains can be contacted via jeepney drivers at the market and at restaurants.

The following tour is beginning to get popular, although you have to be fit to do it (the terrain is tough at times) and only experienced trekkers should attempt it off their own bat. It starts in Banaue and takes you to the View Point (two hrs), then to Pula (eight hrs) and via Cambulo (two hrs) to Batad (two hrs). From there you go back to the road (two hrs) which takes you back to Banaue (five hrs).

Getting There & Away

Info for Self-drivers: The best route from Manila to Banaue is via Angeles and Tarlac, so don't take the turn-off to Cabanatuan on the North Expressway, but carry straight on to Mabalacat, the end of the North Expressway. From Mabalacat take the ordinary highway via Tarlac to Gerona, turn off right there and through Guimba to the other highway that takes you to North-east Luzon. The road from Guimba joins the highway between Muñoz and Talvera, turn off left there. In Bagabag, about 140 km north, the road leads off to Banaue.

Angeles

Bus: It's best to travel from Angeles to Banaue in three stages. With waiting, the trip lasts about ten hours in all, so start as early as possible. Start off with a bus from Dau to Tarlac (every bus heading towards Baguio, La Union, Vigan and Laoag goes through there), which takes one hour. In Tarlac, take a tricycle to the Baliwag Transit Bus Terminal (P5) and from there the next bus to Cabanatuan (1½ hrs). In Cabanatuan, don't carry on to the bus terminal but get out beforehand at the McDonald's at the highway and stop a bus heading north, eg to Roxas, Tuguegarao or Aparri, which you then take to Solano (four hrs). Carry on from the Mountain Lodge & Restaurant in Solano by jeepney to Banaue (two hrs). The last departure from Solano to Banaue is around 4pm. You can also take a jeepney from Solano to Lagawe and change there into a jeepney heading for Banaue. The

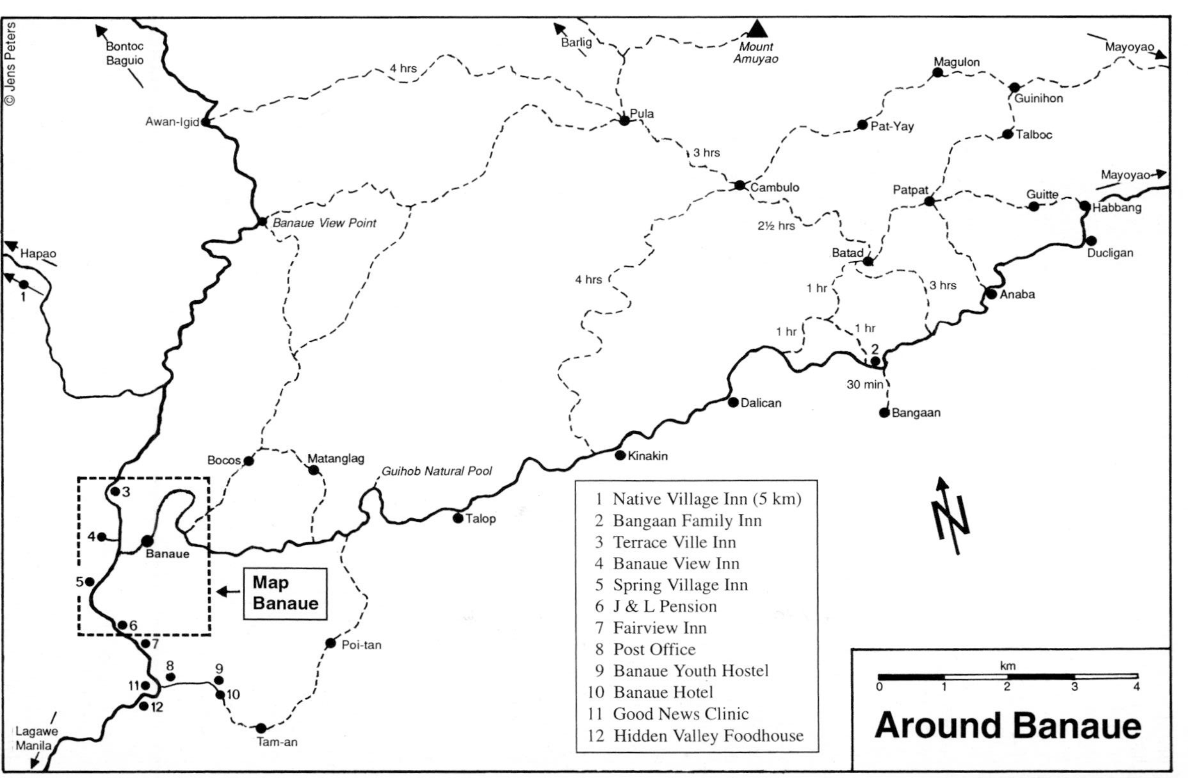
Around Banaue
km
0
1
2
3
4
1 Native Village Inn (5 km)
2 Bangaan Family Inn
3 Terrace Ville Inn
4 Banaue View Inn
5 Spring Village Inn
6 J & L Pension
7 Fairview Inn
8 Post Office
9 Banaue Youth Hostel
10 Banaue Hotel
11 Good News Clinic
12 Hidden Valley Foodhouse
Map Banaue
© Jens Peters
Bontoc
Baguio
Awan-Igid
4 hrs
Barlig
Mount Amuyao
Pula
Magulon
Mayoyao
Guinihon
Pat-Yay
Talboc
3 hrs
Cambulo
Patpat
Guitte
Mayoyao
Habbang
Ducligan
Banaue View Point
Hapao
2½ hrs
Batad
4 hrs
1 hr
3 hrs
Anaba
1 hr
1 hr
30 min
Dalican
Bangaan
Kinakin
Bocos
Matanglag
Guihob Natural Pool
Talop
Banaue
Poi-tan
Tam-an
Lagawe
Manila

last departure from Lagawe to Banaue is around 5.30pm.
From Banaue to Angeles see Central Luzon: *Angeles - Getting There & Away*.

Baguio

Bus: From Baguio to Banaue buses leave daily at 7pm (KMS) and 8pm (Ohayami Trans), taking the southern route via Carmen, San Jose and Bayombong (nine hrs). Dangwa Tranco usually used to leave at 10am but as of the beginning of 2004 had (temporarily?) cancelled the route; info at Tel (074) 4422449.

You have to be at the bus terminal early, as the bus will leave up to an hour early if it's full, especially at Easter. The departure times are often altered, so it's a good idea to check the day before leaving.

Departure from Banaue: Dangwa Tranco (if at all) between 6 and 7.30am, KMS 3pm, Ohayami Trans 4pm.

Northern route: A Norton Trans bus goes from Baguio to Bambang every day at 7am, via La Trinidad and Bangao. Carry on from Bambang by bus or jeepney to Solano and take another jeepney from there to Banaue. The whole trip takes nine hours and you may have to change in Lagawe.

If you want to go from Baguio to Banaue via Bontoc, you will have to stay the night in Bontoc, as there is no direct connection.

A good idea for self-drivers would be to spend the night in the pleasant Mt Data Hotel, about half-way there (see 'Bontoc' above in this chapter).

Bontoc

Bus: Immanuel Trans and Vonvon Trans buses leave Bontoc for Banaue every day at 8 and 8.30am (two hrs).

Departure from Banaue for Bontoc at 10.30 and 11am.

Bulul the Rice Protector
Wood carving is an important element in the Ifugao culture of the Central Cordillera. Particular favourites are sacred figurines, depicting people in various poses. The best-known wooden figurines are the Bulul, pensive-looking male and female deities usually in a crouching position. After the rice harvest has been stored away, these god figures are placed at the entrance to the storehouses and act as guards. The belief is that rice gods who have been enticed there by a special ceremony make themselves at home in the figurines and are happy to stay there. They then ensure that the rice has not been used up by the next harvest, and may even by some miracle increase the stock.

Jeepney: Several jeepneys leave Bontoc for Banaue every day between 7am and 12 noon (2½ hrs).
Last departure from Banaue for Bontoc at about 12 noon.

Manila
Bus: An Autobus Transport air-con bus leaves Manila for Banaue daily at 10pm (P250; eight hrs). The Filipino Travel Center handles reservations in Manila (Adriatico St, Ermita, Tel 5284507-09), in Angeles, on Boracay and in Sabang/Puerto Galera. However, tickets can only actually be picked up at the head office in Manila.
Departure from Banaue to Manila at 5.30pm. Board the bus as early as possible as it gets full quickly. It's best to buy your ticket the day before at Niclyn's Store next to the Sanafe Lodge and reserve your seat at the same time.
From Manila to just before Banaue you can also take buses belonging to Autobus Transport, Baliwag Transit (from their Cubao terminal) and Victory Liner (from their Kamias and Sampaloc terminals). Make sure they're heading for Tuguegarao or Aparri. Get off in Solano just before the turn-off to Banaue, take a jeepney to Lagawe and then carry on by jeepney to Banaue. The last bus leaves Lagawi for Banaue at 5.30pm.
From Banaue to Manila you can also do the trip in stages, taking a bus (heading for Baguio) or a jeepney via Lagawe to Bagabag, Solano or San Jose. Once you're there, get on one of the many buses heading for Manila (including aircon buses), eg those originating in Cauayan or Tuguegarao.

San Fernando (La Union) - Bauang
Bus: To go from San Fernando and Bauang to Banaue, take a bus at about 5 or 6am headed for Manila and get off at the turn-off to Rosario. From there catch the bus from Baguio to Banaue (see above) which gets there about an hour after leaving Baguio. The bus is likely to be jam-packed, but perhaps some of the passengers will get off there.

Tuguegarao - Aparri
Bus: From Banaue to Tuguegarao and Aparri take one of the buses mentioned from Banaue to Manila or Baguio, and get off at Bagabag, Solano or Bayombong. Then wait for the Manila to Tuguegarao or Aparri bus. The trip takes four or six hrs respectively.

Around Banaue

Uhaj, Hapao & Hungduan

Between Banaue and Banaue View Point a seldom-used track turns off to Uhaj (pronounced Oha; nine km), Hapao (15 km) and Hungduan (25 km). It runs through magnificent countryside with scores of rice terraces all around, an ideal area for taking extended hikes. It is said that General Yamashita, the commander in chief of the Japanese Imperial Army, held his last stand in Hungduan at the end of WWII, before finally surrendering in Kiangan, a few km south-east of there.

Places to Stay
Native Village Inn, Uhaj. SR/DR P1000. Rustic, but clean accommodation in original Ifugao houses, standing on the terraces looking for all the world like a little native village. Managed by Graham from Britain and his Filipina wife Monina, this attractive place is built on a hillside with a beautiful panoramic view of the rice terraces on all sides. The restaurant has an open fire in the centre.

Getting There & Away
Jeepney: Several jeepneys make the trip from Banaue to Hungduan via Uhaj

and Hapao daily between 11am and 6pm, taking 40 min (Uhaj), one hr (Hapao) and 1½ hrs (Hungduan) respectively.

Tricycle: A tricycle from Banaue to Uhaj costs P80.

Batad & Cambulo

The wonderful village of Batad is about 16 km north-east of Banaue. It is surrounded by breathtakingly beautiful rice terraces which are in the shape of an amphitheatre. It is an impressive sight to see them slowly emerge from the low-lying cloud early in the morning. Many Ifugao houses now have corrugated iron roofs, but luckily these have not yet been generally accepted. Batad must be one of the most impressive places in Central Cordillera and is a 'must see' spot.
About an hour's walk from Batad there's an impressive waterfall called Tappia Falls, which plunges 30m into a natural, refreshing swimming pool. It's hard to find and the path to it is a bit steep in places. It would be better to stay overnight in Batad rather than try to make it there and back on a day trip from Banaue.
It's about two hours on foot from Batad to Cambulo, a typical little Ifugao village, sits in the midst of rice terraces. From there a trail, which takes about four hours, leads to Kinakin on the main road, where a jeepney might pass by on its way to Banaue (P20). It is another eight km back to Banaue.

Places to Stay

Accommodation is basic throughout the area, but the atmosphere is always very friendly. You can stay the night in Batad for about P100 at the ***Batad Pension***, ***Cristina's Guest House***, ***Shirley's Inn***, ***Foreigner's Inn***, ***Rita's Mount View Inn***, ***Summer Inn***, or ***Simon's Inn*** and ***Hillside Inn***, where the food is also good.
In Cambulo you can spend the night for about P80 in the basic rooms at the ***Riverside Guest House*** belonging to Lydia Domanglig or at Lolita's ***Cambulo Friends Inn***. Both will cook for their guests, and drinks such as mineral water and beer are available, although obviously costing a bit more than in Banaue.

If you want to photograph villagers in Batad, you should do so from a distance if possible, or ask them for permission first. The people here either don't want any photos taken of them, or else will demand payment. The children of Batad have also developed the habit of wheedling a few pesos out of visitors if they can.

Getting There & Away

It's about 16 km from Banaue to Batad. If you take a bus or one of the regular jeepneys heading for Anaba, you should get off after 12 km at the Batad turn-off (referred to locally as the 'junction'), between Dalican and Bangaan. Starting out from there, it's a two-hour trek up the steep path over the saddle. It's more convenient to charter a jeepney in Banaue that'll take you up to the saddle. From there, it's only a one-hour trek.
Another path leads from Bangaan (50m before the Bangaan Family Inn, coming from Banaue) up to the saddle. At first it takes you up a steep path through high grass, further on you can walk in the shade of lush vegetation if you're there in the forenoon. The view of Bangaan valley from the path is magnificent.
On the way back to Bangaan, there is a path that takes you the longer way, but it has the advantage of not having any steep bits to negotiate. The path leads along the mountain chain you climbed

over on the way there. It later rejoins the road to Mayoyao about one km east of Bangaan. This path is in the shade in the afternoons and is difficult to make out in its early stages. Best ask one of the local boys from the first little village (you can see where it is from Batad) to act as guide for you. For a few pesos he'll accompany you for about half an hour, until the path can clearly be made out. The place where it joins up with the road to Mayoyao can be identified by the white painted wall in the rice terraces.
An attractive alternative for the return trip to Banaue is to go from Batad via Cambulo and Kinakin; it takes six hrs.

Jeepney: Jeepney trips as far as the 'junction' and to the saddle can be organised by the Tourist Information Center and several guesthouses for P1000 to P1200. This is for up to 14 people, and the driver will come back to pick up his passengers at an agreed time in the late afternoon, or maybe not, if he's already been paid the full fare in advance! One-way costs P500 to P800. A tricycle to the junction costs around P400 for the round trip.
Several regular jeepneys heading for Anaba and Ducligan leave daily between 1 and 5pm in the direction of Batad; P35 per person. If there are enough passengers there, one more will leave between 7 and 8am (ask the driver at the People's Lodge).

Bus: There may be a bus from Banaue to Mayoyao between 10am and noon, which stops at the 'junction' to Batad. On the way back, it passes by between 9 and 11am.

Bangaan

Not quite two km east of the 'junction' to Batad, a track takes you in the opposite direction down from the road to the picturesquely located village of Bangaan. You can see it from the road, and it's easier to reach than Batad. There too, the scenery is magnificent, with countless rice terraces forming a backdrop to the village.

Places to Stay

Bangaan Family Inn. SR/DR and Ifugao house P150. Expect a family atmosphere. The inn is not in the village of Bangaan itself, but on the main road before it goes downhill. The view from the big, half-open restaurant next to the house is breathtaking.

Getting There & Away

Bus/Jeepney: Buses and jeepneys from Banaue to Mayoyao go via Bangaan (one hr). A Special Ride by jeepney costs about P400.

Tricycle: A Special Ride by tricycle costs about P150 to P200.

Mayoyao

Situated about 30 km east of Bangaan, Mayoyao is a rather unattractive place with a small recognisable centre and numerous houses spread higgledy-piggledy over the valley. You can see that a silver-tongued ironware salesman must have made a killing here, as almost all of the traditional Ifugao houses in this area are roofed not with the original thick covering of grass, but with boring corrugated iron.
The rice terraces in Mayoyao were built with masonry walls. An incredible feat, when you think that they had to drag millions of stones up the mountain from the river beds to do it.

Places to Stay

Only private accommodation is available in Mayoyao. The nice lady who owns the ***Travelers Canteen*** will be glad to fix you up.

Getting There & Away

Bus/Jeepney: A few buses and jeepneys travel every day from Banaue to Mayoyao (4½ hrs). You get the best view if you sit on the right-hand side of the bus.

If you don't want to go back to Banaue, you can get a bus from Mayoyao to Santiago at 7am (five hrs).

The North-West

Vigan

Vigan is 130 km north of San Fernando (La Union) and, next to Intramuros in Manila, is the second greatest architectural legacy of the Spaniards. The difference is that many of the old houses in Vigan are still standing. In the latter half of the 16th century, after the young conquistador Juan de Salcedo won a naval battle against the Chinese, Legaspi, his grandfather, gave him the commission to govern Ilocos Province. Vigan thus became a Spanish base.

In planning the layout of the town, Salcedo was no doubt influenced by the secure fortifications of Intramuros. Today Vigan is the best preserved Spanish town in the Philippines. You can almost smell the history here. It is well known as the birthplace of several national heroes, including Diego Silang and his brave wife, Gabriela, Padre Jose Burgos, Isabelo de los Reyes, Leona Florentina and Elipido Quirino.

Vigan is especially impressive in the early morning, when the diffused light transforms the old town with its colonial houses and calesas into a scene reminiscent of the 17th century, eg Mena Crisologo St is particularly beautiful. The old town is closed off to normal traffic until 10am, after which however the exhaust fumes are blasted out again with a vengeance. UNESCO has already approved money for the redevelopment of the old town centre, also known as 'Vigan Heritage Village', with its over 180 so-called Vigan houses.

Along Rizal St as it crosses Liberation Blvd there are potteries where you can observe the traditional production of water containers. The fat-bellied pots with the small lid are called burnay, a pottery is called pagburnayan.

The Cathedral of St Paul near Plaza Burgos, built in 1641, is one of the oldest and biggest churches in the country. If you're interested in churches, take a tricycle for a few pesos to the district of Bantay and visit the Bantay Church. The belltower, which is a few metres off to the side, used to serve as a watchtower for spying out possible attackers.

Mindoro Beach, about four km southwest of Vigan, is grey and not particularly recommended for swimming, although it is quite suitable for a lonely walk along the ocean. On the way, there is a tobacco factory and a small pottery. It's a good idea to make this short trip (in a way fitting for Vigan) by calesa, which should be possible for around P150 (including a one-hour stop at the sea). A tricycle to Mindoro Beach costs about P30.

Museum

In addition to the partially restored old town, the birthplace of Padre Jose Burgos, who was executed by the Spaniards in 1872, is well worth a visit. The house in which he was born was taken over by the Ayala Museum (aka National Museum Padre Burgos) in 1975. You can also get information there about the Tingguian, who live east of Vigan. Open Mon-Fri 8.30-11.30am and 1.30-4.30pm; admission P10.

In the Crisologo Memorabilia Museum, Liberation Blvd, there are mainly antiques belonging to the Crisologo family on display. Open Mon-Fri 8-11.30am and 1.30-4.30pm; admission free.

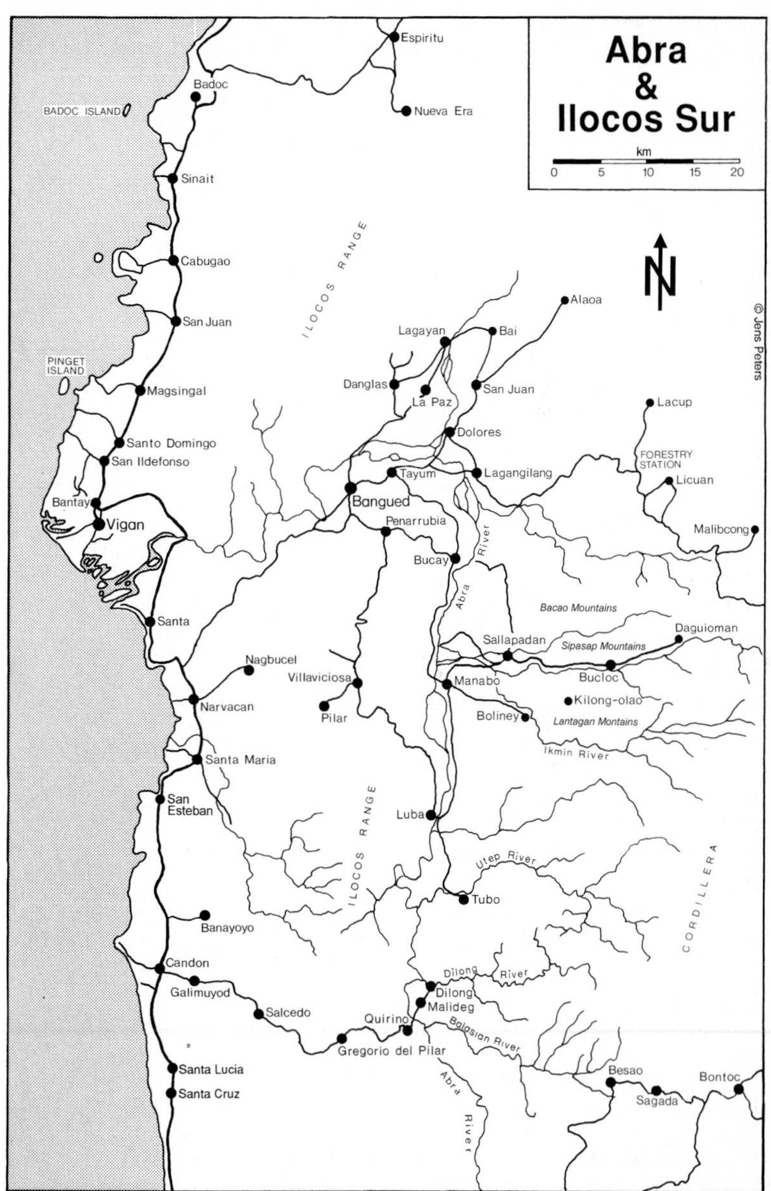
Abra
&
Ilocos Sur
km
0 5 10 15 20
© Jens Peters
Espiritu
Badoc
BADOC ISLAND
Nueva Era
Sinait
Cabugao
San Juan
ILOCOS RANGE
PINGET ISLAND
Magsingal
Santo Domingo
San Ildefonso
Bantay
Vigan
Alaoa
Lagayan
Bai
Danglas
La Paz
San Juan
Lacup
Dolores
FORESTRY STATION
Tayum
Lagangilang
Licuan
Bangued
Penarrubia
Malibcong
Bucay
Abra River
Bacao Mountains
Santa
Sallapadan
Daguioman
Sipasap Mountains
Nagbucel
Villaviciosa
Manabo
Bucloc
Narvacan
Pilar
Kilong-olao
Boliney
Lantagan Montains
Ikmin River
Santa Maria
San Esteban
Luba
ILOCOS RANGE
Utep River
CORDILLERA
Tubo
Banayoyo
Candon
Galimuyod
Dilong River
Dilong
Malideg
Salcedo
Quirino
Balasian River
Gregorio del Pilar
Abra River
Besao
Bontoc
Sagada
Santa Lucia
Santa Cruz

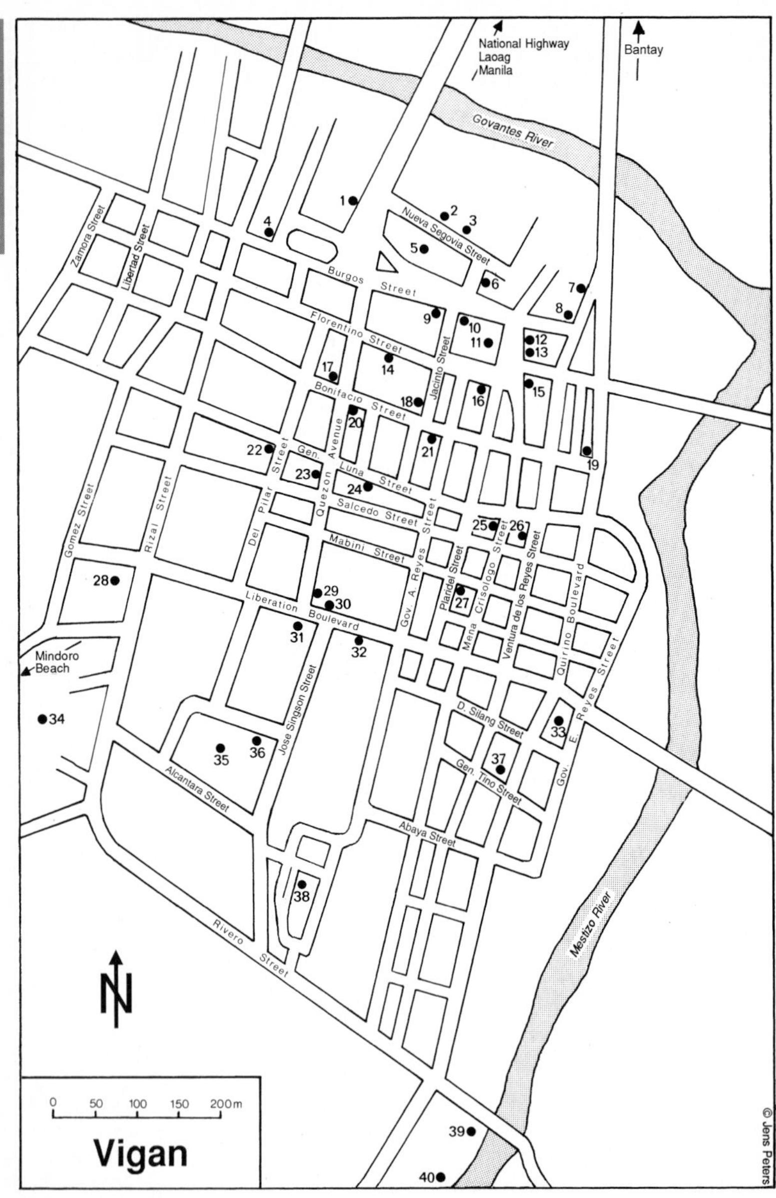
National Highway
Laoag
Manila
Bantay
Govantes River
Nueva Segovia Street
Burgos Street
Zamora Street
Libertad Street
Florentino Street
Jacinto Street
Bonifacio Street
Gen. Luna Street
Del Pilar Street
Quezon Avenue
Salcedo Street
Gomez Street
Rizal Street
Mabini Street
Gov. A. Reyes Street
Plaridel Street
Mena Crisologo Street
Ventura de los Reyes Street
Quirino Boulevard
Liberation Boulevard
Mindoro Beach
Jose Singson Street
D. Silang Street
Gov. E. Reyes Street
Gen. Tino Street
Alcantara Street
Abaya Street
Rivero Street
Mestizo River
0 50 100 150 200 m
Vigan
© Jens Peters

Getting There & Away
24 Philippine Rabbit Bus Terminal
30 Dominion Bus Terminal
36 Partas Bus Terminal
38 Minibus & Jeepney Terminal

Places to Stay
8 Vigan Hotel
12 RF Aniceto Mansion
13 Vigan Plaza Hotel
19 Grandpa's Inn
25 Cordillera Inn
26 Gordion Inn
27 Ferdinandina Hotel
33 El Juliana Hotel
37 Villa Angela Heritage House

Places to Eat
7 Cool Spot 500 Restaurant
9 Greenwich
Jollibee
McDonald's
15 Café Leona
16 Vigan Plaza Restaurant
18 Café Marina
22 8.88 Restaurant
23 Giacomino's
29 Mister Donut

Miscellaneous
1 Provincial Capitol
2 St Paul's College
3 Arzobispado
Museo Nueva Segovia
4 Ayala Museum
5 Plaza Salcedo
6 Cathedral of St Paul
10 Tower
11 Plaza Burgos
14 Philippine National Bank (PNB)
15 Leona Florentina Building
17 Equitable OCI Bank
20 Metrobank
21 Post Office
28 Potteries
31 Simbaan a Bassit Cemetery Chapel
32 Crisologo Memorabilia Museum
34 Mira Hill Park
35 New Market
39 University of Northern Philippines
40 Gabriela Silang General Hospital

The Museo Nueva Segovia is housed in the Arzobispado (Palace of the Archbishop), which was finished in 1783, on Plaza Salcedo. It is exclusively dedicated to church matters, including a collection of precious liturgical objects and portraits of former bishops. Open Mon-Fri 8.30-11.30am 1-4pm; admission P10.

Places to Stay

If you're interested in catching a bit of historical atmosphere - and there's nowhere in the Philippines better for this than Vigan - then check in at one of the restored colonial-style hotels and soak in the atmosphere. Expect Spanish colonial houses still with their original historical tile roofs, the sound and feel of solid hardwood floors, ballustradas you could imagine Zorro jumping from, and azoteas in various Spanish-Mexican styles.

Vigan Hotel, Burgos St, Tel 7221906, Fax 7223001, @. SR/fan P475, DR/fan P675, SR/DR/ac/bath P1375 and P1575 (quite spacious, includes breakfast). An old, cosy building with fairly good accommodation, although some of the rooms seem a bit stuffy.

Grandpa's Inn, Bonifacio St, Tel 7222118. SR/DR/fan P500, SR/DR/fan/bath P600, SR/DR/ac/bath P1000 and P1300. The more expensive rooms have TV and include breakfast. Fairly basic, but friendly accommodation with creative ideas: some of the rooms have quite unusual beds, eg one has been made

from a remodelled calesa (traditional carriage). Coffee Shop (Café Uno).
El Juliana Hotel, Liberation Ave corner Quirino Blvd, Tel 7222994. SR/DR/ac/bath P700 and P800. All rooms (some have no windows) with TV, the more expensive ones also have a refrigerator. Unfortunately no longer in the best of condition, but frequently booked out nevertheless. Friendly service. Swimming pool (P40 admission also for hotel guests). In a quiet area south of the town centre.
Cordillera Inn, 29 Mena Crisologo St, Tel 7222727, Fax 7222739. SR/DR/fan/bath P950, SR/DR/ac/bath P1400. Including breakfast. Reasonable rooms with TV. Restaurant.
Villa Angela Heritage House, Quirino Blvd, Tel 7222914, Fax 7222755, @. SR/DR/fan P970, SR/DR/ac/bath P1800 and P2100. Including breakfast. There are only four rooms available in this gourgeous old villa which was built in 1870. The interior is excellently preserved, with antique fittings and furniture dating from colonial times, and the garden is magnificent. Food can be prepared if ordered beforehand. In January 1989, Tom Cruise was a guest in this delightful place while shooting the film *Born on the 4th of July*. Located near the El-Juliana Hotel.
RF Aniceto Mansion, Mena Crisologo St, Tel 7222383, Fax 7222384. SR/DR/ac/bath from P1000. Situated on the Plaza Burgos diagonally across from the cathedral, with numerous quite good rooms, all with TV but not all with hot water. Restaurant.
Gordion Inn, Salcedo St corner Ventura de los Reyes St, Tel 7222526, Fax 7222840, @. SR/DR/ac/bath P1200, suite P4000. Including breakfast. Neat rooms with TV, pleasant atmosphere. Coffee shop. Reservations in Manila: Tel (02) 4260392, Fax: (02) 4261014.
Vigan Plaza Hotel, Mena Crisologo St, Tel 7228552, Fax 7228552, @. SR/DR/ac/bath P1600 and P1800, suite P2800 and P3000. Comfortably furnished rooms with TV, the suites also have a refrigerator. Vigan's best hotel, located on Plaza Burgos. Good restaurant.

Places to Eat

The unpretentious ***Victory Restaurant*** on Quezon Ave offers inexpensive Filipino food, but closes early in the evening. The ***Cool Spot 500***, a lovely half-open restaurant adjacent to the Vigan Hotel, used to be justifiably proud of its Ilocano food, but the prices are way over the top now. Worth recommending on the other hand are the very popular ***Café Leona***, in Mena Crisologo St at Plaza Burgos, where you can sit outside at the weekends, and ***Giacomino's*** in Quezon Ave, where they serve inexpensive food, including pizzas. You can also sit outside in the pleasant ***Café Marina*** in Jacinto St. The fast food restaurants ***McDonald's***, ***Jollibee*** and ***Greenwich*** are all in Burgos St near the carillon.
While you're in Vigan you should try empanadas at least once; these are tasty vegetable-filled pasties of Spanish origin. You can get them from around 4pm until quite late at night at the Plaza Burgos for pennies each.

Miscellaneous

Festivals: Town Fiesta on 25 January. Viva Vigan Festival in the first week in May (street dancing, calesa parade etc).
Money: Equitable PCI Bank, Quezon Ave, and Philippine National Bank, Florentino St, have ATMs.
Population: 50,000.
Post & Telephone: Post Office in Bonifacio St.
Post code: 2700. Area code: 077.

Getting There & Away

Aparri

Bus: From Aparri to Vigan there are only a few buses a day (nine hrs).

Dagupan
Bus: Getting from Dagupan to Vigan works like this: First, take a minibus to Damortis or San Fernando, change there into a bus from Manila heading for Vigan or Laoag (six hrs).

Laoag
Bus: From Laoag to Vigan, there are many minibuses daily as well as Autobus Transport, Fariñas Trans, Partas and Philippine Rabbit buses bound for Manila or San Fernando (two hrs). You may have to get off the bus in Bantay on the highway outside the town and complete the last stretch to Vigan by tricycle (P5) or walk the remaining 500m (10 min).

Manila - San Fernando (La Union)
Bus: From Manila to Vigan, there are several Autobus Transport, Dominion Bus Line, Fariñas Trans, Partas and Philippine Rabbit buses daily (P400; 9½ hrs). From San Fernando several Philippine Rabbit buses go to Vigan daily, leaving from the plaza (2½ hrs). You can also board a bus from Manila to Vigan or Laoag there.
Some buses continuing north to Laoag bypass the town, in which case you will have to take a tricycle from the highway in Bantay (P5) or walk the remaining 500m (10 min).

Bangued

Bangued was founded in 1598 by Augustinian monks and is the capital of Abra, which has been a province since 1917. From little Victoria Park, on Casmata Hill, you can get a good view of the town and of the Abra River flowing through the wide valley.
Every year in March, Bangued celebrates the Arya Abra Festival with parades, colourful cultural presentations and folklore displays, including some from the Tingguian.

Places to Stay

Tingguian Lodge, Calaba, Tel 7528384. SR/DR/fan P350, SR/DR/ac/bath P500. An unpretentious place, located just outside of town.
Diocesan Pastoral Center, Rizal St, Tel 7528092. SR/DR/fan/bath P200/300, SR/DR/ac/bath P450/600. Make enquiries at the convent near the church if you are interested in staying there. The Center is not a hotel but church-run accommodation.
King David Palace Hotel, Capitulacion St. SR/DR/fan/bath P500, SR/DR/ac/bath P800 (TV). Good rooms. The best hotel in town.

Places to Eat

The Filipino food in the ***Payospi Restaurant*** near the plaza is good, while ***Uncle Pete's*** is a popular fast food restaurant in Taft St, with spaghetti etc.

Miscellaneous

Festival: Arya Abra Festival from 5 to 10 March.
Population: 35,000.
Post & Telephone: Post code: 2800. Area code: 074.

Getting There & Away

Baguio
Bus: Four Philippine Rabbit buses go from Baguio to Batad daily (five hrs).

Manila
Bus: From Manila to Bangued there are Dominion Bus Line, Partas and Philippine Rabbit buses daily (P360; nine hrs).

Vigan
Bus: From Vigan to Bangued there are several minibuses daily from the terminal at the new market (three hrs). Large Dominion Bus Line buses are also likely to be there.

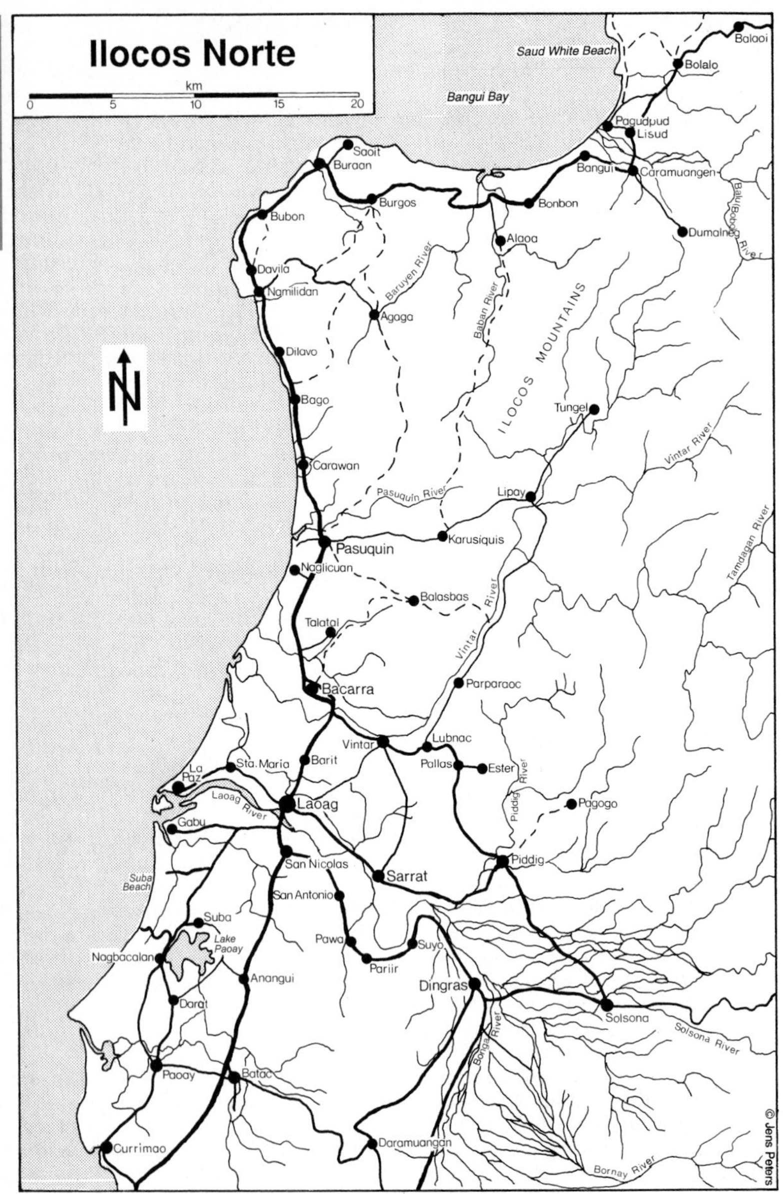

Ilocos Norte
km
0
5
10
15
20
Saud White Beach
Bangui Bay
Balaoi
Bolalo
Pagudpud
Lisud
Saoit
Buraan
Bangui
Caramuangen
Burgos
Bonbon
Bubon
Alaoa
Dumalneg
Davila
Ngmilidan
Baruyen River
Baban River
ILOCOS MOUNTAINS
Agaga
Dilavo
Bago
Tungel
Vintar River
Carawan
Pasuquin River
Lipay
Pasuquin
Karusiquis
Tamdagan River
Naglicuan
Balasbas
Talatal
Vintar River
Parparaoc
Bacarra
Vintar
Lubnac
Barit
Pallas
Ester
La Paz
Sta. Maria
Laoag
Laoag River
Piddig River
Pagogo
Gabu
San Nicolas
Sarrat
Piddig
Suba Beach
San Antonio
Suba
Lake Paoay
Pawa
Suyo
Nagbacalan
Pariir
Anangui
Dingras
Darat
Solsona
Solsona River
Bonga River
Paoay
Batac
Daramuangan
Currimao
Bornay River
© Jens Peters

Laoag

In 1818, when Ilocos Province was divided in two, Laoag, on the Laoag River, became the capital of Ilocos Norte, one of Luzon's most beautiful provinces.

Worth seeing is St William's Cathedral, which was built between 1650 and 1700, and is one of the many old Spanish churches in this province. Also interesting are the mighty 'Sinking Belltower', which stands a little apart from the cathedral and the tidy plaza with the Ilocos Norte Capitol, Marcos Hall of Justice and the Tobacco Monopoly Monument. The latter was built in 1882 in gratitude to the Spanish King Alfonso XII, who had lifted the tobacco monopoly the previous year which for a hundred years had forced the Ilocanos to plant tobacco to the exclusion of everything else.

Day trips into the nearby countryside are recommended. (See the Around Laoag section later in this chapter.)

Museum

The Museo Ilocos Norte in General Antonio Luna St provides a good overview of the history and culture of the Ilocanos as well as information on the ethnic minorities in the region. Open Mon-Sat 9am-noon and 1-5pm. Admission 20 P.

Places to Stay

Texicano Hotel, Rizal St, Tel 7720606, Fax 7720896. SR/fan/bath P220, DR/fan/bath P250, SR/ac/bath P600 and P700, DR/ac/bath P700 to P1500. Fairly good for this price category. The more expensive rooms are in the annex. Restaurant. The actual entrance to the hotel is on General Hizon St.

Hotel del Norte, 26 Fonacier St, Tel 7721697. SR/fan/bath P225, SR/ac/bath P600, DR/ac/bath P650 and P750. Clean, practically furnished rooms, the more expensive ones have a TV.

Hotel Tiffany, Gen Segundo Ave corner MH del Pilar St, Tel 7703550. SR/ac/bath P480, DR/ac/bath P730 and P1000 (refrigerator). Immaculate rooms with TV, all decorated in different candy colours.

La Elliana Hotel, Jose Rizal St corner Ablan St, Tel & Fax 7714876. SR/DR/ac/bath P650 and P750. Impeccable rooms with TV. Good value. Restaurant. Located about 300m west of the Texicano Hotel.

Fort Ilocandia Resort Hotel, Calayab, Tel 7721166, Fax 7721411, @. SR/DR/ac/bath P4600 to P8700, suite P18,000 and P45,000. Including breakfast. An exclusive hotel on Suba Beach, south of the airport. They have four restaurants, a disco with live bands, casino, fitness room and a swimming pool. You can get there from Laoag by taking a jeepney heading for Calayab.

Places to Eat

The aircon ***Macy's Diner*** in the Hotel Tiffany, Gen Segundo Ave, serves good, inexpensive fast food such as pizzas, tacos and so-called combos (combination plates, eg with spaghetti, pizza and roast chicken with a drink on the side) as well as really delicious fruit shakes (eg green mango or avocado tapioca). It's decorated 50s style and is open from 8am to 8pm. ***Giacomino's*** in Rizal St corner Gen Segundo Ave, serves good pizzas and ***Sizzles Restaurant*** right next door lives up to its name with sizzling steaks, 24 hours a day. ***Magic Bunny*** in Jose Rizal St is popular, and the ***Town Bakery*** right next door has tasty cakes.

Also in Jose Rizal St, across from the Texicano Hotel, the pleasant, friendly furnished and aircon ***La Preciosa Restaurant*** can be highly recommended for its excellent, inexpensive local Ilocano food, choice of daily specials, international specialities and great breakfast.

Getting There & Away
1 Florida Liner Bus Terminal
2 Partas Bus Terminal
5 Minibuses to Pagudpud
6 Jeepneys & Minibuses to Bacarra & Pasuquin
9 Philippine Rabbit Bus Terminal (100m)
11 Jeepneys to Airport
13 Autobus Transport Bus Terminal (350m)
15 Jeepneys to Batac & Paoay
22 Jeepneys to San Nicolas
28 Fariñas Trans Bus Terminal
36 Jeepneys to Sarrat & Dingras
39 Jeepneys to Suba & Fort Ilocandia Resort Hotel
43 Airport (5 km)

Places to Stay
3 Pichay Lodging House
4 Casa Llanes Pension
8 Hotel Tiffany
12 Texicano Hotel
13 La Elliana Hotel (300m)
22 Hotel del Norte
43 Fort Ilocandia Resort Hotel

Places to Eat & Entertainment
7 Hotstuff Foodhouse
8 Macy's Diner
14 La Preciosa Restaurant
16 Town Bakery
17 Magic Bunny Restaurant
20 Mister Donut
21 Giacomino's Sizzles Restaurant
26 Discoland
29 Colonial Fast Food
30 Goldilocks
38 Chowking
39 Jollibee

Miscellaneous
10 Museo Ilocos Norte
18 Equitable PCI Bank
19 Provincial Capitol
23 Bank of the Philippine Islands
24 Equitable PCI Bank
25 Philippine National Bank (PNB)
26 Cockpit
31 Marcos Hall of Justice
32 Plaza
Tobacco Monopoly Monument
33 Sinking Belltower
34 Metrobank
35 Market
37 City Hall
Post Office
40 Ermita Hill
42 St William's Cathedral

Entertainment

Cockfighting takes place on the outskirts of town on Sundays and public holidays from 2pm onwards. Next door, you will find Laoag's nightlife at ***Discoland***, consisting of about a dozen clubs and discos.

Miscellaneous

Festival: Pamulinawen Festival from 7 to 10 February.
Money: The Bank of the Philippine Islands and the Equitable PCI Bank, both in Jose Rizal St, have ATMs.
Population: 100,000.
Post & Telephone: Post Office in City Hall.
Post code: 2900. Area code: 077.

Getting There & Away

By Air: The Laoag International Airport is at Gabu, about five km southwest of Laoag. Jeepneys to the airport leave from the corner of AM Regidor St and General Luna St (15 min).
Air Philippines, Fort Ilocandia Resort Hotel, Tel 7721166 (ext 2878).
Destination: Manila.

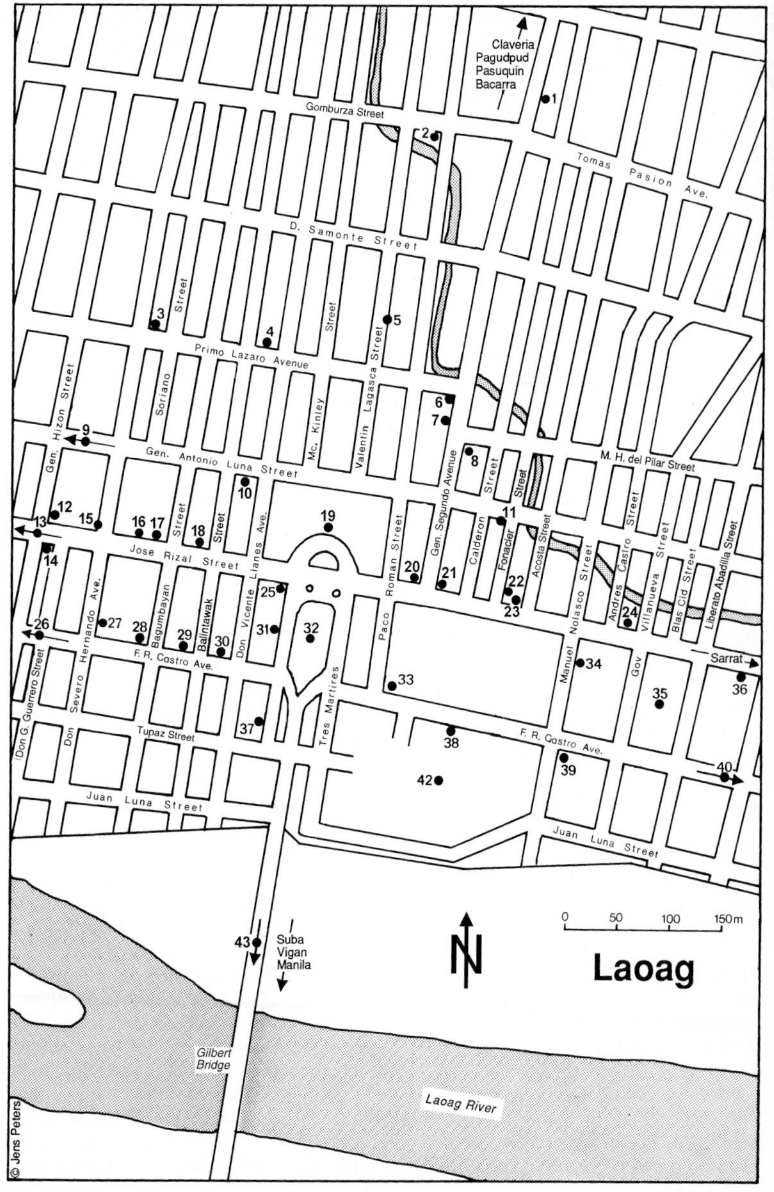
Claveria
Pagudpud
Pasuquin
Bacarra
Gomburza Street
Tomas Pasion Ave.
D. Samonte Street
Primo Lazaro Avenue
Soriano Street
Mc. Kinley Street
Valentin Lagasca Street
Gen. Hizon Street
Gen. Antonio Luna Street
M. H. del Pilar Street
Gen. Segundo Avenue
Calderon Street
Fonacier Street
Acosta Street
Nolasco Street
Andres Castro Street
Villanueva Street
Blas Cid Street
Liberato Abadilla Street
Jose Rizal Street
Don Vicente Llanes Ave.
Paco Roman Street
Don Severo Hernando Ave.
Bagumbayan Street
Balintawak Street
F. R. Castro Ave.
Manuel
Gov
Sarrat
Tres Martires
Don G. Guerrero Street
Tupaz Street
Juan Luna Street
Suba
Vigan
Manila
Gilbert Bridge
Laoag River
0 50 100 150m
Laoag
© Jens Peters

Chemtrad Aviation, Laoag International Airport, Tel 6070167.
Destination: Basco (Batanes Islands).
China Southern, LGS General Services, Laoag International Airport, Tel 7721888.
Destination: Guangzhou (China).
CR Airways, LGS General Services, Laoag International Airport, Tel 7721888.
Destination: Hong Kong.
Far Eastern Air Transport, LGS General Services, Laoag International Airport, Tel 7721888.
Destination: Kaohsiung (Taiwan).
Pacific Airways, Laoag International Airport, Tel 7720663.
Destination: Basco (Batanes Islands).

By Boat: Between Currimao, 30 km south of Laoag, and Basco (Batanes Islands) there is a weekly boat route. See the Getting Away from Luzon section of the Manila chapter.

Getting There & Away

Aparri - Calveria - Pagudpud
Bus: From Aparri to Laoag there are only a few buses, all via Pagudpud, some of which are bound for Vigan. You will probably have to take a jeepney to the new Marcos Bridge on the highway and catch a Florida Liner bus there coming from Tuguegarao and going to Laoag or Vigan. But go by day so you can see the spectacular landscape and the beautiful views over the South China Sea. The view between Claveria and Pagudpud is especially worth seeing (five hrs).

Baguio
Bus: From Baguio to Laoag via San Fernando and Vigan, Philippine Rabbit buses go every hour. (six hrs).

Manila - San Fernando (La Union) - Vigan
Air: Air Philippines flies irregularly (only charter) possibly on Monday, Thursday and Saturday from Manila to Laoag and vice versa (one hr).

Bus: From Manila to Laoag, there are many Autobus Transport, Fariñas Trans, Partas and Philippine Rabbit buses daily (P450; 11½ hrs). The routes go via San Fernando and Vigan. Vigan is off the highway and not all drivers make the detour into town. If you are in a hurry, get a tricycle for P5 to the highway and stop one of the buses there. There are also many minibuses travelling from Vigan to Laoag daily (three hrs).
Buses from Laoag to Manila via Vigan and San Fernando leave roughly hourly between 7am and 11pm.

Tuguegarao
Bus: From Tuguegarao to Laoag you can take one of eight Florida Liner buses; they leave daily between 4am and 7pm (eight hrs).

Around Laoag

North

North of Laoag, Bacarra has a massive belltower which stands next to the town's church. It dates back to 1783 and was partly destroyed in the severe earthquake of 1930. The top of the spire was crooked and, until 1984, was held in place solely, as they said then, by 'the hand of God'. Another earthquake then caused its complete collapse.
Ten km farther north is Pasuquin; from there you can go to Seksi Beach, which is four km outside the town and can be reached by tricycle. From December to March there you can see women strenuously at work harvesting salt in the late afternoon. At low tide, the top layer of salt, mixed with sand, is scraped together and put in a light hanging basket. Water is then poured in and runs out through the bottom of the basket into an earthenware pot, now with a very

Bamboo *(Bambusa vulgaris)*
The many kinds of bamboo *(kawayan)*, which mostly grows in damp places, are used in many different ways, eg as a building material or for weaving. The shoots *(labong)* closest to the ground are finely chopped and boiled, to be used as a basic vegetable in many local dishes.

high salt content. This water is taken to the village and boiled in a large pot until it has almost completely evaporated. The remaining slurry is then ladled out of the pot into a hanging basket, which the remaining water seeps through to form a long, hanging white cone of the finest salt.

West

The nearest good beach to Laoag is in La Paz, a peaceful, long drawn-out community at the mouth of the Laoag River. Hardly any vegetation exists on the wide beach, but there are very extensive sand dunes that eventually end up in a beautiful pebble beach at the north end.

South-East

A fine country road leads to Sarrat, the birthplace of former president Marcos. In the centre of town is the restored Sarrat Church & Convent, built in 1779 by Augustinian monks.
Only ruins remain of the church in Dingras, which was destroyed by fire in 1838.

South

There is a church in San Nicolas which was built in the latter part of the 17th century and restored in the 19th century. About 15 km further south, in Batac, another building attracts the attention of the Filipinos: Marcos Museum is full of memorabilia on the subject of the former president (open daily from 9 am until noon, and 1 to 4pm). Directly next door there is a mausoleum where visitors can pay their respects to the body of the former president which has lain in state there since 1994 (and will continue to do so until permission is granted for his burial in the Heroes' Cemetery in Manila). If the door is locked, one of the museum staff will open it for you. On entering, the visitor is greeted by a Gregorian chant, and the platform with the glass sarcophagus is illuminated by a white beam of light, standing out impressively against the dark background of the otherwise empty room.
A few km to the south-west is the fortress-like Paoay Church, which is worth a stop. Its side walls are supported by strong posts. Styled in 'earthquake baroque', this church is probably the most famous in Ilocos Norte. You can also see the scenically attractive Lake Paoay. Going from Paoay through bamboo forests, along the western shore of the lake to Suba, you could make a detour to Suba Beach. The road there is hilly and winding and there are high, extensive sand dunes, more imposing than those at La Paz, where many Philippine films have been shot. It is usually windy on this wide beach and there is good surf.

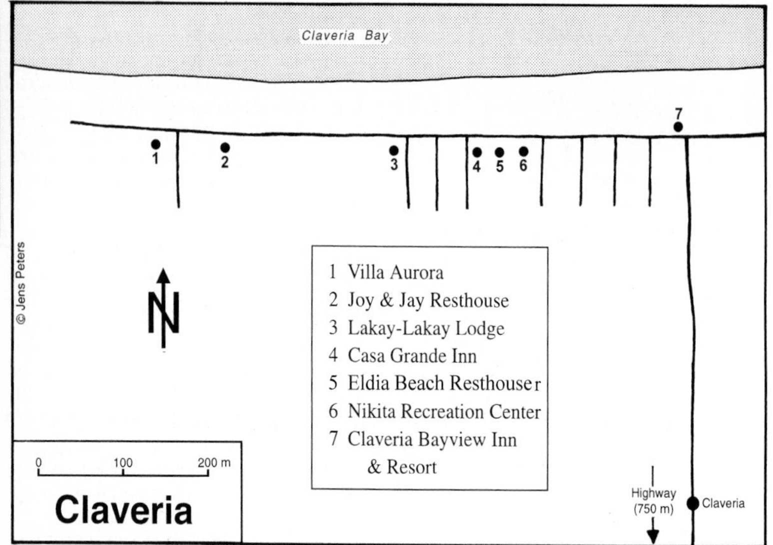

If you have come up the roughly eight km to Nagbacalan from Paoay by tricycle (Special Ride, costing about P100) and want to return to Laoag by jeepney, you can board one at the small restaurants on the beach, at the Fort Ilocandia Resort Hotel, or at the Suba Golf Course. The last regular jeepney leaves the hotel at about 4pm and passes the golf course on the way back to Laoag. The exclusive hotel is about five km south of Gabu, where Laoag International Airport is located. Marcos had it built especially for guests on the occasion of the wedding of his daughter Irene to Greggy Araneta in 1983. The tables and seats under cover on the beach belong to the hotel and there is a P100 charge for their use.

Pagudpud

Pagudpud lies on scenic, palm-lined Bangui Bay, about 60 km north of Laoag, and could become a tourist destination in the near future. The beautiful, stretched out Saud White Beach is probably the best and most attractive in North Luzon and has been used as the backdrop for many a Philippine film. It's about five km from Pagudpud. Unfortunately, there is not a large enough selection of resorts at reasonable prices to really get the place going.
If you have a tricycle bring you to Saud Beach, don't forget to have the driver wait until you've negotiated an acceptable room price before he leaves.

Places to Stay

Arinaya White Beach Resort. SR/DR/fan P900, SR/DR/ac/bath P1500. Basic, clean rooms. Restaurant.
Terra Rika Beach Resort, Tel (077) 7641009, Cellphone 0920-5740136, @. SR/DR/fan P1000 and P1800, SR/DR/ac/bath P2500. A variety of different buildings, all with several rooms each, the aircon ones with refrigerator and cooking facilities. Restaurant.

Villa del Mar Ivory Beach Resort. SR/DR/fan/bath P1300, SR/DR/ac/bath P1600. Popular with locals, some of the rooms are a bit small. Restaurant, swimming pool.
Saud Beach Resort, Tel (077) 7641005. SR/DR/ac/bath P2400 to P3800. Good, generously sized rooms with refrigerator. Extensive grounds with a big, attractive building. The best resort on the beach. Restaurant.

Getting There & Away

Bus: Buses from Vigan and Laoag to Aparri and Tuguegarao go via Pagudpud. From Laoag there are several minibuses which travel to Pagudpud daily and leave from McKinley St (two hrs).

Claveria & Babuyan Islands

The long beach of Claveria is located on a picturesque bay, but there's not a tree to be seen, let alone palm trees.
Trips can be made out to the Babuyan Islands from Claveria. Once a week a passenger boat sails to Calayan Island, taking five hours. From Calayan Island, boats sail to Babuyan Island (four hrs). People live there more or less cut off from the benefits of civilisation. Visitors are advised to take a few presents along for their hosts.
Worth seeing on Babuyan is the 837-metre high Babuyan Claro volcano with its two craters. Fuga Island is said to be the most beautiful of the Babuyan Islands. It's the private property of a Chinese man, whose plans to turn it into a little 'Hong Kong' apparently came to nothing. Around 2,000 Ilokanos live on the island in conditions of extreme poverty.
The Canadian Karie Garnier, @, and his Filipina wife Violeta organise one-week Fuga Island Tours, leaving from Claveria in April and May when the sea in the Babuyan Channel is at its quietest.

Places to Stay

The following accommodation is all on the beach. It's practically impossible to find a vacant room during Easter week. Prices are hiked at that time by up to 50%.
Joy & Jay Resthouse. SR/fan P100, DR/fan P150. Small, unpretentious rooms, but OK for the money.
Lakay-Lakay Lodge. Cottage P100, SR/DR/fan/bath P300. Spartan cottages (totally bare) and basic rooms. Friendly place with a family atmosphere. No restaurant, but it's possible to have a meal with the owner.
Casa Grande Inn. SR/DR/fan/bath P150/300. Attractive, big building with spacious, friendly rooms. Restaurant.
Claveria Bayview Inn & Resort. SR/DR/fan/bath P300, SR/DR/ac/bath P800 (with TV). Clean, basic rooms at reasonable prices. Friendly, family atmosphere. Restaurant (order food beforehand if possible).
Eldia Beach Resthouse, Tel (078) 8661072. SR/DR/fan/bath P500, SR/DR/ac/bath P800. Basic, but good accommodation. Small restaurant.

It's possible to find accommodation for the night on Babuyan Island at the priest's or the mayor's house.

Getting There & Away

By Bus: Claveria itself is about 750m from the highway (turn-off at the Petron filling station); it's about 400m from Claveria to the beach. A tricycle costs P3 per person.

Tuguegarao
Bus: Buses from Tuguegarao to Laoag and Vigan go via Claveria (four hrs).

Vigan - Laoag
Bus: Buses from Vigan and Laoag to Tuguegarao go via Claveria, taking five hrs from Vigan, and three hrs from Laoag.

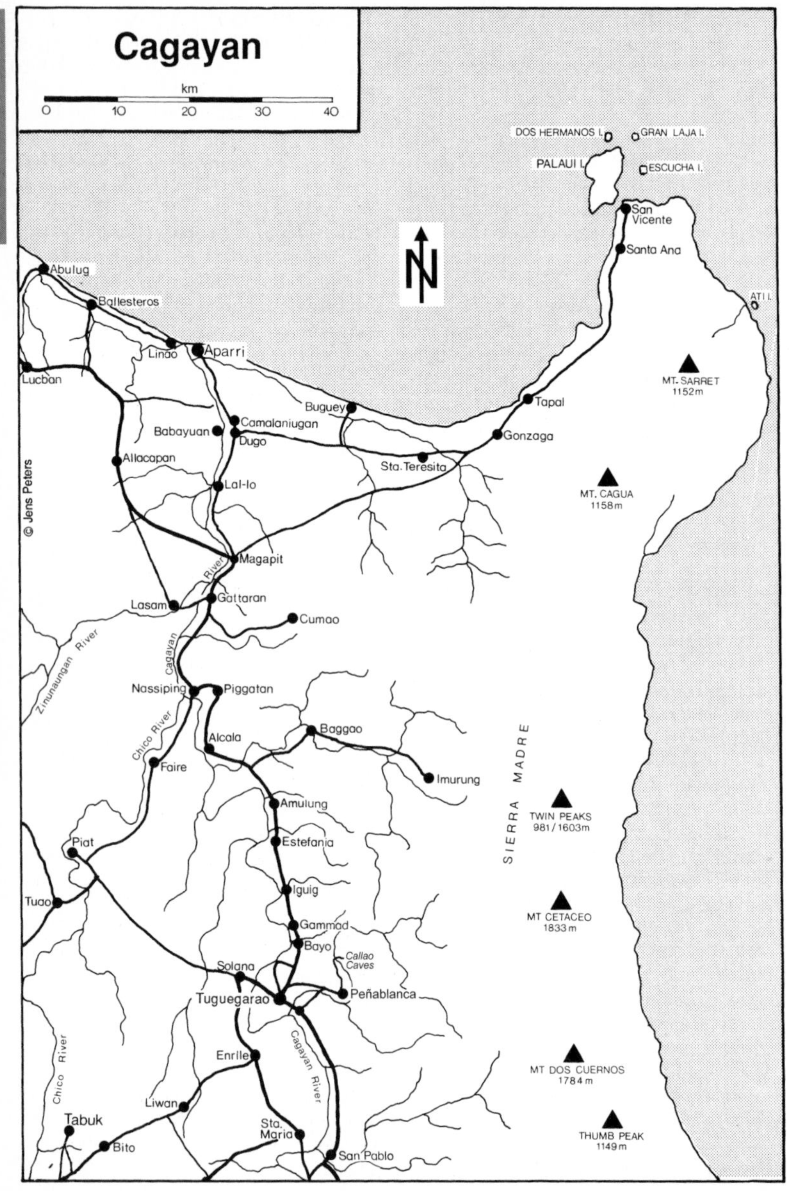
Cagayan
km
0
10
20
30
40
© Jens Peters
DOS HERMANOS I.
GRAN LAJA I.
PALAUI I.
ESCUCHA I.
San Vicente
Santa Ana
ATI I.
Abulug
Ballesteros
Linao
Aparri
Lucban
MT. SARRET
1152m
Tapal
Buguey
Camalaniugan
Babayuan
Dugo
Gonzaga
Allacapan
Sta. Teresita
MT. CAGUA
1158m
Lal-lo
Magapit
River
Lasam
Gattaran
Cumao
Cagayan
Zinunaungan River
Nassiping
Piggatan
Baggao
Alcala
Chico River
Faire
Imurung
SIERRA MADRE
Amulung
TWIN PEAKS
981/1603m
Estefania
Piat
Iguig
Tuao
MT CETACEO
1833 m
Gammad
Bayo
Callao Caves
Solana
Peñablanca
Tuguegarao
Cagayan River
Chico River
Enrile
MT DOS CUERNOS
1784 m
Liwan
Tabuk
Sta. Maria
THUMB PEAK
1149m
Bito
San Pablo

Cagayan Valley & East Coast

Aparri

It's not worth staying for any length of time in Aparri, unless you want to do some big-game fishing, which is popular in the Babuyan Channel, north of Luzon, especially in April and May. The waters around Point Escarpada, near San Vicente, are well known as the best Philippine fishing grounds for marlin. However, not infrequently big game anglers have disappeared here and never turned up again, which is why the Babuyan Channel is known as the Bermuda Triangle of the Philippines.
If you want to explore this north-eastern corner of Luzon, you should take the bus from Aparri to Santa Ana. You will have to continue by tricycle to San Vicente if there is no bus or jeepney. From there you can get somebody to take you across to Palaui Island by outrigger boat.

Places to Stay

Pipo Hotel, Macanaya St. SR/DR/fan P150/300, SR/DR/fan/bath P300/400. Basic. Restaurant. Before you get to Aparri, on the right hand side. Jeepney drivers will halt if requested.
Ryan Hotel, Rizal St, Tel 8228210. SR/DR/fan/bath P350, SR/DR/ac/bath P700 and P750. OK rooms. Restaurant.

Miscellaneous

Population: 40,000.
Post & Telephone: Post code: 3515. Area code: 078.

Getting There & Away

By Bus: Only a few buses go to or from Aparri directly. Most of them stop 30 km further south at the big Marcos Bridge at Magapit. There is a jeepney route between Magapit and Aparri. If you want to go from Aparri to Laoag, for example, you have to go to Marcos Bridge first and then wait for a bus coming from Tuguegarao.

Manila - Tuguegarao - Gattaran
Bus: From Manila to Aparri, Autobus and Baliwag Transit buses leave daily from their Cubao terminals between 6 and 11am and 6 to 11pm roughly hourly. They go via Ilagan, Tuguegarao and Gattaran (12 hrs).
From Aparri to Tuguegarao via Gattaran, during the day there are minibuses in addition to the buses heading to Manila (to Gattaran one hr; to Tuguegarao two hrs).

Vigan - Laoag
Bus: From Vigan and Laoag, only a few buses go to Aparri. The trip takes seven and five hrs respectively (see the Getting There & Away sections under Vigan and Laoag earlier in this chapter).

Gattaran

If you are coming from Manila or Tuguegarao, you can break the journey to Aparri in Gattaran and make a lengthy detour to the Tanlagan Falls, which have a drop of over 100m. You would have to be a dedicated lover of waterfalls, however, to make the trip, as this natural spectacle is almost 40 km to the east, beyond Cumao, which you can only reach by jeepney from Gattaran. The last part of the trip can only be done by vehicle in the dry season, as there are several rivers to be crossed.

Tuguegarao

Tuguegarao, the bustling capital of Cagayan Province, is the starting point for the Callao Caves which are about 15 km north-east of Tuguegarao and nine km north of Peñablanca. Jeepneys go there (take the 'Callao' jeepney from the terminal in the Santo Domingo part of town the whole way to the terminus at the river). The river crossing to the cave entrance costs P3 per person; admission P10. By car, the caves can be reached directly by taking the road along the other side of the river.

If you want to make more than a day trip of it, you can stay the night at the Callao Caves Resort. All together, there are roughly 300 caves at Peñablanca, of which the Callao Caves are the best known.

Apart from speleology, this cave country also offers very interesting treks to the distant villages of the Sierra Madre. Some villages can only be reached by boat on the Pinacanauan River or on foot. A boat to the next point where you can start hiking along the river bank costs P30, further trips costs P50. It's cheaper to take one of the boats which travel at irregular intervals from the jetty at the Callao Cave Resort and the various villages in the area. As a hike along the river involves crossing the river at various places, it's essential to wear appropriate shoes and pack away your valuables so they're watertight.

It takes about 30 min by boat from the Callao Caves Resort to a 'mineral water' waterfall.

In Iguig, just north of Tuguegarao, there are 14 large statues which represent the Stations of the Cross to Calvary. It is an important place of pilgrimage, especially during Easter week (Semana Santa at Iguig Calvary Hills).

Museum

The Cagayan Museum & Historical Research Center next to the Provincial Capitol, exhibits archaeological finds, historical and cultural artefacts, liturgical items and ethnographic objects of the province. It's divided into the Provincial Museum and the National Museum (prehistoric and early history). Open Mon-Fri 8am-4pm, at the weekend only by arrangement. The Provincial Museum also organises guides for tours all around Cagayan (P250 per day), including cave exploration and river trekking.

Places to Stay

Hotel Candice, Blumentritt St, Tel 8442001, Fax 8442003. SR/ac/bath P430, DR/ac/bath P600 (in the annex, cold water), SR/DR/ac/bath P650/700 and P900/1000. Immaculate, spacious rooms with TV, the more expensive with refrigerator. Restaurant.

Hotel Delfino, Gonzaga St, Tel 8441314. SR/ac/bath P450, DR/ac/bath P550. With TV. Good rooms for the money. Restaurant, disco.

Hotel Lorita, Rizal St, Tel 8441390. SR/ac/bath P500, DR/ac/bath P770 to P920. Very nice rooms and a good value suite for P1350 which can be recommended. Coffee shop. They also offer an airport service.

Pensione Roma, Luna St corner Bonifacio St, Tel 8441057, Fax: 8447658. SR/DR/ac/bath P500 to P1800, suites P2400 and P2700. Pleasant, friendly hotel with immaculate rooms of various different sizes with TV, the more expensive ones also with refrigerator. Restaurant.

Callao Cave Resort, Peñablanca. Dorm P100, SR/DR/fan/bath P450 and P850, cottage/ac/bath P1500. Located at the river across from the cave entrance (jeepney terminus) and managed by the Provincial Tourist Office.

Places to Eat

The ***Pampangueña Restaurant***, opposite Pensione Abraham, changes its menus daily and has a surprisingly large choice of cakes. The ***Adri Nelo Restaurant*** in Rizal St can also be recommended, as well as ***Café Michelle*** in the Pensione Roma. At the corner of

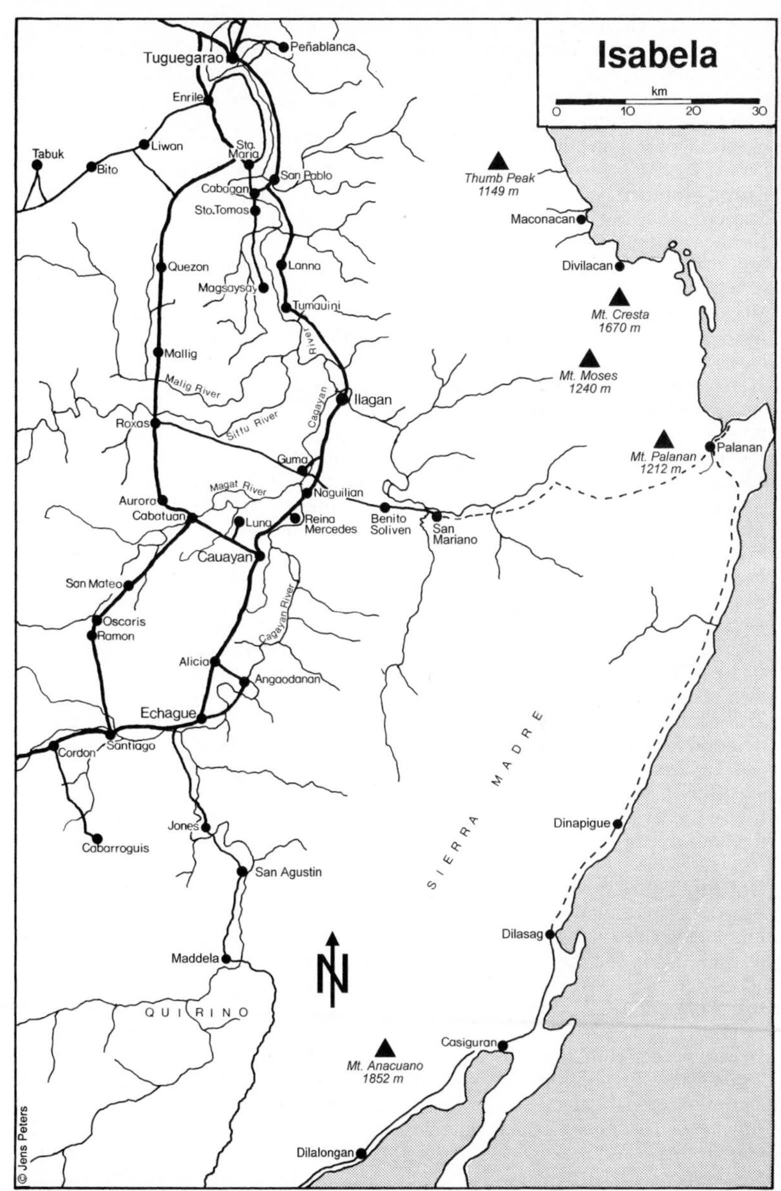
Isabela
km
0
10
20
30
Tuguegarao
Peñablanca
Enrile
Tabuk
Bito
Liwan
Sta. Maria
San Pablo
Cabagan
Sto.Tomas
Quezon
Lanna
Magsaysay
Tumauini
Mallig
Malig River
River
Cagayan
Ilagan
Roxas
Siffu River
Guma
Magat River
Aurora
Naguilian
Cabatuan
Luna
Reina Mercedes
Benito Soliven
San Mariano
Cauayan
San Mateo
Oscaris
Ramon
Cagayan River
Alicia
Angadanan
Echague
Santiago
Cordon
Cabarroguis
Jones
San Agustin
Maddela
QUIRINO
Thumb Peak
1149 m
Maconacan
Divilacan
Mt. Cresta
1670 m
Mt. Moses
1240 m
Mt. Palanan
1212 m
Palanan
SIERRA MADRE
Dinapigue
Dilasag
Casiguran
Mt. Anacuano
1852 m
Dilalongan
N
© Jens Peters

Rizal St and Gomez St you'll find the two-storey, aircon ***Griselda's Snack House*** with its noodles, burgers, spaghetti, pizzas, siopao etc. It's open 24 hours - most of the other restaurants close at 8 or 9 in the evening.

Entertainment

There are a few ***Discos*** and ***Beer Houses*** on the main road to Manila. The Hotel Delfino has its ***Astro Disco***.

Miscellaneous

Festival: Tuguegarao City Patronal Fiesta from 15 to 17 August.
Money: The Equitable PCI Bank and the Philippine National Bank, both in Bonifacio St, have ATMs.
Population: 120,000.
Post & Telephone: Post code: 3500. Area code: 078.
Tourist Office, Gonzaga St (across from the Hotel Delfino on the first floor from the market). Tel 8441621, Fax 8442435. Open Mon-Fri 8am-noon and 1-5pm.
Provincial Tourist Office, Provincial Capitol, Tel 8467576. Open Mon-Fri 8am-noon and 1-5pm.
Travel Agency: Adventures & Expeditions Philippines, 29 Burgos St, Tel 8441298, Cellphone 0917-5327480, @, offers: Cave exploration, wild water trips with kayaks and dinghies, Kalinga trekking.

Getting There & Away

By Air: Tuguegarao's airport is about four km outside the centre of town. It is possible to do the trip by tricycle for about P20.
Air Philippines, Airport Office, Tel 8441201.
Destination: Manila.
Asian Spirit, Rizal Street, Tel 8448141.
Destination: Manila.
Chemtrad Aviation, Tuguegarao Airport, Tel 8443113.
Destinations: Batanes, Pandanan.

Baguio
Bus: Three Autobus Transport nightbuses run daily from Baguio to Tuguegarao (P320; 10 hrs).

Bontoc
Jeepney: From Bontoc to Tuguegarao you go in three stages via Tinglayan and Tabuk. See also below.

Laoag - Pagudpud - Claveria
Bus: Eight Florida Liner buses leave Laoag for Tuguegarao daily between 4am until 7pm (seven hrs). The countryside is beautiful along this route, especially between Pagudpud and Claveria.

Manila
Air: Air Philippines flies on Monday, Wednesday and Friday from Manila to Tuguegarao and vice versa (P2390; 50 min).
Asian Spirit flies on Monday, Tuesday, Thursday, Saturday and Sunday (P2350).

Bus: From Manila to Tuguegarao there are several Autobus Transport, Baliwag Transit (from their Cubao terminal) and Victory Liner buses (from their Kamias and Sampaloc terminals; however, only two departures daily from the latter) daily (P360; 10 hrs). Almost all take the route via Santa Fe, Cauayan and Ilagan, only a few of them going via Roxas instead of Ilagan.
The Manila-Aparri buses also go via Tuguegarao.
In addition to others, some buses leave from the Hotel Delfino in Tuguegarao for Manila at 7am, 7.30pm and 8.30pm.

Palanan
Air: Chemtrad Aviation flies daily from Tuguegarao to Palanan and vice versa (P1250; 40 min).
Note: Chemtrad only flies if there are enough passengers (eight to Palanan, six for the return journey to Tuguega-

Palanan: The Last Wilderness

The Northern Sierra Madre Natural Park in Isabela Province in the north-east of Luzon is the largest protected area in the country (close to 360,000 hectare all together, of that about 248,000 hectare is terrestrial area and 72,000 marine). The relative isolation and the difficulty in reaching this territory (also known as the Palanan Wilderness) have had the positive spin-off that the flora and fauna have survived unusually well by Philippine standards. An apparently endless vista of lowland and hill evergreen forests blankets the foothills of the Sierra Madre all the way down to the Pacific Ocean. The incredible variety of species in this biotope includes up to 50m high giant trees that form a closed roof to the forest, and there's rattan, bushes, ferns, mosses, herbs and orchids. Nipa palms and mango trees grow in profusion on river estuaries, in lagoons and tiny bays. Amongst the innumerable species of animals here are the critically endangered Philippine Eagle (*Pithecophaga jefferyi*) and the Philippine Crocodile (*Crocodylus mindorensis*). Whales and dolphins have been observed in Palanan Bay.

Palanan itself, with its 15,000 inhabitants the main community in the Northern Sierra Madre National Park, is located about eight km inland on the eponymous river. The most important coastal towns are Maconacon (6,000), Divilacan (3,000) and Dinapigue (3,000). The Palaneños are well aware of the historical significance of their town, because it was here that Emilio Aguinaldo was taken prisoner on 23rd March, 1901 by the Americans under the leadership of General Frederick C Funston. Aguinaldo was the leader of the Philippine rebels who could not come to terms with the American annexation of the Philippines after the Spanish-American War. He had declared Philippine independence in 1898 and announced that he was the first president of the Philippine Republic. A stone marker keeps the memory of his arrest alive.

When to go: The best time to visit the Palanan Wilderness is during the dry months from March until June.

Where to Stay: Accommodation is thin on the ground, but a courtesy visit to the Mayor's Office when you arrive in Palanan opens up doors, eg to the Park Administration Dormitory or to Dicotcotan Beach Resort (about an hour by boat from Palanan). Otherwise, you can simply pitch your own tent on the beach, possibly right next to the simple huts belonging to the Dumagat (Negritos). Information is available from the Palanan Mayor's Office in Cauayan, Tel (078) 6521061.

Getting There: There's no road leading either from Cauayan or Ilagan to Palanan from the west. In the south the road from Baler ends in Dilasag. Palanan can be reached on foot from San Mariano (50km), by boat from Baler (irregular, and the trip might only go as far as Dilasag), and by light aircraft from Cauayan and Tuguegarao, but only if the weather is good and there are enough passengers.

Cyclone Airways flies several times daily from Cauayan to Palanan and back, with six-seater aircraft (P1200; 30 min). To charter the whole plane costs P10,800.

Further information available from Cyclone Airways, Cauayan Airport, Tel (078) 6520913.
Chemtrad Aviation flies daily with eight-seaters from Tuguegarao to Palanan and back (P1250; 40 min). To charter the whole plane costs P17,500. Further information available from Chemtrad, Tuguegarao Airport, Tel (078) 8443113.
Up to five kg of baggage are free, each additional kg costing P12.

rao) and the weather is good. Timely reservation is a must. See also the text box on 'Palanan: The Last Wilderness'.

Tinglayan - Tabuk
Jeepney: Several jeepneys leave Tinglayan daily between 6 and 11am for Tabuk, although there is only one on Sunday. In Tabuk there's a connection by bus or jeepney to Tuguegarao. The trip takes four hrs.

Roxas

Roxas is in Isabela Province. You can enjoy real Philippine country life here, far from tourists and rucksack roads. The mayor will be happy to make his resthouse available.
There is a connection by bus from Roxas to Manila.

Cauayan

Cauayan is a busy town on the National Highway with a large market which is worth seeing, and a surprising number of restaurants. There are flights from here to Palanan (see also text box on 'Palanan: The Last Wilderness').

Solano

Solanao is located a few km south of Bagabag, where the road turns off the National Highway for Banaue and the rice terraces.

Places to Stay

Sheila Marie's Resort & Hotel, Bintawan Rd, San Luis, Tel 3265135, Cellphone 0916-2000738. SR/DR/ac/bath P800 and P1000. Good, friendly rooms with TV. Attractive grounds with a pleasant atmosphere. Next to the three swimming pools there are Ifugao houses which can also be rented.

Places to Eat

In the ***Dutch Pancake Restaurant*** in General Santos St you can enjoy not only 40 (yes, forty!) different kinds of pancake but also excellent European and Philippine food.

Miscellaneous

Information: Koert the Dutchman at the Dutch Pancake Restaurant is a mine of information on the local area.
Money: Equitable PCI Bank and Metrobank, both on National Highway, have ATMs.
Population: 50,000.
Post & Telephone: Post code: 3709. Area code: 078.

Getting There & Away

Bus/Jeepney: All buses from Manila to Aparri, Banaue, Roxas and Tuguegarao go via Solano.
Jeepneys make the trip between Solano and Banaue (two hrs).

Salinas

In Salinas, deposits of salt springs have created a white hilly landscape. If you want to go there, you have to break the journey about halfway between Manila and Tuguegarao in Bambang, south of Bayombong. From there you can get a jeepney to Salinas.

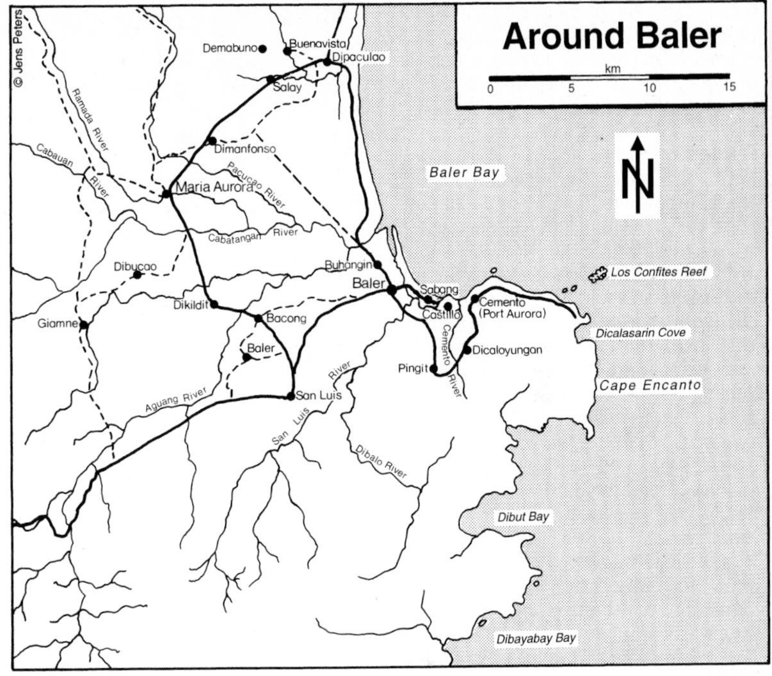

Santa Fe

Santa Fe is in the mountains of Nueva Vizcaya Province and has a pleasant, dry climate. You can buy all sorts of handicrafts there, especially basket ware.

Baler

Baler is the capital of Aurora Province on the wild east coast of North Luzon where the famous "Charlie don't surf" scene in Francis Ford Coppola's *Apocalypse Now* was shot. After the filming had been completed, Coppola handed the surfboards over to the youth of Baler and single-handedly started a surfing craze.

In December the strong surf should be enough for the most avid of surfers. Surfing season is from September/ October to February. The season is declared open every year on the beach at Sabang with the three-day competition for the Aurora Surfing Cup.

The town itself is not very interesting, but you can go on excursions to the surrounding mountains, visit the Negritos tribes (Dumagat), or spend a few days snorkelling or just lazing on the beach. You may also be able to go on fishing trips in the open Pacific in small fishing boats if you can talk the Baler fishermen into taking you. If you want to, you can hire a fully equipped boat.

On the way from Baler to the radar weather station on Cape Encanto there are several refreshing springs, such as the Digisit Springs. In Dibut Bay, a bit farther south, you can find beautiful coral. You can get there by boat, or on foot across the mountains. Dipaculao, north of Baler, is a starting point for mountain treks; some Ilongot tribes live in the mountains.

Places to Stay

Various places offer accommodation along the beach in Sabang, although there are a few loud karaoke bars which are open till late in the evening.

MIA Surf & Sports Resort. SR/fan P150, DR/fan P250, SR/fan/bath P300, DR/fan/bath P400. You can hire surfboards there and take surfing lessons. If you want bigger surf than that at Sabang Beach, you can get a surf guide to take you to another beach.

Angara's Beach House. SR/DR/fan/bath P300 to P500. Friendly, family style accommodation. Restaurant. Garden.

Amco Beach Resort. SR/DR/fan/bath P350, SR/DR/ac/bath P550. Pleasant, quiet accommodation under English management about 100m from the beach.

Bay's Inn. SR/DR/fan/bath P400, SR/DR/ac/bath P600. Decent accommodation on the beach; good value. Their restaurant can be recommended.

Miscellaneous

Festival: Suman Festival from 13 to 20 February.

Population: 27,000.

Post & Telephone: Post code: 3200. Area code: 042.

Getting There & Away

Manila - Cabanatuan

Bus: Several Baliwag Transit and a few Five Star buses make the trip from Manila to Cabanatuan daily (P130; three hrs). You can either take a direct bus or one indicating San Jose, Tuguegarao or Aparri. Departure for Aparri and Tuguegarao every hour from 6 until 11am and 6 until 11pm (from the Baliwag Transit Cubao terminal).

The only direct route from Manila to Baler (via Cabanatuan) is with Genesis Transport Company aircon buses, leaving at 4 and 5am from their Pasay Terminal and 6am from the Santa Cruz Terminal (eight hrs).

The last bus from Cabanatuan to Baler leaves at 3pm and is a Sierra Madre Transit bus (five hrs). The road across the Sierra Madre is bumpy but the views are gorgeous along the twisting road. If you are heading for Baler, you'll get the best view sitting on the left-hand side of the bus. Roughly halfway you'll come to the entrance to the Aurora Memorial Park, where there are a few restaurants. The bus stops there for half an hour.

Olongapo - San Fernando (Pampanga)

Bus: Several Baliwag Transit and E Jose Trans buses go daily from Olongapo to Cabanatuan and also stopping in San Fernando (Pampanga). The last bus connection from Cabanatuan to Baler is at 3pm.

South Luzon

The south of Luzon, with its distinctive contour of innumerable bays and inlets, twists and winds itself south from Manila in the direction of Samar, the furthest east island of the Visayas. It is blessed with an impressive, volcano-studded landscape which includes the Mayon Volcano. Mayon's symmetrical cone is said to be the most perfect in the world. It's one of the symbols of the Philippines and the most imposing feature of South Luzon. North of Mayon, the slopes of Mt Isarog, near Naga, and Mt Iriga, near Iriga, are home to several Negrito tribes. Between Sorsogon and Matnog, Mt Bulusan, with its long spurs, has earned the area the name 'Switzerland of the Orient'.

Forget the little-known beach resorts from Atimonan to Gumaca on Lamon Bay east of Lucena; those at Daet and San Miguel Bay are better. However, compared with other Philippine coastlines, dream days on the beach are rare occasions here, as the Pacific climate is almost always rough. The best time to travel is in April and May.

Getting There & Away

Most transport from Luzon to other islands goes through Manila. See Getting There & Away in the Manila chapter.

Bus: A wide selection of Eagle Star and Philtranco buses go south from Manila as far as Legaspi, via Naga. Some take the usual route via Daet for the middle section of the journey, others use the new Quirino Highway which branches off 22 km after Calauag, in Tabugon just before Santa Elena, rejoining the Philippine Highway two km south of Sipocot. Both stretches of road are in good condition, the one via Daet is, however, longer and has more bends in it.

If you want, you could take one of the Eagle Star and Philtranco buses and follow the Philippine Highway all the way to Matnog at the southern tip. There you could take the ferry to Samar. Some of the Philtranco buses even carry on to Tacloban, Ormoc and Maasin on Leyte, Naval on Biliran, Cagayan de Oro and Davao on Mindanao, and Cebu City.

For journeys from Manila to South-Luzon (Daet, Naga, Iriga, Legaspi, Tabaco, Donsol and Sorsogon/Bulan) Philtranco runs so-called Gold Service buses in addition to the regular buses. These buses carry around 30 passengers, only make a few stops, are equipped with toilets and have stewardesses on board who serve free snacks and also provide blankets. The fare to Legaspi is P630 (normal aircon bus P490) and the trip takes 12 hrs. Reservation recommended.

Tip: The Philtranco Gold Service buses in Manila only leave from their Cubao Terminal (Araneta Center), where the ticket and reservations counter is also located. On arrival in Manila the Gold Service buses first go to the Cubao

Terminal and then to the Pasay Terminal.

Train: The journey by train from Manila to South Luzon is quite an experience, although only for genuine railway freaks, as the coaches are well past their youth, and the tracks they travel on are also museum pieces at over 100 years old!
Philippine National Railways (PNR) runs one train every day bound for Legaspi, taking 15 hrs. It leaves at 4.30pm from Tayuman Station (Tel 3190050), with a boarding stop at Pasay Rd Station (Tel 8447755). Reservations are a must. The fare to Legaspi is P283 for economy, and P326 for aircon (P369 for a reclining seat).

Atimonan & Gumaca

There are a few beach resorts along the Maharlika Highway near Atimonan and Gumaca. They are not the kind of places you'd want to hang around in, but they could be important for self drivers heading south as it's difficult to find anywhere reasonable to spend the night between Gumaca and Daet.

Places to Stay

Rosarian Hotel, Maharlika Highway, Gumaca, Tel (042) 3176767, Fax: 3176899, @. SR/DR/fan/bath P300 and P400, SR/DR/ac/bath P600 to P1800. Good, quiet rooms, OK for the money. Next to the Shell petrol station on the way into town in the west.

Daet & Apuao Grande Island

Daet is a good overnight stop if you're heading to San Miguel Bay for a few days on the beach. About 3½ km from Daet, Bagasbas Beach is said to be the best in the area, and is very popular with the locals for day trips. Don't expect a white, palm-lined dream beach though, it's wide, grey and devoid of vegetation. A surfing competition is held there every August.
You can also visit the gold fields of Paracale and Mambulao. In Capalonga, farther west, the Black Nazarene Festival takes place every year on 12 and 13 May.
Early risers should catch the remarkable fish market in Mercedes from 6 to 8 in the morning. Mercedes is a small coastal town about 10 km north-east of Daet (tricycle P25) from where you can reach beautiful Apuao Grande Island in San Miguel Bay, where the beach is white (OK for a day trip).

Places to Stay

Wiltan Hotel, Vinzons Ave, Tel. 7212525, Fax: 5712907. SR/DZ/fan/bath P250, SR/ac/bath P500, DR/ac/bath P600 and P1100. Basic, reasonable rooms with TV. Restaurant. Located on the east side of town.
Dolor Hotel, Vinzons Ave, Tel 7212167, Fax 5112603. SR/fan/bath P220, DR/fan/bath P400 and P550, SR/ac/bath P450, DR/ac/bath P650, P850 (TV) and P1100 (refrigerator and TV). Fairly good, clean rooms on the third floor of the building; those facing the street are loud. Restaurant.

Places to Eat

The ***Golden House Restaurant*** has fairly good food, as does the ***Sampaguita Restaurant*** upstairs in the Sampaguita Department Store. Worth a mention is the pleasant ***Sandok at Palayok***, which also serves very good food. About 1½ km outside of Daet heading for Bagasbas (P5 per person by tricycle) you'll find the popular open-air ***Excelsa*** restaurant, which offers excellent, good value food from 11am to midnight. They mainly serve barbecued dishes from bangus to prawns, and tuna to chili chicken.

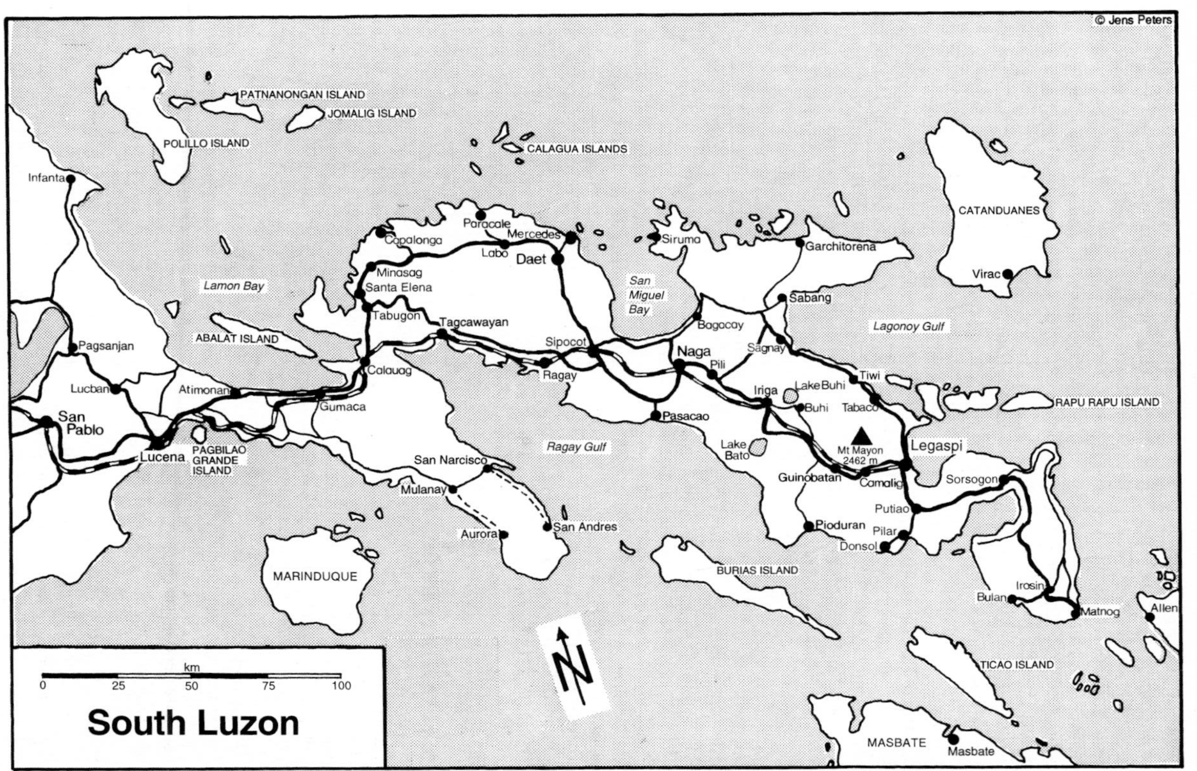
© Jens Peters
PATNANONGAN ISLAND
JOMALIG ISLAND
POLILLO ISLAND
CALAGUA ISLANDS
Infanta
CATANDUANES
Virac
Paracale
Mercedes
Capalonga
Labo
Daet
Siruma
Garchitorena
Minasag
Santa Elena
Lamon Bay
San Miguel Bay
Sabang
Tabugon
Tagcawayan
Bagacay
Lagonoy Gulf
ABALAT ISLAND
Pagsanjan
Sipocot
Naga
Sagnay
Pili
Calauag
Ragay
Tiwi
Lucban
Atimonan
Iriga
Lake Buhi
Buhi
Tabaco
RAPU RAPU ISLAND
Gumaca
San Pablo
Pasacao
Lucena
PAGBILAO GRANDE ISLAND
Ragay Gulf
Lake Bato
Mt Mayon 2462 m
Legaspi
San Narcisco
Guinobatan
Camalig
Sorsogon
Mulanay
Putiao
Aurora
San Andres
Pioduran
Pilar
Donsol
MARINDUQUE
BURIAS ISLAND
Irosin
Bulan
Matnog
Allen
km
0
25
50
75
100
South Luzon
N
TICAO ISLAND
MASBATE
Masbate

Miscellaneous

Festivals: Pinyasan Festival (Pineapple Festival) from 18 to 24 June. Mercedes Festival from 6 to 11 August (in the coastal town of Mercedes).
Money: The Equitable PCI Bank, Governor Ponates Ave, has an ATM.
Population: 80,000.
Post & Telephone: Post code: 4600. Area code: 054.

Getting There & Away

By Air: Daet Airport is in Bagasbas, about four km north-west of the town. At the moment there is no service (2004). Nearest airport: Naga (1½ hrs by bus).

Legaspi - Naga
Bus: Several buses go from Legaspi to Daet via Naga daily, some going through to Manila, taking three hrs. You can get minibuses from Naga (P70).

Manila
Bus: Several Philtranco buses run between Manila and Daet every day (P335; eight hrs).

Naga

Naga is an amiable, noticeably clean town, which is famous for its late-September Peñafrancia Festival on the river.
You can make day trips from Naga to the Inarihan Dam, the Malabsay Falls at Mt Isarog and the Nabontalan Falls.

Shopping

Pili nuts are a popular favourite of the Bicol region. There's a shop in the market at Naga which sells all varieties of this local delicacy.

Places to Stay

Naga draws in loads of visitors during the Peñafrancia Festival and the hotels are booked solid in spite of the increased prices (twice to three times as much as usual). Rooms should be booked by the middle of August at the latest.
Sampaguita Tourist Inn, Panganiban Dr, Tel 4738893. SR/fan/bath P225 (good value), DR/fan/bath P350, SR/ac/bath P400, DR/ac/bath P500. Friendly and fairly good hotel with a large selection of small but well-kept rooms, the aircon ones with TV. Restaurant.
Aristocrat Hotel, Elias Angeles St, Tel 4738832, Fax 8116605. SR/DR/fan P280/300, SR/DR/fan/bath P400/450, SR/DR/ac/bath P650 and P700, suite for six people P1600. TV P100 extra. Reasonable rooms, but nothing special. Restaurant, coffee shop.
Moraville Hotel, Dinaga St, Tel 4731247, Fax 8111685. SR/DR/fan/bath P330, SR/DR/ac/bath P580 to P730. Quiet, comfortably furnished rooms with TV, the more expensive ones also have a refrigerator. Good value. Restaurant, free airport service.
Grand Imperial Plaza, Burgos St, Tel 736534, Fax 8116886. SR/DR/ac/bath P950 and P1300, suite from P2500. Comfortable and cosily furnished rooms. The suites are quite spacious and are equipped with fridge and TV. Restaurant, coffee shop, free airport service.
Crown Hotel, Burgos St, Tel 4738305, Fax 8112241. SR/ac/bath P1250 and P2000, DR/ac/bath P1750 and P2500, suite P3000. Very good rooms with TV, but a bit pricey. Free service to the airport. Restaurant.

Places to Eat

You'll find a fresh menu every day at the ***New China Restaurant*** on General Luna St. The Chinese food in the pleasant ***Wok Food Garden***, by the river next to the bridge, is outstanding; however, they do not serve beer. The ***Oyster Villa Restaurant*** at the south end of Elias St mainly serves seafood, but also has Chinese food on the menu. The

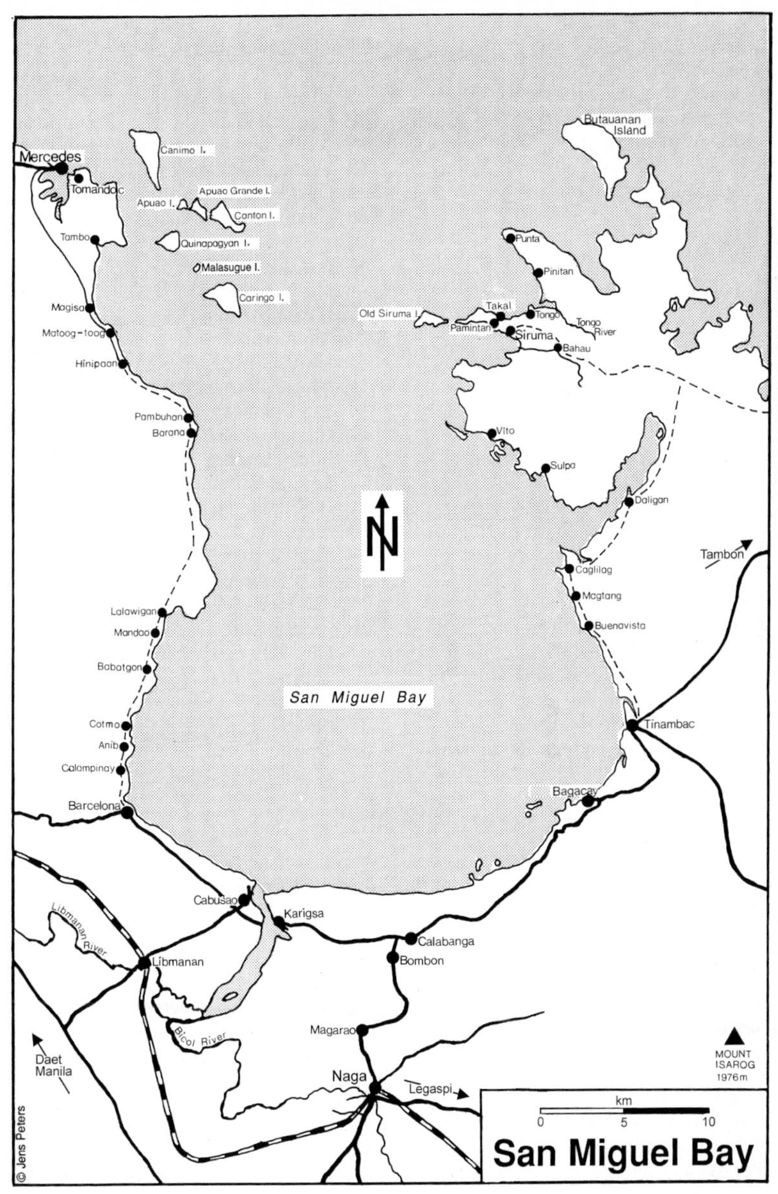
Butauanan Island
Mercedes
Canimo I.
Tomandoc
Apuao Grande I.
Apuao I.
Canton I.
Tambo
Quinapagyan I.
Malasugue I.
Punta
Pinitan
Magisa
Caringo I.
Old Siruma I.
Takal
Tongo
Tongo River
Pamintan
Siruma
Matoog-toog
Bahau
Hinipaan
Pambuhan
Barana
Vito
Sulpa
Daligan
Tambon
Caglilog
Magtang
Lalawigan
Mandao
Buenavista
Babatgon
San Miguel Bay
Tinambac
Cotmo
Anib
Calampinay
Bagacay
Barcelona
Cabusao
Karigsa
Libmanan River
Calabanga
Bombon
Libmanan
Bicol River
Magarao
Daet
Manila
MOUNT ISAROG 1976m
Naga
Legaspi
km
0
5
10
San Miguel Bay
© Jens Peters

Getting There & Away
2 Jeepney Terminal
13 Philippine Airlines
25 Peñafrancia Travels (PAL Agent)
26 Airport (12 km)
Central Bus Terminal (500m)
40 Railway Station

Places to Stay
6 Rodson Garden Hotel
8 Grand Imperial Plaza Hotel
16 Crown Hotel
21 Sampaguita Tourist Inn
24 Moraville Hotel
32 Aristocrat Hotel
35 Fiesta Hotel

Places to Eat; Entertainment
7 Baker's Plaza
9 Geewan Restaurant
Lolo's Music & Resto Bar
10 Chowking
Dunkin' Donuts
Jollibee
13 Greenwich Pizza & Pasta
15 East & West Bar
The Park Restaurant
16 Graceland
19 Planet B Sports Bar & Café
22 Wok Food Garden Restaurant
23 Naga Garden Restaurant
24 The Powerstrip
27 McDonald's
28 Bigg's Diner
29 Café Candice
30 New China Restaurant
32 Shakey's Pizza
33 Oyster Villa Restaurant
36 Chinoy Restaurant

Miscellaneous
1 Naga Cathedral
3 Police Station
4 Metrobank
5 University of Nueva Careres
11 Plaza Martinez
12 San Francisco Church
13 Galleria de San Francisco
14 Lucky 9 Store
17 Equitable PCI Bank
Philippine National Bank (PNB)
18 Plaza Rizal
19 Cody's Store
20 Mercury Drug
31 Shopper's Mall
26 Bicol Medical Center (1.5 km)
City Hall (2 km)
Tourist Office (2 km)
34 Market
37 Equitable PCI Bank
38 Metrobank
39 LCC Mall (300m)

stylish ***Park Restaurant*** in the Crown Hotel has fairly upmarket prices, while the big karaoke restaurant ***The Powerstrip*** in the Moraville Hotel is better value.

You can get local-style turo-turo food in the pleasantly decorated ***Chinoy Restaurant*** in Caceres St, and the ***Geewan Restaurant*** in Burgos St also has a wide selection of pots with Philippine food to choose from.

Bigg's Diner at Plaza Rizal is a 1950s-style fast-food restaurant and is clean, inexpensive and popular. It serves a wide choice of sandwiches, pizzas and various dishes of the day. The ***Chowking*** in Burgos St has inexpensive Chinese and Philippine fast food. Right next door, ***Jollibee*** will serve you hamburgers, as will ***Graceland*** and, of course, ***McDonald's***, both in General Luna St. If you feel like a pizza, there's ***Shakey's*** at the south end of Elias Angeles St and ***Greenwich*** in Peñafranca Ave.

A tip for those who like cakes is ***Baker's Plaza*** in Burgos St at the corner of General Luna St, with its clean bakery and little café on the premises.

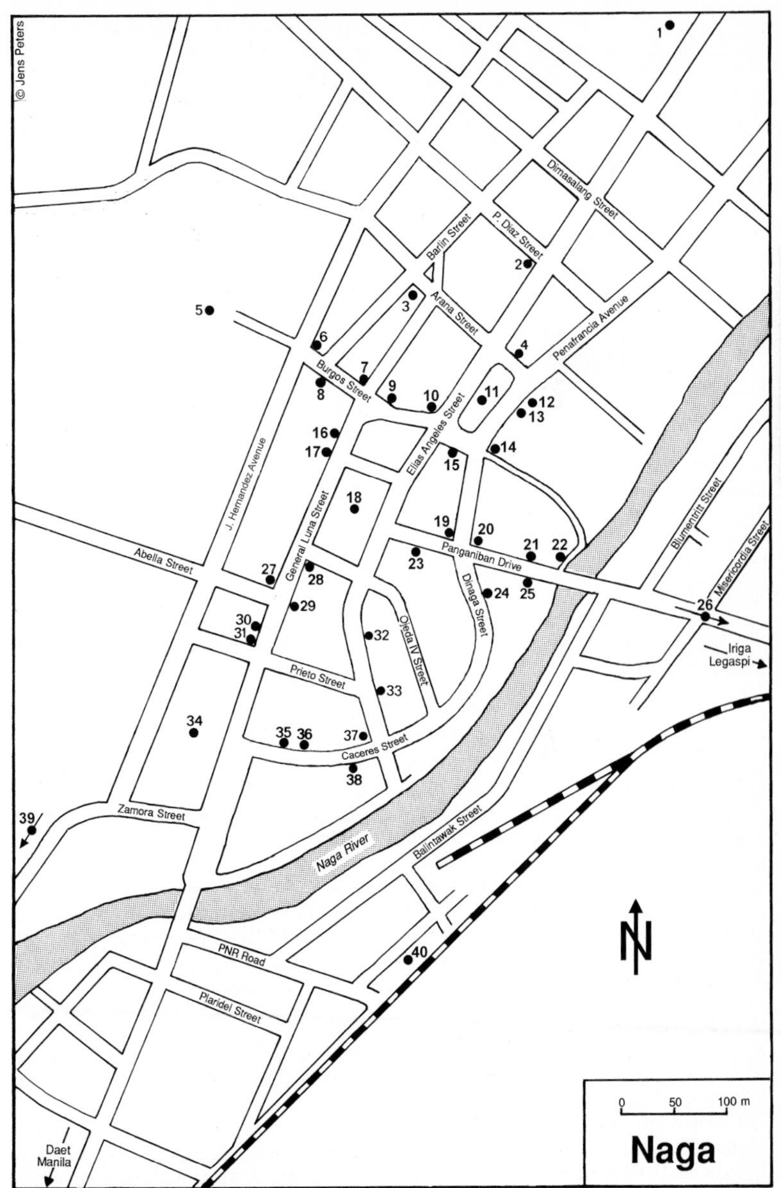
© Jens Peters
Dimasalang Street
P. Diaz Street
Barlin Street
Arana Street
Penafrancia Avenue
Burgos Street
Elias Angeles Street
J. Hernandez Avenue
General Luna Street
Abella Street
Panganiban Drive
Dinaga Street
Ojeda IV Street
Blumentritt Street
Misericordia Street
Prieto Street
Caceres Street
Zamora Street
Naga River
Balintawak Street
PNR Road
Plaridel Street
Iriga
Legaspi
Daet
Manila
N
0
50
100 m
Naga

South Luzon

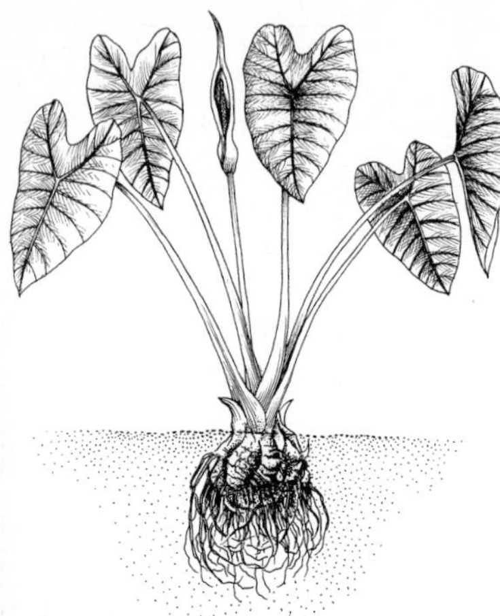

Cocoyam *(Cococasia esculenta)*
In Bicol cooking the large, protein-rich leaves of the yam are combined with onions, garlic and coconut milk and served as a side vegetable *(pinangat na gabi)* with `Bikol Express' a local specialty prepared with green and red hot chili peppers.

Entertainment

The best place to go for excellent entertainment in the evening has to be ***Planet B Sports Bar & Café*** in Peñafrancia Ave (above Cody's Store) with lots on offer, including live music and three billiard tables. An alternative would be ***Lolo's Music & Resto Bar*** in Burgos St. Both ask for P100 cover charge, but it's offset against the bill. If you're looking for something a bit quieter and more up-market, then you'd probably feel more at home at the ***East & West Bar*** in the Crown Hotel.

Miscellaneous

Festivals: Peñafranca Festival on the third Saturday in September. Town Fiesta on 27 December.
Medical Services: The Bicol Medical Center, Panganiban Dr, Tel 8111463, is 1½ km east of the centre.
Money: Equitable PCI Bank and Philippine National Bank, both in General Luna St, have ATMs.
Population: 135,000.
Post & Telephone: Post Office, City Hall Complex, J Miranda Ave.
Post code: 4400. Area code: 054.
Tourist Office, Tourist Office, City Hall Complex, J Miranda Ave, Tel 4734432. Open Mon-Fri 8am-noon and 1-5pm.

Getting There & Away

By Air: Pili Airport is about 12 km south-east of Naga, just off the road to Pili. All the hotels will arrange airport service for you (P200). Otherwise jeepneys (Naga-Pili) are an alternative, although they don't go directly to the airport but stop at the turn-off to the airport on the main road.
Philippine Airlines, Galleria de San Francisco, Peñafrancia Ave, Tel 4732277.
Destination: Manila.

By Bus: The Central Busterminal is located about one km east of the centre. A tricycle costs P4 per person, a Special Ride P20.

By Train: The railway station is in the outskirts in the south of the town. A tricycle to the centre costs P4 per person, a Special Ride P20.
Philippine National Railways (PNR), Tel 4739615.

Daet

Bus: From Daet, several buses leave daily, either for Naga only or for Legaspi or Matnog via Naga (1½ hrs). There are also minibuses.

Legaspi

Bus: From Legaspi, several buses go daily to Naga or through Naga on the way to Daet or Manila (two hrs).

Train: From Legaspi to Naga daily at 3.30pm (P60; three hrs).

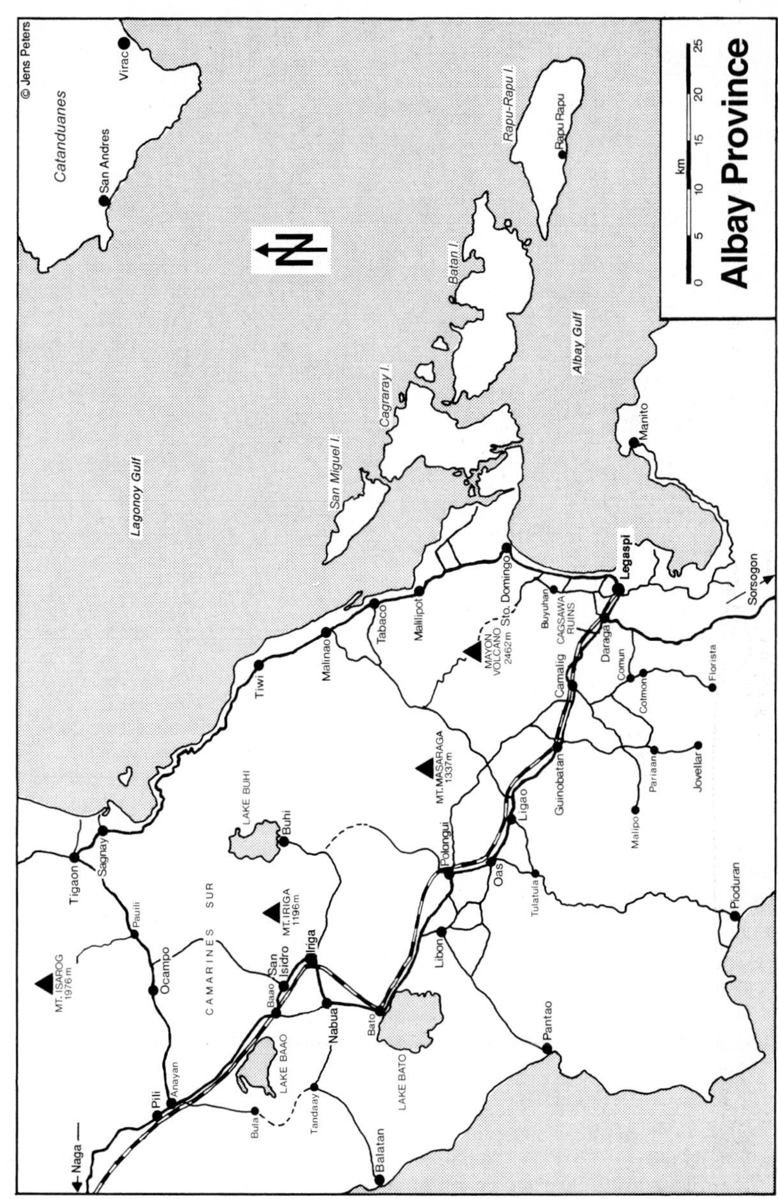
Albay Province
km
0 5 10 15 20 25
© Jens Peters
Catanduanes
San Andres
Virac
Rapu-Rapu I.
Rapu Rapu
Batan I.
Cagraray I.
San Miguel I.
Albay Gulf
Lagonoy Gulf
Manito
Legaspi
Sorsogon
Sto. Domingo
Buyuhan
CAGSAWA RUINS
Daraga
MAYON VOLCANO 2462 m
Malilipot
Tabaco
Malinao
Tiwi
Camalig
Comun
Cotmon
Florista
Guinobatan
Pariaan
Jovellar
Malipo
MT. MASARAGA 1337m
LAKE BUHI
Buhi
Ligao
Polangui
Oas
Tulatula
Pioduran
Libon
Pantao
Sagnay
Tigaon
Pauili
CAMARINES SUR
MT. IRIGA 1196m
Iriga
San Isidro
Ocampo
MT. ISAROG 1976 m
Baao
Nabua
Bato
LAKE BATO
LAKE BAAO
Anayan
Pili
Naga
Bula
Tandaay
Balatan

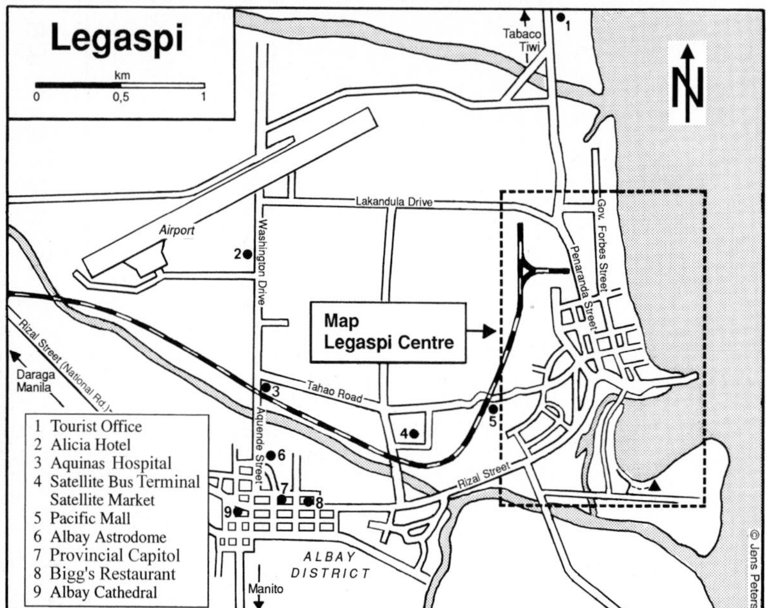

Departure from Naga to Legaspi at 5am.

Manila

Air: Philippine Airlines flies Monday, Wednesday, Friday, Saturday and Sunday and vice versa (P2030; 50 min).

Bus: From Manila, Eagle Star and Philtranco buses run to Naga daily (P350; 7½ hrs).

Train: From Manila to Naga daily at 4.30pm (economy P223, aircon P291; 12 hrs).
Departure from Naga to Manila at 7pm.

Iriga & Lake Buhi

Iriga is the turn-off point for visits to Lake Buhi, the 16½ sq km lake 15 km away where, thanks to intervention by the Bureau of Fisheries and Aquatic Resources (BFAR), the smallest edible fish in the world has at least a chance of survival. Called *sinarapan*, they, like the *tabios* in Lake Bato, were previously threatened with extinction. The short-sighted methods of the fishermen were to blame for this, as they were overfishing the lake with their *sakags* (large fine-mesh V-shaped nets), often destroying the spawn as well. You can see this interesting, tiny species close up at the aquarium in the Municipal Building.

Boat trips on Lake Buhi are rather expensive if you hire a boat at the market right on the lake. The ferry which leaves from there and runs to the other side of the lake is much cheaper.

A tribe of Negrito, the Agta, live on Mt Iriga - also called Mt Asog - between Iriga and Lake Buhi.

Places to Stay

Parkview Hotel, San Roque, Tel 2992450. SR/DR/fan/bath P400, SR/DR/ac/bath P800 and P1000. Quite basically furnished rooms. Restaurant. Quiet location near the Plaza Rizal (in the same building as the Equitable PCI Bank).
Ibalon Hotel, San Francisco St, Tel 2992352. SR/DR/ac/bath P550 and P920, suite P1200. Reasonable rooms, if not the newest. Beautiful old building on the plaza. Restaurant.

Places to Eat

Bigg's Diner at the plaza is a good clean place for inexpensive fastfood.

Miscellaneous

Festivals: Tinagba Festival (thanksgiving festival) on 11 February, and Town Fiesta on 13 June in Iriga. Town Fiesta on 25 May in Buhi.
Money: The Equitable PCI Bank, San Roque, has an ATM.
Population: 85,000.
Post & Telephone: Post code: 4431. Area code: 054.

Getting There & Away

Jeepney: Jeepneys to Lake Buhi leave from opposite the Petron petrol station diagonally across from the church. Going back to Iriga, they do not leave from the centre of town but from the entrance to Buhi, also opposite the Petron petrol station. The last one leaves for Iriga at 7pm.

Legaspi

Legaspi is the capital of Albay Province and is actually divided into two parts: the centre or downtown area around the port and, further inland, the Albay District. The two areas are linked by Rizal St.
There are no outstanding sights in the town itself. The only ones worth mentioning at all are the headless statue in front of the post office, a monument to the unknown heroes who died at the hands of the Japanese in WWII, and the altar of the St Rafael Church, opposite the Plaza Rizal, which was made from a 10-ton chunk of volcanic rock from Mayon.
However, there are many interesting sights to see in the area around Legaspi, including the ruins of Cagsawa, the Hoyop-Hoyopan Cave in Camalig, and of course the mighty Mayon Volcano. In the rainy season the volcano is unfortunately often draped with clouds; however, even on days like this a full, clear view of it can be obtained at sunrise.
From the top of the Kapuntukan Hill you can get a fascinating panoramic view of the port area, with the impressive Mayon in all its glory in the background. The best time to view the volcano is in the early morning hours and at sunset, which is also the best time for taking photographs. A tricycle from the centre of town to the hill costs about P25; negotiate the fare beforehand. On foot, the following route should be taken. Go down Quezon Ave in the direction of the wharf and cross over the little bridge opposite the beginning of Elizondo St; this takes you to the idyllic fishing village of Victory Village. At the south end of the village next to the barangay toilet turn left, then after about 50m at the sari sari store, turn left again and up the modest steps. A few metres before the concrete path at the top leads down to the water, you will see an almost hidden, fairly overgrown path on the right, which will take you to the top of the hill.
Just to the north-west of Legaspi Airport you'll find the Albay Park & Wildlife, a 17 hectare area with around 250 species of bird, over 60 species of reptile and over 80 species of mammal, including lots of apes and even tigers. Admission: P10. A tricycle from the town centre costs P20.

Getting There & Away
3 Airport
4 Caltex Petrol Station
9 Railway Station
11 Shell Petrol Station
15 Taxis
29 Satellite Bus Terminal (800 m)
32 Wharf
37 Airport

Places to Stay
5 Albay Hotel
6 Casablanca Hotel
7 Shirman Lodge
10 Magayon Hotel
19 Hotel Rex
20 Hotel Xandra
22 Hotel La Trinidad
31 Legaspi Tourist Inn
34 Victoria Hotel
35 Tanchuling International House
36 Sampaguita Tourist Inn

Places to Eat & Entertainment
1 Waway Restaurant
7 Lady Ann Nightclub
8 Small Bars
16 Benjo's Pizza & Pasta
17 Mister Donut
Wah Foo Chan Restaurant
18 Graceland
19 South Ocean Villa Restaurant
21 Four Seasons Restaurant
23 Wendees
24 Shangrila Restaurant
25 LCC Food Garden
33 New Legaspi Restaurant

Miscellaneous
2 Tourist Office (1 km)
12 A Bichara Silverscreen Entertainment Center
13 Plaza Rizal
14 St Rafael Church
17 LCC Express Mart
23 Philippine National Bank (PNB)
26 Bank of the Philippine Islands
27 Equitable PCI Bank
28 LCC Department Store
29 Pacific Mall (100m)
Satellite Market (800m)
30 Post Office
Headless Monument
31 Bicol Adventure & Tours

Places to Stay

Sampaguita Tourist Inn, Rizal St, Tel 4806258. SR/fan P125, DR/fan P225, SR/fan/bath P225, DR/fan/bath P325, SR/ac/bath P400 and P450, DR/ac/bath P500 and P550. Nearly all rooms have TV. Basic, but pleasant, good-value accommodation on the road to the Albay District. Small restaurant (breakfast).

Magayon Hotel, Peñaranda St, Tel 2143121. SR/fan P150, SR/ac/bath P350 and P500, DR/ac/bath P650 and P1000. TV costs P100 extra. Reasonable, clean rooms, although a bit spartanly furnished. Located next to the station.

Tanchuling Hotel, Jasmin St, Imperial Subdivision, Tel 4806003. SR/DR/fan/Bad P400, SR/DR/ac/bath P550 and P650 (TV). Basic, but clean and spacious rooms, and there is a pleasant roof garden with a beautiful view of Mayon. Located in a quiet area south of the town centre (10 mins on foot). The atmosphere is friendly and the place is good value for money.

Legaspi Tourist Inn, Quezon Ave corner Lapu-Lapu St, Tel 4806147. SR/fan/bath P450, DR/fan/bath P510, SR/ac/bath P700 abd P800, DR/ac/bath P800 and P900. Really good rooms of various sizes, the aircon ones with TV. Small restaurant. Located on the 3rd floor of the V & O Building opposite the post office.

Hotel La Trinidad, Rizal St, Tel 4807469, Fax 2143148. SR/DR/ac/bath P920/1020, suite P1700 and P2000.

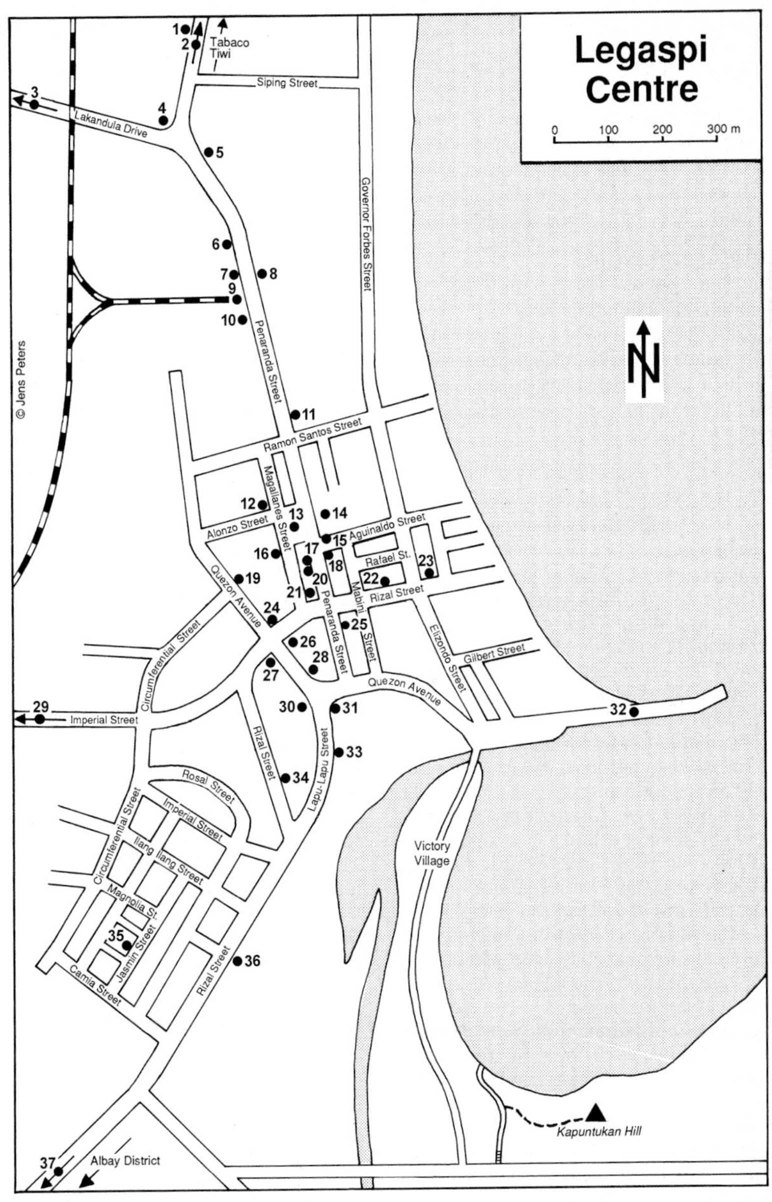

Legaspi
Centre
0 100 200 300 m
Tabaco
Tiwi
Siping Street
Lakandula Drive
Governor Forbes Street
Penaranda Street
Ramon Santos Street
Magallanes Street
Alonzo Street
Aguinaldo Street
Rafael St.
Rizal Street
Quezon Avenue
Mabini Street
Penaranda Street
Circumferential Street
Elizondo Street
Gilbert Street
Quezon Avenue
Imperial Street
Rizal Street
Lapu-Lapu Street
Rosal Street
Imperial Street
Circumferential Street
Ilang Ilang Street
Magnolia St.
Jasmin Street
Camia Street
Rizal Street
Victory Village
Kapuntukan Hill
Albay District
© Jens Peters
1
2
3
4
5
6
7
8
9
10
11
12
13
14
15
16
17
18
19
20
21
22
23
24
25
26
27
28
29
30
31
32
33
34
35
36
37

Reasonable rooms with TV, but you can feel what used to be the best hotel in town is beginning to show its age. Restaurant.

Casablanca Hotel, Peñaranda St, Tel 4808334, Fax 4808338, @. SR/DR/ac/bath P1200 and P1800, suite P2400 (refrigerator). Good rooms with TV, some also with balcony. Restaurant, coffee shop (24 hrs), car hire, free service to the airport.

Albay Hotel, Peñaranda St, Tel. 4808660, Fax: 2143364. SR/DR/ac/bath P2020 and P2320, suite P2720, all including breakfast. Comfortable rooms with TV. Restaurant, coffee shop, disco, swimming pool, car hire, free airport service.

Places to Eat

Good Chinese and Filipino food is served in the ***Shangrila Restaurant*** in Peñaranda St, in the ***Four Seasons Restaurant*** in Magallanes St, in the ***South Ocean Villa Restaurant*** on Quezon Ave, and in the ***New Legaspi Restaurant*** in Lapu-Lapu St, where the special meal is to be recommended. The food is basically Chinese with some Filipino dishes.

The native food in the ***LCC Food Garden*** in the department store of the same name is good value, as is the case in the little ***Wah Foo Chan Restaurant*** next to the Xandra Hotel in Peñaranda St. Right across the road you'll find the ***Graceland*** fast food restaurant.

The ***Waway Restaurant*** in Peñaranda St Extension in the north of town serves good Filipino dishes. The spicy local specialities à la 'Bicol Express' and the vegetarian meals can be recommended. Fastfood restaurants such as ***Jollibee*** can be found in the new Pacific Mall in the outskirts in the west end of town.

Miscellaneous

Festivals: Bicol Arts Festival from 21 to 28 February. Albay Fiesta on 2 and 3 September. Ibalong Festival in the second week of October.

Medical Services: Amec Hospital, Rizal St, Albay District, Tel 8201520, and Esteves Memorial Hospital, Guevarra Subdivision, Tel 4802135, are the two best hospitals in Legaspi.

Money: Bank of the Philippine Islands and Equitable PCI Bank, both in Rizal St corner Quezon Ave, have ATMs.

Population: 150,000.

Post & Telephone: Post Office, Lapu-Lapu St.

Post code: 4500. Area code: 052.

Travel Agency: Bicol Adventure & Tours, Suite 20, V & O Building, Quezon Ave corner Lapu-Lapu St, Tel 4802266, Fax 8201483, @. Their programme includes island hopping, diving trips, cave exploration, climbs up Mayon (two days P3900 if there are two participants, including guide and porters, not including food and supplies) as well as day trips to Donsol (whale shark watching; P7150 per person if there are two participants).

Tourist Office: Regional Center Site, Rawis, Tel 4820712, Fax 8205066, @. Open Mon-Fri 8am-noon and 1-5pm.

Getting Around

Car: Various hotels have cars with driver for rent.

Taxi: There is a taxi rank in Aguinaldo St at the corner of Peñaranda St.

Tricycle: For a short journey within the town you should pay P3 per person.

Getting There & Away

By Air: Legaspi Airport is about three km north-west of the town centre. A tricycle costs P20. You can also take a jeepney heading to Daraga from the centre, get out in the Albay District and take a tricycle from there to the airport for P10.

Philippine Airlines, Legaspi Airport, Tel 2455024, 4810779.

Destination: Manila.

By Bus: The Satellite Bus Terminal is about 1½ km west of the centre. A tricycle costs P10 or P5 per person.

By Train: The railway station is in Peñaranda St. Tickets can be purchased during the day.
Philippine National Railways (PNR), Tel 8204419.

Manila
Air: Philippine Airlines flies daily from Manila to Legaspi and vice versa (P2220; 50 min).

Bus: Several Eagle Star and Philtranco buses run from Manila to Legaspi (P482; 12 hrs).

Train: From Manila to Legaspi daily at 4.30pm (economy P283, air-con P326; 15 hrs).
Departure from Legaspi to Manila at 3.30pm.

Naga
Bus: From Naga, several buses go daily to Legaspi (two hrs).

Train: From Naga to Legaspi daily at 5am (P60; three hrs).
Departure from Legaspi to Naga at 3.30pm.

Tabaco
Bus/Jeepney: Minibuses and jeepneys run frequently from Tabaco to Legaspi every day (one hr).

Tacloban
Bus: A few buses run daily from Legaspi to Tacloban via Matnog and along the west coast of Samar. They come from Manila, pulling in to Legaspi for a short stop. However, it is possible that they will be fully booked. It could be less stressful to make the trip in stages, eg changing in Sorsogon or Irosin.

Around Legaspi

Mayon Volcano

Mayon stands 2462m above sea level and is famed for its perfectly symmetrical cone. The name Mayon is a derivation of the Bicolano word *magayon*, which means beautiful. Beauty can also become dangerous, as the clouds of smoke rising from the crater indicate.
The last serious eruption was in February 2000 when the volcano spewed ash and steam seven km into the atmosphere. Rivers of glowing hot mud, rocks and stones rushed down the south-east slope, totally destroying villages and farmland on the way. Nearly 100,000 people had to be evacuated. Only after a series of smaller eruptions lasting until March did the volcano calm down again, but weeks later the glowing lava was still flowing, offering a fascinating spectacle at night. The most recent, albeit less dramatic, eruptions occured in July 2000, February 2001 and June/July 2001.
The most violent eruption to date took place on 1 February 1814 when many communities were totally destroyed, including those of Camalig, Cagsawa and Budiao. An estimated 1200 people lost their lives in this natural catastrophe. There were reports of ash raining down as far away as the Chinese coast.
If you want to climb Mayon, the tourist office will supply detailed information and they also organise two-day climbs. The usual cost for one or two people is P5500 for guide, porter, tent and food; each additional person costs P1500. Anyone thinking of saving a few pesos by carrying everything themselves would definitely regret the decision later, although it is normal in the Philippines for climbers to carry their own personal items.
You can save a few pesos and try hiring a guide in Buyuhan yourself, eg Gregorio

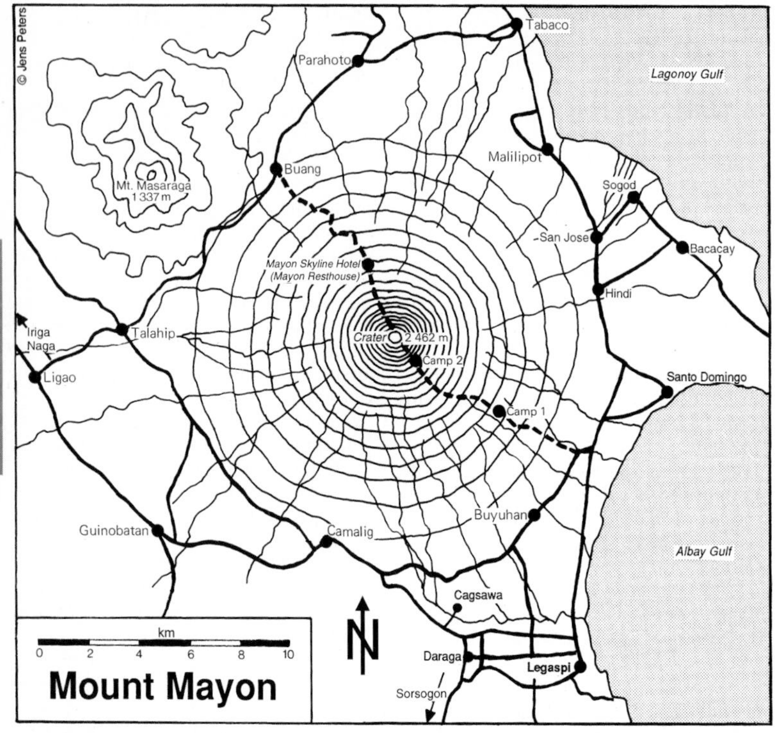

Azores, Cellphone 0919-4655374. To try the ascent without a guide is reckless and irresponsible, as it's easy to get lost at the foot of Mayon. Many of the harmless-looking canyons turn out to be dead ends with sheer drops.

To reach Mayon, you get a jeepney in the market to Buyuhan from where it is a two hour climb to Camp 1 (Camp Amporo) at about 800m. If you start late, you will have to spend the night at the simple hut there; there is a spring nearby.

It's another four hours to Camp 2 (Camp Pepito) at about 1800m. Here you have to use a tent, as there is no hut and the nights can be fairly cold. In the morning you have another four-hour climb to the summit. Since the last eruption it has been impossible to reach the crater itself. The climb ends about 150m below the summit at the so-called Knife Edge, where it is possible to look into the crater if the weather conditions are right.

The last 200m is a scramble through loose stones and over steep rocks, and it is advisable for climbers to be roped. Going down it takes about three hours from the crater to Camp 2, almost two hours from Camp 2 to Camp 1 and over two hours from Camp 1 to the road.

Take warm clothing, a sleeping bag and provisions for two days. On some days you'll need sunscreen lotion as well.

Getting There & Away

Bus/Jeepney: To get from Legaspi to the Mayon Skyline Hotel (still known locally as the Mayon Resthouse; temporarily closed) on the northern slope, where there is a beautiful view, take a bus or jeepney to Tabaco, then a bus or jeepney to Ligao. Get off at the turn-off about halfway to Ligao. From there you've got about an eight-km walk up to the hotel. You could ask at the turn-off if there is a tricycle available which would then run you up for about P100 (or even there and back for P150).

You can hire a jeepney in Tabaco but it's cheaper to persuade the regular Ligao jeepney drivers to make a small detour to the Mayon Skyline Hotel and drop you there.

The tourist office advises people not to climb the north slope of the volcano as it is apparently too dangerous.

Daraga & Cagsawa

The magnificent baroque church in Daraga, built by Franciscan monks in 1773, offers an excellent view of Mayon from its vantage point on the top of a hill overlooking the town. On Sunday and public holidays Daraga is the scene of heated cockfights which take place in the cockpit at the edge of town, near the petrol station. The atmosphere at Daraga's night market is very pleasant with its sounds and smells of frying and cooking. Along the road between Daraga and Cagsawa you can find small workshops where they make whole furniture suites from used car tyres.

The catastrophic eruption of Mayon on 1 February 1814 totally destroyed the villages of Camalig, Cagsawa and Budiao on the southern side of Mayon. About 1200 people perished as ash fell as far away as the China coast. Many local residents took shelter in the church at Cagsawa, only to be smothered by falling ash. Today, only the church tower stands as a reminder of 'The Beautiful One's' terrible powers. The rest of the village was buried under ash and lava. These days, plants, including orchids, are offered for sale near this solitary tower, and there is also a restaurant and even a little swimming pool. With the grandeur of Mayon in the background the scene is idyllic. Admission to the Cagsawa ruins is P5.

Getting There & Away

Bus/Jeepney: From Legaspi, several jeepneys leave from downtown Legaspi or the Satellite Bus Terminal daily for Daraga. The turn-off to the Cagsawa ruins is on the right, two km west of Daraga. A tricycle from Daraga to the ruins shouldn't cost more than P20.

Buses and jeepneys for Camalig, Guinobatan, Ligao, Polangui and Naga also drive through Daraga, directly past the turn-off to the Cagsawa ruins where you can get out. (Don't forget to tell the driver in good time!) From there, it is about 10 min to the ruins on foot.

Camalig

The town of Camalig is famous for the Hoyop-Hoyopan limestone caves which are in Cotmon, about eight km to the south. There is an admission fee of P100. The name Hoyop-Hoyopan means 'blow-blow' from the sound of the wind rushing through. Bones have been found in the caves as have potsherds, which are over 2000 years old. They are now on display in a small museum in the Camalig Catholic church.

Ask for the experienced guide, Alfredo Nieva, who will guide you to the Calabidogan Cave, about two or three km (a 45-minute walk) away from the Hoyop-Hoyopan caves. The guided tour through the cave lasts up to three hours and costs around P500. Take swimming gear along as a few metres have to be swum. The best idea is to have a word with Alfredo the day before, to work out times and prices. He himself may not be the guide as he may give the job to one of his sons. In the months from November to February it is possible that the water level will be too high, making a cave visit impractical.

The Pariaan Cave, known as the 'Fountain of Youth', is near Pariaan. Eduardo (Eddie) Nalasco is an experienced guide - he lives opposite the Town Hall in Camalig.

To get there take a jeepney or a bus, either from Legaspi or Camalig to Guinobatan, where you can get a jeepney heading for Jovellar and get off at Pariaan. Ask the driver to drop you at the path for the cave and, after a 10-minute walk, you will come to a hut where the cave's 'owner' lives. For a few pesos he'll look after excess clothing - it's very hot and humid inside the cave. A strong torch or, even better, a kerosene lamp is necessary onced you're inside. The cave contains a natural pool with warm water, watched over by ancient stalactites. After some time in stuffy subterranean surroundings, it's a pleasure to dip into the privately owned swimming pool on the left side of the road towards Jovellar; admission is P5. The property is in an idyllic setting, in the midst of palm-covered hills. There are actually three pools, all at different heights.

Getting There & Away

Bus/Jeepney: Camalig is about 14 km north-west of Legaspi. Jeepneys and buses go there from the Satellite Bus Terminal, either directly or en route to Guinobatan, Ligao, Polangui or Naga.

Tricycle: From Camalig, you have to take a tricycle to the cave. Occasionally it is possible to find a jeepney in the market going to Cotmon. After 6pm the only way to return to Camalig is to arrange a Special Ride.

Santo Domingo

About two km outside of Santo Domingo town, 15 km north-east of Legaspi, is a long, black, lava-sand beach which occasionally has quite high surf. The beach resorts on the so-called 'Mayon Riviera' vary considerably in size and price. The *Reyes Beach Resort* (admission: P10) with its inexpensive restaurant is popular; the *Sirangen Beach Resort* is basic and nicely laid out. Local day trippers like to use the beach at Santo Domingo for long, drawn-out picnics, but it is not really suitable for bathing and is actually quite disappointing.

Places to Stay

Costa Palmera Resort, Cellphone 0918-9098838. SR/DR/ac/bath P800 and P980. Nicely furnished rooms with TV. Quite good value. Friendly accommodation. Pleasant restaurant on the water.

Getting There & Away

Jeepney/Tricycle: To get to Santo Domingo, take a jeepney from the Satellite Bus Terminal in Legaspi or ask if there's a direct bus to Santo Domingo, as some of the Tabaco buses take the route around the outskirts. Tricycles go from Santo Domingo to the beach resorts.

Malilipot

For lovers of waterfalls in more or less unspoiled nature a day trip from Legaspi to Malilipot can be warmly recommended. From here, on the north-east foothills of Mayon, there is a path leading in the direction of the volcano to the Busay Falls, also known as the Malilipot Falls; admission P5. These

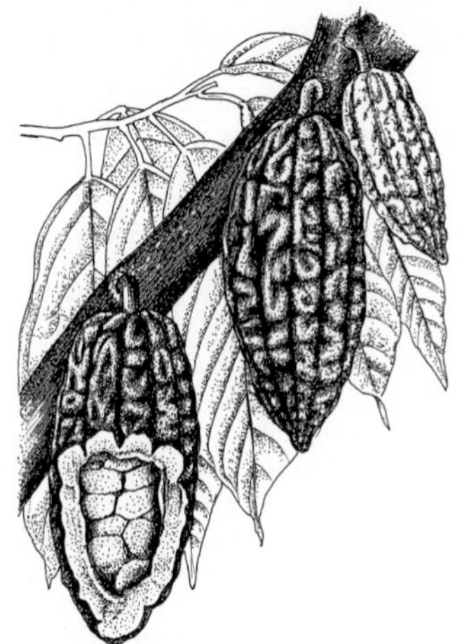

Cocoa *(Theobroma cacao)*
The cocoa tree is indigenous to the northern regions of South America. Presumably the Spaniards brought the first cocoa fruits to the Philippines early in the 18th century.

falls descend in stages from a height of 250m, flowing into seven pools on the way that tempt you to swim in them. If you don't want to jump straight into the first pool, then turn off onto the path on the right just before it. After about a 15-minute walk this will take you to the second pool. The waterfalls are popular with day-trippers at the weekends.

Getting There & Away

Bus/Jeepney: Go from Legaspi to Malilipot by a jeepney or bus travelling to Tabaco. Then it's about another hour on foot. It would be a good idea to have a guide show you the way for about P20.

Tabaco

Tabaco is the main departure point for the boat to San Andres and Virac, both on Catanduanes Island. Probably the only thing worth seeing in Tabaco itself is the two-storey market, where some really interesting knives can be found amongst the bargains on offer. You can't miss the hordes of pedicabs used for short journeys.

Places to Stay

Casa Eugenia Hotel, Tagas, Tel 8300425. Suite P1300 to P2600. Immaculate suites with TV, almost all with a living room, kitchen and small balcony. Restaurant.

Miscellaneous

Festival: Tabak Festival from 20 to 24 March. Town Fiesta on 24 June.
Population: 90,000.
Post & Telephone: Post code: 4511. Area code: 052.

Getting There & Away

Legaspi

Bus/Jeepney: Plenty of buses and jeepneys from Legaspi to Tabaco daily (45 min).

Manila

Bus: Several Philtranco buses go from Manila to Tabaco daily. A few go via Legaspi (10 hrs).
From Tabaco to Manila, the last aircon bus will leave at 5pm.

Tiwi

Jeepney: Jeepneys run frequently between Tiwi and Tabaco in about half an hour.

Tiwi

North of Legaspi, Tiwi is noted for its hot springs, which were for many years a small health resort or spa. Some of the springs were so hot that the locals stood their pots in them to cook their dinners. Nowadays six geothermal power stations have reduced the underground water pressure and most of the springs have dried up. It would be a

waste of time to go there just to see the few remaining springs.
Two well-known but not particularly good beaches, with black sand, are Sogod Beach and Putsan Beach. If you walk to Putsan, take a look at the primitive potteries on the way.

Places to Stay

Baño Manantial de Tiwi Youth Hostel & Mendoza's Resort. SR/DR/fan P200, DR/fan/bath P400, SR/DR/ac/bath P500 and P600 (with own minipool). Fairy tale accommodation with modest rooms. There's a swimming pool that can get really busy at the weekends, and a pretty good restaurant. Located about three km north of Tiwi; P30 by tricycle.
Tiwi Hot Springs Resort. SR/DR/fan/bath P300, SR/DR/ac/bath P600, P700 and P850. Reasonable rooms, the more expensive ones also have a refrigerator and TV. Restaurant, two swimming pools. Right next door to the Youth Hostel.

Miscellaneous

Festival: Town Fiesta on 10 August.
Post & Telephone: Post code: 4513. Area code: 052.

Getting There & Away

Legaspi - Tabaco
Bus/Jeepney: To get from Legaspi to Tiwi, take a minibus or a jeepney, and from Tabaco continue on by jeepney. From the centre of Tiwi to the resort - a distance of about three km - take a tricycle. The whole trip takes about 1½ hrs. Leaving Tiwi, if you want to go beyond Legaspi to Matnog the same day, you must depart early in the morning or you'll have connection problems in Irosin.

Manila
Bus: For Manila, two Philtranco buses leave Tiwi market daily (10 hrs).

Donsol

Whale sharks seem to have taken a shine to the dreamy little coastal town of Donsol. Between February and May, but especially in the months of March and April, shoals of them cruise around the waters where the Burias and Ticao Passages meet. In 1998 the Philippine government declared this region to be a protected area for whale sharks, and since that time more and more friends of nature have visited Donsol to catch a glimpse of these gentle giants from close up.
With the support of the World Wildlife Fund (WWF), the so-called Butanding Interaction Tours were initiated - *butanding* is the local word for whale sharks - which take observers out to approach these imposing creatures with care. Only one boat is allowed per whale shark and no more than six swimmers with snorkelling equipment may approach a fish at one time. Swimmers should not come closer than three to four metres to an animal, and flash photography and touching the animals are not permitted at all. A day trip can be booked at the Visitor Center Center (Cellphone 0918-2315420) next to the Town Hall on the plaza. The price for a boat, crew, tour guide and spotter is P2500, plus P300 per person registration fee (P100 for Filipinos).

Places to Stay

Visitor's Inn. SR/DR/fan P150/300, SR/DR/ac P200/400. Guesthouse belonging to the Belmonte family, with four clean rooms and one communal living room.
Amor Farm Beach Resort, Cellphone 0917-8233802. Cottage/fan P450, cottage/fan/bath P600. Small place with good cottages. Located on the other side of the river directly on the ocean.
Woodland Beach Resort, Cellphone 0921-9699544. SR/DR/fan/bath P800, SR/DR/ac/bath P1500. A few cottages

Whale Sharks - the Gentle Giants

Whale sharks are, funnily enough, sharks the size of whales. They grow up to 18 metres long and with a weight up to 40 tons are the biggest fish on the planet (whales are, of course, not fish but mammals). They swim their majestic way through all the oceans of the world, but prefer the warm waters of the tropics. They can best be recognised by the numerous white spots and stripes on their dark backs as well as several long, clearly prominent ridges on their bodies. In spite of their massive size, whale sharks are as harmless as house pets. They feed on plankton, krill and small fish, by sucking them into their huge mouths which can be as large as two metres across.

There has been a total ban on catching whale sharks in Philippine waters since 1998, after the animals had been mercilessly hunted down and cut up for years before. To this day, whale shark meat and fins are still considered a delicacy in some countries.
Depending on the region, whale sharks are known in the Philippine variously as *butanding*, *balilan*, *kulwano*, *tawiki* and *toki*. Their numbers have increased noticeably since the hunting ban was introduced. The prospects for these gentle giants in Philippine waters will make further progress if the eco-tourism industry continues to develop as it has been doing recently. Another positive spin-off of this is that it also provides former fishermen with a new way of earning a living and feeding their families.

with neat, clean rooms. Pleasant little resort in a quiet location on the beach. Restaurant, garden, diving.

Miscellaneous

Festival: Arribada Festival (whale shark festival) on 28 and 29 January. Town Fiesta on 19 May. Gugurang Festival from 26 to 29 October.
Population: 37,500.
Post & Telephone: Post code: 4715. Area code: 056.

Getting There & Away

Legaspi
Bus: Donsol Transit buses run roughly half-hourly from Legaspi to Donsol (P50; two hrs).

Taxi: A taxi from Legaspi to Donsol costs P500 to P600.

Note for Self-drivers: Leaving Legaspi, drive in the direction of Sorsogon via Daraga. Near Putiao, 20 km south of Daraga, turn right and head for Pilar and Donsol. After 28 km of mostly twisting road, turn off right at the entrance to Pilar. From there, it's another 26 km to Donsol.

Manila
Bus: A Philtranco bus leaves Manila for Donsol daily at 5.30pm (P530; 13 hrs).

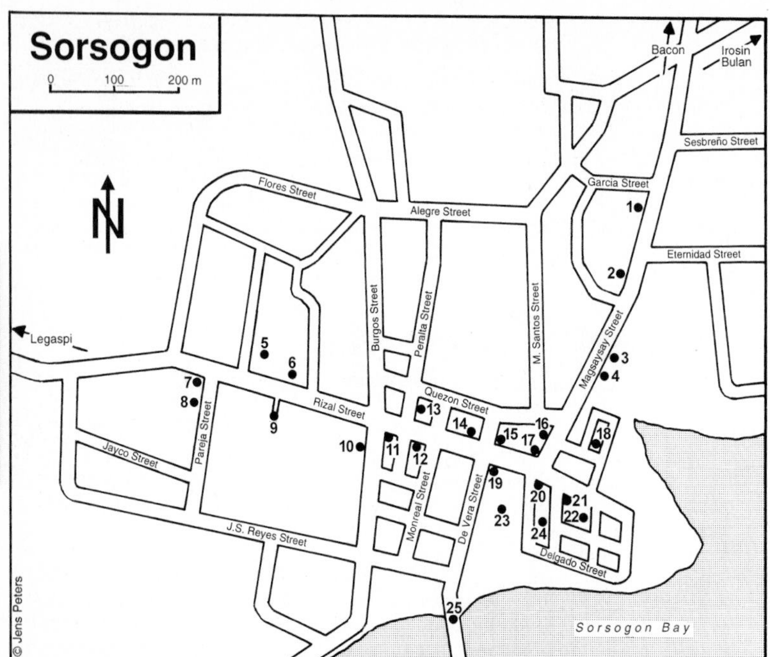

Getting There & Away

11 Shell Petrol Station
19 Petron Petrol Station
22 Philtranco Bus Terminal
24 Bus & Jeepney Terminal
25 Wharf

Places to Stay

8 Fernandos Hotel
9 Villa Kasanggayahan Pensione
10 Olympus Hotel

Places to Eat

1 Kristina's Restaurant
4 Jollibee
7 Kalundan Restaurant
12 Tajji's Fast Food
13 Acacia Restaurant
14 Jana's Fast Food
16 Quick n' Hearty
19 Brownie's
21 Graceland

Miscellaneous

3 Metrobank
4 Allied Bank
5 Provincial Capitol
6 Philippine National Bank (PNB)
8 Sorsogon Adventure & Tours
15 Post Office
16 Jomil Department Store
17 Equitable PCI Bank
Mercury Drug
18 Market
20 Police Station
23 Church

Sorsogon & Gubat

Sorsogon is the capital of Sorsogon Province, an area at the eastern tip of South Luzon which is subject to frequent violent typhoons.
From there, you can make a little detour to Gubat and the long, broad Rizal Beach on the Pacific. A jeepney or tricycle will take you the five km south from Gubat to Rizal Beach for P5.

Places to Stay

Sorsogon
Villa Kasanggayahan Pensione, Rizal St, Tel 2111275. SR/DR/ac/bath P950 and P1600 (good for six people), with TV. Reasonable, clean rooms with veranda. Pleasant lodging house with a small garden about 80m off the road.
Fernandos Hotel, Pareja St, Tel 2111357, Fax 2111573, @. SR/ac/bath P1150 to P2160, DR/ac/bath P1350 to P2360. Friendly, inviting place with good, well-kept rooms, all with TV. Restaurant, car hire.

Gubat
Rizal Beach Resort Hotel, Gubat, Tel 31111829-30. SR/DR/fan/bath P700 and P750, SR/DR/ac/bath P960 and P1200 (good for three people). Basic, acceptable rooms in a long, two-storey building, which is beginning to show its age. The restaurant here is open until 10pm.
Veramaris Resort, Gubat, Tel 3111825, @. SR/DR/fan/bath P770, SR/DR/ac/bath P1090 und P1700 (good for five people). Modest, but good rooms, all furnished differently, the more expensive ones with a sea view and TV. A good alternative to the Rizal Beach Resort Hotel. Restaurant.

Places to Eat

The Philippine food - mostly seafood - is very tasty at the ***Kalundan Restaurant***, Rizal St corner Pareja St (near Fernandos Hotel). Good, fairly inexpensive Chinese food and barbecues is on offer at the big ***Acacia Restaurant*** in Peralta St. ***Kristina's Restaurant*** in Magsaysay St is the place to head for if you want a pizza, and ***Jollibee*** in the same street for hamburgers. ***Brownie's***, Rizal St corner De Vera St, will serve you roast chicken.

Miscellaneous

Festivals: Sorsogon Pili Festival in the last week of June, Town Fiesta on 29 June, and Kasanggayahan Festival (foundation of the province) from 10 to 17 October in Sorsogon. Town Fiesta in Gubat on 13 June.
Money: The Equitable PCI Bank, Rizal St corner Magsaysay St, has an ATM.
Population: 85,000.
Post & Telephone: Post code: 4700. Area code: 056.
Travel Agency: Sorsogon Adventure & Tours in the Fernandos Hotel, Pareja St, Tel 2111357, offers various tours around the area, as well as diving and whale shark watching.

Getting There & Away

Bus: From Legaspi, Eagle Star and Philtranco buses run to Sorsogon (1½ hrs), but not very frequently. The route originates in Manila, and the buses carry on via Matnog to Samar and Leyte.
In addition, aircon minibuses leave from the Pacific Mall in Legaspi for the jeepney terminal in Sorsogon (P40; one hr).

Bulan

Bulan, a little coastal village on the west coast, is simply a departure point for a daily boat to Masbate. (See the Getting Away from Luzon section on the Manila.)

Places to Stay

Mari-El's Lodging House. SR/DR/fan P100/200. Very basic place by the pier.

South Luzon

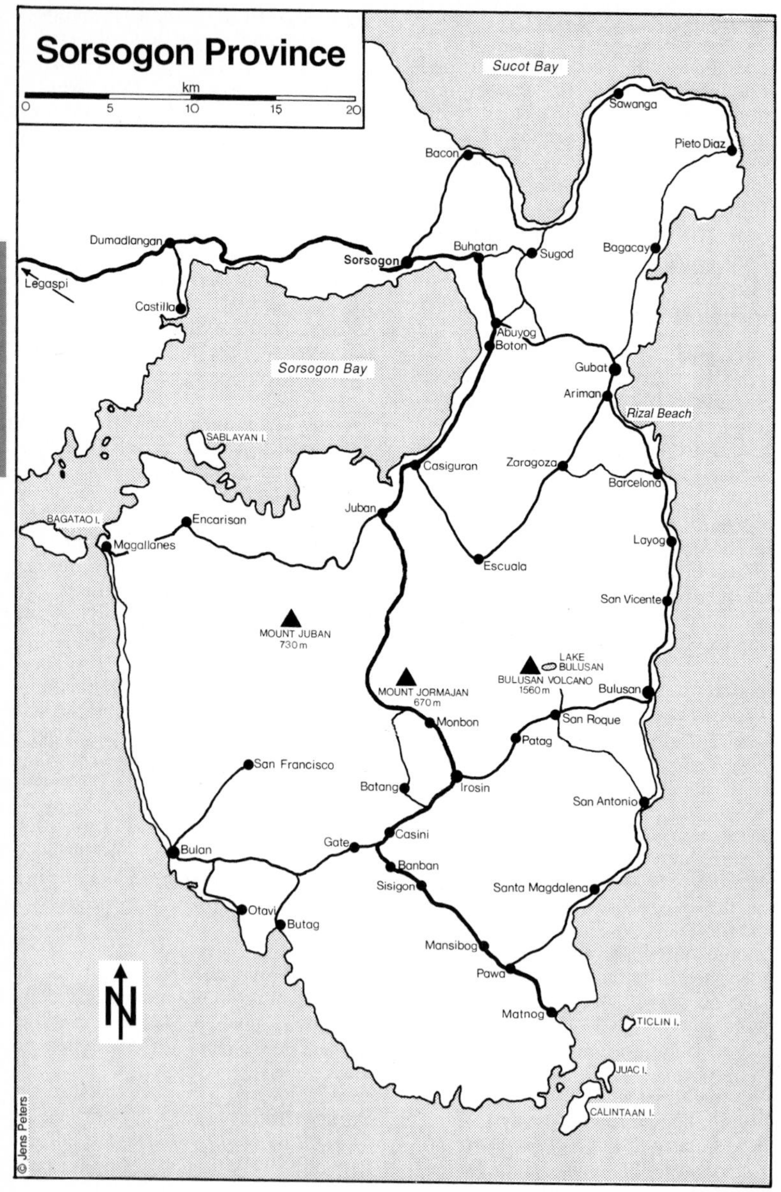

Sorsogon Province
km
0
5
10
15
20
Sucot Bay
Sawanga
Pieto Diaz
Bacon
Dumadlangan
Sorsogon
Buhatan
Sugod
Bagacay
Legaspi
Castilla
Abuyog
Boton
Sorsogon Bay
Gubat
Ariman
Rizal Beach
SABLAYAN I.
Casiguran
Zaragoza
Barcelona
Juban
BAGATAO I.
Encarisan
Magallanes
Escuala
Layog
San Vicente
MOUNT JUBAN
730 m
LAKE
BULUSAN
BULUSAN VOLCANO
1560 m
MOUNT JORMAJAN
670 m
Bulusan
Monbon
San Roque
Patag
San Francisco
Batang
Irosin
San Antonio
Casini
Gate
Bulan
Banban
Sisigon
Santa Magdalena
Otavi
Butag
Mansibog
Pawa
Matnog
TICLIN I.
JUAC I.
CALINTAAN I.
© Jens Peters

Miscellaneous

Festival: Bandalaan sa Bulan Festival and Town Fiesta on the last weekend in May.

Getting There & Away

Legaspi

Bus: From Legaspi, Philtranco buses run to Bulan daily, but they are not so frequent. Take a bus at the latest by 9am if you want to be on time for the boat to Masbate. It takes 3½ hrs.

Sorsogon

Jeepney: Several jeepneys make the trip during the day from Sorsogon to Bulan (two hrs).

Bulusan & Irosin

You can't help but see Mt Bulusan, the 1560m high volcano at the centre of the Juban-Bulusan-Irosin triangle. Nearby, surrounded by lush vegetation, is a small crater lake of the same name, at a height of 600m with a three-km-long path around it called Lovers' Lane. For the walk around the lake, which in parts is fairly difficult and tiring, you will need 1½ hours, including rests.

From Bulusan to Lake Bulusan is about eight km. Only a very few jeepneys make the trip between Bulusan and Irosin, the first one leaving at 7am, the last one at 4pm. They will stop at the turn-off for the crater lake if requested to. The walk up to it is very pleasant.

The refreshingly cool Masacrot Springs, complete with big swimming pool, are in the southern foothills of the volcano, near San Roque. Unfortunately, the way there is not signposted.

Apart from Bulusan, there is another two pleasant bases for a stay in the so-called 'Switzerland of the Orient': the Mateo Hot & Cold Springs Resort and the Guest World Resort & Inn, both north of Irosin.

Places to Stay

Bulusan

Bartilet's Lodging House, 262 Dapdap. SR/DR/fan P150/300. Basic, but good rooms belonging to the friendly teacher Mrs Nerissa Bartilet. Located directly behind the Town Hall.

Villa Luisa Celeste Resort, Dancalan, Tel 2111083. SR/DR/fan/bath P500, SR/DR/ac/bath P700 and P800. Immaculate, spacious rooms in a beautiful building. Appealing place on the Pacific coast about three km north of Bulusan - to be recommended. Good restaurant, swimming pool.

Irosin

Mateo Hot & Cold Springs Resort, San Benon, Monbon. SR/DR/fan P150/300, SR/DR/fan/bath P300, cottage/fan/bath/kitchen P350. The rooms are basic, but acceptable. The resort has two pools (one lukewarm, and one hot) and there is a small restaurant and a variety of cottages set in a peaceful location in the forest. You'll find a signpost at the point where the path leaves the road, three km north of Irosin, and the resort is about two km from the highway.

Guest World Resort & Inn, Gulang-Gulang, Cellphone 0918-4417396. Cottage/ac/bath P850. Great accommodation, well worth the money. Really beautiful garden with a view of the Bulusan volcano. Restaurant. Three big swimming pools. Easy to reach, located as it is on the highway, about five km north of Irosin.

Miscellaneous

Festivals: Town Fiesta on 24 July in Bulusan and on 29 September in Irosin.

Post & Telephone: Post code: 4704 (Bulusan), 4707 (Irosin). Area code: 056.

Getting There & Away

Bus: From Legaspi, Eagle Star and Philtranco buses run to Irosin (2½ hrs).

They come from Manila, go via Matnog to Samar, some carrying on to Leyte.

Jeepney: Several jeepneys run during the day from Irosin to Bulusan (one hr).

Matnog

Matnog is the last stop on Luzon. This little coastal town, on the south-eastern side of Sorsogon, is the departure point for ferries to Allen and San Isidro on Samar, the next big island. During bad typhoons all shipping is stopped, so you could be held up in Matnog for a few days - not a cheerful prospect. It's better to wait somewhere like Bulusan or Legaspi until the seas settle down.
On sunny days, a trip to the little offshore island of Ticlin, with its palms and beautiful white sand beach, would be well worthwhile.

Places to Stay

Primo Lodging House. SR/DR/fan P180, SR/DR/fan/bath P250. Basic accommodation with a restaurant.

You could always do what many Filipinos do when they've missed the last ferry: sleep on a bench in the big waiting room.

Miscellaneous

Festival: Town Fiesta on 19 July.
Post: Post code: 4708.

Getting There & Away

Irosin
Jeepney: Several jeepneys run daily from Irosin to Matnog (one hr).

Legaspi
Bus: In Legaspi, you could try boarding an Eagle Star or Philtranco bus arriving from Manila and going through Matnog en route to Samar, Leyte or Mindanao (3½ hrs). However, these buses are usually full and it might be better to do the trip in stages using other means of transport, eg with an aircon minibus from the Pacific Mall as far as Sorsogon, carrying on from there by jeepney to Matnog.

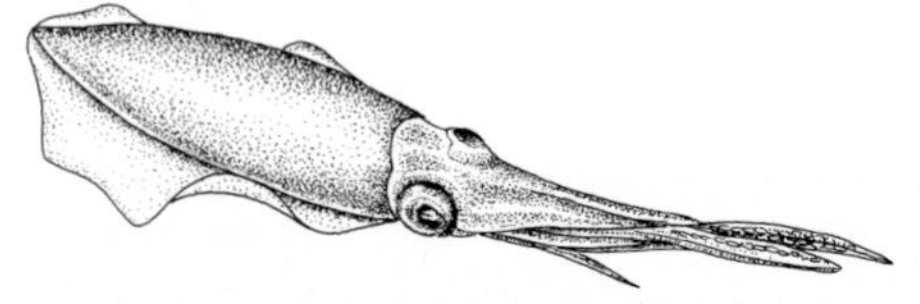

Islands Around Luzon

Several islands around the main island of Luzon are also generally grouped with Luzon. They include the Batanes, which are scattered off the far northern coast of Luzon; Catanduanes, off the south-eastern coast near Legaspi; the smaller islands of Lubang, Marinduque and the larger island of Mindoro, all off the western coast; and Masbate and Romblon in the south. There are air and/or sea routes connecting all of the islands with Luzon.

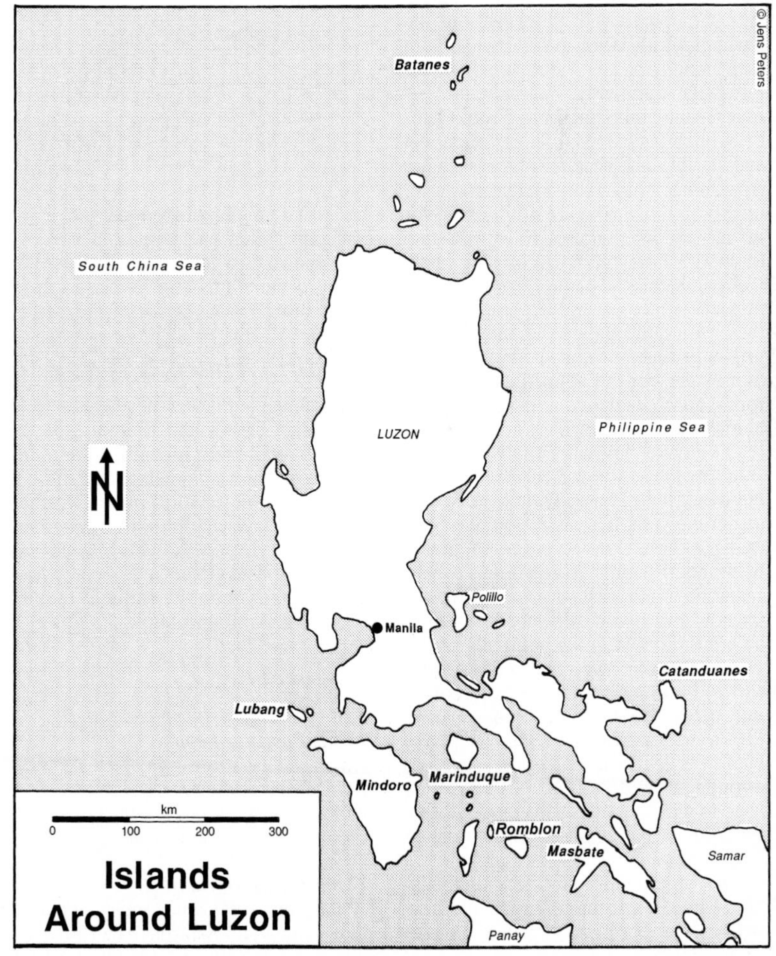

Batanes

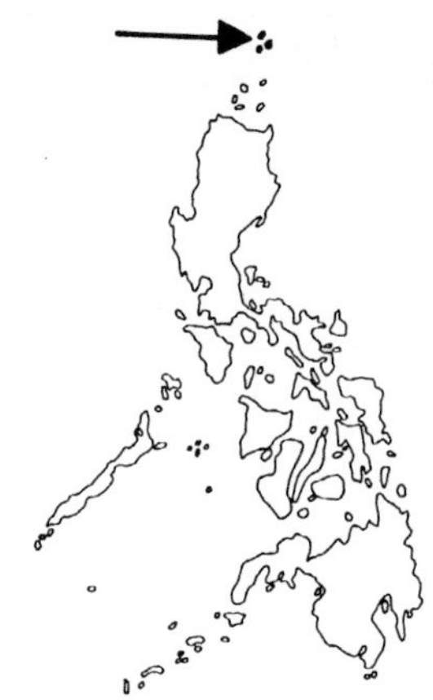

The Batanes Islands are the northernmost islands of the Philippines. Y'ami is only 100 km from Taiwan. The biggest and economically most important islands are Batan, Itbayat and Sabtang. Dinem Island is uninhabited. The climate of the Batanes Islands is fairly changeable. Compared with other parts of the Philippines all 10 of these islands, with their population of 14,000 souls, are hit relatively frequently by typhoons between June and September. From October to February or March it is often wet and stormy. The best months to visit are April and May. The Batanes appeal mostly to those who are not looking for luxury, and love nature - those who like to hike around with a tent on their back. Geographically isolated from the big important islands and archipelagos of the country, the Batanes Islands are surprisingly unspoilt and different. Many houses are built of solid rock and have roofs thickly thatched with cogon grass to resist the weather. They are low, with few windows, and are usually found in small groups in niches protected from the wind. If you know your Asterix, you sometimes feel here as if you had been transported back to a village populated by stubborn Gauls. You would probably not be in the least surprised if around the next corner you came across a venerable druid brewing his potions.

People here protect themselves from sun and rain with a *suot*, a head-covering made from *abaca* and *voyavoy* leaves which reaches right down the back. The leaves are first processed into a rough, straw-like fibre, which is then used to make the hats. (In some villages this protective headwear is also called *vakul* or *bakul*.)

Goods which aren't produced on the islands are slightly more expensive here than they are in Luzon, as they have to be flown in or shipped on the occasional freighter. The main crops are garlic, onions, taro yams and camotes. The main occupations are cattle farming and fishing.

Getting There & Away

You can get to the Batanes Islands from Currimao, Laoag and Manila (see the Getting Away from Luzon section of the Manila chapter). Travel in and out depends first and foremost on the weather. On rainy days, if the partly concreted runway at Basco is wet, planes can neither land nor take off. Delays may also occur even in the summer months of March, April and May.

To Luzon

Air

From Basco to Laoag

Chemtrad Aviation and Pacific Airways fly daily (P2300).

Note: The flight may be cancelled if there are not enough passengers.

From Basco to Manila

Asian Spirit flies on Monday, Wednesday, Friday and Saturday (P3750).

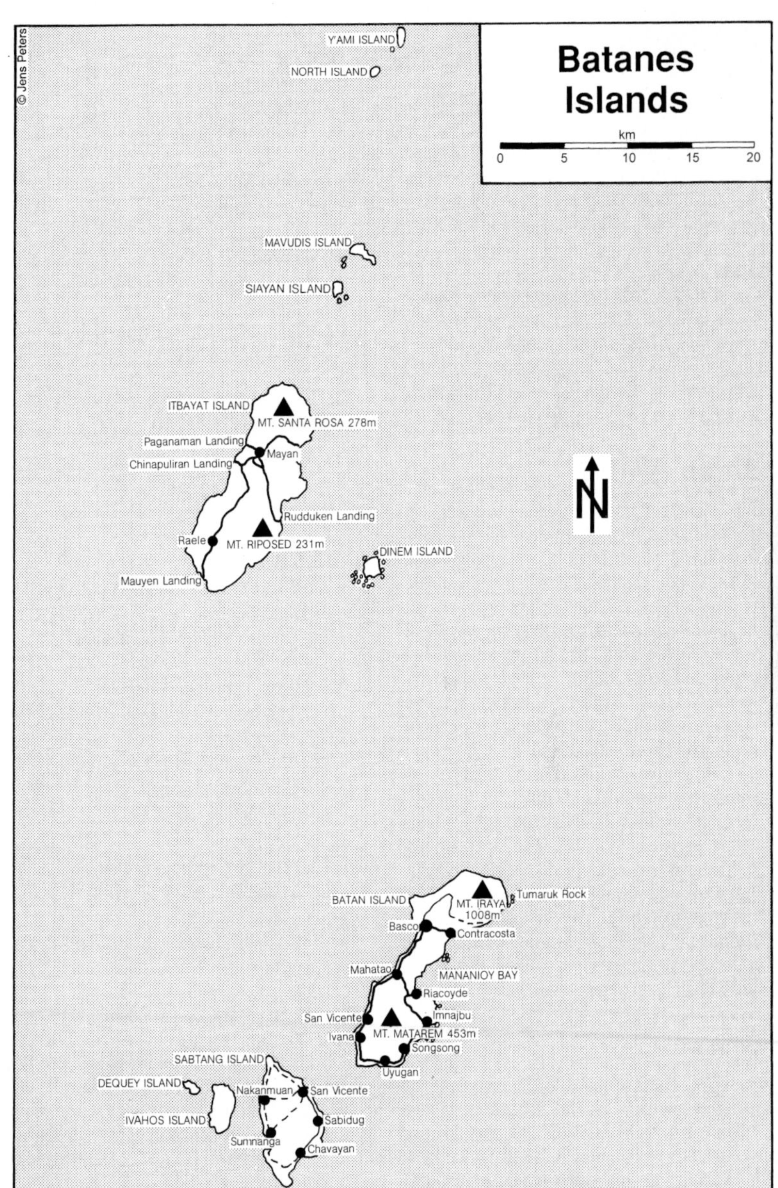
© Jens Peters
Batanes Islands
km
0
5
10
15
20
Y'AMI ISLAND
NORTH ISLAND
MAVUDIS ISLAND
SIAYAN ISLAND
ITBAYAT ISLAND
MT. SANTA ROSA 278m
Paganaman Landing
Mayan
Chinapuliran Landing
Rudduken Landing
Raele
MT. RIPOSED 231m
DINEM ISLAND
Mauyen Landing
N
BATAN ISLAND
MT. IRAYA 1008m
Tumaruk Rock
Basco
Contracosta
Mahatao
MANANIOY BAY
Riacoyde
Imnajbu
San Vicente
MT. MATAREM 453m
Ivana
Songsong
Uyugan
SABTANG ISLAND
DEQUEY ISLAND
Nakanmuan
San Vicente
Sabidug
IVAHOS ISLAND
Sumnanga
Chavayan

From Basco to Tuguegarao
Chemtrad Aviation flies Monday, Wednesday and Friday (P2450).
Note: Chemtrad flies with Britten Norman Islanders (only room for eight passengers), so be sure to reserve a seat about a week in advance. In the summer months from March to May, two to three weeks in advance would be better.

Boat

From Basco to Currimao (Ilocos Norte)
Saturday with the MV *Ivatan Princess* (P1200; 19 hrs); via Calayan Island.
Note: This route is dependent on the weather, especially during the rainy season from May to November.

Batan Island

Don't expect very much in the way of sights; in fact, this is part of the island's charm. About the only activity is the Sunday cockfight. There are a couple of white beaches on the western coast; the southern and eastern coasts are rocky. To the north the landscape of this green and hilly island is dominated by the raw beauty of the 1008m high Iraya Volcano, which can be climbed in about five hours from Basco.
A seldom-travelled and only partly surfaced road runs from Basco to Riacoyde (via Mahatao, Ivana and Uyugan) and then straight across the island back to Mahatao. It's a good track for walking and you come across lovely little villages inhabited by friendly Ivatan, the natives of Batan Island. The road is at its most impressive along the coast between Basco and Uyugan.

Basco

Basco is the capital of the province of Batanes, which is the smallest in the Philippines, both in area and population. Next to the big church, with its beautiful façade, are numerous governmental buildings which dominate this neat town at the foot of Mt Iraya.

Getting There & Away
17 Airport
Asian Spirit
Chemtrad Aviation

Places to Stay
9 Troy Lodge
10 Mama Lily's Inn
13 Iraya Lodge
16 Ivatan Lodge
17 Shanedel's Inn
19 Seaside Lodge (700m)
Batanes Resort (1 km)

Places to Eat
5 St Dominic College Canteen
15 Casa Napoli
17 Shanedel's Café
19 Seaside Restaurant (700m)

Miscellaneous
1 Philippine National Bank (PNB)
2 Basco Cathedral
3 Philtel (Public Telephone Office)
4 Police Station
5 St Dominic College
6 Town Hall
7 Batanes General Hospital
8 Provincial Capitol
11 Post Office
12 Land Bank
14 Batanes Connect Internet

Places to Stay

Iraya Lodge, Amboy St. SR/DR/fan P100/200. Unpretentious place, yet OK.
Troy Lodge, Babat St. SR/DR/fan P100/200. Basic, clean accommodation near the airport. Communal room with cable TV. No restaurant, but coffee and snacks are available.

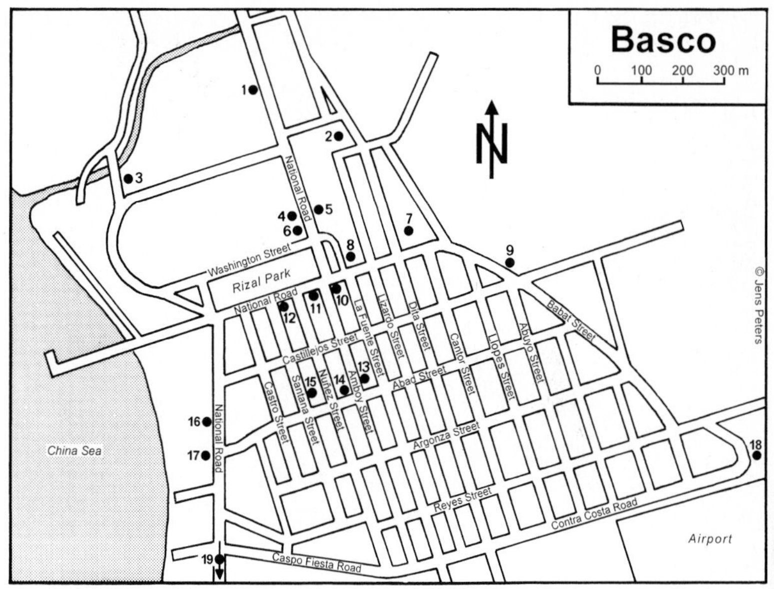

Ivatan Lodge, National Rd, @. Dorm/fan P100, DR/fan/bath P400. Straightforward accommodation near the harbour (beautiful view). Restaurant.

Mama Lily's Inn, National Rd. SR/DR/fan P100/200, or P500 per person including three meals. Centrally located, modest accommodation with a family atmosphere. Guests can use the living room and patio. Restaurant.

Shanedel's Inn, National Rd, Cellphone 0920-4470737, @. SR/DR/fan P250/500 (there'll be aircon rooms from 2005). Pleasant, family-run place with decent rooms. Restaurant.

Batanes Seaside Lodge, National Rd. SR/DR/fan P300/450, SR/DR/ac P750/1000. Good rooms, some will accommodate three people. Restaurant. Billiards.

Batanes Resort, National Rd. SR/DR/fan/bath P600/700. Friendly rooms with TV in stone houses typical for the islands, at the foot of a hill about one km south of Basco.

Places to Eat

You can eat inexpensively at the ***St Dominic College Canteen*** diagonally across from the Town Hall. In the restaurants belonging to the various places to stay you can also expect some culinary delights for very little money, especially from March to May when the fishermen have an easier time of it. Specialties here are coconut crabs (*tatus*), flying fish (*dibang*), dorado (*arayo*) and lobster (*payi*), served with yellow rice (rice boiled with yellow ginger). It's best to order in good time beforehand, eg in the cosy little ***Shanedel's Café*** which in addition to its excellent cooking offers a beautful sea view.

If it's Italian you're looking for, then the ***Casa Napoli*** in the Old Dominican

Stone houses on Batan Island with roofs thatched with cogon grass

House in Santana St serves surprisingly good pasta and pizzas.

Miscellaneous

Festival: Fisherman's Festival in the third week of March. Batanes Day on 26 June. Palo-Palo Festival on 4 and 5 August.
Money: The Philippine National Bank will cash traveller's cheques.
Online: The Batanes Connect Internet Station in Abad St charges P50/hr.
Population: 5000.
Post: Post code: 3900.

Getting Around

You can hire private jeepneys, motorcycles and bicycles. Enquire at Mama Lily's Inn.

Getting There & Away

By Air: Basco Airport is to the east of town. A tricycle to one of the hotels costs from P20 to P30.

Asian Spirit, Basco Airport, Tel (02) 5354851-55, 5333444.
Destination: Manila.
Chemtrad Aviation, Basco Airport, Cellphone 0920-5145274.
Destinations: Itbayat Island, Laoag, Tuguegarao.

Sabtang Island

In contrast to Batan Island, there are no cars on Sabtang apart from an old vehicle belonging to the government. It is worth the effort to go around the island on foot and visit the four villages. It can be done in a day, but if you take your time and take lots of breaks, a few days will pass before you know it. The mayor will place at your disposal a guide who knows the paths and the shortcuts. With his help you will find it easier to get to know the villagers and to see how things such as *suots*, typical headwear on the Batanes

Islands, are made. Sabtang Island is also well-known for its traditional boat-building.
On the eastern coast of the neighbouring island of Ivahos there is a largely intact coral reef. You can get there by boat from Nakanmuan or Sumnanga.

Places to Stay

There are no hotels on Sabtang, but it is possible to stay with the mayor or the director of the Fishery School. You can also get something to eat there, but since no-one will charge you money or accept it, it is nice to 'happen' to have a small gift on hand.

Getting There & Away

Boat: A boat goes once a week from Basco to Sabtang Island. If you don't want to wait, you will have to go to Ivana by jeepney, leaving early in the morning. From there, if the weather's good a boat leaves at 6.30 or 8.30am for San Vicente (Centro) on Sabtang Island (there can even be further crossings at 1 and 4pm). The trip takes 45 min.

Itbayat Island

Itbayat is the largest island of the group. It has few beaches and a rocky coast. A feature of the island is the *tatus*, the coconut crab, which is so fond of coconuts that it will climb trees to get them. You can stay the night, and eat, at the mayor's place.

Getting There & Away

Air: Chemtrad Aviation flies daily from Basco to Itbayat Island and vice versa (P700; 15 min). East of Raele, about ten km south of Mayan, the main town on the island, there's a landing strip for light aircraft.
Note: Flights can be cancelled because of bad weather or lack of passengers.

Boat: The boat service from Basco to Paganaman Landing or Mauyen Landing on Itbayat leaves daily at 8am and costs P100. Travel time is about four hrs, however the boats only go in good weather and are fairly unpredictable - not really suitable if you are on a tight schedule.

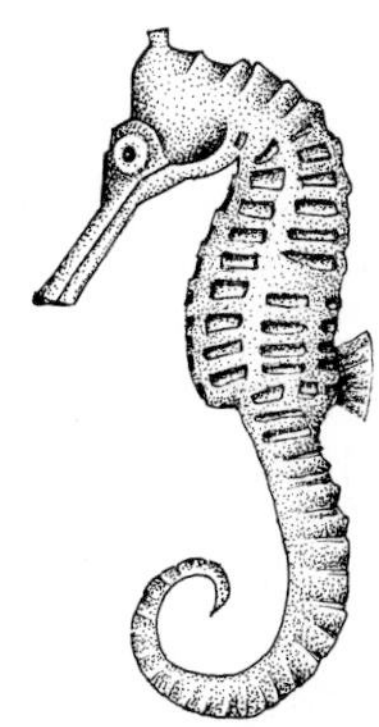

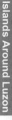

Catanduanes

Also known as the 'land of the howling winds', this kidney-shaped island lies in the Pacific Ocean, separated from South Luzon by the Maqueda Channel and the Gulf of Lagonoy. The province consists of the main island and a few smaller ones, the most important of which are Panay to the north-east and the Palumbanes Islands to the north-west. The Palumbanes Islands are made up of Palumbanes, Porongpong and Calabagio.

Catanduanes is mostly hilly. The only flat land is found east of the capital, Virac, and around Bato and Viga. The climate has shaped the landscape. As a result of typhoons, several coastal hills are barely covered with grass, many palms are uprooted or broken off, and steep cliffs and deeply indented bays are typical of the eastern and north-eastern coasts. The typhoons blast into this part of the Philippines straight off the Pacific. In Catanduanes you have to expect rain throughout the year, particularly from November to January, with not quite so much from April to June.

The main industries are fishing and farming. The most prolific fishing grounds are the Maqueda Channel, the Gulf of Lagonoy and Cabugao Bay. The main agricultural products are abaca (Manila hemp), rattan and coconuts, rice, sweet potatoes, cassava and fruits such as avocados, jackfruit, papayas and oranges. Mining has not been developed much, although there are deposits of coal, gold, silver, manganese and copper.

Many islanders have left Catanduanes in search of work, most settling in Manila. The greatest migrations take place after typhoons when houses and crops have been destroyed. People only come back then to visit on important occasions like festivals or family gatherings.

The people are friendly and very religious. They are Bikolanos, and speak Bikolano, the language of South Luzon. English is also spoken and understood. Visitors are nearly always invited into homes, and you'll have to depend on this hospitality because, with few exceptions, there is no commercially run accommodation on the islands.

Getting There & Away

You can travel to Catanduanes Island from Manila and Tabaco (see the Getting Away from Luzon section of the Manila chapter).

To Luzon

Air

From Virac to Manila
Asian Spirit flies on Monday, Wednesday, Friday, Saturday and Sunday (P2200).

Boat

From San Andres to Tabaco
Daily at 7 and 9am with Regina Shipping Lines (P90; three hrs).

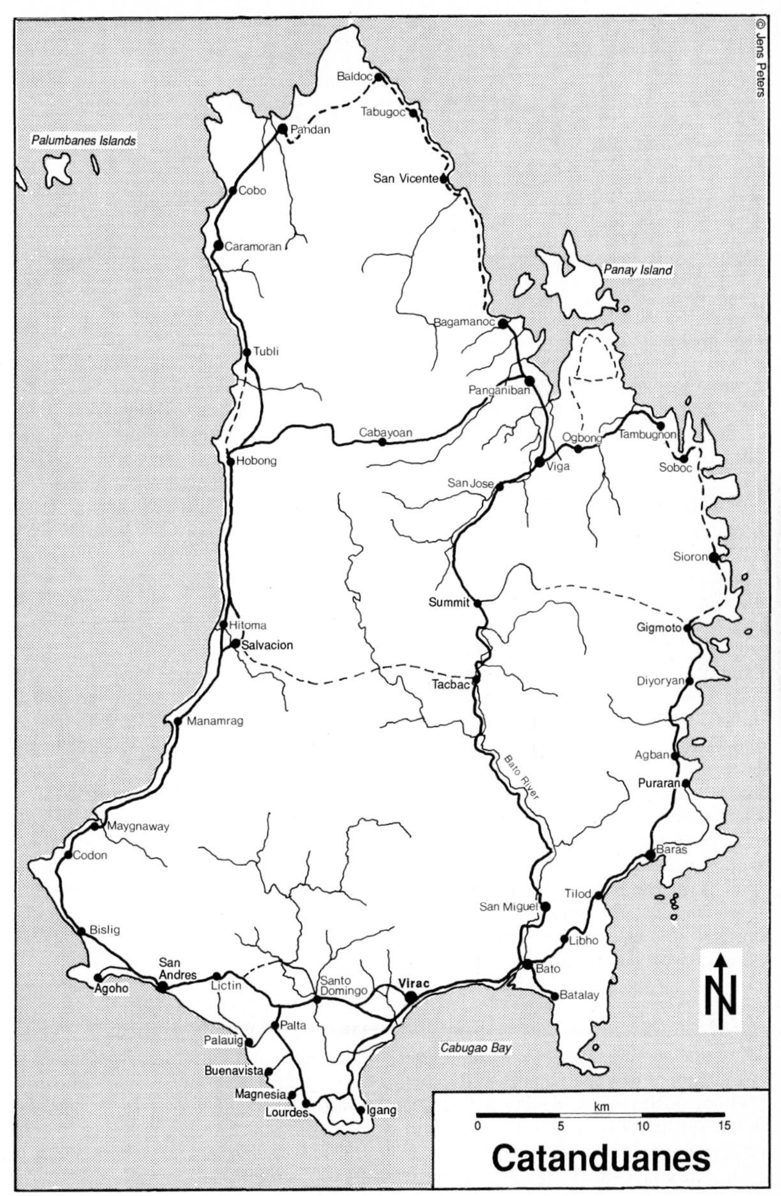
© Jens Peters
Palumbanes Islands
Baldoc
Tabugoc
Pandan
San Vicente
Cobo
Caramoran
Panay Island
Bagamanoc
Tubli
Panganiban
Cabayoan
Ogbong
Tambugnon
Hobong
Viga
Soboc
San Jose
Sioron
Summit
Hitoma
Salvacion
Gigmoto
Tacbac
Diyoryan
Manamrag
Bato River
Agban
Puraran
Maygnaway
Codon
Baras
Tilod
San Miguel
Bislig
Libho
San Andres
Bato
Agoho
Lictin
Santo Domingo
Virac
Batalay
Palta
Palauig
Cabugao Bay
Buenavista
Magnesia
Lourdes
Igang
km
0
5
10
15
Catanduanes
N

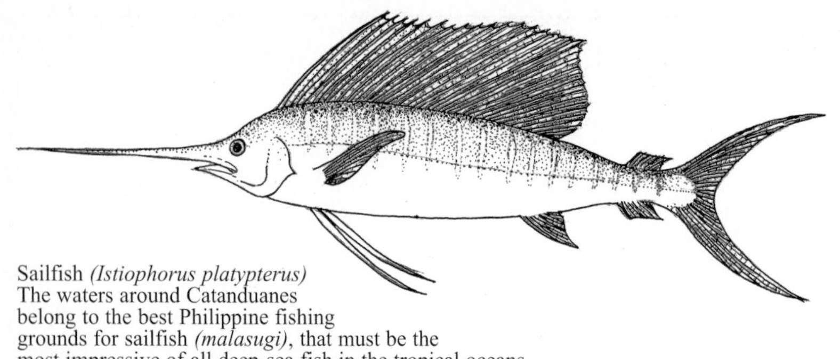

Sailfish *(Istiophorus platypterus)*
The waters around Catanduanes belong to the best Philippine fishing grounds for sailfish *(malasugi)*, that must be the most impressive of all deep-sea fish in the tropical oceans.

From Virac to Tabaco
Daily at 7am (possibly 9am) and 12.30pm with a Starferry Lines car ferry (P100; four hrs).

Getting Around

Bus/Jeepney: Transport connections within Catanduanes are fairly limited. Three jeepneys run daily from Virac market to Pandan, north of the island, and back. One jeepney runs daily from Virac to Tambugnon via Viga, leaving there at 9am and returning at midnight. Two jeepneys go from Virac to Gigmoto via Puraran, leaving between 9 and 10am and returning between 2 and 3am. A regular service of jeepneys and buses runs between Virac and Baras. The bumpy but scenic road from Virac to Gigmoto follows the coast and winds around one bay after another. The dirt road from Bato to Viga, goes through forest and little villages in the centre of the island. This and the Virac to Gigmoto coast road are good for hiking.

Virac

The cosy and clean little town of Virac is the capital of Catanduanes Province. Popular destinations for day trips from there are the Luyang Cave at Lictin (15 km west), which is said to reach as far as the coast and even has lighting at the beginning, Igang Beach, eight km south-west, and the Binanuahan Falls in Cabugao, a little south of Bato; they are easily reached by tricycle and a short walk. A trip to the Balongbong Falls in Bato is, however, hardly worth the effort, especially because they are not easily accessible.

Places to Stay

Virac

Virac Latri Lodge, Pier Site, Tel 8111499. SR/fan P130, DR/fan 230 P, SR/DR/fan/bath P350 (with TV). Basic, small rooms. Restaurant. Located at the wharf.

Marem's Pension House, Rizal Ave corner Rafael St, Tel 8111104, @. SR/DR/fan P125/150, SR/DR/ac/bath P650/775. Modest, not too large rooms with fan, and really good aircon rooms with TV. Restaurant. Located in the northern outskirts of town near the Capitol.

Nito's Lodge, Eastern Cabinitan, Tel 8111056. SR/DR/fan/bath P350, SR/DR/ac/bath P600. Good, clean accommodation in the western outskirts of town near the airport. Restaurant.

Catanduanes Midtown Inn, San Jose St, Tel 8110527, Fax 8111526, @. SR/ac/bath P700, DR/ac/bath P900 to P1800, suite P2500. Impeccable rooms

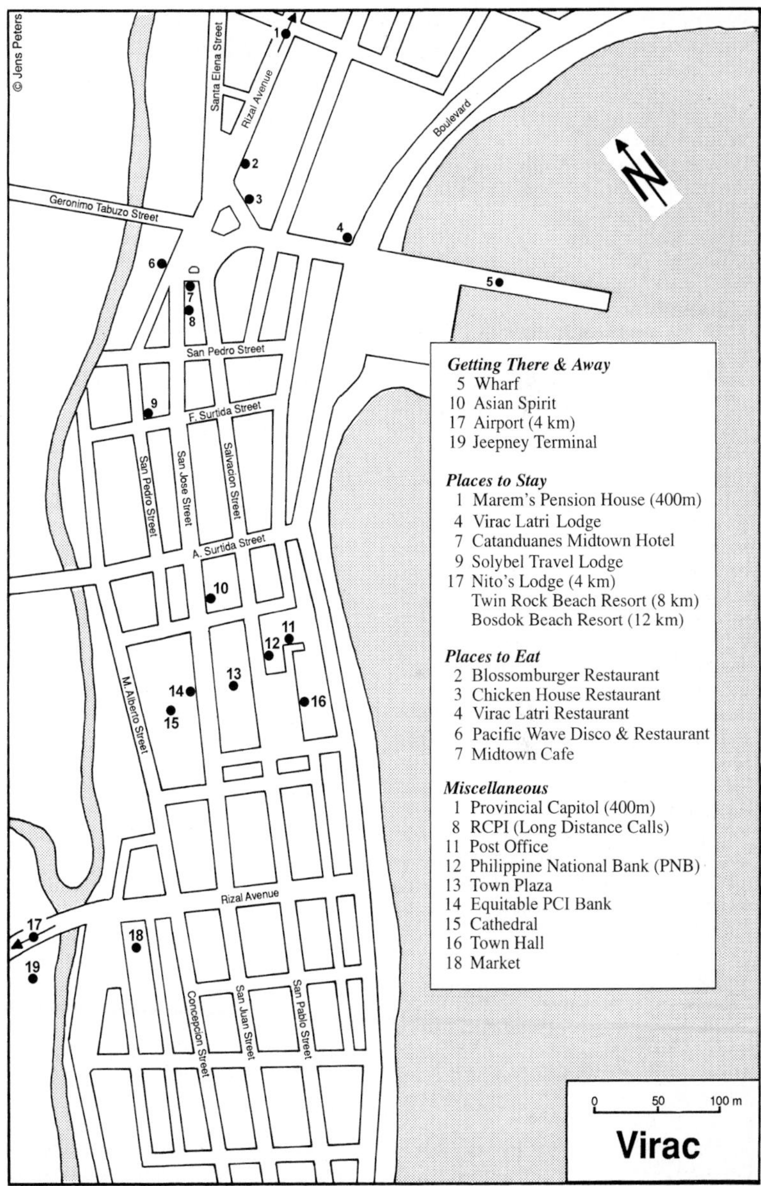
© Jens Peters
Santa Elena Street
Rizal Avenue
Boulevard
Geronimo Tabuzo Street
San Pedro Street
F. Surtida Street
San Pedro Street
San Jose Street
Salvacion Street
A. Surtida Street
M. Alberto Street
Rizal Avenue
Concepcion Street
San Juan Street
San Pablo Street
N
0
50
100 m
Virac
Getting There & Away
5 Wharf
10 Asian Spirit
17 Airport (4 km)
19 Jeepney Terminal
Places to Stay
1 Marem's Pension House (400m)
4 Virac Latri Lodge
7 Catanduanes Midtown Hotel
9 Solybel Travel Lodge
17 Nito's Lodge (4 km)
Twin Rock Beach Resort (8 km)
Bosdok Beach Resort (12 km)
Places to Eat
2 Blossomburger Restaurant
3 Chicken House Restaurant
4 Virac Latri Restaurant
6 Pacific Wave Disco & Restaurant
7 Midtown Cafe
Miscellaneous
1 Provincial Capitol (400m)
8 RCPI (Long Distance Calls)
11 Post Office
12 Philippine National Bank (PNB)
13 Town Plaza
14 Equitable PCI Bank
15 Cathedral
16 Town Hall
18 Market

with TV, the more expensive ones also with a refrigerator. The best hotel in town, not far from the wharf. Restaurant.

Around Virac

Twin Rock Beach Resort, Igang, Cellphone 0918-7361168. SR/DR/fan/bath P800, SR/DR/ac/bath P1000. Comfortable rooms. The cottages were unfortunately destroyed by a typhoon. Restaurant, swimming pool. Located on Igang Beach (very stony, especially when the tide's out) eight km south-west of Virac.

Bosdok Beach Resort, Magnesia. Solidly built, roomy, clean cottages on the side of a hill. The resort covers an extensive area in an idyllic bay and has a beautiful little sandy beach with a gorgeous view of Mayon volcano in the distance. There is also a big restaurant and a swimming pool. Bosdok Beach is a bit out of the way, 12 km south-west of Virac. A Special Ride by tricycle costs P200. A service jeep belonging to the resort leaves daily from Virac (near the market) and also meets the plane and the ferry boat.

Note: This resort was closed in 1998 after a devastating typhoon, but should be opening again in 2005.

Places to Eat

You can eat good, inexpensive Filipino food at the pleasant ***Midtown Café*** in the Catanduanes Midtown Hotel, at the ***Blossomburger Restaurant*** and at the ***Pacific Wave Restaurant***.

Miscellaneous

Festivals: Catanduanes Festival from 22 to 24 October. Kagharong Festival from 16 to 25 December.

Money: The Philippine National Bank at the town plaza will change travellers' cheques.

The Equitable PCI Bank in San Juan St has an ATM.

Population: 50,000.

Post & Telephone: Post code: 4800. Area code: 052.

Getting Around

Car: The Catanduanes Midtown Hotel rents out a nine-seat Toyota for P1000 per day.

Getting There & Away

By Air: The airport is about four km south-west of Virac. The trip into town by tricycle should normally cost P5 per person. The least they will charge, however, is P20.

Asian Spirit, Greypac Corporation, San Jose St, Tel 8111056.

Destination: Manila.

Puraran

Puraran is a small place on the wild Pacific coast about 30 km north-east of Virac. It is a good stopover on a journey to the north of the island. However, many of the few foreigners who have visited Catanduanes up till now take one look at its long white beach and decide to finish the journey right there. Surfers especially like to stay in Puraran for the excellent breakers which usually start at the beginning of July. In September and October the surfing is good, while from November to January the particularly high breakers even provide a challenge for experts.

It is safe to swim at high tide in front of the reef, but be careful: there is a dangerously strong current near the beach, and especially over the reef itself - you have been warned! Even excellent swimmers have been known to get into serious trouble in this current. Only when the water is calm is it worth snorkelling. Typhoons can put an end to all thoughts of water sports. So, unless you're a surfer, the best time to stay would probably be from the middle of March until the middle to end of June.

Places to Stay

Pacific View Beach Resort. SR/DR P300. Basic cottages.

Puting Baybay Resort. SR/DR P300. A basic place with rustic cottages at the bottom of the slope.

Getting There & Away

Jeepney: Two jeepneys leave Virac market for Puraran between 9 and 10am daily, going on to Gigmoto. Another may leave after the arrival of the boat from Tabaco. You can also go to Baras by jeepney and then travel the next five km by tricycle (about P30). A tricycle for the whole trip from Virac costs at least P250. There is a pathway leading from the street in Puraran down to the beach which takes about five minutes on foot.

From Puraran to Virac, there is a regular jeepney service at about 3.30am (it can even be as late as 4.30am). This jeepney comes from Gigmoto.

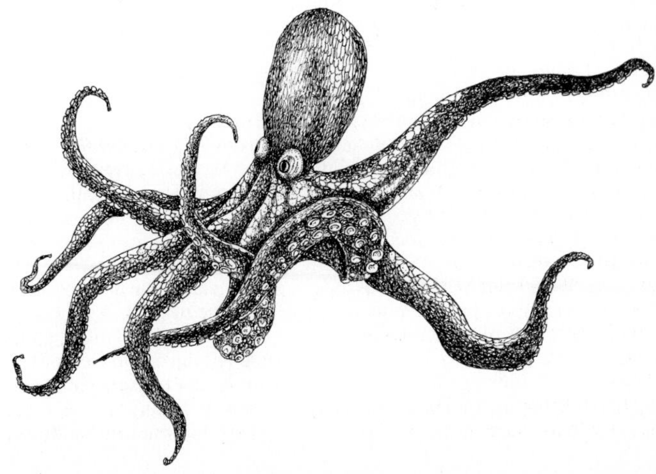

Lubang

The Lubang Islands are part of the province of Mindoro Occidental. They hit the world headlines in 1974 when the Japanese soldier Hiroo Onoda, who had been hiding in the mountains of Lubang for 30 years, finally decided it was time to bring WWII to an end for himself. Fumio Nakahura, a captain in the Japanese Imperial Army, held out for another six years before being discovered in April 1980 on Mt Halcon on Mindoro. When the 74-year-old Hiroo Onoda paid a sentimental return visit to his island hideout in 1996 after many years, he was confronted over and over again by blunt hostility. Either some people still had a chip on their shoulder, or a few badly mannered yobos grasped the opportunity to let off steam about their former enemy. Perhaps they felt reason to, because they didn't only suffer at the hands of the Japanese during the war: until a few years ago Lubang was a popular place with Japanese friends of the gun (and womanisers). They came with their hostesses in charter planes from Manila and took up residence in the World Safari Club on the beach on Lubang. They then proceeded to shoot at targets, clay pigeons and wild boar, although the latter were unfortunately not genuinely wild. Just before a group of hunters turned up, the tame pigs were bought up in surrounding villages (the wilder they looked the more was paid for them), and let loose into the countryside to be shot at. Surrounded by this mayhem, local beaters risked life and limb for a few pesos a day. The World Safari Club was later seriously damaged by a typhoon, although there are plans to rebuild and reopen it.

The people of Lubang earn their income mainly from the sale of garlic. They would like to share in the profits from tourism but seem at present most likely to inspire only one wish in visitors: to leave for Manila or Mindoro as soon as possible. The author found people in Tilik and farther south-east to be less forthcoming than elsewhere. As you go from Tilik towards Lubang, attitudes become noticeably more relaxed.

Getting There & Away

You can get here from Luzon (see the Getting Away from Luzon section of the Manila chapter).

To Luzon

Boat

From Tilik to Manila

Tuesday and Friday with San Nicolas Shipping Lines (P250; seven hrs).

Tilik

You can't travel around much here because of the lack of transport, but the country around Tilik is good for walks, such as the one to Como Beach near Vigo. It's no tropical paradise, but there's some real surf and it's not crowded. There's a beautiful sandy beach at Tag-

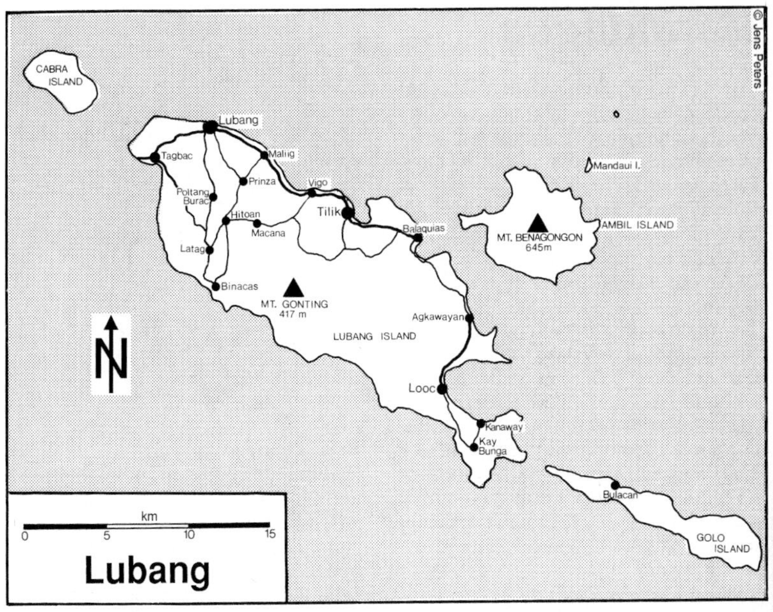

bac, west of Lubang, but the sea floor is muddy. If you go by paddle boat from Tilik to the other side of the bay, make sure there is at least a 15 cm clearance above the water line. The centre of the bay is exposed and even a light wind can blow water into the boat. It's easy to get thoroughly drenched.

Places to Stay

There is no commercial accommodation available in Lubang, so you will have to find a family who will rent you a room. Just ask the mayor or the local priest.

Getting Around

Transport costs on Lubang are at least twice those on other islands. This applies also to the short trip by banca from Balaquias south-east of Tilik across to Ambil Island, for which they now allegedly ask P300. It's not worth it, especially if you are expecting to look for and find the jade which the Philippine technical literature claims is there.

Getting There & Away

By Air: The airport is on the road from Lubang to Tagbac in the north-west of the island. A *carretela* (a calesa or horse-drawn carriage) to Vigo or Tilik costs P80 to P100 and takes one hour.

By Boat: Tilik is the port for this area. When a boat docks, a regular jeepney runs to Lubang and a truck takes freight and passengers to Looc.

Marinduque

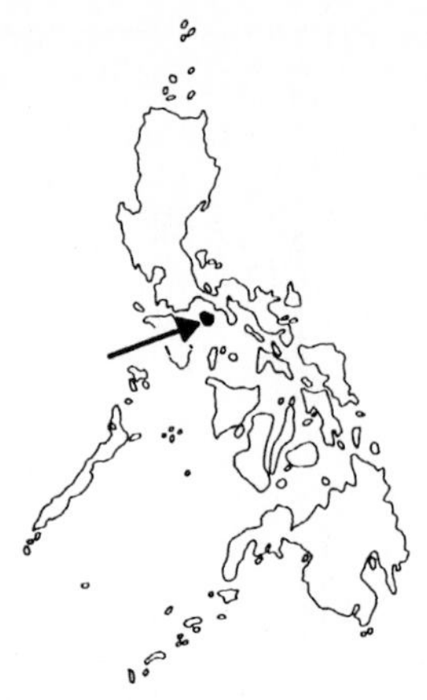

Marinduque is the near-circular island between South Luzon and Mindoro. The Marinduqueros are Tagalogs and most of them come from Batangas and Quezon provinces.

Coconuts and rice are the main agricultural products. Two mining companies extract iron ore and copper; there are large copper deposits at Labo near Santa Cruz.

The main tourist attraction is the Moriones Festival at Easter, which is great fun and everyone joins in with good humour (see the Public Holidays & Special Events section of the Country & People chapter earlier in this book). This is when Marinduque gets most of its tourists. At other times there aren't many around, as the tourist industry here is just getting going.

Getting There & Away

You can get to Marinduque from Luzon and Mindoro (see Getting Away from Luzon in the Manila chapter and Getting There & Away in the Mindoro chapter).

To Luzon

Air

From Boac to Manila

Asian Spirit flies Monday, Wednesday, Friday and Sunday (P1430).

Boat

From Balanacan to Lucena

Daily at 4 and 8am, 12 noon and 4pm with a Montenegro Shipping Lines car ferry (P90; 2½ hrs).

Daily at 7am and 2.30pm with a Blue Magic Ferries fast ferry (P170; 1¾ hrs).

Daily at 2.30pm with Blue Magic Ferries (P150; 2½ hrs).

From Cawit to Lucena

Daily at 12 noon and midnight with a Phil-Nippon Kyoei Corporation car ferry (P130; three hrs).

Note: The Phil-Nippon Kyoei Corporation car ferries are noticeably better than those belonging to Montenegro Shipping Lines.

From Santa Cruz to Lucena

Daily at 5am with a fast ferry (P160; 2½ hrs).

Daily at 1pm with a Montenegro Shipping Lines car ferry (four hrs).

Departure from the Santa Cruz wharf in Buyabod.

To Mindoro

Boat

From Gasan to Pinamalayan

Daily at 8.30am with a big outrigger (P120; 3½ hrs).

Boac

Boac, on the Boac River, is the capital of Marinduque Province. It is a pretty little town towered over by a massive church built on a hill, with a richly decorated altar. Of the passion plays

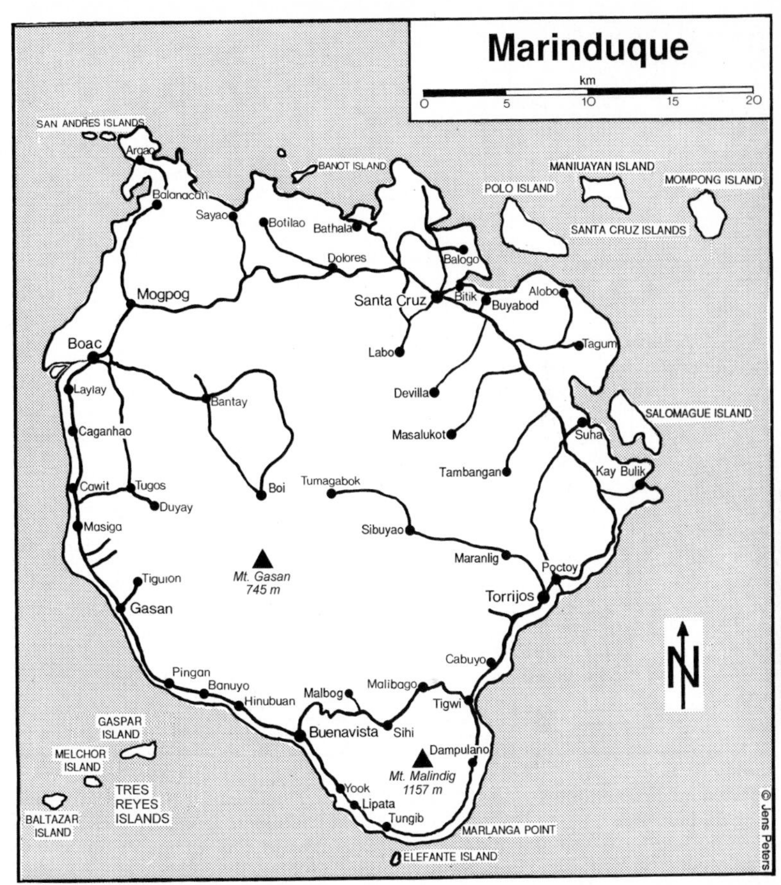

performed all over the island at Easter, each claiming to be the best, the star production of the Moriones Festival is the one staged in Boac.

Next to the Capitol, on the way out of town heading for Gasan, the Butterfly Park has a collection of different species of butterfly. Admission free.

Museum

The National Museum in Moreno St at the plaza maintains a collection on the history of Marinduque as well as an exhibition of selected Moriones masks and costumes. Open daily 8am-4pm. Admission free.

Places to Stay

Boac

Boac Hotel, Nepomuceno St, Tel 3221121, Fax 3322065. SR/DR/fan/bath P250, SR/DR/ac/bath P600/800; with TV P100 extra. Basic, centrally

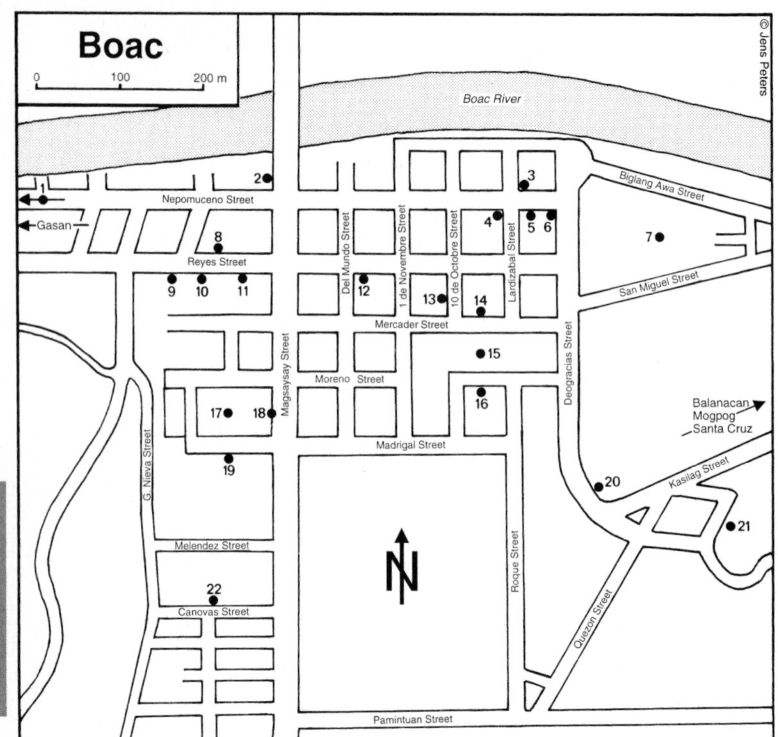

located hotel. The rooms with fan have a small balcony.

Cely's Lodging House, 10 de Octobre St, Tel 3321519. SR/DR/fan P200/300, SR/DR/ac P500. Very basic, family accommodation. Restaurant.

Tahanan sa Isok, Canovas St, Tel 3321231. SR/fan/bath P400, SR/DR/ac/bath P800/1100. Good value. Bright, pleasantly furnished rooms with TV in a well-kept hotel with beautiful garden. To be recommended. Quiet location. Restaurant.

Beach Resorts South of Boac

There are several beach resorts between Boac and Cawit (eight km) along the ring road. Even if the beaches are not picture-perfect on the west coast of Marinduque (brown sand with pebbles and stones), the water is clean and clear. From north to south:

A & A Beach Resort, Laylay, Tel 3322817. SR/DR/fan/bath P600, SR/DR/ac/bath P900 to P1300 (depending on size). Good rooms, all with TV, for up to four people. Restaurant.

Villa Carlos, Ihatub, Tel 3321881. SR/DR/ac/bath P1300 to P1800. Reasonable rooms with two and four beds. With TV. Roomy stone building. Restaurant.

Castaways Beach Inn, Baraling, Tel 3321384. SR/DR/fan/bath P500. Big,

Getting There & Away
1 Airport (12 km)
2 Jeepneys to Gasan, Buenavista & Santa Cruz
6 Asian Spirit
18 Jeepneys to Balanacan

Places to Stay
6 Boac Hotel
13 Cely's Lodging House
22 Tahanan sa Isok

Places to Eat
3 Foodworld Restaurant
12 Krisna Restaurant
14 Kusina sa Plaza

Miscellaneous
1 Hospital (1 km)
Provincial Capitol (1km)
Tourist Office (1 km)
4 Nets Internet Cafe
LBC
5 JED Computer Center
7 Kirche und Kloster
8 Philippine National Bank (PNB)
9 Supermarket
10 Landbank
11 Sound Bytes Computer Center
15 Plaza
16 Museum
17 Market
19 Police Station
20 Post Office
21 Town Hall

cosy rooms in a long beach house. Friendly, well-kept place with a garden and a terrace. British management. Restaurant and bar (Friday and Saturday with live music). Diving.
El Mannuel Beach Resort, Baraling, Tel 3321305. SR/DR/fan/bath P400. Four rooms in a stone building and two cottages. Basic accommodation.
Aurora Beach Resort, Caganhao. SR/DR/fan/bath P300 and P600. Basic rooms, the more expensive ones with three beds and a kitchen.
Pyramid Beach Resort, Caganhao, Tel 3321328. SR/DR/fan/bath P250, SR/DR/ac/bath P650. Basic but adequate rooms for up to four people. Meals should be ordered in advance if required.
3 E's Love Bay Beach Resort, Amoingon, Tel 3221440. SR/DR/fan/bath P600 and P800, SR/DR/ac/bath P1500 to P3000. Big selection of different, attractive rooms for two to six people. Some have TV, the more expensive have a kitchen. Well-kept place with tennis courts. Advanced orders are required for any meals.
Blue Sea Beach Resort, Amoingon, Tel 3221334. SR/DR/fan/bath P400, SR/DR/ac/bath P600 to P1,000 (depending on size). Reasonable rooms in beautiful beach houses. Good value. Attractive grounds. Restaurant.
Sea View Hotel, Cawit, Tel 3322840. SR/DR/fan/bath P500. Fairly good standard rooms. Restaurant. This hotel may only be open during high season.

Places to Eat

Good value Philippine food is available in the basic, but acceptable restaurants ***ALB Foodworld***, Nepomuceno St, ***Kusina sa Plaza***, Mercader St, and in the ***Krisna Restaurant*** in Reyes St. The pleasant ***Café Elias*** and ***Paula's Garden***, both in the Hotel Tahanan sa Isok in Canovas St, will serve you good Philippine and international food.

Miscellaneous

Festival: Moriones Festival in Easter week, mainly from Maundy Thursday to Easter Sunday.
Money: The Philippine National Bank in Reyes St has an ATM.
Online: Sound Bytes Computer Center, Reyes St, JED Computer Center, Nepomuceno St, and Nets Café, Lardizabal Street; all P60/hr.
Population: 45,000.

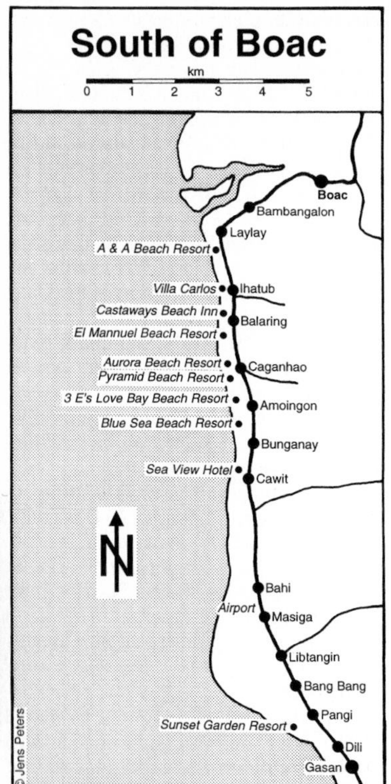

Post & Telephone: Post Office, Deogracias St.
Post code: 4900. Area code: 042 (for all Marindunque).
Tourist Office, Provincial Capitol, Tel 3321018, Cellphone 0920-2490201. Open Mon-Fri 8am-noon and 1-5pm.

Getting Around

Tricycle: A ride within the town boundaries costs P5 per person.

Getting There & Away

By Jeepney: Jeepneys leave for Balanacan (pier) from the market; to Gasan, Buenavista and Santa Cruz from Nepomuceno St at the corner of Magsaysay St (next to the bridge over the river).

By Air: Boac Airport is 12 km to the south of Boac, near Masiga. To get there by jeepney costs P30, a Special Ride with a tricycle costs P100.
Asian Spirit, Boac Hotel, Nepomuceno St corner Deogracias St, Tel 3321121.
Destination: Manila.

Balanacan

This small town in north-west Marinduque has a little harbour in a very picturesque, sheltered bay which provides shipping services to and from Lucena (Dalahican Port) on Luzon.

Places to Stay

LTB Lodge. SR/DR P100/200, SR/DR/fan P200/350. Very basic place, on the left as you come into town (coming from the pier).

Getting There & Away

Jeepney/Bus: There aren't many jeepneys between Boac and Balanacan daily (P20; 30 min). It's safer to rely on those that meet the boats, as they head off in all directions, even directly to Torrijos (via Santa Cruz), and there are also aircon minibuses to Boac, Buenavista and Santa Cruz.

Santa Cruz

Boac might be the capital of Marinduque, but Santa Cruz has the most inhabitants. Its magnificent church, built in 1714, is very impressive with its old paintings and sculpture.
There are boat routes between Santa Cruz and Lucena (Dalahican Port) on Luzon.

Places to Stay

Rico's Lodging House, Recalde St, Tel 3211029. SR/DR/fan P150/300. Basic, but clean accommodation in a private house. Enquire in the restaurant Rico's Inn.

Santa Cruz Hotel *(Fantasia)*, Tavera St, Tel 3211031. SR/DR/ac/bath P1200 and 1400; half price for only twelve hours' stay. Adequate rooms, if a bit expensive. The best hotel in town.

Places to Eat
Of the handful of restaurants in town, probably the best place to eat is ***Rico's Inn***, opposite the Town Hall in Pag-asa St. They serve good value Philippine food as well as a few international dishes.

Getting There & Away
By Boat: Buyabod is the pier for Santa Cruz and is a few km to the east.

Boac
Jeepney: Several jeepneys run daily from Boac to Santa Cruz via Mogpog.

Torrijos
Jeepney: Several jeepneys run daily from Torrijos to Santa Cruz (one hr).

Ipil

The Bathala Caves, about 10 km north-west of Santa Cruz in Barrio Ipil, are a complex of seven caves in all, only four of which are accessible. They are on the private property of the Mendoza family, so before visiting you should ask for their permission (admission costs P50; guided tours P150).

You may be able to swim in the natural pool behind the house - you'll find a swim very welcome after visiting the bats in the caves!

Places to Stay
The Mendoza family rents a fairly big cottage for five to six people.

Getting There & Away
Jeepney/Tricycle: Only a few jeepneys run daily between Santa Cruz and Ipil. A tricycle costs P30 per person.

Maniuayan Island

On the three Santa Cruz islands of Polo, Maniuayan and Mompong north-east of Santa Cruz, there are long beaches and good snorkelling, particularly on Maniuayan Island.

Places to Stay
Lucita Perlada offers a room in a cottage on the beach for P350 per day, including meals. Her sister Julieta also rents out a room in her house on the beach.

Getting There & Away
Boat: A boat leaves Bitik, on the north-eastern coast of Marinduque, daily at about 7 or 8am (45 min).

After the ferry from Lucena arrives, boats leave Buyabod for the islands of Maniuayan and Polo.

Torrijos

Although not the most picturesque, the scenic White Beach at Poctoy near Torrijos is probably the best beach on Marinduque. It has a magnificent view of Mt Malindig, and the outlying coral reef is good for snorkelling.

Tumagabok, Maranlig and Sibuyao, all north-west of Torrijos, make good day trips into the interior of the island. A jeepney runs every day to Maranlig. There is only one to Sibuyao and Tumagabok, and that's on Saturday, market day in Sibuyao. Maranlig has cockfights on Sunday; Sibuyao is on a plateau with rice terraces; not far from Tumagabok you'll find noteworthy virgin forests.

There's a good view from the Pulang Lupa Shrine, a memorial to a battle between Philippine independence fighters and American soldiers at the beginning

of the 20th century. It's about 1½ hours' walk there from White Beach.
You can reach the white beach on Salomague Island by boat in an hour.

Places to Stay

Rendezvous Cottages, Poctoy. Cottage P200, Cottage/fan/bath P400. Very basic, unimaginative huts on White Beach, although the ones with a bath are a bit better. Located about 500m off the ring road (turn off at the sign for White Beach). Billiards. Karaoke.
Marilou's Private Beachhouse, Poctoy, Cellphone 0919-4850531. SR/DR/fan/bath P500. Friendly, spacious rooms. Guests have to feed themselves (kitchen and refrigerator are available). Hosts Hanspeter, who's Swiss, and his Filipina wife Marilou, also do some farming (cattle breeding). Located on a small, very quiet private beach about 500m east of White Beach. To get there, follow the directions for the Rendezvous Cottages, then go left along the beach and cross the grounds to the Beachhouse. There is also a private entrance from the ring road.
Jovita's Paradise, Cagpo. SR/DR/fan/bath P700, SR/DR/ac/bath P1200. Spacious rooms in a two-storey, stone building. Well-kept place on a bay with a light sand beach. Food can be prepared to order. Located three km north-east of White Beach, about 500m off the ring road.

Getting There & Away

Buenavista
Jeepney: A few jeepneys run daily from Buenavista to Torrijos via the hill town of Malibago (you may have to change there). But be careful, as from late afternoon they don't go beyond Malibago.
A Special Ride with a tricycle from Malibago to Torrijos costs P100.

Santa Cruz
Jeepney: Several jeepneys run daily from Santa Cruz to Torrijos (one hr). The last departure is at about 4.30pm. Anybody wanting to go to the White Beach near Poctoy could ask the jeepney driver to make a short detour there.

Note: The route from Boac via Santa Cruz to Torrijos is better than the one via Buenavista.

Buenavista

This town, on the south-east coast of Marinduque, is the departure point for Mt Malindig at Marlanga Point, a 1157m high dormant volcano on which a telegraph station has been built.
The Buenavista market is especially worth seeing at weekends, when mountain people from all around bring their wares. Pigs and goats are sold, slaughtered and cut up on the spot.
About five km by road inland from Buenavista are the Malbog Hot Springs - sulphur springs which are claimed to heal certain skin complaints.

Places to Stay

Susanna Hot Spring Resort, Malbog, Tel 3321997. SR/fan P200, SR/DR/fan/bath P400 (bathroom with bathtub and hot spring water). Well-kept place with a nice garden and picnic tables. There are two small swimming pools with water at least 40°C. Located three km east of Buenavista, about 100m off the ring road.

Getting There & Away

Jeepney: Several jeepneys run daily between Boac and Buenavista via Cawit and Gasan.

Elefante Island

High up on the little Elefante Island to the south of Marinduque, Japanese investors built the Fantasy Elephant Club with extensive facilities set in its own grounds. The place was originally designed to be exclusive, with its golf course, tennis courts and water sports facilities only available to club members. However, clearly the idea didn't work, and it has since been closed down.

Tres Reyes Islands

It's a 30-minute trip in an outrigger boat from Buenavista to the outlying Tres Reyes (Three Kings) Islands. Balthazar and Melchor islands are rocky and uninhabited. However, on the east coast of the third, Gaspar, there's a beach with a small village and, on the side facing away from Marinduque, beautiful little peaceful sandy bays which are great for swimming and lazing around.
In 1980 the wreck of a Chinese junk that sank 200 years ago was discovered about 100m north of Gaspar Island in 38m of water. Although most of its rich cargo of porcelain has already been salvaged, from time to time local divers bring up a few more finds. The waters around Gaspar Island have since been declared a Marine Sanctuary.

Gasan

Like Boac and Mogpog, Gasan is heavily involved in the Easter passion play. Handcrafted basket ware and ornaments are made here; in the UNI Store, for example, you can see how the carved wooden birds are painted.
There is a boat service between Gasan and Pinamalayan on Mindoro.

Places to Stay

Amigo's Lodge, Rizal St corner Del Pilar St. SR/DR P100/200. Family-style accommodation with very basic rooms.
Sunset Garden Resort, Pangi, Tel 3421004, Fax 3421003, @. Cottage/fan/bath P530, cottage/ac/bath P730. Reasonable cottages with veranda in friendly grounds with lots of plants. Austrian management. Restaurant, tennis court. Located about two km north of Gasan.
Katala Beach Resort, Bacong Bacong, Tel 3331079, @. SR/DR/fan/bath P700, SR/DR/ac/bath P900. Big, two-storey building with good rooms. Restaurant. Austrian management. Quiet resort, located four km south of Gasan with a breathtaking view of the offshore Tres Reyes Islands.
Southwest Bay Resort, Bacong Bacong, Tel 3337220. Cottage/fan/bath P2500. Very roomy cottages with four beds, kitchen, refrigerator and big veranda. More suitable for families. Well-kept garden. Located three km south of Gasan.
Casa de Azul, Banuyo, Tel 3341020, @. SR/DR/ ac/bath P1200. Generous, well-furnished rooms in a private holiday home by the sea. Full board available. Swimming pool. Located about seven km south-east of Gasan.

Places to Eat

The ***Sunset Garden Restaurant*** and the ***Katala Restaurant*** belonging to the resorts of the same names have European and Filipino food. Tasty Philippine and German food is available at the cosy little ***Barbarossa Pub*** on the main street in Gasan. At the market in Gasan, market ladies prepare tasty corn pudding and rice and banana cake.

Masbate

The province of Masbate includes Masbate Island and the smaller Ticao and Burias islands. Although the island group is officially part of the Bicol region, the influence of the Visayas is unmistakable, so the Cebuano and Hiligaynon languages are also frequently spoken.
Before WWII, Masbate was a leading gold field. Today it is noted for its meat production, having some herds of cattle as large as 4000 head. That's why the island is also known in the Philippines as 'Cattle Country'. Fishing is also important economically.
Tourism doesn't mean much here, as few foreigners come to these islands, which are off the main traffic routes, so visitors accustomed to rusticity will have a pleasant time here. Even basic commercial overnight accommodation is really only available in the towns of Masbate, Cataingan, Esperanza, Mobo, Aroroy and Mandaon. Lovers of tuba should try the white variety, which is a speciality of Masbate (tuba is the Philippine palm wine).

Getting There & Away

You can get to Masbate from Cebu, Leyte, Luzon and Romblon (see Getting Away from Luzon in the Manila chapter and Getting There & Away in the chapters on the other islands).

To Cebu

Boat

From Cataingan to Cebu City
Tuesday with Super Shuttle Ferry (car ferry), taking 10 hrs.

From Placer to Bogo
Apparently a boat makes the trip three times weekly, probably Monday, Wednesday and Friday (six hrs). The boat originates in Cawayan.

From Esperanza to Maya
Tuesday, Thursday and Saturday at 10am with a big outrigger (three hrs). The boat originates in Pio V Corpus.

From Masbate to Cebu City
Tuesday, Thursday and Saturday with Trans-Asia Shipping Lines (P350; 14 hrs).

To Leyte

Boat

From Masbate to Ormoc
Saturday with Sulpicio Lines (P340; 13 hrs).

From Masbate to Palompon
Wednesday with WG & A (P420; eight hrs).

To Luzon

Air

From Masbate to Manila
Asian Spirit has daily flights (P2505).

Boat

From Aroroy to Manila
Monday with MBRS Lines (20 hrs); via Romblon/Romblon.

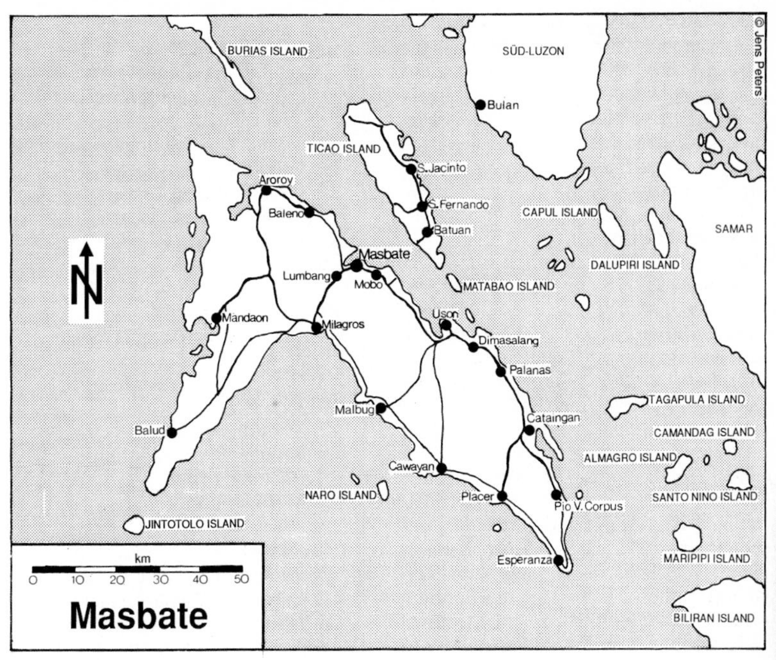

From Masbate to Bulan
Daily at 6 am with San Pablo Shipping Lines (four hrs); probably via San Fernando/Ticao Island.

From Masbate to Lucena
Tuesday, Thursday and Sunday with a Bluewater Ferry car ferry (P400; 12 hrs).

From Masbate to Manila
Monday and Wednesday with Sulpicio Lines (P540; 19 hrs).
Thursday with WG & A (P500; 19 hrs).

From Masbate to Pilar
Daily at 5 and 8am, noon, and at 2pm, with a Montenegro Shipping Lines fast ferry (P210; two hrs).
Daily at 7am (big outrigger; P80; four hrs) and at 11am (wooden boat; P120; three hrs).

Buses and minibuses run between Pilar and Legaspi (1½ hrs).

To Romblon

Boat

From Aroroy to Romblon/Romblon
Monday with MBRS Lines (five hrs); possibly via San Agustin/Tablas Island.

From Mandaon to Cajidiocan/ Sibuyan Island
Three times weekly, probably at 8am with a big outrigger (five hrs). You can only find out the exact departure time in Mandaon.

Masbate

The town of Masbate is the capital of the province but hasn't a great deal of note beyond the harbour, the market and numerous stalls which line the streets. Due to the hordes of tricycles the town is loud and the air is badly polluted. If you feel the need to breathe in deeply, head for one of the two beach resorts at the Punta Nursery north-east of the airport.

Getting There & Away
9 Trans-Asia Shipping Lines
11 Sulpicio Shipping Lines
WG & A
12 Montenegro Shipping Lines
13 Gold Line
14 CAA Shipping Lines
15 Minibuses to Cataingan
20 Asian Spirit
25 Bus & Jeepney Terminal

Places to Stay
4 Rendezvous Hotel & Beach Resort
5 West Wind Waters Resort
10 Jade Hotel
17 St Anthony Hotel
18 Sampaguita Tourist Inn
22 Rancher's Hotel
27 Masbate Lodge

Places to Eat
1 Lantau Restaurant
2 Shimmery Land Restaurant
3 Bulalo-an sa Boulevard
19 Xia Men Restaurant
24 Masbate Snack House
26 D'San Restaurant

Miscellaneous
6 City Hall
Police Station
7 Plaza
8 Post Office
16 Church
21 Philippine National Bank (PNB)
22 Mercury Drug
23 Market

Places to Stay

Sampaguita Tourist Inn, Quezon St, Tel 3334729. SR/DR/fan P120/240, SR/DR/fan/bath P200/300, SR/DR/ac/bath P400 to P650 (TV). Good rooms, OK for the money. Restaurant.

Masbate Lodge, Quezon St, Tel 3332184. SR/DR/fan P180/340, SR/DR/ac P350/500. Basic, fairly clean accommodation near the airport.

Jade Hotel, Quezon St, Tel 3332293. SR/DR/fan/bath P200/400, SR/DR/ac/bath P800. Fairly good, friendly accommodation. Most of the aircon rooms (with TV) have no window, however; those in the back part of the building are quiet. Beautiful view of the town and harbour from the roof terrace.

St Anthony Hotel, Quezon St, Tel 3332180. SR/DR/fan/bath P300/400, SR/DR/ac/bath P400 to P600. The rooms are no longer the newest, some have TV. Restaurant.

Rancher's Hotel, Tara St, Tel 3333931. SR/DR/fan/bath P250, SR/DR/ac/bath P500, P600 and P800 (with TV). Unimaginative, not very inviting rooms; each bath is shared by two rooms. Loud live music until midnight. Food can be prepared to order.

Rendezvous Hotel & Beach Resort, Punta Nursery, Tel 3334751. SR/DR/ac/bath P850. Reasonable rooms with TV. Small resort just outside of town (behind the airport). Very busy at the weekend. Restaurant.

Places to Eat

The half open-air ***Xia Men Restaurant*** in Rosero St serves inexpensive Chinese food. The aircon ***D'San Restaurant*** and ***Masbate Snack House***, both in Tara St, offer good value Philippine food.

Shimmery Land on the boulevard north of the airport is air-conditioned and to be recommended. They have a wide selection on their menu and specialise

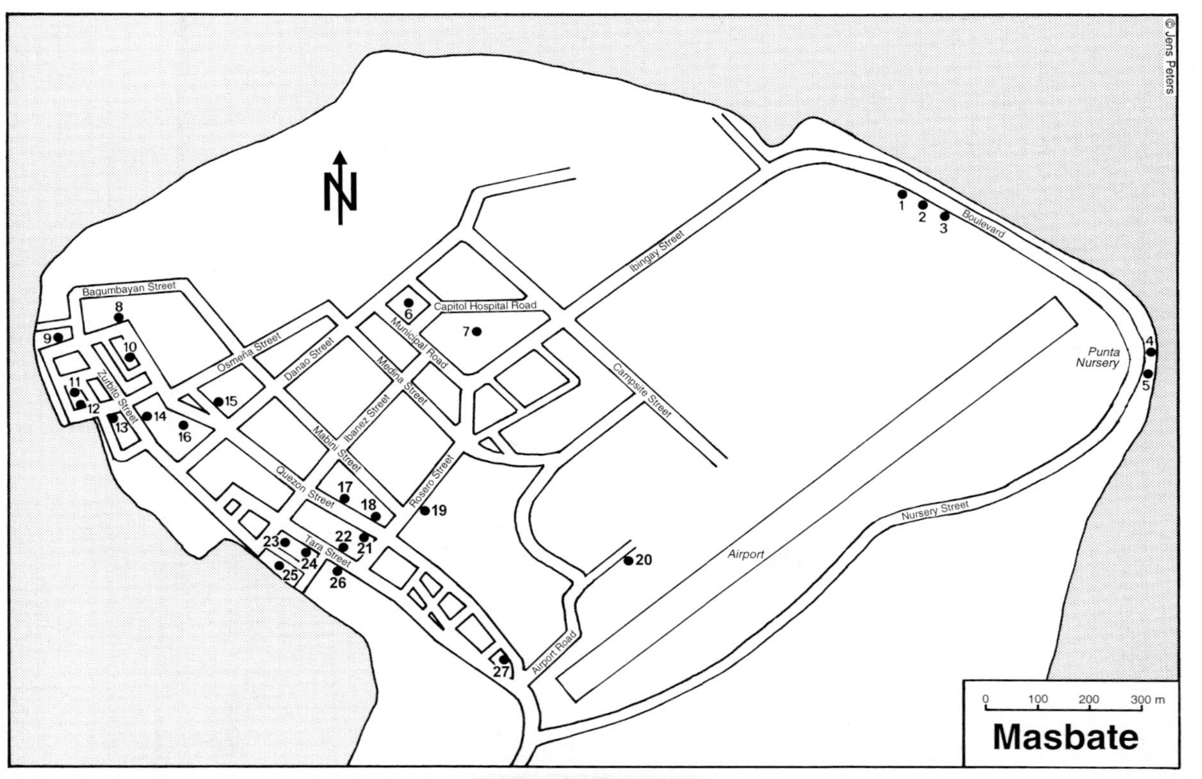
© Jens Peters
Masbate
0
100
200
300 m
Punta Nursery
Boulevard
Nursery Street
Airport
Ibingay Street
Campsite Street
Capitol Hospital Road
Municipal Road
Medina Street
Rosero Street
Ibanez Street
Mabini Street
Quezon Street
Tara Street
Airport Road
Danao Street
Osmeña Street
Bagumbayan Street
Zurbito Street
1
2
3
4
5
6
7
8
9
10
11
12
13
14
15
16
17
18
19
20
21
22
23
24
25
26
27

in steaks and seafood at humane prices, and they offer a good sea view. Right next door in the half open-air ***Bulalo-an sa Boulevard*** and in ***Lantau*** you'll find Philippine dishes and barbecue. The same holds for the two beach resorts ***Rendezvous*** and ***West Wind Waters*** somewhat further east at the Punta Nursery.

Miscellaneous

Festivals: Rodeo Masbateño on three days in April (sometimes in other months). Pagdayao Festival on 11 and 12 June.
Money: Philippine National Bank, Quezon St changes travellers' cheques.
Population: 75,000.
Post & Telephone: Post code: 5400. Area code: 056.

Getting Around

Tricycle: A journey in town costs P3 per person.

Getting There & Away

By Air: Masbate Airport is about one km east of the town centre.
Asian Spirit, Airport Office, Tel 3333937.
Destination: Manila.

By Jeepney/Bus: Jeepneys, multicabs and buses leave from the market for all destinations. Minibuses heading south (as far as Cataingan) leave from Quezon St (across from the church).

By Boat: It's only a short stroll from the town centre to the harbour.
Bluewater Ferry, Port Area.
Destination: Lucena.
Montenegro Shipping Lines, Port Area.
Destination: Pilar.
Sulpicio Lines, Port Area, Tel 3332476.
Destinations: Leyte, Manila.
Trans-Asia Shipping Lines, Port Area, Tel 3278025, 3812025.
Destination: Cebu.
WG & A, Port Area, Tel 3332211.
Destinations: Leyte, Manila.

Bagacay

The small town of Bagacay is about 14 km south-east of Masbate. Roughly 1½ km from the main road you can find Bitu-on Beach, a popular destination locally at the weekends. To get there on foot would take just under half an hour from the turn-off (no signpost, no tricycles). The beach is far from being a 'must'.

Places to Stay

Bitu-on Beach Resort, Tel 3332342. SR/DR/fan/bath P500, SR/DR/ac/bath P800. Fairly basic rooms in plain cottages and a big house set back a little from the beach. Good restaurant with inexpensive Philippine food. Small swimming pool (P40 for non-residents).

Getting There & Away

Jeepney: Several jeepneys make the trip from Masbate to Bagacay daily, heading for Uson and Cataingan (30 min).
Minibuses also cover this route.

Cataingan

Cataingan is a small harbour town at the head of a narrow bay which reaches quite a way inland, on the south-east of the island. Boats leave there for Cebu.

Places to Stay

Extasy Food Square. SR/DR P100/200. Very basic accommodation on the road between the market and the pier. Small restaurant.

Getting There & Away

Jeepney: Several jeepneys run daily from Masbate to Cataingan (two hrs).
Minibuses also cover the route, one an hour, the last one leaving at 4pm.

Esperanza

Esperanza is a small community at the south-east tip of Masbate. The area has a fine selection of white sand beaches and picturesque bays, just waiting for tourists to discover them.

Places to Stay

Esperanza Beach Resort, Talisay. Cottage/bath P250. Small place with four basic, ageing cottages on a white beach about 500m south-east of the pier. Cooking facilities are available.

Getting There & Away

Jeepney: Two jeepneys leave Masbate for Esperanza daily between 6 and 7am, taking four hrs. (The road from Cataingan to Esperanza is in sad need of repair.)

The last jeepney from Cataingan to Esperanza leaves at 3pm.

Mandaon

Boats go from Mandaon to Sibuyan Island in Romblon Province. Near the town is Kalanay Cave, where numerous archaeological finds have been made.

Places to Stay

Mesa's Lodging House. SR/DR/fan P100/200. Very basic accommodation near the pier. Small restaurant.

Getting There & Away

Jeepney: Several jeepneys and buses run daily from Masbate to Mandaon (two hrs).

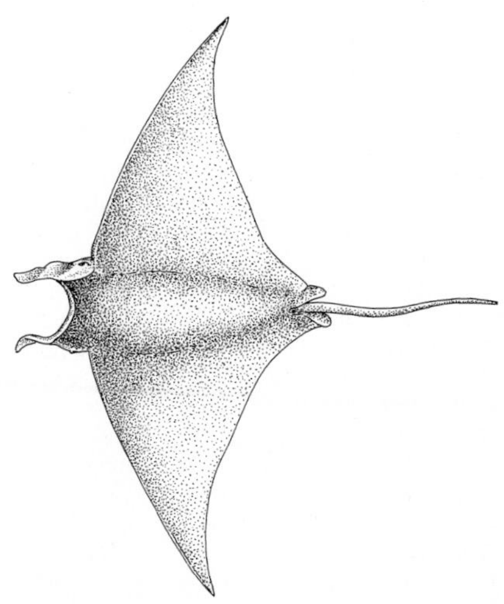

Mindoro

Mindoro is the next big island to the south of Manila, 150 km away, and is the fifth largest in the Philippines. This close, there was no way it could remain completely undiscovered, and the beautiful bays and beaches of the former galleon harbour of Puerto Galera developed into a popular holiday destination. However, tourism did not spread much further than that, and the rest of the island has remained in a surprisingly natural state - perhaps because it is not easily accessed. In small villages well off the beaten track, Mangyan people still live their traditional lives, clad in loincloths. It's a rare event for these peaceful native Mindoro dwellers to leave their mountain forests and venture into the coastal cities, where the wheeling and dealing of modern business is totally alien to them (see the Cultural Minorities section in the Country & People chapter earlier in this book).

Mindoro is divided into the provinces of Mindoro Occidental, which is the western part, and Mindoro Oriental, the eastern part. Fishing and the cultivation of rice and coconuts are the main economic activities, with some cattle raising around San Jose. Although the name Mindoro is a contraction of the Spanish *Mina de Oro*, meaning 'gold mine', no major gold discovery has yet been made. The difficult terrain of the island has also limited Mindoro's potential for copper and iron-ore mining, and the main mining activity has been the quarrying of marble. There has, however, been some promising oil prospecting in the south-west.

The usual tourist route on Mindoro is from Puerto Galera to Roxas, via Calapan. In and around Puerto Galera there are popular beaches and still mostly intact coral reefs. Roxas is the starting

point for boat trips to the islands of Tablas and Boracay. It's a fair bet that it will not be long before the northern stretch of coastline from Mamburao to Sablayan in Mindoro Occidental becomes an important centre of tourism. Unfortunately, there is still no regular shipping route from Sablayan or San Jose to Coron on Busuanga in the north of Palawan. Such a route would really add to the attractions of island hopping in the region.

Getting There & Away

Several JAM Transit and Tritran buses leave their bus terminals in Manila daily for Batangas. Aircon buses leave the Citystate Tower Hotel and the Swagman Hotel in Ermita every day. You can get combined bus and boat tickets to Mindoro from an office in those hotels.

There are boats daily from Batangas to Abra de Ilog, Calapan and Puerto Galera. For more information about getting to Mindoro from Luzon, see the Getting Away from Luzon section of the Manila chapter.

You can also get to Mindoro from Marinduque, Panay and Romblon (see the

Throughout the year, colourful festivals take place on all the bigger islands. The most impressive one has to be the spectacular Ati-Atihan, where people celebrate with comical masks and magnificent costumes.

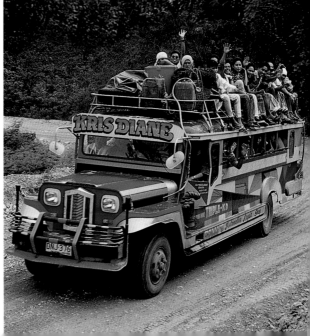

The sturdy jeepney is the favourite means of transport for shorter journeys, being mechanically reliable and able to take a lot of punishment. They are often decorated in a riot of colour, with traditional motifs, banks of gleaming chrome mirrors, and well-polished horses.

The Philippines are the only Christian country in Asia. Clear signs of this are the massive churches wherever you go, and the fanatical, blood-drenched, self-flagellating believers during Holy Week with its hugely popular processions.

Church in Paoay, North Luzon

Flagellant in San Fernando, Pampanga

Black Nazarene Procession in Quiapo, Manila

Countless buildings and monuments in the historical centre of Manila attest to the colonial Spanish past.

North Luzon is blessed with a gorgeously varied topography: sand dunes in Ilocos Norte; Hundred Islands National Park; Sierra Madre.

The nomadic Dumagat live on the Pacific coast.

The impressive rice terraces of the Central Cordillera in North Luzon are a masterpiece fashioned by hand over the centuries.

The inhabitants of the Batanes Islands wear wig-like headgear to protect themselves from the sun and rain in the capricious local climate.

The Philippines contain at least 37 members of the Asiatic "Ring of Fire" chain of volcanoes, including the classic cone of Mt Mayon, and merciless killers such as Mt Pinatubo.

A hike through the ravines of ash and sand near Mt Pinatubo is an unforgettable experience.

Known as the "Land of Howling Winds", the island of Catanduanes also likes to charm visitors with its sunny side.

Manila hemp is an important agricultural product on Catanduanes.

The cultural minorities who live on Mindanao maintain their traditions and local customs.

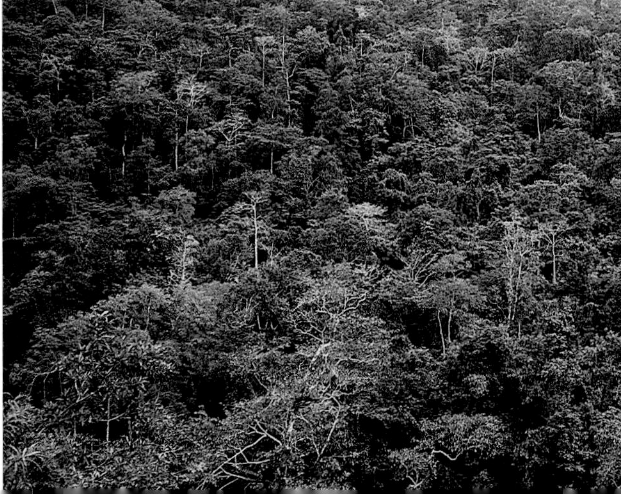

Getting around Palawan is not without its hazards, but the magnificent natural surroundings more than make up for this.

Throw away your watch and relax while island hopping.

The islands of Bantayan and Malapascua in the north of Cebu are becoming more and more popular with tourists.

Working at home, families produce little works of art made from sea shells.

Getting There & Away sections of the individual island chapters).

To Luzon

Air

From San Jose to Manila

Asian Spirit flies Monday, Wednesday, Thursday, Saturday and Sunday (P1400). Air Philippines has flights on Tuesday and Friday (P1600).

Boat

From Abra de Ilog to Batangas

Two times daily, probably at 6.45am and 4.45pm, with the fast ferry *Supercat* (P180; one hr).
Three times daily, probably at 6.30 and 10.30am, and at 4.30pm, with a Montenegro Shipping Lines car ferry (P110; 2½ hrs).

From Calapan to Batangas

Seven times daily with the *Supercat* fast ferry (P240; 45 min).
From 5am to midnight, roughly every hour with a car ferry (two hrs).

From Puerto Galera to Batangas

Daily at 6.30am with a Starlite car ferry from the pier in Balatero, 2½ km west of Puerto Galera. and an additional departure on Friday, Saturday and Sunday at 1pm (P100; two hrs). A Special Ride with an outrigger from Sabang to Balatero costs P300.
Daily at 1.15pm with the fast ferry *Supercat* from the pier in Balatero (P150; one hr).
Daily at 8.30am with an Island Cruiser ferry (150 P; two hrs). Carry on with an aircon minibus to the Swagman Hotel in Ermita, Manila. A combination ticket costs P450.
Daily at 9am with the fast ferry *Blue Eagle* (one hr). An aircon bus waits at the dock in Batangas for the boat to arrive, and goes direct to the Citystate Tower Hotel in Ermita, Manila. Combined bus and boat tickets can be bought at the Si-Kat office at the docks. Fare: P150 (ferry), P500 (ferry and bus).
Daily at 6, 7, 8, 9 and 11.30am with a big outrigger from Sabang (P130; 1½ hrs).
Daily at 9.30am and 2pm with a big outrigger from White Beach, at the weekend also at 8am and 4pm (P110; 1½ hrs).
A Special Ride from Puerto Galera to Batangas with an outrigger should not cost more than P2000, although up to P3000 can be demanded.

Beware! The buses between Manila and Batangas are especially popular with pickpockets; they work on regular bus routes (JAM Transit, Tritran) and usually in threes. So don't take your eyes off your baggage, a nap during the trip can end up costing you a lot.
In Batangas harbour fairly pushy porters try to part arriving passengers from their baggage to carry it to the ferry or bus. They will then stubbornly demand up to P100 per piece of baggage.

From San Jose to Batangas

Daily except Monday with Montenegro Shipping Lines (12 hrs).

From San Jose to Manila

Monday at 6pm with Moretta Shipping Lines (P330; 14 hrs).

To Marinduque

Boat

From Pinamalayan to Gasan

Daily at 8.30am with a big outrigger (P120; 3½ hrs).

To Panay

Jeepney/Bus/Boat

From Puerto Galera to Boracay

One stretch of the Nautical Highway leads from Mindoro to Panay (see the

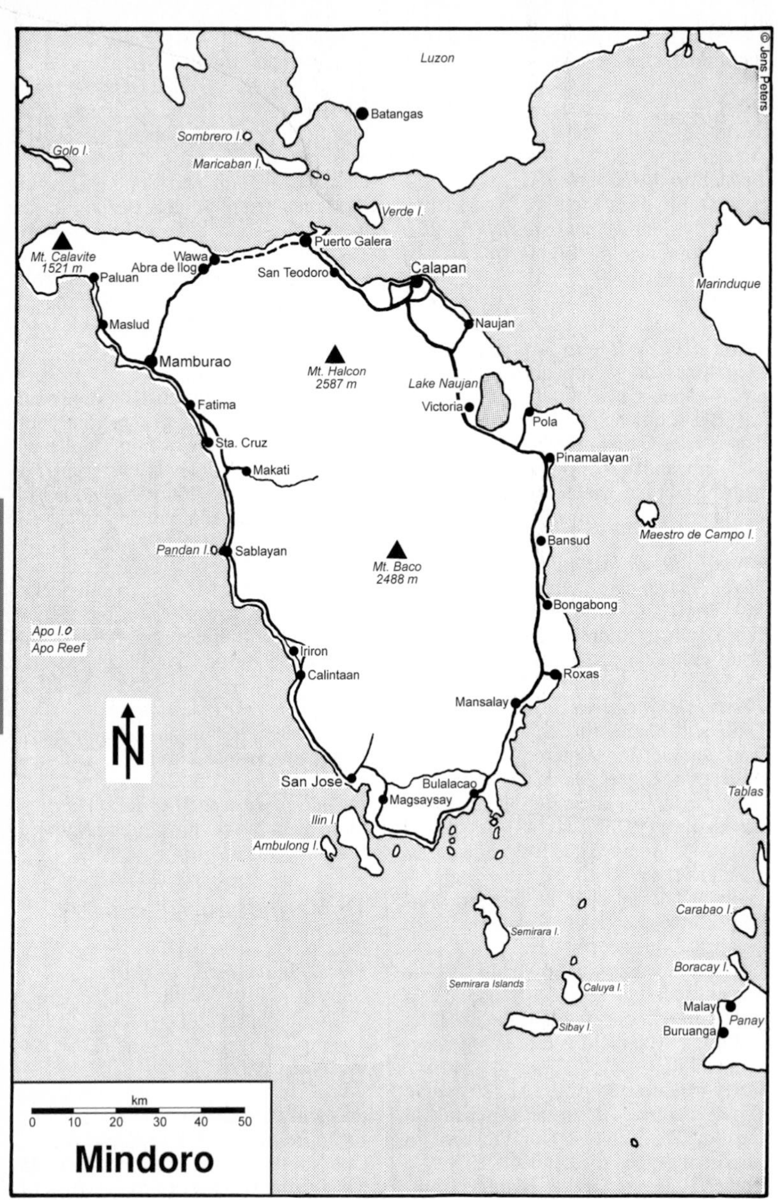
© Jens Peters
Luzon
Batangas
Sombrero I.
Golo I.
Maricaban I.
Verde I.
Mt. Calavite
1521 m
Puerto Galera
Wawa
Abra de Ilog
San Teodoro
Calapan
Paluan
Marinduque
Maslud
Naujan
Mamburao
Mt. Halcon
2587 m
Lake Naujan
Victoria
Fatima
Pola
Sta. Cruz
Pinamalayan
Makati
Maestro de Campo I.
Bansud
Pandan I.
Sablayan
Mt. Baco
2488 m
Bongabong
Apo I.
Apo Reef
Iriron
Calintaan
Roxas
Mansalay
San Jose
Bulalacao
Magsaysay
Tablas
Ilin I.
Ambulong I.
Carabao I.
Semirara I.
Boracay I.
Semirara Islands
Caluya I.
Malay
Panay
Sibay I.
Buruanga
km
0
10
20
30
40
50
Mindoro

Getting Away from Luzon section of the Manila chapter). To be sure to catch the afternoon ferry at 2pm from Roxas to Caticlan, you should leave around 9am by jeepney from Puerto Galera to Calapan and then take a bus from there on to Roxas.

Boat

From Puerto Galera to Boracay

First by ferry from Puerto Galera to Batangas. A Shipshape Ferry or Montenegro Shipping Lines ship leaves there every day except Tuesday at 5pm, heading for Odiongan on Tablas Island in the Romblon Archipelago (see Manila chapter: *Getting Away from Luzon - To Romblon*). When the ship docks at about 1 am there are jeepneys already waiting at the pier with the destination 'Santa Fe' (two hrs). At 10.30am a big outrigger goes from Santa Fe either direct to Boracay or to Caticlan/Panay, where boats leave for Boracay (1½ hrs).

On Tuesday, Thursday and Saturday, the early morning sees the arrival in Odiongan from Manila of either the *Mary the Queen* or the *Virgin Mary* (good ships belonging to MBRS Lines), which carry on at about 5am to Caticlan (three hrs). If you can make the connection, this is a good way to complete your trip to Boracay.

A comfortable way to make the trip from Puerto Galera to Boracay is by the dive cruise ship the *Coco Explorer* (60 metres long, 56 cabins) which leaves the Coco Beach Island Resort at 7pm every Thursday from October to July (route: Puerto Galera - Boracay - North Palawan - Apo Reef - Pandan Island - Puerto Galera). Arrival in Boracay: Friday at 7am. Fare for this section of the route is US$78. Reservations in Puerto Galera at the Coco Beach Island Resort, Cellphone 0918-5954191; in Manila: Tel (02) 5215260, Fax (02) 5266903.

Warning

In bad weather the sea in the Tablas Strait is very rough and the crossing by outrigger - even larger ones - is not to be recommended. Small outriggers do sometimes make the crossing, but they would not appear to be suitable for this trip and, to cap it all, are often dangerously overloaded as well.

From Roxas to Caticlan (Boracay)

Daily at 2 and 8am, and 2pm with a Starlite Ferry or Montenegro Shipping Lines car ferry (P210; 3½ or five hrs, depending on the boat).

From San Jose to Buruanga

Thursday and Sunday with a big outrigger (eight hrs).

From San Jose to Libertad

Tuesday and Saturday with a big outrigger (11 hrs). On the way, the boat drops anchor at Semirara Island and Caluya Island.

From San Jose to Lipata

Once or twice a week, taking 24 hrs. The trip goes via Semirara Island and Caluya Island, where they lie up to 10 hrs at anchor.

Lipata is a small place five km north of Culasi on the west coast of Panay.

To Romblon

Boat

From Bongabong to San Agustin/ Tablas Island

From Bongabong, a big outrigger runs irregularly to San Agustin on Tablas Island, possibly on Sunday. It takes six hrs and continues on to Romblon town on Romblon Island.

From Pinamalayan to Sibali Island
A big outrigger runs irregularly from Pinamalayan to Sibali Island (the local name for Maestro de Campo Island) and then continues to Banton Island.

From Roxas to Looc and Odiongan/ Tablas Island
Three times a week, most likely Tuesday, Friday and Sunday at 10am, with a big outrigger from Melco Beach (P160; three hrs).

Mindoro Oriental

Puerto Galera

Puerto Galera, with its beautiful bays, fine beaches and excellent underwater conditions for snorkelling and diving, has developed into a widely popular travel destination. As early as the 1930s it was regarded by zoologists, botanists and students of the University of the Philippines as an ideal place to study the ecostructure of animals, plants and micro-organisms in almost undisturbed natural conditions. The UP Marine Biological Station was established back in 1934. Forty years later, the United Nations Man & Biosphere Program International declared Puerto Galera a nature centre. It was at this time that the media also discovered the attractions of Puerto Galera as a tourist resort, and the place took off.

Considering the tourism potential of this little beauty spot, the development of the infrastructure has so far been kept mercifully within bounds. Although it must be admitted that the prices and quality of accommodation have improved markedly over the years, there are still no luxury hotels, in spite of demand for them in some quarters. The old adage that tourism is like fire - it can cook your food but it can also burn down your house - is obviously being heeded in Puerto Galera.

Puerto Galera has a most beautiful natural harbour, and the view from the deck of the ferry as you come through the Batangas Channel or the Manila Channel is a delight. Spanish galleons once sought shelter here from typhoons, and the name dates from that era, when this was the gateway for Spanish traders on their way to China, India, Sumatra and Java.

In the hinterland there are some interesting alternatives to beach living, such as the Tamaraw Falls, about 15 km in the direction of Calapan. You can also visit a marble quarry, or climb Mt Malisimbo and explore the nearby jungle.

The journey from Manila to Puerto Galera by bus and boat is comfortable by Philippine standards and only lasts about five hours. Although it can be rainy and somewhat cool, most visitors come to Puerto Galera in December and January. Tourist numbers have usually declined by mid-March, but sunny and exceptionally calm weather can still be enjoyed between June and October.

Places to Stay

Puerto Galera

Bahay-Pilipino, Concepcion St, Tel 4420266, @. SR/DR/fan P180 to P280. Straightforward lodging house belonging to 'Dr Fritz' from Germany, with basically furnished rooms which are OK at this price. Restaurant.

Melxa's Greenhill Nipa Hut, Concepcion St, Cellphone 0919-5692972. SR/-DR/fan P200, SR/DR/fan/bath P600 (with kitchen and TV). Simple, family accommodation.

Melxa's Beach House, Balete Beach. SR/DR/fan/bath P300, with kitchen and TV P500. Modest, spacious rooms in a stone building. Monthly rates available.

Coco Point, Tel 4420191. SR/DR/fan/bath P400 and P500. Basic, but good value, tidy rooms. Pleasant accommodation right at the pier. Restaurant.

Hotel California, E Brucal Street, Tel 4420256, @. SR/DR/fan/bath P500. Four good rooms, appropriately priced. The restaurant serves American and Mexican food, and pizzas. Located next to the post office.
Won Dive Resort Hotel, Tel 4420271, @. SR/DR/ac/bath P1000 to P1500. A big place with really comfortable rooms with TV. Beautiful view of Muelle Bay. Restaurant. Swimming pool. Diving.

Around Puerto Galera
Won Dive Resort, Santo Niño, Tel 4420264. SR/DR/fan/bath P500. Small place with good, well-kept rooms in a stone building. Korean restaurant. Swimming pool. Diving.
Nagura Beach Resort, Balatero, Cellphone 0917-6411705. Cottage/fan/bath P600 to P700 (depending on size and furnishings), SR/DR/fan/bath P850 (with kitchen and TV). Basic place, popular with local tourists. Located about four km west in the direction of White Beach.
Garden of Tabinay, Small Tabinay, Cellphone 0917-9110482, @. SR/DR/fan/bath P800 and P900 (with TV). Immaculate rooms with kitchen and refrigerator. A small, well-maintained, family place belonging to a German-Philippine couple. Located on Tabinay Beach, about two km south in the direction of Calapan.
Fishermen's Cove Beach & Dive Resort, Santo Niño, 0917-5332985, @. SR/DR/fan/bath P1000. Good accommodation, located on a quiet bay (no beach) about one km out of town towards White Beach. Under Italian management, it's no surprise they have an Italian restaurant. They also have windsurfing and diving facilities here.
Kalaw Place, Palangan, Cellphone 0917-5322617, @. SR/DR/fan/bath P980, P1520 and P2480 (two rooms, kitchen), cottage/fan/bath P1320 and P2400, with kitchen, the more expensive one (good for up to six people) also has a refrigerator, apartment/fan/bath P2520 and P3360. An appealing place with well-kept rooms, attractive, generously sized apartments and stylishly designed cottages, spread well out in natural surroundings. Run by a Swiss woman and her Filipino husband. Located about two km east in the direction of Sabang.
Pirate Cove, Palangan, Tel 4420310, @. Cottage/fan/bath P800 and P900. Excellent, roomy cottages on the side of a hill; good value. A friendly place near the Kalaw Place, but not suitable if you're unfit, as access is only via a steep staircase. Their restaurant serves

Puerto Galera Beaches
In almost every bay with a beach that's at all usable, you'll find cottages for local and foreign tourists. To the east, resorts have sprung up at Sabang Beach, Small La Laguna Beach and Big La Laguna Beach. To the south, they go as far as Tabinay Beach. To the west, Talipanan Beach is about the limit at the present. Besides Puerto Galera the main beaches also have had electricity connected. However, considering the number of power failures, it's a good idea to have a torch handy.
Beaches just outside Puerto Galera, such as Balete Beach and Hondura Beach, are rather undeveloped and may disappoint some pampered beachlovers. Most travellers prefer the ones a few km farther away.
The reefs at Big La Laguna Beach, Small La Laguna Beach, Balete Beach, Long Beach and Halige Beach are also good for snorkelling, but careful: strong currents can make Boquete Beach dangerous for swimmers.

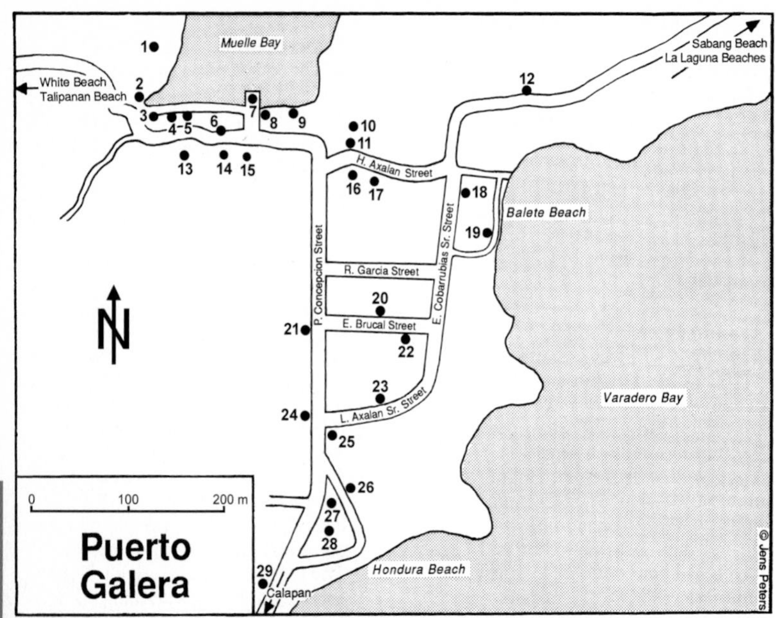

American, European and Philippine cooking. Quiet location with a view of 'Pirate Bay'. No beach, but they are glad to take guests over to nearby beaches.

Franklyn Highland Beach Resort, Palangan, Tel 2873132, Fax 2873183, @. SR/DR/fan/bath P800 and P1000, depending on size and furnishings. Pleasant place, high over Varadero Bay (no beach). Restaurant, swimming pool.

Tanawin Bay Resort, Palangan, Tel & Fax 4420112, @. Cottage/fan/bath P1500 to P3800; depending on furnishings. Located about one km out of town on the way to Sabang, near Encenada Beach (a short descent). It has beautiful little fully-furnished two-storey houses with living rooms and bedrooms, all individually styled. The atmosphere is like staying with friends, and there is a restaurant and a swimming pool with bar. The grounds are possibly the nicest in Puerto Galera, with a beautiful view of Varadero Bay. Reservations in Manila: Tel (02) 5517307.

Encenada Beach Resort, Palangan, Tel 2873082, @. SR/DR/fan/bath P1200, SR/DR/ac/bath P1800. Spacious rooms, about two km out of town towards Sabang. It's a pleasant, beautifully laid out place with its own beach. Restaurant, diving. Reservations in Manila: Tel (02) 5240861.

Blue Crystal Beach Resort, Palangan, Cellphone 0917-5620129, @. SR/DR/fan/bath P2000, SR/DR/ac/bath P2500. Tidy rooms in a big, attractive building directly on the water (not exactly a dream beach though). Restaurant with a beautiful view of the bay. Located about 2½ km out of town in the direction of Sabang.

Marco Vincent Villa, Tel 4419235, Fax 4410240, @. SR/DR/ac/bath P2400 to

Getting There & Away
3 Si-Kat Ferry Office
4 Island Cruiser Office
6 Jeepneys to White Beach & Talipanan Beach
7 Wharf
12 Jeepneys to Sabang
29 Jeepneys to Calapan

Places to Stay
1 The Moorings
8 Coco Point
13 Won Dive Resort Hotel
18 Melxa's Greenhill Nipa Hut
19 Melxa's Beach House
22 Hotel California
25 Bahay Pilipino Pension

Places to Eat & Entertainment
3 Pier Pub Pizza
4 Harbour Point
8 Coco Point Restaurant
25 Bahay Pilipino Restaurant
28 Discobra

Miscellaneous
2 Puerto Galera Yacht Club
4 Bretto's Deli Shop
5 Money Changer
7 Tourist Information
9 Badladz Adventures
10 Church
11 Excavation Museum
14 Virgie's Shopping Arcade
Dalcan Internet
15 Park Way Mini Mart
16 Rural Bank
17 Immigration Office
Police Station
Town Hall
20 Kaisser Internet Café
21 Islandline.net Internet Café
Puerto Galera Pharmacy
22 Post Office
23 Suzara's Pharmacy
24 Candava Supermarket
26 Namuco-Suzara Dental Clinic
27 Betty Tolentino-Wilson Dental Clinic
Hondura Mall
28 Market, LBC

P3100 P. Charming little place with six immaculate, tastefully furnished rooms with TV. Small swimming pool. Located at Markoe Cove not far from the Blue Crystal Beach Resort.

Places to Eat
Around the docks at Puerto Galera various restaurants serve European and Filipino dishes. Among these are the ***Harbour Point Restaurant*** and the ***Pier Pub Pizza,*** where they don't just make pizzas, but also tasty seafood. You'll find good German and Philippine food in the ***Bahay-Pilipino*** in Concepcion St.

Entertainment
The modern décor and equipment at the ***Discobra*** in the Market Building are popular with the locals; admission P50.

Miscellaneous
Diving: See page 440.
Festival: Town Fiesta on the first Saturday in December.
Golf: The Ponderosa Golf & Country Club is run by members and has a nine-hole golf course. It is south-west of Puerto Galera at about 600m above sea level. There is a tremendous view, and guests are welcome. It's about five km from the village of Minolo up to the club. Transport can be requested at the Ponderosa waiting station in Minolo.
Immigration Office, Town Hall, H. Alaxan Street. May not be open every day.
Medical Services: The Palm Medical Clinic is a little out of town on the way to Sabang. It's open Monday to Friday from 8am to 5pm.

Diving

Puerto Galera is one of the most popular areas for diving in the whole Philippines. Conditions are excellent throughout the year for beginners to the most advanced. Dive shops with experienced diving instructors from all over the planet have been established on the beaches, most of them in Sabang. The dive shops all have the best facilities and equipment; nearly every one has its own dive boat. Most diving takes place near Puerto Galera. Many shops also undertake diving trips from February until May, to places like Busuanga in the north of Palawan and the Apo Reef to the west of Mindoro.

You'll pay US$27 for a dive, including equipment, boat and guide. Night dives cost about 30% more. All sorts of diving courses are available: a four-day course costs about US$280; nitrox-diving courses for beginners come to around US$300.

Dive Shops

Action Divers, Sabang and Small La Laguna Beach, Cellphone 0917-7494516 @. Courses in English, French and German.

Asia Divers, Tel 7248530, @. Small La Laguna Beach. Courses in English, French, German, Japanese and Swedish.

Atlantis Dive Resort, Sabang, Tel & Fax: 2873066, @. Courses in Dutch, English, French, German, Spanish and Swedish.

Big Apple Dive Resort, Sabang, Tel 2873134, @. Courses in English.

Capt'n Gregg's, Sabang, Cellphone 0917-5404570, @. Courses in English, German and Swedish.

Cocktail Divers, Garden of Eden, Sabang, Cellphone 0917-8135392, @. Courses in Danish, English and German.

Coral Cove Resort & Dive Centre, Sinandigan Beach, Cellphone & Fax 0919-5693228, @. Courses in English.

Dive Center Scubaplus, Small La Laguna Beach, Tel 2873204, @. Courses in English and German.

Eco Divers, White Beach. Courses in English, German and Swedish.

Fishermen's Cove Beach & Dive Resort, Santo Niño, Cellphone 0917-5332985, @. Courses in English and Italian.

Frontier Scuba, Sabang, Cellphone 0917-5408410, Courses in English, Japanese and Spanish.

Hammer Head Shark Divers, White Beach, Cellphone 0920-2366744, @. Courses in English and Korean.

Korean Dive Park, Starfish Inn, Big La Laguna Beach. Courses in Korean.

La Laguna Dive Centre, Big La Laguna Beach, Tel 7248520, @. Courses in English.

Mabuhay Dive Resort, Club Mabuhay La Laguna, Small La Laguna Beach, Tel 2873232, @. Courses in English and German.

Nikita Divers, White Beach, Cellphone 0917-9981939, @. Courses in English.

Octopus Divers, Villa Sabang, Sabang Beach Cellphone 0919-3790811, @. Courses in Dutch, English, German and Swedish.

Pacific Divers, White Beach, Cellphone 0917-4309995, @. Courses in English, French, German, Italian, Japanese and Spanish.

Philippine Divers, Coco Beach, Cellphone 0917-6981230, @. Courses in Danish, German and English.

Prince Diving, Sabang, Cellphone 0919-4813729, @. Courses in Korean.

Rudy's Dive Center, Small La Laguna Beach, Cellphone 0919-3916399, @. Courses in German, English and Dutch.

Sabang Inn Dive Resort, Sabang, Tel 2873198, @. Courses in Danish, English, German, Swedish and Tagalog.

Scandinavian Divers, Big La Laguna Beach, Cellphone 0917-9037582, @. Courses in Danish, English, German and Swedish.

Scuba World, Sabang, Cellphone 0917-7955664, @. Courses in English.

Sea Divers, Sabang, Tel 2873167, @. Courses in English.

Sinandigan Lodge, Sinandigan, Tel 2873222, @. Courses in English.

South Sea Divers, Sabang, 2873052, @. Courses in English, French, Japanese and Spanish.

Triton Divers, Sabang, Tel 7248517, @. Courses in Dutch, English and German.

Tropicana Castle Dive Resort, Sabang, Tel 7248560, @. Courses in English and German.

Water World, Sabang, Tel 2873052. Courses in English, French, Japanese and Spanish.

The Rural Health Center, about one km outside town on the way to Calapan, is a very basic clinic with only limited medical equipment.

Dr. Delos Reyes, Balatero (GP, recommended by ex-pats), Cellphone 0917-2431939.

Dentists: Betty Tolentino-Wilson Dental Clinic, Hondura Mall (near the market), Cellphone 0919-2125060; Namuco-Suzara Dental Clinic, across from the Hondura Mall, Cellphone 0916-3626990.

Money: The Rural Bank in Puerto Galera changes cash and may also change travellers' cheques, albeit at a less favourable rate than the money changers and banks in Manila.

Online: Kaisser Internet Café, E Brucal St, Islandline.net, Concepcion St, and Dalcan Internet in Virgie's Shopping Arcade near the pier; all P100/hr.

Population: 8000.

Post & Telephone: Post Office on E Brucal St.

Post code: 5203. Area code: 043.

Getting Around

Boat: It costs P150 to P200 per hr to hire an outrigger (including fuel).

Motorcycle: Badladz Adventure, near the pier in Puerto Galera, Tel. 2873184, @, and Pit Stop (Swiss management), Santo Niño (one km west of Puerto Galera), Tel. 2873256, rent from P500 per day.

Tricycle: The fare within Puerto Galera is P5 per person.

Getting There & Away

By Air: Seaplanes can be chartered from Subic Seaplane, Frontier Scuba, Sabang, for flights to Boracay, Manila, Palawan and Subic.

By Boat: Combined bus and ferry tickets from Puerto Galera to Manila can be obtained from the Si-Kat Ferry Office and the Island Cruiser Office at the pier. Bus seats should be reserved at least one day in advance.

Calapan

Jeepney: Several jeepneys run from Calapan to Puerto Galera every day between 6am and 5.30pm, leaving from the market (P50; 1½ hrs).

Departure from Puerto Galera for Calapan roughly every hour from 6am to 1pm, from the Petron filling station in the south on the way out of town.

Manila - Batangas

Bus/Boat: Several JAM Transit and Tritran buses (Pasay Terminal for both

plus Kamias Terminal for the latter) leave Manila daily for Batangas roughly every half hour. Note: 'Batangas Pier' buses which go via the Calabarzon Expressway/Star Tollway (check the destination on the front of the bus) avoid the heavy traffic in Santo Tomas, Tanauan and Lipa (P120; 2½ hrs). Aircon minibuses also leave both terminals in Pasay for the pier in Batangas (P120).
An aircon minibus makes the trip daily at 8am, leaving from the Swagman Hotel in Ermita. Bus-ship tickets are on sale at the gift shop in the hotel (P450); Tel 5238541. Arrival in Puerto Galera about 1pm. Departure from Puerto Galera: 8.30 am.
A coach leaves the Citystate Tower Hotel in Ermita every day at 8am. You can get combined bus and ferry tickets (P500) at the Si-Kat Ferry Office in the hotel; Tel (02) 5213344. Arrival in Puerto Galera at about noon. Departure from Puerto Galera: 9am.
From Batangas to Balatero the fast ferry *Supercat* sails daily at noon (P150; one hr; departure from Balatero at 1.15am). The car ferry MV *Starlite* leaves at 4pm (P100; two hrs; departure from Balatero at 6.30am), with an additional departure on Friday, Saturday and Sunday at 9.30am and 1pm from Batangas and Balatero respectively. Balatero is 2½ km west of Puerto Galera; P5 by jeepney. A Special Ride with an outrigger from Balatero to Sabang costs P300.
Big outriggers go from Batangas to Sabang daily at 9.30 and 10.30am, noon, 1.30 and 2.30pm, to White Beach at 10.30am and 4pm, at the weekend also at noon and 6pm (P130; 1½ hrs).
Note: The departure times are changed frequently, but if you are at Batangas Pier around noon you won't have to wait long for a boat.
A Special Ride with an outrigger from Batangas to Puerto Galera should not cost more than P2000; they will ask for up to P3000.
See also the chapter Manila: *Getting Away from Luzon - To Mindoro*.

Beware: The service buses (Tritran, JAM Transit) between Manila and Batangas are especially popular with pickpockets.

Mamburao - Abra de Ilog

Jeepney/Boat: From Mamburao to Abra de Ilog and on to the wharf at Wawa at least one jeepney runs daily at about 6am (two hrs). From Abra de Ilog (wharf at Wawa), a Special Ride to Puerto Galera costs about P1200 (2½ hrs).
There is another route to Puerto Galera from Abra de Ilog, via Batangas: Catch the morning ferry at 8.30 from Wawa to Batangas (P50; three hrs) and carry on at noon or in the afternoon, with the ferry to Puerto Galera.

Note: The road between Puerto Galera and Abra de Ilog, shown on many maps of the Philippines, doesn't exist yet. As a result, it's not possible at the moment to go the whole way round the island by car or motorbike. But - good news - the construction of the road is well under way and should be completed in 2005.

Roxas

Bus/Jeepney: A big bus takes you from Roxas to Calapan in four hrs. You then go from Calapan to Puerto Galera by jeepney (1½ hrs); the last jeepney leaves at about 5.30pm.

Around Puerto Galera

Sabang

Sabang is a more 'happening' place for the visitor, especially after dark, although it might not be everybody's scene. It can

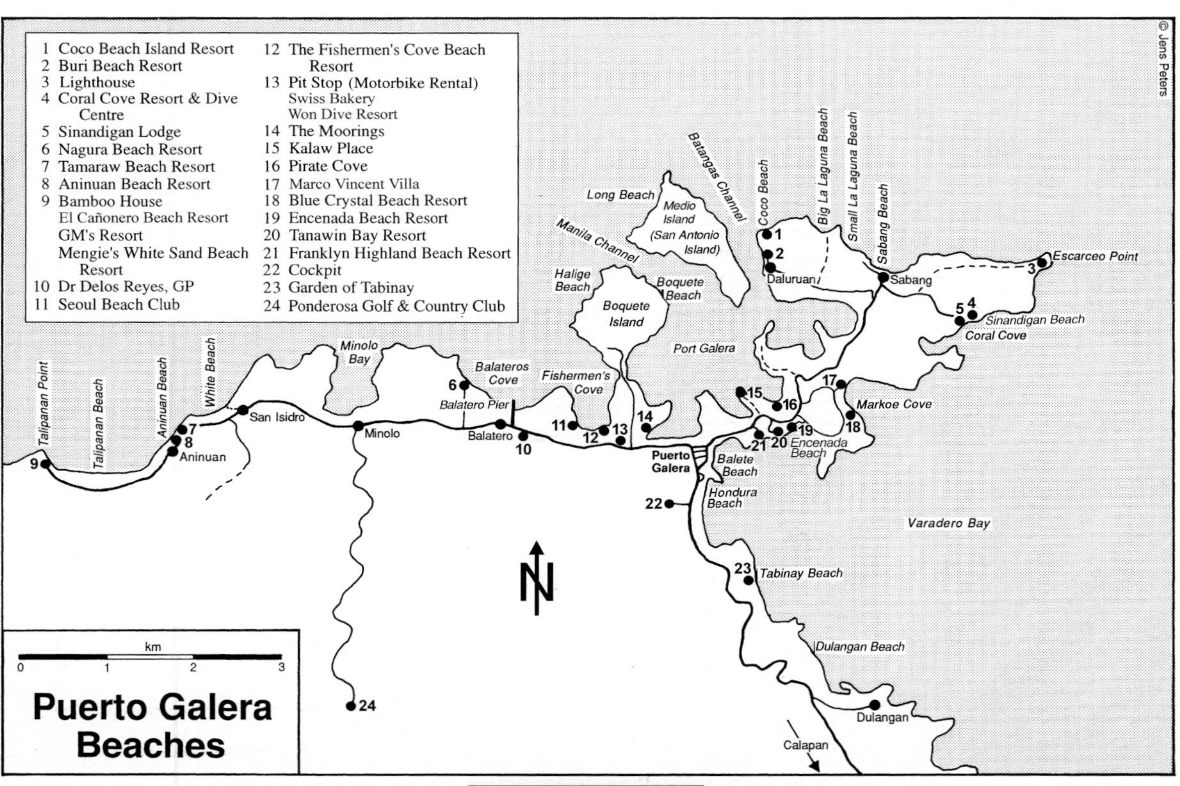
© Jens Peters
1 Coco Beach Island Resort
2 Buri Beach Resort
3 Lighthouse
4 Coral Cove Resort & Dive Centre
5 Sinandigan Lodge
6 Nagura Beach Resort
7 Tamaraw Beach Resort
8 Aninuan Beach Resort
9 Bamboo House
El Cañonero Beach Resort
GM's Resort
Mengie's White Sand Beach Resort
10 Dr Delos Reyes, GP
11 Seoul Beach Club
12 The Fishermen's Cove Beach Resort
13 Pit Stop (Motorbike Rental)
Swiss Bakery
Won Dive Resort
14 The Moorings
15 Kalaw Place
16 Pirate Cove
17 Marco Vincent Villa
18 Blue Crystal Beach Resort
19 Encenada Beach Resort
20 Tanawin Bay Resort
21 Franklyn Highland Beach Resort
22 Cockpit
23 Garden of Tabinay
24 Ponderosa Golf & Country Club
Long Beach
Medio Island (San Antonio Island)
Batangas Channel
Coco Beach
Big La Laguna Beach
Small La Laguna Beach
Sabang Beach
Escarceo Point
Daluruan
Sabang
Sinandigan Beach
Coral Cove
Manila Channel
Halige Beach
Boquete Beach
Boquete Island
Port Galera
Minolo Bay
Balateros Cove
Fishermen's Cove
Markoe Cove
Talipanan Point
Talipanan Beach
Aninuan Beach
White Beach
San Isidro
Balatero Pier
Minolo
Balatero
Aninuan
Puerto Galera
Balete Beach
Encenada Beach
Hondura Beach
Varadero Bay
Tabinay Beach
Dulangan Beach
Dulangan
Calapan
N
km
0
1
2
3
Puerto Galera Beaches

get very hectic and loud at night around the discos and bars. Some restaurants have been built on sites close to the water and the remaining beach is almost completely blocked by outrigger boats. A hill path takes you through a palm grove and over a meadow to Escarceo Point, two km east of Sabang. There you can go to the top of the 14m high lighthouse where the view is gorgeous, especially at sunrise and sunset.

Small La Laguna Beach
Similar to the neighbouring Sabang Beach, there is also some action to be found on Small La Laguna Beach, although it's possibly a bit more relaxed. The beach itself is not particularly impressive. The most popular activities during the day are snorkelling and diving.

Big La Laguna Beach
The lively Big La Laguna Beach is located in a picturesque little white sand bay to the west of Small La Laguna Beach. Just offshore there's a coral reef which offers excellent snorkelling.

Places to Stay
Prices can vary, depending on how successful the season is. Especially around Christmas time, Chinese New Year (one week in January or February) and during the Easter week price hikes of up to 100% are possible, while the off-season from June until November is occasionally good for big discounts.

Sabang Beach
Reynaldo's Upstairs, Cellphone 0917-4895609. Cottage/fan/bath P350 to P600, the more expensive ones have a kitchen, refrigerator and TV. Monthly rates available. The cottages are basic but good, some of them on a hill with a beautiful view. Quiet location.
Gold Coast Cottages, Cellphone 0919-8104009. SR/DR/fan/bath P400 to P600. Basic rooms with balcony in a stone building. Fairly good value accommodation.
Action Divers VIP Dive Resort, Cellphone 0917-7959062, @. SR/DR/fan/bath P450 (with TV) and P750 (with refrigerator and TV), SR/DR/ac/bath P1200 (with refrigerator and TV). Good, very good value rooms in a two-storey stone building. The restaurant offers a beautiful sea view.
Bellevue Cottages, Tel 7248527, @. Cottage/fan/bath P500 to P700. Green all round in the grounds, and pleasant cottages. Warm atmosphere. A bit higher up than other places around, which provides a superb view. Restaurant. Steps leading up here next to Villa Sabang.
Villa Sabang, Tel 2873019, @. SR/DR/fan/bath P500 to P700, SR/DR/ac/bath P800 and P1000. Attractive place with immaculate rooms, nearly all with refrigerator and TV. Restaurant, swimming pool, diving (Octopus Divers).
Sonny's Inn, Tel 2873217. SR/DR/fan/bath P500 to P700, SR/DR/ac/bath P1500. Spacious rooms with balconies, and the cottages are good quality, all with kitchen, refrigerator and TV. Good value.
Red Coral Beach Resort, Tel. 2873124. SR/DR/fan/bath P500 and P700, SR/DR/ac/bath P1500. Basic rooms with TV, the more expensive ones with kitchen and refrigerator. Two-storey stone building.
Big Apple Dive Resort, Tel 2873134, @. Cottage/fan/bath P550 and P600, cottage/ac/bath P950 to P1350. Well-maintained cottages with refrigerator and TV. A big place set in pleasantly landscaped grounds. There is a restaurant, and they have billiards, a fitness room, mini golf, diving, and a swimming pool with poolside bar.
Lopez Lodge, Cellphone 0917-4803469. SR/DR/fan/bath P600. All have a kitchen, refrigerator and TV. Acceptably priced rooms in stone buildings at the west end of the beach.

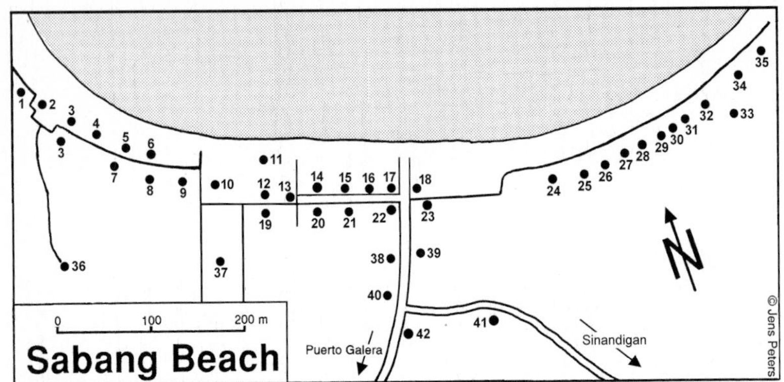

Tina's Sunset Cottages, Cellphone 0917-3691033. SR/DR/fan/bath P600 to P800, SR/DR/ac/bath P1500. A variety of good rooms and cottages, the more expensive with TV, kitchen and refrigerator.

Capt'n Gregg's Divers Resort, Cellphone 0917-5404570, @. SR/DR/fan/bath P600, SR/DR/ac/bath P1000. Good rooms a few with balconies and a view of the sea. A favourite with divers. Restaurant. Reservations in Manila: Tel (02) 8497435.

Angelyn's Beach Resort, Cellphone 0917-3742276, Fax 4420038, @. Cottage/fan/bath P600, cottage/ac/bath P1200 to P1500 (with TV, some with kitchen). Some cottages have a pleasantly large veranda. This is a quiet place, parts of the grounds are on the slope of a hill. Restaurant.

Seashore Lodge, Tel. 2873021, @. Cottage/fan/bath P700 and P800, cottage/ac/bath P1500 to P1800. Immaculate cottages, each with kitchen, refrigerator and TV. Restaurant.

Sabang Inn, Tel 2873198, @. SR/DR/fan/bath P400, SR/DR/ac/bath P1000 to P1300 (depending on size). Pleasant, brightly decorated rooms with TV, refrigerator, kitchen and balcony. Good value. Swimming pool, diving.

Steps & Garden Resort, Cellphone 0917-4623370. Cottage/fan/bath P700 and P900, SR/DR/ac/bath P2000. An attractive, peaceful place with small buildings set among the lush growth of tropical plants on a slope above Sabang. Restaurant.

At-Can's Inn, Cellphone 0917-4638233. SR/DR/fan/bath P800 and P900. Three, two-storey buildings with good rooms, and several really spacious cottages with refrigerator and TV, the more expensive ones also have a kitchen.

Triton Divers Lodge, Tel 7248517, @. SR/DR/ac/bath P1200 and P1500. Spotless rooms with TV in a two-storey stone building, the more expensive ones have a sea view.

Tropicana Castle Dive Resort, Tel 7248560, @. SR/DR/ac/bath P14500 to P1650, bed and breakfast. Well-maintained, attractive rooms with refrigerator and TV, that make you feel at home. The more expensive ones even have four-poster beds, appropriate for this impressive building, built like a medieval castle complete with tower. Excellent value for the money. Restaurant, swimming pool, diving. Located on the way into Sabang.

Garden of Eden, Tel 2873096, @. Cottage/fan/bath P1500, cottage/ac/bath

Getting There & Away
2 Seaplane Charter

Places to Stay
1 Lopez Lodge
Triton Divers Lodge
3 Angelyn's Beach Resort
7 Atlantis Dive Resort
9 Big Apple Dive Resort
10 Red Coral Cottages
11 Capt'n Gregg's Dive Resort
24 Garden of Eden
25 At Can's Inn
26 Action Divers VIP Dive Resort
27 Juling's Place
28 Seashore Lodge
29 Sabang Inn Dive Resort
30 Riseros Guest House
31 Gold Coast Cottages
32 Villa Sabang
33 Bellevue Cottages
34 Sonny's Inn
35 Reynaldo's Upstairs
Tina's Sunset Cottages
36 Steps & Garden Resort
37 AAA Apartment
38 Club Mabuhay Sabang
40 Tropicana Castle Dive Resort
42 Mermaid Resort

Places to Eat & Entertainment
5 Tamarind Restaurant
9 Big Apple Bar
12 The Lounge
13 The Pub
15 Centrum Super Umbrella Disco
16 Philippine Village Disco
18 McRom's Restaurant
19 Relax Thai Restaurant
20 It's OK Bar
21 Sabang Disco
23 Sunset Disco
26 Broadway
Broadway Disco
Le Bistrot
33 Viewpoint Restaurant
38 Sabang Fastfood
39 Lucky's Saloon
40 Tropicana Restaurant

Miscellaneous
1 Triton Divers
2 Frontier Scuba
4 Sea Divers
7 Water World
8 South Sea Divers
10 Sabang Gym
14 Sabang Busines Center
Swiss Bakery
17 Philippine Village Mini Mart
18 Internet Café
Scuba World
22 Dental Clinic Jonna C de Chavez
23 Tarzan Treks
24 Cocktail Divers
26 Action Divers
28 Metropolitan Doctors Clinic
32 Octopus Divers
39 Dutch Bakery
Filipino Travel Center
Going Places Tours
Tourist Center
41 Market

P1900 and P2200. Lots of tastefully furnished cottages, all with refrigerators, the aircon ones also with TV. Set in large grounds with loads of greenery. Restaurant, swimming pool, diving (Cocktail Divers).

Club Mabuhay Sabang, Tel 2873097, @. SR/DR/ac/bath P1700 to P2200, suite P3300. Two-storey stone building with good rooms with veranda or balcony as well as a refrigerator and TV, the suites also have a kitchen. Although this well-run place is in the centre of Sabang, it's quite quiet. Restaurant, small swimming pool, diving.

Mermaid Resort, Tel 2873301, Fax 2873302, @. SR/DR/ac/bath P1800 to P2300. Friendly, well-kept rooms, all

with refrigerator and TV. New hotel under Danish management just as you enter Sabang. Restaurant, swimming pool, diving.
Atlantis Dive Resort, Tel & Fax: 2873066, @. SR/DR/ac/bath P1800 to P4200, with refrigerator and TV. Very appealing rooms in an attractive building in the Spanish-Mexican style. Restaurant, swimming pool with waterfall, diving. Located across from the Tamarind Restaurant.

Sinandigan Beach
Sinandigan Lodge, Tel 2873222, @. SR/DR/fan/bath P700, SR/DR/ac/bath P850. Well-kept rooms with kitchen, refrigerator and terrace in a Mediterranean style building, run by a German-Philippine couple. Quiet location about 1.2 km south-east of Sabang. Restaurant (good, international cuisine), diving.
Coral Cove Beach Resort, Cellphone 0919-5693228, @. SR/DR/fan/bath P750 to P1200, SR/DR/ac/bath P1500. This is a big, tastefully designed building in a small, remote bay, about one km from Sabang. There is a restaurant and diving available, and staff can arrange day trips by boat. This is a great place if you want to get away from it all.

Small La Laguna Beach
Marelex Beach Resort, Cellphone 0917-5620019. SR/DR/fan/bath P350 and P500 (with refrigerator and TV). Basic rooms.
Sha-Che Inn, Cellphone 0917-6410112. Cottage/fan/bath P400 and P600 (with kitchen). Good cottages with TV.
Deep Blue Sea Inn, Cellphone & Fax 0917-5620209, @. SR/DR/fan/bath P500 to P900, SR/DR/ac/bath P1000 to P1600. Good rooms with refrigerator, the aircon ones also have TV. A big place on a rise right on the beach with a beautiful view of the sea. German management. Restaurant, billiards.

Nick & Sonia's Cottages, Cellphone 0917-4567824. SR/DR/fan/bath P600, SR/DR/ac/bath P1500. Monthly rates are available. All rooms have kitchen, refrigerator and TV. Friendly accommodation, own restaurant.

Sunsplash Resort, Cellphone 0917-4598639, @. Cottage/fan/bath P1000. Monthly rates available. Pleasant place with roomy, attractive cottages with refrigerator and TV. Restaurant, diving.

Carmrob Inn, Cellphone 0917-3630550. SR/DR/ac/bath P1000 and P2000. Spick and span, spacious rooms with TV, the more expensive ones also have a kitchen. Well-maintained, two-storey stone building.

El Galleon Beach Resort, Cellphone 0917-8145107, @. SR/DR/fan/bath P1240, SR/DR/ac/bath P1950 and P2400. Immaculate, well equipped rooms with refrigerator. Restaurant, beach bar, swimming pool, kayaks, diving.

Club Mabuhay La Laguna, Tel 2873098, @. SR/DR/ac/bath P1700 and P2000, suite P3800 and P6000. Quiet, attractively laid-out resort with stylishly furnished rooms, all with refrigerator and TV, the suites also have a kitchen. Restaurant. Swimming pool. Diving.

Portofino, Tel 7248567, @. SR/DR/ac/bath P2250 to P5500. Weekly rates available. Comfortable, generously sized rooms with kitchen. An attractive hotel with a small swimming pool.

Big La Laguna Beach

Cataquis Lodge, Cellphone 0916-3169877. Cottage/fan/bath P500 to P800, cottage/ac/bath P1500. Friendly place at the east end of the beach with several good cottages and stone buildings, some with kitchen and TV.

Miller's Corner, Tel 7248572. Cottage/fan/bath P750, SR/DR/fan/bath P950, SR/DR/ac/bath P1500. Attractively lo-

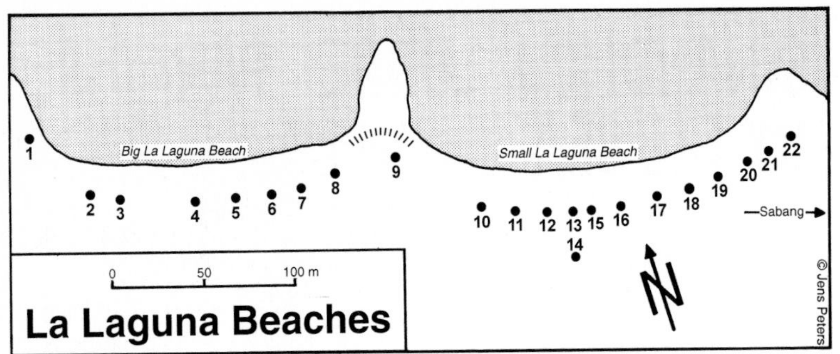

Places to Stay

1 Miller's Corner
2 Scandinavian Divers Beach Resort
3 Lony's Cottage
4 Fernando's Beach Resort
5 Starfish Inn
6 La Laguna Beach Club
8 Cataquis Lodge
9 Red Sun Resort
10 Deep Blue Sea Inn
11 Portofino
12 Marelex Beach Resort
14 Nick & Sonia's Cottages
15 Sha-Che Inn
17 Club Mabuhay La Laguna
18 Sunsplash Resort
19 Carmrob Inn
Roelyn's Inn
20 El Galleon Beach Resort

Places to Eat & Entertainment

7 Kaye en Em Fast Food
16 Full Moon Restaurant
22 The Point Pub

Miscellaneous

2 Scandinavian Divers
5 Korean Dive Park
6 La Laguna Dive Centre
12 Rudy's Dive Center
13 Action Divers
17 Mabuhay Dive Resort
18 Scubaplus Dive Center
21 Asia Divers

cated hotel with a big terrace, at the west end of the beach.

Starfish Inn, Cellphone 0919-3101390. SR/DR/fan/bath P800 to P1500. Spacious rooms, all differently furnished, with wide beds. Pleasant, well-run place right next to La Laguna Beach Club. Restaurant.

Scandinavian Divers Beach Resort, Cellphone 0917-9037582, @. SR/DR/ac/bath P1000. Good rooms with TV. Restaurant. Small swimming pool. Diving.

La Laguna Beach Club & Dive Centre, Cellphone 0917-7940323, @. SR/DR/fan/bath P1500, SR/DR/ac/bath P1800. Comfortable, pleasantly furnished rooms. Restaurant, swimming pool, diving.

Coco Beach

Coco Beach Island Resort, Cellphone 0918-5954191, @. SR/DR/fan/bath P3200/4200; including breakfast. Attractively furnished rooms. Well-maintained, extensive grounds with a restaurant, big swimming pool you just want to jump into, and a quiet private beach with drop-off. Windsurfing, sailing, diving and tennis are available. Reservations can be made in Manila at the

Coco Beach Booking Office, Baywatch Tower, MH del Pilar St, Malate, Tel (02) 5264594, Fax (02) 5266903.
Buri Beach Resort, Cellphone 0917-4838106, @. Cottage/fan/bath P3000 and P5000. Very well-kept, generously laid-out resort with attractive, traditionally furnished cottages with TV, the more expensive ones also have a refrigerator. Restaurant. Swimming pool. Located a few minutes' walk from Coco Beach. Own boat service. Reservations in Manila: Tel (02) 8120722, Fax: (02) 8402245.

Places to Eat

Practically every resort has its own restaurant. There are also various places at the beaches that offer international specialities.
In Sabang, ***Le Bistrot*** can be recommended, with its excellent pizzas and good French food. The tasty Philippine and European food is good value at ***Sabang Fastfood***.
The ***Tropicana Restaurant*** on the way into town offers tasty, international food in cosy surroundings. Lovers of Thai cooking will enjoy the food in the ***Relax Thai Restaurant,*** and ***McRom's Restaurant*** is the place for good steak or seafood.

Entertainment

If you enjoy night life just as much as life on the beach, then Sabang is the place to go. There they have open-air bars like the ***It's OK Bar*** where karaoke gets the atmosphere going. In spite of their names, the ***Broadway Disco***, ***Centrum Super Umbrella Disco***, ***Sunset Disco, Sabang Disco*** and ***Philippine Village Disco*** are not so much discos, but nightclubs with go-go dancers. The laid-back ***Big Apple Bar*** (with billiards) in the Big Apple Dive Resort is a popular place to meet in the evening, as is ***Broadway*** with billiards and live music.

Miscellaneous

Diving: See page 440.
Medical Services: Metropolitan Doctors Clinic in the Seashore Lodge, Sabang, Tel 2873156. General practice, and they also treat diving accident cases. Dentist: Jonna C de Chavez, Tel 2873032, across from the Philippine Village Mini Mart. A practice with up-to-date equipment. Recommended by expats.
Money: Travellers' cheques and all better-known currencies can be exchanged at the Tropicana Castle Dive Resort in Sabang. They also give cash advances on Visa cards, as does the Tourist Center in Sabang (all popular credit cards, albeit for an 8% fee).
Online: Several Internet Cafés, eg in the Sabang Business Center opposite the It's OK Bar; P60 to P120/hr.
Sea Kayaking: Various resorts rent out one-seater and two-seater kayaks for P150 or P250 an hour. It's a bit better value if you rent for the half or full day.
Travel Agencies: You can make bookings and confirm national and international tickets at the Filipino Travel Center, Tel 2873108, @, at the Tourist Center in Sabang.
Trekking & Tours: In Sabang, Going Places, Cellphone 0918-3432899, @, and Tarzan Trek, Cellphone 0919-4101020 offer visits to the Mangyans, trips to the Tamaraw Waterfalls, mountain trekking, jungle river kayaking, beach hopping etc.

Getting There & Away

Jeepney: Jeepneys run between Puerto Galera and Sabang (P10). Departure from Puerto Galera about 500m east of the pier on the road to Sabang. Last departure at about 5.30pm.
The last jeepney back to Puerto Galera leaves Sabang in the late afternoon. The unsealed road can be impassable after heavy rains.
It's only a short walk along the beach from Sabang to Small La Laguna

Beach, and after negotiating a few more rocks you can get to Big La Laguna Beach in about 15 min.

Tricycle: A Special Ride from the pier in Puerto Galera to Sabang costs P100.

Boat: A Special Ride by outrigger from Puerto Galera to Big La Laguna Beach costs P180, to either Small La Laguna Beach or Sabang, P200.

White Beach

There's not much action on the beaches between San Isidro and Talipanan Point, a few km west of Puerto Galera. They are good beaches for bathing, although - unlike the beaches mentioned above - snorkelling is not particularly interesting there. White Beach is the busiest one and is also popular for long and loud nights at the 10 or so beach bars, mainly at the weekend, especially in the Philippine summer months of April and May. But watch out, the water gets very deep a few metres from shore - too deep for children and non-swimmers.

Aninuan Beach & Talipanan Beach
In the long stretch of the bay adjoining White Beach, the two beautiful white sand beaches of Aninuan and Talipanan join together seamlessly. If it's peace and quiet you're looking for, this is the place.

Places to Stay

White Beach
Manolo's Lodge, Cellphone 0917-6096072. Cottage/fan/bath P250, SR/DR/fan/bath P300 (with kitchen P600 to P800), SR/DR/ac/bath P800 to P1000 (with kitchen). Big rooms in a two-storey stone building. Restaurant.
Sheryll's Inn, Cellphone 0917-9877358. Cottage/fan/bath P300. Basic cottages, beginning to show their age.

Places to Stay
1 Summer Connection
2 Villa Anastacia
4 Lodger's Nook
5 Cherry's Inn
6 Sheryll's Inn
8 White Beach Lodge
9 White Beach Nipa Hut
11 Buena Lynnes
12 Manolo's Lodge
Traveller's Beach Delight
15 Las Villas del Natividad Resort
16 Mindorinne Oriental
17 White Coral Garden Resort
18 Lenly's Beach Resort
19 White Beach Resort
20 Simon's Resort
21 Marco Vincent Resort
22 Jun Resort
23 Orchids Lodge
24 Agbing's Beach Resort
27 South of the Border Resort

Places to Eat & Entertainment
3 Coco Aroma Snack Bar
7 Beach Bars
10 Puerto Ria Disco
12 Traveller's Beach Delight Restaurant
13 City Echo Disco
20 Simon's Disco
22 Jun Restaurant
26 Arcobalena Restaurant

Miscellaneous
11 Money Changer
Shopping Center (small)
Telephone
14 Nikita Divers
17 Hammer Head Shark Divers
25 Pacific Divers

Buena Lynne's, Cellphone 0917-6473389. SR/DR/fan/bath P300, SR/DR/ac/bath P500 and P800. Adequate rooms, some with cooking facilities, in a solidly built, two-storey building. Restaurant.

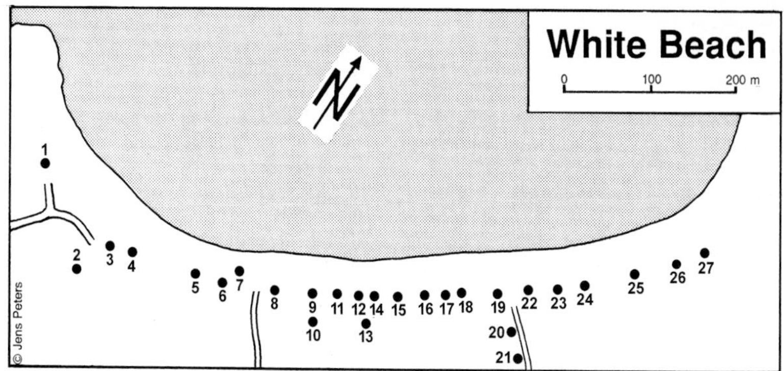

Travellers Beach Delight, Cellphone 0917-4911848. Cottage/fan/bath P300, SR/DR/fan/bath P500 (with TV), SR/DR/ac/bath P1500 (with refrigerator and TV). Building with good rooms and a few cottages as well.

Cherry's Inn, Cellphone 0917-7888239. SR/DR/fan/bath P350 to P500. Big, long building with basic rooms. Restaurant.

Lenly's Beach Resort, Cellphone 0918-2720775. Cottage/fan/bath P350 to P500. Basic, but adequate cottages. Restaurant.

Orchids Lodge, Cellphone 0918-2720775. SR/DR/fan/bath P500. Friendly accommodation with spotless rooms. Restaurant.

South of the Border Resort, Tel 7272791, @. Cottage/fan/bath P500 and P600, SR/DR/ac/bath P800 to P1000. Basic accommodation at a quiet location.

Agbing's Beach Resort, Cellphone 0917-7953899. Cottage/fan/bath P500, SR/DR/fan/bath P500, SR/DR/ac/bath P800. Small place with basic cottages and a stone building with OK rooms. Restaurant.

Las Villas del Natividad Resort, Cellphone 0917-4820505. SR/DR/fan/bath P500 and P700, SR/DR/ac/bath P800 to P1500. A big building with several quite comfortable rooms, and a few basic cottages at the back. Restaurant.

White Beach Nipa Hut, Cellphone 0918-2720774. Cottage/fan/bath P500, SR/DR/ac/bath P800 and P1200 (with refrigerator and TV). A big place with lots of little, really good cottages tightly packed together. The aircon rooms are in the bigger of the buildings. Restaurant.

White Beach Lodge, Cellphone 0917-7327674. Cottage/fan/bath P500 to P800 (TV), SR/DR/ac/bath P1500 (with refrigerator and TV). Popular place with a good variety of fairly roomy cottages, the expensive ones also have a kitchen. Good restaurant.

Lodger's Nook, Cellphone 0917-8377478. Cottage/fan/bath P500 to P1000. Several basic single and double cottages in a row along the beach. They also have a solidly built little stone building (fairly good value). Restaurant, billiard hall.

Summer Connection, Cellphone 0919-3267782. Cottage/fan/bath P500 and P1200. Pleasant, quiet little place at the west end of White Beach. Some of the attractive cottages are on the side of the hill. Nice restaurant. Reservations in Manila: Tel (02) 8217354.

Jun Resort, Cellphone 0917-3950295. Cottage/fan/bath P600, SR/DR/fan/bath P600, SR/DR/ac/bath P1000.

Well-maintained rooms decorated with taste. Restaurant.
Simon's Resort, Cellphone 0917-4565491, @. SR/DR/fan/bath P800, SR/DR/ac/bath P1500. Basically furnished rooms in a two-storey building. Restaurant. Disco.
White Coral Garden Resort, Cellphone 0912-8433064, @. SR/DR/ac/Bad P800 and P2000. Acceptable rooms in a stone building. Swimming pool. Diving.
White Beach Resort, Cellphone 0918-2720774. SR/DR/fan/bath P800, SR/DR/ac/bath P1000 and 1200. Really good cottages as well as good, spacious air-con rooms in a two-storey building. Free shuttle service to and from Puerto Galera.
Mindorinne Oriental, Cellphone 0917-4426929. SR/DR/ac/Bad P2000 and P2500, depending on size. Friendly, well-kept rooms with refrigerator in a big, two-storey stone building.
Marco Vincent Resort, Cellphone 0919-5895854. SR/DR/ac/bath P2500 and P2750. Three-storey building with tastefully decorated rooms, all with refrigerator and TV. Restaurant, swimming pool. Reservations in Manila: Tel (02) 8920309.

Aninuan Beach
Tamaraw Beach Resort, Cellphone 0917-6976802. Cottage/fan/bath P400 to P1000. This is a popular place shaded by trees and with several pleasant cottages, some of them on the side of a hill. Restaurant.
Aninuan Beach Resort, Cellphone 0920-2268808, @. Cottage/fan/bath P500, SR/DR/fan/bath P800, SR/DR/ac/bath P1500. Fairly comfortable rooms and cottages. Small place with a private atmosphere. German management. Restaurant, beach bar.

Talipanan Beach
Mengie's White Sand Beach Resort, Cellphone 0916-3000068. SR/DR/fan/bath P250 to P500. A larger place with basic cottages and rooms in terraced houses. Restaurant.
Bamboo House, Cellphone 0916-3731294. Cottage/fan/bath P350 to P500. Pleasant little place with a family atmosphere. Restaurant.
El Cañonero Beach Resort, Cellphone 0916-6600227. SR/DR/fan/bath P500, SR/DR/ac/bath P1000. Basic, well-kept rooms in a stone building at the west end of the beach. Very quiet location. Italian restaurant.
GM's Resort, Cellphone 0917-7323195. SR/DR/fan/bath P500, SR/DR/ac/Bad P1000. Two-storey stone buildings with basic but OK rooms, some with veranda. Good restaurant, value for money.

Places to Eat

At White Beach you can acquaint yourself with Korean food at the ***Jun Restaurant***. The Philippine and international food can be recommended in the restaurants belonging to the resorts ***Buena Lynne's*** and ***Manolo's***. The latter also has flambéed specialities on the menu. The cosy little ***Coco Aroma Snack Bar*** at the west end of the beach serves international food and first-class milk shakes; jam sessions here on Saturdays.

Getting There & Away

Jeepney: Several jeepneys run daily between Puerto Galera and White Beach in San Isidro, and charge P10. Some of them go on to Talipanan Point, which costs P15. The last one back from San Isidro to Puerto Galera leaves at about 5pm. The fare for a Special Ride is between P100 and P150.
You can walk from White Beach to Talipanan Beach along the beach in about 45 min.

Tricycle: A tricycle from Puerto Galera to White Beach costs at least P50 (15 min).

Boat: A Special Ride by outrigger from Puerto Galera to White Beach costs P450, and to Talipanan Beach P500.

Calapan

Calapan is the capital of Mindoro Oriental Province. The Sanduguan Festival was held here for the first time in May 1981. *Sanduguan* means 'brother' or 'friendship' in the Mangyan language. At the festival the locals re-enacted the first meeting between seafaring Chinese traders and the indigenous Mangyan at Aroma Beach. It was such a success, it is now a yearly event in the middle of November.

Places to Stay

Riceland 1 Inn, JP Rizal Street, Tel 2884253. SR/fan P150, DR/fan P180, SR/DR/fan/bath P285, SR/DR/ac/bath P650 and P750 (with TV). Basic rooms, all right for the money. Centrally located.

Riceland 2 Inn, Del Pilar St, Tel 2885590. SR/fan/bath P220, DR/fan/bath P280, SR/DR/ac/bath P500/600 and P700/800 (with TV). A fairly good hotel, although some of the rooms have somewhat narrow beds. Restaurant. Located about 250m off JP Rizal St (main street); over the river bridge then 50m down on the left.

Hotel Ma-Yi, JP Rizal St, Tel 2884437. SR/DR/fan P250, SR/DR/fan/bath P400/500, SR/DR/ac/bath P800, with TV. A friendly hotel, with small, but adequate rooms. (The expression Ma-Yi comes from the Mangyan language and means 'beautiful'.) Karaoke bar, roof-top garden.

Calapan Bay Hotel, Quezon Dr, Tel & Fax 2881309, @. SR/DR/ac/bath P750 and P850. Tidy, friendly rooms with TV. Good value for the money. Waterside restaurant. Located about two km north-east of the centre in the direction of the wharf and airport.

Marco Vincent Residence Inn, Bonifacio Dr, Tel 4410235, Fax 4410240, @. SR/DR/ac/bath P1400, suites P1700 and P1900. Charming hotel with five well-kept rooms, all with refrigerator and TV.

Microtel Inn & Suites, Roxas Dr, Tel 2862624, Fax 2862622, @. SR/DR/ac/bath P1850 and P2300, suite P3550. Good hotel with immaculate rooms, all with refrigerator and TV, the suites also with a small kitchen. Restaurant. Swimming pool.

Places to Eat

Considering this is a provincial capital, the choice of restaurants is limited. One of the best is the ***La Paulina Restaurant*** in Leuterio St. The menu offers a wide choice of food, although they specialise in pasta and pizza. The ***L & V Snack Restaurant*** in Del Pilar St is also not bad.

Entertainment

Karaoke bars are popular and there are a few of them in the town centre, eg ***Hanunuo Videoke Bar*** upstairs in the Hotel Ma-Yi. There are also a few more or less basic clubs on the access road at the edge of town, eg the ***Love Birds Disco***.

Miscellaneous

Festival: Sanduguan Festival from 11 to 15 November.

Money: The Equitable PCI Bank, JP Rizal St, has an ATM.

Population: 100,000.

Post & Telephone: Post Office, Bonifacio Dr.

Post code: 5200. Area code: 043.

Getting There & Away

By Air: Calapan Airport is situated at the north-eastern edge of town, about three km from the town centre (not far from the jetty). Unfortunately, Seair has stopped running flights from and to

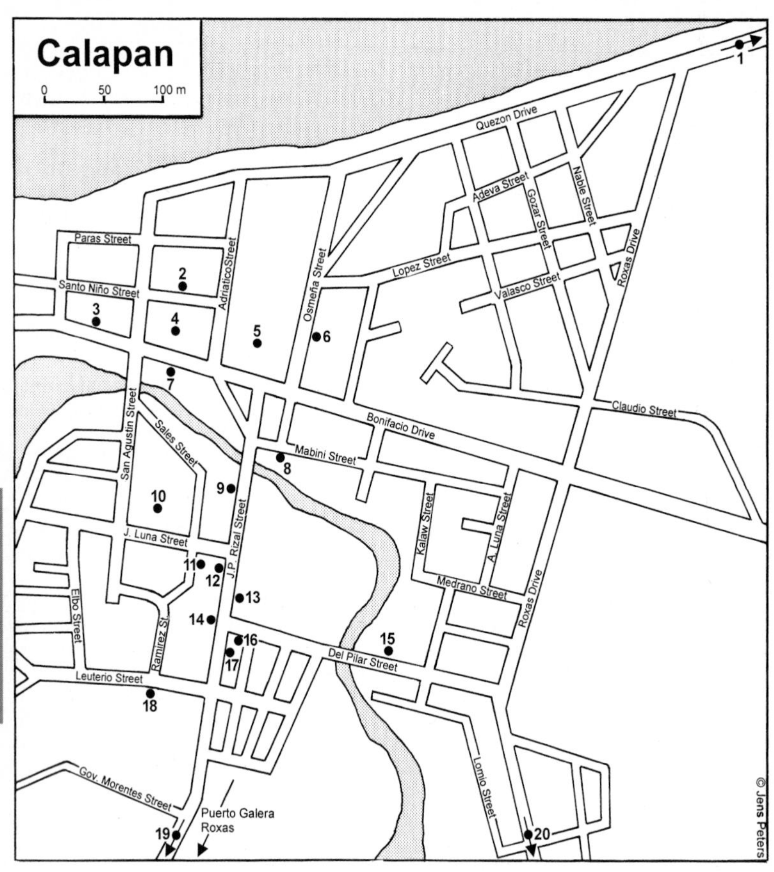

Caticlan (Boracay) and Manila (temporarily?).

By Boat: A tricycle from the pier to the town centre costs P10 per person (10 min).
Starlite Ferry, Pier, Tel 2881088, 2881288.
Destination: Batangas.
Supercat Fast Ferry Corporation, Pier, Tel 2883179, 2883258.
Destination: Batangas.

Puerto Galera
Jeepney: Jeepneys heading for Calapan leave the Petron filling station in the south of Puerto Galera on the way out of town, roughly every hour from 6am until 1pm (P50; 1½ hrs).

Roxas
Bus: From Roxas to Calapan, big buses run hourly until 3pm (P100; four hrs). You can also do it in stages by minibus and jeepney.

Getting There & Away
1 Airport (1.5 km)
Pier (1.6 km)
8 Rodasco (Minibuses to Pinamalayan & Roxas)
10 Jeepneys to Puerto Galera
11 Buses to Roxas

Places to Stay
1 Calapan Bay Hotel (700m)
3 Marco Vincent Residence Inn
12 Riceland 1 Inn
13 Hotel Ma-Yi
15 Riceland 2 Inn
20 Microtel Inn & Suites (700m)

Places to Eat
11 Chowking
12 Jollibee
14 Mister Donut
16 L & V Snack Restaurant
18 Café Nicholas
La Paulina Restaurant

Miscellaneous
2 Land Bank
4 Town Plaza
5 Cathedral
6 Police Station
7 City Hall
Post Office
9 City Mart Island Mall
Bank of the Philippine Islands
10 Market
14 Mercury Drug
Metrobank
17 Equitable PCI Bank
19 Philippine National Bank (PNB) (100m)
Provincial Capitol (300m)

Buses from Calapan to Roxas leave from the jetty (aircon buses) and the market; minibuses also leave from the market.

Pinamalayan

From Pinamalayan boats go to Sibali Island, the local name for Maestro de Campo Island, and to Banton Island, both in Romblon Province. You can also take a boat from here to Marinduque. You can ask about timetables at the coast-guard station, 200m past the market.

Places to Stay

Blue Waves Hotel, Luarca St, Tel 2843399. SR/DR/fan P250, SR/DR/fan/bath P350, SR/DR/ac/bath P700 (with TV). Basic rooms. Quiet location at the southern edge of town.

Oro Beach Hotel, Luarca St, Tel 2843119. SR/DR/fan/bath P350 and P450, SR/DR/ac/bath P600 and P900. Fairly small, but good, friendly rooms with TV, the more expensive ones also have a refrigerator.

Places to Eat

The ***Hong Kong Restaurant*** in the eponymous hotel in Mabini St has inexpensive Philippine and Chinese food.

Getting There & Away

By Boat: A tricycle from the pier to the bus stop costs P10.

Bongabong

Bongabong is a small, not very interesting place. Now and then, boats run from there to Tablas Island in Romblon Province (see the Getting There & Away section at the beginning of this chapter).

Places to Stay

Mabuhay Lodging House, Plaridel St. SR/DR/fan P100/200. Very basic accommodation near the market.

D & J Pension House. SR/fan P120, SR/fan/bath P220, DR/fan/bath P260.

Friendly staff and fairly good, clean rooms. The building has a restaurant and a big patio.

Roxas

Roxas is on the south-east coast of Mindoro, not quite five km off the main road, at the end of a cul-de-sac (dead-end). There's a surprisingly wide selection of good, big, inexpensive fruit at the market.

From Roxas, big outriggers run to Tablas Island in Romblon Province and car ferries to Caticlan (for Boracay) north-west of Panay (see the Getting There & Away section at the beginning of this chapter). Some of the waiting time can be spent at the nearby Melco Beach, where the boats to Boracay arrive and leave from. Apart from that, this is probably one of the less interesting places for tourists.

Places to Stay

Santo Niño Hotel. SR/DR/fan P150/200. Unpretentious place in the town centre at the market. Restaurant.

Dannarosa Hotel, Tel 2892346. SR/DR/fan P150/200, SR/DR/fan/bath P300. Basic accommodation near the Santo Niño Hotel.

Roxas Villa Hotel, Tel 2892026. SR/DR/fan/bath P250/350, SR/DR/ac/bath P500 to P670 (with TV). Good, clean hotel right next to the Santo Niño Hotel (same owner).

Catalina Beach Resort, Bagumbayan. SR/DR/fan/bath P400. Straightforward accommodation 1½ km away from Roxas.

Places to Eat

Good restaurants are pretty thin on the ground in Roxas, which makes it all the more delightful to come across the tastefully furnished ***Segma Café*** with a fair selection of local dishes and pleasant music.

Getting There & Away

By Boat: A tricycle from Melco Beach (pier) to the town centre costs P20.

Calapan - Pinamalayan - Bongabong

Bus: Big buses leave the wharf at Calapan every hour from early morning to 3pm daily, bound for Roxas via Pinamalayan and Bongabong (P10 by tricycle from the centre). It takes two hrs to reach Pinamalayan, three hrs to Bongabong and four hrs to Roxas. Fast minibuses also leave from the market which take 2½ hrs to Roxas (P120).

San Jose - Bulalacao

Jeepney: Two or three jeepneys run daily from San Jose via Bulalacao along the south coast to Roxas, possibly only during the dry season from December to May (taking four hrs).

Bulalacao

Bulalacao is a small fishing village on the bay of the same name in the south-east of Mindoro. The road from here is a really attractive, scenic route with a beautiful view of the Tablas Strait and the little offshore islands, taking you along the south coast via Magsaysay to San Jose. It's mostly unpaved but good to drive on (at least during the dry season from December to May).

There is a second stretch of road that connects Bulalacao with San Jose, but it's hardly used any more. Parts of it are a fairly rough track through the mountains and probably only driveable with a four-wheel drive vehicle. The turn-off for this so-called Old Provincial Road is just north of Bulalacao. It rejoins the coast road between Magsaysay and San Jose.

Places to Stay

San Rosa Inn. SR/DR/fan/bath P800, SR/DR/ac/bath P1300 (four people). Basic, but clean and acceptable accommodation on the way out of town in the south.

Mindoro Occidental

San Jose

Among other things, San Jose is one of the starting points for diving excursions to Apo Reef. It is in the south-western part of Mindoro Occidental and is handy for people with a bit of time to fit in a boat trip to Palawan. (Boats only leave occasionally for Coron on Busuanga and for islands of the Quiniluban Group, which is the northernmost part of the Cuyo Islands.) However, San Jose lacks the kind of appeal that could tempt you to stay longer; the amount of comfortable hotels to choose from is limited, and good restaurants are a rarity.

In Mindoro Occidental there are many cultural minorities, the most remote tribes having little contact with civilisation. Occasionally some come into town and with luck you may meet Mangyans who will guide you to their village.

Queen's Ranch is a good place for a day trip. It is two hours away by jeepney and you can stay there overnight for about P200 per person. From there it takes about eight hours on foot to reach the Mt Iglit Tamaraw Reservation.

Boats can also be hired in San Jose for swimming and snorkelling on the nearby islands of Ilin and Ambulong (P800 to Ambulong). Both islands have white beaches.

Places to Stay

Sikatuna Town Hotel, Sikatuna St, Tel 4911274. SR/DR/fan P140, SR/DR/fan/bath P290 and P370, SR/DR/ac/bath P600 (with TV). Simple, but completely OK for the money.

Plaza Hotel, P Zamore St, Tel 4914661. SR/fan P200, ER/fan/bath P300 and P400, DR/fan/bath P400 and P500, SR/DR/ac/bath P700 and P800. Fairly good rooms, nearly all with TV. Good, small restaurant. The best hotel in the town centre.

Sikatuna Beach Hotel, Airport Rd, Tel 4912182. SR/DR/fan/bath P300, SR/DR/ac/bath P700 (with TV). Basic and definitely acceptable. A good alternative to the hotels in the town. Restaurant. Quiet location on a dark beach about 1.2 km north-west of the town centre; P6 per person by tricycle.

White House Safari Lodge, Airport Rd, Tel & Fax 4911656. SR/DR/ac/bath P1800, suites P2600 and P3000. Attractive, big building with cosy and comfortable rooms with balcony, TV and refrigerator. Restaurant (order meals beforehand). Directly next to the Sikatuna Beach Hotel.

Places to Eat

The ***Kusina ni Lea*** restaurant across from the Sikatuna Town Hotel will serve you deliciously prepared Philippine food. The popular, clean ***Nice & Spice*** on Sikatuna St serves hamburgers, pizzas, ice cream and cakes, starting in the late afternoon, but they don't have coffee.

The food served in the garden restaurant of the ***Sikatuna Beach Hotel*** is good and the portions are generous.

Miscellaneous

Festival: Saknungan Festival from 25 to 27 April.

Money: The Metrobank in Cipriano Liboro St changes travellers' cheques and has an ATM.

Population: 80,000.

Post & Telephone: Post Office, MH Pilar St.

Post code: 5100. Area code: 043.

Getting There & Away

By Air: San Jose Airport is 2½ km north of the town centre; P7 per person by tricycle.

Air Philippines, San Jose Airport, Tel. 4914157.
- Rizal St, Tel 4914158.
Destination: Manila.
Asian Spirit, San Jose Airport Office, Tel. 4914154.
- Santos Building, Rizal St, Tel 4914151, 4911047.
Destination: Manila.

By Boat: Caminavit Port is four km outside of San Jose. A tricycle to the centre of town costs P5 per person.

Mamburao - Sablayan
Bus: Several buses run from Mamburao to San Jose via Sablayan every day (four hrs).

Roxas - Bulalacao
Jeepney: Two to three jeepneys a day go from Roxas via Bulalacao and along the south coast to San Jose, possible only in the dry season from December to May (four hrs).

Boat: A boat leaves Bulalacao for San Jose in the morning at around 8 o'clock. The trip takes six hrs, usually finishing at South Pier, Caminawit Port.
Departure from San Jose to Bulalacao is at 11am every day.

Getting There & Away
1 Airport (1.8 km)
2 North Pier
10 Air Philippines
12 Jeepneys to Bulalacao
15 Asian Spirit
19 Ramadel Express Bus Terminal
23 Caminavit Port (4 km)

Places to Stay
1 Sikatuna Beach Hotel (800m)
White House Safari Lodge (800m)
8 Sikatuna Town Hotel
14 Plaza Hotel
22 Green Drive-In Lodge

Places to Eat & Entertainment
4 Cora's Restaurant
6 Nice & Spice Restaurant
9 Kusina ni Lea Restaurant
13 Emmanuel Panceteria
21 Eduardo's Restaurant & Disco
22 Greenland Disco

Miscellaneous
3 Market
5 Metrobank
7 Mercury Drug
10 Angel's Department Store
11 Movieworld
16 Philippine National Bank (PNB)
17 City Hall
Police Station
Post Office
18 Church
20 Divine Word College

Apo Island & Apo Reef

Right in the middle of the busy Mindoro Strait, which separates Mindoro from the Calamian Group in the north of Palawan, is nestled the flat little island of Apo with the vast Apo Reef stretching out to the east of it. A 36m high lighthouse warns passing ships against getting too close to the reef, where countless rocks and coral heads jut out of the water at low tide. What is for mariners a highly dangerous area, is for divers one of the most spectacular areas in the Philippines for underwater sights, in spite of the enormous number of coral reefs destroyed in recent years by dynamite fishing. In the summer months of March, April and May, several diving expeditions head for Apo Island and Apo Reef. However, this is a paradise not only for divers but also for snorkellers and latter-day Robinson Crusoes.

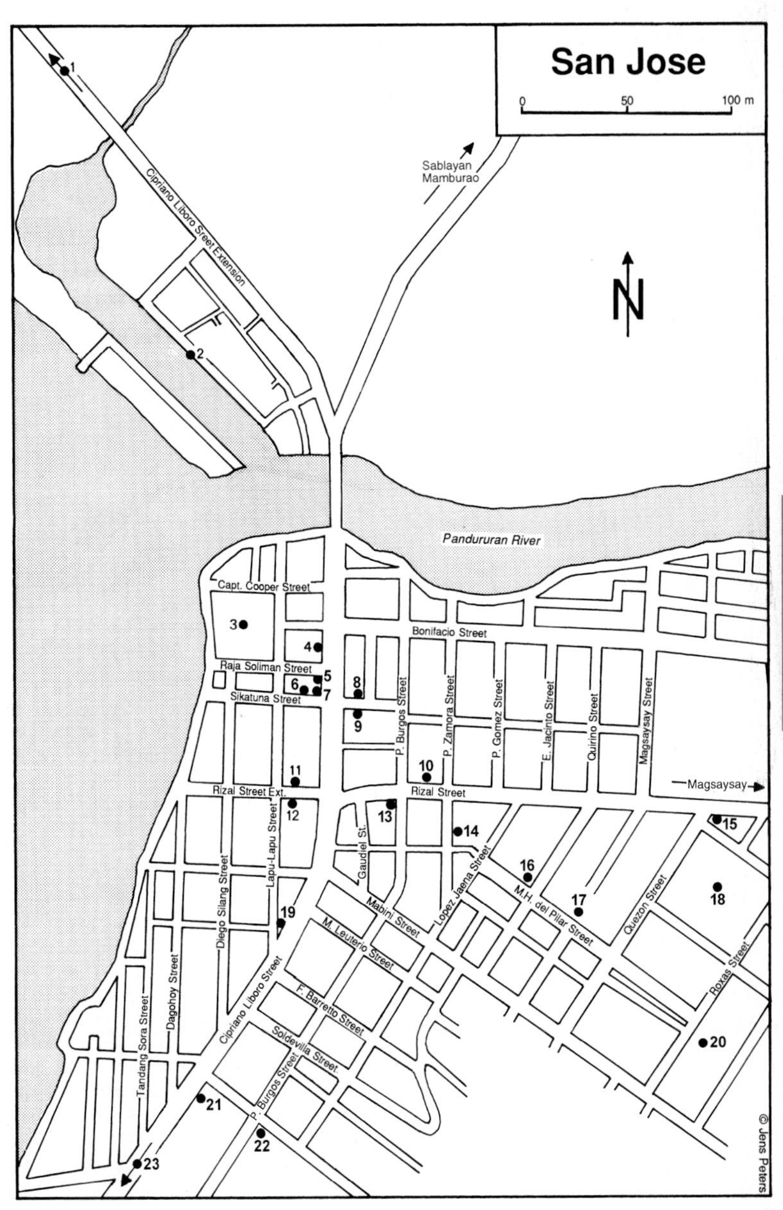
San Jose
0 50 100 m
Sablayan
Mamburao
N
Cipriano Liboro Street Extension
Pandururan River
Capt. Cooper Street
Bonifacio Street
Raja Soliman Street
Sikatuna Street
P. Burgos Street
P. Zamora Street
P. Gomez Street
E. Jacinto Street
Quirino Street
Magsaysay Street
Magsaysay
Rizal Street Ext.
Rizal Street
Lapu-Lapu Street
Gaudiel St.
Lopez Jaena Street
M.H. del Pilar Street
Quezon Street
Roxas Street
Mabini Street
M. Leuterio Street
F. Barretto Street
Soldevilla Street
Cipriano Liboro Street
P. Burgos Street
Diego Silang Street
Dagohoy Street
Tandang Sora Street
1
2
3
4
5
6
7
8
9
10
11
12
13
14
15
16
17
18
19
20
21
22
23
© Jens Peters

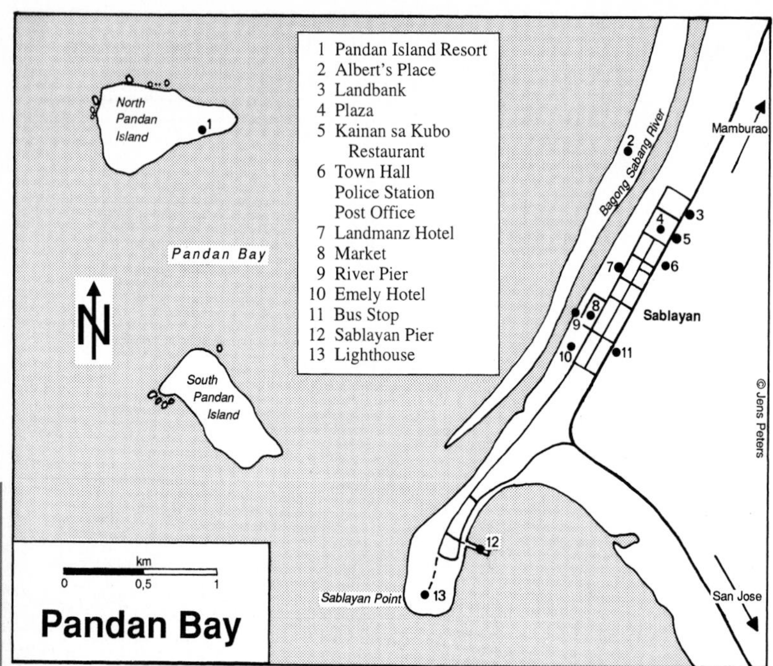

Don't confuse this island with the other Apo Island popular with divers, just off the south-east coast of Negros.

Places to Stay

You'll have to pay P100 per person to the Coast Guard to visit the island. For that, there are basic cottages available free, with bath and cooking facilities (take your own food).

The only place to camp is at the south-eastern end, but make sure your tent is hermetically sealed before sunset or you will be tortured by sandflies. Take your own food and about five litres of water per day.

Getting There & Away

Boat: There is no regular connection to Apo Island so you will have to charter a boat. A return trip in a big outrigger from Sablayan, including a trip round the island, shouldn't cost more than P3000. Arrange a pick-up time beforehand.

Sablayan

This friendly, clean little town is at the mouth of the Bagong Sabang River in the south of Pandan Bay. There are several shops here and a lively market with a few simple local restaurants along the riverside, where boats are tied up which will take you to the islands of Pandan Bay. Larger boats dock at the Sablayan Pier, in a sheltered little bay near the lighthouse.

From Sablayan you can take one-day or several-day motorbike or trekking tours into the mountainous interior of Mindoro, eg to the Mangyan area, Mt Iglit Tamaraw Reservation (where around 150 Tamaraw dwarf buffaloes live) and to the Sablayan Penal Colony (3000 prisoners) next to beautiful Lake Libao. Kayak tours are also possible, eg up the Barahan River (about 20 km north of Sablayan).

Places to Stay

Emely Hotel, Rosario St. SR/DR P100/200, SR/DZ/fan/bath P250. Basic but clean. Restaurant.

Landmanz Hotel, Rosario St. SR/DZ/fan/bath P350, SR/DZ/ac/bath P550 (TV). Good, well-maintained rooms. Restaurant.

Albert's Place, @. SR/DR/fan P250, cottage/fan/bath P650. A pleasant, spread-out place located in a very peaceful area about 1.3 km north of the market, on the opposite side of the Bagong Sabang River on a clean, grey sand beach. They have a restaurant with Philippine and European cooking, and a beach bar.

Getting there: Cross the river by boat (P2), then walk upstream. The boatman will take you the whole way upstream to Albert's Place if you ask him (P50), or directly there along the coast for P100.

Note: This place was closed in mid-2004, possibly only temporarily. Albert's widow, Arlyn, lives in Sablayan and can give more details.

Places to Eat

The restaurant in the Landmanz Hotel is quite good (better to order beforehand). The small restaurants at the market and near the river jetty are good and inexpensive, but close at about 7pm.

Miscellaneous

Festival: Town Fiesta in the third week of January.

Money: The Landbank near the plaza will change US dollars cash. Travellers' cheques and credit cards are worthless in Sablayan.

Population: 12,000.

Post: The Post Office is next to the Town Hall.

Post code: 5104.

Getting Around

Motorcycle: Laurent Bernadette, Cellphone 0918-2946239, rents 200 cc Hondas for P900 per day.

Getting There & Away

Bus/Jeepney: Buses and jeepneys pass through Sablayan on their way to and from San Jose, Abra de Ilog and Mamburao. Jeepneys are more expensive than buses. The trip from Sablayan to Mamburao and San Jose (P80) takes two hrs each leg of the journey.

Fare for a Special Ride with a jeepney to Sablayan: P1800 from Abra de Ilog; P1400 from Mamburao.

North Pandan Island

North Pandan would be near the top of the author's personal Top 10 Philippine islands. In the south this gorgeous spot has a beautiful white sand beach with palms and other tropical trees. The remaining northern part of this roughly triangular island is covered by dense jungle which comes right down to the beach. The animal population of this jungle still appears to be intact.

Places to Stay

Pandan Island Resort, @, Cellphone 0919-3057821. SR/DR/fan P500/600, cottage/fan/bath P1100, big building for four people P1750. The cottages are very roomy and supplied by solar energy. This quiet, rambling establishment is managed by friendly French people. There is a restaurant with a communal buffet for P400, a beach bar, diving (Mariposa Diving), windsurfing, kayaks and shiatsu massage available.

Getting There & Away

Boat: The resort service boat leaves for North Pandan Island around 10am from the river landing place at the market in Sablayan. A Special Ride costs P100 (two people P120), taking 30 min.
Arrangements to be picked up by boat or van either from Mamburao (P8000) or San Jose (P7000); reservations can be made in Manila at Asiaventure Services, Room 305, Sevilla Building, 1153 MH del Pilar St, Ermita, Tel. (02) 5237007, 5266929, Fax: (02) 5251811.

Mamburao

The small town of Mamburao is the capital of Mindoro Occidental Province. Shops and businesses can mostly be found in National Road, which runs from east to west through the town, and at the fish market right on the banks of the Mamburao River. Apart from that, there are only peaceful side streets.
The countryside around offers plenty opportunities for good walks and, one hour's drive north, not far from Paluan and a Mangyan village, you can marvel at the freshwater pools at Calawagan in the foothills of the mountains.

Getting There & Away
2 Jeepneys to Abra de Ilog
3 Shell Petrol Station
11 Jeepneys to Paluan
17 Jeepneys to San Jose
19 Caltex Petrol Station
20 Buses to San Jose
21 Mamburao Airport

Places to Stay
1 Tayamaan Palm Beach Club (2.5 km)
9 Kelsie Hotel
14 La Gensol Plaza Hotel
15 Mindoreños Hotel
17 Travellers' Inn

Places to Eat
14 Goldilocks
16 Food Gallery

Miscellaneous
4 City Hall
Digitel
Police Station
Post Office
5 West Mindoro Academy
6 Church
7 Provincial Capitol
8 River Market
10 Binky's Mini Mart
12 Drugstore
13 Globe Telecom
14 Philippine National Bank (PNB)
18 Market

Places to Stay

Mindoreños Hotel, San Jose St, Tel 7115100. SR/fan/bath P220, DR/fan/bath P280. Basic, reasonable rooms. Restaurant.
Travellers' Lodge, National Rd. SR/DR/fan P100/200, SR/fan/bath P220, DR/fan/bath P300, SR/ac/bath P550, DR/ac/bath P850. Basic accommodation, but acceptable. Restaurant.
La Gensol Plaza Hotel, 95 National Rd, Tel & Fax 7111072. SR/fan/bath P300, SR/DR/ac/bath P850 to P1400. Good rooms, the expensive ones with TV. The best hotel in town. Restaurant.
Tayamaan Palm Beach Club. Cottage/fan/bath P600. Full board is possible. Located four km northwest of Mamburao, the cottages are clean, well-built stone buildings standing under palm trees on a beautiful bay with a sandy beach suitable for bathing. It costs P40 to get there by tricycle from the town centre.

Miscellaneous

Festival: Town Fiesta in May.
Money: The Philippine National Bank next to the La Gensol Plaza Hotel in

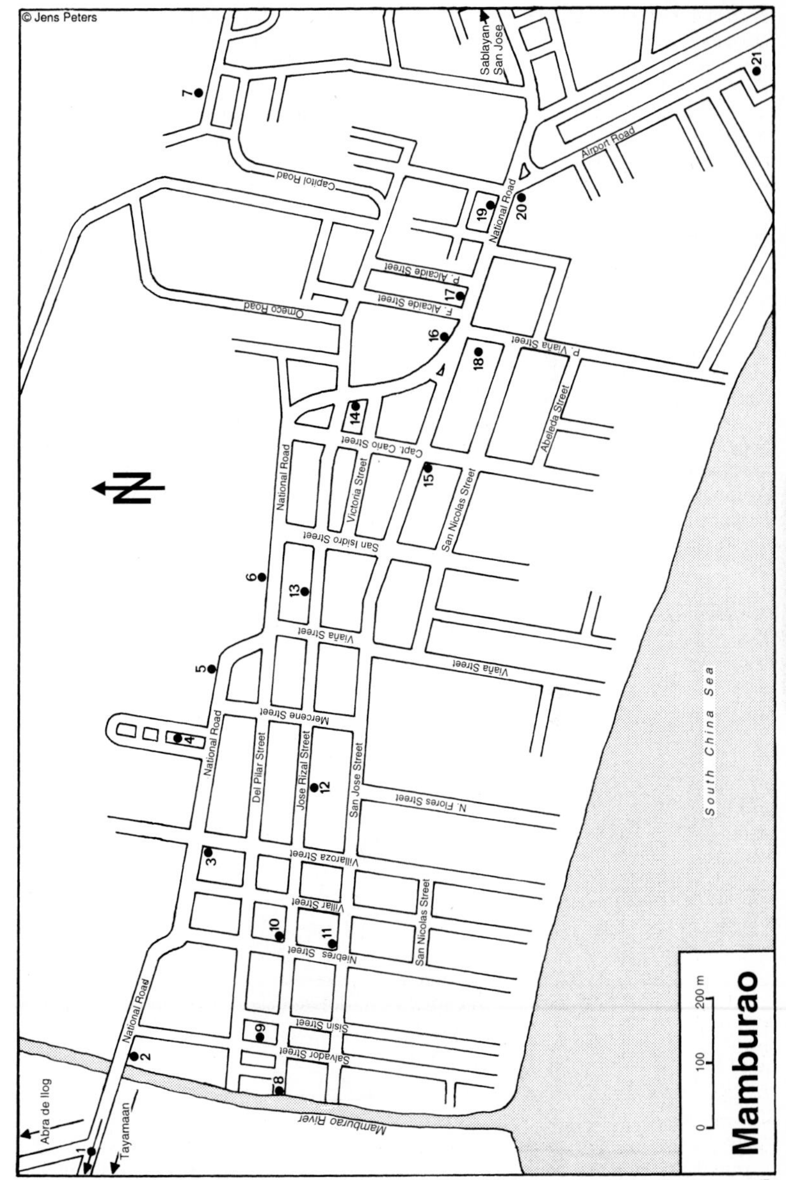
© Jens Peters
Mamburao
0
100
200 m
Sablayan
San Jose
Capitol Road
Airport Road
National Road
P. Alcaide Street
F. Alcaide Street
Omeco Road
P. Viaña Street
Abeleda Street
Capt. Cario Street
Victoria Street
San Nicolas Street
San Isidro Street
Viaña Street
Mercene Street
Del Pilar Street
Jose Rizal Street
San Jose Street
N. Flores Street
Villaroza Street
Villar Street
Niebres Street
Sisin Street
Salvador Street
Mamburao River
Abra de Ilog
Tayamaan
South China Sea
1
2
3
4
5
6
7
8
9
10
11
12
13
14
15
16
17
18
19
20
21

National Rd will change travellers' cheques.
Population: 25,000.
Post & Telephone: Post Office, National Rd (next to City Hall).
National and international calls can be made from Digitel, also in National Rd.
Post code: 5106. Area code: 043.

Getting There & Away

Puerto Galera - Abra de Ilog
Boat/Jeepney: A Special Ride by outrigger from Puerto Galera to Wawa - the landing place for Abra de Ilog - should not cost more than P2000 (2½ hrs).
Another way to get from Puerto Galera to Abra de Ilog is to go via Batangas: take a ferry from Puerto Galera to Batangas and carry on with the ferry to Abra de Ilog.
Jeepneys run between Wawa and Mamburao via Abra de Ilog (1½ hrs).

Note: The road between Puerto Galera and Abra de Ilog, shown on many maps of the Philippines, doesn't exist yet. As a result, it's not possible at the moment to go the whole way round the island by car or motorbike. But - good news - the construction of the road is well under way and should be completed in 2005.
If you are stranded in Wawa, the little port 30 km north-east of Mambuaro, you can spend the night at the *Lodging House*, a basic place about 500m from the pier. Rooms are available for P150/200.

San Jose - Sablayan
Bus: Several buses run from San Jose to Mamburao via Sablayan every day. Some go via Mamburao to Abra de Ilog (pier). The trip takes four hrs from San Jose, and two hrs from Sablayan.

Romblon

Almost in the centre of the Philippine archipelago, Romblon Province comprises around 20 islands and islets, the largest of which are Tablas, Sibuyan and Romblon. All three are hilly, although Sibuyan has more of a forest covering.

Because of its large marble deposits, Romblon is also called 'Marble Country'. Experts consider that Romblon marble is at least equal in quality to Italian marble. It is usually sold as large blocks, but several families make a few pesos by selling handmade ashtrays, chess pieces, vases and statues. Those marble souvenirs are mostly on sale in Romblon/Romblon - that is the town of Romblon on the island of Romblon in the province of Romblon.

Getting There & Away

You can get to Romblon from Luzon, Masbate, Mindoro and Panay (see Getting Away from Luzon in the Manila chapter and Getting There & Away in the chapters on the other islands).

To Luzon

Air

From Tugdan/Tablas to Manila
Seair flies Monday and Thursday (P2790).

Boat

From Cajidiocan/Sibuyan to Lucena
Two times a week, probably Tuesday and Saturday at 4am, with Kalaayan Shipping Lines (26 hrs); via Ambulong/Magdiwang (departure 11am) and Romblon/Romblon.

From Cajidiocan/Sibuyan to Manila
Monday at 2pm with MBRS Lines (P530; 12 hrs).

From Odiongan/Tablas to Batangas
Monday, Thursday and Saturday with Montenegro Shipping Lines (P265; eight hrs).
Tuesday, Friday and Sunday at 5pm with a Shipshape Ferry car ferry (eight hrs).

From Odiongan/Tablas to Manila
Wednesday, Friday and Sunday with MBRS Lines (P530; 11 hrs).

From Romblon/Romblon to Manila
Monday with MBRS Lines (P530; 12 hrs).

From Romblon/Romblon to Batangas
Tuesday, Friday and Sunday at 11am with a Shipshape Ferry car ferry (P330; 14 hrs); via Odiongan/Tablas Island.

From Romblon/Romblon to Lucena
Two times a week, probably Tuesday and Saturday at 6pm, with Kalaayan Shipping Lines (12 hrs). The boat originates in Sibuyan Island.

To Masbate

Boat

From Cajidiocan/Sibuyan to Mandaon
A big outrigger goes three times a week (P130; five hrs).

Warning
In bad weather the sea in the Tablas Strait is very rough, and the following crossings with outriggers are not to be recommended in this case. Small boats sometimes sail over, but they are completely unsuitable and often dangerously overloaded.

From Romblon/Romblon to Aroroy
Sunday with MBRS Lines (five hrs); possibly via San Agustin/Tablas.

To Mindoro

Boat

From Looc and Odiongan/Tablas to Roxas
Daily except Wednesday at 11am with a big outrigger (P160; three hrs). From Looc possibly only on Saturday.

To Panay

Boat

From Cajidiocan/Sibuyan to Dumaguit/Kalibo
Sunday with MBRS Lines (P350; three hrs).

From Looc/Tablas to Boracay
A big outrigger goes daily at 9am (P130; two hrs). The boat carries on to Caticlan.

From Odiongan/Tablas to Caticlan (Boracay)
Tuesday, Thursday and Saturday at 4am with MBRS Lines (three hrs).

From Santa Fe/Tablas to Boracay
A big outrigger goes daily at 10.30am (P150; two hrs). The boat carries on to Caticlan.

Romblon Island

Romblon

The small port town of Romblon is the capital of Romblon Province. In the typhoon season, ships often take cover in its sheltered bay.
The two forts of San Andres and Santiago Hill were built by the Spaniards in 1640 and are said to have underground passages leading to the coast. Today, San Andres is used as a weather station. From the forts (now in ruins) there is a good view of San Joseph's Cathedral and the town with its Spanish-style houses. Dating back to 1726, the cathedral houses a collection of antiques that you can see on request.
In an alleyway next to the Romblon Shopping Center there are several little souvenir shops with workshops, where you can buy art work made of marble (you can watch the artists as they work).
The Romblon Marble Development Multi-Purpose Collective, a Philippine-Italian marble yard, is located about one km north-east of Romblon. There they slice up the marble blocks and then rub and polish them.
The bay of Romblon is protected by the small island of Lugbung, which you can quickly reach by outrigger from the harbour. The island has a beautiful white beach and a few cottages, but you should bring your own provisions. North of Lugbung are the islands of Alad and a bit further out again, Cobrador. This is a beautiful little island with a gorgeous white beach, palm trees and a 250m high mountain in the middle. The water there is crystal clear and good for snorkelling.

Places to Stay

Felmar Pension House *(Marble House)*, Quezon St. SR/DR/fan P150/300, SR/DR/ac/bath P550 (with TV). Modest rooms with fan, and acceptable aircon

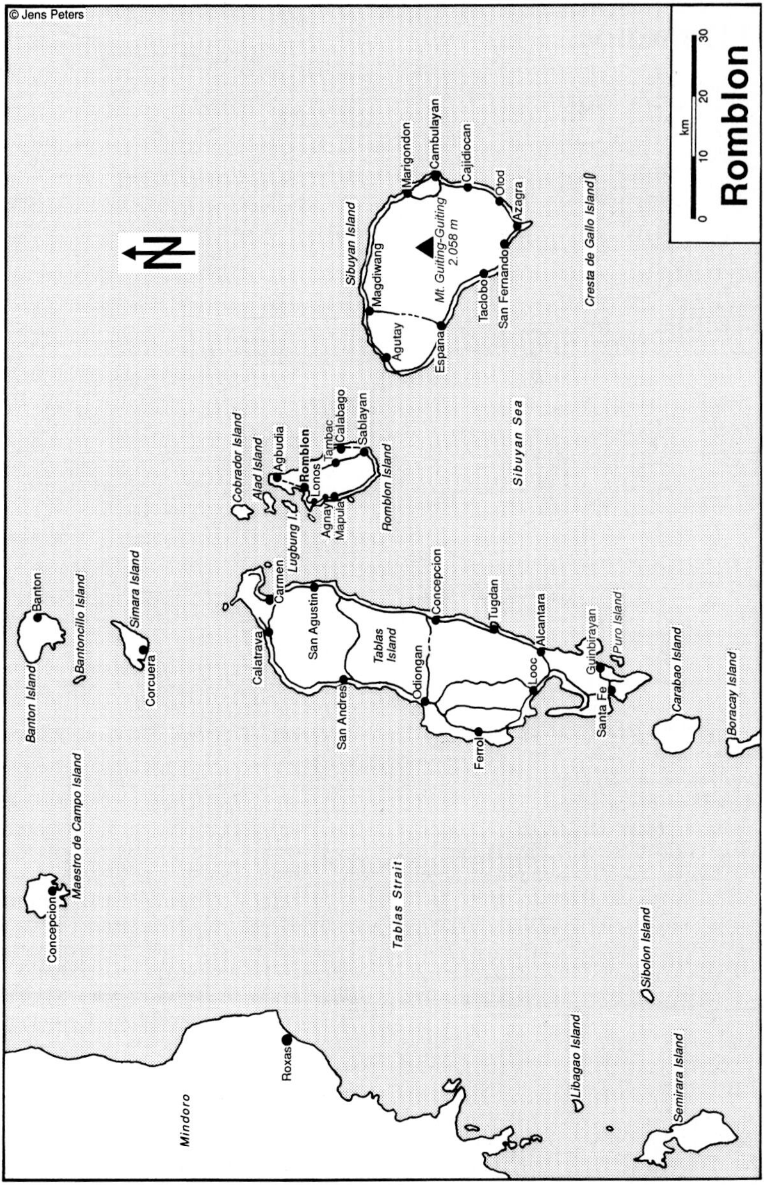

© Jens Peters

Romblon

km
0
10
20
30

Sibuyan Island
Marigondon
Cambulayan
Cajidiocan
Otod
Azagra
Mt. Guiting-Guiting
2.058 m
Magdiwang
Agutay
Espana
Taclobo
San Fernando
Cresta de Gallo Island

Cobrador Island
Alad Island
Agbudia
Romblon
Lonos
Tambac
Calabago
Sablayan
Lugbung I.
Agnay
Mapula
Romblon Island
Sibuyan Sea

Banton
Banton Island
Bantoncillo Island
Simara Island
Corcuera
Carmen
Calatrava
San Agustin
Tablas Island
Concepcion
Odiongan
Tugdan
Alcantara
Looc
San Andres
Ferrol
Guinbirayan
Puro Island
Santa Fe
Carabao Island
Boracay Island

Concepcion
Maestro de Campo Island
Tablas Strait
Sibolon Island
Roxas
Mindoro
Libagao Island
Semirara Island

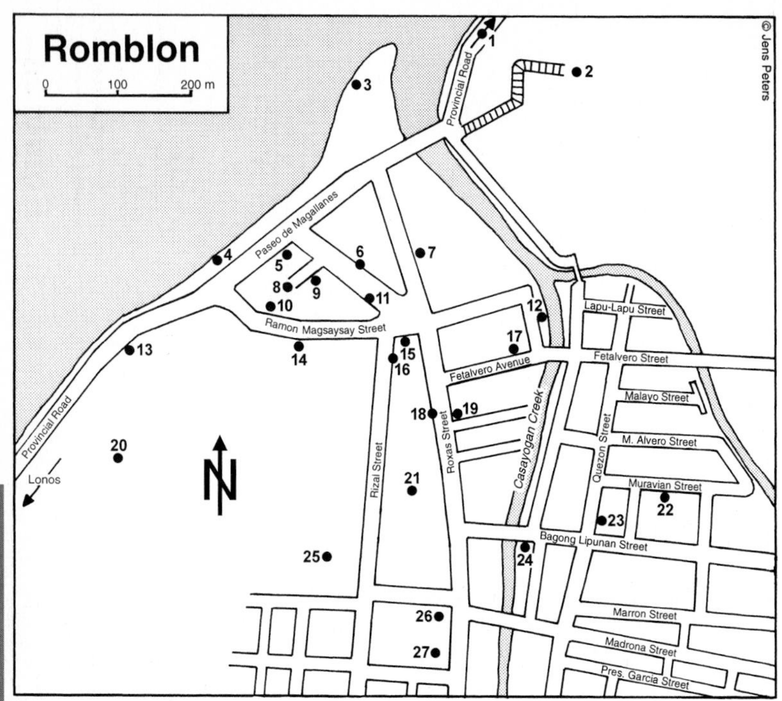

rooms with marble all over the place. Shared balcony. Reception in the hardware store on the ground floor.

Romblon Plaza Hotel, Roxas St, Tel (054) 4728218 (ext 2269), Cellphone 0919-3977924, @. SR/DR/fan/bath P350/400, SR/DR/ac/bath P550/600 (with TV), suite P700 to P1000 (with refrigerator); all including breakfast. Very good, pleasantly furnished rooms, all with a little balcony. Attractive rooftop restaurant with karaoke in the evenings.

Muravian Hotel, Muravian St, (054) 4728218 (ext 2505). SR/DR/fan/bath P400, SR/DR/ac/bath P600. Good value rooms with TV. Located in a small side street set back a bit from Quezon St.

Parc Bay Mansion, Paseo de Magellanes, Tel (054) 4728218 (ext 2408). SR/DR/fan/bath P550, SR/DR/ac/bath P600; all including breakfast. Immaculate, well-kept rooms on three floors, some with a view of the harbour. On the ground floor they have a breakfast room with a refrigerator and cooking facilities, as well as a small bar with TV. 24-hr service. The hotel belongs to a French-Philippine married couple.

Blue Ridge Hotel, Fetalvero St, Tel (054) 4728218 (ext 2274), Cellphone 0919-5183552, @. SR/DR/ac/bath P750 to P1200 (four people). Well-kept, friendly rooms with TV, the more expensive also have a kitchen. Pleasant accommodation in the centre at the market.

Getting There & Away
3 Boats to Magdiwang/Sibuyan
Philippine Port Authority (PPA)
Shipshade Ferry
4 Boats to San Agustin/Tablas
5 MBRS Lines
6 Jeepneys (westbound)
11 Tricyles (downtown)
16 Tricycles (westbound)
18 Jeepneys (eastbound)

Places to Stay
13 Parc Bay Mansion
17 Blue Ridge Hotel
19 Romblon Plaza Hotel
22 Muravian Hotel
23 Felmar Pension House

Places to Eat
10 Jaks Restaurant & Bar
19 Romblon Plaza Restaurant

Miscellaneous
1 Hospital (800m)
Marble Factory (1 km)
2 Fort San Andres
7 Romblon Tel
8 Marble Shops
9 Romblon Shopping Center
12 Market
14 Romblon International Business Center
15 Post Office
19 Supermarket
20 Fort Santiago Hill
21 Plaza
24 Philippine National Bank (PNB)
25 St Joseph Cathedral
26 Police Station
27 Town Hall

Places to Eat

The most popular restaurant with travellers in town has to be ***Jaks Restaurant & Bar***, run by David and Tess Kerchan, a nice British-Philippine couple. They serve Philippine and international dishes, including pizzas and fabulous curries, all at reasonable prices. You can also find good-value Filipino food at ***Eateries*** next to the Romblon Shopping Center at the plaza. People sit outside there in the evenings and soak in the relaxed and pleasant atmosphere. Also on the recommended list is the ***Rooftop Restaurant*** of the Romblon Plaza Hotel. There you can eat Philippine food, seafood, hamburgers and sandwiches, while enjoying the beautiful view of the town, harbour and the picturesque bay.

Miscellaneous

Diving: In the straits between Romblon Island and Alad Island, as well as around Cobrador Island, there are largely intact coral reefs. Dive trips are on offer from Marble Beach Resort, San Pedro.
Festival: Biniray Festival on the second weekend in January.
Online: Romblon International Business Center, Tel. (02) 4122864 (ext 2596, @, diagonally across from Jaks Restaurant & Bar); P40/hr.
Population: 40,000.
Post & Telephone: Post code: 5500. International phone calls and fax service at Romblon Tel in Roxas St.
If calling in from outside Romblon you can only be connected via the numbers (02) 4122864 or (054) 4728218. On Romblon itself you have to add 507 to the number you are dialling.
Tourist Office: The ever-helpful Tourist Information Center, Tel (02) 4122864 (ext 2162), is located in the Provincial Capitol building in the east outskirts of town.

Getting Around

Boat: You can charter outriggers at the harbour wall after the bridge heading for the hospital.
Motorcycle: Bikes can be hired for P350 a day at the Palm Beach Resort in Lonos.

Tricycle: A journey in town costs P5 per person. A three to four-hour trip round the island by tricycle, including a visit to marble quarries and works, can be arranged for P400 (as the road surface can be bad, it would be better to have them dismantle the sidecar and only use the motorbike).

Getting There & Away

By Jeepney: After a ferry arrives, jeepneys leave from the pier for all of the larger communities on the island. Otherwise, they wait for passengers at the plaza.

By Boat: The coastguard, about 700m from the centre heading towards Lonos, has exact information on sailing services to and from Romblon.
Warning: During bad weather the crossing to the further-out islands of Banton, Sibuyan, Simara is not without its dangers!
Kalaayan Shipping Lines, Pier.
Destination: Lucena.
MBRS Lines, Pier.
Destinations: Manila, Masbate.
Shipshape Ferry, Pier.
Destinations: Batangas, Tablas Island.

Banton Island
Boat: From Banton to Romblon on Monday and Thursday with a big outrigger boat (P130; 3½ hrs). Departure from Romblon to Banton on Monday and Friday.

Sibuyan Island
Boat: From Ambulong/Magdiwang to Romblon daily at 8am with a big outrigger (P150; 2½ hrs). Departure from Romblon to Ambulong/Magdiwang at 1pm.

Simara Island
Boat: From Corcuera to Romblon on Monday, Wednesday, Friday and Sunday with a big outrigger boat (P100; two hrs). Departure from Romblon to Corcuera on the same days.

Tablas Island
Boat: A big outrigger leaves San Agustin daily at 8am and 1pm for Romblon (P65; one hr). Departure from Romblon to San Agustin at 8am and 1pm. The boat leaves when it's full, so it's better to be there an hour before scheduled departure.
From Odiongan to Romblon on Tuesday, Friday and Sunday at 2.30am with a Shipshape Ferry car ferry (2½ hrs). Departure from Romblon to Odiongan at 11am.

Agtongo

The little community of Agtongo is located in the north of Romblon Island, directly opposite the island of Alad. The waters there have been declared a fish sanctuary.

Getting There & Away

Boat: A Special Ride by outrigger from Romblon to Agtongo costs P150 and takes 20 min.

Lonos

The village of Lonos, about four km south-west of Romblon, is set back a little from the coast. It's 200m to the white sand of Bonbon Beach (admission: P20). Unfortunately, there is no shade on the beach and no accommodation. However, the resorts are happy to take their guests there by boat.

Places to Stay

Piyapi Resort. Cottage/fan/bath P300. Basic place next to the Palm Beach Garden Resort.
Palm Beach Garden Resort, Cellphone 0919-6437497, @. Cottage/fan/bath P300 and P350, cottage/ac/bath P500. Basic, acceptable cottages with

big veranda. Philippine and European cooking (best order the meal in the morning), motorbike rental, boat trips.
Tiamban Aqua Club, @. SR/DR/fan/bath P700. Reasonable rooms. Pleasant resort on a small bay with a white sand beach. Restaurant, boat trips. Reservations in Manila: Tel (02) 7236710, Fax (02) 7215566.
Diwata Resort. Closed in March 2004 for construction. They are building a prominent, massive, several-storey building with a roof terrace.

Getting There & Away
Tricycle: A tricycle from Romblon to Lonos costs P10 per person - a Special Ride should be available for P40.

Agnay

About eight km south-west of Romblon before Mapula, Agnay has a beautiful beach.

San Pedro

By far the two most comfortable and pleasant establishments in Romblon at the moment are snuggled into peaceful, absolutely idyllic bays two km south of Agnay, in San Pedro.

Places to Stay
Marble Beach Resort, Cellphone 0920-4324710. Cottage/bath P250 and P350. Every cottage has a terrace, a small garden and its own access to the sea. This is a very quiet place with a pleasant, secluded atmosphere, although it's beginning showing its age. Staff will cook for guests on request. Diving (also courses). Located about 1½ km from the ring road.
San Pedro Beach Resort, Cellphone 0920-9055780, @. Cottage/fan/bath P300. Peaceful, very well looked after place with immaculate cottages, their own beach, and greenery all round. To be recommended; good value for money. Restaurant. Located on the way to the Marble Beach Resort, this has to be the best resort on this stretch of the coast.

Getting There & Away
Tricycle: A Special Ride by tricycle from Romblon to San Pedro costs P120 to P150.

Tambac

Tambac is in the mountains in the south-east of Romblon and is home to a pleasant, refreshingly cool resort.

Places to Stay
Buena Suerte Resort. Cottage/fan/bath P300 to P1000. Older cottages with various different furnishings and loads of room between them. Kitchen and barbecue facilities are available, but they will cook for guests on request. Big swimming pool (P50 for non-residents). Enquiries in Romblon handled by Roberto Riano, Cellphone 0921-2141042.

Cobrador Island

Cobrador is a beautiful little island north-west of Romblon. It has a wonderful, palm-lined white beach and a 250m high mountain inland. The water is crystal clear and is great for snorkelling.

Getting There & Away
Boat: A Special Ride by outrigger from Romblon to Cobrador costs P400 (30 min).

Sibuyan Island

Sibuyan is wilder, more mountainous, forested and less explored than Tablas or Romblon, the other two main islands in the Romblon archipelago. This unspoiled island is dominated by the loom-

Mt Guiting-Guiting Natural Park

Mt Guiting-Guiting is 2058m high and right in the middle of the eponymous 15,265 hectare Natural Park. The mountain has a row of small, jagged peaks that look like a gigantic sawtooth, and the slopes are covered to a large extent in thick moss. The densely wooded park is notable for its biodiversity and several plant and animal species are even endemic, i.e. they can only be found on Sibuyan.

Anyone interested in climbing the mountain, which is possible all year round, weather permitting, should plan on taking at least two days. The Mt Guiting-Guiting Natural Park Visitors Center is about eight km inland from Magdiwang. Visitor Permits are issued here (P200) and they also provide information on the park and the 'Green Giant' of Sibuyan. A tricycle there costs between P80 and P100.

The forever-young Jürgen Seyd, who's German, lives halfway between Magdiwang and the harbour (ask the tricycle driver). Although he's now over 80, he still organises tours to Mayo's Peak and Mt Guiting-Guiting. You could also contact Vicky from the Corran Guesthouse who will gladly take care of transportation, tents, guide (P350 per day), porters and supplies.

ing Mt Guiting-Guiting. There are innumerable waterfalls, such as the Cataga and Lambigan Falls near Magdiwang, and the Kawa-Kawa Falls in Lumbang Este near Cajidiocan.

The coral reefs around the white sands of Cresta de Gallo Island just south of Sibuyan Island, are well known for the excellent diving they offer. There are also promising diving areas in the many reefs in the Sibuyan Sea between the islands of Sibuyan and Masbate.

Getting There & Away

Romblon Island

Boat: A big outrigger leaves Romblon daily at 1pm for Ambulang/Magdiwang (P150; 2½ hrs). Departure from Ambulang/Magdiwang to Romblon at 8am.

Magdiwang

Magdiwang is a clean little town on the north coast of Sibuyan Island, the best starting-off point for climbing Mt Guiting-Guiting. The natural pool with crystal-clear water at nearby Lambigan Falls is ideal for a refreshing dip.

Places to Stay

Bridge Lodge, National Highway. Dorm/fan P50, SR/DR/fan P100/200. Very basic, but clean, accommodation at the bridge near the market. Small restaurant.

Corran Guesthouse (better known as *Vicky's Place*). SR/DR/fan P150/300. Basic, clean accommodation next to the elementary school on the way into town coming from the harbour. Vicky the owner is very friendly and is a mine of information on the island's sights. Pleasant garden restaurant with excellent cooking (food to be ordered beforehand).

You can also spend the night in private accommodation in the building shared with Bayantel (round the corner from the market). Clean rooms for up to four people cost P300. Enquire in the hardware store next to Bayantel.

Getting Around

You can hire private jeepneys and motorcycles (P400/day). Ask Vicky from the Corran Guesthouse for information.

Getting There & Away

By Boat: Magdiwang harbour is in barangay Ambulong, about three km from the town centre. After a boat arrives, jeepneys leave from the pier for all larger towns on the island. A tricycle to town costs P10 per person; a Special Ride P30.

Taclobo

Taclobo, on the south-west coast of Sibuyan Island, is a good starting point for trips into the hilly jungles of the interior, such as the wild Cantingas River valley. About 15 minutes outside of Taclobo (take the main road and follow the sign for 'Christ in the Mountain') the little Lagting Falls provide a natural pool where you can cool down in the water.

San Fernando

San Fernando, like Taclobo, is a good base for exploring the interior, for example up the Cantingas River to Mt Guiting-Guiting. You can also make trips from there to the little island of Cresta de Gallo (day trip about P2000; ask at the Seabreeze Inn).

Places to Stay

Seabreeze Inn. SR/DR/fan P200/400, SR/DR/ac/bath P500. Basic, but pleasant, cosy rooms. Guests can use the kitchen. Friendly, family-style accommodation on a pebble beach on the outskirts of the town. Restaurant.

Cantingas River Resort. SR/DR/fan/bath P300. Three not very inviting rooms in the main building, but two new cottages are planned. An older resort on the river of the same name about six km northwest of San Fernando; one km inland from the main road.

Places to Eat

The Filipino food in the ***Starbox Restaurant*** at the market is good value, as it is in the pleasant ***Seabreeze Café*** where you can also enjoy international dishes with a sea view.

Miscellaneous

Online: Internet access in the RCPI Office on the plaza; P95 per hr. Phone also available.

Cresta de Gallo Island

About 15 km south-east of the little village of Azagra in the deep south of Sibuyan there's an unpopulated little island offshore called Cresta de Gallo ('rooster comb'). It has two hills, a white sand beach and excellent snorkelling and diving areas. Anyone wanting to spend the day on the island should take supplies (water) and protection from the sun with them. The best way to get there is from San Fernando or Cajidiocan, which takes 1½ hrs.

Cajidiocan

Big outriggers make the trip from Cajidiocan (pronounced: Kahijockan), on the east coast of Sibuyan, to Masbate. The trip isn't without its perils during windy weather as the waves can get quite high. Big boats sail to Dumaguit/Kalibo on Panay and Manila.

The Marble House arranges day trips to Cresto de Gallo Island (P2500 to P3500).

Places to Stay

Marble House, Magsaysay St, Cellphone 0920-8972103. SR/DR/fan P200/400. Acceptable rooms. Food can be prepared for guests on request.

Laura's Store, Cambijang (three km south of Cajidiocan), Cottage/fan P400. Duplex cottage with shared bathroom and small kitchen. Restaurant.

Places to Eat

The good-value ***JP's Restaurant***, Magsaysay St next to the Marble House, can be recommended for its tasty Philippine and European cooking. ***Laura's Store*** in Cambijan serves Philippine food and also a few European dishes; if you order in advance they'll cook something a bit more substantial. This is where the expat community, mostly Germans, hang out.

Miscellaneous

Online: Internet access in the RCPI Office on the main road near the Marble House; P95 per hr. They also have a phone.

Getting There & Away

Jeepney: There are only two jeepneys that make the trip from Magdiwang to Cajidiocan every day (two hrs).

Tablas Island

Tablas is the largest island in the Romblon archipelago. A tree-covered chain of mountains stretches across the north and the east of the island, reaching up to 600m on occasion. In contrast, the south is flat, as is the west coast with its many bays where most of the villages and small towns can be found.

Getting There & Away

Romblon Island

Boat: Large outriggers leave Romblon town daily at 8am and 1pm for San Agustin (P65; one hr).
From Romblon town to Odiongan on Tuesday, Friday and Sunday at 11am with a Shipshape Ferry car ferry (2½ hrs).

San Agustin

San Agustin is a pleasant little town and has a wharf for boats to and from Batangas (Luzon) and Romblon town. You can also take a day trip to the Bitu Falls near Dabdaban and the Cajbo-aya Ruins.

In Binonga-an, about three km south of San Agustin, there's a pebbly beach (tricycle P10 per person).

Places to Stay

August Inn, Faigao St, Cellphone 0919-5922495. SR/DR/fan P150/300, SR/DR/fan/bath P350. Very good rooms for the money. Friendly place to stay.
Kamilla Lodge, Faigao St, Cellphone 0920-8450467. SR/fan P150, SR/DR/fan/bath P250, SR/DR/ac/bath P450. Fairly good rooms. Pleasant accommodation on the plaza near the pier.

Places to Eat

Lyn's Snack House & Restaurant is a popular place in Morales St at the market, which serves inexpensive Filipino food.

Getting There & Away

Looc

Jeepney: Several jeepneys run from Looc to San Agustin daily (2½ hrs).

Romblon Island

Boat: Large outriggers go daily from Romblon town to San Agustin on Tablas Island at 8am and 1pm (P65; one hr). Departure from San Agustin for Romblon town at 8am and 1pm.

Calatrava & San Andres

Near Calatrava, in Kabibitan, you will find Tinagong Dagat, the 'hidden lake', where the water is salty, apparently due to being connected to the ocean somehow. Not far away there is another, slightly smaller lake with the same properties. A track runs from San Andres (Despujols) to the high Mablaran Falls.

Odiongan

From Odiongan (pronounced: Ojonggan) there are shipping services to Manila and Batangas on Luzon, Caticlan (Boracay) on Panay and Roxas on Mindoro. Only large outriggers run to Mindoro.

Places to Stay

Shellborne Hotel, Zamora St corner Magsaysay St, Tel 5675029. SR/DR/fan P150/300, SR/DR/fan/bath P200/400, SR/DR/ac/bath P500/750. Modest accommodation at the market. Coffee shop.
Poctoy Beach Resort, Tel 5675386. SR/DR/fan P150/300, SR/DR/ac/bath P600 to P800, depending on size (with TV). Good rooms. Restaurant. Quiet location on an uninviting beach, about 1½ km from the town centre on the way to the pier.
Haliwood Inn, Laurel St, Tel 5675292. SR/DR/fan P500, SR/DR/ac/bath P935 (with TV). Good hotel in a quiet location with comfortable rooms. Restaurant.
Odiongan Plaza Lodge, Rizal St, Tel 5675760. SR/DR/ac/bath P1000 and P1500 (three people). Well-kept, spacious rooms. Located at the plaza, over Lyn's Snack Bar.

Places to Eat

There are several small, basic restaurants at the plaza that serve Filipno food, including the aircon ***Lyn's Snack Bar.*** The ***Haliwood Inn Restaurant*** in the hotel of the same name serves Philippine and Chinese food in a pleasant ambience at good prices.

Miscellaneous

Money: The Philippine National Bank, Laurel St at the corner of Formilleza St, changes travellers' cheques.
Online: There's an internet café at the plaza.
Population: 35,000.
Post & Telephone: You can make long-distance phone calls at Bayantel, Zamora St, and PLDT, Laurel St corner Formilleza St.
Post code: 5501. Area code: 042.

Getting Around

Car: The retired police chief Didimo E. Javillo, Fabriag Apts, Barangay Ligaya, has a van for hire with driver at P2500 per day.

Getting There & Away

By Boat: Odiongan's little harbour is three km from the town. A tricycle costs P5 per person; special ride P40.

Romblon Island
Boat: From Romblon town to Odiongan on Tuesday, Friday and Sunday at 11am with a Shipshape Ferry car ferry (2½ hrs).

San Agustin
Jeepney/Bus: Several jeepneys run from the San Agustin wharf to Odiongan daily, via Calatrava and San Andres, taking two hrs. Minibuses also take this route.

Looc

The small port of Looc is located in the south-west of Tablas on the northern shore of Looc Bay. There are boat routes from there to many places, including Boracay. The town has set up a local tourist office at the plaza that is also responsible for the Looc Bay Marine Refuge and Sanctuary, which was established in 1999 (a snorkelling tour costs P50 per person).

Places to Stay

Marduke Hotel, Martinez Arcade. SR/DR/fan/bath P300, SR/DR/ac/bath P400/500. Friendly little hotel with fairly good rooms. Near the plaza (behind the Koop Drug Store; entrance at the back).
Hotel Napoleon, Proviner St corner Bonifacio St, Tel 5094143. SR/DR/fan/bath P350, SR/DR/ac/bath P500 and P800 (four beds). Relatively quiet hotel with reasonable rooms.
Roda Beach Resort, Kawat, Camandag. Cottage/fan/bath P300, cottage/ac/bath

P500 and P600. Reasonable cottages on a sandy beach three km north-west of Looc (tricycle P50). Restaurant.

Places to Eat

The aircon ***Pacific Garden Restaurant*** at the plaza serves good, inexpensive Philippine and Chinese food. ***Robert's Bar*** (karaoke) has a pleasant garden and is a popular meeting place in the evening.

Getting There & Away

Jeepney: Several jeepneys run from Odiongan to Looc daily (two hrs).

Santa Fe

One outrigger makes the trip daily from Santa Fe in the south of Tablas to Caticlan on Panay, via Carabao and Boracay islands (two hrs). The fare to Boracay is P100/150 per person (Filipinos/foreigners).

Places to Stay

Mely Asis Lodging House. SR/DR/fan P100. Rooms are all different, some with bath. Very basic accommodation at the front. Restaurant.

Getting There & Away

Jeepney: There are several jeepneys daily from Looc to Santa Fe. They leave from the plaza and take 1½ hrs.

Tugdan

Tablas Island airport is in Tugdan. Seair has had a flight service to and from Manila since March 2004.

Puro Island

This hilly little island lies off the south coast of Tablas. It's sparsely populated and an ideal place for people looking for peace and quiet who don't consider it boring to spend a day on a tropical island where nothing happens.

Places to Stay

Puro Island Resort. Cottage/bath P250, reduced to P200 for more than three nights stay. A quiet little place with three pleasant, roomy cottages under palms on a white beach in a sheltered, crescent bay on the east coast of the island. Guests have to feed themselves; an adequate kitchen is available. You can do your shopping in Guinbirayan on Tablas Island.

Getting There & Away

Boat: The crossing from Guinbirayan only takes a few minutes. Ask for Edison at the pier, he'll take you over for P50. Jeepneys go to Guinbirayan from Santa Fe and Tugdan.

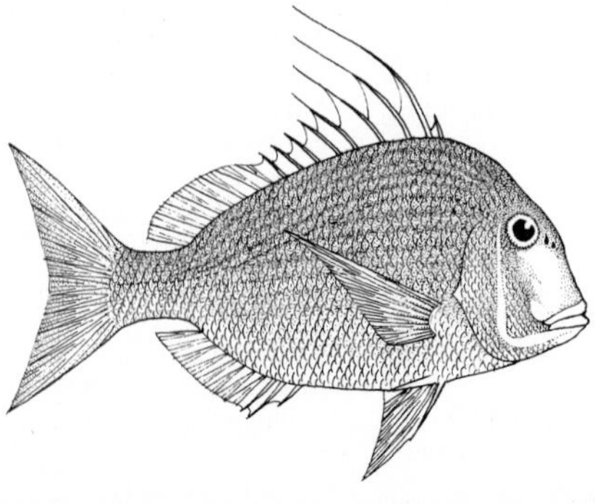

Visayas

South of the island of Luzon, north of Mindanao and east of Palawan is the main island group of the Philippines, the Visayas. The major islands in this group are Bohol, Cebu, Guimaras, Leyte, Negros, Panay, Samar and Siquijor, and there are countless little islands scattered between them. The Visayas offer by far the best possibilities for island hopping in the Philippines. Observant travellers will notice the way the islands differ from each other, whether it be in their topography, state of economic development, nature of the locals or even in the design of the tricycles.

Island Hopping

Suggested Route 1

A possible circuit of the Visayas could take you to most of the places of interest with minimal backtracking. Starting from Manila, you could travel down to the Bicol region and, from Matnog at the southern tip of Luzon, there are ferries every day across to Allen, at the northern end of Samar. The good road down the west coast of Samar provides a quick and relatively easy trip through Calbayog and Catbalogan across the bridge to Tacloban on the island of Leyte. This was where MacArthur returned in 1944 to free the country from the Japanese occupying forces. From Tacloban or Ormoc there are regular ships to Cebu City. You can also take one of the larger outrigger boats from San Isidro to Maya in the north of Cebu, from where boats leave for the little island of Malapascua. If you first want to get from Leyte to Bohol, however, best take a boat from Maasin or Bato to Ubay.

Bohol's main attraction are the Chocolate Hills; a popular destination is also the little island of Panglao, which is just offshore from the capital, Tagbilaran. Ships travel daily from Tagbilaran to Cebu City, the third largest city in the Philippines and the centre of the Visayas.

Cebu was where Magellan arrived in the Philippines, and you can still find a number of reminders of the Spanish period. From Cebu City there are connections by air and sea to nearly all of the important places in the country, including Caticlan (for Boracay) on Panay and Puerto Princesa on Palawan.

Several small ferries make the trip every day between Toledo on the west coast of Cebu and San Carlos on the east coast of Negros. Buses from San Carlos take the route along the coast north to Bacolod, where ferries leave for Iloilo City on Panay. The bus trip from Iloilo City via Kalibo to Caticlan only takes a few hours, and in just another half an hour from there you're on Boracay.

Suggested Route 2

If, however, you're looking for something a shade more adventurous yet still easy to manage, the following trip through the Visayas will fit the bill. Starting off in Manila, take a bus heading south to Batangas or Lucena, from where boats leave more or less regularly for Romblon on Romblon Island. Although this island is well known for its marble and does boast a few beautiful beaches, travellers are still fairly thin on the ground. Boats leave from Romblon daily for the adjacent island of Tablas and on from there to the popular little island of Boracay. (If you are in a hurry and want to avoid some of the hassles of travel, you can fly direct from Manila to Caticlan and cross over from there by outrigger to Boracay.)

After a few lazy days on the beach you can carry on by bus right across Panay to Iloilo City and from there take the ferry to Bacolod on Negros, the sugar island of the Philippines. Take a bus or jeepney to Cadiz, a small harbour town on the north coast of Negros and from there a boat to Bantayan Island, which is already in Cebu Province. This friendly island in the centre of the Visayas can best be explored by bicycle. The ferry from Santa Fe to Hagnaya on Cebu is met on arrival by a bus or jeepney which will take you to Maya, the most northerly settlement on Cebu Island. From there, outrigger boats will take you to the offshore island of Malapascua. If you find Boracay a bit too overrun with tourists, you'll feel at home on this beautiful little island. You could also charter an outrigger to take you directly from Bantayan to Malapascua.

Next stop is the island of Leyte. From San Isidro in the north-west you can carry on in two or three stages by bus via Ormoc and Baybay along the scenic coastal route south to Bato or Maasin, where a boat will take you to Bohol. After you've visited the bizarre Chocolate Hills, the smaller islands of Cabilao, Balicasag and Panglao west of Bohol are good for a few days relaxation. From Cabilao Island you can have yourself taken over to Argao on the south-east coast of Cebu and take a bus from there to Bato, where several ferries leave daily for the big island of Negros. The pleasant provincial capital of Dumaguete is a departure point for trips over to Siquijor Island where, according to many Filipinos, witchcraft flourishes. If you can drag yourself away from the magic of the island, it is possible (seven days a week) to take a ferry to Cebu City via Dumaguete so you can fly from there to Palawan or make your way back to Manila. Alternatively, you could continue the trip from Dumaguete, eg to Mindanao or to Bacolod via Sipalay and from there get back to Manila.

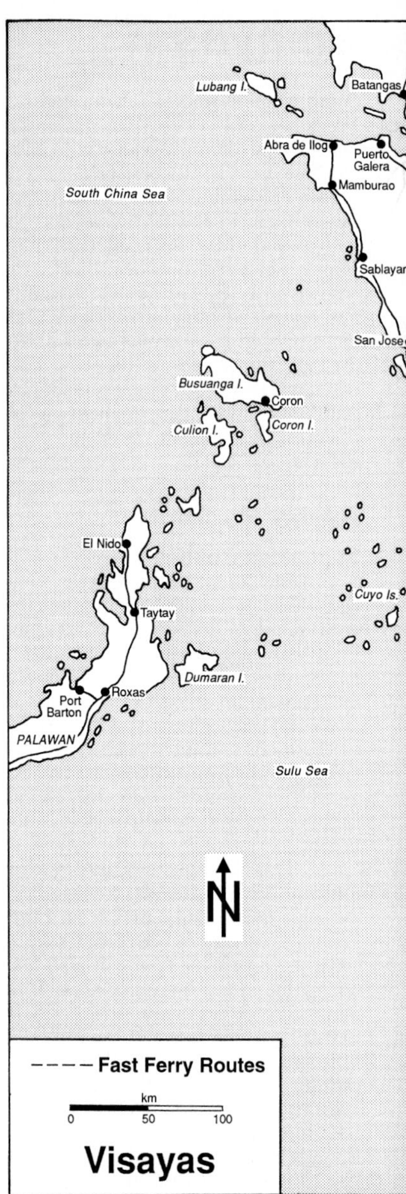

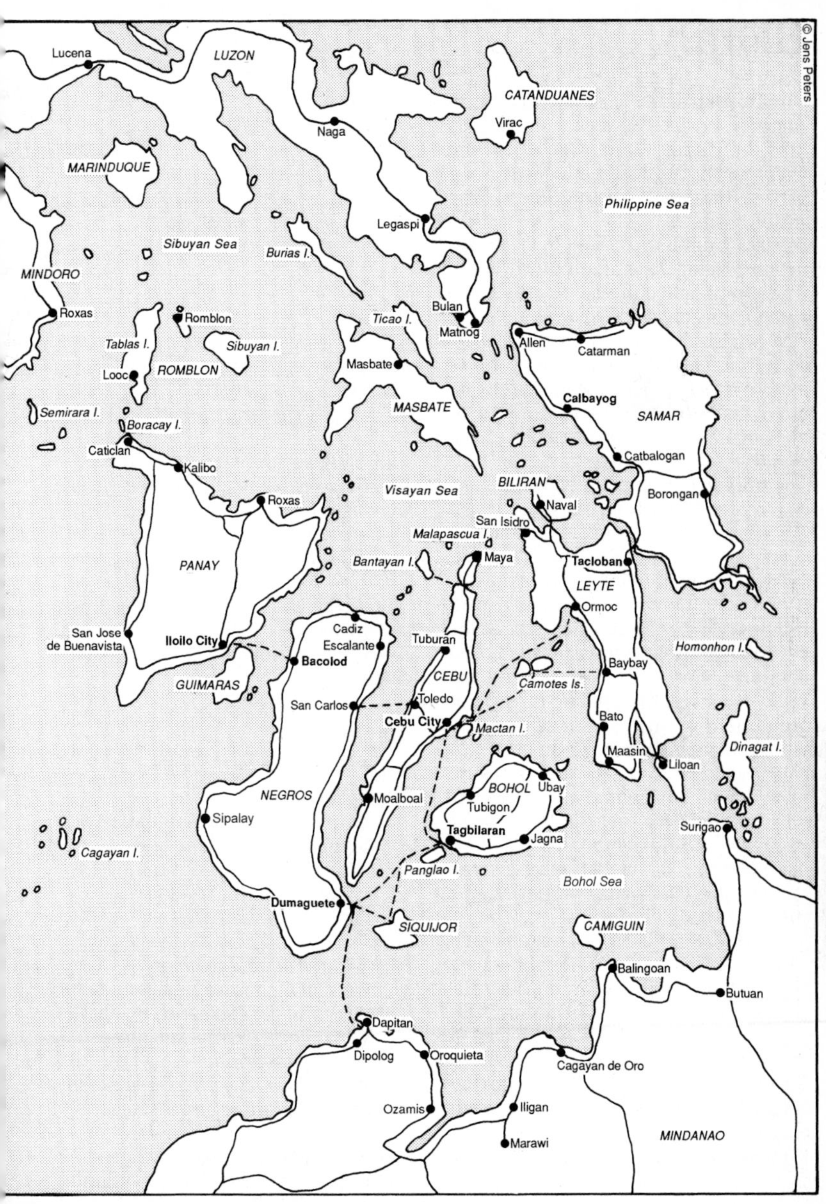
© Jens Peters
Lucena
LUZON
CATANDUANES
Virac
Naga
MARINDUQUE
Philippine Sea
Legaspi
Sibuyan Sea
Burias I.
MINDORO
Roxas
Romblon
Bulan
Ticao I.
Matnog
Tablas I.
Sibuyan I.
Allen
Catarman
Looc
ROMBLON
Masbate
Semirara I.
MASBATE
Calbayog
Boracay I.
SAMAR
Caticlan
Catbalogan
Kalibo
BILIRAN
Visayan Sea
Roxas
Naval
Borongan
San Isidro
Malapascua I.
PANAY
Bantayan I.
Maya
Tacloban
LEYTE
Ormoc
Cadiz
San Jose de Buenavista
Iloilo City
Escalante
Tuburan
Bacolod
Homonhon I.
CEBU
Baybay
GUIMARAS
Camotes Is.
Toledo
San Carlos
Cebu City
Mactan I.
Bato
Maasin
Dinagat I.
Liloan
BOHOL
Ubay
NEGROS
Moalboal
Tubigon
Sipalay
Tagbilaran
Jagna
Surigao
Cagayan I.
Panglao I.
Bohol Sea
Dumaguete
SIQUIJOR
CAMIGUIN
Balingoan
Butuan
Dapitan
Dipolog
Oroquieta
Cagayan de Oro
Ozamis
Iligan
MINDANAO
Marawi

Visayas

Biliran

Biliran Island lies just off the north coast of Leyte. Between both islands runs the Biliran Strait, only a few km wide, which is bridged at its narrowest part in the south, connecting Biliran with Leyte.

In 1992 Biliran succeeded in establishing itself as a separate political entity from its neighbour and has been an autonomous province since that date. It was a wise decision to go for this, as economic aid from Manila now flows directly and without deductions into the provincial coffers. This has proved to be a boon for the development of the island.

The provincial capital is Naval, a busy little harbour town on the west coast. All of the other larger towns on the island are also on the coast. They are connected by a bumpy coastal road which is only surfaced in parts as yet; it'll probably take another few years until the entire stretch is finished. The interior of this 32 km long and 18 km wide island is mountainous terrain, rough, densely overgrown and dotted with extinct volcanoes. Biliran is noticeably green, a pleasure for nature lovers, with an abundance of waterfalls, countless streams and several hot springs. Most of the rainfall takes place in December, but January also gets its fair share. According to statistics, the sun shines most in April.

In addition to a few small, uninhabited islands just off the coast, the somewhat more remote islands Maripipi and Higatangan also belong to Biliran province. There are regular boat services to them.

The locals live mainly from catching fish, but there is some agriculture, principally rice and vegetables. They have also specialised in producing coconut oil.

The language spoken here is Waray-Waray, except on the west coast, where Cebuano is spoken by the majority.

Getting There & Away

You can get to Biliran from Cebu, Leyte and Samar (see the Getting There & Away sections of the individual island chapters).

To Cebu

Boat

From Naval to Cebu City

Tuesday, Thursday and Sunday with MY Shipping (P200; nine hrs).

To Leyte

Bus

From Caibiran to Tacloban

There is a daily bus leaving early in the morning or in the forenoon (five hrs).

From Naval to Ormoc

JD buses leave daily at 5.30 and 8am, noon and 3pm (three hrs).

From Naval to Tacloban

There are about 10 buses belonging to

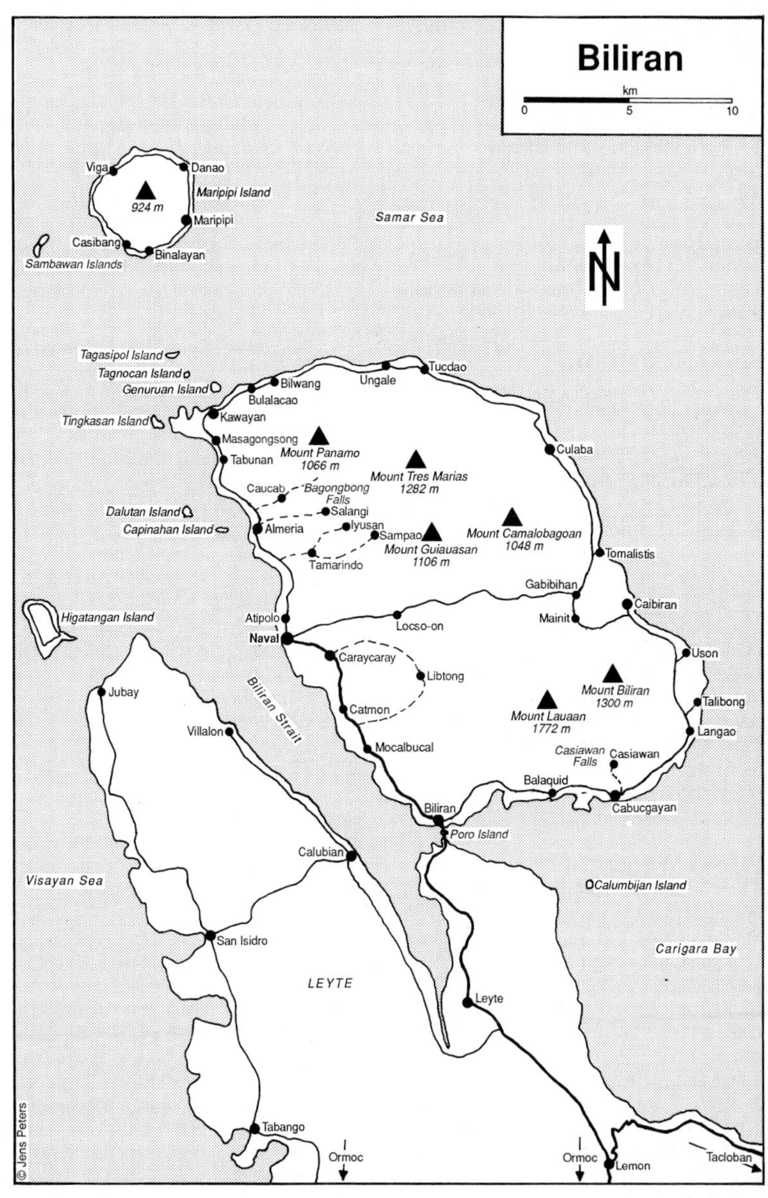
Biliran
km
0
5
10
Viga
Danao
924 m
Maripipi Island
Maripipi
Casibang
Binalayan
Sambawan Islands
Samar Sea
N
Tagasipol Island
Tagnocan Island
Genuruan Island
Tingkasan Island
Tucdao
Ungale
Bilwang
Bulalacao
Kawayan
Masagongsong
Mount Panamo
1066 m
Tabunan
Mount Tres Marias
1282 m
Culaba
Caucab
Bagongbong
Falls
Dalutan Island
Capinahan Island
Salangi
Almeria
Iyusan
Sampao
Mount Guiauasan
1106 m
Mount Camalobagoan
1048 m
Tamarindo
Tomalistis
Gabibihan
Caibiran
Mainit
Higatangan Island
Atipolo
Naval
Locso-on
Caraycaray
Libtong
Uson
Jubay
Biliran Strait
Catmon
Mount Biliran
1300 m
Mount Lauaan
1772 m
Talibong
Langao
Villalon
Mocalbucal
Casiawan
Falls
Casiawan
Balaquid
Cabucgayan
Biliran
Poro Island
Calubian
Calumbijan Island
Visayan Sea
San Isidro
Carigara Bay
LEYTE
Leyte
Tabango
Ormoc
Ormoc
Lemon
Tacloban
© Jens Peters

various companies leaving daily (three hrs).

Boat

From Naval to Calubian

An outrigger goes daily at 9am (one hr).

To Luzon

Bus/Boat

From Naval to Manila

Daily with Liberty Transport and Philtranco aircon buses (P970), taking 29 hrs including the ferry from Alegria/ San Isidro to Matnog.

To Samar

Boat

From Maripipi Island to Calbayog

Practically daily with big outriggers from Danao, Viga and Maripipi (three hrs).

Naval

Legend has it that Naval was founded in the early 18th century by Cebuanos. Later, settlers from Bohol, Negros and Panay joined them. This modest little town did not become provincial capital until 1992. Apart from various official buildings, there are a few shops, a hospital and a Philippine National Bank. There is a daily market at the jetty.

Places to Stay

There's only a handful of places in Naval offering accommodation with one exception in the basic category, most of them disappointing.

LM Lodge, Vicentillo St. SR/DR/fan P100/200, SR/DR/fan/bath P150/300. Expect real hospitality and a family atmosphere. The rooms are clean, and worth the money.

Rosevic Lodging House, Vicentillo St, Tel 5009377. SR/DR/fan P250, SR/DR/ac P350/400. Quiet rooms, although a bit pricey. There is a small inner courtyard, and they have a restaurant.

Brigida Inn, Castin St, Tel 5009379. SR/DR/fan/bath P350, SR/DR/ac/bath P450 (TV). Quite acceptable rooms. There is a small patio on the first floor.

Marvin Seaside Inn, Atipolo, Tel 5009171, Cellphone 0917-5286363. SR/DR/ac/bath P600. Good rooms in a well-kept, yellow building. Attractive day lounge. Nice garden. Swimming pool (on the other side of the road). All in all, a pleasant place on the beach about two km north of Naval.

Places to Eat

Naval has several inexpensive restaurants. The friendly ***Armelan's Coffee Shop***, about 100m into town from the jetty, offers Filipino food and a small selection of cakes. They are open until 8.30pm. The ***Marvin Seaside Inn Restaurant*** has good cooking, especially the seafood can be recommended.

Miscellaneous

Festival: Hudyaka Festival on 11 May.

Money: The Philippine National Bank, Caneja St corner Ballesteros St, will change travellers' cheques.

Population: 30,000.

Post & Telephone: Post code: 6543. Area code: 053

Getting There & Away

Bus: All buses from Tacloban to Kawayan and further to Tucdao and Culaba (and return) go via Naval.

Almeria

The place most travellers head for on Biliran is the small town of Almeria, about eight km north of Naval. To be more precise, the attraction is the Agta Beach Resort, not quite three km north of Almeria on a bay with a modest, but clean, palm-fringed beach. This is a pleasant place to relax for a few days. If it's swimming you're after, take a boat

over to nearby Dalutan Island with its white beach. Or you could always head for Masagongsong, two km north of Agta Beach, where a big swimming pool with fresh, cool spring water invites you to jump in.
Based in Almeria, you could make a few short trips into the interior. For example, to Bagongbong Waterfall about two hours north-east of Caucab on foot (admittedly a bit hard to find), or to the rice terraces at Iyusan, Salangi and Sampao.

Places to Stay

Agta Beach Resort, Cellphone 0916-3322117. SR/DR/fan P120/240, SR/DR/fan/bath P200/360, SR/DR/ac/bath P500. Quiet accommodation with basic rooms. You can eat well in their restaurant and the owner, Clemencio Sabitsana, will gladly try to meet any special orders. Paddleboats for hire cost P30 a day. The resort is popular with day visitors at the weekends.

Getting There & Away

Jeepney: Jeepneys from Naval to Kawayan in the north of the island, go through Almeria and pass the resort (20 min). There are only a few a day so you might have a long wait.

Bus: Several buses travel daily from Naval to Almeria heading for Kawayan, Tucdao or Culaba (30 min).

Cabucgayan

This dot on the map on the south coast of Biliran is the starting point for getting to the Casiawan Waterfall, perhaps the highest on the island. Set in a picturesque location, it is surrounded by rich, green vegetation and forms a natural pool. For P20 a motorcycle will take you as close as possible.
The name Cabucgayan is derived from bucgay, the word for the edible mussels which can be found on the river bank, and means 'a place where lots of bucgay mussels can be found'.

Caibiran

Caibiran is the largest town on the east coast. A climb up to the Biliran volcano can be arranged from there. The barrio captain will help organise the hire of a jeep up to the camp. It takes just over one hour from there to the summit.

Places to Stay

Felans Pension House. SR/DR/fan P300, SR/DR/ac P500. Friendly accommodation with pleasant rooms at a fair price.

Getting There & Away

Bus: A bus originating in Tacloban makes the journey daily from the town of Biliran along the south and east coasts via Cabucgayan and Caibigan to Caluba.
There is a daily jeepney connection between Naval and Caibiran, which goes straight across the island via Locso-on.

Higatangan Island

Apparently, the future President Marcos temporarily took refuge during WWII on this little island off the north-west tip of Leyte. That's why the highest point on the island (46m) is still called Marcos Hill to this day. Approaching Higatangan Island from Naval, the first thing you notice is a roughly 200m long, blindingly white sandbank, stretching out like a gigantic tongue from the little town of Mabini. Along the south coast you'll come across attractive little white stretches of sand tucked in between decorative, angular cliff faces.

Getting There & Away

Boat: Several outriggers travel daily from Naval to Mabini (45 min).

Maripipi Island

Once you have made it to Biliran Island, you should make a detour to Maripipi Island. There is no closer point of departure for there. Because of its relatively remote location, about eight km north-west of Biliran, this exceptionally beautiful island has so far not been affected very much by civilisation. There is no telephone, and only a few villages have electricity for a few hours in the evening. The hospitable inhabitants seem to be happy with their simple and caring way of life.

This exotic island is dominated by an extinct volcano that is almost 1000m high and partly covered by dense jungle. A narrow road circles around the island, connecting picturesque little villages - ideal hiking or cycling territory. Maripipi is less suitable for lazing around on the beach, as the coast is almost entirely rocky and offers few bathing opportunities. In the villages of Casibang and Binalayan on the south coast, the women make clay utensils, which are renowned for their good quality, to sell to other islands.

Getting There & Away

Danao

Boat: A big outrigger leaves at 10am Monday to Friday from Naval heading for Danao (two hrs). Departure time from Danao to Naval is 5am.

Viga

Boat: A big outrigger makes the trip from Naval to Viga, leaving daily except Sunday at 10am (three hrs).

Departure time from Viga to Naval is 2am. Because of the frequent stops, it may be 7am before it arrives in Naval.

Sambawan Islands

These two elongated, rocky islands lie close together to the west of Maripipi. The northern one turns into three even smaller islands at high tide. You can see the dazzlingly white coral beach from quite a distance away.

There are no palms and therefore no shade on the islands, so if you're going there for the day don't forget to take along means of protecting yourself from the sun.

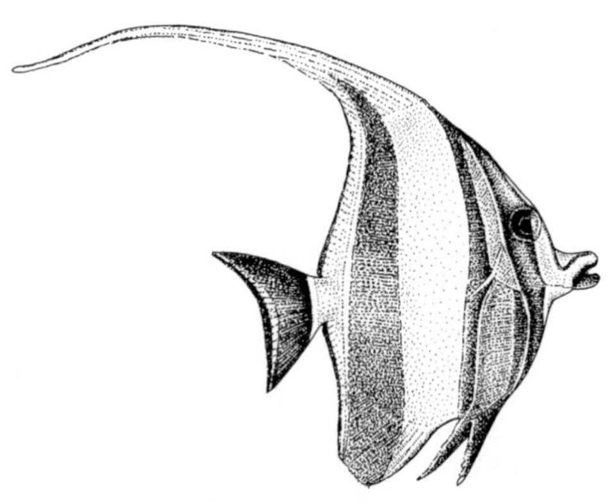

Bohol

Situated between Leyte and Cebu, in the south of the Visayas, Bohol is the 10th largest island of the Philippines. Its historical significance goes back to the blood compact between the Spanish conqueror Legaspi and the Boholano chieftain Sikatuna.

Today most visitors go to Bohol to see the Chocolate Hills: more than 1000 mysterious humps covering 50 square km on a plateau in the interior of the island. The Swiss author Erich von Däniken would have a field day with this strange hilly landscape and its as yet not fully explained origins.

Another 72 small islands belong to the province of the same name. Agriculture is the main source of income of the Boholanos. The main crop is coconut, but maize and rice are also grown. They even have small rice terraces near Lila, 25 km east of Tagbilaran. The Manila souvenir shops are well stocked with woven and plaited goods and basket ware from Bohol, but the prices are much lower in Tagbilaran and other places on Bohol itself. A start has recently been made on establishing facilities for tourism on this sophisticated, scenic island with its friendly inhabitants.

A few km north-east of Tagbilaran, near Corella, live the rare, extremely shy tarsier (*Tarsius syrichta*), the smallest primates in the world with their large, round eyes. These animals, which are found in the Philippines in Leyte, Samar and Mindanao in addition to Bohol, are scarcely larger than a rat. They belong to the prosimians and live mainly on lizards and insects, which they catch after nightfall.

Getting There & Away

You can get to Bohol from Cebu, Leyte, Luzon, Mindanao and Negros (see the Getting Away from Luzon section of the Manila chapter and the Getting There & Away sections of the individual island chapters).

To Cebu

Boat

From Catagbacon/Loon to Taloot/Argao

Tuesday to Saturday at 6am, 10am, and 2pm as well as Sunday and Monday at 9am and 1pm with a Lite Shipping Corporation car ferry (two hrs). Possibly several departures per day.

Tip for self-drive customers: The turn-off for the ferry jetty is to the north-east of Catagbacon. Coming from Tagbilaran, drive through the town, then keep an eye open for the fish ponds on the left. The first road between the fish ponds will take you to the jetty.

From Tagbilaran to Cebu City

Daily with the fast ferries *Oceanjet* (4x; P310) and *Supercat* (3x; P400), taking 1½ hrs.

Daily with Cokaliong Shipping Lines and Lite Shipping Corporation (P150; 3½ hrs).

Monday, Wednesday and Friday with Palacio Shipping Lines (P115; four hrs).
Sunday with Trans-Asia Shipping Lines (P145; four hrs).

From Tubigon to Cebu City
Five times daily with the fast ferry *Oceanjet* (P210; one hr).
Daily with Lite Shipping Corporation (2½ hrs).

To Leyte

Boat

From Ubay to Bato or Maasin
Daily between 9 and 10am with a big outrigger, taking three hrs to Bato (possibly via Lapinin Island which then takes four hrs), and four hrs to Maasin.

To Luzon

Air

From Tagbilaran to Manila
Asian Spirit and Philippine Airlines fly daily (P2950).

Boat

From Tagbilaran to Manila
Monday with Sulpicio Lines (P1095; 28 hrs).
Monday and Wednesday with WG & A (P1390; 26 hrs).
Tuesday and Saturday with Negros Navigation (P1390; 27 hrs).

To Mindanao

Boat

From Jagna to Butuan/Nasipit
Sunday with Cebu Ferries (P240; six hrs).
Thursday with Sulpicio Lines (seven hrs).

From Jagna to Cagayan de Oro
Wednesday and Sunday with Cebu Ferries (P280; five hrs).
Saturday with Sulpicio Lines (P290; eight hrs).

From Tagbilaran to Cagayan de Oro
Monday, Wednesday and Friday with Trans-Asia Shipping Lines (P400; eight hrs).
Saturday with Cebu Ferries (P390; eight hrs).

From Tagbilaran to Dipolog
Daily with the fast ferry *Supercat* (P700; six hrs); via Dumaguete/Negros.
Sunday with WG & A (P400; seven hrs).

To Negros

Boat

From Tagbilaran to Dumaguete
Daily with the fast ferries *Oceanjet* (P300) and *Supercat* (P430; 1½ hrs).
Wednesday with WG & A (P315; three hrs).

To Siquijor

Boat

From Tagbilaran to Larena
Daily with the fast ferries *Oceanjet* (P300; 1½ hrs) and *Supercat* (P565; 3½ hrs; via Dumaguete/Negros).
Monday, Wednesday and Saturday with Palacio Shipping Lines (P135; three hrs).

Tagbilaran

There are no special sights worth mentioning in Tagbilaran, the capital of Bohol Province on the south-west coast of Bohol. The best beach near the city is Kaingit Beach, behind the Hotel La Roca, but it's nothing to write home about. The main street is Carlos P Garcia Ave, or CPG Ave for short. During the day it is populated by a seemingly never-ending stream of noisy tricycles. Here you will find several hotels and restaurants as well as a good selection of shops.
A popular meeting place at sunset is the Jaycee Promenade at the K of C Pier (Knights of Columbus Pier).

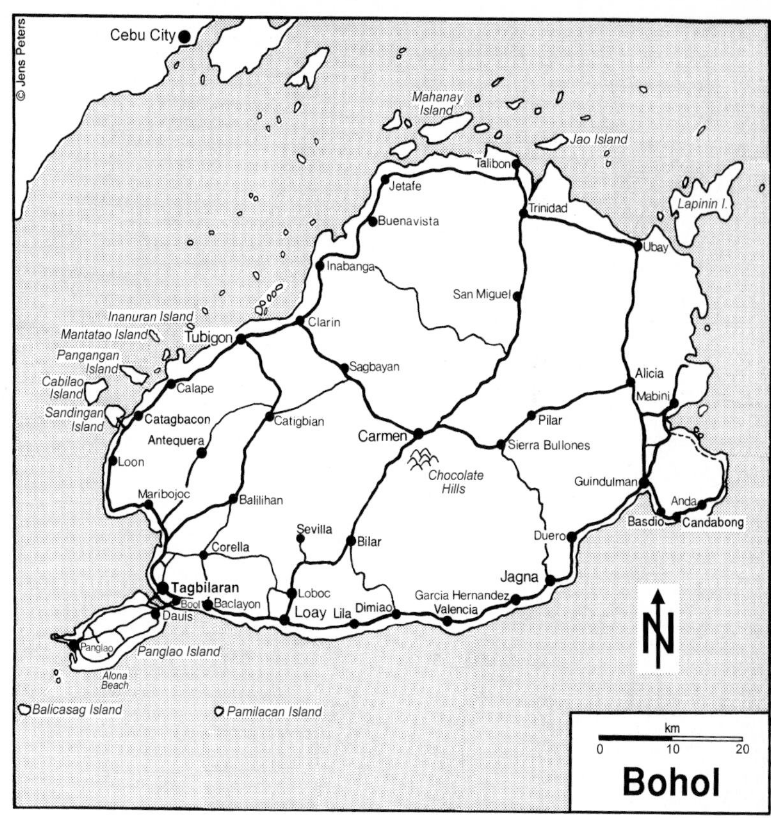

Some interesting trips are possible, eg from Tagbilaran to Panglao Island, or along the western and southern coasts of Bohol.

Museum

The little Bohol Museum in A Hontanosas St exhibits models and pictures of church facades and watchtowers on the island, objects found in caves such as pots and plates, as well as pottery, old money and stuffed birds and tarsiers. Open Mon-Fri 8am-noon and 1-5pm. Admission (donation) P10.

Shopping

Arts and crafts and local articles are available at the Torralba Market in Carlos P Garcia Ave. Bohol Products in VP Inting St also has a good selection of handicrafts. They are about one km outside of Tagbilaran between the two bridges over to Panglao Island (next to the Villa Alzhun Tourist Inn).

Places to Stay

LTS Lodge, Carlos P Garcia Ave, Tel 4113310. SR/DR/fan P100/160, SR/DR/ac P200/300, SR/ac/bath P300, DR/

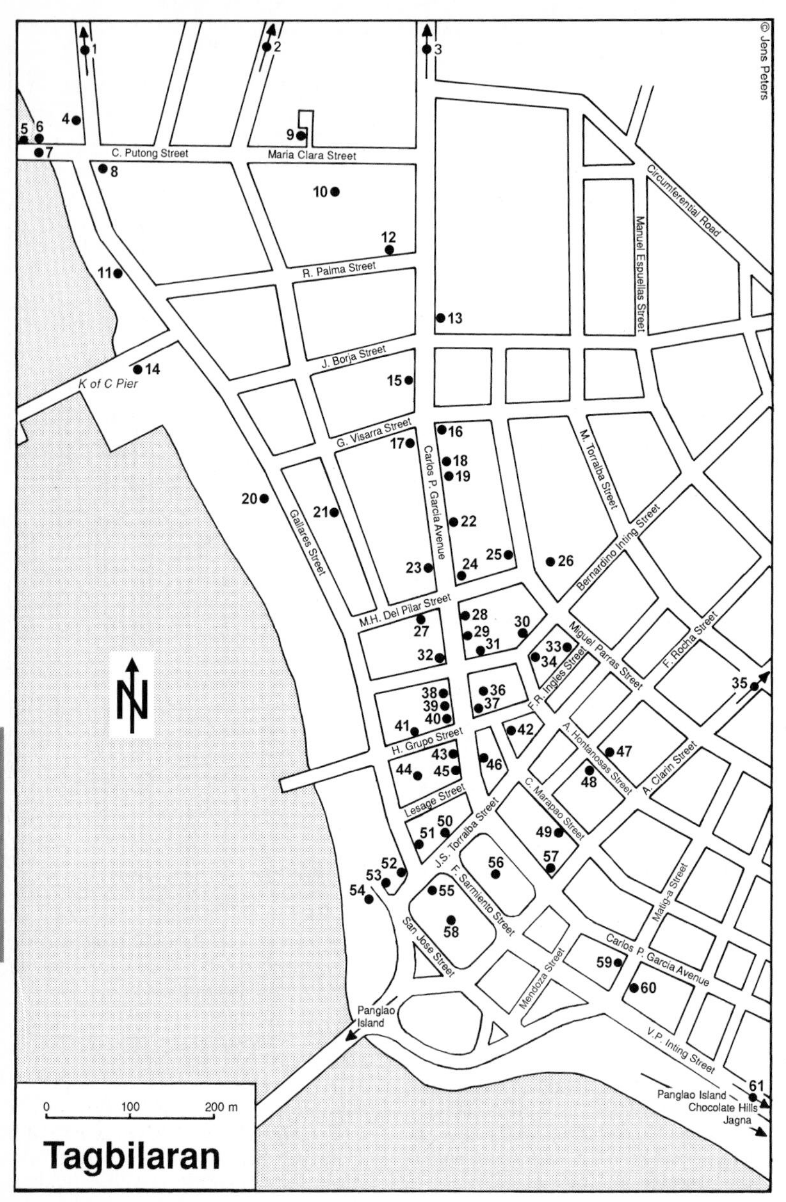
© Jens Peters
C. Putong Street
Maria Clara Street
Circumferential Road
Manuel Espuellas Street
R. Palma Street
J. Borja Street
K of C Pier
G. Visarra Street
M. Torralba Street
Carlos P. Garcia Avenue
Gallares Street
Bernardino Inting Street
M.H. Del Pilar Street
Miguel Parras Street
F. Rocha Street
F.R. Ingles Street
H. Grupo Street
A. Hontanosas Street
A. Clarin Street
Lesage Street
C. Marapao Street
J.S. Torralba Street
F. Sarmiento Street
Matig-a Street
San Jose Street
Carlos P. Garcia Avenue
Mendoza Street
Panglao Island
V.P. Inting Street
Panglao Island
Chocolate Hills
Jagna
0
100
200 m
Tagbilaran

Getting There & Away
3 Airport (700m)
7 Wharf
12 Trans-Asia Shipping Lines
21 Cebu Pacific
24 Caltex Petrol Station
33 Jeepneys to Dao Bus Terminal
35 Dao Bus Terminal (2 km)
38 Aboitiz Express
41 Sulpicio Lines
43 Negros Navigation
48 Buses to Panglao Island

Places to Stay
1 Bohol Tropics Resort Club (400m)
Hotel La Roca (450m)
Coralandia Resort (500m)
8 Everglory Lodge
9 Villa Camilla
11 Sea Breeze Inn
15 Wregent Plaza Hotel
19 Casa Juana Lodging House
21 Taver's Pension House
22 Metro Centre Hotel
25 The East Coast Tourist Inn
27 Gie Garden Hotel
28 LTS Lodge
33 Slim Pension House
45 Charisma Lodge
46 Nisa Travelers Inn
51 Chriscent Ville Pension House
60 Meridian Hotel
61 Villa Alzhun Tourist Inn (1 km)

Places to Eat
3 Rene's Swiss Restaurant (500m)
5 M-R Restaurant
6 Joving's by the Sea Restaurant
14 JJ's Seafood Village
17 Café Cielito
19 JJ's Dimsum & Restaurant
34 Greenwich
Jollibee
40 McDonald's
52 McJac on the Green
55 Garden Café
59 Payag Jo's Chicken Inato

Miscellaneous
2 Cogon Market (200m)
3 Governor's Mansion (200m)
Provincial Capitol (1 km)
Rene's Swiss Gourmet Shop (500m)
St Jude General Hospital (400m)
4 Tarsier Tours & Travel
10 University of Bohol (UB)
13 LBC
16 Bank of the Philippine Islands
18 Metrobank
20 Ramiro Hospital
23 Bohol Travel & Tours
26 Provincial Hospital
29 Metrobank
30 Alturas Department Store
31 Bombay Bazaar (Money Changer)
32 Mercury Drug
36 Tagbilaran City Public Market
37 City Tourist Office
39 Bohol Quality Superstore
42 Shopper's Mart
44 Divine Word College
46 Equitable PCI Bank
47 Bohol Museum
49 PLDT Philippine Long Distance Telephone Company
50 Torralba Market
53 Post Office
54 Police Station
56 Plaza
47 Philippine National Bank (PNB)
58 St Joseph Cathedral

ac/bath P450. Good value. Pleasant accommodation, some of the rooms are quite generous, those overlooking the street are a bit loud however. Good value. Coffee shop.

Nisa Travelers Inn, Carlos P Garcia Ave, Tel 4113731. SR/DR/fan P140/150, SR/DR/ac/bath P500. Basic, but reasonable for the money. Lounge, restaurant.

Villa Camilla, Maria Clara St, Tel 4114966. SR/DR/fan P175/250, SR/DR/ac P280/350, SR/DR/ac/bath P350/500 (with TV). Friendly guesthouse with clean rooms. Across from the University of Bohol.

Casa Juana Lodging House, Carlos P Garcia Ave, Tel 4113331. SR/fan/bath P180, SR/ac/bath P300, DR/ac/bath P375 and P525. Fairly basic, but good value rooms.

Gie Garden Hotel, MH del Pilar St, Tel 4113182. SR/DR/fan/bath P300, SR/ac/bath P490, DR/ac/bath P590. Older, little hotel. The rooms facing the inner courtyard are a lot quieter than those facing the street. Restaurant.

Coralandia Resort, Graham Ave, Tel 4113445. Cottage/fan/bath P375 and P650, cottage/ac/bath P525 and P725. Reasonable cottages with two or three rooms set in quite large grounds on the ocean. Their Veranda Carolina Restaurant serves good pulutan, eg calamares. Located at the northern edge of town near the airport.

The East Coast Tourist Inn, Miguel Parras St, Cellphone 0916-4161793. SR/ac/bath P520, DR/ac/bath P640. Small, clean rooms with TV up on the closet. Coffee shop.

Taver's Pension House, Remolador St, Tel 4114896, Fax 4114790, @. SR/ac/bath P600 and P800, DR/ac/bath P750 and P1000. Excellent rooms with TV, the more expensive ones also have a refrigerator. Good value. No restaurant, only room service.

Villa Alzhun Tourist Inn, VP Inting St, Tel 4113893, Fax 4114143, @. SR/DR/ac/bath P650 to P1500. Beautiful, well-maintained rooms with TV, the more expensive ones also have a refrigerator, balcony and sea view. Attractive building with a tastefully decorated lobby and a pleasant garden restaurant. Located about one km outside of Tagbilaran between the two bridges over to Panglao Island.

Chriscent Ville Pension House, Gallares St, Tel 4114029, Fax 4114028. SR/DR/ac/bath P650/750 to P950/1200. Pleasant accommodation with well-appointed rooms, all with TV, the expensive ones also have a refrigerator. Small restaurant.

Meridian Hotel, Matig-a St, Tel 4113060, Fax 2355793, @. SR/DR/ac/bath P750 to P1150. Appealing place with immaculate, friendly rooms with TV, the more expensive ones also with refrigerator. Restaurant, swimming pool.

Wregent Plaza Hotel, Carlos P Garcia Ave, Tel 4113144, @. SR/ac/bath P800 and P1000, DR/ac/bath P900 and P1200, suite P1400 to P2000. Good, attractive rooms with TV, the more expensive also have a refrigerator. Coffee shop. Free airport service.

Hotel La Roca, Graham Ave, Tel 4113797, Fax 4113009, @. SR/DR/ac/bath P840 to P1680. Older hotel with tidy, but acceptable rooms with TV. Restaurant, swimming pool. Located not far from the Coralandia Resort.

Bohol Tropics Resort, Graham Ave, Tel 4113510, Fax 4113019, @. SR/DR/ac/bath P1265 to P2200, suite P3850. With refrigerator and TV, the suites also have a jacuzzi. Very pleasant rooms in extensive grounds with cottages directly on the ocean. Restaurant, three swimming pools, tennis courts. Near the Hotel La Roca a little bit out of town to the north.

Metro Centre Hotel, Carlos P Garcia Ave, Tel 4112599, Fax 4115866, @. SR/DR/ac/bath P1250 to P1950, suites P4100 and P6100. Comfortable rooms with refrigerator and TV, the cheaper ones have no windows. The best hotel in town. Centrally located, restaurant, disco, swimming pool, fitness room, jacuzzi, sauna, car hire, airport service.

Places to Eat

The aircon ***Garden Café*** next to St Joseph's Cathedral, which is run by

mute, hearing-impaired people comes highly recommended. It's a two-storey restaurant with a wide selection of Philippine dishes, including breakfast, sandwiches, pizzas, cakes and ice cream - all of which are tasty and inexpensive. Across and down a bit, ***McJac on the Green*** is home to several little inexpensive but good restaurants with varied menus, which also goes for ***JJ's Dimsum & Restaurant*** in Carlos P Garcia Ave (next to the Metro Center Hotel) which has Chinese and Philippine food. The atmosphere is really pleasant at ***Payag Jo's Chicken Inato*** in Matig-a St where, predictably, excellent chicken dishes are served. European specialities and baked goods are available in ***Rene's Swiss Gourmet Shop & Restaurant*** in Carlos P Garcia North Ave next to the Calape Bank, not far from the airport.
Around the wharf you'll find some rustic, but good, seafood restaurants, eg the ***M-R Restaurant*** built on piles in the water. At K of C Pier on the other hand, ***JJ's Seafood Village*** is a bit more sophisticated, but the direct contact with the sea is missing.
For friends of fast food there's a ***McDonald's*** in Carlos P Garcia Ave across from the tourist office, and a ***Jollibee*** and a ***Greenwich*** in Bernardino Inting St corner A Hontanosas St.

Miscellaneous

Festivals: Tagbilaran City Festival on 1 May. Sandugo Festival in the third week in July.
Medical Services: The best hospital in town is the Ramiro Hospital, Gallares St, Tel 4113515.
Money: The money changers at the Bombay Electronics and Indian Bazaar in Bernardino Inting St offer good exchange rates for cash and travellers' cheques.
Equitable PCI Bank, Metrobank and Philippine National Bank, all in Carlos P Garcia Ave, have ATMs.
Online: Several Internet cafés in Carlos P Garcia Ave and the side streets going off it, eg in MH del Pilar St.
Population: 70,000.
Post & Telephone: The Post Office is in JS Torralba St. There's a small branch office in the BQ Complex on Carlos P Garcia Ave. The PLDT office in Noli Me Tangere St offers inexpensive fax and long distance phone facilities.
Post code: 6300. Area code: 038.
Tourist Office: City Tourist Office, Carlos P Garcia Ave, Tel 2355497. Open daily 8am-5pm.
Provincial Tourist Office, Provincial Capitol, Tel 4113666. Open Mon-Fri 8am-noon and 1-5pm.
Travel Agencies: Aboitiz Express, Carlos P Garcia Ave, Tel 4114906, are agents for Cebu Pacific and Western Union and also sell tickets for Cebu Ferries, WG & A and Supercat.
Bohol Travel & Tours, Carlos P Garcia Ave, Tel 4113840, Fax 4112984, will arrange Bohol tours and take care of ticket and visa formalities. Their office is one flight up.

Getting Around

Car: Nena's Car Rental Services, R. Palma St, Tel 4114080, rents cars with driver.
Tricycle: A journey within the city costs P5 per person.

Getting There & Away

By Air: The airport is at the northern edge of the city. A tricycle to the city centre costs about P5 to P10 and to Alona Beach P100 to P150. Private taxis will make the run to Alona Beach for between P200 and P250, even if they start off by asking for P400. Taxis with meters demand a 50% surcharge on trips to Panglao Island, making the fare about P250 in all.
Asian Spirit, Airport Office, Tel 4113615, 4115701.
Destination: Manila.

Cebu Pacific, Remolador Street, Tel. 2356215.
Destinations: Manila (from Cebu City and Dumaguete), Davao (from Cebu City).
Philippine Airlines, Metro Centre Hotel, Carlos P Garcia Ave, Tel 4113553.
- Tagbilaran Airport, Tel 4112232, 4114226.
Destination: Manila.

By Bus: Most of the transport on the island is taken care of by the St Jude Trans and Dory Lines. Their buses leave from the Dao Bus Terminal at the north-east edge of town, about two km from the centre. Get there with jeepneys from the Alturas Department Store.
JG Trans Company buses go to Panglao Island, leaving from the Panglao Bus Terminal in A Hontanosas St, across from the Bohol Museum.

By Boat: From the wharf to the city centre is only one km and costs P5 by tricycle.
Cebu Ferries, Aboitiz Express, Carlos P Garcia Ave, Tel 4114906.
Destination: Mindanao.
Cokaliong Shipping Lines, Pier, Tel 4114706, 4115242, 4113066.
Destination: Cebu.
Lite Shipping Corporation, Soledad St, Tel 4113079, 4112874.
Destination: Cebu (from Catagbacon/ Loon).
Negros Navigation, Carlos P Garcia Ave, Tel 4112645, 2355657.
Destination: Manila.
Ocean Fast Ferries, Starlite Terminal, Pier, Tel 2353562.
Destinations: Cebu, Negros, Siquijor.
Palacio Shipping Lines, Pier, Cellphone 0916-8213870.
Destinations: Cebu, Siquijor.
Sulpicio Lines, H Grupo St, Tel 4113079.
Destination: Manila.
Supercat Fast Ferry Corporation, Aboitiz Express, Carlos P Garcia Ave, Tel 4114906.
Destinations: Cebu, Negros.
Trans-Asia Shipping Lines, R Palma St, Tel 4113168, 4113234.
Destinations: Cebu, Mindanao.
WG & A, Aboitiz Express, Carlos P Garcia Ave, Tel 4114906.
Destinations: Manila, Mindanao.

Around Tagbilaran

There are some historical sights to the north and east of Tagbilaran. It's best to hire a car and do a round trip, possibly starting at Alona Beach on Panglao Island. There would also be time to include a detour to the Chocolate Hills. The following places can be reached by public transport from Tagbilaran.

Maribojoc

About 15 km north of Tagbilaran near Maribojoc stands the old Punta Cruz Watchtower, built in the time of the Spaniards in 1796 to look out for pirates. It gives a good view over other islands of the Visayas.

Loon

Loon, a few km north-west of Maribojoc, has a beautiful old church dating back to 1753. It has noteworthy ceiling frescoes. There is a daily connection by car ferry between Catagbacon/Loon and Taloot/Argao on Cebu (see Getting There & Away section earlier in this chapter).

Antequera

Various kinds of basketware are for sale on Sunday in the market at Antequera, about 10 km north-east of Maribojoc. Little more than a km out of town and situated in a forest you will find the beautiful Mag-Aso Falls with a deep natural pool to swim in. The last bus from Antequera to Tagbilaran departs at 3pm.

Corella

The woods around Corella are home to the rare, monkey-like tarsier, which is an endangered species. These tiny primates have extraordinary, immobile eyes and jump from branch to branch with an almost frog-like motion. Also known locally as *maomag*, they are nocturnal hunters and are seldom seen during the day. In Barrio Cancatac, about four km east of Corella, a few tarsier are being held for study purposes in a generously proportioned cage where they can move around freely. Visitors are welcome at this project, run by the Department of Environment and Natural Resources (DENR), although any sleeping animals should not be disturbed during the day. Donations are also welcome.

Bool

The monument at Bool, barely three km east of Tagbilaran, is a reminder of the blood compact between Legaspi and Sikatuna, who sealed their bond of friendship on 16 March 1565 by making a cut in their skin, letting the blood drip into a cup of wine and then emptying the cup together. At Bool there is also the Ilaw International Center, with its open-air restaurant, bar and disco. Big weddings are often held here on Saturdays.

Baclayon

About four km to the east of Bool is Baclayon, the oldest town in Bohol. It is the location of one of the oldest churches in the Philippines, the Parish Church of the Immaculate Conception, built in 1595. The small museum adjoining it is open Mon-Sat 9-11am and 2-4pm. Admission is P10.

There are a few inexpensive restaurants in the market, and boats go from Baclayon to Pamilacan Island, 13 km away.

Loay & Loboc

At Loay, where the Loboc River flows into the Mindanao Sea, there is an old church with an adjoining convent school which are worth seeing.

In Loboc itself it's worth going to see the large Loboc Church with its remarkable naive painting on the ceiling. The church was built in 1734 next to the first stone church at the site, built in 1602 and subsequently destroyed, which now houses a small museum (admission P20).

About one km north of Loboc the boat companies Sarimanok and Supercarp run a small jetty where you can take a chartered outrigger for an exciting river trip to a small waterfall (P300).

Places to Stay

Nuts Huts, Loboc, Tel (038) 5379008, @. Dorm P165, cottages P385 and P550. This is a row of basic cottages under palm trees on the bank of the Loboc River. Run by Belgians, it's an idyllic, peaceful place, perfect for nature lovers. The restaurant and reception are located above the grounds on the side of the mountain (beautiful view). Mountainbikes are available for rent at P330 per day. Herbal sauna (P100 for two people). Get there by outrigger from the jetty mentioned above (P50), or walk from the turn-off two km north of here, taking the 800m path until you come to the stairway which leads to the restaurant and cottages (277 steps in all).

Sevilla & Bilar

A few km north of Loboc, roughly between the turn-off to Sevilla and the small town of Bilar, the road leads through a dark mahogany forest, which was planted a few years ago by students. Near Sevilla a primitive hanging bridge spans the Loboc River. From this bridge you can jump into the water from a height of several metres.

Jagna

Jagna is a clean, busy little town about 60 km east of Tagbilaran. About three ships a week sail from here to various destinations in north Mindanao. Don't miss having a look at the old church, with its ceiling frescoes. Ilihan Hill, four km north from Jagna, can be reached by a winding road and is frequently a place of pilgrimage.

Getting There & Away

Chocolate Hills
Bus: There are buses from the Chocolate Hills area going to Jagna, leaving from Carmen, but no longer direct. You have to take the bus to Tagbilaran, get off in Loay and then wait for a bus or jeepney from Tagbilaran to Jagna.

Tagbilaran
Bus: Several St Jude Trans buses leave Tagbilaran daily for Jagna (two hrs).

Tubigon
Bus: There are several buses a day to Jagna via Talibon. They go along the coast instead of going through Carmen.

Anda

Anda is a clean, somewhat sleepy little community on a peninsula in the southeast of Bohol. Right on the doorstep there is a long, wide beach with white sand that strangers seldom happen onto. With three exceptions there is no commercial accommodation available, a situation that could change in the future considering the attractions of this coastline.
The picturesque scenery begins just outside Guindulman, where lonely bays with little white beaches and crystal-clear water tempt the visitor to stay. The ideal way to explore here is by boat, as the unsurfaced road which runs about 500m from the ocean has few paths offering access to the coast. One of these idyllic bays is Bugnao Beach near Candabong, which has little stretches of white sand sectioned off by rocky cliffs eaten away at their bases by the sea.

Places to Stay

Dapdap Beach Resort, Candabong, Tel 5282011, @. Cottage/fan/bath P400 to P600, cottage/ac/bath P1500. An older, friendly, quiet little place with cottages of various sizes and a handful of picnic huts. About three km west of Anda.
Bituon Beach Resort, Basdio, @. Cottage/fan/bath P1850 per person; including three meals. This family-style establishment has attractive bungalows just up some steps from a little beach. Under German-Philippine management, they have diving facilities here, as well as boat trips. Restaurant. Located five km west of Anda.
Cocowhite Beach Resort, Basdio, Cellphone 0919-3331215, @. Cottage/ac/bath P3950 (one person) and P5150 (two people); including three meals. Well-equipped cottages of various sizes with a beautiful sea view. Swiss-Filipino run, on a cliff top overlooking a little bay with a sandy beach. Restaurant. Diving.

Miscellaneous

Post & Telephone: Post code: 6311. Area code: 038.

Getting There & Away

Jeepney: There are only a few jeepneys that go from Jagna to Anda, taking

1½ hrs for the 40-km trip. The last trip back to Jagna is at about 5pm. A Special Ride costs about P250 one way. Coming from Tagbilaran, instead of stopping at Jagna, you can carry on in the direction of Ubay, get out at Guindulman and take a tricycle from there (P100).

Panglao Island

Several beach resorts have been opened in the last few years on Panglao Island. There are two bridges you can use to cross over to the island from Bohol. The older bridge is near Tagbilaran City Hall. The newer one is almost two km south-east of Tagbilaran and connects the district of Bool on Bohol with Dauis on Panglao.

The lake in Hinagdanan Cave at Bingag on the north-east of the island has refreshingly cool water. However, as all kinds of disease-spreading bacteria thrive in still waters, it is best to do without that tempting swim. For a few coins the caretaker will switch on the light in the cave. Admission P10.

The white sand Alona Beach is the most beautiful, most popular and the most developed beach on the island in terms of tourism. Spread along the beach for about one km there are small, individually designed resorts, cosy restaurants, rough-and-ready beach bars, and several dive shops. The bathing is unfortunately hampered a bit by knee deep sea grass. It is inhabited by sea urchins, so you can't go in for more than a few metres without having to be careful. Still, this beach is good for snorkelling if you swim out to about 100m from the shore and especially (with a bit of luck) for watching sea snakes. There are several places to stay at Alona Beach in different price categories.

Situated on a beautiful part of Dumaloan Beach, about two km east of Alona

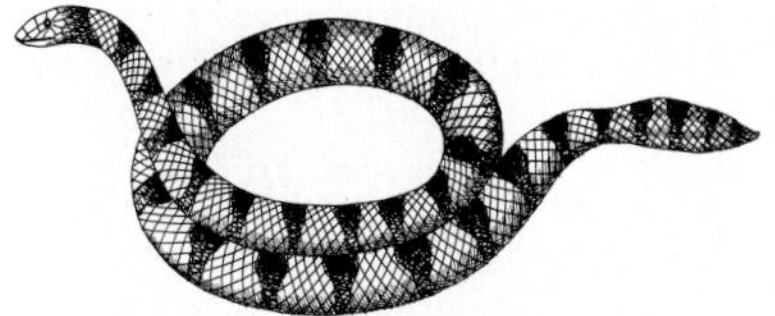

Sea Snakes
It is safe to assume all of the sea snakes *(walo walo)* in the Philippines are poisonous. Fortunately, they are seldom aggressive and only have a tiny mouth. These reptiles, with their richly-patterned skin and paddle-like tail, apparently like to congregate at certain times of year around the Cervera Shoal, between Panglao Island and Pamilacan Island.

Beach, the exclusive Bohol Beach Club is open for business. Just under three km west of Alona Beach you'll find the peaceful, broad, gently sloping Danao Beach.

Doljo Beach is also good, although the water there is pretty shallow; however, it's largely clear of sea grass. From there you can have someone take you over to Pungtud Island in Panglao Bay (30 min).

Places to Stay

Alona Beach

Casa-Nova Beach, Tel 5029189. SR/DR/fan/bath P300. Four basic rooms directly on the beach.

Alonaville Beach Resort. SR/DR/fan P300, cottage/fan/bath P500. Basic accommodation. Pleasant place with loads of older, little cottages. The resort restaurant has a good view of the beach and the sea. They also have motorcycles for hire.

Playa Blanca, Tel 5029015. SR/DR/fan P300 and P400, cottage/fan/bath P500 to P800. Only a few rooms and cottages have survived the fire here in November 2002.

Alonaland, Tel 5029007. Cottage/fan/bath P300 and P800, cottage/ac/bath P1200. Nice place with good cottages

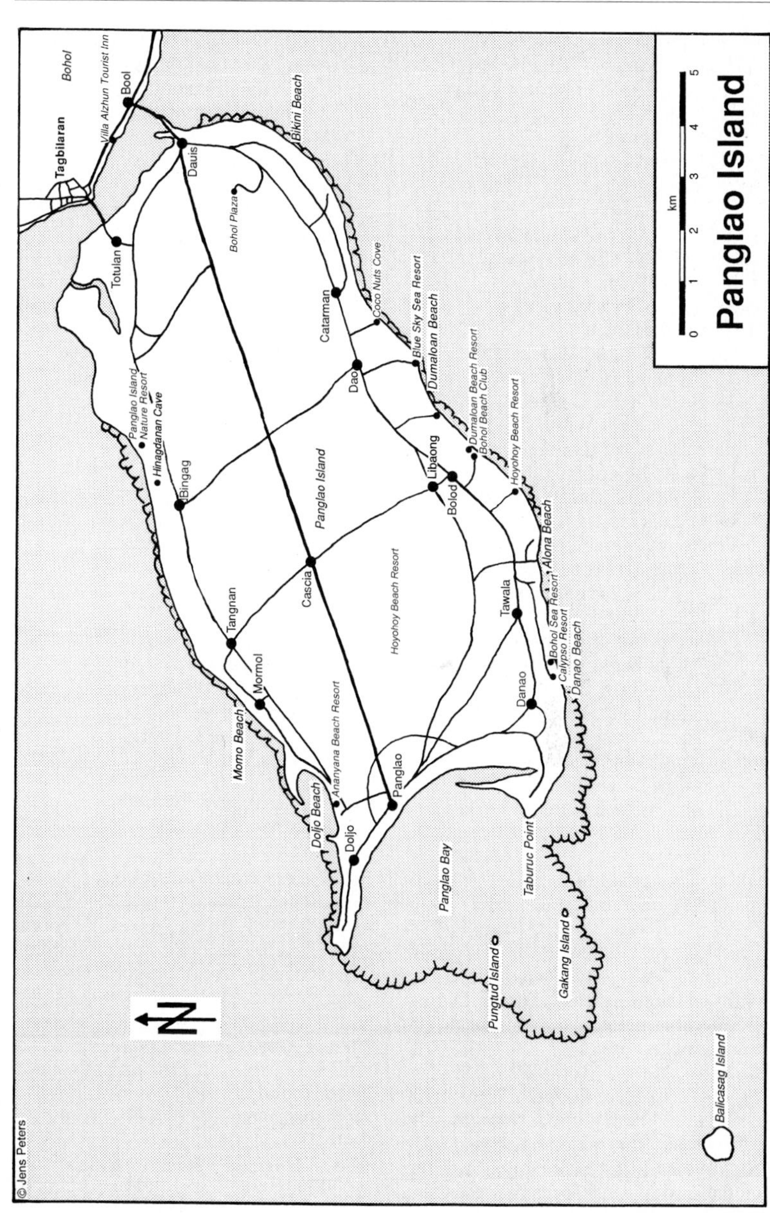
Panglao Island
km
0
1
2
3
4
5
Tagbilaran
Bohol
Villa Alzhun Tourist Inn
Bool
Dauis
Totulan
Bikini Beach
Bohol Plaza
Catarman
Coco Nuts Cove
Blue Sky Sea Resort
Dumaloan Beach
Dao
Dumaloan Beach Resort
Bohol Beach Club
Hoyohoy Beach Resort
Libaong
Bolod
Alona Beach
Panglao Island
Nature Resort
Hinagdanan Cave
Bingag
Panglao Island
Hoyohoy Beach Resort
Cascia
Tangnan
Tawala
Bohol Sea Resort
Calypso Resort
Danao Beach
Mormol
Danao
Momo Beach
Ananyana Beach Resort
Panglao
Doljo Beach
Doljo
Taburuc Point
Panglao Bay
Gakang Island
Pungtud Island
Balicasag Island
© Jens Peters

Places to Stay
1 Alona Secret Garden Resort
2 Rene's Place
3 Sun Apartelle
4 Flower Garden Resort
6 Banana Land
7 Alonaland
11 TGH- Casa Nova Garden
12 Kalipayan Beach Resort
13 Tierra Azul
14 Bohol Divers Resort
15 Playa Blanca
16 Lost Horizon Beach Resort
22 Aquatica Beach Resort
24 Beach Rock Lodge
28 Alona Kew White Beach
29 Casa-Nova Beach
32 Oasis Resort
35 Alonaville Beach Resort
39 Peter's House
40 Alona Palm Beach Resort
41 Alona Tropical Beach Resort
43 Crystal Coast Resort

Places to Eat & Entertainment
5 Alona Bar & Restaurant
10 Flying Fish Bar
Kamalig Restaurant
20 Trudis Place
21 Ging Ging Bistro
23 Aquatica Restaurant
24 Beach Rock Café
28 Alona Kew Restaurant
29 Casa-Nova Beach Café
Tawala Seaside Restaurant
30 Barflies Bar
33 Safety Stop Bar
34 Safety Stop Bistro
36 Alonaville Restaurant
37 Oops Bar
40 Alona Palm Beach Restaurant
41 Alona Tropical Restaurant

Miscellaneous
2 Rene's Swiss Gourmet Shop
8 Bohol Island Cybernet Café
Panglao Island Travel & Tours
9 Rona's Corner
14 Philippine Island Divers
Pro Safari Diving
17 Sierra Madre Divers
18 Alona Divers
19 Baywatch Dive Center
25 Sunseeker Divers
26 Bohol Tourist Center
Internet Café
27 Money Changer
Sunshine Travel
31 Seaquest Dive Center
36 Sharky's Diver
38 Atlantis Dive Center
39 Genesis Divers
42 Sea Explorers
43 Scuba World

which have cooking facilities. A bit off the beach, next to Banana Land.

Peter's House, Cellphone 0918-7708434. SR/DR/fan P400 and P500. Pleasant, family-style accommodation with spacious, clean rooms. Diving. Good-value breakfast with muesli and freshly baked bread.

Banana Land, Tel 5029068, Fax 2353007. Cottage/fan/bath P500, P700 and P1100. Fairly good cottages with refrigerator, the better ones also have cooking facilities. Set in quiet, spacious grounds, with plenty space between them.

TGH-Casa Nova Garden, Tel 5029101. SR/DR/fan/bath P500 and P650, SR/DR/ac/bath P800. Basic, clean little rooms. A well-kept place. Restaurant, billiard, tennis court, swimming pool. They will arrange motorcycle hire on request. Located about 250m from Alona Beach.

Beach Rock Café & Lodge, Tel & Fax 5029034, @. SR/DR/fan/bath P600, SR/DR/ac/bath P1500. Small place with basic but good rooms (only one with aircon). Restaurant.

Lost Horizon Beach Resort, Tel 5029099, Fax: 2324893. SR/SR/fan

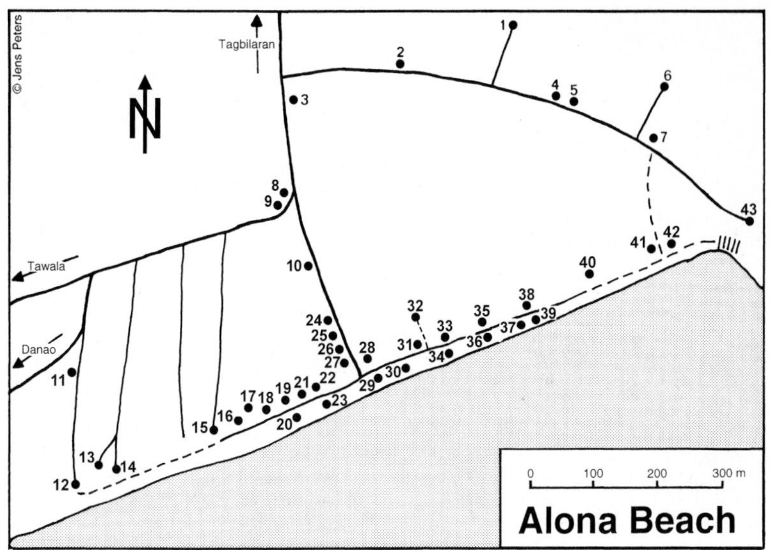

P650, SR/DR/ac/bath P2000. Good aircon rooms in a solid stone building. The rooms with fan are in the dive shop building.

Tierra Azul, Tel 5029065, @. SR/DR/fan/bath P700, SR/DR/ac/bath P1300. Quite good rooms. Restaurant, bicycle and motorbike hire.

Rene's Place, Tel 5029149, @. Cottage/ac/bath P800. Tidy, sprucely-furnished cottages with kitchen. Weekly and monthly rates are available. Located near Flowers Garden Resort. Rene's Swiss Gourmet Shop on the premises.

Alona Tropical Beach Resort, Tel 5029024, Fax 2353326, @. Cottage/fan/bath P800 and P1200, SR/DR/ac/bath P1800. Pleasant, quiet, well-maintained resort at the east end of the beach. The garden is beautifully laid out. Noticeably friendly service. Very good, popular restaurant. Diving.

Aquatica Beach Resort. Cottage/fan/bath P850, SR/DR/ac/bath P1600. Spacious, clean rooms and pleasant cottages.

Alona Kew White Beach, Tel 5029042, Fax 5029027, @. SR/DR/fan/bath P1240, cottage/fan/bath P1440, cottage/ac/bath P2340 to P2740. Beautiful, quite extensive grounds with good cottages furnished in a variety of ways. Well-tended garden, good restaurant, swimming pool.

Flower Garden Resort, Tel 5029012, @. SR/DR/fan/bath P1200 and P1400, SR/DR/ac/bath P1500. Well-tended garden grounds with attractive, two-storey stone buildings (downstairs kitchen and small living rooms with terrace, upstairs bedrooms with balcony). Good value.

Bohol Divers Resort, Tel 5029047, 5029005, @. SR/DR/fan/bath P1300 and P1700, SR/DR/ac/bath P2300 and P2950. Big place with lots of differently furnished rooms, the aircon ones are quite spacious and have a little seating area, some also have a refrigerator and

TV. Good restaurant, tennis court, swimming pool, diving, day trips by boat or jeep on request.

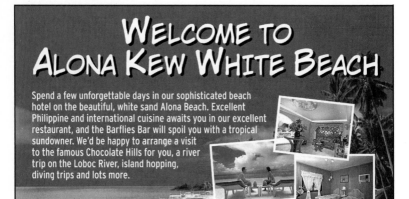

Crystal Coast Resort, Tel 4113179, Fax 4113009, @. SR/DR/ac/bath P2000 to P5400. Good rooms with TV in a big, two-storey building, plus roomy stone cottages, so-called cabanas with two bedrooms, living room, dining room, kitchen and TV. Restaurant, big swimming pool, diving. This peaceful place is spread out over a flat cliff top at the eastern end of the beach.

Kalipayan Beach Resort, @. SR/DR/ac/bath P1600. Solid stone buildings with tidy, spacious rooms. The grounds cover a large area and are well looked after. Restaurant, swimming pool, diving.

Oasis Resort, Tel & Fax 5029083, @. SR/DR/fan/bath P2200/2450, SR/DR/ac/bath P2750/3000. Including breakfast. Beautiful, quiet place with well-kept rooms in double cottages, each with its own terrace. Restaurant. Garden with swimming pool. Diving. Access next to the Seaquest Dive Center, up a few stairs.

Sun Apartelle, Tel 5029063, Fax 5029064, @. SR/DR/ac/bath P3850 to P4600. Spacious, comfortably furnished rooms with TV and kitchen. An attractive building set in well-kept grounds, about 500m from the beach. Restaurant. Inviting swimming pool.

Alona Palm Beach Resort, Tel 5029141, Fax 5029142, @. SR/DR/ac/bath P5700/6000; including breakfast. Very attractively designed resort with comfortably furnished rooms in 'villas', all with refrigerator, TV and terrace. The best accommodation on Alona Beach. Good restaurant. Big swimming pool with bar.

Other Beaches

Calypso Resort, Danao, Tel 5028184, @. Cottage/fan P350, SR/DR/fan/bath P600. Basic rooms in a stone building with a garden. Small, family-style place

about 50m from the beach. Restaurant has Swiss and Philippine cooking. Small swimming pool, diving (Frog Fish Divers), motorbike hire.

Dumaloan Beach Resort, Liboang, Tel 5029081. Cottage/fan/bath P600, cottage/ac/bath P1600; including breakfast. Nicely built cottages set in peaceful grounds on a beautiful part of the beach next to the Bohol Beach Club. Restaurant, swimming pool, diving.

Bohol Plaza, Dauis, Tel 5000882, Fax 5000970. SR/DR/ac/bath P1100 to P1800. Friendly rooms with refrigerator and TV. This is not a beach resort, but a hotel with grounds in the form of a terrace up on Hayo Hill. There is a wonderful view from here of Tagbilaran about six km away, and of Bohol. Restaurant, swimming pool.

Bohol Sea Resort, Danao, @. SR/DR/ac/bath P1300, cottage/ac/bath P1900; including breakfast. Well-equipped rooms and cottages with refrigerator. Big, very comfortable place. Restaurant with German and Filipino food. Swimming pool. Diving. Bicycle and motorbike rental.

Bohol Beach Club, Bolod, Tel 4115222, Fax 4115225, @. SR/SR/ac/bath P2500 to P7500, suites P12,500. Restaurant, swimming pool, tennis courts, sauna, diving, windsurfing. Attractive resort, located on its own beach about 2½ km east of Alona Beach.

Ananyana Beach Resort, Doljo Beach, Tel & Fax 5028101, @. SR/DR/ac/bath P4500, suite P7500 (for four people). Spacious rooms with refrigerator and balcony. Appealing, spread out place under German management. Restaurant, swimming pool, diving, windsurfing, bicycle and motorbike hire.

Places to Eat

Good, inexpensive Philippine food is on offer in the ***Tawala Seaside Restaurant,*** the ***Ging Ging Bistro*** and ***Trudis Place***. Well worth recommending is the ***Tropical Resort Restaurant*** with its tasty seafood dishes. The ***Bohol Divers Resort Restaurant*** on the other side of the beach serves excellent sizzling plates. You can enjoy grilled food fresh on your plate at the ***Safety Stop Bistro***.

The menu at the attractive ***Alona Kew Restaurant*** includes a breakfast buffet, and the spruce ***Alona Palm Beach Resort Restaurant*** does a good job with its excellent international dishes. Great sandwiches are available at the ***Alonaville Restaurant*** accompanied by a beautiful view of the sea. About 200m from the beach you'll find the popular ***Kamalig Restaurant*** with its excellent Italian cuisine.

Miscellaneous

Diving: There are several dive shops on Alona Beach, including the Alona Divers, Tel 5029043; Atlantis Dive Center, Tel 5029058, @; Baywatch Dive & Fun Center, Tel 5029028; Genesis Divers, Tel & Fax 5029056, @; Philippine Island Divers, Tel 5029048, @; Pro Safari Diving, Tel 5029122, @); Scuba World at the Crystal Coast Resort, Tel 5029003; Seaquest Dive Center, Tel 5029069, @; Sea Explorers 5029035, @; Sharky's Divers, Tel 5029025; Sunseeker Divers, Tel 5029800, @. Average prices include one dive at the drop-off for US$20; a dive from a boat for US$23; and two dives from a boat, eg off Balicasag Island, for US$40. A five-day diving course (PADI) costs US$300.

Money: Travellers' cheques and cash can be changed at the Bohol Tourist Center across from the Alona Kew White Beach. They will also make a cash advance on all popular credit cards (for an 8% fee).

Post & Telephone: Post code: 6340. Area code: 038.

Tours: Several resorts organise, or will arrange for you, half-day trips round Panglao Island for P300 (tricycle) or whole day trips by jeepney (including a boat trip on the Loay River and lunch at

the Chocolate Hills) for about P800 per person.
Travel Agencies: Tickets for air and sea travel are available at the Bohol Tourist Center, Tel 5029100, and at Sunshine Travel & Tours Services, Tel 5029030.
Whale Watching: Although whales and dolphins can be seen all year in the Bohol Sea south of Bohol, the best time to take a trip to watch these wonderful creatures is from March to June. A few resorts and dive shops on Alona Beach organise such trips. The Island Leisure Inn, Tagbilaran, Tel 4112482, also offers tours lasting one day or more, (ask for Juny Binamira). See also Pamilacan Island further below.

Getting Around

Car: A car with driver for a day trip to Bohol (Chocolate Hills etc) will cost P1300 to P1500, eg at Sunshine Travel & Tours Services.
Motorcycle: Many resorts have 125 cc motorbikes available for P500 to P600 per day (eight hrs maximum).

Getting There & Away

Bus: Several JG Trans buses go from Tagbilaran to Panglao Island daily, roughly every hour, leaving from the Panglao Bus Terminal in A Hontanosas St, across from the Bohol Museum. Not all go to Alona Beach. Those marked 'Panglao' go right across the island to Panglao town near Doljo Beach. Those marked 'Panglao-Tawala' go along the southern coast and detour to Alona Beach. The first departure is at about 7am, but it may be advisable to confirm. The trip as far as Alona Beach takes 30 min (P14), the last bus leaving about 5pm.
The first bus from Alona Beach to Tagbilaran leaves between 6 and 6.30am, while the last leaves at about 3pm. This is important if you are just making a day trip as normally there are no tricycles waiting for passengers at the beach.

Taxi: Private cars will make the journey from the airport to Alona Beach for between P200 and P250, taking 30 min. A taxi will cost about P200, eg from Varescon, Tel 4115999, 4112548, or Nena's Rental Car Services, Tel 4114080, 4114102.

Tricycle: From Tagbilaran to Alona Beach by tricycle costs P100 to P150, but you'll often be asked for twice as much (45 min).

Balicasag Island

The small island of Balicasag lies about 10 km south-west of Panglao Island and is surrounded by a coral reef which offers excellent diving and snorkelling. The underwater world here is a marine sanctuary which the local fishermen know and respect.

Places to Stay

Balicasag Island Dive Resort. Cottage/fan/bath P1300, cottage/ac/bath P1500, including breakfast. Pleasantly furnished duplex cottages, as well as a mediocre restaurant which is expensive to boot. Diving costs US$40 for two dives, plus P150 for the boat. A diving course costs US$300 and diving equipment can be hired. Reservations in Manila: Philippine Tourism Authority, Tel (02) 5242502, Fax (02) 5256490, and in Tagbilaran at the PTA, Lugod Building, Carlos P Garcia Ave, Tel (038) 4112192.
It is possible to find basic, good value private accommodation on Balicasag, eg for about P300 (it's up to you what you offer) including three meals in Ester's house on the other side of the island (about 10 min on foot from the resort).

Getting There & Away

Boat: Alona Beach Resort proprietors offer Special Rides from P1000 to

From Whale Catching to Whale Watching

Daring whalers row their small, open whaling boats, battling their way through mountainous seas until they get threateningly close to the giant monster. Standing with spread-eagled legs in the bow, the fearless harpooner waits for his chance to deal the death blow with his deadly dart. Such nineteenth-century pictures of whales and whale catching show us vividly what whales were to mankind back then: they were monsters, profitable booty, only there to be slaughtered. Even in Melville's novel *Moby Dick* published in 1851, the white whale ends up as a terrible monster which is to be mercilessly hunted down, regardless of any hint of respect shown towards it.

All sorts of lucrative business emanated from whale products back then: spermaceti, a wax-like substance from the head of the sperm whale, was sought after as a base for cosmetics and for the production of candles; the oil was used to produce soap and margarine; lubricating grease was made from the lard; ambergris provided the foundation for expensive perfumes; the baleen were used to make the bones for corsets and umbrella frames; the bones were processed into manure, and the skin was used to make laces and bicycle saddles.

A whole industry was established around whaling, culminating in the introduction of factory ships and improved hunting techniques. This resulted in an alarming over-exploitation of the whales, which finally led to whale researchers and nature conservationists demanding the immediate introduction of quotas. In 1946 the International Whaling Commission (IWC) was founded to bring about the non-depletive use of the remaining whale population. Initially, the Commission only regulated the cull quota, but in 1979 the decision was finally reached to ban whaling completely. In the meantime stocks have recovered somewhat, in spite of countries like Japan and Norway riding roughshod over international agreements.

In the mid 60s a change in people's perception of the importance of whales took place as ocean mammals were introduced to the public in various oceanariums and delphinariums. Television series also gave world-wide publicity to the loveable nature of these remarkable creatures. The obviously playful nature and intelligence of whales and dolphins made people look at them in a whole new way, and awareness grew that these animals had to be protected. As a natural consequence of this, people also became more and more interested in seeing them in their natural surroundings instead of in captivity.

Whales and dolphins are no strangers to Philippine waters; however, they do seem to prefer the deep water south of Bohol. Various species appear in this area all year round, although mainly between the months of April and June. The little island of Pamilacan is home to several smart ex-whalers who obviously know where and when the most magnificent specimens can be found. They say the best time is just after dawn or just before sunset. There is no question that they have learnt how to show care and consideration in approaching the animals. If you want to profit from their years of experience and hire one of them as a guide and spotter, there's no better way to ensure success in your whale spotting.

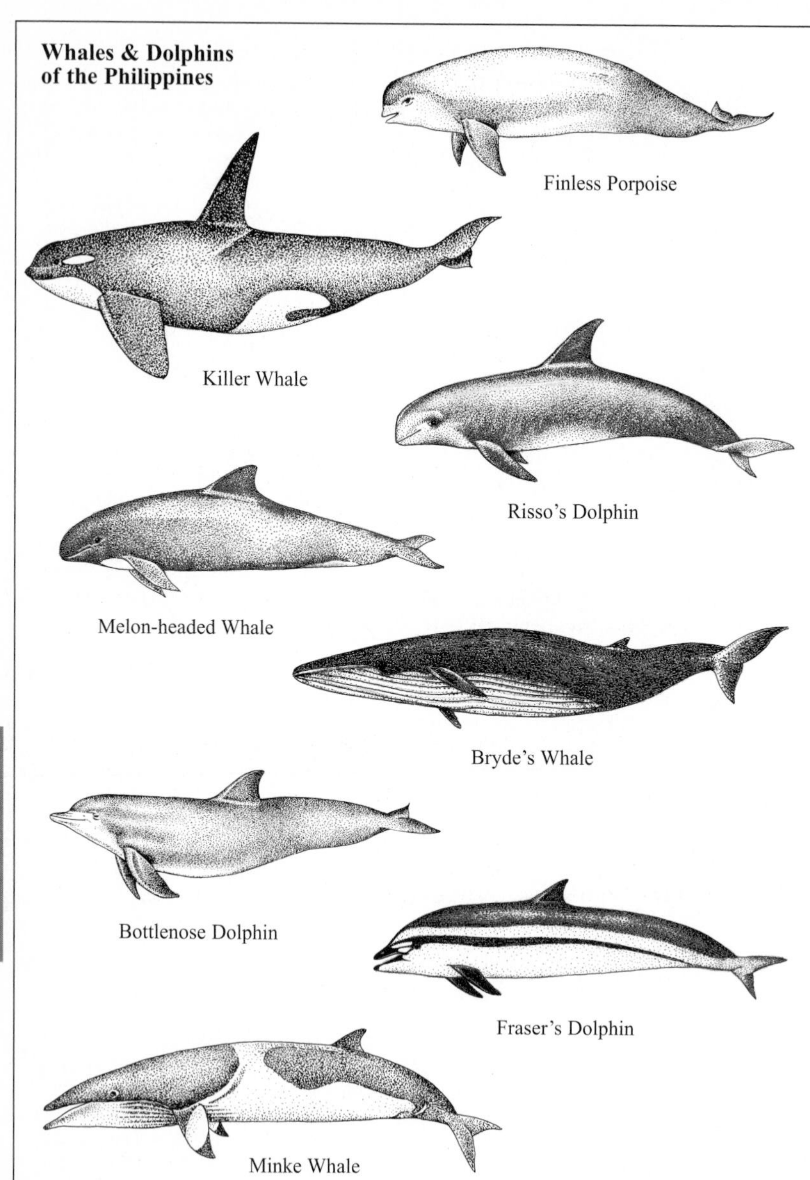
Whales & Dolphins
of the Philippines
Finless Porpoise
Killer Whale
Risso's Dolphin
Melon-headed Whale
Bryde's Whale
Bottlenose Dolphin
Fraser's Dolphin
Minke Whale

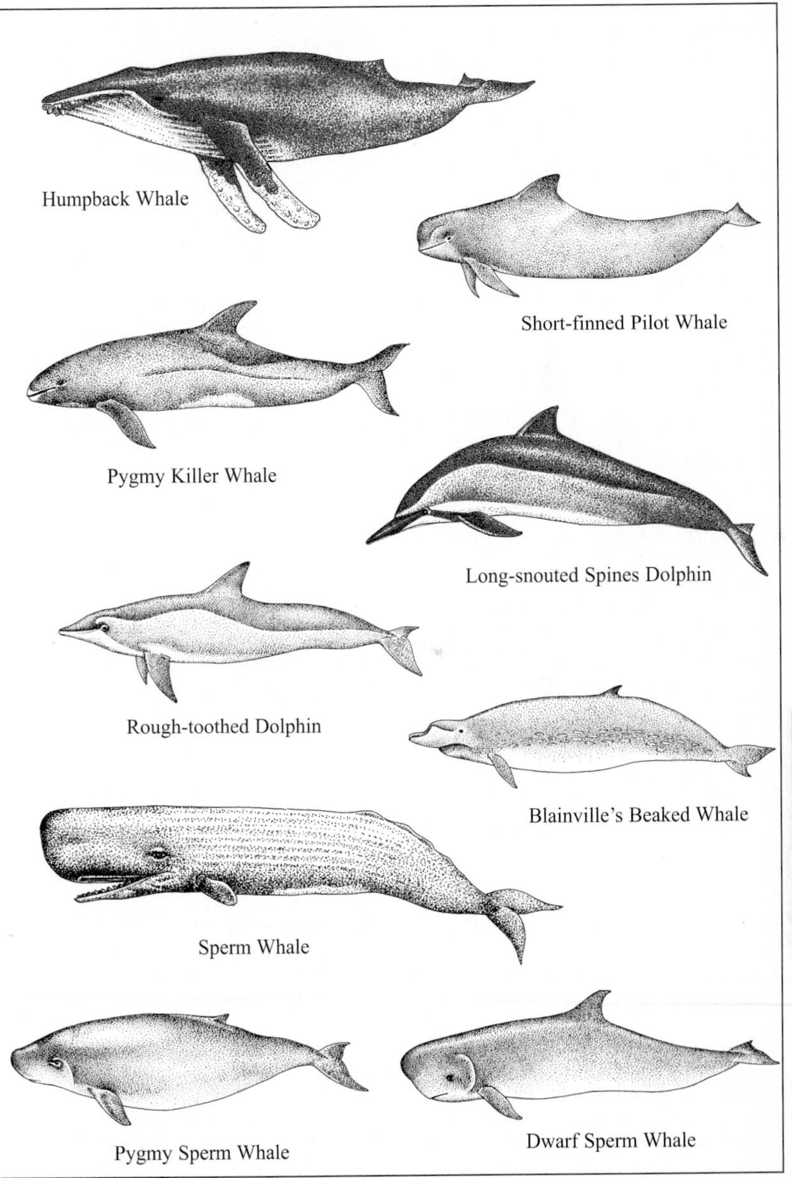
Humpback Whale
Short-finned Pilot Whale
Pygmy Killer Whale
Long-snouted Spines Dolphin
Rough-toothed Dolphin
Blainville's Beaked Whale
Sperm Whale
Pygmy Sperm Whale
Dwarf Sperm Whale

Whale watching
The former whalers have set up the Pamilacan Island Dolphin & Whale Watching Tours (PIDWWT) and now take turns at heading out to sea in their modified whale boats (*canter*) for peaceful purposes only. Prices: P1800 per person (small boat, up to three passengers, P3000 if there's only one passenger) and P1250 per person (big boat, up to six passengers). That might sound a bit expensive, but this activity provides an essential part of the islanders' income and the fares should be seen as a contribution to the protection of the local environment. A tour lasts from about 6am to 3pm. The passengers are collected from their hotel at around 5.30am and dropped off again about 3.30pm. Lunch on the beach is included in the price. Swimming and snorkeling are also on the programme. When planning such a trip, please bear in mind that the organisers cannot actually guarantee any whales will be around on a given day.
Reservations can be made at Joselino 'Jojo' S Baritua, PIDWWT Dolphin & Whale Watching Tours Booking Office, 6301 Baclayon, Tel (038) 5409279, Cellphone 0919-7306108, @.

P1500 (depending on the size of boat). Traders often travel between Balicasag Island and Panglao Island and are happy to take passengers with them to their island.

Pamilacan Island

The beautiful little island of Pamilacan lies about 18 km south-east of Tagbilaran and is surrounded by an extensive coral reef which unfortunately has been severely damaged by dynamite fishing. Strangers don't come here often. If you want to cross over for a few days, you should take provisions for the first day, as the locals are unlikely to be prepared for visitors. From the second day on, you should be able to arrange for supplies from the fishermen.
Pamilacan is also known as a whalers' island. Up until a few years ago the 235 families who live here made their living from hunting dolphins, whales and rays, but these species now enjoy the protection of a hunting ban introduced by the Philippine government. You can still see fishermen's huts decorated with the jawbones and other bones from these marine mammals.
If you want to observe dolphins and whales in the Bohol Sea you'll find experienced boatsmen among the islanders who know where and when they can be spotted. The best time of day for whale watching is in the early morning hours, preferably at dawn. Although various dolphins and small whales can be observed all through the year, the months of March to June are the most populous. During this period the following species can be seen: Fraser's dolphins, bottlenose dolphins, melon-headed whales, Risso's dolphins, pantropical spotted dolphins, long-snouted spines dolphins, Bryde's whales, short-finned pilot whales, sperm whales, Blainville's beaked whales and pygmy sperm whales.

Places to Stay

Nita's Nipa Hut. Cottage P150 per person; P400 including full board. Very basic huts. Extremely friendly, family-style accommodation set in the northern part of the island, on a white beach near the old Spanish watchtower.

Getting There & Away

Boat: There are boats almost daily from Baclayon to Pamilacan Island (one hr).

Your best chance of a cheap trip over is on Wednesday, which is market day, and Sunday when the fishermen and their families return home from church. That will only cost you P20 per person. Even on weekdays there are often people from Pamilacan in Baclayon. They always anchor their boats on the right-hand side of the landing stage looking towards Pamilacan and leave for home shortly before 3pm. If you can wait for them, you won't have to pay the P500, which is about what a Special Ride would cost.
A Special Ride from Alona Beach on Panglao Island to Pamilacan Island and back costs around P1500.

Cabilao Island

Cabilao Island is 30 km as the crow flies, north-west of Tagbilaran in Cebu Strait between Bohol and Cebu. A fairly flat island, it is widely covered in palms and has five villages spread around it. The nearby reef offers excellent snorkelling and diving. Several large beach resorts on Cebu prefer these diving grounds for their guests and send diving boats, usually full of Japanese tourist groups, practically every day.

Places to Stay

Cabilao Beach & Dive Resort. SR/DR P100 per person. Unpretentious, but inexpensive, accommodation without water or electricity. Located under palms on the next beach north of La Estrella Beach Resort, the place is beginning to show its age. Diving, diving courses (the Swiss-run Sea Explorers; @).
La Estrella Beach Resort, Tel. (038) 5054114, Cellphone 0918-9044859, @. Cottage/fan/bath P650 to P1300 (for four people). Beautiful single and double cottages with terrace in pleasant, well-maintained and quiet grounds with an orchid garden and hammocks.

Located in the north-west of the island, south of the lighthouse. There is a good restaurant which serves Filipino and German cuisine, as Babie, the owner, spent several years in Germany. Diving, diving courses (Sea Explorers).

Polaris Beach & Dive Resort, Cellphone 0918-9037187, @. tree house/fan/bath P1000, cottage/fan/bath P1100, SR/DR/ac/bath P1450, two-storey house/ac/bath for four people P2200. Restaurant. Diving. Well-run resort on the west coast of Cabilao, about 100m south of the La Estrella Beach Resort.

Cabilao Beach Club, Cellphone 0917-4545897, @. SR/DR/fan/bath P1200. Spacious rooms in double cottages on a hillock and at the beach. A two-storey house, a few minutes away, with a kitchen terrace and big balcony costs P2500 (good for four people). Restaurant. Mountainbike rental. Diving (Sea Explorers). This friendly little resort is in the north-east of Cabilao.

Getting There & Away

Bus/Tricycle/Boat: From Tagbilaran by bus to Loon (one hr), then carry on by tricycle (P15; 30 min) over a causeway to Mocpoc, Sandingan Island, from there with a regular boat (P10; 10 min) to Talisay, Cabilao Island, and then by tricycle (P50; 10 min) or on foot (one hr) eg to the La Estrella Beach Resort.

It's more comfortable to take a taxi from Tagbilaran to Mocpoc, Sandingan Island (about P400) and from there go by boat (Special Ride P350) direct to one of the beach resorts.

A Special Ride from Alona Beach on Panglao Island to Cabilao Island costs around P2800.

If you go by car ferry from Taloot near Argao on Cebu to Bohol, carry on after the ship has arrived in Loon by tricycle (P15) to Mocpoc, Sandingan Island, where boats leave for Cabilao Island.

Up to three outriggers leave Argao (Looc)/Cebu every Tuesday and Saturday between noon and 3pm heading for Cabilao Island. They tie up at the lighthouse (P35 per person; 1½ hrs). Departure from Cabilao Island to Argao (Looc)/Cebu Tuesday and Saturday between noon and 3pm.

Chocolate Hills

Exactly 1268 in number (so they say!), the Chocolate Hills are on average between 30 and 50m high and covered in grass. At the end of the dry season the grass is quite dry and chocolate coloured, hence the name. If you are not in a hurry, you should spend the night in the Chocolate Hills Complex and experience the bizarre effect of the sunrise in this mysterious landscape the following morning from the observation hill (213 steps). Admission to the complex is P10 for non-residents.

According to some geologists, Bohol lay under water in prehistoric times. Volcanic eruptions caused unevenness on the bottom of the sea which was gradually smoothed and rounded by the movement of the water. Most serious geologists, however, regard such an explanation as nonsense. Even though the geological origin of the hills has not yet been explained beyond doubt, the consensus is that they are weathered formations of a kind of marine limestone lying on top of impermeable clay soils. Comparisons have been made with the Hundred Islands of North Luzon. On the top of the observation hill there are plaques containing what is probably the correct explanation of the hills' origin in relief lettering on them.

Places to Stay

Chocolate Hills Complex. Dorm P75, SR/DR/fan/bath P350, SR/DR/ac/bath P600 and P800. The rooms are unpretentious but OK; they have balconies and an impressive view. The aircon ones are newer and better. Canisters of cold water are available for showers. There is a restaurant and a swimming pool (which is unfortunately unusable a lot of the time).

Getting Around

Motorcycle: Amiable motorcycle riders wait at the turn-off for the Chocolate Hills Complex to take people on half or whole day tours for between P300 and P500 (don't pay until the tour's finished!). Usually the tour will include the mahogany forest at Bilar, the bamboo bridge over the Lopoc River at Sevilla, a boat trip on the Lopoc River, old churches and the Blood-Compact plaque in Bool. You could arrange for the trip to end in Tagbilaran or Panglao Island (P500 to P700). A one to two-hour trip on small trails through the Chocolate Hills costs P150.

Tricycle: The tricycle operators in Carmen ask for at least P50 for the four km to the Chocolate Hills Complex, P30 only to the turn-off. They like to claim that neither buses nor jeepneys make the journey, which is of course absolute rubbish.

Getting There & Away

Tagbilaran

Bus: There are several St Jude Trans buses a day, practically hourly, from Tagbilaran to Carmen (two hrs). As you have to get out four km before Carmen, don't forget to tell the driver. It is about another one km walk from the main road up to the Chocolate Hills Complex or you can have a motorbike take you up there for P5 (a good idea if you have heavy baggage with you). The last bus leaves Carmen for Tagbilaran at about 4pm.

Tubigon

Bus/Jeepney: From Tubigon to Carmen, there are several buses a day which leave fairly reliably after the arrival of a ship from Cebu (two hrs). They may continue beyond Carmen and pass the turn-off to the Chocolate Hills Complex. Otherwise, take the next bus or jeepney going to Bilar, Loay or Tagbilaran to the turn-off. From there it is about a one km walk.

If there are no more regular buses about in the late afternoon, you can take the school bus at 5pm or the jeepney to Sagbayan where you can charter a tricycle to the Chocolate Hills (about P30).

Giant Legends

There are two legends concerning the origin of the Chocolate Hills, and two geological explanations. The first legend tells of a fight between two giants who threw stones and sand at each other for days, until they were so exhausted and tired of fighting they made friends and left the island. However, they didn't tidy up the battlefield, leaving the Chocolate Hills.

The second legend is a lot more romantic. Arogo, a young and unusually strong giant, fell in love with an ordinary mortal, Aloya. After Aloya's death, Arogo cried bitterly. The Chocolate Hills are proof of his grief, for his tears turned into hills.

Tubigon & Inanuran Island

Tubigon is a small place with an important wharf for ships to and from Cebu. A few miles north-west of Tubigon is the island of Inanuran with its white sand beach fringed by palm trees. The small, but exclusive Inanuran Beach resort there has been closed down.

Places to Stay
Cosare Lodging House, Tubigon. SR/DR/fan P100/200. Basic, but reasonable rooms.

Getting There & Away
Bus: There are several buses from Carmen to Tubigon daily (1½ hrs), the last one leaving at about 2pm.

Talibon

Talibon is located on the northern coast of Bohol and has a wharf for ships to and from Cebu City. You can also cross to nearby Jao Island from here.

Places to Stay
Lapyahan Lodge, M Revilles St. SR/DR P100/200, SR/DR/fan/bath P160/240. Basic, reasonable rooms in a pleasant, family-style atmosphere.
Talibon Pension House, National Highway. SR/fan P180, SR/DR/ac P300 to P600. Good rooms, some of the aircon ones have no windows. Restaurant. Located in the south of the city, about one km from the wharf.
La Vicenta Lodge. SR/fan P180, SR/DR/ac P350. Friendly accommodation with a sea view. Near the wharf and the market.

Getting There & Away

Chocolate Hills Complex
Bus: Several buses coming from Tagbilaran leave daily from the Chocolate Hills Complex turn-off to Talibon between 8am and 4pm (2½ hrs).

Tagbilaran
Bus: From Tagbilaran to Talibon via Carmen, there are several St Jude Trans buses (possibly also JG Express buses) daily between 6am and 2pm (4 hrs).

Ubay

From Ubay on the east coast of Bohol boats leave for Bato and Maasin on Leyte.

Places to Stay
J & N Lodge. SR/DR P70/140, SR/DR/ac/bath P300 and P400.
Casa Besas Pension House. SR/fan/bath P250, SR/DR/ac/bath P500.

Getting There & Away

Chocolate Hills Complex
Bus: From Carmen to Ubay via Sierra Bullones, there are several buses daily. They either come from Tagbilaran (you can board these at the turn-off on the main road) or from Carmen. Alternative routes would be: take a bus from Carmen heading for Talibon and change in Trinidad for Ubay, or from the turnoff for the Chocolate Hills head first to Loay and change into a bus there heading along the coast to Ubay.

Tagbilaran
Bus: From Tagbilaran to Ubay, there are a few buses going via Jagna or via Carmen and Sierra Bullones daily (four hrs). A few buses travel daily from Ubay to Tagbilaran via Sierra Bullones and Carmen or via Jagna, the last one via Carmen departing at 2pm.

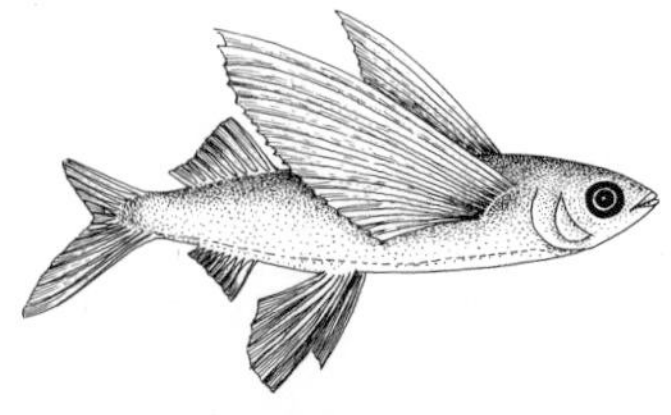

Cebu

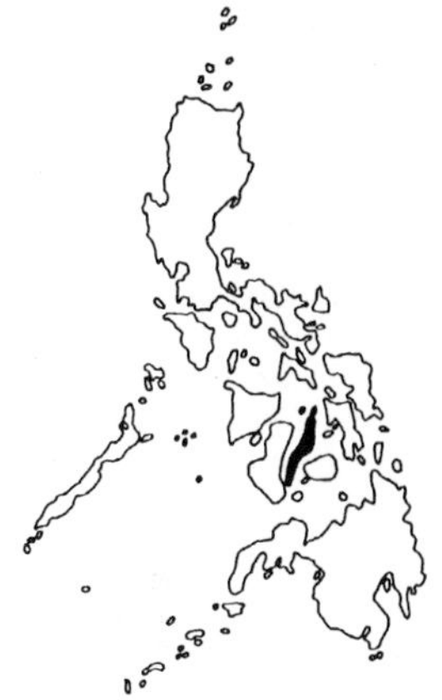

This island, more than 200 km long and just 40 km across at its widest point, is at the centre of the Visayas, locked between Negros, Leyte and Bohol. It is the main island of Cebu Province and the location of the capital, Cebu City. Of the smaller islands which are also part of the province, the most important are Mactan, Bantayan and Camotes. Cebu is a hilly island and flat areas are only to be found on the coast and in the north.

When the Spaniards arrived in Cebu, it was called Sugbu and trade was already being carried on with China. Today, many different industries contribute to the province's economic importance. Cement has been produced in Cebu for some years, but oil is the hope of the future. At the moment, Cebu supplies the West with fashionable shell and coral jewellery and also with rattan furniture.

The cultivation of maize is the dominant agricultural activity. However, there are also sizeable sugar cane plantations in the north and more are planned. The mangoes of Cebu are famous; they only cost a few pesos each during the harvest season, which is in March, April, May and June.

The people of Cebu are all very friendly. They speak Cebuano, the main dialect of the Visayas. Many Chinese live in Cebu City, and they speak Chinese among themselves. Visitors, though, can get by quite well with English.

Cebu has many expensive beach resorts which are always promoted in the island's tourist literature. Those who can do without luxury, however, will feel more comfortable on the less touristically developed beaches, such as those on Bantayan Island or Malapascua Island for example. The coral gardens at Pescador Island near Moalboal and around Sumilon Island are worth seeing, as are the guitar factories on Mactan Island. Treks into the interior are growing in popularity, coupled with a few lazy days near the refreshing waterfalls.

The road from Argao to Bato in the south of Cebu is arguably the most beautiful coast road in the whole Visayas. Especially south of the unfortunately named Oslob, the trip through the luxuriant bougainvillea bushes on either side of the road is simply breathtaking.

Getting There & Away

You can get to Cebu from Biliran, Bohol, Camiguin, Leyte, Luzon, Masbate, Mindanao, Negros, Palawan, Panay, Samar and Siquijor (see the Getting Away from Luzon section of the Manila chapter and the Getting There & Away sections of the individual island chapters).

To Biliran

Boat

From Cebu City to Naval

Monday, Wednesday and Friday with MY Shipping (P200; nine hrs).

To Bohol

Boat

From Argao to Cabilao Island
Tuesday and Saturday at 2pm with a big outrigger (1½ hrs).

From Argao/Taloot to Catagbacon/Loon
Tuesday to Saturday at 4am, 8am and noon, as well as Sunday and Monday at 7 and 11am with a Lite Shipping Corporation car ferry (two hrs).

From Cebu City to Tagbilaran
Daily with the fast ferries *Oceanjet* (4x; P310) and *Supercat* (3x; P400), taking 1½ hrs.
Daily with Cokaliong Shipping Lines and Lite Shipping Corporation (P150; 3½ hrs).
Monday, Wednesday and Friday with Palacio Shipping Lines (P115; four hrs).
Monday with Trans-Asia Shipping Lines (P145; four hrs).

From Cebu City to Tubigon
Five times daily with the fast ferry *Oceanjet* (P210; one hr).
Daily with Lite Shipping Corporation (2½ hrs).
Monday, Wednesday and Friday with Maypalad Shipping Corporation (2½ hrs).

To Camiguin

Air

From Cebu City to Mambajao
Seair flies on Friday and Sunday (P1300).

Air/Boat/Bus

From Cebu City to Mambajao
An alternative connection is from Cebu City via Cagayan de Oro by air or ship, then by bus to Balingoan and by ferry to Benoni, where jeepneys wait at the wharf for passengers to Mambajao.

Boat

From Cebu City to Benoni
Friday with Super Shuttle Ferry (car ferry), taking 11 hrs (P450).

To Leyte

Bus/Boat

From Cebu City to Isabel and Tacloban
The trip takes six hrs to Isabel and 11 to Taclaban.
See below: *To Luzon - From Cebu City to Manila*

Boat

From Camotes Islands to Baybay
~~From Poro [illegible] daily with the fast ferry *Oceanjet* (P250; 1½ hrs).~~
discontinued

From Camotes Islands to Ormoc
From Bukog daily with a big outrigger (three hrs).

From Carmen to Isabel
Daily at 8am with a big outrigger (four hrs).

From Cebu City to Bato
Daily with Kinswell Shipping Lines (P235; four hrs).

From Cebu City to Baybay
~~Two times daily with the fast ferry *Oceanjet* [illegible], 2½ hrs); via Camotes Islands.~~
discontinued

From Cebu City to Hilongos
Two times daily with the fast ferry *Oceanjet* (P440; two hrs).

From Cebu City to Liloan
Monday and Friday with Maypalad Shipping Corporation (P170; six hrs).

From Cebu City to Maasin
Monday, Tuesday, Thursday and Sunday with Cokaliong Shipping Lines (P380; six hrs).

Visayas - Cebu

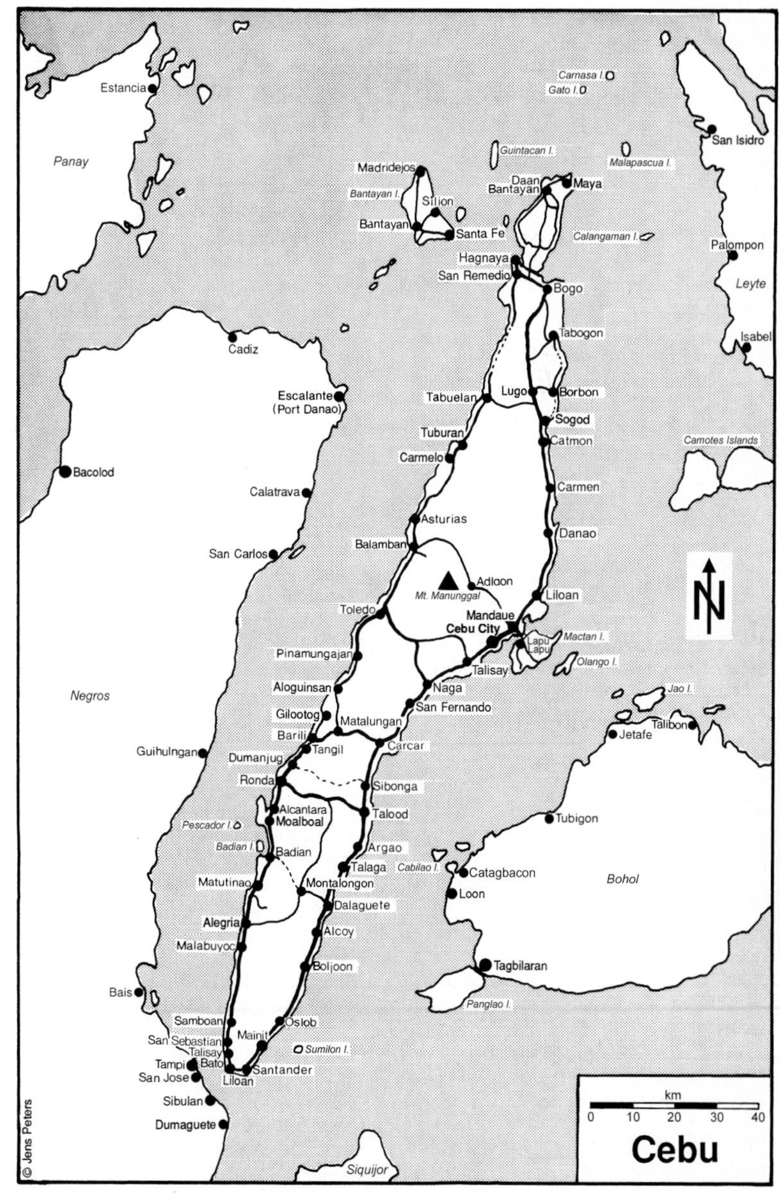
Estancia
Panay
Carnasa I.
Gato I.
San Isidro
Guintacan I.
Malapascua I.
Madridejos
Bantayan I.
Silion
Daan Bantayan
Maya
Bantayan
Santa Fe
Calangaman I.
Palompon
Hagnaya
San Remedio
Bogo
Leyte
Tabogon
Isabel
Cadiz
Escalante
(Port Danao)
Tabuelan
Lugo
Borbon
Sogod
Tuburan
Catmon
Camotes Islands
Carmelo
Bacolod
Carmen
Calatrava
Asturias
Danao
Balamban
San Carlos
Adlaon
Mt. Manunggal
Liloan
Toledo
Mandaue
Cebu City
Lapu Lapu
Mactan I.
Pinamungajan
Olango I.
Talisay
Negros
Aloguinsan
Naga
Jao I.
San Fernando
Gilootog
Matalungan
Talibon
Barili
Carcar
Jetafe
Guihulngan
Tangil
Dumanjug
Ronda
Sibonga
Alcantara
Talood
Moalboal
Tubigon
Pescador I.
Badian I.
Argao
Badian
Talaga
Cabilao I.
Catagbacon
Matutinao
Montalongon
Bohol
Loon
Dalaguete
Alegria
Alcoy
Malabuyoc
Tagbilaran
Boljoon
Bais
Panglao I.
Samboan
Oslob
San Sebastian
Mainit
Talisay
Sumilon I.
Tampi
Bato
San Jose
Santander
Liloan
Sibulan
Dumaguete
Siquijor
km
0 10 20 30 40
Cebu
© Jens Peters

From Cebu City to Ormoc
Three times daily with the fast ferry *Supercat* (P500; two hrs).
Daily except Saturday with Cebu Ferries and Super Shuttle Ferry (car ferry), taking six hrs (P220).
Monday with Sulpicio Lines (P155; six hrs).

From Cebu City to Tacloban
Tuesday, Thursday and Saturday with Maypalad Shipping Corporation (P230; 12 hrs).

From Danao to Isabel
Daily at 7am with Aznar Shipping Corporation (P150; four hrs).

From Maya (North Cebu) to San Isidro
Daily at 10am with a big outrigger (P50; two hrs). On arrival in San Isidro a bus leaves for Ormoc and Tacloban.

To Luzon

Air

From Cebu City to Angeles
Seair flies on Wednesday and Friday.

From Cebu City to Manila
Air Philippines, Cebu Pacific and Philippine Airlines fly daily (P2900).

Bus/Boat

From Cebu City to Manila
Daily at 5am with a Philtranco aircon bus from the Northern Bus Terminal (35 hrs). The fare is P1240 plus P150 for the ferry from Cebu to Leyte (Danao-Isabel) and P70 for the ferry from Samar to Luzon (Allen-Matnog).

discontinued

Boat

From Cebu City to Manila
Monday, Tuesday, Wednesday, Friday and Sunday with Sulpicio Lines (22 hrs).
Monday, Wednesday, Thursday and Friday with WG & A (P1410; 22 hrs).

To Masbate

Boat

From Bogo to Placer
A boat is said to make this run twice a week.

From Cebu City to Cataingan
Monday with Super Shuttle Ferry (car ferry), taking 10 hrs.

From Cebu City to Masbate/Masbate
Monday, Wednesday and Friday with Trans-Asia Shipping Lines (P350; 14 hrs).

From Maya to Esperanza
Monday, Wednesday and Friday with a big outrigger (two hrs).

To Mindanao

Air

From Cebu City to Cagayan de Oro
Asian Spirit flies Monday, Wednesday, Friday, Saturday and Sunday (P2310).
Seair flies on Tuesday, Thursday and Sunday (P1750).

From Cebu City to Cotabato
Seair flies on Monday and Friday (P2650).

From Cebu City to Davao
Air Philippines and Philippine Airlines fly daily (P2590).
Cebu Pacific flies daily except Saturday and Sunday.

From Cebu City to Dipolog
Asian Spirit flies Monday, Wednesday, Friday and Saturday (P2350).

From Cebu City to General Santos
Air Philippines flies daily (P2640).

From Cebu City to Siargao Island
Seair flies on Tuesday and Saturday (P1990).

From Cebu City to Surigao
Asian Spirit flies on Tuesday, Thursday, Saturday and Sunday (P1430).

From Cebu City to Tandag
Asian Spirit flies on Monday, Wednesday, Friday and Saturday (P2350).
Seair flies on Tuesday and Saturday (P2190).

From Cebu City to Zamboanga
Cebu Pacific flies on Monday, Wednesday, Friday and Saturday (P2650).

Boat

From Cebu City to Butuan/Nasipit
Tuesday with WG & A (14 hrs); via Surigao.
Monday, Wednesday, Thursday and Saturday with Sulpicio Lines (seven hrs).
Tuesday, Thursday and Saturday with Cebu Ferries (P250; 11 hrs).

From Cebu City to Cagayan de Oro
Daily with Cebu Ferries and Trans-Asia Shipping Lines (P390; 10 hrs).
Monday, Wednesday and Friday with Sulpicio Lines (10 hrs).

From Cebu City to Dapitan/Dipolog
~~Daily with the fast ferry *Supercat* (P680; six hrs); via Tagbilaran/Bohol and Dumaguete/Negros.~~ discontinued
Daily with Cokaliong Shipping Lines and George & Peter Lines (P400; 13 hrs); via Dumaguete/Negros.

From Cebu City to Davao
Monday and Friday with Sulpicio Lines (P1190; 28 hrs); Monday via Surigao.

From Cebu City to Iligan
Monday, Wednesday and Saturday with Cebu Ferries (P520; 15 hrs); via Ozamis.
Saturday with Sulpicio Lines (nine hrs).

From Cebu City to Ozamis
Monday, Tuesday, Wednesday, Friday and Saturday with Cebu Ferries (P520; 11 hrs).
Monday, Wednesday and Friday with Trans-Asia Shipping Lines (10 hrs).
Saturday with Sulpicio Lines (seven hrs).

From Cebu City to Surigao
Daily except Sunday with Cokaliong Shipping Lines (P385; 11 hrs); Tuesday and Thursday via Maasin/Leyte.
Monday with Sulpicio Lines (P420; nine hrs).
Tuesday with WG & A (P500; seven hrs).

From Cebu City to Zamboanga
Monday and Friday with George & Peter Lines (24 hrs); via Dumaguete and possibly Dapitan.

To Negros

Air

From Cebu City to Bacolod
Air Philippines, Cebu Pacific and Philippine Airlines fly daily (P1880).

Bus/Boat

From Cebu City to Bacolod
Several Ceres Liner buses leave Cebu City daily for Bacolod from the Southern Bus Terminal. They meet the ferry going from Tabuelan to Escalante (Port Danao) and go on to Bacolod. The trip, including the ferry ride, takes eight hours. Reserved tickets with seat number must be purchased in good time before departure.
See also below: *From Tabuelan to Escalante*.

From Cebu City to Dumaguete
See below: *From Bato to Tampi* and *From Oslob to Sibulan and Tampi*.

Boat

From Batanyan to Cadiz
Daily with Island Shipping (depending

From Cebu City to Bacolod/ Negros

The following route is recommended for self-drive visitors: Take the Trans Central Highway from Cebu City to Toledo via Balamban, carry on with a car ferry to San Carlos/ Negros, from there on to the Translink Highway north of the Kanlaon volcano via Don Salvador Benedicto and Murcia to Bacolod. Including the ferry, this trip takes about five hours.
From Cebu City you get to the Trans Central Highway along Cebu Veterans Drive, which runs from the Lahug area of town past the Cebu Plaza Hotel to Busay. Don't take the turn-off for the Tops viewpoint, but stay on the main road.
In San Carlos head for the National Highway from the wharf and then in the direction of Dumaguete. On the way out of town in the south the Translink Highway forks off to the right for Don Salvador Benedicto and Bacolod.
Both routes across their respective islands are good stretches of road with relatively little traffic, plus the scenery's beautiful.

on the tide, but usually at 7am), taking two hrs.
After the ship arrives, jeepneys are waiting which will go as far as Bacolod. Anyone wanting to carry on to Dumaguete should take a tricycle from the wharf to the Ceres Liner Bus Terminal.

From Bato to Tampi
Frequent service (13x daily) with Rovi Navigation from the Passenger Terminal, last departure at 7.30pm (P40; 30 min). In addition, eight car ferries set out every day from the Car Ferry Terminal 300m away, the last one leaving at 11.30pm.
Ceres Liner buses go from Cebu City to Bato, leaving from the Southern Bus Terminal (three hrs). These buses make a direct connection with the ferry from Bato to Tampi.

From Cebu City to Dumaguete
Daily with the fast ferries *Oceanjet* (1x) and *Supercat* (2x; P520), taking 3½ hrs; via Tagbilaran/Bohol.
Daily with Cokaliong Shipping Lines and George & Peter Lines (P265; six hrs).
Sunday with Aleson Shipping Lines (P265; six hrs).

From Liloan to Sibulan
Several times daily with a big outrigger, last departure at around 3pm (20 min). Jeepneys make the trip from Sibulan to Dumaguete.

From Oslob to Sibulan and Tampi
Several times daily with a car ferry, last departure at around 5pm (one hr).

From Tabuelan to Escalante
Daily at 8am, 4 and 10pm with an Aznar Shipping Corporation car ferry (two hrs).

From Tangil to Guihulngan
Daily at 5, 6, 8 and 10am with a small ferry (1½ hrs).

From Toledo to San Carlos
Daily from 6am to noon, roughly every hour with an Aznar Shipping Corporation fast ferry (P120; one hr), and at 10.20am and 3pm with a regular Aznar Shipping Corporation ship (P110; 1½ hrs).
Daily at 7.30am, 1 and 6pm with a Lite Shipping Corporation car ferry (P100; two hrs).

To Palawan

Air

From Cebu City to Puerto Princesa
Cebu Pacific flies on Tuesday, Thursday, Friday and Sunday (P2900).

To Panay

Air

From Cebu City to Caticlan (Boracay)
Asian Spirit and Seair fly daily (P2200).

From Cebu City to Iloilo City
Air Philippines, Cebu Pacific and Philippine Airlines fly daily (P2100).

Boat

From Cebu City to Iloilo City
Daily with Trans-Asia Shipping Lines (P550; 15 hrs).
Tuesday, Thursday and Saturday with Cokaliong Shipping Lines (15 hrs).
Tip for those carrying on directly to Boracay: The boats leave in the early evening from Cebu City (probably at 7pm), so that you can continue your journey by bus practically straight away in the forenoon from Iloilo City to Caticlan (boats for Boracay).

To Samar

Bus/Boat

From Cebu City to Catbalogan and Calbayog
See: *To Luzon - From Cebu City to Manila.*

Boat

From Cebu City to Calbayog
Monday, Wednesday and Friday with Palacio Shipping Lines (P310; 10 hrs).

To Siquijor

Boat

From Cebu City to Larena
Two times daily with the fast ferry *Oceanjet* (P600; 3½ hrs); via Tagbilaran/Bohol.
Daily with the fast ferry *Supercat* (P690; 4½ hrs); via Tagbilaran/Bohol and Dumaguete/Negros. discontinued
Daily except on Saturday with Palacio Shipping Lines (P200; seven hrs); Monday, Wednesday and Friday via Tagbilaran/Bohol (eight hrs).

Central Cebu

Cebu City

Cebu City is the capital and the main town on Cebu, with a population of about 700,000. Even though it's a fairly big city, the so-called 'Queen City of the South' is easy to get to know. The busy city centre near the harbour, known as Downtown, includes Colon St, the oldest street in the Philippines.
In contrast to the rundown charm of Downtown, Uptown - roughly the area north of the Rodriguez St, Fuente Osmeña, Maxilom Ave axis - is clearly enjoying a boom in its prosperity. New hotels, smart restaurants, a variety of entertainment and a well tended townscape provide a marked contrast with the lively Colon area, particularly in the late afternoon.
The densely populated outer suburbs and adjoining barrios are gradually joining up with Cebu City. According to the projections of the city's progressive town planners, its appearance will change considerably in the near future. An imposing new city is being planned in the Reclamation Area in the harbour, with numerous skyscrapers, shopping centres, leisure and recreation centres and a new city hall.
Life in Cebu City is more leisurely than in Manila. There are, of course, many jeepneys and taxis and even a few *tartanillas* (horse-drawn carriages), but you can get almost anywhere in this city on foot. Hotels, restaurants and cine-

mas are widely available, and the nearby beaches are great for leisure activities. Transport facilities to other islands are excellent.

Museums

Casa Gorordo Museum, 35 Lopez Jaena St (big iron gate). Open Mon-Sat 8.30am-noon and 1-5pm. Admission P25; students P10. The Parian district in today's Downtown area was the residential home of Cebu's wealthy at the turn of the century. Of the remaining four houses, the Gorordo residence has been restored and furnished in the style of the period. The Gorordo family produced the first Bishop of Cebu. Apart from furniture, you can see porcelain, liturgical items, clothes and old photographs of Cebu. New exhibits and written material on the same theme are being added all the time. Photography is not allowed.

University of San Carlos Museum, Del Rosario St. Open Mon-Fri 9am-noon and 2-5pm, and Sat 9am-noon. It is closed during vacations. The museum of the University of San Carlos (founded 1595) was opened in 1967. Its divisions cover ethnography, archaeology, natural sciences and the Spanish colonial period. Filipino objects from different epochs and exhibits from other Asian countries are also displayed.

Fort San Pedro

Legaspi himself turned the first sod of earth on 8 May 1565 for this fort, which was built to keep out the marauding pirates who were giving the Spanish quite a bit of bother. He gave it the name of the ship in which he crossed the Pacific. At the end of the Spanish era, in 1898, it was taken over by the freedom fighters of Cebu. Later, it served as a base and barracks for the Americans, and from 1937 to 1941 it was used for training purposes. In WWII the fort was used as a prison camp by the Japa-

Getting There & Away

9 Cebu Pacific
29 Singapore Airlines
31 Northern Bus Terminal
34 WG & A
35 Cokaliong Shipping Lines
36 Southern Bus Terminal
37 Super Terminal (Supercat)
39 Oceanjet Terminal

Places to Stay

1 Cebu Plaza Hotel
4 Ford's Inn Hotel
7 Montebello Villa Hotel
11 Metropolis Court Hotel
12 Cebu Acropolis Hotel
15 La Nivel Hotel
17 La Guardia Hotel
18 Cebu Northwinds Hotel
21 Waterfront Cebu City Hotel
28 Cebu City Marriott Hotel
30 Kiwi Lodge

Places to Eat & Entertainment

2 Sand Trap
3 La Tegola Restaurant
4 Vienna Kaffeehaus
6 Club Circus Disco
10 Ginza Restaurant
15 Seafood City Restaurant
16 La Chapelle Restaurant
18 Golden Cowrie Restaurant
19 The Village
20 Crossroads
21 Cebu Casino
22 Mikado Restaurant
25 Ayala Entertainment Center

Miscellaneous

5 Taoist Temple
8 Gaisano Country Mall
13 Phu Shian Temple
14 Heavenly Temple of Charity
20 Tinder Box
21 International Convention Center
23 Provincial Capitol
24 Century Game Club
26 Citibank
27 Ayala Center
32 Equitable PCI Bank
33 SM City

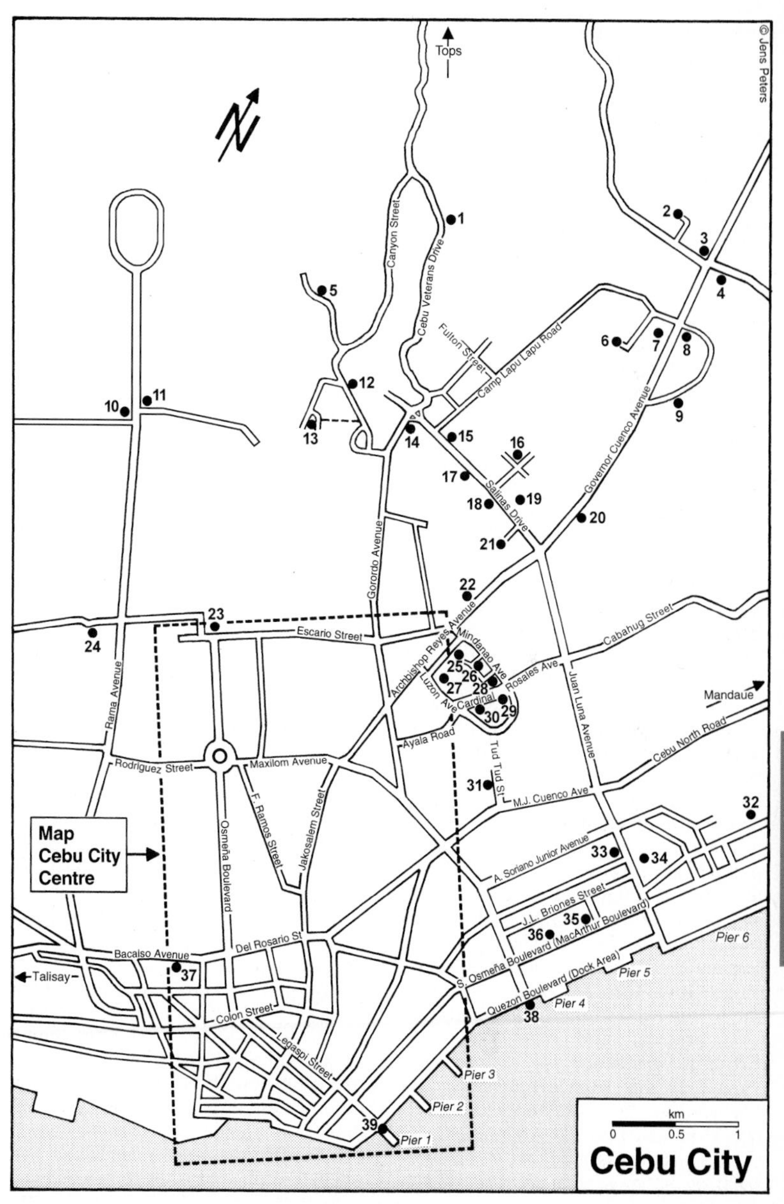
© Jens Peters
Tops
Canyon Street
Cebu Veterans Drive
Fulton Street
Camp Lapu Lapu Road
Governor Cuenco Avenue
Salinas Drive
Gorordo Avenue
Archbishop Reyes Avenue
Mindanao Ave
Luzon Ave
Cardinal
Rosales Ave
Escario Street
Cabahug Street
Juan Luna Avenue
Rama Avenue
Rodriguez Street
Maxilom Avenue
Ayala Road
Tud Tud St.
M.J. Cuenco Ave
Cebu North Road
Mandaue
F. Ramos Street
Jakosalem Street
Osmeña Boulevard
Map Cebu City Centre
A. Soriano Junior Avenue
J.L. Briones Street
S. Osmeña Boulevard (MacArthur Boulevard)
Quezon Boulevard (Dock Area)
Del Rosario St
Bacalso Avenue
Talisay
Colon Street
Legaspi Street
Pier 1
Pier 2
Pier 3
Pier 4
Pier 5
Pier 6
km
0 0.5 1
Cebu City

Visayas - Cebu

nese. The bitter liberation struggle towards the end of the war took its toll, and much of Fort San Pedro was destroyed. Restoration work began in the late 1960s and a well-tended garden was laid out in the inner courtyard - a beautiful little place of refuge not too far from the hustle and bustle of the harbour. In addition, in the mid-90s the little Fort San Pedro National Museum was built; admission P15.

Magellan's Cross

The first Catholic Mass on Cebu was celebrated on 14 April 1521, when Rajah Humabon, his wife, sons and daughters and 800 islanders had themselves baptised by Father Pedro de Valderrama. Magellan marked this beginning of Christianity in the Philippines with the erection of a cross. The original cross is said to be inside the present, hollow cross, which stands in a pavilion near the Cebu City Hall.

Basilica Minore del Santo Niño

The present basilica - formerly San Agustin Church - was finished in 1740, three earlier wooden structures having been destroyed by fire. Undoubtedly, the focal point of the slightly weathered stone church is Santo Niño, a statue of the infant Jesus, but if you want to admire this valuable object on the left of the altar you either need a telescope or have to wait in a long queue. In 1565 this treasure, with its jewelled crown and gem-covered clothes, was found undamaged by Juan de Camus, one of Legaspi's soldiers, in a hut near the basilica. Since then Santo Niño has been the patron saint of the Cebuano.

Caretta Cemetery

A visit to this large cemetery on MJ Cuenco Ave is probably only of significance on 1 November - All Saints Day - or perhaps the night before, when everyone is pretty wound up. Opposite is the Chinese Cemetery. To get there, catch a jeepney from Colon St going towards Mabolo.

Taoist Temple

Some six km from the city centre lies Beverly Hills, the millionaires' quarter of Cebu City. The impressive, highly ornate temple of the Taoist religious community is also located here. Its size and architecture are evidence that a considerable part of the population of Cebu is Chinese. You can get a good view of the city from this magnificent temple.

The taxi fare to the temple from the Downtown area should be about P150 (including 30 min waiting time), but agree on the fare first. It is cheaper by Lahug jeepney, which will get you fairly close. Catch it in Jakosalem St and get off at the Doña M Gaisano Bridge in Lahug (don't forget to tell the driver in good time), cross the small bridge, turn right and walk for another 1½ km or so. At the split in the road behind the guard-post, take the left fork (Canyon Rd).

Cebu Heavenly Temple of Charity

On the way to the Taoist Temple you will see on your left the Cebu Heavenly Temple of Charity. It is built on a hill which provides a stunning view. A natural spring flows underneath the building. The middle altar of this beautiful temple houses the statues of the Supreme God and of Milagrosa Rosa, the temple's patron saint.

To get there, take a jeepney from the Downtown area just as you would to the Taoist Temple. Just after the little bridge go right, then after 200m there's a path leading off to the left in the direction of the temple. You could also carry on in the direction of the Taoist Temple until you come to Justice St, which breaks off just across from the Phu Shian Temple and leads to the temple.

Tops

To enjoy probably the best panoramic view of Cebu City, with Mactan Island and Bohol in the background, you have to make the trip to Tops. This is a lavishly built viewpoint on the 600m high Busay Hill, around eight km north of the Cebu Plaza Hotel and 15 km from Downtown. The view is particularly impressive at sunset, when the lights of the city below come on. At this time of day, however, it can get cool, so you would be well advised to take a pullover or a jacket with you. But beware: there is no public transport back to Cebu City in the evening! The place is owned by the Lito Osmeña family, whose domed, glittering silver residence is not far away. Admission to Tops is P50.

You can get there by taking a Lahug jeepney as far as the La Nival Hotel, changing across the road from there at the turn-off for the Cebu Plaza Hotel to a jeepney heading in the Tops direction. Some of the jeepney drivers turn back 500m after the Cebu Plaza Hotel, so ask before you get in if he actually does go to Tops. Leaving from the Cebu Plaza Hotel the road first takes you past the Chateau de Busay restaurant and the Residence Inn. After 6½ km get out right at the top of the pass (Busay Hill turn-off), and walk up the last stretch (1200m) to the summit. If you don't take a break, the walk should take about 30 min up this rather steep, but well-maintained road.

The trip by taxi from the Downtown area to Tops is decidedly more comfortable and should cost around P300 to P500 including waiting time (agree on the fare first).

About 200m before the pass summit and the Busay Hill turn-off you'll find the charming La Tegola restaurant, where there's a gorgeous view of Cebu City from the terrace. Apart from good Italian food there's also ice cream and refreshingly tart kalamansi juice.

Shopping

It's worth going to see the big, colourful Carbon Market between Magallanes St and Quezon Blvd. Here you will find on offer both agricultural produce and the varied handicrafts of Cebu Province. There are also products from other Visayan islands, such as basketware from Bohol.

Amongst the biggest and best shopping centres are SM City in the Reclamation Area, the Ayala Center in the Cebu Business Park and the Gaisano Country Mall in Talamban Rd. You can also shop till you drop at Gaisano Main and Gaisano Metro, both Downtown on Colon St; and Robinsons on Fuente Osmeña. At the weekends in the Ayala Center, they have Farmers Day with fruit, vegetables and flowers on sale.

A first-class place to go for all sorts of top quality equipment from knives to rucksacks is Habagat Outdoor Equipment, Ramon Aboitiz St. The friendly people there will contact all sorts of outdoor clubs for you, and also organise trekking tours. In the building behind the shop they offer a reliable maintenance and repair service for mountain-bikes.

There is a good branch of the National Book Store on Maxilom Ave. Bookmark has a branch on Osmeña Ave.

Places to Stay

The choice of hotels in Cebu City has increased enormously in the last few years, especially in the middle range. However, it's clear that supply has outstripped demand in the meantime, and prices have plummeted due to lack of guests. As a result, not everyone always charges for breakfast any more and it's always a good idea to ask if a discount or promo rates are available.

Places to Stay - bottom end

Ruftan Pensione, Legaspi St, Tel 2562613, Fax 4121475. SR/DR/fan P165

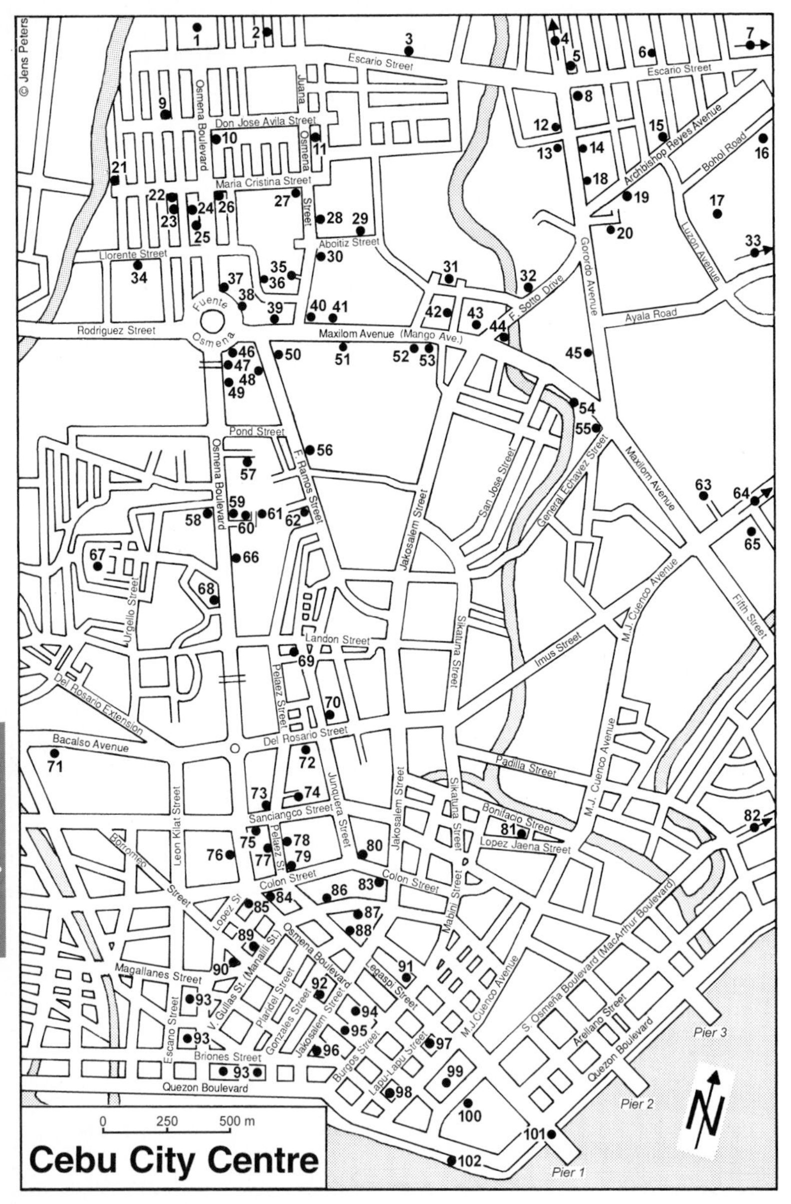

Visayas - Cebu

Getting There & Away

3 Seair
13 Northwest Airlines
Qatar Airways
Thai Airways International
19 Avis
34 Asian Spirit
33 Silkair
Singapore Airlines
40 Air Philippines
44 Cathay Pacific Airways
65 Philippine Airlines
71 Southern Busterminal
82 Northern Busterminal
101 Oceanjet Terminal

Places to Stay

2 Mayflower Pension House
3 Cebu Grand Hotel
The Apartelle
4 Cebu Northwinds Hotel
Hotel La Nivel
La Guardia Hotel
5 Kukuk's Nest Pension House
Tonros Apartelle
7 Montebello Villa Hotel
Waterfront Cebu City Hotel
8 Century Golden Peak Hotel
9 Hotel Asia
11 Vacation Hotel
12 West Gorordo Hotel
15 City Park Inn
20 St. Moritz Hotel
21 Dynasty Tourist Inn
22 Jasmine Pension
23 Verbena Pension House
24 Casa Loreto Pension House
Westpoint Inn
27 Executive Royal Inn
La Casita Pension
28 C'est La Vie Pension
30 NS Royal Pension
32 Richmond Plaza
33 Cebu City Marriott Hotel
35 Century Plaza Hotel
36 Fuente Pension House
37 Elegant Circle Inn
38 Garwood Park Hotel
42 Eddie's Hotel
46 Cebu Midtown Hotel
48 Kan-Irag Hotel
50 Holiday Plaza Hotel
54 Mango Park Hotel
57 Jasmine Pension
60 Arbel's Pension House
61 Pacific Pensionne
62 Diplomat Hotel
64 Kiwi Lodge (500m)
66 YMCA
69 Teo-Fel Pension House
70 Cebu Elicon House
74 Golden Valley Inn
75 Cebu View Tourist Inn
Sogo Hotel
78 Hotel de Mercedes
McSherry Pension House
79 Century Hotel
80 Cebu Business Hotel
84 Cebu Hallmark Hotel
86 Hope Pension
87 Hotel Victoria de Cebu
88 Ruftan Pensione
89 Pacific Tourist Inn

Places to Eat & Entertainment

4 Golden Cowrie Restaurant
Seafood City
7 Crossroads
Ginza Restaurant
Mikado Restaurant
5 Kukuk's Nest Restaurant
12 Family Choice Restaurant
16 Ayala Entertainment Center
18 Royal Concourse Restaurant
26 KFC
31 Lone Star
39 McDonald's
41 Café Italia
Vienna Kaffehaus
45 Grand Majestic Restaurant
48 Love City Disco
Thunderdome
Volvo Bar
49 Silver Dollar Bar

↗

51 Mister Donut
52 La Dolce Vita Restaurant
Vienna Kaffee-Haus
53 Black Hole Bar
Puerto Rico Bar
Viking Bar
54 Lighthouse Restaurant
55 Steve's Music Bar
56 Beehive Restaurant
59 La Buona Forchetta Ristorante
60 Firehouse Bar
73 Our Place Restaurant
76 Snow Sheen Restaurant
77 Pete's Kitchen
Pete's Mini Food Center
87 Visayan Restaurant
98 Eddie's Log Cabin

Miscellaneous
1 Provincial Capitol
4 Beverly Hills
Taoist Temple
Heavenly Temple of Charity
Tops
6 Cebu Holiday & Fitness Center
7 Grand Convention Center
Casino
International Convention Center
10 Cebu Doctors Hospital
13 QC Pavilion
Scuba World
14 Equitable PCI Bank
US Consulate
17 Ayala Center
25 Rizal Memorial Library
& Museum
29 Habagat Outdoor Shop
33 Citibank
40 National Book Store
43 Iglesia Ni Kristo Church
44 The Rivergate Mall
46 Robinsons Department Store
47 Metrobank Plaza
58 Philippine National Bank (PNB)
63 Caretta Cemetery
65 Chinese Cemetery
67 Sacred Heart Hospital
68 Bookmark
72 University of San Carlos
& Museum
78 Metrobank
81 Casa Gorordo Museum
82 SM City
83 Gaisano Main Department Store
85 Gaisano Metro Department Store
90 Equitable PCI Bank
91 Cebu Cathedral
92 Equitable PCI Bank
93 Carbon Market
94 Basilica Minore del Santo Niño
95 Magellan's Cross
96 City Hall
Bank of the Philippine Islands
Philippine National Bank (PNB)
97 Tourist Office
99 Plaza Independencia
100 Fort San Pedro
102 General Post Office

and P250. Basic accommodation. The rooms looking out on to the courtyard are the quietest. 'Wash-up' (only use of the bathroom) available to passing travellers for P40.

Kukuk's Nest Pension House, 157 Gorordo Ave, Tel & Fax 2315180. SR/fan P200, DR/fan P300, SR/DR/ac/bath P450 and P500 (TV). Pleasantly furnished aircon rooms in a fine old bourgeois house. Restaurant.

Elicon House, General Junquera St, Tel 2539189, Fax 2530367. SR/fan P200, DR/fan P290, SR/ac/bath P450, DR/ac/bath P575. Reasonable for the money.

YMCA, 61 Osmeña Blvd, Tel 2534057. SR/DR/fan P150/300, SR/DR/fan/bath P300/400, SR/DR/ac/bath P500. Uninspiring rooms, but OK for the money. Couples may be accepted (it's worth a try). Check-in time = check-out time. Restaurant, swimming pool, billiards, table tennis and bowling. YMCA membership costs P100 per year.

McSherry Pension House, Pelaez St, Tel 2544792. SR/DR/fan/bath P300,

SR/DR/ac/bath P400. Basic, practical rooms. Monthly rates available. Centrally located in a quiet lane next to the Hotel de Mercedes.

Mayflower Pension House, East Capitol Site, Tel 2552800, Fax 2552700, @. SR/fan P230, DR/fan P300, SR/ac/bath P460, DR/ac/bath P580. Quiet rooms, although a bit small; the aircon ones have TV. Fairly good accommodation near the Provincial Capitol. Restaurant.

Pacific Tourist Inn, V Gullas St corner Balintawak St, Tel 2532151-59, Fax 2545674. SR/ac/bath P385, DR/ac/bath P570, suite P1350. Rooms of varying degrees of comfort, almost all with TV; some have no windows. A refrigerator will cost you P100 extra. Restaurant.

Verbena Pension House, 584-A Don Gil Garcia St, Tel 2534440, Fax 2533430. SR/ac/bath P400, DR/ac/bath P460. Friendly accommodation with good rooms of various sizes; TV costs P50 extra. Coffee shop.

Cebu Century Hotel, Pelaez St corner Colon St, Tel 2551341-47, Fax 2551600, @. SR/ac/bath P450, SR/DR/ac/bath P500 to P600. Reasonable rooms with TV (P50 extra for a refrigerator). The singles on the 4th floor are good for two, while those on the 5th floor next door to the disco nightclub are noisy. Centrally located in Downtown.

Hotel de Mercedes, Pelaez St, Tel 2531105-10, Fax 2533880. SR/ac/bath P465 and P680, DR/ac/bath P720 and P960, suites P1230 and P1500. Older hotel with acceptable rooms, the expensive ones with TV, the suites also have a refrigerator. Restaurant.

C'est La Vie Pension, Juana Osmeña St, Tel 2532376. SR/DR/ac/bath P500 and P550. Fairly good rooms with TV, OK for the money.

Pacific Pensionne, 313-A Osmeña Blvd, Tel 2535271, Fax 2611792, @. SR/ac/bath P500, DR/ac/bath P600 and P700. Tidy rooms with TV. Coffee shop. Located in a little side-street.

Teo-Fel Pension House, Junquera St, Tel 2532482, Fax 2532488. SR/ac/bath P500, DR/ac/bath P750. With TV. Pleasant accommodation with well-maintained rooms. Check-out time 1pm. Small restaurant.

Cebu View Tourist Inn, Sanciangco St, Tel 2548333, Fax 2549777. SR/ac/bath P500 and P600, DR/ac/bath P700 to P950. Good, well-kept rooms with TV, albeit mostly without windows. Coffee shop.

Cebu Business Hotel, Colon St corner Junquera St, Tel 2556010, Fax 2556013, @. SR/ac/bath P500, DR/ac/bath P700 to P1000, suites P1200 and P1400. Good rooms at this price, although the single rooms are a bit cramped. All rooms have TV, the more expensive ones also have a refrigerator. Restaurant.

Golden Valley Inn, 155-A Pelaez St, Tel 2538660, Fax 2538482, @. SR/ac/bath P600, DR/ac/bath P700 to P1040. Neat rooms, the more expensive ones also have a refrigerator and TV. Pleasant, friendly accommodation in a quiet location in a little side-street. Coffee shop.

Fuente Pension House, Don Julio Llorente St, Tel 2534133, Fax 2544365, @. SR/ac/bath P600, DR/ac/bath P700 and P975, suite P2150. With TV, the suites also have a refrigerator. Nice rooms in a natty little lodging house. They have a roof-top coffee shop. Quiet location near Maxilom Ave and Fuente Osmeña.

Westpoint Inn, Don Gil Garcia St, Tel 2543433, Fax 2544524, @. SR/ac/bath P650 and P750, DR/ac/bath P P750 and P850. Tidy rooms, some really small and others a bit bigger with TV. Restaurant.

Richmond Plaza Hotel, F Sotto Dr, Tel 2320361, Fax 2321974, @. SR/ac/bath P680, DR/ac/bath P800 to P1175, suites P1500 to P2300; with refrigerator and TV. Attractive rooms, some are a bit small though. Restaurant.

Diplomat Hotel, F Ramos St, Tel 2546342, Fax 2546346, @. SR/DR/ac/bath P700 and P900, suite P1200. Attractive, well-kept rooms with TV, the better ones also have a refrigerator. Good value. Restaurant.

Kan-Irag Hotel, F Ramos St, Tel 2531151, Fax 2536935, @. SR/DR/ac/bath P770 to P880. Acceptable rooms with TV and refrigerator, the ones overlooking the street are, however, a bit on the noisy side. Their restaurant is open round the clock.

Kiwi Lodge, Tud Tud St, Tel & Fax 2329550, @. SR/DR/ac/bath P800 and P1000. Excellent, well-kept rooms with refrigerator and TV. Restaurant. Located in a side street about 100m off M J Cuenco Ave.

Places to Stay - middle

NS Royal Pensione, Juana Osmeña St, Tel 2545358, Fax 2551556. SR/DR/ac/bath P800 to P1400. With TV, the more expensive ones also have a refrigerator. Pleasant accommodation with well-furnished rooms. Restaurant.

City Park Inn, Archbishop Reyes Ave, Tel 2327311, Fax 2327382. SR/ac/bath P800, DR/ac/bath P1000 to P1900. Friendly, clean rooms. Restaurant. Conveniently located for the Ayala Center.

Vacation Hotel, Juana Osmeña St corner Avila St, Tel 2532766, Fax 2536554, @. SR/ac/bath P800, DR/ac/bath P900 to P1500. Friendly, really comfortable rooms with refrigerator and TV. Good value. Restaurant, swimming pool.

West Gorordo Hotel, Gorordo Ave, Tel 2314347, Fax 2311158, @. SR/ac/bath P840, DR/ac/bath P1320 and P1560, suite P3000, all including breakfast. Comfortable rooms with TV, some with a refrigerator. Immaculately run hotel. Restaurant, fitness room, sauna.

Hotel Asia, Don Jose Avila St, Tel 2558536, Fax 2533805. SR/ac/bath P890 to P1300, DR/ac/bath P1190 to P1600. Attractive, pleasantly furnished, cosy rooms with refrigerator and TV. Restaurant.

Mango Park Hotel, General Maxilom Ave, Tel 2331511, Fax 2335695, @. SR/DR/ac/bath P890 to P1400 P. Pleasant hotel with well-furnished rooms, all with TV, the more expensive ones also with refrigerator. Restaurant, swimming pool on the roof.

Eddie's Hotel, Manalo St corner Queens Rd, Tel 2548570, Fax 2548578, @. SR/DR/ac/bath P1480 to P1880. Including breakfast. Tidy rooms with TV; P100 extra for a refrigerator. Restaurant. Located near the Iglesia Ni Kristo church.

St Moritz Hotel, Gorordo Ave, Tel 2311148, Fax 2312485, @. SR/DR/ac/bath P1550 and P1900, suite P2500. Inviting, tastefully furnished rooms with refrigerator and TV. Restaurant, disco nightclub.

Garwood Place Hotel, Fuente Osmeña, Tel 2531131, Fax 2530118, @. SR/DR/ac/bath P1600 to P2000. Including breakfast. Pleasant rooms with TV, some have no windows, however. Restaurant, coffee shop.

The Golden Peak Hotel, Gorordo Ave corner Escario St, Tel 2338111, Fax 2315611, @. SR/ac/bath P1100 and P1400, SR/DR/ac/bath P1200 and P1500, suite P2300 and P2400. Including breakfast. Immaculate, well-appointed rooms. Restaurant.

Montebello Villa Hotel, Banilad, Tel 2313681, Fax 2314455, @. SR/DR/ac/bath P1400 and P1900, suites P2600 and P3600; including breakfast. Good rooms with TV, the more expensive ones and the suites also have a refrigerator. Restaurant, coffee shop, swimming pool, tennis courts, beautiful garden. A charming, slightly ageing place on the north-eastern outskirts of town, near Gaisano Country Mall.

Cebu Grand Hotel, Escario St, Tel 2546361, Fax 2546363, @. SR/DR/ac/

bath P1400 to P2000, suite P3500 and P4000; including breakfast. Nice, big rooms with TV. Restaurant, small roof-top swimming pool, fitness room.
Holiday Plaza Hotel, F Ramos St, Tel 2549880, Fax 2547646, @. SR/DR/ac/bath P1700 and P2000, suites P3000 and P4000; including breakfast. Well-furnished rooms with refrigerator and TV, although some are a bit small. Restaurant.

Places to Stay - top end

Cebu Midtown Hotel, Fuente Osmeña, Tel 2539711, Fax 2539765, @. SR/DZ/ac/bath P2300, suite P5000 to P12,000. Restaurant, swimming pool, jacuzzi, massage, sauna and fitness room. Located above Robinsons.
Cebu City Marriott Hotel, Cardinal Rosales Ave, Tel 2326100, Fax 2326101, @. SR/DZ/ac/bath P2800, suite P5300. First-class hotel with restaurant, swimming pool.
Waterfront Cebu City Hotel, Salinas Dr, Tel 2326888, Fax 2326880, @. SR/ac/bath P3800 to P5100, DR/ac/bath P4450 to P5720, suites P14,310. Restaurant, fitness room, casino, disco. A luxury hotel, you can't miss this impressive building, built in a neo-classical style with several turrets worth popping by to see if you are interested in architecture.

Places to Eat

Cebu City has an amazing number and variety of restaurants. Apart from enjoying local and Chinese food, the Cebuanos have also taken to Italian cooking in a big way. There's also a surprising variety of restaurants to be found in shopping centres such as the Ayala Center, Gaisano Country Mall and SM City.

Filipino

Pete's Kitchen, Pelaez St. Clean, and with amazingly inexpensive food - probably why it's crowded from the early morning hours on.
Pete's Mini Food Center, Pelaez St. A big, semi-enclosed place where the guests can choose their food at a long buffet and have it warmed up if they want.
Royal Concourse, Gorordo Ave. Big, very clean self-service restaurant with inexpensive Filipino, Japanese and Chinese dishes. Disco on Fridays and Saturdays from 10.30pm.
Golden Cowrie, Salinas Dr, Lahug. Open Mon-Sat 11am-2pm and 6-10pm. This restaurant with its great atmosphere has been a long-time favourite with gourmets. Their inexpensive seafood dishes can be heartily recommended. Popular orders are baked mussels (*tahong*) and green mango shakes.
Lighthouse Restaurant, Maxilom Ave. Open daily 10.30am-2pm and 5.30-10.30pm. Apart from Filipino dishes - mostly seafood -, standard Japanese dishes such as tempura and sushi are also served.
Seafood City, Gorordo Ave corner Salinas Dr. Open daily 11am-2pm and 6-10pm. Two-storey restaurant next to the La Nivel Hotel. It's like a market here, with the guests choosing their own fish, vegetables etc, which they then have cooked according to their wishes. Highly recommended, if a bit pricey.

Chinese

Snow Sheen Restaurant, Osmeña Blvd. Has been deservedly popular for years for its good cooking.
Visayan Restaurant, V Gullas St. Worth checking out, this place has earned a good reputation for providing excellent, inexpensive food, big portions and friendly service.
Robinsons, Fuente Osmeña. There's a really good-value dim sum restaurant downstairs which is worth giving a try.
Gaisano Metro, Colon St corner Lopez St. In the *Food Center* on the top floor

Food & Entertainment

A combination of food, drink and entertainment is drawing more and more people into so-called 'resto bars' and 'sport bars'. They can mainly be found in the following complexes: Ayala Entertainment Center (Bohol St corner Mindanao Dr, between Ayala Center and Citibank); Crossroads, Governor Cuenco Ave; and The Village (Salinas Dr, across from the Waterfront Cebu City Hotel in Lahug).

***Ayala Entertainment Center**:* Bigby's Café (pizzas, salads); Bo's Coffee Club (freshly brewed coffee); Brix (café, billards); Café Adriatico (bistro); Don Henrico's (pizzas); Hap Japs (fusion cuisine); Max's (grilled chicken); Ratzky (disco, live bands; P100 admission; P150 at the weekend); Sharro (pizzas, pasta); Tequila Joe's (tacos, pasta, margaritas, fruit shakes); The Dessert Factory (cake, ice cream); Timezone (fruit machines and video games).

***Crossroads**:* Banri Noodle House (Japanese noodles); Café Adriatico (bistro); Chicken House Bacolod (grilled chicken Bacolod-style); Cue Café (freshly brewed coffee, billiards, pizzas); High Life (live bands; P50 admission; P100 at the weekend); Ice Castle (ice cream, halo-halo); Krua Thai (Thai food); La Marea (coffee and pastries); Persian Palate (Indian and Persian dishes); Tsai Asia Restaurant (huge variety of teas); Vudu (bar and restaurant).

***The Village**:* B.O.P. (Karaoke); D's Bar; Il Sole Ristorante (Italian cuisine); Lucy's French Restaurant (French cuisine and seafood); Pulip Korean Restobar; Yo Latino (bar and restaurant, live music).

of the department store you have the opportunity to wander round and try something different. A variety of self-service restaurants serve excellent food like dim sum, but also cakes and ice cream etc. A pleasant place to eat, especially if you're shopping anyway.

Ayala Center, Cebu Business Park, has several small self-service restaurants on the fifth floor with a wide selection of well-cooked, inexpensive food (Chinese and Filipino).

Indian

Persian Palate, Crossroads, Governor Cuenco Ave. Indian and Persian food with excellent curries and samosas - the kebabs are good as well.

Japanese

Mikado, Mahogany Court, Archbishop Reyes Ave. Open daily 11am-2.30pm and 6-10pm. Serves inexpensive standard dishes; favourites are sushi and sashimi. There's another *Mikado* in SM City.

Ginza, J Panis St, Banilad. Open daily 10am-2pm and 6-10pm. Good restaurant in the mid-price range with friendly service. They also prepare Korean food.

Thai

Krua Thai Restaurant, Crossroads, Governor Cuenco Ave. Open daily 11am-2.30pm and 5.30-9.30pm. To be recommended for its excellent Thai food at reasonable prices.

American & European

Sand Trap, Maria Luisa Rd, Banilad (set back from the street a bit). Open daily 10am-1am. Specialities here are lamb cutlets, daily specials, and a bar-

becue in the evening from Wednesday until Saturday. A veritable oasis in the north of the city - more than just a restaurant, it's a sports complex as well - with a swimming pool (P100 for non-members), tennis courts (P85 per hour, P200 per hour in the evening; lessons for P150 per hour), billiards and darts.
Our Place, Pelaez St. Open Mon-Sat 9am-10pm. Relatively cheap Filipino, US and European meals. A narrow staircase leads up to this popular pub/restaurant above street level.
Kiwi Lodge Restaurant, Tud Tud St. Open daily 7am-11pm. Big, airy restaurant with standard fare from hamburgers to steaks.
Eddie's Log Cabin, MC Briones St. Open Mon-Sat 9am-2pm and 6-10pm. Old, established restaurant downtown, near the Plaza Independencia, with good American and Filipino food. Worth trying out are the steaks with salad, and the inexpensive specials of the day.
Beehive Restaurant, F Ramos St. Open daily 11am-10pm. Pleasant, well-established restaurant, known for its Spanish cooking and great steaks.
Kukuk's Nest, Gorordo St corner Escario St. Open daily 10am-2am. Good European and Filipino food, served in a pleasant garden setting.
Idea Italia, Ayala Center. Open daily 10am-9pm. Very popular restaurant. Apart from Italian cuisine, Alfredo the owner and chef also cooks local dishes in the Italian style.
Café Italia, Maxilom Ave. Open daily 9.30am-10pm. Good Italian cooking with a plethora of pastas.
La Buona Forchetta, Osmeña Blvd. Open daily 11am-3pm and 6-11pm. Outstanding Italian food in the medium price range (pizza and pasta at around P200/250).
La Tegola, Governor Cuenco Ave, Banilad. Open daily 11am-3pm and 6-11pm. Definitely the best Italian restaurant in Cebu City; high-end price range. Located in the north of the city. There's a small branch with a gorgeous view a few km outside of the city in Busay Hills.
The French Baker, SM City. Popular café in the biggest shopping centre in Cebu. The menu includes salads, tasty sandwiches etc, and you can even get a cup of real coffee.
Vienna Kaffeehaus, Banilad, between Cebu City and Mandaue, in the Ford's Inn Hotel. Not surprisingly, they pride themselves in Austrian specialities here. Breakfast, cakes and several sorts of coffee are available. The prices are a bit on the high side, but worth it. There is another *Vienna Kaffeehaus* in the Mango Square on Maxilom Ave.

Fast Food

Well-known franchises such as ***Jollibee***, ***McDonald's, Pizza Hut, Chowking*** and ***Goldilocks*** can be found all over, but are well represented in the two big shopping centres Ayala Center and SM City. There is a ***KFC*** on the corner of Osmeña Blvd and Maria Cristina St, while Maxilom Ave has a ***Mister Donut***.

Entertainment

Expats and foreign visitors congregate in pubs such as ***Our Place*** in Pelaez St and the ***Kiwi Lodge Bar*** in Tud Tud St. Also popular are the nightclubs ***Lone Star*** (billiards) in Queen's Road near Eddie's Hotel, ***Papillon***, ***Viking's Bar*** and the ***Black Hole Bar*** in Maxilom Ave and the ***Silver Dollar Bar*** and ***Firehouse*** on Osmeña Blvd.
The Ayala Entertainment Center offers a range of entertainment to suit all tastes. The ***Ratsky*** disco is especially busy with people enjoying their live music.
From Tuesday to Sunday evening you can catch live pop and R & B bands at ***High Life***, Crossroads, Governor Cuenco Ave. It's wall-to-wall people after about 10pm in the popular ***Sunflower***

City disco (with live music) on Salinas Dr in the Lahug area of town. The ***Nasa Disco Club*** in AS Fortuna St in Mandaue - Cebu's biggest disco (with live music) - is also a popular place to hang out.

It's a safe bet that gamblers would prefer the ***Casino*** in the Waterfront Cebu City Hotel, where there is a full house every evening until the wee small hours.

On Sunday in the ***Century Game Club*** in M Velez St near the Provincial Capitol in Banawa you may get a chance to watch 'high rollers' place their bets. The first cockfights take place in the forenoon.

Miscellaneous

Consulates: Thai Consulate, Eastern Shipping Lines Building, MJ Cuenco Ave (near the Plaza Independencia), Tel 2537012, 2537078. A visa for Thailand can be processed within 24 hours. United States Consulate, Equitable PCI Building, Gorordo Ave, Tel 2311261.

The following countries also have consulates here: Austria, Tel. 3210605; Belgium, Tel 2315333; Canada, Tel 2563320; China, Tel 2563400; Denmark, Tel 2331328; France, Tel 2320936; Japan, Tel 2550287; Mexico, Tel 2332758; Netherlands, Tel 3461823; Norway, Tel 2323133; Spain, Tel 2311329; Sweden, Tel 2333106; Turkey, Tel 2544624; and UK, Tel 3460525.

Diving: The following dive shops sell diving equipment: Aquaventure Cebu, Mercedes Commercial Complex, A Cortez Ave, Mandaue City, Tel 3451571, @; Liquid Assets, Cebu Grand Hotel Complex, Escario St, Tel 2546359; Scuba World, Maria Cristina St, Capitol Site, Tel 2549591; White Tip Divers, Borromeo Arcade, F Ramos St, Tel 2542623.

Diving infos also from Sea Explorers, Archbishop Reyes Ave, Knights of Columbus Compound, Tel 2340248, @.

Festival: On the third weekend in January every year, the colourful and crowded Sinulog Festival takes place in Cebu City. As the festival draws large crowds into the city, most hotels are booked up at this time.

Information: *What's on in The Visayas and Mindanao* is a monthly tourist bulletin with interesting articles and useful advertisements which is handed out free at the airport and in various hotels and restaurants.

The advertising pages of the Cebu City daily *Sun Star* contain up-to-date information on entertainment and shipping connections.

Immigration Office, J Burgos St, Mandaue, Tel 3546442-44. Open Mon-Fri 8am-noon and 1-5pm.

Medical Services & Wellness: Cebu Doctors Hospital, Osmeña Blvd, near the Provincial Capitol Building, Tel 2537511.

Dentist: Dr Lorna Tipon-Sabandal, Osmeña Building (room 209), Colon St corner Pelaez St, Tel 2544821, Cellphone 0917-7638854, consults Mon-Sat 8am-6pm, Sun by appointment.

The Meddah Spa, Crossroads, Governor Cuenco Ave, Tel 2342080, @, offers an all-round wellness programme (massages from P150) in a peaceful, relaxing atmosphere. To be recommended: 1½-hour stone massage for P850. Open daily 10am-11pm.

A professionally administered shiatsu massage costs P400 plus tip (P100 to P150) at the Cebu Holiday Health & Fitness Center, Molave St, Tel 2310408, open daily 1-11pm. Also worth recommending is the inexpensive Guardo Shiatsu & Reflexology Center in F Ramos St, Tel 2537963 (shiatsu massage P250). Open daily 1-10pm.

Money: Department stores like Gaisano Metro and Robinsons will also change cash, even at the weekends, and sometimes even at a better rate than the banks will offer.

The best place to change American Express travellers' cheques is at American Express itself (Adventure International Tours), Ayala Center (second floor at the back), Cebu Business Park, Tel 2322970. Open Mon-Fri 8.30am-5.30pm (no cash advances after 4.30pm); Sat 9am-noon.
Thomas Cook Travel has an office on the ground floor of the Metrobank Plaza on Osmeña Blvd, where you can change your Thomas Cook travellers' cheques.
ATM available at: Bank of the Philippine Islands, Magallanes St corner Burgos St; Citibank, Ayala Life/SGU Center, Mindanao Ave corner Biliran Rd; Equitable PCI Bank, Juan Luna Ave (across from SM City), and their two downtown branches on Gonzales St corner Magallanes St, and on Borromeo St corner Magallanes St; HSBC, Cardinal Rosales Ave; Metrobank, Osmeña Blvd and Palaez St; Philippine National Bank, Briones St and Osmeña Blvd.
Online: There are various Internet cafés spread around the city (P20 to P50/hr).
Post & Telephone: The GPO is on Plaza Independencia. The poste restante service is apparently not very reliable here. There are branch offices in the Cebu City Hall, Briones St, at the University of the Visayas (UV), Colon St, and at the University of San Carlos, Del Rosario St.
Post code: 6000. Area code: 032.
Tourist Office, LDM Building., Lapu-Lapu St, Tel 2542811, 2546650, Fax 2542711, @. Open Mo-Fri 8am-noon and 1-5pm.
There is also a service counter at Mactan International Airport, where room reservations and other travel arrangements can be made; Tel 3408229, 3402486 (ext 2450).
Tourist Police: The so-called Task Force Turista can be reached at Tel 4155910 (24 hrs).

Personal Safety
A big city and traffic crossroads such as Cebu City is obviously a lucrative field for pickpockets. They usually work in the late afternoon and evening in the vicinity of Colon St and Osmeña Blvd, and in the harbour area during the arrival and departure of big passenger ships.
Even in Cebu City it is not wise to take apparently friendly invitations at face value!
Our friends the money changers, who always offer a seductively high rate of exchange but more or less never stick to it, are active at the Plaza Independencia in front of the tourist office.

Getting Around
Car: About a dozen local companies offer car hire. The most reliable places would probably be Avis on Archbishop Reyes Ave, Lahug, Tel 2310941 and at Mactan International Airport, Tel 3402486 (ext 1141).
Jeepney: Of the many jeepney routes available, the following ones are probably the most important for tourists: Capitol (Uptown at the end of Osmeña Blvd), Lahug (Lahug district in the north of the city), Carbon (Carbon Market, Downtown) and Colon (Colon St, Downtown).
Taxi: Flag-down is P30. Mind you, not every taxi driver switches on the meter if it is not pointed out to him. It is worthwhile trying to negotiate a fare in advance for longer trips (eg P800 to P1000 to Moalboal). If your journey is at night to a place off the beaten track, then the driver will usually ask for a surcharge of about 20-30% as he has to deadhead on the return journey. If you're leaving by ship, remember that taxis have to pay a fee of P10 to get into the dock area.

Walking: If you get caught jay-walking in Cebu City it can cost you P20. On the other hand, for that money an official ticket issued by the Republic of the Philippines could make a neat souvenir for somebody.

Orientation
Recently several streets in Cebu City were renamed, but people also still use the following names in brackets: Osmeña Blvd (Jones Ave, Juan Luna St), Maxilom Ave (Mango Ave), V Gullas St (Manalili St), Bacalso Ave (Rizal Ave, South Expressway) and Fuente Osmeña (Osmeña Circle).

Getting There & Away

By Air
Mactan International Airport is on Mactan Island, about 15 km from Cebu City. Inland flights use this airport, as do the few international flights from places such as Hong Kong, Malaysia, Singapore and Japan (see the Getting There & Away section of the Travel Planning chapter). On the day of departure, it's a good idea to leave Cebu City in plenty time, as traffic jams often cause delays and are frequently to blame for people missing their flights. If you have an early plane to catch, it could pay to spend the night near the airport instead of in town (see Lapu-Lapu in the following Mactan Island section).
The airport tax for inland flights is P100 and P550 for international flights!

From Mactan International Airport to Cebu City: An aircon taxi or aircon limousine from Mactan International Airport to the city should cost P150, but make sure the price is agreed upon before departure (they will ask from P250 to P400). Hardly any taxis will switch on their meters, unless they have been fixed beforehand. From the town to the airport you might get away with paying P120. If there are no traffic jams a taxi should take around 20 min for the journey.
Tricycles are prohibited in the airport area, but you will find them waiting nearby. They cost about P30 as far as the jeepney terminal, where you can board a jeepney to Cebu City (destination: SM City, change there into a jeepney heading for example to Downtown/Colon).

Airlines in Cebu City: As a result of the opening of Mactan International Airport, not only inland airlines but also several foreign airlines have opened offices in Cebu City.
Air Philippines, Mactan International Airport, Tel 3410920 (open daily 7am-8pm).
- Maxilom Avenue, Tel. 2562969, 2558492 (open Mon-Sat 8.30am-5.30pm).
- SM City, Reclamation Area, Tel 4128833, 2331383 (open daily 10am-8pm).
Destinations: Bacolod, Davao, General Santos, Iloilo City, Manila.
Asian Spirit, Mactan International Airport, Tel 3410226 (open daily 6am-6pm).
- Llorente St, Tel 2544661.
Destinations: Cagayan de Oro, Caticlan (for Boracay), Dipolog, Surigao, Tandag.
British Airways, Ayala Center, Cebu Business Park, Tel 2320006.
Cathay Pacific, The Rivergate Mall, Maxilom Ave, Tel 2540821, 2540476.
Cebu Pacific, Mactan International Airport, Tel 3405360 (open daily 5am-9pm).
- Governor Cuenco Ave (across from the Gaisano Country Mall), Banilad, Tel 2312868.
- Robinsons, Fuente Osmeña, Tel 2557831 (open daily 9.30am-8pm).
- SM City, Reclamation Area, Tel 2334983-85 (open daily 10am-8pm).

Destinations: Bacolod, Davao, Iloilo City, Manila, Puerto Princesa, Zamboanga.
Malaysia Airlines, Ayala Center, Cebu Business Park, Tel 2313887.
Northwest Airlines, QC Pavilion, Gorordo Ave, Tel 2322401.
Philippine Airlines, Mactan International Airport, Tel 3400191, 3400422 (open daily 3.30am-6.15pm).
- Osmeña Blvd, Tel. 2544655 (open Mon-Fri 8.30am-5pm, Sat 8.30am-noon).
- SM City, Reclamation Area, Tel 2328412 (open daily 8.30am-7pm).
Destinations: Bacolod, Davao, Iloilo City, Manila.
Qantas Airways, Ayala Center, Cebu Business Park, Tel 2320004.
Qatar Airways, QC Pavilion, Gorordo Ave, Tel 3231000.
Seair, Mactan International Airport, Tel 3413022-23, 3414879 (reservations).
- Capitol Commercial Complex, Escario St, Tel 2548232.
- SM City, Morning Star Travel & Tourist, Tel 2338263, 2324996.
Destinations: Cagayan de Oro, Camiguin, Caticlan (for Boracay), Cotabato, Siargao Island, Tandag.
Singapore Airlines, Silkair Office, Cebu Holdings Center, Cardinal Rosales Ave, Cebu Business Park, Tel 2326211.
Thai Airways International, QC Pavilion, Gorordo Ave, Tel 2322402, 2311227.

By Bus

There are two important bus terminals in Cebu City: the Northern Bus Terminal in Soriano St, Mabolo, for trips in a northerly direction (note: the buses also stop at the Ayala Center and SM City); and the Southern Bus Terminal on Bacalso Ave for trips in a southerly direction.

By Boat

The piers are not far away from the city centre, so a taxi to a hotel in Downtown should cost P30. If you want to stay in Uptown a taxi should cost about P40. It is not unusual to be charged P100; after the arrival of a bigger ship you will scarcely find a taxi driver who will switch on his meter.
When leaving by boat, remember that taxis have to pay a P10 fee to enter the harbour area.

Shipping Lines in Cebu City: The shipping lines in Cebu City are especially relaxed about keeping to their timetables. Ships are cancelled and others put on without any notice. Even the people on the ticket counters seem to be quite clueless. The announcements in the daily *Sun Star* are more or less reliable. Information from the shipping lines is more accurate, but probably only if you phone and say you are a foreign tourist.
Aleson Shipping Lines, R Palma St, Tel 2556277, 2555673.
Destinations: Mindanao, Negros.
Aznar Shipping Corporation, T Padilla St, Tel 2335915-18.
Destinations: Leyte, Negros (from Tabuelan and Toledo).
Cebu Ferries, Pier 4, Tel 2332611, @.
Destinations: Leyte, Mindanao.
Cokaliong Shipping Lines, S Osmeña Blvd, Tel 2327211-18.
Destinations: Bohol, Leyte, Mindanao, Negros, Panay.
George & Peter Lines, Jakosalem St, Tel 2545404, 2545154.
Destinations: Mindanao, Negros, Siquijor.
Kinswell Shipping Lines, GK Chua Building, MJ Cuenco Ave, Tel 2557572.
Destination: Leyte.
Lite Shipping Corporation, L Lavilles St, Tel 2536857, 2561410.
Destination: Bohol, Negros (from Toledo).
Maypalad Shipping Corporation, Palma St, Tel 2535435, 2537004.
Destination: Leyte.

MY Shipping Lines, Reclamation Area, Tel 2541398, 2541389.
Destination: Biliran.
Ocean Fast Ferries, Pier 1, Tel 2550115, @.
Destinations: Bohol, Camotes Islands, Leyte, Negros, Siquijor.
Palacio Lines, Mabini St corner Zulueta St, Tel 2546629, 2537700.
Destinations: Bantayan Island, Bohol, Camotes Islands, Samar, Siquijor.
Sulpicio Lines, 1st St, Reclamation Area, Tel 2325361-80.
Destinations: Leyte, Manila, Masbate, Mindanao.
Supercat Fast Ferry Corporation, Pier 4, Tel 2324511-16.
Destinations: Bohol, Leyte, Mindanao, Negros, Siquijor.
Super Shuttle Ferry, Gorordo Ave, Tel. 2323150.
Camiguin, Leyte, Masbate.
Trans-Asia Shipping Lines, MJ Cuenco Ave, Tel 2546491-98.
Destinations: Bohol, Leyte, Masbate, Mindanao, Panay.
WG & A, S Osmeña Blvd, Tel 2320491, 2320421.
Destinations: Manila, Mindanao.

Mactan Island

When people talk about the boom in tourism on Cebu, they are usually talking about Mactan Island, which is connected with Cebu by the two Mandaue-Mactan bridges which are over 800m long. On the south-east coast of the island there is a row of exclusive beach hotels like nowhere else on the Philippines. No expense was spared during the building of these resorts. They even constructed beaches with tons of imported sand, although the result is not a continuous beach, but small sections of beach belonging to their respective hotels. About 80% of the guests are Asian, especially Japanese, who fly in direct from Narita (Tokyo), avoiding Manila completely. In the meantime, convenient non-stop flights to Mactan International airport are available from Hong Kong, Malaysia and Singapore.
There is a memorial on the beach at Punta Encaño in the north-east of the island, dedicated to Chief Lapu-Lapu, who killed Ferdinand Magellan in the battle of Mactan Island on 27 April 1521.

Places to Stay

2 Bella Vista Hotel
Hotel Cesario
4 Days Hotel
5 Waterfront Airport Hotel
9 Shangri-La's Mactan Island Resort
10 Tambuli Beach Club
11 Cebu Beach Club
12 Costabella Tropical Beach Hotel
13 Maribago Bluewater Beach Resort
14 Cebu White Sands
15 Quantum Resort
16 Club KonTiki
17 Hadsan Cove
18 Bahia Resort Hotel
20 MB's Tavern
21 Lapu-Lapu Cottages
23 Haruhay Dream Resort
24 Coral Reef Hotel
25 Plantation Bay
26 Cordova Reef Village

Places to Eat

6 Seafarm Market
7 Kaishu Seafood Japanese Restaurant
20 MB's Tavern
22 Lami-ah Filipino Seafood Restaurant

Miscellaneous

1 CebuYacht Club
3 Gaisano Mactan
8 Lapu-Lapu Monument
Magellan Marker

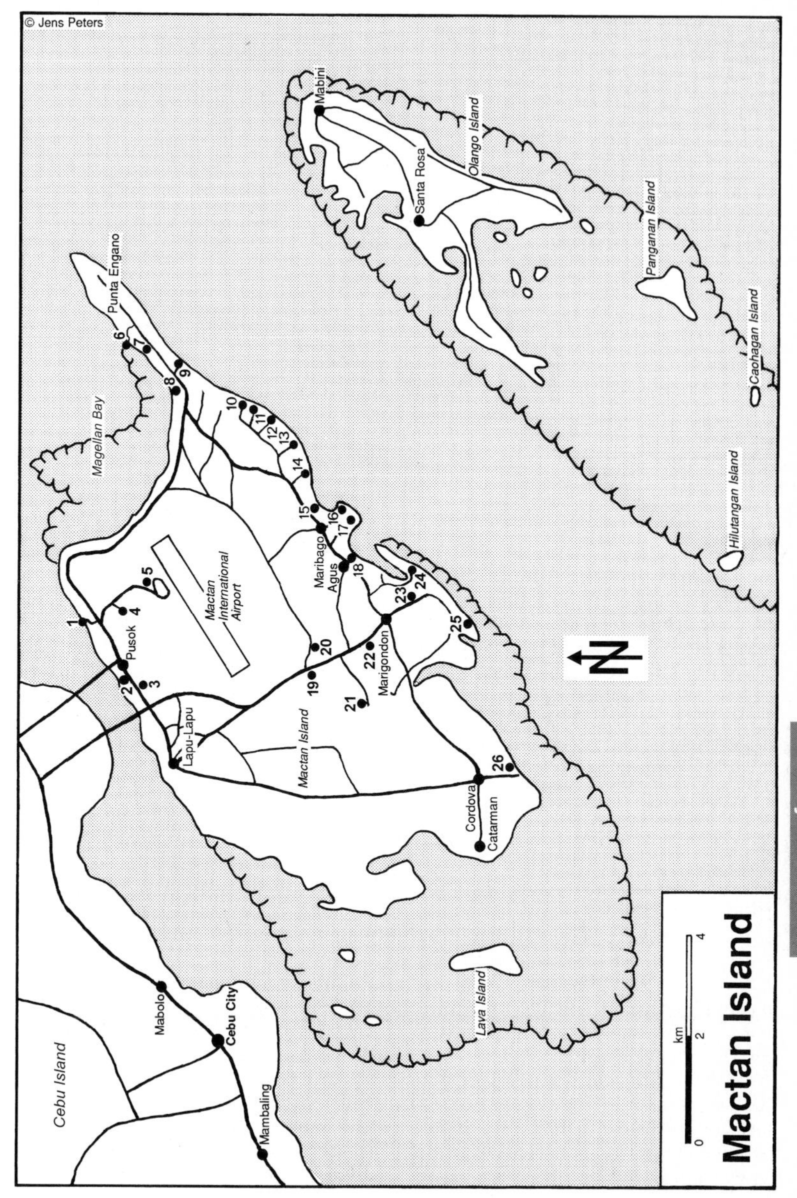
© Jens Peters
Mactan Island
km
0
2
4
Cebu Island
Cebu City
Mabolo
Mambaling
Lapu-Lapu
Pusok
Mactan International Airport
Mactan Island
Magellan Bay
Punta Engano
Maribago
Agus
Marigondon
Cordova
Catarman
Lava Island
Olango Island
Mabini
Santa Rosa
Panganan Island
Caohagan Island
Hilutangan Island
1
2
3
4
5
6
7
8
9
10
11
12
13
14
15
16
17
18
19
20
21
22
23
24
25
26

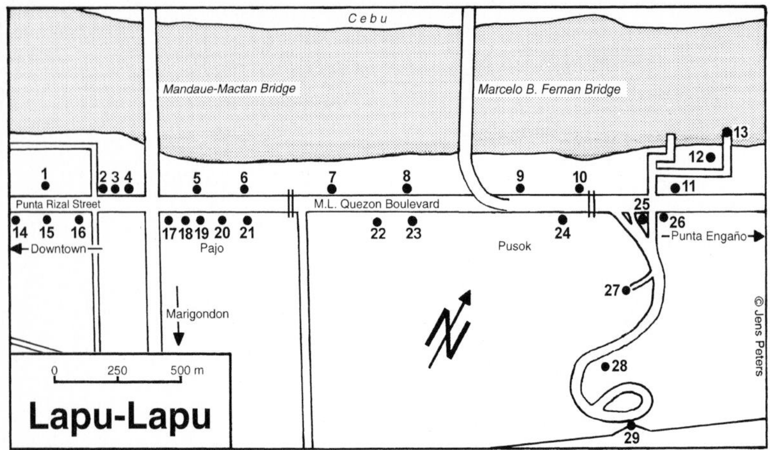

Lapu-Lapu

Lapu-Lapu was founded in 1730 by Augustinian monks. About 150,000 people live today in the former administrative centre of Opon. The city is experiencing a boom, and is clearly profiting from the arrival of a whole range of processing companies in the Mactan Export Processing Zone (MEPZ). All along the ML Quezon Highway, in the areas of Pajo and Pusok between the centre of Lapu-Lapu and MEPZ, there are dozens of banks, hotels, restaurants, bars and even a big Gaisano department store.

Places to Stay

Capt'n Gregg's Hotel, Pajo, Tel 3401530, Fax 3407307, @. SR/DR/fan/bath P450, SR/DT/ac/bath P650 and P750. Great rooms for the money, all with TV. Restaurant. Located next to the Heidelberg Pension.

Heidelberg Pension, Pajo, Tel 3401829. SR/DR/ac/bath P650. Fairly good value for Mactan Island. Restaurant. Motorcycle rental. Located near the Mandaue-Mactan Bridge.

ACE Penzionne, Pajo, Tel 3411140. SR/DR/ac/bath P700 and P800. Excellent rooms at the right price, with TV. Refrigerator P100 extra. Restaurant (downstairs in the building). Located across from Gaisano Mactan.

Mactan Pension House, Pajo, Tel 3405524, Fax 3405528, @. SR/DR/ac/bath P690 to P890. Reasonable rooms with TV. Coffee shop. Check-out time 6pm. Located next to the ACE Penzionne.

Hotel Cesario, Pusok, Tel 3400211, Fax 3400615, @. SR/DR/ac/bath P850 to P1150. With TV and including breakfast. Tidy rooms of different sizes and a variety of furnishings. Coffee shop, free airport service. Located right next door to the Bella Vista Hotel, set back a bit from the road.

Philippine Dream, Cebu Yacht Club, Tel 3403888, Fax 3404090, @. SR/DR/ac/bath P1500 (no window) to P2750 (two big beds), all with TV. Trim rooms. This is a former cruise ship which is permanently anchored only a few minutes from the airport. Good restaurant. There is also a casino and a disco on board.

Getting There & Away
4 Motorcycle Rental (Crash Pub Heidelberg)
9 Petron Petrol Station
10 Shell Petrol Station
14 Jeepney Terminal
16 Shell Petrol Station
21 Cebu Pacific
22 Fast Rent-a-Car
WG & A
29 Mactan International Airport

Places to Stay
3 Capt'n Gregg's Hotel
4 Heidelberg Pension
6 ACE Penzionne
Mactan Pension House
8 Bella Vista Hotel
Hotel Cesario
13 Philippine Dream Hotel & Entertainment Center
27 Days Hotel
28 Waterfront Airport Hotel

Places to Eat & Entertainment
3 Capt'n Gregg's Bar & Restaurant
Lucy's French Restaurant
4 Crash Pub Heidelber
5 Mermaid Bar
7 Miss Asia Disco
11 Shark Cave
15 Evening Bar
Heart Beat
Magic Disco
T-Back Paradise
16 Happy Go Lucky Nightclub
20 McDonald's
21 KFC
Jollibee
22 Manukan sa Sugbu
25 Krua Thai Restaurant
Majestic Restaurant
26 Café de France

Miscellaneous
1 The Arcade
- Molecule Internet Café
- Rose Pharmacy
2 Philippine National Bank (PNB)
5 Money Changer
12 Cebu Yacht Club
17 Inday Guitar Shop
18 Landbank
19 Lilang's Guitar Display Center
Opon Guitars
20 Bank of the Philippine Islands
21 Gaisano Mactan
23 Allied Bank
24 Metrobank

Note: The hotel was closed in mid-2004 but may open again soon.
Bella Vista Hotel, Pusok, Tel 3407821, Fax 3407823, @. SR/DR/ac/bath P1980 and P2200, suites P2750 and P3850; including breakfast. Comfortable, spacious rooms with refrigerator and TV. Roof-top restaurant with a gorgeous view. Beautiful swimming pool on the fifth floor. Free airport service.
Days Hotel, Airport Rd, Tel 3410476, Fax 3410477, @. SR/DR/ac/bath P2500, suites P3300 to P3800. Pleasant rooms with TV, the suites also have a refrigerator. Restaurant.
Waterfront Airport Hotel, Airport Rd, Tel 3404888, Fax 3405862, @. SR/DR/ac/bath P7250 to P9250, suites P12,500 to P90,000. Including breakfast. First-class hotel with fittings to match. Eight restaurants, swimming pool, 24-hour casino.

Places to Eat
The ***Capt'n Gregg's Restaurant*** near the Mandaue-Mactan Bridge serves a fairly wide selection of Philippine and European dishes. The ***Majestic Restaurant*** in the Marina Mall at the turn-off for the airport has Chinese food and

seafood on its menu. In the same mall you'll find the well-recommended, inexpensive ***Krua Thai Restaurant***.
McDonald's, Jollibee and ***KFC*** all have outlets next to the Gaisano Mactan Department Store.

Entertainment
There is a whole selection of more or less basic nightclubs in Lapu-Lapu, including the ***Happy Go Lucky***, ***Club UK***, ***T-Back Paradise***, ***Heart Beat***, ***Mermaid*** and the ***Shark Cave***.

Miscellaneous
Money: The Philippine National Bank on the ML Quezon Highway changes travellers cheques. On the same road you will also find Landbank, Bank of the Philippine Islands (BPI), Allied Bank and Metrobank.
Online: Molecule Internet Café at The Arcade, Punta Rizal St.
Post & Telephone: Post code: 6015. Area code: 032 (for all of Mactan Island).

Getting Around
Car: Avis, Mactan International Airport, Tel 3408527.
Motorcycle: The Crash Pub Heidelberg, Tel 3401829, @, near the Mandaue-Mactan Bridge, rents motorbikes (125 cc) for P850 per day or P600 per day if rented for a week. MB's Rents Bikes, Tel 3404069, in Marigondon/Basak (see below) rents 200 cc Hondas for P550 per day, P1400 for three days and P2600 per week.

Visayas - Cebu

Getting There & Away
Jeepney: A lot of jeepneys go from Cebu City to Lapu-Lapu daily - just listen for the 'opon-opon' call. They leave from the SM City shopping center. The seats next to the driver are best, as the ones behind get very crowded. You can take a jeepney from Colon St to SM City.

The last jeepney from Lapu-Lapu to Cebu City leaves at 11pm, and the next does not go till about 4am the following morning. The jeepney terminal is a bit outside of town, 200m west of the Mandaue-Mactan Bridge.

Taxi: A taxi from Cebu City to Lapu-Lapu costs about P100, but if you want to go to the beach you have to pay another P30 to P50 .

Tricycle: At the Lapu-Lapu Market the tricycles wait for passengers going farther, perhaps to the beaches (P40 to P60).

Marigondon

The next public beach you come to after Cebu City is Marigondon Beach. It is a favourite with the locals and is especially popular at the weekends. However, the beach itself is not too exciting but will do at a push. You could always hire a boat and go out to Olango Island for a bit of snorkelling. Fix the price beforehand.

Places to Stay
MB's Tavern, Basak, Tel 3404069, Fax 3413610, @. SR/DR/ac/bath P600. Good rooms, invitingly furnished, with TV. Discount possible for weekly stays. German-Filipino owners (Michael and Marlene). Popular restaurant. Motorbike rental. Airport service. Located a bit off the main road (turn off at Ester's Pharmacy). It's three km to Marigondon Beach.
Haruhay Dream Resort, Tel 3409790. Cottage/fan/bath P500, cottage/ac/bath P750 and P1000. Friendly little place, belonging to Wolfgang from Austria, and his Filipina wife, Evelyn. Restaurant with Philippine and European cooking.
Lapu-Lapu Cottages, Basak, Tel 3404648, Fax 3405831, @. Cottage/fan/bath P900 (no TV), cottage/ac/bath P1100 and P1300. Well-kept, stone

buildings, each with living room, bedroom, TV and big veranda. Good value. Quiet, extensive grounds with a garden about three km from Marigondon Beach. German-Philippine management. Good restaurant.

Plantation Bay, Marigondon, Tel 3405900, Fax 3405988, @. SR/DR/ac/bath P8200 and P9400, suites P12,500 to P26,000. Excellently furnished rooms with balcony, and so-called Honeymoon Villas for P14,250 (private little buildings with their own small swimming pool and garden). It's worth having a look at this extensive, elaborately designed, well-maintained resort with its huge swimming pool (an artificial lagoon), several restaurants, tennis courts, diving, windsurfing and Hobie Cats.

Places to Eat

You can get good, inexpensive European food at the popular ***MB's Tavern*** in Basak, including big pizzas and various specials of the day. Guests at the ***Lami-ah Filipino Seafood Restaurant*** are entertained with a free Cultural Show (12.30, 6.30, 8 and 9pm), open daily 11am to 11pm.

Getting There & Away

Tricycle: Lapu-Lapu to Marigondon Beach by tricycle usually costs no more than P6 per person, though sometimes you can't get the price down to that figure no matter how hard you bargain. However, a fair price for a tricycle is P40. It would be advisable to agree on a pick-up time for the return.

Maribago

At Maribago, between Marigondon and Punta Engaño, you can inspect some guitar factories. The biggest is probably Lilang's Guitar Factory, but the smaller factories also make quite good and well-priced guitars; it pays to compare them. If you want a guitar that will last, it is worth spending a few pesos more and buying an export guitar, as the ones that are made for the local market are dirt cheap but give up the ghost quickly once out of the tropics. You can get a good export guitar from P5000. Since many airlines will not accept them as hand luggage, at least beyond Cebu, they have to go in the hold, so have them well packed. It is even better to invest in a strong guitar case which will set you back another P1000.

Maribago has several fine hotels by the beach. Day visitors have to pay admission, some of which is deducted from the bill later.

Places to Stay

Club KonTiki, Maribago, Tel 4952434, Fax 3409934. SR/DR/fan/bath P600, SR/DR/ac/bath P800 and P1500. The rooms are very good, the more expensive ones also have a refrigerator and TV. Restaurant, diving. The grounds are fine for what they are, but there is almost no vegetation or beach here. A favourite with divers.

Hadsan Cove, Buyong, Tel 3405937, Fax 4125401. SR/DR/ac/bath P1050 to P2530. The cheapest rooms are getting on a bit, while the more expensive, and newer, ones are facing the sea. Restaurant, swimming pool, diving, windsurfing, small beach. Admission for day visitors P20.

Bahia Resort Hotel, Agus, Tel & Fax 4952352. SR/DR/ac/bath P1120 with TV. Pleasantly designed resort. Restaurant, sea-water swimming pool (P50 for non-residents).

Quantum Resort, Maribago, Tel 2323111, Fax 2334173, @. SR/DR/ac/bath P2500, including breakfast. Immaculate rooms, all with refrigerator, TV and balcony, in a several storey hotel. Restaurant, swimming pool, diving, boat and car hire.

Tambuli Beach Club, Buyong, Tel 4921888, Fax 2324913, @. SR/ac/bath

P3300 to P5000, DR/ac/bath P3600 to P5300. A wonderful place to stay, consisting of two distinct sections, with a well groomed garden and an attractive landscaped area with swimming pools. The more expensive rooms belong to the Tambuli West Wing. They are very spacious, tastefully decorated and noticeably better than the cheaper ones in the older Tambuli East Wing. Admission for day visitors is P200, of which P150 are later deducted from the bill. Further attractions are good restaurants, whirlpool, sauna, tennis courts, Hobie Cats, windsurfing and diving.

Costabella Tropical Beach Resort, Buyong, Tel 3405932, Fax 3405308, @. SR/ac/bath P3000 and P5000, DR/ac/bath P3400 and P6000, suite P6150 to P9000. Good, comfortably furnished rooms with refrigerator and TV. Their restaurant is a bit expensive. There is also a swimming pool and tennis court, and windsurfing and diving are offered, as well as lots of different leisure time facilities (table tennis, darts, billiards etc). The resort appears to be popular with Japanese tourists.

Cebu Beach Club, Buyong, Tel 3407994, Fax 3409981, @. SR/DR/ac/bath P3500 to P4500. Several long buildings with pleasantly furnished rooms, all with refrigerator and TV. Large grounds, restaurant, two beautiful swimming pools, diving, small beach.

Cebu White Sands, Maribago, Tel 4959000, Fax 4952220, @. SR/DR/ac/bath P6300 to P11,600. Attractive, well-kept rooms with refrigerator and TV. Beautiful garden grounds. Restaurant, big swimming pool, small beach.

Maribago Bluewater Beach Resort, Maribago, Tel 4920100, Fax 4920128, @. SR/DR/ac/bath P9500, cottage/ac/bath P16,5000. All with refrigerator and TV. Pleasant rooms and spacious cottages with living room and bedroom. Attractive restaurant, beautiful swimming pool, tennis court, diving, water skiing and windsurfing. This is a pleasant, generously laid out establishment with a remarkably clean beach. Admission for day visitors is P350.

Getting There & Away

Tricycle: A tricycle from Lapu-Lapu to Maribago costs P6 per person. A Special Ride costs P40, but you will have to do some hard bargaining as the drivers are used to guests at the beach resorts paying around P100.

Punta Engaño

Punta Engaño is the north-eastern tip of Mactan Island. On 27 April 1521, the conquering explorer Ferdinand Magellan lost his life in battle while attempting to make a landing here. In 1866 a memorial, the Magellan Marker, was erected to commemorate the spot where he fell. A few metres away, a statue of a bold-looking Chief Lapu-Lapu, complete with sword and shield, keeps the memory of this popular hero alive.

The historic battle for Mactan (Kadaugan sa Mactan) is re-enacted each year on the beach at Magellan Bay by amateur actors, providing a sponsor can be found. The Tourist Office should be able to provide you with up-to-date information.

Places to Stay

Shangri-La's Mactan Island Resort, Tel 2310288, Fax 2311688, @. SR/DR/ac/bath P13,500 to P19,000; suites P24,000 to P120,000. Big, first-class hotel with very spacious rooms. Restaurant, disco, swimming pool, tennis court, diving, water skiing, windsurfing, beautiful beach. Airport service is also provided.

Places to Eat

In the northeast of Mactan Island a 200-metre stretch of bumpy road leads to Magellan Bay and the modest ***Seafarm Market***. In this rustic restaurant built over the water guests can fish live seafood from the pools and have it prepared by the cook (prices per 100 grams: fish P20-50, crabs P38, lobster P80; mussels (called shells' on the menu) P6 each; cooking charge P50-75). Open Sun-Wed 10am-9pm, Thu-Sat 10am-10pm.

Getting There & Away

Tricycle: A tricycle from Lapu-Lapu to Punta Engaño costs P5 per person. You should be able to get a Special Ride for P50 by bargaining skilfully.

Olango Island

Olango Island is the long island visible from Maribago and Marigondon. It has small white beaches and beautiful stands of palms providing shade. The bungalow hotel Santa Rosa by the Sea, which is closed at present, is in the south-western corner. North of the village of Santa Rosa there is an extensive lagoon which was declared a sanctuary for migratory birds in 1992, the first of its kind in the Philippines. Plovers, sandpipers and egrets are some of the birds which can be seen here, stopping over on their flight from the rigours of the Siberian winter on their way to Australia, so the best time for birdwatching is in October and November. Their return journey in the spring also brings them to this area as they rest their wings from the exhausting flight. Boardwalks have been built throughout the sanctuary which connect the various hides. The island is surrounded by a reef stretching another 10 km in a south-westerly direction, where the islands of Panganan, Caohagan, Lassuan (Kalassuan) and Hilutangan mark the drop-off. Much of the coral has unfortunately been destroyed by dynamite fishing.

Getting There & Away

Boat: The trip from Maribago to Olango Island costs P20 per person by outrigger boat, so a Special Ride should cost about P200. However, operators have been known to ask up to P500.

Talisay

If you have some time to kill, this is a nice day trip from Cebu City but not much more. The Talisay beaches, such as Tangque Beach and Canezares Beach, are anything but impressive. Next to the Dumlog Bridge in the Biasong part of town, there is a nature park called Crocolandia with exotic birds, fish, turtles, snakes, wildcats, tarsiers and

Plover Egret Sandpiper

about 30 crocodiles. Open daily 9am-5pm. Admission: P50.

Places to Stay

Tourist Seaside Hotel, Tel & Fax 2727813. SR/DR/fan/bath P400, SR/DR/ac/bath P500 and P680. The place was obviously at its best a few years ago. Restaurant, swimming pool.

Getting There & Away

Jeepney: A lot of jeepneys make the trip from Cebu City to Talisay daily (P8; 30 min).

Taxi: From Cebu City to Talisay by taxi costs around P100.

Toledo

Toledo is on the west coast of Cebu and has a population of about 120,000, many of whom used to be economically dependent on the Atlas Consolidated Mining & Development Corporation copper mine which has closed down. The mine, which was one of the biggest in the world, often provided employment for several members of one family. You can go by ship from Toledo to San Carlos on Negros (see Getting There & Away earlier in this chapter).

Places to Stay

You can enquire at the Vizcayno Restaurant near the wharf whether the basic ***Lodging House*** has rooms available. However, you'd probably be better off at the:

Sailor's Cabin, Abucayan, Tel & Fax 4652816, @, 18 km to the north in the Abucayan Barangay near Balamban. SR/DR/ac P250, SR/DR/ac/bath P700 to P1000. Different sizes of rooms and apartments with a living area, TV and kitchen, all simply squeaky clean. Extensive, quiet, well-maintained grounds set in a garden. Restaurant with Philippine, German and international cooking.

Getting There & Away

Bus: Several buses leave the Southern Bus Terminal in Cebu City for Toledo daily (two hrs).

If you want to get from Cebu City to Balamban, best take the minibus from the Southern Bus Terminal which goes via the new Trans Central Highway. P75; one hr.

Liloan

The road from Cebu City along the east coast heading north takes you through several clean, inviting little provincial towns. It's about 20 km to Liloan, not to be confused with the other Liloan at the southernmost tip of Cebu.

Places to Stay

Franziska's Beach Resort, Jubay, Tel 5643192. SR/DR/fan/bath P700, SR/DR/ac/bath P950. A friendly place. Restaurant, swimming pool. This is especially handy for people who don't want to spend the night in Cebu City and want to carry on to North Cebu. Located a bit outside of town, about one km north of the town centre (the market). Unfortunately, the beach here isn't very inviting.

Getting There & Away

Bus: There are several buses from Cebu City to Liloan daily, leaving the Northern Bus Terminal (30 min).

Buses for Cebu City and North Cebu (Bogo, Hagnaya, Maya) stop at Titay's Bakery.

Danao

About 20 km north of Liloan you come to the town of Danao, the gun town of the Philippines. Under the shadow of the big, old colonial style church, in quiet back rooms, skilful hands busily work away at producing illegal weapons. The production consists mostly of revolvers, but exact copies of well-known makes of pistol are also made to order here.

Basically, Danao is a peaceful place, and the casual observer would never even notice the obscure activities going on behind the scenes. As it is, probably only one hundredth of the population of 75,000 is involved in the clandestine production of weapons, but that's enough to keep Danao's dubious reputation alive all over the country.

Boats leave daily for the Camotes Islands from the jetty near the hospital. There is also a daily car ferry connection to Isabel on Leyte.

Places to Stay

El Salvador's Beach Club, Tel 2003622. SR/DR/fan/bath P600, SR/DR/ac/bath P750 to P1500. Immaculate rooms, the aircon ones also have a TV. Restaurant, swimming pool. Located on the way into town coming from Cebu City.

Intosan Resort, Tabos, Tel 2003476. SR/DR/ac/bath P650 to P850. Pleasant rooms of various sizes, all with TV and balcony. Considering the location, this is surprisingly good accommodation. Restaurant. Attractive, beautifully laid-out, landscaped swimming pool. Located north of Danao, about 1½ km from market in the town centre, 700m from the turn-off on the coast road.

Places to Eat

The Philippine cooking is quite good at ***Roxanne's Restaurant***, where you can also sit outside in a little garden. At the weekend you might catch a rock band performing there. In Rizal St, one block behind the big Gaisano department store, you'll find the inexpensive little ***German Delicatessen***, with its small beer garden. The menu includes good steaks, a variety of German sausages and cold meats, and freshly baked bread.

Mango Tree *(Mangifera indica)*
The majestic mango tree produces the most important fruit grown on Cebu. The fruit, which grows at the magnificent top of this tree, is one of the tastiest sources of vitamins in the tropics.

Miscellaneous

Post & Telephone: Post code: 6004. Area code: 032.

Getting Around

Motorcycle: The restaurant German Delicatessen in Rizal St, Cellphone 0919-7705264, rents motorbikes for P500 per day.

Getting There & Away

Cebu City

Bus/Jeepney: Several buses and jeepneys make the trip daily from Cebu City to Danao, leaving from the Northern Bus Terminal or SM City shopping centre (one hr).

Camotes Islands

Boat: A few big outriggers cross daily from the Camotes Islands to Danao, eg at 8 and 11am from Consuelo and Puertvilla (P40; two hrs).

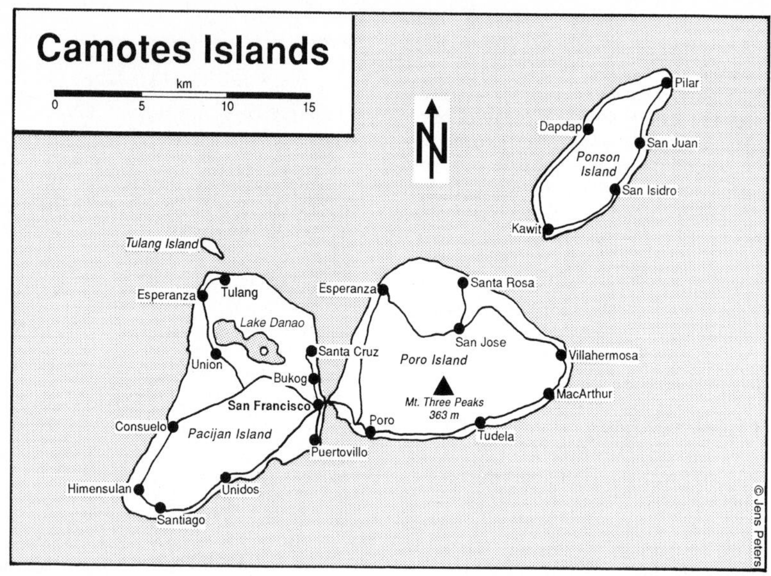

Camotes Islands

The Camotes Islands are located in the middle of the Camotes Sea, about halfway between Cebu and Leyte. The two main islands, Pacijan and Poro, are connected by a causeway. North-east of Poro lies Ponson Island, known locally as Pilar, after the largest town on the island. Tulang (Diyot), the smallest of the four Camotes islands, is located just north of Pacijan Island and populated by fishermen. It boasts a gorgeous white beach which is probably why a few years ago a group of Japanese investors were so impressed they bought the island, although since then they have remained reticent to develop its business potential. The best way to get there is by boat from the small settlement of Tulang on the north coast of Pacijan Island.

All along its west and south coasts, Pacijan Island is also adorned with a row of very attractive white sand, palm-lined beaches interrupted every now and then by rocky promontories. The most beautiful of these beaches must be Bakhaw Beach, which is not far from Esperanza. In the interior of the island, Lake Danao is a fairly large, fresh-water lake that is up to four metres deep in places.

The Camotes Islands are also riddled with scores of caves, eg at Poro and MacArthur (Bukilat Cave) on Poro Island and Consuelo on Pacijan Island. They can also be found between Consuelo and Himensulan on Pacijan Island (about one km from the coast), the ones at the latter location being particularly impressive in size and containing a small lake and swarms of bats. Not far from Himensulan there is also a small patch of rainforest complete with apes and flying dogs.

From San Francisco (San Fran') a road leads over to Poro on Poro Island, curving past the Boho Rocks, a deeply fissured, craggy stretch of coastal rock with roofed picnic facilities every now and then.

The paucity of commercial accommodation and the inadequate infrastructure between the towns have left the Camotes Islands pretty well untouched by tourism up till now. However, it would not be a bad idea to include this attractive group of islands in your island hopping itinerary, as there are boats not only to Cebu, but to Ormoc and Baybay on Leyte.

Places to Stay

Pacijan Island

Multi-Purpose Cooperative (Coop), San Francisco, Pacijan Island. SR/DR/fan P100 per person. Two basic rooms with bunk beds. Located at the market in the town centre.

Santiago Bay Garden Resort, Santiago. SR/DR/fan P500, SR/DR/ac/bath P1000. Basic, but clean. The more expensive, aircon rooms are better furnished and are equipped with refrigerator and TV. Attractive, well-kept place with lots of greenery. On a raised location on the south coast with a beautiful view of Santiago Bay with its wide, bright, and very gently sloping beach. Restaurant. Reservations in Cebu City: Tel. (032) 3458599, 4258053.

Ponson Island

Rosita Pension House, Pilar, Ponson Island. SR/DR/fan/bath P200/400. Friendly little place with basic rooms. Located a few minutes from the pier.

Miscellaneous

Festival: Soli-Soli Festival in San Francisco on 18 and 19 March.

Money: There is neither a bank nor a money changer on the islands, so make sure you have enough pesos with you.

Population: 77,000.

Getting Around

Motorcycle: Although jeepneys travel between Poro, where the fast boat from Cebu City arrives, and San Francisco (P10), for transport you will usually have to depend on relatively expensive motorcycles, eg from San Francisco to Esperanza will cost around P150.

An outrigger from Poro to Taliwang Bas near Esperanza costs about P50 per person (30 min).

The owner of the Seabreeze Restaurant in San Francisco knows Pacijan Island like the back of his hand and will drive guests around the island for between P300 and P400.

The roads on Pacijan Island are noticeably worse than on Poro Island.

Getting There & Away

Cebu City

Boat: ~~From Poro to Cebu City and vice versa twice daily with the fast ferry *Oceanjet* (P300; one hr).~~ discontinued

Monday and Saturday with Palacio Shipping Lines. Departure from Poro to Cebu City: Tuesday and Sunday (P110; four hrs).

Danao

Boat: A few big outriggers make the trip daily from Danao to the Camotes Islands: at 5.30 and 11am to Esperanza and Consuelo; at 7.30 and 11.30am to Santiago and Puertovillo (P80; two hrs).

North Cebu

Sogod

The Cebu Club Pacific Beach Hotel in Sogod was one of the few beach resort hotels on the north-east coast of Cebu for many years. It's closed now and the exclusive Alegre Beach Resort is the unchallenged number one in North Cebu.

Places to Stay

Alegre Beach Resort, Calumboyan, Tel 2311198, Fax 2434345, @. SR/DR/ac/bath P14,500, suite P23,200 (locals pay about a third of that); including breakfast. Luxury rooms with refrigerator and TV. A very comfortable place with a beautiful white beach. Restaurant, swimming pool, tennis court, water skiing, windsurfing, diving, mountainbike rental.

Getting There & Away

Bus: There are several buses daily from Cebu City to Sogod, leaving from the Northern Bus Terminal (two hrs).

Bantayan Island

Located in the north-west of Cebu Province a little off the usual tourist route, Bantayan Island basks in the sunshine with its beautiful beaches. Especially on the southern coast between Santa Fe and Maricaban, Sugar Beach, Paradise Beach and the picturesque beach near Tingting-on all beckon the visitor. Near Paradise Beach you will find the small Ogtong Cave with its freshwater spring.

So far, only a few tourists have come to this pleasant island with its friendly locals. There are only a few beach resorts, which can be comfortably reached on foot from Santa Fe, where the ferries from Hagnaya on Cebu arrive. The problem is, at the weekend and at Easter visitors from Cebu City crowd onto the island, making it difficult to find accommodation.

A small airport was built about two km east of Santa Fe, which it is hoped will encourage a tourism boom to the island. However, in the meantime local fishermen are still making a living supplying squid to the Cebu mainland, while the farmers use their land for raising poultry. They ship millions of eggs to other islands.

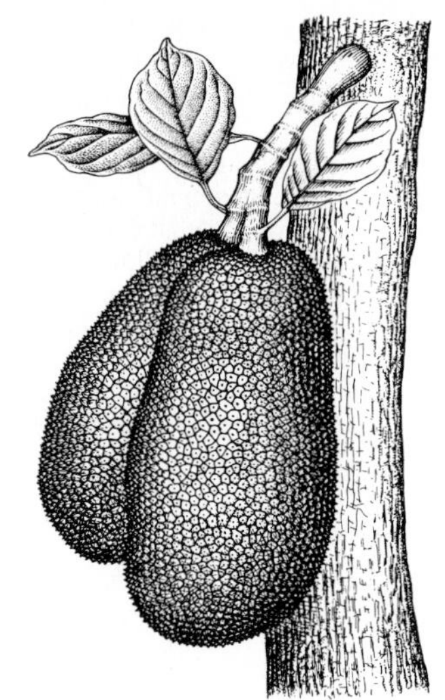

Jackfruit *(Artocarpus heterophyllus)*
The mighty jackfruit, which can be up to a metre long, grows on the trunk and the older branches of the tree.

Bantayan

With its 60,000 inhabitants, Bantayan is the largest town on the island of the same name. It has a nice plaza, a clean and lively market (mercado), a picturesque port, a hospital, three lodges to stay at and some simple restaurants at the pier. However, there are no beaches worth talking about near this friendly little harbour town.

There is a boat service at least every two days, and possibly daily, between Bantayan and Cadiz on Negros, so you can include Bantayan Island in a round trip through the Visayas.

Places to Stay

Island Pension House, Rizal Ave. SR/DR/fan P90/180. Plain rooms, OK for the money. Located on the way out of town in the direction of Santa Fe.

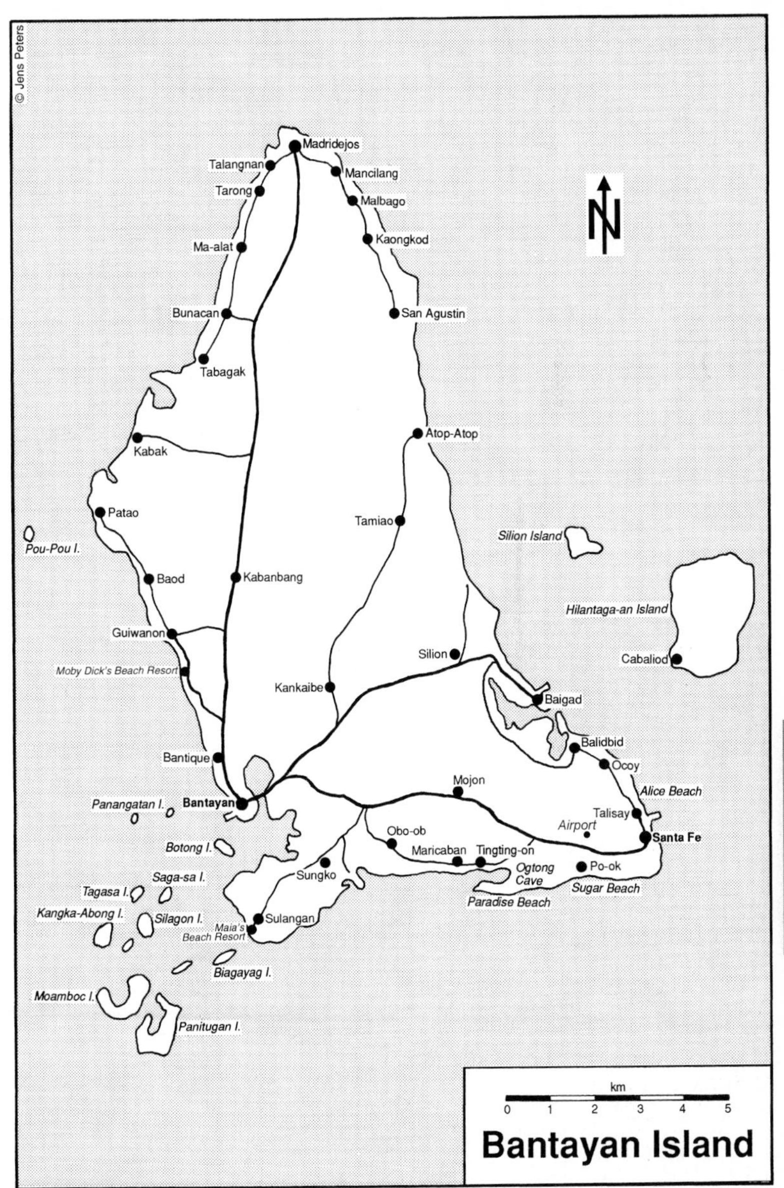
© Jens Peters
Madridejos
Talangnan
Mancilang
Tarong
Malbago
Kaongkod
Ma-alat
Bunacan
San Agustin
Tabagak
Atop-Atop
Kabak
Patao
Tamiao
Pou-Pou I.
Silion Island
Baod
Kabanbang
Hilantaga-an Island
Guiwanon
Silion
Cabaliod
Moby Dick's Beach Resort
Kankaibe
Baigad
Balidbid
Bantique
Ocoy
Mojon
Alice Beach
Panangatan I.
Bantayan
Talisay
Airport
Santa Fe
Obo-ob
Botong I.
Maricaban
Tingting-on
Ogtong Cave
Po-ok
Sungko
Saga-sa I.
Sugar Beach
Tagasa I.
Paradise Beach
Kangka-Abong I.
Silagon I.
Sulangan
Maia's Beach Resort
Biagayag I.
Moamboc I.
Panitugan I.
km
0 1 2 3 4 5
Bantayan Island
Visayas - Cebu

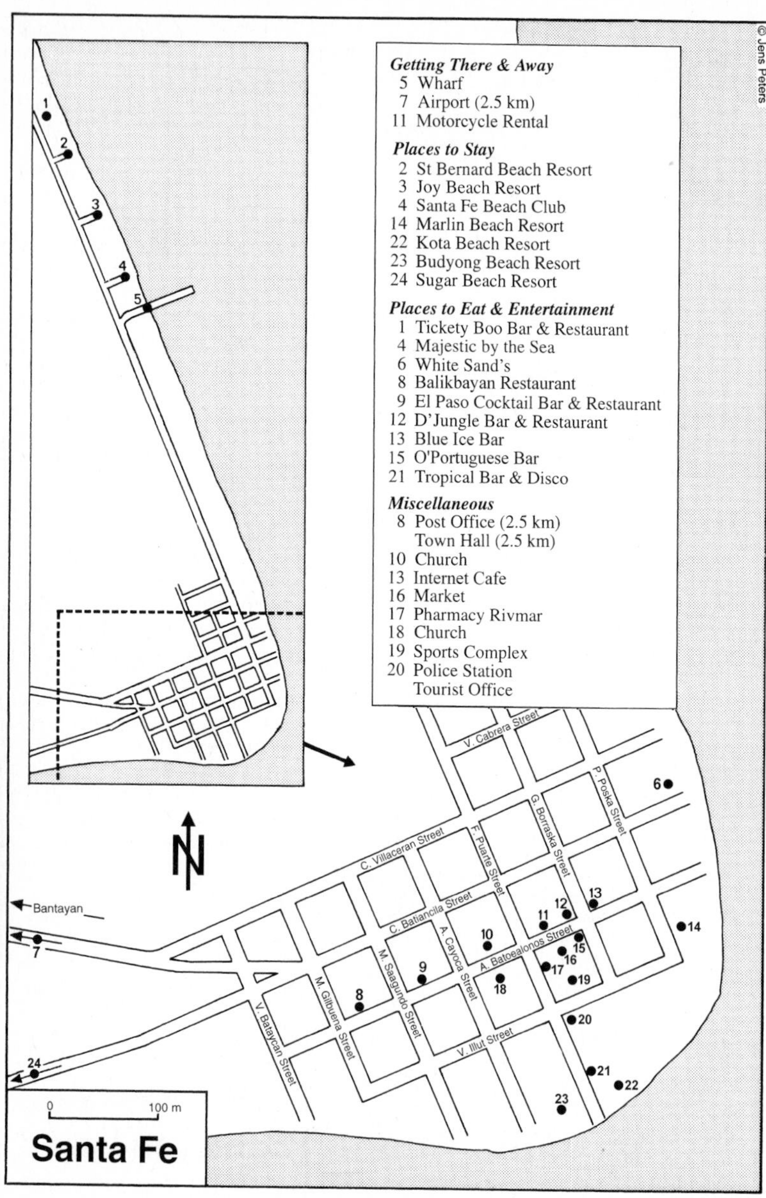
© Jens Peters
Getting There & Away
5 Wharf
7 Airport (2.5 km)
11 Motorcycle Rental
Places to Stay
2 St Bernard Beach Resort
3 Joy Beach Resort
4 Santa Fe Beach Club
14 Marlin Beach Resort
22 Kota Beach Resort
23 Budyong Beach Resort
24 Sugar Beach Resort
Places to Eat & Entertainment
1 Tickety Boo Bar & Restaurant
4 Majestic by the Sea
6 White Sand's
8 Balikbayan Restaurant
9 El Paso Cocktail Bar & Restaurant
12 D'Jungle Bar & Restaurant
13 Blue Ice Bar
15 O'Portuguese Bar
21 Tropical Bar & Disco
Miscellaneous
8 Post Office (2.5 km)
Town Hall (2.5 km)
10 Church
13 Internet Cafe
16 Market
17 Pharmacy Rivmar
18 Church
19 Sports Complex
20 Police Station
Tourist Office
V. Cabrera Street
P. Poska Street
G. Borraska Street
F. Puarte Street
C. Villaceran Street
C. Batiancila Street
A. Cayoca Street
A. Batoealonos Street
M. Saagundo Street
M. Gilbuena Street
V. Bataycan Street
V. Illut Street
Bantayan
N
0
100 m
Santa Fe

Kharuya Pension House, Osmeña St, Tel 3525634. SR/DR/fan P100/200. Basic accommodation with good, fairly big rooms. Check in at the Hardware Store. Located in the north on the way out of town.

Moby Dick's Beach Resort, Guiwanon, Tel 3525269, @. Cottage/fan/bath P500 to P700. Well-kept, tastefully designed cottages. Restaurant, sea-water swimming pool. Very quiet location about three km north of Bantayan, or 10 mins by tricycle, in a rural setting directly on the beach.

Maia's Beach Resort, Basawon, Tel 4380077, @. Cottage/bath P500, P550 and P600, depending on size. Well-kept place with solidly built, concrete cottages that look as if they were built using wood and bamboo. Restaurant, beautiful beach bar. Located near Sulangan in the south-west of the island, about four km from Bantayan. Owners are Klaus, a German, and Maia, his Filipina wife. Good value here.

Santa Fe

Santa Fe is the third-largest community on Bantayan. Day trips can be made from there to the small offshore islands of Hilantaga-an, Jibitnil, Guintacan and other destinations. In and around Santa Fe there is a cottage industry producing lampshades and hanging decorations made from tiny sea shells.

Places to Stay

Bantayan Island is popular for short visits, especially in the Easter week when, unfortunately, prices can actually double.

Sugar Beach Resort. Cottage/fan/bath P400 to P1500, depending on size. Good, basic cottages with verandas, in generously laid-out grounds on Sugar Beach near Po-ok; popular place for picnics at the weekend. No restaurant, but cold drinks and snacks are available.

St Bernard Beach Resort, Ocoy, Cellphone 0917-9636161, @. Cottage/fan/bath P550 and P850. Attractive, friendly resort with out of the ordinary, round, stone cottages which are cosily furnished. Under Danish management. Good restaurant. Located on the white sand Alice Beach, a few 100m north of the Santa Fe Beach Club.

Budyong Beach Resort, Tel 4389040. Cottage/fan/bath P350 to P700, cottage/ac/bath P1000 and P1200. Fairly basic cottages on a beautiful section of the beach right next door to the Kota Beach Resort. Restaurant. Mountain-bike and motorbike rental at P150/day and P500/day respectively.

Kota Beach Resort, Tel 4389042, @. SR/DR/fan/bath P550 and P610, cottage/fan/bath P840, cottage/ac/bath P1200. Attractive cottages. Good restaurant. Trim place at the south-eastern tip of Bantayan, about 1.3 km south of the pier in Santa Fe. The beach here is beautiful.

Marlin Beach Resort, Tel 4389093, Fax 4389094, @. SR/DR/fan/bath P1300, SR/DR/ac/bath P2200 nd P3480. Spacious, immaculate rooms with balcony in a big, two-storey stone building on the beach. Restaurant, windsurfing.

Santa Fe Beach Club, Talisay, Tel 4380031, @. Cottage/fan/bath P1000, SR/DR/ac/bath P1920 to P3200. Well-kept rooms and cottages. The service is attentive and they have a good restaurant. Located in the idyllic village of Talisay, just north of Santa Fe.

Ogtong Cave Beach Resort, Tel 4380165. Cottage/fan/bath P1000, cottage/ac/bath P2880 to P4000, depending on size and furnishings. Attractively furnished stone buildings, the more expensive ones have a refrigerator, and some also have a kitchen. Extensive, well-maintained grounds with a big swimming pool; built around the Ogtong Cave near Paradise Beach. Run by the Santa Fe Beach Club. Tricycle from Santa Fe: P15.

Places to Eat
The excellent restaurant, ***Majestic By the Sea*** at the Santa Fe Beach Club, is probably the best on the island and fairly good value for the money too. The ***D'Jungle Bar & Restaurant*** is also very popular, with its high standard of Philippine and international food. It's located diagonally across from the market. You can enjoy tasty Philippine and German food in the ***Balikbayan*** garden restaurant on the eastern edge of town, where you might be lucky to still find them open late now and then.
The ***White Sand's*** is an open beach restaurant next to the Marlin Beach Resort, with Philippine and Italian fare (good pizzas) and a barbecue, while the ***El Paso Cocktail Bar and Restaurant*** will serve you Thai food.
The guests at the ***Tickety Boo Bar & Restaurant*** (100m behind the St Bernard Beach Resort) run by an Englishman, Bill, are occasionally entertained by live music after dinner (international food).

Miscellaneous
Money: Various resorts will change cash. The banks in Bantayan Town also change travellers cheques.
Online: There's a small Internet café across from D'Jungle Bar & Restaurant.
Post & Telephone: Post code: 6047. Area code: 032.

Getting Around
Boat: Ask at the wharf for Dadoy. He rents outriggers, eg to Malapascua for P1200 (small) and P1500 (big).
Bus: A bus leaves from Santa Fe to Bantayan after the ferry arrives. There are also a few buses daily from Bantayan to Madridejos on the northern tip of the island.
Bicycle: The roads are fairly good on this mostly flat island, and the amount of traffic is minimal, so riding a bike is a great way to do some exploring. They can be hired at D'Jungle Bar & Restaurant and other places.
Motorcycle: The hardware store across from the market rents out motorbikes (125 cc) for about P500/day.
Tricycle: A tricycle from Bantayan to Santa Fe costs P50, or P10 per person.

Getting There & Away
By Air: The little Bantayan Airport is located about 2½ km west of Santa Fe. Unfortunately, Seair has stopped running flights from and to Cebu City (temporarily?).

By Boat: There is a pier in Bantayan Town (boats to and from Cadiz/Negros) and Santa Fe (boats to and from Hagnaya/Cebu). A tricycle from the pier in Santa Fe to the beach resorts of Kota and Budyong (1.3 km) costs P5 per person.

Cebu City
Bus: There are several buses a day from Cebu City's Northern Bus Terminal to Hagnaya (P80; 3½ hrs).

Boat: From Cebu City to Santa Fe Tuesday and Thursday at 9pm, and Sunday at 12 noon with Palacio Lines (P175; nine hrs).
Departure from Santa Fe to Cebu City Wednesday, Friday at 9pm and Sunday at midnight.

Hagnaya
Boat: From Hagnaya to Santa Fe there are *Island Express* ferries daily at 7.30 and 9.30am, and at 12.30 and 6.30pm (P70; 1½ hrs). A bus leaves from Santa Fe to Bantayan after the ferry has arrived. There are daily departures from Santa Fe to Hagnaya at 5.30 and 9.30am, and at 12.30 and 2pm.
The departure times of the *Fastcraft* fast ferry 1-2x daily from Hagnaya to Santa Fe and back depend on the tides (P85 and P120 (aircon); 30 mins).

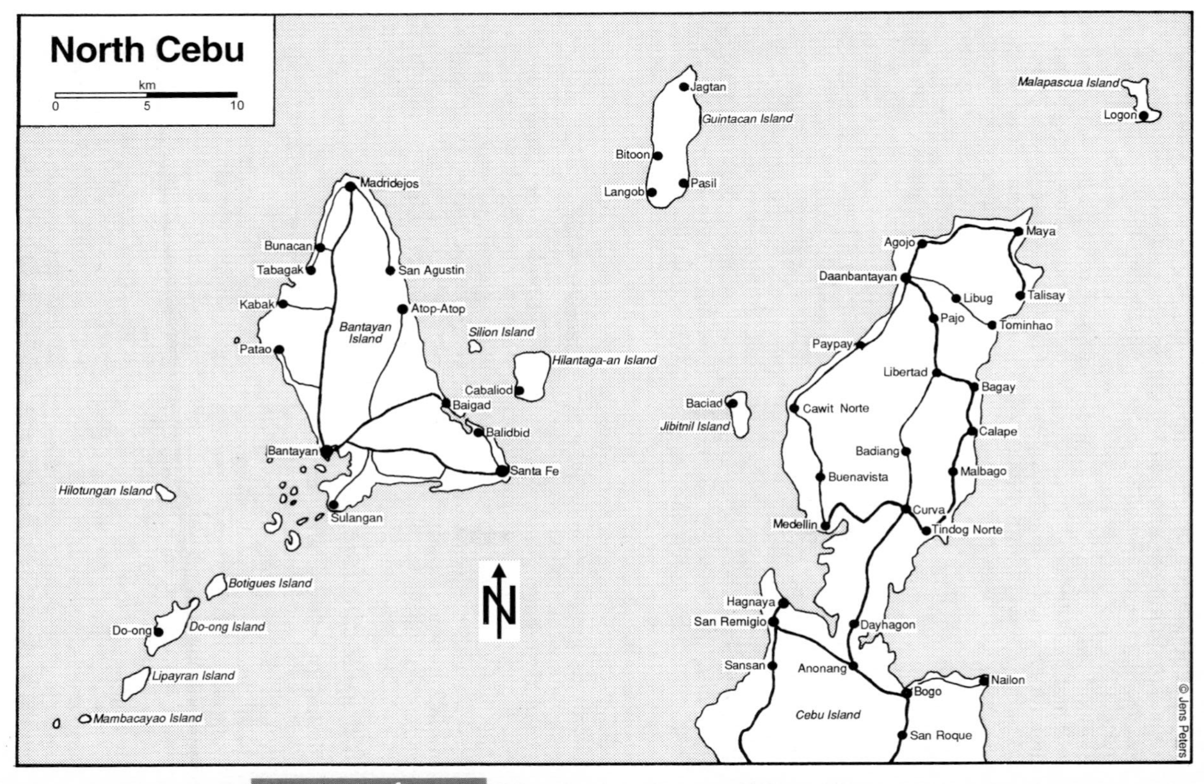
North Cebu
km
0
5
10
Malapascua Island
Logon
Jagtan
Guintacan Island
Bitoon
Pasil
Langob
Madridejos
Bunacan
San Agustin
Tabagak
Kabak
Atop-Atop
Bantayan Island
Silion Island
Patao
Hilantaga-an Island
Cabaliod
Baigad
Balidbid
Bantayan
Santa Fe
Hilotungan Island
Sulangan
Botigues Island
Do-ong
Do-ong Island
Lipayran Island
Mambacayao Island
Maya
Agojo
Daanbantayan
Libug
Talisay
Pajo
Tominhao
Paypay
Libertad
Bagay
Baciad
Jibitnil Island
Cawit Norte
Calape
Badiang
Buenavista
Malbago
Curva
Medellin
Tindog Norte
Hagnaya
San Remigio
Dayhagon
Sansan
Anonang
Nailon
Bogo
Cebu Island
San Roque
© Jens Peters

A Special Ride with an outrigger from Hagnaya to Santa Fe costs around P800 (the crossing can be a bit on the rough side!).

Malapascua Island
Boat: A Special Ride from Santa Fe to Malapascua costs P1200 to P2000 (big outrigger). The trip takes 2½ hrs.

Maya

From Maya outriggers leave for the islands of Malapascua, Masbate and Leyte. If you arrive too late in Maya and want to avoid crossing over to Malapascua in the dark, accommodation is available.

Places to Stay

Abba Lodge, Tel 4370082. SR/DR/fan P300. Basic accommodation at the jetty with small rooms, OK for one night.
Monsanto Beach Resort. SR/DR/fan/bath P600. Good, spacious rooms, priced right. Restaurant, swimming pool, mini-zoo. Located about one km outside of Maya (coming from Cebu City, turn off right before entering the town).
And if you don't make it as far as Maya, there's always the pleasant *Bogo Pension House* with restaurant, in Bogo about 40 km south.

Malapascua Island

Malapascua Island is about eight km north-east of Cebu and 25 km west of Leyte. It is sometimes referred to as Logon, after Barangay Logon, the main community in the south of the island. A walk around the island, which is 2½ km long and about one km wide, will take you to friendly little fishing villages and deserted bays in idyllic locations.
In 1994 a lighthouse was built on the island, and the panoramic view from the top is a sight worth seeing. If he is around, no doubt the lighthouse keeper would not be averse to letting you up there for a small tip. There is a cloud on the horizon, however. It's a pity the fishermen in this area have still not grasped the simple fact that fishing with dynamite is a wanton act of destruction. Maybe the dollars brought in by tourism will bring them to their senses, so the coral reefs can have a chance to regenerate as has been known to happen elsewhere in the Philippines.
The best snorkelling area can still be found around the craggy little offshore island of Lapus-Lapus. A boat there costs P400 for half a day, including a trip round the island.
White sand Bounty Beach on the south coast has seen most development for the tourism industry. There you'll find a good selection of restaurants, beach bars, dive shops and basic, but pleasant place to stay. All together there are about a dozen beaches scattered round the island.

Places to Stay

Ging Ging's Flower Garden. DR/bath P250 (two rooms share a bathroom). Basic guesthouse set back from the beach; behind the Cocobana Beach Resort.
The Palm Place. SR/DR/fan P250/500 and P300/600, depending on size. Pleasantly furnished rooms in a solidly built place a good 200m back from the beach.
Kuan Ba. Dorm/fan P100 (four-bed room), SR/DR/fan P250, SR/DR/fan/bath P800. Basic rooms, some of them quite small. Pleasant place, a fair distance from the beach, under English management. Restaurant. Swimming pool.
White Sand Bungalows, Cellphone 0927-3187471, @. Cottage/fan/bath P400. OK cottages on Logon Bay not far from the popular Maldito Restaurant. Danish owner. Restaurant.

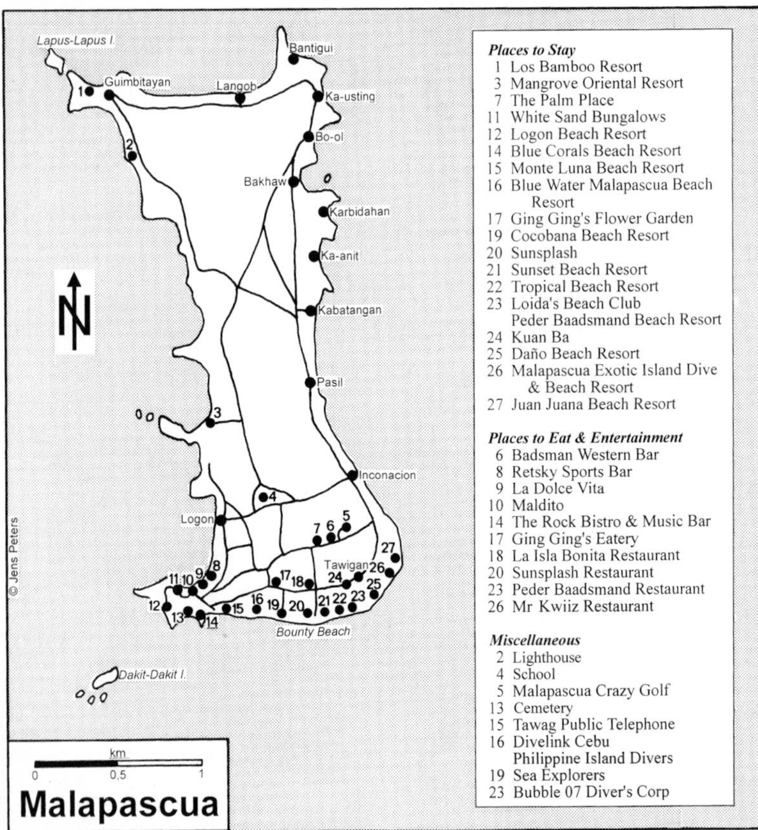

Malapascua Exotic Island Dive & Beach Resort, Cellphone 0919-6903947, Tel. 4370983, Fax: 4370984, @. Cottage/fan P300 (divers) and P400, cottage/fan/bath P900. Small, pleasant place with well-kept rooms and cottages. The owners are Dik the Dutchman and his Filipina wife Cora. Restaurant.

Peter Baadsmand Beach Resort. SR/DR/fan P350, SR/DR/fan/bath P550 and P750. Three-storey building with basic, but adequate rooms with veranda and gorgeous sea view.

Daño Beach Resort. Cottage/fan/bath P400 nad P600. Good cottages of different sizes.

Tropical Beach Resort. Cottage/fan/bath P500. Friendly place with only a few cottages. Restaurant.

Cocobana Beach Resort, Cellphone 0918-3050583, Tel. 4371040, @. Cottage/fan P650/900, cottage/fan/bath P1000/1200 and P1100/1350 (depending on location, in the garden or right on the beach), cottage/ac/bath P1900/2200. Spacious cottages with big ve-

randas. This extensive resort belongs to Freddy from Switzerland, and his Filipina wife Noravilla. Restaurant, beach bar, billiards, table tennis.
Loida's Beach Club, Tel 4371030, @. Cottage/fan/bath P750. Well-kept place with a beautiful garden. Restaurant.
Logon Beach Resort, Cellphone 0919-8913584. Cottage/fan/bath P800. Good, practically furnished cottages on a slope in a little bay, with steps leading down to their own beach. Beautiful view (especially at sunset). Swedish owner. Restaurant. Reachable on foot from the White Sand Bungalows (next bay, near Maldito).
Blue Water Malapascua Beach Resort, Cellphone 0919-8300139, @. SR/DR/fan/bath P500, cottage/fan/bath P700. Tidy rooms and good, spacious cottages. A big resort right next door to the Cocobana Beach Resort. Restaurant.
Sunsplash, Cellphone 0927-2741756, Tel 4370982, @. SR/DR/fan/bath P1400. SR/DR/ac/bath P2000. Comfortable, invitingly furnished rooms in a stone building behind the Sunsplash restaurant.
Blue Corals Beach Resort, Tel 4371020, Fax 4371021. SR/DZ/fan/bath P2200, SR/DR/ac/bath P3500. Good rooms big enough for four people, even if rather spartanly furnished at this price, with veranda and super view (those facing Bounty Beach). You can't miss this place, built prominently as it is on a cliff at the west end of the beach.
Mangrove Oriental Resort, Cellphone 0919-4811861, @. Cottage/fan/bath P3500 (big enough for four people). Attractive place, built on a hill on the west coast of the island, with very tastefully furnished stone cottages. Apparently they're building a few cottages down at the beach which will go for only around P600. Quiet location about 15 minutes on foot from Bounty Beach. British owner. Restaurant.

Places to Eat

A friendly welcome awaits you at ***Ging Ging's Flower Garden*** restaurant with their inexpensive fish dishes (which they would like you to order beforehand) - to be recommended. Breakfast is accompanied by bread baked in their own ovens.
About 100m away from the beach, ***Mr Kwiiz Restaurant*** serves excellent, good value Philippine food; you have to get your pre-order in early here, otherwise it's all gone.
A bit away from the beach, the ***La Isla Bonita Restaurant*** will feed you outstanding local and international fare as well as having pizzas, pasta, wines and filter coffee on the menu. Reservations are a must here.
You can also enjoy good Filipino and European food at the restaurant belonging to the ***Cocobana Beach Resort***. In the ***Kuan Ba Restaurant*** belonging to the resort of the same name you can enjoy roast beef and roast pork with mashed potatoes on Sundays.
The ***Sunsplash*** belonging to Matthias, a German, offers European and Asian food as well as videos, billiards and music. If the weather's right and there are enough people interested, his ***Floating Bar*** is hooked onto a tow-line and then pulled around the island at a leisurely pace - a popular event and a lot of fun.
A pleasant and airy place to have a sundowner with a beautiful view is the ***The Rock Bistro & Music Bar*** at the west end of the beach.
A popular round the clock meeting place is the ***Maldito*** on the beach at Logon Bay, which covers all tastes: they have a good selection of international, Philippine and Thai food, a salad bar, billiards, disco at the weekends, deli shop and bakery. Right next door, there's the ***Retsky Sports Bar*** and the restaurant ***La Dolce Vita*** with good Italian food.

Miscellaneous

Diving: Among the favourite diving destinations around Malapascua are the two Philippine and three Japanese wrecks, the submerged island of Monad, Lapus-Lapus Island and the tiny little Gato Island. The latter offers something quite unusual for divers: underwater caves with swarms of sea snakes. Another attraction which draws in lots of divers are the rare Thresher Sharks which there's a good chance of observing near the submerged island of Monad, 20 minutes by boat from Malapascua.

There are five dive shops to choose from: Bubble 07 Diver's Corp, Cellphone 0919-3229102, @; Divelink Cebu, Cellphone 0919-7487810, @; Malapascua Exotic Island Dive & Beach Resort, Cellphone 0919-6903947, @; Philippine Island Divers, Cellphone 0920-7039421, @; Sea Explorers, Cellphone 0919-4479030, @.

A dive costs P1300, diving courses cost P11,000 for two days and P16,000 for four days. Nitrox diving is available (also courses).

Mini Golf: If you're looking for a change from the beach, then Torsten and An-an's Malapascua Crazy Golf Bar is just what you're looking for (18 lanes; P100, children P50).

Money: There are no banks or ATMs on Malapascua so bring enough pesos along. You can change cash and travellers cheques in all popular currencies at the Cocobana Beach Resort, and at Maldito.

Online: Maldito, Tel & Fax 4371001, @, offers both internet and fax service.

Population: 3000.

Post & Telephone: Almost all resorts have a phone or mobile phone.

Post code: 6013 (Daanbantayan). Area Code: 032.

Sea Kayaking: The Sunsplash rents out two-seater kayaks for P150/hr or P500/day.

Visayas - Cebu

Getting There & Away

Bantayan Island

Boat: A Special Ride by outrigger from Malapascua to Santa Fe on Bantayan Island costs around P1300 to P1500 (2½ hrs).

Cebu City

Bus: If possible take a direct bus to Maya, because buses that make a detour to Hagnaya allow for 30 min extra. Cebu Autobus and D'Rough Riders buses from Cebu City to Maya leave from the Northern Bus Terminal near SM City between 5 and 11am (four hrs). Some buses only go as far as Daanbantayan. From there you can carry on to Maya by jeepney or tricycle.

There's also a minibus service between Cebu City and Maya, although you have to book at least one day in advance: Tel (032) 4371040, Cellphone 0919-4306473. Reservations on Malapascua in the Cocobana Beach Resort. The trip takes three hrs; P2100 (one to three people), P2400 (four to six people).

Taxi: A taxi from Cebu City or Mactan International Airport to Maya costs about P1200 (haggle with them). The trip takes three hrs.

Maya

Boat: Two or three outriggers leave Maya for Malapascua daily between 10 and 11.30am, with the possibility of more leaving during the day. They go directly to Bounty Beach (P50; 30 min). A Special Ride costs between P300 and P400.

Boats from Malapascua to Maya leave between 7.30 and 9.30am.

A big outrigger leaves Maya for San Isidro on Leyte daily at 10am (P50; two hrs). Departure from San Isidro to Maya is around 7 to 8am.

Calangaman Island

One hour by boat south of Malapascua lies the beautiful little island of Calangaman, with a long, dazzlingly white sandbank stretching out to sea on its east side. The turquoise coloured water on both sides of this sandbank is crystal clear and just asks to be swum and snorkelled in.
On the so-called Bird Island (the name Calangaman stems from the word *langgam*, the Cebuano word for bird), there are maybe two to three dozen fishermen living in modest huts. If you make a trip there, take along provisions.

South Cebu

Carcar

In Carcar, 33 km south of Cebu City, the road forks. One road leads along the east coast south to Bato, the other first twists and winds its way through the mountains in the direction of Barili and then along the west coast, also ending up in Bato.
Carcar is known for its many well-preserved buildings from the colonial era and the Parish Church of St Catherine of Alexandria, built between 1860 and 1875.

Getting There & Away

Bus: All buses from Cebu City heading for Bato or Moalboal go via Carcar (one hr).

Moalboal

The small town of Moalboal is located on Badian Bay in the south-west of Cebu, about 90 km by road from Cebu City. Most tourist activity involves the neighbouring, flat Copton Peninsula, mainly on Panagsama Beach in the barangay of Basdiot, about three km from Moalboal. Many of the guests are divers, attracted there by the excellent facilities: loads of dive shops, low prices and over 20 places to dive, including a beautiful house reef and, as a highlight, the teeming underwater world of the Pescador Island Marine Park just offshore.
If it's a sandy beach you're looking for, it takes about 15 min by outrigger from the mainly rocky Panagsama Beach to the nearby White Beach (P600), or you can take a tricycle for P150. Both include a pick-up service. Another idea would be a trip to the white beach at Lambug, near Badian (10 km south of Moalboal; tricycle P150).
If you need a change from the village life on Panagsama Beach, trips are possible to the Orchid Gallery, an orchid farm with swimming pool (out of town in the direction of Cebu City, 300m off the road, admission P10, bathing in the pool costs P30) and to the Kawasan Falls near Matutinao (20 km south; admission P10).
As well as seeing itself as a base for diving outfits, Moalboal is trying to get established as a start-off place for mountain biking, terrain riding, climbing (river climbing) and spelunking (cave exploration). There are already exciting tours on offer; see 'Miscellaneous' further below.

Places to Stay

Accommodation in Moalboal is almost all to be found at Panagsama Beach. There is a fairly wide variety available, ranging from the simplest of huts to places with comfortable rooms with air-conditioning and ceiling fans with remote control. They all have their own restaurants. On season is from December to March, after that the prices drop. If you want to stay longer, you can usually negotiate a cheaper monthly rate.
The northern part of Panagsama Beach from the Moalboal Reef Club to the

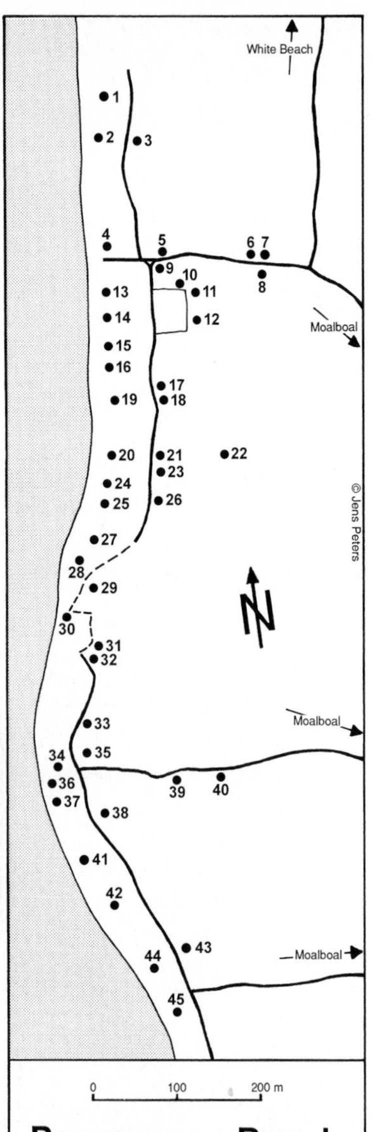

Places to Stay

2 Hannah's Lodge
3 Cor-isa's Cottages
11 Eve's Kiosk
14 Sumisid Lodge
15 Cora's Palm Court
16 Cabana Beach Club Resort
20 Savreda Beach Resort
22 Marina Village
30 Pacita's Nipa Huts
35 Marcosas Cottages
37 Quo Vadis Beach Resort
38 Mollie's Place
39 Sunshine Pension House
40 Nido's Garden
43 Casa Blanca Lodge
44 Love's Lodge
45 Gabunila's Cottages

Places to Eat & Entertainment

4 Hannah's Restaurant
5 New Red Banana Restaurant
6 Lloyd's Music Lounge
7 Lea's Fastfood
8 Chief Mau's Station
9 "D" Bestro
10 The Italian Corner
17 Marina Italiana Ristorante
18 Surface Interval Restaurant
Tabu Bar
23 Chili Bar
24 Seaview Restaurant
25 Balay Bar
Sunset View Restaurant
Visaya Bar & Restaurant
27 Sea Side Restaurant
28 Last Filling Station
31 Roxy Music Lounge
32 Roxy Italian Restaurant
33 Planet Action Bar
36 Arista Seafood Restaurant
38 Mollie's Restaurant
39 Swiss Restaurant
41 Mollie's Ocean View Garden
42 Emma's Store
44 Love's Restaurant

Miscellaneous

1 Aquarium
7 Lea's Minimart
12 Ocean Safari Philippines - Nelson's Scuba Diving School
13 Sequest Dive Center
19 Submaldive Dive Center
21 Cebu Photo Express
Cebu-Travel
Dive Silver
Savreda Dive Center
26 Neptune Diving Adventure
29 Ocean Globe Dive Center
33 Planet Action Adventure
34 Blue Abyss Dive Shop
37 Visaya Divers
38 Philippine Dive & Tour
44 Sea Explorers

Last Filling Station is heavily built-up. There you'll find most of the resorts, restaurants, bars and dive shops. South of there, as far as Gabunila's Cottages, it's quieter and greener. A path connects both sections; a bit hidden away, it takes you behind and past the restaurant at Pacita's Nipa Huts.
Quiet accommodation can also be found at White Beach, about three km north of Panagsama Beach, and at Tongo Point (no beach), about two km south of Panagsama Beach.

North Panagsama Beach
Eve's Kiosk. Cottage/fan/bath P350, cottage/ac/bath P700 to P2000. Really good value. A bigger place with a garden and lots of different cottages. Restaurant, swimming pool, motorbike hire, diving, taxi service.
Sumisid Lodge, Tel 4740005, @. SR/DR/fan/bath P450/550, SR/DR/ac/bath P950; including breakfast. Comfortably furnished rooms. Diving.
Cora's Palm Court. SR/DR/fan/bath P500, SR/DR/ac/bath P700 and P800. Fairly good value.
Marina Village. Cottage/fan/bath P550, SR/DR/fan/bath P950, SR/DR/ac/bath P1400. Basic cottages and very good rooms with refrigerator. Well-run, Italian-Philippine place with a beautiful garden.
Savedra Beach Resort, Tel & Fax 4740011, @. SR/DR/ac/bath P1600. Good rooms with refrigerator in comfortable, spacious stone buildings. Diving.
Cabana Beach Club Resort, Tel 4740034, Fax 4740035, @. SR/DR/ac/bath P3500 to P5250. Beautiful place with neatly furnished, comfortable rooms with refrigerator and TV.
Hannah's Lodge, Tel 4740091, Fax 3460592, @. SR/DR/ac/bath P3000/4000; including three meals. Attractive building with pleasant, spacious rooms with refrigerator set in nice garden grounds. Diving.

South Panagsama Beach
Mollie's Place, Cellphone 0917-2547060, @. SR/DR/fan P100/125, cottage/fan/bath P200 to P400, SR/DR/ac/bath P600. Clean rooms and cottages of differing styles (basic to more comfortable).
Gabunila's Cottages. Cottage/fan/bath P250 and P350. Basic cottages right on the ocean front.
Pacita's Nipa Huts. Cottage/fan/bath P250 and P350, cottage/ac/bath P700 and P1000. Modest cottages in a lush garden.
Sunshine Pension House, Tel & Fax 4740049, @. Cottage/fan/bath P400 and P700, SR/DR/fan/bath P500. Spacious rooms. Quiet location, under Swiss management. Good restaurant, swimming pool.
Nido's Garden. SR/DR/fan/bath P450. Good, pleasantly furnished rooms. Small place next to the Sunshine Pension House.
Love's Lodge, @. SR/DR/fan/bath P450 and P550, SR/DR/ac/bath P1400.

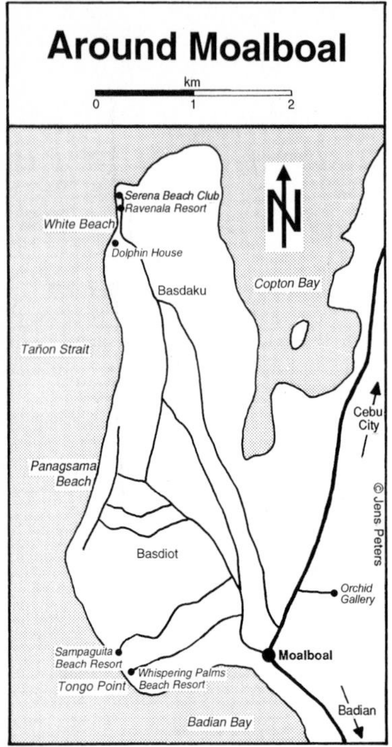

Pleasant place with homey, tastefully decorated rooms. Popular restaurant, diving.

Marcosas Cottages, Cellphone 0916-3042717, Fax 4740064, @. Cottage/fan/bath P600 and P700 (with kitchen), cottage/ac/bath P850 to P1300. Low monthly rates available. Pleasantly decorated, spotless, stone-built cottages in the garden and at the sea, with refrigerator. German-Philippine owners (Michael and Marcosa).

Quo Vadis Beach Resort, Tel 4740018, Fax 4740019, @. Cottage/fan/bath P600, SR/DR/ac/bath P1800. Well-kept place with tidy cottages and comfortably furnished rooms, some with refrigerators and sea view. Sunbathing lawn, swimming pool (P50 for non-residents), diving.

White Beach

Dolphin House, Basdaku, Cellphone 0916-3216533, Tel & Fax 4740073, @. SR/DR/fan P900/1100, cottage/fan/bath P1500/1800, cottage/ac/bath P2000/2400 (with refrigerator). Attractive cottages in a tropical garden and a big, beautiful building with fairly good rooms in a pleasant, friendly atmosphere. This well-kept little resort belongs to Rudy from Luxemburg and his Filipina wife, Luzviminda. Quiet location on a flat clifftop at the southern end of White Beach. Restaurant with good Asian cuisine, seafood and wine. Beach bar, diving (Visaya Divers).

Places to Eat

Most of the restaurants here offer similar fare and the prices don't vary much either. And remember, this is not the big city: service is not always snappy, and your order may take a while to arrive.

You can eat Filipino food cheaply and well at ***Emma's Store*** and in the ***New Red Banana Restaurant***. Several restaurants offer reasonably priced international food, eg ***"D" Bestro*** (good steaks and pizzas) and the following restaurants right on the water: ***Love's Restaurant***, ***Sea Side Restaurant*** (fresh grilled fish), ***Arista Seafood Restaurant*** (nicely decorated), and the ***Sunset View Restaurant***.

The garlic dishes at ***Hannah's Restaurant*** are a bit more expensive, but excellent. The ***Swiss Restaurant*** belonging to the Sunshine Pension House is a good address for tasty Swiss cuisine. Last but not least, if you want to give your system a rest from bacon and eggs, the ***Last Filling Station*** will serve you a healthy breakfast with freshly roasted coffee, home-made muesli, pita bread and other goodies.

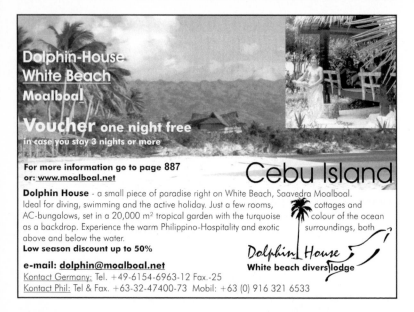

Entertainment
Well-frequented watering holes after sunset are ***Lloyd's Music Lounge***, ***Chief Mau's Station*** and ***Chili Bar***.

Miscellaneous
Activities: Jochen Hanika of Planet Action Adventure, Tel 4740024, @, has a six metre high climbing wall with an overhang, rents kayaks (P500 per day) and offers a selection of activities, such as cave exploration, volcano climbing (Mt Kanlaon on Negros), river climbing, horseback riding (rides into the mountains of South Cebu) as well as one-day or longer cycling tours through the interior of the island, eg:
- hill trip to Batat Batat (30 km, highest point 400m, 2½ hrs cycling time)
- trip to the Busay Caves (26 km, highest point 350m, four hrs cycling and walk through the caves)
- panorama tour of Moalboal via Ronda, Argao, Dalaguete and Badian and back to Moalboal (120 km, highest point 1800m, 14 hrs cycling time)

Aquarium: The result of years of patient work, Hans' Aquarium houses a fine collection of sea creatures such as an octupus and cleaner shrimps. It is open to visitors daily between 5 and 6pm.

Diving: Diving and diving instruction are very cheap in Moalboal. A one-day introduction costs US$70 including equipment. You'll pay US$20 for a diving trip, which includes the hire of a boat. A diving course lasting several days will cost you about US$250. Almost all dive operators offer nitrox-dives. Equipment is available at the various diving centres, but, as usual, it is best to have your own. You can hire a mask, snorkel and flippers for P150 per day.

An extremely popular diving destination is the Pescador Island Marine Park. There are twelve other dive sites in the immediate area of Moalboal which are regularly visited, including trips to the submerged two-seater aircraft not far from White Beach, as well as to Alegria Marine Park, where Father Ray, a priest who is a keen diver, will marry couples underwater if they wish (taking the plunge?!).

Further information on the subject of diving can be obtained at: Blue Abyss Dive Shop, Tel & Fax 4740031, @; Dolphin House, Basdaku, Tel 4740073, Fax 4740074, @; Ocean Globe Dive Center, Tel. 4740071; Nelson's Scuba Diving School next to Eve's Kiosk, Tel. 4740010 @; Neptune Diving Adventure, Tel & Fax 4740087, @; Savedra Dive Center, Tel 4740014, Fax 4740011, @; Sea Explorers at Love's Lodge, Tel 4740061, @; Seaquest Dive Center at Sumisid Lodge, Tel 4740004, @; Submaldive Dive Center, Tel 4740046, @; Visaya Divers at the Quo Vadis Beach Resort, Tel 4740019, @.

Festivals: Basdiot Fiesta in the last week in April. Moalboal Town Fiesta on 15 and 16 May.

Money: Practically every resort will change cash, although not always at the best rates. It would be better to take enough pesos with you. Only a few dive shops and the more expensive hotels and resorts will accept credit cards (with at least 7% surcharge).

Population: 5,000.

Post & Telephone: There is a post office in the Town Hall in Moalboal. It's not unusual for them to be out of postage stamps there. You can make phone calls from the telephone exchange in the same building, although most resorts now have a telephone as well as e-mail and fax facilities.

Post code: 6032. Area code: 032.

Snorkelling: There are good places to snorkel at the drop-offs at Panagsama Beach and White Beach. However, they can't really compete with Pescador Island's coral reef. A trip with one of the dive boats that go there every day costs P70.

Travel Agency: Cebu-Travel, Tel 4740014, will arrange tickets for Air Philippines, Asian Spirit, Cebu Pacific and Supercat.

Buoy oh Buoy!

In 1998, the environmentally minded dive shops of Moalboal initiated a project that could set an example to others: with money they had obtained from sponsors they bought 26 buoys and anchored them at each of the dive sites around Moalboal. Dive boats can now tie up to them without having to drop their own anchor, giving divers the opportunity to contribute to the preservation of the fragile coral reefs by refusing to patronise boats unless they use those buoys.

Getting Around

Boat: The daily rental fee for an outrigger is around P1000.

Bicycle: Planet Action Adventure rents out mountainbikes that are in top shape mechanically for P50 per hour or P300 a day.

Motorcycle: It costs P400 per day to hire a small motorbike; a 200cc bike costs P700 per day (eg at the Roxy Music Pub).

Getting There & Away

Argao

Bus: To go from Argao to Moalboal, first take a bus in the direction of Cebu City to Carcar, then get a bus from Cebu City to Moalboal. The trip takes two hrs.

Cebu City
Bus: Several Ceres Liner buses (leaving from the Southern Bus Terminal) go from Cebu City to Moalboal daily, roughly every hour (2½ hrs). Tricycles go from the main road in Moalboal to Panagsama Beach, charging P5 per person or P20 for the tricycle.

Taxi: A taxi from Cebu City to Moalboal costs between P800 and P1200 (haggle). Make absolutely sure the driver knows where Moalboal actually is.

Toledo
Bus: The connection between Toledo and Moalboal along the west coast is a bit frustrating. You have to allow for three changes of bus, and waiting around. It's better to go from Toledo to Naga and get the next bus from Cebu City to Moalboal.

Badian & Badian Island

About 10 km south of Moalboal you will find the small community of Badian. Just offshore in a lagoon-like bay is Badian Island, a peaceful island with a white sand beach where the Badian Island Resort & Spa is located. This hotel can be found in more and more tour catalogues these days.
In Lambug, about two km south of Badian and a further two km from the main road, there is a peaceful, palm-lined white sand beach with excellent snorkelling opportunities. It can be reached by tricycle from the main road.

Places to Stay
Badian Island Resort & Spa, Badian Island, Tel 4751103, Fax 4751101, @. SR/ac/bath P6000, DR/ac/bath P7600 and P13,400. An attractive place with tastefully furnished rooms; under Philippine-German management. Restaurant, swimming pool, windsurfing, diving.

Matutinao & Kawasan Falls

In the midst of lush tropical vegetation in the mountains near Matutinao you can find the refreshingly cool, crystal-clear Kawasan Falls. They are probably the best waterfalls on Cebu, and the natural pools are great for swimming. This idyllic place is a good starting point for mountain treks. There is a P10 entrance fee, and they charge P50 for the use of the tables, even if you order a drink with the owner.

Places to Stay
There are a number of cottages near the waterfalls which you can rent for P100 to P250. A small restaurant provides cold drinks as well as simple meals. As these cottages may be booked out, it's probably a good idea to organise a day trip first to check them out.

Getting There & Away
Bus/Jeepney: There are no problems getting from Moalboal to Matutinao by jeepney or bus during the day, but you could have trouble getting transport in the late afternoon. The trip takes 45 min. Get off at the church in Matutinao and follow the trail upriver on foot. This will take you about 15 min.

Motorcycle: Motorcycles can be parked at the church for a few pesos.

Samboan

Samboan got its first claim to fame from the 'Escala de Jacob' (Jacob's Ladder), built there in 1878. This flight of stone stairs leads up to an old watchtower on a plateau about 65m above the town. From that vantage point there is a magnificent view over the Tañon Strait, the narrows between Cebu and the neighbouring island of Negros. Whales and dolphins can often

be seen passing by through the straits. A roughly four-hour spotting trip by boat with a fisherman from Samboan will cost about P1000 (for six to eight participants).
Directly off Samboan there is a majestic coral reef, some say easily one of Cebu's best, which stretches from Ginatilan to Bato and is ideal for snorkelling. The coast itself is fairly rocky, with occasional small bays and a few pebbly beaches.

Getting There & Away

Bus: Ceres Liner buses travel from Cebu City to Samboan with a destination of Bato via Barili (three hrs). You can also take a bus to Bato via Oslob and carry on to Samboan by jeepney.

San Sebastian & Bato

Several ships go from San Sebastian and Bato to San Jose or Tampi on Negros daily (see Getting There & Away earlier in this chapter).

Getting There & Away

Cebu City - Argao
Bus: Several Ceres Liner buses leave the Southern Bus Terminal in Cebu City for Bato every day. They either go along the east coast via Argao, Dalaguete, Mainit and Lilian, or along the west coast via Barili, Moalboal, Samboan and San Sebastian to Bato, where there is a direct transfer to a boat heading to Tampi on Negros.

Sumilon Island

Sumilon Island, off Cebu's south-eastern coast, is a favourite with divers and snorkellers. On the western side of this little island south of the sandbank the water is only two to five metres deep and 200m wide, which makes it ideal for snorkelling, while drop-off plunges into the darkness are only about 100m off the south-west coast. Unfortunately, the contract with Silliman University at Dumaguete on Negros for the preservation of wildlife was not renewed by the authorities in Oslob. The Marine Research Center no longer exists, and the former Sumilon Marine Park is being fished day and night. That could mean the end of the coral reef: fishing with dynamite is so easy. But perhaps tourism will help to put a stop to this senseless destruction.

Places to Stay

Sumilon Island Resort. Was closed mid-2004 for renovation work. Information on reopening from the office of the Maribago Bluewater Resort, Mactan Island, Tel (032) 2310437.

Getting There & Away

Boat: For about P500 you can get from Mainit to Sumilon Island by small outrigger and be picked up again. You pay almost twice that for a round trip from Liloan or Santander, although the boats are bigger and therefore safer.

Argao

Argao is a small provincial town on the southern coast of Cebu which became better known when the exclusive Argao Beach Club opened, a few km from the town centre, at the beginning of the 1980s. However, a good 10 years later, the Club was closed down again. Just along the coast is the Dalaguete Public Beach, which is free. Showers are available and the daily rent for sun shelters is P50, or P75 on Sundays and holidays. You can also eat cheaply here.
There is a daily car ferry between Taloot (nine km north of Argao) and Catagbacon (6½ km north of Loon) on Bohol (see Getting There & Away earlier in this chapter).

Places to Stay

Luisa's Place. DR/fan/bath P400. A friendly place with a good restaurant.

Mahayhay Beach Resort, Tel 4859516, @. Cottage/fan/bath P600, cottage/ac/bath P1500 and P2500 (with children's room). Small, family-run place with well-kept stone cottages on the brownish public beach of Mahayhay, about 200m off the road. Restaurant.

Bamboo Paradise Beach Resort, Tel 3677271, @. SR/DR/fan/bath P780, SR/DR/ac/bath P1000, apartment/fan P1100, apartment/ac P1350. Pleasant accommodation with well-maintained rooms. Cosy, family-style atmosphere. German management (Irene and Günther). Good restaurant, diving. They will organise trips round the island and boat trips on request.

Kingfishers Beach Resort, Tel 4858855, @. Apartment P1800. Beautifully furnished apartments with three bedrooms, kitchen, living room and dining room. Japanese owner. Restaurant, diving. The beach is not very inviting.

Places to Eat

You can eat well and cheaply at ***Luisa's Place***. At ***Carmen's Kitchen*** the food is good and inexpensive and they'll be glad to cook any fish you've bought at the market for you.

The ***Bamboo Paradise Beach Resort*** has outstanding German and Filipino cuisine.

Miscellaneous

Post & Telephone: Post code: 6021. Area code: 032.

Getting There & Away

Bus: There are several Ceres Liner buses daily from Cebu City going to Argao (1½ hrs). They leave from the Southern Bus Terminal and are the ones with the destination 'Bato' or 'Oslob' on front.

Guimaras

Lying between Panay and Negros is the island of Guimaras, with its 138,000 inhabitants. Until 1992 Guimaras was a sub-province of Iloilo Province but then became an independent province. The capital is San Miguel, better known locally as Alibhon. Several smaller islands off the south and south-east coasts of Guimaras also belong to the province, such as Inampulugan and Nagarao, which have both already been developed for tourism.

On Bondulan Point, about 40 minutes on foot from Jordan, there is a giant cross (Balaan Bukit Shrine) which attracts many pilgrims during Easter week. You will get a good view from here of Iloilo City and the Iloilo Strait. Originally only a local attraction, Ang Pagtaltal sa Guimaras, an impressive passion play performed in Jordan in the local language on Good Friday, is now pulling in tourists from much further afield.

Among the attractions is Daliran Cave, just outside Buenavista. Mind you, the walk there is more interesting than the cave itself. Tricycles are the only means of transport between Jordan (pronounced Hordan) and Buenavista; the trip should cost about P70.

Near San Miguel, between Jordan and Nueva Valencia, there is a small Trappist monastery which is not really worth going out of your way to visit (it's a boring, modern building).

Carabao-mangoes, also known as 'Super Manilas', have become the most important source of income for Guimaras and several big plantations are dedicated to this tasty tropical fruit. Powerful companies made the Guimarasnons tempting offers to build factories on the island which would have brought a windfall of jobs for the local people, coupled however with the inevitable other side of the coin: pollution. The offers were politely turned down. The people of Guimaras did not want to gamble the intact nature on their island for the sake of industrial development which could endanger the future of their children. With this kind of far-sighted attitude, it would appear that sustainable eco-tourism would fit perfectly into the economic planning for the young province.

The best beaches on the island are south-west of Nueva Valencia, where several resorts have already established themselves. Tourists rarely visit the small village of Cabalagnan, in the deep south of the island. A couple of idyllic islands lie offshore.

Located where it is, the island makes a good day trip from Iloilo City. Loads of boats make the crossing over to Jordan every day. Only about 10 percent of the island's roads are surfaced, the rest are tracks, so this is ideal country for hikers and mountain bikers. The Iloilo Mountain Bike Association (IMBA) came to the same conclusion, and they started to run the Guimaras International Mountain Bike Festival here in February 1995 as an annual event.

Getting There & Away

You can get to Guimaras from Negros and Panay (see the Getting There & Away sections of the individual island chapters).

To Negros

Boat

From Cabalagnan to Valladolid

A small boat leaves Cabalagnan for Valladolid in the early morning around 3 to 4am, stopping at several different islands en route. It will also pick up passengers on Nagarao Island. As there is no jetty in Valladolid the boat anchors a bit out to sea, and the passengers have to wade ashore.

From Suclaran to Pulupandan

Twice a day a boat sails to Pulupandan, a little north of Valladolid (P40; one hr).

To Panay

Boat

From Buenavista to Iloilo City

Daily, roughly every hour from 5am to 5.30pm with a small ferry from the Buenavista wharf (MacArthur Wharf) in Santo Rosario to the Parola wharf at Rotary Park in Iloilo City (one hr).

From Jordan to Iloilo City

Several small ferries run daily, roughly every hour between 5am and 5.30pm to the river wharf near the Post Office (30 min).

An outrigger travels daily about every half an hour between 5am and 5.30pm from Jordan to the Ortiz wharf, near the Iloilo City Central Market (P7; 15 min). A Special Ride costs P250.

Four times daily, possibly at 8.30 and 10.30am, and at 3 and 5.30pm with a FF Cruz Shipping car ferry to the river wharf on Rizal St (P20; 1½ hrs).

Getting Around

Jeepneys run between Jordan and Nueva Valencia, a few going as far as Cabalagnan. They only return to Jordan in the morning, ie not the same afternoon. The last departure from Neuva Valencia to Jordan is at 4pm.

Several jeepneys a day run from Jordan to San Isidro, where you can cross to Nagarao Island. The ride costs P15, but the asking price for a Special Ride is at least P400. Very few regular jeepneys cover this route in the late afternoon. There's a small signal post in San Isidro which you have to wave to get the boat to come across. The crossing costs P100 per boat.

Guimaras only has a few aircon minibuses. You'll pay at least P500 for a Special Ride from Jordan to San Isidro.

Boat Trip around Guimaras

The best way to do this trip is by outrigger, which can take two to three days, depending on the number of stops. It is essential to take along drinking water and food, and make sure your boat is equipped with a roof for sun protection. The trip could start in Iloilo City and continue around the island in an anticlockwise manner. All along the southwest coast, between Lusaran Point and Tandug Island, there are scores of tiny little bays which are perfect for snorkelling. Plans have been mooted to turn this coral-rich section of coastline into a nature reserve. The various little coral islands with white sand beaches to the south and south-west of Guimaras are well worth a visit, especially at high tide, as large areas usually dry out at low tide.

Malingin Island, a good 10 km south of Guimaras, is ideal for spending the night in the open air; Guiuanon Island (pronounced Giwanon) is good for hiking; Ususan Island (pronounced Usu-usan) which houses a handful of hermits, has a passable beach; and Nagarao Island

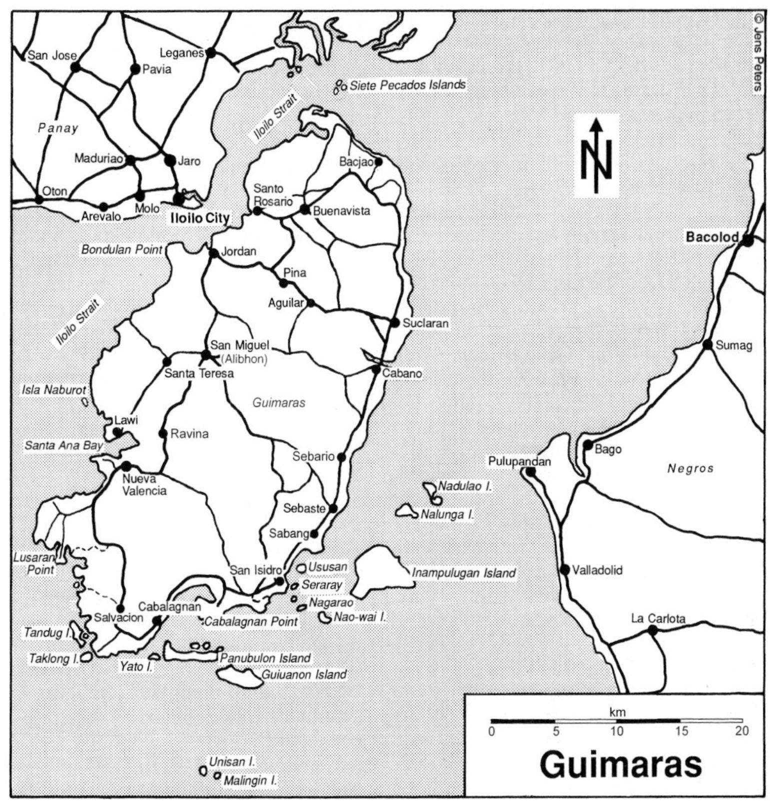

('Island of the Tree Spirits'), is the location of the beach resort of the same name, run by Martin Stummer, a German who has been active there for years in encouraging environmental protection and looking after endangered plants and species. He has even set up a 'tree spirit pathway' to give his guests some idea of the traditional Philippine belief in the spirits of Nature.

On the south coast, between San Isidro and Sebaste, primitive wind turbines have been constructed to pump sea water into flat basins from which salt is later extracted.

Places to Stay

Colmenares Hotel & Beach Resort, Hoskyn, Cellphone 0917-9868735. SR/DR/fan/bath P300 and P400, SR/DR/ac/bath P500 and P1200 (for up to six people). Spacious rooms. Restaurant and disco in a building on stilts. The three swimming pools are unfortunately usually empty or blocked with algae. The beach is not suitable for bathing. This place is about two km west of Jordan, halfway to Bondulan Point.

Valle Verde Mountain Spring Resort, Ravina, Cellphone 0918-7303446. Cottage/bath P300 and P500 (four persons),

SR/DR/fan/bath P600. Friendly place with basic, but pleasant cottages. Beautiful view down to Lawi Bay. Food can be pre-ordered. Swimming pool with spring water. Mountain bike and motorbike hire organised by Luisa the owner. The resort is about 500m west of the road from San Miguel to Nueva Valencia (there's a signpost). Can be reached directly from Jordan by chartered tricycle (P100) or jeepney (P150). The scheduled jeepney from Jordan to Nueva Valencia only stops at the turn-off.

Baras Beach Resort, Lawi, Cellphone 0917-9387159, @. Cottage/bath P750 to P900, depending on size. Beautifully situated resort, albeit not quite the newest. There's a great view down onto the sea from the cottages which are spaced a pleasantly discreet distance apart and surrounded by lush green vegetation in a slightly raised location. The restaurant on a little white beach serves seafood and a selection of Western and Philippine dishes. The easiest way to get there is to call them from Iloilo City and they will send a boat to pick you up (P1100; one hr). You could also hire a jeepney from Jordan to Lawi (P200; 45 min). It's a 10-minute Special Ride by boat from Lawi to the resort (P250; 10 min).

Isla Naburot Resort, Sinapsapan. Cottage/bath P6500 per person, including meals. This is a small, rustic establishment with no electricity, on the island of the same name.

Raymen Beach Resort, Nueva Valencia. SR/DR/fan P300 and P500, cottage/fan/bath P600, cottage/ac/bath P900. A discount can be negotiated for a longer stay. It's pretty quiet here on normal weekdays, otherwise it's a favourite with day trippers - Iloilo City is not far away. Located on the pristine white Alubihod Beach.

Nagarao Island Resort, @. Cottage/bath from P800. Arrangements for long-stay guests are possible. Attractive, roomy cottages. Restaurant, swimming pool, sailing and boat trips. For further information, ask at the Nagarao Island Office, 113 Seminario St, Jaro, Iloilo City, Tel 3206290, Fax 3292139.

Costa Aguada Island Resort, Inampulugan Island, @. SR/fan/bath P2500 to P3000, DR/fan/bath P3000 to P3500. Spacious and nicely decorated cottages with terraces. This extensive, well-maintained property is located on the white Bamboo Beach on a beautiful island east of Guimaras. Restaurant, swimming pool, tennis court, horseback riding, mountainbike and outrigger sailboat rental. Reservations in Manila: Tel (02) 8905333, Fax (02) 8905543.

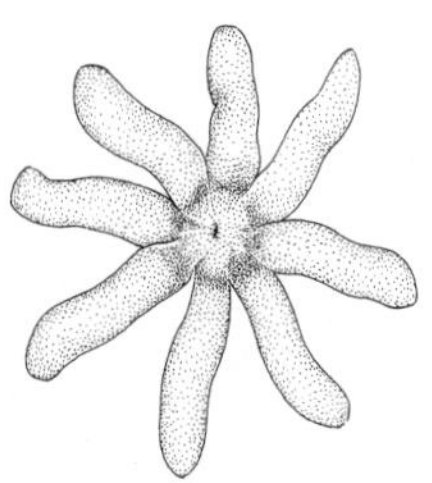

Leyte

Leyte is located in the eastern part of the Visayas and lies between Bohol, Cebu, north-east Mindanao and Samar. The San Juanico Bridge joins the islands of Leyte and Samar across the San Juanico Strait and stands 41m over the water. Built in 1975, and at 2.16 km the longest bridge in the Philippines, it is said to be one of the most beautiful bridges in south-east Asia. Central and southern Leyte are somewhat mountainous, with plains in the northern and western parts of the island. Administratively, it is divided into the province of Leyte, where the capital is Tacloban, and Southern Leyte, with its capital Maasin. Copra is Leyte's most important export product. More than 30% of cultivable land is planted with coconut palms. Other important agricultural exports are rice, maize, sugar cane and abaca. These are mostly shipped directly from Tacloban, making it unnecessary to send exports via Manila.

Leyte is particularly remembered as the place where General MacArthur fulfilled his 'I shall return' pledge. On 20 October 1944, US troops landed at Red Beach in Palo, a little south of Tacloban, and started pushing the Japanese out of the Philippines. A little further south, Tolosa is a town also sure of a future place in history, as the birthplace of the former First Lady, Imelda Marcos. Another place of historical significance here is the little island of Limasawa in the deep south of Leyte. The famous explorer Ferdinand Magellan landed there after a long voyage of discovery and celebrated his first holy mass on Philippine soil on Easter Sunday, 1521.

The main dialect in and around Tacloban is Waray-Waray, whereas in the north-west and the south it is Cebuano, but English is still widely spoken.

Getting There & Away

You can get to Leyte from Biliran, Bohol, Cebu, Luzon, Mindanao and Samar (see the Getting Away from Luzon section of the Manila chapter and the Getting There & Away sections of the individual island chapters).

To Biliran

Bus

From Ormoc to Caibiran

Buses leave from the bus terminal at the wharf daily in the early morning (three hrs). You may have to change in Lemon.

From Ormoc to Naval

JD Company buses go every day, leaving at 4.30 and 5.30am, and possibly noon (three hrs).

From Tacloban to Caibiran

A bus leaves every day between 9 and 11am from the bus terminal (five hrs).

From Tacloban to Naval

Buses belonging to various companies leave from the bus terminal every day (three hrs). Last departure is 3pm.

JD Bus Company buses may leave from their terminal in Real St. Some of them may carry on as far as Almeria, Kawayan, Tucdao or Culaba. You can also take a bus heading for Ormoc and change in Lemon to a bus for Naval.

To Bohol

Boat

From Bato or Maasin to Ubay

Daily between 8 and 10am with a big outrigger, taking three hrs from Bato (possibly via Lapinin Island which then takes four hrs), and four hrs from Maasin.

To Cebu

Bus/Boat

From Tacloban to Cebu City

discontinued

Daily at 7am with a Philtranco bus, taking [illegible] hrs, including the ferry from Isabel to Danao.

Boat

From Bato to Cebu City

Daily with Kinswell Shipping Lines (P235; four hrs).

From Baybay to Camotes Islands

discontinued

Two times daily with the fast ferry *Oceanjet* (one hr).

From Baybay to Cebu City

discontinued

Two times daily with the fast ferry *Oceanjet* (P550; 2½ hrs); via Camotes Islands.

From Hilongos to Cebu City

Two times daily with the fast ferry *Oceanjet* (P440; two hrs).

From Isabel to Carmen

Daily with a big outrigger (three hrs).

From Isabel to Danao

Daily at 1pm with the Aznar Shipping Corporation (P150; four hrs).

From Liloan to Cebu City

Thursday and Sunday with Maypalad Shipping Corporation (P170; six hrs).

From Maasin to Cebu City

Tuesday, Wednesday, Friday and Sunday with Cokaliong Shipping Lines (P380; six hrs).

From Ormoc to Camotes Islands

Daily with a big outrigger to Bukog (three hrs).

From Ormoc to Cebu City

Three times daily with the fast ferry *Supercat* (P500; two hrs).
Daily except Sunday with Super Shuttle Ferry (car ferry), taking six hrs (P220).
Tuesday, Wednesday, Friday and Sunday with Cebu Ferries (P230; six hrs).

From San Isidro to Maya (North Cebu)

Daily at 7 or 8am with a big outrigger (P50; two hrs). If the boat is not too crowded it will call in to Malapascua Island for an extra charge of P200. A special ride from San Isidro to Malapascua Island shouldn't cost more than P1200.
After the boat arrives in Maya others leave for Malapascua Island and a bus leaves for Cebu City.

From Tacloban to Cebu City

Wednesday, Friday and Sunday with Maypalad Shipping Corporation (P230; 12 hrs).

To Luzon

Air

From Tacloban to Manila

Air Philippines, Cebu Pacific and Philippine Airlines fly daily (P2570).

Bus/Boat

From Tacloban to Manila

Liberty Transport buses leave from the bus terminal daily. Philtranco buses make

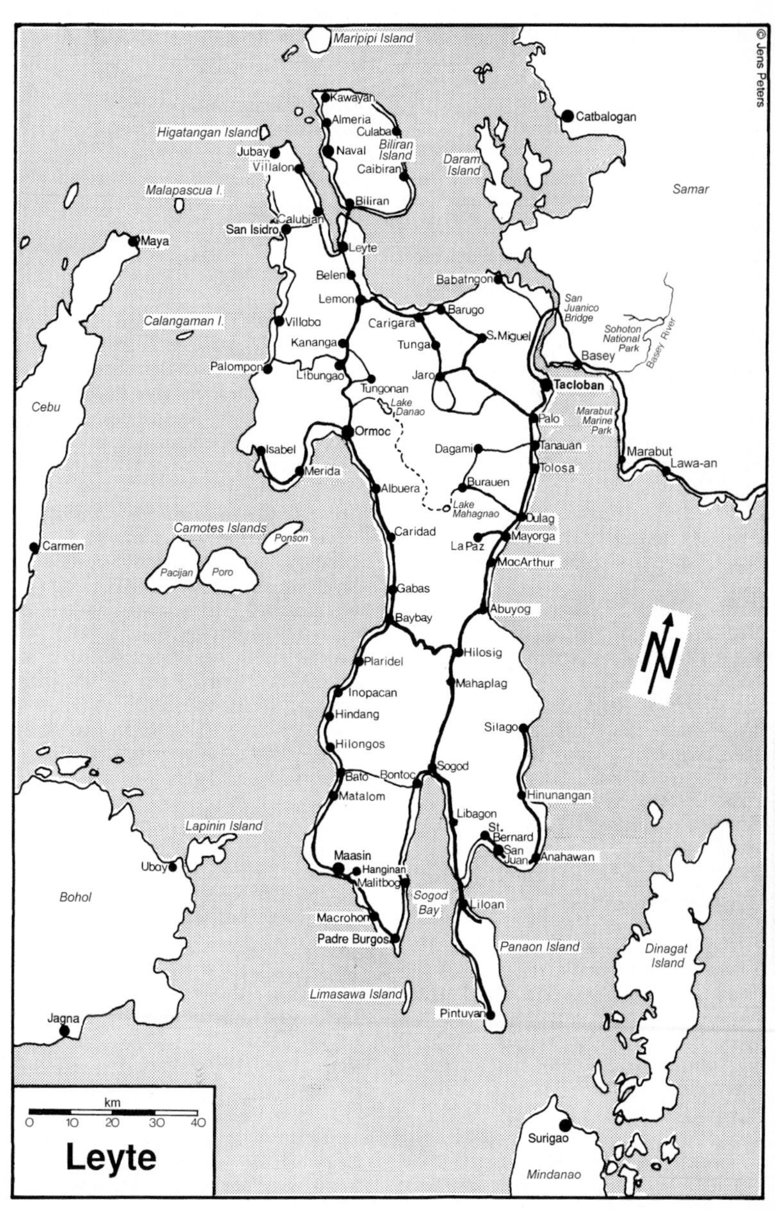

Visayas - Leyte

the trip daily from the Philtranco Bus Terminal. It is advisable to reserve a seat (P860; 28 hrs, including the ferry from Alegria/San Isidro to Matnog).

Boat

From Ormoc to Manila
Tuesday with Sulpicio Lines (P865; 49 hrs); via Masbate/Masbate.

From Palompon to Manila
Thursday with WG & A (P820; 27 hrs); via Masbate/Masbate.

To Masbate

Boat

From Baybay to Masbate
Sunday with Sulpicio Lines (18 hrs); via Calubian.

From Calubian to Masbate
Sunday with Sulpicio Lines (six hrs).

From Maasin to Masbate
Sunday with Sulpicio Lines (24 hrs); via Baybay and Calubian.

From Ormoc to Masbate
Tuesday with Sulpicio Lines (P340; 12 hrs).

From Palompon to Masbate
Thursday with WG & A (P420; eight hrs).

To Mindanao

Bus/Boat

From Tacloban to Davao
Two Philtranco buses leave daily at about midnight, sometimes a little later; it comes from Manila. The trip, including the Liloan-Lipata/Surigao ferry, takes 16 hrs.

Boat

From Liloan to Lipata/Surigao
Daily at 1, 5 and 11.30am and 5pm with a car ferry (three hrs). Lipata is 10 km north-west of Surigao.

From Maasin to Surigao
Wednesday and Friday with Cokaliong Shipping Lines (four hrs).

To Samar

Bus

From Tacloban to Catbalogan and Calbayog
Philtranco buses leave for Pasay City/ Manila daily, going through Catbalogan and Calbayog. Travel time to Catbalogan is three hrs and five hrs to Calbayog. It is advisable to book. You can also take Liberty Transport buses from the bus terminal.

From Tacloban to Borongan and Guiuan (Eastern Samar)
Roughly one bus an hour during the day from the bus terminal taking four hrs (Borongan) or six hrs (Guiuan); via Buray (Western Samar) and Taft.
Several minibuses make the trip in the forenoons, leaving from various petrol stations. Travel time to Borongan is 3½ hrs via Basey and Lawa-an (South Samar).

Boat

From Tacloban to Guiuan (Eastern Samar)
Monday, Wednesday and Friday at 11pm with K & T Shipping Lines (Maypalad Shipping Corporation), taking six hrs.

Tacloban

Tacloban is the provincial capital of Leyte. The colourful market at the western end of the wharf is full of life. A large relief on the wall of the Provincial Capitol depicts MacArthur's return to the Philippines in October 1944 at Palo, just south of Tacloban, from where he proceeded to liberate the country from the Japanese occupation. This historic event is celebrated each year on 19 and 20 October with parades and cockfights.

As a reward for climbing the many steps (decorated with 14 statues representing the Stations of the Cross) to the base of the statue of Christ, you will get a beautiful view over Tacloban and its busy port. You can get there from the market along Torres St.

If you are keen on history, you should visit MacArthur Park on Red Beach, where General MacArthur landed. Nature lovers will enjoy a day trip to Sohoton National Park near Basey on the neighbouring island of Samar.

Museum

Well worth the visit, the Santo Niño Shrine & Heritage Museum gives you an idea of the state of luxury the Marcos clan lived in. A guided tour for up to five persons costs P200. If you are on your own, there are usually other people to join in with. Tours start every hour from 8 to 11am and 1 to 4pm. Next door is the equally large People's Center, with its Library for Samar and Leyte.

Places to Stay - bottom end

Cecilia's Lodge, 178 Paterno St, Tel 3212815. SR/DR/fan P150/300, SR/fan/bath P180, DR/ac/bath P600 (with TV). Basic, quiet and fairly good. A bit hard to find as there's only a small sign.

Rosvenil Pensione, Burgos St, Tel 3212676. SR/DR/fan P210/250, SR/DR/fan/bath P260/310, SR/DR/ac P320/390, SR/DR/ac/bath P370/450. Pleasant, well-kept accommodation in a quiet location. Good value. Restaurant.

Primerose Hotel, Zamora St corner Salazar St, Tel 3212248. SR/DR/fan/bath P300, DR/ac/bath P700 to P1000. OK rooms, the aircon ones have a TV, and some have a refrigerator. Restaurant.

Manabó Lodge, Zamora St, Tel 3213727. SR/fan P300, SR/DR/fan/bath P450 (two rooms share a bath). Not bad for the money. Quiet location in a courtyard at the back.

LNU House, Paterno St corner Santa Cruz St, Tel 3213175. SR/DR/ac/bath P400 to P600. Good accommodation with spacious rooms, the more expensive ones also have a refrigerator and TV.

Tacloban Plaza Hotel, Justice Romualdez St, Tel 3212444. SR/ac/bath P480 and P800, DR/ac/bath P650 and P985. Somewhat worn rooms with TV. Restaurant.

Manhattan Inn, Rizal Ave, Tel 3214170. SR/DR/ac/bath P465 to P730. Comfortable rooms with TV, the more expensive ones also have a refrigerator. Popular place, if not exactly the newest. This well-run hotel is often booked out, so it is advisable to make reservations. Restaurant.

Places to Stay - top end

Asia Stars Hotel, Zamora St, Tel 3214952, Fax 3255889. SR/DR/ac/bath P750/900, suite P1350. Pleasant rooms with TV in a centrally-located hotel.

Hotel Alejandro, Paterno St, Tel 3217033, Fax 5237882. SR/DR/ac/bath P855 to P1380. Attractive building with that special touch of traditional Philippine elegance. Friendly rooms with TV, some also have a refrigerator. Good restaurant.

Leyte Park Resort Hotel, Magsaysay Blvd, Tel 3256000, Fax 3255587, @. SR/DR/ac/bath P2250 to P4800 (promotion rates possible). The best hotel in Tacloban with well-furnished rooms and cottages (so-called villas), all with refrigerator and TV. Beautifully located, directly on San Pedro Bay, it has a restaurant, fitness room, swimming pool and airport service.

Places to Eat

The restaurant ***Yam Yam Fast Food*** is a McDonald's look-alike but they have a good choice of breakfasts (you can find

Getting There & Away
8 Wharf
9 Cebu Pacific
11 K & T Shipping Lines
Maypalad Shipping Corporation
13 Bus Terminal
35 Philippine Airlines (Ticketing Office)
43 Philtranco Bus Terminal
44 Airport (10 km)

Places to Stay
2 Leyte Park Resort Hotel
18 Manhattan Inn
21 Primerose Hotel
25 Traveller's Lodge
26 Manabó Lodge
27 Asia Stars Hotel
32 Tacloban Plaza Hotel
36 Hotel Alejandro
38 Cecilia's Lodge
39 Rosvenil Pensione
41 LNU House

Places to Eat & Entertainment
3 San Pedro Bay Seafood Restaurant
5 The Entertainment Plaza
15 McDonald's
17 Alpha Bakery
19 Jollibee
24 Yam Yam Fast Food
31 Good Morning Food Complex
35 Giuseppe's
40 Dahil Sa Iyo Fastfood
44 Agus Restaurant (1.5 km)

Miscellaneous
1 Children's Park
4 Tourist Office
6 Plaza Libertad
7 Provincial Capitol
10 Post Office
12 Buddhist Temple Paseo de Legaspi
San Juanico Bridge
14 Market
16 Gaisano Department Store
18 Bank of the Philippine Islands
20 Bank of the Philippine Islands
22 Equitable PCI Bank
23 Mercury Drug
28 Equitable PCI Bank
29 Philippine National Bank (PNB)
30 Stations of the Cross (Calvary Hill)
32 Family Internet Café
33 Philippine National Bank (PNB)
34 City Hall
37 Santo Niño Church
42 People's Center & Library
Santo Niño Shrine & Heritage Museum

the real thing two streets further on). You can also start the day right at the ***Alpha Bakery*** in Rizal Ave.

The ***Good Morning Food Complex*** in Gomez St has a wide selection on its menu, mainly seafood and Chinese dishes. ***Dahil Sa Iyo Fastfood*** on the corner of Burgos and Real Sts is clean and popular, but closes at 8pm. The menu has a wide selection of tasty Philippine dishes, and the house specialty is pakdol, a hearty dish similar to meat stew.

As you could guess from the name, ***Giuseppe's*** in Avenida Veteranos is a cosy place for pizzas and other Italian favourites, but they also have Philippine food and seafood.

Highly recommended is the ***San Pedro Bay Seafood Restaurant***, built on stilts in the water near the Leyte Park Resort Hotel. Guests can compose their own meals from the fish and various seafoods available and have them cooked to their taste. They also have a few meat-based meals.

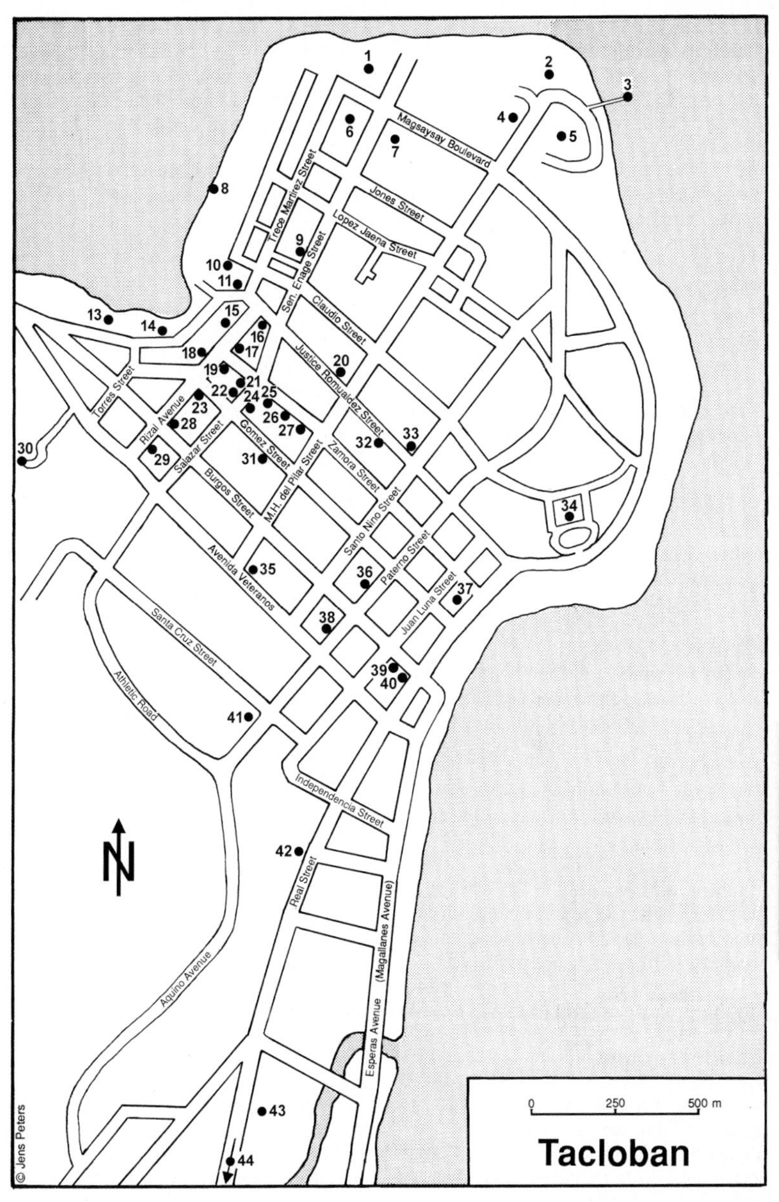
Magsaysay Boulevard
Jones Street
Lopez Jaena Street
Trece Martirez Street
Sen. Enage Street
Claudio Street
Justice Romualdez Street
Torres Street
Rizal Avenue
Salazar Street
Gomez Street
M.H. del Pilar Street
Zamora Street
Burgos Street
Santo Nino Street
Paterno Street
Juan Luna Street
Avenida Veteranos
Santa Cruz Street
Athletic Road
Independencia Street
Real Street
Esperas Avenue (Magallanes Avenue)
Aquino Avenue
0
250
500 m
Tacloban
© Jens Peters

Another good place to go for seafood is the ***Agus Restaurant***, a bit outside of town on the south side (tricycle P20), and directly on San Pedro Bay. Look forward to enjoying excellent, inexpensive food here with a wonderful sea view.

Entertainment

The nightlife is fairly limited in Tacloban. One very popular place is the ***Saint-Tropez Disco*** in the Leyte Park Resort Hotel, and a few steps further on ***The Entertainment Plaza*** offers live music in the evenings.

Miscellaneous

Festivals: Kasadya-an Festival on 10 March. Subiran Regatta on 28 June. Pintados Festival on 29 June. City Fiesta on 30 June.
Money: Bank of the Philippines Islands on Rizal Ave and in Justice Romualdez St, Equitable PCI Bank in Salazar St and on Rizal Ave corner Burgos St, and Philippine National Bank in Justice Romualdez St have ATMs.
Online: Family Internet Café on the ground floor of the Tacloban Plaza Hotel, Justice Romualdez St, and Asahi Internet Access, Zamore St, both charge P25/hr.
Population: 180,000.
Post & Telephone: Post code: 6500. Area code: 053.
Travel Agency: The Ticketing Office, Avenida Veteranos, Tel 3257000, Fax 3255807, sells Cebu Pacific and Philippine Airlines tickets and others.
Tourist Office, Magsaysay Blvd, Tel 3212048, Fax 3255279, @. Open Mon-Fri 8am-noon and 1-6pm.

Getting Around

Car: FMC Rent-A-Car, Tel 3214097, and Jun Encina, Cellphone 0919-4285960, rent cars with driver.
Tricycle: A journey in the central area of the city costs P4 per person.

Getting There and Away

By Air: It is 11 km from Romualdez Airport to the centre of town. The trip should not cost more than P20 per person by jeepney; going back, the trip should cost a little less. A taxi from the airport into town costs P120 to P150.
Air Philippines, Gomez St, Tel 3217800, 3217900.
- Romualdez Airport, Tel 3236800, 3236900.
Destination: Manila.
Cebu Pacific, Senator Enage St, Tel 3257747-48, 3219410.
- Romualdez Airport, Tel 3258486.
Destination: Manila.
Philippine Airlines, Romualdez Airport, Tel 3212212-13.
Destination: Manila.

By Bus: Philtranco aircon buses are often booked out when heading for Manila, so it is worthwhile booking a seat at least one day before leaving. Philtranco (Tel 5231968) has its own terminal in the south of the city. All other buses leave from the bus terminal near the market. The ride from the Philtranco Bus Terminal to a hotel in the city with a tricycle should cost P5.

By Boat: Tacloban harbour is very near the city centre.
Note: K & T Shipping Lines and Maypalad Shipping Corporation have merged.
K & T Shipping Lines, Justice Romualdez St, Port Area, Tel 3213580.
Destination: Samar.
Maypalad Shipping Corporation, Justice Romualdez St, Port Area, Tel 3213580.
Destination: Cebu.

Around Tacloban

Basey & Sohoton National Park

Although Sohoton National Park (also known as Sohoton Natural Bridge National Park) is on the island of Samar, the simplest way to get there is from Tacloban via Basey. It has waterfalls, underground waterways and a labyrinth of caves, which are also called 'wonder caves' because of their glittering stone formations. The biggest and most beautiful are Panhulugan I, Bugasan III and Sohoton. The best time to see the caves is from March to July, as you can only visit them when the water level is low, and not after prolonged rainfall.

Basey is well known for its colourful woven goods, mainly mats made of dried leaves of the buri palm *(banig)* and other woven goods, which are sold at the markets in Tacloban.

Getting There & Away

Staff at the tourist office in Tacloban should be able to help you arrange trips to Sohoton National Park, although making your own arrangements is also no problem - and probably even cheaper. You should try to be in Basey by 8am at the latest; otherwise time will get tight, as there is a chance of the last jeepney back to Tacloban leaving as early as 3pm. The first jeepney leaves Tacloban for Basey at about 6am, the second not till 9.30am, each taking over an hour. There is a chance that communal taxis will leave at 7am.

First you have to go to the DENR Office in the Municipal Building in Basey and get yourself a DENR permit (P8 per person). Then you head for the Tourism Authority at the pier where you have to pay the following fees: P700 for the boat (for 12 people max); P200 for the guide (a maximum of seven people per guide); P100 for a kerosene lamp (they recommend at least two lamps); P20 per person for a mayor's permit; P8 per person for admission.

The beautiful trip upriver to the park takes about 1½ hrs. There you will be met by the guide, who will collect your offical papers from you (he needs them to prove he has done his job, so he'll get paid). You have to leave the park by 3 pm at the latest. If you want to spend overnight in the park you have to clear this with the Tourism Authority first.

Palo

A monument (Leyte Landing Memorial) and a plaque on Red Beach at Palo commemorate the return of General MacArthur to the Philippines on 20 October 1944 after a major naval battle. He liberated the country from Japanese occupation roughly 2½ years after fleeing from the island fortress of Corregidor in Manila Bay.

Palo Cathedral, built in 1596 with an altar covered in gold leaf, was temporarily converted to a hospital by the Americans during the early days of the liberation of the Philippines.

On the outskirts of Palo, Guinhangdan Hill looks down on the town. Also known as Hill 522 (because it is 522 feet above sea level), this was the scene of bitter fighting in 1944 when many American and Japanese soldiers lost their lives. A huge wooden cross now graces the top of the hill, with a path leading up to it. From up there you can get a good view of the historic area and of Palo Cathedral.

Places to Stay

City Lodge Pension. SR/DR/ac/bath P400. Fairly good and clean, and you can rent rooms by the hour.

MacArthur Park Beach Resort, Tel 3233015. SR/DR/ac/bath P1700 and P2200, suite P4500. Including breakfast. The rooms are comfortable and tastefully furnished. Good restaurant, swimming pool. With its extensive grounds, the resort is about 300m south of the Leyte Landing Memorial, directly on San Pedro Bay. Reservations in Manila: Philippine Tourism Authority, Tel (02) 5242502, Fax (02) 5256490.

Getting There & Away

Jeepney: Several jeepneys leave the bus terminal in Tacloban for Palo daily, but not all make the detour to MacArthur Park about 1½ km from the main road (tricycle P5 per person from the main road to the park).

San Isidro

San Isidro is a small community in the north-west of Leyte, with boat connections to northern Cebu. You can also go to the small island of Malapascua from San Isidro (see Getting There & Away earlier in this chapter). The wharf is a bit out of town (P10 per person by motorbike).

Places to Stay

San Isidro Pension House. Dorm/fan P100, SR/DR/ac P350, SR/DR/ac/bath P600. Friendly, family accommodation with a cosy lounge.

Places to Eat

At the market you can have fish prepared for you at an ***Eatery***. There's another eatery at the Caltex filling station.

Getting There & Away

Ormoc

Bus/Jeepney: One bus and some jeepneys leave Ormoc in the early morning for San Isidro (4½ hrs).

Tacloban

Bus: Buses go from Tacloban to San Isidro via Calubian five times a day, leaving at 6, 7 and 10am, noon and 3pm (3½ hrs including a short stopover in Calubian). A Special Ride by motorcycle from Calubian to San Isidro costs P100.

Palompon

Palompon is a coastal town north-west of Ormoc and three hours away by jeepney. Ships go from Palompon to Cebu and Panay. If you follow the road from Palompon northwards along the coast, you will reach Jubay (pronounced 'hoo-bye'), where you can get a boat to small Higatangan Island, which is off the usual routes and belongs to Biliran province.

Places to Stay

Russell Lodging House, Rizal St. SR/fan P100, DR/fan P150, SR/ac/bath P300, DR/ac/bath P450. Not far from the pier; basic, fairly clean accommodation.

There is one more clean, inexpensive lodging house at the entrance to PIT (Philippine Institute of Technology).

Getting There & Away

Jeepney: Several jeepneys travel from Ormoc to Palompon daily (2½ hrs).

Ormoc

This port town is connected to Cebu by ship. The wharf area is always lively, especially in the late afternoons and evenings, when a lot of people meet for a gossip on the wall of the wharf at the beautifully laid-out harbour promenade.

On 5 November 1991 Ormoc experienced the blackest day in its history, when the typhoon Uring stormed over Leyte, leaving in its wake massive quantities of water raging down into the town from the mountains, taking everything with it that couldn't get out of its way. Over 5000 people died from injuries or drowned, while almost 50,000 lost their homes. There is no doubt these floods were made possible by the activities of illegal logging operators who for many years got away scot-free with denuding the slopes, leaving them stony and barren as a result. There is a memorial to the tragedy in the cemetery at Ormoc.

Places to Stay

Pongos Hotel, Bonifacio St, Tel 2552211, Fax 5619721. SR/fan/bath P220, DR/fan/bath P340, SR/ac/bath P420, SR/DR/ac/bath P600 to P1450, suite P1600 and P2400. Good rooms, especially the newer, more expensive ones, which are tastefully furnished, with TV. Quiet place. Restaurant.

Buenas Pension Plaza, Lopez Jaena St corner Mabini St, Tel 2552640. SR/DR/fan/bath P350/400, SR/DR/ac/bath P500/600. Good rooms with TV, well worth the money. Restaurant.

Don Felipe Hotel, Bonifacio St, Tel 2552460, Fax 2554306, @. SR/fan/bath P360, DR/fan/bath P420, SR/ac/bath P480 to P1600, DR/ac/bath P630 to P1800, suite P2100 and P2400. There is an old building and a new one which houses the better and more expensive rooms with TV. The rooms across from the bus terminal are loud in the morning. Restaurant, disco. Located beside the wharf.

Zenaida's Chateau Tourist Inn, Navarro St corner Lopez Jaena St, Tel 2552517. SR/DR/ac/bath P500 to P800. Friendly hotel with pleasant rooms, all with TV. Good value. Restaurant.

Ormoc Villa Hotel, Obrero St, Tel 2555006, Fax 5614065, @. SR/ac/bath P1800, DR/ac/bath P2220, suite P3000, all including breakfast. Spacious, well furnished rooms with TV, refrigerator and balcony, the suites also with jacuzzi. An attractively laid-out hotel near the Ormoc Superdome (community hall). Restaurant, swimming pool (P100 charge for non-residents), tennis court. The best hotel in town.

Sabin Resort Hotel, Bantique, Tel 2553802, Fax 2554906, @. SR/DR/ac/bath P1400 to P1800, suite P2200 and P3200. Sophisticated hotel on the ocean with well-maintained rooms, all with TV. At the weekends this is a popular place for family celebrations, so don't expect to get any peace! Restaurant, beautiful, big swimming pool right on a not particularly inviting beach. Located about three km south of Ormoc (P5 per person by tricycle).

Places to Eat

Chito's Chow Bar & Restaurant on the harbour promenade is airy and open and a good place to sit. It offers a fine selection of inexpensive dishes. The same owner runs the attractively decorated ***Sal's Restaurant*** on Hermosa Drive at the northern edge of the city (tricycle P4 per person), which also has an extensive menu.

There's an extensive menu at ***Big Roy's Resto*** in Real St, where in addition to standard Philippine fare and wonderful salads you can eat your fill with well-priced European specialties such as pasta and garlic bread, lamb, sausages, and schnitzel. The ***Bahia Coffee Shop*** in the Hotel Don Felipe in Bonifacio St, and the ***Filipino Fastfood Restaurant*** on the ground floor of the Gaisano department store in Lopez Jaena St can also be recommended.

Entertainment

The most popular dancing spot in the city is the ***Swing Disco*** in the Don Felipe Hotel at the wharf. There is also the ***Music Vision Disco*** in the Ormoc Sugarland Pension in Rizal St.

Miscellaneous

Medical Services: The OSPA Farmers Medical Center, Can-adieng, Tel 2553194, is the best hospital in the city.

Money: Equitable PCI Bank, Rizal St corner Burgos St, and Philippine National Bank, Bonifacio St corner Cataag St, have ATMs.

Online: Ormoc Net Café, Lopez Jaena St, Webasia, Bonifacio St, and Sevilla Internet Café, Cataag St, charge P30/hr.

Population: 140,000.

Post & Telephone: Post code: 6541. Area code: 053.

Getting There & Away
5 Air Philippines
6 Cebu Pacific
26 Philippine Airlines
27 Jeepney Terminal
28 Bus Terminal
Sulpicio Lines
32 Cebu Ferries
Supercat
WG & A

Places to Stay
4 Ormoc Sugarland Pension
8 Zenaida's Chateau Tourist Inn
9 Buenas Pension Plaza
12 Pongos Hotel
16 Pongos Lodging House
19 Sabin Resort Hotel (3 km)
23 Ormoc Villa Hotel
27 Don Felipe Hotel

Places to Eat & Entertainment
1 Sal's Restaurant (500m)
2 Big Roy's Resto
4 Music Vision Disco
15 Greenwich
Jollibee
30 Chito's Chow Bar & Restaurant

Miscellaneous
3 Mercury Drug
7 Ormoc Net Café
10 Gaisano Department Store
11 Fruit Stalls
13 Philippine National Bank (PNB)
14 Sevilla Internet Café
17 Police Station
Post Office
18 St Peter & Paul Church
19 OSPA Farmers Medical Center (500m)
20 Ormoc Centrum Shopping Center
21 City Hall
Tourist Office
22 Equitable PCI Bank
24 Cityfair Supermarket
25 Webasia
26 Ormoc Superdome
31 Market

Tourist Office, City Hall, Tel 5614556. Open Mon-Fri, 8am-5pm.

Getting Around

Car: J-L Rent-a-Car, Aurelia Village, Linao, Tel 2555416, 5612681 rents cars with driver. (P1500 to Tacloban).
Tricycle: A journey within the city costs P4 per person.

Getting There & Away

By Boat: It's only a few hundred metres from the wharf to most of the hotels.
Sulpicio Lines, in the bus terminal.
Destinations: Cebu, Manila, Masbate.
Supercat Fast Ferry Corporation, Port Area, Tel 2553511.
Destination: Cebu.
Super Shuttle Ferry, Port Area, Tel. 2558367.
Destination: Cebu.

San Isidro
Bus: After the arrival of the boat from Maya on Cebu, a bus leaves San Isidro around noon for Ormoc (4½ hrs).

Tacloban
Bus: Buses for Ormoc leave Tacloban bus terminal daily from 4am until the early afternoon, in a roughly hourly rhythm (2½ hrs).
The first bus leaves Ormoc for Tacloban from the jetty at about 5.30am.

Around Ormoc

Tongonan

In Tongonan, a little north of Ormoc, a hot spring has been developed to provide geothermal energy and is well on the way to making Leyte much less depen-

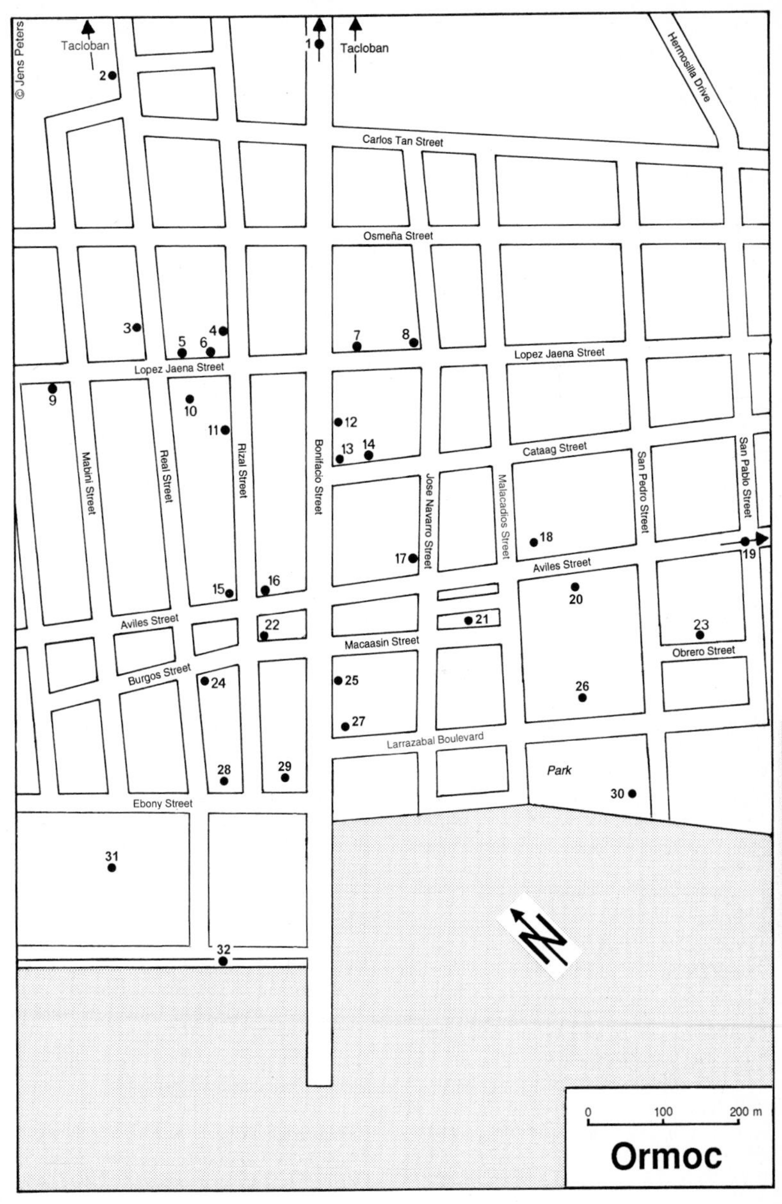

© Jens Peters
Tacloban
Tacloban
Hermosilla Drive
Carlos Tan Street
Osmeña Street
Lopez Jaena Street
Lopez Jaena Street
Cataag Street
Mabini Street
Real Street
Rizal Street
Bonifacio Street
Jose Navarro Street
Malacadios Street
San Pedro Street
San Pablo Street
Aviles Street
Aviles Street
Macaasin Street
Obrero Street
Burgos Street
Larrazabal Boulevard
Ebony Street
Park
0
100
200 m
Ormoc

dent on energy imports. If you want to visit the geothermal project, you need a permit which you have to apply for in writing two weeks beforehand to the Project Manager at the following address: PNOC EDC Geothermal Project, Tongonan, 6504 Ormoc City.

Lake Danao

North-east of Ormoc at 700m above sea level, lies Lake Danao, where the 40 km long Leyte Mountain Trail begins. The trail ends at Lake Mahagnao in Mahagnao National Park near Burauen, after snaking across the mountains of Central Leyte. Jeepneys make the journey up to Lake Danao from the terminal at the jetty in Ormoc, but not on a regular basis. On the way there through the barren hills denuded of trees, it becomes plain what causes led to the flooding of Ormoc. The three km long lake itself is, however, still surrounded by rainforest. The water is clean and refreshingly cool.
If you want to hike the Leyte Mountain Trail from the east coast of Leyte to Lake Danao, first take the bus from Tacloban south to Burauen via Tanauan and Dagami. You can then have yourself driven by motorcycle (P100) from Burauen to the entrance to Mahagnao Volcano Mountain Park, where the hike finally begins. It's about 1½ km to Lake Mahagnao.
The last bus from Burauen to Tacloban leaves about 3pm.

Baybay

Baybay is a little harbour town on the central west coast of Leyte. With mountains in the background and an old Spanish church dominating the town, it makes a most attractive picture seen at dawn from a ship just arriving in port.
About seven km north of Baybay is the modern Visayan State College of Agriculture (VISCA) which was financed by the World Bank. This is a surprisingly clean, well looked-after establishment.
If they have rooms available, travellers can spend the night in the guesthouse called the Visca Hostel.

Places to Stay

Ellean's Lodge, A Bonifacio St. SR/DR/fan P100/200. Very unpretentious place to stay near the jetty.
Visca Hostel. SR/fan/bath P200, DR/fan/bath P300, SR/DR/ac/bath P500. OK rooms. Restaurant. Seven km north of Baybay.
Palermo Hotel, A, Mabini Street, Tel. 5639718, Fax: 3352442, @. SR/DR/fan P220, SR/DR/ac P460, SR/DR/fan/bath P550, SR/DR/ac/bath P770, suite P1650. Neat hotel with quite good rooms. Restaurant.
Uptown Plaza Hotel, Magsaysay Ave, Tel 3352412. SR/DR/fan/bath P300, SR/DR/ac/bath P450 to P1500. Acceptable rooms, the more expensive ones also have a refrigerator and TV.

Miscellaneous

Post & Telephone: Post code: 6521. Area code: 053.

Getting There & Away

Bus: Several buses go from Tacloban to Baybay daily between about 8.30am until 4.30pm (2½ hrs).

Bato & Hilongos

Bato and Hilongos are small ports about halfway between Baybay and Maasin. A fairly big outrigger makes the trip between Bato and Bohol every day. Hilongos is home to a tall bell-tower from Spanish times.

Places to Stay

Casa Verde Lodging House, Rizal St, Bato. SR/DR/fan P100/200, SR/DR/ac

P400. Basic place with big, reasonable rooms. The owner is friendly. Food can be prepared on request.
Chi-Chi Lodging House, Rizal St, Bato. SR/DR/fan P100/200, SR/DR/ac P400. Straightforward accommodation.

Getting There & Away

Ormoc
Bus: From Ormoc to Bato, the first bus leaves at 6am (three hrs).

Tacloban
Bus: Several buses go from Tacloban hourly to Bato every day between about 8.30am and 4.30pm (5½ hrs).

Maasin

Maasin is on the south-west coast of Leyte and is the capital of Southern Leyte Province. If you're feeling active, hikes can be taken from here into the mountainous hinterland. The more religious traveller can also take part in the Friday morning pilgrimage by the faithful up to the Shrine of St Francis Javiar in Hanginan.
There are connections by ship from here to Bohol, Cebu and Mindanao.

Places to Stay

Ampil Pensionne, Tomas Oppus St, Tel 3812628. SR/DR/fan P300, SR/DR/ac/bath P400 and P450 (TV). Basic stay in the centre. Food can be prepared on request.
National Pensionne House, Kangleon St corner Del Pilar St, Tel 5708424. SR/DR/ac/bath P450. Clean, big rooms with up to eight beds. Entrance in Del Pilar St.
Maasin Country Lodge, Mambajao, Tel 3812102. SR/DR/fan/bath P250, SR/DR/ac/bath P450 to P950. The aircon rooms are OK, some have TV. Modest accommodation not far from the Provincial Capitol (five min by tricycle from downtown). Beautiful garden restaurant on the river.
Southern Comforts Pensionne, Demetrio St, Tel 3812552. SR/DR/ac/bath P500 to P750. Spacious, friendly rooms with TV. Good value. The best place to stay in town.

Places to Eat

The ***Avenue Restaurant*** in Tomas Oppus St serves good Philippine and Chinese food. The ***Humming Tune Bar & Restaurant*** also in Tomas Oppus St is a popular, relatively inexpensive aircon restaurant with an extensive menu (Philippine dishes and seafood) which also offers karaoke and disco.

Miscellaneous

Online: Surf the Net, Tomas Oppus St, Country House Internet Café, Demetrio St, and My @ Café, E Rafols St, charge P35/hr.
Population: 65,000.
Post & Telephone: Post code: 6600. Area code: 053.

Getting There & Away

Bus: Several buses leave Tacloban for Maasin hourly every day roughly between 8.30am and 4.30pm (four hrs). The last bus leaves Maasin for Tacloban around 1pm.

Padre Burgos

Burgos, as the locals call it, is a tidy little place about 23 km south-east of Maasin. It's not on the regular tourist circuit yet, but that could change soon. The visitor can expect first-class diving areas and close-up views of peaceful whale sharks, plus caves and waterfalls in the mountainous interior as well as a few average quality beaches.

Places to Stay

Southern Leyte Divers, San Roque, Macrohon, Tel. 5724011, @. SR/DR/fan

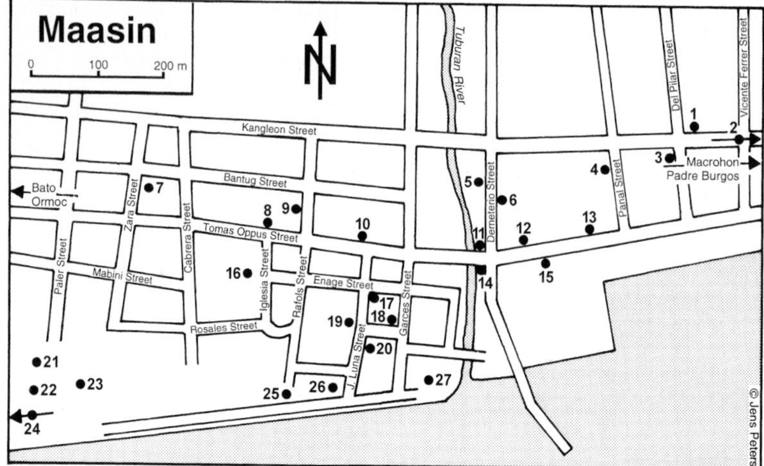

P350/400, cottage/fan/bath P700. Basic, but clean rooms and cottages. Friendly guesthouse belonging to the German-Philippine couple Günter and Alona Mosch (good source of information). They have a garden restaurant with excellent Philippine and German cooking. Diving (also courses), hire of snorkelling equipment and boat trips, including one to Limasawa Island. Located about two km north of Padre Burgos.

Peter's Dive Resort, Lungsodaan, Tel 5730015, Cellphone 0920-7984658, @. SR/DR/fan P300/600, cottage/fan/bath P650 and P750. Pleasant, good, cottages. Friendly little place with a view of Sogod Bay. Restaurant, diving.

Miscellaneous

Diving: A surprisingly intact underwater world (scarcely any dynamite damage) with magnificent coral reefs and great drop-offs is attracting more and more divers to South Leyte. From February to April there is also a chance of a close-up view of whale sharks. A boat trip for diving costs P1200, a diving course P14,000 (eg at Southern Leyte Divers).

Population: 8000.

Post & Telephone: Post code: 6001. Area Code: 053.

Getting There & Away

Bus: Buses with the destinations of Sogod and Liloan leave Maasin for Burgos about every half hour (30 min). Several multicabs also leave from Tomas Oppus St at the corner of Demetrio St (near the pier).

Limasawa Island

About 10 km south of Padre Burgos and 20 km west of Panaon Island you will find the somewhat remote island of Limasawa. Ferdinand Magellan landed here at the end of March 1521 after setting foot for the first time on the Philippines two weeks earlier on the island of Homonhon, to the east of Leyte. A huge cross dominates Limasawa in memory of this event. Every year on 31 March the islanders also commemorate

Getting There & Away
1 Cebu Pacific Ticket Office
4 Philtranco Bus Terminal
14 Multicabs to Macrohon & Padre Burgos
21 Multicab Terminal
22 Jeepney Terminal
23 Bus Terminal
24 Boats to Ubay/Bohol

Places to Stay
2 Maasin Country Lodge (1.3 km) Verano Pension House (700m)
3 National Pensionne House
5 Southern Comforts Pensionne
12 Ampil Pensionne
18 ESFA Lodge

Places to Eat
6 Country House I Café
10 Avenue Restaurant
13 Orange Brutus Fast Food
15 Humming Tune Bar & Restaurant

Miscellaneous
7 Church
8 Surf the Net Internet Café
9 My @ Café
11 Candy's Supermarket
16 Maasin Cathedral
17 Mercury Drug
19 Police Station
20 Philippine National Bank (PNB)
25 Town Hall
26 Post Office
27 Market

the event by getting dressed up and celebrating mass on the beach at Triana in a riot of colour.
The inhabitants of Butuan on the north coast of Mindanao are not at all pleased at the goings-on north of them. The way they see it, the conquering hero did not land at Limasawa, but right round the corner at Masao, on the Agusan river estuary. They simply reject the claim made by later historians that Pigafetta (Magellan's chronicler) was referring to a place on Limasawa when he mentioned the landing at 'Mazauna'.

Places to Stay
In honour of the 475th anniversary of Magellan's landing, a small guesthouse was erected on Limasawa. Visitors may stay there if they don't want to use private accommodation.

Getting There & Away
Boat: One or two outriggers leave Padre Burgos every day for Limasawa. They drop anchor at Triana, the main port on the island, and Magallanes (45 min).

Liloan

Liloan is at the northern tip of Panaon Island in the south of Leyte. The two islands are connected by a 300m long bridge. The waters there are good for diving and snorkelling. Whale sharks can be seen close up in the nearby Tagbak Marine Park between February and April. A ferry service operates between Liloan and Lipata, 10 km northwest of Surigao in north-east Mindanao.

Places to Stay
Liloan Hillside Lodge. SR/DR/fan P100/200. Don't expect luxury here, and it can get loud. Located in the port area behind the ferry terminal.

Places to Eat
The ***Annie & Boys Carenderia*** on Quezon St offers tasty, cheap food.

Getting There & Away

Maasin
Bus: Several buses travel from Maasin to Liloan between 4 and 7.30am (3½ hrs).

Tacloban
Bus: There are several buses daily from Tacloban to Liloan (five hrs). They may terminate in Sogod, however, or carry on from there to Maasin. In that case, you can finish the journey by jeepney from Sogod to Liloan.

Alternative: Take a bus from Tacloban heading for Hinunangan on the southeast coast of Leyte and get off at the turn-off for Liloan. Carry on by motorbike (there will be several waiting for passengers) to Liloan harbour (P10) or to Liloan itself 1½ km further on.

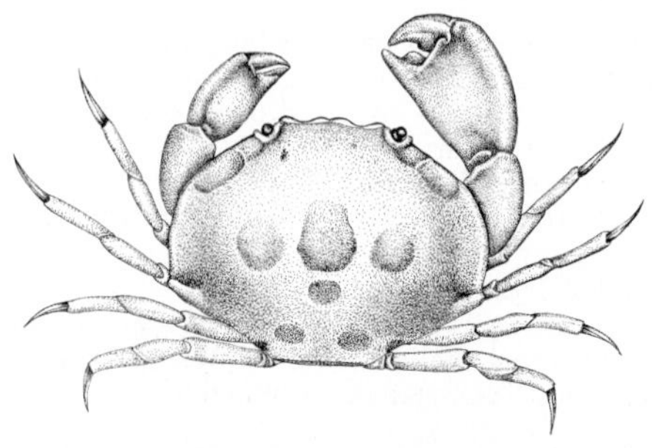

Negros

Sandwiched in between Cebu and Panay in the south-west of the Visayas, Negros consists of the provinces of Negros Occidental and Negros Oriental, which are separated by mountain chains in the centre of the island. The south takes its character from the extended Tablas plateau and the wide plains west of an imaginary line from Ilog to Cadiz. The Negritos are the aboriginal people of Negros, hence the name of the island. Some tribes of this cultural minority still live in the mountain regions. The main dialect in Negros Occidental is Ilongo (Hiligaynon), whereas Cebuano is spoken in Negros Oriental.

Negros is the sugar island of the Philippines. Around 450,000 hectares, or more than half of the total land area, is used for the production of sugar. About 60% of the total sugar production of the country comes from here. There are big sugarcane plantations and refineries in Victorias and Binalbagan. Sugar exportation began in the middle of the 19th century, when the production from the first plantations was shipped to Japan, China, Australia, the UK, Canada and the USA. From then on it brought great wealth and political power to the few sugar barons living on their haciendas. Only during the years of the sugar boom did the seasonally employed plantation workers (known as *sacada*) earn enough to support their families. This irresponsible system of exploitation and social indifference existed until 1985, when the world market price of sugar fell so drastically that it wasn't even worth cutting the cane. Negros, with its single product economy, was economically at rock bottom. About a quarter of a million sacada found themselves out of work. Because of the absence of any government relief programme and the unwillingness of most *hacienderos* to make some land available for grain planting by their needy workers, many desperate Negrenses took to the mountains in 1986 and '87 to join the anti-government NPA in its underground fighting.

If government figures are to be believed, conditions on Negros have improved with rising sugar prices in the last few years. An important part in this improvement is due to the by now widespread prawn cultivation (Black Tiger Prawn, *Penaeus monodon*) and the manufacture of rattan furniture. Both economic activities are strongly export oriented.

'Sugarland', of course, also aims to develop tourism, but leisure facilities like the Mambukal Mountain Resort in the central part of the island for instance, are still too rarely visited to talk about a boom yet. Kanlaon Volcano may, it is hoped, become an attraction similar to the famous Mayon Volcano in South Luzon. The east and south-east coasts of Negros offer Spanish-style charm - perhaps a reason why foreign tourists often spend a few days in the pleasant little town of Dumaguete. Pretty good beaches can be found around Sipalay in the south-west of the

island, where a good start has been made to providing amenities for tourists. The coast there is quite stunning and offers good diving opportunities, while the mountainous inland areas with their numerous waterfalls are positively riddled with caves.
Among the main attractions of Negros are the old steam locomotives, some of which were still being used until recently to bring home the sugar cane, side by side with modern diesel locomotives. During the milling season between October and April, it used to be possible to hitch a ride on one of these working museum pieces; today, however, there are only a few steam locomotives left, but you can see them near the sugar mills. The best of these oldtimers belong to the Hawaiian-Philippine Sugar Co in Silay; Vicmico in Victorias; Central Azucarera de la Carlota in La Carlota; and the Ma-ao Sugar Central in Bago. Also worth seeing are the ones that belong to Biscom in Binalbagan; Sagay Sugar Central and Lopez Sugar Central in Toboso; and San Carlos Milling Co in San Carlos. Colin Carraf describes the engines and all their technical details in his book *Iron Dinosaurs*.

Getting There & Away

You can get to Negros from Cebu, Guimaras, Luzon, Mindanao, Panay and Siquijor (see the Getting Away from Luzon section of the Manila chapter and the Getting There & Away sections of the individual island chapters).

To Bohol

Boat

From Dumaguete to Tagbilaran
Daily with the fast ferries *Oceanjet* (1x) and *Supercat* (2x; P430), taking 1½ hrs. Wednesday with WG & A (P320; three hrs).

To Cebu

Air

From Bacolod to Cebu City
Air Philippines, Cebu Pacific and Philippine Airlines fly daily (P1880).

Bus/Boat

From Bacolod to Cebu City
Several Ceres Liner buses leave daily from the Ceres Liner North Terminal in Bacolod for the ferry from Escalante (Port Danao) to Tabuelan and on to Cebu City. The trip, including the ferry, takes eight hrs.
See also below: *From Escalante to Tabuelan.*

From Dumaguete to Cebu City
See below: From *Sibulan and Tampi to Oslob* and *From Tampi to Bato.*

Boat

From Cadiz to Bantayan
From Cadiz on the north coast of Negros to Bantayan town on Bantayan Island in northern Cebu, daily with Island Shipping (depending on tides; usually at 1pm). The trip takes two hrs.
The river port in Cadiz is several km long, so it's best to take a tricycle from the bus terminal to the wharf.

From Dumaguete to Cebu City
Daily with the fast ferries *Oceanjet* (1x) and *Supercat* (2x; P520), taking 3½ hrs); via Tagbilaran/Bohol.
Daily with Cokaliong Shipping Lines and George & Peter Lines (P265; six hrs).
Saturday with Aleson Shipping Lines (P265; six hrs).

From Escalante to Tabuelan
Daily at 6am, 2 and 8pm with an Aznar Shipping Corporation car ferry (two hrs).

From Guihulngan to Tangil
Daily at 7, 9 and 10.30am and 1pm with a small ferry (1½ hrs).

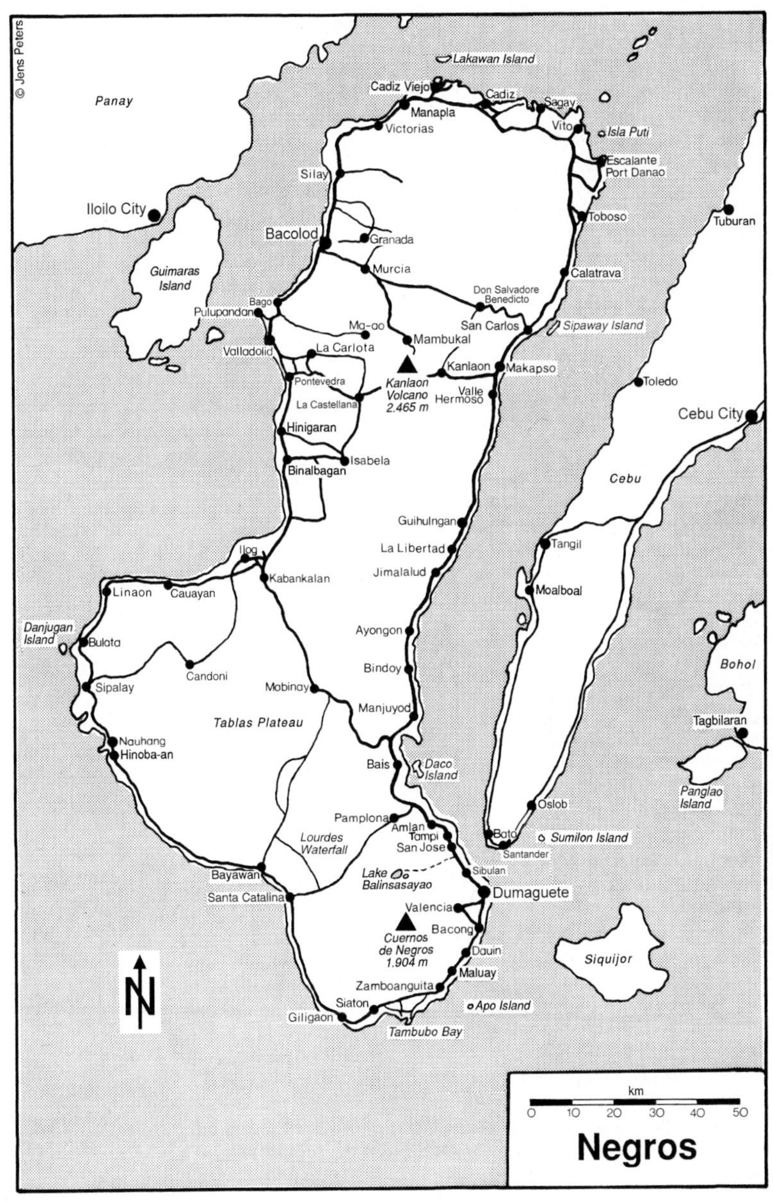
© Jens Peters
Panay
Lakawan Island
Cadiz Viejo
Manapla
Cadiz
Sagay
Vito
Isla Puti
Victorias
Escalante
Port Danao
Silay
Iloilo City
Toboso
Tuburan
Bacolod
Granada
Guimaras Island
Murcia
Calatrava
Don Salvadore Benedicto
Bago
Pulupandan
San Carlos
Sipaway Island
Ma-ao
Mambukal
Valladolid
La Carlota
Kanlaon
Makapso
Pontevedra
Kanlaon Volcano 2.465 m
Valle Hermoso
Toledo
La Castellana
Cebu City
Hinigaran
Isabela
Binalbagan
Cebu
Guihulngan
Tangil
La Libertad
Ilog
Jimalalud
Kabankalan
Linaon
Cauayan
Moalboal
Danjugan Island
Bulata
Ayongon
Bohol
Candoni
Bindoy
Sipalay
Mabinay
Manjuyod
Tablas Plateau
Tagbilaran
Nauhang
Hinoba-an
Bais
Daco Island
Panglao Island
Oslob
Pamplona
Amlan
Tampi
Lourdes Waterfall
San Jose
Bato
Sumilon Island
Santander
Lake Balinsasayao
Sibulan
Bayawan
Dumaguete
Santa Catalina
Valencia
Bacong
Cuernos de Negros 1.904 m
Dauin
Siquijor
Maluay
Zamboanguita
Siaton
Apo Island
Giligaon
Tambubo Bay
km
0 10 20 30 40 50
Negros
Visayas - Negros

From Bacolod to Cebu City

The following route is recommended for self-drive travellers: First head from Bacolod to Murcia and then via the Translink Highway north from the Kanlaon volcano via Don Salvador Benedicto to San Carlos. Carry on with a car ferry to Toledo/Cebu. From there head north along the coast to Balamban and then take the new Trans Central Highway to Cebu City. Including the ferry this trip takes about five hours.
See also *Getting There & Away - To Negros* in the Cebu chapter.

From San Carlos to Toledo
Daily from 5.30am to 1pm, roughly every hour with an Aznar Shipping Corporation fast ferry (P120; one hr), and at 12.30 and 4.30pm with a regular Aznar Shipping Corporation ship (P110; 1½ hrs).
Daily at 5 and 10am and 3.30pm with a Lite Shipping Corporation car ferry (P100; two hrs).

From Sibulan to Liloan
Several times daily with a big outrigger. The last departure is at about 3pm (20 min).

From Sibulan and Tampi to Oslob
Several times daily with a car ferry (one hr).

From Tampi to Bato
Frequent service (13x daily) with Rovi Navigation (P40; 30 min). In addition, eight car ferries run every day.
Jeepneys leave from San Jose St corner Real St in Dumaguete, to the wharf (P10).
After the arrival of ferries, Ceres Liner buses leave Bato for Cebu City (three hrs).

To Guimaras

Bus/Boat

From Bacolod to Calabagnan
As an alternative to the popular connection by boat from Bacolod via Iloilo City on Panay, you can go to Guimaras Island by boat from Valladolid, about 30 km south of Bacolod. Coming by bus or jeepney from Bacolod, you have to get off at the first bridge. A boat goes daily from Valladolid to Cabalagnan on Guimaras at about 11am, stopping at several small islands on the way, including Nagarao Island (P60; two hrs).

From Pulupandan to Suclaran
Twice a day a boat sails from Pulupandan, a little north of Valladolid, to Suclaran on Guimaras (P40; one hr).

To Luzon

Air

From Bacolod to Manila
Air Philippines, Cebu Pacific and Philippine Airlines fly daily (P2780).

From Dumaguete to Manila
Air Philippines and Cebu Pacific fly daily (P2900).

Boat

From Bacolod to Manila
Wednesday, Thursday, Friday and Saturday with Negros Navigation (P1460; 19 hrs).
Wednesday and Sunday with WG & A (P1460; 21 hrs).

From Dumaguete to Manila
Tuesday with Negros Navigation (P1390; 38 hrs); via Tagbilaran/Bohol.
Wednesday and Saturday with WG & A (P1390; 30 hrs); Wednesday via Tagbilaran/Bohol.

To Mindanao

Air

From Bacolod to Davao
Air Philippines flies daily; via Cebu City (P3645).

From Bacolod to General Santos
Air Philippines flies daily; via Cebu City (P3645).

Boat

From Bacolod to Cagayan de Oro
Tuesday with Negros Navigation (P1330; 13 hrs).

From Bacolod to Iligan
Monday with WG & A (P1360; 13 hrs).

From Bacolod to Ozamis
Monday with WG & A (P1390; 17 hrs); via Iligan.

From Dumaguete to Cagayan de Oro
Friday with WG & A (P600; seven hrs).

From Dumaguete to Dapitan/Dipolog
Daily with the fast ferry *Supercat* (P425; 1½ hrs).
Daily with George & Peter Lines (four hrs). On Tuesday the ship carries on from Dapitan to Zamboanga.
Daily except on Monday with Cokaliong Shipping Lines (four hrs).

From Dumaguete to Zamboanga
Tuesday and Friday with George & Peter Lines (14 hrs); Tuesday via Dapitan/Dipolog.
Sunday with Aleson Shipping Lines (P650; 17 hrs); via Dapitan/Dipolog. The ship carries on from Zamboanga to Sandakan (Sabah/Malaysia).

To Panay

Boat

From Bacolod to Iloilo City
Daily with the fast ferries *Bullet Xpress* (8x), *Royal Express* (8x) and *Supercat* (4x; P290) from Bredco Port (Reclamation Port), taking one hr.
Daily except on Sunday at 4am and 12 noon with a Millennium Shipping Corporation car ferry (3½ hrs).

To Siquijor

Boat

From Dumaguete to Larena
Daily with the fast ferry *Supercat* (P190; 45 min).

From Dumaguete to Siquijor
Four times daily with the fast ferry *Delta* (P100; one hr).

North Negros

Bacolod

Bacolod is both the capital of Negros Occidental province and the sugar capital of the Philippines. The name Bacolod is derived from the word *buklod*, or hill, which refers to a rise on which the town's first church stood.
Next to the old San Sebastian Cathedral is the City Plaza, with benches under shady trees, where cultural events are often held on Sunday afternoons and special occasions.
In South Capitol Road only a few steps away from the Negros Museum in the NFEFI Biodiversity Conservation Center, a group of active nature conservationists dedicate themselves to the survival of endangered species which are at home in Negros.
You can take quite a few interesting day trips from Bacolod, eg to Silay and Victorias. Lovers of old locomotives especially will not be disappointed.

Museum

The former Provincial Capitol in Lacson St, known as the *capitolio* and built in the neo-classicist style in the 1930s, has housed the informative Negros Museum since 1996. The main exhibits are objects and machinery closely connected with the development of the sugar industry in Negros Occidental, including models of a steam locomotive and a transport boat, as well as original furniture from a hacienda. Worth seeing are the large paintings with scenes taken from village life on Negros before the arrival of the Spaniards. Open Tue-Sat, 10am-6pm. Guided tours available at 10 and 11am, 3.30 and 5.30pm; admission P40.

Shopping

The ANP Showroom, in Lacson St at the corner of 9th St, has several floors where local Negros craftspeople have the opportunity to present their wares. Here you will find a whole range of products, from arts and crafts, T-shirts and souvenirs to rattan furniture.

About three km north of the centre, also in Lacson St, the huge shopping centre Robinsons Place offers well over 100 shops, six cinemas and fully automatic bowling lanes. You can get there by jeepney (destination 'Bata') from the centre of town.

There are four branches of Lopue's department store, in the centre in Araneta St and San Sebastian St.

The Central Market near the City Plaza is bigger than both Burgos Market and Libertad Market. On sale amongst other things are fruit and arts and crafts.

NB: The Goldenfield Commercial Complex at the southern edge of town is not much use for shopping as it specialises in food, drink and entertainment.

Places to Stay - bottom end

Pension Bacolod, 11th St, Tel 4347065, Fax 4346065. SR/fan P125, DR/fan P145, SR/fan/bath P145, DR/fan/bath P200, SR/ac/bath P280, DR/ac/bath P350. Peaceful location, north of the town centre, most of the rooms are immaculate and really good value for the money. The best in this category, no wonder it's often fully booked. Inexpensive restaurant.

Star Plus Pension, Lacson St corner Rosario St, Tel 4332949. SR/DR/fan P250, SR/DR/fan/bath P345, SR/DR/ac/bath P395 and P445 (with TV). Basic, but reasonable accommodation with small rooms.

K'mas Pension House, Lacson St, Tel 4354293, Fax 7098527. SR/DR/fan/bath P250, SR/DR/ac/bath P500 to P850. Immaculate rooms, the aircon ones have TV. Restaurant, car hire. Located in the north of the city near Robinsons Place.

Places to Stay - middle

Bascon Hotel, Gonzaga St, Tel 4354071-73, Fax 4331393, @. SR/fan/bath P300, DR/fan/bath P400, SR/ac/bath P520, DR/ac/bath P600 to P950. Clean, comfortable rooms well worth the money (the more expensive ones have TV, some also have a refrigerator). Centrally located. Restaurant.

Bacolod Pension Plaza, Cuadra St, Tel 4334547, Fax 4332203. SR/DR/ac/bath P490, P690 and P850, depending on size and furnishings. Comfortable, quiet rooms, the more expensive ones have a TV, some also have a refrigerator. Coffee shop. Central location.

King's Hotel, San Sebastian St corner Gatuslao St, Tel 4344500, Fax 4330572, @. SR/DR/ac/bath P600 to P1200. A good hotel with acceptable quality of rooms, all with TV, the better and bigger ones also have a refrigerator. Coffee Shop.

Sea Breeze Hotel, San Juan St, Tel 4333907, Fax 4337994. SR/DR/ac/bath P670 to P1100 (with TV). Reasonable rooms; don't be put off by the lobby and the restaurant.

Business Inn, Lacson St, Tel 4338877, Fax 4342114, @. SR/DR/ac/bath P790 to P1790. Clean rooms, although some

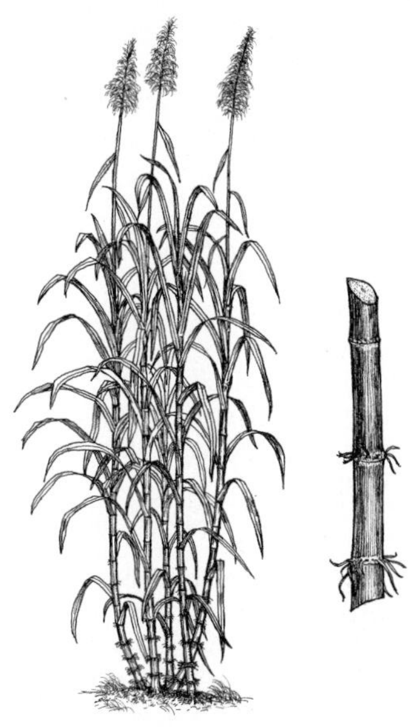

Sugar Cane *(Saccharum officinarum)*
Sugar cane *(tubo)* belongs to the genus of sweet grasses. Juice is pressed out of the metres long stalks and then boiled. The brown sugar which then crystallises out can be processed later in a refinery.

a little small, all with TV; if you pay more, you also get a refrigerator. Often fully booked. Good restaurant.
Alhambra Hotel, Galo St corner Locsin St, Tel 4334021, Fax 4334023, @. SR/DR/ac/bath P800 and P1300, suite P1260. Pleasant rooms in an attractive hotel with a friendly atmosphere. Cosy restaurant.
Bacolod Executive Inn, San Sebastian St, Tel 4337401, Fax 4337442, @. SR/ac/bath P830 to P1100, DR/ac/bath P940 to P1370. Clean, attractively furnished rooms with TV, and a refrigerator in the pricier ones. Friendly service. Popular hotel offering good value for money. Restaurant.
Kundutel, Lacson St, Tel 4337211, Fax 4337202, @. SR/DR/ac/bath P850 and P950, suite P1500 to P2200. Comfortable rooms with TV, the more expensive ones also have a refrigerator. Near the Goldenfield Commercial Complex. Restaurant.
Palmas Del Mar Village & Beach Club, JR Torres Ave, Tangub, Tel 4353527, Fax 4357972, @. SR/DR/ac/bath P1000. Excellent rooms with TV. Attractively built, spread-out resort by the sea west of the airport. Good restaurant. Several swimming pools of various sizes (one is 50m long). Billiards. Fitness room. Admission for day guests: P25; swimming pool P40 extra. Get there from the centre (City Hall) with the 'Airport Subdivision' jeepney.
Sugarland Hotel, Araneta St, Singcang, Tel 4352690-99, Fax 4332645, @. SR/DR/ac/bath P1300 and P1500, suite P1725 and P2000. Comfortable hotel about three km south of the centre. Handy for the airport and the Goldenfield Commercial Complex. Restaurant.

Places to Stay - top end

Casino Filipino Hotel, Goldenfield Commercial Complex, Tel 4348901-10, Fax 4344433, @. SR/ac/bath P1750, DR/ac/bath P2000, suites P3850 to P6000. With TV and refrigerator. Very comfortable, spacious rooms in a well-run hotel about one km from the airport. Restaurant, casino, swimming pool.
Bacolod Convention Plaza Hotel, Magsaysay Ave corner Lacson St, Tel 4344551, Fax 4333757, @. SR/ac/bath P1980 and P2500, DR/ac/bath P2400 and P3000, suites P3900 and P4900; including breakfast. A large hotel at the southern edge of town with inviting rooms with refrigerator and TV. Restaurant, swimming pool, tennis courts. Free airport service.
L'Fisher Hotel, Lacson St corner 14th St, Tel 4333731-39, Fax 4330951, @. SR/ac/bath P2300 and P2980, DR/ac/bath P2900 and P3475, suites P5100 to

Getting There & Away

1 Banago Port (5 km)
7 Ceres Liner North Terminal
11 Negros Navigation
14 Northern Bus Terminal
17 Bredco Port (Reclamation Port; 500m)
25 Cebu Pacific
27 Negros Navigation
33 Air Philippines
41 Ceres Liner South Terminal
Southern Bus Terminal
52 Jeepneys to Airport
55 Jeepneys to Mambucal
57 Airport (2.5 km)

Places to Stay

2 K'mas Pension House (1.2 km)
4 L'Fisher Hotel
6 Pension Bacolod
21 Alhambra Hotel
26 Business Inn
30 Bacolod Pension Plaza
32 Bascon Hotel
33 Sea Breeze Hotel
43 Check Inn
49 King's Hotel
51 Bacolod Executive Inn
53 Star Plus Pension
57 Casino Filipino Hotel (2 km)
Palmas Del Mar Village & Beach Club (3 km)
Sugarland Hotel (1.5 km)
58 Bacolod Convention Plaza Hotel (750m)
Kundutel (1.5 km)

Places to Eat

13 McDonald's
18 El Camino II
19 Imbiss Snack Restaurant (600m)
23 Manokan Country
31 McDonald's
33 Dodong's Fast Break
35 Chowking
38 McDonald's
45 Greenwich
Jollibee
47 Mira's Café

Miscellaneous

2 Robinsons Place (1 km)
3 Doctor's Hospital (300m)
Riverside Hospital (750m)
5 Mayfair Plaza
Le Cafnet Internet Café
8 ANP Showroom
9 Provincial Tourist Office
10 Philippine National Bank (PNB)
12 Negros Museum
15 NFEFI Biodiversity Conservation Center
16 Post Office
20 Burgos Market
22 Equitable PCI Bank
24 San Sebastian Cathedral
28 City Tourist Office
29 City Plaza
34 Equitable PCI Bank
36 Lopue's Department Store
37 Philippine National Bank (PNB)
39 Central Market
40 Foodman Bakery
42 Immigration Office
44 City Hall
45 Mercury Drug
46 Gaisano Department Store
Metrobank
48 Bank of the Philippine Islands
50 Lopue's Department Store
54 Equitable PCI Bank
56 Libertad Market
57 Goldenfield Commercial Complex (2 km)

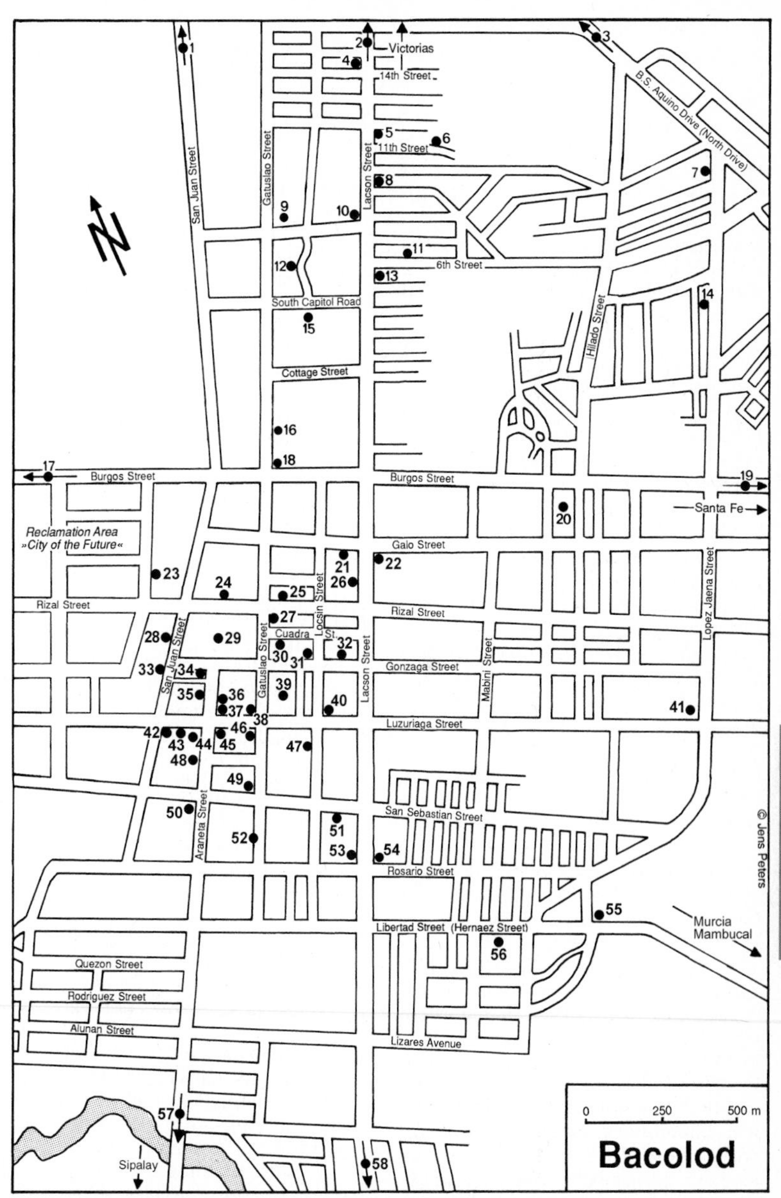
Victorias
14th Street
B.S. Aquino Drive (North Drive)
11th Street
San Juan Street
Gatuslao Street
Lacson Street
6th Street
South Capitol Road
Hilado Street
Cottage Street
Burgos Street
Santa Fe
Reclamation Area
»City of the Future«
Galo Street
Rizal Street
Locsin Street
Cuadra St.
Lopez Jaena Street
Gonzaga Street
Mabini Street
Luzuriaga Street
San Sebastian Street
Araneta Street
Rosario Street
Murcia
Mambucal
Libertad Street (Hernaez Street)
Quezon Street
Rodriguez Street
Alunan Street
Lizares Avenue
Sipalay
0
250
500 m
Bacolod
© Jens Peters

P8200, with TV. Pleasantly decorated, cosy rooms. An elegant, tastefully decorated hotel in the northern part of town. This must be the best accommodation in the city. Restaurant, car hire.

Places to Eat

The friendly, squeaky clean ***Dodong's Fast Break*** in the Bascon Hotel, Gonzaga St, will serve you inexpensive Philippine food. There's another branch in ***Robinsons Place***, where you can find several other good restaurants.

There's no shortage of customers in ***El Camino II***, Burgos St, at the corner of Gatuslao St, where the friendly servers will keep you happy with grilled chicken to the sound of live music in the background. The restaurants at the ***Manokan Country*** in the Reclamation Area are also busy every evening until late at night. This is an ideal place to try *inasal*, the speciality of Bacolod (grilled chicken, marinated with coconut vinegar, soy sauce, ginger, garlic and other spices).

The ***Imbiss Snack Restaurant*** in Burgos St Extension is a very popular German restaurant on the eastern edge of town, a special favourite with the locals.

You can breakfast in style at the ***Café Marinero*** on the ground floor of the L'Fisher Hotel on Lacson St, at the corner of 14th St. ***Mira's Café*** on Locsin St will brew you a cup of so-called native coffee. If you want cakes with your coffee, you can get them at the Foodman Bakery on the corner.

The fastfood franchises ***Greenwich***, ***Jollibee*** and ***McDonald's*** can be found at the corner of Gatuslao St and Luzuriaga St.

Within the Goldenfield Commercial Complex there is a whole raft of different restaurants, including the very popular Philippine restaurant ***Aboy's Kamalig***, the ***Old West Steakhouse***, with its cosy atmosphere, ***Kristin's Steak-***

Getting There & Away
35 Airport (500m)

Places to Stay
2 Sugarland Hotel
24 Casino Filipino Hotel
25 Kundutel

Places to Eat & Entertainment
3 Simple A Restaurant
4 Vajaar Café
5 Old West Steakhouse
Tanoshi Karaoke
6 15 Balls
7 Cat Eyes
Disco 2000
Malagueña Restaurant
8 Alexis KTV
Mardils Place
9 Young at Heart
10 Knights Hall
11 Carlo Restorante Italiano
12 Aboy's Kamalig Restaurant
13 Wild Cats Nightclub
14 Veranda (small restaurants)
15 Carlo Restorante Italiano
16 Shakey's Pizza
18 Nice Café
19 Seafood Market Restaurant
21 Korean Restaurant & Billiard
20 MO2
22 Pizza-o
23 Chicken Alley
Red Castle Club
24 Casino Filipino
Ground Zero Disco
26 Plexus MTV Bar
28 Big Ken Karaoke
29 Camarada Karaoke
30 Moky's Café
31 Hill Haven
32 Rain Gate Bar
33 Ka Na Karaoke

Miscellaneous
1 Bacolod City Plaza (3 km)
15 Equitable PCI Bank
17 Car Park
27 Massage Center
34 Super Bowling Lanes

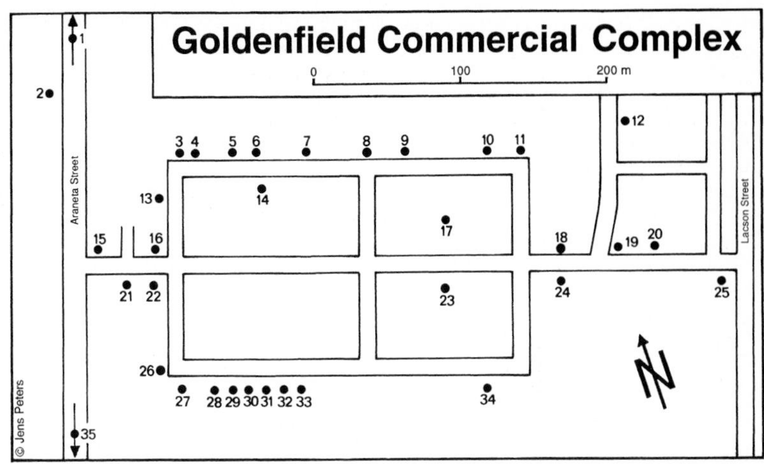

house & Restaurant (in the hotel Kundutel), ***Shakey's***, ***Carlo Restorante Italiano*** and the wonderfully clean, but somewhat expensive ***Seafood Market Restaurant***. Here you will also find ***MO2***, a restobar with Mexican specialities like tostadas, nachos and enchiladas, and 20 ceiling-mounted, oversized fans which rhythmically sway to keep you cool.

The ***Casa Noble Restaurant*** in the Palmas Del Mar Village & Beach Club by the sea offers excellent, surprisingly inexpensive Philippine and international food in attractive surroundings.

Entertainment

Bacolod's night scene can mostly be found just outside the city in the Goldenfield Commercial Complex (although there's nothing doing during the day there). Within the complex, popular entertainment venues are the ***Super Bowling Lanes***, the ***Casino Filipino*** (admission P150), Disco ***MO2*** (relaxed, party mood), ***Disco 2000***, and the small, open restaurants of the ***Veranda***, which is also a good place to watch the (night) world go by.

One popular disco in town itself is ***Upperground*** at the top of the building opposite L'Fisher Hotel, Lacson St, not least because of the humane prices.

Miscellaneous

Festivals: Masskara Festival on the third weekend in October. On the Saturday they have a military parade, and on the Sunday afternoon there is street dancing with all sorts of costumes being worn. Panaad sa Negros in the third week in April is the 'Festival of Festivals' during which over 30 towns from all over Negros Occidental Province exhibit their cultural and commercial achievements in the Panaad Park at the south-eastern edge of town.

Immigration Office, San Juan St corner Luzuriaga St, Tel 7089501. Open Mon-Fri, 8am-noon, 1-5pm.

Medical Services: Riverside Hospital, Tel 4337331, is the best hospital in Bacolod, followed by Bacolod Doctor's Hospital, Tel 4332741. Both are on BS Aquino Dr (North Dr).

Money: The Philippine National Bank on Lacson St and the branches of the Equitable PCI Bank on Araneta St cor-

ner Gonzaga St, Lacson St corner Rosario St, and Lacson St corner Galo St, have ATMs.
A few money changers in Araneta St offer good rates.
Online: Le Cafnet Internet Café, Mayfair Plaza, Lacson St corner 12th St; Cyber Heads Café, L&D Centre, Lacson St corner 7th St; and at Business Place, Cuadra St (opposite Bacolod Pension Plaza).
Population: 460,000.
Post & Telephone: Post Office, Gatuslao St.
Post code: 6100. Area code: 034.
Tourist Office: The City Tourist Office, San Juan St (on City Plaza), Tel & Fax 4346751, Fax: 7077748, mainly supplies information on Bacolod and connecting travel from there. Open Mon-Fri, 8am-6pm.
The Provincial Tourist Office, South Capitol Rd, Tel 4332515, is responsible for the province of Negros Occidental. Open Mon-Fri, 8am-noon, 1-5pm.

Getting Around

Car: Crismart Rent A Car, Pedrosa Subdivision, Tel 7077690, Cellphone 0919-3345373. Self-drive hire for P1500 to P2500 per day, depending on car model and length of hire (it's possible to negotiate).
Parmon Transportation & Tours, 6th St, Tel 4347230.
Rent A Car, Lapu-Lapu St, Gonzaga Subdivision, Tel 4347230.

Getting There & Away

By Air: Bacolod's airport is about four km south of the city. Cebu Pacific have their own terminal about 200m further on. On leaving the terminal, turn left to go towards the city. You can stop a passing jeepney, as they all go to the Central Market. Jeepneys from the city passing the airport are marked 'Tangub' and leave from Gatuslao St. A taxi from the airport to the city centre should cost no more than P50, but it is best to agree on a price with the driver beforehand as they will ask for P150.
Air Philippines, Bacolod Airport, Tel 4339211-12.
- Sea Breeze Hotel, San Juan St, Tel 4339204.
Destinations: Cebu City, Davao (via Cebu City), General Santos (via Cebu City), Manila.
Cebu Pacific, Bacolod Airport, Tel 4342052-53.
- Summit World, Victorina Arcade, Rizal St, Tel 4342020-23.
Destinations: Cebu City, Manila.
Philippine Airlines, Bacolod Airport, Tel 4341595-96.
Destinations: Cebu City, Manila.

By Bus: Buses from Dumaguete (following the east and north coast routes) and San Carlos arrive at the Northern Bus Terminal or at the Ceres Liner North Terminal about 200m farther on. Jeepneys marked 'Libertad' leave these two bus terminals for the city centre and both the Southern Busterminal and the Ceres Liner South Terminal. In the other direction the destination is marked 'Shopping'. A taxi from the bus terminal to the city centre should cost no more than P30.
Buses from South Negros and Dumaguete via Mabinay (the west coast route) arrive at the Southern Bus Terminal in Lopez Jaena St, which is also the location of the Ceres Liner South Terminal.

By Boat: Bacolod has two wharfs: Banago Port and Bredco Port (Reclamation Port).
Banago Port is about seven km north of the city centre. It's mostly ships belonging to Negros Navigation shipping. A jeepney will cost you P10, and a taxi P50 to P70, but determine the price first. After the arrival of a ferry from

Iloilo City the following Negros Navigation aircon buses go into town: 'Plaza' to the city centre, 'Libertad' to the Southern Bus Terminal, and 'Shopping' to the Northern Bus Terminal and Ceres Liner North Terminal. Shuttle buses belonging to Tours & Transport Corporation go directly to the hotel requested. All charge P25.
The new Bredco Port (Reclamation Port) is located one km west of the city centre in Burgos St, Reclamation Area. Ships belonging to Aleson Shipping Lines, Millennium Shipping Corporation and WG & A call in there in addition to the fast ferries *Bullet Xpress*, *Royal Express* and *Supercat* to and from Iloilo City. A taxi there should not cost more than P30 to P40.
Aleson Shipping Lines, Bredco, Reclamation Area, Tel. 4348404.
Destination: Iloilo City.
Bullet Xpress, Bredco, Reclamation Area.
Destination: Iloilo City.
Millennium Shipping Corporation, Bredco, Reclamation Area, Tel. 4339360.
Destination: Iloilo City.
Negros Navigation, Banago Port, Tel 4410652.
- Doll Building, 6th St, Tel 4344291-98, 4345334.
- Gatuslao St corner Rizal St, Tel 4351417.
Destinations: Manila, Mindanao, Panay.
Royal Express, Bredco, Reclamation Area.
Destination: Iloilo City.
Supercat Fast Ferry Corporation, Bredco, Reclamation Area, Tel 4342350-53.
Destination: Iloilo City.
WG & A, Bredco, Reclamation Area, Tel 4330558, 4354965.
Destinations: Manila, Mindanao.

Dumaguete
Bus: Ceres Liner express buses leave Dumaguete for Bacolod via San Carlos in the early morning and forenoon; seat reservations are possible. The trip takes nine hrs.
Several Ceres Liner buses travel from Dumaguete via Mabinay and then along the west coast to Bacolod (5½ hrs).

Hinoba-an
Bus: Several Ceres Liner buses travel from Hinoba-an to Bacolod daily, roughly one an hour, taking five hrs.

San Carlos
Bus: Several Ceres Liner buses go from San Carlos to Bacolod daily. The last one will probably leave after the last ship arrives from Toledo, Cebu. The trip takes 3½ hrs by the coastal road and two hrs by the Translink Highway which crosses the island via Don Salvador Benedicto and Murcia.

Mambukal & Mt Kanlaon

Mambukal is 31 km south-east of Bacolod at 400m elevation in the north-west foothills of the Kanlaon volcano. With its hot sulphur springs, Mambukal is the best known spa resort on Negros, although only rarely visited by tourists. The so-called Mountain Resort (admission: P30) covers 24 hectares, has several swimming pools (P50), picnic huts (P300) and the Blue Lagoon with boats for hire, all set in luscious subtropical vegetation. Other attractions of this beautifully laid-out resort are the Canopy Walk through centuries old trees (a total of 145m of hanging bridges that allow you to get up close to ancient trees 13m up in the air; P50), the Slide for Life (a 4½m high cable which you can safely slide down with a harness to the Blue Lagoon; P50), a rock climbing wall (P25), Ishiwata Bathhouse (P30), hiking paths and seven waterfalls (the first three are fairly easy to get to, although a guide is recommended for the other four; depending on the weather, non-slip footwear is definitely a good idea, especially if you want to climb all the waterfalls).

If you want to climb the 2465m high Kanlaon, you need to allow three to four days for the round trip. The City Tourist Office (Tel 4347472) in Bacolod can organise guides from the Negros Mountaineering Club (NMC). Those who intend to climb the volcano or visit the national park for bird-watching or whatever are advised to inform the club or the tourist office beforehand for co-ordination and safety purposes. There is a serious reason behind this, as the volcano can by no means be described as benign. In August 1996 it suddenly erupted without any warning, catching a group of mountaineers totally by surprise. Quite a few of the party were injured, some fatally.

A tour for two people organised by NMC will cost around P6000 (via Mambukal) or P5000 (via La Carlota). You can also find knowledgeable guides on your own in Mambukal who will also provide a tent and cooker.

Places to Stay

Mambukal Resort, Tel 7100800. SR/DR/ac/bath P600 and P750, cottage/ac/bath P900 and P1200. Reasonable rooms in the slightly out-of-the-way Tourist Lodge, and solid stone cottages with cooking facilities. Restaurant. Reservations in Bacolod: Tel (034) 7090990.

Miscellaneous

Festival: Mudpack Festival on 23 and 24 June, the high point being provided by exuberant dance performances by participants covered in mud and clay.

Post & Telephone: Post code: 6129. Area code: 034.

Getting There & Away

Jeepney: Several jeepneys and mini-buses go from Bacolod to Mambukal daily, leaving from Libertad St (one hr). The last jeepney back leaves at 5pm.

Ma-ao

The sugarcane fields of Ma-ao stretch to the foot of the Kanlaon Volcano, criss-crossed by about 280 km of railway tracks. Just as exciting as the bridges that cross the rivers and ravines are the old steam locomotives, which were used until recently for harvesting. These old-timers were recently pensioned off and pushed on to the old-timer tracks of the Ma-ao Sugar Central (MSC), where they may possibly still be available for inspection (check at the City Tourist Office in Bacolod). There are two American Locomotive Company (Alco) 2-6-0: one is the TS 1-3, dated 1921, and the other is the BM 5, dated 1924.

Getting There & Away

Jeepney: Several jeepneys go from Libertad St in Bacolod to Ma-ao daily (one hr). The last trip back is at 4 or 5pm.

Silay

Located about 15 km north of Bacolod, Silay can boast of being the city with the richest culture in all of Negros Occidental. The town is dominated by the San Diego Cathedral, built in 1925, with its large, gleaming silver dome.

A little outside Silay is the Hawaiian-Philippine Sugar Company, one of the largest plantations on Negros, which has a rail network that is about 180 km long. Nicknamed 'Red Dragons', the steam engines used here are in excellent condition. The name goes back to the time when they were bright red, but today they are blue-black in colour. In WWII, most of them were hidden from the Japanese by being run on special rails into the wooded mountains. They include a 1920 Henschel 0-6-0 and six Baldwin 0-6-0 built in 1919, 1920 and 1928. It is possible to view these steam engines during the harvest from November to March, however visitors must first have a permit issued by the tourist office.

Museum

An excellent way to get a picture of life on Negros in its heyday at the turn of the century is to visit the Balay Negrense Museum in 5-Novembre St. Providing a glimpse particularly of the lifestyle and culture of the upper classes back then, the museum is open every day except Monday from 10am until 6pm. This building is one of the 31 grand old, upper-class dwellings in Silay which were declared to be part of the cultural heritage by the National Historical Institute. The Bernadino-Ysabel Jalandoni Ancestral House was also turned into a Lifestyle Museum.

Miscellaneous

Festival: Kansilay Festival (City Fiesta) from 7 to 13 November.
Population: 25,000.
Post & Telephone: Post code: 6102. Area code: 034.
Tourist Office, City Hall, Tel. 4950061, Fax: 4950587, @.

Getting There & Away

Bus/Jeepney: Several jeepneys leave from Lacson St, on the corner of Libertad St, in Bacolod for Silay daily (30 min). Buses and jeepneys from the Northern Bus Terminal also go through Silay.
Jeepneys leave from the market in Silay to go to the Hawaiian-Philippine Sugar Company.

Victorias

The Victorias Milling Company, Vicmico, is open for inspection from Tuesday to Friday. It's part of a large industrial complex where sugar is processed in several stages for the consumer. Guided tours are possible from Tuesday to Friday, from 9am until noon, and from 2 until 6pm (P15 per person). To get permission for a guided tour, first you have to go to the Public Relations Office next to the Urban Bank on the factory grounds. Men wearing shorts and women wearing shorts or miniskirts will be refused admission. Sandals and thongs (flip-flops) are not permitted for safety reasons.
Vicmico's 349-km railway track is the longest on Negros and possibly the longest two-foot gauge track in the world. As with the Hawaiian-Philippine Sugar Company in Silay, the diesel and steam locomotives are directed by radio remote control from a central point, but the dark-green old-timers are now used only during the peak season from January to February. The rolling stock includes eight Henschel 0-8-0T, dating back to 1926 to 1928, and two Bagnall 0-4-4T, which were built for the Kowloon (Hong Kong) to Canton Line in China.
Apart from the sugar mill, the Chapel of St Joseph the Worker is worth seeing. The unusual coloured mural showing an angry Filipino Jesus, the 'Angry Christ' has received international attention after an article about it appeared in *Life* magazine.

Miscellaneous

Festivals: Kadalag-an Festival on 21 March. Malihaw Festival on 26 April.
Population: 35,000.
Post: Post code: 6119.

Getting There & Away

Bus/Jeepney: Several buses and jeepneys run every day at irregular intervals from Bacolod's Northern Bus Terminal to Victorias (P15; 45 min).
Several jeepneys marked VMC' run daily from Victorias market to the Vicmico sugar mill (15 min).

Cadiz

The little port of Cadiz lies at the estuary of the river of the same name on the north coast of Negros. There is a daily boat connection from there to Bantayan Island in the north of Cebu.

Places to Stay

RL Apartelle, Abelarde St, Tel 4930253. SR/DR/fan P75/100, SR/DR/fan/bath P500, SR/DR/ac/bath P550 (TV). Good value accommodation with basic, but clean rooms.
EC Pension House, Villiana St, Tel 4931711. SR/DR/fan/bath P200 and P350, SR/DR/ac/bath P500. The rooms are of an acceptable quality and almost all have TV.
Cadiz Hotel, Villiana St, Tel & Fax 4931785. SR/DR/fan/bath P350, SR/DR/ac/bath P400 to P600. Best hotel in town with really good rooms, all right for the money; the aircon ones with TV, some with refrigerator. Restaurant.
Laura's Beach Resort, Daga, Tel 4930565. SR/fan/bath P300, SR/DR/ac/bath P500 and P1500. Decent rooms. Restaurant, swimming pool. A credible alternative to the hotels in town. Located five km west of Cadiz, about 10 min by tricycle.

Places to Eat

The big ***Terrace Garden Restaurant*** in Abelarde St near the church serves good Chinese and Philippine food. The best restaurant in town.

Miscellaneous

Festival: Ati-Atihan Festival on the third Sunday in January.
Online: CDZnet, Santa Maria Building, Cabahug St; P30/hr.
Population: 35,000.
Post & Telephone: Post code: 6103. Area code: 034.
Tourist Office, Cabahut St, Tel 4930269. Open Mon-Fri, 8am-noon and 1-5pm.

Getting There & Away
2 Ceres Liner Bus Terminal
5 Shell Petrol Station
18 Wharf

Places to Stay
6 Carmel's Inn
8 A & C Pension House
9 Chamar Pension House
12 Skyland Hotel
15 Coco Grove Hotel

Places to Eat
3 Barbecue Stalls
6 Carmel's Inn Restaurant
11 Flamingo Restaurant
12 Skyland Restaurant

Miscellaneous
1 City Hall (100m)
4 Gaisano Department Store
7 Market
10 Philippine National Bank (PNB)
13 Town Plaza
14 Police Station
16 Hospital
17 Lighthouse

Getting There & Away

Bus: Several Ceres Liner buses make the trip daily from Bacolod to Cadiz (1½ hrs).

Escalante

Every year on 20 September, Escalante commemorates the 1985 massacre of sugar cane workers, with speeches, street theatre and memorial services. The striking workers were marching through the streets in protest when soldiers suddenly opened fire, killing 20 of them at random.
There is a daily boat service between Escalante and Tabuelan on the northwest coast of Cebu. The harbour (Port Danao) is a little bit out of town.

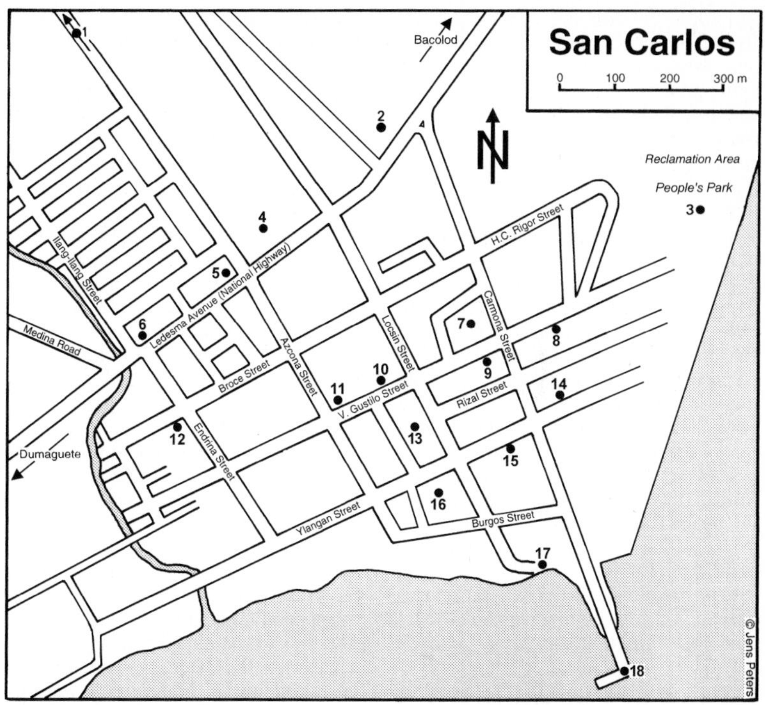

Places to Stay

Laida's Lodge. SR/DR P100/200. Basic rooms. Across from the bus terminal at the market. Restaurant.

Bonista Beach Resort, Buenavista, Cellphone 0917-3609087, @. SR/DR/ac/bath P1200 to P1600 (good for four people). Immaculate rooms with broad beds. Big, attractive swimming pool. Restaurant. The resort is located 17 km south-east of Escalate (about 12 km from the highway); a special ride by tricycle costs P100. Reservations in Escalante: Tel 4540065.

Miscellaneous

Festivals: Manlambus Festival on 30 May. Feast of Our Lady of Mt Carmel on 16 July.

Population: 15,000.

Post & Telephone: Post code: 6124. Area Code: 034.

Getting There & Away

Bus: Several Ceres Liner buses go from Bacolod to Escalante daily from the Ceres Liner North Terminal (2½ hrs).

San Carlos & Sipaway Island

San Carlos is a friendly, homely kind of small town on the north-eastern coast of Negros. A shipping service connects San Carlos with Toledo on Cebu. There is also an historical connection with the neighbouring island: About 200 years ago a group of Negritos under the leader-

ship of the enterprising Cebuano Carlos Apurado moved lock, stock and barrel over to Negros and settled there. Their new home was initially given the name of Nabingkalan, after Nabingka, a beautiful princess and ruler for many years. Around the middle of the 19th century during a time of political change, the town was renamed San Carlos.
The offshore island of Sipaway (geographical name: Refugio Island) is a popular destination for day trips, especially with ornithologists (there are over 30 kinds of birds there). It's about five km long and 400m broad. A well constructed road connects the two communities of Ermita and San Juan, where altogether 4000 people live. There is a reasonable beach at the Ermita pier, otherwise just loads of mangroves. You'll find several Sari-Sari stores on the island, but their stock is limited, so it's advisable to bring your own provisions from San Carlos. Fresh fish is on sale at the piers and the sari-sari stores will cook it for you. Pedicabs on the island cost P5 per person.

Places to Stay

Chamar Pension House, V Gustilo St, Tel 3125170. SR/DR/fan P100/200, SR/DR/fan/bath P200/300, SR/DR/ac/bath P400/500. Basic, friendly accommodation with a family-style atmosphere.
Skyland Hotel, Broce St, Tel & Fax 3125589, @. SR/DR/fan/bath P345 and P470, SR/DR/ac/bath P495 and P595. Good rooms (the more expensive ones have TV); while some are a bit small, the new ones are larger. Well-kept place run by the Australian John and his Filipina wife Virginia. Good restaurant.
A & C Pension House, V Gustilo St corner Dos Hermanos St, Tel 3125563. SR/DR/ac/bath P500 to P750. Spacious, pleasant rooms, all with TV, the expensive ones also have a refrigerator and balcony. Located near the Reclamation Area. Restaurant.
Carmel's Inn, Ledesma Ave (National Highway), Tel 3125976, Fax 7299242. SR/DR/ac/bath P650 and P1.050. Well-kept rooms with TV. Restaurant, beer garden.
Whispering Palms Island Resort, Sipaway Island, Cellphone 0916-2019402, @. SR/DR/fan/ bath P1000 and P1200 (six beds), SR/ DR/ac/bath P1500 and P2000 (six beds), cottage/ac/bath P2500 (with lounge and two bedrooms). Well-maintained, pleasantly furnished rooms with veranda, the aircon ones with TV. Spread-out grounds with a small bay for bathing. Restaurant, billards, swimming pool, mini-zoo.

Places to Eat

The outstanding Philippine food in the attractive and friendly ***Carmel's Inn Restaurant*** on Ledesma Ave at the corner of Ilang-Ilang St is good value. They also have an excellent beer garden. The ***Skyland Restaurant*** in Broce St will serve you juicy steaks as well as other good things to eat.
The finest restaurant in town (albeit expensive), is the tastefully decorated, fully air-conditioned ***Flamingo Restaurant*** in V Gustilo St. The popular ***Barbecue Stalls*** directly on the water at the Reclamation Area are inexpensive and open from 6pm until midnight.

Miscellaneous

Festivals: Pintaflores Festival on 1 July (people paint their skin with floral motifs and dance in the streets wearing colourful, ethnically-styled costumes). Feast of St Charles Borromeo (patron saint of the town) on 4 November.
Money: The Philippine National Bank in V Gustilo St has an ATM and will change travellers' cheques. Bank of the Philippine Islands, Rizal St corner Locsin St, and Metrobank, Carmona St, have ATMs.
Information: A good source of information of interest to tourists is John, the

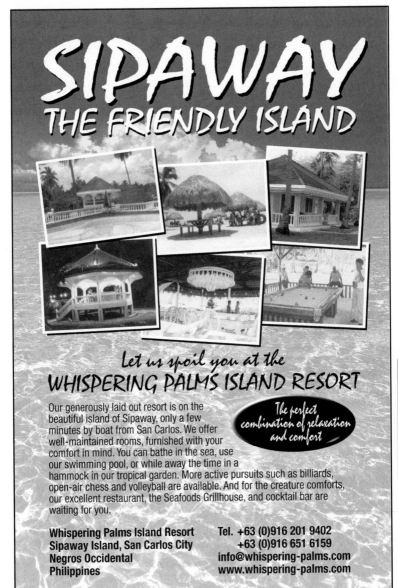

Australian who owns the Skyland Hotel.
Population: 30,000.
Post & Telephone: Post code: 6172. Area code: 034.

Getting Around

Boat: Outriggers sail from San Carlos to the following destinations on Sipaway Island: Ermita Wharf (P6; 30 min); Dapdap Wharf near San Juan (P4; 10 min - a Special Ride costs P50 to P100).

Getting There & Away

By Boat: The following shipping line is represented in San Carlos:
Aznar Shipping Corporation, Port Area. *Destination:* Cebu.

Bacolod

Bus: Ceres Liner buses make the trip from Bacolod to San Carlos every day, either direct or heading for Dumaguete, leaving roughly every half-hour. The trip takes 3½ hrs by the coastal road or two hrs by the Translink Highway which crosses the island via Murcia and Don Salvador Benedicto.

Dumaguete

Bus: From Dumaguete there are Ceres Liner buses to San Carlos, either direct or heading for Bacolod, leaving daily between 3am and 4.30pm every half-hour. Additional departures are at 8 and 10pm. The trip takes four hrs.

South Negros

Bais

The small town of Bais is located about 50 km north-east of Dumaguete and is a popular departure point for whale and dolphin watching trips. Large numbers of these friendly sea mammals pass through the narrow Tañon Strait between the islands of Negros and Cebu, especially from March until June. A whale watching tour from eight in the morning until four in the afternoon with an experienced boatsman costs P2500 for up to 15 people, or P3000 for up to 20. Also included is a bathing stop at a white sand bank and a detour to the Talabong Mangrove Forest in the bay of Bais. The forest has 14 different kinds of mangrove and is a huge nature sanctuary, home to many Philippine birds, including several colourful species of kingfisher. Long boardwalks lead through the sanctuary, providing a perfect platform for observing the various flora and fauna.

It's normally no problem to find a boat for a day trip, but they can also be booked through the Tourist Office (P500 fee), who will also provide a guide.

Places to Stay

Bahia de Bais Hotel, Cellphone 0916-6468844. SR/DR/ac/bath P1000. Basically furnished, but really good rooms. Restaurant. The hotel is located a few km outside Bais on a rise on Dewey Island (aka Daco Island), which provides a good view of Tañon Strait. The island, which splits the Bay of Bais in two and is actually connected to the mainland, is reachable by a roadway. It's best to phone them and have them pick you up in Bais, or you can get AJ Car, Mabini St, to take you there for P200.

Miscellaneous

Festival: Hudyaka sa Bais City on 7 September.
Population: 65,000.
Post & Telephone: Post code: 6203. Area code: 035.
Tourist Office, Aglibay St, Tel 5415161 (on Saturdays and Sundays: Cellphone 0919-4731047, ask for Jun). Open Mon-Fri 8am-noon and 1-5pm.

Getting There & Away

Bus: Buses which travel between Dumaguete and Bacolod go via Bais. From Dumaguete the trip takes one hr.

Dumaguete

Dumaguete is a very pleasant city with neat little park areas and what must be the cleanest market in the Philippines. Especially at the weekends, the atmosphere is friendly and relaxed south of the harbour, where friends and families get together for a drink or a picnic at the quay wall along the promenade (Rizal Blvd) as evening approaches.
Dumaguete is the capital of Negros Oriental Province and also a university town. Silliman University, whose extensive campus is on the northern edge of the city, is the only Protestant university in the Philippines and was named after its founder, Dr Horace B Silliman. For further information about the university, ask at the Administration Building.
Silliman Beach near the airport is not a particularly impressive bathing beach at first sight, but it's actually not bad and is quite popular with students.

Museum

Located in an attractive building on the campus of Silliman University, the Silliman Hall Museum specialises in anthropology and is a mine of information on the subject.

Shopping

Delightful craft work is on sale at Handuman Native Products in Predices St.
There's a European delicatessen in Le Gourmet Swiss Deli Shop in Santa Rosa St at the corner of Real St.
Chang's Department Store and Lee Super Plaza are not open after 7pm.

Places to Stay

Dumaguete

Vintage Inn, Legaspi St, Tel. 2251076. SR/fan/bath P220, DR/fan/bath P330, SR/ac/bath P330 and P440, DR/ac/bath P500 and P600. Basic, practical rooms, some have no windows. Located at the market.
Harold's Mansion, Hibbard Ave, Tel 2258000, Fax 2250439, @. SR/fan/bath P275, DR/fan/bath P385 to P610, SR/ac/bath P500, DR/ac/bath P600 to P1100. Good rooms for the money, the aircon ones have a TV. Quiet location on the university campus in the northern outskirts of the city.
OK Pensionne House, Santa Rosa St, Tel 2255702, @. SR/DR/fan/bath P275, SR/ac/bath P550, DR/ac/bath P770, suite P1320. Wide choice of rooms (the aircon ones with TV), albeit of varying quality and some with no window. Popular accommodation in the south of the city.
Opeña's Hotel, Katada St, Tel 2255214. SR/fan/bath P350, DR/fan/bath P400, SR/ac/bath P470, DR/ac/bath P560. Clean, good-value rooms with TV, the ones at the back are quiet. Restaurant.
The Worldview Pension Plaza, Perdices St, Tel 2254110, Fax 2254112. SR/ac/bath P500, DR/ac/bath P600 to P950. Trim and tidy, pleasant rooms with TV and a refrigerator if you pay more. Well-run, quiet place. Small restaurant.
C & L Suites Inn, Perdices St corner Pinili St, Tel 2256219, Fax 2253103. SR/ac/bath P500, DR/ac/bath P700 to P875, suite P1200. Immaculate rooms with TV, priced just right, the suites also have a refrigerator. To be recommended, in the south of the town. Coffee Shop.
Plaza Maria Luisa Suites Inn, Legaspi St, Tel 4227382, Fax 2257994, @. SR/DR/ac/bath P650/850, suites P1200 and P1300. Including breakfast. Reasonable rooms with TV, the suites also have a refrigerator. Small restaurant.
Bethel Guesthouse, Rizal Blvd, Tel 2252000, Fax 2251374, @. SR/ac/bath P700, DR/ac/bath P900 to P1700, with TV, the more expensive ones also have a refrigerator. Friendly, very well-kept

Getting There & Away
1 Airport
7 WG & A
11 Aleson Shipping Lines
14 Cokaliong Shipping Lines
George & Peter Lines
15 Delta Fast Ferries
21 Negros Navigation
28 Jeepneys & Minibuses to Sibulan & Tampi
39 Aboitiz Express
WG & A
44 Air Philippines
46 Negros Navigation
60 Motorcycle Rental
64 Jeepneys to Valencia
68 Jeepneys to Maluay, Zamboanguita & Siaton
70 Ceres Liner Bus Terminal

Places to Stay
1 Panorama Beach Resort
2 South Sea Resort Hotel
3 Harold's Mansion
5 Coco Grande Hotel
12 Opena's Hotel
19 Hotel El Oriente
21 Home Quest Lodge
25 The Wordview Pension Plaza
29 Aldea Lodge
30 La Residencia Al Mar Hotel
44 Honeycomb Tourist Inn
45 Vintage Inn
47 Plaza Maria Luisa Suites Inn
52 Bethel Guesthouse
59 C & L Suites Inn
62 OK Pensionne House
67 Rose Garden & Pension House
Private Country Club
El Oriente Beach Resort
Santa Monica Beach Resort

Places to Eat; Entertainment
2 Baybay Restaurant
6 El Camino Blanco
Hayahay Restaurant
Lab-as Seafood Restaurant
13 Dock Side
17 Silliman University Cafeteria
22 Scooby's Restaurant
23 Jo's Restaurant
Silliman Avenue Café
24 El Amigo
Thrifty Chicken Alley
26 Rosante Restaurant
27 Coco Amigos Restaurant & Bar
30 Don Atilano Restaurant
Café Fernando Grill House
32 The City Burger
33 Jollibee
34 Chowking
36 Chin Loong Restaurant
38 Dunkin' Donuts
42 Mamia's Bar & Restaurant
43 Chicco's Snack Bar
Le Chalet
Why Not Music Box
48 North Pole Restaurant
Shakey's
62 Kyosco Restaurant
66 Mei-Yan Restaurant

Miscellaneous
1 Provincial Hospital
4 Silliman University Medical Center
6 Silliman Beach
8 Silliman University
9 Aquino Freedom Park
10 Provincial Capitol
15 Silliman Post Office
18 Administration Building
Silliman Hall Museum
20 Philippine National Bank (PNB)
21 Brightwash Laundry
Planetarium Internet Café
27 Paradise Travel Center
31 Handuman Native Products
34 Chang's Department Store
35 Dumaguete Outdoors
37 Lee Super Plaza
39 Metrobank
40 Immigration Office
41 Manson's Place Internet Café
43 Cyberbox Internet Café
46 Maganda Travel & Tours ↗

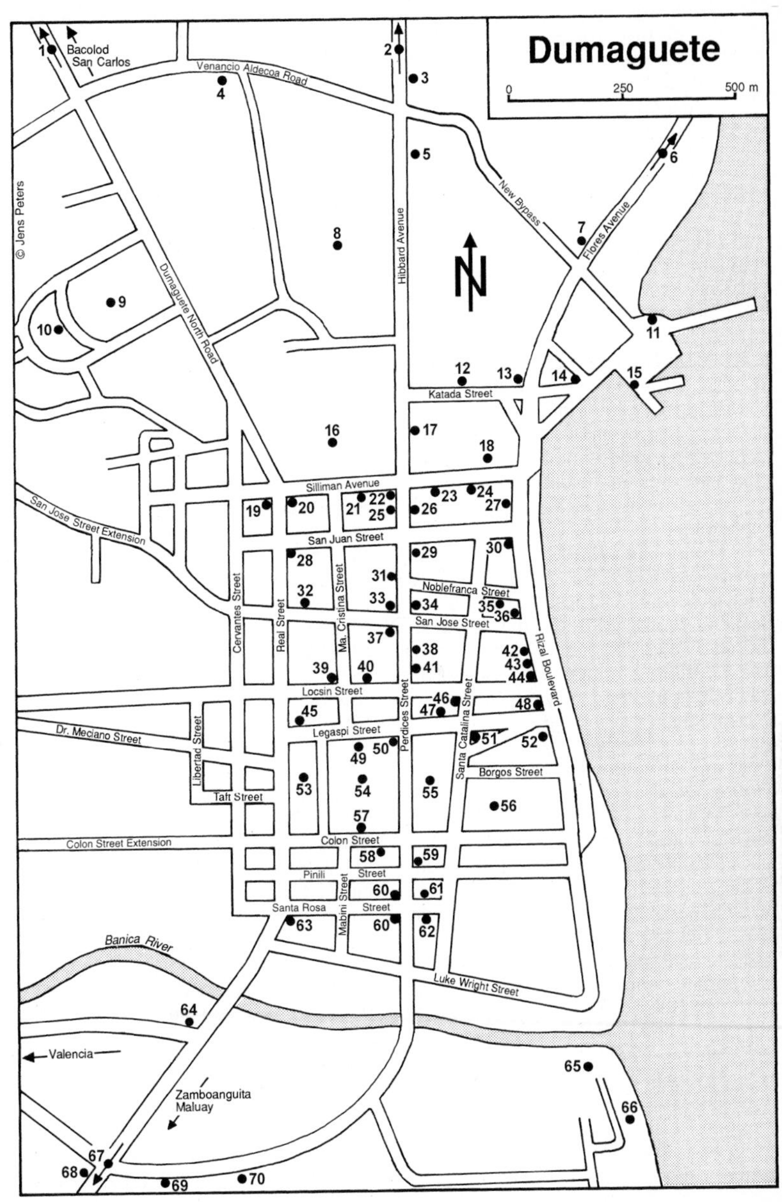

Dumaguete
0
250
500 m
© Jens Peters
Bacolod
San Carlos
Venancio Aldecoa Road
New Bypass
Flores Avenue
Hibbard Avenue
Dumaguete North Road
Katada Street
Silliman Avenue
San Jose Street Extension
San Juan Street
Noblefranca Street
San Jose Street
Cervantes Street
Real Street
Ma. Cristina Street
Rizal Boulevard
Locsin Street
Perdices Street
Santa Catalina Street
Legaspi Street
Dr. Meciano Street
Libertad Street
Borgos Street
Taft Street
Colon Street Extension
Colon Street
Pinili Street
Mabini Street
Santa Rosa Street
Banica River
Luke Wright Street
Valencia
Zamboanguita
Maluay

47 Gate Way Travel & Tours	56 City Hall
49 Holy Child Hospital	Tourist Office
50 Bank of the Philippine Islands	57 Fruit Market
51 Post Office	58 Equitable PCI Bank
53 Market	63 Swiss Gourmet Deli Shop
54 Church	65 Chinese Temple
55 Quezon Park	69 Cockpit

and pleasantly furnished hotel - to be recommended. Located right next to a Shakey's restaurant. Smoking and alcohol consumption are not allowed in the rooms.

Coco Grande Hotel, Hibbard Ave, Tel & Fax 2250833, @. SR/DR/ac/bath P1000 and P1400. Pleasant, spacious aircon rooms, some with small balcony and TV, in a tasteful ambience. Located in a quiet area on the university campus on the northern edge of the city. Small restaurant.

La Residencia Al Mar Hotel, Rizal Blvd, Tel 2257100, Fax: 2254724. SR/DR/ac/bath P1150 to P1490. Comfortable rooms with TV, the more expensive ones have a refrigerator. An older building which has been accurately remodelled in the Spanish style. Restaurant.

Around Dumaguete

South Sea Resort Hotel, Bantayan, Tel 2252409, 4225442, Fax 2250491, @. SR/fan/bath P940, DR/fan/bath P1070, SR/ac/bath P1200 to P1650, DR/ac/bath P1380 to P1590, suites P3475. The more expensive rooms have a refrigerator and TV. Quiet and comfortable place with a well-tended garden. Good restaurant, swimming pool. Located by the sea near Silliman Beach, about two km north of the city centre.

El Oriente Beach Resort, Mangnao, Tel 2250668, Fax 2255544, @. Cottage/fan/bath P350, SR/DR/ac/bath P600 to P1200. Basic cottages and fairly good rooms, some with refrigerator and TV. Located about three km south of Dumaguete. Restaurant, swimming pool.

Rose Garden & Pension House, Noreco Rd, Mangnao, Tel 2250658, @. SR/DR/fan P300, SR/DR/fan/bath P550, SR/DR/ac/bath P700. Pleasant, spacious rooms, the more expensive ones have a kitchen, refrigerator and TV. Under German management. Good restaurant with German and Philippine cuisine. Billiards. Motorcycle hire, diving (Dumaguete Divers), airport service. Located directly on the beach (not too inviting), about three km south of Dumaguete.

Private Country Club, Baptist Rd, Mangnao, Cellphone 0918-7941679. SR/DR/fan/bath P500, SR/DR/ac/bath P700. Reasonable rooms with TV, refrigerator and cooking facilities. Small place (only four rooms) with a garden. Swiss management. Restaurant, mini swimming pool. Located one block south of the Rose Garden & Pension House, 200m from the beach.

Santa Monica Beach Resort, Banilad, Tel 2250704, Fax 2257801, @. SR/ac/bath P1265, DR/ac/bath P1520. Well-equipped cottages and spruce rooms with TV. Quiet place on a dark part of the beach, about four km south of Dumaguete. Restaurant. Big swimming pool with poolside bar.

Places to Eat

There's excellent Chinese food in the ***Chin Loong Restaurant*** on Rizal Blvd; the special menu is really good value. Another good, although slightly more expensive Chinese restaurant is the

Visayas - Negros

Mei-Yan Restaurant in the southern outskirts of Dumaguete, south of the Banica River, directly on the sea next to a little Chinese temple. They also serve Philippine food.

Jo's Restaurant on Silliman Ave has what is probably the best chicken dish in town: the delicious Chicken Inato. Next door, in the ***Silliman Avenue Café*** you'll mostly bump into local and international students. Just round the corner on Percides St, the busy ***Rosante Restaurant*** prepares tasty Filipino dishes.

The selection of inexpensive Philippine food on offer at the ***Kyosco Restaurant*** in Santa Rosa St across from the OK Pensionne House is to be recommended, and they're open round the clock.

A good choice of food is available in the department store ***Lee Super Plaza***, where several local restaurants have fast-food stalls on the first floor. Inexpensive Filipino food is available in several small, clean restaurants in the covered market near the church.

If you get the munchies late at night, then the ***Dock Side*** near the jetty is the place to go. It's a bit functionally furnished, but really good value, and you don't have to wait long. They are closed during the day.

The little ***Chicco's Snack Bar*** in the Why Not Music Box disco on Rizal Blvd serves Philippine and European snacks (also has deli sales and freshly baked bread). This is a popular meeting place, especially for expat Europeans. Right next door in the pleasantly laid-out ***Le Chalet*** you can enjoy excellent international food (good steaks), Thai specialities, fondues and a salad bar.

You can eat the best steaks in town in the air-conditioned comfort of the ***Don Atilano Restaurant*** on Rizal Blvd, where the ambience is Spanish and the service superb. A few buildings along the street heading towards the wharf, you'll come to the inviting, colourfully decorated ***Coco Amigos*** where they serve tasty Mexican dishes, pizzas and cracking cocktails (there's live music after 9pm on Thursday, Friday and Saturday).

For those who like seafood, the attractively decorated ***Lab-as Seafood Restaurant*** can be recommended; on Friday evening they have an inexpensive buffet. They are located on the corner of Flores Rd and El Blanco Dr, two km north of Silliman Ave along the water. Right next door you'll find the popular, two-storey, airy ***Hayahay Restaurant*** with a wide selection of great food, including excellent good-value pizzas. Another good restaurant for seafood, which also serves Filipino and Western cuisine, is the rustically romantic ***Bay-bay Restaurant*** in the South Sea Resort Hotel near Silliman Beach.

Entertainment

The nightlife in Dumaguete is hardly worth mentioning, as there are few places still open in the late evening. One honourable exception is the big, popular ***Why Not Music Box***, Rizal Blvd, which is under Swiss management and can get really busy, although not until after 10pm, when most people start arriving. In ***El Amigo*** in Silliman Ave, the clientele is mostly students who obviously like the loud music.

If you prefer live music, then the ***El Camino Blanco*** is the place for you. It's located about two km north of the centre at the junction of Flores Rd and El Blanco Drive, within easy reach of the restaurants and evening meeting places Hayahay and Lab-as.

Miscellaneous

Diving: Members of the Marine Laboratory near Silliman Beach run diving courses there twice a year. They also use a boat that you can charter for diving excursions. Favourite destina-

tions are Sumilon Island in southern Cebu, and Apo Island, south of Dumaguete.
In Dauis, 15 km south of Dumaguete, Atlantis Dive Resort, @, Dive Society, @, in the El Dorado Beach Resort, and Sea Explorers, @, in the Pura Vida Beach & Dive Resort offer a wide range of diving programmes.
Festivals: Santacruzan Festival in May. Buglasan Festival in October. Sandurot Festival on 23 November. City Fiesta on 25 November. Kasadya-an Festival from 12 to 14 December.
Immigration Office, Locsin St, Tel 2254401. Visa extensions are efficiently taken care of in this friendly office. Open Mon-Fri, 8am-noon, 1-5pm.
Medical Services: The medical care at the Holy Child Hospital, Legaspi St, Tel 2254841, and at the Silliman University Medical Center (SUMC), Tel 2250841, is better than at the Provincial Hospital.
Money: Bank of the Philippine Island, Perdices St corner Legaspi St, and Equitable PCI Bank, and Philippine National Bank, Silliman Ave corner Real St, Colon St, have ATMs.
Online: Planetarium Internet Café, Silliman Ave, and Manson's Place, Perdices St; both P30/hr. The Cyberbox Internet Café (P70/hr; with individual cubicles) is in the Office Centre of the Why Not Music Box on Rizal Blvd, where you can also make copies, send faxes, etc.
Population: 110,000.
Post & Telephone: Post Office, Legaspi St corner Santa Catalina St. There is another, smaller post office on the campus of Silliman University.
Post code: 6200. Area code: 035.
Tourist Office: The City Tourist Office is at the City Hall on Santa Catalina St, Tel 2250549, Fax 2250386, @.
Travel Agency: Dumaguete Outdoors, Noblefranca St, Tel 2256079, Cellphone 0921-2072727, @, all-round service plus organised tours in south-east Negros, eg 'Dolphin & Whale Watching in Bais' and 'Hiking at Lake Balinsasayao'.
Maganda Travel & Tours, Locsin St corner Santa Catalina St, Tel 2258256, Fax 2256565, @, will take care of hotel reservations, visa extensions as well as booking and reconfirmation of national and international flights.
Paradise Travel Center, Rizal Blvd, Tel & Fax 2255490, @, will book air and sea tickets, and will reconfirm national and international flights.

Getting Around

Car: R & R Rent-a-Van, Rovira Rd, Bantayan, Tel. 2251786.
Motorcycle: Small machines are available for P300/day at the corner of Santa Rosa St and Perdices St. The Why Not Music Box on Rizal Blvd has 200 cc machines for P700/day (24 hrs).
Tricycle: Dumaguete has what are probably the roomiest, most comfortable tricycles in the Philippines. A journey within the city costs P4 per person.

Getting There & Away

By Air: The airport is at the northern edge of the city. A tricycle to the city centre shouldn't cost more than P40.
Air Philippines, Dumaguete Airport, Tel 4196020, 2254266.
- Honeycomb Tourist Inn, Rizal Blvd, Tel 2251181.
Destination: Manila.
Cebu Pacific, Dumaguete Airport, Tel 2258758-60.
Maganda Travel & Tours, Locsin St corner Santa Catalina St, Tel 2258256.
Destination: Manila.

By Bus: Buses heading north (San Carlos, Bacolod) and south (Bawayan, Hinoba-an) leave from the Ceres Liner Bus Terminal on the southern outskirts of the city.
A tricycle from the towncentre costs P5 per person.

By Boat: The following shipping lines are represented in Dumaguete:
Aleson Shipping Lines, San Juan St, Tel 2258169, 2258569.
Destinations: Cebu, Mindanao, Sandakan (Sabah, Malaysia).
Cokaliong Shipping Lines, Port Area, Tel 2253588.
Destinations: Cebu, Mindanao.
Delta Fast Ferries, Port Area, Tel 2253128.
Destination: Siquijor.
George & Peter Lines, Port Area, Tel 2254337.
Destinations: Cebu, Mindanao.
Negros Navigation, Silliman Ave, Tel 2255210.
- Maganda Travel & Tours, Locsin St corner Santa Catalina St, Tel 2258256.
Destinations: Bohol, Manila.
Ocean Fast Ferries, Port Area, Cellphone 0917-3208524.
Destinations: Bohol, Cebu.
Supercat Fast Ferry Corporation/ Aboitiz Express, Port Area, Tel 2255811, 2255799.
- Maria Cristina St, Tel 2251540.
Destinations: Bohol, Cebu, Mindanao, Siquijor.
WG & A, Maria Cristina St, Tel 2251540.
Destinations: Bohol, Manila, Mindanao.

Bacolod - Mabinay
Bus: Several buses travel every day from the Ceres Liner South Terminal in Bacolod to Dumaguete (5½ hrs); via Mabinay.

Bacolod - San Carlos
Bus: Several Ceres Liner express buses leave daily to Dumaguete via San Carlos from the Ceres Liner North Terminal in Bacolod, about one an hour. The trip takes 7½ hrs from Bacolod and four hrs from San Carlos.
Bacolod - Hinoba-an
Bus: Several buses go daily to Dumaguete via Hinoba-an, leaving from the Ceres Liner South Terminal in Bacolod. The trip takes 10 hrs.

Hinoba-an
Bus: Several Ceres Liner buses go daily to Dumaguete from the Nauhang bus terminal near Hinoba-an. The trip takes four hrs, possibly with a one-hour stop in Bayawan.

Around Dumaguete

Twin Lakes

About 25 km west of Dumaguete there are two crater lakes surrounded by dense rain forest: Lake Balinsasayao and the smaller, adjoining Lake Danao, at a height of about 800m. They are also known as the Twin Lakes, although they are not identical twins as a hydroelectric power station has been built on Lake Danao.

Getting There & Away
Bus/Jeepney: You can get to Twin Lakes from Dumaguete by bus or jeepney going north. Get off about two km before San Jose, or travel back from San Jose by tricycle to the small track leading from the road up to Twin Lakes. You have to walk the remaining 15 km or so as it is impossible for jeepneys or tricycles. Motorcyclists without cross-country experience would have great difficulty too because of the steep slope and dangerous ruts.
Apparently, it is possible to go as far as San Antonio (west of Sibulan) by jeepney. From there, take the sloping path up to where it forks into two, then again take the right-hand, uphill path which will lead you to the Twin Lakes. The last part of the walk is hardest, down a difficult, very steep hill.

Sibulan & Tampi

Several ships go from Sibulan and Tampi to Bato and Oslob on Cebu daily.

Visayas - Negros

Getting There & Away
Jeepney: Jeepneys for Sibulan and Tampi leave Dumaguete from Real St corner San Juan St.

Valencia

Valencia has a pleasantly laid-out town park, and is the suburb of Dumaguete where people live in upmarket housing comfort, under the shade of the many trees. From there, you can take a tricycle for about P100 (return journey, including waiting time) up to Camp Look-out at the extinct volcano Cuernos de Negros. Unfortunately, what was a beautiful view of Dumaguete, Cebu and Siquijor Island has become more and more hampered as the viewing area has become almost completely overgrown.
In Terejo, about two km out of Valencia, you'll find the Banica Valley Resort, which has a small creek, a swimming pool and a few rest houses (admission P10). It's popular with the locals, especially at weekends. If you want to go there on foot, ask for the swimming pool, which is near a shrine. Further upstream from the swimming pool you can have a wonderful dip in the natural pool at the Casiroro waterfall, surrounded by huge rocks and unspoilt vegetation. The turnoff from the road is hard to find so it would be best to have someone point it out to you. There are steps leading down to the pool.

Getting There & Away
Jeepney: Several jeepneys run daily to Valencia from Dumaguete from the Valencia turnoff south of the Banica River. A tricycle from the city centre to the turnoff costs P5 per person.

South-East Coast

Along the coast from Dumaguete to the southern tip of Negros there are several places that will tempt you to stay a bit longer.

Getting There & Away
Bus/Jeepney: Several jeepneys leave Dumaguete every day from the first road junction south of the Banica River and head along the south coast via Dauin (30 min), Maluay and Zamboanguita (45 min) as far as Siaton (one hr). You can also take any Ceres Liner bus heading for Bawayan or Hinoba-an.

Bacong

In the small coastal village of Bacong, about seven km south of Dumaguete, they have a beautiful church with an old altar and organ, and the beach is clean here.

Dauin

Dauin was founded back in the 18th century and is one of the oldest communities in the province. The charming church was built back then, as were a few watchtowers where they used to keep a lookout for plundering pirate ships. The quality of the beach here, about 15 km south of Dumaguete, is quite good.

Places to Stay
El Dorado Beach Resort, Tel (035) 4240094, Fax 4240238, @. Dorm/fan P450, cottage/fan/bath P1400 (with cooking facilities), SR/DR/ac/bath P935 to P4700 (including breakfast). Rebated weekly and monthly rates are available. Pleasant cottages and good rooms with TV, the more expensive ones also have a refrigerator. Attractive, lushly planted grounds. The excellent restaurant offers outstanding Philippine and European cuisine round the clock. They have a swimming pool and also offer diving (Dive Society; diving instruction can be arranged). Admission for day visitors

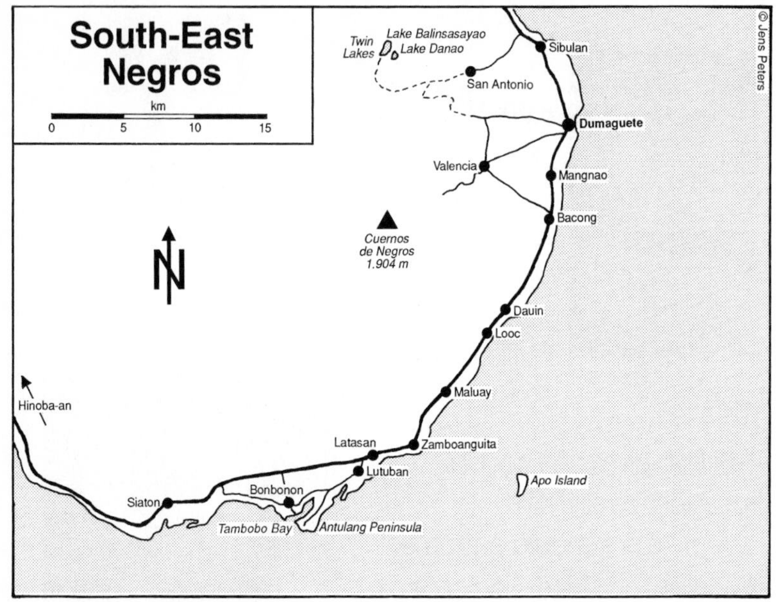

is P80 (your bill is reduced by this amount if you consume anything). The management is Swiss. A free shuttle bus runs between the resort, airport, wharf and the Why Not Music Box disco in Dumaguete several times daily (20 min).

Pura Vida Beach & Dive Resort, Tel (035) 4252085, Fax: 4252284, @. Cottage/fan/bath P1600, SR/ac/bath P2400, DR/ac/bath P2700. This is mainly a resort for divers. Well-equipped cottages and rooms, all with charging stations for diving lamps. The restaurant has a beautiful sea view. Beach bar. Swimming pool. Diving (Sea Explorers; also diving courses). Located about 150m south of the El Dorado Beach Resort.

Atlantis Dive Resort, Tel (035) 4240578, Cellphone 0917-8515126, @. Cottage/ac/bath P2500 to P4100. Tastefully furnished stone cottages, some with two storeys, with refrigerator and TV. Set in well-tended garden grounds directly on the water, about 800m north of El Dorado Beach Resort. Restaurant, diving (also courses).

Maluay

On Wednesdays in Maluay (Malatapay) there's a large market held under palms on the beach, the Malatapay Market, which is considered a highlight of the area. Crowds of farmers come in from the mountains, and fishermen from the coast and nearby islands tie their boats up there. The market trades in agricultural produce, livestock and seafood. Chickens and fish are grilled, and even whole pigs roasted, amid much chattering, gossiping, laughing, eating and drinking.

Although the sand is black on the beaches near Maluay and Zamboanguita, the water is clean and clear. You can get to the offshore island of Apo from either place.

Places to Stay

Hans & Nenita's Malatapay Cottages, Tel (035) 4261087, @. Cottage/fan/bath P750. A friendly place, with roomy cottages right on the beach. Helpful German-Philippine management. Very good restaurant. Mountain hikes and diving trips can be organised by request. Located near the jetty for boats to and from that island. Get out at Malatapay Crossing, head towards the sea for 200m, then 100m to the right.

Wellbeach Resort, Mojon, Tel (035) 4262195, @. SR/DR/ac/bath P1250. Good, well-maintained rooms with a big veranda. Restaurant (Swiss and Philippine cooking). Swimming pool. Garden. The resort is located two km before Maluay coming from Dumaguete, about 200m back from the main road on the beach (signposted).

Tambobo Bay

Also known as Tambobo Yacht Harbour and Port Bonbonon, this bay in the deep south of Negros is only 300m wide at its broadest point, but is 2½ km long. The mouth of the Paliohan River is at the head, that of the Talocoy nearer the entrance to the bay. The eastern end of the bay is marked by the elongated Antulang Peninsula, which, helped by the shape of its narrow sound, provides a sheltered anchorage all year round. Sailors circumnavigating the globe have been known to appreciate the calm anchorage as well as the skilful handiwork of the local boat builders. The first beach resorts have already been opened on the shores of this picturesque bay.

An excellent idea for a day trip is to hire a motorbike and head for the secluded Lourdes Waterfalls near Bayawan, roughly half-way to Hinoba-an.

Places to Stay

Tongo Sail Inn, Cellphone 0918-7400129, @. SR/DR/fan P150, cottage/fan P300, cottage/fan/bath P500 and P800 (two-storey). Well-tended garden grounds with basic, but very tastefully furnished, inviting cottages. Idyllically located on the stony beach near the village of Tambobo at the entrance to the bay. Their restaurant serves good, inexpensive European and Philippine food. Snorkelling equipment and paddle boats are available for hire. Take a jeepney as far as Siaton, carry on from there by motorbike (habal-habal) or tricycle over the occasionally bumpy road to Tambobo (P20 per person, or P50 for the tricycle).

Kookoo's Nest Resort, Cellphone 0919-6958085, @. Cottage/bath P650. Basic, but attractive cottages with a beautiful sea view. The British couple Jamie and Nikki run this charming little place, which is situated on a peaceful stretch of white sand beach at the tip of the Antulang Peninsula, not far from the mouth of the bay. Good restaurant. Diving. Hammocks and paddlebancas are available for guests, and a nearby intact reef is just perfect for snorkelling.

How to get there: As for the Tambobo Beach Resort, then have yourself taken over there by boat from Tambobo. You could also get a taxi from Dumaguete airport; fare: P1000, one hr. (You'll have to cover the last 100m on foot.) Guests can also be picked up in Dumaguete on request.

Antulang Beach Resort, Tel (035) 4270112, Fax 4270115, @. Cottage/ac/bath P1400 to P3900, depending on furnishings and location. Stylish stone cottages, beautifully decorated and clean as a new pin. The luxurious pool villa with private swimming pool, jacuzzi, TV and refrigerator costs P14,000. Good restaurant with a terrace. Perched on top of cliffs, looking down on a

coral beach, this resort provides a view you'll never forget. Reservations in Dumaguete: Tel (035) 2258899, Cellphone 0917-3732766.
Get there by motorbike (habal-habal) from Zamboanguita or Tambobo (P100) or by taxi from Dumaguete (P1000).

Places to Eat
An excellent alternative to the restaurants at the beach resorts is the unpretentious, very popular ***Dorothy's Eatery*** in Tambobo, where a sumptuous meal is put on the table every evening and the guests can eat their fill for a set amount of money (around P75). The ***Ne-Ar-Ne Store & Nicki's Yacht Service***, @, is a bustling restaurant well worth the visit. It's built on piles in Tambolo Bay and is a great favourite with yachtsmen who can tie up there with their dinghies even when the tide's out.

Apo Island

Apo island, about eight km south-east of Zamboanguita, has about 700 inhabitants. The beautiful little island is slightly hilly, and in the north can get as high as 120m. Here they erected a lighthouse which provides a beautiful panoramic view. In the flatter, southern part of the island near the village there's a little lagoon which is separated from the sea by a sandy beach. To protect some unusual coral formations and rare fish, the waters up to 300m around Apo Island have been declared a sanctuary and placed under the protection of Silliman University in Dumaguete. A part of this Apo Island Marine Reserve is the strictly regulated 'Fish Sanctuary' off the lagoon at the south coast of the island, where even anchoring is not allowed. The conditions here are excellent for diving and snorkelling, although the strength of the currents and undertow should not be underestimated.

Snorkelling in the Fish Sanctuary costs P75; divers have to pay P150 a day into the 'island kitty'. This money is used to improve the public facilities of the island.

Places to Stay
Liberty's Resort & Paul's Diving, Tel. 4240888, Cellphone 0917-6039987, @. Dorm/fan P250, SR/DR/fan P650, SR/DR/fan/bath P880 and P1400. Spacious rooms with a view of the beach from the balcony. The resort belongs to Paul, an Englishman, and his Filipina wife Liberty. Restaurant. Diving (courses). Postal address: PO Box 1, 6217 Dauin, Negros Oriental, Philippines.
Apo Island Beach Resort. Cottage/bath P1040 to P1300. An attractive resort, five minutes on foot from the village, set under palms on a hill with really comfortable cottages with a magnificent view. The little white sand beach is framed by decorative rock formations. The restaurant here is good, if a bit expensive, and they offer diving. Reservations in Dumaguete: Paradise Travel Center, Rizal Blvd, Tel (035) 2255490.
It is also possible to spend the night in private accommodation, eg at Roberto and Lusina Mendez' place near the church. They charge P100 per person or P300 including three meals. If you like eating good fish, Lusina will prepare it just the way you like it.

Miscellaneous
Festival: Apo Island Fiesta on 4 and 5 April.
Post & Telephone: Post code: 6218. Area code: 035.

Getting There & Away
Boat: A few fish boats make the trip from Apo Island to Maluay and back at irregular intervals every day. They charge P50 to P100 (locals only pay P20).

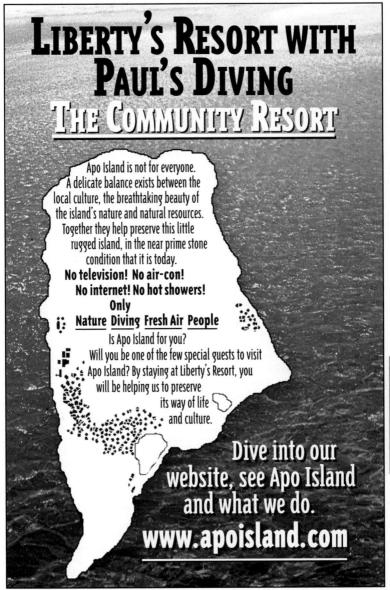

Visayas - Negros

You can hire Special Rides in Zamboanguita and Maluay from about P600 to P800 to go to Apo Island. It's better to leave before 8am and return after 4pm because of the swell.

West Negros

Binalbagan

Binalbagan is on the west coast of Negros, about 65 km south of Bacolod. This is where you will find one of the biggest sugar refineries and plantations in the world. It is called Biscom, which is short for Binalbagan Sugarmill Company. The two Baldwin locomotives 2-6-2T No 6, dated 1924, and Davenport 0-4-0T No 28, dated 1929, are no longer used, but you may inspect them.

Kabankalan

Kabankalan is about 30 km south of Binalbagan and is the most important town in the south-west of Negros in terms of its economy. The town itself was founded over 100 years ago, but the decisive impetus for the upswing in its modern prosperity was given with the opening of two sugar mills only 30 years ago.

The road from Kabankalan to Hinoba-an is now in excellent condition. After the improvements had been at long last carried out, the road is now called 'Love Avenue' and no longer 'Abortion Road' as it was known in the days of its potholed glory.

Places to Stay

Gemms Pension House, Guanzon St, Tel 4713362. SR/DR/fan/bath P350, SR/DR/ac/bath P550. Reasonable rooms, OK for the money. Restaurant. Located next to Lopue's department store on the northern edge of town.

Justine's Guest House, Roxas St, Tel 4713135. SR/DR/ac/bath P700 to P900. Immaculate rooms with TV. Friendly accommodation near the Allied Bank. Coffee Shop.

Places to Eat

Next to Gemms Pension House, ***Pasta & Noodles*** in Guanzon St is a pleasant, inviting restaurant with good value dishes on its menu.

Miscellaneous

Festival: Sinulog sa Kabankalan on the third weekend in January. The Kabankalañons maintain that their Sinulog Festival is older and more authentic than the better known one in Cebu City.

Money: Cash advance (Visa, MasterCard) at the Equitable PCI Bank. The Bank of the Philippine Islands has an ATM. Both banks in Guanzon St.

Online: Knet Internet Café, Cayco-Weill Building, Guanzon St; P30/hr.

Population: 20,000.

Post & Telephone: Post code: 6111. Area code: 034.

Getting There & Away

Bus: All buses that travel between Bacolod and Dumaguete (the southern route via Mabinay) as well as Hinoba-an, go via Kabankalan (two hrs from Bacolod; three hrs from Dumaguete).

Sipalay

The friendly little town of Sipalay is situated on the south-west coast of Negros, about 180 km south of Bacolod and 20 km north of Hinoba-an. It's a perfect place to base yourself for a few days on your way around the sugar island. Not far from Sipalay you'll find several beautiful, palm-lined, white sand beaches which are just in the process of being developed for tourism. Good examples of this are the long Sugar Beach just to the north (a great bathing beach also known locally as Langub Beach), and Punta Ballo White

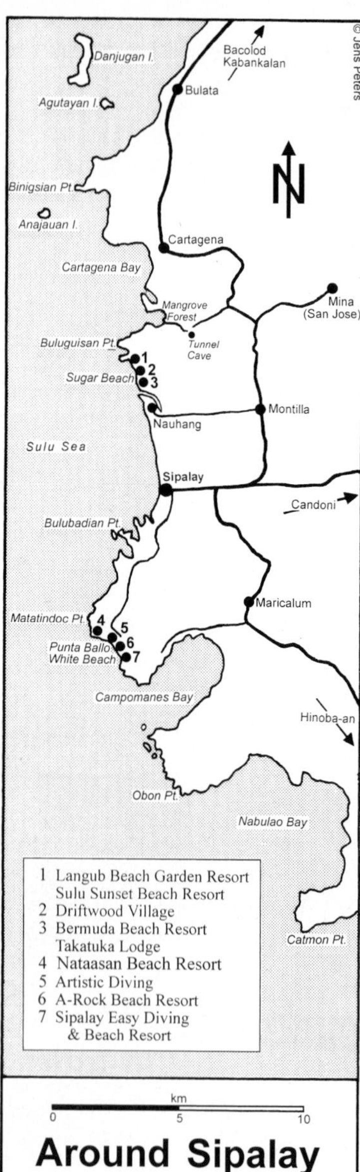

Beach, seven km to the south-west. The stretch of coast on both sides of Sipalay is wonderfully scenic and is interspersed with numerous attractive little bays. Especially impressive is Campomanes Bay which cuts deeply into the coastline, providing excellent snorkelling and diving (there are two wrecks here: the SS *Panay* and the MS *Jojo*). Just off Cartagena Bay there is another wreck only a few feet below the surface which is swarming with big fish. It's about 20 minutes by boat from Sugar Beach and simply tailor-made for diving and snorkelling.

Places to Stay

Sipalay

Langub Pension, Alvarez St corner Lacson St. SR/DR P120/240, SR/DR/fan/bath P300, SR/DR/ac/bath P600. Basic accommodation with practically furnished rooms. Restaurant.

Punta Ballo White Beach

Artistic Diving, Cellphone 0919-4095594, @. SR/DR/fan P400, SR/DR/fan/bath P700, SR/DR/ac/bath P900 and P1500. Modest rooms, and some with better fittings, in two buildings. Restaurant, billiard, diving (also courses).

Sipalay Easy Diving & Beach Resort, Cellphone 0918-3455072, @ SR/DR/fan/bath P700, SR/DR/ac/bath P850, cottage/ac/bath P1300. Good rooms and well-appointed stone cottages. Beautifully laid out resort on a slope about 600m south of Artistic Diving. Swiss owner. Restaurant. Diving.

Nataasan Beach Resort, Cellphone 0919-3657863. SR/DR/fan/bath P1200/1400, cottage/fan/bath P1400/1600, cottage/ac/bath P1700/1900. Spacious rooms in a big building, and pretty cottages, all attractively furnished. The resort is located on a hill above the beach which can be reached by a flight of steps. Restaurant.

Mother Nature on Danjugan Island

The little island of Danjugan is about 125 km south-west of Bacolod, 15 km north of Sipalay and three km west of Bulata. It's 1½ km long and 500m across at its widest point, hilly and covered with a thick blanket of green. Seven different kinds of mangrove grow in lagoons here. On the south-east coast you can find deserted sandy bays, and on the west coast beautiful white beaches which are visited by hawksbill turtles during egg-laying season. Several caves provide shelter and roosting places for lively swarms of bats, and the rain forest echoes exotically to the cries of about 50 species of bird, including white breasted sea eagles, grey headed fishing eagles, herons and kingfishers as well as providing a welcome rest stop for many migratory birds. In 2000 the island and the waters surrounding it were designated a nature reserve (Danjugan Island Marine Reserve and Sanctuaries - DIMRS), but there was a tortuous build-up to this, to say the least:

In the mid-1980s, the gold and copper mines run by the Maricalum Mining Corporation east of Sipalay began to spiral deeper and deeper downwards into financial difficulties. As a result, many of the miners who had been made redundant were forced to change their job and become fishermen. However, in their desperate struggle to make a living, the thoughtless use of dynamite and cyanide in their fishing caused enormous damage to the underwater world round the coast. Danjugan Island, surrounded by coral and with an extensive reef to the west of the island, was especially badly hit by this wanton destruction.

Active conservationists from Bacolod sounded the alarm and managed to bring about the end of these illegal fishing practices. With the financial support of the British World Wide Land Conservation Trust (WWLCT) they bought the island in 1994 and handed it over to the Philippine Reef and Rainforest Conservation Foundation, Inc (PRRCFI), which had been set up to save Danjugan Island. Their first move was to build a camp for caretakers and ecologists on this precious and endangered natural haven for wildlife. One year later, the London-based company Coral Cay Conservation Ltd (CCC) allied itself with this exemplary project for the effective protection of the environment and ever since then has sent volunteers to research and conduct surveys of the local marine life. Keenly interested Philippine students are also often guests at the camp to learn what they can about the ecosystem of this tropical island in workshops lasting several days. As there is only room for 20 visitors, it's necessary to register first with the PRRCFI in Bacolod; Tel. (034) 4411658, @. An overnight stay at the camp costs P2556, including meals. Day visitors pay P1050.

Sugar Beach

Takatuka Lodge, Cellphone 0920-2309174, @. SR/DR/fan P350, SR/DR/fan/bath P450, cottage/fan/bath P800 (for up to five people with cooking facilities and a big veranda). Pleasant accommodation with a few clever ideas in the decoration. Restaurant (international cuisine), diving (also with instruction), boat trips.

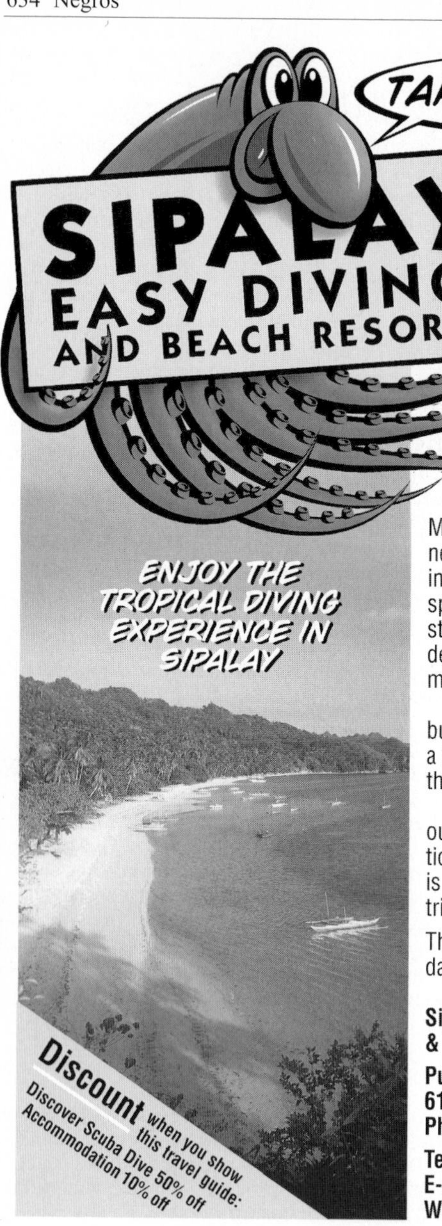
TAKE IT EASY!
SIPALAY
EASY DIVING
AND BEACH RESORT
ENJOY THE TROPICAL DIVING EXPERIENCE IN SIPALAY
Discount when you show this travel guide:
Discover Scuba Dive 50% off
Accommodation 10% off

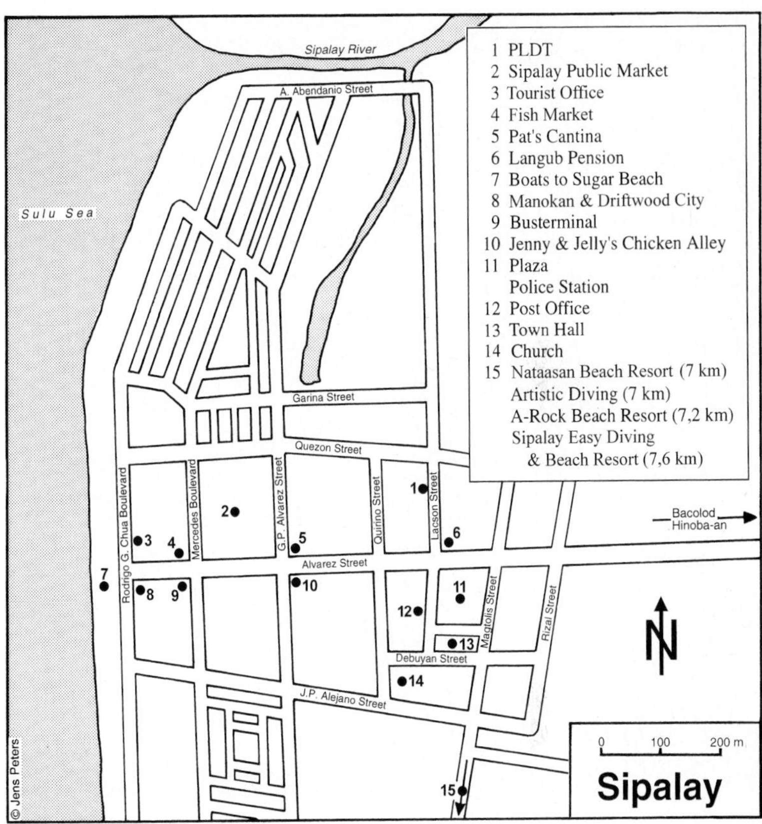

Sulu Sunset Beach Resort, Cellphone 0919-7167182, @. Cottage/bath P400 and P600. A friendly place on Sugar Beach with nicely built cottages where the attention to detail is obvious (light switch at the bed, reading lamp, etc). The restaurant offers German and Philippine cooking and freshly baked bread. Billiards. Motorbike hire (P800/day). Snorkelling equipment and paddlebancas are also available for hire. Diving can be arranged on request.

Driftwood Village, Cellphone 0920-2529474, @. Cottage/fan P400, cottage/fan/bath P700 to P1200. Basic, but good, cottages. Restaurant (Thai and international food) with a novel beach bar made of driftwood. Motorbike hire (P800/day).

Bermuda Beach Resort, Cellphone 0919-4856141, @. Cottage/fan/bath P400, P800 and P1400, depending on size and location. Good value. Well-maintained resort with roomy, really comfortable cottages (generous verandas, caringly decorated, big bathrooms), all creatively and individually furnished. Attractive restaurant with Philip-

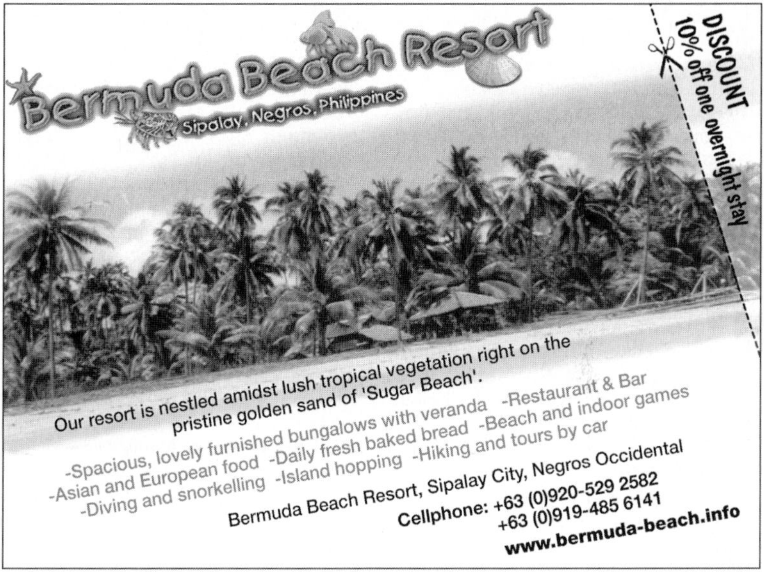
Bermuda Beach Resort
Sipalay, Negros, Philippines
DISCOUNT
10% off one overnight stay
Our resort is nestled amidst lush tropical vegetation right on the pristine golden sand of 'Sugar Beach'.
-Spacious, lovely furnished bungalows with veranda -Restaurant & Bar
-Asian and European food -Daily fresh baked bread -Beach and indoor games
-Diving and snorkelling -Island hopping -Hiking and tours by car
Bermuda Beach Resort, Sipalay City, Negros Occidental
Cellphone: +63 (0)920-529 2582
+63 (0)919-485 6141
www.bermuda-beach.info

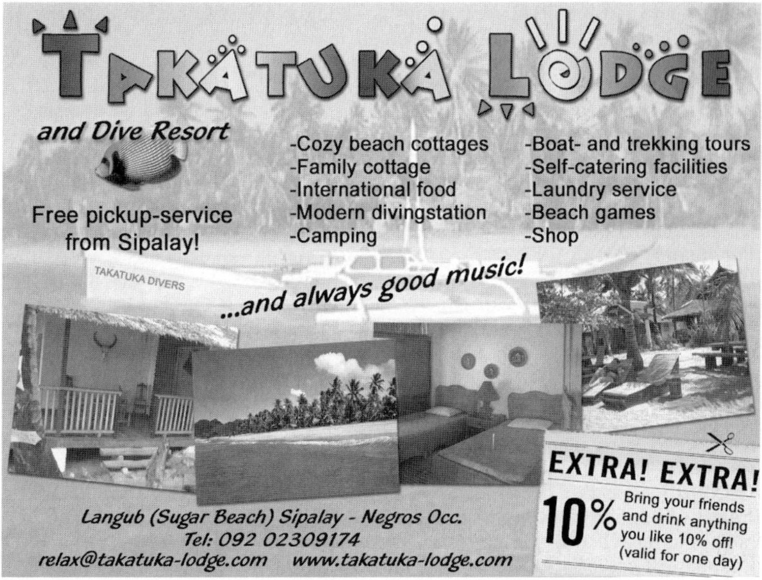
TAKATUKA LODGE
and Dive Resort
Free pickup-service from Sipalay!
-Cozy beach cottages
-Family cottage
-International food
-Modern divingstation
-Camping
-Boat- and trekking tours
-Self-catering facilities
-Laundry service
-Beach games
-Shop
TAKATUKA DIVERS
...and always good music!
EXTRA! EXTRA!
10%
Bring your friends and drink anything you like 10% off!
(valid for one day)
Langub (Sugar Beach) Sipalay - Negros Occ.
Tel: 092 02309174
relax@takatuka-lodge.com www.takatuka-lodge.com

pine and Swiss cooking, and freshly baked bread. Beach Bar.
Langub Beach Garden Resort. SR/DR/fan/bath and cottage/fan/bath P500, cottage/ac/bath P1000. Simple cottages. Communal kitchen. Located right next to the Sulu Sunset Beach Resort.

Places to Eat
Both ***Pat's Cantina*** in Alvarez St and ***Jenny & Jelly's Chicken Alley*** across the road will serve you good, inexpensive Philippine food. On the beach near the bus terminal there's also the ***Manokan*** with several basic, open restaurants, including the Swiss-run ***Driftwood City*** that offers pizzas, pasta and a few international dishes.

Miscellaneous
Diving: The Swiss diving instructor Arthur Müller of Artistic Diving, Punta Ballo White Beach, has reconnoitred 30 diving locations and includes wreck and cave diving in his programme. Other diving outfits with modern equipment include Sipalay Easy Diving, also on Punta Ballo White Beach, and Takatuka Divers on Sugar Beach.
Festival: Pasaway Festival on 20 December.
Money: The nearest place is in Kabankalan, 80 km away, at the Equitable PCI Bank and the Bank of the Philippine Islands.
Population: 10,000.
Post & Telephone: Lacson St (in the same building as the police). Long distance and overseas calls can be made at PDLT, Lacson St.
Post code: 6113.
Tourist Office, Rodrigo G Chua Blvd. Open Mon-Fri, 8am-noon, 1-5pm. May not be open every day.

Getting Around
Boat: A Special Ride with an outrigger boat from the wharf at the bus terminal to Sugar Beach costs P150 (15 min). If none is waiting, you can order a boat from one of the resorts by cellphone or radio at the nearby Driftwood City restaurant or at the Langub Pension. You'd be better off phoning the resort or sending an SMS before you arrive, to arrange pick-up.
Motorcycle: The trip from the bus terminal to Punta Ballo White Beach costs P100.
Tricycle: A tricycle from Sipalay to Nauhang via Montilla costs P100 (from Montilla P50). In Nauhang you can have yourself rowed across the little river for P5 per person; then it's only a few minutes on foot to the south end of Sugar Beach.

Getting There & Away
Bus: Ceres Liner buses leave from the Ceres Liner South Terminal in Bacolod roughly every hour during the day for Sipalay (four hrs).

Taxi: A taxi from Bacolod to Sipalay should not cost more than P1500.

Hinoba-an

As an interesting alternative to the usual route from Bacolod via San Carlos and Toledo, you can travel along the west and south coasts via Hinoba-an and Dumaguete. The last section from Bayawan to Zamboanguita is particularly scenic, although the road between Hinoba-an and Bayawan is not in the best condition for about 20 km. Apart from Sipalay, Hinoba-an is not a bad place for a stopover. The beach there stretches for kilometres and might not be white as snow, but the fine sand is light and of pretty good quality.

Places to Stay
Mesajon Lodging House, Gatuslao St. SR/DR/fan P100/200. Basic romms.
Estrella del Sur. SR/DR/ac/bath P1000. Beautiful little place set in a garden,

Golden Times

Early in 1982 Hinoba-an experienced a real gold rush. Both the national and international press published daily reports about new finds which brought numerous adventurers and optimists. Gold fever broke out in earnest when it was reported that a Filipino had found gold to the value of P23,000 in a single day. Soon afterwards an estimated 20,000 people were trying their luck along a 17-km stretch of the Bacuyongan River and many did find gold. The average daily yield at the peak of the rush is said to have been one gram per person; this sold at P80.Unfortunately, there were disastrous events, too. Within eight weeks one digger was buried alive in a landslide and another three died in fights over claims. Altogether, 17 victims were counted in two months. The most lucrative gains were those made by the gold dealers, merchants and traders, who soon turned the sleepy village of Nauhang into a lively trading centre with a wild-west character. From the Crossing Golden Southbend (a junction near Nauhang), jeepneys ran about seven km inland to Spar III at Sitio Sangke, where the well-trodden path to the bountiful river begins. Government bore holes to a depth of 300m were only completed at the end of 1982. The result surpassed all expectations, indicating a probable 10 million tonnes of rock with a content of three grams of gold per tonne. This was the biggest discovery of all. On hearing this, the government put an embargo on freelance gold prospecting, putting an end to the era of wild adventure.

with only three rooms to let. Family atmosphere. The living room and kitchen can be used by guests. Located at the southern exit to the town.

Happy Valley Beach Resort, Po-ok, @. Cottage/fan/bath P500 and P1000, cottage/ac/bath P1000 to P5000. Cottages and houses of various sizes with up to four bedrooms, some also with living rooms and kitchens. An attractive resort with a garden about 300m south of the edge of town.

Brazaville Beach House, Po-ok, @. SR/DR/ac/bath P1000 to P5000. Friendly place with well looked after rooms. Restaurant. Located next to the Happy Valley Beach Resort.

Miscellaneous

Festival: Town Fiesta on 14 February.
Population: 5000.
Post: Post code: 6114.

Getting There & Away

Bacolod

Bus: Several Ceres Liner buses run daily, roughly every hour, from Bacolod to Hinoba-an from the Ceres Liner South Terminal. They are either direct or continue on to Dumaguete. The trip takes 4½ hrs.

Dumaguete

Bus: Several Ceres Liner buses run daily, roughly every hour, from Dumaguete to Hinoba-an (four hrs). The bus may stop for an hour in Bayawan.

Bayawan

By area, Bayawan is the biggest town in the Province of Negros Oriental. It spreads as far as Mabinay and is about twice the size of the island of Siquijor.

However, only about one fifth of the population live in the urban area. About 15 km east of this beautiful little town the Lourdes Waterfalls are well worth a visit; for the last 1½ km they can only be reached by a narrow pathway.

Places to Stay
Casa Rosario Pension House, Cellphone 0920-6217420. SR/DR/fan/bath P300 and P350, SR/DR/ac/bath P500 to P800. Great rooms, all with TV, the more expensive ones also have a balcony. Located only a few meters off the main road across from the Petron filling station, not far from the market and the bus terminal.

Places to Eat
In a side street near the Philippine National Bank you'll find the ***Freeza Restaurant*** with a good choice of Philippine food.

Miscellaneous
Festival: Town Fiesta on 18 February. Tawo-Tawo Festival on 21 December.
Population: 22,000.
Post: Post code: 6221.

Getting There & Away
Bus: All buses that run between Dumaguete and Hinoba-an go via Bayawan (three hrs to Dumaguete; one hr to Hinoba-an).

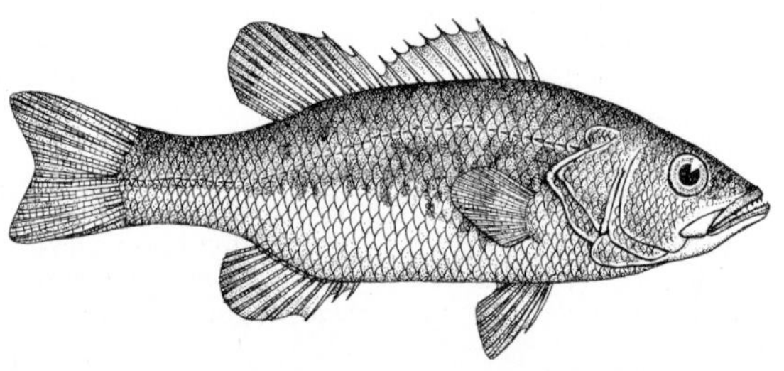

Panay

Panay is the large triangular island in the west of the Visayas. It is subdivided into the provinces of Iloilo, Capiz, Aklan and Antique. The western half of the island is mountainous; the highest mountains being Mt Madja-as (2090m) and Mt Nangtud (2049m), both in the province of Antique. Iloilo City is the biggest city on the island.

The economy is predominantly agricultural, although there is also a small amount of textile industry in Iloilo City. Fabric made from piña, the fibres of the pineapple leaf, is used to make Filipino barong tagalog shirts.

Among the main tourist attractions in Panay are the Ati-Atihan Festival in Kalibo and the Dinagyang Festival in Iloilo City. Along the south coast there are also several massive old churches dating from colonial times.

The little dream island of Boracay is extremely popular, not only with the 'international travel set' but also with quite 'normal' holidaymakers. Travel agents can make reservations at several different resorts on the island offering above-average facilities.

The islands off the north of Panay's east coast have not yet been developed for tourism, although there would be every reason to do so. At least a few of these islands have that certain something about them and compare favourably with many a well-known tourist destination. The mountains in the west of Panay have everything friends of the great outdoors could ask for.

Getting There & Away

You can get to Panay from Cebu, Guimaras, Luzon, Mindanao, Mindoro, Negros, Palawan and Romblon (see the Getting Away from Luzon section of the Manila chapter and the Getting There & Away sections of the individual island chapters).

To Cebu

Air

From Caticlan (Boracay) to Cebu City
Asian Spirit and Seair fly daily (P2200).

From Iloilo City to Cebu City
Air Philippines, Cebu Pacific and Philippine Airlines fly daily (P2100).

Boat

From Iloilo City to Cebu City
Daily with Trans-Asia Shipping Lines (P550; 15 hrs).
Wednesday, Friday and Sunday with Cokaliong Shipping Lines (15 hrs).

To Guimaras

Boat

From Iloilo City to Buenavista
Daily, roughly every hour from 5am to 5.30pm with a small ferry from the Parola wharf at Rotary Park to the Buenavista wharf (MacArthur Wharf) in Santo Rosario (one hr).

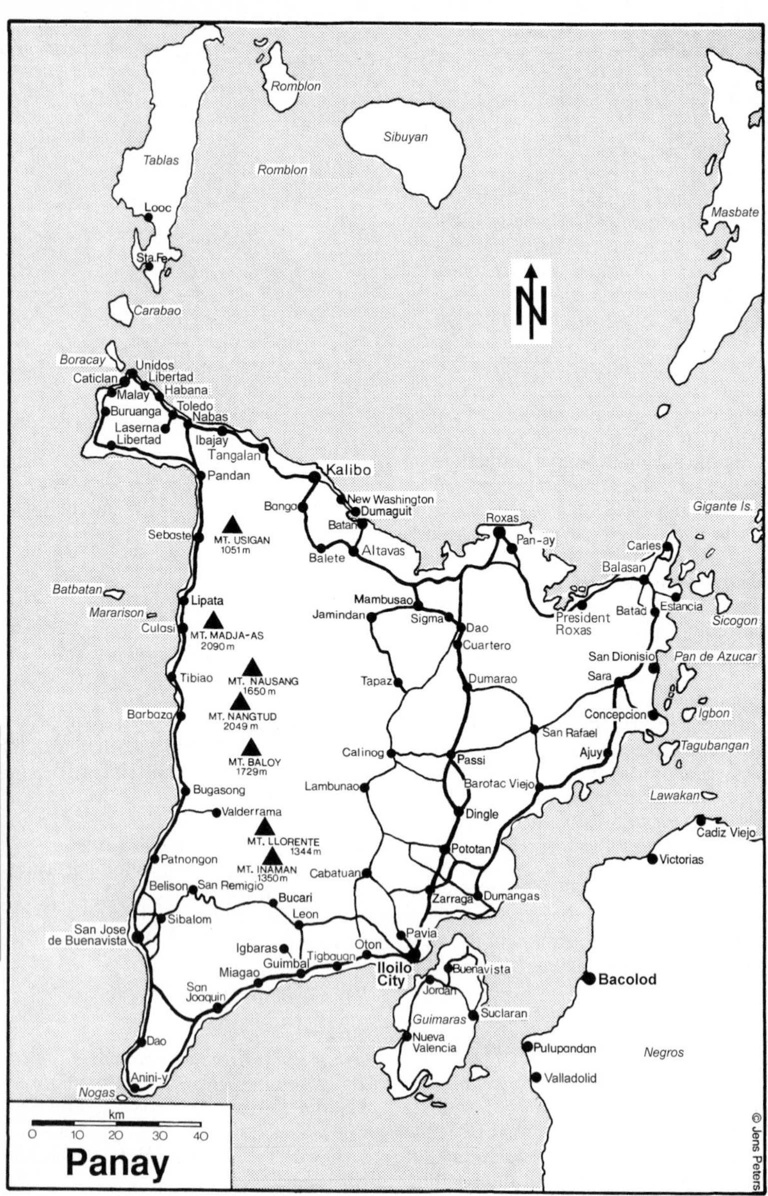
Romblon
Sibuyan
Tablas
Romblon
Looc
Masbate
Sta.Fe
Carabao
Boracay
Unidos
Caticlan
Libertad
Malay
Habana
Buruanga
Toledo
Nabas
Laserna
Libertad
Ibajay
Tangalan
Kalibo
Pandan
New Washington
Dumaguit
Bongo
Batan
Gigante Is.
MT. USIGAN
1051 m
Sebaste
Roxas
Pan-ay
Carles
Balete
Altavas
Balasan
Batbatan
Mambusao
Lipata
Jamindan
Sigma
Dao
Batad
Estancia
Mararison
President
Roxas
Sicogon
Culasi
MT. MADJA-AS
2090 m
Cuartero
San Dionisio
Pan de Azucar
MT. NAUSANG
1650 m
Tapaz
Dumarao
Sara
Tibiao
Igbon
MT. NANGTUD
2049 m
Concepcion
Barbaza
San Rafael
MT. BALOY
1729m
Calinog
Passi
Ajuy
Tagubangan
Bugasong
Lambunao
Barotac Viejo
Lawakan
Valderrama
Dingle
Cadiz Viejo
MT. LLORENTE
1344 m
Pototan
Victorias
Patnongon
MT. INAMAN
1350 m
Cabatuan
Belison
San Remigio
Zarraga
Dumangas
Bucari
Sibalom
Leon
San Jose
de Buenavista
Pavia
Oton
Igbaras
Tigbauan
Guimbal
Iloilo
City
Miagao
Buenavista
Bacolod
San
Joaquin
Jordan
Guimaras
Suclaran
Nueva
Valencia
Dao
Pulupandan
Negros
Valladolid
Anini-y
Nogas
km
0 10 20 30 40
Panay
© Jens Peters

From Iloilo City to Jordan
Several small ferries run daily, roughly every hour between 5am and 6pm, from the river wharf near the Post Office (30 min).
An outrigger leaves daily, roughly every 30 minutes, from the Ortiz wharf near the Central Market (P7; 15 min). A Special Ride costs P250.
Four times daily, possibly at 7.30 and 9.30am, and at 2 and 4pm with an FF Cruz Shipping car ferry from the river wharf on Rizal St (P20; 1½ hrs).

To Luzon

Air

From Caticlan (Boracay) to Angeles
Seair flies daily except Saturday and Sunday; possibly via Manila (P2400).
Asian Spirit flies Monday, Wednesday and Friday (P2950); via Manila.

From Caticlan (Boracay) to Manila
Asian Spirit, Pacific Airways and Seair fly daily (P2400).
See also Boracay: *Getting There & Away*.

From Kalibo to Manila
Air Philippines, Cebu Pacific and Philippine Airlines fly daily (P2900).

From Iloilo City to Manila
Air Philippines, Cebu Pacific and Philippine Airlines fly daily (P2780).

From Roxas to Manila
Cebu Pacific and Philippine Airlines fly daily (P2540).

From San Jose de Buenavista (Antique) to Manila
Asian Spirit flies Monday, Wednesday, Friday and Saturday (P2750).

Bus/Boat

From Caticlan (Boracay) to Manila
Daily at 8am and 3pm with an aircon or ordinary Philtranco bus. Travel time including the Caticlan-Roxas/Mindoro and Calapan-Batangas ferries: 14 hrs.
The trip is a bit cheaper under your own steam (see also the Manila chapter: *Getting Away from Luzon - On the Nautical Highway to Boracay*).

Boat

From Caticlan (Boracay) to Batangas
First, take the big outrigger leaving Caticlan at 9am for Santa Fe on Tablas Island in the Romblon archipelago (two hrs). Carry on from Santa Fe by jeepney to the Odiongan pier (two hrs).
On Wednesday, Friday and Sunday a MBRS Lines ship leaves at noon from Caticlan to Odiangan (three hrs).
A Shipshape Ferry or Montenegro Shipping Lines ship leaves from Odiongan daily except Wednesday for Batangas (see also the chapter Romblon: *Getting There and Away - To Luzon*).

From Caticlan (Boracay) to Manila
Wednesday, Friday and Sunday at noon with MBRS Lines (P560; 15 hrs); via Odiongan (Tablas Island)/Romblon.

From Dumaguit/Kalibo to Manila
Monday with MBRS Lines (P850; 17 hrs); via Cajidiocan/Sibuyan Island (Romblon).
Tuesday, Thursday and Sunday with WG & A (P1010; 14 hrs).
Saturday with Negros Navigation (P1010; 17 hrs).

From Estancia to Manila
Monday with Negros Navigation (P845; 23 hrs); via Roxas.
Thursday with Sulpicio Lines (P815; 18 hrs).

From Iloilo City to Manila
Monday, Wednesday, Thursday, Saturday and Sunday with Negros Navigation (P1460; 21 hrs); Saturday via Bacolod/Negros (24 hrs).

Tuesday, Wednesday and Sunday with WG & A (20 hrs).
Thursday and Sunday with Sulpicio Lines (P1090; 19 hrs); Thursday via Estancia (29 hrs).

From Lipata to Manila
Wednesday, Friday and Sunday with MBRS Lines (19 hrs); via Caticlan/ Boracay and Odiongan (Tablas Island)/ Romblon.

From Roxas to Manila
Monday with Negros Navigation (18 hrs; P1080).
Tuesday, Thursday and Sunday with WG & A (P1000; 19 hrs); via Dumaguit.

From San Jose de Buenavista (Antique) to Manila
Friday with MBRS Lines (P880; 16 hrs).

To Mindanao

Air

From Iloilo City to Davao
Air Philippines and Cebu Pacific fly daily; via Cebu City (P3645).

From Iloilo City to General Santos
Air Philippines has daily flights; via Cebu City (P3645).

Boat

From Iloilo City to Cagayan de Oro
Saturday with Negros Navigation (P1325; 14 hrs).

From Iloilo City to Cotabato
Saturday with WG & A (P1210; 29 hrs); via Zamboanga.
Sunday with Sulpicio Lines (P960; 31 hrs); via Zamboanga.

From Iloilo City to Davao
Sunday with WG & A (P1450; 36 hrs); via General Santos.

From Iloilo City to General Santos
Wednesday with Sulpicio Lines (P1130; 41 hrs); via Zamboanga.
Sunday with WG & A (P1450; 24 hrs).

From Iloilo City to Iligan
Monday with Negros Navigation (P1350; 13 hrs).

From Iloilo City to Zamboanga
Wednesday and Sunday with Sulpicio Lines (P705; 18 hrs).
Saturday with WG & A (P970; 16 hrs).

To Mindoro

Bus/Boat

From Caticlan (Boracay) to Puerto Galera
Via Batangas: see *To Luzon* above. Boats travel from Batangas to Puerto Galera (see chapter Manila: *Getting Away from Luzon - To Mindoro*).
Via Roxas: With the 8am ferry from Caticlan to Roxas, carrying on by bus to Calapan and from there by jeepney to Puerto Galera. Arrival in Puerto Galera around 6pm.

Boat

From Caticlan (Boracay) to Roxas
Daily at 8am and 3pm with a Starlite Ferry or Montnegro Shipping Lines car ferry (P210; 3½ or five hrs, depending on the boat).

From Buruanga to San Jose
Wednesday and Saturday at 7am with a big outrigger (eight hrs).

From Libertad to San Jose
Monday and Friday at 3am with a big outrigger (11 hrs). The boat calls in to Caluya Island and Semirara Island on the way.

From Lipata to San Jose
There are one or two departures per week, on Saturday at 6pm and possibly

on Sunday at 3am (24 hrs). They go via Semira Island and Caluya Island, where they lie up to 10 hrs at anchor. Lipata is a small place five km north of Culasi on the west coast of Panay.

To Negros

Boat

From Iloilo City to Bacolod
Daily with the fast ferries *Bullet Xpress* (8x), *Royal Express* (8x) and *Supercat* (4x; P290) from the river pier at Muelle Loney, taking one hr.
Daily except on Sunday at 5am and 12 noon with a Millennium Shipping Corporation car ferry (3½ hrs).

To Palawan

Air

From Iloilo City to Puerto Princesa
Seair plans to fly the route in the near future.

Boat

From Iloilo City to Cuyo and Puerto Princesa
Monday and Thursday with Milagrosa Shipping Lines to Cuyo (P220; 12 hrs) and Puerto Princesa (P500; 36 hrs, including an eight-hour stopover in Cuyo).

From San Jose de Buenavista (Antique) to Cuyo
Thursday with MBRS Lines (four hrs).

To Romblon

Boat

From Boracay to Looc/Tablas Island
Roughly twice a week with a big outrigger, depending on demand (two hrs).

From Caticlan (Boracay) to Santa Fe/ Tablas Island
Daily at 9am with a big outrigger (two hrs).

Warning
In bad weather the sea in the Tablas Strait between Mindoro and Panay is very rough and the crossing by outrigger - even larger ones - is not to be recommended. Small outriggers do sometimes make the crossing, but they would not appear to be suitable for this trip and, to cap it all, are often dangerously overloaded as well.

From Caticlan (Boracay) to Looc/ Tablas Island
Tuesday, Friday and Saturday with a big outrigger (two hrs).

From Caticlan (Boracay) to Odiongan/Tablas Island
Wednesday, Friday and Sunday with MBRS Lines (three hrs).

From Dumaguit/Kalibo to Cajidiocan/ Sibuyan Island
Monday with MBRS Lines (P350; three hrs).

Iloilo City

Apparently the name Iloilo stems from the expression 'Ilong-Ilong', which means 'like a nose'. This refers to the outline of the city centre, which lies between the mouths of the Iloilo and Batiano rivers. Iloilo City is not very different from other Philippine port towns of a similar size, although there are some lovely old houses in the side streets which noticeably improve the image of this capital of the eponymous province.
Six km west of the city is the suburb of Arevalo. Until a few years ago, it was well known as a centre for the production of woven fabrics from *jusi* and piña. Today only one loom still exists at the Sinamay Dealer on Osmeña St. You

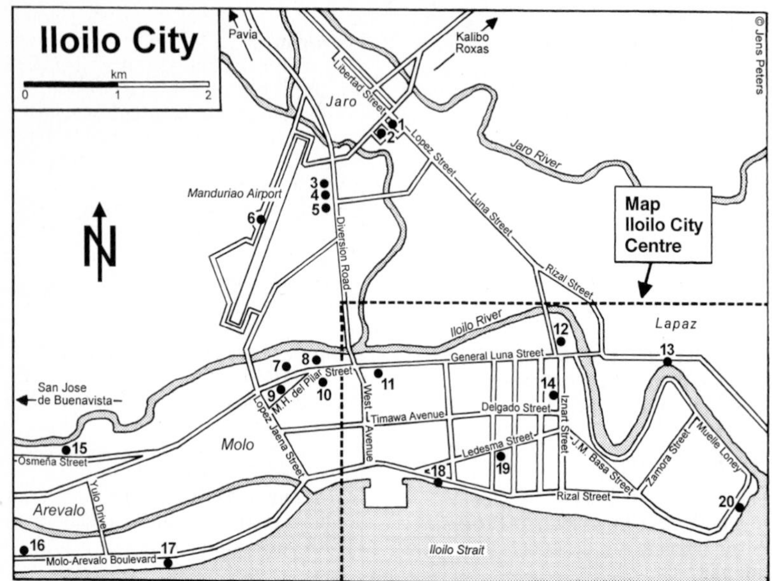

can buy clothes and fabrics here. It is in a beautiful old house partly furnished with valuable carved furniture - something that only wealthy Filipinos can afford. On the way to Arevalo, you pass through Molo, which has a 19th-century church constructed from blocks of coral.

Museum

The small 'Window on the Past' Museo Iloilo on Bonifacio Dr is worth a visit. They have on display old tools, jewelry, pottery, sculptures etc, but also modern objects produced by Ilonggo artists. On request, visitors are shown videos of the attractions of Panay and various Philippine festivals. Open Mon-Sat 9am-noon and 1-5pm. Admission P15; students P5.

Shopping

Diversion Rd, the extension of Infanta St (West Ave) north of the Iloilo River heading towards the airport, is home to the giant SM City shopping centre. The centre is filled with a variety of well-stocked shops, dozens of restaurants and a handful of excellent little cafés. Also north of the river, in Luna St near the Forbes Bridge, you cannot miss Gaisano City, their competition. Both companies run large branches in the city centre (SM Shoemart and Gaisano Iloilo) but have to share the market there with Atrium, Marymart Mall and Robinsons Place.

Places to Stay - bottom end

Family Pension House, General Luna St, Tel 3350070. SR/fan/bath P250, DR/fan/bath P350, SR/DR/ac/bath P675 to P900. Popular inexpensive accommodation with reasonable rooms.

Madia-as Hotel, Aldeguer St, Tel 3372756-59. SR/fan/bath P290, SR/ac/bath P395, DR/ac/bath P485. Decidedly better than the modest entrance stuck in a hallway off Aldeguer St would lead

Getting There & Away
6 Airport Terminal
7 Seventy Six Bus Terminal
13 Car ferries to Bacolod/Negros & Guimaras
18 Tanza Bus Terminal
20 Port of Iloilo Passenger Terminal

Places to Stay
2 Iloilo City Inn
8 Hotel Del Rio
10 La Fiesta Hotel
11 Barceló Sarabia Manor Hotel
14 Amigo Hotel
17 Villa Rosa by the Sea

Places to Eat & Entertainment
2 Bavaria Restaurant
3 Barracks
4 O'Shanghai Restaurant
16 Tatoy's Manokan & Seafood

Miscellaneous
1 Jaro Cathedral
5 SM City
9 Molo Church
12 Tourist Office
15 Sinamay Dealer
19 Robinsons Place

you to expect. Worth the money charged, the rooms are clean and fairly comfortable.

Iloilo City Inn, 113 Seminario St, Jaro, Tel 3206278, @. SR/DR/ac/bath from P540/600. Excellent value for the money. Weekly and monthly rates are available. Comfortable rooms with TV. Cosy accommodation in the Jaro (pronounced Haro) area of town. Well located for the airport. Restaurant.

Chito's Hotel, De Leon St near the corner with Jalandoni St, Tel 3376135, Fax 3381186, @. SR/ac/bath P500, DR/ac/bath P550 and P650. Good, quiet rooms with TV, the more expensive ones also have a refrigerator. Restaurant, small garden with swimming pool, airport service. Located near the Tanza Bus Terminal.

Villa Rosa by the Sea, Calaparan, Tel 3376953. SR/DR/ac/bath P770, with TV. A quiet beach hotel with reasonable rooms. Restaurant, swimming pool. The beach is not particularly inviting here. Located about six km west of Iloilo City. A taxi here from the airport should cost about P100.

Fine Rock Hotel, Jalandoni St, Tel 3369075, Fax 3369080, @. SR/DR/ac/bath P400/540 (with TV), suites P650 (with refrigerator). A good hotel with small, though windowless rooms. Good value. Restaurant.

The Castle Hotel, Bonifacio Dr, Tel & Fax 3381021. SR/ac/bath P500, DR/ac/bath P550 and P650. With TV. Small rooms in an older, refurbished building with an impressive façade. Restaurant.

Places to Stay - middle

Iloilo Midtown Hotel, Yulo St, Tel 3368888, Fax 3380888, @. SR/ac/bath P730, DR/ac/bath P850 to P1100, suite P1830. Small, but tidy rooms with TV. Good restaurant.

Harbor Town Hotel, JM Basa St corner Aldeguer St, Tel 3372384, Fax 3361438, @. SR/ac/bath P750 and P850, DR/ac/bath P850 and P950, suite P1350. Small, pleasantly furnished rooms with TV, the suites also have a refrigerator. The hotel is located at a busy road intersection.

The Residence Hotel, General Luna St, Tel 3381091, Fax 3372454. SR/ac/bath P750 to P1560, DR/ac/bath P980 to P1800. With TV. Attractive rooms overlooking the Iloilo River. Beautiful restaurant on the river. Coffee shop, car hire.

La Fiesta Hotel, MH del Pilar St, Tel 3380044, Fax 3379508, @. SR/DR/ac/bath P880 to P2200. Immaculate rooms with TV, the more expensive ones also

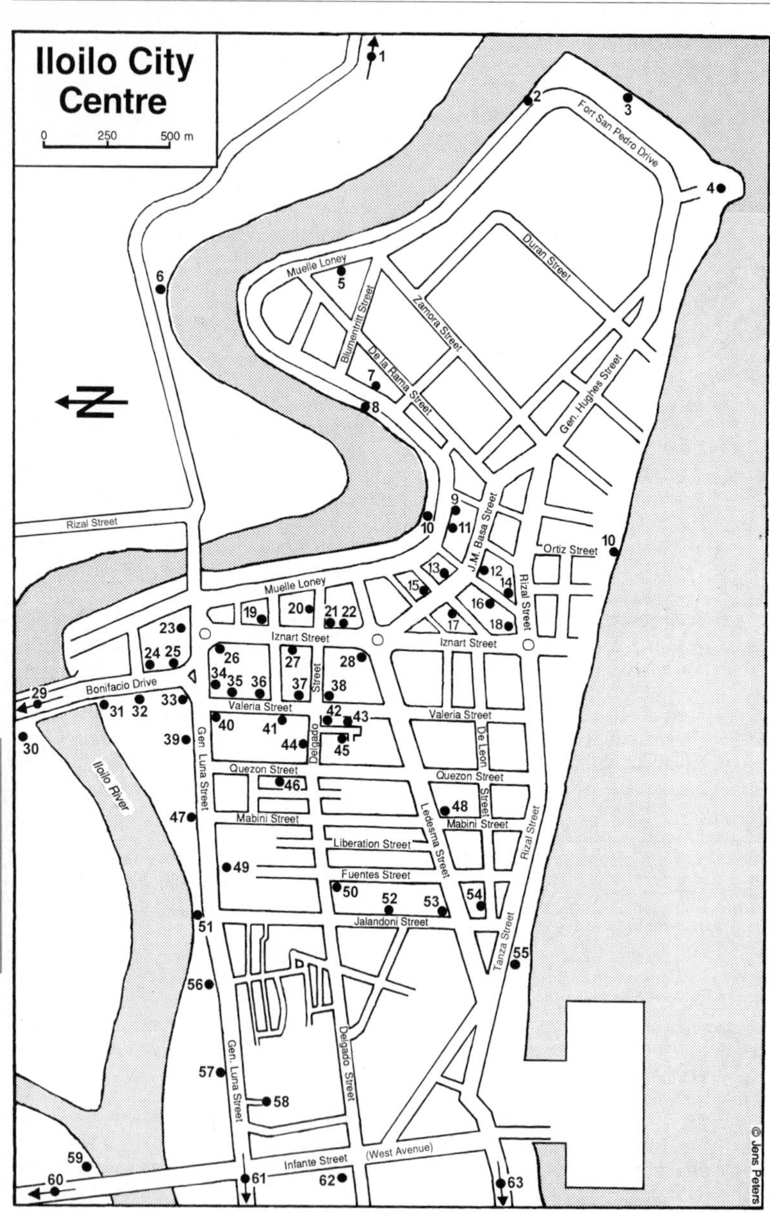
Iloilo City Centre
0
250
500 m
Fort San Pedro Drive
Duran Street
Muelle Loney
Blumentritt Street
Zamora Street
De la Rama Street
Gen. Hughes Street
Rizal Street
J.M. Basa Street
Ortiz Street
Iznart Street
Bonifacio Drive
Valeria Street
Delgado Street
Quezon Street
De Leon Street
Gen Luna Street
Iloilo River
Mabini Street
Liberation Street
Ledesma Street
Fuentes Street
Jalandoni Street
Tanza Street
Infante Street
(West Avenue)
© Jens Peters

Getting There & Away

1 International Port (600m)
2 Boats to Buenavista
3 Port of Iloilo Passenger Terminal
5 Cokaliong Shipping Lines
6 Car ferries to Bacolod/Negros & Guimaras
7 Negros Navigation
Supercat
8 Ships to Bacolod/Negros
10 Boats to Jordan (2 x)
11 Aleson Shipping Lines
Bullet Xpress
Royal Express
21 WG & A
34 Atrium (Airline & Shipping Tickets)
41 Jeepneys to Pavia
43 Air Philippines
Negros Navigation
45 Cebu Pacific
55 Tanza Bus Terminal
60 Airport (3 km)
61 Seventy Six Bus Terminal (400m)

Places to Stay

15 Harbor Town Hotel
17 Madia-as Hotel
20 Iloilo Midtown Hotel
27 Amigo Hotel
29 Iloilo City Inn (2.5 km)
31 The Original River Queen Hotel
32 Castle Hotel
34 Days Hotel
47 Family Pension House
50 Four Season Hotel
51 Residence Hotel
52 Fine Rock Hotel
53 Centennial Plaza Hotel
54 Chito's Penn Hotel
58 Barceló Sarabia Manor Hotel
61 Hotel Del Rio (200m)
La Fiesta Hotel (250m)
63 Villa Rosa by the Sea (6 km)

Places to Eat & Entertainment

4 Fort San Pedro Drive Inn
12 S'Table Restaurant & Snack Bar
13 Kong Kee Restautrant
20 The Summer House Restaurant
22 Chowking
Dunkin' Donuts
26 Ted's Oldtimer Lapaz Batchoy
27 Tivoli Disco
28 Jollibee
29 Bavaria Restaurant (2.5 km)
34 Atrium (McDonald's etc)
35 Surio Thai Restaurant
37 Ted's Oldtimer Lapaz Batchoy
42 La Veranda de Fatima Restaurant
McDonald's
44 Greenwich
Jollibee
Shakey's Pizza
45 Lola Maria Restaurant
51 Waterfront Grill & Restaurant
56 Nena's Manokan & Seafood Restaurant
57 Ocean City Seafood Restaurant
58 Base Disco
59 Zuba Restaurant
60 Barracks (1.5 km)
O'Shanghai Restaurant (1.3 km)
63 Tatoy's Manokan & Seafood (6 km)

Miscellaneous

9 Immigration Office
Post Office
13 Metrobank
14 Gaisano Iloilo
16 Metrobank
18 Central Market
19 Bank of the Philippine Islands
21 Equitable PCI Bank
23 Provincial Capitol
24 Tourist Office
25 Museum (Museo Iloilo)
27 Amigo Plaza Shopping Center
30 Gaisano City

↗

33 Tibiano Bakery	42 Mercury Drug
34 Atrium	46 Equitable PCI Bank
Iloilo Supermart	48 Robinsons Place
36 Equitable PCI Bank	49 Universidad de San Agustin
38 Marymart Mall	60 SM City (1 km)
39 St Paul's Hospital	61 Molo Church (1 km)
40 Philippine National Bank (PNB)	62 Iloilo Doctor's Hospital
41 SM	

have a refrigerator. A good hotel with a traditional atmosphere. Restaurant.

Four Season Hotel, Delgado St corner Fuentes St, Tel 3361070, Fax 5093888, @. SR/ac/bath P780 and P880, DR/ac/bath P880 and P980, suites P1400. Immaculate rooms with TV, the more expensive ones also have a refrigerator. Restaurant.

Centennial Plaza Hotel, Jalandoni St corner Ledesma St, Tel 3372277, Fax 3364444, @. SR/ac/bath P900, DR/ac/bath P1050, suite P1650. Good, pleasantly furnished rooms with refrigerator and TV. Restaurant. Located near the Tanza Bus Terminal.

Places to Stay - top end

Hotel del Rio, MH del Pilar St, Tel 3351171, Fax 3370736, @. SR/ac/bath P1050, and P1320, DR/ac/bath P1210 to P1540, suites P1760 to P3850. A charming, though ageing, hotel with tidy rooms of varying quality. All have TV, the suites also have a refrigerator. Friendly service. Restaurant, swimming pool. Beautifully located on the Iloilo River, a short way from the city centre.

Amigo Hotel, Iznart St, Tel 3350908, Fax 3350610, @. SR/DR/ac/bath P1300 to P1800, suites P1900 and P2000. Including breakfast. The accommodation is comfortable and roomy. All rooms have TV, the more expensive ones and the suites also have a refrigerator. Restaurant, swimming pool. Special offer: If you check in after 6pm, you'll only pay P850 for a standard room (without breakfast).

Barceló Sarabia Manor Hotel, General Luna St, Tel 3351021, Fax 3379127, @. SR/ac/bath P2650, DR/ac/bath P3140, suites P3900 to P9360. A well-run establishment with pleasantly furnished rooms with TV. The more expensive rooms and the suites also have a refrigerator. Restaurant, disco, swimming pool.

Days Hotel, Atrium (4th floor), General Luna St, Tel 3373297, Fax 3368000, @. SR/DR/ac/bath P2650 and P3200, suites P4420 to P7300. Breakfast included. Very comfortable rooms with refrigerator and TV, the suites also have a small kitchen and jacuzzi. Restaurant.

Places to Eat

The most popular, and probably the best, native restaurant is called ***Tatoy's Manokan & Seafood***, at Villa Beach on the western edge of town, about eight km from the city centre. Especially if it's a relaxed atmosphere you're looking for, the short drive there by jeepney or taxi will be well worth the effort. Hundreds of Filipinos make the trek there every day, many of them only because of the tasty chicken, which gave Tatoy's its reputation in the first place. But the other items on the menu are also excellent. First you go to the buffet and pick out your food, then you wash your hands and wait only a few minutes until the waitress serves the tasty morsels. Here the food is eaten

with the fingers, a struggle the locals particularly enjoy watching from the neighbouring tables.
However, there are also some cosy little rustic restaurants to be found nearer the city centre, which also serve Filipino dishes. These include ***Nena's Manokan & Seafood Restaurant,*** where the food is eaten with the fingers too (open until 6am), and the ***Ocean City Seafood Restaurant***, both in General Luna St. If the weather's good, the open-air restaurant ***Fort San Pedro Drive Inn*** is popular for beer and barbecues in the evening.
It's a real pleasure to sit outside on the river terrace of the ***Waterfront Grill & Restaurant*** belonging to The Residence Hotel in General Luna St, and in the ***Zuba Restaurant***, which stands in the river on stilts a few metres off Division Road near the river bridge.
Iloilo City has several batchoy restaurants, including ***Ted's Oldtimer Lapaz Batchoy*** in Iznart St and Valeria St. (Batchoy is a speciality of the western Visayas consisting of beef, pork and liver in a noodle soup.)
Around the area of the Marymart Mall there are a few pleasant restaurants serving Filipino food, including the ***Lola Maria Restaurant*** (a beautiful corner building), and ***La Taverna de Fatima*** with its inexpensive budget meals.
You can get good Chinese meals in ***The Summer House*** (well recommended) in the Iloilo Midtown Hotel, Yulo St, and the ***Kong Kee Restaurant*** in JM Basa St, as well as in the ***O'Shanghai Restaurant*** in Diversion Road between SM City and Barracks. Thai food fans are recommended to pay a visit to the excellent ***Surio Thai Restaurant*** in Valeria St. Japanese specialities are available in the ***Tempura Restaurant*** in the Amigo Hotel (buffet on Friday and Saturday evenings).
There's a warm welcome at ***Bavaria*** in Seminario St in the Jaro part of town, where you'll find Bavarian and European cooking as well as wheat beer (Weissbier). It's developed into a popular place for ex-pats. Not surprisingly, they serve Italian food in the ***Al dente Ristorante Italiano*** in the Barceló Sarabia Manor Hotel.
If you're interested in trying the Viennese specialities of Sachertorte and Wiener Schnitzel, then the place to go is the ***Vienna Kaffeehaus*** in Robinsons Place in Ledesma St corner Mabini St.
The Atrium in General Luna St houses several good restaurants, eg ***Kusina Ni Neneng*** (Filipino food), ***Jungle*** (bar and grill), ***Champs*** (pizza and pasta) and ***Salads Et Cetera***. You will also find ***McDonald's*** and ***Chowking*** here.
If you have a sweet tooth, don't miss the ***S'Table Restaurant & Snack Bar*** in JM Basa St, which probably has the best selection of cakes in Iloilo. ***Dunkin' Donuts*** is open 24 hours in Iznart St, and ***Shakey's***, ***Greenwich*** and ***Jollibee*** have branches in Delgado St.

Entertainment

Iloilo City has a wider selection of good quality entertainment than you might expect. There is a good number of music bars and pubs with live music, whose popularity varies wildly according to which bands are appearing. At the moment the undoubted favourite is ***Barracks*** in Diversion Rd, which has been styled after a military camp.
The most popular discos in Iloilo City are ***Tivoli*** in the Amigo Hotel and the ***Base Disco*** in the Barceló Sarabia Manor Hotel.

Miscellaneous

Festivals: Every year on the fourth weekend in January (one week after the Ati-Atihan Festival in Kalibo), the people of Iloilo City celebrate the Dinagyang Festival, the city's biggest, with lots of noise and brightly coloured costumes. The Jaro area of town also

has the Feast of Our Lady of Candles on 2 February.
The Paraw Regatta, a race between fast outrigger sail boats in the Iloilo Strait between Iloilo City and Guimaras Island, is held on the second Sunday in February or March.
In Pavia, a little north of Iloilo City, water buffalo races (Carabao Carroza) take place each year on 3 May from 8 am. To get there, take a jeepney from the SM Shoemart in Valeria St.
Immigration Office, Muelle Loney. Open Mon-Fri 8am-noon and 1-5pm.
Medical Services: There are several good hospitals in Iloilo City, two of the best being the Iloilo Doctor's Hospital, Infante St, Tel 3377702, and St Paul's Hospital, General Luna St, Tel 3372741.
Money: You can change cash at reasonable rates the moneychanger in the Atrium in General Luna St. The Philippine National Bank, General Luna St corner Valeria St, and the branches of the Equitable PCI Bank in Quezon St and Iznart St, have ATMs.
Online: There are lots of Internet Cafés scattered around the town, especially in shopping centres.
Population: 350,000.
Post & Telephone: Post Office, Muelle Loney.
Post code: 5000. Area code: 033.
Tourist Office, Bonifacio Dr, Tel 3375411, Fax 3350245, @. Open Mon-Fri 8am-5pm.

Getting There & Away

By Air: It's about seven km from the Manduriao Airport to the centre of town. If you take a taxi, it should cost about P100. Private cars cost about half.
There are ticket counters in the Atrium, General Luna St, for Air Philippines, Cebu Pacific and Philippine Airlines.
Air Philippines, Manduriao Airport, Tel 3208048.
- Robinsons Place, Mabini Street, Tel. 3350593.
- Valeria St, Tel 3351348.
Destinations: Cebu City, Davao (via Cebu), General Santo (via Cebu), Manila.
Cebu Pacific, Marymart Mall, Delgado St, Tel 5087144, 3361846.
- Airport Office: Tel 3206889.
Destinations: Cebu City, Davao (via Cebu), Manila.
Philippine Airlines, Iloilo Airport, Tel. 3203131.
Destinations: Cebu City, Manila.

By Bus: Buses heading north leave from the Tanza Bus Terminal in Tanza St near the corner of Ledesma St; buses heading west leave from the Seventy Six Bus Terminal in MH Pilar St.
In addition to the bus routes mentioned below, minibuses run between Iloilo City and various destinations on Panay. They leave fairly frequently, are fast, and most of them are even non-stop. Examples are Iloilo City to Caticlan (five hrs), Kalibo (3½ hrs), Estancia (two hrs), Roxas (three hrs), San Jose de Buenavista (1½ hrs). Buses for Aklan (Caticlan, Kalibo) leave from the Tanza Bus Terminal, Tanza St; for north-east Panay (Estancia, Roxas) across the road from Gaisano City; for Antique (San Jose de Buenavista) from the Seventy Six Bus Terminal in Pilar St.

By Boat: Boats belonging to Negros Navigation, Sulpicio Lines, Trans-Asia Shipping Lines and WG & A leave from the Port of Iloilo Passenger Terminal on Fort San Pedro Dr.
Boats belonging to Aleson Shipping Lines, Cokaliong Shipping Lines, Milagrosa Shipping Lines, fast ferries to Bacolod and ferries to Guimaras use the river wharf Muelle Loney (various places).
FF Cruz Shipping car ferries (from and to Jordan/Guimaras) and Millennium

Shipping Corporation car ferries (from and to Bacolod/Negros) berth at the north river wharf on Rizal St (on the way to the International Port) in the district of Lapaz.

Tickets: At the Port of Iloilo Passenger Terminal, Fort San Pedro Dr, there are ticket counters for Negros Navigation, Sulpicio Lines, Trans-Asia Shipping Lines and WG & A.
There are ticket counters in the Atrium, General Luna St, for Negros Navigation, Supercat, Trans-Asia Shipping Lines and WG & A, and in Robinsons Place, Ledesma St corner Mabini St for Milagrosa Shipping Lines. There are also ticket sales outlets in the SM City and Gaisano City shopping centres and elsewhere.
Aleson Shipping Lines, Muelle Loney, Tel 3373108-09.
Destination: Bacolod/Negros.
Bullet Xpress, Muelle Loney, Tel 3380618.
Destination: Bacolod/Negros.
Cokaliong Shipping Lines, Muelle Loney, Tel 3361122, 3363322.
Destination: Cebu.
FF Cruz Shipping, Lapaz, Tel 3371187, 3369329.
Destination: Guimaras.
Milagrosa Shipping Lines, Jarfel Building, Lapaz, Tel 3378627, 3350955.
Destination: Palawan (Cuyo, Puerto Princesa).
Millennium Shipping Corporation, no office in Iloilo City, Cellphone 0920-2180004 (ask for Kurt),
Bacolod Office, Tel. (034) 4339360.
Destination: Bacolod/Negros.
Negros Navigation, Muelle Loney, Tel 3370472.
- Atrium, General Luna St, Tel 3368910, 3350095.
Destinations: Manila, Mindanao.
Royal Express, Muelle Loney, Tel 3361802.
Destination: Bacolod/Negros.
Sulpicio Lines, Rizal St, Lapaz, Tel 3372202, 3379051.
Destinations: Manila, Mindanao.
Supercat Fast Ferry Corporation, Muelle Loney, Tel 3361316, 5099675.
Destination: Bacolod/Negros.
Trans-Asia Shipping Lines, Fort San Pedro Dr, Tel 3372247.
Destination: Cebu.
WG & A, Rizal St, Lapuz, Tel 3372567.
- Atrium, General Luna St, Tel 3374353.
- Fort San Pedro Dr, Tel 3362110.
Destinations: Manila, Mindanao.

Kalibo - Caticlan - Boracay
Bus: Ceres Liner and GM's Liner buses leave from the Tanza Bus Terminal, travelling from Iloilo City to Kalibo and Caticlan. GM's Liner aircon buses leave at 7.30, 9 and 11.30am for Caticlan via Kalibo, at 2.30pm only going as far as Kalibo. Ceres Liner aircon buses leave at 5, 7 and 10.30am and 12 noon for Caticlan, and from 3am to 3pm every half hour for Kalibo. The trip takes four hrs to Kalibo, and six hrs to Caticlan. The buses are sometimes super-punctual, so it's better to get there early.
Tip: You will hardly find a regular boat leaving Caticlan for Boracay after 5pm.

South Coast

Although there are several beach resorts with cottages along the south coast between Arevalo and San Joaquin, the beaches are not up to much. A good base for short trips to other coastal places or the Nadsadan Falls near Igbaras is the *Coco Grove Beach Resort* at Tigbauan. It has cottages for P500 (fan) and P800 (aircon).

Getting There & Away

Iloilo City - South Coast - San Jose de Buenavista
Bus: Several buses belonging to the Seventy Six company and Ceres Liner

run daily from Iloilo City to San Jose de Buenavista, leaving from MH del Pilar St in the Molo district of town and the Tanza bus terminal respectively (2½ hrs), as do some minibuses (L300 vans). Although buses travel along the south coast, they don't go via Anini-y and Dao.

Guimbal

'Home of the sweetest mangoes in Iloilo province', Guimbal has a sandstone church dating back to the time of the Spaniards. It also has three watchtowers built in the 16th century, from which smoke signals used to be sent to warn against pirates.

Miagao

Miagao, 40 km west of Iloilo City, has a mighty church resembling a fortress that dates back to 1787. Although it was declared part of the world cultural heritage by UNESCO, its main attractions are the unusual reliefs on the façade mixing European elements (St Christopher) and Philippine plants (coconut palms and papaya trees).

San Joaquin

The most 'military' church in the Philippines is in San Joaquin. The façade, built of blocks of coral, shows the battle of the Spanish against the Moors in Tetuan, Morocco, in 1859. Every second Saturday in January water buffalo fights are held in San Joaquin.

Places to Stay

San Bernardino Mountain Resort, New Gumaran, Cellphone 0916-4555687. SR/DR/fan/bath P500. Comfortable resort, located at a fair altitude (pleasant temperature) with four friendly rooms. Restaurant with a beautiful view. Garden. Swimming pool.

Talisayan Beach Resort. Cottage/fan/bath P800, Cottage/ac/bath P1000. Although basic, this is a pleasant resort; the staff can arrange meals for you.

Anini-y & Nogas Island

Anini-y has a massive old church of white coral built by Augustinian monks during the Spanish colonial period. Private overnight accommodation is available with Mrs Magdalena Cazenas.
From Anini-y you can go to Nogas Island, which has white beaches and excellent diving areas. You can get a paddle banca to take you across for about P50.

Getting There & Away

Iloilo City
Bus: There is a daily bus through Anini-y that goes as far as Dao, leaving from the corner of Fuentes and De Leon Sts in Iloilo City at 7am. There may also be others leaving at 11am and noon (three hrs). The return bus leaves Anini-y at 12.30pm; there are sometimes others at 4.30 and 6.30am.

San Joaquin
Jeepney: A daily jeepney goes from San Joaquin to Anini-y at 10am, taking one hour and possibly going on to Dao. The return jeepney from Anini-y leaves at 1pm.

West Coast

San Jose de Buenavista

San Jose de Buenavista is the capital of Antique Province, so Filipinos know the town not by its official name but as San Jose Antique.

Places to Stay

Susana Guest House, Tobias Fornier St. SR/DR/fan P100/200. Basic accommodation. Restaurant.

Barrio House Resort & Training Center, Madrangca, Tel 5407024. Cottage/fan/bath P500, cottage/ac/bath P750. Reasonable accommodation about two km outside of town.
Adelaide Pension, Bantayan St, Tel 5407160. SR/DR/ac/bath P650/800 to P1000 P, including breakfast. Centrally located accommodation with really good rooms, all with TV. Restaurant.
Binirayan Cottages, Santillan, Binirayan, Tel 5409004, @. SR/DR/ac/bath P700/1000 P, including breakfast. Two attractive cottages, with two friendly rooms each.

Places to Eat

The handful of restaurants in the city close very early in the evening. In Tobias Fornier St, ***Regina's Restaurant & Ice Cream House*** is open till about 9pm, serving inexpensive Chinese and Philippine food. After that, you may be lucky to find ***Casa Linda Pizza House & Restaurant*** still open, also in Tobias Fornier St.

Miscellaneous

Festival: Binirayan Festival from 28 to 30 December.
Population: 30,000.
Post & Telephone: Post code: 5700. Area code: 036.
Tourist Office, Provincial Capitol, Tel 5409765. Open Mon-Fri 8am-5pm.

Getting There & Away

By Air: San Jose Airport is located about four km north of the city; P20 with a tricyle.
Asian Spirit, San Joseph Building, Town Plaza, Tel 5408742.
Destination: Manila.

By Boat: The following shipping line is represented in San Jose:
MBRS Lines, Trade Town Building 3, Cellphone 0919-2864712.
Destinations: Cuyo (Palawan), Manila.

Culasi - Pandan - Libertad
Bus/Jeepney: There are few jeepneys and Ceres Liner buses from San Jose to Culasi (three hrs), Pandan (five hrs) and Libertad (six hrs). Some jeepneys only go as far as Culasi. From Pandan you can get connections to Kalibo, and from Libertad to Malay and Caticlan.

Caticlan - Kalibo
Bus: There is a chance that the two companies BL Transit and RM Bus line will have buses leaving early in the morning from San Jose to Kalibo, via Caticlan.

Iloilo City
Bus: Not only big buses belonging to the companies Ceres Liner and Seventy-Six, but also minibuses (L300 vans), make the trip from San Jose to Iloilo City (2½ hrs).

Culasi

You may like to break the trip along the west coast of Panay at Culasi and spend a few days on Mararison Island. Although there is no regular boat service there, one or two crossings a day are possible. A Special Ride costs around P200 and takes 30 min.
A boat makes the trip from Lipata, about five km north of Culasi, once or twice a week to San Jose, Mindoro, via the Semirara Islands. A tricycle takes 10 min and costs P5 per person.

Places to Stay

Balestramon Lodging House. SR/DR/fan P100/200. Basic accommodation with a restaurant.
Casa Juancho Tourist Inn (Xavier Hotel), Tel. 2888012. SR/DR/ac/bath P500 and P600. Immaculate rooms.

On Mararison Island there is only private accommodation, at about P250 per night, including three meals.

Getting There & Away

Bus: From Culasi to San Jose the last bus of this daily service might leave as early as 1.30pm.

The North-East

Concepcion, San Dionisio & Pan de Azucar Island

Concepcion and San Dionisio are small places on the east coast of Panay with quite big markets. There is a string of beautiful islands lying offshore which you can reach quickly by outrigger.
The most conspicuous island is Pan de Azucar - its 573m high 'sugar loaf' can be seen from a long way off. For the time being, it will continue only to attract visitors who are prepared to put up with its basic amenities.
Little Agho Island, a bit farther southeast, is also among the more attractive of the islands. However, it is privately owned by the mayor of Concepcion and visitors must first obtain a permit from him. The caretaker will not allow anyone on the island without this permit.

Places to Stay

SBS Iyang Beach Resort, Concepcion. Cottage/fan/bath P400 and P600. It also has a restaurant, and the owners, Sandy and Betty Salcedo, will organise trips to offshore islands on request (for P2500 a day). The beach at the resort is not the most attractive.
You can only stay in private houses in San Dionisio, for example with the Jun Magsongsong family on JM Basa St; it's about P150 per person.
On Pan de Azucar Island you also have to depend on private hospitality, but as the locals are friendly, this should not be too difficult. You could ask for Anidlina de Julian who is glad to put up travellers (about P100 per person). She doesn't mind preparing the fish you bought from the fishermen at the beach for your meal. If you turn up unannounced, take provisions with you, including drinking water. There's only room for two people, unless you are willing to sleep in the open.

Getting There & Away

Iloilo City

Bus: From Iloilo City to Concepcion, there are a few Ceres Liner buses (2½ hrs).
There is no direct bus from Iloilo City to San Dionisio. The best way to get there is by Ceres Liner bus from the Tanza Bus Terminal to Estancia. They leave every hour from 4am to 4pm. To go to San Dionisio, get off no later than the turnoff in Deveria and wait for a jeepney coming from the larger town of Sara. As an alternative, you can get off at Sara, which is more pleasant than Deveria.

Pan de Azucar Island

Boat: Outriggers leave from Dionisio to Pan de Azucar Island between 9 and 11am (P20; 45 min). Apparently the boats leave on Thursday from Concepcion, where there is a market on that day. A Special Ride should cost around P500.

Estancia

This unassuming little town serves mainly as a jumping-off point for the offshore islands. Boats cross from here to Sicogon Island, the Gigante Islands and other destinations.

Places to Stay

Fuentes Lodging House, Inventor St, Tel 3970264. SR/DR/fan/bath P120/240. Basic, fairly good accommodation.
Pa-on Beach Resort, Pa-on, Tel 3970444. SR/fan/bath P260, DR/fan/

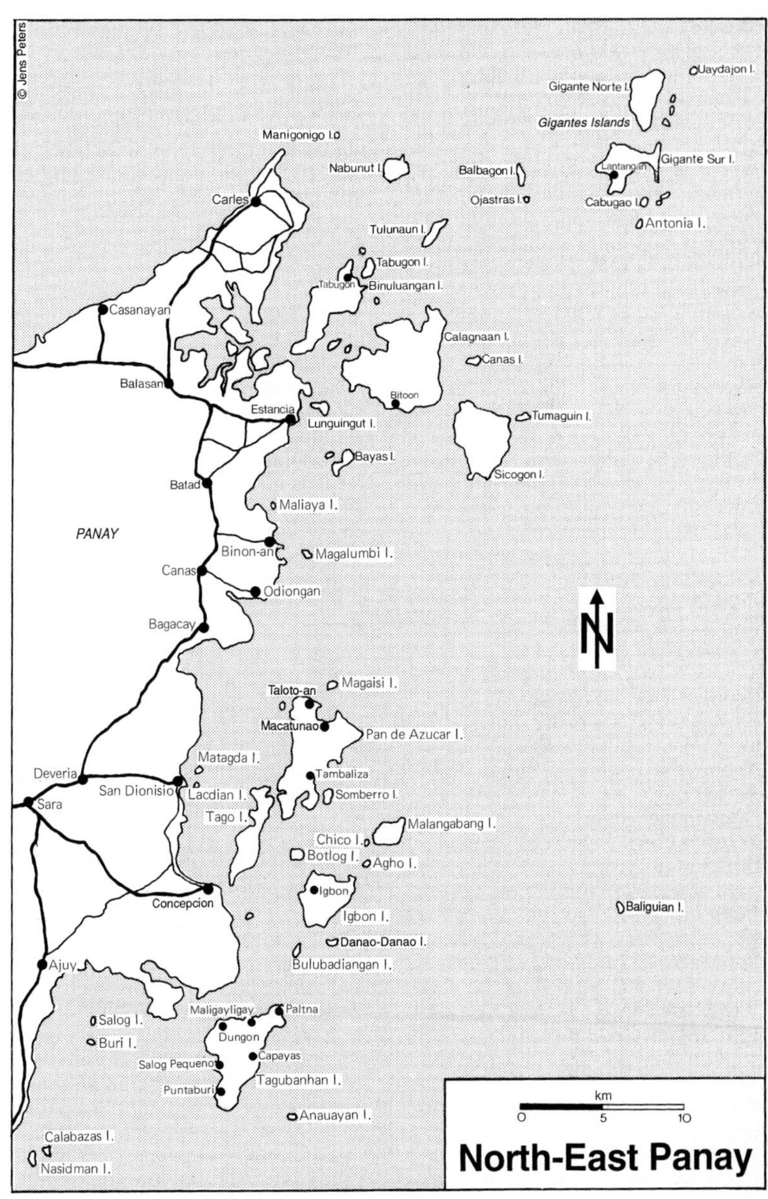
© Jens Peters
Uaydajon I.
Gigante Norte I.
Gigantes Islands
Manigonigo I.
Nabunut I.
Balbagon I.
Lantangan
Gigante Sur I.
Carles
Ojastras I.
Cabugao I.
Antonia I.
Tulunaun I.
Tabugon I.
Tabugon
Binuluangan I.
Casanayan
Calagnaan I.
Canas I.
Balasan
Bitoon
Estancia
Lunguingut I.
Tumaguin I.
Bayas I.
Sicogon I.
Batad
Maliaya I.
PANAY
Binon-an
Magalumbi I.
Canas
Odiongan
Bagacay
N
Taloto-an
Magaisi I.
Macatunao
Pan de Azucar I.
Matagda I.
Deveria
Tambaliza
San Dionisio
Lacdian I.
Sara
Somberro I.
Tago I.
Malangabang I.
Chico I.
Botlog I.
Agho I.
Igbon
Concepcion
Igbon I.
Baliguian I.
Danao-Danao I.
Ajuy
Bulubadiangan I.
Maligayligay
Paltna
Salog I.
Dungon
Buri I.
Capayas
Salog Pequeno
Tagubanhan I.
Puntaburi
km
0
5
10
Anauayan I.
Calabazas I.
Nasidman I.
North-East Panay

bath P330, SR/ac/bath P450 and P550, DR/ac/bath P800 (with TV). Well-kept grounds with clean rooms and a pleasant atmosphere. Restaurant. Located about two km outside of Estancia (P4 by tricycle).
Vila Lily Beach Resort, Pa-on, Tel 3970980. SR/DR/fan/bath P340, SR/DR/ac/bath P650, cottage/ac/bath P750. This is a fairly large establishment on a hill with a beautiful view. Restaurant. Located next to the Pa-on Beach Resort. Reservations in Iloilo City: Tel (033) 3296232, 3294876.

Places to Eat
Estancia's few restaurants close very early. ***Kate's Pizza & Ice Cream House*** in Reyes St serves good, inexpensive food. The ***Friends Restaurant*** across from the Ceres Liner Bus Terminal is good and fairly inexpensive.

Miscellaneous
Population: 20,000.
Post & Telephone: Post code: 5017. Area code: 033.

Getting There & Away
By Boat: The following shipping lines have a presence in Estancia.
Negros Navigation, E Reyes St, Tel 3971113.
Destination: Manila.
Sulpicio Lines, Pier, Tel 3970460.
Destination: Manila.

Iloilo City
Bus: Ceres Liner buses leave daily from Iloilo City to Estancia every hour between 4am and 4pm from the Tanza Bus Terminal (5½ hrs). Aircon minibuses only need 2½ hrs and charge P120.

Roxas
Bus/Jeepney: From Roxas to Estancia, there are several jeepneys or minibuses every morning. You may have to change at President Roxas. Apparently two Ceres Liner buses leave between 7.30 and 9am (three hrs).

Sicogon Island
On the idyllic island of Sicogon, on the magnificent white sand Bantill Beach, stand the buildings of the Sicogon Island Club, one of the first beach resort hotels in the Philippines to achieve international recognition. It's hard to believe it, but this luxurious establishment with its 120 cottages, swimming pool, tennis court etc, has been closed for quite some time. Amongst many factors contributing to its demise, perhaps its peculiar policy of trying to minimise all contact between locals and tourists had a lot to do with it. (Sicogon's 3000 inhabitants were strictly forbidden to let rooms to tourists. They were also not allowed to sell anything either, so the island's only restaurant was the one belonging to the resort. To cap it all, locals were not even allowed to bring strangers to the island unless they were guests of the resort.) Any touristic venture that excludes the locals has to end up creating social tensions, not the kind of background considerate holidaymakers are looking for. Apparently, all of this belongs to the past now on Sicogon Island.

Gigantes Islands
The Gigantes Islands belong to Iloilo Province and are located between northeast Panay and Masbate. Apart from Balbagon Island none of the 18 islands and islets have any infrastructure for tourism.
Gigante Norte and Gigante Sur are both very rugged. Massive rocks, commonly known as the 'enchanted rocks', contain lots of caves which have given rise to many mysterious tales. It is rumoured that the complex system of tunnels between the caves used to serve as a hide-

out for pirates. There may be something to this. And perhaps this also explains the unusually large, three-metre long coffins from the 15th century discovered by archaeologists just after WWII. Made for giants, or gigantic loads perhaps?

Of the 10 caves on Gigante Sur, only three have been explored. Most islanders are too scared and superstitious to enter them and many are just not interested. Turtle Cave, also called Pawikan, has a huge antechamber where white monkeys swing on roots hanging down from the top of the opening. Tiniphagan and Elephant caves have been even less explored than Turtle Cave and they may have connecting tunnels to other caves. A good departure point for visiting the caves is Barrio Lantangan. It's recommended that you hire a guide and take stout shoes, torches, candles and drinking water. There is a natural swimming pool near the caves, also called the Tank. In Lantangan itself in 1997, locals came across the remains of a cemetery from pre-Spanish times. Burrowing in their gardens they uncovered grave urns, little pots, and human bones. Not exactly great treasures, but valuable enough to awaken the interest of antique dealers.

On Gigante Norte you can easily get to Langub Cave from the barrio Piagao. A beautiful beach with crystal clear water stretches all along the barrio.

Just south of the two Gigante Islands are the small islands of Cabugao Norte and Cabugao Sur. Cabugao Norte has a few huts, a small cave and a pretty good swimming beach. The settlement on Cabugao Sur is slightly larger and there also is a good swimming beach with very fine sand.

Places to Stay

Apart from Balbagon Island which has a resort, you will have to find your own accommodation on the Gigante Islands, eg at the Barrio Lantangan on Gigante Sur. But this should present no problems. How much you pay is up to you.

Getting There & Away

Boat: From Estancia to the Gigante Islands daily at 2pm by outrigger (2½ hrs). The return journey to Estancia leaves daily at 8.30am.

Roxas

Roxas is the capital of Capiz Province and is therefore usually just called Capiz by the natives. There are no tourist attractions of note, and the only reason for most people to go there is as a stopping point on the way to Manila. A beach life of sorts can be found at the dark sand Baybay Beach a few km west of Roxas heading for the harbour (P20 by tricycle), which is home to several resorts and restaurants.

Pan-ay, about seven km south-east of Roxas, is home to the Pan-ay Church dating from the Spanish period. Over 200 years old, it was built like a fortress and contains the largest bell in South-East Asia. Over two metres in radius, it weighs 10.4 metric tons. According to legend, the bell was made from the metal from melting down 76 sacks of coins donated by citizens of the town.

Museum

The Ang Panublion (Roxas City Museum), originally a giant water tank, houses mementoes of famous Capizeños such as President Manuel A Roxas, the author Fernando Aranetas, opera singer Jovita Fuentes and ballerina Josefa Arnaldo Villaneuva.

Places to Stay

Plaza Central Inn, Gomez St, Tel 6213061. SR/fan/bath P370, SR/DR/ac/bath P530/670 (TV). Basic accommodation on the Plaza with very good rooms. restaurant.

Halaran Plaza Hotel, on Rizal St corner Gomez St, Tel 6210649. SR/DR/fan/bath P440, SR/DR/ac/bath P500 and P600 (TV). Although not outstanding, the rooms are acceptable for the money. Located on the river near the Plaza and City Hall. Restaurant.
Villa Patria Cottages, Baybay, Tel 6210180. SR/ac/bath P850, DR/ac/bath P950 and P1150 (refrigerator). Really good rooms for the money. Restaurant. Located a little out of town on Baybay Beach (P20 by tricycle from the town centre).
Roxas President's Inn, Rizal St corner Lopez Jaena St, Tel 6210208, Fax 6211040, @. SR/ac/bath P950, DR/ac/bath P1300 and P1450, suite P1600 (all including breakfast). Pleasant, very comfortable rooms with TV. Restaurant, car hire.
La Hacienda Hotel, Arnaldo Blvd, Tel 6215129. SR/DR/ac/bath P1560 and P2000, suites P2400. Comfortable, well-kept rooms with TV, the suites also with refrigerator. Restaurant. Swimming pool. Probably the best hotel in town, located near the Gaisano department store.

Places to Eat

Capiz Province is well-known for its abundant fishing grounds, reason enough for Roxas to be known as 'Seafood Capital of the Philippines'. And the best place to try the seafood is on Baybay Beach, where by midday at the latest the air is filled with the smell of various ***Eateries*** preparing tasty dishes of oyster, crab, prawn, octopus and all kinds of fish from bangus to tuna. For carnivores, there's also roast chicken, pork steaks and spare ribs. And by way of variety, the ***Wayfarer*** even has a billiards table.
Amongst the wide range of restaurants to be recommended in the town itself can be included ***D'Squatters*** in the La Hacienda Hotel and the pleasant ***Roxas President's Inn Restaurant*** in the eponymous hotel, both offering a good variety of native dishes.
If you're reading this and thinking 'All very well, but where's the fast food?' don't worry, the Gaisano department store on Arnaldo Blvd has a ***Chowking***, ***Greenwich***, and a ***Jollibee***.

Miscellaneous

Festivals: The Halaran Festival on the first weekend in October is Roxas' biggest festival, with music and dancing in the streets. The Sinadya Festival takes place from 5 to 8 December.
Money: Equitable PCI Bank, Roxas Ave corner Pavia St, and Philippine National Bank, MH del Pilar St corner CM Recto St, have ATMs.
Population: 80,000.
Post & Telephone: Post code: 5800. Area code: 036.

Getting Around

Car: Roxas President's Inn, Rizal St corner Lopez Jaena St, Tel 6210208, hires out a minibus (L300 van) with driver for P2200 for 10 hrs.

Getting There & Away

By Air: Roxas Airport is about four km west of Roxas.
Cebu Pacific, Legaspi Street, Tel. 6210307.
- Roxas Airport, Tel, 6210663, 6210511.
Destination: Manila.
Philippine Airlines, Roxas Airport, Tel 6210618, 6210618.
Destination: Manila.

By Boat: Culasi Port is about six km west of Roxas. The ride by tricycle from there to the city takes 10 min and costs P20.
Negros Navigation, Roxas Ave, Tel 6211473, 6213822.
Destinations: Dumaguit/Kalibo, Manila.
WG & A, Rizal Street, Tel. 6215567, 6215572.
Destinations: Dumaguit/Kalibo, Manila.

Estancia
Boat: From Estancia to Roxas on Monday with Negros Navigation (four hrs).

Iloilo City
Bus: From Iloilo City to Roxas, Ceres Liner buses leave every 30 minutes from 4am to 5.30pm from the Tanza Bus Terminal (four hrs). Minibuses only take three hrs (P150).

Kalibo
Bus: Only a few buses and minibuses go from Kalibo to Roxas daily (1½ hrs).

Boat: From Dumaguit/Kalibo to Roxas on Tuesday, Thursday and Sunday with WG & A and on Saturday with Negros Navigation (two hrs).

Aklan Province

Kalibo

The oldest town in Aklan, Kalibo is also the capital of the province. Well known for the piña textiles and intricately woven abaca shoes and handbags manufactured there, Kalibo is even more renowned for the annual Ati-Atihan Festival held in January. This is the Mardi Gras of the Philippines. Long before the show begins, the people of Aklan can think of nothing but the vibrant tom-toms, the sound of which dominates the festival's activities from the beginning to the end. Other villages and towns in the Philippines hold similar festivals but the one in Kalibo is the most popular.
About 20 km north-west of Kalibo are the Jawili Falls, which cascade down the valley, forming several pools where you can have a refreshing swim. To get there, take a bus or jeepney from Kalibo going to Nabas or Caticlan, get off at Tangalan and go on by tricycle.
Just under 20 km south-west of Kalibo, there is a long, grey beach with fine sand called Aroma Beach. Overnight accommodation is available. You can get there from Kalibo by taking a jeepney or tricycle to Dumaguit (30 min), then by boat over the bay to Batan (10 min), then another tricycle from Batan on to Aroma Beach (10 min).

Places to Stay

During the Ati-Atihan Festival, prices in Kalibo may triple, and it can be almost impossible to find a hotel room.
RB Lodge, G Pastrana St, Tel 2627460. SR/DR/fan P150/200, SR/DR/ac/bath P400. Basic rooms, but all right for the money. Quiet place.
Glowmoon Hotel, S Martelino St, Tel 2623073. SR/fan P250, DR/fan P350, SR/DR/ac/bath P650/750. Reasonable rooms. Restaurant.
Hotel Casa Felicidad Alba, Archbishop Reyes St corner S Marcelino St, Tel 2684320. SR/DR/fan/bath P500, SR/DR/ac/bath P800. Good rooms. Central location on the plaza.
Apartel Marietta, Roxas Ave, Tel 2623353. SR/DR/fan 400, SR/DZ/fan/bath P600, SR/DR/ac P600, SR/DR/ac/bath P1000. Modest, somewhat noisy accommodation. Restaurant.
Garcia Legaspi Mansion, Roxas Ave, Tel 2625588, @. SR/fan P350, SR/DR/fan/bath P550, SR/DR/ac/bath P650 to P1350. You can be sure of a warm welcome at this good, clean accommodation in the town centre. Pleasant rooms, three floors up; the aircon rooms have TV. Coffee shop, billiards.
Beachcomber Inn, Roldan St, Tel & Fax 2684765. SR/DR/ac/bath P950 to P1500. Well-kept rooms with TV in a pleasant little building in a quiet part of town.
La Esperanza Hotel, Osmeña Ave, Tel 2623989. SR/DR/ac/bath P900 and P1300, suite P2500. Comfortable rooms with TV, the suites also have a refrigerator. Restaurant. Located on the southern edge of town near the bus terminals.

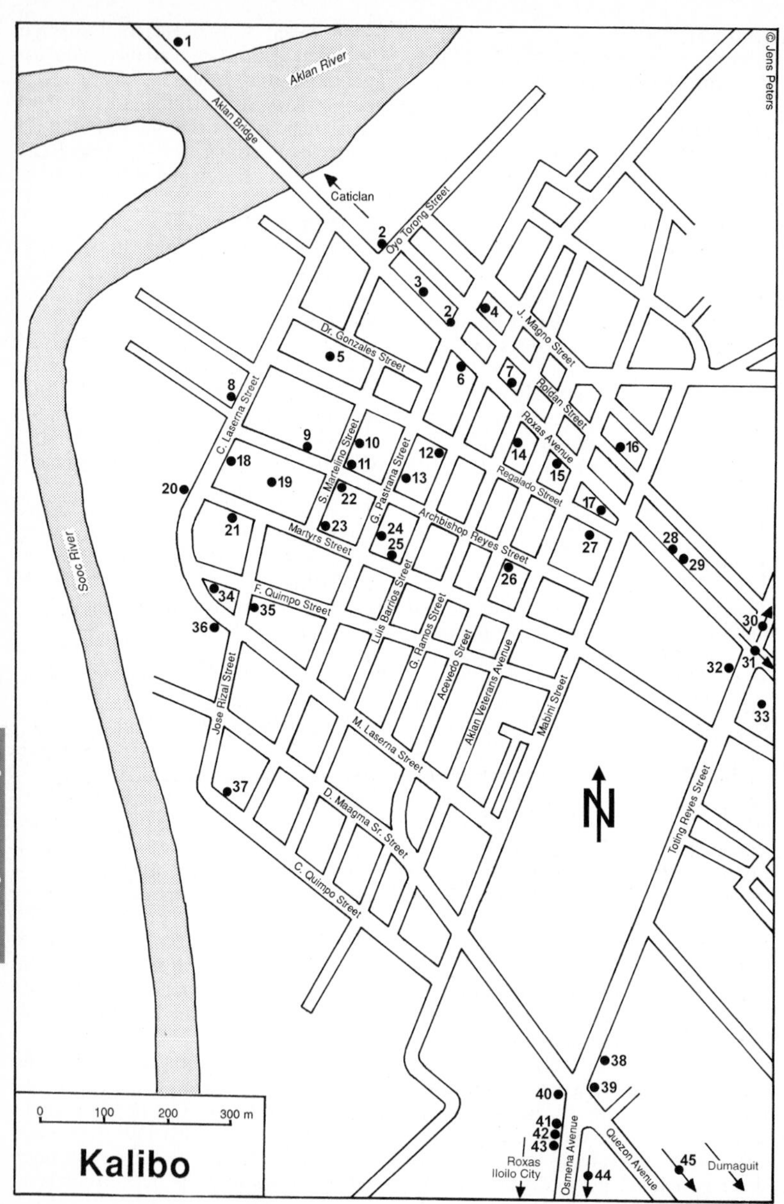

Kalibo
© Jens Peters
Aklan River
Aklan Bridge
Caticlan
Sooc River
Oyo Torong Street
J. Magno Street
Roldan Street
Roxas Avenue
Dr. Gonzales Street
C. Laserna Street
S. Martelino Street
G. Pastrana Street
Regalado Street
Archbishop Reyes Street
Martyrs Street
F. Quimpo Street
Luis Barrios Street
G. Ramos Street
Acevedo Street
Aklan Veterans Avenue
Mabini Street
Jose Rizal Street
M. Laserna Street
D. Maagma Sr. Street
C. Quimpo Street
Toting Reyes Street
Osmena Avenue
Quezon Avenue
Roxas
Iloilo City
Dumaguit
0
100
200
300 m

Getting There & Away

2 Jeepneys & Buses to Caticlan & Malay
8 Negros Navigation
9 RCPI (Air Philippines & Philippine Airlines Ticket Office)
14 Jeepneys to Dumaguit & New Washington
17 MBRS Shipping Lines
26 WG & A
38 Cebu Pacific Ticket Office
39 Shell Petrol Station
41 GM's Liner Bus Terminal
Minibuses to Iloilo City & Roxas
43 Ceres Liner Bus Terminal
45 Airport (3 km)

Places to Stay

4 RB Lodge
6 Garcia Legaspi Mansion
10 Glowmoon Hotel
15 Apartel Marietta
16 Beachcomber Inn
22 Hotel Casa Felicidad Alba
24 Gervy's Lodge
30 Queen Inn (100m)
35 B & H Traveller's Inn
36 Villa Atong Atang Hotel
42 La Esperanza Hotel

Places to Eat & Entertainment

1 Mariana's Restaurant
Ramboy's Restaurant
20 MM Italian Pizza Haus
22 Jollibee
25 Peking House Restaurant
30 Greenwich
Jollibee
Ted's Lapuz Batchoy
32 RML Chicken House
37 San Mig Nightclub
40 Chowking

Miscellaneous

3 Equitable PCI Bank
5 Shopping Center
7 Mercury Drug
9 Church
11 Aklan Museum
12 RCPI
13 Philippine National Bank (PNB)
18 Information Center
19 Plaza (Pastrana Park)
21 Aklan Shopper's Mart
23 Bank of the Philippine Islands
27 City Hall
Immigration Office
Kalibo Tourism Center
28 Royal Supermarket
29 Mercury Drug
31 Gaisano City (100m)
33 Market
34 St Jude Hospital
44 Aklan Provincial Tourist Office (500m)
Provincial Capitol (500m)

Places to Eat

Enjoy good Chinese food at the ***Peking House Restaurant*** on Martyrs St, where the set menu can be recommended. Tasty roast chicken and grilled fish are the specialities at the ***RML Chicken House*** in Toting Reyes St. The restaurants ***Ramboy's*** and ***Mariana's*** on the highway on the other side of the river both offer inexpensive Philippine food (turo-turo style), as does ***Ted's Lapaz Batchoy*** in Gaisano City department store in Roxas Ave. The local food in ***Alexa's Restaurant*** in La Esperanza Hotel, Osmeña Ave, comes highly recommended.

If it just has to be fast food, then ***Jollibee*** and ***Greenwich*** in Gaisano City, the latter also in S Matelino St on the plaza, ***Chowking*** in Quezon Ave corner Osmeña Ave and the ***MM Italian Pizza House*** in C Laserna St will do the trick.

Miscellaneous

Festival: Ati-Ahan Festival on the third weekend in January.
Immigration Office, Regalado St, Tel 2621912. Open Mon-Fri 8am-noon and 1-5pm.
Money: Bank of the Philippine Islands, Martelino St, and Philippine National Bank, Pastrana St, have ATMs.
Population: 30,000.
Post & Telephone: Post Office, Capitol Site.
Post code: 5600. Area code: 036.
Tourist Office: Kalibo Tourism Center, Regalado St, Tel 2621020. Open Mon-Fri 8am-noon and 1-5pm. There's a small Tourist Information Center in C Laserna St on the plaza.
The Aklan Provincial Tourist Office is in the Provincial Capitol, Tel 2624692.

Getting There & Away

By Air: It's only a few km from the airport to town from where jeepneys go to Caticlan/Boracay. Normally, a tricycle costs P5 per person, and a Special Ride for two people P20 (however, you could be asked for P50 or more).
The flights from Kalibo to Manila are occasionally hopelessly overbooked, so you would be well advised to confirm your return flight as soon as you arrive.
Air Philippines and Cebu Pacific have their offices in the big Coco Bar Restaurant across from the parking area. It is worth noting there are opportunities on Boracay to confirm flights and make changes of itinerary.
Tickets for Air Philippines and Philippine Airlines are available from RCPI, Regalado St corner Luis Barrios St. In Toting Reyes St near the bus terminals there is a Cebu Pacific ticket office.
Air Philippines, Kalibo Airport, Tel 2625555.
Destination: Manila.
Cebu Pacific, Kalibo Airport, Tel 2625409.
Destinations: Cebu City, Manila.
Philippine Airlines, Kalibo Airport, Tel 2623263.
Destination: Manila.

By Bus: The Ceres Liner Bus Terminal and GM's Liner Bus Terminal are located next to each another at the southern edge of town. Minibuses also leave from there for Iloilo City and Roxas.
A tricycle from the bus terminal to the jeepney departure point for Caticlan/Boracay costs P5 per person.

By Boat: Jeepneys travel between Dumaguit port and Kalibo (P15; 30 min). A minibus from Dumaguit to Caticlan/Boracay costs P200 per person.
MBRS Lines, Roxas Ave, Tel 2686850.
Destinations: Manila, Romblon (Sibuyan Island, Romblon Island).
Negros Navigation, C Laserna Street, Tel 2684903, 2623127.
Destination: Manila.
WG & A, Archbishop Reyes St corner Acevedo St, Tel 2624943.
Destinations: Manila, Roxas.

Caticlan - Boracay

Jeepney: Several jeepneys make the trip from Kalibo to Caticlan daily from Roxas Ave (P40; 2½ hrs).

Bus: After flight arrivals, comfortable aircon buses (and less comfortable minibuses) of the companies 7107 Boracay Shuttle and Southwest Tours leave the airport for Caticlan, where boats for Boracay depart (P175; two hrs). Tickets are on sale outside the airport, and include the boat transfer which costs P18.

Iloilo City

Bus: From Iloilo City to Kalibo, Ceres Liner and GM's Liner buses leave Tanza Bus Terminal every hour from 3am to 3pm (P100; four hrs). Minibuses take 3½ hrs (P150).
From Kalibo, several Ceres Liner and GM's Liner buses leave from their re-

spectice bus terminals on the southern edge of town daily for Iloilo City. Last departure at 3pm.

Roxas
Bus: Only a few big buses and mini-buses run daily from Roxas to Kalibo (1½ hrs).

Boat: From Roxas to Dumaguit/Kalibo on Tuesday with WG & A and Saturday with Negros Navigation (P190; two hrs).

Ibajay

Ibajay (pronounced Eebahigh) is a small town halfway between Kalibo and Caticlan. Each year on the weekend after the Kalibo festival, the 'really original' Ati-Atihan Festival (according to the locals) is held here. It is more authentic and traditional than the commercialised Kalibo festival. Sunday is the main day. The festival is very colourful and offers great photo opportunities.

Laserna

About 15 km west of Ibajay and two km off the coast road, you'll find barangay Laserna. It's a good start-off point for trips into the largest remaining tropical lowland rain forest in the western Visayas, which covers a wide area of the north-western peninsula of Panay. It's the habitat of several endangered endemic species of birds, mammals and reptiles including the writhed-billed hornbill (*Aceros waldeni*; local name: *dulungan*), and the recently discovered Panay monitor (*Varanus mabitang*; local name: *mabitang*).
One km inland from the Hula Hoop Lodge the road ends in Hurom-Hurom. From there you can only continue on foot on an uphill trail through the rainforest, reaching after about two km the little Sakaan Waterfall with its natural pool.
Between the Hula Hoop Lodge and Hurom-Hurom there are four natural pools: Fern Valley Spring, Basang Spring and on the other side of the Gibon (pronounced Hibon) River, Manyuko Spring and Hurom-Hurom Spring in its picturesque setting. Near Basang Spring you'll come across the entrance to the Basang Cave. Although not explored in its entirety, the cave is said to be several kilometers long and may possibly lead to yet another cave system.

Places to Stay

Hula Hoop Lodge, Cellphone 0919-2925765. Cottage/fan/bath P500, SR/DR/ac/bath P1000. Neat little place with three sturdily built, well-equipped cottages (including one tree house) and one aircon room. An attractive oasis surrounded by green, run by the German Horst and the Filipina Amy. Good restaurant with local and European cooking. Swimming pool.

Getting There & Away

Jeepney/Tricycle: Jeepneys and buses which run between Kalibo and Caticlan pass through the village of Toledo. Get out there at Toledo Crossing, and continue the remaining two km to Laserna by tricycle (P20). Travel time from Caticlan to Toledo Crossing: 30 min. Fare: P20.

Caticlan

This small town in the north-west corner of Panay is the starting point for outriggers to offshore Boracay Island. Apart from the wharf, Caticlan also has an airstrip for small planes, which are being used increasingly to go to and from Manila and Cebu City.
The best day for day trips from Boracay to Caticlan is Sunday, when the market and the cockfights take place.
About 25 km south-east of Caticlan the Ignito Cave (Elephant Cave), a drip

stone cave, was discovered as late as 1966. It is open to the public and can be crossed in half an hour (admission P150). Tours are on offer on Boracay. If, however, you want to make a day trip under your own steam, eg by mountainbike, then take the coast road from Caticlan to about five km past Buruanga. At that point, a track breaks off from the road to the left and takes you up the three km to the cave. Wooden steps take you the last few metres up to the cave entrance.

Getting There & Away

By Air: A tricycle between the small Malay Airport and the Caticlan wharf 500m away costs P30.

Boracay

Boat: Several large outriggers make the trip from Caticlan to Boracay daily until late in the afternoon (P18; 30 min). They tie up at three places, the so-called boat stations on White Beach, provided for them by the tourist office.

Kalibo - Iloilo City

Bus: There are direct daily Ceres Liner buses to Iloilo City via Kalibo departing from Caticlan at around 6.30am and noon. GM's Liner buses also make the trip, leaving at 7.30 and 9.30am. It takes two hrs to reach Kalibo and six hrs to reach Iloilo City. Aircon minibuses take five hrs (P150).

Boracay

Boracay Island is a great place for just lazing around. Seven km long, it is only one km wide at its narrowest point. Boracay's largest villages or *barangays* are Yapac, Balabag and Manoc-Manoc. They, and several smaller hamlets called *sitios*, are connected by a confusing network of paths and tracks, so the map of Boracay can only serve as a general guide. Slightly more than half the 16,000 population live in Manoc-Manoc.

Every day seems to be a holiday on Boracay - all you need to do is relax and enjoy yourself. Just get up, make some coffee and decide whether to go sailing, windsurfing or perhaps snorkelling and looking at corals. If you're curious you may get as far as the 'Caves of the Flying Dogs of Yapak' Bat Caves (admission P25) on the other side of the island, where there are still fishermen unaffected by tourism, except that they too have to pay higher prices in the stores.

There is a beautiful, long beach with gleaming white sand on the west coast. The sand is particularly fine near Balabag although the water is quite shallow there. It's deeper at the southern end, and you can even find coral now and then near the shoreline. For snorkelling the east coast is better but beware of rips. There are scores of little sandy bays scattered around the island; they make an attractive alternative to the ever popular White Beach, which loses some of its allure in the warmer, windless months of February to May due to the appearance of green algae.

The atmosphere on Diniwid Beach just to the north of White Beach, is also pleasant and peaceful. There are a few places offering inexpensive accommodation there that would cost you twice as much at White Beach. Also well worth the visit is the immaculate Punta Bunga Beach.

For years puka shells were dug out of the beautiful beach at Yapak in the north of the island, and sold all over the world. The claim is made that the now very rare, gleaming white puka shells are of the finest quality ever.

Bulabog Beach, which stretches a fair way along the east side of Boracay, might not be as impressive as White Beach on the opposite side of the island, but makes up for it by being noticeably less spoiled by tourism. It's a favourite with windsurfers and kiteboarders who enjoy the favourable wind conditions there from October until May. At the top of Mt Luho, which is all of 100m asl, there's a viewpoint with a refreshment kiosk which provides a beautiful panorama of the entire Bulabog Bay.

For many people, Boracay is the typical Pacific island paradise. Whether this will remain so in the future depends on how much building development goes on, which will inevitably change the face of the island out of all recognition. Although the emphasis nowadays seems to be on concrete instead of bamboo, up till now most architects have succeeded in designing buildings which do not dominate their environment and fit in with the island around them.

There's no doubt this island has lost its innocence. But, in spite of the odd incident and various sins against the environment, it still has that certain something about it. Amongst its good points, the friendly locals being one of them, are the carefully tended gardens, the individually designed resorts, and the tastefully decorated cottages.

Shopping

Imported delicatessen items, red and white wine can all be found in the Aloja Shop behind the hospital. Ralph's Liquor Store also has a large selection of wines and spirits at the D'Mall D'Boracay. Right next to the Tourist Office in the same complex, Paulo Collections sells modern surfwear, swimming trunks and bikinis in most sizes (four shops on Boracay all together). Talipapa Market, an alleyway lined with shops on both sides, is the place to go for souvenirs of all kinds.

Places to Stay

Most of the accommodation is on White Beach, between Balabag and Angol. Usually it consists of rooms and cottages furnished with either two single beds or a double bed. Almost all of them have their own veranda and bathroom. For P500 you can have a basic, practically furnished hut with toilet and shower (cold water). Most places offer aircon, TV and hot water from P1500 up. Prices can vary, depending on how successful the season is. Especially around Christmas time price hikes of up to 200% are possible, while the off season from June until November is good for what can be big discounts. It's not unusual to get cottages for P300 at this time of year, while during the on season you'll be hard pushed to find any accommodation on White Beach for under P500.

There are mini high seasons with large numbers of visitors, such as Christmas and New Year, the week of Chinese New Year (January/February) and the first two weeks in April when students in Japan, South Korea and Taiwan have their spring vacation.

Out of about 300 beach resorts, a selection has been made of some 50 clean and comfortable places to stay. The prices shown are for cottages or rooms for two people. It would be worthwhile comparing the resorts, because there is sometimes a big difference in what is being offered for the same money (size, furnishing and setting of a cottage, for instance).

Places to Stay - up to P500

Sand Castles, Balabag, Tel 2883207, Fax 2883449, @. Dorm/fan/bath P250 per person. So-called backpacker rooms are available in a larger building in the garden at the back, behind the comfortable cottages (see below).

Sea Side Cottages, Angol, Tel 2883138. Cottage/fan/bath P400. Basic accommodation near the Sulu Bar.

Moreno's Place, Angol, Tel 2883182. Cottage/fan/bath P400. Small place with three basic, good value cottages.

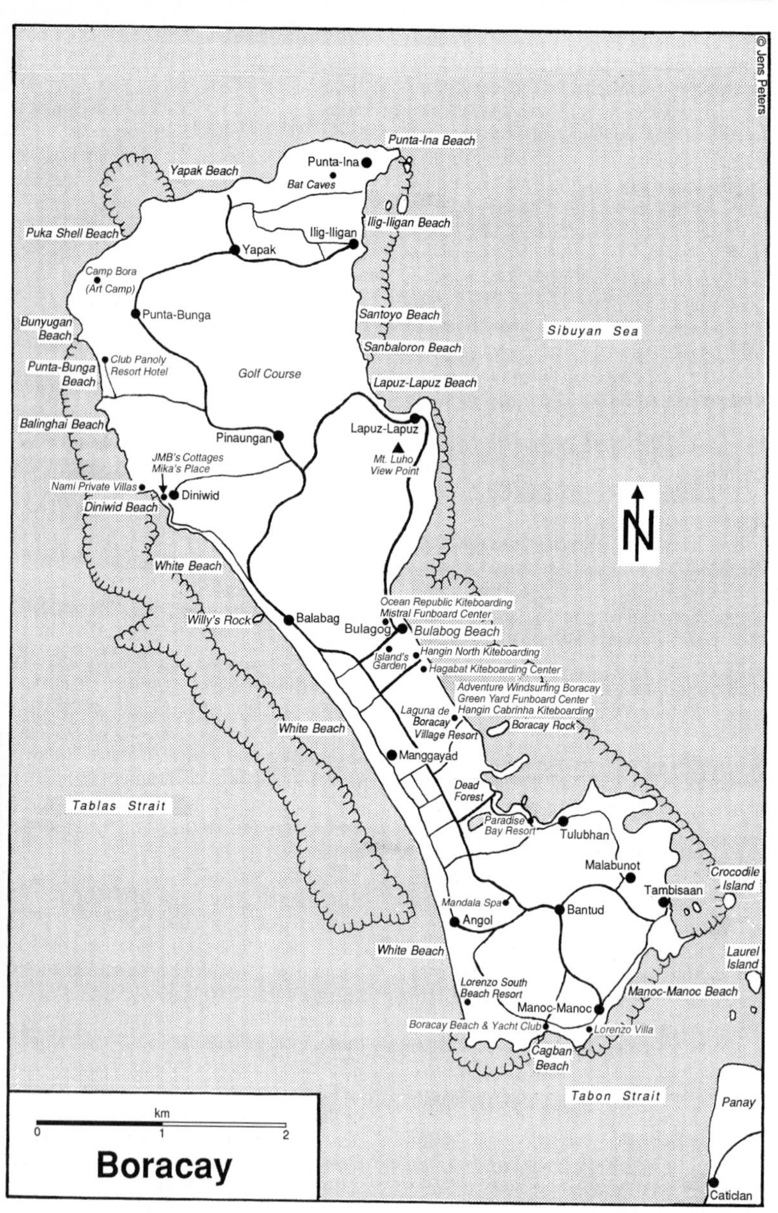
© Jens Peters
Punta-Ina Beach
Punta-Ina
Yapak Beach
Bat Caves
Ilig-Iligan Beach
Puka Shell Beach
Ilig-Iligan
Yapak
Camp Bora
(Art Camp)
Punta-Bunga
Bunyugan Beach
Santoyo Beach
Sibuyan Sea
Sanbaloron Beach
Club Panoly Resort Hotel
Punta-Bunga Beach
Golf Course
Lapuz-Lapuz Beach
Balinghai Beach
Lapuz-Lapuz
Pinaungan
Mt. Luho View Point
JMB's Cottages
Mika's Place
Nami Private Villas
Diniwid
Diniwid Beach
White Beach
Ocean Republic Kiteboarding
Mistral Funboard Center
Willy's Rock
Balabag
Bulagog
Bulabog Beach
Island's Garden
Hangin North Kiteboarding
Hagabat Kiteboarding Center
Adventure Windsurfing Boracay
Green Yard Funboard Center
Hangin Cabrinha Kiteboarding
Laguna de Boracay Village Resort
Boracay Rock
White Beach
Manggayad
Dead Forest
Tablas Strait
Paradise Bay Resort
Tulubhan
Malabunot
Crocodile Island
Tambisaan
Mandala Spa
Bantud
Angol
White Beach
Laurel Island
Lorenzo South Beach Resort
Manoc-Manoc Beach
Manoc-Manoc
Boracay Beach & Yacht Club
Lorenzo Villa
Cagban Beach
Tabon Strait
Panay
km
0
1
2
Boracay
Caticlan

JMB's Cottages, Diniwid, Tel 2883934. Cottage/fan/bath P400. Very basic accommodation.
St Vincent Cottages, Manggayad. Cottage/fan/bath P400 and P500. Good enough place in the centre of the island.
Melinda's Garden, Angol, Tel 2883021, @. Cottage/fan/bath P400 to P1200. Pleasant place, set back a little from the beach.
Austria Pension House, Angol, Tel 2883406. SR/DR/fan/bath P500. Friendly place at the south end of Angol.

Places to Stay - P500 to P1000

Casa Camilla, Angol, Tel 2883051, @. SR/DR/fan/bath P500 to P1000, SR/DR/ac/bath P1400 and P1400. This is a small place, conveniently located just off the beach.
Mika's Place, Diniwid, Tel & Fax 2883475. Cottage/fan/bath P500, SR/DR/fan/bath P1500, SR/DR/ac/Bad P3500. Friendly accommodation with OK cottages and spacious rooms.
Ati-Atihan Resort, Manggayad, Tel 2883226. Cottage/fan/bath P600. Basic, quiet place about 100m from the beach.
Michelle's Bungalows, Manggayad, Tel 2883086, @. SR/DZ/fan/bath P600. Basic, but OK for the money. Located a few metres back from the beach.
Trafalgar Garden & Cottages, Manggayad, Tel 2883711, @. Cottage/fan/bath P600. Small, basic place in the middle of the island near Talipapa Market. Cooking facilities are available.
Morimar Boracay Resort, Manggayad, Tel 2883120. Cottage/fan/bath P600, cottage/ac/bath P1500. Quite large rooms in peaceful grounds located about 150m from the beach.
Fiesta Cottages, Balabag, Tel 2883818. Cottage/fan/bath P600 and P1000. Fairly good value cottages of various vintages.
Serina's Place, Balabag, Tel 2883224. Cottage/fan/bath P800. Small place with reasonable cottages.
Sunshine Place, Balabag, Tel 2883221. Cottage/fan/bath P800, SR/DR/ac/bath P2500 (TV). Well-kept cottages, good value for the money.
Villa Lourdes Resort, Balabag, Tel 2883448. SR/DR/fan/bath P700 to P1000. Decent rooms in double cottages with refrigerator and cooking facilities. Good value.
A-Rock Resort, Angol, Tel 2883201, Fax 2883526. Cottage/ac/bath P800, cottage/ac/bath P1500. Cottages are of varying standard. Located in the second row of buildings a bit off the beach.
Bamboo Beach Resort, Manggayad, Tel 2883109, Fax 2885047. Cottage/fan/bath P800, SR/DR/ac/bath P1500. Basic cottages as well as reasonable rooms in a larger building. Located in a lane just off the beach.
Dalisay Village Resort, Manggayad, Tel 2883266. Cottage/fan/bath P800, cottage/ac/bath P1500. Roomy cottages. The service is very friendly and helpful.
GP's Beach Resort, Balabag, Tel 2883139. Cottage/fan/bath P800, cottage/ac/bath P1500. Fairly good value cottages. Located next to Lapu-Lapu Diving.
Roque's Place, Manggayad, Tel 2883356. Cottage/fan/bath P800, cottage/ac/bath P1500. Well-run, OK for the money.
Paradise Bay Resort, Tulubhan, Tel 2885124, Fax 2885127, @. SR/DR/ac/bath P800 to P2400, depending on size and furnishings. Attractive, spacious rooms with refrigerator and TV. Garden with swimming pool. Located on a small bay in the south-east of the island.
La Luna Court, Manggayad, Tel 2883657, Fax 2883766, @. SR/DR/fan/bath P900, SR/DR/ac/bath P1500. Big, stone building with very good rooms. Located a few metres off the beach, behind Victory Divers.

Bans Beach Resort, Balabag, Tel 2883156. Cottage/fan/bath P1000. A long row of reasonable cottages.
Frendz Resort, Balabag, Tel 2883803. Cottage/fan/bath P1000. Family-style place with pleasantly furnished cottages, set back a bit from the beach (a few minutes' walk).
Saigon Beach Resort, Angol, Tel 2883203, Fax 2883532. Cottage/fan/bath P1000. Reasonable accommodation.

Places to Stay - P1000 to P2000

Boracay Beach Resort, Balabag, Tel 2883208, @. Cottage/fan/bath P1500, Cottage/ac/bath P2000 to P2800. Spacious cottages, both old and new, the more expensive ones have a TV.
Boracay Hideaway Resort, Balabag, Tel 2883548. Cottage/fan/bath P1000, cottage/ac/bath P2000. Pleasant place with only a few cottages. A little hidden away, a few metres from the beach (next to the El Toro Restaurant).
B & B Beach Resort, Manggayad, Tel & Fax 2883235, @. Cottage/fan/bath P1000, cottage/ac/bath P2000. Spacious, well furnished stone cottages set in well-kept grounds in the centre of the island.
Tirol & Tirol Resort, Balabag, Tel & Fax 2883165, @. Cottage/fan/bath P1000, cottage/ac/bath P2300 and P2800. Depending on occupancy, they can be flexible with their pricing. Roomy cottages, the aircon ones with TV.
Mona-Lisa Beach Resort, Manggayad, Tel & Fax 2883205, @. Cottage/fan/bath P1200, cottage/ac/bath P2000. Garden grounds on the beach with reasonable cottages.
Villa de Oro, Manggayad, Tel 2885456, Fax 2603070, @. Cottage/fan/bath P1200, cottage/ac/bath P2500. Pleasant resort with immaculate cottages.
Boracay Plaza Beach Resort, Balabag, Tel & Fax 2883702, @. SR/DR/fan/bath P1500, SR/DR/ac/bath P2200 and P3800. Pleasant, well-furnished rooms with balcony.
Seabird International Resort, Balabag, Tel 2883047, Fax 2883816, @. SR/DR/fan/bath P1600, SR/DR/ac/bath P2800 and P3800. Tidy, quite basically furnished rooms in a building a bit off the beach (behind the Red Coconut Beach Hotel).
Villa Camilla, Angol, Tel 2883354, Fax 2883106, @. SR/DR/fan/bath P1600 to P3800, SR/DR/ac/bath P3200 to P4900. Attractive building with inviting rooms. Swimming pool.
Cocomangas Hotel Beach Resort, Balabag, Tel 2883409, Fax 2883061, @. Cottage/ac/bath P1900. Popular, comfortable accommodation in spacious cottages with TV.
Angol Point, Angol, Tel 2883107. Cottage/fan/bath P2000. There are only six of these tastefully furnished cottages, all with big verandas, set in generously laid-out grounds.

Places to Stay - P2000 to P4000

El Centro Island Beach Resort, Manggayad, Tel 2886352, Fax 2886055, @. SR/DR/ac/bath P2000 to P2600. Well furnished rooms with TV in a two-storey building set in a garden.
Red Coconut Beach Hotel, Balabag, Tel 2883507, @. SR/DR/fan/bath P2000, SR/DR/ac/bath P4000 to P6500. Pleasant, appealingly furnished rooms with refrigerator and TV, the more expensive ones with a balcony and sea view. Well-kept place with a main building on the beach and a second, tidy little place with a garden, set back a little. Swimming pool.
Lorenzo Main Resort, Manggayad, Tel & Fax 2883808, @. Cottage/fan/bath P2400, cottage/ac/bath P5400. Big cottages in pleasant grounds with lots of plants. Swimming pool. The sister resorts *Lorenzo South*, *Lorenzo Villa* and *Lorenzo Grand Villa* (all around P6000) are located in the south of Boracay.

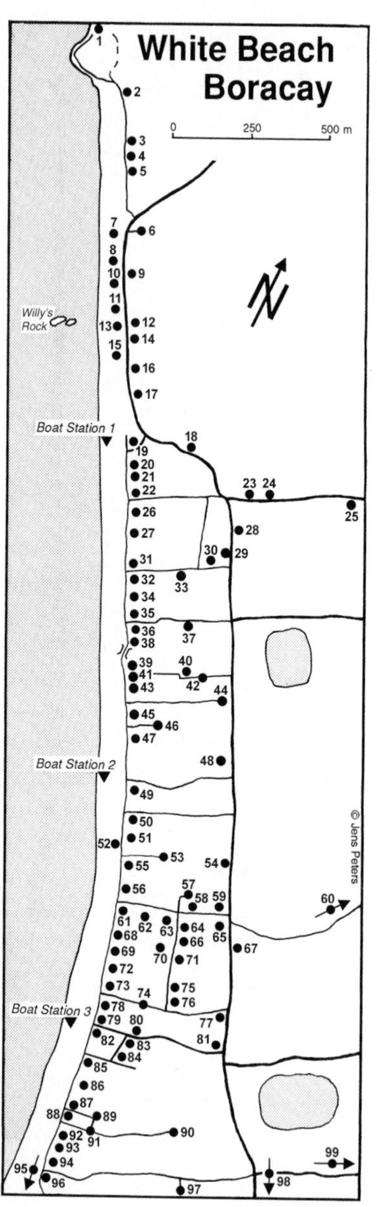

Getting There & Away
28 Air Philippines
41 Seair
61 Cebu Pacific
Pacific Airways
67 Dante's Welding Shop
(MBRS Tickets)
85 Asian Spirit
87 Philippine Airlines

Places to Stay
1 JMB's Cottages
Mika's Place
Nami Private Villas
2 Boracay Terraces
3 Robinson Beach House
Tête-à-Tête
4 Reynaldo's Beach Resort
5 Cottage Queen
Friday's
7 Chalet Tirol
Tyrol Beach Resort
White House Beach Resort
8 Sea Wind
9 Boracay Shores
10 Pearl of the Pacific
Nigi Nigi Too
Waling-Waling Beach Resort
11 Boracay Plaza Beach Resort
Willy's Beach Resort
13 True Home Hotel
14 Cocomangas Hotel Beach
Resort
17 Jony's Beach Resort
19 Royal Park Hotel
Sea Gaia Divers Lodge
20 Boracay Gold Crowne Club
21 Boracay Hideaway Resort
22 Bans Beach Resort
23 Nena's Paradise Inn
25 Island's Garden
26 Jomar's Place
27 Fiesta Cottages
Serina's Place
Sunshine Place
28 Pink Patio Resort
30 Frendz Resort
31 Sand Castles

32 Boracay Beach Resort
33 Club 10
34 Crystal Sands Resort
35 La Reserve Resort
36 Red Coconut Resort
37 Seabird International Resort
38 Bamboo Bungalows
39 Sea Lovers Cottages
40 Villa Lourdes Resort
44 Nirvana Beach Resort
45 GP's Beach Resort
46 Dalisay Village Resort
47 Le Soleil de Boracay
49 Boracay Peninsula
Hotel Seraph
La Playa Blanca
50 Boracay Regency Beach Resort
El Centro Island Beach Resort
Tirol & Tirol Beach Resort
51 La Luna Court
Nigi Nigi Nu Noos
Sunset Beach Resort
Villa Mare Cottages
53 Ati-Atihan Resort
Benross Cottages
55 Boracay Beach Chalets
Villa de Oro
56 Alice in Wonderland
57 Pinjalo Resort Villas
58 Shangrila Oasis Cottages
59 Rainbow Villa Resort
60 Laguna de Bay Boracay Village Resort
61 Serge's Palace Beach Resort
63 Morimar Boracay Resort
64 Roque's Place
St Vincent Cottages
65 B & B Beach Resort
66 Alice in Wonderland Beach Resort
68 Bamboo Beach Resort
70 Lorenzo Main Resort
71 Boracay Imperial Beach Resort
Tonglen Beach Resort
73 Casa Pilar
75 Paradise Garden Resort Hotel
76 Holiday Homes
Trafalgar Garden & Cottages
78 La Isla Bonita
Michelle's Bungalow
Mona-Lisa Beach Resort
79 Oro Beach Resort
Paradise Lodge
Queen's Beach Resort
Saigon Beach Resort
80 Tropical Cottages
83 M & E Guest House
84 A-Rock Resort
86 Boracay Horizon Resort
87 Marzon Beach Resort
89 Melinda's Garden
Roy's Rendezvouz
90 Mountain View Inn
The Orchids Resort
91 Moreno's Place
92 Angol Point
93 Villa Camilla
94 Alyssa Resort
Boracay Surfside Resort
Casa Camilla
357 Boracay Resort
95 Austria Pension House
Boracay Beach & Yacht Club
Lorenzo South Resort
Lorenzo Villa
The Sun Village Beachfront Resort
97 The Music Garden Resort
99 Paradise Bay Resort

Places to Eat & Entertainment
12 Mañana Restaurant
13 Blossoms Crepes House
14 Dos Mestizos
Ice Rock Café
KO Lechon House
Moondog's Shooter Bar
15 Pier One
Déjà Vu Bar & Restaurant
Jonah's Fruit Shake, Jony's Bar
20 El Toro Restaurant
22 Zorbas
24 English Bakery & Tea Room
27 Caribo Restaurant
Jay Jay's Movie Bar
Steakhouse Boracay

31 Café Sun Tha
32 Café Breizh
Café del Mar
35 La Reserve Restaurant
36 Red Coconut Restaurant
39 Sea Lovers Restaurant
Stables Coffee & Tea Bar
41 Gasthof Café & Deli
Hey Jude Pub
Mrs Moon
Pasta & Pizza
43 Club Paradiso
44 Viking Inn Restaurant
45 Shenna's Restaurant
Mango Ray
True Food
47 Chez Deparis Restaurant
Summer Place Bar & Restaurant
50 Seoul Korean Restaurant
Wave Disco
51 Barracuda Sports Bar
Siam Thai Restaurant
52 Carlh's Bar
53 Ati-Atihan Restaurant
61 La Capannina Italiano Restaurant
Serge's Palace
The Wreck Bar & Restaurant
68 Bamboo Guitar Bar
Dalisay Bar & Restaurant
Pizza de Buffo
69 English Bakery
Titay Theater Restaurant
72 Vinju Indian Restaurant
73 Banza Portuguese Restaurant
74 Alvarez Restaurant
Honey Bee Restaurant
Lolit's Restaurant
Nene Bell Food's House
78 Beach Life Club
Scuba Libre Diving
82 Sulu Bar
Sulu Thai Restaurant
Swiss Inn Restaurant
85 Pahar Restaurant
Star Fire Restaurant
88 Kurt & Macz Restaurant
89 Melinda's Garden Restaurant
93 Jazzed Up Café
English Bakery
Outer Space Pub
95 Fischfang Restaurant
Sundown Restaurant
96 Dutch Pub
97 Music Garden

Miscellaneous
5 Red Coral Diving School
6 Boracay Horse Riding Stables
12 Post Office
13 Aqua Sports Beach Rental
14 Boracay Safari Divers
16 Bada Scuba Diving
18 Boracay Medical Clinic
19 Sea Gaia Divers School
22 Allied Bank
Landbank
26 Scuba World
27 Fisheye Divers
29 Pa-ama Minimart
Pantelco
31 Tribal Adventures Tours
32 Aquarius Diving
34 Swagman Travel
41 D'Mall D'Boracay
Bank of the Philippine Islands
Paulo Collections
Ralph's Liquor Store
Tourist Office
42 D'Mall Palengke
43 Nautilus Diving
45 Lapu-Lapu Diving Center
Sea World Dive Center
47 K-Dive Center
48 Aloja the Shop
Hospital
49 Red Coral Diving School
51 Victory Divers
54 Allied Bank
61 Boracay Tourist Center
Filipino Travel Center
Calypso Diving
Char-Sea Water Sports
Diamond Garden Diving School

62	Police Station	81	Metropolitan Doctors Medical Clinic
72	Boracay Scuba Diving School Fausto's Shiatsu Massage Vibes Shiatsu Center	85	Water Colors Boracay Diving Adventures
73	Aqualife Divers Academy	87	Dive Gurus
74	Talipapa Market	93	Immigration Office White Beach Divers
77	Abram's Supermart	94	Island Staff Dive Shop
78	Beach Life Diving Center	98	Mandala Spa
79	Allied Bank		

Sand Castles, Balabag, Tel 2883207, Fax 2883449, @. Cottage/ac/bath P2500 and P3500; including breakfast. Beautiful place, in a garden with quite comfortable cottages.
Nirvana Beach Resort, Manggayad, Tel 2883140, Fax 2883083, @. SR/DR/ac/bath P2800 to P4000. Well-designed resort with beautifully furnished cottages. Located in the interior of the island, about five minutes from the beach.
Crystal Sands Resort, Balabag, Tel 2883149, Fax 2883087, @. SR/DR/ac/bath P2900 to P4800. Tastefully decorated rooms with TV, some also with refrigerator.
Pink Patio Resort, Balabag, Tel 2883888, @. SR/DR/ac/bath P3000 and P4000. Well-kept, invitingly furnished rooms with refrigerator and TV. Restaurant. Fitness room. Rock wall for climbing (apparently the only one on Boracay). Located on the road in the centre of the island.
Sea Wind, Balabag, Tel 2883091, Fax 2883425, @. SR/DR/ac/bath P3500 to P4500, including breakfast. Cosy cottages and rooms, furnished using a lot of natural materials; all with refrigerator and TV. An agreeable, generously proportioned place.
Jony's Place, Balabag, Tel 2883119. Cottage/fan/bath P3000, cottage/ac/bath P3700. Pleasant grounds with lots of plants.
Nigi Nigi Nu Noos, Manggayad, Tel 2883101, Fax 2883112, @. Cottage/fan bath P3700, cottage/ac/bath P4700. Including breakfast. Negotiable room rates. Pleasant cottages of different sizes in a green setting. A second branch, *Nigi Nigi Too*, is to be found in Balabag next to Willy's Beach Resort.

Places to Stay - P4000 to P7000

Boracay Gold Crowne Club, Balabag, Tel 2883942, Fax 2883637, @. SR/ac/bath from P4250, DR/ac/bath from P5250. Well-kept rooms in a kind of Spanish atmosphere.
Willy's Beach Resort, Balabag, Tel 2883395, Fax 2883016, @. SR/DR/ac/bath P4300 to P5000; including breakfast. Attractive rooms with TV, the more expensive ones also have a refrigerator.
Tête-à-Tête, Balabag, Tel 2883631, @. P5000 to P10,000, depending on season. Big building with three bedrooms and kitchen, aircon, TV, maid service. Quiet place near Friday's. Ideal for families with children.
Waling-Waling Beach Resort, Balabag, Tel 2885555, Fax 2884555, @. SR/DR/ac/bath P5000 to P12,000. Reasonable rooms with refrigerator and TV; only the expensive ones have a sea view, however.
Le Soleil de Boracay, Manggayad, Tel 2886209, Fax 2886118, @. SR/DR/ac/bath P5300 and P5950, suites P6700 and P7700. Including breakfast. Comfortable rooms with refrigerator and TV, the suites also have a jacuzzi.

Paradise Garden Resort Hotel, Manggayad, Tel 2883411, Fax 2883557, @. SR/DR/ac/bath P5500 to P8000. Exclusive, well-maintained resort with tastefully decorated rooms, all with refrigerator and TV. They have a beautiful garden with two swimming pools. Located in the interior of the island near the Talipapa Market.

Boracay Regency Beach Resort, Balabag, Tel 2886111, Fax 2886777, @. SR/DR/ac/bath P5500 and P6000, suite P8250; including breakfast. A larger hotel with well-kept, pleasantly furnished rooms, all with refrigerator and TV. Swimming pool.

Seraph Hotel, Balabag, Tel 2886633, Fax 2886663. SR/DR/ac/bath P5900 and P6300. Amiably furnished rooms with refrigerator and TV. Fairly big hotel and grounds, set back a few metres from the beach. Restaurant, fitness room. Garden with swimming pool.

Pinjalo Resort Villas, Manggayad, Tel 2883206, Fax 2883478, @. SR/DR/ac/bath P6000 to P10,000. Attractive stone building with 11 gorgeous rooms decorated to make you feel at home, with TV and big veranda. Quiet location only a few minutes from White Beach.

Pearl of the Pacific, Balabag, Tel 2883220, Fax 2883961, @. SR/DR/ac/bath P6000 to P10,000. Elegant, comfortably furnished rooms with TV. Attractive beach hotel with an overhead walkway to the annex on the other side of the street.

Club Panoly Resort Hotel, Punta-Bunga, Tel 2883011, Fax 2883134, @. SR/DR/ac/bath P7000 and P7500. Comfortable rooms with refrigerator and TV. Restaurant, swimming pool. First-rate place, although a bit out of the way in the north of the island.

Friday's, Balabag, Tel 2886200, Fax 2886222, @. Cottage/ac/bath P9500 and P10.800. Neat and tidy cottages with refrigerator and TV. Well-maintained, long established place (in fact, it was the first ever in this category on Boracay).

Places to Eat

There are so many restaurants on Boracay that some have to tempt customers with surprisingly inexpensive, yet quite sumptuous buffets, ranging from P150 to P250. Others have concentrated on one particular kind of food to attract the customers in.

Angol

In Angol the ***Starfire*** can be recommended for its inexpensive menu of the day. ***Melinda's Garden Restaurant*** is a pleasant place with Filipino cooking and typical European dishes. The ***Sundown Restaurant*** has good German, Austrian and Swiss food, while at the ***Swiss Inn***, not surprisingly, Swiss food features prominently on the menu. Right next door, the Thai food in the ***Sulu Thai Restaurant*** is very tasty. Next to Asian Spirit, try the Indian and Italian cooking at the ***Pahar Restaurant***. For about P75 you can eat marvellous Philippine food in the ***Honey Bee Restaurant*** and ***Nene Bell Food's House***, both in the alleyway of Talipapa Market St.

Manggayad

Manggayad seems to have more European restaurants than anything else. ***Chez Deparis*** is the place for French food, and the ***Bamboo Guitar Bar*** for Swiss. The excellent dinner menu at ***Nigi Nigi Nu Noos*** and ***Alice in Wonderland*** is available every night of the week. Savour both the décor and the good Thai and European food at the ***Siam Thai Restaurant*** next to Victory Divers. If you can find the place, the Filipino food at the ***Ati-Atihan Restaurant*** is good value, as is the Mongolian BBQ (all you can eat) in ***The Wreck Bar & Restaurant.*** Right on the beach, ***Carlh's Bar*** is an excellent location to enjoy the sunset with cold drinks and good music (happy hour from 5 until 9.30 in the evening).

Balabag

In Balabag, the modest ***Sea Lovers Restaurant*** next to the little bridge serves excellent Filipino dishes. The pleasant ***Steakhouse Boracay*** will serve you good international cuisine, as will the popular ***Jay Jay's Movie Bar***. Greek and Filipino food is on the menu at ***Zorbas***, while ***El Toro Restaurant*** offers Spanish food, and ***La Reserve*** prepares genuine French cuisine (wines and cognac too), as well as cooking an excellent lobster. ***Café Breizh*** right next to Aquarius Diving will tempt you with a large selection of tasty crepes for P40 to P150. For good Thai food go to ***Café Sun Tha*** in the Sand Castles Resort. The ambience is part of what makes ***True Food*** popular; they are near the Club Paradiso and offer Indian and vegetarian food.

In D'Mall D'Boracay, Chinese food is what to expect at ***Mrs Moon***, and the ***Gasthaus*** has a wide selection of good fish every evening. Elsewhere, the ***Red Coconut*** serves Chinese and European dishes, ***Mañana*** (near the post office) has Mexican food, while ***Jonah's*** is popular for its wonderful fruit juices. A superb breakfast can be had at the ***English Bakery & Tea Room*** who also have establishments in Angol and Manggayad.

Entertainment

There are lots of opportunities for entertainment and amusement on Boracay. Now that there is also the possibility of using a tricycle, for example from the Sulu Bar to the Pier One, even those of us too lazy to walk can indulge in the pleasure of 'bar-hopping'.

After dinner many guests like to listen to music or go dancing at their favourite place. ***Moondog's Shooter Bar*** in the Cocomangas Beach Resort in Balabag is popular at happy hour. From there, many people move later on to the beach disco ***Pier One*** (formerly Beachcomber) right next door, where the dancing can become very animated when things warm up. Others prefer the attractions of the ***Summer Place*** bar one km farther south, as well as their neighbours, the big ***Club Paradiso*** disco (formerly Club Bazzura). A Filipino band plays live every night in the basement disco bar ***Wave*** in the Boracay Regency Beach Resort.

The atmosphere in the ***Baracuda Bar*** next to the Nigi Nigi Nu Noos is pleasant. Also popular in Angol are the ***Sulu Bar***, with billiards and videos, as well as the ***Jazzed Up Café***. In the season from October to May, the latter features live entertainment in the shape of music from blues to Dixieland and Latin, every evening except Monday. For a change of pace, the ***Beach Life Club*** and ***Mango Ray*** show videos after dark.

Miscellaneous

Art Camp: Camp Bora is a small, open, artists' colony not far from Puka Shell Beach in the north of Boracay. Several Philippine and international artists support this project by donating their time to teach various forms of art. Four-day courses are available, covering for example design, film, photography, painting, meditation, music and yoga. Price per participant: P3,400.

Diving: A diving trip will cost you P1250 (Nitrox P1500); four-day courses cost P14,000 and two-hour taster courses P2000. The equipment at the different dive shops is of varying quality; it's worthwhile shopping around and paying particular attention that the equipment is new. For further information, check with Aqualife Divers Academy, Tel 2883276; Aquarius Diving, Tel 2883132, @; Beach Life Diving Center, Tel 2885211; Boracay Safari

Divers, Tel 2883260; Calypso Diving, Tel 2883206, @; Diamond Garden Diving School, Tel 2883619; Dive Gurus, Tel 2885486, @; Fisheye Divers, Tel 2886090, @; Island Staff Dive Shop, Tel 288316; Lapu-Lapu Diving Center, Tel 2883302, @; Nautilus Diving, Tel 2883432; Red Coral Diving School, Tel. 2883486; Scuba World, Tel 2883310, @; Sea Gaia Diving School, Tel 2883661, @; Sea World Dive Center, Tel 2883033, Victory Divers, Tel 2883209, @; Water Colors Boracay Diving Adventures, Tel 2885166; and White Beach Divers, Tel 2883809, @.

Immigration Office, Angol (at Villa Camilla). Open Mon-Fri 8am-noon and 1-5pm.

Kitesurfing: See *Windsurfing*.

Medical Services & Wellness: The Boracay Medical Clinic in Balabag, Tel 2883147, is open round the clock, as is the Metropolitan Doctors Medical Clinic in Angol, Tel 2886357 (also house calls). Near the Titay Theater Restaurant in Manggayad, Vibes Shiatsu Center and Fausto's Shiatsu Massage will take care of you. For about P200 an hour well-trained, licensed blind masseurs will provide acupressure and reflexion zone massages. These professional massages should not be confused with the ones available at the beach for P150!

The beautifully decorated Mandala Spa, Angol, Tel. 2885858, @, provides massages and other upmarket wellness treatment from 10am until 10pm.

Money: Travellers' cheques and cash can be changed at the Boracay Tourist Center (Tel 2883704), Swagman Travel (who are also agents for Western Union), as well as at the foreign exchange counters run by the Allied Bank, Landbank and the Boracay branch of the Allied Bank (Tel 2883026, 2883048). At the latter, you can open a peso or dollar account (minimum opening balance of P1000 or US$200).

Cash Advance: The Boracay Tourist Center will make a cash advance on all popular credit cards (for a 8% fee). The Allied Bank will only accept American Express.

Allied Bank and Bank of the Philippine Islands (in D'Mall D'Boracay) have ATMs.

Online: There are by now quite a few Internet cafés on Boracay, eg Internet Station, Pantelco Webquest and the fast connection in the Boracay Tourist Center (P70/hr).

Post & Telephone: There is a small post office in Balabag at the basketball court. It would be a good idea to have some change on you. Better still, bring your own stamps with you, from Manila for example. There is no parcel service.

Long-distance calls (national and international) can be made from the Boracay Tourist Center in Manggayad, at Pantelco in Balabag and the RCPI office in Angol, where fax facilities are also available. In the meantime, nearly all resorts have their own telephone and fax links.

Post code: 5608. Area code: 036.

Safe Deposit Boxes: The Boracay Tourist Center in Manggayad, Tel. 2883704, rents out safe deposit boxes for P150 a month.

Sailing: On White Beach you can hire a *paraw* (a small, fast outrigger sailboat given to capsizing). It costs about P400 an hour.

Sea Kayaking: Aqua Sports Beach Rental, Tel 2883369, and Char-Sea Water Sports, Tel. 2885119, rent one-person kayaks for P150 or P200 an hour. The charges for a half day, or a whole day, are a bit more reasonable.

Snorkelling: There are good snorkelling areas at Ilig-Iligan Beach in the north-east and at little Crocodile Island just off the south-east coast. But beware of the strong currents that can often be encountered on the east coast of Bora-

Visayas - Panay

cay. Especially off Crocodile Island and Laurel Island the undertow has been known to put the wind up even strong swimmers. Laurel Island offers a unique attraction for snorkellers. Through an opening in the rocky floor, an iron ladder leads into a partly flooded cave. The cave is open to the sea, and fish and coral can be observed.
Tennis: Tennis is available at the Tirol & Tirol Resort, Manggayad for P150 an hour, including rackets and balls.
Tourist Office, D'Mall D'Boracay, Balabag, Tel 2883689. Open Mon-Fri 8am-5pm.
Travel Agencies: You can make bookings and confirm national and international tickets at Swagman Travel, Balabag, Cellphone 0919-6045383, and at the Filipino Travel Center at the Boracay Tourist Center in Manggayad, Tel 2883704, @. Swagman also take care of visa extensions.
Tribal Adventure Tours at Sand Castles, Balabag, Tel 2883207, Fax 2883449, @, offers adventure tours, eg kayaking in Tibiao, Antique Province, on the neighbouring island of Panay.
Windsurfing: It costs P500 an hour to rent a board. Beginners' courses (3x 1½ hrs) cost around P3500. Rental and courses are available on Bulabog Beach on the east of the island from places like Adventure Windsurfing Boracay, Tel 2883182, @, Greenyard Funboard Center, Tel. 2883449, @, and Mistral Funboard Center. Bulabog Beach is also the venue every January for the Boracay Funboard Cup, one of the leading windsurfing competitions in Asia.
Kitesurfen (Kiteboarding): Kite and board rental as well as courses at Bulabog Beach at Green Yard's kiteboarding schools Hangin Cabrinha and Hangin North, Tel 2883663, @, in the Habagat Kiteboarding Center, Tel 2885352, @, and at Ocean Republic (in the Mistral Funboard Center), Cellphone 0916-5117534, @. Prices: Introductory course P3500 P, two-day course P10,000.
Wind conditions: North-east (*amihan*) from October to February, east-north-east from March until May, south-west (*hagabat*) from June until September.

Getting Around

Bicycle: Various resorts along White Beach rent out bikes. A mountainbike costs P50 an hr, P200 for six hrs, or P300 per day.
Boat: An unhurried trip around the island by outrigger boat can be arranged for about P500. A day trip, including the nearby Carabao Island with its equally beautiful white sand beaches - still unspoiled by tourism - would cost a bit more. There are skilful artisans on Carabao who not only build snazzy *paraw*, but also have mastered the art of sailing them well.
Now and then, boat trips to several interesting snorkelling areas are available, for example with the MB *Blue Dolphin,* which cost P150 per person for four hrs. It's not a good idea to arrange snorkel trips with boatsmen who are not from Boracay and who know neither the water current conditions nor the good places for coral.
Horseback Riding: A one-hour ride, with a guide if necessary, costs about P500 at the Boracay Horse Riding Stables, Balabag, near Friday's, Tel 2883311. Riding lessons are available.
Motorcycle: It costs about P150/hr to hire a motorbike.
Tricycle: Several tricycles make the ride along the narrow road which runs through the middle part of the island from Manoc-Manoc in the south to Yapak Beach in the north. They charge from P5 to P50, depending on the distance and number of passengers. There is a stop for tricycles at the turn-off to Boat Station 3, the first stop for boats from Caticlan.

Getting There & Away

By Air: Two airports serve Boracay: Caticlan (across on Panay) for small aircraft (Asian Spirit, Pacific Airways, Seair) and Kalibo (70 km south-east) for larger aircraft (Air Philippines, Cebu Pacific, Philippine Airlines).

A tricycle from Caticlan Airport to the wharf costs P30 (it's only 500m). After an aircraft arrives in Kalibo there are air-con buses from there to Caticlan. The trip with a Boracay Star Express, Southwest Tours or 7107 Boracay Shuttle bus costs P175. The fare includes the boat transfer from Caticlan to Boracay.

It can happen that there is a repeated announcement in one of the booking offices on Boracay that 'everything is booked out'. The best thing to do in that case is make your reservation by telephone immediately with the head office in Manila, note the flight and computer number, take them to the Boracay office and have them issue the ticket and necessary stickers. Philippine Airlines are the only company with a computer system capable of giving immediate information on flights.

Air Philippines: Reservations at the Pink Patio Resort, Balabag, Tel 2886868.
Destination (from Kalibo): Manila.

Asian Spirit: Office in Angol, next to the Pahar Restaurant, Tel 2883465-66.
Destinations (from Caticlan): Cebu City, Manila.

Cebu Pacific: Reservations at the Filipino Travel Center in the Boracay Tourist Center, Tel 2883704.
Destination (from Kalibo): Manila.

Pacific Airways: Reservations at the Filipino Travel Center in the Boracay Tourist Center, Tel 2883704.
Destination (from Caticlan): Manila.

Philippine Airlines: Office in Angol, next to the Marzon Beach Resort, Tel 2883502. Apart from taking care of changes in itinerary and flight confir-

mations, Philippine Airlines also sells tickets for P175 for the aircon bus from Caticlan to Kalibo, which includes the boat trip from Boracay to Caticlan. Open daily 8.30am-noon and 2-4pm.
Destination (from Kalibo): Manila.
Seair: D'Mall D'Boracay, Tel. 2885502.
Destinations (from Caticlan): Cebu City, Manila.

By Boat: There are three so-called boat stations on White Beach for boats to and from Caticlan: Boat Station 1 at the Boracay Gold Crowne Club, Boat Station 2 at the Boracay Regency Beach Resort and Boat Station 3 at the Sulu Bar. From June to Setember, during the south-west monsoons (*habagat*), the sea on the west side of Boracay can grow too rough for outriggers. They then have to leave from Tabon (to the east of Caticlan) instead of from Caticlan itself, and drop anchor on the east coast in the bay near the Dead Forest, or near Bulabog, where there are probably tricycles already waiting. The crossing takes 30 minutes and costs P18.
The car ferries to and from Mindoro and the big MBRS Lines ships dock in Caticlan. The crossing to Boracay is taken care of by outriggers.
The next harbour is located in Dumaguit (east of Kalibo). The WG & A superferries also berth there. A jeepney to Kalibo costs P15, an aircon bus to Caticlan P200 per person.

Tip: As almost all passengers have to wade through the water to get to the boats or back to shore, patent-leather boots and well-pressed long trousers are definitely not the things to wear. As a general rule it's a good idea to pack everything as watertight as possible, eg in a plastic rubbish bag.

Tickets: The Filipino Travel Center in the Boracay Tourist Center sells tickets for passages with WG & A. Dante's Welding Shop on the Main Road across from the Brent International School issues tickets for MBRS Lines.

Caticlan - Kalibo - Iloilo City
Boat/Jeepney/Bus: Many boats cruise along White Beach heading for Caticlan; just wait at one of the boat stations if you want to go there. The first boat comes along between about 5.30 and 6am. On arrival in Caticlan, you can get a jeepney or bus to Kalibo (two hrs).
The first bus leaves Caticlan for Iloilo City via Kalibo at around 6.30am (six hrs). Anyone wanting to take this bus will have to take either the first boat or a Special Ride for about P300 from Boracay.
Aircon buses make special trips from Caticlan to Kalibo Airport, timed to catch the departures of flights. Tickets for the Southwest Tours bus can be obtained at the Philippine Airlines office on Boracay; the Boracay Star Express office is located in the Pink Patio Resort.

Cebu
Air: Asian Spirit and Seair fly from Caticlan to Cebu City (P2450).

Manila
Air: The quickest connection between Manila and Boracay via Caticlan is by Asian Spirit, Pacific Airways and Seair; the one-way fare is about P2400.
Air Philippines, Cebu Pacific and Philippine Airlines fly from Manila to Kalibo on Panay.

Bus /Boat: Two Philtranco buses run daily from Caticlan via Mindoro (Roxas-Calapan) and Batangas to Manila. The trip takes 14 hrs, including car ferries.

Boat: There are shipping services between Manila and Caticlan as well as to Dumaguit near Kalibo on Panay.
The ships *Mary the Queen* and *Virgin Mary* belonging to MBRS Lines sail on

Monday, Wednesday and Friday at 5pm on the dot from Manila, so don't turn up at the last minute. Arrival in Caticlan is between 6 and 7am. Departure from Caticlan to Manila is on Wednesday, Friday and Sunday at 1pm.
(See also Manila chapter: *Getting Away from Luzon - To Panay*; and *Getting There & Away - To Luzon* at the beginning of this Panay chapter.)

Mindoro
Boat: Car ferries sail twice daily from Caticlan to Roxas (5 hrs). There's a connection in Roxas with buses and aircon minibuses to Caticlan, the latter possibly carrying on to Puerto Galera if there are enough passengers.
(See also *Getting There & Away - To Mindoro* at the beginning of this Panay chapter.)

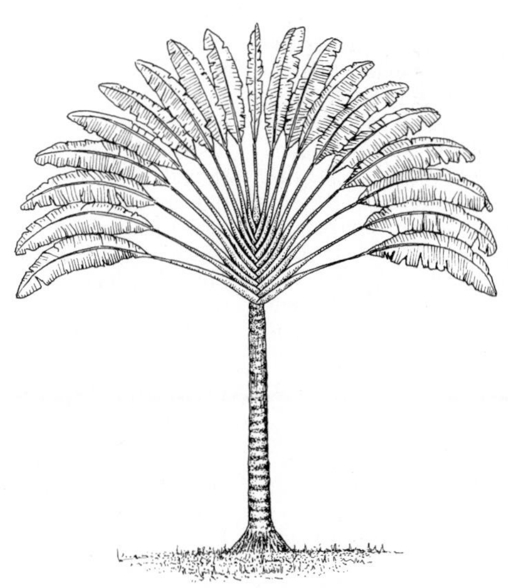

Samar

The biggest island in the Visayas, Samar lies between South Luzon and Leyte and is connected with Leyte by the two-km long San Juanico Bridge, which spans the San Juanico Strait. The island is divided into the three provinces of Eastern, Northern and Western Samar and is surrounded by about 180 small islands. One of these is Homonhon, where Ferdinand Magellan is reputed to have set foot for the first time on Philippine soil on 16 March 1521. Samar's landscape is hilly and steep and the greater part of the island is thickly wooded. Plains exist only along the coast and in the north, around Catarman.

Samar's climate is different from that of other islands in the Philippines, with dry periods only occurring occasionally in May and June. Apart from that, rainfall is possible throughout the year, although never for long periods. Most rain falls from the beginning of November until February. In early October to December there can be fierce typhoons. The best and sunniest time to visit Samar is from May to September, although surfers would probably prefer the time of the north-east monsoon, from November to February on the Pacific coast, when the surf is at its best.

The main crops are rice, maize and sweet potatoes, although Samar does not produce near enough of these to be self-sufficient. On the other hand, there are abundant harvests of abaca and coconuts, and Borongan in Eastern Samar is a leading copra producer.

The cleanliness of the towns and villages is striking. Thanks to pedicabs, which have largely replaced the otherwise ubiquitous tricycles, air pollution is at a reasonable level. It's also encouraging to see that the rainforest has not been totally cut down, but still covers a substantial area of the island. 'Preserve our Forests, Preserve our Lives' is the environmentalists' slogan which can be seen on signs all over the place - obviously to good effect.

Sohoton National Park, near Basey in Southern Samar, is Samar's outstanding natural attraction. The best way to reach it is from Tacloban on Leyte which is why it is described in the Leyte chapter.

Rather less exciting are the Blanca Aurora Falls near Gandara, between Calbayog and Catbalogan. The potential tourist attractions of Northern Samar should not be underestimated (beautiful little islands), although the infrastructure will have to be improved before people start taking notice of them.

The inhabitants of Samar are Visayans who call themselves Waray and speak the Waray-Waray dialect.

Getting There & Away

You can get to Samar from Biliran, Cebu, Leyte, Luzon and Masbate (see the Getting Away from Luzon section of the Manila chapter and the Getting There & Away sections of the individual island chapters).

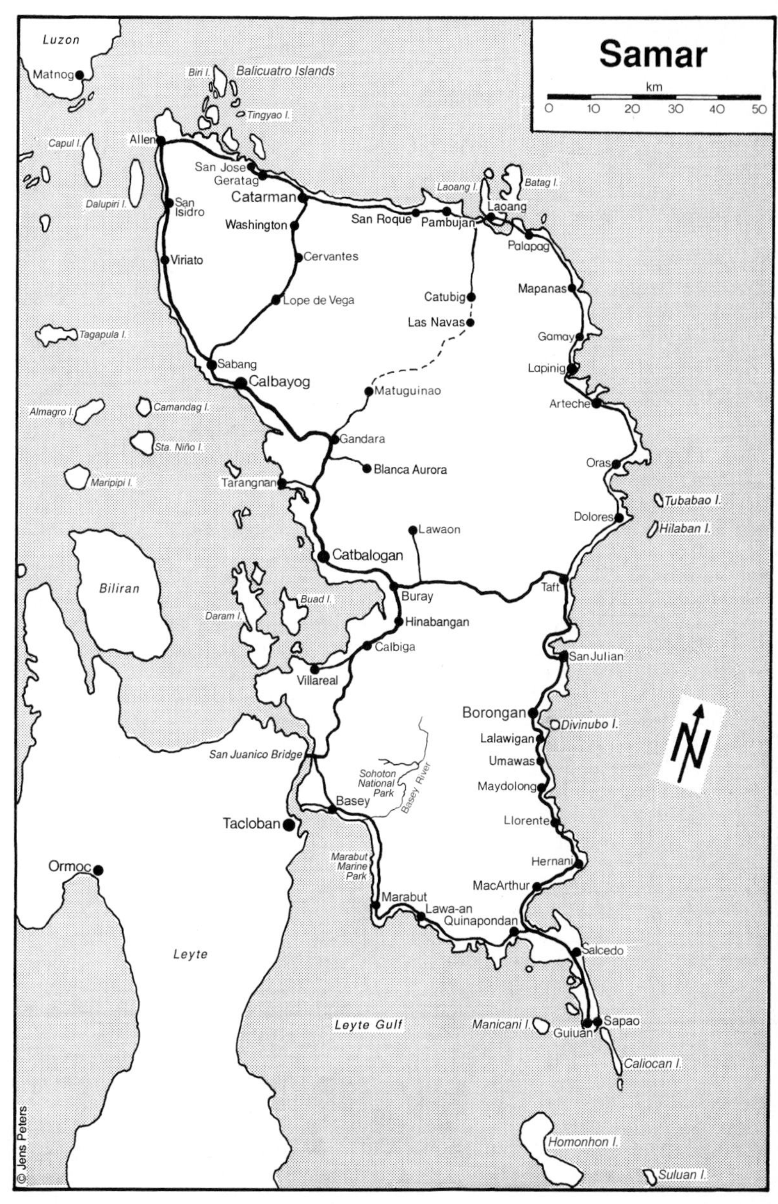
Samar
km
0 10 20 30 40 50
Luzon
Matnog
Biri I.
Balicuatro Islands
Tingyao I.
Capul I.
Allen
Dalupiri I.
San Jose
Geratag
Catarman
San Isidro
Washington
Viriato
Cervantes
Lope de Vega
Laoang I.
Batag I.
Laoang
San Roque
Pambujan
Palapag
Mapanas
Catubig
Las Navas
Gamay
Lapinig
Tagapula I.
Sabang
Calbayog
Matuguinao
Arteche
Almagro I.
Camandag I.
Sta. Niño I.
Gandara
Blanca Aurora
Oras
Maripipi I.
Tarangnan
Tubabao I.
Hilaban I.
Dolores
Lawaon
Catbalogan
Biliran
Taft
Buray
Buad I.
Daram I.
Hinabangan
Calbiga
San Julian
Villareal
Borongan
Divinubo I.
Lalawigan
Umawas
San Juanico Bridge
Sohoton National Park
Basey River
Maydolong
Basey
Llorente
Tacloban
Ormoc
Marabut Marine Park
Hernani
MacArthur
Marabut
Lawa-an
Quinapondan
Salcedo
Leyte
Leyte Gulf
Manicani I.
Guiuan
Sapao
Caliocan I.
Homonhon I.
Suluan I.
© Jens Peters
Visayas - Samar

To Biliran

Boat

From Calbayog to Danao/Maripipi Island
Wednesday and Saturday with a big outrigger (three hrs).

To Cebu

Boat

From Calbayog to Cebu City
Tuesday, Thursday and Saturday with Palacio Shipping Lines (P200; 10 hrs).

To Leyte

Bus

From Catarman, Calbayog and Catbalogan to Tacloban
Several Eagle Star and Philtranco buses run daily along the west coast of Samar, either to Tacloban itself or on the way to Ormoc. The trip takes 2½ hrs from Catbalogan to Tacloban.

From Borongan to Tacloban
Roughly hourly during the day with buses from various companies. First departure very early in the morning, The trip takes four hrs via Taft and Buray. Several Duptours and Eagle Star aircon minibuses run daily along the south coast via Lawa-an and Basey, taking 3 hrs. First departure is at 5am.

From Guiuan to Tacloban
A few buses leave at about 7.30am from the bus terminal, taking six hrs via Borongan. There are also various hopelessly overloaded minibuses which leave from different streets. Travel time is two hrs via Lawa-an and Basey (South Samar).

Boat

From Guiuan to Tacloban
Tuesday, Thursday and Saturday at 10pm with K & T Shipping Lines (Maypalad Shipping Corporation), taking six hrs.

To Luzon

Air

From Calbayog to Manila
Asian Spirit flies on Tuesday, Thursday and Sunday (P2750).

From Catarman to Manila
Asian Spirit flies on Monday, Wednesday and Friday (P2640).

Bus

From Catarman to Manila
Daily with Philtranco aircon buses (P650; 23 hrs, including the Allen-Matnog ferry).

From Calbayog and Catbalogan to Manila
Daily with Eagle Star and Philtranco aircon buses (P670 and P740; 25 and 27 hrs respectively, including the ferry from Algeria/San Isidro to Matnog).

From Borongan and Guiuan to Manila
Daily with Eagle Star and Philtranco buses (via Catbalogan and Calbayog). Including the ferry from Algeria/San Isidro or Allen to Matnog the trip takes 29 hrs from Borongan and 32 hrs from Guiuan.

Boat

From Allen to Matnog
Daily at 2, 3, 7 and 7.30am, 12 noon, 3, 6 and 9pm with a car ferry ((P74, including terminal fee; 1½ hrs).

From Algeria/San Isidro to Matnog
Daily at 5, 8 and 11am and 1, 5 and 9pm with a car ferry (2½ hrs).
The wharf in San Isidro is about 14 km south of Allen; 30 min by jeepney.

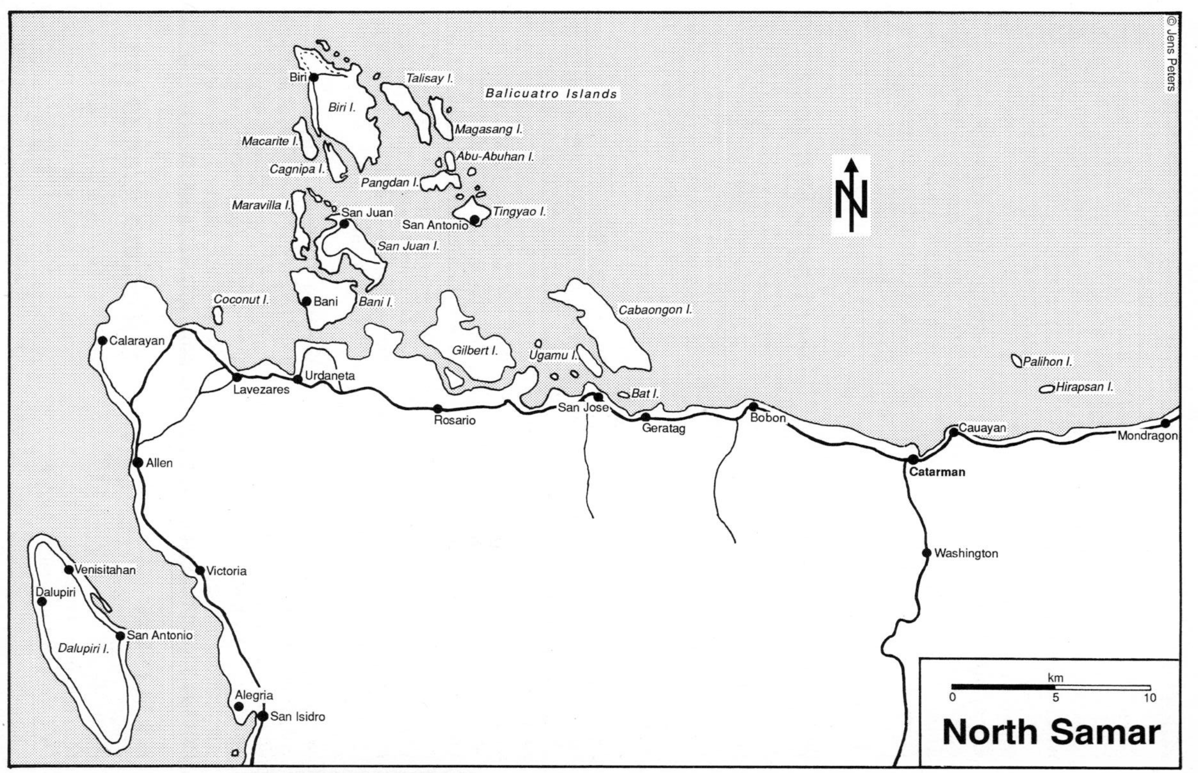
© Jens Peters
Biri
Talisay I.
Balicuatro Islands
Biri I.
Magasang I.
Macarite I.
Abu-Abuhan I.
Cagnipa I.
Pangdan I.
Maravilla I.
San Juan
Tingyao I.
San Antonio
San Juan I.
Coconut I.
Bani
Bani I.
Cabaongon I.
Calarayan
Gilbert I.
Ugamu I.
Palihon I.
Hirapsan I.
Urdaneta
Lavezares
Bat I.
San Jose
Rosario
Bobon
Geratag
Cauayan
Mondragon
Catarman
Allen
Washington
Venisitahan
Victoria
Dalupiri
San Antonio
Dalupiri I.
Alegria
San Isidro
km
0
5
10
North Samar

Allen

Allen has a wharf for ferries to and from Matnog on Luzon. There are also boats for Capul and Dalupiri islands, which lie offshore to the west.

Places to Stay

Mary Ann Lodge. SR/DR P100/200. Basic accommodation.
Kinabranan Lodge. SR/fan/bath P375, DR/fan/bath P475, SR/DR/ac/bath from P750. Fairly good rooms. Good restaurant. A bit out of town.
Wayang Wayang Beach Resort, Cellphone 0918-3388756. Cottage/ac/bath P1200, SR/DR/ac/bath P1950. With TV. Rooms for up to four people. Restaurant. Located about two km outside of Allen heading for San Isidro; P10 by tricycle from the jetty.

Getting There & Away

Bus: Several buses go from Catbalogan to Allen via Calbayog daily. The trip takes 3½ hrs from Catbalogan and 1½ hrs from Calbayog.

Dalupiri Island

South-west of Allen, not far off the Samar coast, is the pleasant little Dalupiri Island. It's known locally as San Antonio, after the village of the same name. If you want to relax for a few days and get away from the more popular tourist destinations, then you'll really enjoy your time on Dalupiri.
To get to know Dalupiri and its beaches better, you can have a motorcycle take you round the island. This costs about P200, including many stops.

Places to Stay

Flying Dog Resort, @. Cottage/bath P700. Friendly, older place with basic cottages. Restaurant.
Octopussy Bungalow Resort, @. Cottage/fan/bath P1350 to P3150, depending on size and facilities. Nice resort with sold stone cottages on a long, palm-lined white-sand beach about 500m from the Flying Dog Beach Resort. The Philippine-Swiss owners offer monthly contracts with half or full board.

Getting There & Away

Boat: Outriggers make the short trip over to Dalupiri Island from San Isidro in the morning (P30; 20 min). A Special Ride is possible for P200 to P250, if you can haggle them down.

Geratag & San Jose

Three km west of Geratag on the north coast of Samar, San Jose is a starting point for several boats which cross to the Balicuatro Islands offshore. Boats are available in both places to hire for island hopping.

Places to Stay

House Schiefelbein (Mendoza), Geratag, Cellphone 0920-2166895, @. SR/DR/fan P400, SR/DR/fan/bath P600. Also known as the House of Mr Hans, near the beach at Geratag, this place offers family-style accommodation. The rooms are quite comfortable. Food can be supplied on demand, and guests can do their own cooking if they want. Motorcycle hire.

Getting There & Away

Bus/Jeepney: Several buses and jeepneys depart from Allen daily and go through San Jose and Geratag on the way to Catarman and Rawis (for Laoang). The trip takes one hour.

Balicuatro Islands

Biri and Bani islands are reckoned to be two of the most attractive diving areas in the eastern Philippines. With an eye to the effect of publicity on tourists, the Northern Samar Tourism Council has applied to the Philippine Congress to have the Balicuatro Islands declared a protected area. In addition, the northern section of the Biri Island coast, with its small offshore limestone islands jutting out of the water by up to 37m, is to be declared a national marine park. During WWII, Biri Island had a Japanese garrison whose job was to observe the maritime traffic in the San Bernardino Straits.

Every two or three days, an outrigger goes from Biri on Biri Island to Gubat in south Luzon.

Places to Stay

There is no commercial accommodation as yet on the Balicuartro Islands, so visitors have to look for private alternatives. If you want to spend a few days in the picturesque village of San Antonio on Tingyao (Tinau) Island, you can organise an overnight stay at House Schiefelbein (Mendoza) in Geratag. See Places to Stay in the previous Geratag & San Jose section for further information.

Getting There & Away

Lavezares

Boat: An outrigger travels daily from Lavezares to Biri on Biri Island (one hr).

San Jose

Boat: Outriggers travel daily from San Jose to San Antonio on Tingyao Island and San Pedro on Pangdan Island, leaving between 9am and noon (45 min to 1½ hrs). Departure from the islands is around 7am.

Catarman

Catarman, the capital of Northern Samar Province, is the starting point for travel in the north-east, for example, to the Laoang or Batag islands. It should soon be possible to carry on from Catarman along the east coast to Guiuan in south Samar, as the coastal road from Laoang to Arteche via Palapag, Mapanas, Gamay and Lapinig is already partly finished. Up till now, the communities of Mapanas, Gamay and Lapinig could only be reached by boat.

An easy river cruise is to go along the Catarman River from Catarman as far as Washington, although there is nothing spectacular to be seen on the way. A boat leaves at 1pm and takes less than two hours for the nine-km trip. You can go back to Catarman by jeepney.

A lot more interesting is the trip up the Catubig river from Laoang to Las Navas via Catubig. It starts in the estuary, where several kilometres of mangrove thicket have to be negotiated, then continues upstream where the river is framed on both sides by breathtaking mountainous territory and mixed vegetation. The trip is meant to finish at the beautiful Pinipisacan Falls near Las Navas. However it would also be possible to carry on from there, hiking right across the mountains to Matuguinao. Plan for another three days if you intend to do this.

Places to Stay

Mijares Pensionne House, Balite St, Tel 2194229. SR/DR/fan P150/300, SR/DR/fan/bath P250/500, SR/DR/ac/bath P600. Good rooms, all with TV. Restaurant, car hire.

Aileen's Lodging House, Bonifacio St, Tel 3541568. SR/DR/fan P200. Suite P750. Basic, but clean accommodation. The one suite, with aircon, refrigerator and cooking facilities, is especially good value. Restaurant.

DCC, Bonifacio St corner Osmeña St. SR/DR/fan P200/400. Basic, but fairly good. Restaurant. Diocesan Catholic Center, next to the Catholic church.

Riverview Hotel, JP Rizal St, Tel 3541096. SR/DR/fan P200, SR/DR/

fan/bath P350, SR/DR/ac/bath P500 to P700, depending on size. Modest rooms, those with a bath are just acceptable. Restaurant. The hotel is decidedly showing its age, and is located near the bridge over the Catarman River which takes you to the University of Eastern Philippines (UEP) three km away at White Beach.

Places to Eat
There are several small restaurants in town that offer Philippine food. The stylishly decorated ***Casa de Coco*** in Balite St is definitely one of the best, with a wide variety on the menu. ***D'Nest*** in Garcia St is good value, and ***Mitz's Café*** in Jacinto St can be recommended for pizzas and pasta.

Miscellaneous
Festival: Embajada Festival on 22 January.
Medical Service: The Leoncio Uy Memorial Hospital, Del Pilar St, Tel 3541208 is better than the Northern Samar General Hospital, Balite St.
Money: Philippine National Bank in Garcia St corner Jacinto St will change travellers' cheques.
Population: 60,000.
Post & Telephone: Post code: 6400. Area code: 05540.
Tourist Office, Provincial Capitol, Tel 3541233.

Getting Around
Car: A van with driver can be hired at the Mijares Pensionne House.
Pedicab: A short trip in town costs P3 per person.

Getting There & Away
By Air: Catarman Airport is at the north-west edge of town on the road to Allen. A tricycle to the centre (four km to get there) costs P50.
Asian Spirit, Magsaysay St, Tel 3541378.
Destination: Manila.

Getting There & Away
6 Irosin Tours (Buses to Manila)
9 Bus Terminal
17 Asian Spirit

Places to Stay
7 Mijares Pensionne House
11 River View Hotel
13 DCC
14 Aileen's Lodging House
21 Joni's Lodging House

Places to Eat
3 Casa de Coco
10 The Nest Restaurant
22 Michz Café

Miscellaneous
1 City Hall
2 Northern Samar General Hospital
4 Park
5 Police Station
8 University of Eastern Philippines (UEP)
12 Catarman Cathedral
15 Metrobank
16 Post Office
18 Mercury Drug
19 Camille Shopping Center
20 Philippine National Bank (PNB)
23 Market
24 Leoncio Uy Memorial Hospital

Allen - Calbayog - Catbalogan
Bus: Every hour between 5 and 8am Eagle Star buses leave from Catarman for Catbalogan, going via Allen and Calbayog. The trip takes one hr to Allen, two hrs to Calbayog, and four hrs to Catbalogan. The buses carry on to Tacloban and Ormoc on Leyte.

Rawis (Laoang)
Jeepney: Several jeepneys run from the market at Catarman to Rawis (for Laoang) daily from 4am until about 5pm (1½ hrs).

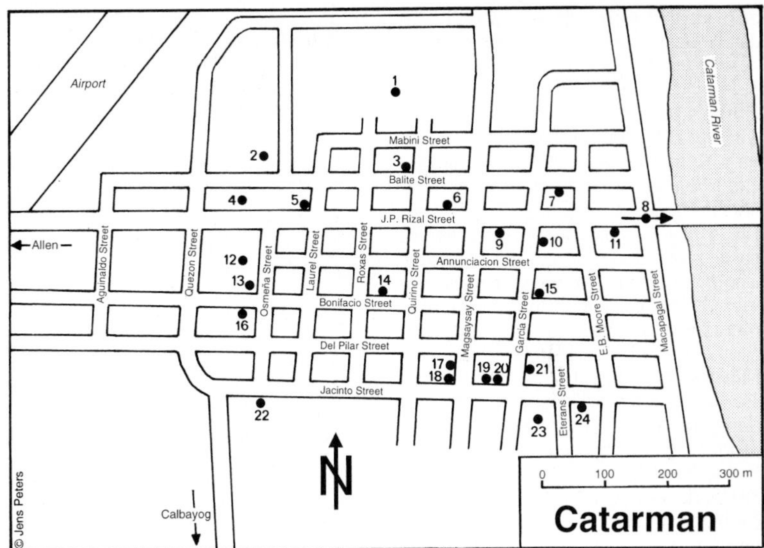

Calbayog

Calbayog, with its lively, picturesque harbour, is at one end of what is probably one of the most scenic coastal roads in the Philippines; at the other end is Allen. The road runs almost the entire length of the coast and is especially impressive near the village of Viriato (about halfway between Calbayog and Allen), with mountains, steep cliffs, distant islands and little bays with colourful boats.

There is a large waterfall near Viriato that can be seen as far back as the bridge near the river mouth. The area around Viriato is good for a day trip and could include a hike along the coast. Getting back to Calbayog or Catarman shouldn't be a problem. The next jeepney will be coming round the corner any minute.

Approximately 50 km south-east of Calbayog, the 20-metre wide and two-metre high Blanca Aurora Falls are the best known on Samar. To get there take the bus going to Catbalogan from Calbayog. Get out at the little community of San Jorge (pronounced San Horhay) about five km beyond Gandara. From there, you can carry on by tricycle to the waterfalls. A few km north-west of Calbayog there are more waterfalls, eg Pan-as Falls near the community of Pilar.

Places to Stay

San Joaquin Inn, Nijaga St corner Orquin St. SR/DR/fan P100/180, SR/DR/fan/bath P350/400, SR/DR/ac/bath P500 and P650. Basic accommodation at the market. Restaurant.

Central Inn, Navarro St. SR/DR/ac/bath P500 and P700 (two double beds and TV). Fairly basic, but loud, rooms. The restaurant is upstairs. Disco.

Eduardo's Tourist Hotel, Pajarito St corner Rosales Blvd, Tel 2091558. SR/DR/ac/bath P500, P700 and P1200. Practically furnished rooms of various sizes with TV, the more expensive ones also have a refrigerator. Centrally located. Basic hotel, but nevertheless the best in town. Restaurant.

Places to Eat

The big ***Eduardo's Diner*** in the Eduardo's Tourist Hotel is very good and inexpensive, with a wide variety of food on the menu. In the ***Plaza Café***, Pajarito St corner Avelino St, sandwiches, pasta, salads and fresh coffee are served. The ***Bread Mix***, Avelino St corner Gomez St, has basic Philippine fast food, pizzas and burgers.

Miscellaneous

Festival: Sarakiki Festival from 1 to 8 September.
Money: The Metrobank, Rosales St corner Umbria St, and the Philippine National Bank, Maharlika Highway, change travellers' cheques.
Online: Swig Cyber Café, Magsaysay Blvd (P40/hr), and Calbayog Online in the PLDT office near the bus terminal (P50/hr).
Population: 125,000.
Post & Telephone: Post Office, Gomez St. There is a sub post office in the City Hall, Avelino St.
Post code: 6710. Area code: 055.

Getting Around

Pedicab: A trip in town, including one to the bus terminal, costs P3 per person.

Getting There & Away

By Air: Calbayog Airport is about seven km north-west of the town, on the road to Allen. Jeepneys and buses are always driving by.
Asian Spirit, Riverview Cinema Building, Gomez St, Tel 2091189.
Destination: Manila.

Catarman - Allen
Bus: Eagle Star buses run almost every hour between 5 and 9am from Catarman to Calbayog via Allen daily. The trip takes 2½ hrs to Catarman and 1½ hrs to Allen. The buses go on to Tacloban and Ormoc on Leyte.

Jeepney: Several jeepneys make the trip every day from Catarman to Calbayog via Allen, taking 3½ hrs from Catarman and two hrs from Allen.

Getting There & Away
5 Cebu Pacific Ticket Office
12 Bus & Jeepney Terminal
13 Airport (7 km)
18 Asian Spirit
24 SF Transport Bus Terminal
25 Palacio Shipping Lines
26 Wharf

Places to Stay
2 Riverside Inn
4 Central Inn
7 San Joaquin Inn
16 Eduardo's Tourist Hotel

Places to Eat & Entertainment
16 Eduardo's Diner
17 Bread Mix
19 Plaza Café
25 Moonlight Nightclub

Miscellaneous
1 Post Office
3 Market
6 Calbayog Online (PLDT)
8 Mercury Drug
9 Swig Cyber Café
10 Christ the King College
11 Calbayog General Hospital
14 Philippine National Bank (PNB)
15 Landbank
16 Metrobank
20 Plaza
21 Sts Peter & Paul Cathedral
22 City Hall
Post Office
23 Police Station

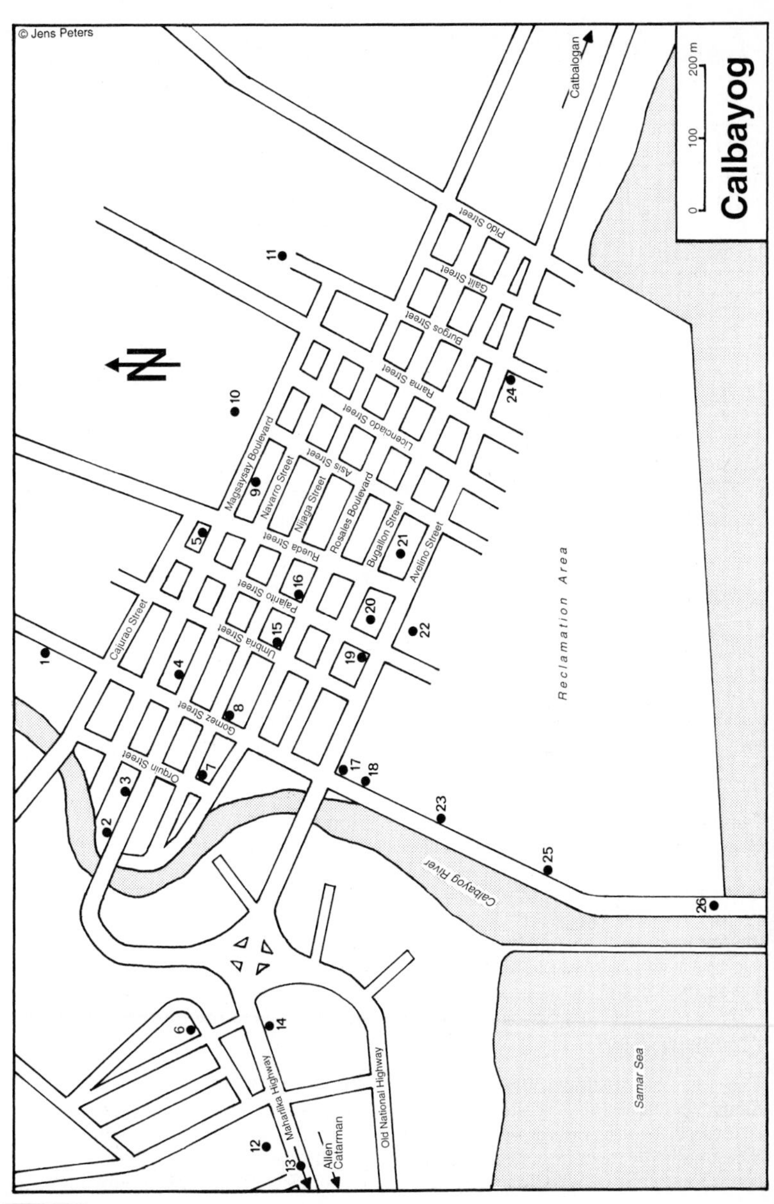
© Jens Peters
Calbayog
0
100
200 m
Catbalogan
Pido Street
Galli Street
Burgos Street
Rama Street
Licenciado Street
Asis Street
Magsaysay Boulevard
Navarro Street
Nijaga Street
Rosales Boulevard
Bugallon Street
Avelino Street
Rueda Street
Pajarito Street
Umbria Street
Cajurao Street
Gomez Street
Orquin Street
Reclamation Area
Calbayog River
Samar Sea
Maharlika Highway
Old National Highway
Allen
Catarman

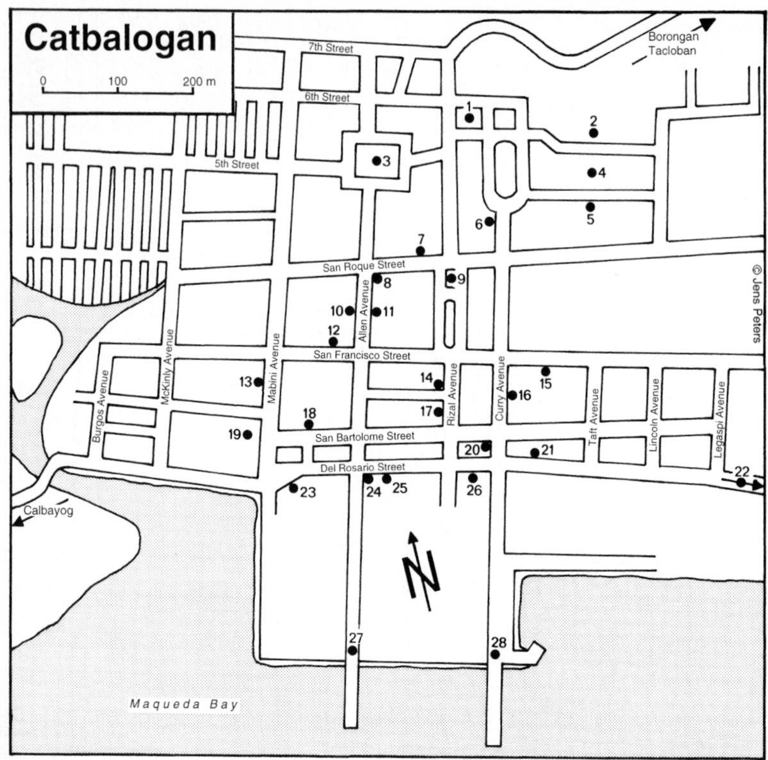

Catbalogan
Bus: Several buses go from Catbalogan to Calbayog daily (two hrs), with the destinations Allen and Catarman.

Jeepney: Several jeepneys make the trip every day from Catbalogan to Calbayog (two hrs).

Catbalogan

The port of Catbalogan, the capital of Samar Province (also Western Samar), is located on the central west coast of Samar. It is the most important business centre on the island. You can get buses from here that go across the island to the east coast.
Calbiga is located almost 50 km south of Catbalogan. In 1987 a group of Italians discovered a cave here, the Calbiga Cave (locally known as Langun-Gobingob). Said to be 27 km long, it is the biggest cave in Asia. Also worth seeing are the Literon Rapids and the Lulugayan Falls.

Places to Stay

Rose Scent Pensionne House, Curry Ave, Tel 3561199, Fax 3561312, @. SR/DR/fan P200 and P300, SR/DR/ac P500, SR/DR/ac/bath P600. Immacu-

Getting There & Away
7 Eagle Star Bus Terminal
10 Bus & Jeepney Terminal
18 Philtranco Bus Terminal
21 Cebu Pacific Ticket Office

Places to Stay
16 Rose Scent Pensionne House
17 Traveler's Home
20 Kikay's Hotel
22 Maqueda Bay Hotel (1 km)
25 Fortune Hotel

Places to Eat & Entertainment
13 Samariño Fast Food
22 Maqueda Bay Restaurant (1 km)
Site & Sounds (300m)
25 Fortune Restaurant
26 Songs & Sounds

Miscellaneous
1 Provincial Capitol
2 Provincial Hospital
3 Market
4 Imelda Park
5 Philippine National Bank (PNB)
6 Post Office
8 Metro Plaza Supermarket
9 City Hall
11 Mercury Drug
12 Net Zone Internet Café
14 Metrobank
15 Wevsite Internet Café
19 Church
23 Police Station
24 Equitable PCI Bank

late rooms, almost all with TV, many however without windows. Good value at a central location.
Fortune Hotel, Del Rosario St, Tel 2512147. SR/DR/fan P180/250, SR/DR/fan/bath P350, SR/DR/ac/bath P650 (with TV). Good rooms, but not all have windows. The best accommodation in the centre of Catbalogan.Restaurant.

Maqueda Bay Hotel, Del Rosario St, Tumalistis, Tel 2512386. SR/DR/ac/bath P525 and P625 (with TV). Spacious rooms. Slightly aging hotel at the southern end of the town right on the ocean front, 1½ km from the centre (tricycle P6 per person). Restaurant.

Places to Eat
The ***Fortune Restaurant***, Del Rosario St, is very popular for its Chinese and Philippine food and aircon dining room. ***Samarino Fastfood*** in Mabini Ave serves Philippine food, pizzas and pasta. There's a gorgeous view of the sea from the ***Maqueda Bay Restaurant*** in the hotel of the same name. Specialities are seafood and international dishes.

Entertainment
You can enjoy live music and karaoke in the ***Songs & Sounds*** in Del Rosario St. In the same street, south of the centre, the ***Site & Sounds*** is a cosy karaoke bar right on the ocean front.

Miscellaneous
Festivals: Kaadlawan Han Samar Festival on 11 August. Town Fiesta on 23 and 24 August.
Money: The Equitable PCI Bank, Del Rosario St, changes up to US$200 travellers cheques per day per customer.
Online: Net Zone and Wevsite Internet Café, both on San Francisco St; P30/hr.
Population: 75,000.
Post & Telephone: Post code: 6700. Area code: 055.

Getting Around
Pedicab: A short trip in town costs P3 per person.

Getting There & Away
Bus/Jeepney: Several buses and jeepneys run daily from Catarman to Catbalogan via Allen and Calbayog, which leave almost every hour between 5 and

9am. Going to Catbalogan, the trip takes five hrs from Catarman, four hrs from Allen and two hrs from Calbayog.

Borongan

Borongan, the capital of Eastern Samar, is an important trading post for copra, rattan and bamboo. Situated as it is, near the mouth of the Loom River and surrounded by numerous coconut palms at the edge of the jungle, Borongan could have just been taken out of one of the adventure stories from bygone days.

Five minutes by tricycle heading south on the road to Guiuan you'll come to the beautiful Cabong Beach. The only problem is that it remains shallow a long way out and is not really suitable for swimming.

Out on the bay, with the Pacific stretching out to the horizon in the background, the little island of Divinubo can be reached in 30 minutes. It could end up being a favourite with the surfers, as could several places south of Borongan, like Lalawigan (seven km), Umawas (17 km) and Llorente (26 km).

Places to Stay

Borongan Pensionne, National Highway, Tel 2612109. SR/DR/fan/bath P180/330, SR/DR/ac/bath P400/700 (10% discount for surfers). Basic, good rooms with TV. Located about one km south of the town centre.

Domsowir Hotel, Real St, Tel 2612133. SR/fan P125, SR/DR/fan/bath P255/385, SR/DR/ac/bath P455/755. Rooms are right for that price and have TV. The best place to stay in town. Restaurant.

Pirate's Cove Beach & Surf Resort, Bato, @. Cottage/fan/bath P500, SR/DR/ac/bath P1500 and 2500. Stylishly furnished cottages, the aircon ones have a refrigerator and TV, some also have a kitchen. Good accommodation three km south of the town (P5 by tricycle). The American owner is friendly and helpful. It is possible to use the kitchen, although they will cook for guests on request. Two swimming pools, surfboards, diving.

Places to Eat

The Philippine food in the ***Domsowir Hotel Restaurant*** is really good. The ***Nipa Hut Restaurant*** near the Metrobank is also good value.

At the beach - the area is known locally as Baybay - there are several restaurants with local food and cold drinks. There you will also find the pleasant ***Boulevard*** with live music in the evenings.

Miscellaneous

Festival: Padul-ong on 7 September.

Money: The Philippine National Bank changes travellers cheques, although their rate is not the best. The Metrobank changes American Express travellers cheques and they also have an ATM.

Online: Borongan Cyb Internet Center (in the courtyard behind Mercury Drug); Space Probe Internet Café, E Cinco St; both charge P40/hr.

Population: 50,000.

Post & Telephone: Post code: 6800. Area code: 055.

Surfing: The Samar Surfriders, San Francisco St, Cellphone 0919-3332387, @, organise the Samar Surfing Competition every year in September and run the small Surfrider Island Resort.

Getting Around

Multicab: Multicabs for journeys to the area around Borongan (heading north to San Julian, or south towards Llorente) can be found at the night market across from the Domsowir Hotel.

Tricycle: A trip within town costs P3.50 per person.

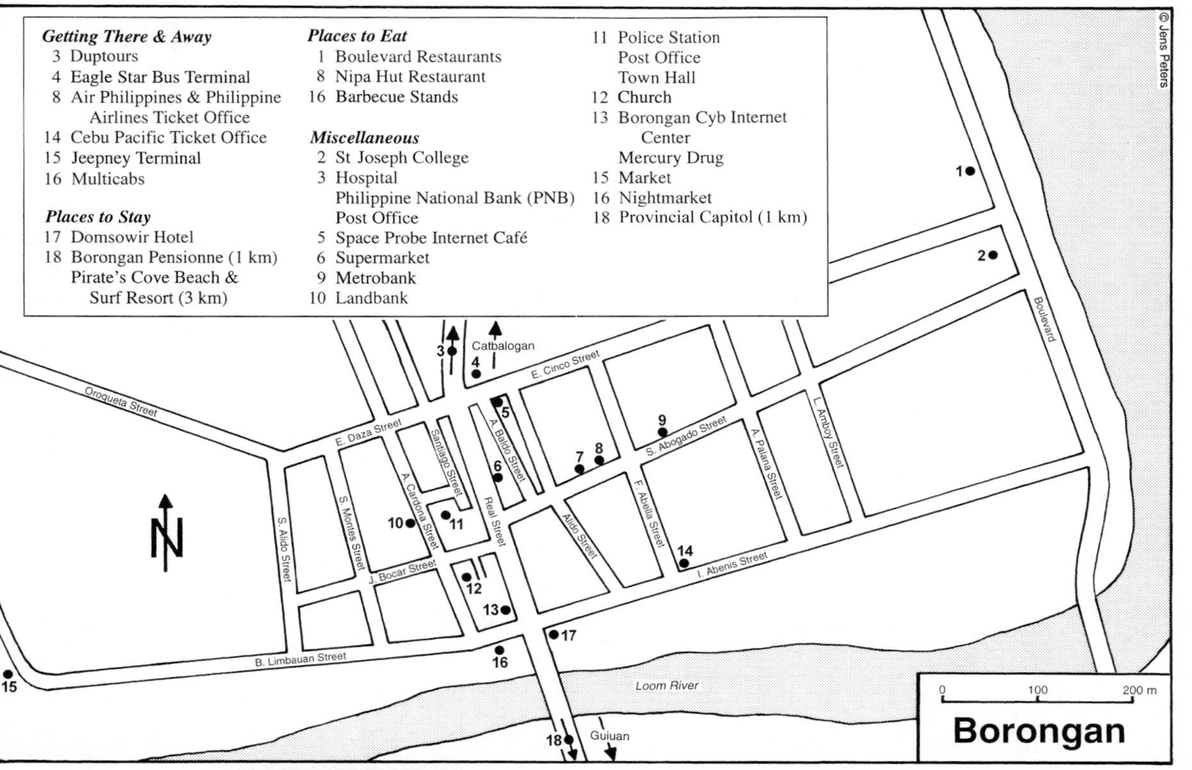

Visayas - Samar

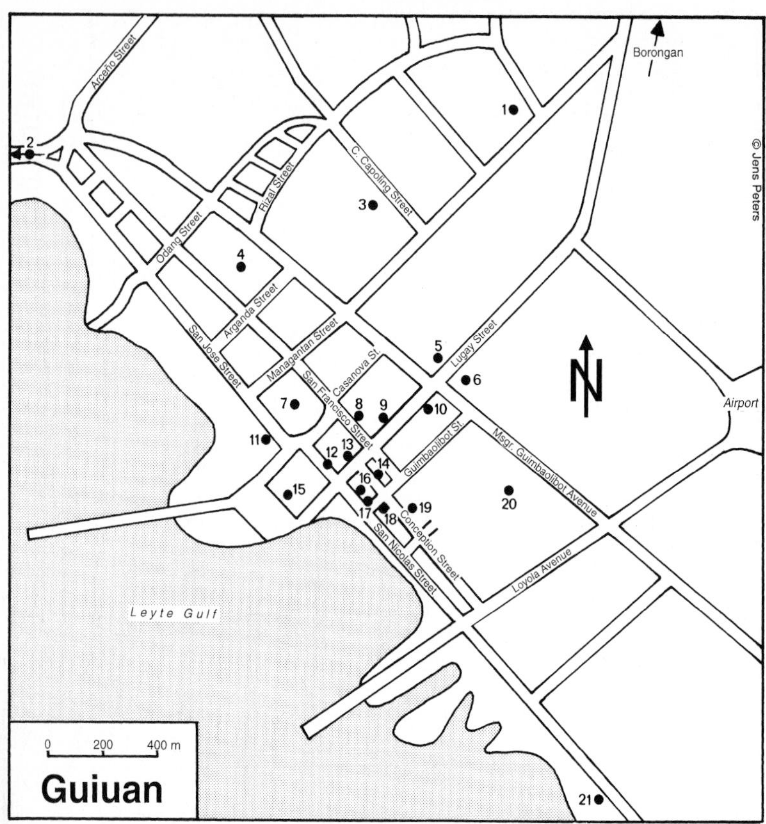

Getting There & Away

Catbalogan
Bus: From 8am onwards, Eagle Star buses leave Catbalogan for Borongan (three hrs). The buses carry on to Guiuan.

Guiuan
Bus/Jeepney: Minibuses and jeepneys leave from early morning until midday from the market in Borongan to go to Guiuan (2½ hrs).

Guiuan & Homonhon Island

Guiuan (pronounced: Geewan) is a friendly little town on a peninsula in south-east Samar. In WWII, the Americans started their aerial attacks on the Japanese from here and the giant airport at the eastern edge was once one of the biggest US bases in the Pacific. Nowadays, the two-km long runway is partially overgrown with vegetation; it's no longer in use.

Getting There & Away
5 Ran-Mar Transport Service Minibuses to Tacloban
6 Eagle Star Bus Terminal
10 Bus Terminal
12 Jeepneys to Borongan
13 Minibuses to Tacloban
17 Torres Transport Service Minibuses to Tacloban

Places to Stay
2 Tanghay View Lodge (1 km)
9 Guiuan Pension House
18 Kevin's Pension House
19 Blue Star Lodge

Places to Eat & Entertainment
14 Sporks Corner Restaurant
21 DJ Disco-Restaurant

Miscellaneous
1 Cockpit
3 Southern Samar General Hospital
4 Town Hall
7 Church
8 Post Office
11 B Hayes Internet Café
13 Police Station
15 Market
16 Philippine National Bank (PNB)
20 Plaza

One of the most beautiful churches of the eastern Visayas can be seen in the centre of Guiuan. Its wonderfully carved doors, one of its most precious treasures, once caught the eye of a certain Imelda Marcos who was not averse to increasing her list of possessions. Thank God, even an offer of two million pesos didn't persuade the men of the cloth to give them up.

Near Guiuan are a couple of attractive beaches which hardly anyone ever visits, as well as numerous small islands west of Guiuan in Leyte Gulf. In 2005 a beach resort should be opening on the beautiful, palm-lined Ngolos Beach on Caliocan Island, a few km south-east of Guiuan.

About 20 km south of Guiuan, the island of Homonhon was the first Philippine ground to be touched by the Portuguese explorer Ferdinand Magellan who was there on behalf of his Spanish paymasters. A memorial plaque reminds visitors of this event which took place on 16 March, 1521.

Places to Stay

Kevin's Pension House, Guimbaolibot St. SR/DR/fan P150, Very basic accommodation.

Guiuan Pension House, Lugay St. SR/DR/fan P100/200, SR/DR/ac P500 (with TV). Basic, but reasonable rooms. The better ones are located at the back of the building. Central location.

Tanghay View Lodge, Campongo. SR/fan P150, DR/fan P320 and P350, SR/ac/bath P450, DR/ac/bath P680 to P800. Squeaky clean rooms of various sizes with TV. Friendly accommodation at the sea front, about one km west of the town centre (tricycle P4 per person). Highly recommended. Restaurant, small beach.

Places to Eat

You can get very cheap meals at the clean ***Sporks Corner Restaurant*** on Concepcion St. The excellent ***Tanghay View Restaurant*** in the lodge of the same name is a pleasant garden restaurant under palms by the sea. A very popular place to go is the ***DJ Disco-Restaurant***, which is built out over the sea. They offer seafood specials in the evening (P30 admission).

Miscellaneous

Online: B Hayes Internet Café, San Jose St; P50/hr.

Population: 35,000.

Post: Post code: 6809.

Getting Around

Pedicab: A trip in town costs P3 per person.
Tricycle: Tricycles for journeys around the Guiuan area can be found in front of the market on the plaza. A trip within town costs P4 per person.

Getting There & Away

Catbalogan - Borongan
Bus/Jeepney: Several buses travel daily from Catbalogan to Guiuan via Borongan (six hrs). Jeepneys also make the trip between Borongan and Guiuan; the last one leaves at about 2 to 3pm.

Homonhon Island
Boat: On good weather days, an outrigger leaves the wharf at the market in Guiuan for Homonhon Island daily at 9am (P30; 1½ hrs).

Marabut

Marabut is on the south coast of Samar, where the scenery is graced by chalk cliffs and little offshore islands with secluded little sandy nooks. This so-called Marabut Marine Park is about 15 km north of Marabut, and with its phalanx of rocky outcrops thrusting out of the water is a popular local beauty spot.

Places to Stay

French Kiss, Amambucale. SR P500, DR P700. Uninspiring accommodation on Jasmin Beach.
Jasmin Beach Resort, Amambucale, Tel (055) 5550012, @. SR/DR/fan P600 (toilet in the restaurant, which is quite a hike), SR/DR/ac/bath P1000 and P1250 (four people). Fairly basic rooms. A bigger resort under palms directly on the beach, with no view of the Marine Park however. Restaurant. Billiards. Kayaks (P120 per hr). Located about two km south of Marabut.
Marabut Marine Park Beach Resort, Tel (053) 5200414. SR/DR/fan/bath P2000; including three meals, P2000 per person. Amiably furnished rooms in tastefully designed duplex cottages. An attractive resort, even if getting on a little now. Idyllically located on a white sand bay. Good restaurant. Kayaks. Located 14 km north of Marabut. This resort belongs to the Leyte Park Resort Hotel in Tacloban, where reservations can also be made.
Ferienhaus Jasmin, Lawa-an, @. Cottage/fan/bath P1300. Neat, pleasantly decorated spacious cottage in the garden. A complete house with living room, bedroom, kitchen and terrace costs P2000. They will cook for guests if requested. This little private bed and breakfast place is 15 km east of Marabut.

Getting There & Away

Bus: Those buses and minibuses which run between Tacloban and/or Borongan and Guiuan taking the south coast route from Samar, go via Marabut. Time from Tacloban: 1½ hrs.

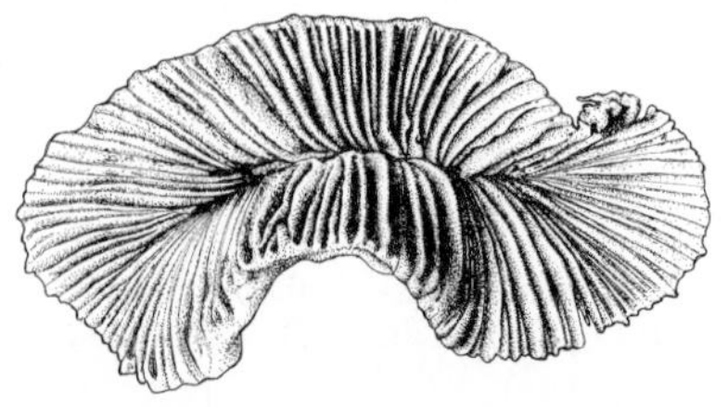

Siquijor

The island of Siquijor is about 25 km east of southern Negros and is one of the smallest provinces in the Philippines. Until 1971 it was a sub-province of Negros Oriental. The 100,000 population of this likeable little island celebrate their Independence Day (Araw ng Siquijor) every year on 17 September. The Siquijodnons are remarkably friendly, but at the same time not in any way pushy.

The largest towns in the province are Siquijor, Larena, Enrique Villanueva, Maria, Lazi and San Juan. Siquijor is the capital, and Larena and Lazi have ports with connections to other islands. A surfaced road encircles this hilly island, connecting its well-kept villages and small towns.

The main industries are agriculture and fishing. Manganese mining north-west of Maria reached its peak before WWII, and deposits of copper and silver have not yet been mined. The economic prosperity of the island is due to a large extent to the money sent back home by Siquijidnons working overseas.

Tourism is still not a major industry on Siquijor, although the potential is obviously there for it. Their palm beaches, waterfalls and caves are just as worth seeing as the historical churches and old houses.

When the Spaniards discovered the island, they called it Isla del Fuego, which means island of fire. This suggests that they saw a large fire as they sailed past. It is believed that what they saw were countless glow-worms.

There is a legend that millions of years ago Siquijor lay completely under water. It emerged from the sea amid crashing thunder and flashing lightning. Fossils of mussels, snails and other underwater creatures can still be found in the mountainous interior and are quoted as evidence for this belief.

You can sense that there is something mysterious about Siquijor when you tell Filipinos that you intend to travel there. They will warn you of witches and magicians and healers with wondrous powers. Many strange events are said to take place on this singular island and are enhanced by the practice of voodoo and black magic. Filipinos will warn you that it is better to avoid it for your own safety's sake...

Getting There & Away

You can get to Siquijor from Bohol, Cebu, Mindanao and Negros (see the Getting There & Away sections of the individual island chapters).

To Bohol

Boat

From Larena to Tagbilaran

Daily with the fast ferries *Oceanjet* (P300; 1½ hrs) and *Supercat* (P565; 3½ hrs; via Dumaguete).

Tuesday, Thursday and Sunday with Palacio Shipping Lines (P135; three hrs).

To Cebu

Boat

From Larena to Cebu City
Two times daily with the fast ferry *Oceanjet* (P600; 3½ hrs); via Tagbilaran/Bohol.
Daily with the fast ferry *Supercat* (P690; 4½ hrs); via Dumaguete/Negros and Tagbilaran/Bohol. discontinued
Monday, Wednesday and Friday with Palacio Shipping Lines (P200; seven hrs).

To Mindanao

Boat

From Larena to Plaridel
Tuesday, Thursday and Sunday with Palacio Shipping Lines (four hrs).

To Negros

Boat

From Larena to Dumaguete
Daily with the fast ferry *Supercat* (P190; 45 min).

From Siquijor to Dumaguete
Four times daily with the fast ferry *Delta* (P100; one hr).

Siquijor

The small town of Siquijor is the capital of the island. It has a Provincial Capitol, a church, a hospital, a post office and the St Francis de Assisi Church with its old belltower, which you can climb up.
At Cangalwang, a little west of Siquijor, there is a small airstrip. The beach there is not recommended.

Places to Stay

Swiss Stars Guest House, Pangi, Tel 4809028, @. SR/DR/fan/bath P320, SR/DR/ac/bath P620 and P780. Great rooms, attractively and cosily furnished, the more expensive with TV. Generous discount for weekly and monthly rates. Very good value for the money. Restaurant. Located about two km east of Siquijor.
Kevin's Beach House, Candanay Sur, Cellphone 0927-4092987, @. SR/DR/ac/bath P500. Sturdily built guesthouse with only a few rooms. Family atmosphere. Small restaurant. Located about 2.3 km east of Siquijor, 500m off the ring road; paved driveway.
The Norwegian Dream Beach Resort, Candanay Norte, Tel. 4809095, Fax: 4809094, @. SR/DR/fan/bath P600/800, cottage/fan/bath P1200. Well-kept place with good rooms and attractive cottages. Restaurant. Located about three km east of Siquijor.
Tikarol Beach Resort, Candanay Sur, Tel 4809047. Cottage/fan/bath P750, P1200 and P1500, depending on size. An idyllic little resort about 2½ km east of Siquijor, with pleasantly decorated, roomy cottages, well tended garden and a good restaurant. A narrow footpath leads from the ringroad to the beach (about 300m from the signpost). The place is run by two women, one from Switzerland, the other from the Philippines. If all you want is just to relax and feel good, this is the place for you.
Dondeezco Beach Resort, Dumanhug, Tel 4809066. SR/DR/ac/bath P850 and P1500. Spacious, pleasantly furnished rooms with TV and balcony in a long stone building. Restaurant. Two swimming pools (one for children) and jacuzzi. This friendly place is located on a long bay with a wide, white sand beach about two km west of Siquijor, 200m off the main road.

Places to Eat

'Mine hosts' in the cosy garden restaurant ***Swiss Stars*** belonging to the eponymous guest house in Pangi, are Geri from Switzerland and his Filipina wife Rea. They serve good European

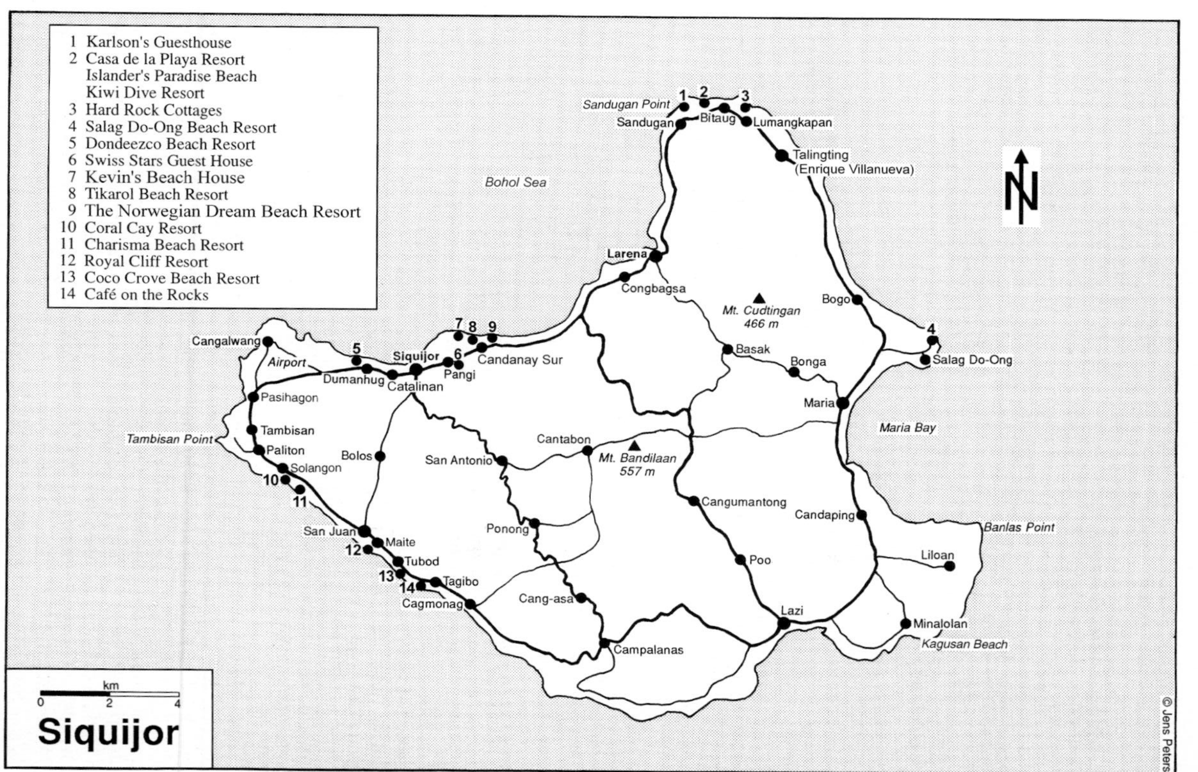

1 Karlson's Guesthouse
2 Casa de la Playa Resort
Islander's Paradise Beach
Kiwi Dive Resort
3 Hard Rock Cottages
4 Salag Do-Ong Beach Resort
5 Dondeezco Beach Resort
6 Swiss Stars Guest House
7 Kevin's Beach House
8 Tikarol Beach Resort
9 The Norwegian Dream Beach Resort
10 Coral Cay Resort
11 Charisma Beach Resort
12 Royal Cliff Resort
13 Coco Crove Beach Resort
14 Café on the Rocks
Sandugan Point
Sandugan
Bitaug
Lumangkapan
Talingting
(Enrique Villanueva)
Bohol Sea
Larena
Congbagsa
Mt. Cudtingan
466 m
Bogo
Salag Do-Ong
Basak
Bonga
Maria
Maria Bay
Cangalwang
Airport
Dumanhug
Siquijor
Catalinan
Pangi
Candanay Sur
Pasihagon
Tambisan
Tambisan Point
Paliton
Solangon
Bolos
San Antonio
Cantabon
Mt. Bandilaan
557 m
Cangumantong
Candaping
Banlas Point
Liloan
San Juan
Maite
Tubod
Tagibo
Cagmonag
Ponong
Cang-asa
Poo
Lazi
Minalolan
Kagusan Beach
Campalanas
km
0
2
4
Siquijor
© Jens Peters

and Philippine dishes at a reasonable price; try their excellent pizza.

Getting There & Away

Tricycle: Short journeys from Siquijor with a tricycle cost P4 per person, P6 to Larena and San Juan. A Special Ride to Sandugan costs between P100 and P150.

Larena

Larena is a quiet little place with a few beautiful buildings. The place only comes to life when a boat docks or departs.

If you walk to Congbagsa and go on along the road that branches off to the right about 100m west of the large, white National Food Authority building, you end up taking some steps down to a peaceful bay with a white beach. If there weren't so many sharp-edged stones in the water, the place would be perfect. There is even a refreshing fresh-water spring flowing out of the rocks here.

Places to Stay

Luisa & Son's Lodge. SR/DR/fan P150/200, SR/DR/ac/bath P500. Basic, friendly accommodation near the noisy wharf. If you can only sleep if it's absolutely quiet, this is not the place for you. However, Luisa and Douglas are very helpful and can provide useful information on the area. They have a restaurant and you can hire a motorcycle.

North Haven Lodge, Capitol Circle, Tel 3772358. SR/DR/fan P150, P200 and P375, SR/DR/ac P400, P450 and P500, depending on size. Small, clean rooms, some with refrigerator. OK for the money. Next to the Old Capitol Building not far from the jetty.

Mykel's Garden Pension House, Roxas St, Tel 3772048. SR/DR/fan P225, SR/DR/ac P575. Basic, family accommodation in the centre (formerly Garden Orchid Pension House). Restaurant.

Getting There & Away
1 Wharf
3 Boat Tickets
13 Tricycles
14 WG & A
20 Multicabs

Places to Stay
6 Luisa & Son's Lodge
7 North Haven Lodge
16 Mykel's Garden Pension House

Places to Eat
6 Luisa & Son's Restaurant
16 Mykel's Garden Restaurant

Miscellaneous
2 Philippine Port Autority
4 Post Office
5 LBC
8 Old Capitol Building
9 Rural Bank
10 Church
11 Police Station
Town Hall
12 Siquijor State College (SSC)
15 Land Bank
17 Allied Bank
18 Market
19 Larena Computer Center
21 Cemetery
22 Cockpit

Places to Eat

There is a fairly large restaurant near the market, where jeepneys wait for passengers. ***Luisa & Son's Restaurant*** near the wharf serves good and relatively inexpensive Philippine food, especially seafood. ***Mykel's Garden Restaurant***, across from the Allied Bank near the market, is also good and inexpensive.

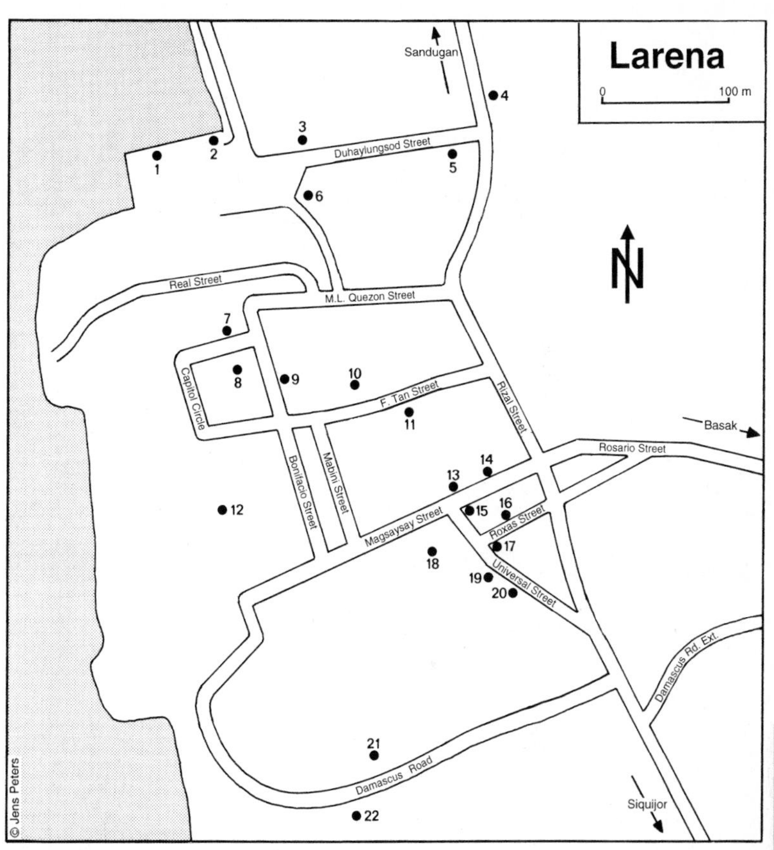

Miscellaneous

Festival: Fiesta of Saint Vecente Ferer on 3 May.

Post & Telephone: The Post Office can be found on the way out of town heading towards Sandugan.

Post code: 6226. Area code: 035 (for all of Siquijor).

Getting There & Away

Jeepney: Numerous jeepneys leave the market in Larena to go to various places around the island. Always ask about the last trip back or you may have to walk, hire a tricycle or stay the night.

Sandugan

Sandugan Point is a fairly deserted beach, six km outside of Larena, with a coral reef just offshore. 'Fairly deserted' because a few resorts have already established a modest infrastructure. If you want peace and quiet but still don't want to be completely alone, then the northernmost tip of Siquijor will just fit the bill.

Places to Stay

Kiwi Dive Resort, Tel & Fax 4240534, Cellphone 0917-3615997, @. Dorm P170, cottage/fan/bath P390 and P450, with refrigerator and cooking facilities P690. A small, cosy place run by Bruce from New Zealand and his Philippine wife Maritess, the atmosphere here is warm and inviting. They offer diving facilities (with their own dive shop and boat), and motorcycle and bicycle hire. Good restaurant.

Islander's Paradise Beach, Cellphone 0919-4469982, @. Cottage/fan/bath P300 to P550 (depending on size), cottage/ac/bath P800, with refrigerator P850. OK cottages right at the beach; good value for the money. They offer a price rebate for longer stays. Pleasant accommodation next to the Kiwi Dive Resort. Restaurant.

Karlson's Guesthouse, Tel 3772242. Cottage/fan/bath P350 and P700 (big, stone building). Small, very quiet place run by Mats the Swede and his Filipina wife Nonnette, who is glad to cook for guests if they order in advance. Boat and motorcycle rental.

Casa de la Playa Resort, Tel & Fax 4841170, Cellphone 0917-3232656, @. Cottage/fan/bath P750 to P1200, cottage/ac/bath P1350 and P1450. Peaceful accommodation in sturdily built, beautifully decorated cottages, on the beach and on a slope. Some have a refrigerator and cooking facilities. The resort is built on a little rise that provides an unobstructed view of the sea below. It is managed by the Filipina Emily, and Terry, who's German. You can hire a motorcycle, bicycle or paddle boat here. Restaurant (including vegetarian food and yoghurt).

Hard Rock Cottages, Bitaug, Tel 4803389, @. Cottage/fan/bath P600 and P700, depending on size. Weekly and monthly rates available. Friendly place with a few pleasant cottages on a rocky

Visayas - Siquijor

section of the coast, with a small beach. Just the place for peace and quiet. Restaurant with a beautiful sea view. Located two km east of Sandugan, just before Talingting (Enrique Villanueva), about 100m off the ring road.

Getting There & Away

Tricycle: A tricycle from Larena to Sandugan costs P5 per person; a Special Ride down to the beach costs P30 (P50 at night).

Salag Do-Ong

Salag Do-Ong is on the east coast of Siquijor at the northernmost point of Maria Bay. With its small swimming beach it is probably the most popular holiday resort with the Siquijodnons.

Places to Stay

Salag Do-Ong Beach Resort. SR/DR/fan P150, DR/ac/bath P800. Basic rooms in stone buildings.

Getting There & Away

There is no regular jeepney service and you have to walk the two km from the road to the beach. The last trip back to Larena is at about 4pm.

Lazi

Lazi is a quiet little port on the south coast. Across from the massive St Isidore Parish Church built in 1884, behind a gnarled stand of acacias, the St Isidore Labradore Convent can be seen. Built in 1891, it's said to be the biggest and oldest in the country.

The coral beaches a little to the east are unsuitable for either swimming or snorkelling. Lapac Beach, north-east of Lazi on Maria Bay, opposite Salag Do-Ong, is said to be better. A few km inland from Lazi, at a place called Po-o set amidst beautiful scenery, you'll find the Kambugahay waterfall with its natural pool.

San Juan

Just outside of the little town of San Juan, on the west coast of Siquijor, you will find several white sand beaches. A few km north-west of there, the palm-lined Paliton Beach is one of the best beaches on the island.

Places to Stay

Charisma Beach Resort, Solangon, Tel 4815033, @. SR/DR/fan/bath P500, SR/DR/ac/bath P750, cottage/ac/bath P1000. Very good rooms in a long stone building and big cottages. Restaurant. Swimming pool, boat and motorbike rental. Located about two km north-west of San Juan.

Royal Cliff Resort, Maite, Tel 4815038, @. SR/DR/fan/bath P600, with refrigerator P700. Gorgeously built place on the impressive rocky coastline of Maite, about 1½ km south-east of San Juan. Quiet, well-tended grounds with plants all around, ideal if you want peace and quiet. The friendly hosts, Arlene and Erich (Filipina and a German) are happy to grant long-term guests a hefty rebate. Good restaurant (seafood specialities). Mountain bike and motorbike rental, tours of the island.

Coral Cay Resort, Solangon, Tel 4815024, @. Cottage/fan/bath P700 to P1200, cottage/ac/bath P1800 and P2300. Spacious, well-furnished cottages, some with refrigerator and TV. A pleasant, well-looked after place under American-Philippine management. Good restaurant, swimming pool. Mountain bike and motorbike rental. Located three km north-west of San Juan.

Coco Grove Beach Resort, Tubod, Tel 4815008, Fax 4815006, @. SR/DR/fan/bath P1200, cottage/ac/bath P1700 and P1900 depending on size, (with refrigerator). The grounds are generously laid out, and the comfortably furnished cottages (each with two rooms) all stand well apart from one another. The garden is a delight, and they have a swimming pool. The restaurant is beautifully laid out. All this, plus attentive service, makes this easily the best place on the island. They have diving facilities (Sea Explorers, Tel 4815007, @), and hire out motorcycles, jeepneys and outriggers. Located two km south-east of San Juan about 100m from the road.

Getting There & Away

Tricycle: A tricycle from Siquijor to Paliton Beach costs P5 per person; a Special Ride from Larena should be available for P100.

San Antonio

San Antonio is in the mountainous interior of the island and has the reputation as a centre for nature healers, also known locally as *mananambals*. But don't expect to find any witches' cauldrons there. The work of these healers has nothing to do with magic, but is a novel attempt to effect cures through the use of coconut oil, herbs and other natural ingredients. By rubbing in the oils and lotions they try to relieve the most common complaints of the sufferers who consult them, mostly people with headaches and stomach pains. One of the best known medicine men in San Antonio is Jose Ponce, who lives in the woods in a simple hut.

A visit to the region during Holy Week should be interesting. That's when various quacks and 'druids' of the southern Philippines gather to exchange information and create dubious herbal potions accompanied by obscure rites. The necessary ingredients are collected during Holy Week, then on Good Friday a brew is brought to the boil in a large cauldron, sorry - vessel, known as a *kawa*, under a specially selected balete tree. Only after a long night of repeated communal praying and much discussion is the deed considered to be done and the healers share out the precious liquid amongst each other, filling up bottle after bottle with it. This is their ration for yet another year to come.

Cantabon

About three km east of San Antonio the small township of Cantabon is located, which is known for its impressive dripstone cave. Coming from Siquijor, the road to Cantabon turns off left after San Antonio market; straight on would take you to Cang-asa and Campalanas. The cave entrance is about 200m north of the market in Cantabon, off the road. Ask at one of the sari-sari stores across from the market if they know a guide.

The way down into the cave is a narrow, steep hole that leads about five to six metres deep into the mountain. After that you can work your way more or less upright, through the dripstones, to the end of the cave several hundred metres away. A crystal clear stream runs through the cave and you have to wade through it in places. Obviously, sturdy shoes and a torch (flashlight) are a 'must' here. Another good idea would be to take along a dry towel, which the guide could keep for you, because spelunking's a dirty business!

In Cantabon you're quite close to the point of highest elevation on the island, Mt Bandilaan, at 557m. It's good for a mountain hike. In the Mt Bandilaan Camp Park there is a small area of luxuriant rain forest through which trails lead to various observation points.

Mindanao & Sulu

If you look at a map, the large land mass south of the Visayas, the island of Mindanao, seems to represent weight and stability, as does Luzon in the north. In comparison, the rest of the Philippine archipelago appears like a jumbled mass of confusion. But the 'Promised Land', as Mindanao is often called, is anything but a pillar of strength and calming influence. For years, the island has been the scene of constant upheaval as different ethnic groups, religions, economic interests and political ambitions have jockeyed for position. Not quite part of the land of promise, but still snuggled into the protection of Mindanao's northern coastline with its many bays, the little volcanic island of Camiguin goes its own unhurried, provincial way.

Basilan and the countless little islands of the Sulu archipelago lie in the water like stepping stones between Mindanao and Borneo. Islands right in the middle of it, by no means free of conflict, but incredibly exciting to visit.

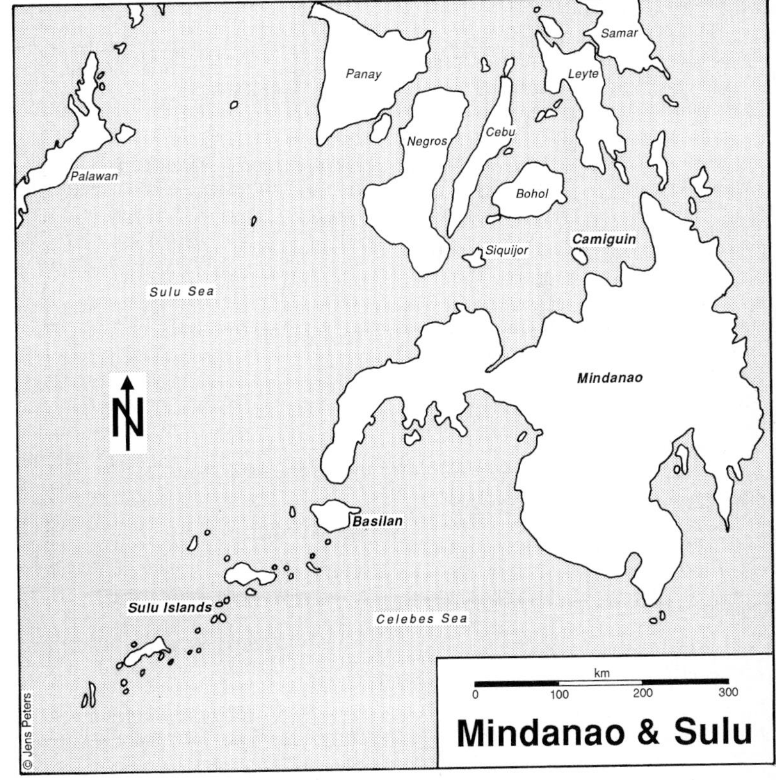

Mindanao & Sulu

Camiguin

Camiguin lies off the north coast of Mindanao. Though relatively small, it has no less than seven volcanoes, as well as springs and waterfalls. The best known volcano is Hibok-Hibok, which last erupted in 1951. Camiguin is well known for its sweet *lanzones* fruit (called buahan on Camiguin), which grows on the slopes of Hibok-Hibok and is the best in the Philippines.

The volcanoes seem to attract clouds like magnets, and from December to mid-March short rain showers can be expected. The sunniest months are April, May and June.

The 70,000 Camigueños are famous for their impressive hospitality. It is certainly one reason why so many of the visitors who have discovered it so far tend to come back again. (Camiguin is pronounced almost like 'come again'...) Unlike on other islands, strangers here are greeted not with 'Hi Joe', but with 'Hi friends'.

Tourism is only just beginning to struggle to its feet on Camiguin. There are no plans as yet for incentives from the state, as other islands are obviously considered a priority. This is not necessarily a bad thing. If you're a friend of nature and can do without glittering hotels, your stay on Camiguin will definitely be a pleasure.

Getting There & Away

You can get to Camiguin from Cebu and Mindanao (see the Getting There & Away sections in the individual island chapters).

To Cebu

Air

From Mambajao to Cebu City
Seair flies on Friday and Sunday (P1300).

Otherwise, the nearest airport for flights to Cebu is in Cagayan de Oro on Mindanao.

Boat

From Benoni to Cebu City
Sunday with Super Shuttle Ferry (car ferry), taking 11 hrs (P450).

Otherwise, the nearest port for crossings to Cebu is in Cagayan de Oro on Mindanao.

To Luzon

Air

The nearest airports for flights to Manila are in Cagayan de Oro and Butuan on Mindanao, in Tagbilaran on Bohol, and in Cebu City on Cebu.

To Mindanao

Boat

From Benoni to Balingoan
A ferry leaves about every hour from 5am to 5.30pm (P50; one hr). A car ferry leaves at 6.45am, 12.30 and 3.30 pm.

From Guinsiliban to Balingoan
Daily at 6.45am, 1.15 and 4.30pm with a car ferry (one hr).

Mambajao

The cosy little town of Mambajao is the capital of Camiguin, which has been a province since 1966. There are still some beautiful old buildings left there. The colourful Lanzones Festival, a sort of thanksgiving festival, takes place here every October.

Places to Stay

Mambajao

GV Pensione House, Burgos St, Tel 3871041. SR/DR/fan/bath P400, SR/DR/ac/bath P600 (TV). Good rooms (spotless). OK for the money.

Casa Grande, Provincial Plaza, Tel & Fax 3870077. SR/DR/ac/bath P1200. Big, well-kept rooms in a beautiful old building across from the Philippine National Bank. Restaurant.

Cabua-an Beach Resort, Balintawak St, Tel 3872103. Dorm/fan P150, cottage/ac/bath P750 and P950, with eight beds P1850. Acceptable cottages with TV. Restaurant. Located at the eastern edge of town.

Around Mambajao

Enigmata Treehouse (*Tarzan's Nest Resort*), Balbagon, Tel 3870273, @. Dorm P150, SR/DR/fan/bath P600 and P800. A unique 'tree house hotel' and art gallery at the same time; one of a kind in the Philippines. It's also home to the group of artists who call themselves the Enigmata Creative Circle. Spread over three storeys, the airy rooms were built from natural materials intertwined around three big trees. You can marvel at this 'must-see' dream house 3½ km south-east of Mambajao, about 500m off the ring road. Restaurant, swimming pool.

Mambajao Beach Resort, Balbagon, Tel 3871059. SR/DR/ac/bath P850, cottage/ac/bath P950. Decent rooms and cottages with TV. Restaurant. Located about three km south-east of Mambajao.

Bahay Bakasyunan sa Camiguin, Balbagon, Tel 3871057, Fax 3870278. Cottage/ac/bath P1650. Good, roomy cottages with TV. Extensive, quiet grounds about 2½ km south-east of Mambajao. Restaurant, swimming pool, car and boat hire.

Camiguin Highland Resort, Sorosoro, Tel 3870515. SR/DR/ac/bath P2000 and P2400, suite P3675 and P8800. Comfortable, well-appointed rooms. Attractive resort about five km south of Mambajao. Restaurant, swimming pool, jacuzzi.

Places to Eat

Inexpensive Philippine food, breakfast and a variety of mouthwatering cakes is available in ***Viola***. They sometimes also have a choice of salads (fruit, potato, pasta) - just ask. A popular expat hangout is ***Sneakers*** next to the Salcedo supermarket.

Miscellaneous

Festivals: Panaad (processions) during Easter Week. San Juan sa Hibok-Hibok on 24 June (all over the island). Lanzones Festival in the third week in October.

Money: You can change travellers' cheques at the Philippine National Bank, Burgos St corner Aranas St, although the rate is not as good as in Cagayan de Oro or Cebu City, for instance. There are no cash advances available on Camiguin (Visa, MasterCard etc); the nearest opportunity would be Cagayan de Oro.

Online: There are Internet cafés at the Shell filling station, Rizal St, at Fatima College and in the Provincial Capitol Planning & Development Office.

Population: 18,000.

Post & Telephone: Post code: 9100. Area code (for the whole of Camiguin): 088.

Travel Agency: Camiguin Action Geckos Tour Service, Mabini St corner Umycco St, Tel 3871266, @, offers various tours on Camiguin (climbing, riding, trekking, diving etc) and takes

care of hotel and transport reservations too.
Fun Trips, VJ Neri Building, Highway corner Llacuna St, Tel 3870380, sells tickets for planes and boats, and will also take care of organising visas.
Tourist Office: There's a tourist information centre behind the Provincial Capitol; Tel 3871097 (ext 119).

Getting Around

Car: Aircon minibus hire with driver for P2500 (eight hrs) in the Bahay Bakasyunan Saturday Camiguin, Balbagon, Tel 3871057, Fax 3870278.

Getting There & Away

By Air: Mambajao Airport is within walking distance from town.
Seair, Airport Office, Tel 3870035.
Destination: Cebu City.

Agoho
Tricycle: A tricycle from Agoho to Mambajao costs P3.50 per person or P30 per tricycle.

Benoni
Jeepney: Several jeepneys run daily from Benoni to Mambajao, the last one leaving at about 5pm (P12; 30 min). A Special Ride costs P150 to P200.

Around Mambajao

Hibok-Hibok Volcano

Hibok-Hibok (1332m) is the most active of Camiguin's seven volcanoes. On 5 December 1951 it erupted without warning, killing over 2000 people. A small collection of photos and newspaper clippings can be seen at the Phivolcs Station (Philippine Institute of Volcanology and Seismology) which monitors volcanic activity. This is about 400m up the mountain and takes a good hour to reach on foot. The staff at the station will be happy to show you around and explain the use of the seismographic instruments. They appreciate small gifts like bread, sweets and cigarettes. Phivolcs employees are not allowed to conduct tours from the station up to the volcano.
For trips to the volcano, the Tourism Office behind the Provincial Capitol in Mambajao or any resort can arrange an experienced guide for about P500. The climb is via Ardent Hot Springs and Esperanza and takes about four hours. It begins with a gentle slope and takes you first through high cogon grass and fern groves, leading to a steeper section which takes you over scree, lava and rock faces to the summit. If you start your climb as early as possible - say 5am, but by 9am at the latest - you should be able to make it back down again before sunset and save an overnight stay on the mountain (allow four hours for the descent). Some of the guides try to make it up and down again in record time and don't like being held up for any reason. The tour loses a lot of its appeal when they do this, of course. So you should not only agree on the price with the guide, but also on the time available. Note: As there are no streams or wells on the way to the summit, take enough water with you.
Once at the top, you can climb down to a moss-encircled crater lake. This takes less than an hour. If you decide to go down to the lake, it would be wise to spend the nights before and after the trek at the Phivolcs Station to save time. In the dry season you can take a tent and camp beside the lake.

Katibawasan Falls

Surrounded by tropical vegetation, the falls thunder down from a height of 50m. The water is refreshingly cool. The best time to go there is from 10am to 2pm, because you can also sunbathe

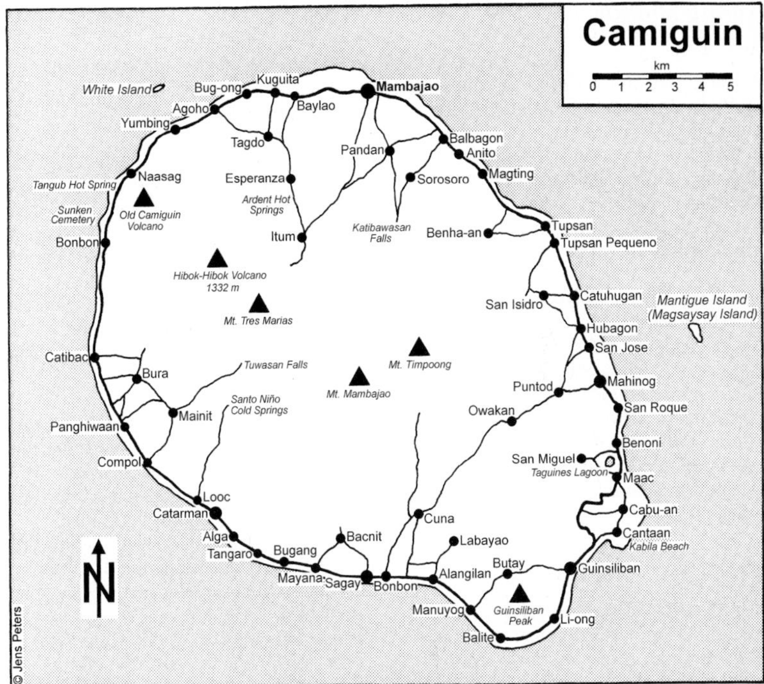

there at that time. You should take your own sustenance with you, although fruit and drinks are available. Admission: P15.

Getting There & Away

Tricycle: To get to the falls, go first from Mambajao to the village of Pandan by tricycle. You then have to do the remaining three km from the fork in the road at the edge of town to the falls on foot. When it's dry, the track to the rest house can be reached by motorcycle.

Ardent Hot Springs

The temperature of the crystal clear water in the beautifully built swimming pools is around 40ºC. The surrounding area is well tended and there are sheltered picnic places. It's a favourite for weekend outings; the pool is cleaned out on Monday from 8am till noon. Admission costs P18.

Places to Stay

Ardent Hot Springs Resort. Dorm P175 to P250 (depending on the number of beds), SR/DR/fan/bath P600, SR/DR/ac/bath P1000. Good restaurant.

Getting There & Away

Tricycle: Including a few hours' waiting time, the trip from Mambajao by tricycle and back costs around P150. There are numerous paths from the ring road to the hot springs, all of which take about an hour on foot.

White Island

White Island is a small island about three km north of Agoho. It consists of nothing but coral and sand, and there's no shade. A parasol or a tent would really come in handy. It's a good place for swimming and snorkelling, although the coral has been decimated in recent years by thoughtlessly destructive fishing methods.

Getting There & Away

Tricycle/Boat: To get to White Island, go by tricycle or jeepney from Mambajao to Agoho, Yumbing or Naasag, then charter a boat. At the White Island terminal in Agoho and in the resorts there, you can organise a round trip for between P200 and P250 per boat. Agree on a time for them to return for you.

Around the Island

You can travel right around the island, which has a circumference of about 65 km, in about three hours by jeepney if you don't make too many stops. For the best connections, go in an anticlockwise direction, as there are not many vehicles between Yumbing and Catarman - the road between Benoni and Mambajao is most travelled by jeepneys and buses and is your best prospect for getting transport on the return trip. Plenty of jeepneys also travel between Catarman, the second largest town on the island, and Benoni. Along the west coast, however, be prepared to walk a few km, as only a few jeepneys run from Mambajao to Catarman and back.

For short distances you may be able to use tricycles but the service is only good in and around Mambajao. A trip around the island by rented motorcycle is a great idea, but remember to check the tank before you leave.

Kuguita

The sandy beach at Mahayahay and Turtles Nest Beach, which has a few corals, are in Kuguita, three km west of Mambajao.

Bug-ong, Agoho & Yumbing

These small coastal towns, five to seven km west of Kaguita, are on most travellers' itineraries and all have their own beach resorts. At Agoho you can get a boat to the offshore White Island for P200 to P250 (see above).

Places to Stay

Jasmine by the Sea Beach Resort, Bug-ong, Tel 3879015. Cottage/fan/bath P500. Friendly place with only a few, but good, cottages in a garden setting. Restaurant, motorcycle hire.

Camiguin Seaside Lodge, Agoho, Tel 3879050. Cottage/fan/bath P500. Roomy cottages, that are unfortunately past their best.

Caves Dive Resort, Agoho, Tel 3879040, Fax 3870077, @. SR/DR P440, SR/DR/fan/bath P550, cottage/fan/bath P770, cottage/ac/bath P1320. and Reasonable rooms and good cottages. Restaurant, diving.

Secret Cove Beach Resort, Yumbing, Tel & Fax 3879084. SR/DR/fan/bath P500 and P600 (depending on size), SR/DR/ac/bath P1000 (with refrigerator and TV). Pleasant accommodation with immaculate rooms. Under Canadian management. Restaurant, billiards, bicycle hire, kayaks, diving.

Camiguin Beach Club, Yumbing, Tel 3879028, @. SR/DR/ac/bath P1000, with refrigerator and TV. OK rooms with verandas in peaceful grounds. Restaurant, swimming pool.

Paras Beach Resort, Yumbing, Tel 3879008, Fax 3879081, @. SR/DR/ac/bath P1700 to P3100, cottage/ac/bath P4950. With TV, some with a refrigera-

tor. Pleasant garden grounds with tasteful rooms and cottages with two bedrooms for up to eight people. Big restaurant, swimming pool, car and boat hire as well as many different watersport facilities.

Places to Eat
There are a few no-frill ***Eateries*** with inexpensive Filipino food on the 'Highway', as the main road from Agoho is called. The ***Jasmine by the Sea Restaurant*** in Bug-ong, and the ***Secret Cove Restaurant*** in Yumbing, will prepare really good European food for you. ***Paras Restaurant***, in the resort of the same name, serves excellent seafood and pizzas.
The food at the popular ***Green Tropical*** garden restaurant in Baylao (half-way between Agoho and Mambajao) is international, and they have a well-stocked bar. Another good place to eat and drink is the ***Paradiso Italian Restaurant***.

Miscellaneous
Diving: A dive costs about P1400, a four to five-day diving course P16,500.
Camiguin Action Geckos Dive Center, Agoho (at the Caves Dive Resort), Tel. 3879140, @.
Johnny's Dive 'n' Fun, Yumbing (at the Secret Cove Beach Resort), Tel. 3879585.
Sea Kayaking: Kayaks can be hired at the Paras Beach Resort and at the Secret Cove Resort, both in Yumbing.

Getting Around
Motorcycle: Various different resorts rent motorbikes (125 cc Enduro) for about P500 per day.

Getting There & Away
Jeepney/Tricycle: A Special Ride by jeepney from Benoni to Agoho is P150. The trip from Mambajao to Agoho by tricycle costs P7 per person; P30 for a Special Ride.

Bonbon

Bonbon is mainly famous for its Sunken Cemetery, which disappeared under the waters after a volcano erupted in 1871. Some years ago, gravestones could be seen poking out of the water at low tide so they say. Now, a large cross in the sea indicates where the Sunken Cemetery is, and that's about all you can see from the coast. If you want to get down to details, then diving would be an interesting way of doing it. Every year on 21 May, the anniversary of the tragedy, Camigueños go to the spot in boats and strew flowers in the water.
A bit north of Bonbon you'll come across the old ruins of the Guiob Church, overgrown with moss. Further north again, starting at the ringroad in a bay, the stations of the cross lead up to the Old Camiguin Volcano (Mt Daan), a favourite with pilgrims during Holy Week. Each of the 14 stations offers a good view. There is a clearly recognisable path which branches off from the way of the cross up to the summit of the volcano (sturdy shoes are a must).

Catarman

At around two and five km north-west of Catarman there are turn-offs leading to the Tuwasan Falls (bad, stony surface), about four to five km from the ringroad. When you get to the Dinangasan River, you have to head upstream a bit to find them. The local people compare the two main falls with two different women: one, Katibawasan, who wears lots of make-up; the other, Tuwasan, who has a natural, unspoilt beauty.
The nearby Santo Niño Cold Springs are refreshingly cool and you can swim in a nice large pool that is one to two metres deep; the pool is cleaned out on Wednesday. There are toilets, a picnic shelter, as well as basic overnight ac-

commodation (cottage/fan P700). The place is also known as the Kiyab Pool and is over two km off the main road. Admission costs P10.

Getting There & Away

Jeepney: Jeepneys leave Mambajao for Catarman at 6 and 9am, noon and 2pm (P15; 1½ hrs). The last one leaves Catarman for Mambajao at 4pm.

Guinsiliban

In Guinsiliban in the south of the island a roughly 300-year old Moro watchtower stands behind the elementary school.

In the village of Cantaan, about four km north-east of Guinsiliban, you'll find Kabila Beach, a beautiful, secluded, 300m long stretch of white sand. If you're travelling by jeepney, have them drop you off on the main road at the Cantaan turnoff and walk the last two km to the beach; turn right when you get to the village. At the east end of the beach the little DENR Center rents flippers and diving goggles and will prepare food for you if you order it beforehand.

Benoni

Benoni (Binone) has a wharf for ferries going to and from Balingoan on Mindanao. From here boats also go to Mantigue (Magsaysay) Island, which lies offshore and is a favourite diving place. About one km south of Benoni there is a beautiful artificial lake, Taguines Lagoon, which is separated from the sea by a causeway.

Places to Stay

J & A Fishpen & Resort, Tel 3874008. Dorm/fan/bath P100, SR/DR/fan/bath P300, SR/DR/ac/bath P600. Basic cottages with large verandas on piles in the water of the Taguines Lagoon. It's a beautiful, cosy and peaceful little place, if somewhat past its best. Good restaurant. A tricycle ride there costs P20.

Mahinog & Mantigue Island

Mahinog lies on the east coast of Camiguin, almost opposite Mantigue (Magsaysay) Island. The beach there is pebbly but Mantigue Island has a white sandy beach and usually offers good snorkelling. If you want to stay for a few days, bring your own provisions and drinking water. The round trip from Mahinog costs about P500 (also possible from Benoni).

Tupsan

Near Tupsan, about one km from the ringroad, you can take a refreshing dip in the cold water of the Macao Cold Spring. The turn-off is sign-posted.

Mindanao

Mindanao is the second largest island of the Philippines. Its landscape is dominated by mountain chains running north-south. Close to Davao is Mt Apo, the highest mountain in the Philippines. Mindanao is one of the Philippines' richest islands, even though little of its mineral wealth has yet been tapped. There is an occasional gold rush sparked off by rumours of a sizeable find, but at present most of the island's income comes from agriculture, with large pineapple plantations in the north near Cagayan de Oro and banana groves in the south near Davao.

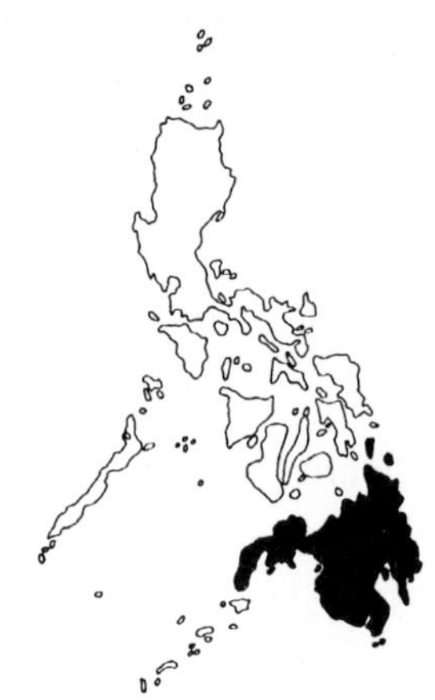

Blood-stained Peace

The struggle of the Moro National Liberation Front (MNLF) for an autonomous Muslim state on Mindanao and the Sulu Islands lasted a quarter of a century. From the perspective of the Philippines government, this was a demand which could never be met. They were, however, prepared to make a concession and established the autonomous region ARMM (Autonomous Region in Muslim Mindanao), comprising the four provinces of Lanao del Sur, Maguindanao, Sulu and Tawi-Tawi. On this basis the government and the MNLF finally signed a peace treaty in 1996, although this by no means brought the fighting to an end. Many Muslims and Christians were, and still are, totally against the treaty and show no desire to take things lying down. Particularly serious are attacks by supporters of the radical Moro Islamic Liberation Front (MILF) and the Abu Sayyaf Group (ASG), splinter groups that broke away from the MNLF because of political differences and are responsible for causing their own brand of trouble. The militant Abu Sayyaf, a group of heavily armed Muslim separatists, use frequent spectacular bombing campaigns and the taking of hostages to draw attention to their demands for an independent Islamic state on Philippine soil. The islands of Basilan and Jolo are pretty much under their control and unsuitable destinations for travel until further notice. It would also be just as well to avoid the provinces of Lanao del Norte, Lanao del Sur and Maguindanao for the time being.

Although some situations are often portrayed as being worse than they are, you should nevertheless enquire about possible crisis spots before making overland trips in western Mindanao. It is not a good idea to get into a bus which is half-filled with soldiers, as these are especially likely to be shot at. The soldiers usually take the cheaper buses and seldom the aircon ones.

Mindanao

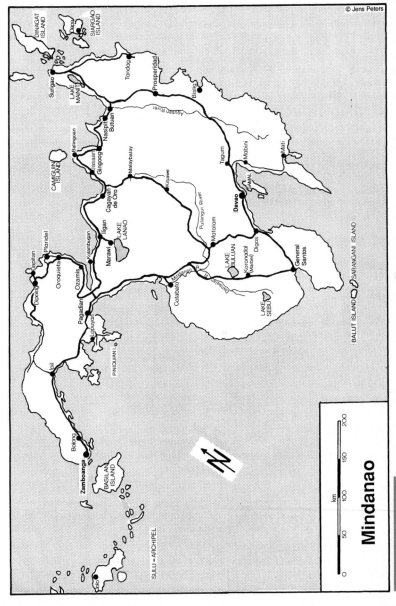

It is not quite true that all of the Mindanao population is Muslim but certainly most of the Muslim Filipinos live there and on the neighbouring Sulu Islands. The area around Lake Lanao in central Mindanao is predominantly Muslim.

Getting There & Away

You can get to Mindanao from Basilan, Bohol, Camiguin, Cebu, Leyte, Luzon, Negros, Panay, Siquijor and Sulu Islands (see the Getting Away from Luzon section in the Manila chapter and the Getting There & Away sections of the individual island chapters).

To Basilan

Boat

From Zamboanga to Isabela
Daily with Basilan Shipping Lines (P35; 1½ hrs).

From Zamboanga to Lamitan
Daily with Basilan Shipping Lines (P35; 1½ hrs). The wharf at Lamitan is on the outskirts of town.

To Bohol

Boat

From Butuan/Nasipit to Jagna
Sunday with Cebu Ferries (P240; six hrs).
Thursday with Sulpicio Lines (seven hrs).

From Cagayan de Oro to Jagna
Wednesday and Sunday with Cebu Ferries (P280; five hrs).
Friday with Sulpicio Lines (five hrs).

From Cagayan de Oro to Tagbilaran
Tuesday, Thursday and Saturday with Trans-Asia Shipping Lines (P400; eight hrs).

From Dapitan/Dipolog to Tagbilaran
~~Daily with the fast ferry *Supercat* (P710; 3½ hrs), via Dumaguete/Negros.~~ discontinued
Sunday with WG & A (P400; seven hrs).

To Camiguin

Boat

From Balingoan to Benoni
A ferry leaves roughly every hour from 6am until 4pm (P50; one hr).

From Balingoan to Guinsiliban
Daily at 6.15 and 11.15am, and 2.30pm with a car ferry (one hr).

To Cebu

Air

From Cagayan de Oro to Cebu City
Asian Spirit flies Monday, Wednesday, Friday, Saturday and Sunday (P2310).
Seair flies on Tuesday, Thursday and Sunday (P1750).

From Cotabato to Cebu City
Seair flies on Monday and Friday (P2650).

From Davao to Cebu City
Air Philippines and Philippine Airlines fly daily (P2590).
Cebu Pacific flies daily except Saturday and Sunday.

From Dipolog to Cebu City
Asian Spirit flies Monday, Wednesday, Friday and Saturday (P2350).

From General Santos to Cebu City
Air Philippines has daily flights (P2640).

From Siargao Island to Cebu City
Seair flies on Tuesday and Saturday (P1990); Saturday via Tandag.

From Surigao to Cebu City
Asian Spirit flies on Tuesday, Thursday, Saturday and Sunday (P1430).

From Tandag to Cebu City
Asian Spirit flies on Monday, Wednesday, Friday and Saturday (P2350).
Seair flies on Tuesday and Saturday (P2190); Tuesday via Siargao Island.

From Zamboanga to Cebu City
Cebu Pacific flies Monday, Wednesday, Friday and Saturday (P2650).

Boat

From Butuan/Nasipit to Cebu City
Monday, Wednesday and Friday with Cebu Ferries (P330; 11 hrs).
Tuesday, Friday and Sunday with Sulpicio Lines (P270; 13 hrs).
Wednesday with WG & A (P580; 16 hrs); via Surigao.

From Cagayan de Oro to Cebu City
Daily with Trans-Asia Shipping Lines (10 hrs).
Daily, except Saturday and Sunday, with Cebu Ferries (P390; 10 hrs).
Tuesday, Thursday and Sunday with Sulpicio Lines (P390; eight hrs).

From Dapitan/Dipolog to Cebu City
Daily with the fast ferry *Supercat* (P875; 5½ hrs); via Dumaguete/Negros and Tagbilaran/Bohol. discontinued
Daily, except Sunday, with Cokaliong Shipping Lines (14 hrs); via Dumaguete/Negros.

From Davao to Cebu City
Wednesday and Sunday with Sulpicio Lines; Wednesday via Surigao (P1190; 28 hrs), Sunday via General Santos (35 hrs).

From Iligan to Cebu City
Tuesday, Thursday and Sunday with Cebu Ferries (P520; 16 hrs); via Ozamis.
Friday with Sulpicio Lines (P430; nine hrs).

From Ozamis to Cebu City
Tuesday, Thursday, Saturday and Sunday with Cebu Ferries (P520; 11 hrs).
Friday with Sulpicio Lines (P430; seven hrs) and Trans-Asia Shipping Lines (10 hrs).

From Surigao to Cebu City
Daily, except Monday, with Cokaliong Shipping Lines (P385; 11 hrs); Tuesday, Wednesday and Friday via Maasin/Leyte.
Thursday with Sulpicio Lines (P420; eight hrs), Trans-Asia Shipping Lines (10 hrs) and WG & A (P500; seven hrs).

From Zamboanga to Cebu City
Wednesday and Saturday with George & Peter Lines (50 hrs); via Dipolog and Dumaguete.
Friday with Aleson Shipping Lines (P850; 23 hrs); via Dumaguete.

To Leyte

Bus/Boat

From Cagayan de Oro to Tacloban
Daily with a Philtranco bus, taking 13 hrs including the ferry Lipata/Surigao-Liloan.

From Davao to Tacloban
Two Philtranco buses daily, taking 16 hrs including the ferry Lipata/Surigao-Liloan.

Boat

From Surigao to Liloan
Daily at 1, 6 and 11.30am and 5.30pm with a car ferry from Lipata, 10 km north-west of Surigao (three hrs).

From Surigao to Maasin
Tuesday, Wednesday and Friday with Cokaliong Shipping Lines (4½ hrs).
Saturday with Sulpicio Lines (P125; four hrs). The ship carries on to Baybay and Calubian.

To Luzon

Air

From Butuan to Manila
Philippine Airlines has daily flights (P3000).

From Cagayan de Oro to Manila
Air Philippines, Cebu Pacific and Philippine Airlines have daily flights (P3645).

From Cotabato to Manila
Philippine Airlines flies daily except Friday (P3838).

From Davao to Manila
Air Philippines, Cebu Pacific and Philippine Airlines have daily flights (P3670).

From Dipolog to Manila
Philippine Airlines flies daily except Saturday (P3838).

From General Santos to Manila
Air Philippines and Philippine Airlines have daily flights (P3670).

From Zamboanga to Manila
Air Philippines, Cebu Pacific and Philippine Airlines have daily flights (P3670).

Bus/Boat

From Cagayan de Oro to Manila
Daily with a Philtranco aircon bus (P1320), taking 39 hrs including the ferries from Lipata/Surigao to Liloan and from Alegria/San Isidro to Matnog.

From Davao to Manila
Two Philtranco aircon buses daily (P1400), taking 42 hrs including the ferries from Lipata/Surigao to Liloan and from Alegria/San Isidro to Matnog.

Boat

From Butuan/Nasipit to Manila
Wednesday and Saturday with WG & A (P1740; 32 hrs); via Surigao.

From Cagayan de Oro to Manila
Tuesday, Friday and Saturday with WG & A (P1790; 35 hrs); Friday via Dumaguete/Negros (39 hrs).
Wednesday and Sunday with Negros Navigation (P1920; 35 hrs); Wednesday via Bacolod/Negros, Sunday via Iloilo City/Panay.
Friday with Sulpicio Lines (P1800; 27 hrs).

From Cotabato to Manila
Monday with WG & A (P1890; 38 hrs); via Zamboanga and Iloilo City/Panay.
Tuesday with Sulpicio Lines (P1500; 56 hrs); via Zamboanga, Iloilo City and Estancia/Panay.

From Davao to Manila
Monday and Wednesday with WG & A (P1870; 54 hrs); Monday via General Santos and Iloilo City/Panay, Wednesday via General Santos and Zamboanga.
Tuesday with Sulpicio Lines (P1500; 66 hrs); via Zamboanga, Iloilo City and Estancia/Panay.

From Dipolog to Manila
Sunday with WG & A (P1250; 41 hrs); via Tagbilaran/Bohol.

From General Santos to Manila
Monday with Sulpicio Lines (P1900; 54 hrs); via Cebu City.
Tuesday and Thursday with WG & A (P1870; 42 hrs); Tuesday via Iloilo City/Panay, Thursday via Zamboanga.

From Iligan to Manila
Tuesday with Negros Navigation (P1610; 37 hrs); via Iloilo City/Panay.
Tuesday and Saturday with WG & A (P1490; 30 hrs).

From Ozamis to Manila
Tuesday with Negros Navigation (P1650; 42 hrs); via Iligan und Iloilo City/Panay.

Tuesday and Saturday with WG & A (P1490; 35 hrs); Saturday via Iligan (39 hrs).

From Surigao to Manila
Thursday and Sunday with WG & A (P1550; 28 hrs); Thursday via Cebu City (33 hrs),
Thursday with Sulpicio Lines (P1540; 40 hrs); via Cebu City.

From Zamboanga to Manila
Monday and Thursday with WG & A (P1460; 27 hrs); Monday via Iloilo City/Panay (39 hrs).
Wednesday and Saturday with Sulpicio Lines (P1270; 46 hrs); Wednesday via Iloilo City and Estancia/Panay, Saturday via Iloilo City.

To Negros

Air

From Davao to Bacolod
Air Philippines flies daily; via Cebu City (P3645).

From General Santos to Bacolod
Air Philippines flies daily; via Cebu City (P3645).

Boat

From Cagayan de Oro to Bacolod
Wednesday with Negros Navigation (P1330; 13 hrs).

From Cagayan de Oro to Dumaguete
Friday with WG & A (P600; seven hrs).

From Dapitan/Dipolog to Dumaguete
~~Daily with the fast ferry *Supercat* (P425; 1½ hrs).~~ discontinued
Daily with George & Peter Lines (five hrs).
Tuesday, Wednesday, Thursday, Friday and Saturday with Cokaliong Shipping Lines (four hrs).

From Iligan to Bacolod
Monday with WG & A (P1360; 13 hrs).

From Ozamis to Bacolod
Saturday with WG & A (P1390; 14 hrs).

From Ozamis to Dumaguete
Sunday with Sulpicio Lines (P320; five hrs).

From Zamboanga to Dumaguete
Wednesday and Saturday with George & Peter Lines (16 hrs); via Dipolog.
Friday with Aleson Shipping Lines (P615; 17 hrs).

To Panay

Air

From Davao to Iloilo City
Air Philippines and Cebu Pacific have daily flights; via Cebu City (P3645).

From General Santos to Iloilo City
Air Philippines has daily flights; via Cebu City (P3645).

Boat

From Cagayan de Oro to Iloilo City
Sunday with Negros Navigation (P1330; 12 hrs).

From Cotabato to Iloilo City
Tuesday with Sulpico Lines (P960; 34 hrs); via Zamboanga.
Sunday with WG & A (P1210; 38 hrs); via Zamboanga.

From Davao to Iloilo City
Monday with WG & A (P1450; 35 hrs); via General Santos.

From General Santos to Iloilo City
Tuesday with WG & A (P1450; 24 hrs); via Zamboanga.

From Iligan to Iloilo City
Tuesday with Negros Navigation (P1350; 13 hrs).

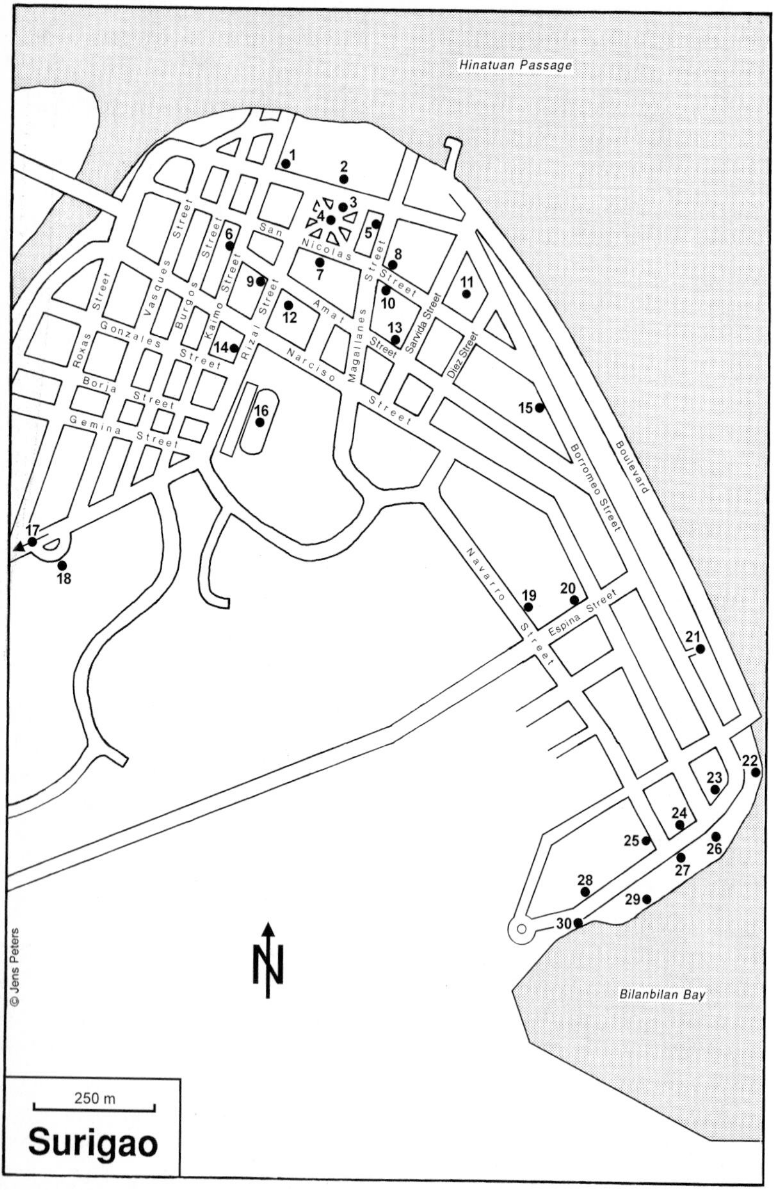

Hinatuan Passage
Bilanbilan Bay
San Nicolas Street
Amat Street
Narciso Street
Vasques Street
Burgos Street
Kaimo Street
Rizal Street
Magallanes Street
Sarvida Street
Diez Street
Roxas Street
Gonzales Street
Borja Street
Gemina Street
Borromeo Street
Boulevard
Navarro Street
Espina Street
1
2
3
4
5
6
7
8
9
10
11
12
13
14
15
16
17
18
19
20
21
22
23
24
25
26
27
28
29
30
N
250 m
Surigao
© Jens Peters

Getting There & Away
6 Sulpicio Lines
17 Airport (3 km)
Bus & und Jeepney Terminal (3 km)
20 WG & A
24 Trans-Asia Shipping Lines
28 Alev Shipping Lines
Aska Shipping Lines
BCT Shipping Lines
Cokaliong Shipping Lines
29 Wharf
30 Boats to Siargao Island

Places to Stay
10 Garcia Hotel
13 SLB Pensionne House
15 Leomondee Hotel
17 Hotel Gateway (1 km)
19 Metro Pension Plaza
21 The Tavern Hotel
23 SLB Pensionne House Annex

Places to Eat
9 Alesandra Chicken House
21 The Tavern Restaurant
22 Adriano's STK by the Sea
25 4 A's Fast Food
27 Barbecue Stalls

Miscellaneous
1 Police Station
2 City Hall
Post Office
3 Tourist Office
4 Plaza (Luneta Park)
5 Surigao Internet Café
7 Church
8 Equitable PCI Bank
9 Alesandra Supermart
11 Market
12 Northeastern Mindanao College
14 Bank of the Philippine Islands
Philippine National Bank (PNB)
16 Grandstand
18 Hospital
26 Philippine Port Authority (PPA)

From Zamboanga to Iloilo City
Monday with WG & A (P880; 15 hrs).
Saturday with Sulpicio Lines (P700; 19 hrs).

To Siquijor

Boat
From Plaridel to Larena
Tuesday, Thursday and Sunday with Palacia Shipping Lines (four hrs).

To Sulu Islands

Air
From Zamboanga to Jolo
Seair flies daily except Sunday (P1290).

From Zamboanga to Tawi-Tawi
Seair flies daily except Friday and Sunday (P2490).

Boat
From Zamboanga to Bongao
Monday, Wednesday and Saturday with Aleson Shipping Lines (P470; 16 hrs).
Monday and Friday with SRN Fast Seacraft (P900; seven hrs - fast ferry).

From Zamboanga to Jolo
Daily with SRN Fast Seacraft (P420; 3½ hrs - fast ferry).
Daily with Aleson Shipping Lines (P180; eight hrs).

North Mindanao

Surigao

Surigao, the capital of Surigao del Norte Province, is the starting point for trips to offshore islands like Dinagat and Siargao. What must be the best beach in the Surigao area, Mabua Beach, 12 km outside the city, is a favourite weekend resort. The water is clear here and the swimming is great, although the beach itself has black pebbles instead of sand.

It's always a bit rainy in north-east Mindanao and in December and January be prepared for heavy downpours. If you can put up with a few drops, however, you will be well rewarded by the magnificent landscape of the east coast. The best time to visit Surigao and its surroundings is from April to June.

Places to Stay

Tavern Hotel, Borromeo St, Tel 2317300, 8268566. SR/DR/fan P120/190, SR/fan/bath P150 and P220, DR/fan/bath P190 and P270, SR/ac/bath P420 to P850, DR/ac/bath P520 to P950. They have a number of different kinds of room of varying quality, the expensive ones in the annex (with refrigerator and TV) are good and acceptable. Restaurant.

Leomondee Hotel, Borromeo St, Tel 8260364. SR/DR/fan P200, SR/DR/ac/bath P400 to P1100 (DR with TV). Reasonable rooms of different sizes, the DR have TV. Fairly new accommodation.

SLB Pensionne House, Amat St, Tel 2326739. SR/DR/fan/bath P275, SR/DR/ac/bath P465, with TV P50 extra. Spacious, well-appointed rooms. Restaurant and karaoke on the ground floor. Good value, as is the more recently opened *SLB Pensionne House Annex* in Borromeo St, Tel 8263564, only a few minutes on foot from the jetty.

Metro Pension Plaza, Navarro St, Tel 2326726, 8266468. SR/ac/bath P350, DR/ac/bath P500, with TV P40 extra. Friendly, family accommodation with clean rooms. Value for money.

Hotel Gateway, Tel 2324257, 8261283, Fax 8261285. SR/DR/ac/bath P800 to P2250, depending on size and furnishings. All rooms have TV, the expensive ones also have a refrigerator. Quality hotel, in fact the best in town. Good restaurant, cellar bar. Located about two km south of the town centre.

Places to Eat

The attractive ***Adriano's STK by the Sea*** can be recommended. Located in the harbour area right on the ocean, they serve quite inexpensive seafood in a great atmosphere. The ***Alesandra Chicken House*** in Rizal St at the corner of Amat St, is air-conditioned and offers good-value Philippine and international dishes. You can get inexpensive Filipino food and barbecued dishes in ***4A's Fast Food*** in Navarro St at the corner of Borromeo St. Not far from there, at the jetty in Borromeo St, you will find lots of ***Barbecue Stalls***.

Miscellaneous

Festivals: Bonok-Bonok Maradjao Festival and City Fiesta on 9 September.

Money: Bank of the Philippine Islands, Rizal St, Equitable PCI Bank, San Nicolas St corner Magallanes St, and Philippine National Bank, Rizal St, have ATMs.

Online: Surigao Internet Café, Magallanes St. P35/hr.

Population: 110,000.

Post & Telephone: Post code: 8400. Area code: 086.

Tourist Office: Tourism Assistance Center, Luneta Park, Borromeo St, Tel 8268064, Fax 8264131. Open Mon-Fri 8am-noon and 1-5pm.

Getting There & Away

By Air: Surigao Airport is about four km from the centre. A tricycle costs P25 to P30. Multicabs cost P6 per person.

Asian Spirit, Airport Office, Tel 8261571. *Destination:* Cebu City.

By Bus: The Surigao Bus terminal is about four km south of the city centre. Jeepneys and comfortable multicabs go from the terminal through downtown (Rizal St, Borromeo St) to the wharf.

By Boat: Most boats use the wharf south of town at the end of Borromeo

St (tricycle costs P3 per person). The ferries to and from Liloan on Leyte use the wharf at Lipata, about 10 km northwest of Surigao. The regular price for a tricycle from the centre of town to Lipata should be about 15 per person. There are also jeepneys and multicabs from the bus terminal (P12).
Aska Shipping Lines, Borromeo St (at the wharf), Tel 8268952.
Destination: Siargao Island.
BCT Shipping Lines, Borromeo St (at the wharf), Tel 2324999.
Destination: Siargao Island.
Cokaliong Shipping Lines, Borromeo St (at the wharf), Tel 8265118.
Destination: Cebu.
Trans-Asia Shipping Lines, Borromeo St (at the wharf), Tel 2326375.
Destinations: Cebu, Leyte.
Sulpicio Lines, Kaimo St, Tel 2317548.
Destinations: Cebu, Davao, Manila.
WG & A, Espina St, Tel 2326625, 8265474.
Destinations: Cebu, Manila.

Cagayan de Oro - Butuan
Bus: Buses belonging to various companies make the trip daily from Cagayan de Oro to Surigao via Butuan. The trip takes six hrs; 2½ hrs from Butuan.

Boat: From Butuan to Surigao on Wednesday and Sunday with WG & A (4½ hrs).

Davao
Bus: Buses belonging to various companies go every day from Davao to Surigao, mainly in the morning. You may have to change in Butuan. The trip takes eight hrs.
Philtranco buses go from Davao to Surigao, carrying on to Tacloban and Manila.

Boat: From Surigao to Davao on Monday with Sulpicio Lines (P975; 17 hrs).

Dinagat Island
Boat: Daily except Saturday from Dinagat to Surigao at 4.30pm with the big outrigger MB *Amelia* (P40; one hr). Departure from Surigao to Dinagat daily at 12.30pm.

Siargao Island
Boat: From Dapa to Surigao daily at 5am and noon with the Aska Shipping Lines' fast ferry *Aska Queen* (P200; 1½ hrs). Departure from Surigao to Dapa at 10am and 2.30pm.
The BCT Shipping Lines' fast ferry *Fortune Jet* leaves Dapa for Surigao daily at 5.45am and 12.15pm (P150; 1½ hrs). Departure from Surigao to Dapa at 8am and 2.15pm.
The BCT Shipping Lines' MV *Fortune Angel* leaves Dapa for Surigao daily at 6.30am (P130; three hrs). Departure from Surigao to Dapa at 11.30am.
A boat travels from Sapao to Surigao daily (though possibly only every second day) at 6.30am (four hrs). Departure from Surigao to Sapao between 9.30 and 11.30am. This boat also takes motorbikes and cars.

Siargao Island

Siargao is the biggest island in the mini-archipelago to the east of Surigao, though still relatively unknown amongst travellers. It is blessed with a tropical backdrop that in places could have come straight out of a picture book, with more palms than you could count, white beaches, an azure ocean and deserted offshore islands. The infrastructure for tourists is still modest, so it's too early to expect much in the way of transport and accommodation. Most resorts can only provide the most basic of facilities, power cuts are frequent, and running water is by no means to be taken for granted (although clean enough spring water is available for showers). Most international visitors chiefly value the island because of its excellent surf, especially from August to October on the east coast which faces the Pacific. At least a dozen breaks have become popular, including Tuason Point, Cloud Nine, Rock Island, and Pilar Point, all north of General Luna and reachable on foot or by boat. Just south of Union there's Pansukian Reef, and further south out on the islands of La Janosa and Antokon huge breakers are just waiting for surfers to experience them. The annual Siargao International Surfing Cup takes place in October.

Getting There & Away

By Air: The little Siak Airport is in the south-west of the island, about half-way between Dapa and Del Carmen. At the moment there are flights to and from Cebu City and Tandag.
Seair: Municipal Hall, General Luna.
Destinations: Cebu City, Tandag.

Surigao

Boat: From Surigao to Dapa daily at 10am and 2.30pm with the Aska Shipping Lines' fast ferry *Aska Queen* (P200; 1½ hrs). Departure from Dapa to Surigao at 5.15am and 12.15pm.
The BCT Shipping Lines' fast ferry *Fortune Jet* leaves Surigao for Dapa daily at 8am and 2.15pm (P150; 1½ hrs). Departure from Dapa to Surigao at 5.45am and 12.15pm.
The BCT Shipping Lines' MV *Fortune Angel* leaves Surigao for Dapa daily at 11am (P130; four hrs). Departure from Dapa to Surigao at 6.30am.
A boat goes from Surigao to Sapao daily (but possibly only every other day) between 9.30 and 11.30am (four hrs). Departure from Sapao to Surigao at 6.30am.

Tandag

Air: Seair flies Saturday from Siargao to Tandag and Tuesday from Tandag to Siargao (P990; 25 min).

Dapa

Dapa is on the south coast of Siargao and is the most important town on the island. There are boat connections from there to Surigao and to Socorro on Bucas Grande Island.

Miscellaneous

Money: There is a bank in Dapa, but you can't change travellers' cheques or cash there, so bring enough pesos with you.

Getting Around

Jeepney: After the arrival of a ferry, jeepneys travel from Dapa to almost all of the coastal towns, most reliably in the mornings. Remember to ask for departure times for the return journey.

General Luna

General Luna, a laid-back small town on the south-east tip of the island, is the most popular destination on Siargao Island, especially for surfers.

Places to Stay

General Luna

Patrick's on the Beach, Cellphone 0920-4024356, @. Cottage/fan/bath P750 and P1000, cottage/ac/bath P1500. Friendly resort with basic, but still alright cottages all on the beach. They also have tents for hire (big, family tents for P500 a day). Restaurant. Located on the northern edge of town.
Cherinicole Beach Resort, Cellphone 0918-2444407, @. Cottage/fan/bath P800, SR/DR/ac/bath P1200, cottage/ac/bath P1400, P1600 (with refrigerator and TV) and P1800 (with cooking facilities). Several pleasant cottages of different sizes and fittings. Restaurant. Beach bar. Billiards. Swimming pool (planned). Located in the northern outskirts of town.

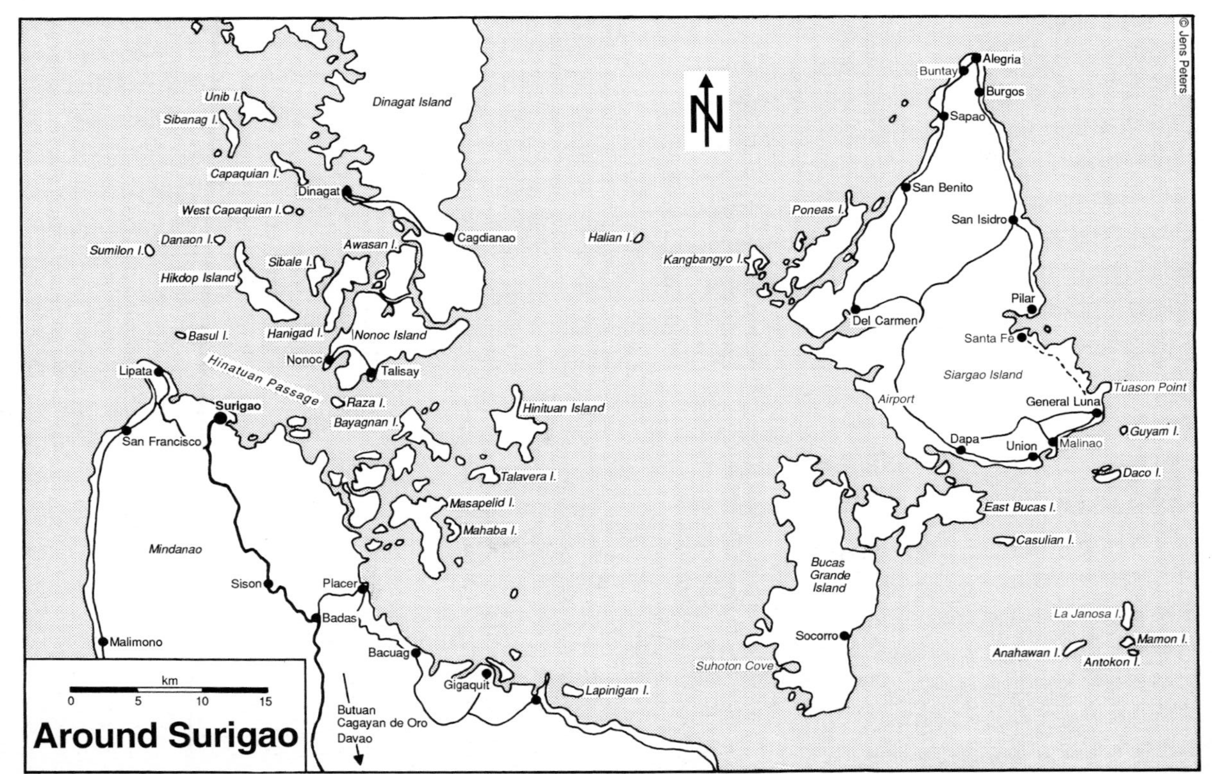

Mindanao & Sulu

Around General Luna

There are a few places stay at the beach about two km west of General Luna. A habal-habal there costs P20 per person (see Getting Around below).

Jadestar Lodge, Cellphone 0919-2344367, @. Cottage/fan/bath P300 and P600 (four people), SR/DR/ac/bath P1200 and P1500. Friendly, very peaceful accommodation, a little out of the way. Hire of outriggers and sailboats.

Villa Ernesto Resort, Fax (086) 8263487. Cottage/fan/bath P350. Family-style place with tidy cottages.

Places to Eat

There are only a few restaurants in General Luna. Good-value Philippine food is available at the popular ***Maridyl*** and ***Lourdes Foodhouse***. Otherwise, most resorts have good restaurants, eg ***Patrick's on the Beach*** that includes on its menu excellent fish dishes and eight different international breakfasts.

A popular place to meet and slake your thirst with an ice-cold beer is ***Matt's Halfmoon Bar*** on the beach in the northern ourtskirts of town.

Miscellaneous

Online: Patrick's on the Beach has the only internet café on the island and charges P50 an hour.

Post & Telephone: A public telephone is available in the Town Hall.

Post code: 8419. Area code: 086.

Surfing: Surfboards can be hired at Dodong (next to the Lourdes Foodhouse).

Tours: Peter the Australian from the Pirate's Bar organises jeepney tours around the island as well as trips with outriggers or sailboats.

Getting Around

Boat: An outrigger costs around P2000 a day, including crew and petrol.

Bicycle: Dodong (next to the Lourdes Foodhouse) hires out mountainbikes for P100 a day.

Motorcycle: The usual means of transport for short trips is the habal-habal, a motorbike with an extended bench for up to four passengers. Depending on the distance and number of passengers the price per person is around P5 to P20. To rent one for the day (with driver) for a trip around the island will cost you P800.

Getting There & Away

Dapa

Jeepney: Four or five jeepneys travel during the day from Dapa to General Luna (P10; 30 min). The last chance to go back might be around noon.

Motorcycle: A Special Ride with a habal-habal costs P100.

Union & Malinao

Located halfway between Dapa and General Luna, Union is a village with lovely beaches, a small bay and outlying islands. It is at the western end of the bay and is connected to Dapa by an eight-km road. There is an irregular jeepney service between the two places. Malinao, a peaceful little place at the east end of the bay, has a beautiful sandy beach.

Places to Stay

Arenas Blancas Resort, Union. Cottage/fan/bath P100 per person. Unpretentious, older resort in a palm garden with a view of the offshore islands. Very peaceful location. Restaurant.

L & B Beach Resort, Malinao. Dorm P100, SR/DR 250, cottage/bath P150 and P250. Fairly good value, peaceful accommodation in an almost unspoilt natural setting. German management. Restaurant with Philippine and European cooking, bicycle hire, table tennis.

Pansukian Tropical Resort, Cellphone 0918-9039055, @. Cottage/ac/bath

P8500 to P13,000 per person. Full board is inclusive. A very attractive luxury resort with all the trimmings you would expect. Well-tended garden. Restaurant, water sport facilities. Known to the locals as 'Rambo's Place' (after its French owner Nicolas Rambeau).

Getting There & Away

Jeepney: A jeepney leaves Dapa for Union every day at 7am and sometimes at noon. Corresponding departure from Union for Dapa is between 10 and 11am and between 1 and 2pm.

Catangnan

Three km north of General Luna, at Tuason Point, Catangnan is the surfers' headquarters. It's also known as Cloud 9 after the offshore reef of the same name.

Places to Stay

Jungle Reef Surf Resort. Dorm P200, cottage/fan/bath P600. Restaurant. Pleasant grounds with tidy cottages in the garden. Goggles and flippers are available for rent, as well as boats.

The Green Room Surf Camp, @. Cottage/fan/bath P350, SR/DR/fan/bath P400. Reasonable rooms and cottages. Restaurant, surfboards for hire

Cloud 9, Cellphone 0918-7970656 Cottage/fan P400, cottage/fan/bath P1000 to P1200, depending on size. Nicely built cottages in pleasant surroundings on the beach. Good restaurant.

Drop Inn, Cellphone 0918-7742467. SR/DR/fan/bath P1500, including breakfast. Appealingly designed place with stylishly furnished rooms and a friendly atmosphere. Restaurant, karaoke, surfboards for hire, boat trips.

Sagana Resort, Cellphone 0919-8095769. Cottage/fan/bath P1500 to P2750, cottage/ac/bath P2500. Attractive resort with tastefully built, well-equipped cottages in a beautiful garden. Restaurant. Billiards.

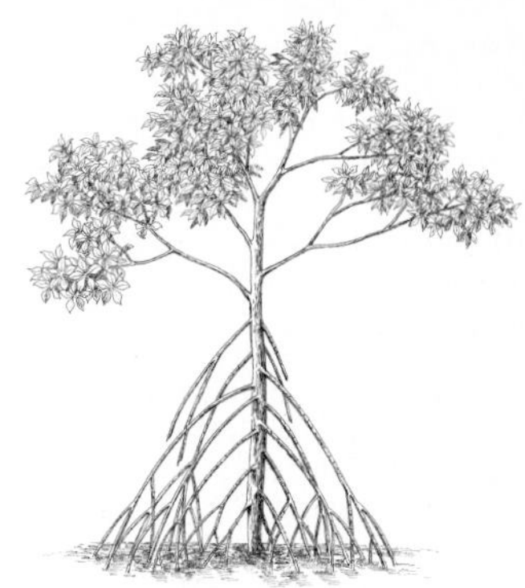

Mangrove *(Rhiziphora mangle)*
Mangrove trees are resistent to the effects of sea water and grow mainly around river mouths in the tidal area of tropical coasts.

Del Carmen

There are said to be crocodiles at Del Carmen (Numancia), 25 km from General Luna, but the reports only seem to come from people who don't happen to be there at the time!

Getting There & Away

Jeepney: At least two jeepneys a day go from Dapa to Del Carmen between 7 and 9am.

Pilar

The little township of Pilar is located on the north side of Port Pilar Bay on the east coast of Siargao Island. Similar to Del Carmen, the countryside around Pilar is covered by extensive mangrove swamps which are criss-crossed by a network of 'water streets'. You can take an interesting day trip there by boat from General Luna and cruise these waterways.

Burgos

Near Burgos on the north-east coast of Siargao Island there are a few reasonable sandy beaches, coral reefs and places to surf.

Alegria

This is the northernmost community on Siargao Island, with a beautiful white sand beach. There is a popular place to surf near Buntay, a bit south-west of Alegria. Otherwise, the area is pretty well deserted.

Getting There & Away

Dapa
Jeepney: A jeepney makes the trip every day between 7.00 and 9.00am from Dapa to Alegria via San Isidro and Burgos (2½ hrs), and back the next day.

Surigao
Boat: A boat makes the trip between Surigao and Sapao every day; see *Siargao Island* above. A habal-habal will take you from Sapao to Alegria (P20, although they'll ask for P50), or Burgos (P50).

Islands Near Siargao

You can reach the lovely little outlying islands of Guyam, Daco, La Janosa, Anahawan, Mamon and Antokon with their magnificent white sand beaches, by outrigger from Dapa, Union and General Luna.
South-west of Siargao, Bucas Grande Island is a 'must see' if you're island hopping.

Bucas Grande Island

The jagged south-west coast of Bucas Grande Island, with its rich vegetation, deserted beaches and craggy little offshore islets, is the location of Suhoton Cove, a labyrinth of fjords only accessible at low tide. There is a Ranger Station at the entrance to the cove where admission is taken (P80 for foreigners, P10 for Filipinos). It's best to have the correct amount ready as there is a shortage of change around here.
The Ranger accompanies the visitors and pilots the boat through the shallows. The trip starts in a natural tunnel (keep your head down if the water is high) then opens into an impressive fjord with countless, ever-changing steep walled ravines off to the sides. The water in this area of untouched nature is crystal clear, the coral appearing near enough to touch. At low tide you can swim into a cave which is home to bats.

La Janosa Island

La Janosa is inhabited. Apart from the village of the same name in the north-east of the island, there is the fishing village of Suyangan where private accommodation is available. In the south of the island there's a beautiful beach with a magnificent coral reef which stretches to the next island, Mamon. It's a popular place to surf (Mamon Reef).
South of the nearby island of Anahawan, a wreck juts out of the water in places.

Butuan

Butuan, on the Agusan River in the north-east of Mindanao, is the capital of the province of Agusan del Norte. Several Filipino historians assert that Butuan could be the site of the oldest urban settlement in the country. This theory seemed to be confirmed in 1976 by the discovery near Butuan of a *balanghai* (a large sea-going outrigger boat) thought to be over 1000 years old. You can see the balanghai in a special-

ly made glass showcase in the place it was found outside the town (known as the 'boat site'), half-way between Butuan and the airport, roughly 1.2 km from the main road.
In 1984, not far from the Agusan River, human bones, including skulls, were found together with death masks, porcelain, pottery and jewellery, which indicated an even earlier occupation of Butuan. The 1984 finds are displayed in the Museum of History next to the Town Hall (two km from the town centre; P5 by tricycle); open Mon-Sat 9am-noon and 1-4.30pm, admission free.

Places to Stay - bottom end

Hensonly Plaza Inn, San Francisco St, Tel 2252040. SR/fan P130, SR/ac/bath P330, DR/ac/bath P500. Basic but neat rooms (some with no windows); the aircon ones have a TV. Restaurant.
Imperial Hotel, San Francisco St, Tel 3415319. SR/fan/bath P200, SR/ac/bath P400, DR/ac/bath P450. Fairly good, OK for the money. The aircon rooms have a TV.
Embassy Hotel, Montilla Blvd, Tel 3425883. SR/ac/bath P400, DR/ac/bath P500. Reasonable, although very small, rooms, all with TV. Friendly service. Peaceful location. Restaurant.
Emerald Villa Hotel, Villanueva St, Tel 2252141. SR/ac/bath P450 and P500, DR/ac/bath P550 and P600. With TV. A well-run hotel in a quiet location with spotless, albeit poorly sound-proofed, rooms (wooden walls). Good restaurant.
Royal Plaza Hotel, T Calo St, Tel 3415125, Fax 3425824. SR/ac/bath P450, DR/ac/bath P550 to P1200. Good, spacious rooms, well worth the money, with TV. Restaurant.
Hotel Karaga, Montilla Blvd, Tel 3415405, Fax 3415260. @. SR/ac/bath P600 and P1300, DR/ac/bath P700 and P1400. Suite P1600 to P2500. Good hotel with immaculate rooms with TV, the suites also have a refrigerator. Restaurant.
Balanghai Hotel, Malvar Subdivision, Doongan, Tel 342064, Fax 3423067. @. SR/DR/ac/bath P700 (with no windows) and P800, suite P1500 and P2500. Cosy rooms with TV, the suites also with refrigerators. An attractive, well-maintained, good-sized place. Restaurant, coffee shop, swimming pool. Peacefully located about two km northwest of the town centre (near City Hall).
Almont Hotel, San Jose St, Tel 3425263, Fax 3415010. SR/ac/bath P800, DR/ac/bath P950, suite P1400 and P1500. Good rooms, all with TV and refrigerator. Restaurant. Central location at the small Rizal Park.

Places to Eat

On Montilla Blvd, the inexpensive restaurant in the ***Embassy Hotel*** is open around the clock. The ***Punta Engano Restaurant*** in the Almont Hotel, San Jose St, serves international dishes. ***D'New Narra Restaurant*** on Juan Luna St has a good reputation for inexpensive Chinese food.
In the Jet's Hotel on Villanueva St, the good, air-conditioned ***Jet's Sinugba*** specialises in seafood. There's a ***Shakey's*** at the corner of Lopez Jaena St and Montilla Blvd.

Entertainment

There are various ***Karaoke Bars*** dotted around the entire town. You can catch live music in the evenings at ***Jet's Pop Garden*** on Montilla Blvd.

Miscellaneous

Festivals: City Fiesta on 19 May. Abayan Festival on the last Sunday in July.
Medical Services: The MJ Santos Hospital, Montilla Blvd, is the best hospital in Butuan.
Money: Bank of the Philippine Islands, Equitable PCI Bank and Philippine National Bank, all on Montilla Blvd,

Getting There & Away
1 Sulpicio Lines
2 Andaya Bus Terminal (2 km)
12 Philippine Airlines
17 Cebu Ferries
WG & A
18 Sulpicio Lines
28 Bancasi Airport (7 km)

Places to Stay
4 Royal Plaza Hotel
5 Balanghai Hotel (2 km)
6 Imperial Hotel
8 Jet's Hotel
9 Butuan Luxury Hotel
11 Hotel Karaga
13 Emerald Villa Hotel
14 Hensonly Plaza Hotel
21 Almont Hotel
Luciana Inn
34 Embassy Hotel

Places to Eat
7 Jet's Pop Garden
8 Jet's Sinugba Restaurant
16 Shakey's Pizza
20 D'New Narra Restaurant
21 Punta Engaño Restaurant
22 Jollibee

Miscellaneous
2 Langihan Market (2 km)
3 Post Office
5 City Hall (2 km)
Museum of History (2 km)
19 Small Market
15 Equitable PCI Bank
19 Bank of the Philippine Islands
22 Otis Department Store
23 Crown & Empress Cinema
24 Crown Thrift Market
25 Urios College
26 St Joseph Cathedral
27 Rizal Park
28 Boat Site (4.7 km)
Gaisano Department Store (2 km)
29 MJ Santos Hospital
30 Web Crawl Internet Café
31 Police Station
32 The Net Café
Web Art Internet Center
33 Tourist Office (100m)
35 Philippine National Bank (PNB)

have ATMs available. ATMs belonging to the first two banks can be found in the Gaisano department store, JC Aquino Ave corner of Jose Rosales Ave.
Online: Web Crawl Internet Café, RC Calo St; Web Art Internet Center and the Net Café, the latter two both on Montilla Blvd. All charge P40/hr.
Population: 230,000.
Post & Telephone: Post Office, Flores Ave.
Post code: 8600. Area code: 085.
Tourist Office, Pili Dr, Tel 2255712, Fax 3418413, @. Open Mon-Fri 8am-noon and 1-5pm.

Getting There & Away

By Air: Bancasi Airport is about seven km west of Butuan. The Butuan-Cagayan de Oro road is about 200m from the airport. To the left it goes to Butuan and to the right to Balingoan (2½ hrs; ferries for Camiguin) and Cagayan de Oro. Buses pass by here. A taxi from the airport to Butuan costs about P80, a multicab P7. Multicabs and jeepneys leave from Aquino Ave in the town centre for the airport showing as their destination 'Aquino-Libertad-Bancasi'.
Philippine Airlines, Villanueva St, on the corner of RD Calo St, Tel 3428576.
- Bancasi Airport, Tel 3415156, 3415257.
Destination: Manila.

By Bus: The Andaya Bus Terminal is about two km north-west of the town centre. A tricycle costs P4 per person.

By Boat: Boats from other islands tie up at the harbour in Nasipit/Lumbacan.

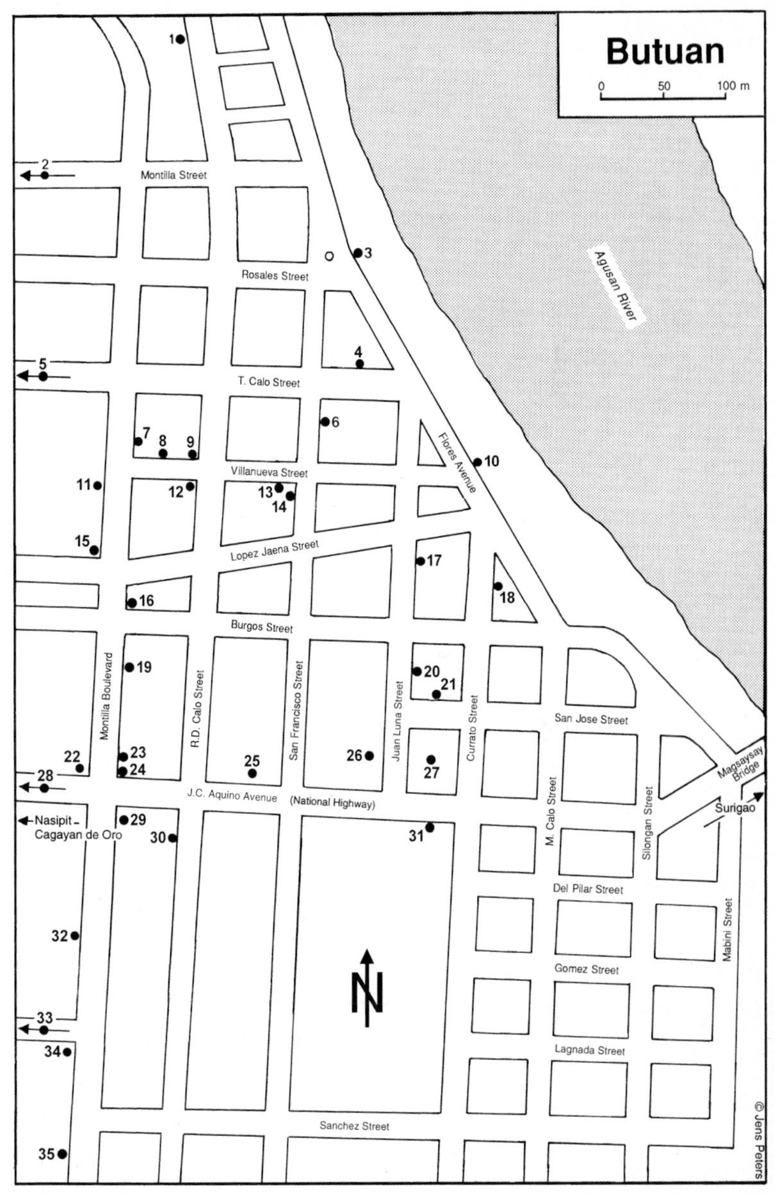
Butuan
0
50
100 m
Montilla Street
Rosales Street
T. Calo Street
Villanueva Street
Lopez Jaena Street
Burgos Street
Flores Avenue
Agusan River
Montilla Boulevard
R.D. Calo Street
San Francisco Street
Juan Luna Street
Currato Street
San Jose Street
M. Calo Street
Silongan Street
Magsaysay Bridge
Surigao
J.C. Aquino Avenue
(National Highway)
Nasipit - Cagayan de Oro
Del Pilar Street
Gomez Street
Lagnada Street
Mabini Street
Sanchez Street
© Jens Peters

Jeepneys run between Lumbacan and Butuan (P15; 20 min). From Butuan to Lumbacan they leave from Aquino Ave showing as their destination 'Nasipit' or 'Lumbacan'.
Cebu Ferries (WG & A), Juan Luna St, Tel 2252822, 3415351.
Destinations: Bohol, Cebu.
Sulpicio Lines, RD Calo St, Tel 3425790, 3425791.
- Currato St (Best Bakery), Tel 3415223.
Destination: Cebu.
WG & A, Juan Luna St, Tel 2252822, 3415351.
Destinations: Cebu, Manila.

Cagayan de Oro
Bus: Several buses travel daily from Cagayan de Oro to Butuan (3½ hrs).

Davao
Bus: Several buses make the trip daily from Davao to Butuan, mainly in the forenoons (6½ hrs).
Philtranco buses go from Davao to Butuan, carrying on via Surigao to Tacloban and Manila.

Surigao
Bus: Several buses from various different companies travel daily from Surigao to Butuan (2½ hrs), either direct or heading towards Davao, Cagayan de Oro or Iligan.

Boat: From Surigao to Butuan on Wednesday and Sunday with WG & A (4½ hrs).

Balingoan

A small coastal town on the road from Butuan to Cagayan de Oro, Balingoan is the departure point for ships going to nearby Camiguin Island (see also the Mindanao Getting There & Away section). The bus terminal is on the highway. It's only a few minutes on foot to the jetty (about 100 m).

Places to Stay

Balingoan Hotel. SR/DR/fan P100 to P120 per person. Very basic place to stay, near the jetty.
Ligaya's Restaurant & Cold Spot. SR/DR/fan P100/200. Unpretentious accommodation with only one room, near the jetty.
Mantangale Alibuag Dive Resort, Tel & Fax (088) 8562324, @. SR/DR/ac/bath P950 and P1500, depending on size. Neat rooms, the more expensive include breakfast. Attractive, quite place. Restaurant, swimming pool, diving. Located 1½ km outside of Balingoan in the direction of Butuan; P5 by tricycle.

Getting There & Away

Bus: Buses displaying the destination of Butuan make the trip roughly every hour from Cagayan de Oro to Balingoan. Comfortable, slightly faster minibuses also cover this route (P50; 1½ hrs).

Cagayan de Oro

Cagayan de Oro, the 'City of Golden Friendship', is the capital of the province Misamis Oriental. It is a clean and friendly university city with numerous schools. Golden Friendship Park, also known as Divisoria, is right at the heart of the city.
An old legend explains how the name Cagayan is derived from the word *kagayha-an*, which means shame. The legend tells of an attack on a Manobo tribe by another tribe. The defeated villagers planned to retaliate, but, before they could, their chieftain fell in love with the daughter of the enemy chieftain and married her. His disgusted subjects referred to their village as a place of shame or Kagayha-an. The Spaniards pronounced it Cagayan and, after they discovered gold in the river, it became Cagayan de Oro.

Museum

The Xavier Museo de Oro on Corrales Ave includes in its displays an overview of the Maranao and Bukidnon cultures as well as other cultural minorities on Mindanao. Open Mon-Fri 8-am-5pm. Admission P10.

Shopping

In the east of the city you will find the Cogon Market (good for fruit and Islamic wares) and several big department stores, including the Oro Rama Super Center, Borja St, and Gaisano, Bora St at the corner of Osmeña St. The Limketkai Shopping Center (LKKC) on Limketkai Dr is a huge shopping centre with various department stores, restaurants and food stalls. The big Gaisano City Mall can be found north of the centre in Corrales Ave Extension.

Places to Stay - bottom end

City Plaza Tourist Inn, Capistrano St, Tel 8572008. SR/fan P120, SR/DR/ac/bath P250/350. Quite clean. Probably the most inexpensive place to stay in the downtown area.

Park View Lodge, Tirso Neri St, Tel 8571197, Fax 726656. SR/DR/fan P240, SR/DR/ac/bath P430 to P780. Perfectly good accommodation, although some of the rooms are a bit small. Restaurant, coffee shop. Quite location on Golden Friendship Park.

Nature's Pensionne, T Chavez St, Tel 8572274, Fax 723718. SR/DR/ac/bath P400 and P500. Reasonable rooms of different size with TV and wide beds. Restaurant.

Hotel Ramon, Burgos St, Tel & Fax 8574804. SR/DR/ac/bath P500 to P800, with TV. Good rooms of different size. Quiet location. Coffee shop. Music lounge with live music at the weekends.

Lamar Inn, Borja St corner Velez St, Tel 723474. SR/DR/ac/bath P530 to P730, depending on size. Pleasant, tidy rooms with TV. Good value.

Places to Stay - middle

Casa Crystalla, Pabayo St corner T. Chavez St, Tel 8561704, Fax 722480. SR/DR/ac/bath P600 to P900. Well-appointed rooms with TV, the more expensive ones also have a refrigerator. Popular hotel in this price class. Restaurant.

VIP Hotel, Velez St corner Borja St, Tel 726080, 8562505, Fax 726441. SR/ac/bath P600 to P1490, DR/ac/bath P720 to P1790, suite P2750 and P3900. Good quality, spacious rooms, the more expensive ones with a refrigerator, TV and include breakfast. Restaurant, airport service.

Grand City Hotel Cagayan, Velez St, Tel & Fax 8571900. SR/DR/ac/bath P820 and P920. With TV, unfortunately some of the rooms have no windows. A comfortable, pleasant hotel in the city centre. Restaurant.

Philtown Hotel, Makahambus St, Tel 8564402, Fax 723104. SR/DR/ac/bath P900 to P1100. Good hotel with really comfortable rooms, all with TV, some also have a refrigerator. Restaurant, disco, airport service.

Maxandrea Hotel, Borja St corner Aguinaldo St, Tel 8572244, Fax 8574129. SR/ac/bath P900, SR/DR/ac/bath P1100 to P1580, suite P2480 and P3000, all including breakfast. Impeccable rooms with TV. Restaurant, music lounge, car hire, airport service.

Places to Stay - top end

The Dynasty Court Hotel, Tiano Brothers St corner Hayes St, Tel 8571250, Fax 727825, @. SR/DR/ac/bath P1000 and P1500, suite P2000, all including breakfast and lunch. Quality rooms with TV, the more expensive ones have refrigerators, as do the suites. Not all the standard rooms have windows. An excellently run hotel in the

Getting There & Away

1 Macabalan Wharf
2 Asian Spirit
Cebu Ferries
Cebu Pacific
Negros Navigation
Sulpicio Lines
WG & A
3 Bus Terminal (2 km)
31 Philippine Airlines
46 Cebu Pacific
54 Air Philippines
LRCL Car Rental
56 Seair (400m)
Lumbia Airport (10 km)

Places to Stay

9 Philtown Hotel
17 VIP Hotel
18 Fem's Lodging House
19 Maxandrea Hotel
24 Mantaring Inn
27 City Plaza Tourist Inn
30 Hotel Ramon
32 Park View Lodge
41 Grand City Hotel Cagayan
42 Nature's Pensionne
43 Casa Crystalla
50 The Dynasty Court Hotel
56 Pryce Plaza (3 km)

Places to Eat & Entertainment

7 Gourmet D'Oro Restaurant
11 Consuelo Restaurant
13 Bulldog
14 Bagong Lipunan Restaurant
21 Mandarin Tea Garden Restaurant
22 Persimmon Fastfoods & Bakeshoppe
25 Café Nona
26 Sunflower Disco
28 Starlet Disco
33 McDonald's
35 Jollibee
40 Chowking
42 Hotfoods Plaza
46 Silver Pond Dimsum & Restaurant
47 Blueberry Coffee Shop
48 Bigby's Café
51 The Site Bar
53 Paolo's Ristorante

Miscellaneous

2 Gaisano City Mall
3 Agora Market (2 km)
4 Northern Mindanao Medical Center
5 Cagayan de Oro Medical Center
6 Provincial Capitol
8 Landbank
10 Pelaez Sports Complex
Tourist Office
12 Limketkai Shopping Center (1 km)
15 Cogon Market (500 m)
20 Cogon Market (500 m)
Oro Rama Super Center (200 m)
23 Bank of the Philippine Islands
29 The Mailbox Internet Café
34 Comlink Internet Café
36 Metrobank
37 Golden Friendship Park
38 Xavier University
39 Bank of the Philippine Islands
41 Equitable PCI Bank
44 Philippine National Bank (PNB)
45 Post Office
49 Xavier Museo de Oro
52 Dot Com Internet Center
54 Internet Avenue
55 City Hall
56 SM City
57 Riverside Park
58 Gaston Park
59 San Agustin Cathedral

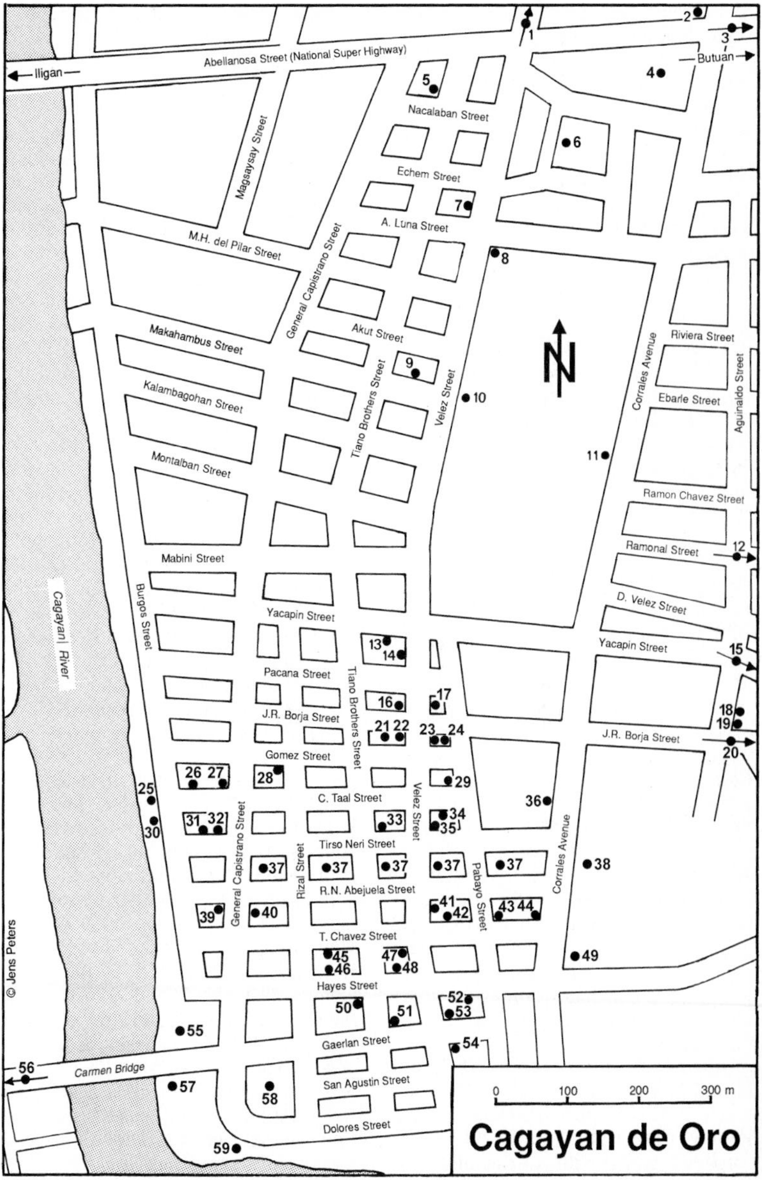

Cagayan de Oro

0 100 200 300 m

Iligan
Abellanosa Street (National Super Highway)
Butuan
Nacalaban Street
Echem Street
A. Luna Street
Magsaysay Street
M.H. del Pilar Street
General Capistrano Street
Makahambus Street
Akut Street
Kalambagohan Street
Tiano Brothers Street
Velez Street
Montalban Street
Corrales Avenue
Riviera Street
Ebarle Street
Aguinaldo Street
Ramon Chavez Street
Ramonal Street
D. Velez Street
Mabini Street
Burgos Street
Cagayan River
Yacapin Street
Pacana Street
J.R. Borja Street
Gomez Street
C. Taal Street
Tirso Neri Street
Rizal Street
R.N. Abejuela Street
Pabayo Street
T. Chavez Street
Hayes Street
Gaerlan Street
Carmen Bridge
San Agustin Street
Dolores Street

1 2 3 4 5 6 7 8 9 10 11 12 13 14 15 16 17 18 19 20 21 22 23 24 25 26 27 28 29 30 31 32 33 34 35 36 37 38 39 40 41 42 43 44 45 46 47 48 49 50 51 52 53 54 55 56 57 58 59

downtown area. Restaurant, coffee shop, music lounge, car hire.

Pryce Plaza, Carmen Hill, Tel 8583595, Fax 726687, @. SR/DR/ac/bath from P2000 to P2700, suite P5000; including breakfast. This is a good hotel of the upper-middle class standard. Restaurant, swimming pool, tennis court, car hire. Situated on a hill about four km south-west of the town centre. From the vantage point of the hill you can get a magnificent view of Cagayan de Oro and the Mindanao Sea beyond.

Places to Stay - Around Cagayan de Oro

Gardens of Malasag, Eco-Tourism Village (see 'Around Cagayan de Oro'. Dorm/ac/bath P200, cottage P150 to P600, SR/DR/ac/bath P680 and P730, cottage/ac/bath P850 and P970 (with refrigerator). Restaurant, swimming pool.

Cha-li Beach Resort, Cugman, Tel 732929, 8552116, Fax 8552108, @. Cottage/ac/bath P960 to P1475, SR/DR/ac/bath P1475. Attractive, quiet place with well-kept cottages and rooms with TV. Restaurant, swimming pool. Crowds of day guests at the weekend (admission P60). Located about seven km east of Cagayan de Oro on Macalajar Bay (no bathing beach).

Lauremar Beach Hotel, Opol, Tel 735411, 8587506, Fax 754497, @. SR/ac/bath P1140, DR/ac/bath P1380, suite P2700. The rooms are well-kept and have balconies with a view of the pool. They all have TV, the suites also have a refrigerator. Pleasantly decorated restaurant with a sundeck to the sea; open 24 hours. All in all, an inviting hotel on the beach at Opol, about seven km west of Cagayan de Oro. A taxi there costs P80 to P100.

Malasag Resort, Alwana Business Park, Cugman, Tel 732182, 8552202, Fax 8552198, @. SR/DR/ac/bath P2090 and P2750, suite P4290. Comfortable rooms with refrigerator and TV. Attractive place. Restaurant, swimming pool, jacuzzi. Situated about seven km east of Cagayan de Oro, set back a bit from the highway.

Places to Eat

You get sandwiches and good, standard Filipino dishes like caldereta, kare-kare and sinigang at the self-service restaurant ***Persimmon Fastfoods & Bakeshoppe*** on Velez St corner JR Borja St. At ***Bigby's Café*** in Hayes St you can get tasty pasta (big portions) and also more unusual dishes like Madras Chicken Curry and Roast Beef Down Under. The prices are decent, and this popular place has a friendly atmosphere.

If you like Chinese food, then there is a good choice of restaurants including ***The Sea King Garden Restaurant*** in the Grand City Hotel Cagayan, the ***Dynasty Court Restaurant*** in the hotel of the same name, the ***Oriental Garden Restaurant*** (inexpensive, large servings) in the Philtown Hotel, as well as the ***Mandarin Tea Garden Restaurant*** in JR Borja St, that includes fast food and dimsum on its menu, and the ***Silver Pond Dimsum & Restaurant*** in Hayes St which is good value for money.

Friends of Japanese food will like the cosy ***Miyuki Restaurant*** in Yacapin St, which is fairly inexpensive. The ***Consuelo Restaurant*** in Corrales Ave has a style of its own and can be highly recommended. They specialise in steaks and sizzling spaghetti. Also known for good steaks is the ***Gourmet D'Oro Restaurant*** at the northern end of Velez St. Romantic candlelight and the gentle sounds of a piano lend a special ambience to ***Paolo's Ristorante***, a garden restaurant located on Velez St near the corner with Gaerlan St. It is a popular place to eat, with not only a good variety of pizzas and pastas, but also Spanish and Japanese food, seafood, steaks and sandwiches.

If you have a sweet tooth, then the ***Blueberry***, on Velez St near the corner with Chavez St, is well worth the visit. It specialises in coffee and cakes and the menu runs from blueberry pie to cappuccino.

Entertainment

There is no shortage of entertainment here, especially if it's karaoke bars you are looking for, eg the ***Bulldog*** in Pacana St (P200 minimum consumption). The ***Picasso Music Lounge*** on the seventh floor of the Dynasty Court Hotel offers excellent music and the atmosphere to go with it. ***The Site Bar*** in Tiano Brothers St at the corner of Gaerlan St, welcomes you with its long counter and waiters wearing hard hats (the 'site' in the name referring to 'building site', geddit?!). The ***Café Nona*** in Burgos St is a pleasant piano bar with singers (it's also a good restaurant). You can enjoy model shows and disco dancing in the ***Starlet Disco*** in Gomez St at the corner of Rizal St.

Miscellaneous

Festivals: Kumbira Festival in the third week of July. City Fiesta and Kagay-an Festival from 26 to 28 August.
Immigration Office, Osmeña St, Tel 726517. Open Mon-Fri 8am-noon and 1.30-5pm.
Medical Services: The best hospital in town is the Cagayan de Oro Medical Center in Tiano Brothers St corner Macalaban St, Tel 722256-57, 8561276.
Money: Bank of the Philippine Islands, Velez St corner Borja St, Equitable PCI Bank, Velez St corner RN Abejuela St, and Philippine National Bank, Corrales Ave corner T Chavez St, have ATMs.
Online: More and more Internet cafés are opening up all the time, including: Comlink, Taal St; Dot Com Internet Center, Hayes St; Internet Avenue, Velez St corner Gaerlan St; The Mailbox, Taal St corner Pabayo St.
Population: 500,000
Post & Telephone: Post Office, T Chavez St. The Dynasty Court Hotel will accept letters and parcels.
Post code: 9000. Area code: 088 and 08822 (for six-digit numbers).
Tourist Office, Pelaez Sports Complex, Velez St, Tel 723696, 8564048, @. Open Mon-Fri 8am-5.30pm, Sat 8am-noon.

Getting Around

Car Hire: LRCL Car Rental, c/o Internet Avenue, Velez St corner Gaerlan St, Tel 724972.
Nissan Rent-a-Car, Pryce Plaza, Carmen Hill, Tel 8583131.

Getting There & Away

By Air: Lumbia Airport is located on a plateau, 185m above sea level, barely 11 km from town. Taxis may ask up to P250, but you can do the trip for P150.
Air Philippines, Lumbia Airport, Tel. 8588880.
- Velez St corner Gaerlan St, Tel 8571124, 8577724.
Destinations: Cebu City, Manila.
Asian Spirit, Lumbia Airport, Tel. 8588300.
- Gaisano City Mall, Tel 8565435.
Destination: Cebu City.
Cebu Pacific, Lumbia Airport, Tel 8588856, 8588857.
- Hayes St, Tel 8576661, 8563936.
- Gaisano City Mall, Tel 727490.
Destination: Manila.
Philippine Airlines, Lumbia Airport, Tel 8588863.
- 21 Tirso Neri St, Tel 726795.
Destination: Manila.
Seair, Vamenta Blvd (at the Petron filling station), Carmen, Tel 8581661.
Destinations: Cebu City, Cotabato, Davao.

By Bus: The bus terminal is on the outskirts in the north-east of the city, next to the Agora Market. Jeepneys going to the centre three km away have the sign 'Cogon - Carmen'. Jeepneys going from the town to the bus terminal will have the sign 'Agora'. A taxi costs about P50. Jeepneys from the bus terminal to the Macabalan Wharf cost P6; they may go via Cogon Market.

By Boat: The Macabalan Wharf is four km from the town centre. There is a jeepney service, which usually goes direct to the bus terminal but may go via Cogon Market. The trip by taxi shouldn't cost more than P40.

Tickets: All the larger shipping lines have ticket counters in the city in addition to their harbour offices. One good place to find them is at the Gaisano City Mall, Corrales Ave Extension.
Cebu Ferries, Gaisano City Mall, Tel 712105.
- SM City, Tel. 8592360.
- Macabalan Wharf, Tel 725406.
Destinations: Bohol, Cebu, Negros, Manila.
WG & A, Gaisano City Mall, Tel 712105.
- SM City, Tel. 8592360.
- Macabalan Wharf, Tel 723982, 725406.
Destinations: Cebu, Negros, Manila.
Negros Navigation, Gaisano City Mall, Tel 8563702.
Destinations: Manila, Negros, Panay.
Sulpicio Lines, Gaisano City Mall, Tel 710902.
- Macabalan Wharf, Tel 724543, 726269.
Destinations: Cebu, Manila.
Trans-Asia Shipping Lines, Gaisano City Mall, Tel 8583920.
- Macabalan Wharf, Tel 8568691.
Destinations: Bohol, Cebu.

Butuan - Balingoan
Bus: Buses leave Butuan almost hourly for Cagayan de Oro (3½ hrs).
The buses go via Balingoan (P50; 1½ hrs), which is the berth for ferries to and from Camiguin.

Davao
Air: Seair flies Tuesday, Thursday and Sunday from Davao to Cagayan de Oro and vice versa (P1850; one hr).

Bus: Several buses from various companies run daily from Davao to Cagayan de Oro (eight hrs via Malaybalay and 10 hrs via Butuan).

Iligan
Bus/Jeepney: Several buses from various companies travel daily between Iligan and Cagayan de Oro (1½ hrs). Jeepneys and minibuses also cover this route.

Pagadian
Bus: Bachelor Bus Liner and Fortune Liner buses leave Pagadian daily for Cagayan de Oro, once an hour between 4.30am and 1pm (4½ hrs).

Zamboanga
Bus: Between 1am and 8.30am, Rural Transit buses leave roughly every hour from Zamboanga, heading for Cagayan de Oro (14 hrs).

Around Cagayan de Oro

Raagas Beach & San Pedro Beach

The beaches around Cagayan de Oro are not particularly good. However, if you really feel you need a swim, try Raagas Beach near Bonbon and San Pedro Beach in Opol, seven km west of Cagayan de Oro. They're nothing special but are OK for a few hours by the water.

Timoga Spring

About half-way between Cagayan and Iligan, Timoga Springs is a refreshing spot at the sea with several swimming pools.

Kahulugan Spring & Twin Hearts Spring

Near Jasaan (pronounced: Hasaan), about 30 km north-east of Cagayan de Oro, the mountain resorts of Kahulugan Spring and Twin Heart Spring can be found about two km off the highway and about 100m apart. Between them they have at least seven swimming pools and loads of picnic huts. Admission is P15 and P10 respectively. The road up to them is bad and barely useable if it's raining.

Sagpulon Cold Spring

About 35 km north-east of Cagayan de Oro (near San Isidro, five km north of Jaasan), a track heads off from the highway into the mountains. It's five km from the highway to Sagpulon Spring, a beautiful waterfall with a few picnic huts. You can get there from San Isidro by motorbike (P15) to a hanging bridge; from there it's about another 200m on foot.

Gardens of Malasag

This Eco-Tourism Village is a project of the Department of Tourism and is an idea well worth taking up elsewhere. It's located about 10 km south-east of Cagayan de Oro (turn off to the right before Cugman, then it's another three km into the mountains). There you will find a nature park constructed on a sprawling, seven-hectare site with a wide variety of attractions, including an orchidarium, an ethnology museum (north Mindanao), a tribal village (with houses belonging to cultural minorities) and an amphitheatre with performances of traditional dances. They also have a restaurant and cottages where you can stay overnight (see Cagayan de Oro). Admission is P20, and P50 for the swimming pool.

Canopy Walk

In Magbais near Claveria, about 40 km north-east of Cagayan de Oro, the flora and fauna of the rain forest are close enough to touch. At a height of 20m above the ground, visitors can walk along hanging bridges from treetop to treetop, where from platforms they can get a close up view of life in the upper reaches of those jungle giants.

This eco-tourism project was developed by the Department of Tourism and could well serve as a model for other places. For safety reasons, people are not allowed to visit the Canopy Walk unaccompanied and have to contact the Tourist Office in Cagayan de Oro first, where a guide will be organised.

Makahambus Cave

The Makahambus Cave is about 14 km south of Cagayan de Oro and can be reached by jeepneys going to Talacag. Make sure you take a powerful torch (flashlight) with you.

Camp Phillips

Even visitors who are not remotely interested in agriculture will enjoy a trip to the huge pineapple plantations at Camp Phillips, 34 km out of Cagayan de Oro. Jeepneys with the destination 'Phillips' go there (one hr). If you're lucky, you may get on a tour of the plantation.

On Wednesday and Saturday, jeepneys run the extra five km from Camp Phillips to the Del Monte Club House, where you can get a good meal in the Golf Club (tender steaks from locally bred cattle).

The Del Monte Canning Factory is at Bugo, 15 km east of Cagayan de Oro, where the finished products are shipped away.

Pineapple *(Ananas comosus)*
The Philippines are the second largest producers of pineapples in the world.

Malaybalay

Malaybalay is the capital of Bukidnon, the largest province in the northern Mindanao region. The city is surrounded by mountain ranges in the valley of a tributary of the Pulangi River. Once a year there they observe the Kaamulan Festival, when the members of the various cultural minorities living in and around Malaybalay get together to celebrate. Dressed in traditional costumes, they meet in Pines View Park, where they perform rousing dances to the rapid rhythms of drums and gongs.

Places to Stay

Haus Malibu, Bonifacio Drive corner Comisio St, Tel 2213318, @. SR/DR/fan/bath P450, SR/DR/ac/bath P800. Good, well-kept rooms, the more expensive with TV and some with a refrigerator. Coffee shop.
Pine Hills Hotel, Fortich Street, Tel 2213211, @. SR/DR/ac/bath P1300 to P2280, suite P3580. Comfortable rooms with TV, the more expensive ones also with refrigerator. Restaurant.

Miscellaneous

Festival: Kaamulan Festival in the first week in March.
Money: The Bank of the Philippine Islands, Fortich St, has an ATM.
Population: 120,000.
Post & Telephone: Post code: 8700. Area code: 088.

Getting There & Away

Cagayan de Oro
Bus: Buses run daily between Cagayan de Oro and Malaybalay, leaving hourly (two hrs).

Davao
Bus: There are regular buses between Davao and Malaybalay (via Kibawe and Valencia.)

Iligan

Iligan is an industrial town with factories in the outskirts. The nearby Maria Cristina Falls will be the main source of power for the neighbouring districts as far as Zamboanga. The hydro-electric power station so dominates the landscape that it's more likely to appeal to the technically minded than to nature lovers. To get to the falls, take a jeepney from the pier to Agus Bridge, about seven km away, turn left after the bridge and walk for about half an hour. You can't swim in the pool as the river is a raging torrent and far too dangerous; the attraction is to look down on the falls from above by going about 200m back towards Iligan from the Agus Bridge, where a path and concrete steps lead straight to the waterfall.
In contrast, the Tinago Falls - also known as the Hidden Falls - have been left in their beautiful natural state and are not marred by construction. They must be amongst the most beautiful waterfalls on Mindanao. It is a real pleasure to go for a dip in the big, natu-

ral pool there. At the entrance to the Tinago Falls you will find the Tinago Residence Inn, a resort with a small zoo, children's play area and overnight accommodation, including a few tree houses. Admission is P30, which includes a soft drink. Steps lead down to the pool from the resort. The easiest way to get to the Tinago Falls is by taxi, or by jeepney as mentioned above. If you do take the jeepney, then go past the Agus Bridge for another two km to the turn-off (which is signposted) and cover the next couple of km on foot.

Places to Stay

Iligan Star Inn, Quezon Ave, Tel 2215272. SR/fan/bath P250, DR/fan/bath P300, SR/ac/bath P400, DR/ac/bath P500. Basic accommodation, beginning to show its age. The rooms onto Quezon Ave are a bit loud. Restaurant.
Maria Cristina Hotel, Aguinaldo St corner Mabini St, Tel 2213352, Fax 2213940. SR/ac/bath P650, DR/ac/bath P865, suite P1300. Reasonable rooms with TV. This is the best hotel in the centre of town. Restaurant.
Elena Tower, Tibanga Highway, Tel 2215995, Fax 2215996. SR/DR/ac/bath P690 to P1320. Tidy rooms with TV. Restaurant. Just outside the town centre.
The Corporate Inn, Sparrow St, Isabel Village, Pala-o, Tel 2214456, Fax 2214459, @. SR/ac/bath P750, DR/ac/bath P1050; including breakfast. Good quality, impeccable rooms with refrigerator and TV. Friendly little hotel with a garden. Located close by City Hall, about 1½ km east of downtown.
Cheradel Suites, Brother Raymund Jeffrey Rd, Villa Verde, Tel 2238118, Fax 2214926. SR/DR/ac/bath P1200 to P3500, depending on size and furnishings. Pleasant, well-kept rooms with refrigerator and TV. Attractive hotel, located in the east of the town, opposite the La Salle School. Restaurant, swimming pool.

Places to Eat

Iligan has quite a few bakeries and restaurants, though most of them close at about 9pm. You have a choice of reasonably priced Chinese meals at the ***Big Dipper Restaurant*** on Quezon Ave. ***Enrico's Restaurant***, also in Quezon Ave, is clean, serves excellent food and the service is friendly. In the evenings there's a good atmosphere at the barbecue stands on the plaza, where the ***Bar-B-Q Inn*** is also located. The ***Bahayan Restaurant*** in General Aguinaldo St is in the mid-range category and serves Filipino food. The only problem with the well-run ***Patio Alejandra***, on the corner of San Miguel and Luna Sts, is making your mind up from the wide choice of food and cuisines available; the seafood festival is highly recommended.

Miscellaneous

Festivals: City Fiesta, Kasadya Festival and Festival of St Miguel the Archangel on 27 September.
Medical Services: Mindanao Sanitarium & Hospital, National Highway, Tibanga, Tel 2213029, 2217199, is in the northern outskirts of town.
Money: Equitable PCI Bank, B Labao St corner Del Pilar St, and Philippine National Bank, B Labao St corner General Aguinaldo St, have ATMs.
Population: 300,000.
Post & Telephone: Post Office, San Miguel St corner Mabini St.
Post code: 9200. Area code: 063.
Tourist Office: City Tourist Office, City Hall, Quezon Ave Extension, Pala-o, Tel 2213426. Open Mon-Fri 8am-noon and 1-5pm.

Getting There & Away

By Air: The airport is located 17 km south of Iligan, about 600m off the road to Marawi. The taxi to Iligan will cost you about P200. At the time of writing (2004) there are however no regular flights from and to Iligan.

By Boat: The following shipping companies are represented in Iligan:
Cebu Ferries, Port Area, Tel 2211375.
Destination: Cebu.
Negros Navigation, Ponce Building, Sabayle St, Tel 2215329, 2219914.
Destinations: Manila, Panay.
Sulpicio Lines, Port Area, Tel 2215681.
Destination: Cebu.
WG & A, Port Area, Tel 2215331.
Destinations: Manila, Negros.

Cagayan de Oro
Bus: From Cagayan de Oro, several Bachelor Bus Liner and Fortune Liner buses run daily to Iligan (1½ hrs). There are also jeepneys and minibuses.

Ozamis
Boat: From Ozamis to Iligan on Tuesday and Saturday with WG & A (2½ hrs).

Pagadian
Bus: From Pagadian, several Bachelor Bus Liner and Fortune Liner buses run daily to Iligan (three hrs). The last bus usually leaves in the early afternoon.

Zamboanga
Bus: Rural Transit buses leave Zamboanga for Iligan daily from 1am until 8.30am, with the destination Cagayan de Oro on the front (12 hrs).

Marawi & Lake Lanao

Marawi on Lake Lanao is the spiritual and cultural centre of the Filipino Muslims (see also the Cultural Minorities section in the Country & People Chapter earlier in this book). It is the location of the Mindanao State University, usually referred to as 'Misyu' because of its initials, as well as the RP-Libya Hospital, one of the biggest and most modern hospitals on Mindanao. Jeepneys make the trip between Marawi and MSU.

Getting There & Away
2 New Wharf
3 North Wharf
4 South Wharf
5 Cebu Ferries
Sulpicio Lines
WG & A
6 Negros Navigation
8 Bus Terminal
10 Minibuses to Marawi
30 Airport (17 km)

Places to Stay
1 Elena Tower
7 Farrah Hotel
12 Iligan Star Inn
13 Cheradel Suites (1 km)
The Corporate Inn (1.2 km)
26 Maria Cristina Hotel

Places to Eat
11 Big Dipper Restaurant
16 Bar-B-Q Inn
Maharaja Restaurant
17 Enrico's Restaurant
20 Bahayan Restaurant
21 Jelo's Ice Cream House
23 Jollibee
27 Niga Restaurant
29 Patio Alejandra Restaurant

Miscellaneous
1 Mindanao Sanitarium & Hospital (1 km)
9 Church
13 City Hall (1,2 km)
14 Gaisano Department Store
15 Equitable PCI Bank
18 Police Station
19 Plaza
22 J & L Supermart
24 Market
25 Philippine National Bank (PNB)
28 Post Office

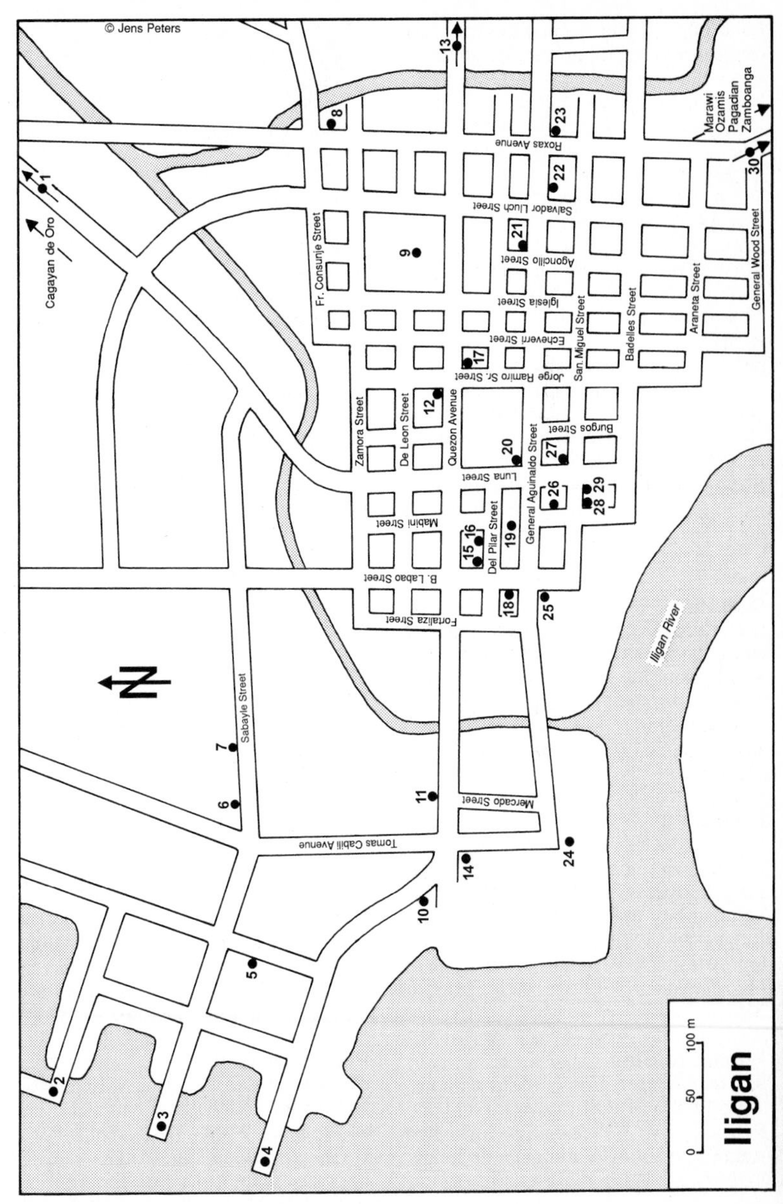
Iligan
0
50
100 m
© Jens Peters
Cagayan de Oro
Marawi
Ozamis
Pagadian
Zamboanga
Fr. Consunje Street
Zamora Street
De Leon Street
Quezon Avenue
Del Pilar Street
General Aguinaldo Street
San. Miguel Street
Badelles Street
Araneta Street
General Wood Street
Roxas Avenue
Salvador Lluch Street
Agoncillo Street
Iglesia Street
Echeverri Street
Jorge Ramiro Sr. Street
Burgos Street
Luna Street
Mabini Street
B. Labao Street
Fortaliza Street
Mercado Street
Tomas Cabili Avenue
Sabayle Street
Iligan River
1
2
3
4
5
6
7
8
9
10
11
12
13
14
15
16
17
18
19
20
21
22
23
24
25
26
27
28
29
30

Lake Lanao is the second largest body of water in the Philippines. During normal conditions it would be 112m deep, but it has often been considerably lower than this in recent years. More than 500,000 Maranao who live in one of the 30 towns around or near the lake, and whose lives depend on it, feel their way of life is being threatened. The culprit is apparently a power station in Marawi, run by the National Power Corporation (Napocor), which draws water from the lake (located 700m above sea level) to generate power. Napocor runs another five power stations along the Agus River, which drains naturally from Lake Lanao. They make use of the river current and would generate less power if the lake were dammed. Slash and burn farming as well as illegal tree felling in the rain catchment area all around the lake have also contributed to the low level of the water.

Museum

On the MSU campus you can find the small but interesting Aga Khan Museum, featuring the Muslim culture of Mindanao. Open Mon-Thu 9-11.30am and 1.30-5pm, and Fri 9-10.30am and 1.30-5pm. They are closed on public holidays.

Shopping

Don't expect an exotic oriental bazaar in Marawi - there is, however, a big market over towards the lake where you can buy brass ware, tapestries and Indonesian textiles. Good hand-woven tapestries at fixed prices are for sale at the Dansalan College Art Shop at MSU.

Places to Stay

Marawi Resort Hotel, MSU campus, Tel 520981. SR/DR/fan/bath P850 and P1000 (TV). Pleasantly furnished rooms and cottages, although no longer in the best condition. Restaurant, swimming pool, tennis court. The hotel is located in extensive, park-like grounds, on a hill outside of Marawi with a beautiful view of Lake Lanao.

Warning

Marawi and the region around Lake Lanao is a crisis area, so think at least twice before visiting the town of Tugaya, famous for its brass ware, or making boat trips to the small islands of Nusa-Nusa and Silangan. You can get an up-to-date situation report in Iligan.
You may give offence if you photograph a Muslim woman without first asking permission.

Miscellaneous

Festival: Kalilang Festival from 10 to 15 April.
Population: 120,000.
Post & Telephone: Post code: 9700. Area code: 063.

Getting There & Away

Bus: Several minibuses go from Iligan to Marawi daily, leaving from Quezon Ave near the Gaisano department store (one hr).

Ozamis

There's not much for the traveller in Ozamis in the south-east of Misamis Occidental Province. It is simply a sea port for ships heading for destinations such as Cebu and Negros. (See also the Mindanao Getting There & Away section earlier in this chapter.)

Places to Stay

Country Lodge, Ledesma St Extension, Tel 5210472. SR/DR/fan/bath P200/250, SR/ac/bath P300, DR/ac/bath P360. Reasonably good, quiet rooms. Located near the Lilian Liner Bus Terminal.

Asian Hotel, Capistrano St corner Parojnog St, Tel 5211424, @. SR/ac/bath P350, DR/ac/bath P450 und P650 (TV). Basic, fairly good rooms, OK for the money.
Executive Hotel, Blumentritt St, Tel & Fax 5210360. SR/ac/bath P450, DR/ac/bath P650. Quite good rooms with TV. Restaurant.
Plaza Beatrix Hotel, Port Rd, Tel 5211394, Fax 5211549. SR/ac/bath P490, DR/ac/bath P640 and P1220, suite P1470. Comfortable rooms with TV. Attentive service. Restaurant. Located about 400m from the harbour.
Naomi's Tourist Inn, Bañadero Highway, Tel 5212441, @. SR/DR/ac/bath P600, P800 und P1200. Amiably furnished rooms with TV. Substantial garden grounds with tropical flowers and plants all over. Restaurant. Located a bit outside the city (five min by jeepney).
Royal Garden Hotel, Burgos St corner Zamora St, Tel & Fax 5210008. SR/ac/bath P500, DR/ac/bath P750, suites P1500. Attractive rooms with TV, the suites also have a refrigerator. With their friendly staff, this is the best hotel in town. Restaurant (till 10pm).

Miscellaneous

Festival: City Fiesta and Subayen Keg Subano Festival on 16 July.
Money: Equitable PCI Bank and Metrobank, both on Rizal Ave, have ATMs.
Online: Sip N' Surf Cybercafé, Tee Building, Jose Abad Santos St, and Lim Building, Las Aguadas St corner Abanil St.
Population: 110,000.
Post & Telephone: Post code: 7200. Area code: 088.
Tourist Office: Tourist Information Center, Port Rd (near PPA), Open Mon-Fri 8am-noon and 1-5pm.

Getting There & Away

By Boat: The following shipping lines are represented in Ozamis:
Cebu Ferries, Port Area, Tel 5210046.
Destination: Cebu.
Negros Navigation, Reymund's Bar & Restaurant, Tel 5211151, 5210824.
- Twins Building, Port Rd.
Destinations: Manila, Panay.
Sulpicio Lines, Port Area, Tel 5210302, 5210305.
Destinations: Cebu, Negros.
Trans-Asia Shipping Lines, Port Area, Tel 5211573.
Destination: Cebu.
WG & A, Port Area, Tel 5211565.
Destination: Negros, Manila.

Dipolog - Oroquieta
Bus: From Dipolog, Lilian Liner buses go daily to Ozamis via Oroquieta, leaving almost hourly. The trip takes 2½ hrs from Dipolog and one hr from Oroquieta.

Iligan - Kolambugan
Bus: From Iligan, several Bachelor Bus Liner and Fortune Liner buses run daily to Kolambugan, some finishing there and some going on to Pagadian (one hr).

Boat: There is a ferry service between Kolambugan and Ozamis almost every hour between 7am and 5pm.
From Iligan to Ozamis on Tuesday and Saturday with WG & A (2½ hrs).

Pagadian
Bus: From Pagadian, several Lilian Liner buses run daily to Ozamis (2¼ hrs). The last bus leaves in the early afternoon.

Oroquieta

Oroquieta is located at the mouth of the Lawayan (Oroquieta) River on Iligan Bay in the north-east of the Zamboangan Peninsula. It is the provincial capital of Misamis Occidental, but most of the region's trade and industry is centred farther south in Ozamis.

Places to Stay

Rhovic's Place, Paseo de Roxas, SR/DR/ac/bath P600. Well-equipped rooms with TV. Friendly accommodation near City Hall. Restaurant, swimming pool.
Tatong Beach Resort, San Vicante Bajo. SR/DR/fan/bath P250, SR/DR/ac/bath P400 and P500, Cottage/ac/bath P850 and P1100. Good rooms and cottages. Restaurant. Swimming pool. Located on Iligan Bay a few km out of town in the direction of Ozamis (tricycle P6 per person).

Places to Eat

A pleasant place to go is ***Rhovic's Restaurant*** in the hotel of the same name. You have the choice of enjoying their Philippine cooking and seafood while sitting outside by the water. On offer at ***Karen's Food House*** in Washington St are barbecues and Filipino food, and in the nearby ***Chopstick Restaurant*** in Independence St they, not surprisingly, serve Chinese food.

Miscellaneous

Festivals: Cabecera Day from 1 to 6 January. Inug-og Festival on 14 October. City Fiesta on 16 October.
Population: 60,000.
Post & Telephone: Post code: 7200, Area code: 088.

Getting There & Away

Dipolog

Bus: Several Lilian Liner buses run daily from Dipolog to Oroquieta, either finishing there or going on to Ozamis or Plaridel (1½ hrs).

Ozamis

Bus: From Ozamis several Lilian Liner buses run daily to Oroquieta, some going on to Dipolog (one hr).

Dipolog

Most people's first impression of Dipolog, the capital of Zamboanga del Norte Province, is of a clean and pleasant town, in spite of hordes of tricycles polluting the place. The offshore Aliguay Island has white beaches and extensive undamaged coral reefs good for snorkelling and diving; you can reach it in about 45 min by outrigger. There's a chance of getting a lift out there with the boats that come in daily to Dipolog and Dapitan to get fresh water.

Places to Stay

Ranillo Pension House, Bonifacio St, Tel 2123536. SR/DR/fan P100/120, SR/DR/fan/bath P200/250, SR/DR/ac/bath P300/350. Basic accommodation with rooms which are all right for the money.
Ragin Pension House, Quezon Ave, Tel 2126320. SR/DR/fan P100/220, SR/DR/fan/bath P250, SR/DR/ac/bath P300 to P450 P (TV). Basic rooms, the better ones on the ground floor.
CL Inn, Rizal Ave, Tel 2123216. SR/DR/fan/bath P150/275, SR/DR/ac/bath P400 to P800, depending on size and furnishings (refrigerator, TV). Spacious rooms, the ones facing the street are on the loud side. Restaurant.
Dipolog Village Hotel, Sicayab, Tel 2122338. SR/DR/fan/bath P250, SR/DR/ac/bath P400, P550 (TV) and P700 (refrigerator). Basically furnished, but well-kept rooms of different sizes. Restaurant. The hotel is in a quiet area, about three km outside of Dipolog towards Dapitan about one km after the airport. A tricycle into town costs P4 per person (Special Ride P30). It's only a few minutes on foot from the hotel to the long, fairly clean, black sand beach.
Hotel Camila, General Luna St, Tel & Fax 2123008, @. SR/DR/ac/bath P600 to P1280. Good quality, well-kept rooms with TV, the more expensive

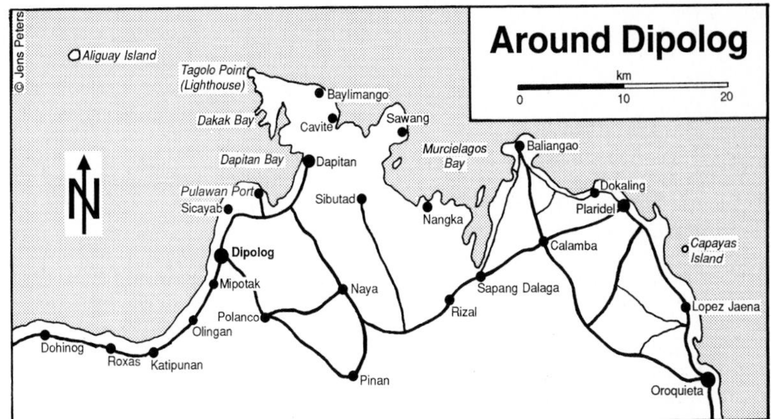

ones also have a refrigerator. Good value. Restaurant (Sunburst Fried Chicken on the ground floor).

Top Plaza Hotel, Quezon Ave corner Echavez St, Tel 2125888, Fax 2125788, @. SR/DR/ac/bath P990 to P1850, suite P3450. Immaculate, well-appointed rooms with TV, the more expensive ones have a refrigerator, as do the suites. Best hotel in town, with remarkably friendly staff. Good restaurant.

Places to Eat

The ***Top Diner*** on Quezon Ave at the corner of Echavez St and the pleasant ***Golden Pot Restaurant*** in General Luna St both serve good Philippine and Chinese food at reasonable prices.

Popular restaurants for Filipino food are ***Mickie's Restaurant***, Rizal Ave, and ***Alison's Food Plaza***, General Luna St; the latter is a pleasantly laid out garden restaurant with sizzling dishes and sea food specialities.

Miscellaneous

Festivals: Pg'Salabok Festival (Linggo ng Dipolog) from 1 to 6 July. Sinulog Dipolog on the third Saturday in January. City Fiesta on 7 October.

Medical Services: The private Hospital ng Kabataan, Padre Ramon St, Tel 2122837 is said to be the best in Dipolog.

Money: Metro Shoppers in Rizal St will change money at a good rate of exchange. The following banks have ATMs: Bank of the Philippine Islands, Rizal Ave corner Garcia St; Equitable PCI Bank, Garcia St; Metrobank, General Luna St corner Garcia St; Philippine National Bank, General Luna St.

Online: Net U See Internet Café, General Luna St.

Population: 40,000.

Post & Telephone: Post Office, Quezon Ave (near the Satellite Bus Terminal). There is also a sub post office in City Hall.

Post code: 7100. Area code: 065.

Travel Agency: Aloha Travel, Rizal Ave corner Quezon Ave, and Sueders Travel, Echavez St corner Quezon Ave will obtain flight and ship tickets.

Getting There & Away

By Air: The airport is about two km north of Dipolog, in Sicayab. A tricycle from the centre of town will cost you P30-50.

Getting There & Away
1 Airport (2 km)
Pulawan Port (7 km)
7 Philippine Airlines
(Aloha Travel)
16 Trans-Asia Shipping Lines
18 Sulpicio Lines
21 Aleson Shipping Lines
Philippine Airlines
(Sueders Travel)
22 George & Peter Lines
24 Aboitiz Express
WG & A
25 Asian Spirit
31 Cokaliong Shipping Lines
38 Satellite Bus Terminal (1 km)

Places to Stay
1 Dipolog Village Hotel (3 km)
3 Ragin Pension House
5 Ranillo Pension House
8 CL Inn
17 Top Plaza Hotel
25 Camila Hotel
32 Pepic's Lodge
37 Nonoy Pension House

Places to Eat
9 Jollibee
17 Top Plaza Diner
20 Mickie's Restaurant
26 Golden Pot Restaurant
27 Alison's Food Plaza

Miscellaneous
2 ZN Provincial Hospital
4 Mercury Drug
6 Market
7 Aloha Travel
10 Jerry's Shoppers World
11 Bank of the Philippine Islands
12 Police Station
13 City Hall
14 Plaza Magsaysay
15 Church
19 Metro Shoppers
21 Sueders Travel
23 Equitable PCI Bank
28 Net U See Internet Café
29 Philippine National Bank (PNB)
30 Metrobank
33 Hospital ng Kabataan
34 Provincial Capitol
35 Cultural Sports Center
36 LBC
38 Post Office (1 km)

Asian Spirit, Dipolog Airport, Tel 2128735.
- General Luna St, Tel 2129086.
Destination: Cebu City.
Philippine Airlines, Dipolog Airport, Tel 2122356, 2122360.
- Aloha Travel, Rizal Ave corner Quezon Ave, Tel 2127412, 2123525.
- Sueders Travel, Echavez St corner Quezon Ave, Tel 2127424.
Destination: Manila.

By Bus: The Satellite Bus Terminal is located on Quezon Ave about 1½ km south of the centre. Minibuses leave from there for nearby places such as Dapitan, and big buses for various destinations on Mindanao. A tricycle there from the centre costs P4 per person.

By Boat: The harbour for Dipolog and Dapitan is called Pulawan Port and is located between the two towns; a tricycle there costs about P30 per person (Special Ride P100).
Aleson Shipping Lines, General Luna St, Tel 2128653.
- Sueders Travel, Echavez St corner Quezon Ave, Tel 2127424.
Destinations: Cebu, Negros, Zamboanga.

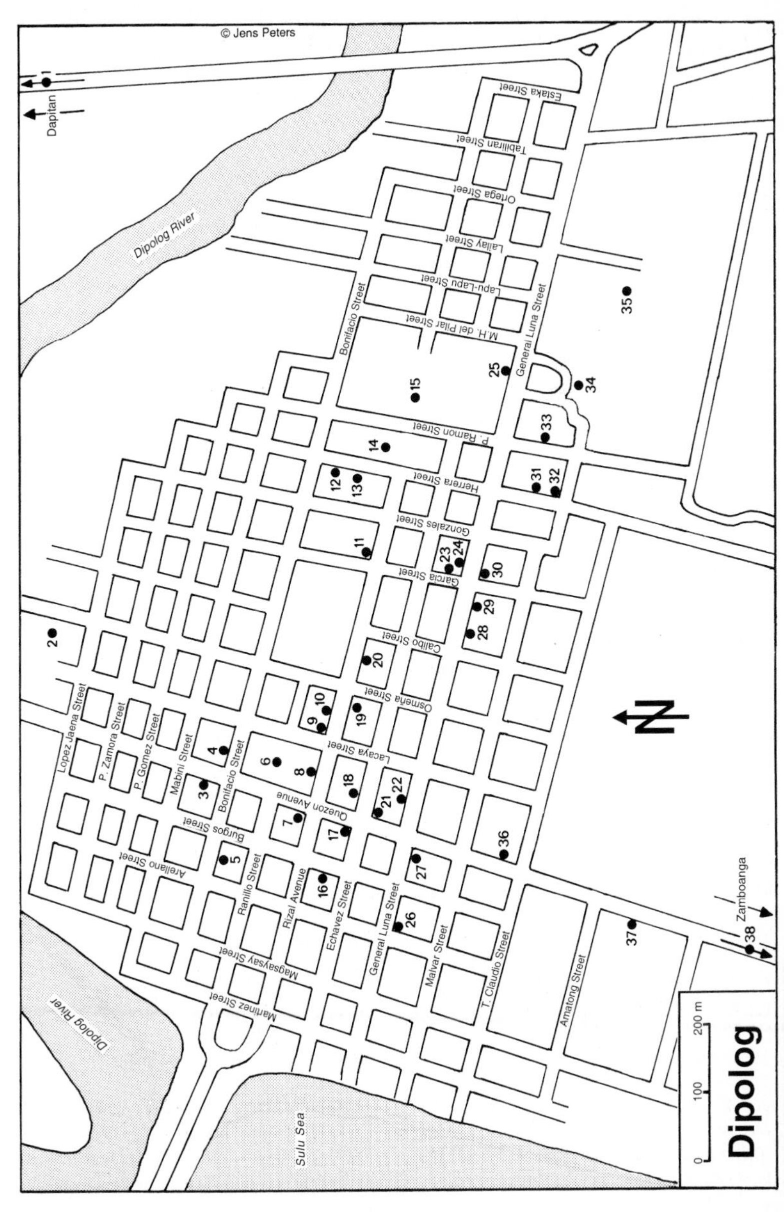
Dipolog
0
100
200 m
© Jens Peters
Dapitan
Zamboanga
Dipolog River
Dipolog River
Sulu Sea
Estaka Street
Tabiliran Street
Ortega Street
Lailay Street
Lapu-Lapu Street
M.H. del Pilar Street
Bonifacio Street
General Luna Street
P. Ramon Street
Herrera Street
Gonzales Street
Garcia Street
Calibo Street
Osmeña Street
Lacaya Street
Quezon Avenue
Burgos Street
Arellano Street
Magsaysay Street
Martinez Street
Lopez Jaena Street
P. Zamora Street
P. Gomez Street
Mabini Street
Bonifacio Street
Ranillo Street
Rizal Avenue
Echavez Street
General Luna Street
Malvar Street
T. Claudio Street
Amatong Street
N

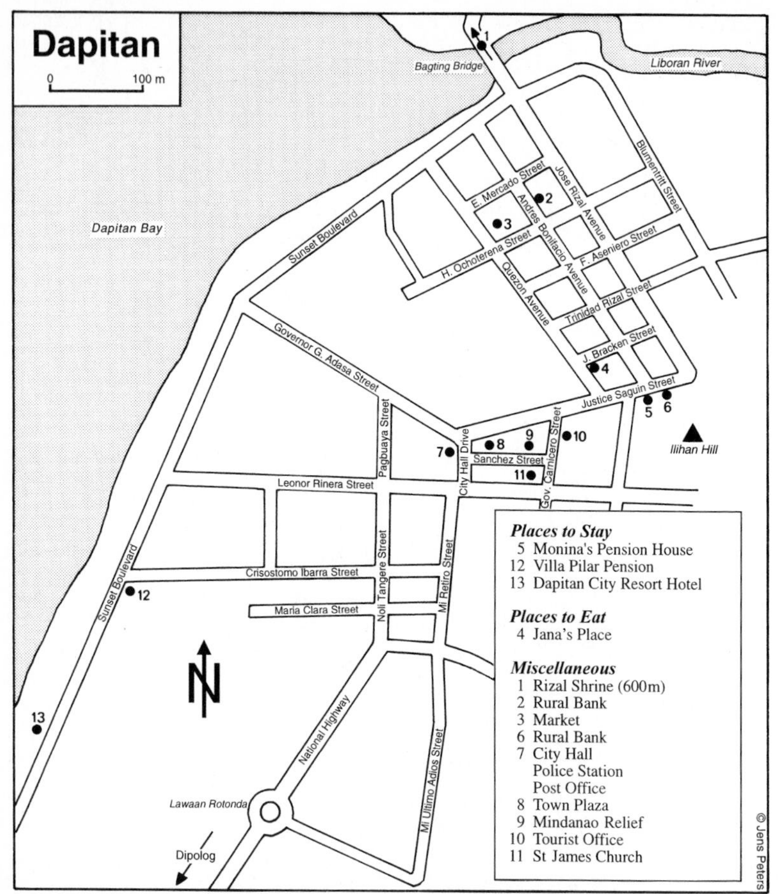

Cokaliong Shipping Lines, Herrera St, Tel 2122461.
Destinations: Cebu, Negros.
George & Peter Lines, General Luna St, Tel 2122664, 2125451.
Destinations: Cebu, Negros.
Supercat Fast Ferry Corporation, General Luna St, Tel 2124998, 2124990.
Destinations: Cebu, Negros.
Sulpicio Lines, Echaves St, Tel 2122344.
Destinations: Bohol, Manila.

Trans-Asia Shipping Lines, Burgos St, Tel 2124460, 2124468.
Destinations: Cebu, Negros.
WG & A, Echavez St corner Quezon Ave, Tel 2125574, 2125578.
Destinations: Bohol, Manila.

Pagadian - Ozamis - Oroquieta

Bus: From Pagadian, several buses belonging to various companies run daily to Dipolog via Ozamis and Oroquieta.

It takes five hrs from Pagadian, 1½ hrs from Ozamis and one hour from Oroquieta.

Zamboanga

Bus: Lilian Liner buses run from Zamboanga to Dipolog daily from 3.30 to 6.30am every half-hour. Another one leaves at 11.00am. The trip takes 13 hrs.

Boat: From Zamboanga to Dipolog on Friday with Aleson Shipping Lines and Saturday with George & Peter Lines (10 hrs).

Dapitan

Dapitan ('Shrine City') is 15 km northeast of Dipolog, and is a peaceful, clean town. The national hero, Jose Rizal, lived in exile here from 1892 to 1896. He created the big relief map of Mindanao in the town plaza, near St James Church (1870). Just northeast of there is Ilihan Hill, once the location of the Spanish-built Fort de Dapitan, which affords a beautiful view of the town and Dapitan Bay.

Rizal Park with the Rizal Shrine is located north of the city centre, about 600m from the Bagting Bridge which crosses over the Liboran River. Also to be found on the grounds of the memorial is the Rizalania Building, which houses a Rizal library.

From the Bagting Bridge you can catch a boat going to Dakak Bay, which boasts a white beach and the luxurious, beautifully laid-out Dakak Park Beach Resort. There is also a road from Dapitan to the bay. You can take a motorcycle taxi to the beach resort for P100. A minibus service for hotel guests is also available.

Places to Stay

Monina's Pension House, Justice Saguin St, Tel 2136715. SR/DR/ac P500. Squeaky-clean, friendly rooms with communal cooking facilities. Family-run accommodation. Reception in the shop on the ground floor.

Villa Pilar Pension, Sunset Blvd corner Crisostomo Ibarra St, Tel 2136579. SR/DR/ac/bath P500 to P850. Big, well-kept rooms, the more expensive ones with two beds, TV and veranda. Quiet location near the beach.

Dapitan City Resort Hotel, Sunset Blvd, Tel 2136413, Fax 2136543. SR/DR/ac/bath P1680, suites P2640 and P4560. Comfortable, well-kept rooms with refrigerator and TV. Pleasant place right on Dapitan Bay, with a beautiful view of the sea and the setting sun. Restaurant, swimming pool near the beach (P50 for non-residents).

Dakak Park Beach Resort, Dakak Bay, Cellphone 0918-5950714. SR/DR/ac/bath P5200 to P13,000. Attractive place with tastefully furnished cottages standing in well-organised grounds. Restaurant, open-air bar, swimming pool, whirlpool, sauna, tennis court and diving. Airport service costs P800 (there and back). They charge day visitors P200, for admission alone.

Places to Eat

Good, inexpensive Filipino food can be found in the very popular ***Jana's Place*** Quezon Ave corner J Bracken St.

Miscellaneous

Festivals: Kinabayo Festival on 24 and 25 July. Pasco sa Dapitan (Festival of Lights) in December.

Population: 26.000.

Post & Telephone: Post Office, City Hall Dr.

Post code: 7101. Area code: 065.

Tourist Office, Governor Carnicero St, Tel 2136203.

Getting There & Away

Jeepney: Several jepneys and minibuses travel every day between Dipolog and Dapitan (30 min).

Pagadian

The province of Zamboanga del Sur is described by the Department of Tourism of Pagadian as a 'land of lakes, caves and waterfalls'. Sounds good, but is perhaps gilding the lilly a bit. What may interest the traveller is that the small town of Lapuian, 40 km from Pagadian, and other parts of the two Zamboangan provinces, are home to the Subanon, which means 'river people' (*suba* = river). American Protestant missionaries brought Christianity and the English language to this cultural minority in their isolated mountain world. The trip by jeepney to Lapuian takes 2½ hrs. Last one back at 1.30pm.

Places to Stay

Zamboanga Hotel, Jamisola St, Tel 2141875. SR/fan/bath P180, DR/fan/bath P220, SR/ac/bath P320 and P350, DR/ac/bath P450 and P500. Basic rooms, OK for the money; the more expensive ones have TV.
Guillermo Hotel, Rizal Ave, Tel 2141471. SR/ac/bath P500 and P750, DR/ac/bath P600 and P700. Quite comfortable rooms with TV. Restaurant.
Hotel Camila, Bonifacio Dr, Tel 2142934. SR/DR/ac/bath P550 to P1280. Attractive rooms with TV. The best hotel in Pagadian. Restaurant.

Miscellaneous

Festivals: Zambulawan Festival and City Fiesta on 17 January.
Money: Bank of the Philippine Islands and Equitable PCI Bank, both in FS Pajares St, and Metrobank, Rizal Ave corner JS Alona St, have ATMs.
Population: 70,000.
Post & Telephone: Post code: 7003. Area code: 062.

Getting There & Away

By Air: Pagadian Airport is on the east edge of town, two km from the centre. At the time of writing (2004) there are however no regular flights from and to Pagadian.

Cotabato
Bus: The road from Cotabato to Pagadian passes through a crisis area and can be interrupted by destroyed bridges. So it's better not to take the bus, even if one is making the trip. It's better to take the daily ship.

Boat: A ship leaves Cotabato at about 6pm for Pagadian (eight hrs).

Iligan
Bus: From Iligan, several Bachelor Liner and Fortune Liner buses run daily to Pagadian (three hrs), the last one possibly leaving at about 2pm.

Ozamis
Bus: From Ozamis, several Lilian Liner buses run daily to Pagadian (2½ hrs).

Zamboanga
Bus: From Zamboanga, Mary May Express and Rural Transport buses leave hourly from 1 to 10am for Pagadian (eight hrs).

Boat: From Zamboanga to Pagadian on Monday, Thursday nad Saturday with Aleson Shipping Lines (P290; 12 hrs).

Zamboanga

Some people find it hard to see why Zamboanga has been praised as 'the exotic pearl of the south Philippines'. A few Muslims in an otherwise Filipino-populated city are not what most people would call exotic, and the colourful - and very expensive - sails of the Vintas are only seen at festivals or when one of these boats is chartered. Plain sails are normally used.
The popular description of City of Flowers comes from the Malay word

jambangan, meaning 'land of flowers' and may have been used when the first Malays settled here. It is more likely that the name comes from *samboangan*, a word made up of *samboang*, meaning 'boat pole', and *an*, meaning 'place'.
As well as speaking English, Filipino, Cebuano, Tausug and Samal, the locals in Zamboanga also speak Chabacano, a mixture of Spanish and Philippine languages ironically known as Bamboo Spanish.

Fort Pilar & Marine Life Museum

On the outskirts of town, to the east of Zamboanga, are Fort Pilar and the Muslim water village of Rio Hondo. The fort was built in 1635 by Jesuit priests as protection against Muslim, Dutch, Portuguese and English attacks. It was then called Real Fuerza de San Jose, but was renamed Fort Pilar after its overthrow by the Americans at the end of the 19th century. For many years the only part of the ruins worth seeing was the altar on the outside, but in the mid-80s a start was made on cleaning up and restoring the building to make it useable again. Today, a visit to the instructive Marine Life Museum is worth the effort. They have also set up botanical, archaeological, anthropological and historical departments. The museum is open daily except Saturday from 9am until noon, 2 to 5pm (closed on public holidays).

Rio Hondo

About 200m east of Fort Pilar, past a shining silver mosque, is a bridge leading to a village built on piles in the mouth of the river. This is Rio Hondo. The houses are linked by footbridges, some looking none too secure. The locals here are very friendly, however for your own safety, it's probably not a good idea to visit Rio Hondo on your own or after nightfall.

Shopping

The fish market at the docks is very lively and colourful in the late afternoons. In the alleys of the Public Market next door, between the fish market and JS Alano St, there are lots of little shops - flea-market style.
The Mindpro Citimall in La Purisma St also contains a number of large and small shops. You will find more department stores and supermarkets in Governor Lim Ave.

Places to Stay - bottom end

Dynasty Pension House, Almonte St corner Tomas Claudio St, Tel. 9914579. SR/DR/fan/bath P250/300, SR/DR/ac/bath P350/500. Small, basic rooms, loud on the street side. Central location.
Mag-V Royal Hotel, San Jose Rd corner Don Basilio Navarro St, Tel 9913054. SR/fan/bath P350, DR/fan/bath P400, SR/ac/bath P500, DR/ac/bath P650. The rooms are tidy and generously sized, but not all of them have windows. The aircon rooms have a TV. The arrival of morning is announced at 6am by very loud jeepneys! Restaurant. Located just outside the city centre.
Hotel Paradise, R Reyes St, Tel. 9912026. SR/ac/bath P400, DR/ac/bath P500. Restaurant. Well-kept rooms with TV. Good value. Friendly service. Central location.
Embassy Pension House, Valera St, Tel 9911697. SR/DR/fan/bath P400, SR/DR/ac/bath P600. Big rooms in a villa. Quiet location. Coffee Shop.
Amil's Pension House, Pilar St, Tel 9924296, Fax 9920730. SR/DR/ac/bath P500 to P800. Wih TV. Small rooms, but absolutely immaculate, and quiet - to be recommended. Located on the first floor of Amil's Tower. There's a supermarket on the ground floor.

Places to Stay - middle

Platinum 21 Pension House, Barcelona St, Tel 9912514, Fax 9912709.

Getting There & Away
2 Bus Terminal (3 km)
12 Aleson Shipping Lines
26 SRN Fast Seacrafts
28 WG & A
38 Buses to San Ramon
41 Negros Navigation
44 George & Peter Lines
47 Basilan Shipping Lines
48 Cebu Pacific
51 Jeepneys to Pasonanca Park & Taluksangay
53 Sulpicio Lines
55 Wharf

Places to Stay
5 Azenith Royale Hotel
7 Hotel Orchid Garden
8 Hotel Marcian Garden
10 Atilano's Pension House
13 L'Mirage Pension House
14 Jardin de La Vina Hotel
16 GC Hotel
King Jesse Pension House
17 Zamboanga Hermosa Hotel
18 Hotel Preciosa
20 New Astoria Hotel
21 Hotel Perlita
25 Dynasty Pension House
26 Amil's Pension House
29 Platinum 21 Pension House
30 Skypark Hotel
31 Mag-V Royal Hotel
33 Hotel Paradise
37 Embassy Pension House
48 Lantaka Hotel

Placeds to Eat & Entertainment
1 Aldea Pasonanca Restaurant
7 Ground Zero Disco
9 Alavar's House of Seafood
18 Savoury Restaurant
19 Abalone Restaurant
27 Sunburst Fried Chicken
32 Hai San Restaurant
33 Food Paradise
34 Dunkin' Donuts
39 Sunflower Food Center
43 Flavorite Restaurant

Miscellaneous
1 Climaco Freedom Park
Pasonanca Park
3 Santa Cruz Market
11 Immigration Office
15 Zamboanga Medical Center
22 Mindpro City Mall
23 Puericulture Center
24 Corner Box Internet Café
Touchline Internet Café
26 Amil's Tower
35 Plaza Pershing
36 Athletic Field
40 Equitable PCI Bank
42 Mosque & Rio Hondo (200m)
45 Philippine National Bank (PNB)
46 City Hall
47 Bank of the Philippine Islands
48 Tourist Office
49 Fort Pilar
50 Public Market
52 Post Office
54 Fish Market

SR/DR/ac/bath P620 and P700. Reasonably comfortable place. Rooms all have TV; the more expensive ones also have a refrigerator. Acceptable for the money. Their restaurant is open 24 hours.

Zamboanga Hermosa Hotel, Mayor Jaldon St, Tel 9912040. SR/ac/bath P650 and P700, DR/ac/bath P750 and P850. Neat hotel with OK rooms, all with TV. Restaurant.

GC Hotel, Tomas Claudio St, Tel 9914752. SR/ac/bath P650, DR/ac/bath P810. Good, well-kept rooms with TV. Restaurant. Quiet location.

Hotel Preciosa, Mayor Jaldon St, Tel 9912020, Fax 9930055. SR/DR/ac/bath P680, suite P1000. Tidy, quite comfortable rooms with TV. Restaurant.

Grand Astoria Hotel, Mayor Jaldon St, Tel 9912510, Fax 9912533, @. SR/ac/

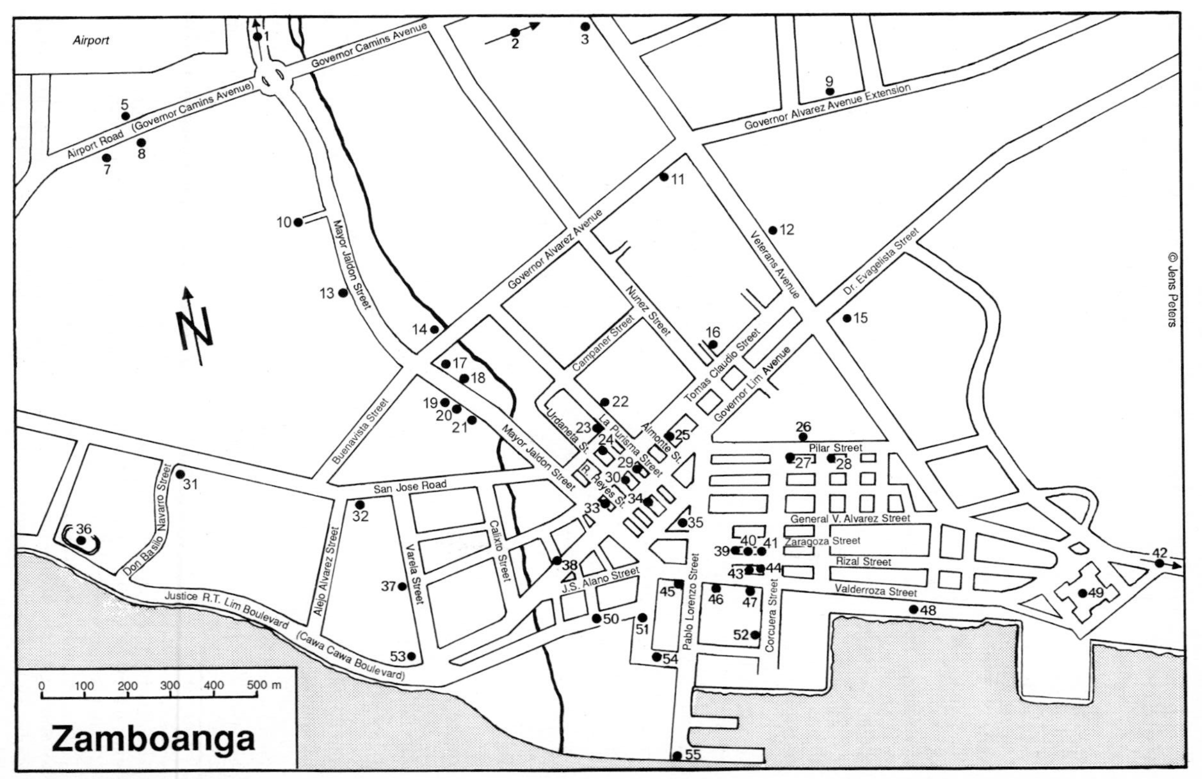
Zamboanga
© Jens Peters
Airport
Airport Road (Governor Camins Avenue)
Governor Camins Avenue
Governor Alvarez Avenue Extension
Governor Alvarez Avenue
Veterans Avenue
Dr. Evagelista Street
Mayor Jaldon Street
Buenavista Street
Tomas Claudio Street
Governor Lim Avenue
Nunez Street
Campaner Street
Almonte St.
La Purisma Street
Urdaneta St.
R. Reyes St.
Pilar Street
General V. Alvarez Street
Zaragoza Street
Rizal Street
Valderroza Street
Corcuera Street
Pablo Lorenzo Street
J.S. Alano Street
Calixto Street
San Jose Road
Varela Street
Alejo Alvarez Street
Don Basilio Navarro Street
Justice R.T. Lim Boulevard
(Cawa Cawa Boulevard)
0 100 200 300 400 500 m

bath P650 and P750, DR/ac/bath P950 and P1300, suites P1600 to P4000. With refrigerator and TV. Long established hotel with comfortable rooms. Restaurant.

Skypark Hotel, Tomas Claudio St corner Urdaneta St, Tel 9920951, Fax 9920869. SR/DR/ac/bath P750 to P950, suite P1350. Spotless rooms with TV, the suites also have a refrigerator. Good, centrally located hotel. Restaurant.

Jardin de La Vina Hotel, Governor Alvarez Ave, Tel Fax 9923748, @. SR/DR/ac/bath P825 and P990, suite P1320. Excellent, generously sized, rooms with TV. Up to 30% discount is possible, which then makes this place the best value for money. Rooftop restaurant. The hotel is on the fourth floor of the Fidela Building.

Hotel Marcian Garden, Governor Camins Ave, Tel 9912519 Fax 9911874. SR/DR/ac/bath P860 and P920, suite P1200. Immaculate rooms with TV. Attractive, good-value accommodation near the airport. Restaurant, swimming pool.

Places to Stay - top end

Don't forget to ask for promotion rates in the two hotels that follow; you can get up to a 50% discount.

Lantaka Hotel, Valderroza St, Tel 9912033, Fax 9911626. SR/ac/bath P1320, DR/ac/bath P1650, suites P2500 and P3300. The rooms are big and have a balcony, half of them with an excellent view of the sea and harbour. Popular hotel set in neat grounds with a garden. Restaurant, swimming pool. Beautiful location on the water.

Garden Orchid Hotel, Governor Camins Ave, Tel 9910031, Fax 9910035, @. SR/ac/bath P3000 to P3750, DR/ac/bath P3750 to P4500, suite P7500. Attractive, comfortable rooms with refrigerator and TV. Restaurant, disco, swimming pool, tennis court, fitness room, sauna. Near the airport.

Places to Eat

You can eat cheaply and well at the ***Flavorite Restaurant*** on Valderroza St. Young Zamboangans meet in the popular ***Food Paradise*** on Mayor Jaldon St, where there are milk shakes and fast food on the ground floor and Chinese meals upstairs. In the Plaza Mall building not far from there, ***Dunkin' Donut*** is the place if you have a sweet tooth, and they're open round the clock. ***Sunburst Fried Chicken***, on Corcuera St near the intersection with Pilar St, specialises in chicken meals.

The ***Barbecue Stalls*** in the Puericulture Center at the corner of La Purisma St and Brillantes St, offering meat, fish and poultry, are good value for money. Across the road in the Mindpro Citimall there are all kinds of air-conditioned ***Fast Food Restaurants***. The self-service ***Sunflower Food Center*** at the plaza is also good value and never short of customers.

Alavar's House of Seafood on Governor Alvarez Ave is known for good Filipino and Chinese dishes, especially seafood, but is rather expensive. Equally good and in the mid-price range is the ***Abalone Restaurant***, beside the Grand Astoria Hotel on Mayor Jaldon St. In the ***Hai San Restaurant*** in San Jose Rd, guests choose their food (fish, shrimp, lobster, mussels, vegetables) in the Seafood Market next door and then have it cooked to order (fried, steamed etc.).

The ***Food Stalls*** that open in the late afternoon along Justice Lim Blvd are a good place for sunset freaks. You can also sit out by the water, by torch light in the evenings, at the Lantaka Hotel's ***Terrace Restaurant***. They often have a reasonably priced dinner buffet, and it's a pleasant place to have breakfast.

Entertainment

In Zamboanga, like most Philippine cities, there's a restricted amount of nightlife in the city centre. The best, and most popular nightclubs are usually on the outskirts of town. In Zamboanga there are also some near the airport. Most clubs have a cover charge of P30 to P100 to get in. This often includes at least one drink.

Alejandras Restobar in Nuñez St offers a wide range of entertainment with a roof bar, music bar with bands and disco, billiards bar, karaoke, as well as a restaurant with live music. A popular destination at the weekends is the ***Ground Zero Disco*** in the Orchid Garden Hotel. And if it all gets too exhausting, you can always take it easy in the soothing atmosphere of the open-air ***Talisay Bar*** at the waterside of the Lantaka Hotel, which is also a perfect place for a sundowner.

Miscellaneous

Festivals: Dia De La Ciudad De Zamboanga on 26 February. Zamboanga Hermosa Festival from 7 to 12 October.
Money: Equitable PCI Bank, Rizal St, and Philippine National Bank, Pablo Lorenzo St corner JS Alano St, have ATMs.
Immigration Office, Governor Alvarez Ave. Open Mon-Fri 8am-noon and 1-5pm.
Medical Services: The Zamboanga Medical Center, Dr Evangelista St corner Veterans Ave, Tel 9919463, is a well-equipped hospital.
Online: Corner Box and Touchline (P30/hr) are both in Barcelona St corner Brillantes St.
Population: 520,000.
Post & Telephone: Post Office, Corcuera St.
Post code: 7000. Area code: 062.
Tourist Office, Lantaka Hotel, Valderroza St, Tel 9910218, Fax 9930030, @. Open Mon-Sat 8am-noon and 1-5pm.

Getting Around

Car: You can rent a car with driver at the ABC Driving Company, Mayor Jaldon St, Tel 9910219, and 3NR Rent-a-Car, Governor Camins Ave, Tel 9932491.

Getting There & Away

By Air: Zamboanga International Airport is two km from the city centre. The regular fare for the jeepney marked 'ZCPM' or 'Canelar – Airport' is P6, or P20 by tricycle, but you rarely get a tricycle under P30, and up to P50 is sometimes asked. Taxi drivers, presumably without a licence, demand up to P100.

Air Philippines, Zamboanga International Airport, Tel 9922575.
Destination: Manila.
Cebu Pacific, Zamboanga International Airport, Tel 9913675.
- Lantaka Hotel, Valderroza St, Tel 9913567.
Destinations: Cebu City, Davao, Manila.
Philippine Airlines, Zamboanga International Airport, Tel 9932957.
Destination: Manila.
Seair, Zamboanga International Airport, Tel 9912225.
Destinations: Cotabato, Jolo, Tawi-Tawi.
South Phoenix Airways, Zamboanga International Airport, Tel. 9915688.
Flugziel: Sandakan (Sabah/ Malaysia).

By Bus: The bus terminal for trips to and from Cagayan de Oro, Dipolog, Iligan and Pagadian is on the National Highway in the Guiwan District of town, about four km north of the city centre. A tricycle costs P30.

By Boat: It's only a few hundred metres from the wharf to the city centre. A tricycle costs P5.
Aleson Shipping Lines, Veterans Ave, Tel 9914258, 9912687.
Destinations: Cebu, Negros, Pagadian, Sulu Islands, Sandakan (Sabah/Malaysia).
Basilan Shipping Lines, Valderroza St, Tel 9917964.
Destination: Basilan.

George & Peter Lines, Rizal St corner Corcuera St, Tel 9911575.
Destinations: Dapitan/Dipolog, Cebu, Negros.
SRN Fast Seacrafts, Amil's Tower, Pilar St, Tel 9923756.
Destinations: Bongao, Jolo, Sandakan (Sabah/ Malaysia).
Sulpicio Lines, Governor Lim Ave corner Valera St, Tel 9915480.
Destinations: Cotabato, General Santos, Manila, Panay.
WG & A, Pilar St, Tel 9910275.
Destinations: Cotabato, Davao, General Santos, Manila, Panay.

Cagayan de Oro - Iligan
Bus: From Cagayan de Oro, several early morning Rural Transit buses run daily to Zamboanga via Iligan, taking 14 hrs from Cagayan de Oro and 12 hrs from Iligan.

Cotabato
Air: Seair flies on Monday, Wednesday and Friday from Cotabato to Zamboanga and vice versa (P1690; 50 min).

Boat: From Cotabato to Zamboanga on Monday with WG & A and Tuesday with Sulpicio Lines (P625; 10 hrs).

Davao
Air: Cebu Pacific flies on Tuesday and Thursday from Davao to Zamboanga and vice versa (P2650; 50 min).

Boat: From Davao to Zamboanga on Wednesday with WG & A (P855; 23 hrs); via General Santos.

Dipolog
Bus: From Dipolog, several early morning Lilian Liner buses run daily to Zamboanga via Ipil (13 hrs).

Boat: From Dapitan/Dipolog to Zamboanga on Sunday with Aleson Shipping Lines (P530; 12 hrs).

General Santos
Boat: From General Santos to Zamboanga on Thursday with WG & A and Friday with Sulpicio Lines (P855; 13 hrs).

Pagadian
Bus: From Pagadian, Mary May Express and Rural Transport buses run about every hour from 4.30 to 10am to Zamboanga (eight hrs).

Boat: From Pagadian to Zamboanga on Tuesday, Friday and Sunday with Aleson Shipping (P290; 12 hrs).

Around Zamboanga

Pasonanca Park & Climaco Freedom Park

Even if the houses of the early settlers really were surrounded by a carpet of flowers, these days the evocative nickname City of Flowers can only be applied to Pasonanca Park, about seven km, or 15 min by jeepney, north of the city centre.
On the way there you pass prize-winning gardens, and in the 58-hectare park itself there are three swimming pools, an amphitheatre and a tree house, where honeymooners can spend one night free. Since the demand is not great, tourists can also stay there by applying to the City Mayor's office.
Also in Pasonanca Park is the once popular Zamboanga Plaza Hotel & Casino. It was one of the possessions of the Marcos family, and was requisitioned and closed by the Aquino government in 1986.
Not far from Pasonanca Park is Climaco Freedom Park, which used to be called Abong-Abong Park. It is now named in memory of a popular mayor, Cesar Climaco, who was murdered by political opponents. From the big cross on Holy Hill, you get a wonderful view over Zamboanga and the Basilan Strait.

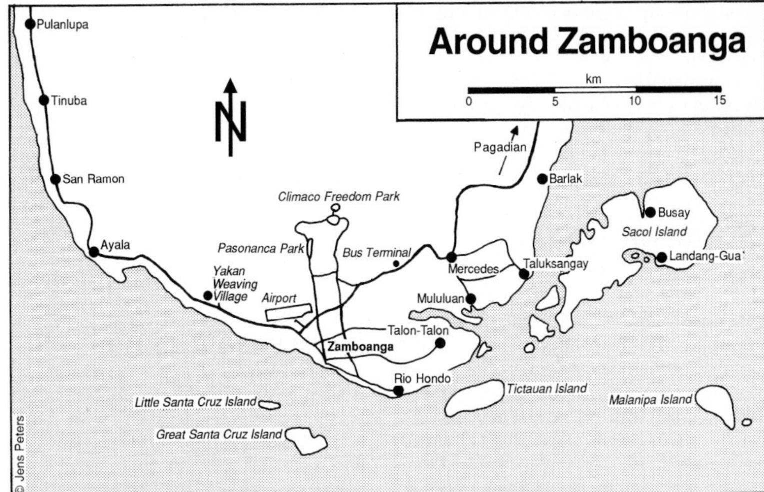

Jeepneys heading for Pasonanca Park leave from the fish market near the wharf.

Santa Cruz Islands

Great Santa Cruz Island has a lightly coloured sandy beach, peppered with fine, red pieces of coral; although it sounds perhaps a bit better than it is. Drinks are available at a small kiosk. Not far from the main beach are a small Samal cemetery tucked away in the bush, and a Muslim village built on piles in a mangrove lagoon. Nearby Little Santa Cruz Island is off limits to visitors. A few soldiers are stationed there and there is an army guesthouse.
Sea gypsies try to sell shells and coral to tourists from their outrigger canoes beside the Lantaka Hotel. From here you can also hire boats to go over to Great Santa Cruz Island. It takes 20 min and the return fare is about P300 per boat. They also charge a landing fee of P10 per person. You must also register beforehand in the Tourist Office.

San Ramon & Yakan Weaving Village

About 20 km west of Zamboanga is San Ramon Prison & Penal Farm - a good place to buy handicrafts made by the prisoners. You can get there by bus. At Pulanlupa, eight km north-west of San Ramon, there is said to be a magnificent coral reef, but it is only suitable for diving from March to June. At other times heavy seas cause poor visibility. On the San Ramon road, seven km from Zamboanga on the right-hand side, is a weaving village of seven Yakan families who make and sell traditional fabrics, which you can see on the looms. You can get a bus there from Governor Lim Ave, near the corner of Mayor Jaldon St.

Taluksangay

This Muslim town, 19 km north-east of Zamboanga, is partly built over the water. The Badjao live in houses on piles, while the Samal have settled on land centred around a minareted mosque.

They make a modest living mainly by fishing and collecting firewood. The children there can get quite aggressive if their begging doesn't produce results. Jeepneys leave Zamboanga for Taluksangay from the public market and the last one back is likely to depart before dark.

South Mindanao

Davao

Davao is the fastest growing city in the Philippines after Manila. There is still plenty room for newcomers here, as it covers 2440 sq km and is one of the most sprawling urban areas in the world. You can't miss the Chinese influence here, especially west of the wharf, where numerous businesspeople have set up little stores. Muslims have also set up the so-called Muslim Fishing Village, not far from the wharf and the nearby Magsaysay Park.
Tamolo Beach and Times Beach, southwest of Davao, are not particularly impressive, but the white Paradise Island Beach on Samal Island makes a good day trip from Davao, as do Talikud Island and Eagle Camp.

Dabaw Museum & Etnika Dabaw

Next to the Waterfront Insular Hotel Davao near the airport, is the Dabaw Museum, featuring the cultural minorities of south Mindanao, such as the Mansaka and the Bagobo; the latter are known as a proud and warlike people. Open Mon-Fri 8.30am-5pm. Admission P20.
Behind the Waterfront Insular Hotel Davao in Etnika Dabaw, Mandaya people demonstrate their traditional skills in dyeing abaca fibres, weaving, and decorating textiles.

Lon Wa Temple & Taoist Temple

The Lon Wa Temple (also known as the Long Hua Temple) on Cabaguio Ave, three km in the direction of the airport, with its statues of the Buddha and its wood carvings is the biggest Buddhist temple in Mindanao and a sight to be seen. Monks and nuns live on the temple grounds and the Philippine Academy of Shakya (a Buddhist religious movement) is also located here. About 300m south of the temple, a Taoist Temple with a beautiful pagoda stands in a side street off Cabaguio Ave. Jeepneys with the sign 'Sasa' will take you there.

Orchid Farms & Banana Platations

A visit to the temples mentioned above would be well rounded off with a tour of the Puentaspina Orchid Gardens, about one km south of the Lon Wa Temple on Cabaguio Ave (there's a sign pointing the way in the side street Bolcan St). Outside of the city, there are numerous banana plantations and orchid farms open to the public, like the Lapanday Banana Plantation near Buhangin, 14 km north-west of Davao, and the Worldwide Derling Orchids Farm near Toril, 12 km south-west of Davao.
The GAP Farming Orchid Resort can be found in Ma-a. Set in a park with a swimming pool, this is a popular place for day trips. They charge P20 for admission, and the swimming pool costs P30. Jeepneys go from Matina Crossing to Ma-a; carry on from there by tricycle or on foot (10 min).

Shrine of the Holy Infant Jesus of Prague

From the Shrine of the Holy Infant Jesus of Prague, there's a good view over the city and the Davao Gulf. This small shrine is in the suburb called Matina, about six km west of Davao. It stands on a hill behind the Davao Memorial Park and can be reached by a road which branches off the MacArthur

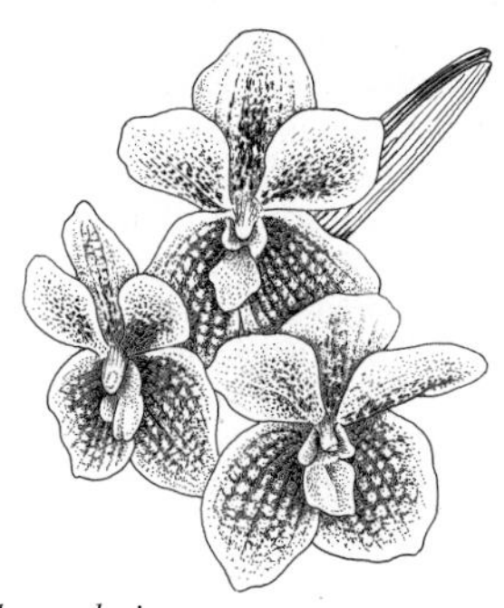

Vanda sanderiana
The *waling-waling* orchid is widespread around Davao.

Highway. Take a jeepney from the NCCC department store, Magsaysay Ave, to the Bankerohan Market and change there to a jeepney heading for Matina. The turn-off to the shrine is easy to miss, so the best thing to do is use the Matina cockpit (cockfighting arena) on the left-hand side as an orientation point. The ride by tricycle up to the shrine costs at least P5 per person.

Shopping

Davao boasts of quite a few attractive markets and shopping centres which have a wide variety of goods on offer. Fruit, vegetables, meat and fish are all sold at the Bankerohan Market near Bankerohan Bridge, and at the Agdao Market on Lapu-Lapu St. The stalls of the Madrazo Fruit Center on P Reyes St offer a wide selection of tropical fruits including, naturally, the infamous durian - a speciality of Davao. There is even a monument to it in Magsaysay Park. This prickly fruit that 'stinks like hell and tastes like heaven', has such a strong smell that it is banned from most hotel rooms, and airlines deliberately won't allow it on their planes.

The leading department stores and shopping centres in Davao are the NCCC department store, Magsaysay Ave; Gaisano City Mall, Duterte St at the corner of Ilustre St; the Gaisano Mall and Victoria Plaza, both on JP Laurel Ave; and SM City in the Ecoland area. The Aldevinco Shopping Center on Claro M Recto Ave offers artwork, antiques, products from cultural minorities, batik and lots more.

Places to Stay

To bring in more guests, some of the hotels below have drastically reduced their prices. For the foreseeable future these reductions will remain in force, and price variations of up to 30% are possible.

Places to Stay - bottom end

Le Mirage Family Lodge, San Pedro St, Tel 2263811. SR/fan P140, SR/DR/fan/bath P250/300, SR/DR/ac/bath P500/650. Very basic, but all right for the price. Coffee shop. Located next to Mercury Drug. Entrance is in the alleyway to the side.

El Gusto Family Lodge, A Pichon St, Tel 2273662. SR/DR/fan P175, SR/DR/fan/bath P250 and 400, SR/DR/ac/bath P700. The rooms are very basic but fairly clean, although some are on the stuffy side. Still, it's OK for the money.

Aveflor Inn, Claro M Recto Ave, Tel 2278152. SR/DR/fan/bath P250, SR/DR/ac/bath P350 and P550 (with TV). Reasonable rooms, however some are louder than you might like. Restaurant.

Royale House, Claro M Recto Ave, Tel 2273630, Fax 2218106. SR/ac/bath P300 and P500, DR/ac/bath P500 and P600. Small, very neat rooms, the more expensive ones with TV. Restaurant. A bit off the main road.

BS Inn, Monteverde St corner Gempesaw St, Tel 2213980, Fax 2210740. SR/ac/bath P400, DR/ac/bath P500 to P800. Nice, differently sized rooms with TV, well worth the money. Tastefully designed coffee shop. Restaurant.

Getting There & Away
1 Airport
5 Cebu Pacific
8 Malaysia Airlines
9 Silk Air
10 WG & A
11 Sulpicio Lines
12 Santa Ana Wharf
31 Philippine Airlines
36 Air Philippines
39 Avis
43 Seair
50 Cebu Pacific
66 Busterminal (500m)

Places to Stay
1 Grand Regal Hotel
Waterfront Insular Hotel Davao
3 Linmarr Apartelle
6 Villa Margarita (500m)
17 BS Inn
27 Regency Inn
28 Trader's Inn
33 The Marco Polo
37 Imperial Hotel
38 Aveflor Inn
39 The Royal Mandaya Hotel
40 Casa Leticia
41 Apo View Hotel
42 Tower Inn
45 Bagobo House Hotel
47 Villa Fontana Inn
53 Le Mirage Family Lodge
55 Royale House
57 Aljem's Inn
The Manor Pension House
61 El Gusto Family Lodge
62 Grand Men Seng Hotel

Places to Eat & Entertainment
1 Casino Filipino
Hagar's Place
Square Circle Disco
5 Ahfat Seafood Plaza
Buffet Palace
Cynthia's Lechon
Mr Buddha
15 Kanaway Restaurant
20 Luz Kinilaw Place
22 Regine's Seafood & Grill
23 Bistro Rosario
Harana Restaurant
Mongolian Garden
Peter Pan Bake Shop
Sarung Banggi Restaurant
26 Venue
29 Shanghai Restaurant
48 McDonald's
51 Tsuru Japanese Restaurant
52 Kusina Dabaw
New Sunya Restaurant
64 Colasa's Bar-B-Q

Miscellaneous
1 Dabaw Museum
Etnika Dabaw
Lon Wa Temple
Taoist Temple
2 Agdao Market
4 University of Southeastern Philippines
5 Victoria Plaza Shopping Center
7 Immigration Office
13 Whitetip Divers Davao
14 Magsaysay Park
15 Tourist Office
16 Equitable PCI Bank
18 NCCC Department Store
19 Salmonan Market
21 Muslim Fishing Village
24 San Pedro Hospital
25 Gaisano Mall
30 Madroza Fruit Center
32 Post Office
34 Equitable PCI Bank
35 Aldevinco Shopping Center
36 Pilman Travel & Tours
43 Pan Asia World Holidays
44 South Gaisano
46 Netconfusion
49 Starex 200 Internet Café
54 St Peter's Cathedral

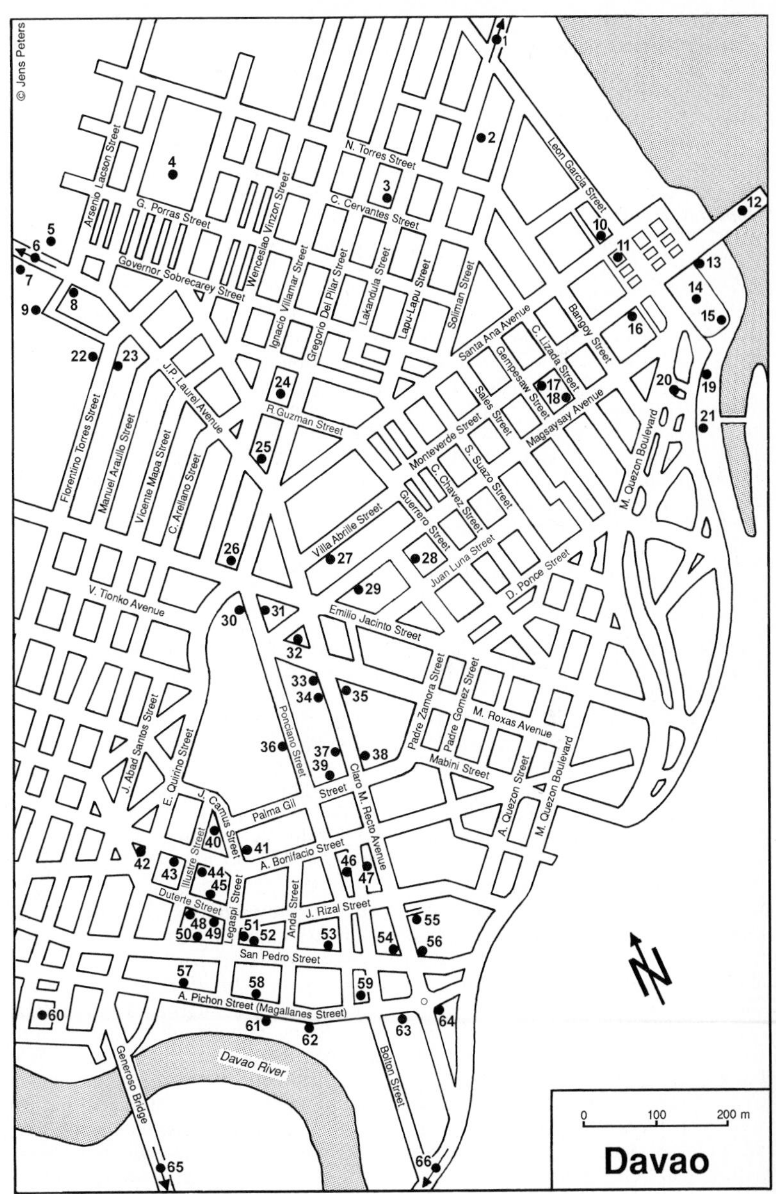
© Jens Peters
Arsenio Lacson Street
G. Porras Street
Governor Sobrecarey Street
Wenceslao Vinzon Street
Ignacio Villamar Street
Gregorio Del Pilar Street
Lakandula Street
Lapu-Lapu Street
Soliman Street
N. Torres Street
C. Cervantes Street
Leon Garcia Street
Santa Ana Avenue
C. Lizada Street
Bangoy Street
Gempesaw Street
Sales Street
Magsaysay Avenue
M. Quezon Boulevard
Monteverde Street
S. Suazo Street
C. Chavez Street
Guerrero Street
Juan Luna Street
D. Ponce Street
Villa Abrille Street
R. Guzman Street
J.P. Laurel Avenue
Florentino Torres Street
Manuel Araullo Street
Vicente Mapa Street
C. Arellano Street
V. Tionko Avenue
Emilio Jacinto Street
Padre Zamora Street
Padre Gomez Street
M. Roxas Avenue
Mabini Street
A. Quezon Street
M. Quezon Boulevard
Ponciano Street
Claro M. Recto Avenue
Palma Gil Street
J. Abad Santos Street
E. Quirino Street
J. Camus Street
Illustre Street
A. Bonifacio Street
Legaspi Street
Duterte Street
Anda Street
J. Rizal Street
San Pedro Street
A. Pichon Street (Magallanes Street)
Davao River
Generoso Bridge
Bolton Street
1 2 3 4 5 6 7 8 9 10 11 12 13 14 15 16 17 18 19 20 21 22 23 24 25 26 27 28 29 30 31 32 33 34 35 36 37 38 39 40 41 42 43 44 45 46 47 48 49 50 51 52 53 54 55 56 57 58 59 60 61 62 63 64 65 66
N
0 100 200 m
Davao

56 Philippine National Bank (PNB)
58 Internet Zone
59 City Hall
60 Bankerohan Market
63 Web Link Internet Café
65 GAP Farming Orchid Resort
Shrine of the Holy Infant Jesus of Prague
66 Indonesian Consulate (1 km)
SM City (1.5 km)

Imperial Hotel, Claro M Recto Ave, Tel 2224930, Fax 2212127. SR/ac/bath P440 (good value), DR/ac/bath P610 and P680. Immaculate rooms with TV, the more expensive also have a refrigerator. Restaurant, fitness room, billiards. The hotel entrance is a bit hard to find.
Regency Inn, Villa Abrille St, Tel 2225819, Fax 2274333, @. SR/ac/bath P650, DR/ac/bath P850, suite P1800. Tidy, pleasantly furnished rooms with TV. Restaurant.
The Manor Pension House, A Pichon St, Tel 2212511. SR/ac/bath P600 and P750, DR/ac/bath P700 and P850. Good-value, pleasantly furnished rooms with TV. Friendly service. Restaurant.

Places to Stay - middle

Bagobo House Hotel, Duterte St, Tel 2224444, Fax 2224440, @. SR/ac/bath P625, DR/ac/bath P835 to P1100. Good, well-kept, quiet rooms with TV, some also have a refrigerator. Restaurant.
Villa Margarita, JP Laurel Ave, Tel 2215674, Fax 2262968, @. SR/ac/bath P655 to P855, DR/ac/bath P750 to P1050, suites P1310, including breakfast. Inviting place with well-maintained rooms, all with TV. Restaurant, swimming pool, free airport service. Located about two km north of the centre.
Casa Leticia, J Camus St, Tel 2240501, Fax 2213585, @. SR/ac/bath P1700, DR/ac/bath P1800, suites P2500 and P3700, all including breakfast. Attractive, friendly accommodation with well-kept, pleasantly furnished rooms, all with TV and refrigerator. Restaurant, free airport service.

Places to Stay - top end

Grand Men Seng Hotel, A Pichon St, Tel 2219040, Fax 2212431, @. SR/ac/bath P1200, DR/ac/bath P1500, suite P2800. Immaculate, comfortable rooms, each with refrigerator and TV. Restaurant, fitness room, swimming pool, airport service.
The Royal Mandaya Hotel, Palma Gil St, Tel 2258888, Fax 2251888, @. SR/ac/bath P1500, DR/ac/bath P1700, including breakfast. Big hotel with quite pleasant rooms, all with TV and refrigerator. Restaurant, swimming pool.
Grand Regal Hotel, JP Laurel Ave, Tel 2350888, Fax 2343858, @. SR/ac/bath P1700 and P2000, DR/ac/bath P2000 and P2300, suites P3000 to P17,000, all including breakfast. Good quality rooms with a well-groomed atmosphere. Restaurant, sauna, fitness room, swimming pool. They also have the in-house Casino Filipino and a Duty Free Shop. Located in the Lanang part of town, about seven km east of the centre.
Apo View Hotel, J Camus St, Tel 2216430, Fax 2210748, @. SR/ac/bath P1500, DR/ac/bath P1750, suites P6000 to P12,000, all including breakfast. Old-established place with comfortably furnished rooms. Restaurant, disco, swimming pool.
Waterfront Insular Hotel Davao, Lanang, Tel 2343050-79, Fax 2350915, @. SR/ac/bath P1500 to P2000, DR/ac/bath P1700 to P2500, suites P5000 and P12,000, all including breakfast. Comfortable rooms. Attractive garden setting; must be the most attractive hotel in Davao. Restaurant, swimming pool, tennis court, diving. Located directly

on the Gulf of Davao about eight km east of the centre in the direction of the airport.

The Marco Polo, Claro M Recto Ave, Tel 2210888, Fax 2250111, @. SR/DR/ac/bath P5800 and P6700, suites P12,000 to P36,000. First-class, centrally located international hotel with top comfort. Restaurant, swimming pool, fitness room, free airport service.

Places to Eat

Enjoyable, inexpensive Chinese meals are available in the ***Shanghai Restaurant*** on Magsaysay Ave. Other popular restaurants are the ***Kusina Dabaw*** which serves Chinese and Filipino dishes, and the ever crowded ***New Sunya Restaurant***, both on San Pedro St.

The seafood restaurant is the ***Luz Kinilaw Place*** next to the Salmonan Market on Quezon Blvd. It might be unassumingly decorated, but they offer a large selection of really tasty fish specialities and seafood - highly recommended. Not far from there, in the same building as the Tourist Office on Magsaysay Park, you can eat Philippine dishes and seafood in the cosy surroundings of the ***Kanaway Restaurant.***

If it's roast chicken or barbecue you're after, then ***Colasa's Bar-B-Q*** next to the Bonifacio Monument in A Pichon St is the place to go, even late at night.

It's also worth making a short detour to Florentino Torres St where there's a whole variety of restaurants in a row near the corner of JP Laurel Ave. Worth mentioning are ***Regine's Seafood & Grill,*** a fairly inexpensive, attractive open restaurant with al fresco tables, the ***Harana*** with good barbecues and Filipino food, the ***Sarung Banggi*** renowned for its delicious steaks, prawns and salads, the ***Mongolian Garden*** specialising in Mongolian barbecue and spare ribs, the ***Bistro Rosario*** with its excellent steaks, and the ***Peter Pan Pie Shop*** which has wonderful cakes.

No smoking in Davao!
Non-smokers will rub their hands in glee, but the smoking fraternity are unhappy at yet another by-law to make their lives miserable: In Davao no smoking is allowed in public areas, on streets and pavements, as well as in public buildings, shopping centres, restaurants, bars etc. A Task Force keeps a sharp eye open to make sure the by-law is respected and will issue a P300 fine for a first offence. Repeat offenders are put in jail.

Near the Victoria Plaza Shopping Center (behind the big parking lot), on JP Laurel Ave, you'll also find several popular restaurants, including the two excellent, if a bit pricey, restaurants ***Ahfat Seafood Plaza*** and ***Mr. Buddha*** (serving seafood as well). Also to be recommended there are the ***Buffet Palace***, where you can eat your fill for P200, and ***Cynthia's Lechon*** with all sorts of barbecued fare and a live band drawing in big, mostly younger, crowds from about 10pm.

A tip for lovers of Japanese food: The ***Tsuru Restaurant*** with sushi bar in Legaspi St serves excellent and pleasantly inexpensive meals.

The European food is very good at ***Hagar's Place*** at the entrance to the Waterfront Insular Hotel Davao in Lanang. They have a garden and billiards and are a popular meeting place for foreign residents, as is ***Picobello*** in the South Gaisano (4th floor), Ilustre St, run by two Swiss. In the latter you can enjoy a good selection of wines, and pizzas from a wood-fired oven.

If it has to be fast food. then ***McDonald's*** can be found next to the Victoria Plaza shopping centre in JP Laurel Ave and in Duterte St, where you'll also find ***Jollibee*** and ***Shakey's***.

Entertainment

There's live music and disco every night in the popular ***Venue*** in E Quirino St opposite the Central Bank; lots going on after about 10pm.

A bit outside the city centre in the direction of the airport, on a side street to the right 300m before the Taoist Temple, is the ***Square Circle Disco***. Also popular is the ***Needle Point Nightclub*** right next door (P200 admission). You can gamble every night at the ***Casino Filipino*** in the Grand Regal Hotel located in JP Laurel St, on the north-west outskirts of the city.

Miscellaneous

Consulates: Indonesian Consulate, Ecoland Dr, Ecoland Subdivision, Tel 2992931, 2263889, Fax 2970139.

Malaysian Consulate, A Bonifacio St, Tel 2214050, 2214014.

Diving: Scuba World, Pro Dive Center, Monteverde St, Santa Ana Wharf, Tel & Fax 2262588, @.

Whitetip Divers Davao, PPA Building, Santa Ana Wharf, Tel 2270234, Fax 2276175, @.

Festivals: Araw ng Dabaw (Foundation Day celebrations) from 10 to 16 March. Kadayawan sa Dabaw Festival in August: A festival in honour of the cultural minorities on Mindanao and in thanks for a good harvest of flowers and fruit.

Immigration Office, JP Laurel Ave (across from the Victoria Plaza shopping centre), Tel 2222427, 3307258. Open Mon-Fri 8am-noon and 1-5pm.

Medical Services: The San Pedro Hospital, Guzman St, Tel 2212731, is the best hospital in the city.

Money: Equitable PCI Bank, Claro M Recto Ave, and Philippine National Bank, San Pedro St corner Claro M Recto Ave, have ATMs.

Online: Almost all Internet cafés charge P30/hr, eg Web Link and Internet Zone, both in Pichon St, Gatesway Online in the Regina Complex, Claro M Recto Ave, Starex 2000, Duterte St, and. Netfusion, Bolton (reduced rate from 10pm to 2am).

Post & Telephone: Post Office, M Roxas Ave.

Post code: 8000. Area code: 082.

Travel Agency: Ekran Tours, Monteverde St, Tel 2220808, Fax 2219989, offers various day trips (City Tour, Countryside Tour, Island Hopping).

Tourist Office, Magsaysay Park Complex, Tel 2216955, 2216798, Fax 2210070, @. Open Mon-Fri 8am-noon and 1-5pm.

Getting Around

Car: Avis, The Royal Mandaya Hotel, Palma Gil St, Tel 2258888.

Getting There & Away

By Air: Davao International Airport is 12 km north-east of Davao, between the districts of Lanang and Panacan. A taxi shouldn't cost more than P100. It's cheaper to take a tricycle (P10), 1½ km along the Airport Rd to the main road, then a jeepney marked 'San Pedro' or 'Bajada' to Davao (P8); you may have to wait a few minutes. The jeepney travelling from the town centre to the airport has the sign 'Sasa'.

Airport tax: For international flights a P550 airport tax is levelled.

Ticket sales outlets for Air Philippines, Cebu Pacific and Philippine Airlines can be found in the Victoria Plaza and Gaisano Mall shopping centres.

Air Philippines, Davao International Airport, 2342969.

- Pilman Travel & Tours, Ponciano St, Tel. 2245869.

Destination: Bacolod, Cebu City, Iloilo City, Manila.

Bouraq Airlines and ***Merpati***, Anstar Travel, Duterte St, Tel. 2211346.

Destination: Manado (North Sulawesi, Indonesia). From there connecting flights to Bali, Jakarta, Ujung Pandang etc.

Cebu Pacific, Summit World, Victoria Plaza, JP Laurel Ave, Tel 2240960-62.
- San Pedro St, Tel 2217446, 2222008.
- Davao International Airport, Tel 2331919-21.
Destinations: Cebu City, Iloilo City, Manila, Zamboanga.
Malaysia Airlines, Landco Center, JP Laurel Ave, Tel 2241897.
Destinations: Kota Kinabalu, Kuala Lumpur.
Philippine Airlines, Villa-Abrille Building, P Reyes St, Tel 22155641, 2215313.
- Davao International Airport, Tel 2340073, 2346434.
Destinations: Cebu City, Manila.
Seair, Pan Asia World Holidays, General Luna St, Tel 2212679.
Destination: Cagayan de Oro.
Silk Air, Pryce Tower, JP Laurel Ave, Tel 2211039, 2216430.
- Davao International Airport, Tel 2211039, 2245608.
Destination: Singapore.

By Bus: The bus terminal for trips to and from Butuan, Cagayan de Oro, Cotabato, General Santos, Manila and Surigao is in the Ecoland district, about two km south of the town centre. Taxis charge P50 and 'Ecoland' jeepneys cost P6.

By Boat: There are two piers you can use: Santa Ana Wharf next to Magsaysay Park and Sasa Pier a few km out of town. A jeepney from Sasa to the town centre costs P8.
Sulpicio Lines, Leon Garcia St, Tel 2217722.
Destinations: Cebu, Manila, Surigao.
WG & A, Santa Ana Ave, Tel 2340973, 2211385.
Destinations: General Santos, Manila, Panay, Zamboanga.

Butuan
Bus: Several buses run by various companies leave Butuan for Davao daily (6½ hrs).

Cagayan de Oro
Air: Seair flies Tuesday, Thursday and Sunday from Cagayan de Oro to Davao and vice versa (P1850; one hr).

Bus: From Cagayan de Oro, several buses run by various companies make the trip to Davao daily (eight hrs via Malaybalay; 10 hrs via Butuan).

Cotabato
Bus: From Cotabato, numerous Mintranco and Weena Express buses run daily to Davao (six hrs).

General Santos
Bus: From General Santos, numerous Yellow Bus Line buses run daily to Davao (four hrs). The last one might leave at about 3pm.

Boat: From General Santos to Davao on Monday and Wednesday with WG & A (P390; eight hrs).

Surigao
Bus: There are several buses run by various companies from Surigao to Davao daily, mainly in the morning (eight hrs via Malaybalay, or ten hrs via Butuan, where it may be necessary to change).

Boat: From Surigao to Davao on Wednesday with Sulpicio Lines (P975; 17 hrs).

Zamboanga
Air: Cebu Pacific flies on Tuesday and Thursday from Zamboanga to Davao and vice versa (P2650; 50 min).

Boat: From Zamboanga to Davao on Tuesday with WG & A (P855; 22 hrs); via General Santos.

Around Davao

Samal Island

Samal used to be the place to find a romantic pearl-diving atmosphere, but no longer. The days of prosperity for the once lucrative Aguinaldo Pearl Farm on the island are over. Nowadays, a first-class hotel complex - the Barceló Pearl Farm Island Resort - spreads along the picturesque bay where only a few years ago thousands of oysters produced cultured pearls. And it is an exclusive resort; uninvited day visitors may not be admitted.

The white Paradise Island Beach on the north-west coast is the best beach on Samal. To the north of the Paradise Island Park & Beach Resort stand the cottages of the Coral Reef Beach Resort, and to the south, a little out of the way, the Costa Marina Beach Resort.

Big and Little Cruz, also known as the Ligid Islands, north-east of Samal, are good for diving. There is another good diving area near the Barceló Pearl Farm Island Resort at Malipano Island, where the wrecks of two WWII ships lie 30m below water.

Once a year in the first week in March, the Island Garden City of Samal, as Samal Island is now also called, celebrates the Pangapog Festival. Highlights of this many faceted festival are the boat races (Bancarera), a sandcastle building competition, and a street parade in Peñaplata with colourful dance and music groups.

Places to Stay

Costa Marina Beach Resort, Tel 2331209, Fax 2330229. Cottage/fan/bath P700 to P900, cottage/ac/bath P1200 to P1500, depending on size and location. The garden is beautifully laid out and the cottages have lots of rooms between them. All have TV. Restaurant.

Samal Island Beach Park, Tel & Fax 2225935. Cottage/ac/bath P780 to P3500, depending on size. Fairly basic cottages for up to eight people. Restaurant.

Paradise Island Park & Beach Resort, Tel 2330252, Fax 2342926, @. Cottage/fan/bath P950, cottage/ac/bath P1300. A pleasant, well-tended place with extremely friendly staff and good service. The restaurant is good and inexpensive. It's quiet around here during the week, although popular at the weekend for day trips. Admission for day visitors is P45.

Barceló Pearl Farm Island Resort, Tel 2219970, Fax 2219979, @. SR/DR/ac/bath P8200. Samal house (standing on piles in the sea) P9600, suite P15,000. All with refrigerators. Cosy, comfortable rooms, and the suites are generously sized. The extensive grounds and facilities include a restaurant (not too cheap), swimming pool, tennis courts, water skiing, windsurfing and diving. Free airport service.

Getting There & Away

Jeepney/Boat: To get from Davao to the Paradise Island Park & Beach Resort on Samal, take a jeepney towards the airport with the destination 'Sasa' for P8. Ask the driver to stop at the Sasa pier next to the Caltex oil tanks. From there it's a few steps to the boat that will take you over to Paradise Island Beach; it costs P5 per person, or P50 for the boat. Boats leave between 5.30am and 5pm.

From Santa Ana Wharf boats leave for Peñaplata on Samal Island roughly every hour (P10; 30 min). From the jetty in Peñaplata you can have a motorcycle take you to Paradise Island Park & Beach Resort for about P80.

Roughly every two hours boats leave Santa Ana Wharf for Kaputian in the south of Samal (P20; one hr).

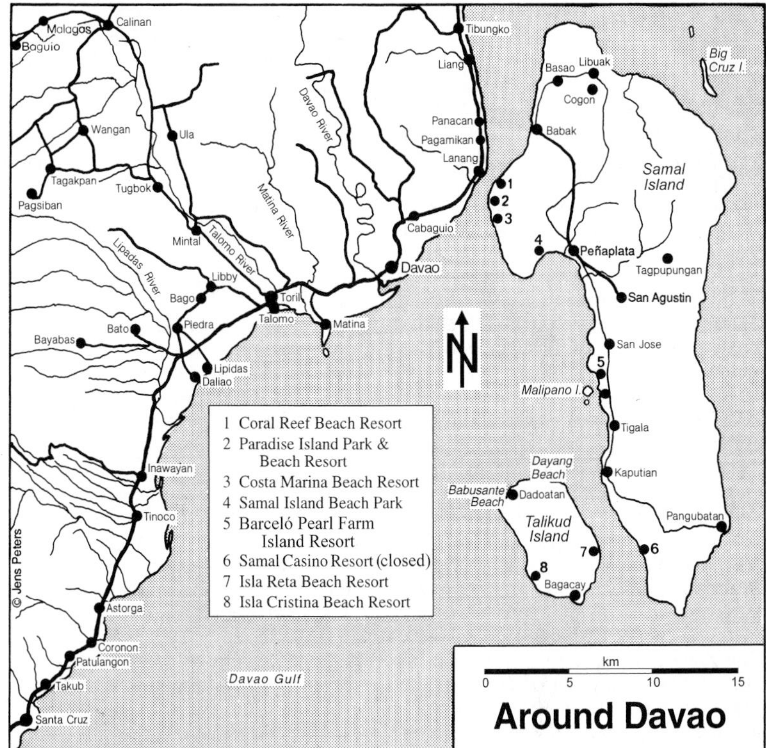

Talikud Island

Talikud Island, which lies south-west of Samal Island, sports several beautiful palm-lined beaches, especially along its west coast. Just off the north coast are two of the best diving areas of the Davao Gulf: Coral Garden and Dizon Wall.

The development of tourism on Talikud did not come up to expectations with the result that Isla Cristina Beach Resort, one of the most attractive places on the island, closed down again. There are picnic huts available on some of the other beaches which can be hired for P150 to P200, eg on Babusanta Beach and Dayang Beach.

Places to Stay

Isla Reta Beach Resort. Cottage/fan P400 and P500. Basic bamboo and stone cottages which are beginning to show their age. Located in a beautiful palm grove on the central east coast. Admission P10.

Getting There & Away

Boat: From Davao to Talikud Island (Isla Reta Beach Resort) by boat from Santa Ana Wharf daily at about 9.30am and 4.30pm (P20; one hr). Return trip to Davao at 6am and 3pm. Departure times are not fixed - you'll have to ask around a lot.

Eagle Camp

This camp (also known as the Philippine Eagle Nature Center) has been set up at Malagos, near Calinan in the Baguio District, about 36 km north-west of Davao by road. A trip to this establishment run by the Philippine Eagle Foundation Inc (PEFI) is really worth the effort (not only for ornithologists). The grounds are very well maintained and laid out like a botanical garden. They also have some typical Philippine animals in a small zoo, which includes the whole range of Philippine eagles (admission P25).

In the whole country there are only 77 confirmed examples of the Philippine eagle, 16 of which live in Eagle Camp. Two of them hatched in the incubator and were successfully raised in the camp. So there is a small spark of a chance that 'the air's noblest flier', as the aviator Charles Lindburgh called the Philippine national bird during a campaign to save the species back in the 60s, will escape extinction.

The people at the camp, who observe the nesting habits of the Philippine eagle, are very friendly and prove to be a mine of information on these birds. For a fee, it may be possible to stay overnight and go trekking in the area, for instance to Mt Apo National Park. You should bring a sleeping bag, provisions and warm clothing, as it gets much colder up there than in Davao.

Two km south of Eagle Camp, you'll find the Malagos Garden Resort with its pleasant restaurant, orchid garden and swimming pool. The resort is open from 9am to 5pm.

Getting There & Away

Jeepney/Tricycle: Several jeepneys leave for Calinan daily from Agdao Market in Davao (P12; you can also board them in San Pedro St or at the Bankerohan Market). Take a tricycle for the remaining five km or so from Calinan to Malagos and the camp entrance (P50). The last jeepney from Calinan to Davao (with the sign 'Agdao') leaves at about 6pm.

Taxi: A taxi from Davao to Eagle Camp and back will cost you P600 (you can always negotiate), including waiting time (total time about five hours).

Mt Apo National Park

The Tourist Office in Davao has detailed information about Mt Apo National Park, the various routes up the mountain, and recommended equipment. The personnel is competent to advise whether the climb is responsible and feasible. In April 1989 when around 300 local and foreign climbers took part in the annual organised climb, members of the NPA made it blatantly clear to the public who was boss on the mountain by seizing the whole group in a surprise raid, only to free them again shortly after.

In Digos, south of Mt Apo, you can obtain further information about climbing and security from the Mt Apo Climber Association at the office of the *Digos Times*. Guides and porters can be hired in Kidapawan for at least P300 a day. A water canteen and boots are essential. A warm sleeping bag is also necessary as the nights are cool - temperatures around freezing point are not uncommon. Take your own provisions, not forgetting salt, to prevent dehydration.

The climb is not easy. Even though sprinters have completed it in one day, five or six days is a more realistic schedule.

Kapatagan Route

Also known as the Davao del Sur-Route, this can be managed in three days, although four would be more comfortable, including travel from and back to Davao.

Day 1: Take a Yellow Bus Line, Mintranco or Weena bus from Davao to Digos from the bus terminal in Ecoland. It can either be a direct bus or one heading for Cotabato or General Santos (one hr). From Digos bus terminal at the market take a tricycle to the jeepney station on Quezon St at the corner of Rizal Ave, then a jeepney the 30 km up to Kapatagan (1½ hrs). A motorcycle will do the last stretch for about P120 (45 min).

Get in touch with a guide in Kapatagan, eg through Guillermo Franco, Sampaguita Chapter. A written request in advance wouldn't harm: 8002 Kapatagan, Davao del Sur.

Buying your provisions is definitely cheaper in Kapatagan than in Digos or Davao, but there's not a big selection of tinned food available.

Around noon, set off for the village of Sabaug (four hrs). Stay overnight in the hut.

Day 2: Start off with only your day pack at dawn. The first part of the route leads through tropical mountain rainforest and the slopes are steep by anybody's definition. The second section takes you through a rocky ravine and after that through lava stone formations to the summit (five hrs).

After a proper midday break on the summit, descend to Sabaug (three hours). Spend overnight in the hut.

Day 3: It'll take about three hrs to get back to Kapatagan in the morning. Go back to Davao via Digos. The last bus from Digos to Davao leaves at around 7pm. Overnight accommodation is available in Digos at the Digos Travel Lodge, Rizal Ave, where a room with fan and bath costs between P300 and P500. You could also stay at the better quality Hotel Ynciert's, Juan Luna St, where a room with aircon and bath will cost between P600 and P900.

Kidapawan Route

This recommended four-day schedule includes travel to and from Davao:

Day 1: Go from Davao to Kidapawan by Mintranco bus headed either for Kidapawan itself or Cotabato. This takes over two hrs. Leave early as the last jeepney from Kidapawan to Lake Agco, via Ilomavis, usually leaves at about 3pm. From Lake Agco it's a good three hrs uphill on foot to the Marbel River Campsite, where you can stay overnight in the shelter.

Day 2: This is six to eight hrs' hard climbing; it's about five hrs to Lake Venado. You will have to sleep outside, so take a plastic sheet, or better still a small tent, as it's uncomfortable if it rains.

Day 3: Allow for two hrs to reach the summit, then return to Lake Venado or the Marbel River Campsite.

Day 4: Return to Kidapawan or Davao.

General Santos

Maguindanao Muslims and B'laans were the sole inhabitants of this city up to the beginning of the 20th century. The first influx of immigrants arrived between 1914 and 1915 and more followed in the 1930s. In 1939 pioneers from Luzon and the Visayas led by General Paulino Santos established a settlement on the Silway River on Sarangani Bay. In 1965 Dadiangas was renamed General Santos ('Gen San') in his honour. The old name is also used today.

The city's economy depends mainly on pineapple, bananas (Dole Pineapple Plantation and Stanfilco Banana Plantation), cattle (Sarangani Cattle Co) and fishing (tuna).

The two islands of Balut and Sarangani, which still belong to the Philippines, lie off the coast of Mindanao, south of General Santos. Indonesia's territorial waters begin only a few miles away.

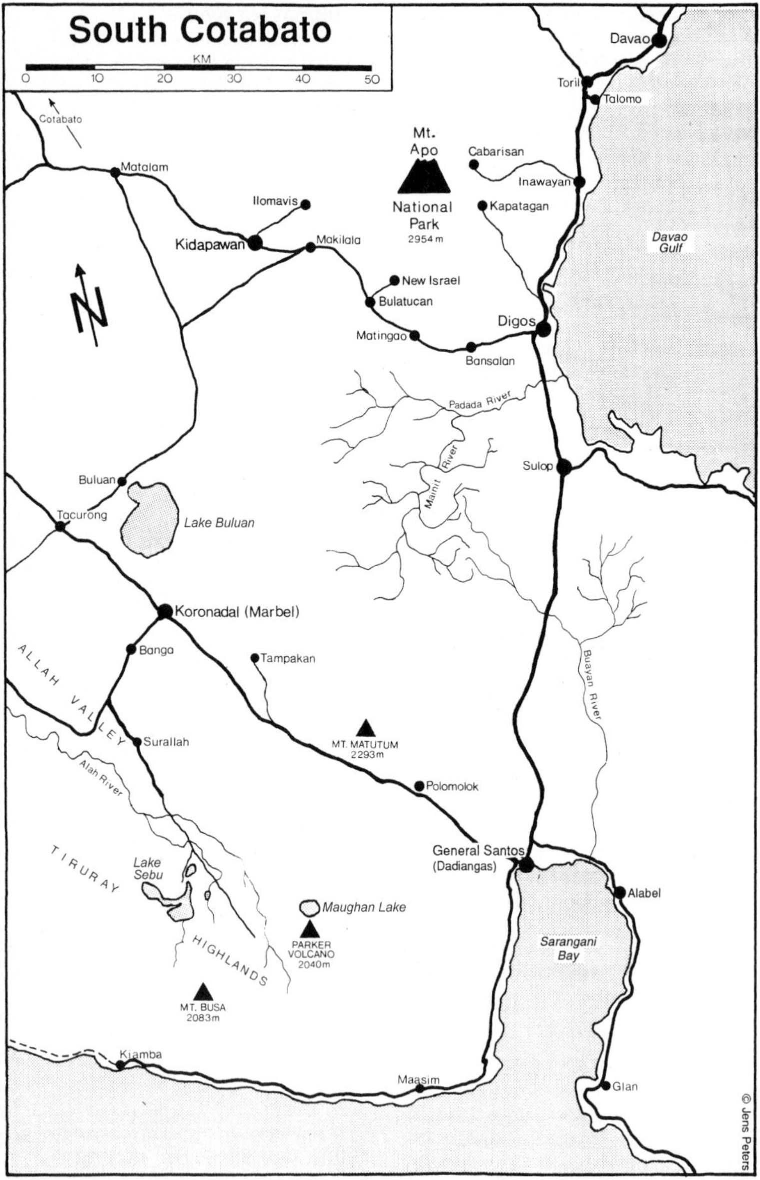

South Cotabato

KM
0 10 20 30 40 50

Cotabato
Matalam
Ilomavis
Kidapawan
Makilala
Mt. Apo
National Park
2954 m
Cabarisan
Inawayan
Kapatagan
Davao
Toril
Talomo
Davao Gulf
New Israel
Bulatucan
Matingao
Bansalan
Digos
Padada River
Mainit River
Sulop
Buluan
Lake Buluan
Tacurong
Koronadal (Marbel)
Banga
Tampakan
ALLAH VALLEY
Surallah
MT. MATUTUM
2293m
Buayan River
Alah River
Polomolok
General Santos
(Dadiangas)
Alabel
TIRURAY
Lake Sebu
HIGHLANDS
Maughan Lake
PARKER VOLCANO
2040m
Sarangani Bay
MT. BUSA
2083m
Kiamba
Maasim
Glan

Although there is a shipping route between Balut Island and Manado in the north of Sulawesi/Indonesia, they will only accept Filipinos and Indonesians as passengers. Other nationalities are not allowed on board, even with a valid Indonesian visa. The Indonesian border officials who check everybody before they leave Balut Island stick to the rules exactly.

The outrigger from General Santos to Balut Island only goes at night, and the trip can be damp and cold (seven hrs). It's more comfortable to take a tour to Balut Island with Tropicana Express who have an office in the Anchor Hotel.

Places to Stay - bottom end

Vince's Pension House, Asencio Building, Magsaysay Ave corner Atis St. SR/fan/bath P220, SR/ac/bath P380 and P420, DR/ac/bath P490 to P900. Inviting rooms, furnished with varying degrees of comfort. The ones facing the street are a bit loud. Coffee shop.

Lea's Pension House, Champaca St corner Rambutan St, Tel 3010055. SR/fan/bath P250, SR/ac/bath P400, DR/ac/bath P600. Pleasant, quiet location, with friendly rooms, some with TV. Restaurant.

Cambridge Farm Pension House, Nuñez St, Purok Malakas, Tel 5536310, @. SR/DR/fan/bath P300, SR/ac/bath P400, DR/ac/bath P500 and P800, suite P980 (including breakfast). Pleasantly furnished rooms with TV. Good value. Excellent accommodation run by the Englishman Chris and his Filipina wife, Ellie. Restaurant, swimming pool, mini zoo, diving. Located about four km north of the town centre (taxi P50 to P70).

Pietro's Hotel, National Highway, Tel 5524831. SR/ac/bath P400, DR/ac/bath P500, suite P1000. Good rooms, OK for the money. They also offer hourly rates and have a disco and restaurant.

Places to Stay - middle

T'Boli Hotel, National Highway, Tel 5537586. SR/ac/bath P450 and P560, DR/ac/bath P750 to P1030. Comfortable rooms, the more expensive ones with refrigerator and TV. Restaurant, music lounge. Located in the outskirts of town.

Tierra Verde Hotel, National Highway, Tel 5524500, Fax 5522802. SR/ac/bath P500, DR/ac/bath P680, suites P850 and P1120. Pleasant, quiet hotel with tidy rooms (with TV) which are all right for the money. Restaurant, disco.

Anchor Hotel, Cagampang St Extension, Tel 5524660, Fax 5524575, @. SR/ac/bath P600 and P650, DR/ac/bath P800 and P850, suite P1200. Neat rooms with TV, the more expensive ones also with refrigerator. Restaurant, coffee shop.

Phela Grande Hotel, Magsaysay Ave, Tel 5524925, Fax 5522990, @. SR/ac/bath P600, DR/ac/bath P850 and P1150, all include Filipino breakfast. Very good rooms, more than adequate. Restaurant, coffee shop.

Places to Stay - top end

Sydney Hotel, Pioneer Ave corner Pendatun Ave, Tel 5525479, Fax 5525478, @. SR/DR/ac/bath P1340, suites P1800 and P2000. Immaculate rooms with TV, the suites also have a refrigerator. The best hotel in the city centre. Restaurant, seafood grill on the roof, piano bar, airport service.

East Asia Royale Hotel, National Highway, Tel 5534119, Fax 5534129, @. SR/DR/ac/bath P1800 and P2160, suite P2880. Comfortable rooms with refrigerator and TV, the suites also have a jacuzzi. An excellent hotel at the northeastern end of town. Restaurant, piano bar.

Places to Eat

The fact that General Santos is home to an important fishing harbour is re-

Getting There & Away
11 Yellow Bus Line Busterminal
14 Jeepneys to Makar Wharf
15 Philippine Airlines
32 Air Philippines
40 Philippine Airlines
41 Bulaong Bus Terminal
42 Makar Wharf
General Santos International Airport (10 km)

Places to Stay
1 East Asia Royale Hotel (200m)
3 Anchor Hotel
10 T'Boli Hotel
12 Tierra Verde Hotel
17 Lea's Pension House
19 Matutum Hotel
24 Concrete Lodge
27 Cambridge Farm Pension House
31 Sydney Hotel
33 Hotel Sansu
34 Phela Grande Hotel
35 Zabala Sanitary Lodge
40 Pietro's Hotel
42 Tropicana Resort Hotel

Places to Eat & Entertainment
3 The Garden Grill
5 Shakey's
13 NR Lechon Manok & Seafoods
16 Tuna Grill & Restaurant
19 Starwars Disco
23 Manukan sa Balanghai
36 Jollibee
37 Ciacomino's
38 Kurdapoy's Litson Manok
39 Disco Rama

Miscellaneous
1 Gaisano (300m)
2 St Elizabeth Hospital
4 Bank of the Philippine Islands
6 Equitable PCI Bank
7 S-Gate Internet Café
8 Market
9 Doctor's Hospital
18 Explorer's Haven
20 Immigration Office
21 Post Office
22 Philippine National Bank (PNB)
26 Metrobank
27 Tuna City Dive Center
28 Notre Dame College
29 Police Station
30 City Hall
36 Kimball Plaza
37 RD Plaza Mall

flected in the high number of good quality, mostly open-air seafood restaurants in the city. In the ***Tuna Grill & Restaurant*** in Quirino St fish and various kinds of seafood are prepared to order. One specialty of this warmly decorated restaurant is deep-fried quail. About 100m from there, in Naranjita St, the very pleasant ***NR Lechon Manok & Seafoods*** will also cook meals according to the customer's instructions, as does ***Kurdapoy's Litson Manok*** in Magsaysay Ave at the corner of Atis St. The ***Manukan Saturday Balnghai*** in Pioneer Ave is a cosy, tastefully furnished restaurant with inexpensive Philippine food. ***The Garden Grill*** on the roof of the Anchor Hotel in Cagampang St offers specialties from the grill (meat and fish). If you want steak, then the place to go is the ***Kalilangan Restaurant*** in the East Asia Royale Hotel on the National Highway. Last, but not least, pizza and pasta can be had at ***Shakey's*** on Santiago Blvd and at ***Ciacomino's*** in the RD Plaza Mall in Pendatun St at the corner of Osmeña St.

Entertainment

You can enjoy first-class live music in the evenings at ***Babes Piano Bar*** in the East Asia Royale Hotel, National High-

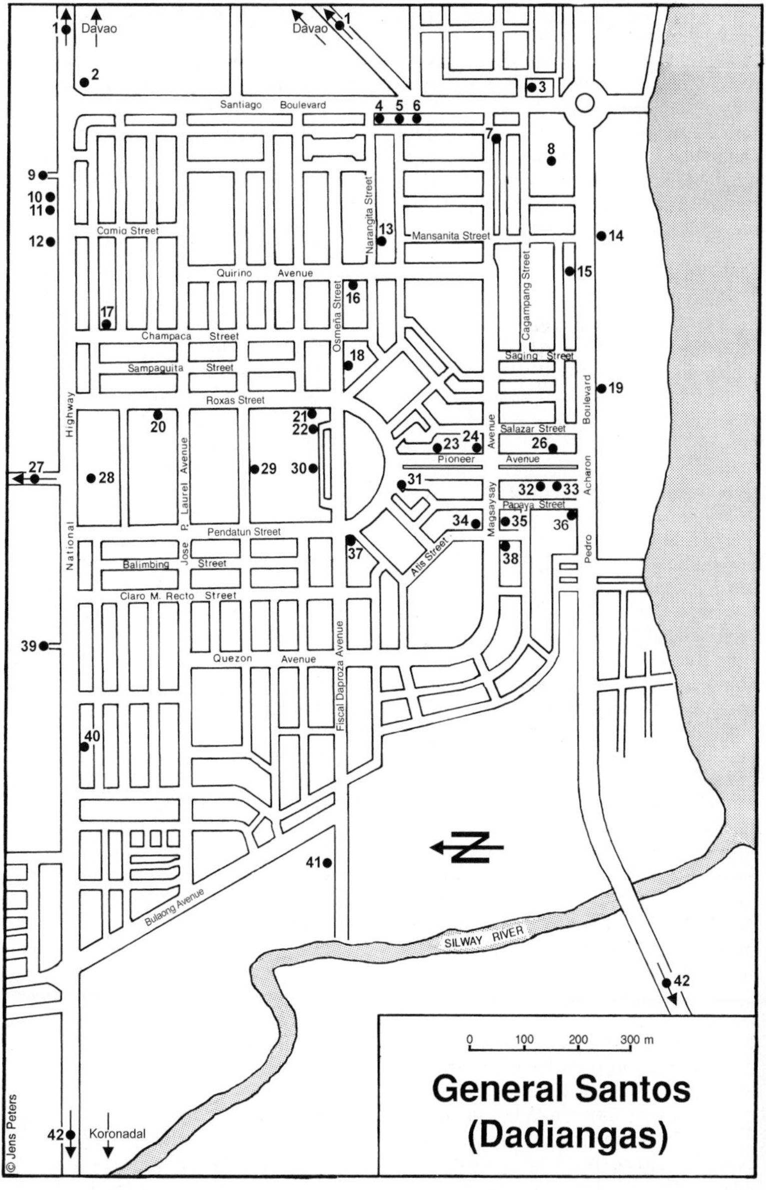

1 Davao
Davao 1
2
3
Santiago Boulevard
4 5 6
7
8
9
10
11
12
Camia Street
13
Narangita Street
Mansanita Street
14
Cagampang Street
15
Quirino Avenue
16
Osmeña Street
17
Champaca Street
18
Saging Street
Sampaguita Street
19
Roxas Street
National Highway
20
21
22
P. Laurel Avenue
23
24
Salazar Street
26
Magsaysay Avenue
Pioneer Avenue
27
28
29
30
31
32
33
Pedro Acharon Boulevard
Papaya Street
34
35
36
Pendatun Street
37
Atis Street
38
Jose Balimbing Street
Claro M. Recto Street
39
Quezon Avenue
Fiscal Daproza Avenue
40
41
Bulaong Avenue
SILWAY RIVER
42
0 100 200 300 m
General Santos (Dadiangas)
42 Koronadal
© Jens Peters

way. Some of the most popular discos in the city are ***Pier 8 Disco*** in Pietro's Hotel, ***Disco Rama***, National Highway (near Pietro's Hotel), and the ***Starwars Disco,*** Acharon Blvd (next to the Matutum Hotel). If you like to trip the light fantastic, then ballroom dancing is available Wednesday, Thursday and Saturday in the ***Tierra Verde Hotel Disco*** on the National Highway.

Miscellaneous

Diving: Tuna City Dive Center, Cambridge Farm Pension House, Tel 5545681, @, and Whitetip Divers, Tel 5536310, Cellphone 0917-3301237, @, arrange individual diving trips.
Festivals: Foundation Day and Kalilangan Festival on 27 February. Pagdidriwang (Charter Day) and Tuna Festival from 1 to 5 September.
Medical Services: The best hospital in General Santos is the Doctor's Hospital on National Highway.
Money: Bank of the Philippine Islands, Santiago Blvd, Metrobank, Pioneer Ave, and Philippine National Bank, City Hall Dr, have ATMs.
Online: S-Gate, Magsaysay Ave, (P60/hr) and in the Kimball Plaza shopping centre, Acheron Blvd at the corner of Papaya St, (P70/hr). The cheapest is Explorer's Haven, Osmeña St, (P40/hr).
Population: 270,000.
Post & Telephone: Post Office, Roxas St. Post code: 9500. Area code: 083.
Swimming: Villa Aurora Swimming Resort, National Highway, (entrance between the Tierra Verde Hotel and the Yellow Bus Line Bus Terminal). Admission is P50.

Getting Around

Tricycle: Swarms of tricycles are responsible for most of the innercity local transport. They ride on established routes and are not too happy to deviate from them (they charge extra if they do). One trip costs P3 per person.

Getting There & Away

By Air: The General Santos International Airport is about 10 km south-west of the city. A taxi from there to the centre costs at least P100.
Air Philippines, General Santos International Airport, Tel 5545611, 5532463.
- RD Building, Pioneer Ave, Tel 5532429.
Destinations: Cebu City, Iloilo City (via Cebu City), Manila.
Philippine Airlines, Acharon Blvd, Tel 5528856.
- Pietro's Hotel: Tel 5527685.
Destination: Manila.

By Bus: The Bulaong Bus Terminal can be found in the western outskirts of the city. Yellow Bus Line buses also start here before going to their own terminal on National Highway.

By Boat: The Makar Wharf is six km south-west of the city centre. A taxi costs between P50 and P100. Jeepneys with the destination 'Tambler' leave for the wharf from Acharon Blvd near the market.
Sulpicio Lines, Makar Wharf, Tel 5525242, 5522181.
Destinations: Cebu, Manila, Panay, Zamboanga.
WG & A, Fremie's Xerox, Pioneer Ave, Tel 5522060, 5524962.
Destinations: Davao, Manila, Panay.

Davao
Bus: From Davao numerous Yellow Bus Line buses run daily to General Santos (four hrs). The last one is likely to leave at about 3pm.

Boat: From Davao to General Santos on Monday and Wednesday with WG & A (P390; eight hrs).

Koronadal (Marbel)
Bus: From Koronadal (Marbel) numerous Yellow Bus Line buses make the

one-hour run to General Santos every day, some going on to Davao. Last departure is around 7pm. There are also minibuses.

Surallah
Bus: Several Yellow Bus Line buses go from Surallah to General Santos every day. You may have to change in Koronadal (two hrs).

Zamboanga
Boat: From Zamboanga to General Santos on Tuesday with WG & A and Thursday with Sulpicio Lines (P855; 13 hrs).

Koronadal (Marbel)

Koronadal, also known locally as Marbel, is the capital of South Cotabato Province. Apart from immigrants from other parts of the Philippines it's mainly Maguindanao and B'laan, members of the original native ethnological groups, who live here. The Maguindanao call the town Koronadal, while the B'laan call it Marbel. It is a good starting point for a trip to Lake Sebu.

Places to Stay

Alabado's Home, Alunan Ave corner Rizal St. SR/DR/fan/bath P200/280, SR/DR/ac/bath P350/400. Basic rooms which are all right for the money. A bit loud though.
Ramona Plaza Hotel, General Santos Dr, Tel 2283284. SR/ac/bath P550 and P650, DR/ac/bath P700 and P850, suite P1450. Quiet rooms with TV, the suites also have a refrigerator. A pleasant, friendly hotel in a central location. Restaurant.
Marvella Plaza Hotel, General Santos Dr, Tel & Fax 2282063. SR/ac/bath P660 to P960, DR/ac/bath P860 to P1250, suites P1350 to P2000. Immaculate rooms, all have TV, and the suites also have a refrigerator. Restaurant.

Places to Eat

Worth a good mention is the self-service restaurant ***Casa Illonga*** in the Ramona Plaza Hotel which has inexpensive Filipino food. They also run the adjoining baker's, ***The Fresh Baker***.
The ***Café Loretta*** in the Marvella Plaza Hotel has good Chinese and Japanese dishes; they also do good breakfasts.

Miscellaneous

Festival: Town Fiesta on 18 July.
Money: Bank of the Philippine Islands, General Santos Dr, and Equitable PCI Bank, Alunan Ave, have ATMs.
Population: 130,000.
Post & Telephone: Post code: 9506. Area code: 083.

Getting There & Away

Davao - General Santos
Bus: From Davao several Yellow Bus Line buses run daily to Koronadal via General Santos, some going on to Tacurong. It takes four hrs from Davao and one hr from General Santos.

Lake Sebu - Surallah
Bus: To go from Lake Sebu to Koronadal via Surallah, you go first by jeepney to Surallah, then to Koronadal in a Yellow Bus Line bus bound for General Santos (two hrs).

Surallah

Surallah is a small town in the southern part of the Allah Valley. It provides access to Lake Sebu, perhaps the loveliest inland sea in the Philippines.
About 15 km south of Surallah are the impressive Seven Falls, which are surrounded by tropical rainforest. These thundering falls can be reached on foot in less than an hour along a well-cleared path which begins at the road from Surallah to Lake Sebu and leads through dense jungle.

The following day trips from Surallah can be recommended: to Buluan, and from there to Lake Buluan with its swamp areas - which is especially interesting for ornithologists. If possible, to the Kimato gold mines in the mountains of the Tiruray Highlands, where the metal of kings is mined under hair-raising conditions. This area might be closed off.

Places to Stay

D'Chateau Lodging, Camia St. SR/DR P100/200, SR/DR/ac P400. Basic accommodation.

Warning

The area around Lake Sebu was extremely dangerous as recently as 1996. Within a period of a few weeks, over twenty foreigners were kidnapped by Moslem extremists and held to ransom. After the military had sent in reinforcements in the shape of battle-hardened soldiers, the situation returned to normal. Nevertheless, it's advisable to check on the latest state of affairs around Lake Sebu, eg in General Santos or Koronadal, before going there.

Lake Sebu

Lake Sebu, which is teeming with fish, and the two smaller neighbouring lakes Sultan and Lahit, are nestled into the southern Tiruray Highlands at an altitude of almost 300m. Around Lake Sebu live the tribespeople called the T'boli who live in almost total seclusion and produce rice, maize and sugar cane as well as breeding tilapia fish. They are well known for the quality of their brassware and weaving. (For more details, see the section on Cultural Minorities in the Country & People chapter.)

Try to arrange your schedule so as to include the colourful Saturday market, or, even better, the annual Lem-Lunay T'boli Festival (Helubong Festival) on the second Friday in November, which climaxes in wild horse fights the following Sunday.

You will only enjoy visiting the Lake Sebu area if you are interested in the traditional life and culture of the T'boli. Those looking for more modern attractions, such as discos, will soon be bored and will not be welcomed by the locals. On the other hand, you should also not expect to come across gloriously folky ethnic groups all decked out in their traditional costume. Time has not stood still for the T'boli any more than anywhere else, and they are just as partial to jeans and T-shirts as the rest of us.

Places to Stay

Lakeview Tourist Lodge. SR/DR P100/200. Basic place near the market. The owners, Carlos and Irene Legaste, also own a souvenir shop, where they sell T'Boli arts and crafts.

Bao Ba-ay Village Inn. SR/DR P125/150. Modest, family-style accommodation, idylically located on the lakeshore. Bao Ba-ay, the owner, is a pure T'boli (in fact, he's a justice of the peace) and can tell you a great deal about the T'boli culture. His wife, Alma, is an Ilokana and is a good cook. They also have their own fish farm and can arrange boats and horses for outings for a reasonable charge.

Artacho Resort, Cellphone 0918-4512685. Dorm P50, SR/DR/fan P150, SR/DR/fan/bath P250 and P400. Unpretentious, but acceptable. Restaurant, swimming pool.

Estares Lake Resort, Cellphone 0918-4502747. SR/DR/fan/bath P200, P250 and P400. Idyllic location on the lake, with neat rooms. Restaurant. They also organise local tours.

Punta Isla Lake Resort. Dorm P50, SR/DR/fan/bath P300 and P500. Friendly rooms in a fairly comfortable resort on a hillside with a beautiful view of the lake. Their cook's speciality is tilapia fish, fresh out of the water, prepared any way you want.

Getting There & Away

Jeepney: Several jeepneys go from the market at Surallah to Lake Sebu daily till about 5pm (P15; one hr).
The last jeepney from Surallah to Koronadal (Marbel) usually leaves at about 3pm.

Cotabato

Cotabato is on the Rio Grande de Mindanao, one of the country's longest rivers. The town appears to be predominantly Muslim, but statistics show that the population is 60% Christian and only 40% Muslim. The people here are known as Maguindanao. Islam came to Cotabato in 1371, when the Arab Sharif Muhammad Kabunsuwan, who is said to be the founder of Cotabato, arrived. The Jesuits didn't arrive until 1872 and settled in Tamontaka, seven km south-west, to build a church and establish Christianity in the area.

Places to Stay

Hotel Filipino, Sinsuat Ave corner Pendatun Ave, Tel 4212307. SR/fan P200, DR/fan P300, SR/ac/bath P560, DR/ac/bath P670 and P850. Basic, but fairly good rooms, some with a good view over the city plaza.
El Corazon Inn, Makakua St, Tel. 4213240. SR/fan/bath P300, SR/ac/bath P500, DR/ac/bath P780. Reasonable rooms.
Hotel Castro, Sinsuat Ave, Tel 4217523, Fax 4216406. SR/fan/bath P350 SR/ac/bath P750, DR/ac/bath P1020. Inviting rooms with TV, well worth the money. Restaurant.
Pacific Heights Hotel, Don Juliano Ave, Tel & Fax 4212249, @. SR/DR/ac/bath P760 to P2500. A friendly hotel with good, well-kept rooms, all with TV. Restaurant. Free airport service.
Estosan Garden Hotel, Governor Gutierrez Ave, Tel 4216777, Fax: 4215488, @. SR/DR/ac/bath P1440, suites P2160 and P3600. Comfortable rooms with TV, the suites also have a refrigerator. This is the best hotel in Cotabato. Restaurant.

Places to Eat

The Chinese and Philippine dishes in the ***Sardonyx Restaurant***, Governor Guiterrez Ave at the corner of Sinsuat Ave, are good value. ***Jay Pee's Dan Restaurant & Snack House*** on Don Rufino Alonzo St has a reputation for tasty, reasonably priced food and generous portions.

Miscellaneous

Festivals: City Fiesta (Araw ng Kutabato) on 19 and 20 June. Shariff Kabunsuwan Festival from 15 to 19 December.
Medical Services: The Cotabato Medical Center, Sinsuat Ave, Tel 4217228, is considered to be one of the best hospitals in the city.
Money: The Equitable PCI Bank, Makakua St, has an ATM.
Population: 160,000.
Post & Telephone: Post Office, Bonifacio St.
Post code: 9600. Area code: 064.
Tourist Office, Cosme Building, Quezon Ave, Tel 4211110, Fax 4217868, @. Open Mon-Fri 8am-noon and 1.30-5pm.

Getting There & Away

By Air: Cotabato Awang Airport is about six km outside the city. A taxi costs P100, the trip by jeepney P8.
Philippine Airlines, Concepcion Building, Don Ramin Vilo St, Tel 4211212.

- Awang Airport: Tel. 4310136.
Destination: Manila.
Seair, 51 Sinsuat Avenue, Tel. 4213788.
Destinations: Cagayan de Oro, Cebu City, Zamboanga.

By Boat: The harbour in Cotabato is called Polloc and is about 20 km north of the city. Minibuses go there for P25 per person.
Sulpicio Lines, Tukahanis, Tel 4212513, 4214072.
Destinations: Manila, Panay, Zamboanga.
WG & A, Salimbao, Tel 4212448, 4214175.
Destinations: Manila, Panay, Zamboanga.

Davao
Bus: Different companies run numerous buses from Davao to Cotabato daily (5½ hrs).

Koronadel (Marbel)
Bus: From Koronadal (Marbel), many Maguindanao Express and JD Express buses run daily to Cotabato (three hrs). Yellow Bus Line buses go at least as far as Tacurong, from where jeepneys run to Cotabato.

Pagadian
Bus: The bus trip from Pagadian to Cotabato by land is not advisable even if one is available. (See the Getting There & Away section under Pagadian earlier in this chapter.)

Boat: A boat leaves Pagadian for Cotabato daily at 5pm (eight hrs).

Zamboanga
Air: Seair flies on Monday, Wednesday and Friday from Zamboanga to Cotabato and vice versa (P1690; 50 min).

Boat: From Zamboanga to Cotabato on Monday with Sulpicio Lines, Sunday with WG & A (P625; 10 hrs).

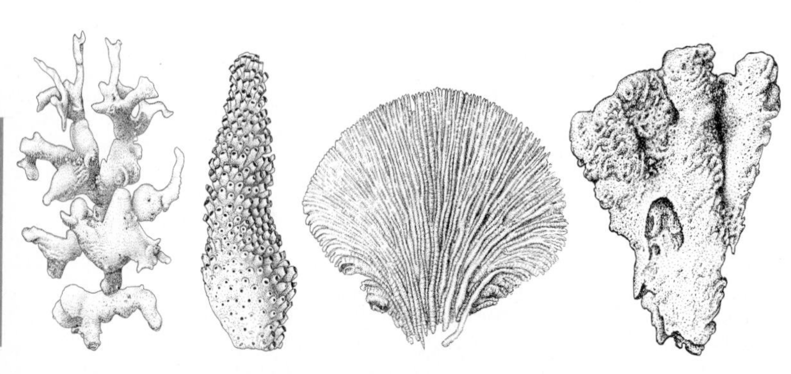

Basilan

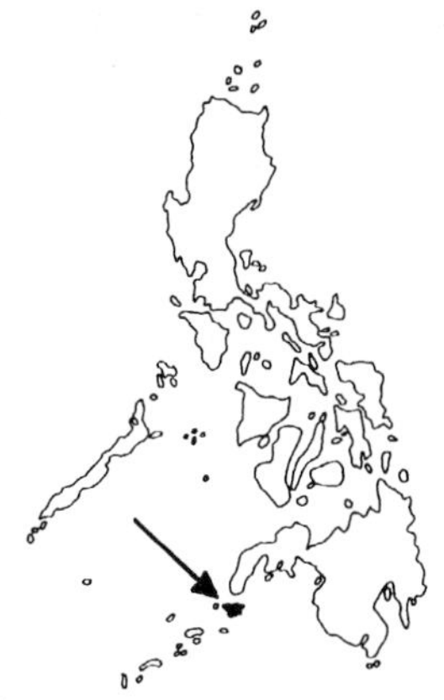

The southern end of Basilan meets the northern end of the Sulu Islands, and its northern end is just across the Basilan Strait from Mindanao. Since 1973, Basilan has been a province, comprising a main island and numerous smaller ones. About 230,000 people live here, roughly one-third of whom are Yakan, an ethnic minority found only on Basilan, except for some families living near Zamboanga on Mindanao. They are peace-loving Muslim farmers and cattle raisers, who are well known for their hospitality towards visitors and for their colourful and elaborate ceremonies, festivals and weddings. As well as the Yakan, Basilan is inhabited by the Chavacano, Visayan, Samal, Tausug and a few Badjao tribespeople.

Basilan is hilly and rugged and its centre is virtually unexplored. In the north of the island, the climate is fairly stable and there is no obviously dry or wet season, for rain may fall at any time of the year. The southern part, by contrast, has a fairly dry season from November to April.

The area's main industry is the processing of caoutchouc for rubber. Basilan rubber is considered among the best in the world, and large international companies have invested in the plantations. Other crops are coffee, cocoa, pepper, African oil (a plant oil extracted from the dates of the African palm tree) and abaca; copper is also mined. Because the waters around Basilan abound with fish, mussels and seaweed, the province is one of the most important suppliers of seafood in the southern Philippines.

Safety Warning

From 1993 until 1995, Basilan frequently hit the headlines in the Philippine press owing to kidnappings and other acts of violence. Many people lost their lives in shoot-outs between the military and members of the Moro National Liberation Front (MNLF) who had set up camp in the Basilan mountains.

In the meantime, the MNLF has come to an arrangement with the government, but dissident elements who have combined into the Moro Islamic Liberation Front (MILF) have taken control of the mountain regions. In the middle of 2001, the extremist Muslim splinter group Abu Sayyaf generated a series of negative headlines when they kidnapped a group of foreign visitors and Philippine nationals, dragging them off into the inpenetrable interior of the island. This led to a massive counter-strike by the Philippine Army. As a result, peace is unlikely to return soon to Basilan.

For your own safety you would be wise to think twice about visiting Basilan. Check with the tourist office in Zamboanga for the latest news on the situation there.

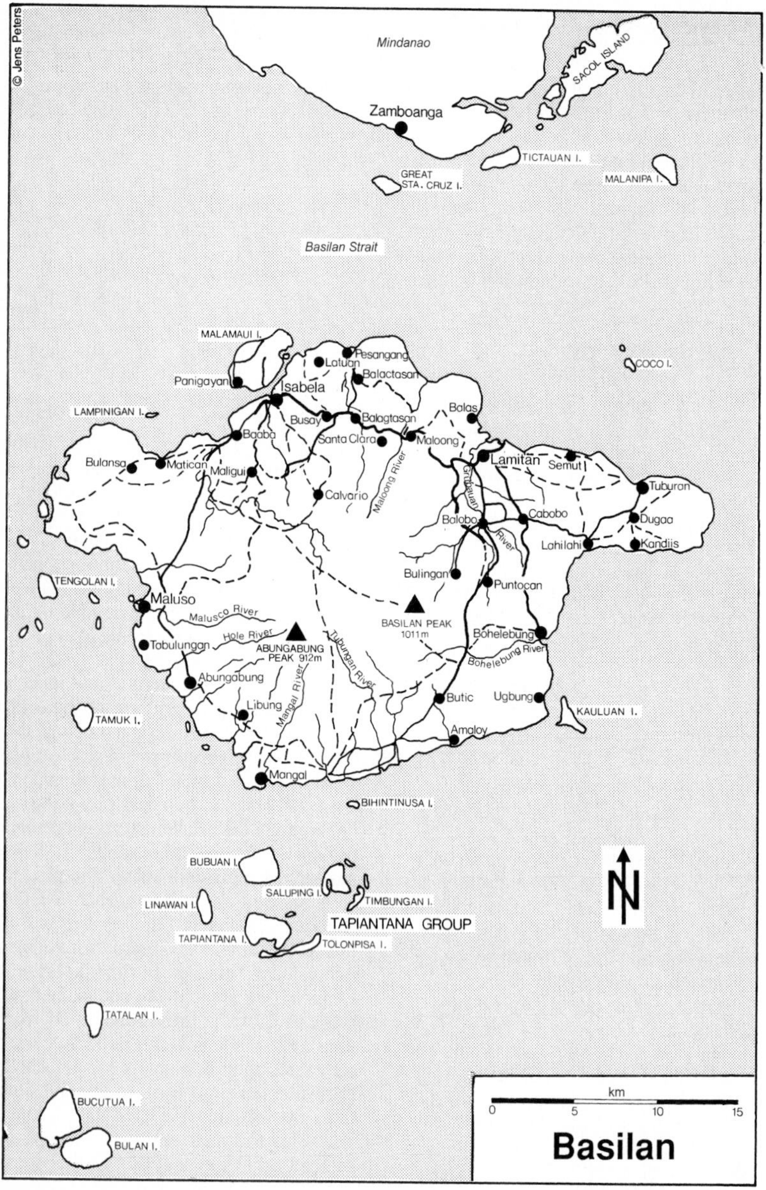

© Jens Peters

Mindanao
SACOL ISLAND
Zamboanga
TICTAUAN I.
GREAT STA. CRUZ I.
MALANIPA I.
Basilan Strait
MALAMAUI I.
Panigayan
Latuan
Pesangang
Balactasan
Isabela
COCO I.
LAMPINIGAN I.
Busay
Balagtasan
Balas
Baaba
Santa Clara
Maloong
Bulansa
Matican
Maligui
Lamitan
Semut
Calvario
Maloong River
Grubauan River
Tuburan
Balobo
Cabobo
Dugaa
Lahilahi
Kandiis
Bulingan
TENGOLAN I.
Puntocan
Maluso
Malusco River
BASILAN PEAK 1011 m
Hole River
Tabulungan
ABUNGABUNG PEAK 912m
Tubungan River
Bohelebung
Bohelebung River
Abungabung
Mangal River
Butic
Ugbung
Libung
TAMUK I.
KAULUAN I.
Amaloy
Mangal
BIHINTINUSA I.
BUBUAN I.
SALUPING I.
TIMBUNGAN I.
LINAWAN I.
TAPIANTANA GROUP
TAPIANTANA I.
TOLONPISA I.
TATALAN I.
BUCUTUA I.
BULAN I.
N

km
0 5 10 15

Basilan

Getting There & Away

To Mindanao

Boat

From Isabela to Zamboanga
Daily with Basilan Shipping Lines (P35; 1½ hrs).

From Lamitan to Zamboanga
Daily with Basilan Shipping Lines (P35; 1½ hrs). The wharf in Lamitan is just outside town.

To Sulu Islands

Boat

Services to the Sulu Islands are irregular. It is probably better to go to Zamboanga and then on from there.

Isabela

The capital of Basilan Province, Isabela, is a small town with not much to see. You can go across the harbour in a few minutes in an outrigger to see Malamaui Island, where a few Badjao live in pile houses. The beautiful White Beach is the best known beach on the island, but, in spite of this, is practically deserted. It's about an hour on foot from the landing place. You can get there by tricycle but there is no regular return service, so you either have to ask the driver to wait, order the tricycle for a fixed time, or walk. The last boat back to Isabela leaves around 4pm.

A few km from Isabela are orange, caoutchouc, coffee, pepper and date plantations belonging to the Menzi family, originally from Switzerland. On the way there you pass the Menzi manufacturing plant, where you can see exactly how rubber is produced from caoutchouc. Coffee beans are roasted there in the open air. It is closed on weekends. Before you reach the factory, you pass a mansion belonging to the wealthy Allano family, who own the electricity plant and a shipping company, among other enterprises.

Places to Stay

New Basilan Hotel, JS Alano St. SR/DR/fan P150/200, SR/DR/fan/bath P200/300. It is not far from the wharf and is better than the nearby *Selecta Hotel.*

Places to Eat

You can eat really well at the ***New International Restaurant***. The food at ***Awin's Icecream House*** on Valderossa St is not exactly cheap, but the price of the beer makes up for it.

Lamitan

Lamitan is a small town that is slightly inland but connected to the sea by an estuary. Every Thursday and Saturday from 6 to 11am there is a large market that's really worth seeing. Ragged Badjao come with their boats to sell seafood, while Yakan bring farm produce and animals down from the hillside villages. Chinese merchants vie with local Chavacano and Visayan merchants in selling household goods and textiles.

In March 1983, the first Lami-Lamihan Festival took place. It was a pure Yakan folk festival to which the Yakan from the surrounding hills came in droves, dressed in their colourful costumes. The festival now takes place every year at the end of March or beginning of April.

Just off the main road, 12 km from Lamitan, you will find the Buligan Falls, which have a big, deep, natural pool - ideal for swimming.

Sulu Islands

The Sulu Islands are at the southernmost tip of the Philippines. They stretch about 300 km from Basilan to Borneo, dividing the Sulu and Celebes seas. A well-known pirate haunt, these waters are avoided by wary sailors whenever possible. Even commercial trading ships have been boarded and plundered. Frequent bloody battles also occur between pirates and smugglers.

The Sulus consist of 500 islands, which are divided into the groups of Jolo (pronounced Holo), Samales, Pangutaran, Tapul, Tawi-Tawi, Sibutu and Cagayan de Tawi-Tawi (Cagayan Sulu). There are two provinces: Sulu with its capital Jolo, and Tawi-Tawi, the capital of which is Bongao.

Attempts by the Spaniards to gain a foothold on these islands failed and the Americans were no more successful. At the moment government troops are attempting to prevent the radical Muslim groups Abu Sayyaf and MILF (Moro Islamic Liberation Front) from achieving their goal of political self-reliance.

Safety Warning

Because of the unstable political situation on the Sulu Islands it is unfortunately extremely dangerous to visit them at the present time. This is especially true of the island of Jolo, which is a stronghold of Muslim extremists.

Before going there it would be advisable to enquire about the current situation in areas of possible unrest. The tourist office in Zamboanga or Southern Command Headquarters should be able to help.

Among the most significant cultural minority groups are the Samal and the Badjao. Both seem very gentle and peaceful. The main islands inhabited by the Samal are Siasi, Tawi-Tawi and Sibutu islands. These people are Muslim and make their living predominantly from fishing, agriculture and small-scale trading. Their houses are always close to the water, often standing in the water on piles.

The Badjao live on boats throughout the entire archipelago, but are concentrated around Tawi-Tawi and Sibutu. They are sea gypsies and their religion is generally thought to be animism. A lot of them, especially those who have ceased to be nomads and live in houses on piles like the Samal, have accepted the new way of life and converted to Islam. Of all the inhabitants of the Sulu Islands, the Badjao are on the lowest rung of the social ladder. Like the Samal, they feel oppressed by the Tausug, the largest and most politically and economically advanced tribe.

The Tausug are Muslim and are considered powerful, aggressive and independent. Quite a few generations have lived by piracy, smuggling and slave-trading. The original inhabitants of the

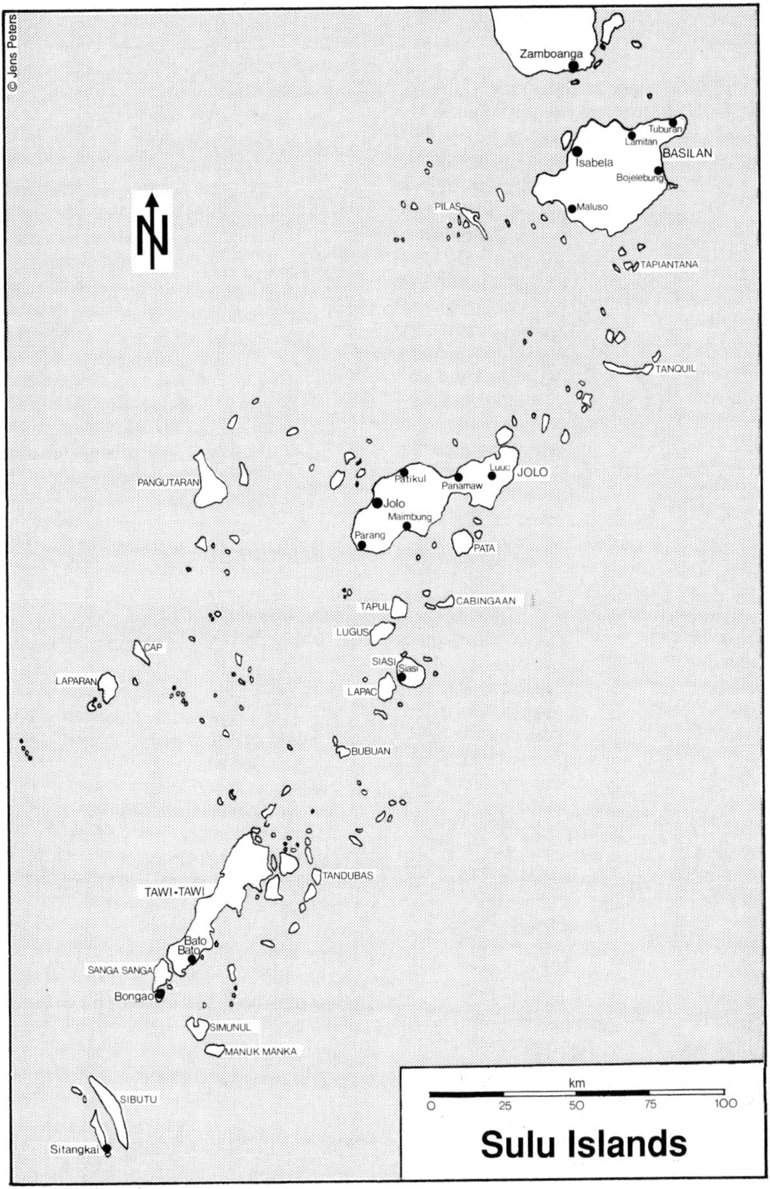

© Jens Peters

Zamboanga
Tuburan
Lamitan
BASILAN
Isabela
Bojelebung
Maluso
PILAS
TAPIANTANA
TANQUIL
PANGUTARAN
Patikul
Panamaw
Luuc
JOLO
Jolo
Maimbung
Parang
PATA
TAPUL
CABINGAAN
LUGUS
CAP
SIASI
Siasi
LAPARAN
LAPAC
BUBUAN
TANDUBAS
TAWI-TAWI
Bato Bato
SANGA SANGA
Bongao
SIMUNUL
MANUK MANKA
SIBUTU
Sitangkai

km
0 25 50 75 100

Sulu Islands

Sulu Islands, the Buranun, are said to have been the forefathers of the Tausug. They too were converted to Islam and their descendants have remained so, except for small communities of Catholics and Buddhists.

From 1974 until the end of 1981, the Sulu Islands were totally out of bounds to tourists. You could sail there from Zamboanga but were not permitted to disembark without a permit. Now, however, foreigners are allowed into the area without permits or restrictions on where they go or how long they stay. This sounds good, but in fact many islands or parts of the islands are still inaccessible because of constant tension, such as that between Tawi-Tawi and Jolo. There are other islands like Laa, near Simunul, or Sipangkot, near Tumindao, which hardly any boat operators will visit because of their fear or dislike of the inhabitants. It is essential to take warnings seriously. When I wanted to cross from Bongao to Bilatan, the boatman only gave a discouraging `Maybe tomorrow'. That evening there was a real shoot out on Bilatan. A few days earlier I had been refused a ride from Bongao to Laa through fear of an ambush. That night you could clearly hear a long fusillade of shots from across the water. There was probably a good reason, too, for the naval escort given to our boat from Sitangkai to Bongao.

Added to this are accommodation and water shortages. Commercial accommodation is available only in Jolo, Bongao and Sitangkai. Elsewhere you have to find private lodgings and you should pay a reasonable price for them. On the southern islands, like Bongao, Sibutu, Tumindao and Sitangkai, there is a severe water shortage. You get a guilty conscience even brushing your teeth! Any washing is done in sea water polluted with sewage and refuse. You can almost feel the hepatitis threatening your liver.

Nevertheless, a trip to the Sulu Islands is a unique experience. The impressions gained are many and varied and well worth the effort.

Getting There & Away

You can get to the Sulu Islands from Mindanao and probably also from Basilan. (See the Getting There & Away section in the Mindanao chapter.)

To Basilan

Boat

From Jolo to Isabela

Connections to Basilan from the Sulu Islands are irregular. However, merchant ships which will also take passengers are said to leave Jolo quite often for Isabela.

To Mindanao

Air

From Jolo to Zamboanga

Seair flies daily except Sunday (P1290).

From Tawi-Tawi to Zamboanga

Seair flies daily except Friday and Sunday (P2490).

Boat

From Bongao to Zamboanga

Tuesday, Thursday and Friday with Aleson Shipping Lines (P470; 16 hrs). Tuesday and Saturday with with SRN Fast Seacraft (P900; seven hrs).

From Jolo to Zamboanga

Daily with SRN Fast Seacraft (P500; three hrs) and Aleson Shipping Lines (P180; eight hrs).

To Palawan

Boat

If you have time, you could try the following route: go from Jolo to Pangu-

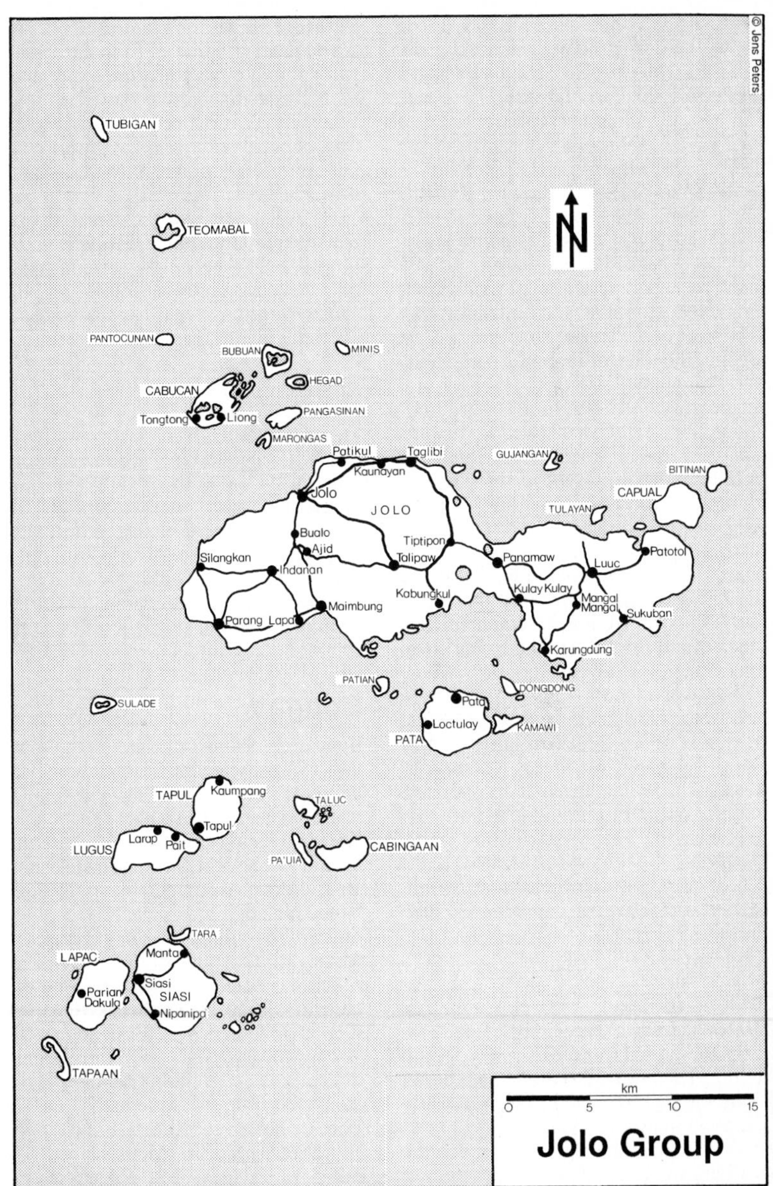
© Jens Peters
TUBIGAN
TEOMABAL
N
PANTOCUNAN
BUBUAN
MINIS
HEGAD
CABUCAN
Tongtong
Liong
PANGASINAN
MARONGAS
Patikul
Taglibi
Kaunayan
GUJANGAN
BITINAN
Jolo
JOLO
CAPUAL
TULAYAN
Bualo
Ajid
Tiptipon
Patotol
Silangkan
Indanan
Talipaw
Panamaw
Luuc
Kabungkul
Kulay Kulay
Mangal Mangal
Maimbung
Sukuban
Parang
Lapa
Karungdung
PATIAN
DONGDONG
SULADE
Pata
Loctulay
KAMAWI
PATA
TAPUL
Kaumpang
TALUC
Tapul
Larap
Pait
LUGUS
PA'UIA
CABINGAAN
TARA
LAPAC
Manta
Siasi
SIASI
Parian Dakula
Nipanipa
TAPAAN
km
0
5
10
15
Jolo Group

taran Island, then on to Cagayan de Tawi-Tawi, where you can occasionally get a freighter to Rio Tuba or Brooke's Point in southern Palawan.

Jolo

Jolo is the capital of the island of the same name and also of Sulu Province. It is the only place in the entire archipelago where the Spaniards, after a relatively short period of 20 years, finally gained a foothold and built a fortress. This was at the end of the 19th century, about 300 years after they first reached the Philippines.

In February 1974, Jolo was partly destroyed in fighting between Muslims and government troops. Even today the military is still present in the city. Although no permit is required for the city itself, foreigners need a military permit to travel around this volcanic island. It is remarkable to see the many trishaws standing around the great mosque. Don't miss the colourful fish market and the Barter Trade Market in the halls next to the harbour, where goods that come mainly from Borneo are sold. The lovely, sandy Quezon Beach is about three km north-east of Jolo. If it's not off-limits for security reasons, you can reach it by jeepney, getting out before Patikul. A little farther east in Taglibi is another wide, sandy beach with crystal clear water.

There may be a curfew on Jolo from seven o'clock every evening, which must be respected.

Places to Stay

Helen's Lodge, Buyon St, Tel 2278. SR/DR/fan P100/600, SR/fan/bath P200, DR/fan/bath P300, SR/DR/ac/bath P500. It is simple and relatively clean and has a restaurant.

Travellers passing through can use the sanitary facilities for a small charge.

Places to Eat

If you have just arrived from Zamboanga, you will have your first experience of the island's coffee shops in Jolo. Whether you order coffee or a Sprite (the popular soft drink in Sulu), you will be offered a large tray of all sorts of cakes.

Good restaurants are the ***Bee Gees*** on Sanchez St, the ***Plaza Panciteria*** on Sevantes St, where they serve a mean milkshake among other things, and the ***Plaza Restaurant*** that has quite passable toilet facilities.

Siasi

This island is a crisis area according to locals. I must admit, the little harbour town of the same name didn't make a particularly good impression on me either. It has lots of damaged or totally burnt-out houses, a boarded-up hotel and there are lots of military personnel around. People are rather unforthcoming and language difficulties could be a problem.

Bongao

Bongao, on Bongao Island, is the most important town in the Tawi-Tawi Island group. It's bigger than Siasi but smaller than Jolo, and has two harbours, a market, two cinemas and a main street with several side streets. The Provincial Capitol Building stands out like a mosque on the hillside.

The Badjao village of Tungkalang, on the south-west tip of Sanga Sanga, which has been described in some old travel books, no longer exists. Sea gypsies have settled near Bongao, in the bay by the hospital, and Notre Dame College. As far as these friendly people are concerned, an 'Americano' isn't a 'Joe' (a holdover from 'GI Joe', popular after American troops helped liberate the islands from Japanese in-

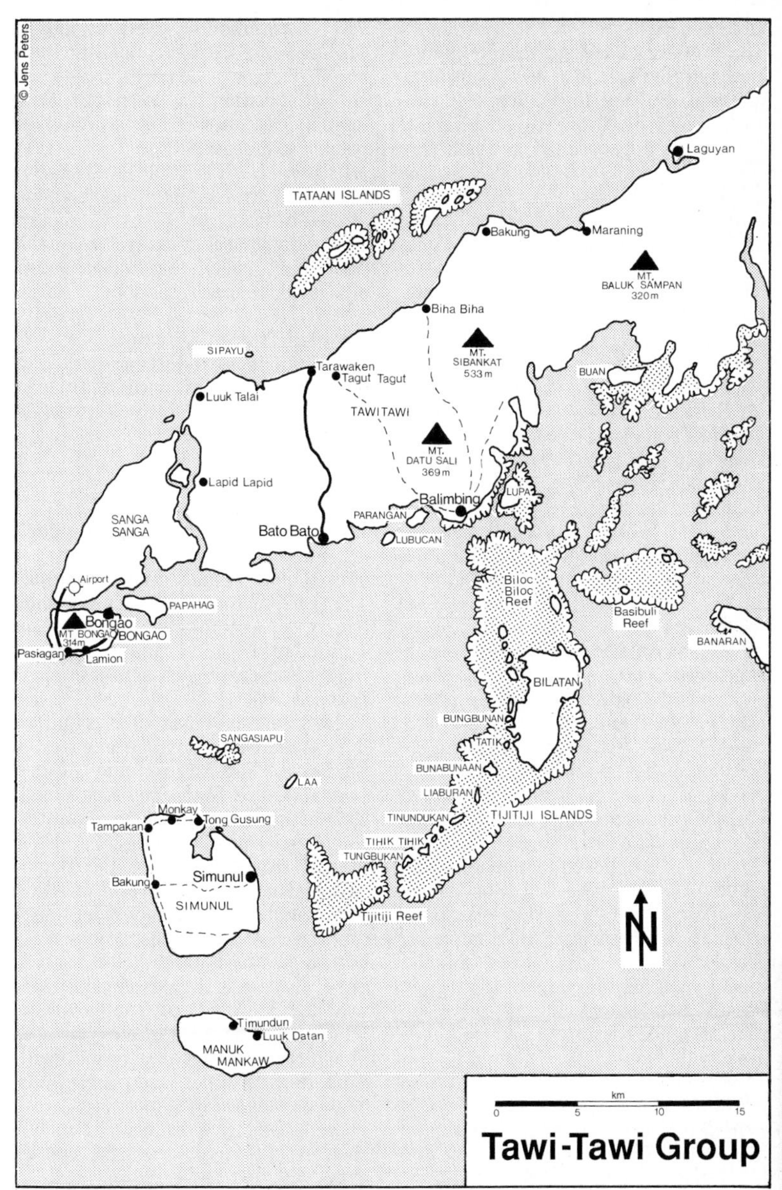
© Jens Peters
Laguyan
TATAAN ISLANDS
Bakung
Maraning
MT. BALUK SAMPAN 320 m
Biha Biha
MT. SIBANKAT 533 m
SIPAYU
Tarawaken
Tagut Tagut
BUAN
Luuk Talai
TAWITAWI
MT. DATU SALI 369 m
Lapid Lapid
Balimbing
LUPA
SANGA SANGA
PARANGAN
Bato Bato
LUBUCAN
Airport
Biloc Biloc Reef
PAPAHAG
Basibuli Reef
Bongao
MT BONGAO 314 m
BONGAO
Pasiagan
Lamion
BANARAN
BILATAN
BUNGBUNAN
SANGASIAPU
TATIK
BUNABUNAAN
LAA
LIABURAN
Monkay
Tampakan
Tong Gusung
TINUNDUKAN
TIJITIJI ISLANDS
TIHIK TIHIK
TUNGBUKAN
Simunul
Bakung
SIMUNUL
Tijitiji Reef
N
Timundun
Luuk Datan
MANUK MANKAW
km
0
5
10
15
Tawi-Tawi Group

vaders in 1944 to 1945) but 'Milikan'. The military camp and the Philippine National Bank are also on the outskirts of town. Beyond them, you come to quite a nice place to swim, where the road meets the shore. At low tide you can walk across to a sandbank that is good for snorkelling.
From Bongao you can catch small boats to the islands of Bilatan, Simunul and Manuk Mankaw. Bunabunaan is the burial island of the Badjao and can only be reached by a Special Ride. When in Bongao, I was constantly advised not to visit Tawi-Tawi.

Mt Bongao

The little village of Pasiagan is five km from Bongao. This is the start of the trail leading up Mt Bongao, a 314m mountain worshipped by both Christians and Muslims. Anjaotals, a member of an old royal family, is buried on the summit. Prayers said in the four-sq-metre enclosure with its wall draped in white cloth are said to be more powerful than any medicine. (If you visit the enclosure, you must take off your shoes.) Paths right and left of the grave lead to good lookout points that are clear of trees. The climb takes about an hour and is hot and tiring.
As this is a holy mountain, you should not defile it in any way and offensive behaviour like swearing should be avoided. It is believed that people who touch a monkey here will soon die or lose their wits. It's as well to take some bananas for these inquisitive animals. There are numerous snakes, though they're not easy to see, so don't grab blindly at trees or vines. In early October, Bongao has a fiesta and the hill is alive with people.

Places to Stay

Peping Cuarema's Residence, Muslimin St. SR/DR P150/200. The rooms are basic, but clean. Friendly people.
The Southern Inn, Datu Halun St. SR/DR P250, DR/fan/bath P400. Basic hotel with two beautiful balconies. However, it's a bit run-down and a shade too expensive. Restaurant. Located opposite the mosque.
Hill Stone Hotel. SR/DR/fan/bath from P250. Beautiful, big building about two km out of town.
It is possible to find really comfortable private accommodation in Bongao, including three meals, for about P300.

Getting There & Away

By Air: The Tawi-Tawi Airport is on Sanga Sanga Island, north of Bongao. The jeepney trip to the town costs P20, or P50 by tricycle.

Sitangkai

It is said that more than 6000 people live in this 'Venice of the Far East', in houses built on piles on the giant reef. The water is so shallow that big ships have to anchor three km away in the Tumindao Channel and ferry their freight and passengers across in small boats.
There are more Badjao villages built on piles scattered over a large area west of Sitangkai. The largest, and furthest away, is called Tong Tong and is made up of 50 houses. It's not far from the Meridian Channel, which is 50 to 100m deep. Here as elsewhere the Badjao have laid out underwater seaweed fields; sea cucumbers are another main source of income. A day trip there by boat can be arranged for P300 to P500.
Small boats run from Sitangkai to the two bigger islands of Tumindao and Sibutu. As the boat routes between Sitangkai and Bongao can be unreliable from time to time, any planned stay may be extended by a few days.
There is neither a bank nor a money changer in Sitangkai, so take enough pesos with you.

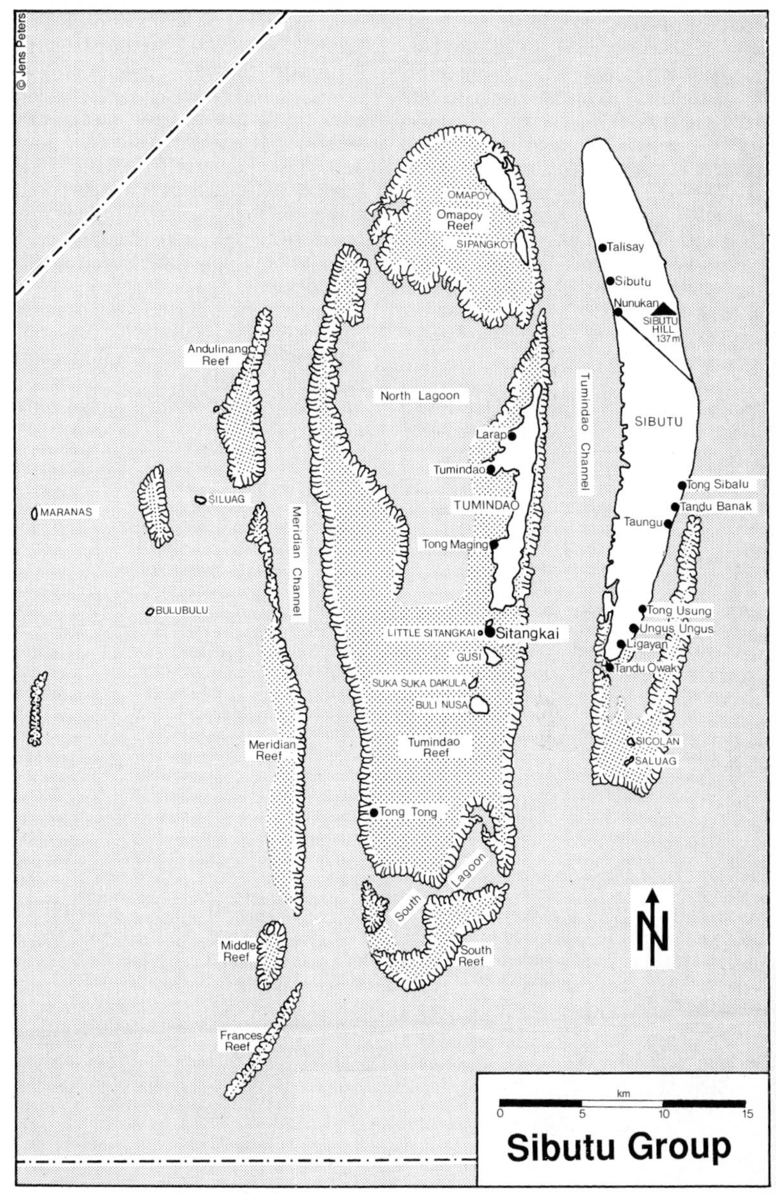
© Jens Peters
OMAPOY
Omapoy Reef
SIPANGKOT
Talisay
Sibutu
Nunukan
SIBUTU HILL 137m
Andulinang Reef
North Lagoon
Tumindao Channel
SIBUTU
Larap
Tumindao
TUMINDAO
Tong Sibalu
Tandu Banak
Taungu
MARANAS
SILUAG
Meridian Channel
Tong Maging
BULUBULU
Tong Usung
Ungus Ungus
LITTLE SITANGKAI
Sitangkai
Ligayan
GUSI
Tandu Owak
SUKA SUKA DAKULA
BULI NUSA
Meridian Reef
Tumindao Reef
SICOLAN
SALUAG
Tong Tong
South Lagoon
Middle Reef
South Reef
N
Frances Reef
km
0
5
10
15
Sibutu Group

Places to Stay

You will have to look for private accommodation if you want to stay in Sitangkai. If you have the chance to stay with the Badjao for a few days, do so but be generous with food and supplies, as these friendly people don't have much. Hadji Musa Malabong, the teacher at Sitangkai, and his brother, Hadji Yusof Abdulganih, can arrange private accommodation for about P300 per person (including three meals). Yusof will also arrange a boat to visit the spread-out Badjao villages, and will take care of accommodation if you want.

Note: Because of the many people who travel illegally on the smugglers' boats from Sitangkai to Sempora on Borneo (in the state of Sabah, East Malaysia), for many years tourists were only allowed to leave the ship at Sitangkai after showing a passport and a valid visa, as well as a permit from the Tawi-Tawi Task Force (TTTF). The TTTF Permit was issued by the appropriate authorities in Bongao, where showing a return ticket (eg from Zamboanga to Manila) cut down the interrogation considerably.

Apparently these checks have been discontinued in the meantime. Nevertheless, it would be worth the effort asking in Bongao whether it is possible to travel to Sitangkai without going through red tape first.

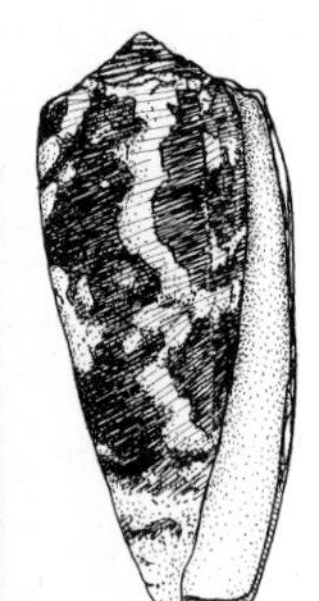
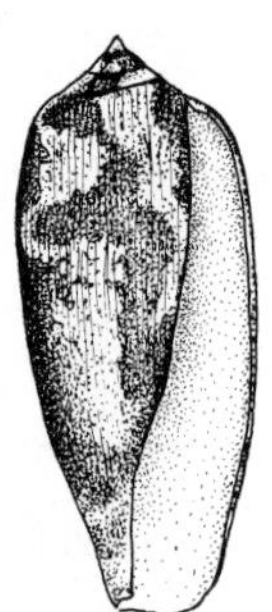
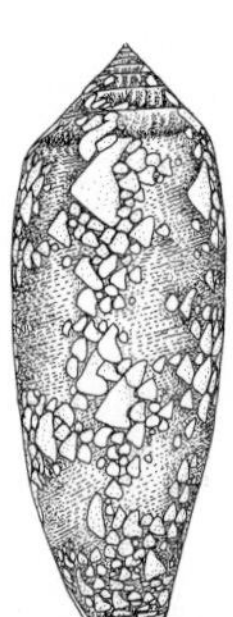
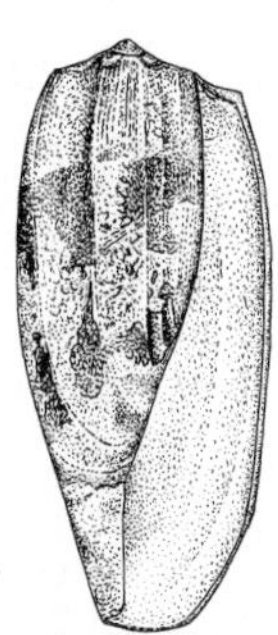
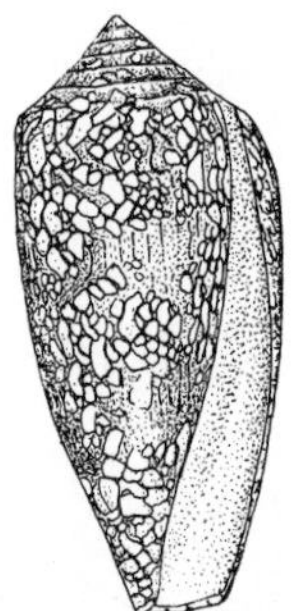

Palawan

Palawan is in the south-west of the Philippines and separates the Sulu Sea from the South China Sea. Although 400 km long, it is only 40 km across at its widest point. Beautiful empty beaches, largly untouched natural scenery and friendly inhabitants make this a very attractive island. A further 1768 islands make up Palawan Province, the most important being Busuanga, Culion, Coron, Cuyo, Dumaran, Bugsuk and Balabac. Most of Palawan consists of mountainous jungle. At 2086m, Mt Mantalingajan is the highest mountain, followed by Mt Gantung at 1788m and Cleopatra's Needle at 1585m.

The El Nido cliffs and the limestone caves of Coron and Pabellones islands, off Taytay, are home to countless swallows' nests. Hotels and Chinese restaurants all over the country get their supplies from these places to make that oriental delicacy, birds' nest soup. If you like fish, you will think this is paradise, as the fruits of the sea are really plentiful here. You could try a different fish dinner every day, choosing from crayfish, mussels, sea urchin, lobster and many others. The jungles harbour plants and animals which are found nowhere else in the Philippines. These include the iron tree, the mouse deer (chevrotain), the king cobra and many rare parrots and butterflies.

With the exception of the Underground River and the Tabon Caves, Palawan has no particularly overwhelming sights to see. On the other hand, what makes the island so attractive and pleasant to visit are the friendly people and the outstanding natural features. Palawan also offers a wide variety of activities for the more adventurous visitor including jungle expeditions, prospecting for gold, cave exploring, diving, hiking, searching for shipwrecks, or even living like Robinson Crusoe if that's what you want.

Population & People

Palawan is thinly populated, with most inhabitants coming from several islands in the Visayas. The Batak and Pala'wan are among the aboriginal inhabitants. Those living in the north are nomads (Negritos) who live by hunting. Attempts to convince them of the benefits of agriculture and of settling the land have nearly always failed. Some of them go to school but then disappear into the jungle again. The Batak are very shy. If you want to find them and visit their villages, you need plenty of time and a competent guide.

In the extreme north of Palawan are the Tagbanua, a seafaring people who rarely settle in one place. There are also Tagbanua who live near the coast and along the rivers of Central Palawan in settled village communities. Like the Hanunoo on Mindoro, they use a syllabic writing system.

The Tau't Batu in the south of Palawan were only discovered in 1978. They live in caves in the Singnapan Basin, a few km east of Ransang, as they have done for about 20,000 years. Their habitat has been declared a protected area and is absolutely off limits. This prohibition must obviously be respected.

Economy
Only a few coastal regions can be used for agriculture. The main crops are rice, coconuts, bananas, groundnuts and cashew nuts. For the economy, however, fishing is by far the most important activity. The richest fishing grounds in the Philippines are off Palawan's northern coast. About 60% of Manila's staple food is caught between Coron, Cuyo and Dumaran islands and especially in Taytay Bay.
Since the discovery of oil off Palawan's north-west coast, the development of that industry looks promising.

Ecology
Between 1979 and 1989, when the Aquino government imposed a logging ban, Palawan lost 20,000 hectares of forest every year. This amounted to about 2½% of the total forest reserves of this island, home to such rich flora & fauna. However, as so often in the Philippines, the letter of the law and the realities of life were at opposite ends of the scale, and the law was initially more often honoured in the breach than in the observance. But the mid-90s finally saw an end to fire clearance and illegal wood felling. Both the authorities and the ordinary people seem to have recognised the mood of the times, and their new awareness of the ecology has prevented the final plundering of Palawan. Even people who fish with dynamite and cyanide are now facing immediate arrest and court appearances.

Health
Outside of the capital, medical services are inadequate. Even if you can find a doctor, you usually won't be able to find a pharmacy which stocks the necessary medication. In case of illness, head straight for Puerto Princesa.
Malaria is widespread on Palawan, so it's important to take antimalarial tablets, always sleep under mosquito netting, and use insect repellent. If you get a fever, remember that it could be malaria and head straight for Puerto Princesa (Malaria Office - Extension Field Office of Department of Health, National Highway, Santa Monica). The doctors there know more about malaria and how to treat it than doctors in Manila. On a more positive note, you won't see a mosquito during the dry season in large parts of Palawan. This is also when most people visit. Mosquitoes are usually only a problem in the rainy season, especially in the south.

Nasty Nik-Niks

Unfortunately many Palawan beaches are also a popular home for *nik-niks*: tiny sandflies which often take pleasure in stinging lightly-clad sun worshippers. An effective way of warding off these annoying little insects is to rub on coconut oil combined with a dash of insect repellent such as Autan or Off.

Getting There & Away

You can get to Palawan from Cebu, Luzon and Panay (see the Getting Away from Luzon section of the Manila chapter and the Getting There & Away sections of the individual island chapters).

To Cebu

Air

From Puerto Princesa to Cebu City
Cebu Pacific flies on Tuesday, Thursday, Friday and Sunday (P2900).

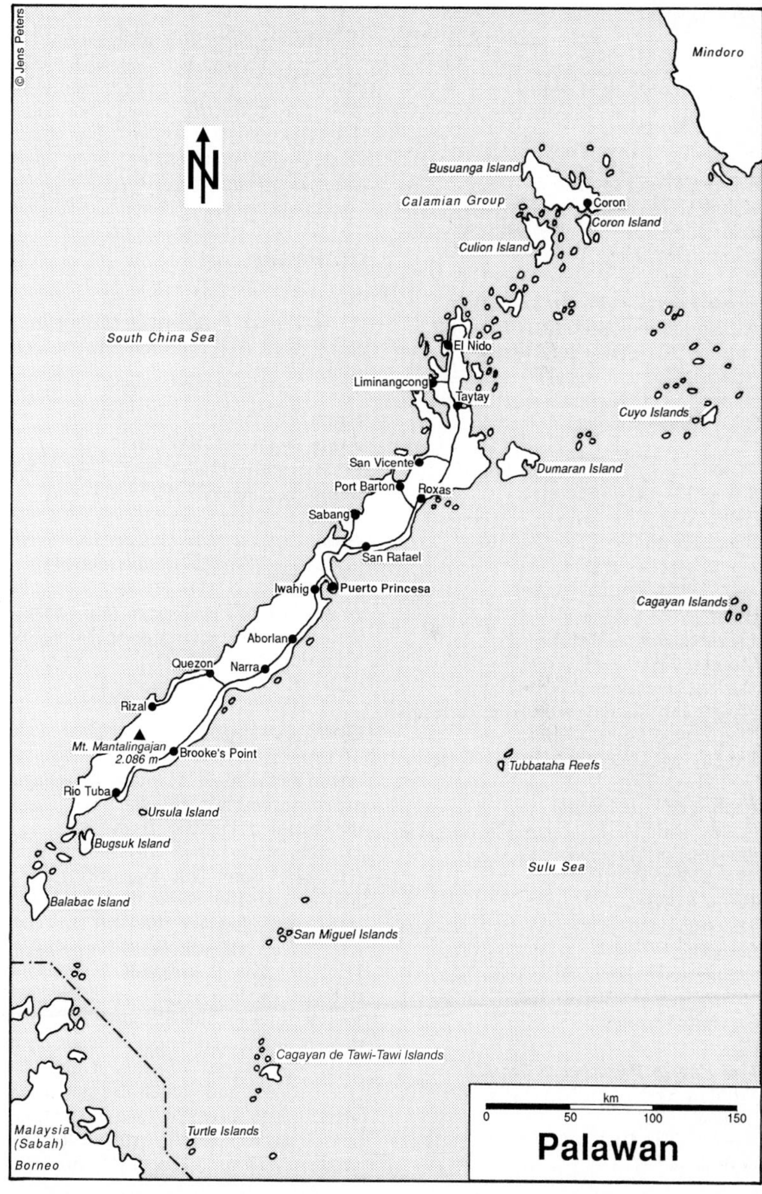
© Jens Peters
N
Mindoro
Busuanga Island
Calamian Group
Coron
Coron Island
Culion Island
South China Sea
El Nido
Liminangcong
Taytay
Cuyo Islands
San Vicente
Dumaran Island
Port Barton
Roxas
Sabang
San Rafael
Iwahig
Puerto Princesa
Cagayan Islands
Aborlan
Quezon
Narra
Rizal
Mt. Mantalingajan
2.086 m
Brooke's Point
Tubbataha Reefs
Rio Tuba
Ursula Island
Bugsuk Island
Sulu Sea
Balabac Island
San Miguel Islands
Cagayan de Tawi-Tawi Islands
km
0
50
100
150
Malaysia
(Sabah)
Turtle Islands
Borneo
Palawan

To Luzon

Air

From Busuanga to Manila
Asian Spirit, Pacific Airways and Seair fly daily (P2300).

From El Nido to Manila
Island Transvoyager has daily flights.
Seair flies three times weekly; via Busuanga (P4400).

From Puerto Princesa to Manila
Air Philippines, Cebu Pacific and Philippine Airlines have daily flights (P2850).
Seair flies three times weekly; via El Nido and Busuanga.

From Sandoval/Taytay to Manila
Seair flies daily (P4400).
Asian Spirit flies Monday, Wednesday, Thursday and Sunday (P4050).

Boat

From Coron to Manila
Monday, Wednesday and Friday with San Nicolas Lines (P650; 22 hrs).
Friday and Sunday with Atienza Shipping Lines (P690; 17 hrs).
Sunday with WG & A (P980; 12 hrs).

From Cuyo to Manila
Friday with MBRS Lines (24 hrs); via San Jose de Buenavista/Panay.

From El Nido to Manila
Thursday and Saturday with Atienza Shipping Lines (42 hrs); via Coron.
Wednesday and Sunday with San Nicolas Lines (P750; 30 hrs); Sunday via Coron (42 hrs).

Von Puerto Princesa to Manila
Friday with Negros Navigation (P1320; 23 hrs).
Sunday with WG & A (P1320; 26 hrs); via Coron.

Note: Almost all the Atienza Shipping Lines and San Nicolas Lines ships are old and rickety freighters, and the trip is only for the adventurous! It is possible that they will soon no longer be allowed to carry passengers.

To Panay

Air

From Puerto Princesa to Iloilo City
Seair plans to fly the route in the near future.

Boat

From Cuyo to Iloilo City
Friday and Monday with Milagrosa Shipping Lines (P220; 13 hrs).

From Cuyo to San Jose de Buenavista
Friday with MBRS Lines (four hrs).

From Puerto Princesa to Iloilo City
Thursday and Sunday with Milagrosa Shipping Lines (P500; 37 hrs); via Cuyo (8-hr stopover there).

Getting Around

Touring is a little bit difficult in Palawan as the roads between the villages are only good in parts. The main road is the so-called 'Palawan Highway', which is only partly surfaced, leading from Brooke's Point via Puerto Princesa, Roxas and Taytay to El Nido. Over most of its distance the road still consists of an unsurfaced, bumpy, dusty track, pitted with potholes. If you want to travel on side roads, you either need lots of time or lots of money. Jeepney drivers and boat operators always try to make you pay for a Special Ride.
It's difficult, and sometimes not possible at all, to travel by road in the rainy season as some of the routes become impassable after a few days' rain. If, as

a result, you can only travel by boat, you will have to pay through the nose to get anywhere.

There is no such thing here as a reliable, fixed departure time for buses and jeepneys; most leave in the early morning between 6 and 8 o'clock when they're full. Your best bet is to make enquiries at the terminal the evening before your departure, find out roughly when they'll be leaving and try to book a seat with your driver or conductor.

The recently introduced shipping route between Manila-Coron-Puerto Princesa has made travelling in North Palawan much more convenient. With the addition of regular flights between Manila-Busuanga, Manila-El Nido, Busuanga-Caticlan (Boracay), Busuanga-El Nido, and El Nido-Puerto Princesa, round trips are now possible without hassle, in an area where up until recently almost every trip ended up in a dead end.

Tips for the Palawan journey

As the electricity supply is extremely unreliable, it's a good idea to take a flashlight with you, maybe a candle as well.

Just as importantly, remember to take enough cash with you (pesos or dollars). It's best to bring it with you from Manila, as changing travellers' cheques in Puerto Princesa is a long and complicated procedure. Outside of Puerto Princesa it's practically impossible to change travellers' cheques, cash advances are not possible and only a few resorts accept credit cards.

Boat Tours

More and more visitors are discovering the pleasures of extended boat trips to Palawan's more interesting places and islands. So it is not surprising to find out that more and more large boats are being built.

A 10-day tour could look something like this: Puerto Princesa - Coco-Loco Island - Elephant Island - Flower Island - El Nido - Port Barton - Underground River. This would cost around P3000 per day per person, with full board.

Mark Bratschi from Switzerland offers such trips from December until March with his live-aboard dive boat MY *Moonshadow*, @. From April until June he offers several trips to the Tubbataha National Marine Park (Tubbataha Reefs). The boat is 20m long and has five cabins for eight to 10 passengers. He can be contacted at the Trattoria Inn in Puerto Princesa.

Longer boat trips are also possible with the MY *Jinn Sulu* and the MY *Talusi* belonging to Queen Anne Divers and Palawan Yacht Charter respectively. See also under Puerto Princesa: *Miscellaneous - Diving*.

The Dutchman Jacob Bakker organises sailing trips with his yacht *La Esperanza* (15m) from Coron/Busuanga. The schooner was built in Portugal in 1974 and has room for six passengers. Prices per day, including full board: US$100 per person (for four to six people) and US$160 per person (for two people). The shortest trip is three days. Bookings can be made at La Esperanza Charters, 5316 Coron, Busuanga, @.

The Cruise & Hotel Center, Manila, offers four and seven-day trips on the catamaran MV *Lagoon Explorer*. This extremely well-equipped ship (10 aircon cabins for 20 passengers in all) sails from Coron through the island world of North Palawan with frequent stops at anchor. Price for four days/three nights: US$450 per person in a double cabin, with full board. Reservations can be made at Blue Horizons Travel & Tours, Trafalgar Plaza, Dela Costa St, Salcedo Village, Makati, Manila, Tel (02) 8483907, Fax (02) 8483909 @.

Central Palawan

Puerto Princesa

At 210,670 hectares, Puerto Princesa is the second largest city in the Philippines after Davao, in terms of area. Even rural Sabang and the St Paul Subterranean National Park, 50 km north of the city centre, belong administratively to the city. It is a relatively new city with about 70,000 inhabitants in the urban area itself and a total population of around 150,000. Although new houses are going up all the time, you can still find impressively beautiful old ones in the traditional style. The dominant buildings in the city are the cathedral and the Provincial Capitol. In complete contrast to them, south of the harbour at the waterfront there are little fishermen's huts which are built on piles in the sea and can be reached by gangplanks (best access is from the basketball court in Reynoso St).

The city is remarkable for its cleanliness, something the mayor Edwin Hagedorn is deservedly praised for. He managed to enthuse the locals with the idea of keeping their city clean. Refuse disposal and street cleaning both function immaculately, and many tricycles even have an ashtray in them (throwing away cigarette butts on the streets incurs a fine of P200!). The most important distinctions garnered by Puerto Princesa in recent vears were the 1993 Earth Day Award and the 1994 Macliing Dulag Environment Award.

The scene on the wharf at sunset is good fun. Puerto Princesa Bay also has some interesting places for diving. For about P700 you can hire an outrigger for a few hours and sail, swim, dive and fish in the bay.

Nasin-Aw White Beach is on the southern edge of town; admission P5. Watch out for sea urchins when you're swimming. It's best to wear shoes for protection. You can get to the Nasin-Aw White Beach by tricycle (about P20).

Winged Wonders

On the outskirts of Puerto Princesa there's a butterfly farm built in an exemplary fashion dedicated to the conservation of Palawan's brightly-coloured butterflies.

Palawan Butterfly Garden, Bunkhouse Rd, Santa Monica, Fax 4335343. In addition to a display of beautiful butterflies, the Filipino Roy Rodriguez and his wife Imee show visitors their collection of beetles, caterpillars, scorpions, millipedes and lizards. They are located about seven km north of the town centre. Turn left after the Elementary School in Santa Monica, and it's another 100m (tricycle P40). Open: 8.30am-4.30pm. Admission P25.

Museum

The Palawan Museum at the Mendoza Park provides a really good overview of the history, art and culture of Palawan, and of the people of the island and their mythology. Open Mon-Sat 8am-noon and 1.30-5pm. Admission P20; students P10.

Shopping

Typical Palawan artwork is available in the Palawan Treasures & Gift Shop next to the City Tourist Office at the airport. Also on sale are T-shirts with Palawan motives and the cassette *Palawan: At Peace with Nature*, which makes an excellent souvenir. It is 'A Musical Journey to the Last Frontier' by Sinika, a group using mostly native instruments.

Places to Stay - bottom end

Payuyo Pension, 200 Manalo St Extension, Tel 4343363. SR/fan P150, DR/fan P250, SR/DR/ac P400, SR/DR/ac/bath P470 and P600 (TV). Modest, fairly inexpensive rooms with fan, those facing the street are a bit loud.

Duchess Pension House, 107 Valencia St, Tel 4332873. SR/DR/fan P150/250, SR/DR/fan/bath P400/450, SR/DR/ac/bath P500/550. Friendly accommodation with basic rooms, some of them on the small side. Restaurant (snacks).

Backpackers, 1212 Valencia St, SR/DR/fan P150/250. Basic rooms. Restaurant. Across from the Duchess Pension House.

Rendez-Vous Lodge, Macasaet St, Tel 4343136. SR/fan/bath P250, DR/fan/bath P300, SR/ac/bath P350, DR/ac/bath P500. Pleasant, clean accommodation with neat rooms, two of them with balcony. Quiet location about 250m east of Backpackers. Good restaurant (also vegetarian).

Banwa Pension & Art House, Liwanag St, Tel. 4347197, Cellphone 0918-7152649, @. Dorm P150, SR/fan P200, DR/fan P350, SR/DR/fan/bath P450. Cosy, imaginatively furnished accommodation. An enchanting little oasis in the south-west of the city - can't recommend this too much. Beautiful garden terrace. Little restaurant.

Tropical Sun Inn, 152 Manalo St, Tel 4336493, Fax 4336526. SR/fan/bath P300, DR/fan/bath P380, SR/ac/bath P550, DR/ac/bath P700 to P1200 (TV). Neat and tidy rooms around a courtyard with lots of plants. Restaurant.

Abelardo's Pension, 63 Manga St, Tel 4332049. SR/fan P175, DR/fan P250, SR/DR/fan/bath P400, SR/DR/ac/bath P600. Friendly, family-style guesthouse with down-to-earth but clean rooms. Good breakfast. The helpful owners can provide lots of tips on Palawan.

Puerto Pension, 35 Malvar St, Tel 4332969, Fax 4334148, @. SR/fan P225, DR/fan P360 (each bath is shared by two rooms), SR/DR/fan/bath P470, SR/DR/ac/bath P660 and P675. Quite good rooms in a building furnished with natural materials. Roof deck with view over Puerto Princesa Bay.

Angela's Farm, San Jose, Tel 4338052, @. SR/SR/fan P250/300, Cottage/fan/bath P600 and P700, cottage/ac/bath P1200 (with TV). Friendly, family-style place in a suburb about 10 km north of the city centre (P50 by tricycle). Restaurant with Philippine, Swiss and Thai food. Swimming pool, garden, tennis court.

Amelia Pensionne, 420 Rizal Ave, Tel 4337029, Fax 4334895, @. SR/fan/bath P350, DR/fan/bath P400, SR/ac/bath P610 and P675, DR/ac/bath P675 and P745. Really good rooms, the more aircon ones with TV. Quiet location about 50m off Rizal Ave.

Casa Linda, Trinidad Rd, Tel 4332606, Fax: 4332309, @. SR/DR/fan/bath P350/450, SR/DR/ac/bath P600/700. Attractive accommodation with pleasant, tastefully decorated rooms and well-tended garden. Attentive, friendly service. All in all, a well-run establishment in a quiet area about 80m off Rizal Ave. Restaurant, airport service.

Badjao Inn, 350 Rizal Ave, Tel 4332761, Fax 4332180, @. SR/fan/bath P350, DR/fan/bath P450, SR/ac/bath P600 to P850, DR/ac/bath P700 to P950. Reasonable, aircon rooms; the better, and more expensive ones with refrigerator and TV. Well-kept, large garden with restaurant.

Paradise Hotel, 200 Manalo St Extension, Tel 4345526. SR/DR/ac/bath P600, P650 and P700. Fairly new hotel. Good, pleasantly furnished rooms with TV. No restaurant, but breakfast is provided. Small garden.

Audissie Pension, 31 Malvar St, Tel 4346430. SR/ac/bath P650, DZ/ac/bath P750. Immaculate accommodation with well-kept rooms, all with TV. Located next to the Puerto Pension.

Getting There & Away
2 Bus Terminal (3 km)
6 Negros Navigation
7 Jeepney Terminal
10 Charing Bus Lines
Puerto Royale Bus Lines
12 Anleger (Wharf)
Milagrosa Shipping Lines
13 Negros Navigation
24 WG & A
33 Seair (Floral Travel & Tours)
Topstar Rent-A-Car
36 Philippine Airlines
50 Cebu Pacific
57 Air Philippines
Layang Layang Aerospace
(Sanctuary Tours & Travel)

Places to Stay
2 Angela's Farm (8 km)
Barceló Asturias Hotel (1 km)
Hillside Pension (5 km)
Kawayanan Resort (600m)
Royal Oberoi Resort Hotel (4 km)
Sheena's Cottage Garden (2 km)
3 The Legend Hotel
4 Asiaworld Resort Hotel Palawan
8 Sierra Apartelle
9 Princesa Inn
11 Audissie Pension
Puerto Pension
18 Rengel Hotel
23 Hotel Fleuris
28 Baragayan Sa Puerto Inn
29 Admiral Hotel
33 Moana Hotel
39 Lola Itang Pension
40 Abelardo's Pension
42 Circon Hotel
46 El-Rey Pensionne House
Manggahan Pension
54 Badjao Inn
55 Casa Linda
56 Palawan Hotel
57 Amelia Pensionne
58 Airport Hotel
59 Tropical Sun Inn
63 Backpackers
64 Duchess Pension House
65 Payuyo Pension
66 Paradise Hotel
67 Yayen's Pension
68 Sonne Gasthaus
69 Banwa Pension & Art House
70 Rendez-Vous Lodge

Places to Eat & Entertainment
1 Nightclubs
2 Café Arturo
16 Roadside Pizza Inn & Folkhouse
14 Mozcom Internet Café
18 Edwin's Food Palace
Good Old Grandma Bakeshop
24 Chowking
26 Cristina's
27 Seven Plates Restaurant
31 Kalui Restaurant
32 Zum Kleinen Anker
33 King's Cross
34 The Backyard Grill
37 Pho Vietnamese Restaurant (1 km)
39 Lola Itang Filipino Restaurant
43 Bruno's Swissfood & Snack Bar
49 Jollibee
51 Hub's Rodeo Grill Restaurant
54 Kinabuchs Restaurant
60 Bisasasayan Grill
61 Tom Tom Club
62 Vegetarian House
67 Chicken Inato
70 Rendez-Vous Terrace Restaurant
71 Badjao Seafront Restaurant
73 Deep Forest Garden Resort

Miscellaneous
2 Cockpit (150m)
Palawan Adventist Hospital (1 km)
New Public Market (3 km)
City Hall (4 km)
Police Station (4 km)
5 Provincial Hospital
15 Market
17 Kawing Internet
Philippine National Bank (PNB)

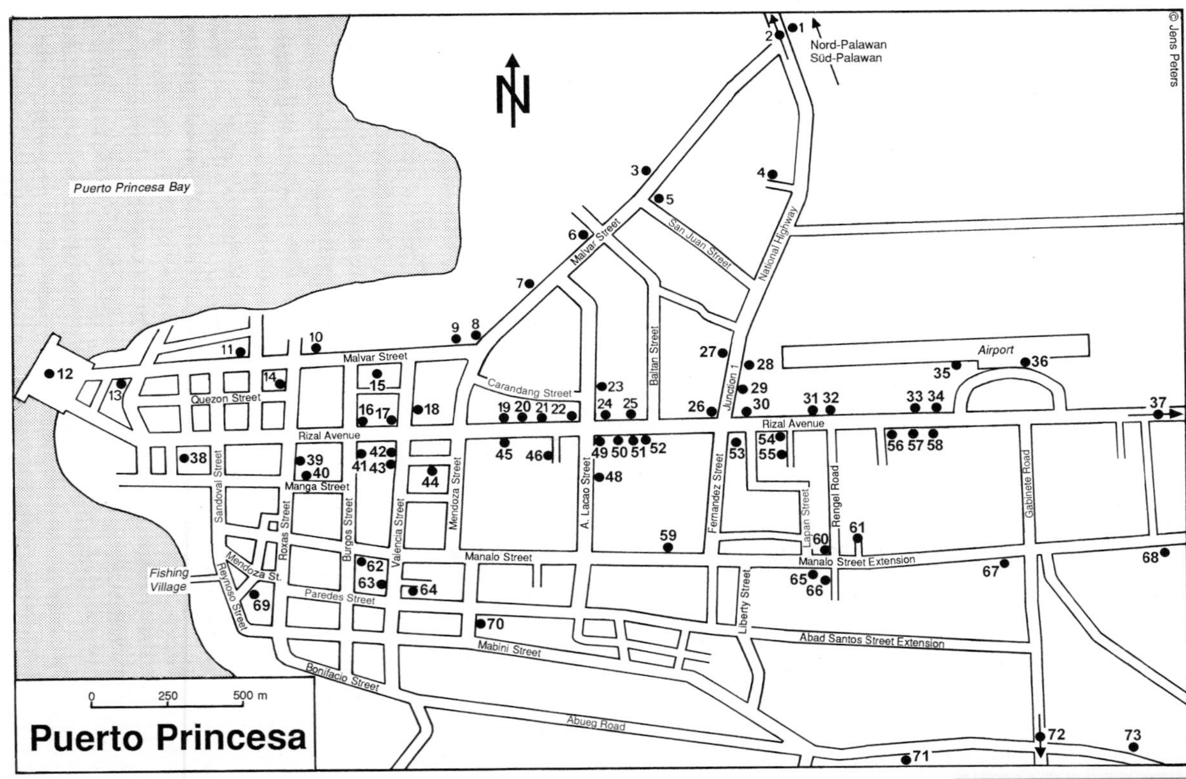
© Jens Peters
Nord-Palawan
Süd-Palawan
Puerto Princesa Bay
National Highway
San Juan Street
Malvar Street
Carandang Street
Baltan Street
Junction 1
Airport
Rizal Avenue
Quezon Street
Sandoval Street
Manga Street
Roxas Street
Burgos Street
Valencia Street
Mendoza Street
A. Lacao Street
Fernandez Street
Lapan Street
Rengel Road
Gabinete Road
Manalo Street
Manalo Street Extension
Liberty Street
Fishing Village
Mendoza St.
Reynoso Street
Paredes Street
Mabini Street
Abad Santos Street Extension
Bonifacio Street
Abueg Road
0 250 500 m
Puerto Princesa

19 Allied Bank
20 Swagman Travel
21 Metrobank
22 Equitable PCI Bank
25 Bayantel/RPCI (Long Distance Calls)
Western Computer Internet Café
30 Palawan Money Changer
33 Floral Travel & Tours
Topstar Travel & Tours
35 City Tourist Office
Palawan Treasures & Gift Shop
38 Cathedral
41 Post Office
44 Palawan Museum
45 Bank of the Philippine Islands
48 NCCC
52 AS Money Changer
53 Provincial Capitol
Provincial Tourist Office
54 Palawan Yacht Charter
57 Immigration Office
72 Nasin-Aw White Beach (500m)

Lola Itang Pension, Roxas St, Tel 4332990. SR/DR/ac/bath P650 and P750 (TV). Neat, fairly big rooms. Quiet location. Restaurant.
Moana Hotel, Rizal Ave, Tel 4344753. SR/DR/fan/bath P650, SR/DR/ac/bath P850 (TV). Cosy place at the airport with neat rooms. Restaurant (24 hrs), coffee shop, swimming pool in a well-kept courtyard, diving.
Admiral Hotel, Junction 1, Tel 4344561, Fax 4344308. SR/ac/bath P720 to P1200, DR/ac/bath P960 to P1500. Reasonable rooms with TV. Coffee shop (live music in the evenings).

Places to Stay - middle

Hillside Resort, Sandiwa, Tiniguiban, Tel 4337318, Fax 4337851, @. SR/DR/ac/bath P880, cottage/ac/bath P1620, suite P1885. Well-kept cottages and rooms with TV. Attractive garden setting with view of Puerto Princesa Bay. Restaurant, swimming pool. Quiet location on the north-west edge of town, about seven km from the centre (P30 by tricycle).
Airport Hotel, 442 Rizal Ave, Tel 4332177, Fax: 4336514. SR/DZ/ac/bath P1000 and P1400. Cosy rooms and comfortable suites with refrigerator and TV. Restaurant, coffee shop, small swimming pool. As the name implies, it is handy for the airport.
Hotel Fleuris, Lacao St, Tel 4344338, Fax 4344343, @. SR/ac/bath P1700, DR/ac/bath P2200, suite P2000 and P2500. Breakfast included. Attractive, comfortable rooms with refrigerator and TV. Centrally located, but quiet. Restaurant, swimming pool, airport service.

Places to Stay - top end

The Legend Hotel, Malvar St, Tel 4339076, Fax 4339077, @. SR/ac/bath P2400 to P3400, DR/ac/bath P2700 to P3700, suite P4600 and P5800, all including breakfast. Upper-middle class of hotel. Comfortable rooms with TV, the more expensive ones also have a refrigerator. Pleasantly furnished restaurant, swimming pool.
Barceló Asturias Hotel, South National Highway, Tel 4343851, Fax 4343750, @. SR/ac/bath from P3000, DR/ac/bath from P3300; including breakfast. Neat rooms with TV in an attractive, Spanish-style building. Restaurant, disco, swimming pool. Located on the northern edge of town, about three km from the centre.

Places to Eat

Well worth a mention is the international cuisine at the ***Trattoria Restaurant & Garden*** in PEO Rd. They offer an excellent breakfast, steaks, pasta dishes and pizzas. A commendable selection of inexpensive vegetarian dishes is on

the menu at the ***Vegetarian House*** on Manolo St corner Burgos St (closed on Sundays).

Definitely to be recommended is the easily-overlooked, charmingly rustic ***Kalui Restaurant*** on Rizal Ave. In addition to having a refreshingly original look about it, there is an area in the restaurant where guests can simply read and relax. It is open daily except Sunday, from 11am to 2pm and 5.30 to 11pm (guests should take their shoes off). Instead of a menu, they have a meal of the day, always seafood, varying according to what has been caught that day. All meals are served with vegetables and rice.

Two km further out of town, near the entrance to the former Vietnamese Refugee Camp, the popular ***Pho Vietnamese Restaurant*** is the place for good, albeit not cheap, Vietnamese food.

The Philippine and international food in the ***Seven Plates Restaurant*** on the National Highway is very good indeed.

Another good tip is the pleasant ***Lola Itang Filipino Restaurant*** in Roxas St, where they pride themselves on preparing the food the traditional Filipino way.

However, probably the best place to find Filipino food is ***Café Arturo***. Their Fisherman's Soup and Bulalo Steak is to be recommended. This pleasant place is a little bit out of the way, five km north of the centre, set in an idyllic grove at the Memorial Park 200m off the National Highway. Still, getting there is well worth the effort; have the tricycle wait for you though, otherwise you could have problems getting back. Open daily 11am-2pm and 6-11pm.

If you're looking for a romantic spot with a light sea breeze and a view of the ocean, then look out for the ***Badjao Seafront*** restaurant. It's located right on the water a short way off Abueg Rd. About 800m east of there, also in Abueg Rd, you'll find the ***Deep Forest Garden Resort***, a big area where various Philippine sights and scenes from Philippine life are presented in miniature (admission: P35, children P25). They have good local and international food in their restaurant.

The ***Tom Tom Club***, a few metres to the side of the Manalo Extension, is both a restaurant and a music bar, with a garden too. Their specialities are steaks, seafood and paella. The German owner, not surprisingly called Tom, organises an outstanding programme of music. About 400m to the east of this, the popular ***Chicken Inato*** will serve you inexpensive and tasty grilled chicken. Also popular are the open-air restaurants ***Balinsasayan Grill***, Manalo Extension corner Rengel St, ***Cristina's***, Rizal Ave corner Junction 1, and above all ***Kinabuchs*** on Rizal Ave.

The ***NCCC Fastfood Restaurant***, on the ground floor in the shopping mall of the same name on A Lacson St, is always busy. It offers a wide choice of Filipino dishes and is self-service.

In Valencia St next to the Chinese restaurant ***Edwin's Food Palace***, the ***Good Old Grandma Bakeshop*** will serve you breakfast and fresh brewed coffee. They also offer expresso, cappuccino, café au lait and mocca, as well as cakes and ice cream.

If you're into self-catering and hanker for ingredients from home, ***Bruno's Swissfood & Snack Bar*** in Valencia St has a selection of European delicacies on offer.

Entertainment

Popular meeting points are the ***Trattoria Bar*** in PEO Rd, and the ***Tom Tom Club***, Manalo Extension, which both have a good selection of music. If you're looking for a place to share a nightcap with someone, then head for the rustic pub ***Zum Kleinen Anker*** on Rizal Ave. Abanico Rd in the north of the city is home to a few basic ***Nightclubs***.

Miscellaneous

Diving: Queen Anne Divers, @, have a 16m-long dive boat, the MY *Jinn Sulu* which has one four-berth and three two-berth cabins and 10 complete sets of diving equipment on board. They offer diving instruction as well as one-day or more diving trips with two dives daily for US$60 per day per person, including equipment and lunch. Also available are five- and seven-day diving trips to the Tubbataha Reefs (Tubbataha National Marine Park) in April, May and June for US$660 and US$900 respectively. Five-day diving trips to Panglima, Costancia or Dumaran are available in July, September and October (US$580). A boat charter without diving is also available on request. For bookings, contact Urs Rechsteiner, c/o Trattoria Inn, PEO Rd, 5300 Puerto Princesa, Palawan; Tel 4334709 (Urs's home number).

Palawan Yacht Charter, Rizal Ave (Badjao Hotel), Tel & Fax 4345818, Cellphone 0918-9131630, @, offers diving trips with the MY *Talusi*, eg to the Tubbataha reef and to Busuanga (wreck diving). This 20-meter long motor boat has 10 aircon double cabins and can also be chartered for daytrips.

The MY *Moonshadow*, @, also has diving equipment on board. They offer several trips to the Tubbataha Reefs from April to June (see Boat Tours earlier in this chapter).

Information on the Tubbataha National Marine Park is available from Tubbataha Management Office, National Highway, 5300 Puerto Princesa, Fax 4345759, @.

Festivals: Tabuan Festival (Foundation Day) from 4 March (lasting one week); Pista Y Ang Kagueban (Feast of the Forest) on the third Saturday in June; City Fiesta on 8 December.

Immigration Office, Rizal Ave, Tel 4332248. Open Mon-Fri 8am-noon and 2-5pm.

Information: Bookshops may have the monthly bulletin *Bandillo ng Palawan*, written and published by local environmentalists, with interesting articles about ecotourism and conservation on Palawan. It is also available at the Kalui Restaurant on Rizal Ave and in many hotels.

The Palawan Museum at the Mendoza Park houses a library specialising in books on Philippine and Palawan history, anthropology, ethnology, flora and fauna.

Medical Services: The treatment, nursing care and medication are apparently much better in the Palawan Adventist Hospital, Tel 4332156, than in the Provincial Hospital, Tel 4332621.

Malaria Office (Extension Field Office of Department of Health), National Highway, Santa Monica, Tel 4337743.

Money: AS Money Changer and Palawan Money Changer will change cash, as will many hotels.

Bank of the Philippine Islands, Equitable PCI Bank, Philippine National Bank and Metrobank, all on Rizal Ave, have ATMs, Equitable PCI Bank and Metrobank also have them in the NCCC shopping centre.

The Philippine National Bank changes travellers' cheques, although only up to US$500 per day. Chances are, only the Allied Bank will change Thomas Cook cheques.

Important Note: Outside of Puerto Princesa there are practically no money-changing facilities on Palawan. This is especially true in Port Barton and El Nido, where many travellers have had to leave early because of lack of available funds.

Online: Mozcom Internet Café, Roxas St, Kawing Internet and Western Computer Internet Café, Rizal Ave (all P40/hr).

Post & Telephone: Post Office, Rizal Ave. International telephone calls can be made at Bayantel/RCPI on Rizal Ave. Post code: 5300. Area code: 048.

Swimming pool: The Royal Oberoi Resort Hotel, Esteban Rd, Santa Monica (right in the north of the city, about six km from the centre) has the biggest and best laid-out swimming pool in the city (with a pool bar). Admission for non-residents: P100.
Tourist Office: There is a City Tourist Office, Tel 4344211, 4332893, @, at the airport which specialises mainly in information on Puerto Princesa and transport connections from there. Open Mon-Fri 8am-noon and 1-5pm, Sat-Sun 8am-noon.
The Provincial Tourist Office in the Provincial Capitol on Rizal Ave corner Fernandez St, Tel 4332968, has information on the whole province of Palawan. Open Mon-Fri 8am-noon and 1-5pm.
Travel Agency: The travel agencies Floral Travel & Tours, Tel 4343839, Fax 4332540, @, and Topstar Travel & Tours, Tel & Fax 4338247, @, both on Rizal Ave, offer various day trips, eg island hopping in Honda Bay and trips to the Underground River. Both will also take care of flight confirmations and visa extensions, as does Swagman Travel on Rizal Ave, Tel 4344902.

Getting Around

Car: Cars (including 4-wheel drive) are only hired out with a driver. Prices depend on the destination, eg to Sabang (Underground River) costs P2500 (round trip), Port Barton P3800, Taytay P6500, or El Bido P10,000. There are several local firms, such as Topstar Travel & Tours, Tel & Fax 4338247, @.
Motorcycle: Various hotels offer motorcycles (125 cc) suitable for off-road riding from P650 to P800 per day. Don't forget: in Puerto Princesa you have to wear a helmet.
Multicabs: There are multicab routes between Puerto Princesa and several suburban areas. Fare for a short trip (up to four km): P6.
Tricycle: A short trip within town by tricycle costs P4 per person (P5 at night). Chartering a tricycle is possible for P60 an hour.

Getting There & Away

By Air: It's a good idea to have your return or continuation flight confirmed immediately after your arrival.
The airport is about two km east of the centre. A tricycle into town costs P5 per person or P20 to P30 if it's not shared.
Air Philippines, Rizal Ave (near the airport), Tel 4337003, 4338045.
Destination: Manila.
Cebu Pacific, Puerto Princesa Airport, Tel 4347038.
- Rizal Ave, Tel 4335541
Destinations: Cebu City, Manila.
Layang Layang Aerospace, Sanctuary Tours & Travel, Corporate Center Building, Rizal Ave, Tel 4348231, Cellphone 0919-3503279, Fax 4348204, @.
Destination: Kota Kinabalu (Sabah, Malaysia).
Philippine Airlines, Puerto Princesa Airport, Tel 4334565.
Destination: Manila.
Seair, Floral Travel & Tours, Rizal Ave, Tel 4332540, Fax: 4345272, @.
Destinations: Cuyo, El Nido, Busuanga, Manila.

By Bus/Jeepney: Departure times from Puerto Princesa are fairly irregular. It's best to make enquiries the night before you leave and head for the terminal at the New Public Market (about four km north of the centre) as early as possible the next day.

By Boat: The wharf is at the western edge of town. The normal price by tricycle to a hotel in the centre should be P5, but P10 is often charged.
Milagrosa Shipping Lines, Port Area (at the entrance), Tel 4334860.
Destinations: Cuyo, Panay.

Negros Navigation, Pier Office, Tel 4337197, 4344533.
- Malvar St, Tel 4337204, 4337165.
Destination: Manila.
WG & A, Rizal Ave, Tel 4334875.
- Pico Building, Port Area, Tel 4345736-37.
Destinations: Coron/Busuanga, Manila.

Irawan

Irawan, halfway between Puerto Princesa and Iwahig, is the location of the Irawan Crocodile Farming Institute, which was founded in 1987 and recently renamed to Palawan Wildlife Rescue & Conservation Center. The goal of this project, financed by Japanese money, is supposed to be to protect endangered species of the Philippine crocodile from extinction. On paper, this is of course a commendable idea. We can only hope that the project does not eventually fall victim to its original objective of making money for its backers. However, up till now it's still true to say that a visit to the 10-hectare farm will give you a good idea of what crocodiles are all about.
Some of the reptiles here are up to five metres long. They also have examples of young animals belonging to different species of crocodile, as well as some impressive skeletons. Numerous notice boards provide information on the biology and habits of the various crocodiles in the collection.
Apart from the crocodile pens and open compounds, the farm also has a small zoo which includes animals that can only be found on Palawan.
They are open Monday to Friday and on public holidays from 1.30 to 5pm, Saturday from 9am to 5pm. Feeding of the crocodiles: Monday and Thursday. Guided tours are available hourly. The farm is closed on Sunday. Admission is free.

Getting There & Away

Bus/Jeepney: Buses and jeepneys for South Palawan go via Irawan (P10).

Tricycle: A tricycle from Puerto Princesa to Irawan costs around P80.

Balsahan

There is a resort by the river in Balsahan which the local Filipinos like to visit on short holidays to relax and celebrate family occasions.

Getting There & Away

Jeepney: No direct connection exists between Puerto Princesa and Balsahan. At about 9.30am a jeepney leaves Valencia St, near the market, for Iwahig. For a couple of extra pesos the driver may make the detour from the highway to Balsahan and pick you up again at about 1.30pm.

Iwahig

The Iwahig Penal Colony is 23 km south of Puerto Princesa. Prisoners live here as in a normal village; there are no walls. They fish, cultivate rice and so on. The warders and administrators have a good time here and are never short of workers. Tourists are welcome as the souvenir shop sells handicrafts made by the prisoners. The prison colony also works as an advertisement for the government's modern and liberal penal policy. At the moment about 2000 prisoners, called colonists, live there. Many of them have their families with them. This penal colony is self-supporting and needs no financial assistance from the state. The rate of recidivism of former prisoners is said to be markedly lower than in traditional prisons.

Getting There & Away

Jeepney: A jeepney leaves Puerto Princesa for the Iwahig Penal Colony at

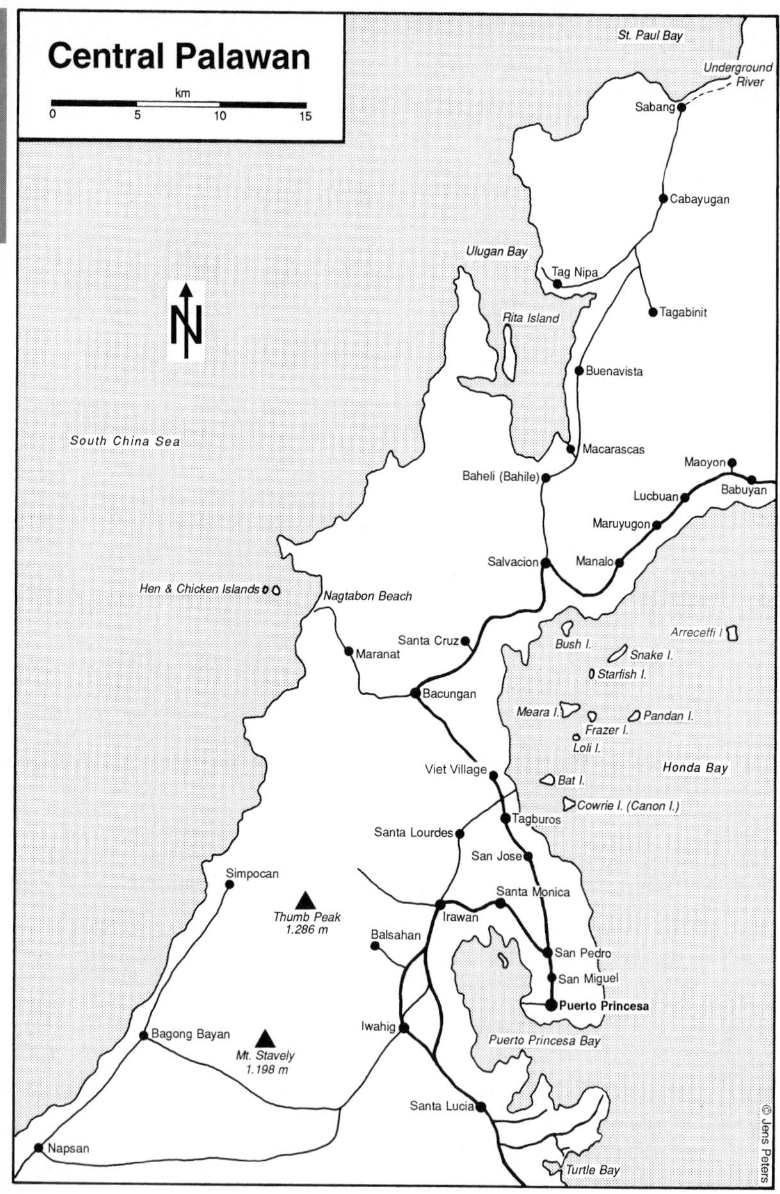

Central Palawan
km
0
5
10
15
St. Paul Bay
Underground River
Sabang
Cabayugan
Ulugan Bay
Tag Nipa
Tagabinit
Rita Island
Buenavista
South China Sea
Macarascas
Maoyon
Baheli (Bahile)
Babuyan
Lucbuan
Maruyugon
Salvacion
Manalo
Hen & Chicken Islands
Nagtabon Beach
Santa Cruz
Arreceffi I.
Bush I.
Snake I.
Maranat
Starfish I.
Bacungan
Meara I.
Pandan I.
Frazer I.
Loli I.
Honda Bay
Viet Village
Bat I.
Cowrie I. (Canon I.)
Tagburos
Santa Lourdes
San Jose
Simpocan
Santa Monica
Thumb Peak
1.286 m
Irawan
Balsahan
San Pedro
San Miguel
Puerto Princesa
Iwahig
Bagong Bayan
Mt. Stavely
1.198 m
Puerto Princesa Bay
Santa Lucia
Napsan
Turtle Bay
© Jens Peters

9.30am from Valencia St, near the market, and returns at 1.30pm. If you want to return later, you can walk to the highway and wait for a bus or jeepney coming from the south.

Tricycle: You can get a tricycle for the half-day trip to the Iwahig Penal Colony, the Balsahan Resort and the crocodile farm. You should pay no more than about P250 to P300 for the round trip.

Napsan

Around 70 km south-west of Puerto Princesa at Labtay near Napsan on the South China Sea, there is a beautiful long beach (unfortunately spoiled in places by the sandflies) where you can find small, family-style accommodation. The somewhat adventure-packed journey there involves travelling right across Palawan, including climbing mountains covered in thick jungle on the second half of the journey.

Places to Stay

Kiao Sea Lodge, Laptay, Satellite Tel 098-5401830 @. Cottage/fan/bath P750 and P1200 (for up to seven people; bunk beds), cottage/ac/bath P1000. Neat cottages, nestled under palm trees. Peaceful location with a pleasant, relaxing atmosphere. Good restaurant.

Getting There & Away

Jeepney: Two or three jeepneys leave Puerto Princesa for Labtay/Napsan between 7 and 9am from the jeepney terminal (3½ hrs). From Labtay to Puerto Princesa the jeepneys leave between 10am and 1pm.

Honda Bay

The islands in Honda Bay make a good day trip from Puerto Princesa. You can also stay there overnight. Pandan Island, populated by large numbers of

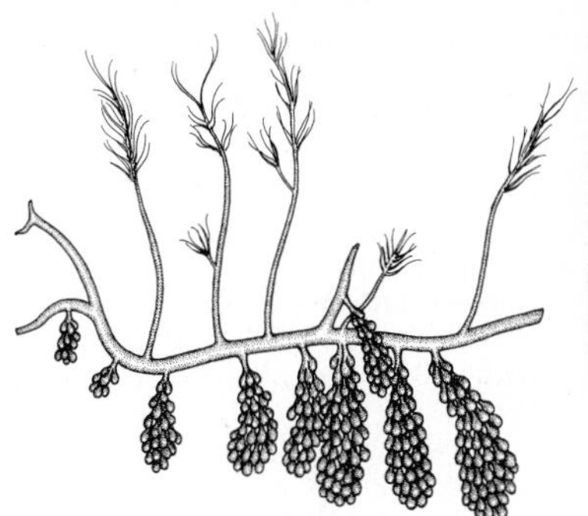

Seaweed *(Caulerpa racemosa)*
Crunchy green bacciform seaweed *(lato)* is one of the tastiest edible plants in the ocean and a mainstay of any maritime vegetarian diet.

fishermen, is one of the best-known islands in Honda Bay, but hardly anyone ever visits it. There is a Coast Guard base on the island. An almost intact coral reef exists between Pandan and Cowrie (Canon) islands. Because fishing is strictly controlled, snorkelling and diving are better in Honda Bay than in many of the areas around Palawan.

Snake Island is one of the most attractive islands for a day trip. It is sandy and has a shallow coral reef on the landward side which is ideal for snorkelling. Take some bread with you to feed the fish - they'll eat it out of your hand! Anyone wanting to camp for a few days on this island where there is no shade, has to take drinking water and food.

A bit south-west of Snake Island is the small Starfish Island, the location of the Starfish Sandbar Resort; admission is P30. It's definitely no Fantasy Island, but a flat, treeless sandbar with a few simple huts. They also sport a modest, rustic restaurant (where the fish is excellent), and loungers for guests. You can hire a boat, snorkel and goggles if you want. There is a small coral reef at

the end of the island where you can go snorkelling.
In the late afternoon swarms of bats fly from Bat Island (where else?) to the mainland.

Places to Stay

Starfish Sandbar Resort, Starfish Isand. SR/DR/bath P500 to P800. Basic accommodation, don't expect an idyllic resort.
Dos Palmas, Arreceffi Island, @. Cottage/ac/bath P9250 to P12,000 per person, including full board. Extensive, exclusive grounds with well-kept, tastefully decorated cottages, some of which are built on piles in the water. Restaurant, swimming pool, tennis court, kayaks, diving. Reservations in Puerto Princesa: NCCC Compound, 89 Lacao St, Tel (048) 4343118, Fax (048) 4343119.

Getting There & Away

Bus/Jeepney/Boat: You can go from Puerto Princesa to Santa Lourdes Pier (on the highway, north of Tagburos) by any jeepney or bus going north. Get off at the big Caltex tank and walk towards the waterfront, where you can hire a boat. Prices range from P600 to P1000, depending on the number and distance of the islands you want to visit. Jollibee Boat Hire has outriggers with plenty of protection from the sun and cold drinks on board.

Tricycle: A tricycle from Puerto Princesa to Santa Lourdes Pier costs P100.

Viet Village

The end of the Vietnam War in 1975 and the subsequent installation of a Communist government there drove thousands of Vietnamese into exile. In small boats they risked their lives to cross the South China Sea to reach Malaysia, Thailand or the Philippines on their way to the United States, Canada, Australia or Europe. However, for many of them the dream of emigrating to the West was not to be fulfilled. Having survived the open sea and murderous pirates, many of these so-called Boat People who made it to the Philippines found themselves accommodated in a refugee camp in Puerto Princesa which had been specially built for them. With the relaxation of the political situation in the 90s, the Philippine government decreed that the refugee camp should be dismantled and the 300 Vietnamese occupants sent back home. The result was a massive protest amongst ordinary Filipinos against this involuntary repatriation. With the active support of concerned locals, the Catholic Bishops' Conference of the Philippines (CBCP) finally managed to secure a residence permit for the refugees and push through the construction of a new residential area, the Viet Village.
Viet Village, with its Catholic and Protestant churches, pagoda and temple, lies 13 km north of Puerto Princesa and belongs to the Santa Lourdes community. The administration is controlled by the Vietnamese population themselves and they maintain economic independence with the help of several projects such as manufacturing noodles, running a bakery, a restaurant, a souvenir shop etc.

Places to Stay

Viet Village Guest House. SR/DR/ac P450. Basic accommodation.

Places to Eat

Right at the entrance to the village, the ***Viet Ville Restaurant,*** Cellphone 0918-7934820, mainly prepares organic food. Their spring rolls (Cha Giò) and the Seafood Fondue (Lâu Biên) are a treat to eat. There are no soft drinks such as Coke or Sprite, but to make up for it they have fresh fruit juices and a tasty, so-called Ginseng tea, made of cogon root extract. Open daily 9am to 9pm.

Getting There & Away

Tricycle: A Special Ride with a tricycle from Puerto Princesa to the Viet Village costs around P100.

Jeepney/Bus: All jeepneys and buses heading in the direction of North Palawan go past the Viet Village.

Nagtabon Beach

White, palm-lined Nagtabon Beach lies on a beautiful calm bay on Palawan's west coast looking out on the Hen & Chicken islands (fishermen will take you over there for P600). Unfortunately, there is a fly in the ointment, literally: sandflies just love it here.

Places to Stay

Georg's Place. Cottage/bath P500 and P800, depending on size. Fairly extensive grounds with reasonable cottages. Restaurant with European and Filipino cuisine.

Getting There & Away

Jeepney: One or two jeepneys are supposed to go from Puerto Princesa to Nagtabon Beach, but this route is not always reliable. They leave between noon and 2pm, taking one hour for the trip. Between 6 and 7am there are meant to be two jeepneys leaving to make the journey between Nagtabon Beach and Puerto Princesa. However, it is possible that only one will actually turn up, and it may leave at 5am! A Special Ride from Puerto Princesa to Nagtabon Beach costs around P1.000.

Underground River

The Underground River, or St Paul Cave to give it its proper name, is Palawan's most fascinating network of caves. Carved out by an underground river, the cave meanders for over eight km. Nature has provided it with a bewildering variety of enormous stalactites, fragile-looking columns, smooth-walled pipes, jagged caverns and big, impressive chambers.
The entrance to the Underground River is set in a picturesque lagoon on the west coast of Central Palawan. You could almost overlook this deeply fissured, yawning opening in the grey limestone face, through which you can enter the dark maw of the cave in small paddle bancas. The light of the lamps reveals countless bats in the cave. You would need a powerful flash to take photographs here.

Getting There & Away

Boat: The easiest and best way to make a short trip to the Underground River is from Sabang. This takes about 20 min and costs P500 there and back (for the boat); P400 for the single trip. It's worth noting that the trip from there is not possible during the south-west monsoon season from June to November, which can get quite stormy, as the waves of the South China Sea are simply too large for outriggers at this time.
If you want to make a day trip to the Underground River from Puerto Princesa it's better to have a travel agent organise it for you, or hire a car and driver (for about P2500). If you take a regular jeepney you'll almost definitely run out of time, as the last one back leaves by 2pm at the latest.
Day trips are also possible by outrigger from Cacnipa Island and Port Barton.

Sabang

The introduction of a regular jeepney service from Puerto Princesa a few years ago brought to an end the role of the tiny community of Sabang as a kind of Sleeping Beauty.

Sabang is situated near the St Paul Subterranean National Park, supported by the World Wide Fund for Nature (WWF); this beautiful piece of nature with its thick covering of jungle lies at the feet of the 1028m Mt St Paul.

There is an amazing number of different varieties of tree; about 100 are marked around the Central Ranger Station and along the so-called 'Monkey Trail'. If you keep your eyes and ears open you will be aware of a rich and vocal community of birds, monkeys by the dozen, and a few majestic 1½-metre-long monitor lizards. The imposing vertical grooves caused by erosion in the limestone cliffs are also well worth seeing. However, the main attraction of this extremely well-run national park is, as the name would suggest, a subterranean one: the Underground River. There is another relatively unknown cave with impressive dripstone deposits which was only discovered a few years ago, called the Ren-Pat Cave. This can be reached from Sabang by outrigger, provided the sea is calm enough.

If you head out from Sabang on foot along the beach in a westerly direction, after about 45 minutes you will come to a little waterfall, arching into the sea from a height of about 10m. You would be well advised to wear sturdy shoes as the beach is quite stony around this side.

Another fascinating trip from Sabang is by paddle boat up the little Poyuy-Poyuy River, the mouth of which is near the national park. For the first few kilometres the banks are lined with dense mangrove thickets. You'll find workers on the Mangrove Paddle Boat Tour project at the bridge near the mouth of the river. During the boat tour they give an expert discourse on the Mangrove ecosystem and turn the trip into a rewarding experience. An adequate tip is expected.

Macaque

From Sabang to the Underground River

The walk to the Underground River from Sabang is well worth the effort, and you'll get a chance to walk through the jungle part of the way. Getting back is no problem: several boats make the journey from the Underground River back to Sabang every day. It's recommended to wear sturdy shoes.

Leaving Sabang by foot, head along the long, palm-lined sandy beach to the right in an easterly direction. After about two km, or one hour through the jungle and over a little mountain, you will come to the park's Central Ranger Station. It's about another two km, or just over an hour on foot from the Ranger Station to the cave entrance. You can either take the so-called 'Monkey Trail', which has been laid out as naturally as possible and has steep, wooden steps in places, or the Jungle Trail, which is a bit longer and has some fairly overgrown stretches.

The permit for the journey into the Underground River is available at the entrance. However, the rangers prefer people to obtain the permit beforehand at the Information Office in Sabang (open from 8am). Admission costs P200 (P150 for Filipinos), including the river trip with a paddle boat. This takes 45 min and will end up in the 60m high 'Cathedral' at a minimum, although they

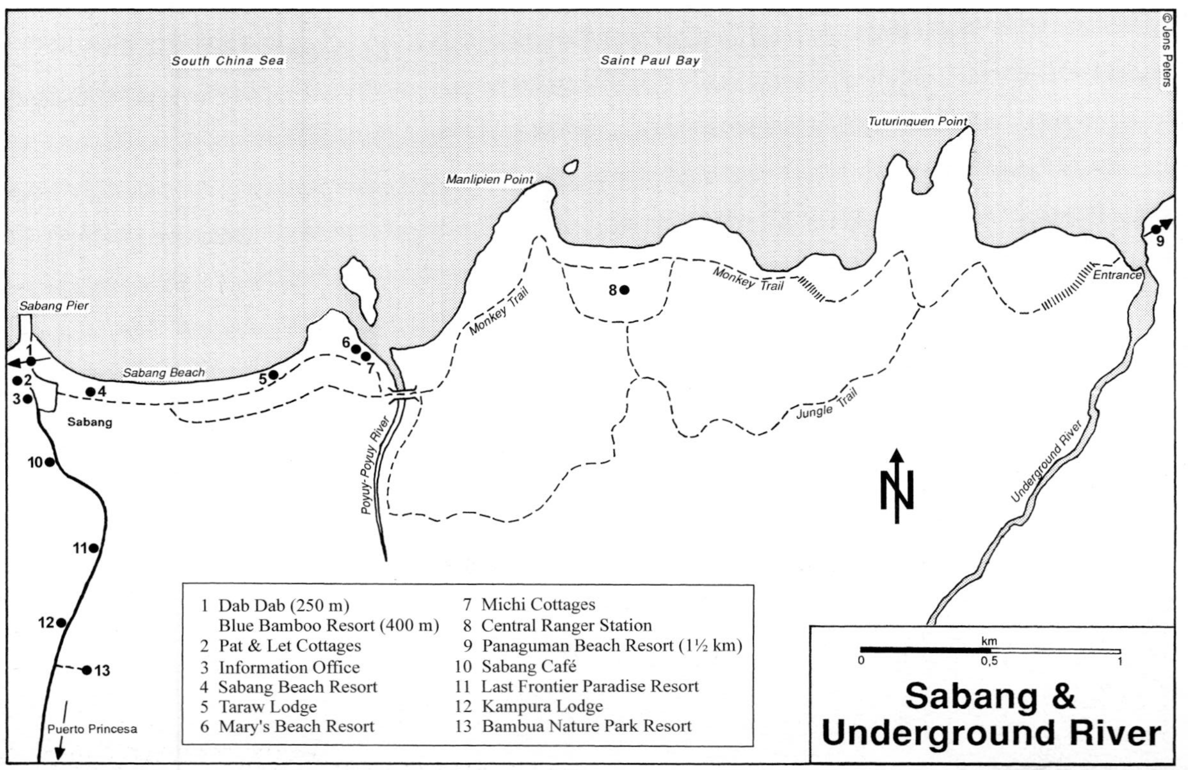
South China Sea
Saint Paul Bay
© Jens Peters
Tuturinquen Point
Manlipien Point
Sabang Pier
Sabang Beach
Sabang
Monkey Trail
Monkey Trail
Jungle Trail
Entrance
Poyuy-Poyuy River
Underground River
Puerto Princesa
1 Dab Dab (250 m)
Blue Bamboo Resort (400 m)
2 Pat & Let Cottages
3 Information Office
4 Sabang Beach Resort
5 Taraw Lodge
6 Mary's Beach Resort
7 Michi Cottages
8 Central Ranger Station
9 Panaguman Beach Resort (1½ km)
10 Sabang Café
11 Last Frontier Paradise Resort
12 Kampura Lodge
13 Bambua Nature Park Resort
km
0
0,5
1
Sabang &
Underground River

may take you further. The trips are usually made between 8am and noon and then from 1 to 4pm. However, the boatmen sometimes pack up for the day in the early afternoon, so it's safer to get there before 1pm.

Places to Stay

Almost all restaurants and places offering accommodation have their own generators which provide electricity until at least 10pm.

Sabang

Blue Bamboo Resort, @. Cottage P200, cottage/bath P300 and P400. Basic, but beautifully built cottages of various sizes about 400m west of the pier. The resort belongs to Yan from Switzerland and his Filipina wife, Lorena. Restaurant.

Pal & Let Cottages. Cottage/bath P300 to P400. Set in garden grounds, with modest cottages of different sizes. Restaurant.

Taraw Lodge. Cottage/fan/bath P350. Inviting resort with good, inexpensive cottages. Restaurant.

Mary's Beach Resort. Cottage/bath P400. Basic cottages, most of which are no longer in the best condition. Situated out of the way, on a small bay at the eastern end of Sabang Beach, just at the entrance to the National Park. The beach itself is graced by a big, impressive tree which has hammocks slung in the shade of its extensive network of gnarled branches.

Sabang Beach Resort. Cottage/bath P400 to P750, depending on location, size and amenities. They have older, relatively basic cottages as well as newer ones which are somewhat better. Right on the beach, they have lots of plants on the grounds. Restaurant.

Dab Dab, Satellite Tel 098-5403961. Tent P150, cottage/bath P450 and P500. Friendly accommodation. At the moment, there are only two cottages (good condition) set in a beautiful garden, although others are to be built. The restaurant here is popular. Located about 250m west of the jetty.

Michi Cottages, Satellite Tel 098-5403869. Cottage/fan/bath P1000, including breakfast. Quite comfortable, roomy cottages. Restaurant with a beautiful sea view. Located at the east end of Sabang Beach, right next to Mary's Beach Resort. Reservations in Puerto Princesa: Tel (048) 4342010.

Around Sabang

Central Ranger Station. If you want to have a closer look at the rugged countryside around the national park, you can spend the night in the Ranger Station. A dorm bed in a simple but clean, four-bed room will cost you P100. You will have to take food and supplies with you. Drinking water is available.

Bambua Nature Park Resort, @. SR/DR P150/300, cottage/bath P600. Half or full board possible. Basic rooms and tastefully furnished cottages with a generous amount of space separating them. The view from their excellent restaurant is beautiful. Located about 20 min on foot from Sabang, in a dream setting at the foot of a mountain with jungle at the back door. A little paradise, with plenty of animals and plants around.

Panaguman Beach Resort. Pleasant resort on a white sand, palm-lined beach at the northern end of the long sweep of Panaguman Bay. It's about 1½ km northeast of the mouth of the Underground River, just outside the National Park. Note: This resort was closed in 2004, but should open again soon. Latest information on this in Puerto Princesa at the Trattoria Inn, PEO Rd.

Places to Eat

The tastefully decorated and wonderfully cosy ***Dab Dab Restaurant*** about

250m west of the pier can be highly recommended for its excellent cooking. The owners, Manja and Dante, are a German-Filipino couple. They prefer you to pre-order.
A good place to have breakfast (providing they're open) is the ***Café Sabang***, just outside Sabang on the road to Puerto Princesa. You can just smell their home-baked French bread and freshly brewed coffee. In the evening they serve superb pizzas in addition to other dishes. About one km further, the beautifully situated ***Bambua Restaurant*** has seafood as well as delicious Oriental and vegetarian food on the menu.

Getting There & Away

El Nido - Port Barton
Boat: The boat route from Sabang and Port Barton to El Nido was discontinued owing to lack of demand. A Special Ride from El Nido to Sabang via Cacnipa Island costs P5000 to P7500, depending on the size of boat (seven hrs; via Port Barton eight hrs). It can get wet out there, so remember to insist on your baggage being covered up. There are possibly no boats venturing out during the rainy season.
A Special Ride with a small outrigger from Sabang to Cacnipa Island or Port Barton costs P2500 (3½ hrs).

Puerto Princesa
Bus/Jeepney: One bus and two to three jeepneys run between Puerto Princesa and Sabang daily. They leave when they're full, so it can be a long wait. The same applies to the 7.30am bus, which is preferable to the cramped jeepneys (P100; 2½ to as much as four hrs). It's a dusty ride! Because of the bad state of the road between Salvacion and Sabang during the rainy season, this route may not always be available. Departure from Sabang to Puerto Princesa is between 6 and 8.30am, at 12.30 and possibly 2pm.

Car: The trip by rental car (with driver) from Puerto Princesa to Sabang costs around P2500, eg from Topstar Travel & Tours, Rizal Ave, Tel (048) 4338247, @. If you're in a hurry, arrange for them to pick you up when you arrive at the airport and you'll be on the road in next to no time.

San Rafael
Walking: You can get to Sabang from San Rafael in a three-day walk right across Palawan (guide P500 per day, porter P250 per day, plus food and drink.

San Rafael

San Rafael has only a few huts, which are strung out along the highway, a school and two small shops, where you can't buy much anyway. From San Rafael you can visit the Batak with a guide. Whether to visit the Batak or not is something you will have to decide for yourself. The few remaining tribes of these nomadic people certainly don't find contact with travellers important.
The Duchess Beachside Cottages and the adjacent Coral Island can be recommended for those seeking peace and quiet. It's also a good starting point for longer hikes, for example right across Palawan to Sabang with its St Paul Subterranean National Park and the Underground River.

Places to Stay

Duchess Beachside Cottages. Cottage/fan P250 and P300. Basic but clean cottages built in a row on the beach. Situated about 500m from the road, this well looked after place also has a good restaurant.
Tarabanan Cottages, Concepcion, @. Cottage/bath P750 and P1000, including breakfast. Attractive, roomy two-

Palawan

storey cottages with living room and bedroom; good for four to six people. Peaceful, nicely built family-style resort on Honda Bay about 10 km east of San Rafael.

Getting There & Away

Bus: Between 6 and 9am, Puerto Royale buses run daily from the market in Puerto Princesa to San Rafael (1½ hrs), going on to Roxas or Taytay.

Jeepney: There are several jeepneys in the morning, leaving from the market or the jeepney terminal in Puerto Princesa heading north through San Rafael.

South Palawan

Aborlan

Near the fishing village of Tigman, about 10 km south-west of Aborlan, there is a beautiful white sand beach which is almost two km long and is lined with countless palm trees. The shallow water is suitable for bathing.

Places to Stay

Camille Del Sol, Tigman, @. Cottage/fan/bath P420, P580 and P690, depending on size. Pleasant beach resort in a quiet location about 300m from the village of Tigman, run by an American-Philippine couple. Restaurant, kayaks, windsurfing. Reservations in Puerto Princesa: Helen Tan Plaza, 233 Rizal Ave, Tel & Fax 4336526.
Princesa Holiday Resort, Tigman, @. Cottage/ac/bath P1700 to P6500. Large grounds with very roomy, comfortably furnished cottages with refrigerator. Restaurant, beach bar, swimming pool, tennis court, billiards, windsurfing, kayaks. Philippine-Belgian management.

Getting There & Away

Bus/Jeepney: Take a jeepney or a bus from Puerto Princesa (or an aircon minibus from Jollibee, Rizal Ave corner Lacao St) in the direction of Narra, get off at the Tigman turn-off in Plaridel, a little south of Aborlan (1½ hrs). It'll cost you P50 from there to take a tricycle to the beach.
Helpful hint: Order your tricycle for the return journey as soon as you get there. The last bus to Puerto Princesa leaves at around 6pm.

Narra

On the way to South Palawan a stopover is possible in Narra. The Estrella Waterfalls are six km north of there at the foot of Victoria Peak. You can get there by taking a tricycle from Narra market to Estrella village.

Places to Stay

Tiosin Lodging House, Panacan Rd. SR/DR/fan P100/P200. Modest, but acceptable accommodation. Restaurant with good, affordable food.
Victoria Peak Inn, National Highway. SR/DR/fan P150/P200. Adequate for the money.
Gardeña Boarding House, Panacan Rd. SR/DR/fan P150/P220. Basic and relatively clean.

Miscellaneous

Festival: Town Fiesta on 18 and 19 March.
Population: 10,000.
Post: Post code: 5303.

Getting There & Away

Bus/Jeepney: Loads of jeepneys and several buses make the trip from Puerto Princesa to Narra every day, either direct or heading on to Quezon and Brooke's Point, taking two hrs.

Quezon

Quezon is a small fishing village on Malanut Bay. It is the departure point

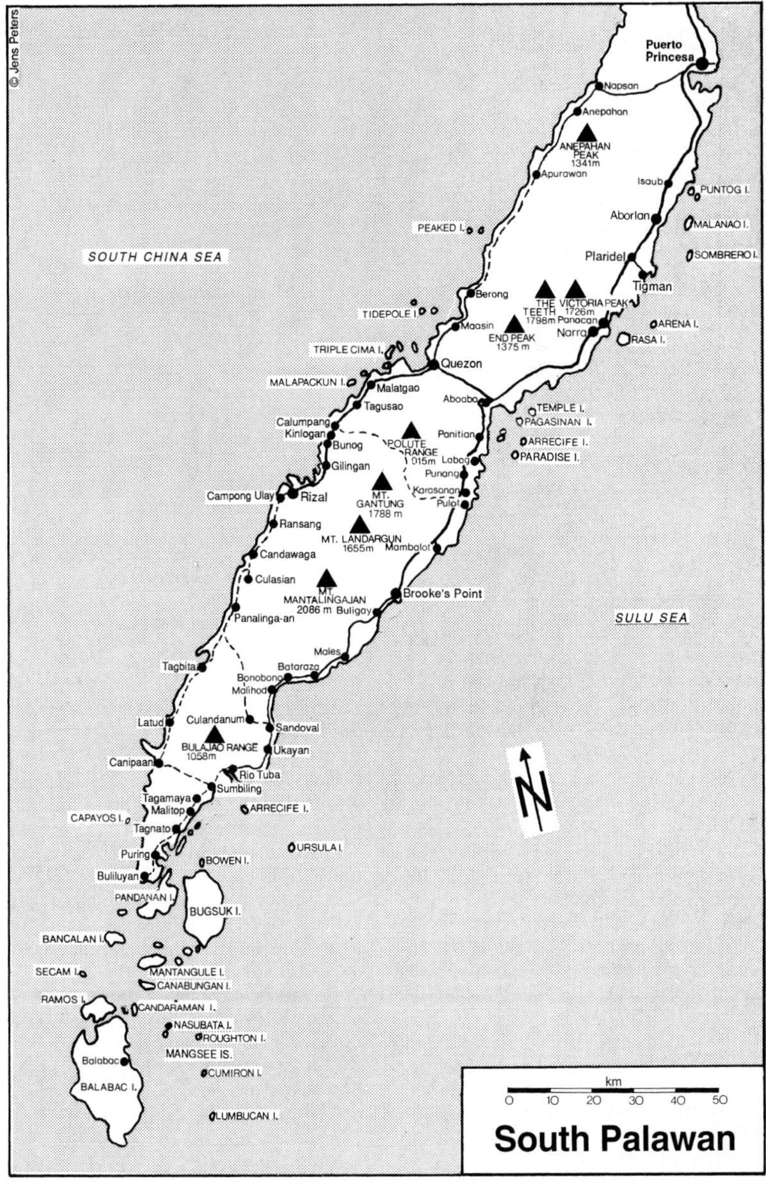
© Jens Peters
Puerto Princesa
Napsan
Anepahan
ANEPAHAN PEAK 1341m
Apurawan
Isaub
PUNTOG I.
Aborlan
MALANAO I.
PEAKED I.
SOUTH CHINA SEA
Plaridel
SOMBRERO I.
Tigman
Berong
THE TEETH 1798m
VICTORIA PEAK 1726m
Panacan
TIDEPOLE I.
Maasin
END PEAK 1375 m
Narra
ARENA I.
RASA I.
TRIPLE CIMA I.
Quezon
MALAPACKUN I.
Malatgao
Tagusao
Aboabo
TEMPLE I.
PAGASINAN I.
Calumpang
Kinlogan
Panitian
ARRECIFE I.
Bunog
POLUTE RANGE 915m
Labog
PARADISE I.
Gilingan
Punang
Karasanan
Campong Ulay
Rizal
MT. GANTUNG 1788 m
Pulot
Ransang
MT. LANDARGUN 1655m
Mambalot
Candawaga
Culasian
MT. MANTALINGAJAN 2086 m
Brooke's Point
Buligay
Panalinga-an
SULU SEA
Moles
Tagbita
Bataraza
Bonobono
Malihod
Latud
Culandanum
Sandoval
BULAJAO RANGE 1058m
Ukayan
Canipaan
Rio Tuba
Sumbiling
Tagamaya
Malitop
ARRECIFE I.
CAPAYOS I.
Tagnato
URSULA I.
Puring
BOWEN I.
Bululuyan
PANDANAN I.
BUGSUK I.
BANCALAN I.
SECAM I.
MANTANGULE I.
CANABUNGAN I.
RAMOS I.
CANDARAMAN I.
NASUBATA I.
ROUGHTON I.
MANGSEE IS.
Balabac
BALABAC I.
CUMIRON I.
LUMBUCAN I.
km
0 10 20 30 40 50
South Palawan

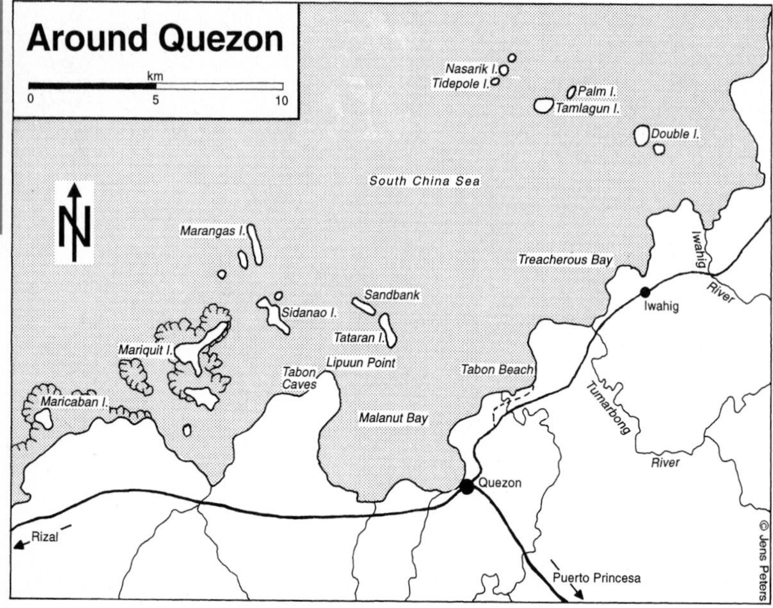

for the Tabon Caves, whose main entrance is on the north-west side of Lipuun Point. By boat the trip to the caves only takes 30 min and should not cost more than P400.

This huge complex contains 200 caves. Only 29 have been explored and only seven are open to the public. Tabon Cave is the biggest and Diwata Cave, 30m above sea level, is the highest and most beautiful. Because of their prehistoric sites, the Tabon Caves are a kind of natural museum. Human bones dating back to the Stone Age have been found here, and it is thought that the original inhabitants, the Pala'wan, may have used the caves as a burial site. Ask at the National Museum in Quezon for an experienced guide, but don't expect too much from the caves, however, as all you can see are some large holes in the mountainside.

After you've gone cave exploring, you might be tempted to hop over to the nearby islands with their white beaches, for example Sidanao, or Tataran with its long sandbank jutting out into the ocean. Far offshore on idyllic Tamlagun Island, a German called Frederick lived a real-life Robinson Crusoe existence surrounded by all kinds of animals until his death in May 1994. A Philippine family now lives in his tropical Garden of Eden. A round trip from Quezon to Tamlagun Island costs around P700.

A Belgian named Theo runs the Tabon Village Resort on Tabon Beach, four km north-east of Quezon. From here it's about an hour's walk to the Tumarbon Waterfall, or you can take a tricycle from Quezon to the river (P50), where a path splits off about 70m before the Tumarbong Bridge. This leads

to the waterfall and will take you about 20 min on foot.
For P300 you could also go by boat up the Tumarbon River through dense jungle. From the Tabon Village Resort it takes 45 min by sea to reach the mouth of the river and another 30 min to reach the waterfall. Overnight accommodation is available (see below).

Places to Stay

Quezon
Villa Esperanza. SR/DR/fan P150/250, cottage/fan/bath P500. Basic rooms and modest cottages, which are perhaps a little overpriced. The neat grounds are basically in good shape. Restaurant where no alcoholic drinks are served. Located about 300m from the bus terminal in the direction of Tabon Beach.

Around Quezon
Tabon Village Resort, Cellphone 0910-2398381. SR/DR P150/180, cottage/bath P450/580. Basic rooms; quite good, roomy cottages. Pleasant resort situated on a beautiful bay, but unfortunately the water at the beach is muddy and full of rocks which makes swimming impossible. Located on Tabon Beach, about four km north-east of Quezon. A tricycle from town to the resort costs P30 or P10 per person.
Tumarbong Paraiso sa Falls. Cottage P250/300. Basic accommodation set in the middle of practically unspoiled nature with a beautiful view of the Tumarbong waterfall. Restaurant. Belongs to the Tabon Village Resort.
Malapackun Island. Theo from the Tabon Village Resort has also set up a four-room cottage on the island of Malapackun, 20 km east of Quezon. If you want to retreat there, take water and food with you. Fish is available from local fishermen, and the cottage has cooking facilities. The boat trip from Quezon takes 1½ hrs and costs around P700.

Places to Eat
The tastefully designed ***Mutya ng Dagak*** (Pearl of the Sea) has very good food. It's part of the Tabon Village Resort and is on an artificial island connected to the beach by a bridge.

Miscellaneous
Festival: Town Fiesta on 30 March.
Population: 9000.
Post: Post code: 5304.

Getting There & Away
Bus: Charing Bus Lines buses depart daily, roughly hourly from 5am until 3pm, from Malvar St in Puerto Princesa to Quezon (P130; 3½ hrs). Some buses continue on from Quezon to Rizal.

Jeepney: Several jeepneys leave early in the morning from both Quezon and Puerto Princesa.

Brooke's Point

Halfway through the 19th century, a British adventurer, James Brooke, had an imposing watchtower built here in the south of Palawan as a warning to the pirates of the Sulu Sea. A few years earlier, pure wanderlust had driven the former officer of the East India Company to leave England for Borneo. At the head of a small private army, Brooke helped the Sultan of Brunei put down a local revolt. As a sign of his gratitude, the sultan made him Rajah of Sarawak. With the weight of his considerable authority behind him the 'white rajah' - as Brooke became known - tried amongst other things to make the Sulu Sea safe for merchant vessels.
On nautical charts and in mariners' handbooks the light at Sir James Brooke Point is listed as a navigational aid. The township of Brooke's Point on the cape at the northern end of Ipolote Bay is, however, more important in terms of growing trade.

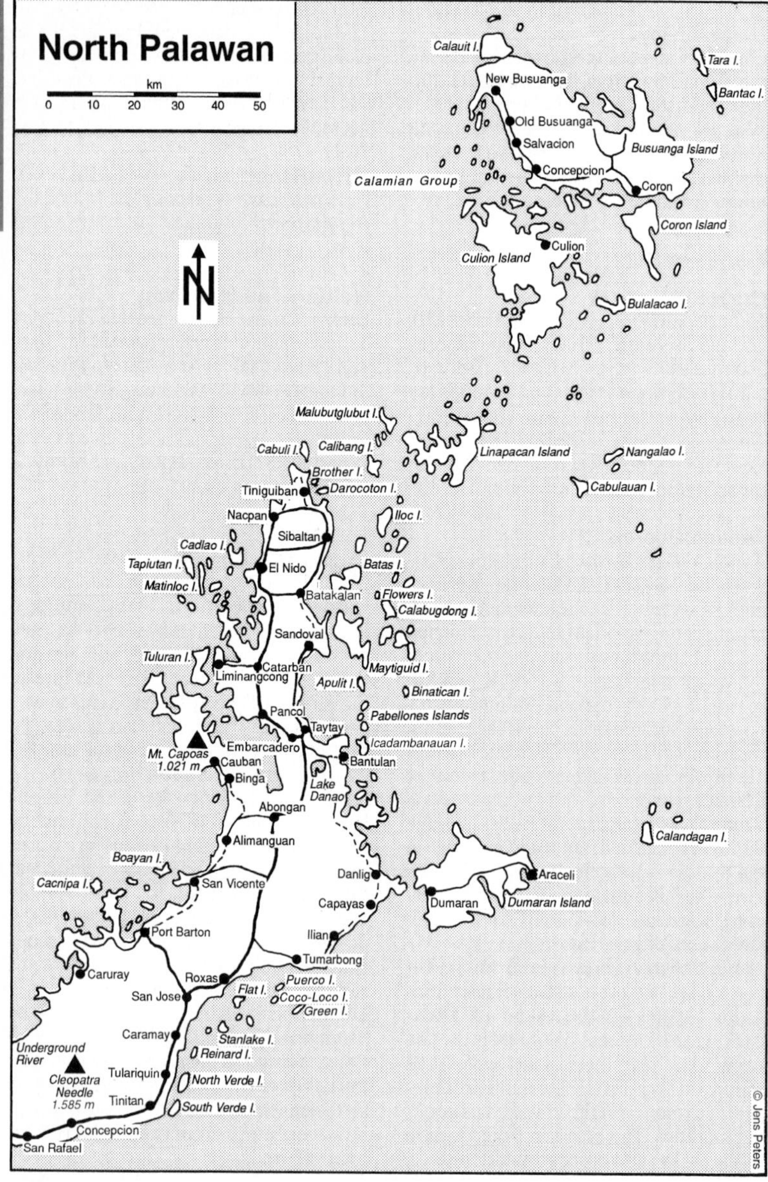
North Palawan
km
0 10 20 30 40 50
Calauit I.
New Busuanga
Tara I.
Bantac I.
Old Busuanga
Salvacion
Busuanga Island
Concepcion
Calamian Group
Coron
Coron Island
Culion
Culion Island
Bulalacao I.
Malubutglubut I.
Cabuli I.
Calibang I.
Linapacan Island
Nangalao I.
Brother I.
Tiniguiban
Darocoton I.
Cabulauan I.
Nacpan
Iloc I.
Sibaltan
Cadlao I.
Tapiutan I.
El Nido
Batas I.
Matinloc I.
Batakalan
Flowers I.
Calabugdong I.
Sandoval
Tuluran I.
Catarban
Liminangcong
Maytiguid I.
Apulit I.
Binatican I.
Pancol
Pabellones Islands
Taytay
Embarcadero
Icadambanauan I.
Mt. Capoas
1.021 m
Cauban
Bantulan
Binga
Lake Danao
Abongan
Alimanguan
Calandagan I.
Boayan I.
Danlig
Araceli
Cacnipa I.
San Vicente
Dumaran
Dumaran Island
Capayas
Port Barton
Ilian
Tumarbong
Caruray
Roxas
Puerco I.
Flat I.
San Jose
Coco-Loco I.
Green I.
Caramay
Stanlake I.
Underground River
Reinard I.
Cleopatra Needle
1.585 m
Tulariquin
North Verde I.
Tinitan
South Verde I.
Concepcion
San Rafael
© Jens Peters

Several km inland there is a range of forested mountains with peaks around 1500m. Mt Matalingajan, Palawan's highest mountain at 2086m, is roughly 25 km west of Brooke's Point.
About 10 km north-west of Brooke's Point, near Mainit, you could visit a small waterfall and hot sulphur springs, but missing them out would be no great loss. You can get there by tricycle (P50 one-way or P150 per day).

Places to Stay

Silayan Lodge. SR/DR/fan P100/150, SR/fan/bath P300, DR/fan/bath P350, SR/ac/bath P350, DR/ac/bath P450. Unpretentious, but clean rooms. Coffee shop.
Sunset Greenland Garden Lodge. SR/DR P100/200, SR/DR/fan/bath P350, SR/DR/ac/bath P500. Although basic, it passes muster. There is a restaurant, disco and quite extensive grounds.

Places to Eat

Most of the few restaurants in town close early at night, but the pleasant, half-open ***Islander*** on the main road serves very good Filipino dishes until 10pm. The food in the basic, clean ***Panciteria*** is tasty and worth the money.

Miscellaneous

Festival: Town Fiesta on 19 March.
Population: 8000.
Post: Post code: 5306.

Getting There & Away

Cagayan de Tawi-Tawi Island
Boat: Freighters occasionally sail from Brooke's Point to Cagayan de Tawi-Tawi Island (Cagayan de Sulu Island), where there are sometimes opportunities for onward travel to Jolo or Zamboanga via Pangutaran Island.

Puerto Princesa
Bus: Puerto Royale buses leave Puerto Princesa for Brooke's Point every 1½ hrs from 5am until 3pm (4½ hrs). Aircon Mic Mac Trail and Princess Transport buses leave in the morning.

Jeepney: Several jeepneys travel daily between Puerto Princesa and Brooke's Point leaving at various times in the early morning and forenoon (five hrs).

Ursula Island

Thousands of birds used to nest on beautiful Ursula Island, where they would return in swarms in the evening after foraging on other islands. However, the depredations caused by hunters with their shotguns have caused most birds to shift their nests, mainly to the faraway Tubbataha Reef. Ursula Island is uninhabited and there is no drinking water.

Getting There & Away

Boat: A Special Ride on an outrigger from Brooke's Point, Bataraza or Rio Tuba to Ursula Island costs at most P2500.

North Palawan

Roxas & Coco-Loco Island

Roxas is a quiet little place right by the sea. Fish and fruit are on sale at reasonable prices in the fair-sized market not far from the jetty. If you want to be dropped off on a desert island in the north of Palawan, you can get things like canisters, buckets and cookers in Roxas, although some equipment is now also available in Taytay and El Nido.
The wide sweep of the bay beyond Roxas contains several small islands worth seeing, including the palm covered Coco-Loco Island (Reef Island), with its white sand beach and offshore coral reef.

Places to Stay

Gemalain's Inn. SR/DR/fan P150/200, SR/DR/fan/bath P250. Very basic accommodation by the jetty.

EN-Jay's Pension House. SR/DR/fan P150/200. Basic, but clean rooms. Quiet location in the street across from the bus terminal.

Rover Pension House. SR/DR/fan/bath P200 and P450, SR/DR/ac/bath P650. The older building has basic rooms (each bath shared by two rooms), better ones in the newer building. It's only a few feet from the bus and jeepney terminal.

Retac Beach Resort. Cottage/fan/bath P350 and P450. Roomy cottages in beautiful, green surroundings with lots of tropical plants and flowers as well as a little orchid garden. Restaurant. About three km north of Roxas, a tricycle will take you there for P10.

Coco-Loco Island Resort, @. Cottage P400, cottage/fan/bath P790. Full board including transfer from and to Roxas costs P1400 per person. The only place on the island with a large number of cottages. Billiards, table tennis, boat trips (several days, with tents), kayaks, diving facilities (including courses), water skiing. Their pleasant restaurant has a thoughtfully prepared menu. Information can be obtained in Roxas at the bus terminal; in Puerto Princesa at the Deep Forest Garden Resort, Abueg Rd, Tel (048) 4333877.

Places to Eat

There are a few modest restaurants at the bus and jeepney terminal where you will be offered a limited choice of simple meals. The ***Tia-Ver Restaurant*** next to the Rover Pension House is a little bit better but you'll already find them putting up the chairs at 9pm.

Miscellaneous

Festivals: Town Fiesta on 14 and 15 March.

Population: 4000.

Post: Post code: 5308.

Getting There & Away

By Bus/Jeepney: It's about 200m from the bus and jeepney terminal to the jetty.

Coco-Loco Island

Boat: Every day between 4 and 6pm, the Coco-Loco Island Resort's outrigger returns to the island after buying supplies in Roxas (P175; 45 min). From December until June there may be another one or two departures. A Special Ride shouldn't cost more than P600.

The first boat from Coco-Loco Island to Roxas leaves at 7am.

Puerto Princesa

Bus: Puerto Royale buses leave Puerto Princesa for Roxas daily roughly every two hours between 5am and 4.30pm (P100; three hrs). Aircon buses also leave at 8am and 2pm. In addition, aircon minibuses leave roughly every hour (P150).

Jeepney: In the morning between 6 and 10am several jeepneys also make the run from Puerto Princesa to Roxas.

Port Barton

Port Barton is a small community on the picturesque Pagdanan Bay with a long, drawn-out beach.

There are several waterfalls in the beautiful countryside around Port Barton. Worth a special mention are those at Pamuayan, which you can reach in about 1½ hrs on foot: Leave Port Barton and head north. About halfway to Pamuayan a path, which looks like the driveway to a house set on its own, breaks off to the right leading to a river which is shallow enough to wade through. Stick close to the river until you come to the first waterfall; just a bit further upstream there is a second waterfall with three pools.

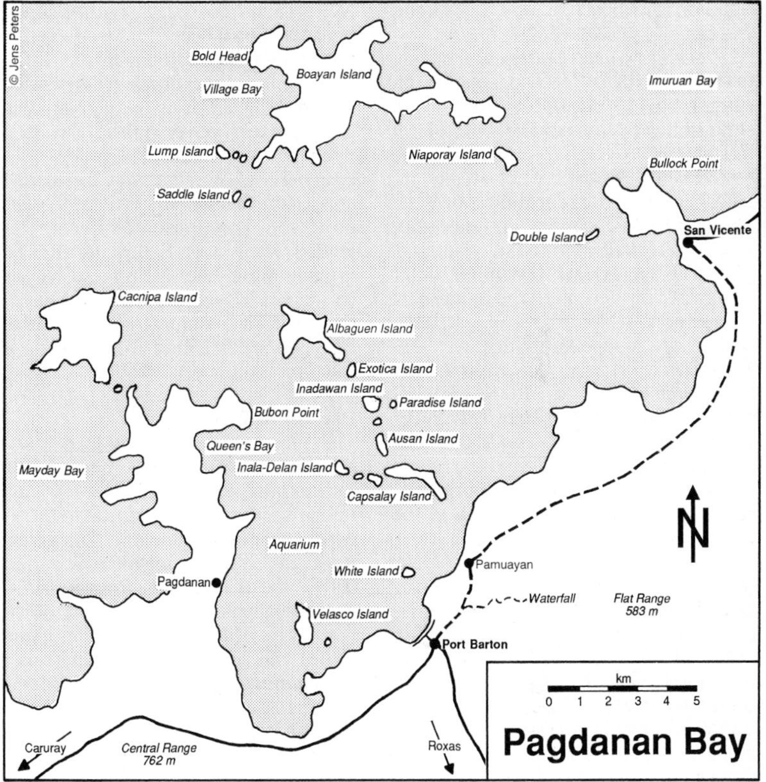

Outriggers can be hired in Port Barton to visit the nearby islands, some of which have strikingly beautiful white beaches. You can enjoy good snorkelling off Inadawan Island (formerly Tomas Tan Island) and in the so-called 'aquarium'. The colourful coral reefs off Exotica and Albaguin islands have unfortunately been largely destroyed by dynamite fishing. However, there is reason to hope that this kind of environmental banditry will soon be a thing of the past, as the authorities in Port Barton have promised to deal harshly with such criminals in future.

Places to Stay

Ausan's Cottages. SR/DR P200/250. Basic accommodation.

Cabungan Cottages. Cottage/bath P200 and P300, depending on size. Small, family-style place with garden grounds and three basic cottages reasonable for the money. Paddle boat.

Elsa's Beach Cottages. Cottage/bath P300 and P450. Pleasant accommodation with small but attractive cottages. Restaurant.

El Busero Inn, Satellite Tel 0985403876. SR/DR P200/300. Cottage/bath P500 to P700. Modest rooms and cottages right on the beach. Good restaurant. Diving.

El Dorado Sunset Cottages. Cottage/fan/bath P350 to P500, depending on furnishing. Comfortable wood and stone cottages. Immaculately run place. Restaurant.

Greenviews Resort, @. Cottage/fan/bath P500 to P700, depending on size. Neat, extensive garden grounds with attractive, well separated cottages. British management. Restaurant. A bit set apart, nestled into the north-east corner of the bay. You can get there over a narrow wooden bridge.

Swissippini Lodge & Resort, @. Cottage/bath P700 to P1.000, depending on furnishings and size. Tidy, nicely built cottages, some with fan. The pleasant, well-tended grounds have lots of plants. Good restaurant, billiards. Reservations in Puerto Princesa at the Moana Hotel, Tel (048) 4344753.

Around Port Barton

Paraiso Beach Resort, Albaguen Island, @. SR/fan P3600 and P3800, DR/fan P5000 and P5400, cottage/fan/bath P4000 and P5800 (two people). Includes breakfast and dinner. Neat rooms in the octagonal guesthouse and stone cottages. Attractive, well-maintained grounds with fine sandy beach and offshore coral reef. Peaceful, friendly, family-style atmosphere. Swiss management. Restaurant. Boat trips. Diving (courses available). Located about 30 min by boat from Port Barton.

Coconut Garden Island Resort, Cacnipa Island, Satellite Tel 098-5408129. SR/DR P360/540, cottage P570, cottage/bath P760 and P780. Long building with several rooms as well as cottages with various different sizes and furnishings. The Swiss owner Henry manages this attractive, quite large place with plants all around. It's located in the south-east of the island on a peaceful, white palm-lined beach with a superb house reef on a beautiful bay. Excellent for bathing. Good, inexpensive restaurant (Henry's the chef). This densely vegetated, natural island is an ideal place for a stopover on the way from Sabang to El Nido.

Every Tuesday and Friday between 9 and 10am the service boat MS *Sahra* goes from Port Barton to Cacnipa Island, as well as on Saturdays after the jeepney from Puerto Princesa has arrived; (P120 per person, 45 min); a Special Ride shouldn't cost more than P500. A Special Ride from Sabang to Cacnipa Island costs P2500.

Places to Eat

The places to stay mentioned above serve good and generous meals, eg the ***Swissippini***, where you can enjoy a few Italian specialities in addition to the inexpensive menu of the day. The village itself has a small, inexpensive eatery called the ***Evergreen Restaurant*** in Rizal St opposite the Petron petrol station. They offer good value Philippine dishes and seafood as does the excellent ***Bamboo House Restaurant*** in Ballesteros St.

The ***Chicago Sunset Water Hole*** bar belonging to the El Dorado Sunset Cottages resort serves a wide variety of cocktails.

Miscellaneous

Diving: Palawan Easy Diving has diving courses in German, English and French, plus snorkel trips, island hopping, water-ski and banca sailing. El Busero Diving offers amongst other things diving courses in German and English. At the Paraiso Resort on Albaguen Island diving courses are also available (Swiss diving instructor).

Money: There is no bank in Port Barton so take enough cash with you.

Population: 5000.

Post: Post code: 5309.

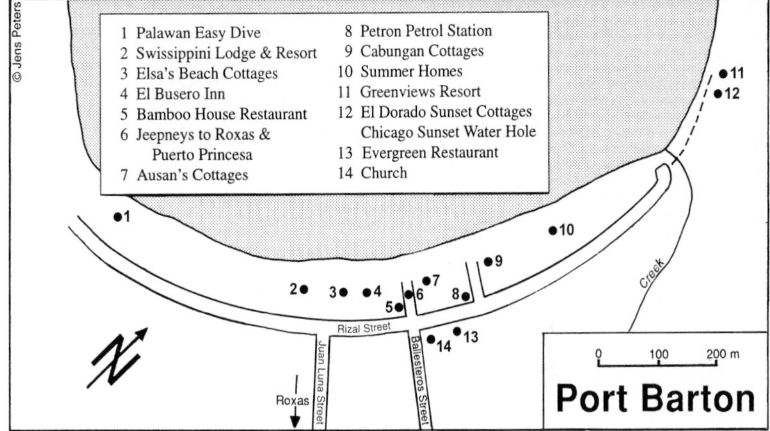

Getting Around

Boat: At the time of this book's preparation in 2004 the following prices were being charged (four/six passengers): Island Hopping P600/1000; San Vicente and Albaguin P600/1000; El Nido P2500/3500; Sabang P2500/3000. The charge for waiting time for the boat is P600 per day.

The boat trip from Port Barton to the Underground River at Sabang takes at least three hours. It is important to leave early or you'll not have much time to see the cave river.

Getting There & Away

El Nido

Boat: The boat route from Sabang and Port Barton to El Nido was discontinued owing to lack of demand. It costs between P2500 and P5000 to charter a boat, depending on the size (five hrs).

Puerto Princesa

Jeepney: At least one jeepney will make the run every day from Puerto Princesa to Port Barton, leaving between 7 and 9am from the jeepney terminal (four hours). You can also go to Roxas first by bus or jeepney and then catch a jeepney going to Port Barton.

A jeepney runs daily to Puerto Princesa from Port Barton at 5am and possibly at 10am; a Special Ride costs P2500.

Roxas

Jeepney: At least one jeepney leaves Roxas for Port Barton every day between 11am and 1pm (1½ hrs).

A jeepney leaves Port Barton for Roxas daily at 6am.

Sabang

Boat: A Special Ride with an outrigger from Port Barton to Sabang costs P2500 (2½ hrs).

San Vicente

San Vicente lies on a peninsula, about 18 km north-east of Port Barton. On the other side of the peninsula, Imuruan Bay with its long beach starts its sweep down to Alimanguan. The beach is actually 14 km long and is only interrupted once, at Bokbok Point. If you appreciate solitude and want to get away from the madding crowd, this is the place for you. A good idea for a day's outing would be a hike to the Little Baguio Waterfall, about six km inland from San Vicente.

Places to Stay

Caparii Beach Resort. SR/DR/fan/bath P1100, SR/DR/ac/bath P2200. Well-run resort two km outside of San Vicente. Restaurant, tennis court. Reservations in Puerto Princesa at the Caparii Booking Office at the airport, Tel (048) 4334868.

Getting There & Away

Port Barton

Boat: Now that the road from Port Barton to San Vicente has been closed for an indefinite period the only way to travel between them is by outrigger (P150 per person, P600 for the boat; one hr).

Roxas

Jeepney: A jeepney goes from Roxas to San Vicente two or three times daily (2½ hrs).

Taytay

Taytay is the old capital of Palawan. You can still visit the ruins of the fort built by the Spaniards in 1667. The church is about 300 years old. There is a hospital and numerous shops with a surprisingly wide range of goods.

Only a few km south of Taytay is Lake Danao, which is 62 hectares in size. It has small islands and is surrounded by unspoiled forest.

From Taytay you can go to the Pabellones Islands by outrigger, taking about one hour. These are three small islands with sheer limestone cliffs. The many caves and cracks yield birds' nests for birds' nest soup. Elephant Island has a lagoon which is good for snorkelling. A round-trip costs about P800.

The new Sandoval Airport is located at the northern end of Taytay Bay. It's expected to bring an enormous boom in tourism to the whole group of islands north-east of Palawan. Guests of the Club Noah Isabelle on Apulit Island are already being flown in here from Manila.

Agpay (Embarcadero) is about six km west of Taytay. In the rainy season if the road is blocked, outriggers go nearly every day, or at least twice a week, down the mangrove river to Malampaya Sound and on to Liminangcong.

Tricycles will take you between Agpay and Taytay for P20 per person or P80 for the tricycle; now and then jeepneys also travel the route.

Places to Stay

Taytay

Pem's Pension House. SR/DR P100/150, SR/DR/fan/bath P150/250, cottage/fan/bath P250 and P550. The place is no longer the newest and has basic rooms and reasonable cottages, the more expensive ones are roomier and better furnished. Good restaurant. Located on Taytay Bay near the fort.

Publico's International Guest House. EZ/DR/fan P150, SR/DR/bath P250. Basic rooms, OK for the money. It has a restaurant (order beforehand). The owner is a helpful soul and the courtyard is green and inviting. Located near the market.

Casa Rosa, Cellphone 0921-2120522. DR/fan P350, cottage/fan/bath P600 and P800 (TV). Two good rooms and pleasant cottages on the hillside in well-kept grounds with a beautiful view. Restaurant, boat trips.

Casa Rosa belongs to Thierry and Rose, the previous owners of the Flower Island Resort. If all goes to plan, they'll open the *Oasis Resort* at the beginning of 2005 in the north-west of Calabugdong Island, the larger island south of

Flower Island (P1000 to P1500 per person, full board).

Around Taytay

Dilis Beach Resort, Icadambanauan Island. Satellite Tel 098-5403971, @. SR/DR/fan/bath P800, cottage/fan/bath P1200. Spacious, thoughtfully furnished rooms in the main building standing on a hill, and pretty cottages on the 150m long, white sand beach. There's a beautiful view from the restaurant, which also has a veranda. The resort is located about one hour by boat (P500) east of Taytay. If the resort's own boat is not available, Pem's Pension House or the Casa Rosa will arrange transport.

Punta Negra Beach Resort, Maytiguid Island. Work in progress. A beautiful white beach on the south-east coast of Maytiguid Island in the north of Taytay Bay impressed the German, Norby, and Janet from the Philippines so much, they decided to build a beach resort there. And they're doing it with an obvious love for detail. At the moment, the choice is limited to a few very basic bamboo huts and two family-size tents. Price: P300 per person, including food. Cold drinks are available. Depending on the size, a boat from Taytay costs P1000 to P1500.

Places to Eat

There are several small restaurants and food stalls at the Taytay public market, where you can eat inexpensive Philippine food. The local dishes in ***Pem's Restaurant*** in the pension house of the same name are also quite cheap.

In a class of its own is the ***Casa Rosa Restaurant*** up on the hill, where you can savour the great pizzas and seafood. From here there's a beautiful view of Taytay Bay and the fort.

Miscellaneous

Festival: Town Fiesta on 3 and 4 May.

Information: The Casa Rosa Restaurant is the place to go for any questions or problems concerning tourism.

Population: 6000.

Post: Post code: 5312.

Getting There & Away

Air: A jeepney leaves from the pier at 6.30am for Sandoval Airport Cesar Lim Rodriguez at the northern end of Taytay Bay (1½ hrs; P150 to P200).

Asian Spirit, Cesar Lim Rodriguez Airport, Cellphone 0916-4528197.

Destination: Manila.

Seair, Cesar Lim Rodriguez Airport, Cellphone 0919-5536094, 0927-3747876.

Destination: Manila.

El Nido

Bus/Jeepney: Several jeepneys make the trip between El Nido and Taytay every day (P150; 3½ hrs) - at least during the dry season, and usually in the morning.

Jeepney/Boat: Daily except Saturday at 8am or 12 noon with a jeepney from El Nido to Batakalan (1½ hrs). Carry on by boat to Taytay (2½ hrs).

Boat: The trip from El Nido to Agpay/Taytay by outrigger boat costs P240 per person or P2400 for a Special Ride (4½ hrs). Departure times are irregular.

Puerto Princesa - Roxas

Bus: Puerto Royale buses leave Puerto Princesa every two hours from 5am to 3pm heading for Taytay via Roxas (from Puerto Princesa the journey takes six hrs; from Roxas 2½). Jeepneys might also make the trip.

Sandoval

Jeepney: A jeepney travels from Sandoval to Taytay twice daily, at around 7am and noon (two hrs). It's about a 15-minute walk from Sandoval Airport to Sandoval.

Apulit Island

In the middle of Taytay Bay, not quite 12 nautical miles north-east of Taytay itself, lies the idyllic Apulit Island. This island deserves the description of enchanting, it's like something out of the backdrop of an overly romantic South Pacific film. Only 1½ km long, Apulit is very narrow and not very high at the southern end, while a jagged 175m high ridge runs along the middle of the wider, northern end of the 'dragon island'. Drawn by its exclusive resort, white beaches, house reef and the Royalist Reef only half a nautical mile east, the island is a favourite with better-off holidaymakers and divers.

Places to Stay

Club Noah Isabelle, @. Comfortably furnished cottages, standing on piles in the sea with aircon and bath cost US$195 per person. For your money you get full board plus boat transfer, windsurfing, water ski and two dives a day. The club has issued strict environmental guidelines for the surrounding waters. Reservations in Manila: Tel (02) 8446688, Fax (02) 8452380.

Flower Island

Flower Island is a dream of a small island, around 50 km north-east of Taytay, with a white sandy beach and a largely intact reef.

Places to Stay

Flower Island Resort, Satellite Tel 0985409027. Cottage/bath P3000 per person, including full board. Roomy, pleasantly decorated cottages.

Getting There & Away

El Nido

Jeepney/Boat: Once or maybe twice a day, jeepneys make the trip from El Nido either right across Palawan or via Nacpan to Sibaltan on the east coast (P60; 1½ hrs). A boat from Sibaltan to Flower Island shouldn't cost more than P800.

There's another, possibly better, route via Batakalan: daily except Saturday at 8am or 12 noon with a jeepney from El Nido to Batakalan (1½ hrs; P90). A boat over to Flower Island costs P600.

The jeepney from Batakalan to El Nido leaves daily except Saturday at 6am. Leave Flower Island for Batakalan by 5am at the latest.

Sandoval

Boat: An outrigger from Sandoval Airport to Flower Island costs at least P1200 (one hr).

Taytay

Boat: An outrigger from Taytay to Flower Island costs P1000 to P1200 (three hrs).

Liminangcong

During the north-east monsoons, Liminangcong becomes a fishing centre. The place itself is surprisingly peaceful as there are practically no cars. Even after the 22 km long access road has been opened there is little likelihood of there being much traffic, apart from a few jeepneys. Many of the well-tended houses have little gardens in the front, with the edge of the property marked by quaint red toadstools made of coconut shells.

From Liminangcong you can go to the small offshore Saddle and Camago islands. You can also get boats to islands farther north. In addition, there are shipping connections to Manila at irregular intervals. Local shopkeepers often know more about departure times than the coastguard.

Places to Stay

Kaver's Inn. SR/DR P250. Good, solid building and the rooms are reasonable for the money The dark blue tub in the communal bath may come as a bit of a surprise.

Places to Eat

The big, two-storey ***Puerto Paraiso Restaurant*** opposite the Lady Bug disco has good Philippine food on the menu. Built right on the water, there is a gorgeous view of the offshore islands.

Getting There & Away

Agapay/Taytay
Boat: From Agpay several outriggers leave for Liminangcong weekly (P200). A Special Ride costs about P1500.

Jeepney: At least once a day there's a jeepney between Taytay and Liminangcong.

El Nido
Boat: A few outriggers make the trip daily from Liminangcong to El Nido (P120; two hrs). A Special Ride costs about P1000.

El Nido & Bacuit Archipelago

Picturesque El Nido is on a beautiful part of the coast, surrounded by rugged, steep limestone cliffs. The houses and streets are clean and well looked after. There are scarcely any vehicles. More and more travellers have been attracted to this beautiful little town in the north of the 'Last Frontier' (as Palawan is often called) since the roads and transport were improved. Inevitably, some of these people will have been disappointed, because the transport and accommodation require not only flexibility, but also a willingness not to expect too much.

Endangered Treasure

El Nido's most important attraction for tourists is provided by its living coral reefs and the multicoloured fish of the Bacuit archipelago. Consequently, if no-one manages to put an end to irresponsible fishermen dynamiting vast areas of the underwater world into oblivion, then tourism in El Nido has no chance of having a future. By the way, the boats that do the damage with dynamite are not from El Nido, but come from further afield to wreak havoc in other people's local waters.

When in El Nido you can take a trip to the fascinating islands of the Bacuit archipelago just offshore. Almost all of these rocky grey islands jut steeply out of the crystal-clear water and have small, sandy bays. Anyone who finds it too expensive to hire a boat for a day or more, or join an excursion group, but who wants to go snorkelling or to the beaches outside of El Nido, would be best advised to go to Corong-Corong Bay, about two km further south. The sunsets there are spectacular. From there it is possible to get a fisherman to drop you off for a few pesos on one of the sandy beaches on the south-west coast of the peninsula, for example on Lapus-Lapus Beach or Seven Commandos Beach.
You can also have a boat take you from El Nido to a beach or nearby island of your choice (don't forget to arrange when they are to pick you up again!). A few suggestions might be: Bocal Island (P350 per boat, up to four passengers), Paradise Beach (P350), Pasandigan Cove (P420; good for snorkelling), Dilumacad (Helicopter) Island (P450), Ipil Beach (P350), Lapus-Lapus Beach (P400), Inabuyutan Island (P600) and

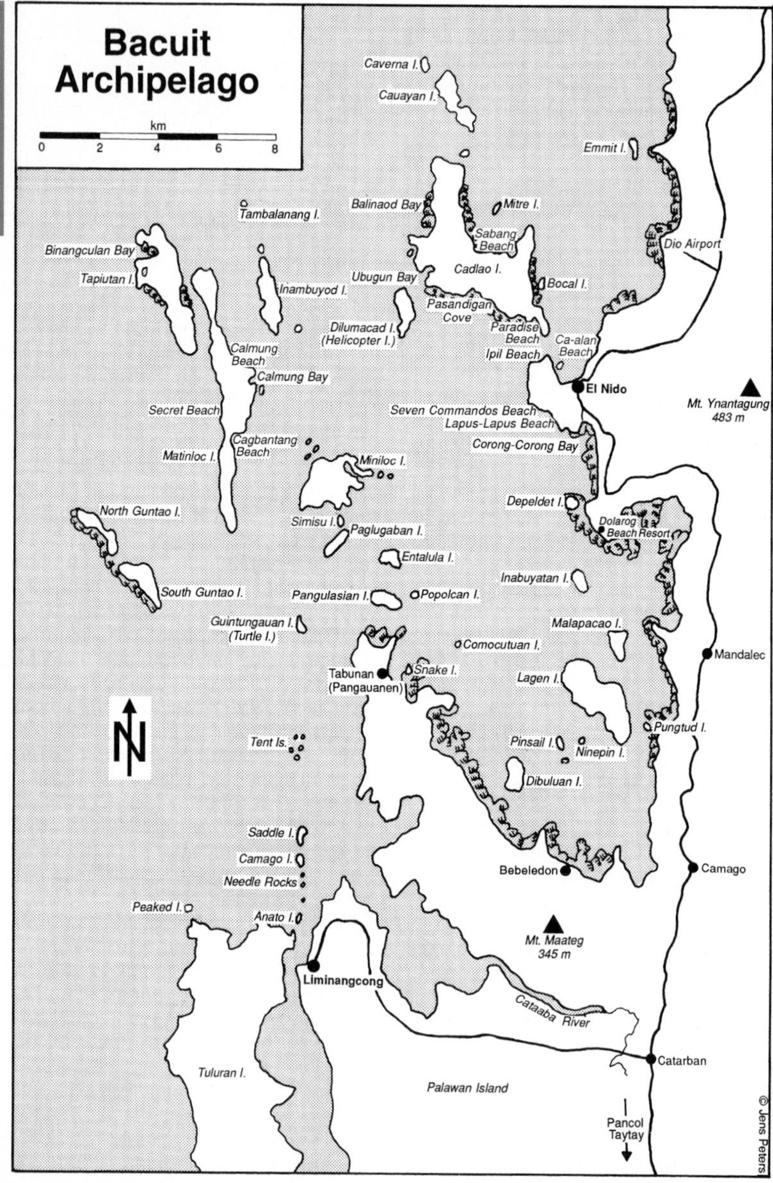
Bacuit Archipelago
km
0 2 4 6 8
Caverna I.
Cauayan I.
Emmit I.
Tambalanang I.
Balinaod Bay
Mitre I.
Sabang Beach
Dio Airport
Binangculan Bay
Tapiutan I.
Cadlao I.
Ubugun Bay
Bocal I.
Inambuyod I.
Pasandigan Cove
Dilumacad I. (Helicopter I.)
Paradise Beach
Ca-alan Beach
Calmung Beach
Ipil Beach
Calmung Bay
El Nido
Mt. Ynantagung 483 m
Secret Beach
Seven Commandos Beach
Lapus-Lapus Beach
Cagbantang Beach
Corong-Corong Bay
Matinloc I.
Miniloc I.
Depeldet I.
North Guntao I.
Simisu I.
Dolarog Beach Resort
Paglugaban I.
Entalula I.
Inabuyatan I.
South Guntao I.
Pangulasian I.
Popolcan I.
Guintungauan I. (Turtle I.)
Malapacao I.
Comocutuan I.
Mandalec
Tabunan (Pangauanen)
Snake I.
Lagen I.
Pungtud I.
Tent Is.
Pinsail I.
Ninepin I.
Dibuluan I.
Saddle I.
Camago I.
Needle Rocks
Bebeledon
Camago
Peaked I.
Anato I.
Mt. Maateg 345 m
Liminangcong
Cataaba River
Catarban
Tuluran I.
Palawan Island
Pancol
Taytay
© Jens Peters

Seven Commandos Beach (P400; excellent for snorkelling). Another excellent snorkelling area can be found at the little Simisu Island between the islands of Miniloc and Paglugaban.
You can find out more about these boat trips from Judith, who's Swiss, in the El Nido Boutique. She also organises a variety of whole-day island-hopping tours (9am to 4pm, P400 and P450 per person, including a barbecue lunch).

Islands of the Bacuit Archipelago

Cadlao Island is the biggest, and at almost 600m, also the highest island in the Bacuit archipelago. Its massive cliff face, in places covered with thick green vegetation, is riddled with caves and fissures. Cadlao is also known as Bird Island.

Miniloc Island, south-west of El Nido, is the island where the well-known Miniloc Island Resort is located (only open to residents). The deeply indented coast a little to the north of this establishment leads to a beautiful lagoon in the island's interior which is only accessible by boat. There are said to be barracuda in the deep centre part of the lagoon, which could possibly be dangerous to snorkellers. Turtles have also been occasionally sighted there. The smaller Small Lagoon is just to the north, from where you can swim to the adjoining Secret Lagoon.

Matinloc Island has numerous little bays along its long coast, with sandy beaches and corals well worth seeing. Calmung Bay on the east side of the island is worth a mention, as well as the Secret Beach on the west coast.

Tapiutan Island runs for half of its length almost parallel and fairly closely to Matinloc Island. On this part of the island there is an attractively situated beach with a reef well suited for snorkelling. The extremely picturesque Binangculan Bay in the north-west of the island has a beach with some vegetation. Occasionally, sailboats drop anchor here. The cliffs sticking out to the south of the bay signal one of the best diving areas in the waters around El Nido. There are several tunnels, archways and fissures that can be swum through; turtles, groupers and barracudas are quite common.

North Guntao Island is the most westerly island of the archipelago. The climb to the top is rewarded with a breathtaking panorama. The little beaches on the west coast and at the south tip of the island are suitable for snorkelling breaks.

Pangulasian Island has a long, white sand beach and is, unlike most of the islands in the archipelago, flat in places and covered with thick vegetation. The expensive Pangulasian Resort used to be located here, but it burnt down in 1999.

Malapacao Island lies just off the coast of Palawan in the south-east of the Bacuit archipelago and surely counts as one of the Gardens of Eden of this group of islands. Coming from the north, Malapacao can be recognised by its two striking giant rock-faces standing sentry at both ends of a flat section of the island, overgrown with palms and other tropical plants on a beautiful beach. Here you will find the little resort called Malapacao Island Retreat & Spa. The once superb resort of Marina del Nido on its palm-lined, white sand beach on the east coast of the island is unfortunately falling to pieces and is temporarily no longer inhabitable.

Inabuyatan Island is another one of the South Seas dream islands in the archipelago. There's no mistaking its steep cliffs rising straight out of the

Getting There & Away
1 Petrol Station
3 Seair
25 Bus & Jeepney Terminal
26 Lio Airport (6 km)
33 Island Transvoyager

Places to Stay
5 Bayview Inn
9 Marina Garden Beach Cottages
10 Og's Lodging House
13 Rico's Beach Cottage
14 Gloria's Beach Cottages
15 Dara Faye Beach Cottages
16 Tandikan Cottage
17 Rosanna's Cottages
18 Lally & Abet Beach Resort
22 El Nido Plaza Cottages
28 Austria's Guesthouse
43 Cliffside Cottages
44 Lualhati Cottage

Places to Eat & Entertainment
2 JND's Restaurant
3 Artcafé
4 Shipwrecked
5 Seaside Restaurant
6 Vicenta's Eatery
7 Blue Karrot Bar
10 Marbers Restaurant
11 Bom Disco
12 Ric Sons Restaurant
19 Hard Rocks Café
21 Squidos Restaurant
28 Austria's Restaurant
31 Florit's Restaurant
34 Comprendio Eatery
39 Mago's Restaurant
41 Elm St Café & Restaurant

Miscellaneous
3 El Nido Boutique
8 El Nido Souvenir Shop
12 Supermarket
13 Ocean Quest Dive Center
20 Nharcelle's Boutique
23 Old Market
24 Palawan Divers
27 Fish Market
29 FU Store
30 Tourist Office
32 Globe Telecom
35 Saint Francis of Assisi Church
36 Post Office
37 Police Station
Town Hall
38 School
39 Market
40 Health Center
42 Cockpit

water; the southern tip is graced with a palm-fringed, white sandy beach.

Pinsail Island. From a distance, Pinsail Island looks like a modest lump of rock until you come to an opening in the cliffs which leads to a cathedral-like cave, impressively illuminated from above by shafts of sunlight.

Lagen Island is the largest island in the south-east of the archipelago and boasts the exclusive Lagen Island Resort. And this is meant literally: non-residents are barred from entering the premises.

Places to Stay

In El Nido itself there are around a dozen places offering basic accommodation, most of them in Hama St right on the beach curving along Bacuit Bay. Some places recently opened up about one km north of El Nido, on the long, deserted Ca-alan Beach, also known as Sunset Lovers Beach (where there's no electricity). They can be reached from El Nido by walking along the beach (past the cemetery).

El Nido

Austria's Lodging House, Real St. SR/DR/fan P150/200. Reasonable for the

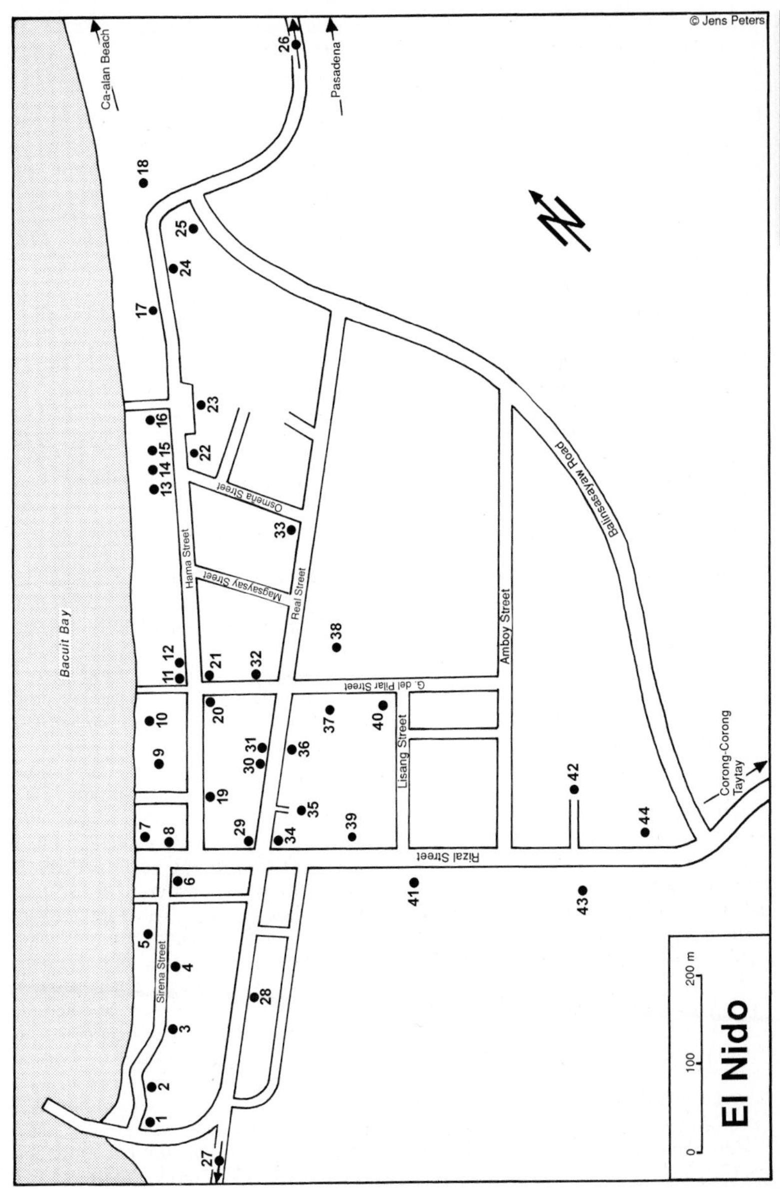
El Nido
© Jens Peters
Bacuit Bay
Ca-alan Beach
Pasadena
Corong-Corong
Taytay
Sirena Street
Hama Street
Osmeña Street
Magsaysay Street
Real Street
G. del Pilar Street
Lisang Street
Rizal Street
Amboy Street
Balinsasayaw Road
0
100
200 m

money. Family-style accommodation with garden. Restaurant. Two streets away from the sea.

Og's Lodging House, Hama St. SR/DR/fan/bath P150 to P800. Relatively new, three-storey building with nice rooms.

El Nido Plaza Cottages, Hama St. SR/DR/fan P250 and P300. Large place with rooms of various sizes. Restaurant.

Lualhati Cottage, Rizal St, Cellphone 0919-3196683. SR/DR P200, SR/DR/fan/bath P300. Peaceful, friendly accommodation with garden. Good value. Cooking facilities, breakfast is available. Located at the southern edge of town heading in the direction of Corong-Corong. Manding, the owner, gives half-hour massages for P150.

New Bayview Inn, Sirena St. SR/fan P300, DR/fan P400. Quite good rooms in a two-storey building with veranda overlooking the sea.

Marina Garden Beach Cottages, Hama St. SR/DR/fan P200/250, cottage/fan/bath P500. A more established place. Friendly, family-style atmosphere.

Tandikan Cottages, Hama St. SR/DR/fan/bath P300, cottage/fan/bath P500. Pleasant little place with tidy rooms and a choice of different sized cottages. Kitchen facilities are available.

Cliffside Cottages, Rizal St. Cottage/fan/bath P250 to P500, depending on size and location. Good cottages at the southern end of town with a huge cliff towering above.

Lally & Abet Beach Resort, Hama St, Cellphone 0919-5839110, @. SR/DR/fan/Bad P380, SR/DR/ac/bath P1650, cottage/fan/bath P880 to P990, depending on furnishings and location. A bigger establishment at the peaceful eastern end of the bay. Restaurant. Reservations in Manila: Tel (02) 7134019.

Dara Faye Beach Cottages, Hama St. SR/DR/fan/bath P400, cottage/fan/bath P500. Friendly little family place in a spruce garden.

Gloria's Beach Cottages, Hama St. SR/DR/fan/bath P400. Good, clean rooms, and a large veranda overlooking the water.

Rico's Beach Cottage, Hama St. SR/DR/fan P400 and P600. Rooms of varying quality, with the bigger, and better, ones on the upper floor.

Rosanna's Cottages, Hama St. Cottage/fan/bath P500. Peaceful little place. Pleasant atmosphere.

Around El Nido - Ca-alang Beach

Hadefe's Cottages. Simple cottages, some with bath, for P250. Use of kitchen possible.

Rhoma Beach Cottages. Cottage/bath P300. Straightforward cottages, right on the beach.

Shipwrecked Cottages, Cellphone 0916-5911563. Cottage/bath P350. Only two cottages, but they are beautiful.

Around El Nido - South

Magos Cottage, Corong-Corong. SR/DR P100/200. Pleasant, family-style accommodation with good-value rooms. Food should be ordered food beforehand. Paddleboat. Located 1½ km south of El Nido, at the northern end of Corong-Corong Bay.

Dolarog Beach Resort, Cellphone 0919-8674360, @. Cottage/bath P1200 and P1400. Full board is possible. Roomy, tastefully decorated cottages with big verandas and beautiful view of the offshore islands as well as the magnificent sunset. Friendly, inviting atmosphere. Good restaurant (home baked bread, Italian cooking; dinner P350), diving and windsurfing. The beach here is best described as second-rate, although there are some nice places to bathe. The resort is owned by Edo, an Italian, and Elena, his Filipina wife, and is not quite five km south of El Nido. It's about 1½ hours' walk along the Corong-Corong Bay beach (at low tide only) and through jungle, or half an hour by boat (P400, pick-up on request).

Around El Nido - Bacuit Archipelago
Miniloc Island Resort, Miniloc Island. Cottage/ac/bath US$228 per person, including three meals. Well-maintained place in front of a steep cliff wall on an attractive bay. Some of the cottages are built on piles in the water. Restaurant, diving and windsurfing, small beach. Reservations in Manila: Tel: (02) 8945644; Fax (02) 8103620.
Lagen Island Resort, Lagen Island. SR/DR/ac/bath US$228, cottage/ac/bath US$276. Prices are per person and include three meals. Comfortable, stylishly furnished rooms and cottages, some of which are built on piles in the water. Restaurant, swimming pool, kayaks, diving. Reservations in Manila: Tel (02) 8945644; Fax (02) 8103620.

Places to Eat

Surprisingly, El Nido has a few excellent restaurants, even if they don't always look too impressive from the outside.
Great for breakfast is the pleasantly run ***Artcafé*** above the El Nido Boutique; during the day you can also pop in for a selection of snacks, pizzas and tasty fruit juices. Open from 6.30am to 9pm.
Good food and value for money can be found at ***Vicenta's Eatery*** with its excellent fish menu. What's available depends on the catch of the day. Also on the recommended list is the modest-looking ***JND's*** near the jetty, where the restaurant doubles as the family living room. Your host, Nelda, cooks wonderfully, European-style if you want. It's a good idea to order your food here well beforehand. You won't have to pay much for good Philippine food at ***Magos Restaurant*** at the market on Rizal St and in the nearby ***Comprendio Eatery***.
European and Asian dishes are on the menu at ***Marbers Restaurant***, and at ***Squidos Restaurant*** a few feet away you'll find Filipino food with a hint of French to it.
After dinner many guests like to visit the tastefully decorated ***Shipwrecked Bar*** with its astounding variety of cocktails, and fine music, the ***Blue Karrot Bar*** at the beach, or the ***Hard Rocks Café*** (Videoke).

Miscellaneous

Diving: Snorkelling and diving equipment can be hired from the Ocean Quest Dive Center. Goggles and snorkel are also available at the El Nido Boutique (P125 per day).
Palawan Divers (Jean Marc, the Frenchman), Cellphone 0919-8546175 offer a four-day diving course for P13,000; one diving trip with two dives costs P1600 (including equipment, food and drink).
Festival: Town Fiesta from 15 to 18 March. Mosquito Net Day on 5 December (unique fiesta involving a procession of people in costumes made of mosquito nets).
Hiking & Climbing: The El Nido Tour Guide Organisation has a programme of short hikes to various places: the lagoon on Cadlao Island as well as to the Makinit Hotspring and the Makalitkalit Waterfall. You have to be fit to make the climb up the El Nido Cliff, but the view from the top is well worth the effort. All tours are with a guide and some also include a barbecue lunch. Put your name down the day before in the El Nido Boutique.
Medical Services & Wellness: The small Health Center in Abdullah St carries out malaria testing.
Relaxing massages are available for P150 to P300 (depending on how long they take) from Rose: Cellphone 0919-4533095.
Money: There is neither a bank nor a moneychanger in El Nido. The best they will do is change cash US dollars (El Nido Boutique) and travellers cheques

(FU Store), albeit at an unfavourable rate. So, remember to bring enough pesos! You might also try to get a cash advance on one of the widely accepted credit cards at the El Nido Boutique (for a 15% fee).
Online: May soon be available at Globe Telecom, Abdulla St.
Post & Telephone: The small post office in Real St, just round the corner from the town hall and police station, is only open sporadically.
You can make phone calls at Globe Telecom, Abdulla St.
Post code: 5313.
Tourist Office, Real St (across from the post office).

Getting Around

Boat: It costs around P900 to P1200 per day to hire a boat, including petrol, eg at Vicenta's Eatery and the El Nido Boutique which also has lists of various tours available. A paddleboat costs P100/day, eg at Ric Sons Restaurant.
Motorcycle: Clifford's Jr Restaurant hires out bikes (125 cc) for P800 a day.
Tricycle: Within the town one journey costs P3 per person, to Corong Corong P5. A tricycle to the airport costs P150 for two passengers.

Getting There & Away

By Air: The small Dio Airport is about four km north of El Nido right on the coast. Tricycles go into town after the arrival of a scheduled flight (P150; 15 min). A Special Ride by boat from El Nido to the airport costs P200.
Island Transvoyager, Real St, on the corner of Osmeña St (White House).
Destination: Manila.
Seair, Artcafé, Sirena St, Cellphone 0918-5066123.
Destinations: Cuyo (via Puerto Princesa), Busuanga, Manila, Puerto Princesa.
By Boat: Almost all the Atienza Shipping Lines and San Nicolas Lines ships are old and rickety freighters, and the trip is only for the adventurous! It is possible that they will soon no longer be allowed to carry passengers. In El Nido they anchor in the bay, and freight and passengers are taken onshore by outriggers.
Atienza Shipping Lines, Malapacao Booking Office, Sirena St.
Destinations: Coron/Busuanga, Manila.
San Nicolas Lines, on the street behind Austria's Lodging House.
Destinations: Coron/Busuanga, Manila.

Busuanga/Coron

Air: Seair flies three times weekly from Busuanga to El Nido and vice versa (P2100; 30 min).

Boat: From Coron to El Nido on Tuesday and Thursday with Atienza Shipping Lines and Friday with San Nicolas Lines (nine hrs).

Cuyo

Air: Seair flies two times weekly from Cuyo to El Nido and vice versa (via Puerto Princesa).

Flower Island

Boat/Jeepney: First take a boat from Flower Island to Batakalan, leaving by 5am at the latest (P600 for the boat). The jeepney leaves Batakalan for El Nido daily except Saturday at 6am (P90; 1½ hrs).

Port Barton - Sabang

Boat: The boat route from Sabang and Port Barton to El Nido was discontinued owing to lack of demand. It costs about P3000 to P5000 to charter a boat from Port Barton to El Nido, depending on the size; five hrs to Port Barton, eight to Sabang.

Puerto Princesa

Air: Seair flies three times weekly from Puerto Princesa to El Nido and vice versa (P1700; 45 min).

Bus: At least one bus of the companies Eulen Joy Bus Line or Sweety Bus Line goes daily from Puerto Princesa to El Nido (P300; eight hrs). Departure from El Nido for Puerto Princesa at 8am.
Puerto Royale buses leave in the morning from Puerto Princesa to Taytay (six hrs). From Taytay to El Nido continue with a jeepney.

Jeepney: At least one jeepney leaves Puerto Princesa daily in the early morning for El Nido (P300; nine hrs - it's a long, hard, sometimes dusty trip!).

Taytay
Bus/Jeepney: One or two buses as well as several jeepneys run between Taytay and El Nido daily - at least in the dry season (P150), taking two hrs (bus) or three hrs (jeepney). Departure either in the forenoon (if there are enough passengers) or in the early afternoon.
Note: The track from El Nido via Taytay to Roxas is very dusty in parts; you would be well advised to take along a rag to put over your mouth as a mask.

Boat/Jeepney: An outrigger from Agpay near Taytay to El Nido costs P2400. Trip takes 4½ hrs.
Now and then boats also make the trip from Taytay to Batakalan and Sibaltan on the east coast of north Palawan (taking 2½ to 3½ hrs). From there you can carry on by jeepney, cutting straight across Palawan or via Nacpan to El Nido (1½ hrs).

Calamian Group

The northernmost part of Palawan consists of the Calamian Group, whose main islands are Busuanga, Culion and Coron. The improvements made to the travel links with other islands and towns, together with the expansion in overnight accommodation, have brought about a modest upsurge in tourism in this beautiful island world. But so far people still live mostly from fishing and selling *kasoy* (cashew nuts), which are mainly harvested on Busuanga and Culion.
The identical names of some of the towns and islands can certainly give the newcomer a headache. For example, there's the island of Busuanga with the towns Old Busuanga, New Busuanga and Coron. South of the town of Coron you can see the island of Coron in the east part of Coron Bay. To the west of the island of Coron the island of Culion is home to the town of Culion. Clear as mud, isn't it?

Busuanga Island

Busuanga is the largest island in the Calamian Group. A partly surfaced road runs from Coron through Concepcion, Salvacion, Old Busuanga and New Busuanga to Quezon. The amount of traffic on the roads is minimal. In the forenoon, two rickety buses and a few jeepneys leave Coron for Salvacion, returning the next morning. That makes Busuanga an ideal spot for nature lovers and hikers.
Located in the centre of the island is the Yulo King Ranch, said to be one of the largest cattle stations in Asia.

Getting There & Away

By Air: Tiny Francisco Reyes Airport (Busuanga Airport) is south of Decalachao in the north of Busuanga. Asian Spirit and Seair aircraft land and take off from there. Several resorts, for example, Club Paradise, pick up their guests with their own vehicles, otherwise all the jeepneys operated by the airlines go to Coron (P150; 45 min to 1½ hrs, depending on time of year). A Special Ride costs P1200. A roof seat guarantees an uninterrupted view of the magnificent scenery.

On the outskirts of Coron, at Coron Airport behind the Kokosnuss Garden Resort, Pacific Airways flights leave and arrive on a daily basis. It's not quite one km from there to the market in the centre of town, and a tricycle costs P5. Another airstrip is available near Old Busuanga in the north-west of the island. The occasional charter flight will arrive or leave from there.
Asian Spirit, National Highway, Coron.
Destination: Manila.
Pacific Airways, Airport Coron.
Destination: Manila.
Seair, Coron Tours, Real St, Coron.
Destinations: El Nido, Manila, Puerto Princesa.

By Boat: The wharf is in Tagumpay, which belongs to Coron, and is not quite three km south-east of the town centre. For P10 per person you can take a tricycle.
Atienza Shipping Lines, Tagumpay Pier.
Destinations: El Nido, Manila.
San Nicolas Lines, Tagumpay Pier.
Destinations: El Nido, Manila.
WG & A, Real St, Coron.
Destinations: Manila, Puerto Princesa.

Coron

The small town of Coron is the second largest community on Palawan. The fishing and trading centre of the Calamian Group, it has a market, a fishing school, a hospital, a discos and several shops. Many of the houses here are built on piles in the sea. There are a few more shops and simple restaurants at the wharf in Tagumpay.
A road leads from Tagumpay to the village of Makinit, four km away. From there it's another 500m to the Makinit Hot Spring (41°C!). Admission P30.
Concrete steps lead from Neuva St up to Mount Tapyas, a hill which provides a beautiful view of Coron Bay. The best time is in the late afternoon, in time for the sunset. It takes about half an hour to get to the top, and it wouldn't harm to take something to drink with you.
It's a bit more difficult to climb the 640m high Mt Tundulara. You have to be fit to make it up there. A path behind the Kokosnuss Garden Resort will take you to the summit. They are happy to give information at the resort, and will even provide a guide if you want one.

Places to Stay

Coron
Sea Coral Lodge. SR/DR/fan P100/200. Straightforward place to stay on the main road not far from the town centre.
L & M Pe Sea Lodge, Cellphone 0918-5145254, @. SR/DR/fan/bath P250 to P350. Pleasant accommodation, with small, but quite good rooms for the money. Attractive building also built on piles over the water, with a cosy veranda. At the market. Popular restaurant, boat trips, beach camping, safari tours, diving.
Darayonan Lodge, National Highway, @. SR/DR/fan P300/500. Peaceful place with cosily decorated rooms and garden. Restaurant. Reservations in Manila: Tel (02) 8232752; Fax (02) 8210163.
Coron Reef Pension House, Cellphone 0919-5933575, @. SR/DR/fan P300, SR/DR/fan/bath P500, SR/DR/ac/bath P600. Small, family place. The rooms are basic but OK. They will prepare food if asked.
Sea Dive Resort, @. SR/DR/fan/bath P350, SR/DR/ac/bath P450. Pleasantly furnished rooms in a building standing on piles in the water. Good restaurant, diving, kayaks. Reservations in Manila: Tel (02) 8040331.
Bayside Divers Lodge. SR/DR/fan P150/250, SR/DR/fan/bath P450, SR/DR/ac/bath P650. Reasonable rooms, some of which are a bit dark however. Good restaurant, large veranda with sea

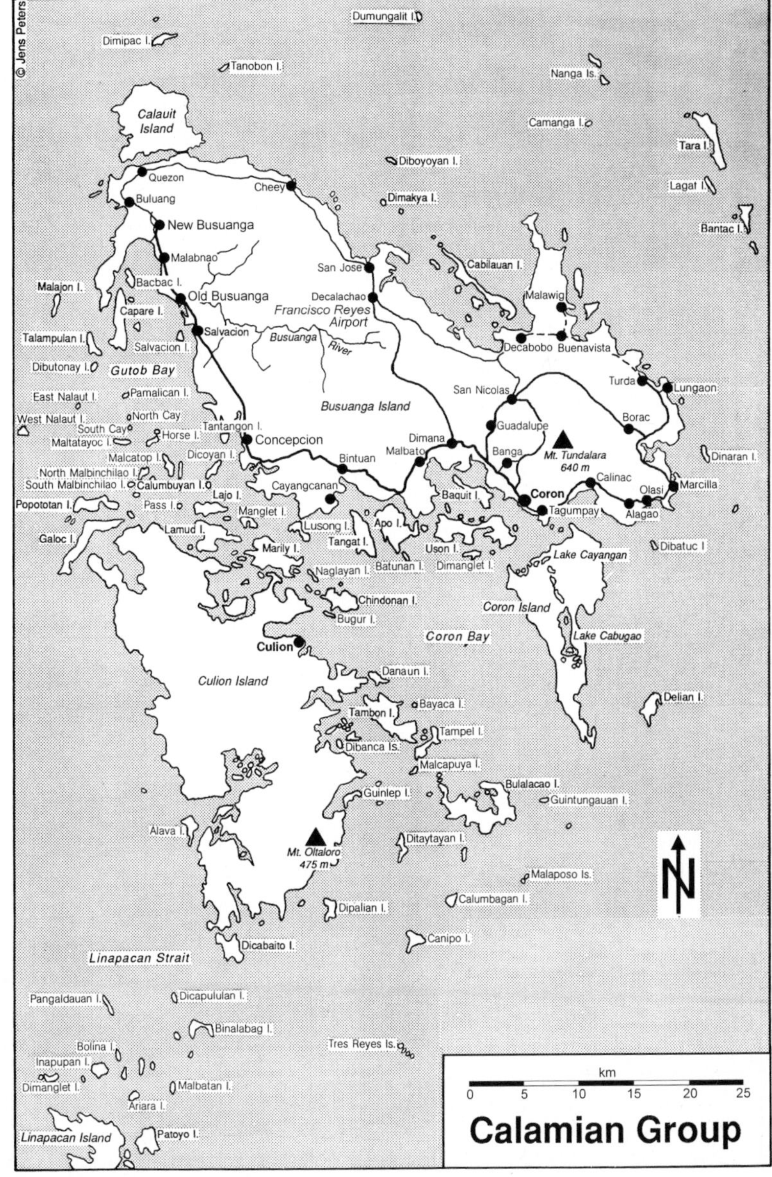
© Jens Peters
Dumungalit I.
Dimipac I.
Tanobon I.
Nanga Is.
Calauit Island
Camanga I.
Tara I.
Diboyoyan I.
Quezon
Cheey
Lagat I.
Buluang
Dimakya I.
New Busuanga
Bantac I.
Malabnao
San Jose
Cabilauan I.
Malajon I.
Bacbac I.
Old Busuanga
Decalachao
Malawig
Capare I.
Francisco Reyes Airport
Salvacion
Busuanga River
Talampulan I.
Salvacion I.
Decabobo
Buenavista
Dibutonay I.
Gutob Bay
Turda
Lungaon
San Nicolas
East Nalaut I.
Pamalican I.
Busuanga Island
Borac
West Nalaut I.
North Cay
South Cay
Tantangon I.
Guadalupe
Maltatayoc I.
Horse I.
Concepcion
Dimana
Mt. Tundalara 640 m
Banga
Dinaran I.
Malcatop I.
Dicoyan I.
Malbato
Bintuan
North Malbinchilao I.
South Malbinchilao I.
Calumbuyan I.
Cayangcanan
Calinac
Marcilla
Lajo I.
Baquit I.
Coron
Olasi
Popototan I.
Pass I.
Manglet I.
Tagumpay
Alagao
Lusong I.
Apo I.
Lamud I.
Tangat I.
Galoc I.
Marily I.
Uson I.
Dibatuc I.
Lake Cayangan
Batunan I.
Dimanglet I.
Naglayan I.
Chindonan I.
Coron Island
Bugur I.
Coron Bay
Lake Cabugao
Culion
Danaun I.
Culion Island
Bayaca I.
Delian I.
Tambon I.
Tampel I.
Dibanca Is.
Malcapuya I.
Bulalacao I.
Guinlep I.
Guintungauan I.
Alava I.
Ditaytayan I.
Mt. Oltaloro 475 m
Malaposo Is.
N
Calumbagan I.
Dipalian I.
Canipo I.
Dicabaito I.
Linapacan Strait
Pangaldauan I.
Dicapululan I.
Binalabag I.
Tres Reyes Is.
Bolina I.
Inapupan I.
Dimanglet I.
Malbatan I.
Ariara I.
Linapacan Island
Patoyo I.
km
0
5
10
15
20
25
Calamian Group

Palawan

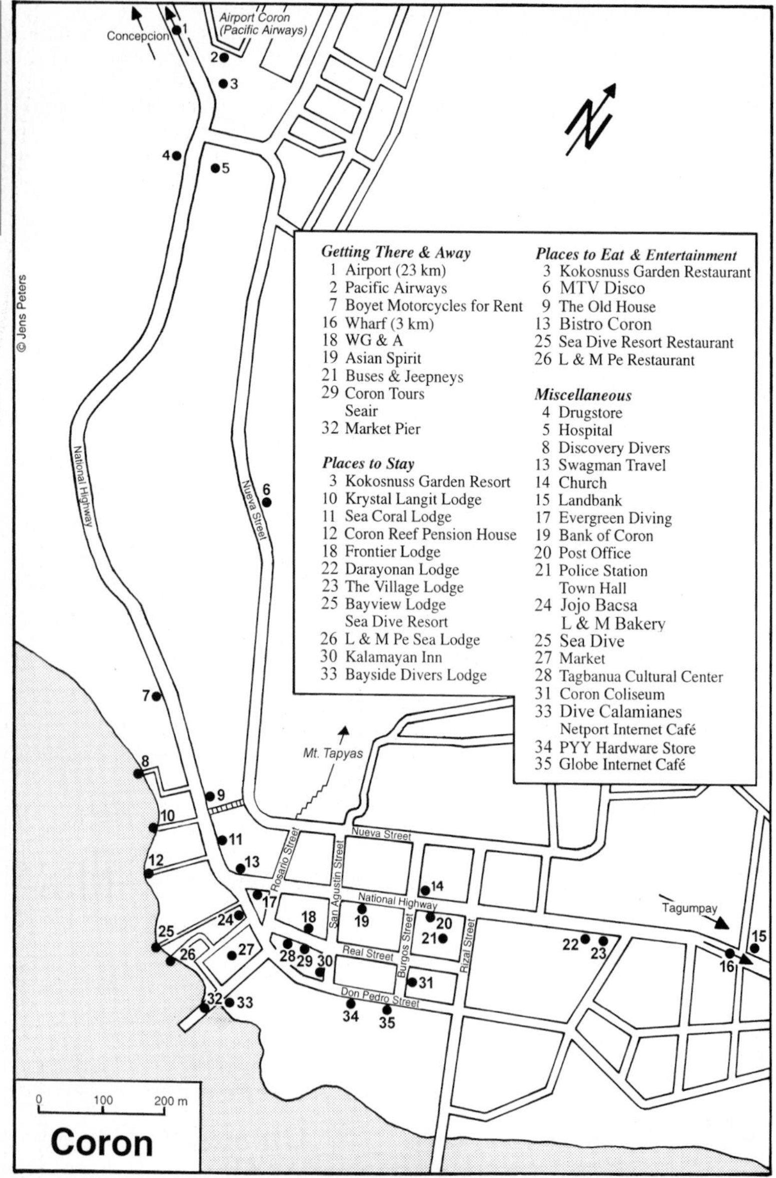

Concepcion
Airport Coron
(Pacific Airways)
Getting There & Away
1 Airport (23 km)
2 Pacific Airways
7 Boyet Motorcycles for Rent
16 Wharf (3 km)
18 WG & A
19 Asian Spirit
21 Buses & Jeepneys
29 Coron Tours
Seair
32 Market Pier
Places to Stay
3 Kokosnuss Garden Resort
10 Krystal Langit Lodge
11 Sea Coral Lodge
12 Coron Reef Pension House
18 Frontier Lodge
22 Darayonan Lodge
23 The Village Lodge
25 Bayview Lodge
Sea Dive Resort
26 L & M Pe Sea Lodge
30 Kalamayan Inn
33 Bayside Divers Lodge
Places to Eat & Entertainment
3 Kokosnuss Garden Restaurant
6 MTV Disco
9 The Old House
13 Bistro Coron
25 Sea Dive Resort Restaurant
26 L & M Pe Restaurant
Miscellaneous
4 Drugstore
5 Hospital
8 Discovery Divers
13 Swagman Travel
14 Church
15 Landbank
17 Evergreen Diving
19 Bank of Coron
20 Post Office
21 Police Station
Town Hall
24 Jojo Bacsa
L & M Bakery
25 Sea Dive
27 Market
28 Tagbanua Cultural Center
31 Coron Coliseum
33 Dive Calamianes
Netport Internet Café
34 PYY Hardware Store
35 Globe Internet Café
National Highway
Nueva Street
Mt. Tapyas
Rosario Street
San Agustin Street
Burgos Street
Rizal Street
Real Street
Don Pedro Street
Tagumpay
0 100 200 m
Coron

view, diving. Located at the market. Reservations can be made in Manila with Swagman Travel: Tel (02) 5266057, Fax (02) 5223663.
The Village Lodge, National Highway, Cellphone 0919-2221161. SR/ac P400, SR/DR/fan/bath P550, SR/DR/ac/bath P750. Family-style accommodation with spacious, well-kept, friendly rooms. Restaurant, garden. Reservations in Manila: Tel (02) 8063932.
Krystal Langit Lodge, @. SR/DR/fan P150/300, SR/DR/fan/bath P350, cottage/fan/bath P500 and P1000 (for up to five people). Modest, but pleasant, quiet place with wooden buildings standing on piles in the water. Small restaurant where they are glad to cook anything you want to order.
Kokosnuss Garden Resort, Cellphone 0919-7769544, @. Cottage/fan P300 to P500 (depending on size and furnishings), cottage/fan/bath P840, cottage/ac/bath P960 (electricity extra). Charmingly furnished cottages set in quiet grounds with a big garden and fountain. Full board is possible. Situated near the hospital about one km from the centre of town, it's only about 15 min on foot from Coron in the direction of the airport (or by tricycle for P5 per person). The management is German. They organise boat trips, motorbike tours, day trips, you name it. Reservations in Manila: Fax (02) 8040331.
Kalamayan Inn, @. SR/DR/ac P700/800, SR/DR/ac/bath P850/1000, including breakfast. OK rooms in a stone building in the centre of town. Good service. Restaurant.

Around Coron

Discovery Island Resort, Decanituan Island, about 10 minutes by boat from Coron, @. Cottage/fan/bath P500 to P1000. Pleasantly furnished cottages in a variety of different styles, each with a good view. The grounds are lavishly planted and the resort has a delightful, very quiet, secluded atmosphere about it. Restaurant, diving, kayaks, windsurfing. Check-in at Discovery Divers in Coron, Cellphone 0920-9012414. Reservations in Manila: Tel (02) 5756254.
Dive Link Resort, Uson Island, @. Cottage/fan/bath P1250 per person, including breakfast. Well-kept, peaceful location. Restaurant, swimming pool. About 15 minutes by boat from Coron. Reservations in Manila at Hotelmasters: Tel (02) 7516279, Fax (02) 7516278.

Places to Eat

A popular meeting place is the ***L & M Pe Restaurant*** with good-value Philippine and international food. In addition to other things on its menu, the ***Sea Dive Resort Restaurant*** serves steaks and great seafood, while in the ***Kokosnuss Garden Restaurant*** near the Coron airport tasty Philippine and European food is served.
Two popular meeting places are the ***Coron Bistro***, run by Bruno the Frenchman, and ***The Old House***, which is a cosy little restaurant, which is a good place to pop into for a late beer.

Miscellaneous

Diving: For many people diving is the only reason to go to Busuanga; the waters between Busuanga and Culion islands are simply a paradise for wreck explorers. In Coron you will be charged about P1000 per dive; day trips (P1400, with two dives) and diving courses (P10,000) are available as well as dives in the so-called Barracuda Lake, an inland lake on Coron Island.
Dive Calamianes, Bayside Divers Lodge, Cellphone 0927-5275799, @. Courses in Dutch, English and German.
Discovery Divers (Günter Bernert), Cellphone 0920-9012414, @. Courses in English, French, German and Tagalog.
Sea Dive, Sea Dive Resort, @. Courses in English.

Live-Aboard Dive Boats

Tartaruga Diving Safaris offer diving trips on their MY *Maribeth* in the island world of the Calamian Group and to Tubbataha Reef. The well-constructed wooden boat can accommodate up to eight people. Diving courses are possible. Contact in Coron at the Bayside Divers Lodge: ABC Dive Coron, @, (ask for Vera, Heinz or Georg), and Dive Calamianes.
The Kokosnuss Garden Resort offers two and three-day diving trips on the 22m MB *Kon-Tiki*.

Festival: Town Fiesta on 28 August.
Money: You would be advised to take as many pesos with you as you think you'll need. The money changer, National Highway at the corner of Rosa St, as well as most places offering accommodation will change cash US dollars, although at an unfavourable rate.
Changing travellers cheques can be a problem; try at the Kokosnuss Garden Resort, at Swagman Travel (who might give you a cash advance on your credit card as well), the PYY hardware store, or at the Landbank.
Online: Globe Internet Café, Don Pedro St, and Netport Internet Café at the Bayside Divers Lodge charge P60/hr.
Population: 9000.
Post & Telephone: Calls can be made by cellphone (Smart, and soon also with Globe).
Post code: 5316.
Travel Agency: Swagman Travel, National Highway, will get airline tickets, take care of visa extensions and is also an agent for various resorts.

Getting Around

Horseback Riding: The Horse Valley Horseback Riding Club about 1½ km north of Coron Town has about a dozen horses available for riding out. They charge P600 for a half day. Further information from Discovery Divers and the Kokosnuss Garden Resort.
Kayak: Sea Dive Resort hires out kayaks for P200 per day.
Motorcycle: Boyet Motorcycles for Rent charges P500 per day rental (125 cc). The Kokosnuss Garden Resort has a bigger machine available (200 cc, P800/day).
Tricycle: A trip within the town costs P5 per person, P10 to the wharf in Tagumpay.

Getting There & Away

Culion
Boat: Two or three big outriggers leave Coron (Tagumpay Pier) heading for Culion every day (P50; 1½ hrs).

El Nido
Air: Seair flies three times weekly from El Nido to Busuanga and vice versa (P2100).

Boat: From El Nido to Coron on Thursday and Saturday with Atienza Shipping Lines and on Sunday with San Nicolas Lines (nine hrs). The ships carry on to Manila. Departure from Coron to El Nido on Tuesday, Thursday and Friday.

Puerto Princesa
Air: Seair flies three times weekly from Puerto Princesa to Busuanga and vice versa, via El Nido (P2200).

Boat: From Puerto Princesa to Coron on Sunday with WG & A (P995; 13 hrs). The ship carries on to Manila. Departure from Coron to Puerto Princesa on Saturday.

Concepcion

This pleasant little community with only a few houses on a mangrove-lined

bay, is a good starting point for boat trips to the offshore islands in Gutob Bay. On the way out of town heading towards Salvacion, just off the road, there is a small waterfall with a natural pool where you can have a relaxing swim.

Places to Stay

Pier House. SR/DR/fan P200/300. This pleasant, quiet accommodation is right at the pier, and is run by a Swede, Michael. Restaurant (food should be ordered beforehand), boat trips to offshore islands.
Concepcion Divers Lodge. Cottage/fan P350 and P500. Basic, but reasonable cottages in a small garden at the pier. Use of the kitchen is possible. Boat trips (P500 to P800), diving.

Getting There & Away

Bus: Two buses leave Coron for Concepcion at around 10am (two hrs). From Concepcion to Coron the buses leave between 4 and 5am and sometimes even earlier.

Jeepney: A few jeepneys make the trip from Coron to Concepcion, but there is no precise timetable. From Concepcion to Coron, the jeepneys leave between 4 and 5am and sometimes even earlier.

Motorcycle: From Coron to Concepcion, the trip costs P500 to P800 by motorcycle.

Old Busuanga

The small town of Old Busuanga is at the mouth of the Busuanga River in the north-west of Busuanga Island. A long beach stretches south of the river mouth. A trip upriver in an outrigger is a wonderful way to experience nature and is highly recommended if you are staying in the area. Old Busuanga is also handy as a base for a short trip to Calauit Island.

Places to Stay

Las Perlas Beach Resort, @. Cottage/fan/bath P1800. Attractive, peaceful place under Swiss management. Restaurant, swimming pool. Reservations in Coron at Swagman Travel or Coron Tours.

Getting There & Away

Bus/Boat: To get from Coron to Old Busuanga, first take a bus or a jeepney to Salvacion, from there it is only a few minutes by outrigger to the beach. The bus leaves Coron around 10am.
The bus leaves Salvacion for Coron between 3.30 and 4.30am.

San Jose

For a long time, the north coast of Busuanga led a Cinderella existence as far as tourists were concerned, but now a few resorts have been established near San Jose on the white sand beach of Maricaban Bay.

Places to Stay

Maricaban Bay Marina-Resort, @. Cottage/ac/bath P5500 per person, including three meals. Amiably furnished cottages with and without aircon (same price). Very attractive place, under German management. Restaurant, floating bar, beautiful swimming pool, Hobie Cats, kayaks, windsurfing, diving, boat trips, sailing trips. Reservations in Manila at Euro-Pacific Resorts, Tel (02) 8384956, Fax: (02) 8384462.

Calauit Island

Large African animals are being raised on this small island, north of Busuanga Island. This experiment, which started in 1977 with eight African species and was carried on for 10 years initially in strict seclusion, can now be pronounced a success. Almost 500 African wild animals, including giraffes, zebras and ga-

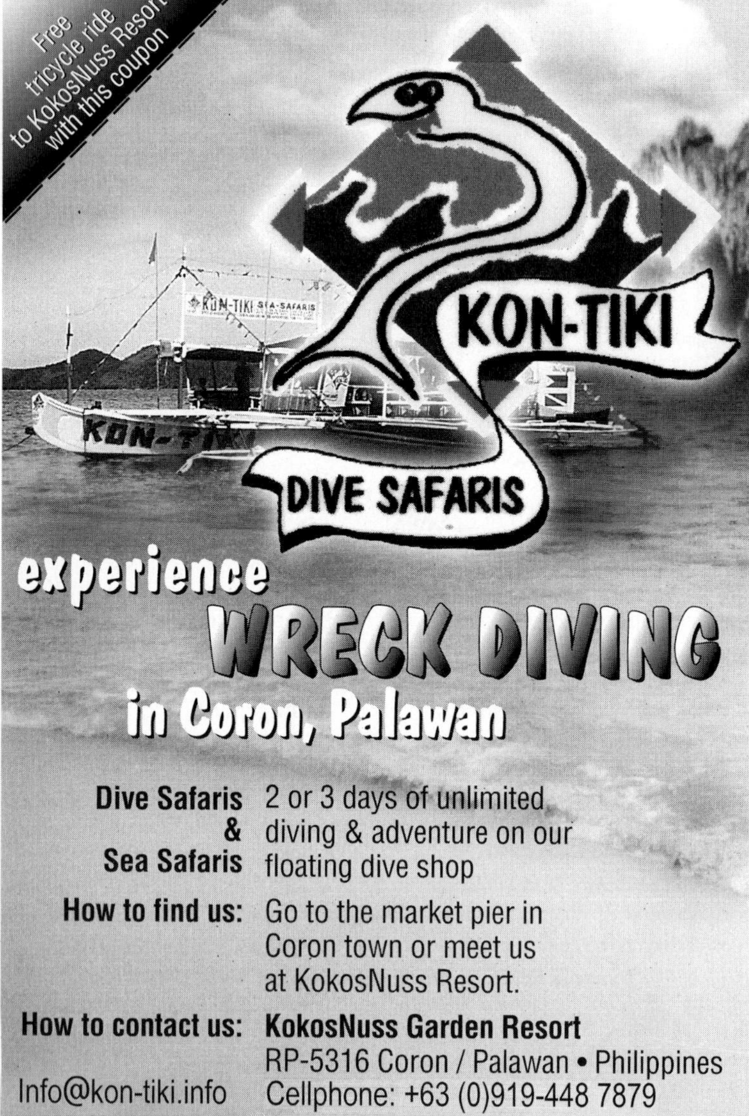
Free
tricycle ride
to KokosNuss Resort
with this coupon
KON-TIKI
DIVE SAFARIS
experience
WRECK DIVING
in Coron, Palawan
Dive Safaris & Sea Safaris
2 or 3 days of unlimited diving & adventure on our floating dive shop
How to find us:
Go to the market pier in Coron town or meet us at KokosNuss Resort.
How to contact us:
KokosNuss Garden Resort
RP-5316 Coron / Palawan • Philippines
Info@kon-tiki.info
Cellphone: +63 (0)919-448 7879
www.kon-tiki.info
Cellphone: +63 (0)919-776 9544

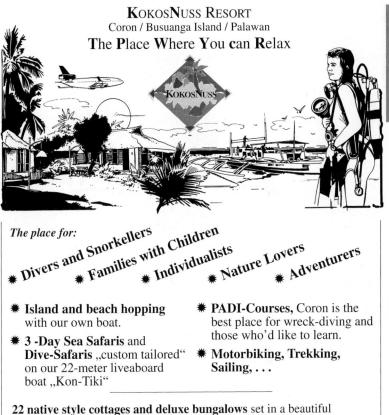

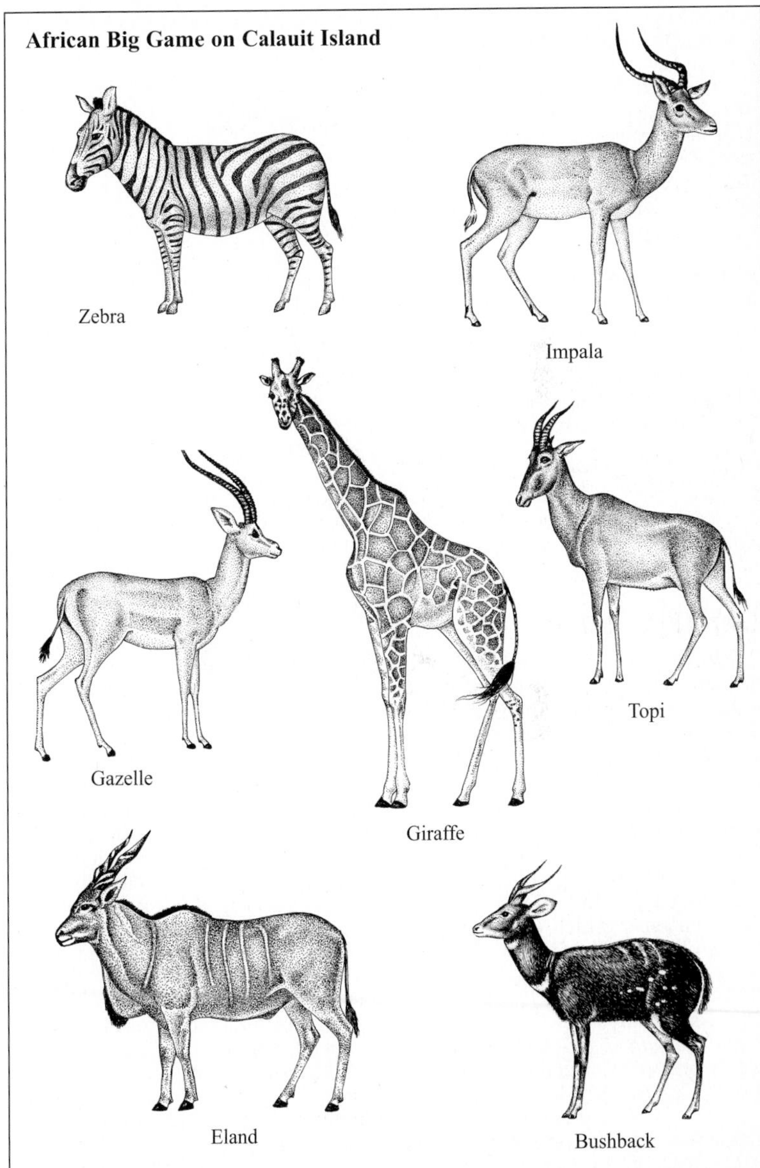
African Big Game on Calauit Island
Zebra
Impala
Gazelle
Giraffe
Topi
Eland
Bushback

zelles, live together with rare Philippine animals such as the mouse deer, bear cat and Philippine crocodile in the 3700-hectare large Calauit Island Wildlife Sanctuary. Visitors are welcome. The manager is happy to drive guests around the national park in his truck. He charges P600 per group and gets right up close to the animals. Admission costs P300 (P100 for Filipinos).

Getting There & Away

Bus: The most comfortable way to travel is by chartered minibus (FX) from Coron to Quezon (there and back P2500), and from there by boat across to Calauit Island (P300). Vehicle hire from Jojo Bacsa next to the L & M Bakery.

Boat: A big outrigger from Coron to Calauit Island and back costs P3500 and can be booked at the L & M Pe Sea Lodge and elsewhere. It takes four hrs one-way.

Dimakya Island

There is a group of beautiful little rocky islands north of Busuanga Island, partially covered with various kinds of vegetation. If palms grew there, they would be veritable treasure islands. One of them is Dimakya Island. It is surrounded by a magnificent coral reef and boasts a beach with blindingly white sand which makes a seductive contrast to the turquoise, crystal clear water. This island is home to the exclusive Club Paradise which amongst other things offers trips to Calauit Island and diving trips.

Places to Stay

Club Paradise, @. Cottage/ac/bath P5500 per person, including three meals. Roomy, cosily furnished cottages. Restaurant. swimming pool, tennis court, Hobie Cats, kayaks, windsurfing, diving. The management is German, and reservations can be made in Manila at Euro-Pacific Resorts, Tel 8384956, Fax 8384462.

Coron Bay

The best way to explore the islands of Coron Bay is from Coron and Culion. Tiny Cagbatan Island, better known as CYC Island, is ideal for picnics, as is the slightly larger Dimanglet Island; both of them are near Coron. I especially liked the small Malcapuya Island amongst those east of Culion Island. It now belongs to a lawyer from Manila who has built a weekend house on it.

In 1944 a convoy of 12 Japanese naval and merchant ships was sunk in Coron Bay in the north-west, most of them in the waters between Lusong Island and Tangat Island, where there are seven wrecks altogether in around 30m depth of water.

Coron Island

Wedge-shaped Coron Island is practically uninhabited and can be reached by boat from Coron in about 30 min. It consists of steep limestone cliffs with caves and numerous lonely sandy bays where you may meet Tagbanua semi-nomads of Negrito extraction. In the interior are hidden mountain lakes such as the turquoise Lake Cayangan, Barracuda Lake (home to a 1½m long barracuda) which can be reached by climbing a sharp-edged chalk rockface, and the large Lake Cabugao which has two islands. If you want to spend more than a few hours on Coron don't forget to take enough drinking water with you.

When exploring the island resist the temptation to have a quick look at Lake Cabugao. It's located in an area reserved for the Tagbanua which is strictly off-limits. Please respect the law! As it is, the Tagbanua are not at all happy about receiving uninvited guests in their little

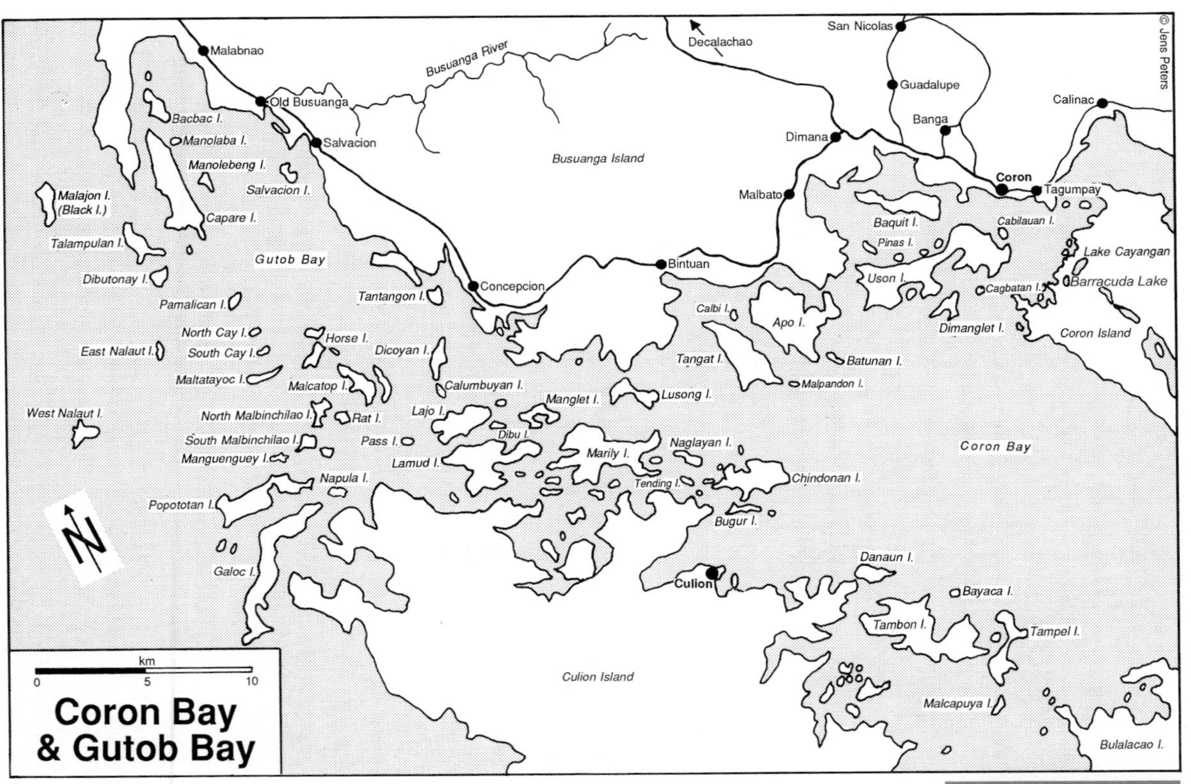

© Jens Peters
Malabnao
Busuanga River
Decalachao
San Nicolas
Guadalupe
Calinac
Old Busuanga
Bacbac I.
Banga
Manolaba I.
Salvacion
Dimana
Busuanga Island
Manolebeng I.
Coron
Tagumpay
Malajon I.
(Black I.)
Salvacion I.
Malbato
Capare I.
Baquit I.
Cabilauan I.
Talampulan I.
Pinas I.
Lake Cayangan
Gutob Bay
Bintuan
Dibutonay I.
Uson I.
Concepcion
Cagbatan I.
Barracuda Lake
Pamalican I.
Tantangon I.
Calbi I.
Apo I.
Dimanglet I.
Coron Island
North Cay I.
Horse I.
East Nalaut I.
South Cay I.
Dicoyan I.
Tangat I.
Batunan I.
Maltatayoc I.
Calumbuyan I.
Malpandon I.
Malcatop I.
Lusong I.
Manglet I.
West Nalaut I.
Lajo I.
North Malbinchilao I.
Rat I.
Dibu I.
Pass I.
Naglayan I.
Coron Bay
South Malbinchilao I.
Marily I.
Manguenguey I.
Lamud I.
Napula I.
Tending I.
Chindonan I.
Popototan I.
Bugur I.
Danaun I.
Galoc I.
Culion
Bayaca I.
Tambon I.
Tampel I.
km
0
5
10
Culion Island
Coron Bay
& Gutob Bay
Malcapuya I.
Bulalacao I.

Cashew Nut *(Anacardium occidentale)*
The kidney-shaped cashew nut *(kasoy)* grows at the end of a thick, fleshy stem which is very juicy and can be eaten as a fruit. But watch out: the refreshing juice can cause stubborn stains on your clothing. Cashew nuts are roasted before eating. Cooking oil can be produced from them.

communities on the east coast, and it's best to simply leave them alone.
In the little Tagbanua Cultural center in Real St, Coron Town, you can find out which beaches and lakes on Coron Island are open to the public. They also issue visitor tickets for Lake Cayangan (P200) and Barracuda Lake (P75).
Tip: On the way to Lake Cayangan mosquitos can make life hell, so don't forget to take along some mosquito repellent.

Tangat Island

Tangat Island (known locally as Sangat Island) is situated about four km south of Busuanga and juts fairly steeply out of the sea. In the southern part it gets as high as 460m. In the little bays dotted around the island you will occasionally come across a shimmering white sand beach. A narrow mangrove glade stretches along roughly the middle of the west coast, and there is a coral reef offshore at this point. The island is home to a teeming, richly varied animal population, including monkeys and monitor lizards.

Places to Stay

Sangat Reserve, Cellphone 0919-2050198, @. Cottage/bath P3000 per person, including three meals. Immaculate, roomy cottages. Nice atmosphere. This pleasant little resort at the southern tip of Tangat Island belongs to the Englishman, Andy. Good restaurant, kayaks, diving. Getting there: It takes about an hour by boat from Coron (it's an idea to get in touch with Swagman Travel in Coron so they can pick you up). Reservations in Manila at Swagman Travel, Tel (02) 5266057, Fax (02) 5223663.

Tending Island

This little island is snuggled between Marily and Chindonan islands. It is also called Isla Migrosa. The coarse sandy beach is only of moderate quality but is good for snorkelling.

Gutob Bay

There are lots of beautiful, deserted islands in Gutob Bay, between Culion and Busuanga islands. Dibutonay Island, Maltatayoc Island and Horse Island are only three amongst the many idyllic spots available.
The larger Talampulan Island is a complete contrast, with a town of 2000 people straggling along the east coast. There are two cinemas, and big ships often drop anchor off the town. Talampulan is a fishing centre, where the catches are brought and shipped to Manila two or three times a week. Note the chance of a ride!

One note of caution: After days and weeks at sea some of the fishermen get carried away with their alcohol consumption. Late afternoons and evenings in the village can get a bit hair-raising.

Lamud Island

Off the north coast of Culion Island, surrounded by the islands of Lajo, Manglet and Marily, lies the hilly, forested island of Lamud. On the west coast of the island, with a great view of the sunset, Joachim (Jojo) and Margie Lorenz run their Lamud Island Resort. A boat over there from Concepcion should not cost more than P400 (20 min).

Places to Stay

Lamud Island Resort, @. SR/DR P400, cottage/bath P800. Good rooms and cottages on the beach in a bay framed by two hills. Guests can relax in comfortable hammocks, shaded by the trees. Restaurant with Philippine and European cooking. Diving (also courses and night dives); two dives from the boat costs P1900. Paddleboats are available free.

Popototan Island

Situated off the north coast of Culion Island, this hilly island reaches a height of 105m. From up there you have a beautiful view of the surrounding islands. The west coast is rocky, the rest of the island is graced with white sand beaches and mangroves.

Places to Stay

Coral Bay Marina Resort, @. Cottage/fan/bath P1750 per person, including three meals. Very peaceful place with roomy cottages on a white sand beach (the house reef is a sight to see). Restaurant. Located about two hours by boat from Coron. A minimum stay of three days is required to qualify for free transport (can be booked at Bayside Divers Lodge). Reservations in Manila: Tel (02) 3719928, Fax (02) 3726031.

Evergreen Diving Resort, @. SR/DR/fan P1400, cottage/fan/bath P1650. Prices are per person, including three meals. Small, pleasant resort with two cottages and four rooms on a beautiful sandy bay with an intact house reef. Restaurant (Philippine food). Diving. German management. Enquiries and reservations at the Evergreen Diving Office in Coron, Cellphone 0920-5343015.

Culion Island

Culion Island is the second largest island of the Calamian Group and is known in the Philippines as Leprosy Island. The colony is in Culion, but only a few lepers live here along with their relatives. Most of the bays on the island, many of them quite deep, are lined with mangroves and are not very attractive when you actually take a good look at them.

Culion

Culion is a tidy, picturesque community on the side of a hill, with a small harbour. Boats leave from there for Manila via Coron.

Places to Stay

New Luncheonette Lodge. SR/DR P150. Basic accommodation with two airy terraces overlooking the water. On the larger one, there is live music (disco-type) at the weekends. It's the second building on the right, coming from the jetty.

Safari Lodge. SR/DR P300. Unpretentious accommodation about 200 metres left of the jetty.

Getting There & Away

Boat: See Coron: *Getting There & Away*.

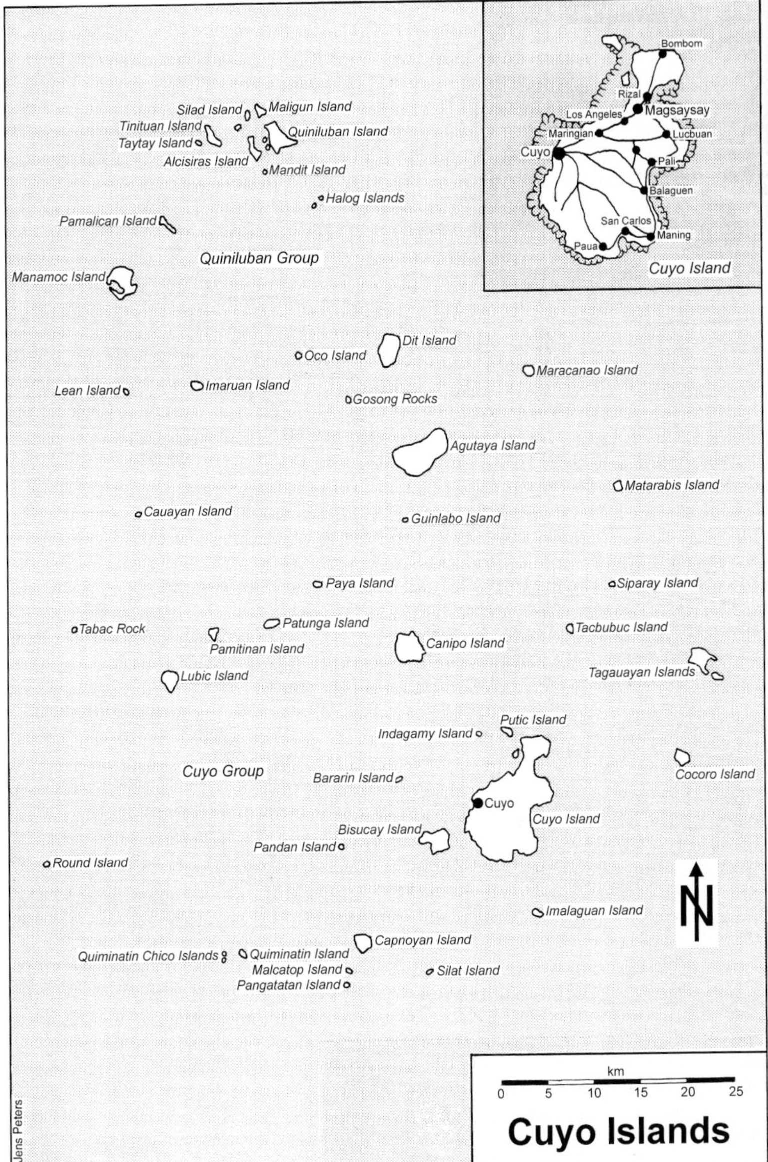
Silad Island
Maligun Island
Tinituan Island
Quiniluban Island
Taytay Island
Alcisiras Island
Mandit Island
Halog Islands
Pamalican Island
Quiniluban Group
Manamoc Island
Bombom
Rizal
Los Angeles
Magsaysay
Maringian
Lucbuan
Cuyo
Pali
Balaguen
San Carlos
Maning
Paua
Cuyo Island
Dit Island
Oco Island
Maracanao Island
Lean Island
Imaruan Island
Gosong Rocks
Agutaya Island
Matarabis Island
Cauayan Island
Guinlabo Island
Paya Island
Siparay Island
Tabac Rock
Patunga Island
Tacbubuc Island
Pamitinan Island
Canipo Island
Tagauayan Islands
Lubic Island
Putic Island
Indagamy Island
Cuyo Group
Bararin Island
Cocoro Island
Cuyo
Cuyo Island
Bisucay Island
Pandan Island
Round Island
Imalaguan Island
N
Capnoyan Island
Quiminatin Chico Islands
Quiminatin Island
Malcatop Island
Silat Island
Pangatatan Island
km
0 5 10 15 20 25
Cuyo Islands
© Jens Peters

Palawan

Cuyo Islands

In the north Sulu Sea, set apart from the large Palawan main islands but still part of Palawan Province, the Cuyo Islands comprise 40 islands, forming the Cuyo Group in the south and the Quiniluban Group in the north. This island world, which has scarcely been touched by tourism, offers an excellent environment for diving and snorkelling, particularly in the reefs around Manamoc, Pamalican and Tinituan islands. The diving areas around the islands of Alcisiras and Quiniluban, as well as Agutaya and Oco are also impressive.

Getting Around

Regular transport between the islands is unfortunately practically non-existent, and it is hard to avoid having to charter a boat. The only half-way reliable routes are those from the main town of Cuyo on Cuyo Island to Bisucay Island, Cocoro Island and Agutaya Island. However, the direct route from Cuyo to the Quiniluban Group, especially from December to March, can be quite rough. It's a good idea to take along your own life jacket if you're thinking of island hopping, for example, from Agutaya Island via Dit Island to Tinituan Island (Concepcion). There is an irregular boat service from Manamoc Island, Tinituan Island and Quiniluban Island to San Jose, Mindoro Occidental.

Cuyo

Cuyo is a pleasant little town with clean streets, beautiful old buildings and a fortress-church built in 1677 by the Spaniards as protection against the Moro pirates. The main sources of income are dried fish, copra and cashew nuts. However, for economic reasons many Cuyonos have moved to Palawan where they make up the largest group of immigrants. Their economic, cultural, social and political influence on the entire province is considerable and is the reason for Cuyo's reputation as a centre of traditional culture.
Tabunan Beach, between Cuyo and Suba, is probably one of the best beaches on Cuyo Island.

Places to Stay

Ireen's Pension House. SR/DR/fan P120/240. Unpretentious accommodation. Restaurant.
Nicky's Pension. SR/DR/fan P150, SR/DR/ac/bath P350. Two-storey building with basic, but acceptable rooms. Has to be the best place to stay in Cuyo. Restaurant.

Miscellaneous

Festival: Town Fiesta on 28 August.
Population: 7000.
Post: Post code: 5318.

Getting There & Away

By Air: ***Seair***, Cuyo Airport.
Destinations: Manila (via Puerto Princesa, El Nido and Busuanga).

By Boat: The following shipping lines have a presence in Cuyo.
MBRS Lines, Port Area.
Destinations: Manila, Panay.
Milagrosa Shipping Lines, Port Area.
Destinations: Panay, Puerto Princesa.

Puerto Princesa
Air: Seair flies two times weekly from Puerto Princesa to Cuyo and vice versa (P2000).

Boat: From Puerto Princesa to Cuyo Thursday and Sunday with Milagrosa Shipping Lines (P320; 16 hrs).

Manamoc Island

There is a broad, shallow lagoon in the south-west of this friendly island which welcomes guests who have a feeling for nature. Mt English, at 220m, is the highest point on the island; a bit of a challenge for hill-climbers, as there is no trail for the final stage of the climb. The coral reef surrounding the island is good for snorkelling. It runs quite some distance from the beach, so a small boat is required to get there.

Pamalican Island

This enchanting little island six km north-east of Manamoc Island belongs to the Soriano Group (the San Miguel Corporation) who have been getting involved in the tourism business. The marine environment in a wide area around the island has been declared a protected area, which means fishing and dropping anchor in this marine sanctuary are strictly forbidden.

Places to Stay

Amanpulo Resort, @. Cottage/ac/bath US$630 to $3000, depending on size and furnishings. In addition to a villa with four bedrooms, three bathrooms, living room and kitchen, your $3300 gets you four more, very comfortable buildings (casitas) each with its own bedroom and marble bathroom. These superbly furnished buildings have a living room, veranda, satellite TV, CD players and other goodies. This is simply ideal for private parties (who don't have to count their pennies). Luxury is considered a necessity here. Savour the food in the restaurant after enjoying the swimming pool, tennis courts, diving, Hobie Cats and windsurfing. This must be the most exclusive beach resort in the Philippines, and they have the awards to back up the claim. They even have their own little airfield. Reservations in Manila, Tel (02) 7594040, Fax (02) 7594044.

Getting There & Away

Air: Island Transvoyager flies from Manila to Pamalican Island and back every day (round trip US$300).

Tinituan Island

This island is one of the northernmost in the Cuyo archipelago. It is better known under the name Concepcion, after Barangay Concepcion, the largest town on the island on the south-east coast. Many of the locals make their living by seaweed farming. The seaweed flourishes in underwater fields cultivated in the extensive neighbouring coral reefs. To protect these profitable plants, fishing with dynamite and poison is not tolerated in the waters around Tinituan Island. So the underwater world can be viewed in all its pristine glory; snorkellers especially can enjoy first-class conditions here.
Anyone wishing to spend a few days on the little island of Taytay with its blindingly white sand beach, just west of Tinituan, should ask the owner Mr Tony de los Angeles, for permission first.

E-mail Directory

A

ABC Dive Coron	abcdive@mozcom.com
Action Divers	info@actiondiversvip.com
Action Divers VIP Dive Resort	info@actiondiversvip.com
Admiral Hotel	admiral@philonline.com.ph
Adventures & Expeditions Philippines	aepi@cagayan.net
Adventure Windsurfing Boracay	mail@adventure-windsurfing-boracay.com
Aileen's Lodging House	aileenteody@hotmail.com
Airport Hotel	airhotel@mozcom.com
Albert's Place	info@grabler.at
Alegre Beach Resort	abrsales@cebu.weblinq.com
Alhambra Hotel	alhambra@mozcom.com
Alliance Française	info@alliance.ph
Aloha Hotel	alohotel@info.com.ph
Alona Kew White Beach	kewbeach@mozcom.com
Alona Palm Beach Resort	info@alonapalmbeach.com
Alona Tropical Beach Resort	alona_tropical@hotmail.com
Amanpulo Resort	reservation@amanpulo.com
Amelia Pensionne	robes64@hotmail.com
America Hotel	amehotel@mozcom.com
Amigo Hotel	amigo@iloilo.net
Amorsolo Mansion	hdlsasia@netasia.net
Ananyana Beach Resort	info@ananyana.com
Anchor Hotel	anchor@gslink.net
Anchorage Inn	cony@mozcom.com
Angela's Farm	angelas_farm@hotmail.com
Angeles City Flying Club	acfc@mozcom.com
Angeles International Travel Center	angtrav@mozcom.com
Angely's Beach Resort	centrum@batangas.i-next.net
Aninuan Beach Resort	aninuanbeachresort@yahoo.com
Antulang Beach Resort	info@antulang.com
Apartelle Royal	apartelleroyal@digitelone.com
Apo Island Liberty's Guest House	paul_on_apo_island@yahoo.co.uk
Apo View Hotel	apoview@interasia.com.ph
Aquarius Diving	aquarius@boracay.i-next.net
Aquaventure Cebu	aquacebu@skyinet.net
Aquaventure Philippines	aqua@skyinet.net
Arizona International Hotel	reservation@arizonasubic.com
Artistic Diving	artisticdiving@lasaltech.com
Asia Divers	admin@asiadivers.com
Asian Hotel	zied@ozamiz.com
Astor Hotel	crs@genesishotels.com
Atlantis Dive Center	info@atlantisdivecenter.com
Atlantis Dive Resort	info@atlantishotel.com
Atrium Hotel	asmanila@skyinet.com

Aussie Hotel	baguio@swaggy.com
Australia Centre	roli.inocencio@dvat.gov.au
Austria Pension House	mail@sundown-boracay.com

B

Baguio Boardriders Club	baguioboardriders@yahoo.com
Bacolod Convention Plaza Hotel	bcphotel@mozcom.com
Bacolod Executive Inn	executiv@lasaltech.com
Badian Island Beach Resort	badiancebu@aol.com
Badladz Adventure	badladz@yahoo.com
Bagobo Beach Resort	info@bagobo.com
Bagobo House Hotel	JHT@weblinq.com
Bahay-Pilipino	bahay_pilipino@hotmail.com
Balanghai Hotel	blhotel@mozcom.com
Bali Hai Beach Resort	balihai@balihai.com.ph
Bali Hai East Resort Hotel	balihaieast@sflu.com
Bamboo Paradise Beach Resort	paradise@maweb.de
Bambua Nature Park Resort	bambua@pal-onl.com
Banwa Pension & Art Café	jane@banwa.net
Baras Beach Resort	pauli@gmx.info
Barceló Asturias Hotel	asturias@barcelo-asia.com
Barceló Eagle Point Resort	eaglepoint@barcelo-asia.com
Barceló Pearl Farm Island Resort	pearlfarm@barcelo-asia.com
Barceló Sarabia Manor Hotel	sarabia@barcelo-asia.com
Barts Resort Hotel	barts@svisp.com
Bascon Hotel	melbas@mozcom.com
Batangas Plaza	bplaza@cybat.sequet.net
Bayview Park Hotel	business.ctr@bayview.com.ph
Baywatch Dive & Fun Center	baywatch@mozcom.com
B & B Beach Resort	mangus@boracay.i-next.net
Beach Rock Café & Lodge	beachrockcafe@yahoo.com
Bella Vista Hotel	xenios@mozcom.com
Bellevue Cottages	bellevue_viewpoint@hotmail.com
Bermuda Beach Resort	info@bermuda-beach.info
Bethel Guesthouse	bethel@mozcom.com
Bicol Adventure & Tours	bicoladventure@digitelone.com
Big Apple Dive Resort	bigapple@pulo.ph
Binirayan Cottages	jubilan@sac.edu.ph
Binocot Beach Resort	binocot_beach@hotmail.com
Binondo Suites	business@binondosuites.com
Bituon Beach Resort	bituon@wtal.de
Blue Abyss Dive Shop	cebuacc@ibm.net
Blue Crystal Beach Resort	bcrystal@globe.com.ph
Bluefields Hotel	frontdesk_bluefields@yahoo.com
Blue Horizons Travel & Tours	bhtt_inc@mozcom.com
Blue Ridge Hotel	blue_ridgehotel@hotmail.com
Blue Rock Resort	bluerocksubic@hotmail.com
Blue Water Malapascua Beach Resort	janetmalapascua@hotmail.com

Bohol Beach Club	bbclub@mozcom.com
Bohol Divers Resort	boholdiv@bohol-online.com.ph
Bohol Sea Resort	tootiger@hotmail.com
Bohol Tropics Resort	info@boholtropics.com
Bonista Beach Resort	bonista@hotmail.com
Boracay Beach Chalets	bbchalet@boracay.i-next.net
Boracay Beach Resort	nenette04@hotmail.com
Boracay Gold Crowne Club	webmaster@boracaygold.com
Boracay Plaza Beach Resort	bplaza@boracay.i-next.net
Boracay Regency Hotel	regency@iloilo.net
Boulevard Mansion	htlsasia@netasia.net
Brazzaville Beach Resort	pgdavid@lasaltech.com
Broadway Court	bcourtapt@yahoo.com
Bubble 07 Diver's Corp	dive@bubble07.com
Bureau of Immigration	bimail@immigration.gov.ph
Buri Beach Resort	buribeach@hotmail.com
Business Inn	businn@marapara.babysky.net.ph
By The Sea Resort	info@bythesearesort.com

C

Cabana Beach Club Resort	cabana@skyinet.net
Cabaña Beach Resort	cabana@sflu.com
Cabanbanan Dive & Beach Resort	cabanbanan@hotmail.com
Cabilao Beach Club	cabilao@skyinet.net
Calapan Bay Hotel	calapanbay@yahoo.com
Calypso Diving	calypso@boracay.i-next.net
Calypso Resort	philippines@gmx.net
Cambridge Farm Pension House	dvgensan@mozcom.com
Camelot Hotel	cameloth@pworld.net.ph
Camiguin Action	camiguinaction@sni.ph
Camiguin Action Dive Center	camiguinaction@sni.ph
Camille Del Sol	motoxp72@yahoo.com
Capt'n Gregg's Dive Resort	captgreg@gmx.net
Capt'n Gregg's Hotel	captgreg@mozcom.com
Casablanca Hotel	lee@globalink.net.ph
Casa Camilla Boracay	bill_lorna@yahoo.com
Casa de Azul	thomasklenke@gmx.net
Casa de la Playa Resort	laplaya@gmx.net
Casa Leticia	stay@casaleticia.com
Casa Linda	casalin@mozcom.com
Casa Velma	alonzogs@aol.com
Casino Filipino Hotel	csedpbac@lasaltec.com
Catanduanes Midtown Inn	catmidinn@yahoo.com
Caves Dive Resort	genesis@skyinet.net
Cebu Beach Club	cbclub@mozcom.com
Cebu Business Hotel	cebubusinesshotel@skyinet.net
Cebu City Mariott Hotel	ccmh1@mozcom.com
Cebu Century Hotel	klg@pacific.net.ph

Cebu Ferries	cfc@cebu-online.com
Cebu Grand Hotel	cghotel@skyinet.net
Cebu Marine Beach Resort	info@cebumarine.com
Cebu Midtown Hotel	cmhsales@skyinet.net
Cebu Mintel	wgoberre@gsilink.com
Cebu Plaza Hotel	cphres@cebu.weblinq.com
Cebu White Sands	whitesands@skyinet.net
Centennial Plaza Hotel	cenplaze@i-iloilo.com.ph
Central Park Hotel	information@centralpark-ac.com
Century Citadel Inn Makati	pctm-ccim8976561@globe.com.ph
Century Park Hotel	century@globe.com.ph
Cha-li Beach Resort	cha-li@cdo.philcom.com.ph
Charina's Travel Service-Center	cts-cltn@comclark.com
Charisma Beach Resort	resortcharisma@yahoo.com
Cherinicole Beach Resort	cherinicole_ph@yahoo.com
Cherry Blossoms Hotel	cbh@surfshop.net.ph
Chico River Quest	nss45@hotmail.com
China Sea Beach Resort	chinasea@sflu.com
Chito's Hotel	chitoshotel@yahoo.com
Circle C Ranch	martial@hotmail.com
City Garden Hotel	garden@iconn.com.ph
City Garden Hotel Makati	ctgarden.mkt@pacific.net.ph
City of Springs Resort Hotel	leo@mozcom.com
City Park Inn	cityparkinn@hotmail.com
Citystate Tower Hotel	tower@i-manila.com.ph
Clarkton Hotel	clarkton_hotel@hotmail.com
Club KonTiki	kontikiph@yahoo.com
Club Mabuhay La Laguna	mabuhaysabang@hotmail.com
Club Mabuhay Sabang	mabuhaysabang@hotmail.com
Club Noah Isabelle	info@clubnoah.com.ph
Club Panoly Resort Hotel	panoly@boracay.i-next.net
Club Paradise	clubpara@pworld.net.ph
Cocktail Divers	cdiver@vasia.com
Cocobana Beach Resort	info@cocobana.ch
Coco Beach Island Resort	resort@cocobeach.com
Coco Crove Beach Resort	info@cocoaporesorts.com
Coco Grande Hotel	paradise.glinesnx.com.ph
Coco-Loco Island Resort	cocoloco@pto-princesa.com
Cocomangas Hotel Beach Resort	cocomangas@boracay.i-next.net
Coconut Grove Beach Resort	resort@coco.com.ph
Cocowhite-Beach Resort	info@cocowhite-beach.com
Concorde Hotel	concorde@mozcom.com
Copacabana Apartment Hotel	copa@skyinet.net
Coral Bay Beach Resort	bookings@coralbay.com.ph
Coral Beach Club	coralbch@skyinet.net
Coral Cay Resort	scoralcayresort@yahoo.com
Coral Cove Resort & Dive Centre	coral-cove@asiagate.net
Coral Reef Hotel	coral@cebu.pw.net.ph

Corcel Car & Van Rental	corcel@hvisions.com
Coron Reef Pension House	coron_ph@yahoo.com
Costa Aguada Island Resort	orinc@evoserve.com
Costabella Tropical Beach Hotel	costa@cnns.net
Crown Peak Garden Hotel	crownht@svisp.com
Crystal Coast Resort	crystal@boholnet.com
Crystal Sand Beach Resort	crystal@boracay.i-next.net

D

Dakota Mansion	htlsasia@netasia.net
Dapdap Beach Resort	dapdap@andabohol.org
Dapitan City Resort Hotel	dcrh@dapitan.com
Darayonan Lodge	darayonan@i-manila.com.ph
Days Hotel Batangas	days@cybat.sequel.net
Days Hotel Lapu-Lapu	dayscebu@dayshotel.ph
Days Hotel Iloilo City	days@skyinet.net
Days Hotel Tagaytay	daystag@mozcom.com
Deep Blue Sea Inn	dbsi@catsi.net.ph
Department of Tourism (DOT)	*see Tourist Office*
Diplomat Hotel	diplomat@cebu.pw.net.ph
Discovery Divers	info@ddivers.com
Discovery Island Resort	ddivers@vasia.com
Discovery Suites	rsvn@discovery.com.ph
Dive Buddies	center@divephil.com
Dive Calamianes	info@divecal.com
Dive Gurus	george@divegurus.com
Divelink Cebu	gary@cebu.weblinq.com
Dive Link Resort	divelink@epic.net
Dive Right	diveright@mozcom.com
Dive Right Boracay	divright@boracay.i-next.net
Diver's Cove	divercov@globe.com.ph
Dive Society	dumaguete@divesociety.com
Dolarog Beach Resort	dolarog@mozcom.com
Dolphin House	dolphin@moalboal.net
Dondeezco Beach Resort	dondeezco@eudoramail.com
Dos Palmas	info@dospalmas.com.ph
Driftwood Village	info@driftwood-village.com
Dryden Hotel	Dryden_Hotel@bigfoot.com
Dumaguete Outdoors	dumagueteoutdoors@eudoramail.com
Durban Street Inn	durbanstinn@edsamail.com.ph
Dusit Hotel Nikko	dusitmnl@dusit.com

E

East Asia Royale Hotel	royale@gslink.net
Eddie's Hotel	reservations@eddieshotel.com
Edsa Shangri-La	esl@shangri-la.com

El Centro Island Beach Resort	elcentroboracay@yahoo.com
El Cielito Tourist Inn	elcielit@mozcom.com
El Dorado Beach Resort	info@eldoradobeachresort.com
El Galleon Beach Resort	admin@asiadivers.com
El Nido Boutique & Artcafé	judithdistal@my.smart.com.ph
El Oriente Beach Resort	jlaguda@cvpc.edu.ph
El-Rey Pensionne House	el-rey@pal-onl.com
Embassies & Consulates (in Manila)	*see also Philippine Embassies & Consulates*
- Australia	manila.consular@dfat.gov.au
- Canada	manil-cs@dfait-maeci.gc.ca
- Belgium	Manila@diplobel.org
- Denmark	mnlconsul@maersk.com
- Finland	sonamat.mni@formin.fi
- France	consulat@ambafrance-ph.org
- Germany	germanembassymanila@surfshop.net.ph
- India	eimani@vasia.com
- Italy	ambitaly@surfshop.net.ph
- Netherlands	man-vz@minbuza.nl
- New Zealand	nzmanila@nxdsl.com.ph
- Norway	emb.manila@mfa.no
- Sweden	ambassaden.manila@foreign.ministry.se
- Switzerland	vertretung@man.rep.admin.ch
- UK	uk@info.com.ph
Encenada Beach Resort	sunlink@mozcom.com
Escapade Marine	escapade@mozcom.com
Estosan Garden Hotel	estosan-hotel@yahoo.com
Euro Apartment	euroapt@skyinet.net
Europhil International Hotel	europhil@mozcom.com
Evergreen Diving Resort	evergreen_diving@yahoo.de
Executive Plaza Hotel	information@executiveplazahotel.com.ph

F

Ferienhaus Jasmin	uw@haus-lawaan.de
Fernandos Hotel	fernandohotel@hotmail.com
Filipino Travel Center	info@filipinotravel.com.ph
Fine Rock Hotel	finerock@hotmail.com
Fishermen's Cove Beach & Dive Resort	info@fishermenscove.com
Fisheye Divers	info@fisheyedivers.com
Floral Travel & Tours	floral@mozcom.com
Flower Garden Resort	flowergardenres@hotmail.com
Flying Dog Beach Resort	cbaloja85@hotmail.com
Fort Ilocandia Resort Hotel	booking@fortilocandia.com.ph
Four Season Hotel	season4@iloilo.fapenet.org
Franklyn Highland Beach Resort	inquiry@franklynresort.com
Friday's	fridays@boracay.i-next.net
Frontier Scuba	fdivers@mozcom.com
Fuente Pension House	fuente@pacific.net.ph

G

Garcia Legaspi Mansion	glgarcia_2000@yahoo.com
Garden of Eden	info@wetexpedition.de
Garden of Tabinay	mindoro_tabinay@yahoo.de
Garden Orchid Hotel	goh@jetlink.com.ph
Gardenville Hotel	gardenville@butuanonline.com
Garwood Park Hotel	sales@garwoodparkhotel.com
Genesis Divers	genesis@cebu.weblinq.com
Georg's Place	gigitrav@hotmail.com
GM's Resort	info@gmresortphil.com
Goethe Institute	goethepr@csi.com.ph
Going Places	uhlam@hotmail.com
Golden Dove Hotel	jopineda@hvisions.com
Golden Valley Inn	goldenv@cnms.net
Gordion Inn	edalcan@skyinet.net
Grand Astoria Hotel	info@grandastoria.com
Grand Men Seng Hotel	grand@menseng.com.ph
Grand Regal Hotel	grhd_dvo@mozcom.com
Great Eastern Hotel	sales@greateasternhotelmanila.com
Greenview Hotel	GVI@mozcom.com
Greenviews Resort	palawandg@clara.co.uk
Greenyard Funboard Center	nenette04@hotmail.com

H

Habagat Kiteboarding Center	nudibranch@hotmail.com
Halfmoon Hotel	halfmoon@svisp.com
Hammer Head Shark Divers	jonathan_naui@yahoo.com
Hangin Cabrinha	info@kite-boracay.com
Hannah's Lodge	hannah@sequestdivecenter.com
Hans & Nenita's Malatapay Beach Resort	hans@negrosbeach.com
Happy Valley Beach Resort	wonderft@skyinet.net
Harbor Town Hotel	harborth@worlddelphil.com
Hard Rock Cottages	hardrockcottages@yahoo.com
Harolds Mansion	haroldsmansion@yahoo.com
Haruhay Dream Resort	haruhay@skyinet.net
Haus Malibu	hmalibu@mozcom.com
Heaven on Earth Club	koeck@heaven-on-earth-club.com
Hidden Vale Sports Club	info@hidden-vale.com
Hillside Resort	hillside@mozcom.com
Holiday Inn	himanila@info.com.ph
Holiday Inn Resort Clark Field	hiclark@portalinc.com
Holiday Plaza Hotel	fo-res@holidayplazacebu.com
Hotel Alejandro	aljandro@mozcom.com
Hotel Asia	kunio@col.net.ph
Hotel California	neneblp@yahoo.com
Hotel Camila	hotelcam@mozcom.com
Hotel Cesario	xenios@mozcom.com
Hotel Del Rio	hdelrio@iloilo.net

Hotel Don Felipe	hdfelipe@ormoc.weblinq.com
Hotel Fleuris	hfleuris@mozcom.com
Hotel Hana	hanabooking@yahoo.com
Hotel Inter-Continental	manila@interconti.com
Hotel Karaga	webadmin@hotelkaraga.com
Hotel Kimberly	reservations@hotelkimberly.com
Hotel La Corona	lacorona@mnl.sequel.net
Hotel La Roca	laroca@bohol-online.com
Hotel Maguindanao	hmsales@mozcom.com
Hotel Marquis	info@hotelmarquis.net
Hotel Mikka	mikka@sflu.com
Hotel Rembrandt	hr_rsrvn@hotelrembrandt.com.ph
Hotel Supreme	supreme@burgos.slu.edu.ph
Hotel Veniz	hotelveniz@skyinet.net
House Schiefelbein	hansundcelly@yahoo.com
Hundred Islands Resort Hotel	hillvertz@yahoo.com
Hyatt Regency	reservations@hyatt.com.ph

I

Iloilo City Inn	info@nagarao.com
Iloilo Midtown Hotel	midtownhotel@iloilo.worldtelphil.com
Immigration Office Manila	bimail@immigration.gov.ph
Inn Suites Hotel	innsuites@pacific.net.ph
Interisland Air Services	info@interislandairservices.com
Interisland Travel & Tours	info@interisland.com.ph
Interisland Tours & Transportation	interislandsubic@yahoo.com
International Diving Center Philippines	info@divesibulan.com
Islander's Paradise Beach	islanders1@ntlworld.com
Iseya Hotel	nick.let.ph@pacific.net.ph
Ivatan Lodge	ivatanlodge@yahoo.com

J

Jadestar Lodge	jadestarlodge@yahoo.com
Jardin de La Vina Hotel	lavina@jetlink.com.ph
Jasmin Beach Resort	jasminbeach@yahoo.com
Jazzed Up Café Hotel	blmccauley@pacific.net.ph
Jenmar Lodge	divertops@hotmail.com
Jimmy Boyd	jimmyboyd@navionair.com
Johan's Adventure & Wreck Dive Centre	johan@subicdive.com
Johan's Dive Resort	johan@subicdive.com
Johansson's Lodge	ronny@hvisions.com

K

Kabayan Hotel	info@kabayanhotel.com.ph
Kalamayan Inn	kalmayan@mozcom.com
Kalaw Place	kalaw@kalawplace.com.ph
Kalipayan Beach Resort	meridian@mozcom.com
Kan-Irag Hotel	kanhotel@cebu.pw.net.ph

Karie Garnier	karie@netidea.com
Katala Beach Resort	katalaresort@gmx.net
Kevin's Beach House	info-siquijor@web.de
Kiao Sea Lodge	info@kiaosealodge.com
Kingfishers Beach Resort	kingfishers@skyinet.net
King's Hotel	kingshtl@babysky.net.ph
Kiwi Dive Resort	info@kiwidiveresort.com
Kiwi Lodge	kiwilodge@pacific.net.ph
Koala Hotel	koalahotel@hotmail.com
Koala Lodge	inquiries@koala.com.ph
Kokosnuss Garden Resort	info@kokosnuss.info
Kookoo's Nest Resort	info@kookoosnest.com.ph
Kota Beach Resort	kota@cebu.i-next.com
Krystal Langit Lodge	krista@pacific.net.ph
Kukuk's Nest	kukuks@nexus.com.ph
Kundutel	kundutel@bcd.weblinq.com

L

La Casa Pension	lacasa@netasia-angeles.net
La Esperanza Charters	sailpalawan@yahoo.com
La Estrella Beach Resort	info@laestrella.ph
La Fiesta Hotel	lafiesta@iloilo.net
Lago De Oro Beach Club	lago-de-oro@westlink.com.ph
La Isla Bonita Restaurant	laislabonita_malapascua@yahoo.com
Lally & Abet Beach Resort	info@lallyandabet.com
La Laguna Beach Club & Dive Centre	lalaguna@llbc.com.ph
La Luna Court	normeth@hotmail.com
Lamud Island Resort	lamudisland@gmx.de
Lapu-Lapu Cottages	lapu-lapucottages@lycos.com
Lapu-Lapu Diving Center	info@lapulapu.com
Las Palmas Hotel	information@laspalmashotel.com.ph
Las Perlas Beach Resort	lasperlas@pacific.net.ph
Las Villas Resort	lasvilla@sflu.com
Lauremar Beach Hotel	lauremar@cdo.weblinq.com
Layang Layang Aerospace	layaero@tm.net.my
Legenda Hotel	fom@legendanet.com
Legenda Suites	fom@legendanet.com
Lemuria Inn	lemuria@philonline.com
Le Soleil de Boracay	lesoleil@boracay.i-next.net
L'Fisher Hotel	lfisher@lasaltech.com
Liberty's Resort & Paul's Diving	paul_on_apo_island@yahoo.co.uk
L & M Pe Sea Lodge	meloupe@my.smart.com.ph
Loida's Beach Club	loida@gmx.de
Lorenzo Main Resort	reservations@boracay-lorenzo.com
Lotus Garden Hotel	lotusgardenhtl@pacific.net.ph
Love's Lodge	diveasia@ozemail.com.au
Lucena Fresh Air Hotel & Resort	freshair@quezon.net

M

Mabini Mansion	htlsasia@netasia.net
Mabuhay Dive Resort	divemabuhay@hotmail.com
Mactan Pension House	mph@cebu.weblinq.com
Maganda Travel & Tours	magtours@speed.com.ph
Maharajah Hotel	mahatel@mozcom.com
Mahayahay Beach Resort	mahayahay@lycos.de
Maia's Beach Resort	maia.becker@gmx.de
Makati Shangri-La	slm@shangri-la.com
Malapascua Exotic I. Dive & Beach Resort	info@malapascua.net
Malate Pensionne	info@mpensionne.com.ph
Malasag Resort	marco@alwana.com
Mandarin Oriental	momnl@wordroom.com
Maldito	maldito@eldoradobeachresort.com
Mandala Spa	info@mandalaspa.com
Mango Park Hotel	mangoparkhotel@yahoo.com
Mangrove Oriental Resort	mangrove@malapascuaisland.info
Manila Hotel	resvn@manila-hotel.com.ph
Manila Diamond Hotel	diamond@cnl.net
Manila Galleria Suites	galleriasuites@netasia.net
Manila Midtown Hotel	mmh_sm@netasia.net
Manila Yacht Club	mycrace@i-manila.com.ph
Mantangale Alibuag Dive Resort	mantadive@col.com.ph
Manureva Beach Resort	manureva@mozcom.com
Marcosas Cottages	relax@marcosas.com
Marble Inn	marbleinn@datelnet.net
Marco Vincent Residence Inn	mvri@dalcan.com
Marco Vincent Resort	mvri@dalcan.com
Marco Vincent Villa	mvri@dalcan.com
Marem's Pension House	marem@euduramail.com
Maribago Bluewater Beach Resort	bluwater@mozcom.com
Maricaban Bay Marine-Resort	maricby@info.com.ph
Marlin Beach Resort	info@marlin-bantayan.com
Mar-Nich	mar-nich@hvisions.com
Marsman Tours & Travel	inquiry@marsman-tours.com.ph
Maryland Beach Resort	beachhouse@cjb.net
Maya-Maya Reef Resort	inquiry@mayamaya.com
Mayflower Pension House	mayflower@cebu.weblinq.com
Matabungkay Beach Resort & Hotel	hruphils@skyinet.net
MBC Serena of Palawan	morgan@societe.ch
MB's Tavern	mbs_tavern@yahoo.com
Meddah Spa	reservations@meddahspa.com
Melinda's Garden	melindasgarden@hotmail.com
Meridian Hotel	meridian@mozcom.com
Mermaid Resort	info@mermaidresort.com
Metro Centre Hotel	metroctr@mozcom.com
Michelle's Bungalows	info@mbungalows.com
Microtel Inn & Suites (Calapan)	filipiniana@microtelphilippines.com

Microtel Inn & Suites (Baguio)	microtelbgo@viacomm.com.ph
Miniloc Island Resort	elnido@mailstation.net
Moana Hotel	moanatel@mozcom.com
Moby Dick's Beach Resort	belbar1111@yahoo.com.au
Mollie's Place	molliesplace@skyinet.net
Mona-Lisa Beach Resort	nneubeck@monalisaresort.com
Montebello Villa Hotel	montebello@skyinet.net
Morimar Boracay Resort	philpages@ukonline.co.uk
Mountain Lodge	mountainlodge@hotmail.com
Mr. Ticket	mrticket@info.com.ph
MY Moonshadow	info@moonshadow.ch

N

Nagarao Island Resort	info@nagarao.com
Naomi's Tourist Inn	mimi@ozamiz.com
Navion Air Service	jimmyboyd@navionair.com
Ne-Ar-Ne Store & Nicky's Yacht Service	nearne@yahoo.com
Neptune Diving Adventure	info@neptunediving.com
New Solanie Hotel	solanie@skyinet.com
New World Hotel	HOTEL@nwrenaissance.com.ph
Nigi Nigi Nu Noos	niginigi@pworld.net.ph
Nirvana Beach Resort	mail@nirvana-resorts.com
Nuts Huts	walterken@hotmail.com

O

Oasis Country Resort	oasis@sflu.com
Oasis Hotel	oasishtl@datelnet.net
Oasis Resort	seaquest@seaquestdivecenter.com
Ocean Deep Diver Training Center	oceandp@sflu.com
Ocean Fast Ferries	oceanjet@skyinet.net
Ocean Republic	info@ocean-republic.com
Ocean Safari Philippines	oceansafariphilippines@hotmail.com
Octopus Divers	info@octopusdivers.org
Octopussy Bungalow Resort	info@octopussy.ph
OK Pensionne House	ok_pensionne@eudoramail.com
Omni Aviation	info@omniaviation.com.ph
Orchid Garden Suites	orchid@mydestiny.net
Orchid Inn Resort	orchid@datelnet.net
Ormoc Villa Hotel	villa@ormocnet.net.ph
Oxford Suites	sales@oxfordsuitesmakati.com

P

Pacific Divers	pacificdivers@yahoo.com
Pacific Heights Hotel	pacific_hotel@hotmail.com
Pacifico's Cottages	aquaload@usa.net
Pacific Pensionne	candy@gsilink.com
Pagsanjan Garden Resort	pgresortlag@yahoo.com

Palawan Hotel	Islapal@mozcom.com
Palawan Yacht Charter	talusi@mozcom.com
Palermo Hotel	palermohtl@philwebinc.com
Palmas Del Mar Village & Beach Club	palmas@bcd.i-next.net
Palm Beach Garden Resort	atoymortos@hotmail.com
Palmera Garden Beach Resort	palmera@mozcom.com
Palm Plaza Hotel	information@palmplazahotel.com.ph
Pandan Island Resort	info@pandan.com
Pangasinan Regency Hotel	pang_regency@yahoo.com
Panorama Beach Resort	panoramabeach@hotmail.com
Pansukian Tropical Resort	travelvision@skyinet.net
Paradise Bay	info@paradisebay.de
Paradise Garden Resort Hotel	info@paradise-garden.com
Paradise Island Park & Beach Resort	paradise@dv.weblinq.com
Paradise Travel Center	paradise.glinesnx.com.ph
Paraiso Beach Resort	hene.buetikofer@gmx.ch
Paras Beach Resort	paras@oronet.com.ph
Park Hotel	parkhotl@parkhotel.com.ph
Patrick's on the Beach	andreas@mojf.org
Pearl of the Pacific	boracay@pearlofthepacific.com.ph
People's Lodge	jerwin_t@yahoo.com
Peter's Dive Resort	infodesk@whaleofadive.com
Phela Grande Hotel	phelainc@gsilink.net
Philippine Divers	tauchtom@batangas.i-next.net
Philippine Dream Hotel	phildream@cebu.nexmil.com
Philippine Embassies & Consulates	
- Bangkok	inquiry@philembassy-bangkok.net
- Beijing	main@philembassy-china.org
- Berlin	Berlinpe@t-online.de
- Berne	berne_pe@bluewin.ch
- Brussels	brusselspe@brutele.be
- Canberra	embaphil@iaa.com.au
- Chicago	phchi@moon.igcom.net
- Guangzhou	gzphcggz@public1.guangzhou.gd.cn
- Hanoi	phv@hn.vnn.vn
- Hong Kong	info@philcongen-hk.com
- Honolulu	honolulupc@hawaii.rr.com
- Jakarta	phjkt@indo.net.id
- Kuala Lumpur	consular@philembassykl.org.my
- London	embassy@philemb.co.uk
- Los Angeles	losangelpc@aol.com
- Madrid	MADRIDPE@terra.es
- Manado	manadopc@manado.wasantara.net.id
- Moscow	moscowpe@co.ru
- New York	philconsulateny@mindspring.com
- Ottawa	embassyofphilippines@rogers.com
- Paris	Ambaphil_Paris@compuserve.com
- Phnom Penh	ph@worldmail.com.kh

- Port Moresby	pomphpem@dg.com.pg
- Pretoria	philemb@mweb.co.za
- Rome	romepe@agora.it
- Riyadh	filembry@sbm.net.sa
- San Francisco	phisf@aol.com
- Shanghai	ShanghaiPC@dfa.gov.ph
- Singapore	php@pacific.net.sg
- Stockholm	ph@swipnet.se
- Sydney	phsydpc@ozemail.com.au
- The Hague	ph@bart.nl
- Tokyo	phjp@gol.com
- Toronto	torontopc@philcongen-toronto.com
- Vancouver	VancouverPC@dfa.gov.ph
- Vienna	ph.vienna@magnet.at
- Washington	info@philippineembassy-usa.org
- Wellington	wgtnpe@paradise.net.nz
Philippine Islands Divers	dive@phildivers.com
Phoenix Hotel	phoenixh@mozcom.com
PIDWWO	pamilacan@yahoo.com
Pine Hills Hotel	pptwnctr@mozcom.com
Pinjalo Resort Villas	calypso@boracay.i-next.net
Pink Patio Resort	pinkpatio@epic.net
Pirate Cove Beach Resort	pirate_betty@yahoo.com
Pirate's Cove Beach & Surf Resort	pirates_cove_surf@hotmail.com
Planet Action Adventure	planet@action-philippines.com
Plantation Bay	rsvns@plantationbay.com
Platinum Lodge	platinumlodge@hotmail.com
Playa Papagayo Inn	reservations@playapapagayo.net
Polaris Beach & Dive Resort	polaris_cabilao@yahoo.com
Portofino	resort@portofino.com.ph
Premiere Hotel	premierh@mozcom.com
Prince Diving Resort	water221@hanmail.net
Princesa Holiday Resort	phresort@skyinet.net
Pro Safari Diving	info@prosafari.com
PRRCFI	prrcfi@mozcom.com
Pryce Plaza Hotel	prycepht@cdo.philcom.com.ph
Puerto del Sol	crs@genesishotels.com
Puerto de San Juan Resort Hotel	psj@puertodesanjuan.com
Puerto Flower Garden	puerto_flower_garden@yahoo.com
Puerto Pension	ppension@pal-onl.com
Pura Vida Resort	dumaguete@sea-explorers.com
Puyo Travels & Tours	puyosurigao@usa.net

Q

Quantum Resort	quantumr@cebu.weblinq.com
Queen Anne Divers	trattori@info.com.ph
Quo Vadis Beach Resort	quovadis@cybercebu.com

R

Rajah Tours	sales@rajahtours.com.ph
Ralph Anthony Suites	ras1988@compass.com.ph
Rama International Beach Resort	Ramabeach@euduramail.com
Red Coconut Beach Hotel	info@redcoconut.com.ph
Regency Inn	add.regency@skyinet.net
Regine's Apartelle	regines@info.com.ph
Rene's Place	renesswiss@yahoo.com
Ricardo's Forest Hills & Resort	butchi8@prodigy.net
Richmond Plaza Hotel	rphcebu@skyinet.net
Rip Curl Board Riders	lizz30_2000@yahoo.com
Riviera Mansion	riviera@pworld.net.ph
Robelle Mansion	robelle@I-manila.com.ph
Rockport	dlrrockport@hotmail.com
Romblon International Business Center	dp_kershaw@hotmail.com
Romblon Plaza Hotel	rphreservation@usa.net
Rontonda Hotel	rontondahotel@philonline.com
Rosarian Hotel	ave-sol@quezon.net
Rosas Garden Hotel	rosart@info.com.ph
Rose Garden & Pension House	lorelie_rosegarden@eudoramail.com
Rose Scent Pensionne House	ginajao@mozcom.com
Roxas President's Inn	presinn@i-rox.net.ph
Royal Cargo	info@royalcargo.com
Royal Cliff Resort	erichmack@eudoramail.com
Royal Taal Inn	info@royaltaal.com
Rudy's Dive Center	rudydive@vasia.com

S

Sabang Inn Dive Resort	sab-inn@mozcom.com
Sabin Resort Hotel	sabin@ormocnet.net.ph
Sagana Resort	sagana@cloud9surf.com
Sailor's Cabin	contact@sailors-cabin.com
Saint Illian's Inn	saintillians@cyberlinq.net
Samal Casino Resort	samal@weblinq.com
Samar Surfriders	info@surfingph.com
Sanctuary Tours & Travel	sanctuarytours@yahoo.com
Sand Castles	nenette04@hotmail.com
San Fabian PTA Beach Resort	sfptabr@pang.pworld.net.ph
Sangat Island Reserve	info@sangat.com.ph
San Juan Surf Resort	landrigan@sflu.com
San Pedro Beach Resort	mina_mingoa@hotmail.com
Santa Fe Beach Club	sfbci@bantayan.net
Santa Monica Beach Resort	stamonica@speed.com.ph
Savedra Beach Resort	info@savedra.com
Savedra Dive Center	info@savedra.com
Scandinavian Divers	pl@scandinaviandivers.com
Scotty's Dive Centre	puerto_galera@divescotty.com
Scubaplus Dive Center	martin@scubaplus.com

Scuba Venture	sventure@mozcom.com
Scuba World	info@scubaworld.com.ph
Scuba World Boracay	swidive@boracay.i-next.net
Scubaworld Coron	swcoron@pacific.net.ph
Scuba World Davao	denz@skyinet.net
Seabird International Resort	seabird@boracay.i-next.net
Sea Canoe Philippines	seacanoe@vasia.com
Sea Dive Center Lodging House	jim@seadive.com.ph
Sea Divers	sead@asiadivers.com
Sea Dive	seadive@starnet.net.ph
Sea Explorers	cebu@sea-explorers.com
Sea Gaia Divers Lodge	seagaia@boracay.i-next.net
Seahorse Inn	seahorse@vasia.com
Sea Park Beach Resort	ssi_sflu@digetelone.com
Seaquest Dive Center	seaquest@seaquestdivecenter.com
Seashore Lodge	seashore_lodge@yahoo.com
Sea Wind	seawind@pacific.net.ph
Sebay Resort Hotel	vida@sflu.com
Shanedel's Inn	aeromite01@yahoo.com
Shangri-La's Mactan Island Resort	srsvn@mac-shangri-la.com
Sheavens Lodge	allen@hvisions.com
Sheena's Cottage Garden	sheenas@mozcom.com
Shraders Travel & Tours	maricel@svisp.com
Sibuyan Asian Diver	tauchbasis@sibuyan_asian_diver.de
Sierra Apartelle	sierotel@mozcom.com
Sierra Vista Beach Resort	sierra@mozcom.com
Simon's	simonsres@hotmail.com
Sinandigan Lodge	info@sinandigan-lodge.de
Sipalay Easy Diving & Beach Resort	diving@sipalay.com
Skyland Hotel	skylandaussie@yahoo.com
Southern Leyte Divers	info@leyte-divers.com
Southern Palms Beach Resort	inquiries@southernpalms.com.ph
Southern Star Hotel	starfox@mozcom.com
South of the Border Resort	roland@southoftheborder.com.ph
South Sea Divers	dive@southseadivers.com
South Sea Lodge	anchor@gslink.net
South Sea Resort Hotel	southsea@philwebinc.com
Sports, Action & Adventure	sportsaa@mozcom.com
Star Boulevard Inn	star.blvdinn@pacific.net,ph
St. Bernard Beach Resort	bernard@bantayan.dk
St. Moritz Hotel	info@stmoritzhotelph.com
Subic Bay Wellness Center	staff@subicbaywellness.com
Subic Mirage Beach Hotel	subicmirage@hotmail.com
Subic Seaplane	info@seaplane-philippines.com
Submaldive Dive Center	info@submaldive.com
Sugarland Hotel	sugarlnd@mozcom.com
Sulo Hotel	bmcc@sulohotel.com.ph
Sulu Sunset Beach Resort	mail@sulusunset.com

Sumisid Lodge	seaquest@sequst.com
Sun Apartelle	sunapartelle@web.de
Sun Cruises	suncruises@magsaysay.com.ph
Sunseeker Divers	marie@sunseekerdivers.com
Sunset Bay Resort	john_gaye@sunsetbayinfo
Sunset Garden Inn	sunsetg@mozcom.com
Sunset Garden Resort	sunsetgarden@vasia.com
Sunset German Beach Resort	info@sunsetgermanbeach.com
Sunshine Pension House	sunshine.pension@yahoo.com
Sunsplash (Malapascua)	mkuehtmann@hotmail.com
Sunsplash Resort	reservations@scubaplus.com
Swagman Hotel	swagman@ibm.net
Swagman Narra Hotel	bookings@swagmanhotelangeles.com
Swiss Chalet	info@swisschaletph.com
Schweizergarten Resort	schweizergarten@gmx.net
Swissippini Lodge & Resort	floral@moscom.com
Swiss Stars Guest House	swissstars@siquijorisland.every1.net
Sydney Hotel	Sydney@gslink.net

T

Taal Vista Hotel	taalvista@barcelo-asia.com
Takatuka Lodge	relax@takatuka-lodge.com
Tambuli Beach Club	resrvations@tambuli.com
Tanawin Bay Resort	vtw@tanawinbayresort.com
Tarabanan Cottages	anfrage@tarabanan.de
Tarzan's Nest Resort	enigmatatreehouse@yahoo.com
Taver's Pension House	tavers@mozcom.com
Teach-on-the-Beach	anfrage@teach-on-the-beach.de
Terra Rija Beach Resort	terrarika@yahoo.com
Tête-à-Tête	info@sprboracay.com
The Blue Wave	bluewaveinn@yahoo.com
The British Council	britishcouncil@britishcouncil.org.ph
The Coco Palace Hotel	info@cocopalacehotel.com.ph
The Corporate Inn (Iligan)	corpo8inn@yahoo.com
The Corporate Inn Hotel	tcihotel@skyinet.net
The Dynasty Court Hotel	dynasty@cdo.philcom.com.ph
The Farm at San Benito	info@thefarm.com.ph
The Garden Plaza	gplaza@universecafe.com
The Golden Peak Hotel	goldenpk@cebu.i-next.net
The Green Room Surf Camp	emmarcon@usa.net
The Heritage Hotel	inquire@heritagehotelmanila.com
The House of Halina	cehalina@quezon.com
The Legend Hotel (Manila)	legend@wpi.webquest.com
The Legend Hotel (Palawan)	salesppc@legendhotels.com.ph
The Leyte Park	leypark@tac.weblinq.com
The Mangrove Hotel	themangrove@hotmail.com
The Marco Polo	davao@marcopolohotels.com
The Norwegian Dream Beach Resort	post@thenorwegiandream.com

The Pan Pacific	rsvnmanila@panpac.com.ph
The Patio	billlyon@datelnet.net
The Peninsula Manila	mnlpen@i-quest.com
The Richmonde Hotel	trh@richmondehotel.com.ph
The Royal Mandaya Hotel	mandaya@mozcom.com
The Spa	thespa@thespa.com.ph
The Sun Village Beachfront/Hilltop Resort	fpni@pacific.net.ph
The Townhouse Hotel	bill_lorna@yahoo.com
The Westin Philippine Plaza Hotel	bscenter@westinmanila.com
Tiamban Aqua Club	tacmnl@benedicto.com.ph_
Tierra Azul	info@tierraazul.com
Tirol & Tirol Beach Resort	tandt@boracay.i-next.net
Tongo Sail Inn	tongosailinn@hotmail.com
Top Plaza Hotel	topplaza@mozcom.com
Topstar Travel & Tours	ted_topstar@yahoo.com
Tourist Office (DOT)	
- Baguio	dotcar@mozcom.com
- Butuan	dot13@butuan.philcom.com.ph
- Cagayan de Oro	dot10@cdo.weblinq.com
- Cebu City	dotr7@cvis.net
- Chicago	pdotchi@aol.com
- Cotabato	dot12@mozcom.com
- Davao	dotr11@mozcom.com
- Dumaguete	ctourism@mozcom.com
- Frankfurt	phildot-fra@t-online.de
- Hong Kong	pdothk@asiaonline.net
- Iloilo City	dot6@pop.cbu.skyinet.net
- Legaspi	dotr5@globalink.net.ph
- London	tourism@pdot.co.uk
- Los Angeles	pdotla@aol.com
- Manila	deptour@info.com.ph
- New York	pdotnyc1@aol.com
- Osaka	dotosaka@osk3.3web.ne.jp
- Paris	dotpar@club-internet.fr
- Puerto Princesa	ppcto@mozcom.com
- San Fernando (La Union)	dotregion1@sflu.com
- San Fernando (Pampanga)	dot3@mozcom.com
- San Francisco	pdotsf@aol.com
- Silay	sil2@babysky.net.ph
- Singapore	philtours_sin@pacific.net.sg
- Sydney	ptsydney@ozemail.com.au
- Tacloban	dotr8@mozcom.com
- Tokyo	dotjapan@gol.com
- Zamboanga	dotr9@jetlink.com.ph
Trafalgar Garden & Cottages	trafalgarboracay@hotmail.com
Trattoria Inn	trattori@info.com.ph
Travelers Inn	hruphils@skyinet.net
Trek Adventures	trekadventures@digitelone.com

Trend Transport	trend_ac@yahoo.com
Tribal Adventure Tours	info@tribaladventures.com
Triton Divers Lodge	tritondivers@mindoro.net
Tropicana Castle Dive Resort	paultropicana@yahoo.com
Tropicana Resort Hotel	anchor@gslink.net
T-Rose Apartments	trose@svisp.com
True Home Hotel	truehomehotel@yahoo.com
Tubbataha Management Office	tmo@mozcom.com
Tuna City Dive Center	dvgensan@mozcom.com
Twins Beach Club	twinsbc@hotmail.com

V

Vacation Hotel	vhcebu@mybizlinks.net
Vian Lodge	vian@comclark.com
Victory Divers	boracay@victory-divers.de
Vigan Hotel	viganhtl@iln.csi.com.ph
Vigan Plaza Hotel	viganplazahotel@msn.com
Villa Alzhun Tourist Inn	villaalzhun@bohol-island.com
Villa Angela Heritage House	gasser@ramnet-ph.net
Villa Camilla	front_desk@villacamilla.com
Villa Estelita Beach & Dive Resort	arnehave@hotmail.com
Villa Estrella Resort Hotel	verh_2000@yahoo.com
Villa Loreto Beach Resort	villa@subictel.com
Villa Margarita	villamar@interasia.com.ph
Villa Sabang	info@villa-sabang.com
Visaya Divers	quovadisb.r@skyinet.net
Vistamar Beach Resort & Hotel	vistamar@pacific.net.ph

W

Waling-Waling Beach Resort	waling@boracay.i-next.net
Waterfront Cebu City Hotel	rsvplahug@waterfronthotel.com
Waterfront Insular Hotel Davao	ichdavao@weblinq.com
Waterfront Airport Hotel	wah@waterfronthotel.com
Waveriderz	waveriderz@ozemail.com.au
Wellbeach Resort	well@hispeed.ch
Westcoast Beach Resort	westcoastbresort@hotmail.com
West Gorordo Hotel	wgorordo@skyinet.net
Westpoint Inn	westside@mozcom.com
Whispering Palms	info@whisperingpalms.com.ph
Whispering Palms Island Resort	info@whispering-palms.com
White Beach Divers	whitebeachdivers@hotmail.com
White Coral Garden Resort	jonathan_naui@yahoo.com
White Rock Resort Hotel	wrh@svisp.com
White Sand Bungalows	whitesandbungalows@hotmail.com
Whitetip Divers Davao	ctshack@dv.weblinq.com
Whitetip Divers General Santos	docdiver@dv.weblinq.com
Whitetip Divers Manila	whitetip@whitetip.com
Whitewater Rafting Adventure	whiterafting@cagayabdeoro.net.ph

Willy's Beach Resort	willys@boracay.i-next.net
Woodland Park Resort Hotel	woodland@mozcom.com
Won Dive Resort Hotel	wondive@hotmail.com
Wregent Plaza Hotel	warrien@mozcom.com

Z

Zanzibar Hotel	zanzibar@svisp.com

Index

Locations

A

B

C

Index

Keywords

www.travelphil.com

Travelling in the

PHILIPPINES

JENS PETERS PUBLICATIONS

Search Site

Embassies
Consulates, Tourist
Offices, Organisations

Travel Agents
Tour Operators
Philippines etc

Airlines
Philippines, International
Airports

Shipping Lines
Passenger Ships
Schedules

Cars & Bikes
Rental, Used Cars
Spare Parts, Traffic

Weather
Forecasts, Web Cams
Satellite Pictures

Money
Exchange Rates, Credit
Cards, Money Transfer

Accommodation
Hotels
Beach Resorts

Pubs & Restos
Bistros, Restaurants
Entertainment

Diving
Dive Areas, Dive Boats
Dive Operators

Activities
Climbing, Hiking
Sailing, Surfing etc

Health
Tropical Diseases, Self-
Help, Medical Terms

Language
Language Courses
Vocabulary

Media
Newspapers, Magazines
Radio, TV, Online

Maps
Towns, Islands
Locations

Mixed Links
Art, Culture, Food
Ecology, Sports etc

Towns & Islands
Cities, Municipalities
Provinces, Regions

Who's Who
Actors, Bands, Models
Painter, Singer, Writer

Search & Find
Post Codes, Area Codes
Time, Telephone

Personal Pages
Traveller's Tales
Impressions

News
Latest Information
Updates

Photos
The Philippines
in Pictures

Shop - Books
Travel Guides
(English & German)

LOGOS FOR LINKS